The GALE ENCYCLOPEDIA *of* SENIOR HEALTH

A GUIDE FOR SENIORS AND THEIR CAREGIVERS

The GALE ENCYCLOPEDIA of SENIOR HEALTH

A GUIDE FOR SENIORS AND THEIR CAREGIVERS

FIRST EDITION

VOLUME
5
S–Z

JACQUELINE L. LONGE, EDITOR

GALE
CENGAGE Learning™

Detroit • New York • San Francisco • New Haven, Conn • Waterville, Maine • London

GALE
CENGAGE Learning

Gale Encyclopedia of Senior Health: A Guide for Seniors and Their Caregivers

Project Editor: Jacqueline L. Longe

Editorial: Donna Batten, Amy Kwolek, Jeffrey Wilson

Product Manager: Kate Hanley

Editorial Support Services: Andrea Lopeman

Indexing Services: Factiva, a Dow Jones Company

Rights Acquisition and Management: Vernon English, Barbara McNeil, Sara E. Teller, and Robyn V. Young

Composition: Evi Abou-El-Seoud

Manufacturing: Rita Wimberley

Imaging: Lezlie Light

Product Design: Pam Galbreath

Library of Congress Cataloging-in-Publication Data

The Gale encyclopedia of senior health: a guide for seniors and their caregivers / Jacqueline L. Longe, editor.
p. cm.
Includes bibliographical references and index.
ISBN 978-1-4144-0383-0 (set : alk. paper) – ISBN 978-1-4144-0384-7 (vol. 1 : alk. paper) – ISBN 978-1-4144-0385-4 (vol. 2 : alk. paper) – ISBN 978-1-4144-4850-3 (vol. 3 : alk. paper) – ISBN 978-1-4144-4851-0 (vol. 4 : alk. paper) – ISBN 978-1-4144-4905-0 (vol. 5 : alk. paper)
1. Older people–Health and hygiene–Encyclopedias. 2. Geriatrics–Encyclopedias. I.
Longe, Jacqueline L.

RC952.5.G3485 2009
618.97003–dc22 2008017305

Gale
27500 Drake Rd.
Farmington Hills, MI, 48331-3535

ISBN-13: 978-1-4144-0383-0 (set) ISBN-10: 1-4144-0383-6 (set)
ISBN-13: 978-1-4144-0384-7 (vol. 1) ISBN-10: 1-4144-0384-4 (vol. 1)
ISBN-13: 978-1-4144-0385-4 (vol. 2) ISBN-10: 1-4144-0385-2 (vol. 2)
ISBN-13: 978-1-4144-4850-3 (vol. 3) ISBN-10: 1-4144-4850-3 (vol. 3)
ISBN-13: 978-1-4144-4851-0 (vol. 4) ISBN-10: 1-4144-4851-1 (vol. 4)
ISBN-13: 978-1-4144-4905-0 (vol. 5) ISBN-10: 1-4144-4905-4 (vol. 5)

This title is also available as an e-book.
ISBN-13: 978-1-4144-4855-8 ISBN-10: 1-4144-4855-4
Contact your Gale, a part of Cengage Learning sales representative for ordering information.

Printed in China
1 2 3 4 5 6 7 12 11 10 09 08

CONTENTS

LIST OF ENTRIES

A

AARP
Abdominoplasty
Acetaminophen
Activities of daily living evaluation
Acupressure
Acupuncture
Acute leukemia
Adjustment disorders
Administration of medication
Adult day care
Advance directives
Advanced practice nurses
Aerobic exercise
Age-related macular degeneration
Aging
AIDS
AIDS counseling
AIDS tests
Alcohol abuse
Allergies
Allergy tests
Aloe
Alopecia
$Alpha_1$-adrenergic blockers
Alpha hydroxy acids
Alzheimer's disease
Ambulatory blood pressure
Americans with Disabilities Act
Aminoglycosides
Amputation
Amyloidosis
Amyotrophic lateral sclerosis
Analgesics
Anemia
Anesthesia, general
Anesthesia, local
Anesthesiologist's role
Aneurysm
Angina pectoris
Angiography
Angioplasty
Angiotensin-converting enzyme inhibitors
Ankle-brachial index
Anoxia
Antacids
Anti-insomnia drugs
Anti-itch drugs
Antiangina drugs
Antianxiety drugs
Antiarrhythmic drugs
Antibiotics
Anticancer drugs
Anticoagulant and antiplatelet drugs
Anticonvulsant drugs
Antidementia drugs
Antidepressant drugs, SSRI
Antidepressants, tricyclic
Antidiabetic drugs
Antidiarrheal drugs
Antifungal drugs, topical
Antihistamines
Antihypertensive drugs
Antiinflammatory diets
Antioxidants
Antiparkinsonian drugs
Antipsychotic drugs
Antiretroviral drugs
Antituberculosis drugs
Antiviral drugs
Anxiety
Aortic dissection
Aortic valve stenosis
Arrhythmias
Arteriovenous fistula
Arteriovenous malformations
Aspiration
Aspirin
Assisted living facilities
Asthma
Atherosclerosis
Audiometry
Autoimmune disease tests
Autoimmune disorders
Autonomic disorders

B

Back and neck pain, physical therapy for
Back curves
Bacteremia
Bacterial Infections
Balance and coordination tests
Barbiturates
Bariatric surgery
Barium enema
Behcet's syndrome
Benzodiazepines
Bereavement counseling
Beta blockers
Biofeedback
Bipolar disorder

Bladder cancer
Bladder infection
Bladder stones
Bladder training
Bladder ultrasound
Blepharoplasty
Blindness
Blood clots
Blood pressure
Blood sugar tests
Body mass index
Boils
Bone density test
Bone marrow aspiration and biopsy
Bone scan
Botox injection
Brain and central nervous system tumors
Breast biopsy
Breast cancer
Breast implants
Breast reconstruction
Breast self-examination
Breathing problems
Bronchitis
Bronchodilators
Bronchoscopy
Bruising
Bursitis

C

Cachexia and wasting
Caffeine
Calcium
Calcium channel blockers
Calcium supplements
Cancer
Cancer fighting foods
Cancer therapy, supportive
Carbohydrates
Cardiac ablation
Cardiac bypass
Cardiac catheterization
Cardiac monitor
Cardiac rehabilitation
Cardiac surgery
Cardiac valve surgery
Cardiomyopathy
Cardiopulmonary resuscitation
Cardioversion
Caregiver
Carotid disease
Carotid ultrasound
Cataracts
Catheterization, female
Catheterization, male
Celiac disease
Cellulitis (infection)
Cephalosporins
Cervical cancer
Cervical spondylosis
Chemotherapy
Chest CT scan
Chest physical therapy
Chest x ray
Chiropractic
Cholesterol test
Chronic kidney failure
Chronic leukemia
Chronic obstructive pulmonary disease
Cinnamon
Circulatory problems
Cirrhosis
Clinical nurse specialist
Code of ethics for nurses
Collagen injection
Colon cancer
Colonoscopy
Colostomy
Colostomy care
Coma
Commercial prescription programs
Common cold
Community health programs
Community nutrition
Community social programs
Complete blood count
Congestive heart failure
Conservatorship
Constipation
Contact dermatitis
Corneal diseases
Coronary artery disease
Cosmetic surgery
Cox-2 inhibitors
CT scans
Cushing's syndrome
Cystitis

D

Death and dying
Deep vein thrombosis
Dehydration
Delirium
Dementia
Dental health and hygiene
Dental implants
Denture care
Depression
Dermatitis
Dermatologist
DHEA
Diabetes insipidus
Diabetes mellitus
Diabetic foot infections
Diabetic nephropathy
Diabetic neuropathy
Diabetic retinopathy
Dialysis technology
Diarrhea
Diet
Diet and lifestyle over 50
Diet and mental health
Dietary assessment
Dietary counseling
Dietary intake and nutrition status
Dietary supplements
Dietetics
Dietician
Discharge from the hospital
Dislocations and subluxations
Diuretics
Diverticulosis and diverticulitis
Dizziness
Do not resuscitate order

Doctor of osteopathy
Driver safety
Drug abuse
Drug interactions
Dry eye
Dry mouth
Dry skin
Dysphasia

E

Ear irrigation
Echocardiogram
Edema
Elder abuse
Electrocardiography
Electroencephalography
Electrolyte balance
Electrolyte tests
Emphysema
Endometrial cancer
Endoscopy
Endotracheal tube management
Enemas
Erectile dysfunction
Esophageal cancer
Euthanasia
Exercise
Eye examination
Eye glasses and contact lenses
Eyedrop instillation
Eyelid disorders

F

Face lift
Fainting
Falls
Family relationships
Fatty liver
Fecal incontinence
Fibromyalgia
Financial management
Finding a surgeon
Floaters
Folic acid
Food allergies
Food intolerance
Foot care
Fungal culture
Fungal infections

G

Gait and balance assessment
Gait and balance problems
Gallbladder cancer
Gallstones
Gambling
Gangrene
Garlic
Gastroenteritis disease
Gastroesophageal reflux disease
Gastroesophageal reflux scan
Generalized anxiety disorder
Geriatric assessment tests
Geriatric nutrition
GI bleeding
GI bleeding studies
Gingivitis
Ginkgo biloba
Glaucoma
Glucosamine
Gluten-free diet
Gout
Gout drugs

H

H-2 receptor blockers
Head injury
Headaches
Health care financing
Health care, quality
Health history
Health Resources and Services Administration
Hearing aids
Hearing loss
Heart attack
Heart disease
Heart valve repair
Heartburn
Heatstroke
Helicobacteriosis
Hematologist
Hemochromatosis
Hemorrhoids
Hepatitis
High cholesterol
High-fiber diet
Hip fractures rehabilitation
Hip replacement
Hip revision surgery
HMOs
Holter monitoring
Home care
Home health aide
Home safety
Homeopathic medicine
Hormone replacement therapy
Hospices
Household management
Hydrotherapy
Hyperlipoproteinemia
Hyperparathyroidism
Hypertension
Hyperthyroidism
Hypertrophic cardiomyopathy
Hysterectomy

I

Immune system
Implantable cardioverter-defibrillator
Independence
Infection control
Infectious diseases
Influenza
Influenza vaccination
Informed consent
Inhalation therapies
Insomnia
Insulin
Intravenous fluid regulation
Intravenous medication administration

Iron deficiency anemia
Iron tests
Irritable bowel syndrome
Ischemia
Isolation
Itching

J

Joint integrity and function
Joint mobilization and manipulation

K

Kidney cancer
Kidney function tests
Kidney nuclear medicine scan
Kidney stones
Kidney transplantation
Kidney, ureter, and bladder x-ray study
Knee joint replacement
Knee problems

L

Lactose intolerance
Laxatives
Lice infestation
Licensed practical nurse
Liposuction
Liver biopsy
Liver cancer
Liver function tests
Liver-spleen scan
Living will
Low back pain
Low-cholesterol diet
Low fat diet
Low sodium diet
Low vision
Lower limb prostheses
Lumpectomy
Lung biopsy
Lung cancer
Lupus
Lyme disease
Lymphedema

M

Magnetic resonance imaging
Malignant lymphomas
Malignant melanoma
Malnutrition
Mammogram
Managed care plans
Marijuana
Massage therapy
Mastectomy
Meals On Wheels
Medicaid
Medical billing
Medical ethics
Medicare
Medicare prescription drug plan
Memory loss
Meningitis
Menopause
Mental retardation
Metastasis
Migraine
Mind/body medicine
Minimally invasive heart surgery
Minoxidil
Mitral valve insufficiency
Mitral valve prolapse
Mitral valve stenosis
Mobility issues
Motor neuron disease
Movement therapy
MRSA infection
Multiple myeloma
Multiple sclerosis
Muscle relaxants
Myocarditis

N

Nail fungus
Nail removal
Naturopaths
Neuralgia
Neurologic examination
Neuromuscular physical therapy
Nonsteroidal anti-inflammatory drugs
Nuclear stress test
Nursing assistant
Nursing homes
Nutrition
Nutrition and healthy aging
Nutrition through an intravenous line
Nutritional supplements
Nutritionist

O

Obesity
Optometry
Oral cancer
Oral hygiene
Organ donation
Osteoarthritis
Osteopathy
Osteoporosis
Ovarian cancer
Overactive bladder
Overdose
Oxygen/ozone therapy

P

Pacemakers
Paget's disease of bone
Pain
Pain management
Pancreatic cancer, endocrine
Pancreatic cancer, exocrine
Panic disorder
Pap test
Paralysis
Parathyroid scan
Parkinson's disease
Patient confidentiality
Patient education
Patient representative

Patient rights
Pericarditis
Periodic limb movement disorder
Peripheral vascular disease
Peripheral vision loss
Persistent vegetative state
Personal hygiene
Personality disorders
Pharmacology
Pharmacy technician
Physical therapist
Physical therapy
Physical therapy assisting
Pleural effusion
Pneumonia
Polymyalgia rheumatica
Polymyositis
Post-traumatic stress disorder in seniors
Postoperative care
PPOs
Prayer and spirituality
Preoperative cardiac assessment
Preoperative care
Presbyopia
Pressure sores
Priapism
Private insurance plans
Probiotics
Prostate biopsy
Prostate cancer
Prostate enlargement
Prostate ultrasound
Proton pump inhibitors
Psoriasis
Psychological and social issues
Psychoses
Pulmonary embolism
Pulmonary fibrosis
Pulmonary hypertension
Pulmonary rehabilitation

Q

Qigong

R

Reconciliation
Recovery at home
Recovery room
Registered nurse
Relationships
Relaxation
Respiratory failure
Retinal detachment
Rheumatoid arthritis
Rheumatologist
Rosacea

S

Sarcoidosis
Sarcomas
Saw palmetto
Scabies
Sciatica
Scleroderma
Seborrheic dermatitis
Seizure disorder
Senior travel
Seniors' health
Sexual dysfunction
Sexually transmitted diseases
Sexually transmitted diseases cultures
Shiatsu
Shingles
Sildenafil citrate
Sjögren's syndrome
Skin cancer
Skin culture
Skin lesion removal
Skin lesions
Sleep apnea in seniors
Sleep disorders
Smoking
Smoking cessation
Snoring surgery
Social work in health care
Sodium
Special dietary needs of cancer patients
Speech problems
Spinal cord injury
Spinal stenosis
Staphylococcal infections
Stomach cancer
Streptococcal disease
Stress
Stress test
Stroke
Substance abuse and dependence
Substance abuse counseling
Suicide
Surgical oncology
Swallowing problems

T

T'ai chi
Talking with your doctor
Teeth whitening
Tendinitis
Testicular self-examination
Tetanus
Therapeutic exercise
Thoracic surgery
Thrombocytopenia
Thrombocytosis
Thrombolytic therapy
Thyroid cancer
Thyroid function tests
Thyroid nuclear medicine scan
Thyroid ultrasound
Tinnitus
Transient blindness
Transient ischemic attacks
Trigger finger
Tube feedings
Tuberculosis

U

Ulcers
Upper GI exam

Upper GI series
Urinary incontinence
Urinary tract infection
Urine culture

V

Vaccinations
Varicose veins
Ventilation management
Ventilators
Ventricular fibrillation
Ventricular tachycardia
Veterans Affairs hospital system
VFW
Viruses
Vision disorders
Visual impairment
Vital signs in the aging
Vitamin B_{12}
Vitamin C
Vitamin D
Vitamin E
Vitamin K
Vitamins

W

Walking problems
Water and nutrition
Water exercise
Weight loss
Wheelchair prescription
Withdrawing support
Wound care
Wrinkles

XYZ

Yoga
Zinc

PLEASE READ—IMPORTANT INFORMATION

The Gale Encyclopedia of Senior Health: A Guide for Seniors and Their Caregivers is a health reference product designed to inform and educate readers about a wide variety of diseases and conditions, nutrition and dietary practices, treatments and drugs, as well as other issues associated with the health of seniors. Cengage Learning believes the product to be comprehensive, but not necessarily definitive. It is intended to supplement, not replace, consultation with a physician or other healthcare practitioners. While Cengage Learning has made substantial efforts to provide information that is accurate, comprehensive, and up-to-date, Cengage Learning makes no representations or warranties of any kind, including without limitation, warranties of merchantability or fitness for a particular purpose, nor does it guarantee the accuracy, comprehensiveness, or timeliness of the information contained in this product. Readers should be aware that the universe of medical knowledge is constantly growing and changing, and that differences of opinion exist among authorities. Readers are also advised to seek professional diagnosis and treatment for any medical condition, and to discuss information obtained from this book with their healthcare provider.

INTRODUCTION

The Gale Encyclopedia of Senior Health: A Guide for Seniors and Their Caregivers is a unique and invaluable source of information. This collection of over 600 entries provides in-depth coverage of cover various issues related to one's aging body, how diseases affect it, and treatment options, including medications, for seniors. The set will cover every major body system, focusing on issues specific to the aging body. These entries constitute over fifty percent of the work, and follow a standard format, including a definition, description, symptoms, treatment options, "questions to ask your doctor," and more. Topics specific to the aging population, but beyond descriptions of medical diagnoses round out the set. Examples of this coverage include use of various adaptive devices and equipment, transportation issues, housing options, maintaining mental acuity, definitions and descriptions of the roles of different care givers (i.e. physical therapist, social worker, hospital discharge planner), nutrition and exercise guidelines, definitions of different types of medical insurance (i.e., private PPOs or HMOs vs. Medicare) and more.

SCOPE

The Gale Encyclopedia of Senior Health covers a wide variety of topics relevant to the user. Entries follow a standardized format that provides information at a glance. Rubrics include:

Disease and conditions

- Definition
- Description
- Demographics
- Causes and symptoms
- Diagnosis
- Treatment
- Nutrition/Dietetic concerns
- Therapy
- Prognosis
- Prevention
- Caregiver concerns
- "Questions to ask the doctor"
- Resources
- Key Terms

Tests and procedures

- Definition
- Purpose
- Description
- Precautions
- Preparation
- Aftercare
- Complications
- Results
- Care team roles
- "Questions to ask the doctor"
- Resources
- Key Terms

Drugs, herbs, vitamins

- Definition
- Description
- Recommended dosage
- Precautions
- Side effects
- Interactions
- Caregiver concerns
- "Questions to ask the doctor"
- Resources
- Key Terms

Nutrition, exercise, diet

- Definition
- Description
- Demographics
- Purpose
- Challenges
- Risks
- Results
- Resources
- Key Terms

Recovery and rehabilitation

- Definition
- Purpose
- Precautions
- Steps of recovery
- Challenges
- Risks
- Results
- Resources
- Key Terms

Professions

- Definition
- Description
- Work settings
- Care team role
- Education/training
- Family teaching
- Resources
- Key Terms

Devices/tools

- Definition
- Description
- Purpose
- Operation
- Maintenance
- Training
- Resources
- Key Terms

Aging and senior issues

- Definition
- Description
- Viewpoints
- Resources
- Key Terms

INCLUSION CRITERIA

A preliminary list of topics was compiled from a wide variety of sources, including senior health books, general medical encyclopedias, and consumer health guides. The advisory board, composed of medical doctors, registered nurses, health educators, and nutritionists, evaluated the topics and made suggestions for inclusion. Final selection of topics to include was made by the advisory board in conjunction with the editor.

ABOUT THE CONTRIBUTORS

The essays were compiled by experienced medical writers, including medical doctors, pharmacists, and registered nurses. The advisers reviewed the completed essays to ensure that they are appropriate, up-to-date, and accurate.

HOW TO USE THIS BOOK

The *Gale Encyclopedia of Senior Health* has been designed with ready reference in mind.

- Straight **alphabetical arrangement** of topics allows users to locate information quickly.
- **Bold-faced terms** within entries direct the reader to related articles.
- **Cross-references** placed throughout the encyclopedia direct readers from alternate names and related topics to entries.
- A list of **Key terms** is provided where appropriate to define terms or concepts that may be unfamiliar to the user. A **glossary** of key terms in the back matter contains a concise list of terms arranged alphabetically.
- The **Resources** section directs readers to additional sources of information on a topic.
- Valuable **contact information** for health organizations is included with each entry. An **appendix of organizations** in the back matter contains an extensive list of organizations arranged alphabetically.
- A comprehensive **general index** guides readers to significant topics mentioned in the text.

GRAPHICS

The *Gale Encyclopedia of Senior Health* is also enhanced by over 370 color photographs, illustrations, and tables.

ADVISORS

A number of experts in the medical community provided invaluable assistance in the formulation of this encyclopedia. Our advisory board performed a myriad of duties, from defining the scope of coverage to reviewing individual entries for accuracy and accessibility. The editor would like to express her appreciation to them.

Kenneth Berniker, M.D.
Attending Physician
Emergency Room
Kaiser Permanente Medical Center
Vallejo, California

Donna Gauthier, Ph.D., R.N., C.N.E.
Assistant Professor of Nursing
Adrian Vega/BORSF Professorship in Nursing
University of Louisiana at Lafayette
Lafayette, Louisiana

Melinda Granger Oberleitner, R.N., D.N.S.
Acting Department Head and Associate Professor
Department of Nursing
University of Louisiana at Lafayette
Lafayette, Louisiana

Sarah Schenker S.R.D., Ph.D., R.P.H.Nutr.
Nutrition Scientist
British Nutrition Institute
London, England UK

Marianne Vahey, M.D.
Clinical Instructor in Medicine
Yale University School of Medicine
New Haven, Connecticut

James E. Waun, M.D., M.A., R. Ph..
Associate Clinical Professor
Department of Family Practice
Faculty
Center for Ethics and the Humanities
Michigan State University
Adjunct Assistant Professor of Clinical Pharmacy
Ferris State University
East Lansing, Michigan

CONTRIBUTORS

Margaret Alic, Ph.D.
Science Writer
Eastsound, Washington

William Asenjo, Ph.D., CRC
Medical writer
Iowa City, Iowa

William Arthur Atkins, Ph.D.
Science Writer
Atkins Research and Consulting
Pekin, Illinois

Linda K. Bennington, C.N.S, M.S.N.
Clinical Nurse Specialist
Virginia Beach, Virginia

Kenneth J. Berniker, M.D.
Attending Physician
Kaiser Permanente Medical Center
Vallejo, California

Mark A. Best, M.D., MPH, MBA
Associate Professor of Pathology
St. Mathew's University
Grand Cayman, BWI

Robert Bockstiegel
Freelance Writer
Portland, Oregon

Maggie Boleyn, R.N., B.S.N.
Medical Writer
Oak Park, Michigan

June G. Borazjani, R.N., M.S.N., C.P.H.Q.
Saint Martinville, Louisiana

Michelle Q. Bosworth, MS, CGC
Writer

Patricia L. Bounds, Ph.D.
Science Writer
Zurich, Switzerland

Rosalyn Carson-DeWitt, M.D.
Durham, North Carolina

Stacy Chamberlin
Freelance Writer
New Albany, Ohio

Lata Cherath, Ph.D.
Science Writer
Franklin Park, New York

Rhonda Cloos, R.N.
Medical Writer
Austin, Texas

David Cramer, M.D.
Medical Writer
Chicago, Illinois

L. Lee Culvert
Freelance Writer
Alna, Massachusetts

Helen Davidson
Freelance Writer
Eugene, Oregon

Tish Davidson, A.M.
Medical Writer
Fremont, California

Douglas Dupler, M.A.
Freelance Writer
Boulder, Colorado

L. Fleming Fallon, Jr., M.D., Dr.P.H.
Professor of Public Health
Bowling Green State University
Bowling Green, Ohio

Diane Fanucchi-Faulkner, C.M.T., C.C.R.A
Medical Writer
Oceano, California

Janie F. Franz
Freelance Writer
Grand Forks, North Dakota

Rebecca Frey, Ph.D.
Research and Administrative Associate
East Rock Institute
New Haven, Connecticut

Jason Fryer
Freelance Writer
Lubbock, Texas

Jill Granger, M.S.
Senior Research Associate
Department of Pathology
University of Michigan
Ann Arbor, Michigan

Laith Farid Gulli, M.D.
Consultant Psychotherapist
Lathrup Village, Michigan

Katherine Hauswirth, APRN
Medical Writer
Deep River, Connecticut

Kevin O. Hwang, M.D.
Medical Writer
Morristown, New Jersey

René A. Jackson, R.N.
Medical Writer
Port Charlotte, Florida

Michelle L. Johnson, M.S., J.D.
Patent Attorney and Medical Writer
Portland, Oregon

Cindy L.A. Jones, Ph.D.
Biomedical Writer
Lakewood, Colorado

Crystal H. Kaczkowski, MSc.
Medical Writer
Montreal, Quebec Canada

David Kaminstein, M.D.
Medical Writer
Westchester, Pennsylvania

Joseph Knight, PA
Medical Writer

Monique Laberge, Ph.D.
Centre for Structural and Functional Genomics, Concordia University
Montreal, Quebec

Lorraine Lica, Ph.D.
Medical Writer
San Diego, California

John T. Lohr, Ph.D.
Utah State University
Logan, Utah

Mary Elizabeth Martelli, R.N., B.S.
Medical Writer
Sebastian, Florida

Jacqueline N. Martin, M.S.
Medical Writer
Albrightsville, Pennsylvania

Richard A. McCartney, M.D.
Fellow, American College of Surgeons
Richland, Washington

Nancy McKenzie, Ph.D.
Public Health Consultant
Brooklyn, New York

Beverly Miller, M.T.(A.S.C.P.)
Technical Writer
Charlotte, North Carolina

Susan M. Mockus, Ph.D.
Medical Writer
Seattle, Washington

Melodie Monahan
Copyeditor and Writer
Rochester, Michigan

Louann W. Murray, Ph.D.
Writer

Bilal Farid Nasser, M.Sc.
Writer

Katherine E. Nelson, N.D.
Nutritionist and Writer

Debra Novograd, B.S., R.T.(R)(M)
Royal Oak, Michigan

Debbie Nurmi, M.S.
Medical Writer, Public Health Researcher
Atlanta, Georgia

Melinda Oberleitner, R.N., D.N.S.
Acting Department Head and Associate Professor
Department of Nursing, University of Louisiana
Lafayette, Louisiana

Teresa Odle
Medical Writer
Albuquerque, New Mexico

Lisa Papp, R.N.
Medical Writer

LeeAnn Paradise
Science Writer
Lubbock, Texas

Jane E. Phillips, Ph.D.
Writer
Chapel Hill, North Carolina

Lisa Piazza, MA
Freelance Writer
Clearwater, Florida

J. Ricker Polsdorfer, M.D.
Medical Writer
Phoenix, Arizona

Elaine R. Proseus, MBA/TM, BSRT, RT(R)

Elizabeth Pulcini, M.Sc.
Medical Writer
Phoenix, Arizona

Kulbir Rangi, D.O.
Medical Doctor and Writer
New York, New York

Esther Csapo Rastegari, R.N., B.S.N., Ed.M.
Registered Nurse and Medical Writer
Holbrook, Massachusetts

Linda Richards, R.D., C.H.E.S.
Flagstaff, Arizona

Nancy Ross-Flanigan
Science Writer
Belleville, Michigan

Mark Damian Rossi, Ph.D., P.T., C.S.C.S.
Medical Writer
Pembroke Pines, Florida

Belinda Rowland, Ph.D.
Medical Writer
Voorheesville, New York

Laura Ruth, Ph.D.
Medical and Science Writer
Los Angeles, California

Joan Schonbeck, R.N.
Medical Writer
Massachusetts Department of Mental Health
Marlborough, Massachusetts

Cathy Hester Seckman, R.D.H.
Medical Writer
Calcutta, Ohio

Kim A. Sharp, M.Ln.
Medical Writer

Lee A. Shratter, M.D.
Medical Writer

Judith Sims, M.S.
Science Writer
Logan, Utah

Genevieve Slomski, Ph.D.
Medical Writer
New Britain, Connecticut

Jane Elizabeth Spear
Medical Writer
Canton, Ohio

Allison Joan Spiwak, MSBME
Circulation Technologist
Ohio State University
Gahanna, Ohio

Lauren L. Stinson
Freelance writer
Los Angeles, California

Amy Sutton
Science Writer
Narvon, Pennsylvania

Liz Swain
Medical Writer
San Diego, California

Deanna M. Swartout-Corbeil, R.N.
Medical Writer
Thompsons Station, Tennessee

Peggy Campbell Torpey, MPT
Medical Writer
Royal Oak, Michigan

Sam Uretsky, PharmD
Pharmacist and medical writer
Wantagh, New York

Ellen S. Weber, MSN
Medical Writer
Fort Wayne, Indiana

Ken Wells
Freelance Writer
Laguna Hills, California

Barbara Wexler, MPH
Medical Writer
Chatsworth, California

Gayle G. Wilkins, R.N., B.S.N., O.C.N.
Medical Writer
Willow Park, Texas

Abby Wojahn, R.N., B.S.N., C.C.R.N.
Medical Writer
Milwaukee, Wisconsin

Kathleen Wright, R.N.
Medical Writer
Delmar, Delaware

S

Sarcoidosis

Sarcoidosis is an inflammatory disease with no known cause and no known cure.

Description

Sarcoidosis is a disease in which inflammatory cells (granulomas) form usually in the lungs but it can affect the heart, liver, lymph nodes, skin, and eyes. Granulomas may collect and grow larger or form groups of granulomas. Granulomas usually affect more than one organ.

During the active phase of the disease, granulomas form and grow and symptoms may develop. Scar tissue may form in the affected organ(s). Sometimes the granulomas change an organ's structure and function.

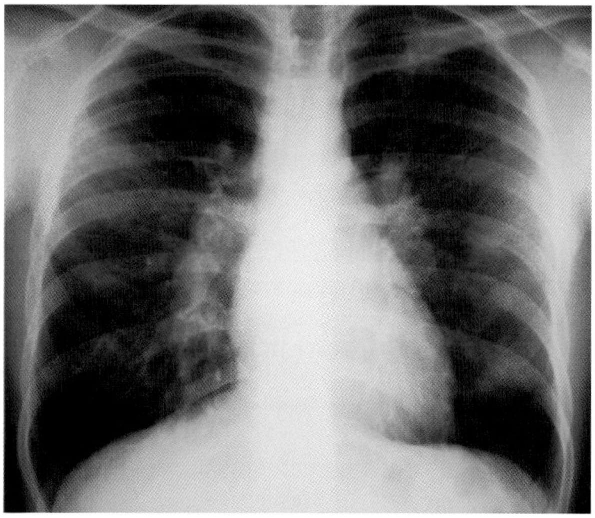

Chest x ray showing sarcoidosis in which inflammation occurs in the lymph nodes, lungs, liver, eyes, skin, and other tissues. *(Garo / Photo Researchers, Inc. Reproduced by permission.)*

During the nonactive phase, the inflammatory response decreases and the granulomas may shrink. Scars may remain and continue to cause symptoms.

The disease may resolve spontaneously within two to three years or there may be only an occasional flare-up of symptoms. In some people, the disease may get worse and cause permanent damage.

Demographics

Women ages 20-40 are more likely to develop sarcoidosis. Sarcoidosis occurs more often in people of African or Scandinavian descent (in particular Swedes and Danes). It occurs more often in nonsmokers than in smokers. In the United States certain groups have a higher percentage of cases of sarcoidosis including health care workers, naval aircraft servicemen, and firefighters.

African Americans have a four to seventeen time chance of developing sarcoidosis compared to Caucasians. Having a brother or sister or parent with sarcoidosis increases the risk of developing the disease five fold.

Causes and symptoms

The cause of sarcoidosis is unknown. It is theorized that sarcoidosis develops when the body's **immune system** responds abnormally to bacteria, **viruses**, dust, or chemicals in the environment. Sarcoidosis may also develop as a result of overactivity of the body's immune system (autoimmune response). There may also be a genetic predisposition to developing sarcoidosis.

Many people have no symptoms. Symptoms depend on which organs are affected. The most common symptoms include shortness of breath, persistent dry cough, wheezing, and reddish bumps or rashes on the skin. Eye symptoms may include vision problems and dry eyes. Other symptoms rarely occur but may include a generalized sick feeling (malaise), loss of appetite, **weight loss**, and fatigue. Blacks tend to have the more severe and chronic form of the disease.

Diagnosis

Evaluation to diagnose sarcoidosis begins with a complete medical history and physical examination. Diagnostic testing may include a chest x-ray, pulmonary function testing, tissue biopsy, an **eye examination**, the Serum Angiotensin Converting Enzyme (S. A.C.E.) blood test, computed axial tomography (C.A. T. scan), Gallium scanning, and **calcium** blood and urine level testing.

Chest x-ray is used to detect the presence of enlarged lymph nodes and granulomas. Pulmonary testing using a special instrument called a spirometer evaluates lung volumes and assesses the lungs' ability to exchange oxygen and carbon dioxide. Tissue biopsy is used to obtain tissue samples to confirm a diagnosis of sarcoidosis. Tissue samples are obtained during a **bronchoscopy** to examine for the presence of granulomas. Bronchoscopy is an outpatient procedure during which a specially trained physician inserts a narrow tube through the nose into the lungs. Bronchoalveolar lavage may also be done during bronchoscopy. During bronchoalveolar lavage, part of the lung is washed (lavaged) then the fluid is examined for cell inflammation characteristic of sarcoidosis. If the physician suspects that other parts of the body are affected by sarcoidosis, e.g. the skin, lymph nodes, or eyes, a tissue sample for biopsy may be taken from these areas.

Eye examination is conducted by an ophthalmologist to evaluate for inflammation or damage to the eyes from sarcoidosis. If the S.A.C.E. blood test result is elevated, it may indicate the presence of sarcoidosis. This blood test may be used at periodic intervals to determine if the disease is getting worse or improving. For some people with sarcoidosis, calcium levels are elevated in the blood and urine therefore, calcium blood and urine testing may be done.

C.A.T. scanning may reveal enlarged lymph nodes and lung scarring that a chest x-ray cannot. During Gallium scanning, a small amount of radioactive material is injected into the bloodstream. The radioactive material collects in inflamed areas of the body which can help to show sarcoidosis in the lungs and other organs.

Treatment

Treatment may be unnecessary if symptoms are mild. If treatment is needed it usually consists of corticosteroids to decrease inflammation. Prednisone is the corticosteroid used most often. The length of time medication is needed is dependent on how severe the disease is and how quickly the symptoms improve. Corticosteroids can reduce symptoms, improve lung function, decrease S.A.C.E. levels, decrease granuloma formation, and may reduce lung scarring.

Corticosteroids can cause serious side effects especially when taken for an extended period of time. These side effects include **osteoporosis** (a disease in which bones become thin and brittle), high **blood pressure**, **cataracts**, diabetes, increased risk of infection, and weight gain with redistribution of body fat. Benefits of using corticosteroids outweigh medication side effects.

Lung function testing and chest x-ray should be done every six to twelve months. An annual eye examination and electrocardiogram (E.C.G.) are recommended.

Nutrition/Dietetic concerns

Maintain a healthy weight. It is important to eat a balanced **diet** and drink adequate amounts of water daily. Foods high in calcium should be avoided. Foods high in calcium include dairy products, oranges, and canned salmon with bones.

Therapy

Don't smoke. Remain physically active without overexertion. Get adequate rest. Avoid exposure to chemicals, dust, toxic fumes, and other environmental lung irritants. Get recommended follow-up testing and regular medical care. Self-help groups are available for people diagnosed with sarcoidosis. Medication should be taken as prescribed.

Prognosis

Many people diagnosed with sarcoidosis do not require treatment and improve spontaneously. Those with advanced lung disease or heart or neurological involvement have a poorer prognosis.

Prevention

Because there is no definitive cause for sarcoidosis, there is no way to prevent it.

Caregiver concerns

Regular follow-up care is vital as new symptoms may occur unexpectedly and the disease may worsen

QUESTIONS TO ASK YOUR DOCTOR

- Will I need treatment?
- What are some of the treatments that may be recommended?
- How will I know if the treatments are working?
- Are there any side effects to the treatment?
- Do I need to see a specialist?

without notice. It is important to remember that sarcoidosis is not contagious.

Ensure that medication is taken as prescribed. Some medications used to treat sarcoidosis can have side effects so it is important to be aware of potential adverse effects. Report them to your health care provider as indicated.

June G. Borazjani R.N., M.S.N., C.P.H.Q.

Sarcomas

Definition

Most primary bone tumors are called sarcomas. A sarcoma is a bone tumor that contains **cancer** (malignant) cells. Sarcomas can also affect muscle, tendons, ligaments, and other tissues in the body. A benign bone tumor is an abnormal growth of noncancerous cells. Sometimes other cancer types (advanced **breast cancer**, **prostate cancer**, and **lung cancer**) will spread to the bone. This is known as metastatic bone cancer. Sometimes other types of cancers, such as **multiple myeloma** and some lymphomas and leukemias that start in the bone marrow, are referred to as "bone cancers". However, these types of cancers are not true bone cancers. The main or true type of primary bone cancer is sarcoma.

Description

A primary bone tumor originates in or near a bone. Most primary bone tumors are benign, and the cells that compose them do not spread (metastasize) to nearby tissue or to other parts of the body.

Malignant primary bone tumors can infiltrate nearby tissues, enter the bloodstream, and metastasize to bones, tissues, and organs far from the original malignancy.

Types of bone tumors

Osteogenic sarcoma, or osteosarcoma, is the most common form of bone cancer, accounts for 6% of all instances of the disease, and for about 5% of all cancers that occur in children. Nine hundred new cases of osteosarcoma are diagnosed in the United States every year. The disease usually affects teenagers, and is almost twice as common in boys as in girls. About 10% of cases of osteosarcoma occur in older adults in their 60s and 70s.

Osteosarcomas, which grow very rapidly, can develop in any bone but most often occur along the edge or on the end of one of the fast-growing long bones that support the arms and legs. About 80% of all osteosarcomas develop in the parts of the upper and lower leg nearest the knee (the distal femur or in the proximal tibia). The next likely location for an osteosarcoma is the bone of the upper arm closest to the shoulder (the proximal humerus).

Ewing's sarcoma is the second most common form of childhood bone cancer. Accounting for fewer than 5% of bone tumors in children, Ewing's sarcoma usually begins in the soft tissue (the marrow) inside bones of the leg, hips, ribs, and arms. It rapidly infiltrates the lungs, and may metastasize to bones in other parts of the body. Ewing's sarcoma is rare in adults over the age of 30.

Chondrosarcomas are cancerous bone tumors that is rarely diagnosed in individuals under the age of 20. The risk of developing this type of bone tumor continues to rise after age 20 until about age 75. It is the second most common type of true bone cancer. Usually originating in strong connective tissue (cartilage) in ribs or leg or hip bones, chondrosarcomas grow slowly. They rarely spread to the lungs. It takes years for a chondrosarcoma to metastasize to other parts of the body, and some of these tumors never spread.

Other types of cancerous bone tumors are fibrosarcomas and malignant fibrous histiocytomas, giant cell tumors of bone, and chordomas. Fibrosarcomas and malignant fibrous histiocytomas, which usually occur in older and middle-age adults, usually start in the soft tissues that surround the bone. The bones of the jaw, arms, and legs are most typically affected. Only about 10% of giant cell bone tumors are malignant tumors. These tumors are most common in young and middle-aged adults and most often appear in the arm or leg bones. Chordomas, which are usually diagnosed in adults over age 30, develop in the base of the skull and bones of the spine. Chordomas tend to grow slowly.

Demographics

Primary bone cancers are relatively rare in the United States and comprise only a very small percentage of all cancers diagnosed in this country

Causes and symptoms

The cause of bone cancer is unknown, but the tendency to develop it may be inherited. Children who have bone tumors are often tall for their age, and the disease seems to be associated with growth spurts that occur during childhood and adolescence. Injuries can make the presence of tumors more apparent but do not cause them.

A bone that has been broken or exposed to high doses of radiation used to treat other cancers is more likely than other bones to develop osteosarcoma. A history of noncancerous bone disease also increases bone-cancer risk.

The amount of radiation in diagnostic x rays poses little or no danger of bone-cancer development, but children who have a family history of the most common childhood cancer of the eye (retinoblastoma), or who have inherited rare cancer syndromes have a greater-than-average risk of developing bone cancer. Exposure to chemicals found in some paints and dyes can slightly raise the risk.

Both benign and malignant bone tumors can distort and weaken bone and cause **pain**, but benign tumors are generally painless and asymptomatic.

It is sometimes possible to feel a lump or mass, but pain in the affected area is the most common early symptom of bone cancer. Pain is not constant in the initial stages of the disease, but it is aggravated by activity and may be worse at night. If the tumor is located on a leg bone, the patient may limp. Swelling and weakness of the limb may not be noticed until weeks after the pain began.

Other symptoms of bone cancer include:

- a bone that breaks for no apparent reason
- difficulty moving the affected part of the body
- fatigue
- fever
- a lump on the trunk, an arm or leg, or another bone
- persistent, unexplained back pain
- weight loss

Diagnosis

Physical examination and routine x rays may yield enough evidence to diagnose benign bone tumors, but removal of tumor tissue for microscopic analysis (biopsy) is the only sure way to rule out malignancy.

A needle biopsy involves using a fine, thin needle to remove small bits of tumor, or a thick needle to extract tissue samples from the innermost part (the core) of the growth. A surgical bone biopsy may be performed to remove a small portion of a large tumor. The procedure may require **general anesthesia**

Bone cancer is usually diagnosed about three months after symptoms first appear, and 20% of malignant tumors have metastasized to the lungs or other parts of the body by that time.

Imaging techniques

The following procedures are used, in conjunction with biopsy, to diagnose bone cancer:

- Bone x rays. These x rays usually provide a clear image of osteosarcomas.
- Computerized axial tomography (CAT scan) is a specialized x ray that uses a rotating beam to obtain detailed information about an abnormality and its physical relationship to other parts of the body. A CAT scan can differentiate between osteosarcomas and other types of bone tumors, illustrate how tumor cells have infiltrated other tissues, and help surgeons decide which portion of a growth would be best to biopsy. Because more than four of every five malignant bone tumors metastasize to the lungs, a CAT scan of the chest is performed to see if these organs have been affected. Chest and abdominal CAT scans are used to determine whether Ewing's sarcoma has spread to the lungs, liver, or lymph nodes.
- Magnetic resonance imaging (MRI) is a specialized scan that relies on radio waves and powerful magnets to reflect energy patterns created by tissue abnormalities and specific diseases. An MRI provides more detailed information than does a CAT scan about tumors and marrow cavities of the bone, and can sometimes detect clusters of cancerous cells that have separated from the original tumor. This valuable information helps surgeons select the most appropriate approach for treatment.
- Radionuclide bone scans. These scans involve injecting a small amount of radioactive material into a vein. Primary tumors or cells that have

metastasized absorb the radioactive material and show up as dark spots on the scan.

Cytogenic and molecular genetic studies, which assess the structure and composition of chromosomes and genes, may also be used to diagnose osteosarcoma. These tests can sometimes indicate what form of treatment is most appropriate.

Laboratory studies

A **complete blood count** (CBC) reveals abnormalities in the blood, and may indicate whether bone marrow has been affected. A blood test that measures levels of the enzyme lactate dehydrogenase (LDH) can predict the likelihood of a specific patient's survival.

Immunohistochemistry involves adding special antibodies and chemicals, or stains, to tumor samples. This technique is effective in identifying cells that are found in Ewing's sarcoma but are not present in other malignant tumors.

Reverse transcription polymerase chain reaction (RTPCR) relies on chemical analysis of the substance in the body that transmits genetic information (RNA) to:

- evaluate the effectiveness of cancer therapies
- identify mutations consistent with the presence of Ewing's sarcoma
- reveal cancer that recurs after treatment has been completed

Staging

Once bone cancer has been diagnosed, the tumor is staged. This process indicates how far the tumor has spread from its original location. The stage of a tumor suggests which form of treatment is most appropriate, and predicts how the condition will probably respond to therapy.

An osteosarcoma may be localized or metastatic. A localized osteosarcoma has not spread beyond the bone where it arose or beyond nearby muscles, tendons, and other tissues. A metastatic osteosarcoma has spread to the lungs, to bones not directly connected to the bone in which the tumor originated, or to other tissues or organs.

Treatment

Since the 1960s, when **amputation** was the only treatment for bone cancer, new **chemotherapy** drugs and innovative surgical techniques have improved survival with intact limbs. Because osteosarcoma is so rare, patients should consider undergoing treatment at a major cancer center staffed by specialists familiar with the disease.

A treatment plan for bone cancer, developed after the tumor has been diagnosed and staged, may include surgery, chemotherapy, and/or radiation therapy. Chemotherapy is usually administered in addition to surgery to kill cancer cells that have separated from the original tumor and spread to other parts of the body.

Surgery, coordinated with diagnostic biopsy, enhances the probability that limb-salvage surgery can be used to remove the cancer while preserving nearby blood vessels and bones. A metal rod or bone graft is used to replace the area of bone removed, and subsequent surgery may be needed to repair or replace rods that have loosened or broken. Patients who have undergone limb-salvage surgery need intensive rehabilitation. It may take as long as a year for a patient to regain full use of a leg following limb-salvage surgery, and patients who have this operation may eventually have to undergo amputation

Radiation therapy is used often to treat Ewing's sarcoma.

Rotationoplasty, sometimes performed after a leg amputation, involves attaching the lower leg and foot to the thigh bone, so that the ankle replaces the knee. A prosthetic is later added to make the leg as long as it should be. Prosthetic devices are not used to lengthen limbs that remain functional after amputation to remove osteosarcomas located on the upper arm. When an osteosarcoma develops in the jaw bone, the entire lower jaw is removed. Bones from other parts of the body are later grafted on remaining bone to create a new jaw.

Follow-up treatments

After a patient completes the final course of chemotherapy, CAT scans, bone scans, x rays, and other diagnostic tests may be repeated to determine if any traces of tumor remain. If none are found, treatment is discontinued, but patients are advised to see their oncologist and orthopedic surgeon every two or three months for the next year. X rays of the chest and affected bone are taken every four months. An annual **echocardiogram** is recommended to evaluate any adverse effect chemotherapy may have had on the heart, and **CT scans** are performed every six months.

Patients who have received treatment for Ewing's sarcoma are examined often - at gradually lengthening intervals - after completing therapy. Accurate growth measurements are taken during each visit and blood is drawn to be tested for side effects of treatment. X rays, CT scans, bone scans, and other imaging studies are generally performed every three months during the first year. If no evidence of tumor growth or recurrence is indicated, these tests are performed less frequently in the following years.

Some benign bone tumors shrink or disappear without treatment. However, regular examinations are recommended to determine whether these tumors have changed in any way.

Alternative treatment

Alternative treatments should never be substituted for conventional bone-cancer treatments or used without the approval of a physician. However, some alternative treatments can be used as adjunctive and supportive therapies during and following conventional treatments.

Nutrition/dietetic concerns

Dietary adjustments can be very helpful for patients with cancer. Whole foods, including grains, beans, fresh fruits and vegetables, and high quality fats, should be emphasized in the **diet**, while processed foods should be avoided. Increased consumption of fish, especially cold water fish like salmon, mackerel, halibut, and tuna, provides a good source of omega-3 fatty acids. **Nutritional supplements** can build strength and help maintain it during and following chemotherapy, radiation, or surgery. These supplements should be individually prescribed by an alternative practitioner who has experience working with cancer patients.

Prognosis

Some types of primary bone cancers can reappear after treatment was believed to have eliminated the cancer.

Likelihood of long-term survival depends on:

- the type and location of the tumor
- how much the tumor has metastasized, and on what organs, bones, or tissues have been affected

More than 85% of patients survive for more than five years after complete surgical removal of low-grade osteosarcomas (tumors that arise in mature tissue and contain a small number of cancerous cells). About 25-30% of patients diagnosed with high-grade osteosarcomas (tumors that develop in immature tissue and contain a large number of cancer cells) will die of the disease.

QUESTIONS TO ASK YOUR DOCTOR

- Is my bone cancer a primary bone cancer or a metastatic bone cancer?
- What type of diagnostic tests will I be required to undergo?
- How will my cancer be treated?
- Does my type of bone cancer usually require amputation?
- Will I have to undergo chemotherapy and/or radiation therapy treatments?

Prevention

There is no known way to prevent bone cancer.

Resources

ORGANIZATIONS

American Cancer Society. 1599 Clifton Rd., NE, Atlanta, GA 30329-4251. (800) 227-2345. http://www.cancer.org.

CancerCare, Inc. 1180 Avenue of the Americas, New York, NY 10036. (800) 813-4673. http://www.cancercare.org.

National Cancer Institute. Building 31, Room 10A31, 31 Center Drive, MSC 2580, Bethesda, MD 20892-2580. (800) 422-6237. http://www.nci.nih.gov.

Maureen Haggerty
Melinda Oberleitner R.N., D.N.S.

Saw palmetto

Definition

Saw palmetto is an extract derived from the deep purple berries of the saw palmetto fan palm (*Serenoa repens*), a plant indigenous to the coastal regions of the southern United States and southern California. There is an estimated one million acres of wild saw palmetto palms in Florida, where the bulk of commercial saw palmetto is grown.

Description

Saw palmetto is used by natural health practitioners to treat a variety of ailments in men and

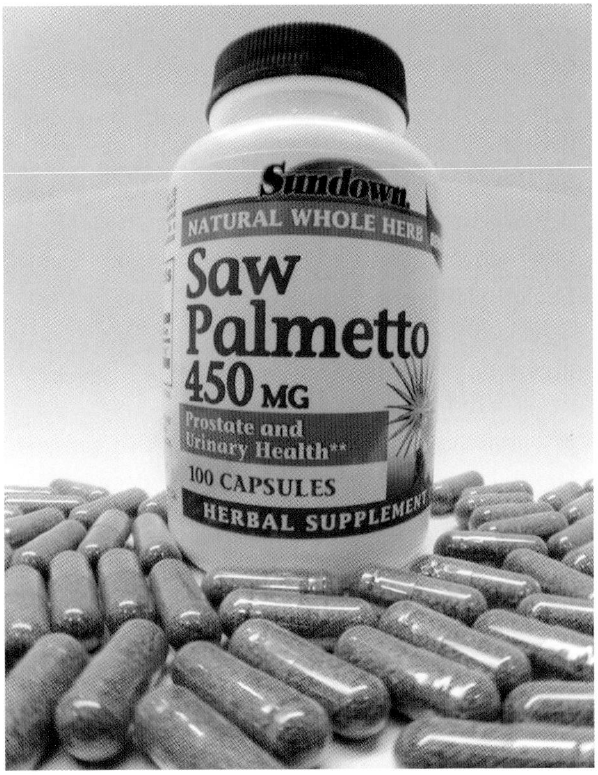

A bottle and pills of the plant extract, saw palmetto used to treat an enlarged prostate. *(AP Images. Reproduced by permission.)*

women, such as testicular inflammation, urinary tract inflammation, coughs, and respiratory congestion. It is also used to strengthen the thyroid gland, balance the metabolism, stimulate appetite, and aid digestion. Most of the evidence supporting these uses is anecdotal and has not been proven by controlled clinical trials. However, there is much scientific documentation outlining the effectiveness of the herb in treating irritable bladder and urinary problems in men with benign prostate hyperplasia (BPH), an enlargement of the prostate gland. BPH results in a swelling of the prostate gland that obstructs the urethra. This causes painful urination, reduced urine flow, difficulty starting or stopping the flow, dribbling after urination, and more frequent nighttime urination. Saw palmetto does not reduce **prostate enlargement**. Instead, it is thought to work in a variety of ways. First, it inhibits the conversion of testosterone into dihydrotestosterone (DHT). BPH is thought to be caused by an increase in testosterone to DHT. Second, saw palmetto is believed to interfere with the production of estrogen and progesterone, hormones associated with DHT production.

In addition to causing **pain** and embarrassment, BPH can lead to serious kidney problems if undiagnosed and left untreated. It is a common problem in men over the age of 40. Estimates are that 50 to 60% of all men develop BPH in their lifetimes. The Agency for Health Care Policy and Research estimates there are six million men between the ages of 50 and 79 who have BPH serious enough to require some type of therapy. Yet only half of them seek treatment from physicians. Health practitioners in both the allopathic and natural medicine communities recommend annual prostate exams for men over the age of 50 and an annual blood test that measures prostate specific antigen, a marker for **prostate cancer**.

In 2006, researchers in San Francisco reported that a year-long study of saw palmetto to treat BPH showed it was no more effective than a placebo in controlling symptoms. The study of 225 men taking 160 mg of saw palmetto twice a day concluded that there clearly was no benefit of using saw palmetto to treat BPH. The researchers said that previous studies that showed saw palmetto effective in treating BPH involved a small number of participants and had a short duration. However, researchers said their study was not conclusive and urged further research. They also noted that other health practitioners believe a higher dose of saw palmetto is needed for it to be effective.

Saw palmetto berries have been used in American folk medicine for several hundred years as an aphrodisiac and for treating prostate problems. Native Americans in the southeast United States have used saw palmetto since the 1700s to treat male urinary problems. In the 1800s, medical botanist John Lloyd (1854–1945) noted that animals that ate saw palmetto appeared healthier and fatter than other livestock. Early American settlers noticed the same effects and used the juice from saw palmetto berries to gain weight, to improve general disposition, as a sedative, and to promote reproductive health. A pungent tea made from saw palmetto berries was commonly used in the early 1900s to treat prostate enlargement and urinary tract infections. It was also used in men to increase sperm production and sex drive, although these uses are discounted in the late 2000s. One of the first published medical recommendations that saw palmetto was effective in treating prostate problems appeared in the 1926 edition of *United States Dispensatory*. In the late 1920s, the use of medicinal plants, including saw palmetto, began to decline in the United States, while at the same time, it was on the rise in Europe.

Uses in women

There is very little documentation or scientific research into saw palmetto use in women. However, several studies in the 1990s show that the BPH drug

QUESTIONS TO ASK YOUR PHARMACIST

- Have you recommended saw palmetto for prostate enlargement in other patients?
- If so, what were the results?
- Will saw palmetto interact with any current medications I'm taking?
- Do you recommend a particular brand and/or dosage. If so, why?

Proscar can be effective in stopping unwanted facial and body hair growth and in treating thinning hair in women. It works by blocking the action of an enzyme called 5-alpha reductase. Anecdotal reports suggest that saw palmetto may be as effective as Proscar in treating unwanted hair growth and thinning hair and in preventing some types of acne. It has also been used to treat urinary tract inflammation and help relieve the symptoms of menstruation. There are claims it can be used to enlarge breasts, but these claims have not been scientifically tested.

Recommended dosage

People taking saw palmetto should use only standardized extracts that contain 85 to 95% fatty acids and sterols. Dosages vary depending on the type of saw palmetto used. A typical dose is 320 mg per day of standardized extract or 1 to 2 g per day of ground, dried, whole berries. It may take up to four weeks of use before beneficial effects are seen.

Precautions

There are no special precautions associated with taking saw palmetto, even in high doses. However, BPH can become a serious problem if left untreated. Men who are experiencing symptoms should be examined by a physician, since the symptoms of BPH are similar to those of prostate **cancer**. Men over the age of 50 should have a yearly prostate exam. Saw palmetto should only be used under a doctor's supervision by people with prostate cancer, **breast cancer**, or any sex hormone related diseases. Women taking estrogen replacement products should consult a physician before taking saw palmetto. Persons taking testosterone or other anabolic steroids should not take saw palmetto without first consulting their doctor.

In rare cases, allergic reactions to saw palmetto have been reported. Symptoms include difficulty breathing, constricting of the throat, hives, and swelling of the lips, tongue, or face. Persons experiencing any of these symptoms should stop taking saw palmetto and seek immediate medical attention.

KEY TERMS

Anabolic steroids—A group of mostly synthetic hormones sometimes taken by athletes to temporarily increase muscle size.

Aphrodisiac—Any substance that excites sexual desire.

Benign prostate hyperplasia (BPH)—Enlargement of the prostate gland.

Estrogen—A hormone that stimulates development of female secondary sex characteristics.

Placebo—An inert or innocuous substance used in controlled experiments testing the efficacy of another substance.

Progesterone—A steroid hormone that is a biological precursor to corticoid (another steroid hormone) and androgen (a male sex hormone).

Testosterone—A male hormone produced in the testes or made synthetically that is responsible for male secondary sex characteristics.

Urethra—The tube that carries urine from the bladder out of the body and in males also carries semen.

Side effects

The only reported minor side effects are rare and include cramps, nausea, **diarrhea**, and headache.

Interactions

Saw palmetto may interfere with hormone-related drugs such as testosterone and estrogen replacements, including Premarin, Cenestin, Vivelle, Fempatch, and Climara. Individuals on these types of medications should consult with their doctor before taking saw palmetto. There are no known restrictions on food, beverages, or physical activity while taking saw palmetto. Some factors that can impair the effectiveness of saw palmetto include beer, cigarette smoke, and some chemical pesticides used on fruit and vegetables. Some physicians recommend using saw palmetto in addition to a prescription medicine for BPH, such as Proscar, Hytrin, or Cardura.

Caregiver concerns

Since saw palmetto is generally considered safe, there is no reason for caregivers to be concerned about its use. They should be aware that saw palmetto can interfere with certain hormone-related drugs, such as testosterone and estrogen replacements.

Resources

PERIODICALS

Altshul, Sara. "Soothe His Prostate Problems." *Prevention* (January 2006): 80.

Bent, S., et al. "Saw Palmetto for Benign Prostatic Hyperplasia." *New England Journal of Medicine* (February 9, 2006): 557–566.

Cooperman, Ted. "Saw Palmetto for Benign Prostatic Hyperplasia." *Townsend Letter: The Examiner of Alternative Medicine* (June 2006): 94.

Ebell, Mark. "Saw Palmetto Ineffective for Prostate Patients." *American Family Physician* (June 1, 2006): 2023.

Helmer, Jodi. "Saw Palmetto: Find Out How This Dwarf Plant May Help Stop Prostate Enlargement." *Better Nutrition* (June 2006): 12.

Sego, Sherril. "Saw Palmetto." *Clinical Advisor* (May 2006): 113.

ORGANIZATIONS

American Association of Clinical Urologists, 1100 E. Woodfield Rd., Suite 520, Schaumburg, IL, 60173, (847) 517-1050, (847) 517-7229, info@aacuweb.org, http://www.aacuweb.org.

American Prostate Society, PO Box 870, Hanover, MD, 21076, (410) 859-3735, (410) 850-0818, ameripros@mindspring.com, http://www.americanprostatesociety.com.

American Urological Association, 1000 Corporate Blvd., Suite 410, Linthicum, MD, 21090, (410) 689-3700, (866) 746-4282, (410) 689-3800, aua@auanet.org, http://www.auanet.org.

Canadian Urological Association, 1155 University, Suite 1155, Montreal, QC, Canada, H3B 3A7, (514) 395-0376, (514) 875-0205, central.office@cua.org, http://www.cua.org.

National Kidney and Urologic Diseases Information Clearinghouse, 3 Information Way, Bethesda, MD, 20892-3580, (800) 891-5390, (703) 738-4929, nkudic@info.niddk.nih.gov, http://www.kidney.niddk.nih.gov.

Urological Society of Australia and New Zealand, 180 Ocean St., Suite 512 Eastpoint, Edgecliff, NSW, Australia, 2027, (61) 2 9362-8644, (61) 2 9362-1433, secretary@usanz.org.au, http://www.usanz.org.au.

Ken R. Wells

Scabies

Definition

Scabies is a relatively contagious infection caused by a tiny mite(*Sarcoptes scabiei*).

Description

Scabies is caused by a tiny insect about 0.3 mm long called a mite. When a human comes in contact with the female mite, the mite burrows under the skin, laying eggs along the line of its burrow. These eggs hatch, and the resulting offspring rise to the surface of the skin, mate, and repeat the cycle either within the skin of the original host, or within the skin of its next victim.

The intense **itching** almost always caused by scabies is due to a reaction within the skin to the feces of the mite. The first time someone is infected with scabies, he or she may not notice any itching for a number of weeks (four to six weeks). With subsequent infections, the itchiness will begin within hours of picking up the first mite.

Causes and symptoms

Scabies is most common among people who live in overcrowded conditions, and whose ability to practice good hygiene is limited. Scabies can be passed between people by close skin contact. Although the mites can only live away from human skin for about three days, sharing clothing or bedclothes can pass scabies among family members or close contacts. In May 2002, the Centers for Disease Control (CDC) included scabies in its updated guidelines for the treatment of **sexually transmitted diseases**.

The itching, or pruritus, from scabies is worse after a hot shower and at night. Burrows are seen as winding, slightly raised gray lines along the skin. The female mite may be seen at one end of the burrow, as a tiny pearl-like bump underneath the skin. Because of the intense itching, burrows may be obscured by scratch marks left by the patient. The most common locations for burrows include the sides of the fingers, between the fingers, the top of the wrists, around the elbows and armpits, around the nipples of the breasts in women, in the genitalia of men, around the waist (beltline), and on the lower part of the buttocks. Babies may have burrows on the soles of their feet, palms of their hands, and faces.

Scratching seems to serve some purpose in scabies, as the mites are apparently often inadvertently removed. Most infestations with scabies are caused by no more than 15 mites altogether.

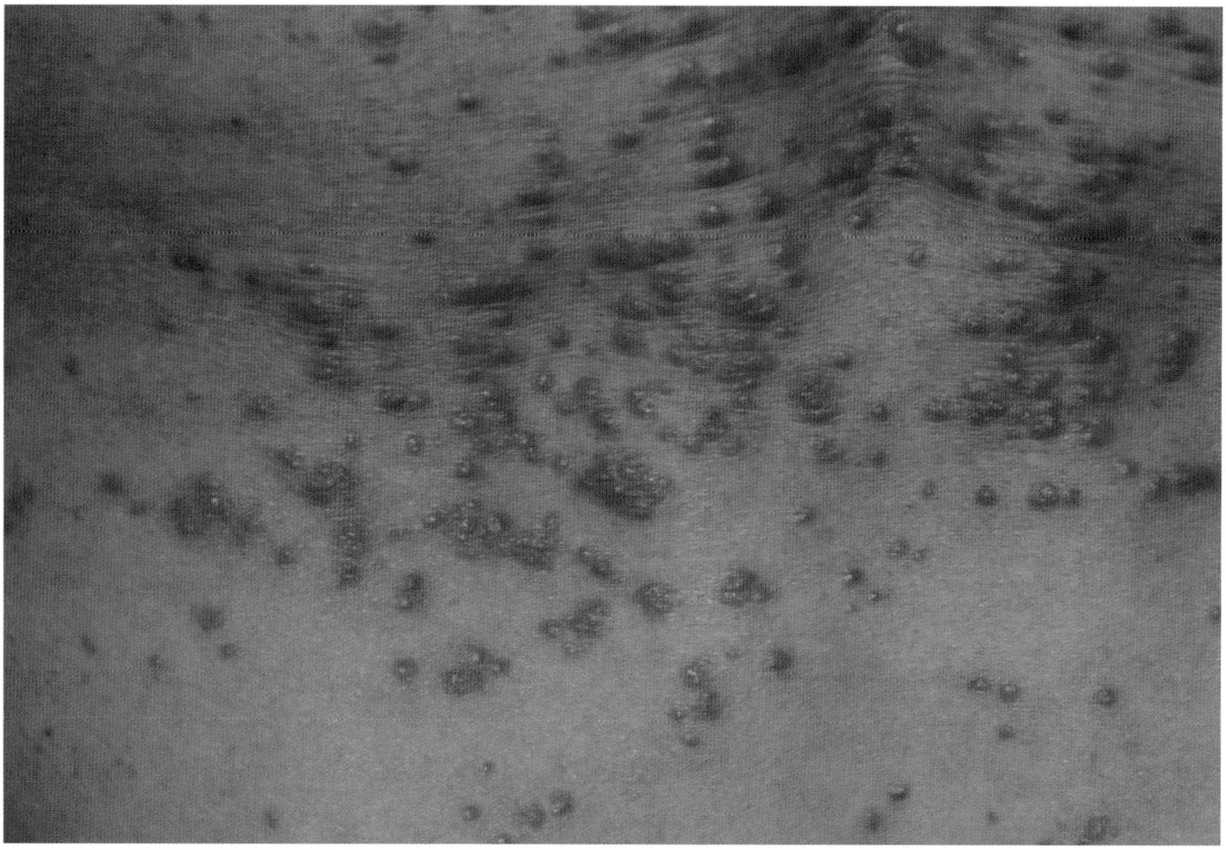

Red papules (lumps) on the skin due to scabies. *(Dr. P Marazzi/Photo Researchers, Inc. Reproduced by permission.)*

Infestation with huge numbers of mites (on the order of thousands to millions) occurs when an individual does not scratch, or when an individual has a weakened **immune system**. These patients include those who live in institutions; are mentally retarded, or physically infirm; have other diseases which affect the amount of sensation they have in their skin (leprosy or syringomyelia); have leukemia or diabetes; are taking medications which lower their immune response (cancerchemotherapy, drugs given after organ transplantation); or have other diseases which lower their immune response (such as acquired immunodeficiency syndrome or **AIDS**). This form of scabies, with its major infestation, is referred to as crusted scabies or Norwegian scabies. Infected patients have thickened, crusty areas all over their bodies, including over the scalp. Their skin is scaly. Their fingernails may be thickened and horny.

Diagnosis

Diagnosis can be made simply by observing the characteristic burrows of the mites causing scabies. A sterilized needle can be used to explore the pearly bump at the end of a burrow, remove its contents, and place it on a slide to be examined. The mite itself may then be identified under a microscope.

Occasionally, a type of mite carried on dogs (*Sarcoptes scabiei var. canis*) may infect humans. These mites cannot survive for very long on humans, and so the infection is very light.

Treatment

Several types of lotions (usually containing 5% permethrin) can be applied to the body, and left on for 12–24 hours. One topical application is usually sufficient, although the scabicide may be reapplied after a week if mites remain. Preparations containing lindane are no longer recommended for treating scabies as of 2003 because of the potential for damage to the nervous system. Itching can be lessened by the use of calamine lotion or antihistamine medications.

In addition to topical medications, the doctor may prescribe oral ivermectin. Ivermectin is a drug that was originally developed for veterinary practice as a broad-spectrum antiparasite agent. Studies done

KEY TERMS

Mite—An insect parasite belonging to the order Acarina. The organism that causes scabies is a mite.

Pruritus—An unpleasant itching sensation. Scabies is characterized by intense pruritus.

Topical—A type of medication applied to the skin or body surface.

in humans, however, have found that ivermectin is as safe and effective as topical medications for treating scabies. A study published in 2003 reported that ivermectin is safe for people in high-risk categories, including those with compromised immune systems.

Prognosis

The prognosis for complete recovery from scabies infestation is excellent. In patients with weak immune systems, the biggest danger is that the areas of skin involved with scabies will become secondarily infected with bacteria.

Prevention

Good hygiene is essential in the prevention of scabies. When a member of a household is diagnosed with scabies, all that person's recently-worn clothing and bedding should be washed in very hot water.

Resources

BOOKS

Beers, Mark H., MD, and Robert Berkow, MD., editors. "Scabies (The Itch)." Section 10, Chapter 114 In *The Merck Manual of Diagnosis and Therapy.* Whitehouse Station, NJ: Merck Research Laboratories, 2004.

PERIODICALS

Burroughs, R. F., and D. M. Elston. "What's Eating You? Canine Scabies." *Cutis* 72 (August 2003): 107–109.

Burstein, G. R., and K. A. Workowski. "Sexually Transmitted Diseases Treatment Guidelines." *Current Opinion in Pediatrics* 15 (August 2003): 391–397.

Fawcett, R. S. "Ivermectin Use in Scabies." *American Family Physician* 68 (September 15, 2003): 1089–1092.

Santoro, A. F., M. A. Rezac, and J. B. Lee. "Current Trend in Ivermectin Usage for Scabies." *Journal of Drugs in Dermatology* 2 (August 2003): 397–401.

ORGANIZATIONS

American Academy of Dermatology (AAD). 930 East Woodfield Road, Schaumburg, IL 60173. (847) 330-0230. http://www.aad.org.

Rosalyn Carson-DeWitt MD
Rebecca J. Frey Ph.D.

Sciatica

Definition

Sciatica refers to **pain** or discomfort associated with the sciatic nerve. This nerve runs from the lower part of the spinal cord, down the back of the leg, to the foot. Injury to or pressure on the sciatic nerve can cause the characteristic pain of sciatica: a sharp or burning pain that radiates from the lower back or hip, possibly following the path of the sciatic nerve to the foot.

Description

The sciatic nerve is the largest and longest nerve in the body. About the thickness of a person's thumb, it spans from the lower back to the foot. The nerve originates in the lower part of the spinal cord, the so-called lumbar region. As it branches off from the spinal cord, it passes between the bony vertebrae (the component bones of the spine) and runs through the pelvic girdle, or hip bones. The nerve passes through the hip joint and continues down the back of the leg to the foot.

Sciatica is a fairly common disorder and approximately 40% of the population experiences it at some point in their lives. However, only about 1% have coexisting sensory or motor deficits. Sciatic pain has several root causes and treatment may hinge upon the underlying problem.

Of the identifiable causes of sciatic pain, lumbosacral radiculopathy and back strain are the most frequently suspected. The term lumbosacral refers to the lower part of the spine, and radiculopathy describes a problem with the spinal nerve roots that pass between the vertebrae and give rise to the sciatic nerve. This area between the vertebrae is cushioned with a disk of shock- absorbing tissue. If this disk shifts or is damaged through injury or disease, the spinal nerve root may be compressed by the shifted tissue or the vertebrae.

This compression of the nerve roots sends a pain signal to the brain. Although the actual injury is to the

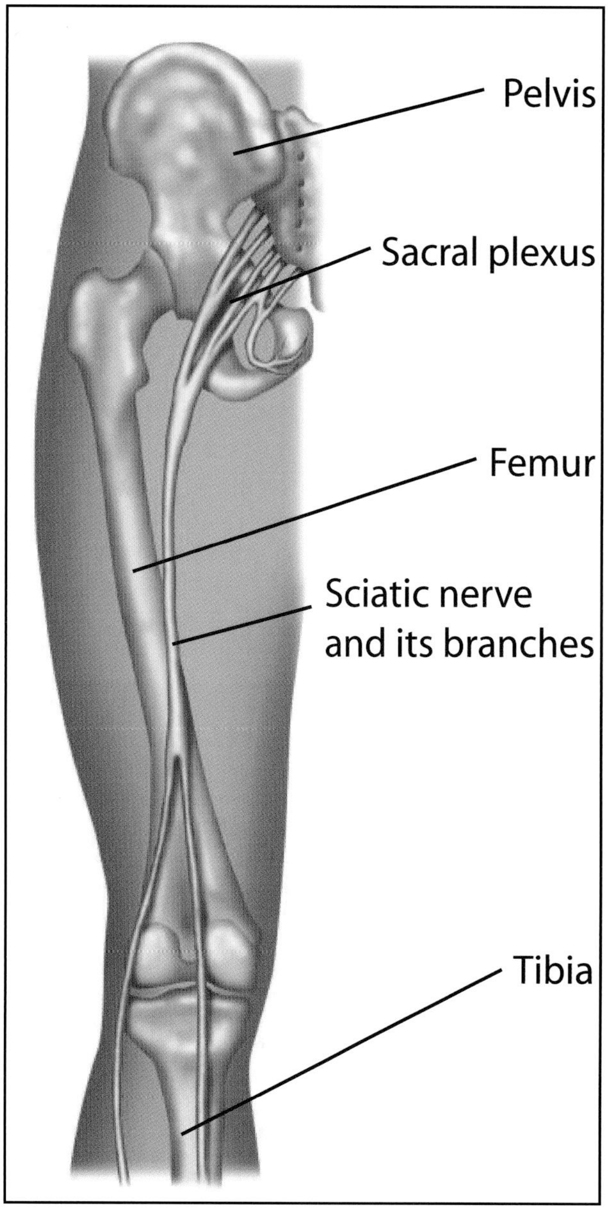

Illustration of a human leg with pointers to the sciatic nerve. *(Cengage learning, Gale.)*

nerve roots, the pain may be perceived as coming from anywhere along the sciatic nerve.

The sciatic nerve can be compressed in other ways. Back strain may cause muscle spasms in the lower back, placing pressure on the sciatic nerve. In rare cases, infection, **cancer**, bone inflammation, or other diseases may be causing the pressure. More likely, but often overlooked, is the piriformis syndrome. As the sciatic nerve passes through the hip joint, it shares the space with several muscles. One of these muscles, the piriformis muscle, is closely associated with the sciatic nerve. In some people, the nerve actually runs through the muscle. If this muscle is injured or has a spasm, it places pressure on the sciatic nerve, in effect, compressing it.

In many sciatica cases, the specific cause is never identified. About half of affected individuals recover from an episode within a month. Some cases can linger a few weeks longer and may require aggressive treatment. In some cases, the pain may return or potentially become chronic.

Demographics

A common disorder, sciatica affects about 40 percent of the population. It is found more frequently in people 30 to 50 years old, but occurs often in the elderly due to degenerative spinal disorders. Most often, sciatica is seen as a result of general wear and tear on the lower lumbosacral spine.

Causes and symptoms

Causes

The most common cause of sciatic pain is pressure on the nerves in the lumbosacral spine. Injury to the pelvis or other trauma can cause sciatica. However, it is most often a disc (a pad of shock-absorbing tissue between each vertebra) that bulges or is herniated, usually near the L4 or L5, and presses on the sciatic nerve and causes pain, numbness, or tingling. This is often called a slipped disc. Degenerative disc disease, a condition where the discs begin to break down or crumble, can irritate the nerves, too. Sometimes, a disc may rupture, causing a jelly-like substance to seep out and press on the sciatic nerve. A bulging disc can form slowly over time. A ruptured disc may be caused by an injury, bone spurs growing from the spine, or aging.

Spondylolisthesis, a condition when one vertebra slips forward over another, can press against the sciatic nerve. This action is similar to a slipped disc, except here it is a vertebra that has moved. Spondylolisthesis is the result of degenerative disc disease.

Back strain can cause the muscles in the lower back to spasm and swell. This can also put pressure against the sciatic nerve.

Some medical disorders can also cause sciatic pain. Lumbar **spinal stenosis**, a narrowing of the spinal canal, is found in adults over 60 years old. This condition can put pressure on the sciatic nerve. Other diseases that can cause sciatica are spinal arthritis, diabetes, and cancer.

Pregnancy can also cause sciatic pain. The growing fetus can shift internal structures so that pressure is placed on the sciatic nerve.

Other conditions such as sacroiliac joint dysfunction or piriformis syndrome can mimic sciatica symptoms, but are not actually sciatica. An irritation of the sacroiliac joint can irritate the nerve at L5 and can cause sciatic-like pain. Piriformis syndrome is a spasm of the piriformis muscle that is located near the sciatic nerve. In some cases, the sciatic nerve runs through the muscle itself. If the piriformis muscle is injured or spasms, it can press against the sciatic nerve. Runners, race walkers, and people who sit for long periods can experience piriformis syndrome.

In a number of cases, no specific cause for the sciatic pain or numbness is discovered.

Symptoms

Pain is the most pronounced symptom of sciatica. It is often accompanied by numbness or a burning or tingling sensation. Often, the pain is felt even during sitting, but may be more pronounced when attempting to stand. Some patients feel pain increase when they walk any distance.

Where that pain is felt, however, is largely a factor of where the sciatic nerve is compressed. Each region affects different parts of the lower extremities and produces characteristic symptoms.

If the nerve is affected in the region of L3-L4, the patient will have pain and/or numbness in the lower leg and foot and can have problems trying to walk on the heel of the foot. The patient may also have reduced knee-jerk reflex.

A sciatic nerve compression near L4-L5 results in pain and/or numbness in the top of the foot, especially near the area between the big toe and the second toe. The patient may present with weakness in the ankle that causes the foot to drop or drag.

Patients who have sciatic compression near L5-S1 experience pain and/or numbness in the outside regions of the foot. The patient has reduced ankle-jerk reflex and has trouble walking on tip toe.

Pressure on the sacral nerves from sacroiliac joint dysfunction produces a deep ache inside the leg, rather than pain in a specific area as in true sciatica. Piriformis syndrome causes pain or numbness most commonly in the buttocks and can radiate downward, mimicking true sciatica.

Diagnosis

Before treating sciatic pain, as much information as possible is collected. The individual is asked to recount the location and nature of the pain, how long it has continued, and any accidents or unusual activities prior to its onset. This information provides clues that may point to back strain or injury to a specific location. Back pain from disk disease, piriformis syndrome, and back strain must be differentiated from more serious conditions such as cancer or infection. Lumbar stenosis, an overgrowth of the covering layers of the vertebrae that narrows the spinal canal, must also be considered. The possibility that a difference in leg lengths is causing the pain should be evaluated; the problem can be easily be treated with a foot orthotic or built-up shoe.

Often, a straight-leg-raising test is done, in which the person lies face upward and the health-care provider raises the affected leg to various heights. This test pinpoints the location of the pain and may reveal whether it is caused by a disk problem. Other tests, such as having the individual rotate the hip joint, assess the hip muscles. Any pain caused by these movements may provide information about involvement of the piriformis muscle, and piriformis weakness is tested with additional leg-strength maneuvers.

Further tests may be done depending on the results of the physical examination and initial pain treatment. Such tests might include **magnetic resonance imaging** (MRI) and computed tomography scans (**CT scans**). Other tests examine the conduction of electricity through nerve tissues, and include studies of the electrical activity generated as muscles contract (electromyography), nerve conduction velocity, and evoked potential testing. A more invasive test involves injecting a contrast substance into the space between the vertebrae and making x-ray images of the spinal cord (myelography), but this procedure is usually done only if surgery is being considered. All of these tests can reveal problems with the vertebrae, the disk, or the nerve itself.

Treatment

Returning the patient to mobility and **independence** is the goal of treatment. Since pain must be managed before further options are considered, the doctor will prescribe over-the-counter NSAIDS (**nonsteroidal anti-inflammatory drugs**) such as naproxen and ibuprofen. Oral steroids may also be prescribed for herniated discs. **Muscle relaxants** may be prescribed, especially for piriformis syndrome.

If a patient is in severe pain, the doctor may inject steroids directly into the area around the sciatic nerve. This decreases inflammation and offers temporary pain relief. Some patients experience relief for up to a year; others are pain-free for a week. Though this procedure does not work for everyone, it can be necessary relief for the patient to be able to complete the physical therapy necessary for recovery.

Bed rest is discouraged, though the doctor may recommend frequent rest periods when the patient can apply heat to the lower back to treat the inflammation of sciatica. Moist heat is the most effective.

The doctor may also begin to treat any underlying condition that may have caused or contributed to the bout of sciatica. Depending on the cause, specific treatment may be postponed until the current sciatic episode has passed.

Once the pain is under control, the doctor often will refer the patient to a **physical therapist** for a regime of **exercise** and education specific to the patient's type of sciatica. Ultrasound, transcutaneous electrical stimulation (TENs), **biofeedback**, and deep tissue massage may also be ordered by the physical therapist.

Braces, splints, or orthopedic shoes may help some patients accommodate for lost impairment. However, these are not permanent solutions. They may help a patient continue to work or go about daily activities until they can strengthen the muscles necessary to support the back.

Occupational therapy may also be helpful to educate patients about proper body alignment when doing daily tasks or work requirements. Other behavioral education may be necessary.

Surgery is only used in extreme cases when the sciatic nerve creates significant weakness or loss of bladder or bowels. However, surgery (diskectomy) is often used to remove part of a herniated disc. This procedure can be done with a microscope (microdisketomy). Surgery for degenerative disc disease does not stop the progression of this disease; it merely relieves the immediate problem. A study in 2007 reported that though disc surgery patients may receive immediate relief, they had similar positive outcomes a year later as those of patients who chose conservative treatment over surgery.

Alternative treatments

The doctor may also recommend alternative treatments to help a patient either manage the pain or treat the underlying cause.

Acupuncture is the Eastern practice of balancing the body's natural energies by inserting thin sterilized needles into specific parts of the body. The procedure is relatively painless, and many patients experience peaceful **relaxation** during the process. The National Institutes of Health has noted that acupuncture is effective in relieving the pain of sciatica and other back discomfort.

Though massage cannot help remove the pressure of a disc against the sciatic nerve, it can relax tense muscles in the lower back and buttocks and stimulate blood flow. This is especially helpful for patients suffering from piriformis syndrome. Massage also is relaxing and can help release endorphins, the body's natural pain relievers.

Chiropractic manipulations can help align the spine. They may be helpful for some disc problems.

Further, **yoga** has been found to be useful for keeping the muscles stretched and the spine flexible. However, care may need to be taken regarding some postures that put stress on the lower back. Those include any type of sitting cross legged or extreme stretches of the spine.

QUESTIONS TO ASK YOUR DOCTOR

What is the cause of my sciatica pain?
What can be done to treat that condition?
What tests will I have to take?
How long will I need to take pain medication?
What can I expect from the physical therapist?
What alternative treatments do you recommend?
What home care do you suggest?
How long before I can go back to my regular activities?
Will I have to have surgery?

Nutrition/Dietetic concerns

There are no dietetic concerns regarding sciatica.

Therapy

Physical therapy is essential to successful recovery from sciatica. Inactivity, especially bed rest, has been found to make sciatic pain worse. Consistent movement keeps the body supple and strengthens critical muscles that support the lower back and legs. Walking and swimming, including pool therapy, are essential long-term exercises necessary to prevent sciatica recurrence.

Prognosis

Most cases of sciatica are treatable with pain medication and physical therapy. After 4-6 weeks of treatment, an individual should be able to resume normal activities.

KEY TERMS

Disc—A tissue between two vertebrae that cushions the spine.

Diskectomy—Surgery to remove part of a herniated disc.

CT—Computerized tomography, a test that uses a dye and a computer to image parts of the body

Coccyx—The tail bone or last four vertebrae of the spine.

Electromyography—An electrical activity test of the nerves and muscles.

Lumbosacral spine—The lower portion of the spine, including the sacrum and the coccyx.

MRI—Magnetic resonance imaging, a test that uses magnets to film parts of the body.

Microdisketomy—A disketomy using a microscope.

Piriformis—A muscle in the pelvic area near the sciatic nerve.

Radicuolpathy—Another name for sciatica.

Sciatic nerve—The largest and longest nerve in the body, running from the lower back to the foot.

Spondylolisthesis—A condition when one vertebra slips forward over another.

Vertebrae—Structures that compose the spine that protect the spinal chord.

Prevention

Some sources of sciatica are not preventable, such as disk degeneration, back strain due to pregnancy, or accidental **falls**. Other sources of back strain, such as poor posture, overexertion, being overweight, or wearing high heels, can be corrected or avoided. Cigarette **smoking** may also predispose people to pain, and should be discontinued.

General suggestions for avoiding sciatica, or preventing a repeat episode, include sleeping on a firm mattress, using chairs with firm back support, and sitting with both feet flat on the floor. Habitually crossing the legs while sitting can place excess pressure on the sciatic nerve. Sitting a lot can also place pressure on the sciatic nerves, so it's a good idea to take short breaks and move around during the work day, long trips, or any other situation that requires sitting for an extended length of time. If lifting is required, the back should be kept straight and the legs should provide the lift. Regular exercise, such as swimming and walking, can strengthen back muscles and improve posture. Exercise can also help maintain a healthy weight and lessen the likelihood of back strain.

Caregiver concerns

Special care should be taken to determine the underlying cause of sciatica and to treat that as well as the presenting symptoms.

Resources

PERIODICALS

Barry, Henry. "Bed rest is bad for back pain, ineffective for sciatica." *American Family Physician* (July 2005):329

Gupta, Sanjay. "Two fixes for bad backs." *Time* (July 2007):74

"How can I treat sciatica." *Natural Health.*(October 2006:30

Markova, Tsveti; Dhilion, Baldev Singh, and Martin, Sandra. "Treatment of acure sciatica." *American Family Physician.*(January 2007):99-100

"Observation is an option for patients with sciatica >6 weeks." *Journal of Family Practice.*(September 2007):704

OTHER

"Sciatica"*Mayo Clinic.* 2008.http://www.mayoclinic.com/health/sciatica/DS00516

Eidelson, Stewart G. "Sciatic Nerve and Sciatica." *Spine Universe*2008. http://www.spineuniverse.com/displayarticle.php/article2524.html

"Sciatica."*Medline Plus*2008.http://www.nlm.nih.gov/medlineplus/ency/article/000686.htm

"Sciatica." *eMedicineHealth*2008. http://www.emedicinehealth.com/script/main/art.asp?articlekey=59259&pf=3&page=1

OTHER

Spine Health. http://www.spine-health.com

ORGANIZATIONS

American Academy of Orthopaedic Surgeons, 6300 North River Rd, Rosemont, IL, 60018-4262, 847-823-7186, 800-346-2267, 847-823-8125, http://www.aaos.org.

Janie F. Franz

Scleroderma

Definition

Scleroderma is a progressive disease that affects the skin and connective tissue (including cartilage, bone, fat, and the tissue that supports the nerves and

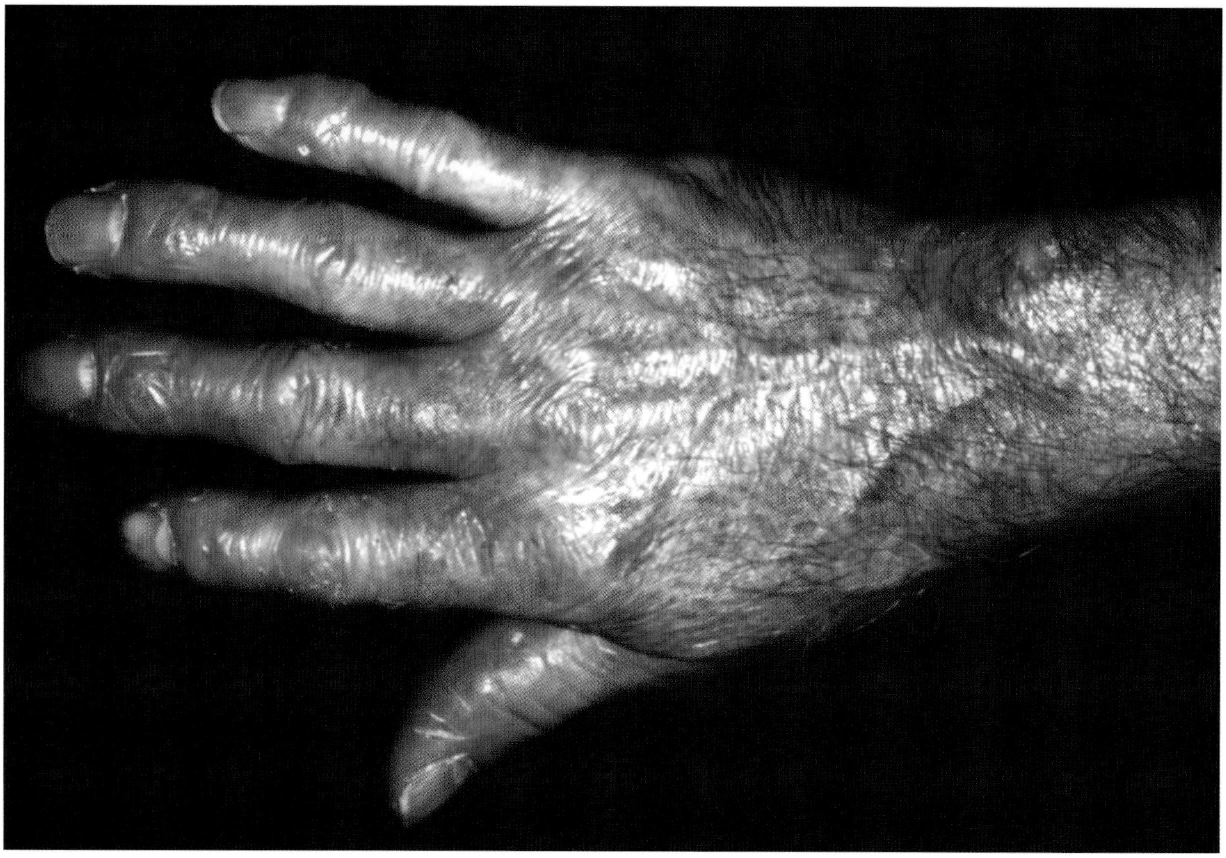

Scleroderma, red, thickened and tough looking skin, also known as systemic sclerosis. *(Dr. P. Marazzi/SPL/Photo Researchers, Inc. Reproduced by permission.)*

blood vessels throughout the body). There are two major forms of the disorder. The type known as localized scleroderma mainly affects the skin. Systemic scleroderma, which is also called systemic sclerosis, affects the smaller blood vessels and internal organs of the body.

Description

Scleroderma is an autoimmune disorder, which means that the body's **immune system** turns against itself. In scleroderma, there is an overproduction of abnormal collagen (a type of protein fiber present in connective tissue). This collagen accumulates throughout the body, causing hardening (sclerosis), scarring (fibrosis), and other damage. The damage may affect the appearance of the skin, or it may involve only the internal organs. The symptoms and severity of scleroderma vary from person to person.

Scleroderma occurs in all races of people all over the world, but it affects about four females for every male. Among children, localized scleroderma is more common, and systemic sclerosis is comparatively rare. Most patients with systemic sclerosis are diagnosed between ages 30 and 50. In the United States, about 300,000 people have scleroderma. Young African-American women and Native Americans of the Choctaw tribe have especially high rates of the disease. In 2003, researchers reported that they had identified 12 different genetic markers associated with scleroderma in the Choctaw population.

Causes and symptoms

The cause of scleroderma is still a puzzle. Although the accumulation of collagen appears to be a hallmark of the disease, researchers do not know why it occurs. Some theories suggest that damage to blood vessels may cause the tissues of the body to receive an inadequate amount of oxygen—a condition called **ischemia**. Some researchers believe that the resulting damage causes the immune system to overreact, producing an autoimmune disorder. According to this theory of scleroderma, the immune system gears up to fight an invader, but no invader is actually present.

Cells in the immune system called antibodies react to the body's own tissues as if they were foreign. The antibodies turn against the already damaged blood vessels and the vessels' supporting tissues. These immune cells are designed to deliver potent chemicals in order to kill foreign invaders. Some of these cells dump these chemicals on the body's own tissues instead, causing inflammation, swelling, damage, and scarring.

Most cases of scleroderma have no recognizable triggering event. Some cases, however, have been traced to exposure to toxic (poisonous) substances. For example, coal miners and gold miners, who are exposed to high levels of silica dust, have above-average rates of scleroderma. Other chemicals associated with the disease include polyvinyl chloride, benzine, toluene, and epoxy resins. In 1981, 20,000 people in Spain were stricken with a syndrome similar to scleroderma when their cooking oil was accidentally contaminated. Certain medications, especially a drug used in **cancer** treatment called bleomycin (Blenoxane), may lead to scleroderma. Some claims of a scleroderma-like illness have been made by women with silicone **breast implants**, but a link has not been proven in numerous studies.

Symptoms of systemic scleroderma

A condition called Raynaud's phenomenon is the first symptom in about 95% of all patients with systemic scleroderma. In Raynaud's phenomenon, the blood vessels of the fingers and/or toes (the digits) react to cold in an abnormal way. The vessels clamp down, preventing blood flow to the tip of the digit. Eventually, the flow is cut off to the entire finger or toe. Over time, oxygen deprivation may result in open ulcers on the skin surface. These ulcers can lead to tissue **death** (**gangrene**) and loss of the digit. When Raynaud's phenomenon is the first sign of scleroderma, the next symptoms usually appear within two years.

SKIN AND EXTREMITIES Involvement of the skin leads to swelling underneath the skin of the hands, feet, legs, arms, and face. Swelling is followed by thickening and tightening of the skin, which becomes taut and shiny. Severe tightening may lead to abnormalities. For example, tightening of the skin on the hands may cause the fingers to become permanently curled (flexed). Structures within the skin are damaged (including those producing hair, oil, and sweat), and the skin becomes dry and scaly. Ulcers may form, with the danger of infection. **Calcium** deposits often appear under the skin.

In systemic scleroderma, the mouth and nose may become smaller as the skin on the face tightens. The small mouth may interfere with eating and **dental hygiene**. Blood vessels under the skin may become enlarged and show through the skin, appearing as purplish marks or red spots. This chronic dilation of the small blood vessels is called telangiectasis.

Muscle weakness, joint **pain** and stiffness, and carpal tunnel syndrome are common in scleroderma. Carpal tunnel syndrome involves scarring in the wrist, which puts pressure on the median nerve running through that area. Pressure on the nerve causes numbness, tingling, and weakness in some of the fingers.

DIGESTIVE TRACT The tube leading from the mouth to the stomach (the esophagus) becomes stiff and scarred. Patients may have trouble swallowing food. The acid contents of the stomach may start to flow backward into the esophagus (esophageal reflux), causing a very uncomfortable condition known as **heartburn**. The esophagus may also become inflamed.

The intestine becomes sluggish in processing food, causing bloating and pain. Foods are not digested properly, resulting in **diarrhea**, **weight loss**, and **anemia**. Telangiectasis in the stomach or intestine may cause rupture and bleeding.

RESPIRATORY AND CIRCULATORY SYSTEMS The lungs are affected in about 66% of all people with systemic scleroderma. Complications include shortness of breath, coughing, difficulty breathing due to tightening of the tissue around the chest, inflammation of the air sacs in the lungs (alveolitis), increased risk of **pneumonia**, and an increased risk of cancer. For these reasons, lung disease is the most likely cause of death associated with scleroderma.

The lining around the heart (pericardium) may become inflamed. The heart may have greater difficulty pumping blood effectively (heart failure). Irregular heart rhythms and enlargement of the heart also occur in scleroderma.

Kidney disease is another common complication. Damage to blood vessels in the kidneys often causes a major rise in the person's **blood pressure**. The blood pressure may be so high that there is swelling of the brain, causing severe **headaches**, damage to the retinas of the eyes, seizures, and failure of the heart to pump blood into the body's circulatory system. The kidneys may also stop filtering blood and go into failure. Treatments for high blood pressure have greatly improved these kidney complications. Before these treatments were available, kidney problems were the most common cause of death for people with scleroderma.

Other problems associated with scleroderma include painful dryness of the eyes and mouth, enlargement and destruction of the liver, and a low-functioning thyroid gland.

Diagnosis

Diagnosis of scleroderma is complicated by the fact that some of its symptoms can accompany other connective-tissue diseases. The most important symptom is thickened or hardened skin on the fingers, hands, forearms, or face. This symptom is found in 98% of people with scleroderma. It can be detected in the course of a physical examination. The person's medical history may also contain important clues, such as exposure to toxic substances on the job. There are a number of nonspecific laboratory tests on blood samples that may indicate the presence of an inflammatory disorder (but not specifically scleroderma). The antinuclear antibody (ANA) test is positive in more than 95% of people with scleroderma.

Other tests can be performed to evaluate the extent of the disease. These include a test of the electrical system of the heart (an electrocardiogram), lung-function tests, and x-ray studies of the gastrointestinal tract. Various blood tests can be given to study kidney function.

Treatment

Mainstream treatments

As of early 2004 there is no cure for scleroderma. A drug called D-penicillamine has been used to interfere with the abnormal collagen. It is believed to help decrease the degree of skin thickening and tightening, and to slow the progress of the disease in other organs. Taking **vitamin D** and using ultraviolet light may be helpful for localized scleroderma. One group of British researchers reported in 2003 that long-wavelength ultraviolet A light is particularly effective in treating localized scleroderma. Corticosteroids have been used to treat joint pain, muscle cramps, and other symptoms of inflammation. Other drugs have been studied that reduce the activity of the immune system (immunosuppressants). Because these medications can have serious side effects, they are used in only the most severe cases of scleroderma.

The various complications of scleroderma are treated individually. Raynaud's phenomenon requires that people try to keep their hands and feet warm constantly. Nifedipine is a medication that is sometimes given to help control Raynaud's. Thick ointments and creams are used to treat **dry skin**. **Exercise** and massage may help joint involvement; they may also help people retain more movement despite skin tightening. An exercise regimen for stretching the mouth opening has been reported to be a helpful alternative to surgery in managing this condition. Skin ulcers need prompt attention and may require **antibiotics**. People with esophageal reflux will be advised to eat small amounts more often, rather than several large meals a day. They should also avoid spicy foods and items containing **caffeine**. Some patients with esophageal reflux have been successfully treated with surgery. Acid-reducing medications may be given for heartburn. People must be monitored for the development of high blood pressure. If found, they should be promptly treated with appropriate medications, usually ACE inhibitors or other vasodilators. When fluid accumulates due to heart failure, **diuretics** can be given to get rid of the excess fluid.

Patients with scleroderma may also benefit from some form of counseling or psychotherapy, as they are at increased risk of **depression**. One study found that 46% of the patients in its sample met the criteria for a depressive disorder.

Alternative treatments

One alternative therapy that some **naturopaths** have used in treating patients with scleroderma is superoxide dismutase (SOD), an antioxidant enzyme used in its injectable form. More research, however, needs to be done on the benefits of this treatment.

Prognosis

The prognosis for people with scleroderma varies. Some have a very limited form of the disease called morphea, which affects only the skin. These individuals have a very good prognosis. Other people have a subtype of systemic scleroderma called limited scleroderma. For them, the prognosis is relatively good. Limited scleroderma is characterized by limited involvement of the patient's skin and a cluster of five symptoms called the CREST syndrome. CREST stands for:

- C=Calcinosis
- R=Raynaud's disease (phenomenon)
- E=Esophageal dysmotility (stiffness and malfunctioning of the esophagus)
- S=Sclerodactyly (thick, hard, rigid skin over the fingers)
- T=Telangiectasias

In general, people with very widespread skin involvement have the worst prognosis. This level of disease is usually accompanied by involvement of other organs and the most severe complications.

KEY TERMS

Collagen—The main supportive protein of cartilage, connective tissue, tendon, skin, and bone.

Connective tissue—A group of tissues responsible for support throughout the body.

Fibrosis—The abnormal development of fibrous tissue; scarring.

Limited scleroderma—A subtype of systemic scleroderma with limited skin involvement. It is somestimes called the CREST form of scleroderma, after the initials of its five major symptoms.

Localized scleroderma—Thickening of the skin from overproduction of collagen.

Morphea—The most common form of localized scleroderma.

Raynaud phenomenon/Raynaud disease—A condition in which blood flow to the body's tissues is reduced by a malfunction of the nerves that regulate the constriction of blood vessels.

Sclerosis—Hardening.

Systemic sclerosis—A rare disorder that causes thickening and scarring of multiple organ systems.

Telangiectasias—Very small arteriovenous malformations, or connections between the arteries and veins. The result is small red spots on the skin known as "spider veins."

Although women are more commonly stricken with scleroderma, men more often die of the disease. The two factors that negatively affect survival are male sex and older age at diagnosis. The most common causes of death include heart, kidney, and lung diseases. About 65% of all patients survive 11 years or more following a diagnosis of scleroderma.

There are no known ways to prevent scleroderma. People can try to decrease occupational exposure to high-risk substances.

Resources

BOOKS

Beers, Mark H., MD, and Robert Berkow, MD., editors. "Systemic Sclerosis." *The Merck Manual of Diagnosis and Therapy.* Whitehouse Station, NJ: Merck Research Laboratories, 2004.

Pelletier, Dr. Kenneth R. *The Best Alternative Medicine, Part II: CAM Therapies for Specific Conditions: Scleroderma.* New York: Simon and Schuster, 2002.

PERIODICALS

Dawe, R. S. "Ultraviolet A1 Phototherapy." *British Journal of Dermatology* 148 (April 2003): 626–637.

Hill, C. L., A. M. Nguyen, D. Roder, and P. Roberts-Thomson. "Risk of Cancer in Patients with Scleroderma: A Population Based Cohort Study." *Annals of the Rheumatic Diseases* 62 (August 2003): 728–731.

Matsuura, E., A. Ohta, F. Kanegae, et al. "Frequency and Analysis of Factors Closely Associated with the Development of Depressive Symptoms in Patients with Scleroderma." *Journal of Rheumatology* 30 (August 2003): 1782–1787.

Mayes, M. D., J. V. Lacey, Jr., J. Beebe-Dimmer, et al. "Prevalence, Incidence, Survival, and Disease Characteristics of Systemic Sclerosis in a Large US Population." *Arthritis and Rheumatism* 48 (August 2003): 2246–2255.

Pizzo, G., G. A. Scardina, and P. Messina. "Effects of a Nonsurgical Exercise Program on the Decreased Mouth Opening in Patients with Systemic Scleroderma." *Clinical Oral Investigations* 7 (September 2003): 175–178.

Zhou, X., F. K. Tan, N. Wang, et al. "Genome-Wide Association Study for Regions of Systemic Sclerosis Susceptibility in a Choctaw Indian Population with High Disease Prevalence." *Arthritis and Rheumatism* 48 (September 2003): 2585–2592.

ORGANIZATIONS

American College of Rheumatology. 60 Executive Park South, Suite 150, Atlanta, GA 30329. (404) 633-3777. http://www.rheumatology.org.

National Organization for Rare Disorders, Inc. (NORD). 55 Kenosia Avenue, P. O. Box 1968, Danbury, CT 06813. (800) 999-6673 or (203) 744-0100. http://www.rarediseases.org.

Scleroderma Foundation. 12 Kent Way, Suite 101, Byfield, MA 01922. (978) 463-5843 or (800) 722-HOPE. Fax: (978) 463-5809. http://www.scleroderma.org..

Rebecca J. Frey Ph.D.

Seborrheic dermatitis

Definition

Seborrheic **dermatitis** is a common inflammatory disease of the skin characterized by scaly lesions usually on the scalp, hairline, and face.

Description

Seborrheic dermatitis appears as red, inflamed skin covered by greasy or dry scales that may be

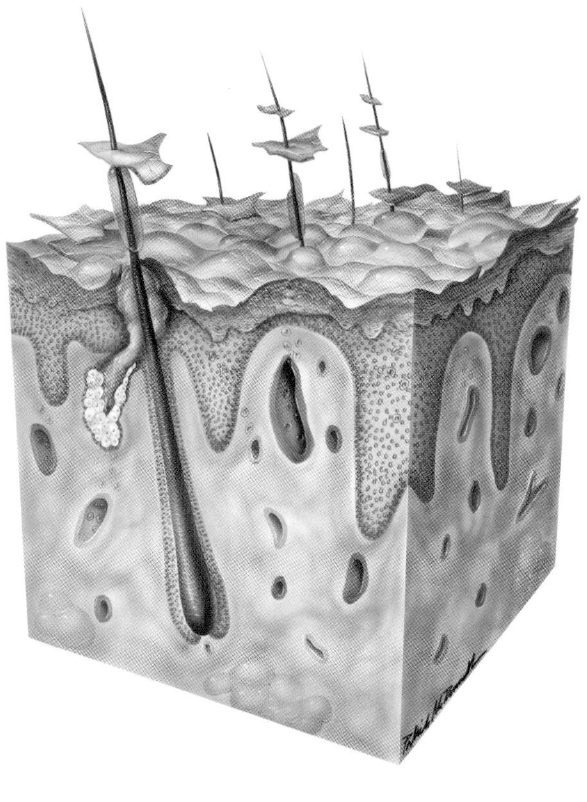

Illustration of skin inflammation. *(Patrick McDonnell / Photo Researchers, Inc. Reproduced by permission.)*

white, yellowish, or gray. It can effect the scalp, eyebrows, forehead, face, folds around the nose and ears, the chest, armpits (axilla), and groin. Dandruff and cradle cap are mild forms of seborrheic dermatitis, and appear as fine white scales without inflammation.

Causes and symptoms

The cause of seborrheic dermatitis is unclear, though it is has been linked to genetic or environmental factors. *Pityrosporum ovale*, a species of yeast normally found in hair follicles, has been proposed as one possible causative factor. A high fat **diet** and alcohol ingestion are thought to play some role. Other possible risk factors include:

- stress and fatigue
- weather extremes (e. g. hot, humid weather or cold, dry weather)
- oily skin
- infrequent shampoos
- obesity
- Parkinson's disease
- AIDS
- use of drying lotions that contain alcohol
- other skin disorders (for example acne, rosacea, or psoriasis)

Mild forms of the disorder may be asymptomatic. Symptoms also disappear and reappear, and vary in intensity over time. When scaling is present, it may be accompanied by **itching** that can lead to secondary infection.

Diagnosis

The diagnosis of seborrheic dermatitis is based on assessment of symptoms, accompanied by consideration of medical history.

Treatment

Treatment consists of vigorous shampoos with preparations that assist with softening and removing the scaly accumulations. For mild cases, a non-prescription shampoo with selenium sulfide or **zinc** pyrithione may be used. For more severe problems, the doctor may prescribe shampoos containing coal tar or scalp creams containing cortisone. The antiseborrheic shampoo should be left on the scalp for approximately five minutes before rinsing out. Hydrocortisone cream may also be ordered for application to the affected areas on the face and body. Application of the hydrocortisone should be discontinued when the condition clears and restarted with recurrence.

Prognosis

This chronic condition may be characterized by long periods of inactivity. Symptoms in the acute phase can be controlled with appropriate treatment.

KEY TERMS

Acne—A chronic inflammation of the sebaceous glands that manifests as blackheads, whiteheads, and/or pustules on the face or trunk.

Psoriasis—A skin disorder of chronic, itchy scaling most commonly at sites of repeated minor trauma (e.g. elbows, knees, and skin folds). It affects up to 2% of the population in Western countries—males and females equally.

Rosacea—A chronic inflammation of the face, with associated scattered round nodules and increased reactivity of the facial capillaries to heat. It is most common in females, aged 30–50 years.

Prevention

The condition cannot be prevented. The severity and frequency of flare-ups may be minimized with frequent shampoos, thorough drying of skin folds after bathing, and wearing of loose, ventilating clothing. Foods that appear to worsen the condition should be avoided.

Resources

BOOKS

Monahan, Frances, and Marianne Neighbors. *Medical Surgical Nursing: Foundations for Clinical Practice.* Philadelphia: W. B. Saunders,1998.

Kathleen D. Wright RN

Second nesters *see* **Family relationships**

Seizure disorder

Definition

A seizure is a sudden disruption of the brain's normal electrical activity accompanied by an alteration in consciousness or other neurological and behavioral manifestations. Epilepsy is a condition characterized by recurrent seizures that may include repetitive muscle jerking called convulsions.

Description

There are more than 20 different seizure disorders. One in 10 Americans will have a seizure at some time, and at least 200,000 have at least one seizure each month.

Epilepsy affects 1–2% of the United States population. Although epilepsy is as common in adults over 60 as in children under 10, 25% of all cases develop before the age of five. One in every two cases develops before the age of 25. About 125,000 new cases of epilepsy are diagnosed each year, and a significant number of children and adults that have not been diagnosed or treated have epilepsy.

Most seizures are benign, but a seizure that lasts a long time can lead to status epilepticus, a life-threatening condition characterized by continuous seizures, sustained loss of consciousness, and respiratory distress. Non-convulsive epilepsy can impair physical coordination, vision, and other senses. Undiagnosed seizures can lead to conditions that are more serious and more difficult to manage.

Types of seizures

Generalized epileptic seizures occur when electrical abnormalities exist throughout the brain. A partial seizure does not involve the entire brain. A partial seizure begins in an area called an epileptic focus, but may spread to other parts of the brain and cause a generalized seizure. Some people who have epilepsy experience more than one type of seizure.

Motor attacks cause parts of the body to jerk repeatedly. A motor attack usually lasts less than an hour and may last only a few minutes. Sensory seizures begin with numbness or tingling in one area. The sensation may move along one side of the body or the back before subsiding.

Visual seizures, which affect the area of the brain that controls sight, cause people to see things that are not there. Auditory seizures affect the part of the brain that controls hearing and cause a person to imagine voices, music, and other sounds. Other types of seizures can cause confusion, upset stomach, or emotional distress. When such phenomena occur prior to the onset of a seizure, they are called auras.

GENERALIZED SEIZURES A generalized tonic-clonic (grand-mal) seizure begins with a loud cry before the person having the seizure loses consciousness and **falls** to the ground. The muscles become rigid for about 30 seconds during the tonic phase of the seizure and alternately contract and relax during the clonic phase, which lasts 30 to 60 seconds. The skin sometimes acquires a bluish tint, and the person may bite the tongue, lose bowel or bladder control, or have trouble breathing.

A grand mal seizure lasts between two and five minutes, and the person may be confused or have trouble talking when consciousness is regained (post-ictal state). There may be complaints of head or muscle aches or weakness in the arms or legs before falling into a deep sleep.

PRIMARY GENERALIZED SEIZURES A primary generalized seizure occurs when electrical discharges begin in both halves (hemispheres) of the brain at the same time. Primary generalized seizures are more likely to be major motor attacks than to be absence seizures.

ABSENCE SEIZURES Absence (petit mal) seizures generally begin at about the age of four and stop by the time the child becomes an adolescent. Absence seizures usually begin with a brief loss of consciousness and last between one and ten seconds. A person having a petit mal seizure becomes very quiet and may blink, stare blankly, roll eyes, or move lips. A petit mal seizure lasts 15 to 20 seconds. When it ends, the person who had the seizure resumes whatever task was being completed before the seizure began. There will be no memory of the seizure, and the person may not realize that anything unusual has happened. Untreated petit mal seizures can recur as many as 100 times a day and may progress to grand mal seizures.

MYOCLONIC SEIZURES Myoclonic seizures are characterized by brief, involuntary spasms of the tongue or muscles of the face, arms, or legs. Myoclonic seizures are most apt to occur when waking after a night's sleep.

A Jacksonian seizure is a partial seizure characterized by tingling, stiffening, or jerking of an arm or leg. Loss of consciousness is rare. The seizure may progress in characteristic fashion along the limb.

Limp posture and a brief period of unconsciousness are features of akinetic seizures, which occur in young children. Akinetic seizures, which cause the child to fall, are also called drop attacks.

PARTIAL SEIZURES Simple partial seizures do not spread from the focal area where they arise. Symptoms are determined by what part of the brain is affected. The person usually remains conscious during the seizure and can later describe it in detail.

COMPLEX PARTIAL SEIZURES A distinctive smell, taste, or other unusual sensation (aura) may signal the start of a complex partial seizure. These seizures start as simple partial seizures but move beyond the focal area and cause loss of consciousness. Complex partial seizures can become major motor seizures. Although a person having a complex partial seizure may appear to be conscious, the person has no knowledge of what is happening and may behave inappropriately. There will be no memory of the seizure and there may be a brief period of confusion after it ends.

Causes and symptoms

The origin of 50–70% of all cases of epilepsy is unknown. Epilepsy is sometimes the result of trauma at the time of birth. Such causes include insufficient oxygen to the brain; **head injury**; heavy bleeding or incompatibility between a woman's blood and the blood of her newborn baby; and infection immediately before, after, or at the time of birth.

Other causes of epilepsy include:

- head trauma resulting from a car accident, gunshot wound, or other injury
- alcoholism
- brain abscess or inflammation of membranes covering the brain or spinal cord
- phenylketonuria (PKU) (A disease that is present at birth, PKU is often characterized by seizures, and can result in mental retardation and other inherited disorders.)
- infectious diseases such as measles, mumps, and diphtheria
- degenerative disease
- lead poisoning, mercury poisoning, carbon monoxide poisoning, or ingestion of some other poisonous substance
- genetic factors

Status epilepticus, a condition in which a person suffers from continuous seizures and may have trouble breathing, can be caused by:

- suddenly discontinuing anti-seizure medication
- hypoxic or metabolic encephalopathy (brain disease resulting from lack of oxygen or malfunctioning of other physical or chemical processes)
- acute head injury
- blood infection caused by inflammation of the brain or the membranes that cover it

Diagnosis

Personal and family medical history, description of seizure activity, and physical and neurological examinations help primary care physicians, neurologists, and epileptologists diagnose this disorder. Doctors rule out conditions that cause symptoms that resemble epilepsy, including small strokes (**transient ischemic attacks** or TIAs), fainting (syncope), pseudoseizures, and sleep attacks (narcolepsy).

Neuropsychological testing uncovers learning or memory problems. Neuro-imaging provides views of brain areas involved in seizure activity.

An electroencephalogram (EEG) is the main test used to diagnose epilepsy. EEGs use electrodes placed on or within the skull to record the brain's electrical activity and pinpoint the exact location of abnormal discharges. A person may be asked to remain motionless during a short-term EEG or to go about normal activities during extended monitoring. Some people are deprived of sleep or exposed to seizure triggers, such as rapid, deep breathing (hyperventilation) or flashing lights (photic stimulation). In some cases, people may be hospitalized for EEG monitoring that can last as long as two weeks. Video EEGs also document what an individual was doing when the seizure occurred and how the seizure altered behavior.

Other techniques used to diagnose epilepsy include:

- Magnetic resonance imaging (MRI) provides clear, detailed images of the brain. Functional MRI (fMRI), performed while a person does various tasks, can measure shifts in electrical intensity and blood flow and indicate the brain region each activity affects.
- Positron emission tomography (PET) and single photon emission tomography (SPECT) monitor blood flow and chemical activity in the brain area being tested. PET and SPECT are very effective in locating the brain region where metabolic changes take place between seizures.

Treatment

The goal of epilepsy treatment is to eliminate seizures or make the symptoms less frequent and less severe. Long-term anticonvulsant drug therapy is the most common form of epilepsy treatment.

Medication

A combination of drugs may be needed to control some symptoms, but most persons who have epilepsy take one of the following medications:

- phenytoin (Dilantin)
- carbamazepine (Tegretol)
- phenobarbital (Barbita)
- primidone (Mysoline)
- valproic acid or sodium valproate (Depakene)
- clonazepam (Klonopin)
- ethosuximide (Zarontin)

Phenytoin, carbamazepine, phenobarbital, and primidone are used to manage or control generalized tonic-clonic and complex partial seizures. Valproic acid (**sodium** valproate), clonazepam, and ethosuximide are prescribed for persons who have absence seizures. Gabapentin (Neurontonin) and lamotrigine (Lamictal) are medications recently approved in the United States to treat adults who have partial seizures or partial and grand mal seizures.

Even a person whose seizures are well controlled should have regular blood tests to measure levels of anti-seizure medication in the blood stream and to check to see if the medication is causing any changes in the blood or liver. A doctor should be notified if any signs of drug toxicity appear, including uncontrolled eye movements; sluggishness, **dizziness**, or hyperactivity; inability to see clearly or speak distinctly; nausea or vomiting; or sleep problems.

Status epilepticus requires emergency treatment, usually with Ativan (Valium), phenytoin, or phenobarbital. An intravenous dextrose (sugar) solution is given to persons whose condition is due to low blood sugar, and a vitamin B_1 preparation is administered intravenously when status epilepticus results from chronic alcohol withdrawal. Because dextrose and thiamine are essentially harmless and because delay in treatment can be disastrous, these medications are given routinely, as it is usually difficult to obtain an adequate history from a person suffering from status epilepticus.

Intractable seizures are seizures that cannot be controlled with medication or without sedation or other unacceptable side effects. Surgery may be used to eliminate or control intractable seizures.

Surgery

Surgery can be used to treat people whose intractable seizures stem from small focal lesions that can be removed without endangering them, changing their personality, dulling their senses, or reducing their ability to function.

Each year, as many as 5,000 new people may become suitable candidates for surgery, which is most often performed at a comprehensive epilepsy center. Potential surgical candidates include people with:

- partial seizures and secondarily generalized seizures (attacks that begin in one area and spread to both sides of the brain)
- seizures and childhood paralysis on one side of the body (hemiplegia)
- complex partial seizures originating in the temporal lobe (the part of the brain associated with speech, hearing, and smell) or other focal seizures (However, the risk of surgery involving the speech centers is that a person will lose speech function.)
- generalized myoclonic seizures or generalized seizures featuring temporary paralysis (akinetic) or loss of muscle tone (atonal)

A physical examination is conducted to verify that a person's seizures are caused by epilepsy, and surgery is not used to treat people with severe psychiatric disturbances or medical problems that raise risk factors to unacceptable levels.

Surgery is never indicated unless:

- The best available anti-seizure medications have failed to control the person's symptoms satisfactorily.

- The origin of a person's seizures has been precisely located.
- There is good reason to believe that surgery will significantly improve the person's health and quality of life.

Every person considering epilepsy surgery is carefully evaluated by one or more neurologists, neurosurgeons, neuropsychologists, and/or social workers. A psychiatrist, chaplain, or other spiritual advisor may help an affected individual and family members family cope with the stresses that occur during and after the selection process.

TYPES OF SURGERY Surgical techniques used to treat intractable epilepsy include:

- Lesionectomy. Removing the lesion (diseased brain tissue) and some surrounding brain tissue is very effective in controlling seizures. Lesionectomy is generally more successful than surgery performed on persons whose seizures are not caused by clearly defined lesions, but removing only part of the lesion lessens the effectiveness of the procedure.
- Temporal resections. Removing part of the temporal lobe and the part of the brain associated with feelings, memory, and emotions (the hippocampus) provides good or excellent seizure control in 75–80% of properly selected individuals with appropriate types of temporal lobe epilepsy. Some people experience post-operative speech and memory problems.
- Extra-temporal resection. This procedure involves removing some or all of the frontal lobe, the part of the brain directly behind the forehead. The frontal lobe helps regulate movement, planning, judgment, and personality, and special care must be taken to prevent post-operative problems with movement and speech. Extra-temporal resection is most successful in people whose seizures are not widespread.
- Hemispherectomy. This method of removing brain tissue is restricted to persons with severe epilepsy and abnormal discharges that often extend from one side of the brain to the other. Hemispherectomies are most often performed on infants or young children who have had an extensive brain disease or disorder since birth or from a very young age.
- Corpus callosotomy. This procedure, an alternative to hemispherectomy in persons with congenital hemiplegia, removes some or all of the white matter that connects the two halves of the brain. Corpus callosotomy is performed almost exclusively on children who are frequently injured during falls caused by seizures. If removing two-thirds of the corpus callosum doesn't produce lasting improvement in a person's condition, the remaining one-third will be removed during another operation.
- Multiple subpial transection. This procedure is used to control the spread of seizures that originate in or affect the "eloquent" cortex, the area of the brain responsible for complex thought and reasoning.

Other forms of treatment

KETOGENIC DIET A special high-fat, low-protein, low-carbohydrate **diet** is sometimes used to treat persons whose severe seizures have not responded to other treatment. Calculated according to age, height, and weight, the ketogenic diet induces mild starvation and **dehydration**. This forces the body to create an excessive supply of ketones, natural chemicals with seizure-suppressing properties.

The goal of this controversial approach is to maintain or improve seizure control while reducing medication. The ketogenic diet works best with children between the ages of one and 10. It is introduced over a period of several days, and most children are hospitalized during the early stages of treatment.

If a child following this diet remains seizure-free for at least six months, increased amounts of **carbohydrates** and protein are gradually added. If the child shows no improvement after three months, the diet is gradually discontinued.

Introduced in the 1920s, the ketogenic diet has had limited, short-term success in controlling seizure activity. Its use exposes people to such potentially harmful side effects as:

- staphylococcal infections
- stunted or delayed growth
- low blood sugar (hypoglycemia)
- excess fat in the blood (hyperlipidemia)
- disease resulting from calcium deposits in the urinary tract (urolithiasis)
- disease of the optic nerve (optic neuropathy)

VAGUS NERVE STIMULATION The United States Food and Drug Administration (FDA) has approved the use of vagus nerve stimulation (VNS) in persons over the age of 16 who have intractable partial seizures. This non-surgical procedure uses a pacemaker-like device implanted under the skin in the upper left chest, to provide intermittent stimulation to the vagus nerve. Stretching from the side of the neck into the brain, the vagus nerve affects swallowing, speech, breathing, and many other functions, and VNS may prevent or shorten some seizures.

First aid for seizures

A person having a seizure should not be restrained, but sharp or dangerous objects should be moved out of reach. Anyone having a complex partial seizure can be warned away from danger by someone calling out his or her name in a clear, calm voice.

A person having a grand mal seizure should be helped to lie down. Tight clothing should be loosened. A soft, flat object like a towel or the palm of a hand should be placed under the person's head. Forcing a hard object into the mouth of someone having a grand mal seizure could cause injuries or **breathing problems**. If the person's mouth is open, placing a folded cloth or other soft object between the teeth will protect the tongue. Turning the head to the side will help breathing. After a grand mal seizure has ended, the person who had the seizure should be told what has happened and reminded of the present location.

Alternative treatment

Stress increases seizure activity in 30% of people who have epilepsy. **Relaxation** techniques can provide some sense of control over the disorder, but they should never be used instead of anti-seizure medication or used without the approval of a person's doctor. **Yoga**, meditation, and favorite pastimes help some people relax and more successfully manage stress. **Biofeedback** can teach adults and older adolescents how to recognize an aura and what to do to stop its spread. Children under 14 are not usually able to understand and apply principles of biofeedback. **Acupuncture** treatments (acupuncture needles inserted for a few minutes or left in place for as long as half an hour) make some people feel pleasantly relaxed. **Acupressure** can have the same effect on children or on adults who dislike needles.

Aromatherapy involves mixing aromatic plant oils into water or other oils and massaging them into the skin or using a special burner to waft their fragrance throughout the room. Aromatherapy oils affect the body and the brain, and undiluted oils should never be applied directly to the skin. Ylang ylang, chamomile, or lavender can create a soothing mood. People who have epilepsy should not use rosemary, hyssop, sage, or sweet fennel, which seem to make the brain more alert.

Dietary changes that emphasize whole foods and eliminate processed foods may be helpful. Homeopathic therapy also can work for people with seizures, especially constitutional homeopathic treatment that acts at the deepest levels to address the needs of an individual.

Prognosis

People who have epilepsy have a higher-than-average rate of **suicide**; sudden, unexplained **death**; and drowning and other accidental fatalities.

Benign focal epilepsy of childhood and some absence seizures may disappear in time, but remission is unlikely if seizures occur several times a day, several times in a 48-hour period, or more frequently than in the past.

Seizures that occur repeatedly over time and always involve the same symptoms are called stereotypic seizures. The probability that stereotypic seizures will abate is poor.

About 85% of all seizure disorders can be partially or completely controlled if a person takes anti-seizure medication according to directions; avoids seizure-inducing sights, sounds, and other triggers; gets enough sleep; and eats regular, balanced meals.

Caregiver concerns

First aid may be provided by trained individuals. Physicians make the initial diagnosis of seizure disorders. Endocrinologists and radiologists may assist in refining a diagnosis. Neurologists, neurosurgeons, neuropsychologists, and social workers may assess persons prior to receiving surgery for a seizure disorder. Neurosurgeons may perform surgery to remove structures in the brain that are known to cause seizures. Psychiatrists, chaplains, or other spiritual advisors may help an affected individual and relations cope with the stresses that occur during and after surgery. Nurses also teach family and friends about emergency care of patient when having a seizure, as well as **home care** following a seizure and hospitalization.

Prevention

Eating properly, getting sufficient sleep, and controlling stress and fevers can help prevent seizures. A person who has epilepsy should be careful not to hyperventilate. A person who experiences an aura should find a safe place to lie down and stay there until the seizure passes. Anticonvulsant medications should not be stopped suddenly; and, if other medications are prescribed or discontinued, the doctor treating the seizures should be notified. In some conditions, such as severe head injury, brain surgery, or subarachnoid hemorrhage, anticonvulsant medications may be given to a person to prevent seizures. Seizures that are caused by ingesting substances such

KEY TERMS

Akinetic seizure—Seizure characterized by limp posture and a brief period of unconsciousness; also called a drop attack.

Aura—A distinctive smell, taste, or other unusual sensation that preceeds the onset of a seizure.

Clonic—Referring to clonus, a series of muscle contractions and partial relaxations that alternate in some nervous diseases in the form of convulsive spasms.

Epileptologist—A physician who specializes in the treatment of epilepsy.

Lesionectomy—Removal of a lesion and surrounding tissue. The term is applied to brain tissue when trying to control seizures.

Myoclonic seizures—Brief, involuntary spasms of the tongue or muscles of the face, arms, or legs.

Petit-mal seizure—Absence seizure.

Post-ictal state—A period of disorientation usually followed by sleep that occurs after a seizure.

Tonic—Characterized by tonus, a state of partial contraction that is maintained at least in part by a continuous bombardment of motor impulses.

as alcohol or drugs can be prevented by discontinuing use of the offending substance.

Resources

BOOKS

Adams, Raymond D., Maurice Victor, and Allan H. Ropper. *Adam's & Victor's Principles of Neurology.* 6th ed. New York: McGraw Hill, 1997.

Chesney, Russell W. "Conditions that Mimic Seizurres." In *Nelson Textbook of Pediatrics.* 16th ed. Ed. by Richard E. Behrman, et al. Philadelphia: Saunders, 2000, pp.1829-1832.

Gates, John R., and A.J. Rowan. *Non-Epileptic Seizures.* 2nd ed. Woburn, MA: Butterworth-Heinemann, 2000.

Haslem, Robert H.A. "Febrile Seizures." In *Nelson Textbook of Pediatrics.* 16th ed. Ed. Richard E. Behrman et al. Philadelphia: Saunders, 2000, pp.1818-1819.

Haslem, Robert H.A. "Generalized Seizures." In *Nelson Textbook of Pediatrics.* 16th ed. Ed. Richard E. Behrman et al. Philadelphia: Saunders, 2000, pp.1815-1818.

Haslem, Robert H.A. "Neonatal Seizures." In *Nelson Textbook of Pediatrics.* 16th ed. Ed. Richard E. Behrman et al. Philadelphia: Saunders, 2000, pp.1825-1827.

Haslem, Robert H.A. "Partial Seizures." In *Nelson Textbook of Pediatrics.* 16th ed. Ed. Richard E. Behrman et al. Philadelphia, Saunders, 2000, pp.1814-1815.

Haslem, Robert H.A. "Seizures in Childhood." In *Nelson Textbook of Pediatrics.* 16th ed. Ed. Richard E. Behrman et al. Philadelphia: Saunders, 2000, pp.1813-1814.

Haslem, Robert H.A. "Status Epilepticus." In *Nelson Textbook of Pediatrics.* 16th ed. Ed. Richard E. Behrman et al. Philadelphia: Saunders, 2000, pp.1827-1829.

Haslem, Robert H.A. "Treatment of Epilepsy." In *Nelson Textbook of Pediatrics.* 16th ed. Ed. Richard E. Behrman et al. Philadelphia: Saunders, 2000, pp.1819-1825.

Lowenstein, Daniel H. "Seizures and Epilepsy." In *Harrison's Principles of Internal Medicine.* 14th ed. Ed. Anthony S. Fauci et al. New York: McGraw-Hill, 1998, pp.2311-2325.

Mizrahi, Eli M., and Peter Kellaway. *Diagnosis and Management of Neonatal Seizures.* New York: Raven Press, 1998.

Pedley, Timothy A. "The Epilepsies." In *Cecil Textbook of Medicine.* 21st ed. Ed. Lee Goldman and J. Claude Bennett. Philadelphia: W.B. Saunders, 2000, pp.2151-2164.

PERIODICALS

Anagnostou, E. "On Absence Seizures and Oculomotor Phenomena. *Clinical Neurophysiology* 112, no. 3 (2001): 563-564.

Beran, R.G. "The Classification of Epileptic Seizures and Syndromes." *Medicine and Law* 19, no. 4 (2000): 753-756.

Browne, T.R., and G.L. Holmes. "Epilepsy." *New England Journal of Medicine* 344, no. 15 (2001): 1145-1151.

Bui, T.T., et al. "Infant Seizures Not So Infantile: Presentations to the Hospital of Children Less Than 6 Months of Age with a First-Time Seizure." *Academy of Emergency Medicine* 8, no. 5 (2001): 438-441.

Dale, M.C. "Distinguishing Between Partial Seizures and Panic Attacks. Psychotic and Behavioural Symptoms Are also Common in Elderly Patients." *British Medical Journal* 322, no. 7290 (2001): 864-865.

Mack, C.J. "Treating the Person." *Lancet* 357, no. 9257 (2001): 724-725.

ORGANIZATIONS

American Academy of Neurology. 1080 Montreal Avenue, St. Paul, MN 55116. (651) 695-1940. http://www.aan.com/.

British Epilepsy Association. http://www.epilepsy.org.uk/ (August 14, 2001).

Epilepsy Foundation. 4351 Garden City Drive, Landover, MD 20785-7223. (800) 332-1000. (301) 459-3700. http://www.efa.org.

OTHER

Epilepsy Ontario. http://epilepsyontario.org/.

Greenstein, Doreen B. "Caring for Children with Special Needs: Seizure Disorders." National Network for Child Care. http://www.nncc.org/Diversity/spec.seiz.html (August 14, 2001).

L. Fleming Fallon Jr., MD, DrPH

Senior nutrition *see* **Nutrition**

Senior travel

Definition

Senior travel or travel by older adults has become a reward of having more free time and more discretionary income. Since aging produces physiological changes as well as increases the probability of having an underlying medical condition, travel for older adults poses special risks that other age groups do not experience. Following certain precautions can help ensure a safe and enjoyable trip.

Demographics

In 2007, the American Association of Retired Persons (**AARP**) and Focalyst released a study of 30,000 Boomers (people born between 1946 and 1964) and Matures (people born prior to 1946). The study indicated that older adults represented a viable target market for the travel industry. Retired adults encompass a large portion of this industry, but the biggest segment is composed of Boomers who travel with their minor children. Boomers also tend to travel in larger groups and spend more money per trip.

Many seniors take advantage of time after retirement to travel. *(Corbis Premium RF / Alamy. Reproduced by permission.)*

Description

Travel contributes to the quality of life and overall health of many older adults. Some seniors may travel to see children and grandchildren or connect with friends, while a number of seniors travel for career-related conferences and personal research or for special interests, including hobbies, sports, education, and spiritual activities. During the later part of life, many adults seek out places they have never seen before, such as the ocean, a tropical locale, or other countries.

Obtaining travel information

Travel opportunities for many older adults is not usually difficult. A travel agent or website can provide suggested destinations, hotels, and methods for travel. Travel magazines, documentaries, or travel presentations at local venues can also inspire travel plans. Many seniors rely on information from organizations such as the AARP or the American Automobile Association (AAA). Once a destination is determined, the senior traveler can plan their itinerary.

One study on the travel habits of seniors found that word of mouth and personal experience were far more important sources of information to older adults when deciding on a travel destination. This was echoed by the AARP and Focalyst 2007 study and emphasized that there was no brand loyalty regarding transportation, accommodations, or even destination activities. The study also found that life stage was a major factor in travel decisions. Finances, work status, and household composition were the most influential factors.

Preparation

Travel can be mind-broadening and soul-expanding, but it can also be stressful, especially if the travelers have an underlying medical condition or **mobility issues**. It is a good idea for older adults to discuss their travel plans with their physician, preferably prior to making travel arrangements. The physician can determine if the senior is fit to travel and engage in the activities they have planned. The physician may suggest changes in destination, transportation arrangements, or activities. For example, if a person with a respiratory disorder plans to hike in the Rocky Mountains, the physician may suggest a different destination. The thinner air of higher altitudes would make breathing more difficult for the patient with lung problems.

Preventive health for cruise ship travelers

- ✓ Consult a health-care provider before embarking on a cruise if you have health conditions that might increase the potential for injury or illness. Special cruises are now available for travelers who have certain medical conditions, including those on dialysis.
- ✓ Inform the cruise line of special medical needs, such as wheelchair access, oxygen tank, dialysis, in advance of travel.
- ✓ Ensure you have adequate medical insurance coverage for receiving healthcare overseas and medical evacuation.
- ✓ Obtain a written summary of your medical history, including pertinent diagnostic data such as EKG and chest x-ray, to facilitate medical care, should it be required.
- ✓ Consult a healthcare provider for destination-specific recommended and required vaccines (e.g., yellow fever), as well as prevention medication (e.g. malaria chemoprophylaxis) if needed; and routinely recommended age- and medical condition-specific immunizations, such as influenza vaccines.
- ✓ Consult a healthcare provider for appropriate options for motion sickness based on your medical history and current medications.
- ✓ Practice good health habits and disease prevention practices during travel by washing hands for at least 20 seconds with soap and water or, if soap and water are unavailable, using an alcohol-based product containing more than 60% alcohol, and using tissue to cover coughs and sneezes.
- ✓ Take food and water intake precautions; checking that foods are thoroughly cooked and the appropriate temperature.
- ✓ Use mosquito prevention (using DEET-containing repellents and wearing clothing that provides coverage over exposed areas of the body), as necessary.
- ✓ Keep a record of your medical pre-travel preparation, medications taken, duration of travel, countries visited, and shoreside activities to facilitate any medical care needed upon your return home.
- ✓ See your healthcare provider if you become ill after returning home, even many months after travel, let your physician know where you have traveled. In particular, a fever after traveling in a malarious area should be considered a medical emergency.

SOURCE: CDC 2008 Yellow Book for the Public, National Center for Preparedness, Detection, and Control of Infectious Diseases, Centers for Disease Control and Prevention, U.S. Department of Health and Human Services

(Illustration by GGS Information Services. Cengage Learning, Gale)

The physician may also suggest ways to manage the **stress** of travel, minimize the **pain** of arthritis or recurrent **bursitis**, or adjust to a different time zone. If there is a chronic disorder such as diabetes or cardiovascular disease, the doctor may suggest how to manage the disease in a different part of the country or part of the world.

Travelers with a heart condition may find it necessary to travel with a copy of a current cardiogram. If the traveler has a symptoms, such as shortness of breath, chest pain, or nausea, which may indicate a heart problem, having a prior reading can help emergency room doctors determine treatment more accurately.

Traveling with medications

Before departure, older travelers should check their current medications and make sure they pack enough for the trip. It is a good idea to keep an extra week of medication on hand in case plans change or a travel emergency occurs. Some physicians give their patients an extra written prescription to take along in case something happens to their medications.

Travelers should pack medications in their carry-on luggage. Medications should remain in the original bottles that clearly identify the patient, the doctor, the type of medication, and how it should be taken. Medications can be transferred to daily pill reminder containers when the traveler arrives at their destination. On the trip home, all medications should once again be packed in their original containers for travel. This is important to determine what medications are being taken if the traveler has a medical emergency.

Some medications must be kept cool. Travelers should put them in a small insulated container with a gel ice pack. If flying, travelers should keep these medicines separate in their carry-on until aboard the plane; then ask the flight attendant for help with keeping the medications cool.

It is very important to keep a written list of all medications (including generic equivalents), dosages, and the medical conditions for which they are being taken. If the patient is traveling with hypodermic syringes, needles, narcotics, or other controlled substances, it is wise to carry a written letter from the patient's physician. Travelers should keep the list of medications and the doctor's letter with their other travel documents and put a copy in their checked luggage.

Traveling by plane

Flying poses some unique challenges for older adults. Increased airport security often causes travelers with **pacemakers**, artificial joints, and implanted cardiac defibrillators (ICDs) to off airport metal detectors. Patients with these devices usually carry a wallet card that identifies the type of devices they have. Travelers with ICDs or pacemakers should present the ID card to the security personnel and ask for a hand search or to use a handheld wand, passing it over the location of the device for no more than a few seconds and to wait thirty seconds before passing it over the device again.

Some international airports use radiation detectors. These are sensitive enough to pick up radioisotopes used in nuclear medicine scans. Patients who plan to fly within thirty days of having a thyroid, bone, or heart scan should carry documentation regarding the date and place that the procedure was done.

Oxygen and air pressure is in lower concentration as the airplane reaches higher altitudes. This thinner air may be problematic for people with serious lung or heart problems. If the person can walk upstairs without becoming short of breath, then flying should not be a problem.

Airline passengers should drink plenty of water. The dry cabin environment can cause symptoms of **dehydration**. Travelers should avoid alcohol because it can further dehydrate the body.

Some people may feel bloated when they fly. This happens because the gases within the intestines are sensitive to air pressure similar to the ears and the sinuses. This is normally a minor inconvenience, but if the traveler has recently had abdominal or chest surgery, the expanded gas can stretch surgical stitches, causing added discomfort.

Travelers who are prone to airsickness should not eat before flying. They should sit upright and minimize movement of the head. Motion sickness can be worsened by reading or watching videos so these activities should be avoided. Over-the-counter motion sickness medications are available, such as dimenhydrinate (Dramine) or meclizine (Bonine). These medications are taken before the flight. Patients should check with their physician prior to taking these medications.

In the event of a medical emergency on board, all airlines have emergency medical kits and automated external defibrillators to treat cardiac arrest.

Avoiding deep vein thrombosis

Sitting for long periods can cause blood to settle in the lower legs and feet, resulting in swelling. Sometimes, sluggish blood flow from the feet back to the heart can cause tiny **blood clots** to form. Often, these clots dissolve via the body's own natural clot busters. For some people, the clot continues to travel up through the leg, blocking blood flow. This is called **deep vein thrombosis** and can cause leg pain. If the clot breaks away and continues to pass through the circulatory system and enters the lungs, it can cause a **pulmonary embolism**, which is life-threatening. This condition can occur in younger travelers, but it is especially problematic in older adults whose circulatory system may already be sluggish due to arteriosclerosis, high **blood pressure**, diabetes, or medications that slow the heart rate. People who have **cancer**, are recovering from surgery or an injury, smokers, women taking estrogen replacement therapy, men taking medication for **prostate cancer**, and those who have had a clot before are at increased risk.

Travelers can avoid deep vein thrombosis by stretching frequently, doing leg exercises, or wearing compression stockings. Alternately flexing and pointing the feet and doing ankle rotations for thirty seconds every half hour are helpful if the traveler does not get up and move around. Passengers may walk up and down the aisle of the airplane or through the cars of a passenger train. If traveling by car, travelers should stop every hour and walk around. Travel by bus may be more problematic, since stops are determined by the bus schedule. Risk of deep vein thrombosis may persist after the plane has landed or the bus has reached its destination. Travelers should continue to walk and **exercise** daily.

Traveling abroad

When traveling outside of the United States, older adults need to make sure their immunizations are up to date. A physician can determine what immunizations are necessary based on the destination. Information is also available from the Center for Disease Control and Prevention (CDC) and the U.S. State Department.

Going through customs with medications or hypodermic syringes and needles is much easier if all medications are kept in their original containers and are carried in carry-on luggage. A written note from the traveler's physician explaining that a medical condition requires the traveler to take narcotics or use hypodermic syringes and needles for injections will make having them in the traveler's possession understandable. A list of medications and the conditions for which they are taken verifies why the traveler has them. This list should also include over-the-counter medicines and supplements. Some countries have different laws about controlled substances than the United States and may regulate what is in some over-the-counter products.

Travelers should take enough medication for their trip, as well as enough extra for a few days in case something happens to their medications or there is a change in plans. Patients taking generic medications may not be able to find equivalent drugs abroad if they run out. In some cases, their physician may not be able to find generic equivalents in other countries or even be able to identify specific equivalents if they are available.

Food and drink can be major sources of illness for travelers. Raw food should be avoided, particularly fish, meat, shellfish, and unpasteurized dairy products. Raw vegetables, salads, and fruit may be eaten only if the traveler is assured that they were washed in clean water and prepared under sanitary conditions. Food from street vendors should be avoided. Travelers should also avoid drinking local water and anything made with water, including lemonade, fountain sodas, fruit juices made from concentrate and mixed with water, alcoholic beverages mixed with water, and ice. Bottled water, bottled soft drinks, beer, and wine are the safest to drink. Coffee and tea made with rapidly boiling water may also be safe. The CDC travel website provides updated information about food-borne and water-borne illnesses in specific countries and how to avoid them.

Seeking medical help away from home

Accidents can occur anytime and at any age, but older travelers with underlying medical conditions should plan for the event of a medical emergency. Before leaving on a trip, the traveler should locate the local clinic or hospital near their accommodations. Academic medical centers are good sources of care. If the traveler has a specific medical condition and will be away from home for more than two weeks, a physician may be able to suggest an appropriate specialist near the traveler's destination.

If older travelers become ill when abroad, they can call the front desk at their hotel. Many large hotels have a physician on call or have a list of physicians who cater to international patients. Travelers can also call the U.S. embassy or consulate in the country where they are staying and ask for a local medical referral.

Insurance

Many major medical insurance policies restrict out of state coverage and may not offer any coverage for treatments outside of the United States. **Medicare** does not pay for medical treatment abroad. Temporary supplemental insurance policies can be purchased for the duration of travel. These are good investments if travelers will be away more than a week or two.

KEY TERMS

Compression stockings—Support hosiery used by men and women to prevent deep vein thrombosis, swelling, or leg pain.

Deep vein thrombosis—A blood clot that forms in a vein in the lower leg or thigh.

Implanted cardiac defibrillators (ICDs)—Small devices placed in the chest below the collar bone that monitor the heart and can send a small jolt of electricity to restore normal rhythm. They are most often prescribed for rapid or irregular heartbeat but can be used as a pacemaker for a slower heart rhythm.

Pulmonary embolism—A blood clot that occurs in the lung and is often fatal.

Radioisotopes—Small amounts of radioactive material used in medical imaging scans.

At the destination

Travel is supposed to be enjoyable, especially as adults grow older. Seniors should pace their daily activities and balance them with healthy meals and rest.

A change in climate often puts stress on the body. As adults grow older, the ability to cool the body and maintain hydration is slowed down. Some older adults may not feel hot when the outside temperature is reaching dangerous levels. They also may not feel thirsty, even if their bodies are already dehydrated. It may be tempting to linger in the sun, but older adults should seek shade and a cool drink, preferably something without alcohol or **caffeine**. In warm climates, wearing a hat and light-colored, lightweight clothing that fits loosely around the body is recommended.

In addition, older adults should try to avoid infection. Frequent hand washing or use of alcohol-based hand sanitizers before eating and after being around crowded places such as the airplane, train, or tour bus helps to avoid disease transmission.

Returning from abroad

Travelers, especially those who visit developing countries or who remain abroad for several weeks or months, should be vigilant when they return to the United States. Travel-related illnesses may take time to develop. This usually depends on the destination, how long the person was out of the country, what kind of accommodations they had, any underlying medical conditions, and exposure to potential infection. A fever of any kind that occurs a few days to several months after a trip abroad is cause to seek medical attention. The traveler should tell the physician where he or she has been and for how long, as well as the activities engaged in or if the traveler had a tattoo, body piercing, or had an injection. The length of time between return home and the appearance of fever can be a crucial indication of a particular infectious disease. Dengue fever, for example, appears three weeks or more after the traveler returns home. Malaria may take 6 to 12 months to show symptoms.

Resources

PERIODICALS

Patterson, Ian. "Information Sources Used by Older Adults for Decision Making about Tourist and Travel Destinations." *International Journal of Consumer Studies* 31, no 5 (September 2007): 528–533.

OTHER

Air Travel and Your Health." *The Harvard Medical School Family Health Guide.* October 2006 [cited April 14, 2008]. http://www.health.harvard.edu/fhg/updates/update1006b.shtml.

"The Sky's the Limit: Travel Trends among the Baby Boom Generation & Beyond." *Focalyst Insight Report* June 2007 [cited April 14, 2008]. AARP. http://www.aarp.org/research/family/travel/travel_trends.html.

"Travel Tips for Older Adults." *Center for Aging Research and Clinical Care.* [Cited April 14, 2008]. Cornell University. http://www.cornellaging.com/tips.html.

ORGANIZATIONS

American Association of Retired Persons (AARP), 601 E Street NW, Washington, DC, 20049, (888) 687-2277, http://www.aarp.org.

Centers for Disease Control and Prevention (CDC), 1100 Clifton Rd., Atlanta, GA, 30333, (404) 639-3311, (800) CDC-INFO, (703) 931-4520, http://www.cdc.gov/travel.

Foundation for Health in Aging, 350 Fifth Avenue, Suite 801, New York, NY, 10118, (212) 755-6810, http://www.healthinaging.org.

Janie F. Franz

Seniors' health

Definition

Seniors' health refers to the physical and mental conditions of senior citizens, those who are in their 60s and older. The proportion of people age 65 years and older in the United States is on the rise and will continue to increase through 2050. As of July 1, 2004, there were 36.3 million Americans age 65 and older, 12% of the total U.S. population, according to the U. S. Census Bureau. This will grow to 86.7 million, or 21% of the total U.S. population by 2050, the Census Bureau estimates. Worldwide, there were nearly 500 million people age 65 and older as of July 1, 2007, according to the United Nations Statistics Division. This represented 7.5% of the world's estimated population of 6.6 billion.

Purpose

For a senior, the aging process and a person's lifestyle will affect health. People who maintain a healthy weight, **exercise** regularly, eat nutritionally, and don't smoke reduce the risk for many health conditions. This wellness allows people to live longer and to remain independent for more years. **Smoking**, **obesity** (excess weight), and lack of exercise shorten life and increase the risk for many health conditions. According to the Centers for Disease Control and Prevention, about 80% of people in the United States age 65 and older have at least one chronic (long-lasting) condition and 50% have two.

Diet and exercise

Proper **diet** and regular exercise form the foundation of senior health. A nutritional diet and physical activity can help prevent diseases such as **cancer**, **stroke**, **heart disease**, and diabetes. A healthy diet also can help manage diabetes, high **blood pressure**, and heart disease.

As people age, there is more of a need to exercise on a regular basis. According to the American Heart Association, the inactive person loses from 3–5% of muscle fiber each decade after age 30. That loss would total 30% of lost muscle fiber at age 60. Exercise helps to boost muscle strength. It can help improve balance and coordination, and therefore help to prevent **falls**.

Organizations including the heart association advise that regular physical activity helps prevent bone loss (**osteoporosis**) and the risk of conditions such as heart disease, Type II diabetes, **colon cancer**, **stress**, and **depression**. In addition, exercise can help extend the lives of people with conditions such as diabetes, high blood pressure, and **high cholesterol**. Good health later in life helps to prevent serious illness or **death** from common infections as well. If a senior catches the flu, for instance, it can have more detrimental effects than in a healthier, younger person. When the SARS outbreak occurred in 2002 and

2003, clinicians expressed concern about the elderly Americans and again expressed the importance of diet and exercise. As people age, their **immune system** response weakens. Seniors need to be proactive in keeping their systems strong.

Osteoporosis

Osteoporosis is a condition in which bones become less dense (solid). Bones become brittle, thinner, and break easily. Although osteoporosis is associated with aging, it is only the risk of osteoporosis that increases as a person ages. It is linked to approximately 70% of bone fractures in people age 46 and older. According to the National Institutes of Health (NIH), one out of two women over age 50 will experience an osteoporosis-related fracture. So will one out of eight men over 50.

Osteoporosis is associated primarily with the changes that occur to women during **menopause**. During menopause, there is a decrease in the level of estrogen, the hormone that helps maintain bone mass. Other causes of osteoporosis include lack of exercise and a diet deficient in **vitamin D**.

Osteoporosis is largely preventable, however, research released in 2003 said that evidence is increasing to suggest that the condition starts as far back as in the womb. If this is true, it still is preventable, but by the behavior of the mother carrying a child. More research needs to be done, but it is clear that childhood growth rates are linked to hip fractures that happen decades later.

Osteoarthritis

Osteoarthritis is a joint disease in which cartilage wears out and bones rub against each other. This condition can occur gradually over time as activities performed throughout the years cause wear on joints. In addition, bones thin as a person ages.

Excess weight and injuries can aggravate this condition. About 16 million Americans experience some form of osteoarthritis. It generally affects the neck, fingers, lower back, knees, and toes. Symptoms include **pain**, stiffness, swelling, and creaking. The pain may disrupt sleep, and joint stiffness may make it difficult for a person to dress.

Falls

More than two million Americans each year fall and experience serious injuries, according to the American Academy of Otolaryngology-Head and Neck Surgery. For seniors, fall-related injuries can reduce mobility and hinder **independence**.

As people age, their reflexes slow down so it may be more difficult to prevent a fall. Deteriorating vision and hearing can affect balance, which can cause an accidental fall. Furthermore, conditions such as arthritis, **dizziness**, and sleeping disorders can increase the likelihood of a fall. In addition, a person may fall at the start of a condition such as a stroke or **heart attack**.

Falls can result in broken bones or fractures because bones are weakened by osteoporosis. In addition, healing takes longer. Head injuries could affect sight and hearing. Injuries sustained during falls could reduce an active person's mobility and independence.

Vision

Eyesight changes as people age. Generally, people are in their 40s when they experience **presbyopia**, a form of farsightedness. This is a progressive condition involving a decrease in the eye's ability to focus on close objects (near vision). By age 65, little near focusing ability remains.

Glaucoma is a condition caused by pressure from the build-up of a large amount of fluid in the eye. This progressive condition is often seen in people in their 50s. It starts with the gradual loss of peripheral vision. If not treated, it can lead to some vision loss.

People in their 60s may experience the first signs of **age-related macular degeneration** (AMD). It is a progressive condition affecting the retina. The macula in the retina distinguishes detail. Degeneration in the macula could cause scarring and a gradual reduction in vision. The person experiences a circle of blindness, an area of sightlessness that grows as the condition progress.

More than half of people age 65 or older will be diagnosed with **cataracts**. Cataract refers to the loss of the transparency in the lens of the eye. As the loss progresses, the person is able to see less detail. This condition generally affects both eyes.

Hearing

Presbycusis, age-related **hearing loss**, is a progressive condition. It usually starts with a difficulty in hearing high-frequency sound such as people talking. A senior has less trouble with low-frequency tones. Background noise will make it even more difficult to hear. Presbycusis affects approximately 25% of people between the ages of 65 and 75 and half of those over 75. Many people diagnosed with this condition say they have lost hearing in both ears. They also report feelings of dizziness and that they experience a ringing in their ears.

Sleep disorders

Sleep patterns change when a person ages. Many people in their 60s and 70s experience less time in the stages of deep sleep known as delta sleep. Despite this change, many healthy older people don't experience **sleep disorders**. Overall health plays a role in whether a senior experiences trouble sleeping.

Obesity is linked to snoring and sleep apnea. Snoring can turn into apnea. A person with apnea stops breathing for up to one minute until the brain restarts the breathing process. This action could be repeated several hundred times each night.

Furthermore, a senior's sleep can be disrupted by conditions such as arthritis, osteoporosis, and Alzheimer's disease. **Insomnia**, or the inability to stay asleep, is a symptom of conditions including depression, **anxiety**, chronic pain, and restless legs syndrome (RLS).

RLS involves movement of legs when a person is at rest. The person moves legs in response to a tingling sensation in the upper leg, calf, or foot. In other cases, legs move involuntarily. Sensations that trigger movement can re-occur within seconds.

A person with RLS is likely to have PLMD (**periodic limb movement disorder**). A sleeping person with this condition will kick legs or move arms repeatedly. These involuntary movements can last from 20 seconds to an hour. Approximately 45% of the elderly have a mild form of PLMD, according to the National Sleep Foundation.

The cause of these disorders is not known. They are thought to be caused by a chemical reaction in the brain. In addition, the conditions may be hereditary.

Mental health

While age has little effect on the mind, social and emotional factors affect an older person's health. After a lifetime of work or raising a family, retirement brings several challenges. A person who has been identified for years by a profession may experience a sense of lost identity.

A senior may find that the thinking process has changed. Learning something new may take longer. However, older people have excellent recall of new information.

Memory loss may be a concern, particularly since this is a symptom of Alzheimer's disease.

Dementia

Alzheimer's disease is a form of dementia, a condition in which mental abilities decline. Symptoms of dementia include memory loss that goes beyond forgetting a word or where an item was placed. The person with dementia may never recognize family members or remember how to perform functions such as preparing a meal. Sometimes they experience a change in personality, with some uncharacteristic aggression or paranoia.

Alzheimer's disease is the most prevalent form of dementia. Although the cause of this condition is not known, the risk of Alzheimer's increases as a person ages. In 2007, the condition affected one in 15 people over the age of 65. The ratio rises to one in three people age 85 and older.

Alzheimer's is a progressive condition. In most cases, after five to eight years, a patient with this condition is unable to perform basic functions. There is no known cure for Alzheimer s. However, as of 2008, the U.S. Food and Drug Administration (FDA) had approved five medications that could help delay the degenerative process.

Precautions

A health condition may result in a doctor recommending against some forms of exercise. However, even if a person can't jog, other forms of exercise include those designed for people in wheelchairs and those who are bedridden.

Treatments for menopause and osteoporosis include Raloxifene, a medication that may cause **blood clots**.

Description

The cost of treatment varies. Cost of medical treatment will be determined by the type of procedure and whether a person has medical insurance. Health plan and **Medicare** coverage and copayments impact an individual's cost for various preventions and treatments.

Nutrition

Nutrition plays an important role in senior health. Not only does a well-balanced diet keep a person from becoming obese, that same diet is a safeguard against health conditions that seniors face. Proper diet can help prevent a condition like diabetes or keep it from worsening.

The senior diet should consist of foods that are low in fat, particularly saturated fat and cholesterol.

A person should choose foods that provide nutrients such as iron and **calcium**. Other healthy menu choices include:

- fish, skinless poultry, and lean meat.
- proteins such as dry beans (red beans, navy beans, and soybeans), lentils, chickpeas, and peanuts.
- low-fat dairy products
- vegetables, especially those that are dark green and leafy
- citrus fruits or juices, melons, and berries
- whole grains like wheat, rice, oats, corn, and barley
- whole grain breads and cereals

Exercise

Physical activity should be rhythmic, repetitive, and should challenge the circulatory system. It also should be enjoyable so that a senior gets in the habit of exercising regularly for 30 minutes each day. It may be necessary to check with a doctor to determine the type of exercise that can be done.

Walking is recommended for **weight loss**, stress release, and many other conditions. Brisk walking is said to produce the same benefits as jogging. Other forms of exercise can include gardening, bicycling, hiking, swimming, dancing, skating or ice-skating. If weather prohibits outdoor activities, a person can work out indoors with an exercise video.

Exercise also offers a chance to socialize. In some cities, groups of seniors meet for regular walks at shopping malls. Senior centers offer exercise classes ranging from line dancing to belly dancing.

Costs for exercise range from the price of walking shoes to the fees for joining a gym.

Osteoporosis

Prevention is the best method of treating osteoporosis. Methods of preventing osteoporosis include regular weight-bearing exercise such as walking, jogging, weight lifting, **yoga**, and stair climbing.

People should not smoke since smoking makes the body produce less estrogen. Care should be taken to avoid falling.

Diet should include from 1,000–1,300 mg. of calcium each day. Sources of calcium include:

- leafy, dark-green vegetables such as spinach, kale, mustard greens, and turnip greens
- low-fat dairy products such as milk, yogurt, and cheeses such as cheddar, Swiss, mozzarella, and parmesan; also helpful are foods made with milk such as pudding and soup
- canned fish such as salmon, sardine, and anchovies
- tortillas made from lime-processed corn
- tofu processed with calcium-sulfate
- calcium and vitamin D tablets

MEDICAL TREATMENT An x ray will indicate bone loss when much of the density has decreased. A more effective way of detecting osteoporosis is the DEXA-scan (dual-energy x-ray absorbtiometry). This whole-body scan will indicate whether a person is at risk for fractures. It could be useful for people at risk for osteoporosis as well as women near the age of menopause or older. People should ask their doctors about whether this test is needed.

During menopause, a woman loses estrogen. A pill or skin patch containing estrogen and progesterone eases symptoms of menopause has been used to treat osteoporosis. This treatment is known as **hormone replacement therapy** (HRT). In 2002, the Women's Health Initiative found that HRT produced harmful effects in postmenopausal women, including increased incidence of **breast cancer**, heart disease and dementia. The effects were bad enough to stop the study. In 2003, researchers were looking for alternatives to HRT for women who had been using the hormones for osteoporosis. Until an alternative is identified, women and physicians have been advised to closely weigh the risks and benefits of hormone therapy. Several drugs are available to help reduce the risk of fractures in seniors with osteoporosis. In 2003, the FDA approved a new treatment option called Teriparatide. Some alternative treatments show promise in studies, including SAMe, (S-adenosylmethionine). However, long-term safety and effectiveness of SAMe have yet to be established.

Osteoarthritis

Treatments for osteoarthritis range from preventative measures such as walking to joint replacement surgery. Treatment costs vary from no cost for soaking a joint in cold water, the price of over-the-counter remedies to fees for surgery.

Preventive and maintenance remedies include low-impact exercise such as swimming and walking, along with maintaining proper posture. Nutritional aids include foods rich in **vitamin C** such as citrus fruits and broccoli. Also recommended is daily consumption of 400 international units of **Vitamin E**.

Cutting back on fats, sugar, salt, cholesterol, and alcohol helps relieve the symptoms of osteoarthritis.

HOME REMEDIES AND PHYSICAL THERAPY The Arthritis Foundation recommends several remedies for easing pain. To treat inflammation, a person should use a cold treatment. Methods include soaking the affected area in cold water or applying an ice pack. To soothe aches and stimulate circulation, a person applies heat to the affected area for 20 minutes. This should be done three times a day.

Over-the-counter (OTC) remedies such as **aspirin** and ibuprofen and salves containing capsaicin can be helpful. Furthermore, a doctor may recommend anti-inflammatory medications.

SURGICAL TREATMENT If osteoarthritis is suspected, a doctor's diagnosis will include an assessment of whether joint pain is part of a patient's medical history. The doctor may take an x ray to determine the presence of cartilage loss and how much degeneration occurred.

Acupuncture may be helpful in treating mild osteoarthritis. Generally, a person should have one to two treatments a week for several weeks. Afterward, one treatment is recommended. An assessment of results should be made after 10 treatments.

In cases of severe osteoarthritis, joint replacement surgery or joint immobilization may be required. Joints are replaced with metal, plastic, or ceramic material.

Fall prevention

Fall prevention starts with regular exercise such as walking. This improves balance and muscles. The walk route should be on level ground. Other methods for preventing falls include:

- when rising from a chair or bed, a senior should move slowly to avoid dizziness
- people who smoke should quit
- shoes with low heels and rubber soles are recommended
- medications should be monitored because of side effects that increase the probability of a fall
- vision and hearing should be checked periodically
- fall-proofing the home, including the installation of lighting, especially on stairways, clearing clutter and electrical cords that can cause falls, and installing handrails and strips in bathtubs and rails on stairs.

MEDICAL TREATMENT FOR FALLS After a fall, a senior may need first aid treatment for cuts or fractures. The doctor may evaluate whether medications cause balance problems. If indicated, the doctor may examine the patient's central nervous system function, balance, and muscle/joint function. A hearing or vision test may be ordered.

Corrective measures could include adjusting prescriptions, vision surgery or having the patient use a cane or walker.

Vision

A person diagnosed with presbyopia may need bifocals or reading glasses to read print that appears too small. These lenses may need to be changed as vision changes over the years. Eventually, a person relies on glasses to focus on items that are near. Other seniors who never needed corrective lenses may need to wear eyeglasses. Publishers aware of this condition produce books with large print.

A senior should schedule periodic vision exams because early treatment helps prevent or lessen a risk of cataracts or glaucoma. Diet also plays a role in vision care. Dark green vegetables like broccoli are said to help prevent cataracts from progressing. Physical exercise is thought to reduce the pressure associated with glaucoma.

Glaucoma can be treated with eye drops. Surgery can remove cataracts. The affected lens is removed and replaced with a permanent synthetic lens called an intraocular lens. Macular degeneration is the leading cause of vision loss and blindness in Americans age 65 and older, affecting 1.75 million Americans. There are two types of macular degeneration: wet and dry. There was no successful treatment for dry macular degeneration as of 2008 but there are three FDA-approved medications for treating wet macular degeneration.

Hearing

An audiologist can administer tests to determine the amount of hearing loss. Although there is no cure for presbycusis, **hearing aids** can help a senior affected by age-related hearing loss. If this treatment is not effective, the person might need to learn to read lips.

Sleep disorders

Losing weight can help with conditions such as snoring and sleep apnea. A doctor may advise the senior to quit smoking, reduce alcohol consumption, or to sleep on his or her side. In some cases, a doctor may refer the senior to a sleep disorder clinic. The senior may be prescribed a continuous positive airway pressure device. Known as a CPAP, the device is placed over the nose. It sends air into the nose.

PLMD and restless leg syndrome may be treated with the prescription drugs Dopar, Requip, and Mirapex. These disorders could be signs of kidney or circulation conditions. Treatment of those conditions should end these sleeping disorders.

Insomnia treatments include exercising and treating depression, stress, and other causes of sleeplessness.

Mental health

After retirement, a senior must find activities and interests to provide a sense of fulfillment. Otherwise, feelings of loneliness and **isolation** can lead to depression and susceptibility to poor health.

Activities that stimulate a person physically and intellectually contribute to good health. A senior can start an exercise program, take up hobbies, take classes, or volunteer. Senior centers offer numerous activities. Lunch programs provide nutritional meals and companionship. This is important because a senior living alone may not feel motivated to prepare healthy meals.

Dementia

Diagnosis of Alzheimer's disease starts with a thorough medical examination. The doctor should administer memory tests. Blood tests may be required, as well as a CT scan or MRI scan of the brain. If Alzheimer's is diagnosed, the doctor may prescribe medication to slow down progression of this form of dementia.

As of 2007, the FDA had approved five prescription medications for treatment of Alzheimer's Disease (AD). Tacrine, donepezil, riviastigmine, and galantamine are cholinesterase inhibitors that enhance memory. Modest improvement was reported in clinical trials on donepezil, riviastigmine, and galantamine. Tacrine's possible side effects include liver damage, so it is seldom prescribed. Namenda (memantine) is approved for moderate to severe AD. It is in a class of drugs called N-methyl D-aspertate (NMDA) antagonists.

Preparation

Before beginning a weight loss or exercise program, seniors should check with their doctors. The doctor will determine whether a patient is at a healthy weight, or needs to gain or lose weight. The medical professional should be informed about a health condition or a family history of a condition like heart disease. The doctor may order a physical exam or recommend a specific exercise program.

Exercise preparation

A senior should select a form of exercise enjoyable enough to become a regular routine. Suitable clothing or equipment such as walking shoes or a bicycle helmet should be purchased. If a person is active for more than a half-hour, the American Heart Association recommends drinking water every 15 minutes.

In addition to packing a water bottle, a person should pick an exercise buddy. Exercising with a friend or a group makes the activity more enjoyable. In addition, a person is more apt to stick with a routine if a buddy is involved.

Before exercising, a warm-up with slow stretching exercises is recommended. This could take longer for a senior because muscular elasticity slows down as a person ages. The exercise session should end with a cool-down that includes slow stretches.

Aftercare

Some recovery time may be needed after surgery. However, a healthy person will heal more quickly. A senior needs to maintain a schedule of regular exercise in order to remain mobile. Otherwise, a minor illness could make them dependent on others for daily care, according to the American Heart Association.

If mobility becomes limited due to a condition such as osteoarthritis, equipment like a walker and devices that make it easier to open bottles and grip cutlery can be helpful.

Risks

Exercising too long or too strenuously can be physically harmful. The over-exertion could cause the person to lose interest in exercise and put off establishing a regular routine. Experts recommend starting out slowly and building up to more intense or longer sessions. This is particularly important for a sedentary person.

Osteoporosis

The long-term effects of hormone replacement therapy have ruled this treatment out for some women.

Results

Seniors who stay active and eat nutritionally will be at less risk for conditions such as diabetes. A senior also should seek mental stimulation and social interaction. These provide enjoyment, boost self-esteem, and help reduce feelings of isolation and depression. Although eyesight and hearing will weaken, glasses and hearing aids help seniors keep the senses of sight and hearing.

When surgery is required for osteoarthritis, **hip replacement** surgery is extremely successful. In about 98% of surgeries, flexibility returns and pain is eased. Knee replacement surgery also is effective.

If a person maintains a healthy lifestyle, the ability to avoid falls and recover from them is increased.

After a fall, seniors needs to build up physical strength and the confidence needed so they don't fear falling again. Care should be taken so that seniors don't feel isolated by their injuries. Isolation could lead to decreased mobility and loss of independence.

There is no cure for Alzheimer's disease. However, several medications have proved moderately effective in stopping memory loss. Since Alzheimer's is progressive, a person diagnosed with this condition should make arrangements for the future. Finances should be taken care of and plans should be made for future care. Family should be brought into the discussion.

After diagnosis, a person should stay active for as long as possible. Not only does this help with enjoying this stage of life, activities can help to fight depression. Alzheimer and other support groups can be helpful. In addition, modifications to environment can be effective.

Resources

BOOKS

Editors of the Johns Hopkins Medical Letter Health After 50.*The Johns Hopkins Medical Guide to Health After 50.*New York: Black Dog & Leventhal Publishers, Inc., 2006.

Fodor, John T.*Maintaining Your Health and Vitality: A Guide for Seniors and Their Families*Bangor, ME: Booklocker.com, 2007.

PERIODICALS

DuVal, Tara, et al. "Preventive Care in Older Adults: What and When?"*Family Practice Recertification*(October 2007): 41(8).

Quinn, Jane Bryant. "The Medicare Drug Plan: How to Help Your Parents: There's a New Prescription Benefit for the Elderly. But Choosing the Right Insurer is Complicated, and Time is Running Out. Here's What to Do."*Good Housekeeping*(April 2006): 79(2).

Reese, Susan. "CTE Plays a Crucial Role in Health Care for the Elderly: The Need for Nurses, for Sure, Is Extremely Severe, but the Need for Health Care Professionals in General is Just as Critical, as Many of These Health Care professionals Support the Proper, Accurate, Timely and Critical Care of Patients."*Techniques* (October 2007): 20(6).

Seppa, N. "Fueling a Flu Debate: Do Vaccinations Save Lives Among the Elderly?"*Science News*(October 6, 2007): 213.

Wellbery, Caroline. "Benefits of Exercise Regimen are Limited in Older Adults."*American Family Physician* (October 15, 2007): 1214.

Zoler, Mitchel L. "Clue Into Suicide Risk Among Elderly Patients."*Family Practice News*(November 1, 2007): 30.

ORGANIZATIONS

Alzheimer's Association. 225 N. Michigan Ave., Suite 1700, Chicago, IL 60601. (800) 272-3900. http://www.alz.org . (Accessed Jan. 8, 2008.)

American Academy of Otolaryngology-Head and Neck Surgery. One Prince St., Alexandria, VA 22314-3357. (703) 836-4444. http://www.ent.org. (Accessed Jan. 8, 2008.)

American Dietetic Association. 120 S. Riverside Plaza, Suite 2000, Chicago, IL 60606. (800) 877-1600. http://www.eatright.org. (Accessed Jan. 8, 2008.)

American Heart Association. 7272 Greenville Ave., Dallas, TX75231. (800) 242-8721. http://www.americanheart.org. (Accessed Jan. 8, 2008.)

Division of Aging and Seniors, Health Canada. Address locator: 1908A1, 200 Eglantine Driveway, Ottawa, ON K1A 1B4 Canada. (613) 952-7606. http://www.publichealth.gc.ca. (Accessed Jan. 8, 2008.)

National Institute on Aging. Building 31, Room 5C27, 31 Center Dr., Bethesda, MD 20892. (800) 222-2225. http://www.nia.nih.gov. (Accessed Jan. 8, 2008.)

National Osteoporosis Foundation. 1232 22nd St., NW, Washington, DC 20037. (800) 231-4222. http://www.nof.org. (Accessed Jan. 8, 2008.)

Liz Swain
Ken R. Wells

Sexual dysfunction

Definition

Sexual dysfunction is broadly defined as the inability to fully enjoy sexual intercourse. Specifically, sexual dysfunctions are disorders that interfere with a full sexual response cycle. These disorders make it difficult for a person to enjoy or to have sexual intercourse. While sexual dysfunction rarely threatens physical health, it can take a heavy psychological toll, bringing on **depression**, **anxiety**, and debilitating feelings of inadequacy.

Description

Sexual dysfunction takes different forms in men and women. A dysfunction can be life-long and always present, acquired, situational, or generalized, occurring despite the situation. A man may have a sexual problem if he:

- ejaculates before he or his partner desires
- does not ejaculate, or experiences delayed ejaculation
- is unable to have an erection sufficient for pleasurable intercourse
- feels pain during intercourse
- lacks or loses sexual desire

A woman may have a sexual problem if she:

- lacks or loses sexual desire
- has difficulty achieving orgasm
- feels anxiety during intercourse
- feels pain during intercourse
- feels vaginal or other muscles contract involuntarily before or during sex
- has inadequate lubrication

The most common sexual dysfunctions in men include:

- Erectile dysfunction: an impairment of the erectile reflex. The man is unable to have or maintain an erection that is firm enough for coitus or intercourse.
- Premature ejaculation: rapid ejaculation with minimal sexual stimulation before, on, or shortly after penetration and before the person wishes it.
- Ejaculatory incompetence: the inability to ejaculate within the vagina despite a firm erection and relatively high levels of sexual arousal.
- Retarded ejaculation: a condition in which the bladder neck does not close off properly during orgasm so that the semen spurts backward into the bladder.

Until recently, it was presumed that women were less sexual than men. In the past two decades, traditional views of female sexuality were all but demolished, and women's sexual needs became accepted as legitimate in their own right.

Female sexual dysfunctions include:

- Sexual arousal disorder: the inhibition of the general arousal aspect of sexual response. A woman with this disorder does not lubricate, her vagina does not swell, and the muscle that surrounds the outer third of the vagina does not tighten—a series of changes that normally prepare the body for orgasm ("the orgasmic platform"). Also, in this disorder, the woman typically does not feel erotic sensations.
- Orgasmic disorder: the impairment of the orgasmic component of the female sexual response. The woman may be sexually aroused but never reach orgasm. Orgasmic capacity is less than would be reasonable for her age, sexual experience, and the adequacy of sexual stimulation she receives.
- Vaginismus: a condition in which the muscles around the outer third of the vagina have involuntary spasms in response to attempts at vaginal penetration.
- Painful intercourse: a condition that can occur at any age. Pain can appear at the start of intercourse, midway through coital activities, at the time of orgasm, or after intercourse is completed. The pain can be felt as burning, sharp searing, or cramping; it can be external, within the vagina, or deep in the pelvic region or abdomen.

Causes and symptoms

Many factors, of both physical and psychological natures, can affect sexual response and performance. Injuries, ailments, and drugs are among the physical influences; in addition, there is increasing evidence that chemicals and other environmental pollutants depress sexual function. As for psychological factors, sexual dysfunction may have roots in traumatic events such as rape or incest, guilt feelings, a poor self-image, depression, chronic fatigue, certain religious beliefs, or marital problems. Dysfunction is often associated with anxiety. If a man operates under the misconception that all sexual activity must lead to intercourse and to orgasm by his partner, and if the expectation is not met, he may consider the act a failure.

Men

With premature ejaculation, physical causes are rare, although the problem is sometimes linked to a neurological disorder, prostate infection, or urethritis. Possible psychological causes include anxiety (mainly performance anxiety), guilt feelings about sex, and ambivalence toward women. However, research has failed to show a direct link between premature ejaculation and anxiety. Rather, premature ejaculation seems more related to sexual inexperience in learning to modulate arousal.

When men experience painful intercourse, the cause is usually physical; an infection of the prostate, urethra, or testes, or an allergic reaction to spermicide or condoms. Painful erections may be caused by Peyronie's disease, fibrous plaques on the upper side of the penis that often produce a bend during erection. **Cancer** of the penis or testes and arthritis of the lower back can also cause **pain**.

Retrograde ejaculation occurs in men who have had prostate or urethral surgery, take medication that keeps the bladder open, or suffer from diabetes, a disease that can injure the nerves that normally close the bladder during ejaculation.

Erectile dysfunction is more likely than other dysfunctions to have a physical cause. Drugs, diabetes (the most common physical cause), Parkinson's disease, **multiple sclerosis**, and spinal cord lesions can all be causes of erectile dysfunction. When physical causes are ruled out, anxiety is the most likely psychological cause of erectile dysfunction.

Women

Dysfunctions of arousal and orgasm in women also may be physical or psychological in origin. Among the most common causes are day-to-day discord with one's partner and inadequate stimulation by the partner. Finally, sexual desire can wane as one ages, although this varies greatly from person to person.

Pain during intercourse can occur for any number of reasons, and location is sometimes a clue to the cause. Pain in the vaginal area may be due to infection, such as urethritis; also, vaginal tissues may become thinner and more sensitive during breast-feeding and after **menopause**. Deeper pain may have a pelvic source, such as endometriosis, pelvic adhesions, or uterine abnormalities. Pain can also have a psychological cause, such as fear of injury, guilt feelings about sex, fear of pregnancy or injury to the fetus during pregnancy, or recollection of a previous painful experience.

Vaginismus may be provoked by these psychological causes as well, or it may begin as a response to pain, and continue after the pain is gone. Both partners should understand that the vaginal contraction is an involuntary response, outside the woman's control.

Similarly, insufficient lubrication is involuntary, and may be part of a complex cycle. Low sexual response may lead to inadequate lubrication, which may lead to discomfort, and so on.

Diagnosis

In deciding when a sexual dysfunction is present, it is necessary to remember that while some people may be interested in sex at almost any time, others have low or seemingly nonexistent levels of sexual interest. Only when it is a source of personal or relationship distress, instead of voluntary choice, is it classified as a sexual dysfunction.

The first step in diagnosing a sexual dysfunction is usually discussing the problem with a doctor, who will need to ask further questions in an attempt to differentiate among the types of sexual dysfunction. The physician may also perform a physical exam of the genitals, and may order further medical tests, including measurement of hormone levels in the blood. Men may be referred to a specialist in diseases of the urinary and genital organs (urologist), and primary care physicians may refer women to a gynecologist.

Treatment

Treatments break down into two main kinds: behavioral psychotherapy and physical. Sex therapy, which is ideally provided by a member of the American Association of Sexual Educators, Counselors, and Therapists (AASECT), universally emphasizes correcting sexual misinformation, the importance of improved partner communication and honesty, anxiety reduction, sensual experience and pleasure, and interpersonal tolerance and acceptance. Sex therapists believe that many sexual disorders are rooted in learned patterns and values. These are termed psychogenic. An underlying assumption of sex therapy is that relatively short-term outpatient therapy can alleviate learned patterns, restrict symptoms, and allow a greater satisfaction with sexual experiences.

In some cases, a specific technique may be used during intercourse to correct a dysfunction. One of the most common is the "squeeze technique" to prevent premature ejaculation. When a man feels that an orgasm is imminent, he withdraws from his partner. Then, the man or his partner gently squeezes the head of the penis to halt the orgasm. After 20–30 seconds, the couple may resume intercourse. The couple may do this several times before the man proceeds to ejaculation.

In cases where significant sexual dysfunction is linked to a broader emotional problem, such as depression or substance abuse, intensive psychotherapy and/or pharmaceutical intervention may be appropriate.

In many cases, doctors may prescribe medications to treat an underlying physical cause or sexual dysfunction. Possible medical treatments include:

- clomipramine and fluoxetine for premature ejaculation
- papaverine and prostaglandin for erectile difficulties
- hormone replacement therapy for female dysfunctions
- Viagra, a pill approved in 1998 as a treatment for impotence

Alternative treatment

A variety of alternative therapies can be useful in the treatment of sexual dysfunction. Counseling or psychotherapy is highly recommended to address any emotional or mental components of the disorder. Botanical medicine, either western, Chinese, or ayurvedic, as well as nutritional supplementation, can help resolve biochemical causes of sexual dysfunction. **Acupuncture** and homeopathic treatment can be helpful by focusing on the energetic aspects of the disorder.

Some problems with sexual function are normal. For example, women starting a new or first relationship may feel sore or bruised after intercourse and find that an over-the-counter lubricant makes sex more pleasurable. Simple techniques, such as soaking in a warm bath, may relax a person before intercourse and improve the experience. **Yoga** and meditation provide needed mental and physical **relaxation** for several conditions, such as vaginismus. Relaxation therapy eases and relieves anxiety about dysfunction. Massage is extremely effective at reducing **stress**, especially if performed by the partner.

Prognosis

There is no single cure for sexual dysfunctions, but almost all can be controlled. Most people who have a sexual dysfunction fare well once they get into a treatment program. For example, a high percentage of men with premature ejaculation can be successfully treated in two to three months. Furthermore, the gains made in sex therapy tend to be long-lasting rather than short-lived.

KEY TERMS

Ejaculatory incompetence—The inability to ejaculate within the vagina.

Erectile dysfunction—Difficulty achieving or maintaining an erect penis.

Orgasmic disorder—The impairment of the ability to reach sexual climax.

Painful intercourse (dyspareunia)—Generally thought of as a female dysfunction but also affects males. Pain can occur anywhere.

Premature ejaculation—Rapid ejaculation before the person wishes it, usually in less than one to two minutes after beginning intercourse.

Retrograde ejaculation—A condition in which the semen spurts backward into the bladder.

Sexual arousal disorder—The inhibition of the general arousal aspect of sexual response.

Vaginismus—Muscles around the outer third of the vagina have involuntary spasms in response to attempts at vaginal penetration, not allowing for penetration.

Resources

ORGANIZATIONS

American Academy of Clinical Sexologists. 1929 18th St. NW, Suite 1166, Washington, DC 20009. (202) 462-2122.

American Association for Marriage and Family Therapy. 1133 15th St., NW Suite 300, Washington, DC 20005-2710. (202) 452-0109. http://www.aamft.org.

David James Doermann

Sexually transmitted diseases

Definition

Sexually transmitted diseases are infections that are highly contagious and are spread through sexual contact.

Description

Aging presents physiological changes that increase the risk of contracting sexually transmitted diseases

(STDs). A woman's vaginal tract thins with age and may be more prone to tears where infections can enter. Sometimes, already having an STD, such as herpes or syphilis, can create ulcers on the genitals. This produces another avenue for HIV infections to enter the body.

Older women are at risk of being infected with the human papillomavirus (HPV), which is responsible for genital warts and **cervical cancer**. Doctors and researchers once thought these HPV infections were flare-ups of older infections but are now realizing that these are new diseases that are appearing in older patients because of unprotected sexual activity.

Moreover, the immune systems of older adults may be slowed simply by aging or compromised by existing medical conditions. A poorly working **immune system** causes sexually transmitted diseases to progress more rapidly than in younger people. These underlying medical conditions may make the disease progression for STDs more complex and treatment more difficult. In addition, there is a higher risk of **drug interactions** between medications used to treat chronic illnesses in the elderly and HIV.

Older adults are also least likely to use a condom during intercourse. Partly, this is because most elderly people, even those who used condoms in their youth, associate them with preventing unwanted pregnancies. Older women, in particular, may feel a sexual freedom in their later years. If they are widowed or divorced, they may feel that they can seek out new partners without the social constraints of their youth. With the advent of medications for **erectile dysfunction**, older men are finding a new lease on their sexuality. Men and women are realizing that their own sexuality continues well into old age. Unfortunately, many are engaging in risky behaviors such as having multiple partners or not using a condom.

Part of the problem with preventing and even treating STDs in older adults is the fact that often patients do not want to talk about their sexual activity or do not know how to broach the subject with their doctors. Moreover, doctors themselves are equally reluctant to initiate discussions about this topic with their elderly patients, and many do not consider older adults to be a high risk group akin to young people. Some doctors also misdiagnose early HIV symptoms of weakness, fatigue, and **memory loss** for normal aging. This delays diagnosis and treatment, placing not only the older patient at risk but all of his or her sexual partners at risk.

Types of STDs

More than twenty different diseases can be transmitted by sexual content, including HIV/AIDS.

ACQUIRED IMMUNE DEFICIENCY SYNDROME (AIDS) First reported in the U.S. in 1981, **AIDS** spread through the homosexual population in epidemic proportions. Today, it is a disease that is appearing among both heterosexual and homosexual populations and among those who share needles for injecting drugs (both legal and illegal). Before 1985, HIV infections were also spread through blood transfusions that were not screened for the virus. It also appears in children born to mothers infected with the disease. HIV is transmitted through unprotected sex and sharing needles.

CHLAMYDIA This STD is the most frequently reported STD in the U.S. Nearly 3 million Americans become infected each year. Adolescents have the highest incidence of this disease. Chlamydia is transmitted through oral, vaginal, and anal sexual contact. It can also be passed to a newborn during birth, causing eye infections and **pneumonia**. Though men can have the disease and can spread it to another woman or man, they do not have serious reproductive complications as women do. The disease can damage a woman's reproductive organs and promote pelvic inflammatory disease and infertility. Having Chlamydia puts a woman at risk factor for **ovarian cancer** and acquiring HIV. The U.S. is also seeing infections of Chlamydia and gonorrhea occurring at the same time.

GONORRHEA Gonorrhea can thrive not just in the vagina in women or the urethra in both men and women, it can multiply deep into the reproductive organs, infecting the cervix, the uterus, and the fallopian tubes, causing pelvic inflammatory disease and even infertility. It can also spread to the bloodstream and become life-threatening. Like Chlamydia, gonorrhea puts the patient at risk for HIV.

SYPHILIS Human beings have been living with this disease for millennia, with incidence rates rising and falling in cycles. In this century, syphilis incidence has increased by 12 percent for the general population, with rates for women decreasing and those for men increasing. This disease is transmitted through direct contact with a syphilis sore, usually through oral, vaginal, or anal sex. Women can also transmit syphilis to their unborn babies. If syphilis is not treated early and it progresses to more advanced stages, it can become systemic, damaging the eyes, heart, liver, bones, joints, nerves, blood vessels, and the brain. People with syphilis have double the risk of contracting HIV.

HUMAN PAPILLOMAVIRUS (HPV) HPV is a group of more than 100 **viruses**. Over 30 of them are sexually transmitted, infecting the skin of the penis, the outside of the vagina, the anus, or the linings of the rectum, the vagina, or the cervix. Some types of HPV cause genital warts, and others cause cervical **cancer** and other genital cancers.

TRICHOMONIASIS Trichomoniasis is a common, very curable STD. It is usually found in young women and can affect men also, but it is less common in older women. This may be because other types of vaginal flora are higher in elderly women and prevent trichomoniasis from developing. Men can contract the disease only from women, but women can acquire it from infected men or women.

GENITAL HERPES This is a highly contagious viral infection caused by two strains of herpes simplex virus, HSV-1 and HSV-2. HSV-2 is more common in women. The virus remains in the body for life and creates episodic symptoms. It is spread by having sexual contact, including oral-genital sex, with someone who has the disease.

Demographics

Though nearly two thirds of all sexually transmitted diseases are found among individuals under the age of 25, the incidence among older adults is on the rise. In some states, such as Michigan, STD incidence in older adults is rising to overshadow the rates found in teenagers. The Center for Disease Control (CDC) has reported that throughout the country people 40 and older are getting STDs at twice the rate as their younger counterparts, and women represent the most dramatic increases. However, in Michigan, STD rate are twice as high for men as women.

HPV exists among half of all sexually active men and women. Eighty percent of all women will have an HPV infection by age 50. Since there is no cure and one strain of HPV causes cervical cancer, these numbers are alarming.

Chlamydia rates have increased throughout all populations in this century. However, the increase among adults age 45 and older has been more than 200 percent. Gonorrhea also has climbed to record numbers, showing a 40 percent increase among older adults, whereas rates among adults in their twenties have increased less than 10 percent. New cases of syphilis, reported between 1995 and 2003, increased by 275 percent among older adults.

Conversely, though the number of cases of HIV has declined among people under 30, they have increased by almost 17 percent among older adults age 60 and older. Approximately 10 percent of all adults 50 years and older have been diagnosed with HIV. This may be due in part to HIV-infected adults living longer because of improved drug therapies. However, when 15 percent of all new HIV/AIDS cases happen to people age 50 and older, with 3 percent of all AIDS cases found in adults over age 60, there is another mechanism at work, probably an increase in risky behaviors.

Of particular concern is that fact that 55 percent of all AIDS cases among older adults who fall within populations of color (African Americans and Hispanics). Though nearly half of all men with AIDS are of color, 73 percent of women with AIDS are Hispanic or African American. These populations are also the fastest growing ethnic groups in the country. The challenges for prevention and treatment for these populations will further increase as these groups age. Therefore, age-appropriate and culture-appropriate STD prevention education programs will need to be created to deal with disease incidence in all populations of older adults.

Causes and symptoms

Causes

The causes of STDs vary depending on the nature of the infection. Some are viral, and some are bacterial. Chlamydia, gonorrhea, and syphilis are caused by distinct bacteria strains. Trichomoniasis is caused by a protozoan parasite. Genital herpes is caused by two strains of herpes simplex virus (HSV). AIDS is caused by the human immunodeficiency virus (HIV) that destroys the body's immune system and its ability to fight off infection. **Death** occurs to AIDS patients because the body cannot fight off illnesses such as pneumonia.

Symptoms

Many cases of sexually transmitted disease may go unreported because many STDs have mild symptoms or none at all during the early stages of the disease. Early symptoms of HIV/AIDS are fatigue and weakness. Chlamydia symptoms may be absent or very mild in women, and men may not even realize that they have it, though some men may experience a discharge from the penis. Women with gonorrhea usually report lower abdominal **pain**, vaginal discharge, and pain when they urinate. Men also experience a discharge from the penis and painful urination. Initial syphilis symptoms are open sores (chancres) that usually appear on the penis or vagina, but can also occur on the hands, the anus, or the mouth.

Men with trichomoniasis do not have any symptoms, though some may have a slight discharge or feel mild burning after urination. Women with trichomoniasis have a frothy, yellow-green vaginal discharge that has a strong odor and may experience vaginal **itching** or pain during urination or intercourse.

Men with genital herpes infections may have sores on the penis, and women can have them around the vaginal area. Both can find them on the buttocks, the thighs, or around the anus. Sometimes, sores appear in other areas of the body, as well as the mouth.

Diagnosis

The doctor will take a medical history and do a physical exam. For most STDs, a blood test can determine the exact type of STD a person has. Some STDs in women require a vaginal swab for slide preparation in order to examine the sample under a microscope.

Treatment

Most STDs can be treated and cured with **antibiotics**. Penicillin is the most effective treatment for syphilis, and metronidazole is used to treat trichomoniasis. Some strains of gonorrhea have become drug resistant, making treatment more difficult and finding a permanent cure allusive. Several new antibiotics and new combinations of drugs are being tried to treat this STD.

A number of drug combinations are now able to prolong the lives of those with HIV/AIDS. But diagnosis must be made early and monitoring begun immediately.

There is no cure for genital herpes, but several antiviral medications have been developed to shorten and prevent outbreaks. Patients need to take the medication for life and can still spread the disease if they engage in risky behaviors.

Prognosis

Many STDs can be cured with antibiotics. The patient will make a full recovery if the disease is identified and treated early. Some diseases, such as gonorrhea, are becoming more difficult to treat, and others such as genital herpes can only be managed. HIV/AIDs is proving to be a challenge, but progress is being made to extend the lives of those who have it and improve their quality of life.

Prevention

One proven way to prevent STDs is to use a condom during every sexual contact. This can prevent most STDs. Oral sexual contact may need to be limited or conduced with a condom or dental dam in the vagina.

WHEN TO SEE THE DOCTOR

Older adults should see the doctor if they have painful urination, genital sores, painful intercourse, or unusual vaginal discharges.

Some retirement communities and even **nursing homes** are supporting residents who wish to continue their sexual lives, often with having single residents housed in private rooms or having a special room available for sexual encounters. These facilities are also initiating education campaigns about condom use and STDs.

The CDC issued new HIV screening recommendations in 2006 that urged doctors to do voluntary blood tests on all patients age 13 to 64. This action hopes to prevent the 50 to 70 percent of new cases that are spread by those who do not know they have HIV.

Likewise, in 2007, New York City launched a new education program in senior centers that urged all older adults to have an HIV test as part of their regular yearly checkups. The state of Florida launched a similar education drive that distributed condoms and literature to community centers, **assisted living facilities**, and bereavement groups.

Another area of great concern is HPV infections. There is no cure for them. The mild forms resolve on their own, but the one causing cervical cancer and other genital cancers has been troubling. In 2006, a new vaccine was developed to prevent cervical cancer and genital warts. Gardasil protects against four types of HPV, which cause 90 percent of all genital warts and 75 percent of all cervical cancers. This vaccine is only available to young girls who are not sexually active.

Caregiver concerns

Healthcare providers should become familiar with the difference between HIV-associated dementia and Alzheimer's. Both mental conditions may present similarly but HIV-associated dementia has a very rapid disease progression, whereas Alzheimer's Disease progresses slowly.

In addition, healthcare providers should monitor elderly patients with herpes simplex viruses. These infections, though they are bothersome and painful, are not necessarily harmful to the body if they are managed. However, for those whose immune systems are compromised, herpes infections can lead to eye problems and neurological disorders, or can be fatal.

KEY TERMS

Acquired Immune Deficiency Syndrome (AIDS)—A disease that is characterized by the body's inability to fight off infection.

Chancres—Open sores

Human immunodeficiency virus (HIV)—The virus that causes AIDS.

Human papillomavirus (HPV)—A group of viruses that are responsible for genital warts and cervical cancer.

Resources

PERIODICALS

"Similarities between HIV infection and aging may aid fight against both."*Immunotherapy Weekly.*(April 7, 2004):46

Levy-Dweck, Sandra. "HIV/AIDS fifty and older: A hidden and growing population."*Journal of Gerontological Social Work.*(October 2005):37-51

Kirkendoll, Shantell. "STDs rising for older adults."*The Flint Journal.*(December 3, 2007):NA

Kotz, Deborah. "Sex ed for seniors: You still need those condoms."*U.S. News and World Report.*(August 5, 2007):NA

Williams, Edith. "Older Americans and AIDS: Some guidelines for prevention."*Social Work.*(April 2002): p105-112

ORGANIZATIONS

National Institute on Aging(NIA), 31 Center Drive, MSC 2292, Building 31, Room 5C27, Bethesda, Maryland, 20892, 301-496-1752, 301-496-1072, www.nia.nih.gov.

Rural Center for AIDS/STD Prevention, Indiana University, 801 E. Seventh St., Bloomington, IN, 47405-3085, 812-855-1718, 800-566-8644, 812-855-3717, aids@indiana.edu, www.indiana.edu.

Janie F. Franz

Sexually transmitted diseases cultures

Definition

Sexually transmitted diseases are infections spread from person to person through sexual contact. A culture is a test in which a laboratory attempts to grow and identify the microorganism causing an infection.

Purpose

Sexually transmitted diseases (STDs) produce symptoms such as genital discharge, **pain** during urination, bleeding, pelvic pain, skin ulcers, or urethritis. Often, however, they produce no immediate symptoms. Therefore, the decision to test for these diseases must be based not only the presence of symptoms, but on whether or not a person is at risk of having one or more of the diseases. Activities, such as drug use and sex with more than one partner, put a person at high risk for these diseases.

STD cultures are necessary to diagnose certain types of STDs. Only after the infection is diagnosed can it be treated and further spread of the infection prevented. Left untreated, consequences of these diseases range from discomfort to infertility to **death**. In addition, these diseases, if present in a pregnant woman, can be passed from mother to fetus.

Description

Gonorrhea, syphilis, chlamydia, chancroid, herpes, human papillomavirus, human immunodeficiency virus (HIV), and mycoplasma are common sexually transmitted diseases. Not all are diagnosed with a culture. For those that are, a sample of material is taken from the infection site, placed in a sterile container, and sent to the laboratory.

Bacterial cultures

In the laboratory, a portion of material from the infection site is spread over the surface of several different types of culture plates and placed in an incubator at body temperature for one to two days. Bacteria present in the sample will multiply and appear on the plates as visible colonies. They are identified by the appearance of their colonies and by the results of biochemical tests and a gram stain. The Gram stain is done by smearing part of a colony onto a microscope slide. After it dries, the slide is stained with purple and red stains, then examined under a microscope. The color of stain picked up by the bacteria (purple or red), the shape (such as round or rectangle), and the size provide valuable clues as to the identity and which **antibiotics** might work best. Bacteria that stain purple are called Gram-positive; those that stain red are called gram-negative.

The result of the gram stain is available the same day or in less than an hour if requested by the physician. An early report, known as a preliminary report, is usually available after one day. This report will tell if any microorganisms have been found yet, and if so, their Gram stain appearance—for example, a Gram-negative rod or a gram-positive cocci. The final report, usually available in one to seven days, includes complete identification and an estimate of the quantity of the microorganisms isolated.

A sensitivity test, also called antibiotic susceptibility test, commonly done on bacteria isolated from an infection site, is not always done on bacteria isolated from a sexually transmitted disease. These bacteria often are treated using antibiotics that are part of a standard treatment protocol.

GONORRHEA *Neisseria gonorrhoeae*, also called gonococcus or GC, causes gonorrhea. It infects the surfaces of the genitourinary tract, primarily the urethra in males and the cervix in females. On a gram stain done on material taken from an infection site, the bacteria appear as small gram-negative diplococci (pairs of round bacteria) inside white blood cells. *Neisseria gonorrhoeae* grows on a special culture plate called Thayer-Martin (TM) media in an environment with low levels of oxygen and high levels of carbon dioxide.

The best specimen from which to culture *Neisseria gonorrhoeae* is a swab of the urethra in a male or the cervix in a female. Other possible specimens include vagina, body fluid discharge, swab of genital lesion, or the first urine of the day. Final results usually are available after two days. Rapid nonculture tests are available to test for GC and provide results on the same or following day.

CHANCROID Chancroid is caused by *Haemophilus ducreyi*. It is characterized by genital ulcers with nearby swollen lymph nodes. The specimen is collected by swabbing one of these pus-filled ulcers. The gram stain may not be helpful as this bacteria looks just like other Haemophilus bacteria. This bacteria only grows on special culture plates, so the physician must request a specific culture for a person who has symptoms of chancroid. Even using special culture plates, *Haemophilus ducreyi* is isolated from less than 80% of the ulcers it infects. If a culture is negative, the physician must diagnose chancroid based on the person's symptoms and by ruling out other possible causes of these symptoms, such as syphilis.

MYCOPLASMA Three types of mycoplasma organisms cause sexually transmitted urethritis in males and pelvic inflammatory disease and cervicitis in females: *Mycoplasma hominis*, *Mycoplasma gentialium*, and *Ureaplasma urealyticum*. These organisms require special culture plates and may take up to six days to grow. Samples are collected from the cervix in a female, the urethra or semen in a male, or urine.

SYPHILIS Syphilis is caused by *Treponema pallidum*, one in a group of bacteria called spirochetes. It causes ulcers or chancres at the site of infection. The organism does not grow in culture. Using special techniques and stains, it is identified by looking at a sample of the ulcer or chancre under the microscope. Various blood tests also may be done to detect the treponema organism.

CHLAMYDIA Chlamydia is caused by the gram-negative baterium *Chlamydia trachomatis*. It is one of the most common STDs in the United States and generally appears in sexually active adolescents and young adults. While chlamydia often does not have any initial symptoms, it can, if left untreated, lead to pelvic inflammatory disease and sterility. Samples are collected from one or more of these infection sites: cervix in a female, urethra in a male, or the rectum. A portion of specimen is combined with a specific type of cell and allowed to incubate. Special stains are performed on the cultured cells, looking for evidence of the chlamydia organism within the cells. A swab can also be taken from the woman's vulva. Men and women can now be screened for Chlamydia with a urine sample. Urine-based screening has increased screening significantly, especially among men.

Viral cultures

To culture or grow a virus in the laboratory, a portion of specimen is mixed with commercially prepared animal cells in a test tube. Characteristic changes to the cells caused by the growing virus help identify the virus. The time to complete a viral culture varies with the type of virus. It may take several days or up to several weeks.

HERPES VIRUS Herpes simplex virus type 2 is the cause of genital herpes. Diagnosis is usually made based on the person's symptoms. If a diagnosis needs confirmation, a viral culture is performed using material taken from an ulcer. A Tzanck smear is a microscope test that can rapidly detect signs of herpes infection in cells taken from an ulcer. The culture takes up to 14 days. In 2004, the FDA approved a blood test to detect the antibodies to herpes virus.

HUMAN PAPILLOMAVIRUS Human papillomavirus causes genital warts. This virus will not grow in culture; the diagnosis is based on the appearance of the warts and the person's symptoms. In late 2003, the U. S. Food and Drug Administration (FDA) approved a human papillomavirus (HPV) DNA test with a Pap smear for screening women age 30 and older. The combined test would help physicians determine which women were at extremely low risk for **cervical cancer** and which should be more closely monitored.

HIV Human immunodeficiency virus (HIV) is usually diagnosed with a blood test. Cultures for HIV are possible, but rarely needed for diagnosis. However, newer rapid tests were developed in 2003 and approved by the FDA in 2004. These tests are cheaper and can deliver results in as little as three minutes. The FDA also approved an HIV test in 2004 that can detect HIV in saliva.

Preparation

Generally, the type of specimen depends on the type of infection. Cultures always should be collected before the person begins taking antibiotics. After collection of these specimens, each is placed into a sterile tube containing a liquid in which the organism can survive while in route to the laboratory. The new rapid HIV tests rely on blood samples collected from a finger stick or vein or on saliva collected from the mouth. Initial results are not sent to a lab but are processed onsite.

Urethral specimen

Men should not urinate one hour before collection of a urethral specimen. The physician inserts a sterile, cotton-tipped swab into the urethra.

Cervical specimen

Women should not douche or take a bath within 24 hours of collection of a cervical or vaginal culture. The physician inserts a moistened, nonlubricated vaginal speculum. After the cervix is exposed, the physician removes the cervical mucus using a cotton ball. Next, he or she inserts a sterile cotton-tipped swab into the endocervical canal and rotates the swab with firm pressure for about 30 seconds.

Vaginal specimen

Women should not douche or take a bath within 24 hours of collection of a cervical or vaginal culture. The physician inserts a sterile, cotton-tipped swab into the vagina.

Anal specimen

The physician inserts a sterile, cotton-tipped swab about 1 inch into the anus and rotates the swab for 30 seconds. Stool must not contaminate the swab.

KEY TERMS

Culture—A laboratory test done to grow and identify microorganisms causing infection.

Gram stain—Microsopic examination of a portion of a bacterial colony or sample from an infection site after it has been stained by special stains. Certain bacteria pick up the purple stain; these bacteria are called gram positive. Other bacteria pick up the red stain; these bacteria are called gram negative. The color of the bacteria, in addition to their size and shape, provide clues as to the identity of the bacteria.

Sensitivity test—A test that determines which antibiotics will kill the bacteria isolated from a culture.

Vulva—The external part of the woman's genital organs, including the vaginal vestibule.

Oropharynx (throat) specimen

The person's tongue is held down with a tongue depressor, as a healthcare worker moves a sterile, cotton-tipped swab across the back of the throat and tonsil region.

Urine specimen

To collect a "clean-catch" urine, the person first washes the perineum, and the penis or labia and vulva. He or she begins urinating, letting the first portion pass into the toilet, then collecting the remainder into a sterile container.

Results

These microorganisms are not found in a normal culture. Many types of microorganisms, normally found on a person's skin and in the genitourinary tract, may contaminate the culture. If a mixture of these microorganisms grow in the culture, they are reported as normal flora.

If a person has a positive culture for one or more of these microorganisms, treatment is started and his or her sexual partners should be notified and tested. Certain laws govern reporting and partner notification of various STDs. After treatment is completed, the person's physician may want a follow-up culture to confirm the infection is gone.

Resources

PERIODICALS

"Answer Back: Is there a Vulval Swwab Test for Chlamydia?" *Pulse* September 13, 2004: 100.

"Approval Sought for HIV-1 Test that Detects Antibodies in Oral Fluid or Plasma." *AIDS Weekly* October 27, 2003: 23.

Boschert, Sherry. "Chlaymdia Urine Test: Males Still Underscreened: Noninvasive Screening Test." *Pediatric News* August 2004: 10–12.

"FDA Approves DNAwithPap for Screening Women (Greater than or Equal to) Age 30)." *Contemporary OB/Gyn* October 2003: 105.

"FDA Approves OraQuick HIV-1/2 Test to Detect HIV-2 in Oral Fluid." *Biotech Week* July 21, 2004: 401.

Kaye, Donald. "FDA Approves Herpes Antibody Test." *Clinical Infectious Diseases* September 15, 2004: 1.

"New HIV Rapid Test Is 100 Percent Accurate." *Health & Medicine Week* September 15, 2003: 194.

"New Three-minute Rapid HIV Test Launched in the United States." *Medical Devices & Surgical Technology Week* September 12, 2004: 102.

"One-step HIV Test May Be Cheaper, Faster, Less Wasteful." *Medical Letter on the CDC & FDA* October 5, 2003: 5.

St. Lawrence, Janet S., et al. "STD Screening, Testing, Case Reporting, and Clinical and Partner Notification Practices: A National Survey of U.S. Physicians." *The American Journal of Public Health* November 2002: 1784.

ORGANIZATIONS

American Social Health Association. PO Box 13827, Research Triangle Park, NC 27709. (800) 227-8922. http://sunsite.unc.edu/ASHA.

Centers for Disease Control and Prevention. National Center for HIV, STD, and TB Prevention. 1600 Clifton Road NE, Atlanta, GA 30333. (404) 639-8000. http://www.cdc.gov/nchstp/od/nchstp.html.

Nancy J. Nordenson
Teresa G. Odle

Shiatsu

Definition

Shiatsu is a manipulative therapy developed in Japan and incorporating techniques of *anma* (Japanese traditional massage), **acupressure**, stretching, and Western massage. Shiatsu involves applying pressure to special points or areas on the body in order to maintain physical and mental well being, treat disease, or alleviate discomfort. This therapy is considered holistic because it attempts to treat the whole person instead of a specific medical complaint. All types of acupressure generally focus on the same pressure points and so-called energy pathways, but may differ in terms of massage technique. Shiatsu, which can be translated as finger pressure, has been described as needle-free acupuncture.

Origins

Shiatsu is an offshoot of anma that developed during the period after the Meiji Restoration in 1868. Traditional massage (anma) used during the age of shoguns was being criticized, and practitioners of *koho anma* (ancient way) displeased with it introduced new practices and new names for their therapies.

During the twentieth century, shiatsu distinguished itself from anma through the merging of Western knowledge of anatomy, koho anma, *ampuku* (abdominal massage), acupressure, *Do-In* (breathing practices), and Buddhism. Based on the work of Tamai Tempaku, shiatsu established itself in Japan and worldwide. The Shiatsu Therapists Association was found in 1925 and clinics and schools followed. Students of Tempaku began teaching their own brand of shiatsu, creating branch disciplines. By 1955, the Japanese Ministry of Health and Welfare acknowledged shiatsu as a beneficial treatment and licensing was established for practitioners.

Benefits

Shiatsu has a strong reputation for reducing stress and relieving nausea and vomiting. Shiatsu is also believed to improve circulation and boost the **immune system**. Some people use it to treat diarrhea, indigestion, constipation, and other disorders of the gastrointestinal tract; menstrual and menopausal problems; chronic pain; migraine; arthritis; toothache; anxiety; and **depression**. Shiatsu can be used to relieve muscular **pain** or tension, especially neck and back pain. It also appears to have sedative effects and may alleviate insomnia. In a broader sense, shiatsu is believed to enhance physical vitality and emotional well being.

Description

Shiatsu and other forms of Japanese acupressure are based on the concept of *ki*, the Japanese term for the all-pervading energy that flows through everything in the universe. (This notion is borrowed from the Chinese, who refer to the omnipresent energy as qi or chi.) Ki tends to flow through the body along special energy pathways called meridians, each of which is associated with a vital organ. In Asian systems of traditional medicine, diseases are often believed to occur due to disruptions in the flow this energy through the body. These disruptions may stem from emotional factors, climate, or a host of other causes including **stress**, the presence of impurities in the body, and physical trauma.

The aim of shiatsu is to restore the proper flow of bodily energy by massaging the surface of the skin along the meridian lines. Pressure may also be applied to any of the 600 or so acupoints. Acupoints, which are supposedly located just under the skin along the meridians, are tiny energy structures that affect the flow of ki through the body. When ki either stagnates and becomes deflected or accumulates in excess along one of these channels, stimulation to the acupoints, which are sensitive to pressure, can unblock and regulate the ki flow through toning or sedating treatment.

Western medicine hasn't proven the existence of meridians and acupoints. However, in one study, two French medical doctors conducted an experiment at Necher Hospital in Paris to test validity of theory that energy is being transported along **acupuncture** meridians. They injected and traced radioactive isotopes with gamma-camera imaging. The meridians may actually correspond to nerve transmission lines. In this view, shiatsu and other forms of healing massage may trigger the emission of naturally occurring chemicals called neurotransmitters. Release of these chemical messengers may be responsible for some of the therapeutic effects associated with shiatsu, such as pain relief.

Preparations

People usually receive shiatsu therapy while lying on a floor mat or massage table or sitting up. The massage is performed through the clothing—preferably a thin garment made from natural fibers—and disrobing is not required. Pressure is often applied using the thumbs, though various other parts of the body may be employed, including fingertips, palms, knuckles, elbows, and knees—some therapists even use their feet. Shiatsu typically consists of sustained pressure (lasting up to 10 seconds at a time), squeezing, and stretching exercises. It may also involve gentle holding as well as rocking motions. A treatment session lasts anywhere from 30 to 90 minutes.

Before shiatsu treatment begins, the therapist usually performs a general health assessment. This involves taking a family medical history and discussing the physical and emotional health of the person seeking therapy. Typically, the practitioner also conducts a diagnostic examination by palpating the abdomen or back for any energy imbalances present in other parts of the body.

Precautions

While shiatsu is generally considered safe, there are a few precautions to consider. Because it may increase blood flow, this type of therapy is not recommended in people with bleeding problems, heart disease , or **cancer**. Massage therapy should always be used with caution in those with **osteoporosis**, fresh wounds or scar tissue, bone fractures, or inflammation.

Applying pressure to areas of the head is not recommended in people with epilepsy or high **blood pressure**, according to some practitioners of shiatsu.

Shiatsu is not considered effective in the treatment of fever, burns, and infectious diseases.

Shiatsu should not be performed right after a meal.

Side effects

When performed properly, shiatsu is not associated with any significant side effects. Some people may experience mild discomfort, which usually disappears during the course of the treatment session.

Research & general acceptance

Like many forms of massage, shiatsu is widely believed to have a relaxing effect on the body. There is also a significant amount of research suggesting that acupressure techniques can relieve nausea and vomiting associated with a variety of causes, including pregnancy and anesthetics and other drugs. In one study, published in the *Journal Of Nurse-midwifery* in 1989, acupressure was shown to significantly reduce the effects of nausea in 12 of 16 women suffering from morning sickness. Five days of this therapy also appeared to reduce anxiety and improve mood. Another investigation, published in the *British Journal Of Anaesthesia* in 1999, studied the effects of acupressure on nausea resulting from the use of anesthetics. Pressure applied to an acupoint on the inside of the wrist appeared to alleviate nausea in patients who received anesthetics during the course of laparoscopic surgery.

Shiatsu may also produce sedative and analgesic effects. The sedative powers of acupressure were investigated in a study published in the *Journals of Gerontology* in 1999, which involved over 80 elderly people who suffered from sleeping difficulties. Compared to the people in the control groups, the 28 participants who received acupressure were able to sleep better. They slept for longer periods of time and were less likely to wake up during the night. The researchers concluded that acupressure may improve the quality of sleep in older adults. The use of acupressure in post-operative pain was investigated in a study published in the *Clinical Journal Of Pain* in 1996. In this study, which involved 40 knee surgery patients, one group received acupressure (15 acupoints were stimulated) while the control group received sham acupressure. Within an hour of treatment, members of the acupressure group reported less pain than those in the control group. The pain-relieving effects associated with acupressure lasted for 24 hours.

Shiatsu may benefit **stroke** victims. The results of at least one study (which did not include a control group) suggest that shiatsu may be useful during stroke rehabilitation when combined with other treatments.

Training & certification

A qualified shiatsu therapist must have completed courses in this form of therapy and should be nationally certified or licensed by the state (most are certified by the American Oriental Bodywork Therapy Association). Asking a medical doctor for a recommendation is a great place to start. It can also be helpful to consult friends and family members who have tried shiatsu. There are several massage-related organizations that offer information on locating a qualified therapist. These include the National Certification Board for Therapeutic Massage and Bodywork, the American **Massage Therapy** Association, the International School of Shiatsu, and the American Oriental Bodywork Therapy Association.

Resources

BOOKS

Cook, Allan R. *Alternative Medicine Sourcebook.*Detroit: Omnigraphics, 1999.

PERIODICALS

Chen, M.L., L.C. Lin, S.C. Wu, et al. "The effectiveness of acupressure in improving the quality of sleep of institutionalized residents." *J Gerontol A Biol Sci Med Sci* (1999): M389-94.

Felhendler, D. and B. Lisander. "Pressure on acupoints decreases postoperative pain." *Clin J Pain* (1996): 326-329.

Harmon, D., J. Gardiner, R. Harrison, et al. "Acupressure and the prevention of nausea and vomiting after laparoscopy." *Br J Anaesth* (1999): 387-390.

Hogg, P.K. "The effects of acupressure on the psychological and physiological rehabilitation of the stroke patient." *Dissertation Abstracts Int* (1986): 841.

Hyde, E. "Acupressure therapy for morning sickness. A controlled clinical trial." *J Nurse Midwifery* (1989): 171-178.

ORGANIZATIONS

Acupressure Institute. 1533 Shattuck Avenue, Berkeley, CA 94709.

American Massage Therapy Association. 820 Davis Street, Suite 100, Evanston, IL.

American Oriental Bodywork Therapy Association. 50 Maple Place, Manhassett, NY 11030.

International School of Shiatsu. 10 South Clinton Street, Doylestown, PA 18901.

National Certification Board for Therapeutic Massage and Bodywork. 8201 Greensboro Drive, Suite 300, McLean, VA 22102.

OTHER

International School of Shiatsu. http://www.shiatsubo.com.

Medline. http://igm.nlm.nih.gov.

Greg Annussek

Shingles

Definition

Also known as *herpes zoster,* or *zoster*, shingles appears as a generally painful and blistered skin rash. It is caused by a reactivation of the varicella zoster virus (VSV) that is also the origin of chicken pox. The name of the condition, *shingles* is derived from the Latin word, *cingulum,* which means "belt" or "girdle"

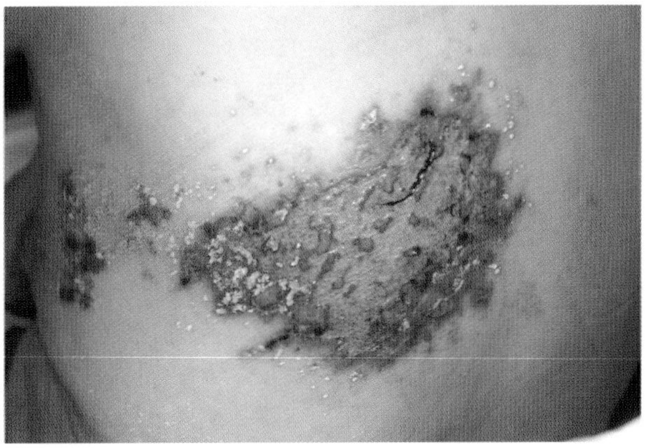

Shingles rash on a patient's back, which has ruptured and caused a further infection. Shingles (herpes zoster) is caused by the infection of sensory nerves with the varicella-zoster virus. *(Dr. MA Ansary/Photo Researchers, Inc. Reproduced by permission.)*

and was adopted due to the way in which the rash seems to spread. The name of the virus, *varicella-zoster* puts the Latin term meaning "little pox" together with the Greek word for "girdle"—and thus, also, comes the derivation for the scientific name for the disease, *herpes zoster.* In Italy, the condition is also known as *St. Anthony's Fire.*

Description

Any person who has had chicken pox is subject to developing shingles. Individuals who have not had chicken pox can contract that disease by being exposed to someone with shingles. Shingles is not contagious among those who have already had chicken pox because every person who has had chicken pox already has the potential for shingles.

When the VSV is reactivated in a person with a history of chicken pox, this virus then moves through the body by way of the nerve fibers. It typically settles in one area, localized on one side of the body or another. Initially individuals experience a burning sensation and sometimes more severe **pain**. Within two to three days the virus reaches the skin, and a rash appears, usually with small blisters that resemble those that come during the early stages of chicken pox. The rash continues to worsen for another three to five days, at which time the blisters open. The open sores usually begin to dry out and form a crust. Another two or three weeks pass before the crust falls off. At that point the skin finally begins to heal. Once the blisters dry out, the contagious stage of the disease is ended.

The trunk is often affected with the belt-like rash that extends from the spine around one side of the chest to the breastbone.

Lesions might appear on the scalp, the neck, or on the face in those areas along the nerve (trigeminal) that is like a three-pronged branch, affecting either the forehead, middle, or lower part of the face. That part of the branch specifically involved is the location where the lesions appear. Shingles also can affect the eyes or mouth if those nerves are affected.

Herpes Zoster Ophthalmicus

If the virus does involve the eye, more serious problems can result such as the scratching of the cornea, increasing the risk of bacterial infection, or inflammation inside the eye. In severe cases, the virus might also affect the optic nerve or retina. When shingles originate in the upper ophthalmic branch of the trigeminal nerve, often a small patch of the rash will appear on the tip of the nose. Medical professionals call this *Hutchinson's sign*; it is an indication of *herpes zoster ophthalmicus,* or HZO. The eye is vulnerable to serious damage in this case, which can result in loss of vision if not treated early.

One important point to note is that this herpes virus is different from the virus that causes genital herpes, which is a sexually transmitted disease.

Demographics

Shingles is most likely to occur in people over the age of 60 who have had chicken pox; those in that age group account for more than 50 percent of the cases. In the U.S. population of those over 85, chances of getting shingles is one out of two, according to statistics determined by the National Institutes of Health, with 50 percent of all Americans suffering shingles by the time they are 80. Of those over 80, for instance, 10.9 people out of every 1,000 people are likely to get shingles as opposed to 4.6 out of every 1,000 people of those between ages 50 to 59. For those younger, the incidence rate plunges even lower.

Though the cause of the reactivation of the virus has not been clearly determined, it also occurs more frequently in people with weakened immune systems, such as the older adult population and those with **autoimmune disorders** such as HIV/AIDS and diabetes. Also, people who are undergoing special medical treatments might be candidates for the illness: those receiving steroid therapy, radiation, or **chemotherapy**; and those who have a history of bone or lymphatic **cancer**.

As of 2008, there were an estimated one million cases of shingles in the United States each year. Although second and third instances have been documented, it is rare for a person to contract shingles more than once in a lifetime.

Causes and symptoms

Shingles is caused by the same virus that causes chicken pox, *herpes zoster.* Once individuals contract chicken pox, most often in childhood, the virus stays latent in certain nerves. When the virus reactivates, more often in older adults than in those under the age of 60, shingles occurs. Though it remains scientifically undetermined as of 2008 exactly what brings on the illness, weakened immune systems appear to be a leading predictor. The disease can begin at any time, but the older the individuals who have it, the longer it lasts.

The onset of shingles can go unheeded because the symptoms resemble those of other conditions such as **allergies**: **itching**, tingling, burning, and even more severe pain. The early stages of the illness might also include fever, a weakened appetite, and fatigue. Within a few days of the onset of these symptoms, a rash of fluid-filled blisters breaks out on the body, usually on one side of the body or face.

The pain of the condition is caused by the inflammation of the nerves. The pain may be mild to severe. In extreme cases, the skin feels like it is burning and excruciating pain comes from the lightest touch or even from air flow in fanning the area. When the pain lingers, often for months after the rash itself is healed, it is referred to as *post herpetic neuralgia* or PHN. This pain is both severe and chronic in some individuals. The natural course of the disease is from three to five weeks with no residual scarring.

Diagnosis

Once the outbreak of the blistered rash occurs in individuals who have had chicken pox and thus have the virus, doctors can diagnose shingles easily. The only circumstance that would slow diagnosis is in the case of individuals who are uncertain about their medical history. As the condition persists, however, in these cases, doctors would recognize the disease. Skin scrapings from the sores can also confirm the condition. In addition, in those individuals who pain without rash, the diagnosis is determined by a blood test.

Treatment

Antiviral medication is used to weaken the virus and also reduce the extent of the nerve damage. In cases that are determined early, individuals are prescribed antiviral pills and painkillers such as *nonsteroidal anti-inflammatory* drugs commonly known as NSAIDs. Other painkillers include **acetaminophen** compounds, narcotics, and steroids. If PHN continues, an anti-seizure drug known as *gabapentin*, pain patches, and **tricyclic antidepressants** can be given to combat pain.

Medical professionals recommend that individuals with shingles keep fingernails cut short in order to prevent secondary **bacterial infections** that might arise due to scratching the infected blisters. Short fingernails are easier to keep clean and bacteria-free, and they reduce scratching.

Bacterial infections are a serious concern in the onset of shingles, in connection to the eyes and in the threat of **pneumonia**. If the rash of the shingles spreads to the upper or lower eyelids, it can cause redness of the mucous membrane covering the white of the eye known as the *conjunctiva*. If it brings about scratches to the cornea, the risk of bacterial infection increases. In these instances, an antibiotic drug may be prescribed.

Nutrition/Dietetic concerns

Individuals suffering from shingles should avoid all foods to which they have an allergic response or which cause itching. A balanced **diet** with an adequate amount of fruits and vegetables is always desirable in helping to maintain a strong **immune system**. Since people with weakened immune systems seem more susceptible to the virus, these individuals need to bolster themselves; a balanced diet, moderate **exercise**, and **relaxation** to relieve **stress** aid individuals while they cope with the illness. No specific foods have been proven to help cure the disease.

Therapy

In addition to drug therapy to calm the effects of the condition, stress management techniques such as exercise and meditation might be recommended therapy while the person is healing from the disease and during the PHN that can linger for months following the outbreak and healing of the rash.

Prognosis

With proper medical treatment, though symptoms can last for several months before a person is free from pain, shingles is treatable; though the virus continues to inhabit the system, seldom does an outbreak occur twice. It is crucial to see a physician or medical professional as soon as symptoms occur in order to support an optimum outcome. Recurrence of outbreaks is more likely in the population over 85, as well as longer duration of the illness.

Prevention

In May 2006, the Federal Drug Administration (FDA) approved the vaccine, *Zostavax*, which was determined to help reduce the risk of getting shingles. It is recommended for any individual 60 years and older who have had chicken pox and is the only licensed vaccine in the United States the reduces the risk of reactivation of the varicella zoster virus. In those individuals over the age of 70, the FDA also determined, who received the vaccine yet still developed shingles, the use of Zostavax reduced the frequency of PHN but does not work to treat PHN. Zostavax is given by injection under the skin, preferably in the upper arm, in a single dose. As of 2008, its safety or effectiveness in people under the age of 60 had yet to be determined. The price of the vaccine is several hundred dollars; however, **Medicare** may cover it under the Part D prescription program.

Studies reported by the FDA in November of 2006 included approximately 38,000 people throughout the Unites States, aged 60 and older. Half of the participants received the vaccine, and half received the placebo. The participants were followed for about three years to determine if they developed shingles, and how long their pain lasted if they did. The studies concluded that the vaccine reduced the occurrence of shingles (in those 60 and older) by approximately 50 percent. The vaccine was most effective (64 percent) in people between the ages of 60 and 69; it declined to 41 percent for the 70 to 79 age group, and to 18 percent for those 80 and older. With regard to the severity and duration of the pain, the pain lasted an average of 20 days for those who received the vaccine and 22 days for those who received the placebo. Nothing indicated that the severity of the pain differed between the two.

As of publication of the study in 2006, adverse effects were still being determined in the administration of the vaccine. In the largest study conducted, however, adverse events were similar between the two groups: Those who received the vaccine and those who received the placebo were both listed at 1.4 percent. Another study within that study was conducted to examine safety aspects more closely. This smaller study showed that serious adverse effects occurred in 1.9 percent of those receiving the vaccine in contrast to 1.3 percent in those receiving the placebo. The number of deaths in each group was similar. This data did not establish, however, that these occurrences are connected to the vaccine. The manufacturer of the vaccine was set to continue a post-market study in order to ensure safety and provide further information. The reported side effects were redness, pain and tenderness, swelling at the site of the injection of the vaccine, and headache. No similar side effects occurred in those who had taken the placebo.

Zostavax should not be taken by individuals who are allergic to neomycin, or any component of that vaccine. Because it is a live vaccine, it should not be taken by people who already have a weakened immune system due to HIV/AIDS; cancer of the lymph, bone, or blood; are taking corticosteroids; or are undergoing radiation treatments. It is also not approved for pregnant women or women who might be pregnant and has not been proven safe for children. It is not a substitute for Varivax, the vaccine used to prevent chicken pox.

With the increased use of the chicken pox vaccine, available since 1995, the incidence of chicken pox has dropped about 70 to 90 percent among those vaccinated, with 95 percent having only mild symptoms. With the effectiveness of the chicken pox vaccine and fewer people developing chicken pox, fewer people will contract shingles in the future.

QUESTIONS TO ASK YOUR DOCTOR

- How will the illness and treatment affect my lifestyle?
- Given my other health concerns or conditions, are there any contraindications with other medicines I am taking or treatments I am receiving?
- Will the blisters scar me?
- Should I stay away from my children or grandchildren during the outbreak of shingles?

Alternative treatment

In April 2007, the National Center for Complementary and Alternative Medicine (NCCAM), a division o the NIH, reported another preventative measures in an article in the *Journal of the American Geriatrics Society.*. In a study conducted by Michael Irwin at the University of California, Los Angeles (UCLA), 112 healthy adults ages 59 to 86 took part in a 16-week program of either **tai chi**, a traditional form of Chinese exercise that combines aerobic activity, relaxation, and meditation, or health education with 120 minutes of instruction weekly. Both groups of people had received a single dose of the chicken pox vaccine, Varivax, and blood tests were done to determine immunity at the completion compared with the beginning levels at the beginning of the study. Tai chi alone was found to increase the participants' immunity to the varicella virus, and the use of the vaccine with the exercise created a significantly higher level of immunity: about 40 percent, double the immunity of the health education group.

Attention to diet and exercise is known to help strengthen the immune system. Those precautions, along with the vaccine, seem to be a significant help in lowering the likelihood of developing shingles.

Caregiver concerns

When caring for older persons with shingles, caregivers need be cautious on various levels, both physical and emotional. Caregivers must maintain

KEY TERMS

Herpes zoster—The virus that causes shingles.

Herpes Zoster Ophthalmicus (HZO)—The condition indicating that shingles has affected a person's eyes.

Post-herpetic neuralgia (PHN)—The pain that continues or recurs after the shingles rash has healed. PHN is generally defined as pain that lingers more than five weeks past the appearance of the first rash.

Trigeminal nerve—The cranial (head) nerve with three branches, which serves one side of the face.

Varicella—The virus that causes chicken pox and remains in a person's system, eventually causing shingles to occur.

contact with a physician or healthcare professional, alerting them to any complications that may arise. Proper bathing, even when the sores are still in their early stages, can be crucial to eliminating or reducing the potential for bacterial infections. Maintaining a hygienic environment is also vital. Creating a calm and stress-free environment can also help reduce the patients' stress in coping with the illness.

Resources

PERIODICALS

"AAFP to Support Immunizing Elderly Against Shingles: Payment under Medicare Remains Murky." *Family Practice News* (November 15, 2006): 1.

"Augmenting Immune Responses to Varicella Zoster Virus in Older Adults: A Randomized, Controlled Trial of Tai Chi." *Journal of the American Geriatrics Society* (April 2007).

"Chicken Pox Vaccine Cuts Deaths but Raises Questions on Shingles." *New York Times* (February 3, 2005).

"Shingles' Fiscal and Physical Burden Is Steep." *Skin & Allergy News* (October 2006): 37.

"Shingles: More Tools Now; Elderly Patients Are at Greatest Risk for Debilitating Post-herpetic Neuralgia, but Antiviral Therapies Ease the Pain and Shorten Its Duration, and a New Vaccine Offers Hope of Prevention." *Cortlandt Forum* (November 2006): 40.

"Visual Clues to the Diagnosis of Infectious Disease: Skin Disorders in Elderly Persons: Identifying Viral Infections." *Infections in Medicine* (November 1, 2007): 479.

OTHER

Elliott, Victoria Stagg. "Immunization Panel Endorses Shingles Vaccine." *Amednews.com* November 13, 2006 [cited April 9, 2008]. http://www.ama-assn.org/amednews/2006/11/13/hlsc1113.htm

"Herpes Zoster." *American Academy of Dermatology* [cited April 9, 2008]. http://www.aad.org/public

"Herpes Zoster (Shingles) Eye Infections." *Steen-Hall Eye Institute* [cited April 9, 2008]. http://www.steen-hall.com/zoster.html

"International Survey Reveals Need for Greater Understanding of Shingles." *Medical News Today* June 4, 2005 [cited April 9, 2008]. http://www.medicalnewstoday.com/articles/25590.php

"Zostavax." *U.S. Food and Drug Administration* May 26, 2006 [cited April 9, 2008]. http://www.fda.govcdc.gov/products/zosmer052506qa.htm

ORGANIZATIONS

American Academy of Dermatology, 1350 I Street NW, #870, Washington, DC, 20005-4355, (202) 842-3555, (202) 843-4355, http://www.aad.org.

American Chronic Pain Association, PO Box 850, Rocklin, CA, 95677-0850, (800) 533-3231, (916) 632-0922, (916) 632-3208, http://www.theacpa.org.

American Diabetes Association, 1701 Beauregard Street, Alexandria, VA, 22311, (800) 342-2383, http://www.ada.org.

Mayo Clinic, 200 First Street NW, Rochester, MN, 55905, (507) 284-2511, http://www.mayoclinic.com.

National Institute on Aging, National Institutes of Health, Building 31, Room 5C27, 31 Center Drive, Bethesda, MD, 20892, http://www.nia.nih.org.

VZV Research Foundation (For Research on Varicella Zoster), 21 East Sixty-fourth Street, 5th floor, New York, NY, 10021, (212) 371-7280, (212) 838-0380, vzv@vzvfoundation.org, http://www.vzvfoundation.org.

Jane Elizabeth Spear

Sildenafil citrate

Definition

Sildenafil citrate (Viagra) is a medication used to treat *erectile dysfunction* (ED), or impotence, in men.

Purpose

Labeled use

Viagra treats **erectile dysfunction**, the inability to achieve and/or maintain an erection of the penis that is adequate for sexual intercourse. Ten to fifteen million men in the United States suffer from ED, and by age 65, up to 25% of men have experienced impotence problems. Erectile dysfunction can be caused by a number of physical and psychological conditions, including diabetes, **depression**, **prostate cancer**, **spinal cord injury**, **multiple sclerosis**, artherosclerosis, and **heart disease**. Injuries to the penis that cause nerve, tissue, or vascular damage can trigger impotence. It is also a common side effect of some prescription medications, including **antihistamines**, antidepressants, antihypertensives, antipsychotics, **beta blockers**, **diuretics**, tranquilizers, appetite suppressants, cimetidine (Tagamet), and finasteride (Propecia).

A study of African American and Hispanic men published in 2002 reported that Viagra appears to be equally safe and equally effective across different racial and ethnic groups in the United States.

Investigational uses

Although not approved for use in women, clinical studies have shown that sildenafil citrate may be effective in relieving female **sexual dysfunction** for some women. In one study, both female and male study participants who suffered from sexual dysfunction related to their use of such psychotropic medications as **benzodiazepines** reported an increase in arousal and overall sexual satisfaction when they began taking Viagra. Several studies have also indicated the drug may be effective in improving libido and arousal in women taking selective serotonin uptake inhibitors (SSRIs).

Another possible use of sildenafil in women is the treatment of infertility. Women who have had repeated failures with in vitro fertilization (IVF) due to poor development of the tissue that lines the uterus may benefit from treatment with vaginal suppositories containing sildenafil. One study reported that 70% of patients had a significant thickening of the uterine lining, with 29% having a successful implantation of a new embryo, and 45% achieving ongoing pregnancies.

Another investigational study conducted by researchers at Johns Hopkins University School of Medicine in Baltimore, and published in the August 2000 issue of the *Journal of Clinical Investigation* found that Viagra may have additional clinical promise for people with diabetes beyond treating ED. In animal studies, Viagra was effective in relaxing the pyloric muscle of stomach, improving digestion and relieving the symptoms of gastroparesis. Up to 75% of people with diabetes suffer from gastroparesis, which causes bloating, nausea, loss of appetite, and vomiting. Further human studies are needed to evaluate Viagra's effectiveness in treating this common diabetic complication.

Because of its capacity to enhance nitric oxide production, sildenafil has been investigated as a possible treatment for other disorders that are caused by impaired nitric oxide production. One such disorder is esophageal motility dysfunction (achalasia), in which the smooth muscles of the esophagus and the cardiac sphincter remain constricted, causing difficulty in swallowing, regurgitation of food, and chest **pain** when eating. A study published in 2000 in the journal *Gastroenterology* found that sildenafil temporarily improved the condition in some patients by relaxing the lower esophageal muscles. An Italian study reported in 2002 that sildenafil shows genuine promise as a treatment for spastic esophageal disorders.

Precautions

Viagra is not labeled or approved for use by women or children, or by men without erectile dysfunction. The medication may also be contraindicated (not recommended for use) in patients with certain medical conditions.

Because sexual activity can **stress** the heart, men who have heart problems should check with their physician to see if sexual activity is recommended. Viagra may trigger temporary hypotension (low **blood pressure**) and is known to increase cardiovascular nerve activity, so it is prescribed with caution in men with a history of **heart attack**, artherosclerosis, **angina**, arrhythmia, and chronic low blood pressure problems. However, a study published in the March 15, 2001, *British Medical Journal* found no evidence that the drug causes a higher incidence of heart attack. A four-year update on the safety of Viagra published in September 2002 corroborated the findings of the British report, and stated that the only absolute contraindication for the use of sildenafil is the concurrent use of nitrates.

Anyone experiencing cardiovascular symptoms such as **dizziness**, chest or arm pain, and nausea when participating in sexual activity after taking Viagra should stop the encounter. They should also not take Viagra again until they have discussed the episode with their healthcare provider.

It is recommended that men with kidney or liver impairments, and men over age 65, start at the lowest possible dosage of Viagra (25 mg). Clinical studies have shown that the drug builds up in the plasma of these patients to a concentration that is three to eight times higher than normal. Caution is also recommended in prescribing the drug to individuals with *retinitis pigmentosa*, a rare genetic eye disorder.

Viagra should not be taken more than once per day by anyone.

Viagra has not been studied for use on patients with stomach ulcers and bleeding disorders, and its safety in these individuals is unknown. Men who have either of these conditions should let their physician know before taking Viagra. It should also be used with caution in men with misshapen or deformed penises, such as those with Peyronie's disease, cavernosal fibrosis, or with angulation of the penis.

Men who take medications containing nitrates (e. g., nitroglycerin, isosorbide mononitrate, isosorbide dinitrate) should never take Viagra, as the interaction between the two drugs may cause a dramatic drop in blood pressure, and possibly trigger a heart attack or **stroke**. This includes illegal recreational drugs such as amyl nitrates (also known as poppers).

Viagra may also interact with other prescription and over-the-counter (OTC) medications, either magnifying or diluting the intended therapeutic effects of one or both drugs. Some drugs that have a known interaction with Viagra include the protease inhibitor ritonavir and the antibiotic erythromycin. For this reason, it is critical that men who are prescribed Viagra let their healthcare providers know all the medications they are taking.

Other medications and therapies for erectile dysfunction, including vacuum or pump devices, drug injections (Caverject), and urethral suppositories (MUSE), should never be used in conjunction with Viagra.

Description

Sildenafil citrate was originally developed in 1991 as a treatment for angina, or chest pain. The drug, marketed under the name Viagra, received FDA market clearance as a treatment for impotence in March 1998, and since that time it has been prescribed for over 10 million men worldwide. It was the first oral medication approved for ED treatment. A newer drug, tadalafil, has been developed to treat men who do not respond to sildenafil. Tadalafil has gained preliminary approval in the European Union (EU), and is in the final stages of regulatory approval in Canada as of November 2002.

Viagra is a vasodilator, a drug that has the effect of dilating the blood vessels. It works by improving blood circulation to the penis, and by enhancing the effects of *nitric oxide*, the agent that relaxes the smooth muscle of the penis and regulates blood vessels during sexual stimulation, allowing the penis to become engorged and achieve an erection.

The average recommended dose of Viagra is 50 mg. For men that do not respond adequately to this amount, the dosage may be increased up to 100 mg or decreased to 25 mg. The medication is taken approximately one hour before sexual activity is planned, and may remain effective for up to four hours.

Viagra does not increase sexual desire. Sexual stimulation and arousal are required for the medication to be effective. Despite its widespread use as a recreational drug, it is not an aphrodisiac and there is no clinical evidence that it improves sexual performance in men who are not suffering from ED.

Many insurance plans provide coverage or reimbursement for sildenafil citrate provided it is prescribed to treat erectile dysfunction. A 1999 report issued by a health insurance consulting group indicated that almost half of the men taking Viagra at least once weekly receive insurance reimbursement for the drug. The pills cost approximately $10 each, and insurers may limit coverage to a specific number of pills each month.

Preparation

Viagra requires time to be absorbed by the body and become effective. The average recommended time frame for taking the drug is one hour before initiating sexual activity, although depending on an individual's response to the drug, this time can vary from four hours to 30 minutes.

Men should always consult with their physician before beginning treatment with sildenafil citrate. The medication is not for everyone, and a healthcare professional needs to evaluate medical history and perform a thorough medical examination before prescribing the drug. In addition, erectile dysfunction may be a symptom of an undiagnosed condition (i.e., diabetes) for which treatment is critical, and may actually reverse the impotence problem.

Risks

The most commonly reported side effects of Viagra are headache, flushing of the face, upset stomach, and nasal congestion.

Other less common side effects include, but are not limited to:

- vision problems, including sensitivity to light, blurred vision, and a color tinge to vision
- urinary tract infection
- diarrhea
- dizziness
- rash

KEY TERMS

Angina—Angina pectoris, or chest pain, caused by an insufficient supply of oxygen and decreased blood flow to the heart muscle. Angina is frequently the first sign of coronary artery disease.

Angulation of the penis—Abnormal bend or angle to the structure of the penis.

Antidepressants—Medications prescribed to relieve major depression. Classes of antidepressants include selective serotonin reuptake inhibitors (fluoxetine/Prozac, sertraline/Zoloft), tricyclics (amitriptyline/Elavil), MAOIs (phenelzine/Nardil), and heterocyclics (bupropion/Wellbutrin, trazodone/Desyrel).

Antihistamines—A drug used to treat allergic conditions that counteracts histamines — a substance in the body that causes itching, vascular changes, and mucus secretion when released by cells.

Antihypertensives—Medications used to treat high blood pressure.

Antipsychotics—A class of drugs used to control psychotic symptoms in patients with psychotic disorders such as schizophrenia and delusional disorder. Antipsychotics include risperidone (Risperdal), haloperidol (Haldol), and chlorpromazine (Thorazine).

Arrhythmia—Irregular heartbeat caused by erratic electrical signals or nerve impulses to the cardiac muscles.

Artherosclerosis—The cause of coronary artery disease, in which the walls of the coronary arteries thicken due to the accumulation of plaque in the blood vessels.

Beta blockers—Drugs that lower blood pressure and reduce stress to the heart by blocking the actions of beta receptors that control the speed and strength of heart muscle contractions and blood vessel dilation.

Cavernosal fibrosis—The formation of abnormal fibrous tissue in the erectile tissue of the penis.

Diuretics—Any substance that increases urine output.

Erectile dysfunction—Impotence; the inability of a man to achieve and/or maintain an erection of sufficient quality for sexual intercourse.

Gastroparesis—Nerve damage of the stomach that delays or stops stomach emptying, resulting in nausea, vomiting, bloating, discomfort, and weight loss.

Peyronie's disease—A disease which causes a hardening of the corpora cavernosa, the erectile tissue of the penis. The penis may become misshapen and/or curved as a result.

Placebo—An inactive substance with no pharmacological action that is administered to some patients in clinical trials to determine the relative effectiveness of another drug administered to a second group of patients.

Priapism—A painful, abnormally prolonged erection (i.e., four or more hours).

Protease inhibitor—A drug that inhibits the action of enzymes.

Retinitis pigmentosa—An inherited degenerative eye disease that impairs night vision and drastically narrows the field of vision.

Selective serotonin uptake inhibitors (SSRIs)—Drugs that regulate depression by blocking the reabsorption of serotonin in the brain consequently raising serotonin levels. SSRIs include fluoxetine (Prozac), sertraline (Zoloft), and paroxetine (Paxil).

Serotonin—One of three major neurotransmitters found in the brain that is linked to emotions.

Side effects may be reduced or eliminated through adjustments to dosage. Men who experience these symptoms should consult their physician.

Priapism, a painful and prolonged erection that lasts for two to six hours, is a rare but potentially serious side effect of Viagra. Because prolonged erection can permanently damage the tissues of the penis, anyone who experiences an erection lasting over four hours should call a healthcare professional immediately.

Men who are taking Viagra and inadvertently or intentionally take a medication containing nitrates may suffer from life-threatening hypotension—a severe drop in blood pressure.

The cardiovascular risks of sildenafil citrate are still under investigation. The drug is known to cause dips in blood pressure and to boost cardiovascular nerve activity. Some cardiovascular-related deaths have been reported in men who use Viagra, but it is unclear whether the fatalities were due to the drug itself or to the underlying heart disease. Further complicating the picture is the fact that the stress of sexual activity may have triggered the fatal cardiac event with or without the use of Viagra. The *BMJ* study, and a report published in the April 18, 2001 issue of the *Journal of the American Medical Association* (*JAMA*) suggest that the drug does not increase the risk of heart attack. However, *JAMA*also notes that further studies are necessary to confirm this finding.

Although it is a prescription drug, as of early 2001 there was still a thriving illicit market for Viagra via the Internet. Aside from the health risks recreational use of the drug poses to individuals with heart conditions and other contraindicated disorders, any adverse effects caused by Viagra cannot be tracked by regulatory authorities if it has been illegally obtained. In addition, the drug appears to be toxic in large doses. In November 2002, a group of French toxicologists reported the case of a 56-year-old male who took a fatal overdose of Viagra.

Results

When used as directed, Viagra allows men with erectile dysfunction to achieve and maintain a penile erection when aroused during sexual activity. Double-blind, randomized clinical trials of sildenafil citrate have shown that the drug has an 63–82% efficacy rate in improving erectile activity among men with ED, depending on the dose administered (between 25 and 100 mg), compared to a 24% improvement in men receiving a placebo.

Resources

BOOKS

Medical Economics Company. *The Physicians DeskReference (PDR).* 55th ed. Montvale, NJ: Medical Economics Company, 2001.

Stolar, Mark. *Viagra & You.* New York:Berkley Books, 1999.

PERIODICALS

Bortolotti, M., N. Pandolfo, M. Giovannini, et al. " Effect of Sildenafil on Hypertensive Lower Oesophageal Sphincter" *European Journal of Clinical Investigation* 32 (September 2002): 682–685.

Boyce, E. G., and E. M. Umland. "Sildenafil Citrate: A Therapeutic Update." *Clinical Therapeutics* 1 (January 2001): 2–23.

Kuan, J., and G. Brock. " Selective Phosphodiesterase Type 5 Inhibition using Tadalafil for the Treatment of Erectile Dysfunction." *Expert Opinion on Investigational Drugs* 11 (November 11, 2002): 1605–1613.

Mitka, Mike. "Studies of Viagra Offer Some Reassurance to Men With Concerns About Cardiac Effects." *The Journal of the American Medical Association* 285, no.15 (April 18, 2001): 1950.

Padma-nathan, H., I. Eardley, R. A. Kloner, et al. " A 4-year Update on the Safety of Sildenafil Citrate (Viagra)." *Urology* 60, no.2, Supplement 2 (September 2002): 67–90.

Shakir, S. A., et al. "Cardiovascular Events in Users of Sildenafil: Results from First Phase of Prescription Event Monitoring in England." *British Medical Journal* 322, no.7287 (March 17, 2001): 651–2.

Sher, G., and J. D. Fisch. " Effect of Vaginal Sildenafil on the Outcome of in vitro Fertilization (IVF) After Multiple IVF Failures Attributed to Poor Endometrial Development." *Fertility and Sterility* 78 (November 2002): 1256–1257.

Tracqui, A., A. Miras, A. Tabib, et al. " Fatal Overdosage with Sildenafil Citrate (Viagra): First Report and Review of the Literature." *Human and Experimental Toxicology* 21 (November 2002): 623–629.

"Viagra Increases Nerve Activity Associated with Cardiovascular Function." *Drug Week* January 26, 2001: 11.

Young, J. M., C. Bennett, P. Gilhooly, et al. " Efficacy and Safety of Sildenafil Citrate (Viagra) in Black and Hispanic American Men." *Urology* 60, no. 2, Supplement 2 (September 2002): 39–48.

ORGANIZATIONS

American Heart Association. American Heart Association. 7320 Greenville Ave. Dallas, TX 75231. (214) 373-630 or (800) 242-8721. inquire@heart.org. http://www.americanheart.org.

U.S. Food and Drug Administration (FDA), Center for Drug Evaluation and Research. Viagra Information. http://www.fda.gov/cder/consumerinfo/viagra/default.htm.

OTHER

Pfizer, Inc. Viagra Information Site. http://www.viagra.com/.

Paula Anne Ford-Martin
Rebecca J. Frey Ph.D.

Sjögren's syndrome

Definition

Sjögren's syndrome is an autoimmune disorder in which the body's immune system inappropriately attacks the glands that are responsible for the production of tears and saliva, leading to decreased secretion. This attack can eventually spread to other organs and tissues. It was first described in 1933 the Swedish ophthalmologist, Henrick Sjögren, who observed a group of women with both dry eyes and mouth, most of whom also had **arthritis**.

Description

The primary symptoms of this disease are dry eyes (xerophthalmia) and dry mouth (xerostomia). Sjörgren's syndrome is considered to be a systemic rheumatic disease, and may progress to cause inflammation in other areas of the body such as the joints, skin, nervous system (nerves), and kidneys, among others. It is often associated with other diseases such as **rheumatoid arthritis** or **lupus**, which are diseases of the connective tissues of the body; groups of cells that support organs and connect parts of the body together.

Demographics

Sjögren's syndrome is one of the most common autoimmune disorders, affecting about four million people in America. The majority of cases are diagnosed in the late 40's, and approximately 90% of these are women. Most of these patients are caucasian women, though this is in no means exclusive, as it can be found in all ethnicities, both sexes, and a wide variety of age groups.

Causes and symptoms

In Sjögren's syndrome, the lymphocytes (white blood cells of the body's immune system) travel to the glands that are responsible for the production of tears (lacrimal glands) and saliva (salivary glands that produce "spit") and begin to attack them in an abnormal "autoimmune response." The reason why this occurs is still a subject of debate and investigation; however it has been suggested that it may be a combination of genetics (inherited tendency), a result of certain viral infections, other dysfunctions of the immune system and nervous system, as well as hormonal influences.

There are two basic types of Sjögren's syndrome: primary and secondary. Half of the cases are primary Sjörgren's, where this is the only autoimmune disease present in the body. The other half of cases are "secondary" Sjörgren's, which occurs in combination with other autoimmune diseases such as systemic lupus erthematatosus, rheumatoid arthritis, polymotositis/dermatomyositis, and systemic sclerosis (**scleroderma**). Sjörgren's may occur in other areas of the body as well, such as in the nerves, lung, and intestines.

The symptoms of this disease may vary greatly, depending upon where the attack occurs, and they may be mild, remain at a certain level (plateau), or progress and become debilitating. These symptoms may include:

- dry mouth
- dental decay (cavities) due to changes in the composition of saliva
- problems with dentures due to changes in tissues in the mouth
- enlarged glands (salivary glands on the side of the jaw)
- trouble swallowing and chewing
- inability to taste properly
- problems speaking
- infections of the mouth (yeast)
- dry eyes (may feel like grit or sand due to reduced lacrimal secretion)
- eye infections, "red eye", ulcers on cornea
- dry skin
- Raynaud's phenomenon (restriction of blood vessels in fingers and toes in response to cold or stress)
- joint **pain**
- gastrointestinal problems such as nausea and pain
- nervous system effects
- problems with the lungs (dry, unproductive cough, infections such as **pneumonia**)
- liver problems (revealed by abnormal results on liver panel tests)
- vaginal dryness (women) with accompanying infections (yeast and/or bacterial)
- fatigue
- lymphoma

Diagnosis

Diagnosis of Sjögren's is difficult, and it is particularly challenging in the elderly, as they frequently have other conditions with similar presentations that might occur, such as chronic fatigue syndrome and menopause, among many others. Due to the variability of symptoms over time, it is often misdiagnosed as another condition or may not be diagnosed at all. On average, it takes approximately six years to achieve an accurate diagnosis.

There has been much debate as to the classification of the different types of this disease, but in 2002, the American-European Consensus Group proposed criteria that is now widely accepted, based upon the following guidelines.

- Positive dry eye tests for the disease (Shirmer's test for tear production and Lissamine Green and Rose Bengal for dryness, slit-lamp tests)
- Dry mouth symptoms
- Specific pathology findings that indicate the presence of the disease
- Affliction of the salivary glands (measurements may be taken to asses salivary function through sialogram and scintagraphy, and the flow of saliva assessed from parotid gland, as well as biopsies)
- Presence of autoantibodies in the blood (Anti-Ro/SSA and/or Anti-La /SSB, though Anti-Ro antibodies have been found in normal elderly patients)

There may also be additional tests performed as well. The blood may be tested for the presence of immunoglobulins (IgG), anti-nuclear antibody (ANA), rheumatoid factor (RF), and ESR (erythrocyte sedimentation rate test for inflammation), though these are found in other conditions besides Sjögren's syndrome. The urine may also be tested to assess kidney function.

The diagnosis may be further divided into primary and secondary Sjörgren's, based upon pathological findings and patient history. As many diseases and medication side-effects are similar to the symptoms of Sjögren's syndrome, it is particularly important that elderly patients bring a complete medical history and medication list to a consultation with their physician. Additionally, some nervous system symptoms may be similar to conditions frequently found in the elderly, such as **Alzheimer's disease**.

In general, patients diagnosed with the disease should be under the care of a team of health care professionals including an eye doctor (ophthalmologist), dentist, and **rheumatologist** (specializing in diseases such as arthritis).

Treatment

As of 2008, there is no cure for Sjögren's syndrome, nor is there any real treatment to stop the damaging effects. Research is underway to explore treatment possibilities.

Actions can be taken, however, to alleviate the symptoms of this disease. Patients may be encouraged to use artificial tears for dry eyes, though some have problems with the preservatives contained in some brands with long-term use. To alleviate the symptoms of dry mouth, they may be instructed to use specific mouthwashes, chew gum to promote salivation, sip water, or use salvia substitutes. Proper dental care is recommended to counteract the tendency for dental effects, with regular visits to a dental professional. Wearing of dentures can be problematic for the elderly who have Sjögren's syndrome, as yeast may accumulate on denture material and oral tissues may not support dentures adequately. Thus a dentist should be consulted regarding denture use.

The patient may also be instructed to take certain medications to assist in alleviating the symptoms of the disease, such as corticosteroids, **non-steroidal anti-inflammatory drugs**, Evoxac (for dry mouth), and immunosuppressants, among others. Also, a surgical procedure may be recommended for relief of dry eyes.

QUESTIONS TO ASK YOUR DOCTOR

- What tests may be needed to diagnosis Sjogren's syndrome, and is any special preparation needed for these tests?
- What type of Sjogren's is suspected?
- What is the extent of the disease and the prognosis?
- What practical steps can be taken to alleviate the symptoms?
- What type of medical and dental monitoring is needed?
- What symptoms should be reported to health care professionals?

Nutrition/Dietetic concerns

There is considerable debate as to the role of diet in autoimmune disease. Some patients have reported improvement by restriction of certain food items, and improvement by inclusion of others. In general, a healthy, well-rounded diet that encompasses good nutrition is helpful in disease states. A nutritionist should be consulted for further information.

Therapy

Different types of therapy may be helpful to assist in the alleviation of symptoms, depending upon the extent of disease. A physician should be consulted for recommendations.

Prognosis

The earlier a patient is diagnosed, the better his/her chances of alleviating symptoms and avoiding

KEY TERMS

Anti-nuclear antibody (ANA)—A test for autoimmune disease, among which Anti-Ro/SSA and/or Anti –La /SSB are specific types.

Autoimmune disease—A type of disease in which a person's immune system inappropriately attacks the body's own cells and tissues.

ESR (erythrocyte sedimentation rate)—A test for inflammation where the rate at which erythrocytes (red blood cells) settle to the bottom of a tube, which often increases during inflammation.

Immunoglobulins (IgG)—A type of protein (antibody) that helps to fight infection, particularly bacterial infections

Lymphocytes—Blood cells of the body's immune system that fight infection.

RF Test—Test for rheumatoid factor, which can be elevated in conditions such as rheumatoid arthritis and Sjorgren's syndrome.

Xerophthalmia—Dry eyes.

Xerostomia—Dry mouth. Dry eyes.

Salivary glands—The glands in the mouth that produce saliva, the parotid, sublingual, and submandibular glands.

complications. The symptoms may remain mild, worsen and plateau, or become debilitating. As there is a higher risk of developing lymphoma associated with this disease, as well as frequent co-existence with other autoimmune conditions, a patient should be under a physicians care for regular monitoring.

Prevention

It is very important to obtain a diagnosis early in the course of the disease, so measures can be taken to alleviate the symptoms and begin monitoring the patient for more serious complications such as lymphoma. Swelling of glands in the facial area, underneath the arms (armpits) or groin area, which may or may not indicate lymphoma, should be brought to a physician's attention.

Caregiver concerns

Caregivers should be aware of the need for the appropriate monitoring of the patient by health-care professionals for the management of disease symptoms. In the case of elderly patients, special care should be given to the use of dentures, proper dental care, infections, effects on eyes, and monitoring for development of lymphoma. Elderly individuals may need special assistance when dealing with the complications of this disease, and if in assisted living, the health care provider staff should be notified of their needs.

Resources

BOOKS

Theofilopoulos, A., and C. Bona, ed. *The Molecular Pathology of Autoimmune Diseases (2nd Edition).* New York, Taylor & Francis, 2002.

Sjögren's Syndrome Foundation. *What is Sjögren's syndrome?* Bethesda,2007 http://www.sjogrens.org/images/SSF%20patient%20brochure.pdf

PERIODICALS

Ng, K.P., and D.A. Isenberg. *Drug Aging* 2008,Vol. 25, No. 1 pp.19-33

Vitali,et al. *Ann Rheum Dis.* 2002, Jun; (61)6, pp.554-8

Mathews, S.A.,et. al. *J. Dent Res* 2008,87(4) pp.308-318

ORGANIZATIONS

Sjögren's Syndrome Foundation, 6707 Democracy Boulevard, Suite 325, Bethesda, MD, 20817, 301-530-4420, 800-475-6473, 301-530-4415, tms@sjogrens.org, http://www.sjogrens.org/.

Jill Granger M.S.

Skin cancer

Definition

Skin **cancer** refers to abnormal cells of the skin that grow uncontrollably. If untreated these cells can grow deeper into the skin and invade other tissues. There are three main types of skin cancer: basal cell carcinoma, squamous cell carcinoma and melanoma. All three types are related to excessive sun exposure.

Description

Cancer which is also called a neoplasm, carcinoma or malignancy is a group of diseases where abnormal cells continuously grow out of control. These cells can spread to other organs and if not controlled can result in **death**. Skin cancer is the most common type of cancer but certainly not the most fatal. Although skin cancer most often occurs on areas of the

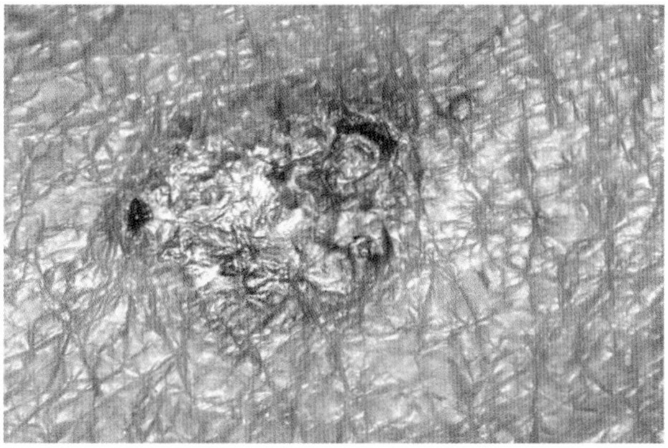

Close up of dark, bruise-like lesion on leg of elderly woman, caused by a rare form of skin cancer called Bowen's disease. *(Dr. P. Marazzi/SPL/Photo Researchers. Reproduced by permission.)*

skin that arc cxposcd to sunlight, this is not always the case.

There are three main types of skin cancer; melanoma, basal cell cancer and squamous cell cancer. Each develops from a different cell type of the skin's epidermal layer. Basal cell carcinoma and squamous cell carcinoma are the most common and most treatable if they are found early. Melanoma is a more serious form of skin cancer affecting deeper layers of the skin and has a higher potential to spread to other parts of the body. Risks of all three types of skin cancer are increasing. The National Cancer Institute estimates that there will be 1,000,000 new cases of non-melanoma cancer in the US in 2008 with less than 1,000 deaths due to these cancers. It is estimated that there will be 62,480 new melanomas cases diagnosed and 8,420 deaths in the US due to melanoma in 2008.

Basal cell cancer is the most common type of skin cancer, accounting for about 75% of all skin cancers. It develops from cells of the lowest layer of the epidermis, the basal cells. These are the cells which produce new skin cells. It occurs primarily on the parts of the skin exposed to the sun and is most common in people living in equatorial regions or areas of high ozone depletion. Light-skinned people are at greater risk of developing basal cell cancer than dark-skinned people. Basal cell cancer grows very slowly; however if it is not treated it can invade deeper skin layers causing extensive damage and can be fatal. This type of cancer can appear as a shiny, translucent nodule on the skin or as a red, wrinkled and scaly area.

Squamous cell cancer is the second most frequent type of skin cancer. It arises from the outer keratinizing layer of skin just below the surface. Squamous cell cancer grows faster than basal cell cancer and is more likely to metastasize to the lymph nodes as well as to distant sites. Squamous cell cancer most often appears on the arms, head, and neck. Fair-skinned people of Celtic descent are at high risk for developing squamous cell cancer. This type of cancer is rarely life-threatening but can cause serious problems if it spreads and can also cause disfigurement. Squamous cell cancer usually appears as a scaly, slightly elevated area of damaged skin. Squamous cell cancer can spear in an area of chronic inflammation on the skin.

Malignant melanoma is the most serious type of skin cancer. It develops from the melanocytes or pigment producing cells of the skin. These cells are found in the lower part of the epidermis. Melanocytes are stimulated by the sun to produce more melanin or pigment. It is this pigment that protects skin cells from sun damage and explains why darker skinned persons have a lower risk of melanoma. Although melanoma is the least common skin cancer, it is the most aggressive. It spreads (metastasizes) to other parts of the body– especially the lungs and liver– as well as invading surrounding tissues. Melanomas in their early stages resemble moles. In Caucasians, melanomas appear most often on the trunk, head, and neck in men and on the arms and legs in women. Melanomas in African Americans, however, occur primarily on the palms of the hand, soles of the feet, and under the nails. Melanomas appear only rarely in the eyes, mouth, vagina, or digestive tract. Although melanomas are associated with exposure to the sun, the greatest risk factor for developing melanoma might be genetic. People who have a first-degree relative with melanoma have an increased risk up to eight times greater of developing the disease.

Besides the three major types of skin cancer, there are a few other less common forms of skin cancer as well as some precancerous skin lesions.

- Kaposi's sarcoma (KS) occurs primarily in people whose immune system is depressed, such as AIDS patients, or those who have had organ transplants. When KS occurs with AIDS it is usually more aggressive.
- Merkel cell carcinoma is a rare skin cancer usually found on sun-exposed areas. Merket cell carcinoma grows more rapidly than basal and squamous cell carcinomas and can spread.
- Sebaceous gland carcinoma is an aggressive cancer that begins in the oil glands of the skin. They are hard, painless nodules that can develop anywhere, but most often on the eyelid.

Precancerous **skin lesions** include:

- Actinic keratosis or AK is also known as solar keratosis. It appears as rough, scaly patches that are red, pink or brown. They appear most often on the face, ears, lower arms and hands. This condition is not cancer but may develop into squamous cell carcinoma.
- Leukoplakia occurs inside the mouth as white patches. It is related to constant irritation as might be caused by smoking, rough edges on teeth, dentures or fillings.
- Actinic chelitis is a type of actinic keratosis or leukoplakia that occurs on the lips.
- Bowen's disease. This is a type of skin inflammation (dermatitis) that sometimes looks like squamous cell cancer. This may be a superficial type of squamous cell carcinoma that appears as a persistent, scaly patch. It can resemble eczema or psoriasis.
- Keratoacanthoma is a dome-shaped tumor that can grow quickly and appear like squamous cell cancer. Although it is usually benign, it should be removed.

Demographics

The biggest risk for skin cancer is excessive exposure to the sun and getting sunburned. The risk of skin cancer is also hereditary, with the risk increasing with a first degree relative having the disease. Those who are fair skinned are more at risk. Age is also a risk factor as skin cancers tend to take years to develop they rarely appear before age 30 or 40. Melanoma is 10 times more likely to occur in whites than in African Americans. People having a high number of moles on their body are also at higher risk.

Exposure to toxic chemicals such as arsenic, tar, coal, paraffin and certain types of oil can increase the risk of non-melanoma skin cancer. Radiation therapy used for cancer as well as drugs used to treat **psoriasis** can also increase the risk of non-melanoma skin cancer. Skin cancer most often develops on areas of the skin that are exposed to the sun. The most common locations are the scalp, face, lips, ears, neck, chest, arms and hands. It can however also occur on areas that do not see much light such as the palms, between the toes and the genital area.

Risk factors for skin cancer include the following

- Excessive exposure to ultraviolet light or a history of sunburns. Severe sunburns as a child increases the risk for skin cancer later in life.
- Having fair skin or less pigmentation in the skin.
- A family history of skin cancer or a personal history of previously having skin cancer.
- Exposure to certain environmental chemicals including arsenic, pitch, creosote, radium or coal tar.
- Age—skin cancer takes years to develop and is more common with age. The sunburn you get as a teen can increase your risk of skin cancer when you are 40.
- A weakened immune system due to HIV/AIDS, leukemia, or drugs that suppress the immune system.
- Having a high number of moles on the body; more than 100.

Causes and symptoms

All three main types of skin cancer are related to excessive sun exposure. Ultraviolet light from the sun damages the DNA found in the cells. This damage to the DNA causes changes in the cell that can lead to increased and out of control growth. Although it was once thought that only UVB rays were responsible for the DNA damage that leads to cancer we now know it is both UVA and UVB rays. Since tanning beds deliver high levels of UVA, they can put people at significant risks.

Basal cell carcinoma appears as a pearly or waxy bump or a flat, flesh colored or brown mark. It is difficult to distinguish this type of mark from a normal mole without performing a biopsy. A basal cell carcinoma can take months or years before it becomes sizable. Squamous cell carcinoma can appear as a firm, red nodule or a flat mark with scaly, crusted surface.

Melanoma, the most serious of the skin cancers, appears as a large brownish spot. This spot can change in color or size or have an irregular border. It can also appear as a shiny, firm, dome-shaped bump. Melanomas can vary greatly in their appearance, but often the first sign is a change in a mole. Early detection of melanoma is important for successful treatment.

Kaposi sarcoma appears as red or purple patches on the skin or mucous membranes. This type of cancer tends to be more common in people with immune suppression such as those with **AIDS** or who have undergone organ transplants.

It used to be the ABCD rule was used as a guide for examining moles. Recently, the American Cancer Society added E to their visual grading system. This ABCDE system provides an easy way to remember the important characteristics of moles when one is examining the skin:

- Asymmetry. A normal mole is round, whereas a suspicious mole is unevenly shaped.
- Border. A normal mole has a clear-cut border with the surrounding skin, whereas the edges of a suspect mole are often irregular or scalloped.
- Color. Normal moles are uniformly tan or brown, but cancerous moles may appear as mixtures of red, white, blue, brown, purple, or black.
- Diameter. Normal moles are usually less than 5 millimeters in diameter. A skin lesion greater than 1/4 inch across may be suspected as cancerous.
- Evolving. A mole that changes over time in color or shape or develops itchiness or bleeding can be suspect.

Diagnosis

A person who finds a suspicious-looking mole, a change in the appearance or texture of a mole, new areas of skin growth or a bothersome area of skin should consult a physician. As with many cancers, early detection and treatment is important in increasing the chances of treating the cancer successfully. A physician can do a thorough inspection of the skin, noting any suspicious looking areas. If any suspect areas are found, the patient's primary care physician will most likely refer him or her to a physician who specializes in skin diseases (a **dermatologist**). A proper diagnosis of skin cancer requires that a biopsy or a small sample of skin be taken and analyzed by a lab. The skin sample is often done in the physician's office under **local anesthesia**.

If cancer is present, the stage of the cancer is then determined. This is a rating of how advanced the cancer is and will help determine the appropriate treatment for the cancer. Stages include stage 0, stage I, stage II, stage III, and stage IV, often with substages as well. Each stage represents a progressively larger sized tumor. Stage 0 refers to a precancerous lesion of suspicious cells and stage IV refers to a more severe tumor that has spread to other parts of the body.

Treatment

Treatment depends upon the type of cancer and the severity. Basal cell carcinoma is fairly easy to treat when detected early as is squamous cell. There are four main types of treatment for skin cancer. They include surgery, radiation therapy, **chemotherapy** and photodynamic therapy. There are always new types of treatment being tested in clinical trials. One new type is biologic therapy which stimulates the patient's **immune system** to remove the cancer.

Surgery is often the best choice if the tumor is localized and easily removable. There are several different surgical procedures used. Excision surgery involves using a scalpel cutting around the tumor to remove it from the skin. This can also be done by shaving the tumor off the surface of the skin. Mohs micrographic surgery involves taking the skin lesion off in small sections and immediately examining it in the microscope to see when the surgery has gone deep enough to remove the cancerous cells. It is a more time consuming surgery though and not always available. Cryosurgery freezes and destroys the tumor cells. Laser surgery uses a laser beam to cut the skin to remove the tumor. Dermabrasion removes the upper layer of skin and can be used for very small superficial tumors.

Radiation therapy uses high energy x rays directed towards the tumor to kill cancer cells. It is often used for cancers that occur on the face or ears where reconstructive surgery would be difficult. It is also used primarily for the elderly since it can increase the long term risk of other types of cancers.

Chemotherapy refers to drugs taken internally either by injection or orally that travel through the bloodstream. Chemotherapy is intended to either stop the growth of cancer cells or to kill the cancer cells. Chemotherapy often has rather serious side effects as it affects other cells in the body besides the cancer cells. Occasionally, for non-melanoma skin cancers, the chemotherapy can be delivered in a cream form to use topically.

Photodynamic therapy uses both a drug and a laser to kill cancer cells. The drug is a photosensitizer which becomes active only after light of a specific wavelength from the laser contacts it. This allows more control over preventing damage to healthy tissue. Photodynamic therapy is relatively new and not always available.

Nutrition/Dietetic concerns

Some studies have found that a **diet** high in antioxidant nutrients such as carotenoids, **vitamins** E and C and selenium can decrease the risk of skin cancer. These nutrients are found in diets high in fruits and vegetables. Low fat diets are also linked to lower rates of skin cancer.

Therapy

None needed.

Prognosis

Prognosis depends upon the type of cancer and its severity. Skin cancer is the most common type of cancer in the US but accounts for less than 1% of cancer deaths. Basal cell carcinoma is fairly easy to treat when caught early. Squamous cell carcinoma also is not usually serious and can be 100% treatable if caught early. If not caught early though it can be more difficult to treat and can cause some disfigurement. A small number of squamous cell carcinomas can spread to other organs.

Melanoma is a more serious type of skin cancer, however, if it is caught early is still curable. Melanoma is the most likely skin cancer to spread to other parts of the body which worsens the prognosis. According to the American Cancer Society, for stage I melanoma, the 5-year survival rates range from 92 to 99%. The 5-year survival rate for stage II melanomas is from 56-78%. The 5-year survival rate for stage III melanoma decreases to 50-68% and for stage IV melanoma, 5-year survival drops to 18%. Patients over the age of 70 typically have 5-year survival rates on the lower side.

Prevention

Although one can never change his genes or hereditary risk of getting any type of cancer, there is a lot one can do to decrease his risk of getting skin cancer. Avoid prolonged exposure to the sun or sunburn. Recently, there has been some controversy in the area of sun exposure and cancer. Although there is a definite relationship to excessive sun exposure and skin cancer, the risk of sensible exposure to the sun may have been over exaggerated. Exposure to sunlight is necessary for our bodies to make **vitamin D** and vitamin D deficiencies have been increasing recently, putting people at risk of vitamin D deficiency diseases. Vitamin D has also been found to decrease the rate of several types of cancer. There is also some evidence that certain sunscreen ingredients may actually contribute to cancer risks. However, recommendations are still to prevent overexposure to the sun.

- Wear protective clothing (long sleeves and hat) while in the sun.
- Use sunscreen of at least 15 SPF when outside.
- Avoid being outside when the sun is brightest, between 10 a.m. and 4 p.m.
- Avoid tanning beds.
- Check your skin periodically for abnormal moles. The American Academy of Dermatologists recommends doing this on your birthday: "Check your birthday suit on your birthday." Although this will not prevent skin cancer, early detection improves prognosis.

QUESTIONS TO ASK YOUR DOCTOR

- What are my various treatment options?
- Are there any clinical trials that would be relevant for my type of cancer?
- What supplements are ok to take during treatment?
- What is your experience in treating this type of cancer?
- What stage or how advanced is my cancer?
- What is the goal of treatment, to eradicate the cancer or to alleviate symptoms?
- Should I go to a specialized cancer center?

Caregiver concerns

A caregiver might want to be observant of moles on a patient in areas that he or she cannot see, such as the back. If a mole looks suspicious, a physician should be consulted.

Resources

PERIODICALS

Moan, J., Porojnicu, A.C., Dahlback, A., Setlow, R.B., Addressing the health benefits and risks, involving vitamin D or skin cancer, or increased sun exposure. PNAS 2008; 105: http://www.pnas.org/cgi/reprint/0710615105v1

Holick, M.F., Sunlight and vitamin D for bone health and prevention of autoimmune diseases, cancers, and cardiovascular disease. Am. Journ. Clin. Nutr. 2004; 80:1678S-1688S. http://www.ajcn.org/cgi/content/full/80/6/1678S

OTHER

National Cancer Institutehttp://www.cancer.gov/cancertopics/pdq/treatment/skin/Patient/page3

Mayo Clinichttp://www.mayoclinic.com/health/skin-cancer/DS00190/DSECTION=7

ORGANIZATIONS

American Cancer Society, 1-800-ACS-2345, http://www.cancer.org.

American Institute for Cancer Research, 1759 R Street NW, Washington, DC, 20009, 1-800-843-8114, aicrweb@aicr.org, http://www.aicr.org.

Skin Cancer Foundation, 149 Madison Avenue, Suite 901, New York, NY, 10016, 1-800-SKIN-490, http://www.skincancer.org.

Cindy L. Jones Ph.D.

Skin culture

Definition

A skin culture removes a small amount of skin, pus, or fluid from an infected wound. The sample is then grown in the lab to identify the organisms responsible for the infection. Sensitivity testing may be done on the organisms to help determine an effective treatment method.

Purpose

A skin culture is performed to help a doctor determine the cause of a skin infection. It is generally done for skin infections that have been present for a significant period of time or that have not responded to treatment. The culture determines if there is, in fact, an infection present, which can help rule out some other causes of the symptoms. In many cases sensitivity testing is also performed on the sample. Sensitivity testing is done to determine which treatment option is going to be most effective at killing the organisms causing the infection.

Precautions

If the patient is taking, or has recently been taking, **antibiotics** he or she should tell the doctor. Antibiotics can interfere with the ability of the infectious organism to grow on the culture. The patient should also inform the doctor if he or she has any **allergies**, as some people are allergic to certain types of local or topical anesthesia. The doctor will take precautions to ensure that the infection is not spread by taking the skin sample.

Description

Skin infections occur when a virus, bacterium, or fungus, that is not native to the skin begins to grow in or on the skin. It can be an organism from outside the body, or even an organism that occurs naturally in another part of the body but does not normally occur on or in the skin. Skin infections can occur on unbroken skin, but they are especially likely to occur on skin that has been broken by an injury or abrasive accident. Although most skin infections are not serious they can be very dangerous if left untreated.

To perform a skin culture a sample of the material from the area believed to be infected must be collected. There are a number of ways this may be collected. It may be swabbed or wiped with a sterile swab to collect any of the pus or excretion given off by the infected area. If the area believed to be infected is covered with a scab sample pus or liquid may be taken using a needle.

QUESTIONS TO ASK YOUR DOCTOR

- What type of organism is suspected?
- How can I help ensure my infection does not spread to other areas of my body?
- If the results come back negative what is the next step?

In some cases a sample of the skin itself, not just the pus or excretion, must be collected. In this case a skin biopsy is performed. There are three main types of biopsy. The first is a called a shave biopsy. In this case a very thin layer of the skin is shaved off and collected. The second type of biopsy is a punch biopsy. Punch biopsies are used when the doctor wants to test all layers of the skin, or the infection of the skin is not on the surface. A small instrument, usually about the size of a pencil eraser, is used to take a small, circular sample of the skin. The third type of biopsy is an excisional biopsy. In this case a section of skin is actually cut out to send for testing. Then the new wound site is either closed with stitches, or in some cases, a skin graft is used to cover the area.

After the sample has been collected it is sent to the laboratory. There a small amount of the sample is placed onto a culture medium and allowed to grow for anywhere from one to two days to a few weeks. The laboratory technician then uses a microscope and a variety of testing procedures to identify any colonies that have formed.

In some cases sensitivity testing is also performed. In that case the laboratory technician exposes colonies that have grown on the sample to a variety of antibacterial, antiviral, or antifungal agents until one is identified that successfully kills the organisms present. This can then be used as an effective treatment for the infection.

Preparation

There is no special patient preparation required before a skin culture. Patients can eat and drink normally, and participate in normal daily activities before the culture is performed.

Aftercare

Most skin culture require little or no aftercare. There may be temporary discomfort at the site if the site is tender from the infection. If a biopsy is needed to collect the sample additional aftercare may be required. If a punch biopsy is performed stitches may or may not be required. If not, the area will be bandaged and allowed to heal on its own, but will require regular cleaning and good would hygiene to promote healing. If the punch biopsy encompasses a large area, stitches may be used to close the wound. In this case the stitches must be kept clean, and the bandage may need to be changed regularly. Most stitches are removed in three to 14 days. If the biopsy is excisional it will also be closed with stitches and will require care to stay clean and dry. The doctor may prescribe antibiotic ointment to be rubbed onto the wound regularly to help prevent additional infection from occurring.

Complications

In most cases of skin culture there are no complications. There is always a small chance of infection, **bruising**, or bleeding, anytime an injection is given. Therefore if **local anesthesia** is given there is a small chance of these complications. If a section of skin needs to be removed there is a chance of new infection, slow healing, scarring, and excessive bleeding at the removal site. There is also a very small chance that the infection could spread, especially if a biopsy is required.

Results

A normal skin culture result shows that no other organisms have grown on the culture medium other than those normally present on or in the skin. A normal result indicates that no infection is present. Abnormal results occur when there is a much larger than normal amount of organism growth on the culture medium, or one type of organism grows much more readily than any other organisms present. Abnormal results indicate a skin infection.

Once it has been determined that a large colony or organisms grow in the culture medium, sensitivity testing often occurs. The results of sensitivity testing indicate the effectiveness of various antibiotics, antiviral, or antifungal agents that were applied to the growing organisms. Positive results from a sensitivity test indicate that the organisms exposed to the agent were successfully killed. Negative results indicate that the agent had little or no effect on the health and reproduction of the organisms present.

Caregiver concerns

The doctor who determined the need for the skin culture often performs the sample or biopsy him or herself. A nurse may perform sample if a swab is performed. The doctor or nurse then labels the sample and sends it to the laboratory, where a laboratory technician performs the culture itself. The laboratory technician also performs the sensitivity testing if required. The results are then sent back to the doctor who ordered the skin culture who determines and prescribes treatment as necessary.

KEY TERMS

biopsy—the diagnostic removal of a sample of tissue from a living body

Resources

BOOKS

Frankel, David H., ed. *Field Guide to Clinical Dermatology*, 2nd Ed. Philadelphia, PA: Lippincott Williams & Wilkins, 2006.

Jablonski, Nina G. *Skin: A Natural History.* Berkeley : University of California Press, 2006.

Noble, W.C., ed. *The Skin Microflora and Microbial Skin Disease.* Cambridge, England: Cambridge University Press, 2004.

PERIODICALS

MacNeil, Jane Salodof. "Shave Biopsy May Impair Accuracy." *Family Practice News* 37.10 (May 15, 2007): 24-25.

Snyder, Robert J. "Clinical Evaluation of Wound Swabbing Versus Tissue Biopsy to Diagnose Infection." *Podiatry Management* 26.7 (Sept 2007): 217-224.

ORGANIZATIONS

American Skin Association, 346 Park Avenue South, 4th Floor, New York, NY, 10010, 800-499-7546, http://www.americanskin.org/.

Robert Bockstiegel

Skin lesion removal

Definition

Skin lesion removal employs a variety of techniques, from relatively simple biopsies to more complex surgical excisions, to remove lesions that range from benign growths to **malignant melanoma**.

Purpose

Sometimes the purpose of skin lesion removal is to excise an unsightly mole or other cosmetically unattractive skin growth. Other times, physicians will remove a skin lesion to make certain it is not cancerous, and, if it proves cancerous, to prevent its spread to other parts of the body.

Precautions

Most skin lesion removal procedures require few precautions. The area to be treated is cleaned before the procedure with alcohol or another antibacterial preparation, but generally it is not necessary to use a sterile operating room. Most procedures are performed on an outpatient basis, using a local anesthetic. Some of the more complex procedures may require specialized equipment available only in an outpatient surgery center. Most of the procedures are not highly invasive and, frequently, can be well-tolerated by young and old patients, as well as those with other medical conditions.

Description

A variety of techniques are used to remove **skin lesions**. The particular technique selected will depend on such factors as the seriousness of the lesion, its location, and the patient's ability to tolerate the procedure. Some of the simpler techniques, such as a biopsy or cryosurgery, can be performed by a primary care physician. Some of the more complex techniques, such as excision with a scalpel, electrosurgery, or laser surgery, are typically performed by a dermatologic surgeon, plastic surgeon, or other surgical specialist. Often, the technique selected will depend on how familiar the physician is with the procedure and how comfortable he or she is with performing it.

Biopsy

In this procedure, the physician commonly injects a local anesthetic at the site of the skin lesion, then removes a sample of the lesion, so that a definite diagnosis can be made. The sample is sent to a pathology laboratory, where it is examined under a microscope. Certain characteristic skin cells, and their arrangement in the skin, offer clues to the type of skin lesion, and whether it is cancerous or otherwise poses danger. Depending on the results of the microscopic examination, additional surgery may be scheduled.

A variety of methods are used to obtain a skin biopsy. The physician may use a scalpel to cut a piece or remove all of the lesion for examination. Lesions that are confined to the surface may be sampled with a shave biopsy, where the physician holds a scalpel blade parallel to the surface of the skin and slides the blade across the base of the lesion, removing a sample. Some physicians use a single-edge razor blade for this, instead of a scalpel. A physician may also perform a punch biopsy, in which a small circular punch removes a plug of skin.

Excision

When excising a lesion, the physician attempts to remove it completely by using a scalpel to cut the shape of an ellipse around the lesion. Leaving an elliptical wound, rather than a circular wound, makes it easier to insert stitches. If a lesion is suspected to be cancerous, the physician will not cut directly around the lesion, but will attempt to also remove a healthy margin of tissue surrounding it. This is to ensure that no cancerous cells remain, which would allow the tumor to reappear. To prevent recurrence of basal and squamous cell skin cancers, experts recommend a margin of 0.08–0.16 in (2–4 mm) for malignant melanoma, the margin may be 1.2 in (3 cm) or more.

Destruction

Not all lesions need to be excised. A physician may simply seek to destroy the lesion using a number of destructive techniques. These techniques do not leave sufficient material to be examined by a pathologist, however, and are best used in cases where a visual diagnosis is certain.

- Cryosurgery. This technique employs an extremely cold liquid or instrument to freeze and destroy abnormal skin cells that require removal. Liquid nitrogen is the most commonly used cryogen. It is typically sprayed on the lesion in several freeze-thaw cycles to ensure adequate destruction of the lesion.
- Curettage. In this procedure, an instrument with a circular cutting loop at the end is drawn across the lesion, starting at the middle and moving outward. With successive strokes, the physician scrapes portions of the lesion away. Sometimes a physician will use the curet to reduce the size of the lesion before turning to another technique to finish removing it.
- Electrosurgery. This utilizes an alternating current to selectively destroy skin tissue. Depending on the type of current and device used, physicians may use electrosurgical equipment to dry up surface lesions (electrodessication), to burn off the lesion (electrocoagulation), or to cut the lesion (electrosection). One advantage of electrosurgery is that it minimizes bleeding.

Mohs' micrographic surgery

The real extent of some lesions may not be readily apparent to the eye, making it difficult for the surgeon to decide where to make incisions. If some **cancer** cells are left behind, for example, the cancer may reappear or spread. In a technique called Mohs' micrographic surgery, surgeons begin by removing a lesion and examining its margins under a microscope for evidence of cancer. If cancerous cells are found, the surgeon then removes another ring of tissue and examines the margins again. The process is repeated until the margins appear clear of cancerous cells. The technique is considered ideal for aggressive tumors in areas such as the nose or upper lip, where an excision with wide margins may be difficult to repair, and may leave a cosmetically poor appearance.

Lasers

Laser surgery is now applied to a variety of skin lesions, ranging from spider veins to more extensive blood vessel lesions called hemangiomas. Until recently, CO_2 lasers were among the more common laser devices used by physicians, primarily to destroy skin lesions. Other lasers, such as the Nd:YAG and flashlamp-pumped pulse dye laser have been developed to achieve more selective results when used to treat vascular lesions, such as hemangiomas, or pigmented lesions, such as café-au-lait spots.

Preparation

No extensive preparation is required for skin lesion removal. Most procedures can be performed on an outpatient basis with a local anesthetic. The lesion and surrounding area is cleaned with an antibacterial compound before the procedure. A sterile operating room is not required.

Aftercare

The amount of aftercare will vary, depending on the skin lesion removal technique. For biopsy, curettage, cryosurgery, and electrosurgery procedures, the patient is told to keep the wound clean and dry. Healing will take at least several weeks, and may take longer, depending on the size of the wound and other factors. Healing times will also vary with excisions and with Mohs' micrographic surgery, particularly if a skin graft or skin flap is needed to repair the resulting wound. Laser surgery may produce changes in skin coloration that often resolve in time. **Pain** is usually minimal following most outpatient procedures, so pain medicines are not routinely prescribed. Some areas of the body, such as the scalp and fingers, can be more painful than others, however, and a pain medicine may be required.

KEY TERMS

Curet—A surgical instrument with a circular cutting loop at one end. The curet is pulled over the skin lesion in repeated strokes to remove one portion of the lesion at a time.

Mohs' micrographic surgery—A surgical technique in which successive rings of skin tissue are removed and examined under a microscope to ensure that no cancer is left.

Shave biopsy—A method of removing a sample of skin lesion so it can be examined by a pathologist. A scalpel or razor blade is held parallel to the skin's surface and is used to slice the lesion at its base.

Risks

All surgical procedures present risk of infection. Keeping the wound clean and dry can minimize the risk. **Antibiotics** are not routinely given to prevent infection in skin surgery, but some doctors believe they have a role. Other potential complications include:

- bleeding below the skin, which may create a hematoma and sometimes requires the wound to be reopened and drained,
- temporary or permanent nerve damage resulting from excision in an area with extensive and shallow nerve branches,
- wounds that may reopen after they have been stitched closed, increasing the risk of infection and scarring.

Results

Depending on the complexity of the skin lesion removal procedure, patients can frequently resume their normal routine the day of surgery. Healing frequently will take place within weeks. Some excisions will require later reconstructive procedures to improve the appearance left by the original procedure.

In addition to the complications outlined above, it is always possible that the skin lesion will reappear, requiring further surgery.

Resources

ORGANIZATIONS

American Academy of Dermatology. 930 N. Meacham Road, P.O. Box 4014, Schaumburg, IL 60168-4014. (847) 330-0230. Fax: (847) 330-0050. http://www.aad.org.

American Society for Dermatologic Surgery. 930 N. Meacham Road, P.O. Box 4014, Schaumburg, IL 60168-4014. (847) 330-9830. http://www.asds-net.org.

American Society of Plastic and Reconstructive Surgeons. 44 E. Algonquin Rd., Arlington Heights, IL 60005. (847) 228-9900. http://www.plasticsurgery.org.

Richard H. Camer

Skin lesions

Definition

A skin lesion is a superficial growth or patch of the skin that does not resemble the area surrounding it.

Description

Skin lesions can be grouped into two categories: primary and secondary. Primary skin lesions are variations in color or texture that may be present at birth, such as moles or birthmarks, or that may be acquired during a person's lifetime, such as those associated with **infectious diseases** (e.g. warts, acne, or **psoriasis**), allergic reactions (e.g. hives or **contact dermatitis**), or environmental agents (e.g. sunburn, pressure, or temperature extremes). Secondary skin lesions are those changes in the skin that result from primary skin lesions, either as a natural progression or as a result of a person manipulating (e.g. scratching or picking at) a primary lesion.

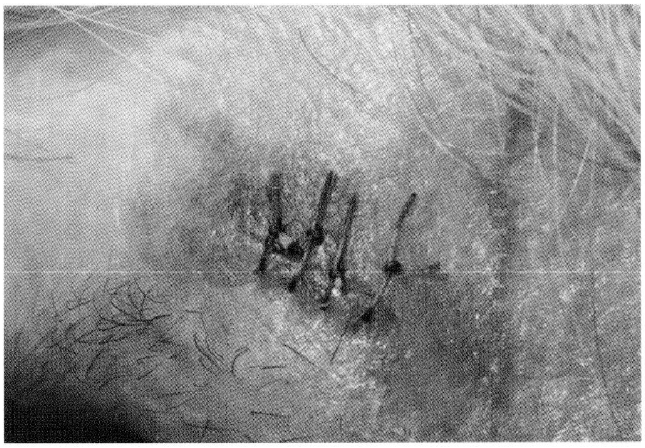

Melanoma biopsy scar. *(Dr P. Marazzi / Photo Researchers, Inc. Reproduced by permission.)*

The major types of primary lesions are:

- Macule. A small, circular, flat spot less than $\frac{2}{5}$ in (1 cm) in diameter. The color of a macule is not the same as that of nearby skin. Macules come in a variety of shapes and are usually brown, white, or red. Examples of macules include freckles and flat moles. A macule more than $\frac{2}{5}$ in (1 cm) in diameter is called a patch.
- Vesicle. A raised lesion less than $\frac{1}{5}$ in (5 mm) across and filled with a clear fluid. Vesicles that are more than $\frac{1}{5}$ in (5 mm) across are called bullae or blisters. These lesions may may be the result of sunburns, insect bites, chemical irritation, or certain viral infections, such as herpes.
- Pustule. A raised lesion filled with pus. A pustule is usually the result of an infection, such as acne, imptigeo, or boils.
- Papule. A solid, raised lesion less than $\frac{2}{5}$ in (1 cm) across. A patch of closely grouped papules more than $\frac{2}{5}$ in (1 cm) across is called a plaque. Papules and plaques can be rough in texture and red, pink, or brown in color. Papules are associated with such conditions as warts, syphilis, psoriasis, seborrheic and actinic keratoses, lichen planus, and skin cancer.
- Nodule. A solid lesion that has distinct edges and that is usually more deeply rooted than a papule. Doctors often describe a nodule as "palpable," meaning that, when examined by touch, it can be felt as a hard mass distinct from the tissue surrounding it. A nodule more than 2 cm in diameter is called a tumor. Nodules are associated with, among other conditions, keratinous cysts, lipomas, fibromas, and some types of lymphomas.
- Wheal. A skin elevation caused by swelling that can be itchy and usually disappears soon after erupting. Wheals are generally associated with an allergic reaction, such as to a drug or an insect bite.
- Telangiectasia. Small, dilated blood vessels that appear close to the surface of the skin. Telangiectasia is often a symptom of such diseases as rosacea or scleroderma.

The major types of secondary skin lesions are:

- Ulcer. Lesion that involves loss of the upper portion of the skin (epidermis) and part of the lower portion (dermis). Ulcers can result from acute conditions such as bacterial infection or trauma, or from more chronic conditions, such as scleroderma or disorders involving peripheral veins and arteries. An ulcer that appears as a deep crack that extends to the dermis is called a fissure.

- Scale. A dry, horny build-up of dead skin cells that often flakes off the surface of the skin. Diseases that promote scale include fungal infections, psoriasis, and seborrheic dermatitis.
- Crust. A dried collection of blood, serum, or pus. Also called a scab, a crust is often part of the normal healing process of many infectious lesions.
- Erosion. Lesion that involves loss of the epidermis.
- Excoriation. A hollow, crusted area caused by scratching or picking at a primary lesion.
- Scar. Discolored, fibrous tissue that permanently replaces normal skin after destruction of the dermis. A very thick and raised scar is called a keloid.
- Lichenification. Rough, thick epidermis with exaggerated skin lines. This is often a characteristic of scratch dermatitis and atopic dermatitis.
- Atrophy. An area of skin that has become very thin and wrinkled. Normally seen in older individuals and people who are using very strong topical corticosteroid medication.

Causes and symptoms

Skin lesions can be caused by a wide variety of conditions and diseases. A tendency toward developing moles, freckles, or birthmarks may be inherited. Infection of the skin itself by bacteria, **viruses**, fungi, or parasites is the most common cause of skin lesions. Acne, athlete's foot (tinea pedis), warts, and **scabies** are examples of skin infections that cause lesions. Allergic reactions and sensitivity to outside environmental factors can also lead to the formation of skin lesions. Underlying conditions can also precipitate the appearance of skin lesions. For example, the decreased sensitivity and poor circulation that accompanies **diabetes mellitus** can contribute to the formation of extensive ulcers on extremities such as the feet. Infections of body's entire system can cause the sudden onset of skin lesions. For example, skin lesions are a hallmark symptom of such diseases as chicken pox, herpes, and small pox. Cancers affecting the skin, including basal cell carcinoma, squamous cell carcinoma, **malignant melanoma**, and Kaposi's sarcoma, are recognized by their lesions.

Diagnosis

Diagnosis of the underlying cause of skin lesions is usually based on patient history, characteristics of the lesion, and where and how it appears on the patient's body (e.g. pustules confined to the face, neck and upper back can indicate acne, while scales appearing on the scalp and face may indicate **seborrheic dermatitis**). To determine the cause of an infection, doctors may also take scrapings or swab samples from lesions for examination under a microscope or for use in bacterial, fungal, or viral cultures. In cases where a fungal infection is suspected, a doctor may examine a patient's skin under ultraviolet light using a filter device called a Woods light–under these conditions, certain species will taken on specific fluorescent colors. Dermatologists may also use contrast lighting and subdued lighting to detect variations in the skin. When involvement of the **immune system** is suspected, doctors may order a immunofluorescence test, which detects antibodies to specific antigens using a fluorescent chemical. In cases of contact **dermatitis**, a condition in which a allergic reaction to something irritates the skin, doctors may use patch tests, in which samples of specific antigens are introduced into the skin via a scratch or a needle prick, to determine what substances are provoking the reaction.

The vast majority of skin lesions are noncancerous. However, doctors will determine whether or not a particular lesion or lesions are cancerous based on observation and the results of an excisional or punch biopsy, in which a tissue sample is excised for microscopic analysis. Since early detection is a key to successful treatment, individuals should examine their skin on a monthly basis for changes to existing moles, the presence of new moles, or a change in a certain area of skin. When examining moles, factors to look for include:

- Asymmetry. A normal mole is round, whereas a suspicious mole is uneven.
- Border. A normal mole has a clear-cut border with the surrounding skin, whereas the edges of a suspect mole may be irregular.
- Color. Normal moles are uniformly tan or brown, but cancerous moles may appear as mixtures of red, white, blue, brown, purple, or black.
- Diameter. Normal moles are usually less than $\frac{1}{5}$ in (5 mm) in diameter, a skin lesion greater than this may be suspected as cancerous.

Treatment

Treatment of skin lesions depends upon the underlying cause, what type of lesions they are, and the patient's overall health. If the cause of the lesions is an allergic reaction, removing the allergen from the patient's environment is the most effective treatment. Topical preparations can also be used to clean and protect irritated skin as well as to remove dead skin cells and scales. These may come in a variety of forms, including ointments, creams, lotions, and solutions.

KEY TERMS

Corticosteroid—A type of steroid medication that helps relieve itching (puritis) and reduce inflammation.

Fibroma—A usually benign tumor consisting of fiborous tissue.

Lesion—A possibly abnormal change or difference in a tissue or structure, such as the skin.

Lipoma—A usually benign tumor of fatty tissue.

Patch test—Test in which different antigens (substances that cause an allergic reaction) are introduced into a patient's skin via a needle prick or scratch and then observed for evidence of an allergic reaction to one or more of them. Also known as a scratch test.

Woods light—Device that allows only ultraviolet light to pass through it.

Topical **antibiotics**, fungicides, pediculicides (agents that kill lice), and scabicides (agents that kill the scabies parasite) can be applied to treat appropriate skin infections. Oral medications may be taken to address systemic infections or conditions. Deeply infected lesions may require minor surgery to lance and drain pus. Topical agents to sooth irritated skin and reduce inflammation may also be applied. Corticosteroids are particularly effective in reducing inflammation and **itching** (puritis). Oatmeal baths, baking soda mixtures, and calamine lotion are also recommended for the relief of these symptoms. A type of corticosteroid may be used to reduce the appearance of keloid scars. Absorbent powders may also be used to reduce moisture and prevent the spread of infection. In cases of ulcers that are slow to heal, pressure dressings may be used. At times, surgical removal of a lesion may be recommended–this is the usual course of therapy for **skin cancer**. Surgical removal usually involves a simple excision under local anesthetic, but it may also be accomplished through freezing (cryotherapy) or laser surgery.

Prognosis

Skin lesions such as moles, freckles, and birthmarks are a normal part of skin and will not disappear unless deliberately removed by a surgical procedure. Lesions due to an allergic reaction often subside soon after the offending agent is removed. Healing of lesions due to infections or disorders depends upon the type of infection or disorder and the overall health of the individual. Prognosis for skin **cancer** primarily depends upon whether or not the lesion is localized and whether or not it has spread to other areas of the body, such as the lymph nodes. In cases where the lesion is localized and has not spread to other parts of the body, the cure rate is 95-100%.

Prevention

Not all skin lesions are preventable; moles and freckles, for example, are benign growths that are common and unavoidable. However others can be avoided or minimized by taking certain precautions. Skin lesions caused by an allergic reaction can be avoided by determining what the offending agent is and removing it from the home or workplace, or, if this is impossible, developing strategies for safely handling it, such as with gloves and protective clothing. Keeping the skin, nails, and scalp clean and moisturized can help reduce or prevent the incidence of infectious skin diseases, as can not sharing personal care items such as combs and make-up with others. Skin lesions associated with **sexually transmitted diseases** can be prevented by the use of condoms. Scratching or picking at existing lesions should be avoided since this usually serves only to spread infection and may result in scarring. Individuals who have systemic conditions, such as diabetes mellitus or poor circulation, that could lead to serious skin lesions should inspect their bodies regularly for changes in their skin's condition. Regular visual inspection of the skin is also a key to preventing or minimizing the occurrence of skin cancer, as is the regular use of sun screens with an SPF of 15 or more.

Resources

BOOKS

Rosen, Theodore, Marilyn B. Lanning, and Marcia J. Hill. *The Nurse's Atlas of Dermatology.* Boston: Little Brown & Co., 1983.

Bridget Travers

Sleep apnea in seniors

Definition

Sleep apnea is the temporary interruption of breathing during sleep, usually lasting less than 30 seconds at a time. However, episodes may occur several times a night.

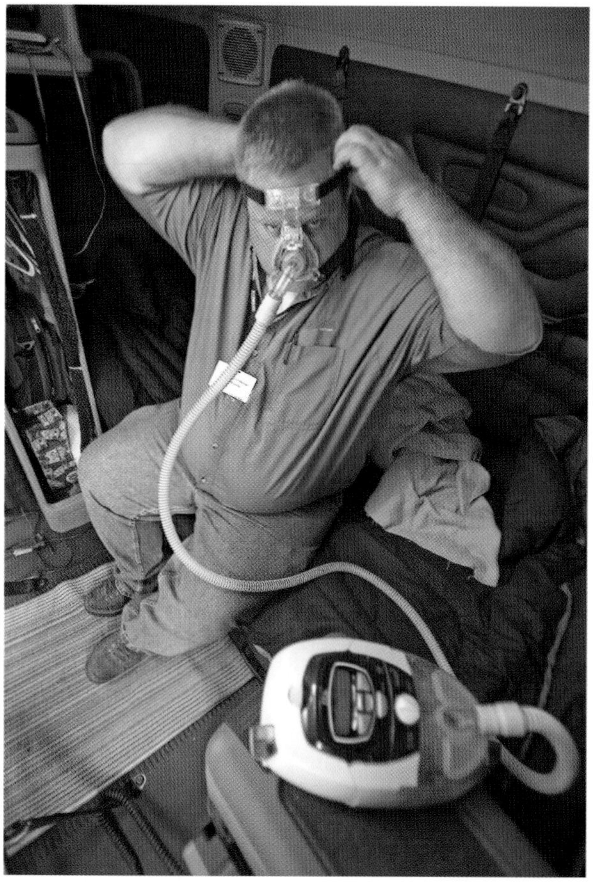

This truck driver demonstrates use of a machine he keeps in the cab of his truck to help him deal with his sleep apnea. *(AP Images. Reproduced by permission.)*

Description

There are two types of sleep apnea—obstructive and central. Obstructive sleep apnea (also called OSA) can be caused by such factors as **obesity** or an obstruction in the mouth or nose that blocks the airway. Central sleep apnea is less common, more difficult to treat, and can be caused by a problem with the brain, nervous system, or spine. Without treatment, either type of sleep apnea can cause other life-threatening conditions, including **pulmonary hypertension**, **stroke**, heart failure, or even **death** when the apnea is severe.

Sleep apnea can result in oxygen deprivation, which may cause seniors to experience personality changes, **depression**, **headaches**, and fogginess. Some researchers believe severe sleep apnea may also lead to high **blood pressure**, stroke, and **heart attack**, which can lead to death.

Most people who have sleep apnea wake in the morning and have no recollection of their apnea. That is why the condition is usually recognized by another person living in the same home or room as the senior with sleep apnea. The housemate may notice a senior exhibits patterns of excessive snoring, followed by 5–30 second intervals of silence, then coughing or gasping for air. This usually occurs several times throughout the night. The senior will usually awaken in the morning with no recollection of the apnea, but may be tired from the recurrent episodes of apnea.

Sleep apnea can lead to daytime sleepiness. Some seniors who don't feel well rested upon waking or who may have difficulty going to sleep will turn to sedatives or alcohol to induce sleep in an effort to feel more rested the next day. This type of behavior is dangerous for a senior with sleep apnea because the sedatives can actually suppress the respiratory functions further, which can hinder waking during episodes of apnea.

When the airway is already somewhat closed, deep breaths can collapse the windpipe, blocking the ability of air to pass. When the airflow is blocked, the blood oxygen level falls, which causes the brain to tell the person to wake to breath. This interrupts rapid eye movement (REM) during sleep, which seniors already have less of as they age. REM is crucial to every person because it makes up for 15 to 25 percent of sleep and is responsible for creating dreams and the internal Circadian rhythm (a biological process which occurs naturally on a daily basis that tells the body when to sleep). More importantly, REM also assists in the regulation of blood pressure, heartbeat, and respiration.

Demographics

Though OSA affects people of all ages, it is the most common type of sleep apnea in senior patients. Studies show that 24% of seniors living independently have OSA. And between 33–42% of seniors living in an institution or facility are affected by the condition. However, it is widely believed that the percentage of seniors with OSA who live independently is potentially higher than these statistics. This is due to the fact that most people with OSA do not realize they have the condition while they are sleeping and, therefore, the condition is underreported.

Causes and symptoms

Men are more likely than women to have sleep apnea. This may be due in part to low testosterone or hypogonadism in men as they age. However, for all seniors, obesity or an obstruction of the nose or mouth may cause sleep apnea.

Sleep apnea is a serious condition that, if left untreated, may result in a host of other conditions or diseases. If daytime drowsiness impairs the senior's ability to drive or function mentally, it may also lead to accidental falls, death or worsening of mental disease, such as increased disorientation in dementia patients.

Snoring or daytime sleepiness alone cannot be used to define sleep apnea in seniors because these are prevalent for much of the population. A senior must also exhibit the following trademark symptoms during sleep on a frequent basis: Severe snoring, then interrupted breathing lasting 5–30 seconds or longer, followed by a gasp for air, choking, or some other indication that the senior is trying to open their airway to breathe again.

More controversial reasons to test for sleep apnea are unexplained **hypertension**, a large neck circumference, obesity, or right ventricular failure.

The diagnostic tool that is used by a doctor to determine whether a senior has sleep apnea is a polysomnogram, which is costly and not always available. It tests the number of episodes of apnea per night and how long each one lasts. This determines what classification of apnea the senior may fall in: mild, moderate, or severe.

If the polysomnogram is not covered by insurance or unavailable, an ambulatory polysomnogram is another option. It costs less, is used at home, and may be more feasible for insurance companies to cover.

Because diagnosis may be costly and insurance may not always cover diagnostic tools without just cause, a second-hand witness to the condition can be crucial. Bed partners and housemates are the ideal reporters for sleep apnea. They are able to view the senior exhibiting the symptoms and are able to offer a full description of the symptoms to medical professionals.

Diagnosis

A proper diagnosis is critical because the consequences of untreated sleep apnea can be dangerous. Seniors with severe, untreated sleep apnea are two to three times more likely to cause or participate in an automobile accident because of their sleep deprivation. They also run the risk of developing pulmonary hyperthyroidism, high blood pressure, heart attack, or stroke. Severe, untreated sleep apnea can also lead to death.

Treatment

Although sleep apnea is a treatable condition, there are only a handful of treatments available. The most common treatment for a moderate to severe case of sleep apnea requires a senior to wear a Continuous Positive Airway Pressure (CPAP) nasal mask while sleeping. Since the pause in breathing during an episode of sleep apnea deprives the senior of oxygen, the CPAP nasal mask ensures a steady stream of oxygen flows throughout the night.

If obesity is a factor in a senior, **weight loss** is always recommended. Slimming down the body will slim a thick neck, which is important since this will reduce weight and pressure surrounding the airway.

If alcohol, **caffeine**, or sedatives are sedatives are being used or abused, doctors usually recommend ceasing their use or only using them earlier in the day. All three substances affect REM sleep and alcohol and sedatives can affect respiration during sleep.

One of the most common remedies for some snorers is to refrain from sleeping on their back. The same is true for seniors who have mild sleep apnea.

Most people must sleep an average of eight hours per night. Seniors are no exception. However, with the naturally occurring decrease in REM sleep as people age, a senior's sleep is already interrupted. And sleep apnea may compound the problem. To increase the amount of REM sleep in seniors, researchers assert that **exercise** and exposure to bright light regulates the Circadian rhythm of the body, which may improve sleep at night. Also, since daytime drowsiness or sleepiness is common, refraining from napping may improve the odds of nighttime sleepiness during bedtime hours.

QUESTIONS TO ASK YOUR DOCTOR

- Do you think I have a sleep disorder? If so, what type?
- If so, do you recommend any sleep studies?
- Do you think I should take a polysomnogram? If so, will you speak to my insurance company about coverage and options?
- Do you think I could have a psychological or physical factor that is causing or contributing to my problem?
- I (choose one or more, if applicable) use sedatives, drink alcohol, drink caffeine. Do you think that could contribute to my problem?
- Do you think my weight could be a contributor?
- What treatment is right for me? Will it have any side affects?

KEY TERMS

Circadian rhythm—A biological process that occurs naturally on a daily basis that signals the body when to sleep.

CPAP (Continuous Positive Airway Pressure)—The most common treatment for a moderate to severe case of sleep apnea requires a senior to wear a CPAP nasal mask while sleeping.

OSA (Obstructed Sleep Apnea)—One type of sleep apnea that may be caused by obesity or an obstruction in the mouth or nose that blocks the airway.

Sleep apnea—The temporary interruption of breathing during sleep, usually lasting less than 30 seconds at a time.

Nutrition/Dietetic concerns

Avoid caffeine, alcohol, and sedatives because they interrupt crucial REM sleep and may cause daytime drowsiness.

Therapy

The most common treatment for a moderate to severe case of sleep apnea requires a senior to wear a Continuous Positive Airway Pressure (CPAP) nasal mask while they sleep.

Prevention

A sleep study or evaluation of sleep patterns in seniors—especially those living alone—can be crucial since seniors will have no recollection of their episodes of apnea upon waking. Some studies show keeping weight at a normal level may prevent the worsening of sleep apnea.

Resources

PERIODICALS

Brunk, Doug. "Serum testosterone could be marker for OSA." *Clinical Psychiatry News 13(1)* (January 2005): 48-58.

Heart Advisor. "Why pauses in breathing during sleep should be a wake-up call." *Gale. Thomson Gale Trial Site. 2007* (Oct 2006): 2(1).

Wexler, Barbara, ed. "Weight in America: Obesity, Eating Disorders, and Other Health Risks." *Gale Virtual Reference Library. Gale. Thomson Gale Trial Site. 2007 ed.* (2006): 23- 50.

OTHER

American Heart Association. "Severe Sleep Apnea and Risk of Ischemic Stroke in the Elderly." 2006. http://www.americanheart.org/presenter.jhtml?identifier=3041799.

American Lung Association. "Sleep Apnea (Sleep- Disordered Breathing)." June 2005. http://www.lungusa.org/site/apps/s/content.asp?c=dvLUK9O0E&b=34706&ct=67313.

Beers, Mark H., MD. "Sleep apnea." *The Merck Manual of Geriatrics Online, 3rd ed.* 2000. http://www.merck.com/mkgr/mmg/sec6/ch47/ch47f.jsp.

National Institute of Neurological Disorders and Stroke. "NINDS Sleep Apnea Information Page." *Nursing Magazine Online* June 22, 2007. http://www.ninds.nih.gov/disorders/sleep_apnea/sleep_apnea.htm.

Neurbauer, David N., M.D. "Sleep Problems in the Elderly." *American Academy of Family Physicians* 1999. http://www.aafp.org/afp/990501ap/2551.html.

Sleep Disorders Channel. "Obstructive Sleep Apnea." 2008. http://www.sleepdisorderchannel.com/osa/index.shtml.

ORGANIZATIONS

American Sleep Disorders Association, 1424 K St NW, Washington, DC, 20005-2410, 202-293-3650, http://www.sleepapnea.org/.

National Sleep Foundation, 1522 K Street, NW, Suite 500, Washington, DC, 20005, 202-347-3471, http://www.Sleepfoundation.org.

American Heart Association, 7272 Greenville Avenue, Dallas, TX, 75231, 1-800-242-8721, http://www.americanheart.org.

American Stroke Association, 7272 Greenville Avenue, Dallas, TX, 75231, 1-800-478-7653, www.strokeassociation.org/.

National Institute of Neurological Disorders and Stroke (NINDS), P.O. Box 5801, Bethesda, MD, 20824, 1-800-352-9424, ninds.nih.gov.

Lauren L. Stinson

Sleep disorders

Definition

Sleep disorders involve a variety of persistent problems that people have with falling asleep, staying asleep, and quality of sleep. They may also involve sleeping too little or too much.

Description

Lack of proper sleep can interfere with memory and learning, compromise the body's **immune system**, play havoc with people's emotional states, and shorten the life span. Inadequate sleep can also increase **pain** in arthritis sufferers and complicate diabetes, as well as increase the risk of diabetes and **heart disease**. Since sleep helps regulate body functions, including hormone production, lack of sleep increases the risk of developing diabetes and is worse if you sleep five hours or less each night.

A 17-year study reported at the British Sleep Society in 2008 revealed that people who had five or fewer hours sleep each night also had increased their risk of **dying** from any cause. These people also doubled their risk of dying from heart disease because lack of sleep elevated **blood pressure**. The study also found that sleeping more than eight hours also increased mortality risk, but not from heart disease.

Further, lack of sleep in the workplace costs employers $50 billion in lost productivity and accounts for $15 billion in medical expenses yearly. Many companies report increased end-of -shift injuries due to lack of sleep.

A study published in 2007 linked sleep deprivation with heightened emotions and impulsive behaviors. Sleep was found to be necessary to restore rational emotional brain pathways.

Types of sleep disorders

Many adults report sleep problems of varying kinds. *The International Classification of Sleep Disorders, Second Edition*lists 81 different sleep disorders. There are ten primary disorders that are common and fall into six areas: **insomnia**, breathing related disorders, movement disorders, circadian rhythm sleep disorders, inadequate sleep hygiene, and parasomnias (sleep disorders marked by night terrors or sleepwalking).

Older adults may experience any of these sleep disorders, however, they also have special needs. They generally require as much sleep as they once did, between 7 and 9 hours every night, but now get sleepy earlier in the evening and get up earlier. They also have trouble falling asleep, staying asleep, and getting back to sleep. This may be due to a sleep-wake cycle that does not work as well as it did or to sleep habits, diseases, or medications. Older adults also may secrete less melatonin, a hormone that promotes sleep.

In addition, sleep disorders may underlie sleep problems in menopausal women. Though these women often report having their sleep interrupted by hot flashes, a 2008 study revealed that sleep disorders may also be occurring. Treating hot flashes, the study emphasized, would not help women sleep better. Doctors need to look at other factors when women report interrupted sleep and feel it is because of hot flashes.

Unfortunately, sleep disorders in older adults are underdiagnosed and undertreated. In 2007, The National Coalition for Sleep Disorders in Older People was formed to develop comprehensive guidelines for diagnosis and treatment of sleep disorders in older Americans. The coalition consists of twelve organizations, including the American Association of Retired Persons (**AARP**), AGS Foundation for Healthy Aging, and the National Sleep Foundation.

INSOMNIA Most sleep disturbances can be lumped under insomnia. This is a broad definition of conditions that interfere with satisfying sleep. Some of these conditions are caused by poor sleep hygiene; others are due to other factors.

Older men have more trouble with sleep, taking longer to fall asleep and waking up more often than older women. Both men and women experience lighter and less restful sleep and have fewer episodes of deep REM (rapid eye movement) sleep where dreams originate.

Insomnia can be temporary. Situational insomnia is the result of stressful life events such as worry over finances, concerns about an ill relative, or a **death** in the family. Sleeplessness or interrupted sleep may last three weeks or less. Normal sleep usually returns when the **stress** is passed or resolved. Some doctors may recommend medications or counseling to help the patient through this stressful time.

Chronic insomnia lasts more than three weeks. It must be treated by dealing with the underlying problem. Sometimes this insomnia is the result of **anxiety** disorders, illness, or chronic stress.

BREATHING RELATED DISORDERS Sleep apnea is the most common breathing related sleep disorder. It is a condition marked by loud snoring interspersed with episodes where a person stops breathing for 10 to 30 seconds during sleep. When the person starts breathing again, the breath is taken as a loud gasp that often wakes the sleeper. Sometimes, the person comes fully awake and wonders what woke him or her up. At other times, the sleeper comes to light wakefulness. In either case, the sleeper does not sleep deeply. Sleep apnea can cause daytime tiredness or drowsiness and can contribute to heart disease because sleep apnea episodes raise blood pressure. A 2005 study showed strong evidence that sleep apnea also caused strokes.

MOVEMENT DISORDERS There are two movement disorders involving poor sleep: restless leg syndrome and **periodic limb movement disorder**. These disorders appear more frequently in older adults than in younger people. Restless leg syndrome is a crawling feeling in the legs that makes the sleeper uncomfortable and want to move the legs. This often keeps the sleeper awake at night. Older adults are more likely to have restless leg syndrome.

People with periodic limb movement disorder kick every 20 to 40 seconds in their sleep, often forcing their bed partners to sleep elsewhere. Some people have both restless leg syndrome and this condition as well.

CIRCADIAN RHYTHM SLEEP DISORDERS These sleep disorders can be temporary. They often deal with circumstances that upset the normal sleep-wake pattern within a 24-hour cycle. Jet lag caused by traveling quickly from one part of the country or world to another can move bedtimes farther from the body's normal bedtime or closer to it.

Though many older people may be retired, some may volunteer or work part-time. If they volunteer at a crisis line or work at a convenience store or all-night retail store, they may work at night for a few days and then have several days off. People who do this often have trouble adjusting to different patterns of sleeping and waking.

PARASOMNIAS These sleep disorders are marked by night terrors or sleepwalking. Though they are most common in childhood, they can still occur in the elderly. Sometimes, vivid nightmares are due to strange surroundings, traumatic stress, or medications. Sleepwalking can also be the result of medications, **food allergies**, or an inherited condition, but usually has occurred previously in the patient's life.

Demographics

The National Sleep Foundation reports that 75 percent of adults in the US have trouble sleeping at least a few nights each week. Nearly half of older adult between the ages of 65 and 79 report mild to severe sleep problems.

Causes and symptoms

Causes

Many conditions can cause sleep disorders. Simple insomnia can be caused by stress or worry, **depression**, anxiety, using **caffeine** or other stimulants, using alcohol or sedatives, poor sleep habits, seasonal factors, pain, or urinary frequency or incontinence. Being overweight can cause **breathing problems** that disturb sleep.

Some medications, especially **diuretics** that cause frequent urination, if taken near bedtime, can interrupt sleep by having the patient get up to go to the bathroom. Taking multiple medications can lead to feeling tired all the time and can sometimes interfere with sleep.

Chronic illnesses such as diabetes can cause pain or restlessness that interrupts sleep. Arthritis pain and stiffness can make falling to sleep difficult. Some Alzheimer's patients sleep less and wake up more often and others sleep too much.

Symptoms

The symptoms of sleep disorders can vary, depending on the condition causing poor sleep. In general, most patients report having trouble getting to sleep. They may wake up often during the night or wake up and not be able to go back to sleep. They also do not feel rested when they wake and may feel tired during the day. Moreover, they may feel anxious around bedtime because of past experience with poor sleep.

Patients with sleep apnea often snore loudly and are startled awake as they gasp for their next breath. Often, bed partners report these episodes clearly though the patient may not be aware of them. Bed partners also report periodic limb movement disorder or restless leg syndrome because their own sleep is disturbed by the movements of their partners. Many restless leg syndrome patients, however, do report feeling crawly or itchy sensations in leg muscles throughout the night.

Diagnosis

The doctor will review the patient's medical history and will ask about the patient's sleep patterns and sleep habits. The patient's bed partner may need to accompany the patient to explain what he or she has observed during the patient's sleep and how that has affected him or her. The doctor will do a physical exam.

Usually, treatment recommendations begin at this stage. However, some doctors may want more details, especially if sleep apnea or movement disorders are suspected. The doctor then may send the patient to a sleep specialist at a sleep center. There, the patient may undergo a polysomnogram, an overnight sleep study. This test measures heart rate, breathing, body movements, and brain waves. The specialist may conduct a multiple sleep latency test instead. This test has the patient nap every two hours in the daytime. If the patient falls asleep quickly, that means the patient is not getting adequate sleep at night.

Treatment

The first line of treatment is usually instilling good sleep hygiene. That means going to bed and rising at the same time every day, trying not to take naps longer than twenty minutes during the day, avoiding caffeinated drinks after lunch, and not drinking alcohol in the evening. Doctors usually recommend having the patient **exercise** during the day, but not within three hours of bedtime. If the person cannot fall asleep within thirty minutes of going to bed, the person should get up and go into another room to do something quite, such as reading or listening to soft music. Then, the person can return to bed and try to fall asleep.

The bedroom should be used only for sleep and romance, not for watching television or reading. The rooms should be kept dark and cool. Soft music may be played to encourage a relaxing mood. Sometimes, a massage or a warm bath before bed helps. Many doctors encourage people who have insomnia to create a bedroom routine, doing the same relaxing things every night about a half hour to an hour before bed, cueing the body and the mind for sleep.

If there are medical conditions that are keeping the person awake, the doctor should make sure that these conditions are under adequate control. The doctor may be able to prescribe pain medications or alter the time of day in which medications are taken in order to ensure uninterrupted sleep.

Doctors may also recommend **relaxation** techniques or counseling to deal with anxiety disorders or stress issues. Physical exercise or **movement therapy** such as **Tai Chi**, **Yoga**, or dance can also help older adults sleep better.

Patients with sleep apnea often wear a nasal mask attached to a machine that provides continuous airway pressure to keep the nasal passages open. This prevents snoring and allows the person to have a deeper sleep experience. Sometimes mouth guards are used instead to keep the airway open.

Restless leg syndrome can sometimes be managed by placing hot or cold packs on the legs or taking a hot or cold bath. Some people massage the legs before bed. Others use relaxation techniques. Exercise during the day may also help. There are medications for this condition as well as periodic limb movement disorder. However, some of these drugs also produce sleep-walking or eating in one's sleep or even addictive behaviors such as gambling.

WHEN TO SEE THE DOCTOR

If a person cannot sleep well every night for two weeks, an appointment should be made to see a doctor.

Medications

New, safer, more effective drugs have replaced the habit-forming sedatives and **barbiturates** of the past. **Benzodiazepines** (estazolam, oxazepam, and temazepam) are older drugs that are still used, especially to treat night terrors or sleepwalking. They are habit-forming. Imidazopyrines (eszapiclone, zaleplon, and zolpidem) work like benzodiazepines but leave the body quickly. They are not likely to be habit-forming or cause daytime drowsiness. They can, however, produce bizarre behaviors. Melatonin receptor agonist (ramelteon) works like the hormone melatonin. It is fast-acting and is flushed from the body quickly. It does not appear to be habit-forming.

Alternative treatments

The most popular supplements used as sleep aids are melatonin and valerian. Melatonin is produced by the pineal gland in the brain. When taken in low doses, it seems to have favorable results when used for temporary relief from jet lag. Valerian, an herb, however, has little research backing its effectiveness.

Bach Flower Remedies Rescue Sleep is another herbal alternative. It is a mixture of six flower essences that are sprayed under the tongue. The aroma and taste are found to be relaxing and therefore sleep inducing.

Nutrition/Dietetic concerns

Caffeine consumption can lead to wakefulness and trouble falling asleep. Many doctors recommend that no coffee, black tea, or sodas with caffeine should be consumed at night or even in the afternoon.

Therapy

Behavioral therapy and cognitive therapy may be helpful to some patients with sleep disorders. Behavioral therapists help patients learn relaxation training, deep breathing, and progressive muscular relaxation. They may even offer ways for patients to meditate. A

KEY TERMS

Circadian rhythm—A body rhythm within a 24-hour cycle

Jet lag—Disruption of the sleep-wake cycle due to travel across several time zones within one day.

Melatonin—A hormone that promotes sleep.

Polysomnogram—An overnight sleep study.

REM sleep—Rapid eye movement sleep phase where dreaming occurs.

Sleep apnea—Repeated episodes of temporary suspension of breathing during sleep.

Sleep center—A clinic where doctors diagnose, treat, and do research on sleep disorders.

relaxed state in body and mind is helpful for drifting off to sleep.

Some behavioral therapists help patients create relaxing environments in the bedroom. They insist that the bedroom be only used for sex and sleep. Stimulus control therapy also has the patient maintain a consistent bedtime and rising time.

Sleep restriction therapy sets a bedtime later that than normal, making sure the patient gets at least five hours sleep. But the patient gets up at the same time each morning. This is done for a week, then the bedtime is moved up 15 minutes earlier each week until the patient can sleep for 7 to 9 hours each night.

Cognitive therapy helps patients reframe their negative sleep experiences. It replaces negative statements about sleep with positive ones.

Prognosis

The prognosis for treatment of most sleep disorders in the elderly depends on the nature of the disorder. Some sleep problems are temporary and resolve with time or little intervention. Some can be corrected with healthy sleep hygiene. Others may be the result of medical conditions that may or may not have a solution that will encourage satisfying sleep. In most cases, therapy, medications, and good sleep habits offer hope to many sleep-deprived older adults.

Prevention

Generally, good sleep habits can prevent many sleep problems. However, for some patients some sleep disorders cannot be prevented but can be managed.

Caregiver concerns

Patients with sleep apnea should be carefully screened for heart disease and **stroke** risk factors and monitored closely. In addition, menopausal patients should also be screened for sleep disorders when they present with interrupted sleep they think is due to hot flashes.

Resources

PERIODICALS

Contie, Vicki. "Lack of sleep disrupts brain's emotional controls."*Research Matters, National Institutes of Health.*(November 5, 2007):NA

Cooper, Phyllis G. "Insomnia (Adult Health Advisor 2007)."*Clinical Reference Systems.*(May 31, 2007):NA

"Help for Insomnia."*Harvard Health Commentaries.*(April 23, 2007):NA

"Insomnia in older adults (Senior Health Advisor 2007)."*Clinical Reference Systems.*(May 31, 2007):NA

Kiefer, Dale. "Lack of sleep increases mortality risk."*Life Extension.*(January 2008):NA

"New coalition to tackle sleep disorders in older adults." *Medical Condition News.*(August 16, 2007):NA

"Nighttime awakenings in menopause may be caused by sleep disorders, not hot flashes."*Harvard Women's Health Watch.*(February 2008):NA

Pallarito, Karen. "Sleep problems plague the older set."*HealthDay.*(November 23, 2007):NA

"Women and sleep: Not always the best of friends."*Harvard Health Commentaries.*(August 21, 2006):NA

Author. "article title."*Journal Name.*(date):page

OTHER

NIH Senior Health *www.nihseniorhealth.gov*

Sleep Educationhttp://www.sleepeducation.com

ORGANIZATIONS

American Insomnia Association (AIA), One Westbrook Corporate Center, Suite 920., Westchester, IL, 60154, 708-492-0939, www.americaninsomniaassociation .org.

American Sleep Apnea Association(ASAA), 1424 K Street, NW, Suite 302., Washington, DC, 20005, 202-293-3650, www.sleepapnea.org.

Better Sleep Council, 501 Wythe Street., Alexandria, VA , 22314, 703-683-8371, www.bettersleep.org.

National Institute on Aging(NIA), 31 Center Drive, MSC 2292, Building 31, Room 5C27, Bethesda, Maryland, 20892, 301-496-1752, 301-496-1072, www.nia.nih .gov.

National Institute on Neurological Disorders and Stroke (NINDS), P.O. Box 5801., Bethesda, MD, 20824, 800-468-9424, www.ninds.nih.gov.

National Sleep Foundation, 1522 K Street, NW, Suite 500., Washington, DC, , 202-347-3471, www.sleepfoundation.org.

Restless Legs Syndrome Foundation, 819 Second Street, SW., Rochester, MN, 55902, 507-287-6465, www.rls.org.

Janie F. Franz

Small cell lung cancer *see* **Lung cancer**

Smoking

Definition

Smoking is the inhalation of the smoke of burning tobacco encased in cigarettes, pipes, and cigars. Casual smoking is the act of smoking only occasionally, usually in a social situation or to relieve **stress**. A smoking habit is a physical addiction to tobacco products. Many health experts now regard habitual smoking as a psychological addiction, too, and one with serious health consequences.

Description

The U.S. Food and Drug Administration has asserted that cigarettes and smokeless tobacco should be considered nicotine delivery devices. Nicotine, the active ingredient in tobacco, is inhaled into the lungs, where most of it stays. The rest passes into the bloodstream, reaching the brain in about 10 seconds and dispersing throughout the body in about 20 seconds.

Depending on the circumstances and the amount consumed, nicotine can act as either a stimulant or tranquilizer. This can explain why some people report that smoking gives them energy and stimulates their mental activity, while others note that smoking relieves **anxiety** and relaxes them. The initial "kick" results in part from the drug's stimulation of the adrenal glands and resulting release of epinephrine into the blood. Epinephrine causes several physiological changes—it temporarily narrows the arteries, raises the **blood pressure**, raises the levels of fat in the blood, and increases the heart rate and flow of blood from the heart. Some researchers think epinephrine contributes to smokers' increased risk of high blood pressure.

Nicotine, by itself, increases the risk of **heart disease**. However, when a person smokes, he or she is

Percentage of adults in the United States age 45 and over who are current cigarette smokers, by selected characteristics, selected years, 2000–2007‡

	Total		White		Black or African American	
Year	45–64	65 and over	45–64	65 and over	45–64	65 and over
			Percent			
Men						
2000	26.4%	10.2%	25.8%	9.8%	32.2%	14.2%
2001	26.4%	11.5%	25.1%	10.7%	34.3%	21.1%
2002	24.5%	10.1%	24.4%	9.3%	29.8%	19.4%
2003	23.9%	10.1%	23.3%	9.6%	30.1%	18.0%
2004	25.0%	9.8%	24.4%	9.4%	29.2%	14.1%
2005	25.2%	8.9%	24.5%	7.9%	32.4%	16.8%
2006	24.5%	12.6%	23.4%	12.6%	32.6%	16.0%
2007‡	22.6%	8.6%	21.5%	8.6%	30.5%	12.8%
Women						
2000	21.7%	9.3%	21.4%	9.1%	25.6%	10.2%
2001	21.4%	†9.1%	21.6%	9.4%	22.6%	9.3%
2002	21.1%	8.6%	21.5%	8.5%	22.2%	9.4%
2003	20.2%	8.3%	20.1%	8.4%	23.3%	8.0%
2004	19.8%	8.1%	20.1%	8.2%	20.9%	6.7%
2005	18.8%	8.3%	18.9%	8.4%	21.0%	10.0%
2006	19.3%	8.3%	18.8%	8.4%	25.5%	9.3%
2007‡	20.0%	8.1%	21.2%	8.6%	21.0%	8.2%

†The value for all women includes other races which have a very low rate of cigarette smoking. Thus, the weighted average for all women is slightly lower than that for white women.

‡The 2007 estimates are based on Early Release National Health Interview Survey (NHIS) data collected January–June 2007, using preliminary weights.

SOURCE: Centers for Disease Control and Prevention, National Center for Health Statistics, National Health Interview Survey

(Illustration by GGS Information Services. Cengage Learning, Gale)

ingesting a lot more than nicotine. Smoke from a cigarette, pipe, or cigar is made up of many additional toxic chemicals, including tar and carbon monoxide. Tar is a sticky substance that forms into deposits in the lungs, causing **lung cancer** and respiratory distress. Carbon monoxide limits the amount of oxygen that the red blood cells can convey throughout your body. Also, it may damage the inner walls of the arteries, which allows fat to build up in them.

Besides tar, nicotine, and carbon monoxide, tobacco smoke contains 4,000 different chemicals. More than 200 of these chemicals are known be toxic. Nonsmokers who are exposed to tobacco smoke also take in these toxic chemicals. They inhale the smoke exhaled by the smoker as well as the more toxic *sidestream smoke*—the smoke from the end of the burning cigarette, cigar, or pipe.

Here's why sidestream smoke is more toxic than exhaled smoke: When a person smokes, the smoke he or she inhales and then breathes out leaves harmful deposits inside the body. But because lungs partially cleanse the smoke, exhaled smoke contains fewer poisonous chemicals. That's why exposure to tobacco smoke is dangerous even for a nonsmoker.

Causes and symptoms

No one starts smoking to become addicted to nicotine. It isn't known how much nicotine may be consumed before the body becomes addicted. However, once smoking becomes a habit, the smoker faces a lifetime of health risks associated with one of the strongest addictions known to man.

About 70% of smokers in the United States would like to quit; in any given year, however, only about 3.6% of the country's 47 million smokers quit successfully.

Although specific genes have not yet been identified as of 2003, researchers think that genetic factors contribute substantially to developing a smoking habit. Several twin studies have led to estimates of 46–84% heritability for smoking. It is thought that some genetic variations affect the speed of nicotine metabolism in the body and the activity level of nicotinic receptors in the brain.

Smoking risks

Smoking is recognized as the leading preventable cause of **death**, causing or contributing to the deaths of approximately 430,700 Americans each year. Anyone with a smoking habit has an increased chance of lung, cervical, and other types of **cancer**; respiratory diseases such as **emphysema**, **asthma**, and chronic **bronchitis**; and cardiovascular disease, such as **heart attack**, high blood pressure, **stroke**, and **atherosclerosis** (narrowing and hardening of the arteries). The risk of stroke is especially high in women who take birth control pills.

Smoking can damage fertility, making it harder to conceive, and it can interfere with the growth of the fetus during pregnancy. It accounts for an estimated 14% of premature births and 10% of infant deaths. There is some evidence that smoking may cause impotence in some men.

Because smoking affects so many of the body's systems, smokers often have vitamin deficiencies and suffer oxidative damage caused by free radicals. Free radicals are molecules that steal electrons from other molecules, turning the other molecules into free radicals and destabilizing the molecules in the body's cells.

Smoking is recognized as one of several factors that might be related to a higher risk of hip fractures in older adults.

Studies reveal that the more a person smokes, the more likely he is to sustain illnesses such as cancer, chronic bronchitis, and emphysema. But even smokers who indulge in the habit only occasionally are more prone to these diseases.

Some brands of cigarettes are advertised as "low tar," but no cigarette is truly safe. If a smoker switches to a low-tar cigarette, he is likely to inhale longer and more deeply to get the chemicals his body craves. A smoker has to quit the habit entirely in order to improve his health and decrease the chance of disease.

Though some people believe chewing tobacco is safer, it also carries health risks. People who chew tobacco have an increased risk of heart disease and mouth and throat cancer. Pipe and cigar smokers have increased health risks as well, even though these smokers generally do not inhale as deeply as cigarette smokers do. These groups haven't been studied as extensively as cigarette smokers, but there is evidence that they may be at a slightly lower risk of cardiovascular problems but a higher risk of cancer and various types of circulatory conditions.

Recent research reveals that passive smokers, or those who unavoidably breathe in second-hand tobacco smoke, have an increased chance of many health problems such as lung cancer and asthma, and in children, sudden infant death syndrome.

Smokers' symptoms

Smokers are likely to exhibit a variety of symptoms that reveal the damage caused by smoking. A nagging morning cough may be one sign of a tobacco habit. Other symptoms include shortness of breath, wheezing, and frequent occurrences of respiratory illness, such as bronchitis. Smoking also increases fatigue and decreases the smoker's sense of smell and taste. Smokers are more likely to develop poor circulation, with cold hands and feet and premature **wrinkles**.

Sometimes the illnesses that result from smoking come on silently with little warning. For instance, coronary artery disease may exhibit few or no symptoms. At other times, there will be warning signs, such as bloody discharge from a woman's vagina, a sign of cancer of the cervix. Another warning sign is a hacking cough, worse than the usual smoker's cough, that brings up phlegm or blood—a sign of lung cancer.

Withdrawal symptoms

A smoker who tries to quit may expect one or more of these withdrawal symptoms: nausea, **constipation** or **diarrhea**, drowsiness, loss of concentration, **insomnia**, headache, nausea, and irritability.

Diagnosis

It's not easy to quit smoking. That's why it may be wise for a smoker to turn to his physician for help. For the greatest success in quitting and to help with the withdrawal symptoms, the smoker should talk over a treatment plan with his doctor or alternative practitioner. He should have a general physical examination to gauge his general health and uncover any deficiencies. He should also have a thorough evaluation for some of the serious diseases that smoking can cause.

Treatment

Research shows that most smokers who want to quit benefit from the support of other people. It helps to quit with a friend or to join a group such as those organized by the American Cancer Society. These groups provide support and teach behavior modification methods that can help the smoker quit. The smoker's physician can often refer him to such groups.

Other alternatives to help with the withdrawal symptoms of kicking the habit include nicotine replacement therapy in the form of gum, patches, nasal sprays, and oral inhalers. These are available by prescription or over the counter. A physician can provide advice on how to use them. They slowly release a small amount of nicotine into the bloodstream, satisfying the smoker's physical craving. Over time, the amount of gum the smoker chews is decreased and the amount of time between applying the patches is increased. This helps wean the smoker from nicotine slowly, eventually beating his addiction to the drug. But there's one important caution: If the smoker lights up while taking a nicotine replacement, a nicotine overdose may cause serious health problems.

The prescription drug Zyban (bupropion hydrochloride) has shown some success in helping smokers quit. This drug contains no nicotine, and was originally developed as an antidepressant. It isn't known exactly how bupropion works to suppress the desire for nicotine. A five-year study of bupropion reported in 2003 that the drug has a very good record for safety and effectiveness in treating tobacco dependence. Its most common side effect is insomnia, which can also result from nicotine withdrawal.

Researchers are investigating two new types of drugs as possible treatments for tobacco dependence as of 2003. The first is an alkaloid known as 18-methoxycoronaridine (18-MC), which selectively blocks the nicotinic receptors in brain tissue. Another approach involves developing drugs that inhibit the activity of cytochrome P450 2A6 (CYP2A6), which controls the metabolism of nicotine.

Results

Research on smoking shows that most smokers desire to quit. But smoking is so addictive that fewer than 20% of the people who try ever successfully kick the habit. Still, many people attempt to quit smoking over and over again, despite the difficulties—the cravings and withdrawal symptoms, such as irritability and restlessness.

For those who do quit, the benefits to health are well worth the effort. The good news is that once a smoker quits the health effects are immediate and dramatic. After the first day, oxygen and carbon monoxide levels in the blood return to normal. At two days, nerve endings begin to grow back and the senses of taste and smell revive. Within two weeks to three months, circulation and breathing improve. After one year of not smoking, the risk of heart disease is reduced by 50%. After 15 years of abstinence, the risks of health problems from smoking virtually vanish. A smoker who quits for good often feels a lot better too, with less fatigue and fewer respiratory illnesses.

Alternative treatment

There are a wide range of alternative treatments that can help a smoker quit the habit, including hypnotherapy, herbs, **acupuncture**, and meditation. For example, a controlled trial demonstrated that self-massage can help smokers crave less intensely, smoke fewer cigarettes, and in some cases completely give them up.

Hypnotherapy helps the smoker achieve a trance-like state, during which the deepest levels of the mind are accessed. A session with a hypnotherapist may begin with a discussion of whether the smoker really wants to and truly has the motivation to stop smoking. The therapist will explain how hypnosis can reduce the stress-related symptoms that sometimes come with kicking the habit.

Often the therapist will discuss the dangers of smoking with the patient and begin to "reframe" the patient's thinking about smoking. Many smokers are convinced they can't quit, and the therapist can help persuade them that they can change this behavior. These suggestions are then repeated while the smoker is under hypnosis. The therapist may also suggest while the smoker is under hypnosis that his feelings of worry, anxiety, and irritability will decrease.

In a review of 17 studies of the effectiveness of hypnotherapy, the percentage of people treated by hypnosis who still were not smoking after six months ranged from 4–8%. In programs that included several hours of treatment, intense interpersonal interaction, individualized suggestions, and follow-up treatment, success rates were above 50%.

One study demonstrated that inhaling the vapor from black pepper extract can reduce symptoms associated with smoking withdrawal. Other essential oils can be used for relieving the anxiety a smoker often experiences while quitting.

A variety of herbs can help smokers reduce their cravings for nicotine, calm their irritability, and even reverse the oxidative cellular damage done by smoking. Lobelia, sometimes called Indian tobacco, has historically been used as a substitute for tobacco. It contains a substance called lobeline, which decreases the craving for nicotine by bolstering the nervous system and calming the smoker. In high doses, lobelia can cause vomiting, but the average dose—about 10 drops per day—should pose no problems.

Herbs that can help relax a smoker during withdrawal include wild oats and kava kava.

To reduce the oral fixation supplied by a nicotine habit, a smoker can chew on licorice root—the plant, not the candy. Licorice is good for the liver, which is a major player in the body's detoxification process. Licorice also acts as a tonic for the adrenal system, which helps reduce stress. And there's an added benefit: If a smoker tries to light up after chewing on licorice root, the cigarette tastes like burned cardboard.

Other botanicals that can help repair free-radical damage to the lungs and cardiovascular system are those high in flavonoids, such as hawthorn, gingko biloba, and bilberry, as well as **antioxidants** such as vitamin A, **vitamin C**, **zinc**, and selenium.

This ancient Chinese method of healing is used commonly to help beat addictions, including smoking. The acupuncturist will use hair-thin needles to stimulate the body's *qi*, or healthy energy. Acupuncture is a sophisticated treatment system based on revitalizing qi, which supposedly flows through the body in defined pathways called meridians. During an addiction like smoking, qi isn't flowing smoothly or gets stuck, the theory goes.

Points in the ear and feet are stimulated to help the smoker overcome his addiction. Often the acupuncturist will recommend keeping the needles in for five to seven days to calm the smoker and keep him balanced.

Nutrition/Dietetic concerns

Smoking seriously depletes vitamin C in the body and leaves it more susceptible to infections. Vitamin C can prevent or reduce free-radical damage by acting as an antioxidant in the lungs. Smokers need additional C, in higher dosage than nonsmokers. Fish in the **diet** supplies Omega-3 fatty acids, which are associated with a reduced risk of **chronic obstructive pulmonary disease** (emphysema or chronic bronchitis) in smokers. Omega-3 fats also provide cardiovascular benefits as well as an anti-depressive effect. Vitamin therapy doesn't reduce craving but it can help beat some of the damage created by smoking. **Vitamin B_{12}** and **folic acid** may help protect against smoking-induced cancer.

Prevention

How do you give up your cigarettes for good and never go back to them again?

Here are a few tips from the experts:

- Have a plan and set a definite quit date.
- Get rid of all the cigarettes and ashtrays at home or in your desk at work.
- Don't allow others to smoke in your house.
- Tell your friends and neighbors that you're quitting. Doing so helps make quitting a matter of pride.

KEY TERMS

Antioxidant—Any substance that reduces the damage caused by oxidation, such as the harm caused by free radicals.

Chronic bronchitis—A smoking-related respiratory illness in which the membranes that line the bronchi, or the lung's air passages, narrow over time. Symptoms include a morning cough that brings up phlegm, breathlessness, and wheezing.

Cytochrome—A substance that contains iron and acts as a hydrogen carrier for the eventual release of energy in aerobic respiration.

Emphysema—An incurable, smoking-related disease, in which the air sacs at the end of the lung's bronchi become weak and inefficient. People with emphysema often first notice shortness of breath, repeated wheezing and coughing that brings up phlegm.

Epinephrine—A nervous system hormone stimulated by the nicotine in tobacco. It increases heart rate and may raise smokers' blood pressure.

Flavonoid—A food chemical that helps to limit oxidative damage to the body's cells, and protects against heart disease and cancer.

Free radical—An unstable molecule that causes oxidative damage by stealing electrons from surrounding molecules, thereby disrupting activity in the body's cells.

Nicotine—The addictive ingredient of tobacco, it acts on the nervous system and is both stimulating and calming.

Nicotine replacement therapy—A method of weaning a smoker away from both nicotine and the oral fixation that accompanies a smoking habit by giving the smoker smaller and smaller doses of nicotine in the form of a patch or gum.

Sidestream smoke—The smoke that is emitted from the burning end of a cigarette or cigar, or that comes from the end of a pipe. Along with exhaled smoke, it is a constituent of second-hand smoke.

- Chew sugarless gum or eat sugar-free hard candy to redirect the oral fixation that comes with smoking. This will prevent weight gain, too.
- Eat as much as you want, but only low-calorie foods and drinks. Drink plenty of water. This may help with the feelings of tension and restlessness that quitting can bring. After eight weeks, you'll lose your craving for tobacco, so it's safe then to return to your usual eating habits.
- Stay away from social situations that prompt you to smoke. Dine in the nonsmoking section of restaurants.
- Spend the money you save not smoking on an occasional treat for yourself.

Resources

PERIODICALS

"AAAAI, EPA Mount Effort to Raise Awareness to Dangers of Secondhand Smoke." *Immunotherapy Weekly* November 30, 2001: 30.

Batra, V., A. A. Patkar, W. H. Berrettini, et al. "The Genetic Determinants of Smoking." *Chest* 123 (May 2003): 1338–1340.

Ferry, L., and J. A. Johnston. "Efficacy and Safety of Bupropion SR for Smoking Cessation: Data from Clinical Trials and Five Years of Postmarketing Experience." *International Journal of Clinical Practice* 57 (April 2003): 224–230.

Janson, Christer, Susan Chinn, Deborah Jarvis, et al. "Effect of Passive Smoking on Respiratory Symptoms, Bronchial Responsiveness, Lung Function, and Total Serum IgE in the European Community Respiratory Health Survey: A Cross-Sectional Study." *Lancet* 358 (December 22, 2001): 2103.

Lerman, C., and W. Berrettini. "Elucidating the Role of Genetic Factors in Smoking Behavior and Nicotine Dependence." *American Journal of Medical Genetics* 118-B (April 1, 2003): 48–54.

Maisonneuve, I. M., and S. D. Glick. "Anti-Addictive Actions of an Iboga Alkaloid Congener: A Novel Mechanism for a Novel Treatment." *Pharmacology, Biochemistry, and Behavior* 75 (June 2003): 607–618.

Richmomd, R., and N. Zwar. "Review of Bupropion for Smoking Cessation." *Drug and Alcohol Review* 22 (June 2003): 203–220.

Sellers, E. M., R. F. Tyndale, and L. C. Fernandes. "Decreasing Smoking Behaviour and Risk through CYP2A6 Inhibition." *Drug Discovery Today* 8 (June 1, 2003): 487–493.

"Study Shows Link Between Asthma and Childhood Exposure to Smoking." *Immunotherapy Weekly* October 10, 2001: np.

Yochum, L., L. H. Kushi, and A. R. Folsom. "Dietary Flavonoid Intake and Risk of Cardiovascular Disease in Postmenopausal Women." *American Journal of Epidemiology* 149, no. 10 (May 1999): 943–9.

ORGANIZATIONS

American Association of Oriental Medicine. 5530 Wisconsin Avenue, Suite 1210, Chevy Chase, MD 20815.

(301) 941-1064 or (888) 500-7999. http://www.aaom.org.

American Cancer Society. Contact the local organization or call (800) 227-2345. http://www.cancer.org.

American Lung Association. 1740 Broadway, New York, NY 10019. (800) 586-4872 or (212) 315-8700. http://www.lungusa.org.

Herb Research Foundation. 1007 Pearl St., Suite 200, Boulder CO 80302. (303) 449-2265. http://www.herbs.org.

National Heart, Lung, and Blood Institute (NHLBI). Building 31, Room 5A52, 31 Center Drive, MSC 2486, Bethesda, MD 20892. (301) 592-8573. http://www.nhlbi.nih.gov.

Smoking, Tobacco, and Health Information Line. Centers for Disease Control and Prevention. Mailstop K-50, 4770 Buford Highway NE, Atlanta, GA 30341-3724. (800) 232-1311. http://www.cdc.gov/tobacco.

OTHER

Virtual Office of the Surgeon General: Tobacco Cessation Guideline. http://www.surgeongeneral.gov/tobacco.

Barbara Boughton

Smoking cessation

Definition

Smoking cessation means "quitting smoking," or "withdrawal from nicotine." Because smoking tobacco is highly addictive, quitting the habit often involves irritability, headache, mood swings, and cravings associated with the sudden cessation or reduction of tobacco use by a nicotine-dependent individual.

Purpose

There are many good reasons to stop smoking; one of them is that smoking cessation may speed post-surgery recovery. Smoking cessation helps a person heal and recover faster, especially in the incision area, or if the surgery involved any bones. Research shows that patients who underwent hip and knee replacements, or surgery on other bone joints, healed better and recovered more quickly if they had quit or cut down their tobacco intake several weeks before the operation. Smoking weakens the bone mineral that keeps the skeleton strong and undermines tissue and vessel health. One study suggested that even quitting tobacco for a few days could improve tissue blood flow and oxygenation, and might have a positive effect on wound healing. If a patient has had a history of heart problems, his chances of having a second **heart attack** will be lowered. Quitting may also reduce wound complications, and lower the risk of cardiovascular trouble after surgery. If surgery was performed to remove cancerous tumors, quitting will reduce the risk of a second tumor, especially if **cancer** in the lung, head, or neck has been successfully treated.

Description

Quitting smoking is one of the best things a person can do to increase their life expectancy. On average, male smokers who quit at 35 years old can be expected to live to be 76 years old instead of 69 years if they were still smoking. Women who quit would live to be 80 years old instead of 74 years.

Effects of smoking on the body

Nicotine acts as both a stimulant and a depressant on the body. Saliva and bronchial secretions increase along with bowel tone. Some inexperienced smokers may experience tremors or even convulsions with high doses of nicotine because of the stimulation of the central nervous system. The respiratory muscles are then depressed following stimulation.

Nicotine causes arousal as well as **relaxation** from stressful situations. Tobacco use increases the heart rate about 10–20 beats per minute; and because it constricts the blood vessels, it increases the **blood pressure** reading by 5–10 mm Hg.

Sweating, nausea, and **diarrhea** may also increase because of the effects of nicotine upon the central nervous system. Hormonal activities of the body are also affected. Nicotine elevates the blood glucose levels and increases **insulin** production; it can also lead to **blood clots**. Smoking does have some positive effects on the body by stimulating memory and alertness, and enhancing cognitive skills that require speed, reaction time, vigilance, and work performance. Smoking tends to alleviate boredom and reduce **stress** as well as reduce aggressive responses to stressful events because of its mood-altering ability. It also acts as an appetite suppressant, specifically decreasing the appetite for simple **carbohydrates** (sweets) and inhibiting the efficiency with which food is metabolized. The fear of weight gain prevents some people from quitting smoking. The addictive effects of tobacco have been well documented. It is considered mood- and behavior-altering, psychoactive, and abusable. Tobacco's addictive potential is believed to be comparable to alcohol, cocaine, and morphine.

Cigarette smoking status of adults in the United States age 45 and over, by sex and age group, 2006

Sex and age group	All current smokers	Every day smokers	Some day smokers	Former smokers	Non-smokers
			Percent		
Both sexes	20.8%	16.7%	4.2%	21.0%	58.2%
Men					
45–64	24.5%	21.1%	3.5%	32.1%	43.4%
65 and over	12.6%	10.4%	2.2%	51.1%	36.2%
Women					
45–64	19.3%	16.5%	2.8%	22.0%	58.7%
65 and over	8.3%	7.0%	1.3%	27.9%	63.8%

SOURCE: Centers for Disease Control and Prevention, National Center for Health Statistics, National Health Interview Survey

(Illustration by GGS Information Services. Cengage Learning, Gale)

Health problems associated with smoking

In general, chronic use of nicotine may cause an acceleration of coronary artery disease, **hypertension**, reproductive disturbances, esophageal reflux, peptic ulcer disease, fetal illnesses and **death**, and delayed wound healing. The smoker is at greater risk of developing cancer (especially in the lung, mouth, larynx, esophagus, bladder, kidney, pancreas, and cervix); heart attacks and strokes; and chronic lung disease. Using tobacco during pregnancy increases the risk of miscarriage, intrauterine growth retardation (resulting in the birth of an infant small for gestational age), and the infant's risk for sudden infant death syndrome.

The specific health risks of tobacco use include: nicotine addiction, lung disease, **lung cancer**, **emphysema**, chronic **bronchitis**, coronary artery disease and **angina**, heart attack, atherosclerotic and **peripheral vascular disease**, aneurysms, hypertension, blood clots, strokes, oral/tooth/gum diseases including **oral cancer**, and cancer in the kidney, bladder, and pancreas. Nicotine is also associated with decreased senses of taste and smell. During pregnancy, nicotine may cause increased fetal death, premature labor, low birth weight infants, and sudden infant death syndrome.

Nonsmokers who are regularly exposed to second hand smoke also may experience specific health risks including:

- Increased risk of lung cancer.
- An increased frequency of respiratory infections in infants and children (e.g. bronchitis and pneumonia), asthma, and decreases in lung function as the lungs mature.
- Acute, sudden, and occasionally severe reactions including eye, nose, throat, and lower respiratory tract symptoms.

The specific health risks for smokeless tobacco users include many of the diseases of smokers, as well as a 50-fold greater risk for oral cancer with long-term or regular use.

In diabetics taking medication for high blood pressure, it has been reported that smoking may increase the risk of kidney disease and/or kidney failure.

Making a plan to quit

Long lead times for elective procedures like joint operations offer a good opportunity for doctors to encourage their patients to quit smoking, but only the smoker has the power to stop smoking. Before a smoker decides to quit, he should make sure he wants to quit smoking for himself, and not for other people. The following are some suggestions the smoker may want to consider:

- Women should set their quit date to begin at the end of their period for best results. The first step is to set a quit date.
- Make a written list of why you want to quit smoking.
- Consider using an aid to help you quit, which can be the patch, nicotine gum, Zyban, nicotine spray, soft laser therapy, nasal inhaler, or some other method. If you plan to use Zyban, set your quit date for one week after you begin to use it.
- Smoke only in certain places, preferably outdoors.
- Switch to a brand of cigarettes that you don't like.
- Do not buy cigarettes by the carton.
- Cut coffee consumption in half. You will not need to give it up.
- Practice putting off lighting up when the urge strikes.

KEY TERMS

Addiction—Compulsive, overwhelming involvement with a specific activity. The activity may be smoking, gambling, alcohol, or may involve the use of almost any substance, such as a drug.

Appetite suppressant—To decrease the appetite.

Constrict—To squeeze tightly, compress, draw together.

Convulsion—To shake or effect with spasms; to agitate or disturb violently.

Depressant—A drug or other substance that soothes or lessens tension of the muscles or nerves.

Detoxification—To remove a poison or toxin or the effect of such a harmful substance; to free from an intoxicating or addictive substance in the body or from dependence on or addiction to a harmful substance.

Endorphins—Any of a group of proteins with analgesic properties that occur naturally in the brain.

Gestational age—The length of time of growth and development of the young in the mother's womb.

Metabolism—The sum of all the chemical processes that occur in living organisms; the rate at which the body consumes energy.

Nicotine—A poisonous, oily alkaloid in tobacco.

Oxygenation—To supply with oxygen.

Paraphernalia—Articles of equipment or accessory items.

Premature—Happening early or occurring before the usual time.

Psychoactive—Affecting the mind or behavior.

Respiratory infections—Infections that relate to or affect respiration or breathing.

Smoking cessation—To quit smoking or withdrawal from nicotine.

Stimulant—A drug or other substance that increases the rate of activity of a body system.

Tremor—A trembling, quivering, or shaking.

Withdrawal—Stopping of administration or use of a drug; the syndrome of sometimes painful physical and psychological symptoms that follow the discontinuance.

- Go for a walk every day or begin an exercise program.
- Stock up on non-fattening safe snacks to help with weight control after quitting.
- Enlist the support of family and friends.
- Clean and put away all ashtrays the day before quitting.

Smokers who are trying to quit should remind themselves that they are doing the smartest thing they have ever done. Because of the preparation for smoking cessation, the smoker won't be surprised or fearful about quitting. The quitter will be willing to do what's necessary, even though it won't be easy. Remember, this will likely add years to the lifespan. The quitting smoker should be prepared to spend more time with nonsmoking friends, if other smokers don't support the attempt to quit.

Since hospitals are smoke-free environments, if a smoking patient is in the hospital for elective surgery, it may be a good opportunity to quit smoking. It might be best to set the quit date around the time of the surgery and let the attending doctor know. As the smoker takes the first step, professional hospital staff will be there to give the support and help needed. Medical staff can start the patient on nicotine replacement therapy to help control the cravings and increase the chances of quitting permanently.

Methods of quitting

Cold turkey, or an abrupt cessation of nicotine, is one way to stop smoking. Cold turkey can provide cost savings because paraphernalia and smoking cessation aids are not required, however, not everyone can stop this way as tremendous willpower is needed.

Laser therapy is an entirely safe and **pain** free form of **acupuncture** that has been in use since the 1980s. Using a painless soft laser beam instead of needles the laser beam is applied to specific energy points on the body, stimulating production of endorphins. These natural body chemicals produce a calming, relaxing effect. It is the sudden drop in endorphin levels that leads to withdrawal symptoms and physical cravings when a person stops smoking. Laser treatment not only helps relieve these cravings, but helps with stress reduction and lung detoxification. Some studies indicate that laser therapy is the most effective method of smoking cessation, with an extraordinarily high success rate.

Acupuncture—small needles or springs are inserted into the skin—is another aid in smoking cessation. The needles or springs are sometimes left in the ears and touched lightly by the patient between visits.

Some smokers find hypnosis particularly useful, especially if there is any kind of mental conflict, such as phobias, panic attacks, or weight control. As a smoker struggles to stop smoking, the conscious mind, deciding to quit, battles the inner mind, which is governed by habit and body chemistry. Hypnosis, by talking directly to the inner mind, can help to resolve that inner battle.

Aversion techniques attempt to make smoking seem unpleasant. This technique reminds the person of the distasteful aspects of smoking, such as the smell, dirty ashtrays, coughing, the high cost, and health issues. The most common technique prescribed by psychologists for "thought stopping"—stopping unwanted thoughts—is to wear a rubber band around the wrist. Every time there is an unwanted thought (a craving to smoke) the band is supposed to be pulled so that it hurts. The thought then becomes associated with pain and gradually neutralized.

Rapid smoking is a technique in which smoking times are strictly scheduled once a day for the first three days after quitting. Phrases are repeated such as "smoking irritates my throat" or "smoking burns my lips and tongue." This causes over-smoking in a way that makes the taste and sensations very unpleasant.

There are special mouthwashes available, which, when used before smoking, alter the taste, making cigarettes taste awful. The aim is for smoking to eventually become associated with this very unpleasant taste.

Smoking cessation aids wean a person off nicotine slowly, and the nicotine can be delivered where it does the least bodily harm. Unlike cigarettes, they do not introduce other harmful poisons to the body. They can be used for a short period of time. However, it should be noted that nicotine from any source (smoking, nicotine gum, or the nicotine patch) can make some health problems worse. These include heart or circulation problems, irregular heartbeat, chest pain, high blood pressure, overactive thyroid, stomach ulcers, or diabetes.

The four main brands of the patch are Nicotrol, Nicoderm, Prostep, and Habitrol. All four transmit low doses of nicotine to the body throughout the day. The patch comes in varying strengths ranging from 7 mg to 21 mg. The patch must be prescribed and used under a physician's care. Package instructions must be followed carefully. Other smoking cessation programs or materials should be used while using the patch.

Nicorette gum allows the nicotine to be absorbed through the membrane of the mouth between the cheek and gums. Past smoking habits determine the right strength to choose. The gum should be chewed slowly.

The nicotine nasal spray reduces cravings and withdrawal symptoms, allowing smokers to cut back slowly. The nasal spray acts quickly to stop the cravings, as it is rapidly absorbed through the nasal membranes. One of the drawbacks is a risk of addiction to the spray.

The nicotine inhaler uses a plastic mouthpiece with a nicotine plug, delivering nicotine to the mucous membranes of the mouth. It provides nicotine at about one-third the nicotine level of cigarettes.

Zyban is an oral medication that is making an impact in the fight to help smokers quit. It is a treatment for nicotine dependence.

The nicotine lozenge is another smoking cessation aid recently added to the growing list of tools to combat nicotine withdrawal.

Withdrawal symptoms

Generally, the longer one has smoked and the greater the number of cigarettes (and nicotine) consumed, the more likely it is that withdrawal symptoms will occur and the more severe they are likely to be. When a smoker switches from regular to low-nicotine cigarettes or significantly cuts back smoking, a milder form of nicotine withdrawal involving some or all of these symptoms can occur.

These are some of the withdrawal symptoms that most ex-smokers experience in the beginning of their new smoke-free life:

- dry mouth
- mood swings
- irritability
- feelings of depression
- gas
- tension
- sleeplessness or sleeping too much
- difficulty in concentration
- intense cravings for a cigarette

- increased appetite and weight gain
- headaches

These side effects are all temporary conditions that will probably subside in a short time for most people. These symptoms can last from one to three weeks and are strongest during the first week after quitting. Drinking plenty of water during the first week can help detoxify the body and shorten the duration of the withdrawal symptoms. A positive attitude, drive, commitment, and a willingness to get help from health care professionals and support groups will help a smoker kick the habit.

Researchers from the University of California San Diego strongly suggest that any of the above cessation aids should be used in combination with other types of smoking cessation help, such as behavioral counseling and/or support programs. These products are not designed to help with the behavioral aspects of smoking, but only the cravings associated with them. Counseling and support groups can offer tips on coping with difficult situations that can trigger the urge to smoke.

Even a new heart can't break a bad habit

Why do some people who have heart transplants continue to smoke? In a three-year study at the University of Pittsburgh of 202 heart transplant recipients, 71% of the recipients were smokers before surgery. The overall rate of post-transplant smoking was 27%. All but one of the smokers resumed the smoking habit they had before the transplant. The biggest reason for resuming smoking was addiction to nicotine. Smoking is a complex behavior, involving social interactions, visual cues, and other factors. Those who smoked until less than six months before the transplant were much more likely to resume smoking early and to smoke more. One of the major causes of early relapse was because of **depression** and **anxiety** within two months after the transplant. Another strong predictor of relapse was having a caretaker who smoked. The knowledge of these risk factors could help develop strategies for identifying those in greatest need of early intervention. According to European studies, the five-year survival rate for post-transplant smokers is 37%, compared to 80% for nonsmoking recipients. Smokers can develop inoperable lung cancers within five years after a transplant, thus resulting in a shorter survival rate. There is an alarming incidence of head and neck cancers in transplant recipients who resume smoking.

Overall, there is a 90% relapse rate in the general population but, the more times a smoker tries to quit, the greater the chance of success with each new try.

Resources

BOOKS

Dodds, Bill. *1440 Reasons to Quit Smoking: 1 For Every Minute of the Day.* Minnetonka, MN: Meadowbrook Press, 2000.

Jones, David C. and Derick D. Schermerhorn, eds. *Yes You Can Stop Smoking: Even if You Don't Want To.* Dolphin Pub., 2001.

Kleinman, Lowell, Deborah Messina-Kleinman, and Mitchell Nides. *Complete Idiot's Guide to Quitting Smoking.* London, UK: Alpha Books, 2000.

Mannoia, Richard J. *NBAC Program: Never Buy Another Cigarette: A Cigarette Smoking Cessation Program.* Paradise Publications, 2003.

Shipley, Robert H. *Quit Smart: Stop Smoking Guide With the Quitsmart System, It's Easier Than You Think!* Quitsmart, 2002.

PERIODICALS

Landman, Anne, Pamela M. Ling, and Stanton A. Glantz. "Tobacco Industry Youth Smoking Prevention Programs: Protecting the Industry and Hurting Tobacco Control." *American Journal of Public Health* 92, no. 6 (June 2002): 917–30.

Ling, Pamela M. and Stanton A. Glantz, "Forum on Youth Smoking, Why and How the Tobacco Industry Sells Cigarettes to Young Adults: Evidence From Industry Documents." *American Journal of Public Health* 92, no. 6 (June 2002): 908–16.

Taylor, Donald H., Jr., Vic Hasselblad, S. Jane Henley, Michael J. Thun, and Frank A. Sloan. "Research and Practice, Benefits of Smoking Cessation for Longevity. " *American Journal of Public Health* 92, no. 6 (June 2002): 990–6.

ORGANIZATIONS

Action on Smoking and Health. 2013 H Street, NW, Washington, DC 20006. (202) 659-4310. http://ash .org.

The American Lung Association. 61 Broadway, 6th Floor, New York, NY. 10006. (800) 586-4872. http://www .lungusa.org.

OTHER

Illig, David. *Stop Smoking.* Audio CD. Seattle: WA: Successworld, 2001.

Mesmer. *Stop Smoking With America's Foremost Hypnotist.* Audio CD. Victoria, BC: Ace Mirage Entertainment, 2000.

Crystal H. Kaczkowski M.Sc.

Snoring surgery

Definition

Snoring is defined as noisy or rough breathing during sleep, caused by vibration of loose tissue in the upper airway. Surgical treatments for snoring include several different techniques for removing tissue from the back of the patient's throat, reshaping the nasal passages or jaw, or preventing the tongue from blocking the airway during sleep.

Purpose

The purpose of snoring surgery is to improve or eliminate the medical and social consequences of

Snoring surgeries (uvulopalatopharyngoplasty)

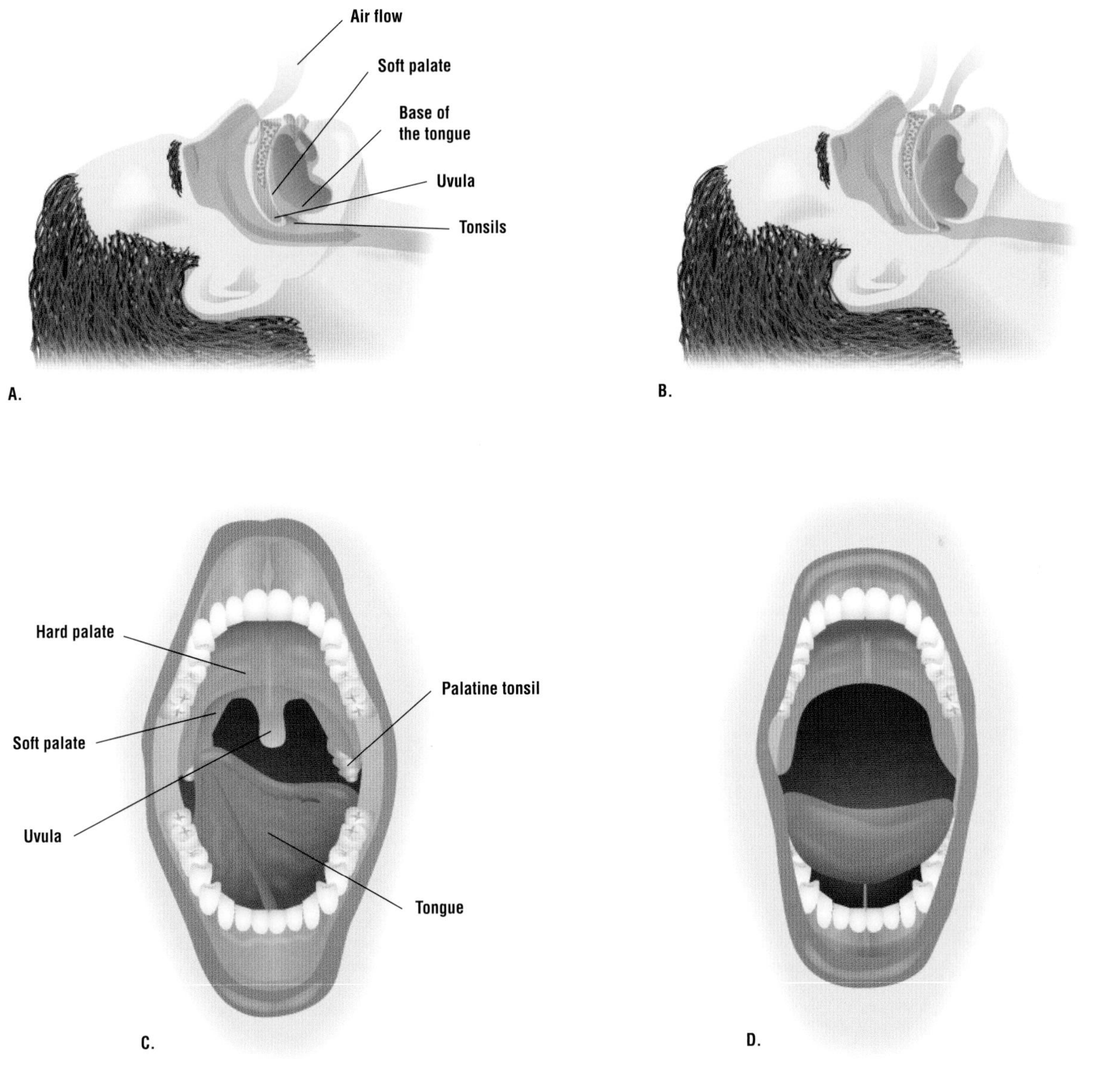

Heavy snorers have their airflow impeded by the structures at the back of the mouth and nose (A and B), which can be alleviated by surgery. In uvulopalatopharyngoplasty, the patient's uvula, soft palate, and tonsils are removed (C and D). *(Illustration by GGS Information Services. Cengage Learning, Gale)*

heavy snoring. Most insurance companies, however, regard surgical treatment of snoring as essentially a cosmetic procedure, which means that patients must cover its expenses themselves. The major exception is surgery to correct a deviated septum or other obstruction in the nose, on the grounds that nasal surgery generally improves the patient's breathing during the day as well as at night.

Snoring as a medical problem

The connection between heavy snoring, breathing disorders, and other health problems is a relatively recent discovery. Obstructive sleep apnea (OSA) is a breathing disorder that was first identified in 1965. OSA is marked by brief stoppages in breathing during sleep resulting from partial blockage of the airway. A person with OSA may stop breathing temporarily as often as 20–30 times per hour. He or she usually snores or makes choking and gasping sounds between these episodes. The person is not refreshed by nighttime sleep and may suffer from morning **headaches** as well as daytime sleepiness. He or she may be misdiagnosed as suffering from clinical **depression** when the real problem is physical tiredness. In addition, the high levels of carbon dioxide that build up in the blood when a person is not breathing normally may eventually lead to high **blood pressure**, irregular heartbeat, heart attacks, and **stroke**. In children, heavy snoring appears to be a major risk factor for attention-deficit/hyperactivity disorder.

Although people with OSA snore, not everyone who snores has OSA. It is thought that OSA affects about 4% of middle-aged males and 2% of middle-aged females. Most adults who snore have what is called primary snoring, which means that the loud sounds produced in the upper airway during sleep are *not* interrupted by episodes of breathing cessation. Other terms for primary snoring are simple snoring, benign snoring, rhythmical snoring, continuous snoring, and socially unacceptable snoring (SUS). Although primary snoring is not associated with severe disorders to the same extent as OSA, it has been shown to have some negative consequences for health. A study published in April 2003 reported that habitual primary snoring is a risk factor for chronic daily headaches.

Snoring as a social problem

As the term SUS suggests, primary snoring can cause the same social problems for a person as does snoring associated with OSA. People who snore heavily often keep other family members, roommates, or even neighbors from getting a good night's sleep, which leads to considerable anger and resentment. Recent studies have found that the nonsnoring partner or roommate loses an average of an hour's sleep each night. According to Dr. Kingman Strohl, head of a **sleep disorders** program in a Veterans Administration hospital, even the average volume of snoring (60 decibels or dB) is as loud as normal speech. Some people, however, snore around 80–82 dB, the sound level of a loud yell; a few have been recorded as reaching 90 dB, the sound level of loud rock music. One study found that 80% of people married to heavy snorers end up sleeping in separate rooms. A group of Swedish researchers reported that heavy snoring has the same level of negative effects on quality of life among adult males as high blood pressure, **chronic obstructive pulmonary disease**, **heart disease**, and similar chronic medical conditions.

Risk factors for snoring

Some people are at higher risk of developing problem snoring than others. Risk factors in addition to sex and age include:

- Genetic factors. The size and shape of the uvula, soft palate, tonsils, and other parts of the airway are largely determined by heredity.
- Family history of heavy snoring.
- Obesity. Severe overweight increases a person's risk of developing OSA.
- Lack of exercise. Physical activity helps to keep the muscles of the throat firm and strong as well as the larger muscles of the body.
- Heavy consumption of alcohol and tobacco.
- A history of frequent upper respiratory infections or allergies.
- Trauma to the nose, face, or throat.

Demographics

Snoring is a commonplace problem in the general population in North America. About 12% of children over the age of five are reported to snore frequently and loudly. Among adults, 45% snore occasionally, while 25% snore almost every night. The problem usually grows worse as people age; 50% of people over age 65 are habitual snorers.

Problem snoring is worse among males than among females in all age brackets. With regard to racial and ethnic differences, a sleep research study published in 2003 reported that frequent snoring is

KEY TERMS

Continuous positive airway pressure (CPAP)—A ventilation device that blows a gentle stream of air into the nose during sleep to keep the airway open.

Deviated septum—An abnormal configuration of the cartilage that divides the two sides of the nose. It can cause breathing problems if left uncorrected.

Injection snoreplasty—A technique for reducing snoring by injecting a chemical that forms scar tissue near the base of the uvula, helping to anchor it and reduce its fluttering or vibrating during sleep.

Obstructive sleep apnea (OSA)—A potentially life-threatening condition characterized by episodes of breathing cessation during sleep alternating with snoring or disordered breathing. The low levels of oxygen in the blood of patients with OSA may eventually cause heart problems or stroke.

Palate—The roof of the mouth.

Polysomnography—A test administered in a sleep laboratory to analyze heart rate, blood circulation, muscle movement, brain waves, and breathing patterns during sleep.

Primary snoring—Simple snoring; snoring that is not interrupted by episodes of breathing cessation.

Somnoplasty—A technique that uses radiofrequency signals to heat a thin needle inserted into the tissues of the soft palate. The heat from the needle shrinks the tissues, thus enlarging the patient's airway. Somnoplasty is also known as radiofrequency volumetric tissue reduction (RFVTR).

Uvula—A triangular piece of tissue that hangs from the roof of the mouth above the back of the tongue. Primary snoring is often associated with fluttering or vibrating of the uvula during sleep.

Uvulopalatopharyngoplasty (UPPP)—An operation to remove the tonsils and other excess tissue at the back of the throat to prevent it from closing the airway during sleep.

more common (in the United States) among African American women, Hispanic women, and Hispanic men than their Caucasian counterparts, even after adjusting for weight and **body mass index** (BMI). African American, Native American, and Asian American males have the same rates of snoring as Caucasian males. Further research is needed to determine whether these differences are related to variations in the rates and types of health problems in these respective groups.

According to international researchers, heavy snoring appears to be more common in persons of Asian origin than in persons of Middle Eastern, European, or African origin.

Description

With the exception of UPPP, all of the surgical treatments for snoring described in this section are outpatient or office-based procedures.

Uvulopalatopharyngoplasty (UPPP)

Uvulopalatopharyngoplasty, or UPPP, is the oldest and most invasive surgical treatment for snoring. It was first performed in 1982 by a Japanese surgeon named S. Fujita. UPPP requires **general anesthesia**, one to two nights of inpatient care in a hospital, and a minimum of two weeks of recovery afterward. In a uvulopalatopharyngoplasty, the surgeon resects (removes) the patient's tonsils, part of the soft palate, and the uvula. The procedure works by enlarging the airway and removing some of the soft tissue that vibrates when the patient snores. It is not effective in treating snoring caused by obstructions at the base of the tongue.

UPPP has several drawbacks in addition to its cost and lengthy recovery period. It can result in major complications, including severe bleeding due to removal of the tonsils as well as airway obstruction. In addition, the results may not be permanent; between 50% and 70% of patients who have been treated with UPPP report that short-term improvements in snoring do not last longer than a year.

Laser-assisted uvulopalatoplasty

Laser-assisted uvulopalatoplasty, or LAUP, is an outpatient surgical treatment for snoring in which a carbon dioxide laser is used to vaporize part of the uvula, a small triangular piece of tissue that hangs from the soft palate above the back of the tongue. The patient is seated upright in a comfortable chair in the doctor's office. The doctor first sprays a local anesthetic—usually lidocaine— over the back of the patient's throat, covering the patient's soft palate, tonsils, and uvula. The second step is the injection of more anesthetic into the muscle tissue in the uvula. After waiting for the anesthetic to take effect, the surgeon uses a carbon dioxide laser to make two vertical incisions in the soft palate on either side of the uvula. A third incision is used to remove the tip of the uvula. The surgeon also usually removes part of the soft palate itself. The total procedure takes about half an hour.

LAUP is typically performed as a series of three to five separate treatments. Additional treatment sessions, if needed, are spaced four to eight weeks apart.

LAUP was developed in the late 1980s by Dr. Yves-Victor Kamami, a French surgeon whose first article on the technique was published in 1990. Kamami claimed a high rate of success for LAUP in treating a condition known as obstructive sleep apnea (OSA) as well as snoring. The procedure has become controversial because other surgeons found it less effective than the first reports indicated, and also because most patients suffer considerable **pain** for about two weeks after surgery. Although some surgeons report a success rate as high as 85% in treating snoring with LAUP, the effectiveness of the procedure is highly dependent on the surgeon's experience and ability.

Somnoplasty

Somnoplasty, or radiofrequency volumetric tissue reduction (RFVTR) is a newer technique in which the surgeon uses a thin needle connected to a source of radiofrequency signals to shrink the tissues in the soft palate, throat, or tongue. It was approved by the Food and Drug Administration (FDA) for the treatment of snoring in 1997. The needle is inserted beneath the surface layer of cells and heated to a temperature between 158°F and 176°F (70° and 80° C). The upper layer of cells is unaffected, but the heated tissue is destroyed and gradually reabsorbed by the body over the next four to six weeks. Somnoplasty stiffens the remaining layers of tissue as well as reducing the total volume of tissue. Some patients require a second treatment, but most find that their snoring is significantly improved after only one. The procedure takes about 30 minutes and is performed under **local anesthesia**.

Somnoplasty appears to have a higher success rate (about 85%) than LAUP and is considerably less painful. Most patients report two to three days of mild swelling after somnoplasty compared to two weeks of considerable discomfort for LAUP.

Tongue suspension procedure

The tongue suspension procedure, which is also known as the Repose™ system, is a minimally invasive surgical treatment for snoring that stabilizes the base of the tongue during sleep, preventing it from falling backward and obstructing the airway. The Repose system was approved by the FDA in 1998. It consists of a titanium screw inserted into the lower jaw on the floor of the mouth and a suture passed through the base of the tongue that is then attached to the screw. The attachment holds the tongue forward during sleep.

The Repose system is done as an outpatient procedure under total anesthesia. It takes about 15–20 minutes to complete. The advantages of the tongue suspension procedure include the fact that it is reversible, since no incision is made; and that it can be combined with UPPP, LAUP, or a tonsillectomy. Its disadvantages include its relatively long healing time (one to two weeks) and the fact that it appears to be more effective in treating OSA than primary snoring. One team of American and Israeli researchers who conducted a multicenter trial concluded that the tongue suspension procedure requires further evaluation.

Injection snoreplasty

Injection snoreplasty was developed by a team of Army physicians at Walter Reed Hospital and introduced to other ear, nose and throat specialists at a professional conference in 2000. In injection snoreplasty, the surgeon gives the patient a local anesthetic and then injects a hardening agent known as **sodium** tetradecyl sulfate underneath the skin of the roof of the mouth just in front of the uvula. The chemical, which is also used in sclerotherapy, creates a blister that hardens into scar tissue. The scar tissue pulls the uvula forward, reducing the vibration or flutter that causes snoring.

Preliminary research indicates that injection snoreplasty is safe, has a higher rate of success than LAUP (about 92%), and is also less painful. Most patients need only one treatment, and can manage the discomfort the next day with a mild **aspirin** substitute and throat spray. The primary drawback of injection snoreplasty is that it treats only tissues in the area of the uvula. Snoring caused by tissue vibrations elsewhere in the throat requires another form of treatment. Injection snoreplasty costs about $500 per treatment.

Diagnosis/Preparation

Diagnosis

The most important task in diagnosing a patient's snoring is to distinguish between primary snoring and obstructive sleep apnea. The reason for care in the diagnosis is that surgical treatment without the recommended tests for OSA can complicate later diagnosis of the disorder.

The sounds made when a person snores have a number of different physical causes. Snoring noises may result from one or more of the following:

- An unusually long soft palate and uvula. These structures narrow the airway between the nose and the throat. They act like noisy flutter valves when the person breathes in and out during sleep.
- Too much tissue in the throat. Large tonsils and adenoids can cause snoring, which is one reason why tonsillectomies are sometimes recommended to treat heavy snoring in children.
- Nasal congestion. When a person's nose is stuffy, their attempts to breathe create a partial vacuum in the throat that pulls the softer tissues of the throat together. This suction can also produce a snoring noise. Nasal congestion helps to explain why some people snore only when they have a cold or during pollen season.
- Anatomical deformations of the nose. People who have had their noses or cheekbones fractured or who have a deviated septum are more likely to snore, because their nasal passages develop a twisted or crooked shape and vibrate as air passes through them.
- Sleeping position. People are more likely to snore when they are lying on the back because the force of gravity draws the tongue and soft tissues in the throat backward and downward, blocking the airway.
- Obesity. Obesity adds to the weight of the tissues in the neck, which can cause partial blockage of the airway during sleep.
- Use of alcohol, sleeping medications, or tranquilizers. These substances relax the throat muscles, which may become soft or limp enough to partially close the airway.

Because snoring may be related to lifestyle factors, upper respiratory infections, seasonal **allergies**, and sleeping habits as well as the anatomy of the person's airway, a complete medical history is the first step in determining suitable treatments. In some cases the patient may have been referred by his or her dentist on the basis of findings during a dental procedure. A primary care doctor can take a history and perform a basic examination of the patient's nose and throat. In addition, the primary care doctor may give the patient one or more short questionnaires to evaluate the severity of daytime sleepiness and other problems related to snoring. The test most commonly used is the Epworth Sleepiness Scale (ESS), which was developed by an Australian physician, Dr. Murray Johns, in 1991. The ESS lists eight situations (reading, watching TV, etc.) and asks the patient to rate his or her chances of dozing off in each situation on a four-point scale (0–3, with 3 representing a high chance of falling asleep). A score of 6 or lower indicates that the person is getting enough sleep; a score higher than 9 is a danger sign. The ESS is often used to measure the effectiveness of various treatments for snoring as well as to evaluate patients prior to surgery.

The next stage in the differential diagnosis of snoring problems is a detailed examination of the patient's airway by an otolaryngologist, who is a physician who specializes in diagnosing and treating disorders involving the nose and throat. The American Sleep Apnea Association (ASAA) maintains that no one should consider surgery for snoring until their airway has been examined by a specialist. The otolaryngologist will be able to determine whether the size and shape of the patient's uvula, soft palate, tonsils and adenoids, nasal cartilage, and throat muscles are contributing factors, and to advise the patient on specific procedures. It may be necessary for the patient to undergo more than one type of treatment for snoring, as some surgical procedures correct only one or two structures in the nose or throat.

A complete airway examination consists of an external examination of the patient's face and neck; an endoscopic examination of the nasal passages and throat; the use of a laryngeal mirror or magnifying laryngoscope to study the lower portions of the throat; and various imaging studies. The otolaryngologist may use a nasopharyngoscope, which allows for evaluation of obstructions below the palate and the tongue, and may be performed with the patient either awake or asleep. The nasopharyngoscope is a flexible fiberoptic device that is introduced into the airway through the patient's nose. Other imaging studies that may be done include acoustic reflection, computed tomography (CT) scans, or **magnetic resonance imaging** (MRI).

In addition to the airway examination, patients considering surgical treatment for snoring must make an appointment for sleep testing in a specialized laboratory. The American Academy of Sleep Medicine recommends this step in order to exclude the possibility that the patient has obstructive sleep apnea. Sleep testing consists of an overnight stay in a special sleep laboratory. Before the patient goes to sleep, he or she will be connected to a polysomnograph, which is an instrument that monitors the patient's breathing, heart rate, temperature, muscle movements, airflow, body position, and other measurements that are needed to evaluate the cause(s) of sleep disorders. A technician records the data in a separate room. As of 2003, some companies are developing portable polysomnographs that allow patients to connect the device to a computer in their home and transmit the data to the sleep center over an Internet connection.

Preparation

Apart from the extensive diagnostic testing that is recommended, preparation for outpatient snoring surgery is usually limited to taking a mild sedative before the procedure. Preparation for UPPP requires a physical examination, EKG, blood tests, and a preoperation interview with the anesthesiologist to evaluate the patient's fitness for general anesthesia.

Aftercare

Aftercare following outpatient snoring surgery consists primarily of medication for throat discomfort, particularly when swallowing. The patient can resume normal work and other activities the same day as the procedure, and speaking is usually not affected.

Risks

In addition to the risk of an allergic reaction to the local anesthetic, snoring surgery is associated with the following risks:

- Severe pain following the procedure that lasts longer than two to three days. This complication occurs more frequently with LAUP than with somnoplasty or injection snoreplasty.
- Causation or worsening of obstructive sleep apnea. LAUP has been reported to cause OSA in patients who had only primary snoring before the operation.
- Nasal regurgitation. This complication refers to food shooting or leaking through the nose when the patient swallows.
- Dehydration. This complication has been reported with the tongue suspension procedure.
- Permanent change in the quality of the patient's voice.
- Recurrence of primary snoring.

Results

In general, surgical treatment for snoring appears to be most effective in patients whose primary problem is nasal obstruction. The results of snoring surgery depend to a large degree on a good "fit" between the anatomy of a specific patient's airway and the specific procedure performed, as well as on the individual surgeon's skills.

Morbidity and mortality rates

Mortality rates for UPPP are related to complications of OSA rather than to the procedure itself. With regard to the outpatient procedures for snoring, mortality rates are very close to zero because these surgeries are performed under local anesthesia. Complication rates, however, are high with both UPPP and LAUP. According to one European study, as many as 42% of patients have complications following UPPP, with 14% reporting general dissatisfaction with the results of surgery. Specific complication rates for UPPP are 15% for recurrence of snoring; 13% for nasal regurgitation; 10% for excessive throat secretions; 9% for **swallowing problems**; and 7% for speech disturbances. Complications for LAUP have been estimated to be 30–40% for recurrence of snoring; 30% for causing or worsening of OSA; 5–10% for persistent nasal regurgitation; 1% for permanent change in vocal quality.

As of early 2003, no morbidity figures have been published for somnoplasty or injection snoreplasty.

Alternatives

Oral devices and appliances

Oral appliances are intended to reduce snoring by changing the shape of the oral cavity or preventing the tongue from blocking the airway. There are three basic types of mouthpieces: those that push the lower jaw forward; those that raise the soft palate; and those that restrain the tongue from falling backward during sleep. To work properly, oral appliances should be fitted by an experienced dentist or orthodontist and checked periodically for proper fit. Their major drawback is a low rate of patient compliance; one German study found that only 30% of patients fitted with these devices were still using them after four years. In addition, oral appliances cannot be used by patients with gum disease, **dental implants**, or teeth that are otherwise in poor condition.

Continuous positive airway pressure (CPAP) devices

CPAP devices are masks that fit over the nose during sleep and deliver air into the airway under enough pressure to keep the airway open. If used correctly, CPAP devices can be an effective alternative to surgery. Their main drawback is a relatively low rate of patient compliance; the mask must be used every night, and some people feel mildly claustrophobic when using it. In addition, patients are often asked to lose weight or stop **smoking** while using CPAP, which are lifestyle adjustments that some would rather not make.

Lifestyle changes

Patients who snore only occasionally or who are light snorers may be helped by one or more of the following changes without undergoing surgery:

- Losing weight and getting adequate physical exercise.
- Avoiding tranquilizers, sleeping pills, antihistamines, or alcoholic beverages before bedtime.
- Quitting smoking.
- Sleeping on the side rather than the back. One do-it-yourself device that is sometimes recommended to keep the patient turned on his or her side is a tennis ball placed inside a sock and attached to the back of the pajamas or nightgown. This approach seems to work for some patients with simple snoring.
- Tilting the head of the bed upward about 4 in (10 cm).

Complementary and alternative (CAM) approaches

There are three forms of alternative treatment that have been shown to be helpful in reducing primary snoring in patients with histories of nasal congestion or swollen tissues in the throat. The first is **acupuncture**. Treatments for snoring usually focus on acupuncture points on the stomach, arms, and legs associated with the production of excess mucus. Insertion of the acupuncture needles at these points is thought to stimulate the body to release the excess moisture or phlegm.

Homeopathy and aromatherapy also appear to benefit some patients whose snoring is related to colds, allergies, or sore throats. Homeopathic remedies for snoring are available as nose drops and throat sprays as well as the traditional pill formulations. Aromatherapy formulas for snoring typically contain marjoram oil, which may be used alone or combined with lavender and other herbs that clear the nasal passages. Some people find aromatherapy preparations helpful alongside mainstream treatments because their fragrance is pleasant and relaxing.

QUESTIONS TO ASK THE DOCTOR

- How often have you performed surgery for primary snoring? Which procedures have you performed most frequently?
- What is your opinion of somnoplasty and injection snoreplasty?
- Am I likely to benefit from lifestyle changes or other less invasive alternatives?
- Should I talk to my dentist about an oral appliance to control snoring?

Resources

BOOKS

American Psychiatric Association. *Diagnostic and Statistical Manual of Mental Disorders*, 4th edition, text revision, "Sleep Disorders." Washington, DC: American Psychiatric Association, 2000.

"Disorders of the Oral Region." Section 9, Chapter 105 in *The Merck Manual of Diagnosis and Therapy*, edited by Mark H. Beers, M.D., and Robert Berkow, M.D. Whitehouse Station, NJ: Merck Research Laboratories, 1999.

Pelletier, Kenneth R., M.D. *The Best Alternative Medicine*, Part I, Chapter 5, "Acupuncture," and Chapter 8, "Homeopathy." New York: Simon & Schuster, 2002.

Price, Shirley. *Practical Aromatherapy*, 3rd ed. London, UK: Thorsons, 1994.

"Sleep Disorders." Section 14, Chapter 173 in *The Merck Manual of Diagnosis and Therapy*, edited by Mark H. Beers, M.D., and Robert Berkow, M.D. Whitehouse Station, NJ: Merck Research Laboratories, 1999.

PERIODICALS

Back, L. J., P. O. Tervahartiala, A. K. Piilonen, et al. "Bipolar Radiofrequency Thermal Ablation of the Soft Palate in Habitual Snorers Without Significant Desaturations Assessed by Magnetic Resonance Imaging." *American Journal of Respiratory and Critical Care Medicine* 166 (September 15, 2002): 865-871.

Blumen, M. B., S. Dahan, B. Fleury, et al. "Radiofrequency Ablation for the Treatment of Mild to Moderate

Obstructive Sleep Apnea." *Laryngoscope* 112 (November 2002): 2086–2092.

Brietzke, S. E., and E. A. Mair. "Injection Snoreplasty: How to Treat Snoring Without All the Pain and Expense." *Otolaryngology and Head and Neck Surgery* 124 (May 2001): 503–510.

Cartwright, R., T. K. Venkatesan, D. Caldarelli, and F. Diaz. "Treatments for Snoring: A Comparison of Somnoplasty and an Oral Appliance." *Laryngoscope* 110 (October 2000): 1680–1683.

Fischer, Y., B. Hafner, and W. J. Mann. "Radiofrequency Ablation of the Soft Palate (Somnoplasty). A New Method in the Treatment of Habitual and Obstructive Snoring." [in German] *HNO* 48 (January 2000): 33–40.

Grontved, A. M., and P. Karup. "Complaints and Satisfaction After Uvulopalatopharyngoplasty." *Acta Otolaryngologica Supplementum* 543 (2000): 190–192.

Hessel, N. S., and N. de Vries. "Diagnostic Workup of Socially Unacceptable Snoring. II. Sleep Endoscopy." *European Archives of Oto-Rhino-Laryngology* 259 (March 2002): 158–161.

Kamami, Y. V. "Laser CO_2 for Snoring. Preliminary Results." *Acta Oto-Rhino-Laryngologica Belgica* 44 (1990): 451-456.

Kyrmizakis, D. E., C. E. Papadakis, J. G. Bizakis, et al. "Sucralfate Alleviating Post-Laser-Assisted Uvulopalatoplasty Pain." *American Journal of Otolaryngology* 22 (January-February 2001): 55–58.

Littner, Michael, M.D., Clete A. Kushida, M.D., Ph.D., Kristyna Hartse, Ph.D., et al. "Practice Parameters for the Use of Laser-Assisted Uvulopalatoplasty: An Update for 2000." *Sleep* 24 (May 2001): 603–609.

Loth, S., B. Petruson, L. Wiren, and L. Wilhelmsen. "Evaluation of the Quality of Life of Male Snorers Using the Nottingham Health Profile." *Acta Oto-Laryngologica* 118 (September 1998): 723–727.

Morgan, Charles E., M.D., and Kenneth Johnson, M.D. "Snoring and Obstructive Sleep Apnea, Surgery." *eMedicine*, May 20, 2002 [cited May 10, 2003]. http://www.emedicine.com/ent/topic370.htm.

Nuñez-Fernandez, David, M.D., and Manuel Fernandez-Muradas, M.D. "Snoring and Obstructive Sleep Apnea, Upper Airway Evaluation." *eMedicine*, June 6, 2002 [cited May 10, 2003]. http://www.emedicine.com/ent/topic410.htm.

O'Brien, L. M., C. R. Holbrook, C. B. Mervis, et al. "Sleep and Neurobehavioral Characteristics of 5- to 7-Year-Old Children with Parentally Reported Symptoms of Attention-Deficit/Hyperactivity Disorder." *Pediatrics* 111 (March 2003): 554–563.

O'Connor, G. T., B. K. Lind, E. T. Lee, et al. "Variation in Symptoms of Sleep-Disordered Breathing with Race and Ethnicity: The Sleep Heart Health Study." *Sleep* 26 (February 1, 2003): 74–79.

Raphaelson, M., and T. S. Hakim. "Diagnosing Sleep Apnea in Dental Patients." *Dental Clinics of North America 45 (October 2001): 797–816.*

Rose, E., R. Staats, J. Schulte-Monting, et al. "Long-Term Compliance with an Oral Protrusive Appliance in Patients with Obstructive Sleep Apnoea." [in German] *Deutsche medizinische Wochenschrift* 127 (June 7, 2002): 1245–1249.

Ryan, C. F., and L. L. Love. "Unpredictable Results of Laser Assisted Uvulopalatoplasty in the Treatment of Obstructive Sleep Apnoea." *Thorax* 55 (May 2000): 399–404.

Scher, A. I., R. B. Lipton, and W. F. Stewart. "Habitual Snoring as a Risk Factor for Chronic Daily Headache." *Neurology* 60 (April 22, 2003): 1366–1368.

Seemann, R. P., J. C. DiToppa, M. A. Holm, and J. Hanson. "Does Laser-Assisted Uvulopalatoplasty Work? An Objective Analysis Using Pre- and Postoperative Polysomnographic Studies." *Journal of Otolaryngology* 30 (August 2001): 212–215.

Truelson, John M., MD, and D. Heath Roberts, DDS. "Snoring and Obstructive Sleep Apnea, Prosthetic Management." *eMedicine*, April 15, 2002 [cited May 10, 2003]. http://www.emedicine.com/ent/topic498.htm.

Woodson, B. T., A. Derowe, M. Hawke, et al. "Pharyngeal Suspension Suture with Repose Bone Screw for Obstructive Sleep Apnea." *Otolaryngology and Head and Neck Surgery* 122 (March 2000): 395–401.

ORGANIZATIONS

American Academy of Medical Acupuncture (AAMA). 4929 Wilshire Boulevard, Suite 428, Los Angeles, CA 90010. (323) 937-5514. http://www.medicalacupuncture.org.

American Academy of Otolaryngology, Head and Neck Surgery, Inc. One Prince Street, Alexandria, VA 22314-3357. (703) 836-4444. http://www.entnet.org.

American Academy of Sleep Medicine (AASM). One Westbrook Corporate Center, Suite 920, Westchester, IL 60154. (708) 492-0930. http://www.aasmnet.org.

American Dental Association. 211 East Chicago Avenue, Chicago, IL 60611. (312) 440-2500. http://www.ada.org.

American Sleep Apnea Association (ASAA). 1424 K Street NW, Suite 302, Washington, DC 20005. (202) 293-3650. http://www.sleepapnea.org.

National Center on Sleep Disorders Research (NCSDR). Two Rockledge Centre, Suite 10038, 6701 Rockledge Drive, MSC 7920, Bethesda, MD 20892-7920. (301) 435-0199. http://www.nhlbi.nih.gov/about/ncsdr/index.htm.

OTHER

American Sleep Apnea Association (ASAA). *Considering Surgery for Snoring?* [May 10, 2003]. http://www.sleepapnea.org/snoring.html.

National Heart, Lung, and Blood Institute (NHLBI). *Facts About Sleep Apnea*. NIH Publication No. 95-3798 [cited April 13, 2003]. http://www.nhlbi.nih.gov/health/public/sleep/sleepapn.htm.

Rebecca Frey Ph.D.

Social issues *see* **Psychological and social issues**

Social work in health care

Definition

Social work in health care helps people who are dealing with a medical problem to function within their situation. The social worker who specializes in health care works with clients and their families to provide services necessary to make their lives easier for the duration of the client's illness, and to help them deal with the consequences directly related to that illness.

Description

According to the code of ethics of the National Association of Social Workers (NASW), the profession of social work is dedicated to a set of core values. These values include social justice, service, dignity and worth of the person, importance of human **relationships**, integrity, and competence, and they form the foundation of social work. Social workers in the medical field provide a wide variety of services to clients who are going through a short-term medical crisis, suffering from chronic illnesses, facing a life-threatening disease, or in need of long-term care or rehabilitation.

The main concern of the social worker is to assist the client and the client's family in coping with their health care situation. Clients are faced with many problems when they have an accident, contract a sudden and debilitating illness, or are diagnosed with a chronic or life-threatening disease. Social workers help them assess these problems, identify their immediate and long term needs, and find resources to supply the needs.

Within the health care setting, the social worker has many responsibilities. The services provided by the social worker depend on the needs of the client. The worker acts as an advocate to secure the client's rights, directly counsels the client and the client's family, and refers the client to other social agencies, community resources, or facilities that can meet the client's immediate and long-term needs. The services provided by the social worker always depend upon the client's needs and the health care setting.

If the social worker is working in a hospital, these duties may include setting up home health care services after the client's discharge, arranging for meals to be delivered to the client's home, and setting appointments for follow-up care. The worker may also make arrangements for transportation to doctor's appointments and community social service agencies, and for long-term care within another facility.

Work settings

Duties of the social worker vary with the health care setting. Medical social workers may work in a hospital, hospice, assisted living center, nursing home, physical rehabilitation center, clinic, home health care agency, or drug rehabilitation or mental health center. Social workers may work in the health care facility or make home visits to work with their clients. They often work with other agencies and have to travel short distances for meetings with the agency members. Social workers confer with other agency workers or with health care team members to assess client needs and to make plans for the client's care.

Hours of work vary for the social worker, depending upon the facility or agency within which he is employed. Usually the work hours are between 8 AM and 5 PM Monday through Friday, but the worker may be required to work hours as needed for emergencies. In larger urban areas or rural areas, the social worker may also be required to work during evening hours and on weekends to better serve the clients.

Education and training

Education, training, and licensing requirements may vary from state to state, but the NASW states that the minimum educational requirement for social workers is a baccalaureate degree in social work (BSW). However, people who hold a bachelor's degree in another discipline such as psychology, sociology, or urban studies may also qualify for entrance level jobs.

BSW programs prepare students for direct care of clients. Students who choose to major in social work must complete courses in social work practice, social work policies, human behavior and social environment, research methods, social work values and ethics, study of populations at risk, and the promotion of social justice. They must also complete 400 hours of supervised field work.

KEY TERMS

BSW—Baccalaureate degree in social work.

Long-term care—Placement of client in a facility that provides nursing and basic needs care when client is no longer able to provide that care at home.

MSW—Master's degree in social work.

NASW—National Association of Social Workers.

Needs assessment—Social worker conducts an interview with client and family, reviews charts, interviews other health workers to determine what specific services are required by client.

Urban studies—Course work in the sociology of urban areas.

An advanced degree is the standard for many positions in social work including positions within the field of health care. A master's degree in social work (MSW) allows the social worker to be certified for clinical and supervisory work.

Advanced education and training

A master's degree in social work qualifies the social worker to make clinical assessments, choose an area of specialization, manage large caseloads, and supervise social workers with lesser degrees. In addition to courses of specialization and assessment, the MSW candidate must complete 900 hours of supervised field work, or an internship.

Social workers may also acquire a Ph.D. or D.S. W. in social work. This is required if they want to teach in an accredited program at a university or to work in a supervisory position as the head of a social service program.

The National Association of Social Workers requires social workers to complete 90 hours of continuing education classes every three years to continue their certification in the profession. Licensed professionals with advanced degrees may be required to complete more than 90 hours of continuing education classes.

Future outlook

Social work is a growing profession. The occupational outlook is optimistic. The national Bureau of Labor Statistics predicts that growth will continue at a rate exceeding that of other occupations until at least 2008. There are several reasons why the field of social work in health care continues to grow:

- the aging population of "baby boomers"
- advanced medical treatment
- longer life expectancy
- growth of home health care due to growing trend of early release of patients from hospitals
- replacement of workers seeking career change
- stress and burnout among social workers causing them to leave profession
- increase in population of people living with AIDS

Resources

BOOKS

Occupation Outlook Handbook, Washington, DC: Department of Labor, 2007.

Peggy Elaine Browning

Sodium

Definition

Sodium is a mineral that exists in the body as the ion Na+. Sodium is acquired through **diet**, mainly in the form of salt (sodium chloride, NaCl). Regulating the amount of Na+ in the body is absolutely critical to life and health.

Purpose

Sodium is possibly the most important mineral in the body. It plays a major role in controlling the distribution of fluids, maintaining **blood pressure** and blood volume, creating an electrical gradient that allows nerve transmission and muscle contraction to occur, maintaining the mechanisms that allow wastes to leave cells, and regulating the acidity (pH) of the blood. Many different organ working together, including the kidneys, endocrine glands, and brain, tightly control the level of Na+ in the body. Researchers estimate that between 20% and 40% of an adult's resting energy use goes toward regulating sodium. Sodium affects every cell in the body, and a major failure of sodium regulatory mechanisms means **death**.

Description

In the body, sodium exists as electrolyte. Electrolytes are ions that form when salts dissolve in water or fluids. These ions have an electric charge. Positively charged ions are called cations. Negatively charged ions are called anions. Electrolytes are not evenly distributed within the body, and their uneven distribution allows many important metabolic reactions to occur. Sodium (Na+), potassium (K+), **calcium** (Ca 2+), magnesium (Mg 2+), chloride (Cl-), phosphate (HPO4 2-), bicarbonate (HCO3-), and sulfate (SO4 2-) are important electrolytes in humans.

Na+ is ten times more concentrated in fluid outside cells (i.e. extracellular fluid and blood) than it is in fluid inside cells. This difference in concentration is maintained through the expenditure of cellular energy, and it is critical to many metabolic functions, including maintaining the proportion of water that exists inside and outside of cells. (See the entry on electrolytes for a more detailed explanation of how this occurs). When Na+ is too high or too low, it is almost never because an individual has eaten too much or too little salt. Instead, it is because organs such as the kidneys or endocrine glands that regulate the conservation or removal of sodium from the body have broken down.

Sodium requirements

Researchers estimate that humans can remain healthy taking in only 500 mg of sodium daily. Salt is 40% sodium by weight, and 500 mg is slightly less than the amount of sodium found in 1/4 teaspoon of salt. Humans almost never take in too little salt; their health problems result from too much salt in the diet.

The United States Institute of Medicine (IOM) of the National Academy of Sciences has developed values called Dietary Reference Intakes (DRIs) for many **vitamins** and minerals including sodium. The DRIs consist of three sets of numbers. The Recommended Dietary Allowance (RDA) defines the average daily amount of the nutrient needed to meet the health needs of 97–98% of the population. The Adequate Intake (AI) is an estimate set when there is not enough information to determine an RDA. The Tolerable Upper Intake Level (UL) is the average maximum amount that can be taken daily without risking negative side effects. The DRIs are calculated for children, adult men, adult women, pregnant women, and breastfeeding women.

The IOM has not set RDAs for sodium, but instead it has set AI levels for all age groups based on observed and experimental information about the amount of sodium needed to replace what is lost by a moderately active individual each day. Sodium is lost in both urine and sweat. IAs for sodium are measured in milligrams (mg). UL levels have not been set. However, the IOM recommends that adults limit their sodium intake to less than 2,400 mg per day, and the American Heart Association recommends an adult daily intake of 1,500–2,300 mg.

The following list gives the recommended daily AL levels of sodium for each age group.

- children birth–6 months: AI 120 mg
- children 7–12 months: AI 370 mg
- children 1–3 years: AI 1,000 mg
- children 4–8 years: AI 1,200 mg
- children 9–13 years: AI 1,500 mg
- adolescents 14–18 years: IA 1,500 mg
- adults age 19–50: AI 1,500 mg
- adults ages 50–70 1,300 mg
- adults 71 years or older: AI 1,200 mg
- pregnant women: IA 1,500 mg
- breastfeeding women: AI 1,500 mg

Sources of sodium

Many people think that the main source of salt in their diet is what they add to food when they are cooking or at the table while eating. In reality, more than three-quarters of the sodium in the average American's diet is added to food during processing. Another 12% is already naturally in the food. For example, 1 cup of low-fat milk contains 110 mg of sodium. About 6% of sodium in the diet is added as salt during cooking and another 5% from salting food while eating.

Although most sodium in diet comes from salt, other sources of sodium include preservatives and flavor enhancers added during processing. Sodium content is required to be listed on food labels of processed foods. Some common "hidden" sources of sodium include:

KEY TERMS

Diuretic—a substance that removes water from the body by increasing urine production

Ion—an atom or molecule that has an electric charge. In the body ions are collectively referred to as electrolytes.

- baking soda
- baking powder
- disodium phosphate
- monosodium glutamate (MSG)
- sodium nitrate or sodium nitrite

Below are some common foods and their sodium content.

- table salt, 1 teaspoon:2,300 mg
- dill pickle, large: 1731 mg
- canned chicken noodle soup, 1 cup: 850–1,100 mg
- ham, 3 ounces: 1,000 mg
- sauerkraut, 1/2 cup: 780 mg
- pretzels, 1 ounce: 500 mg
- potato chips, 1 ounce: 165–185 mg
- soy sauce, 1 teaspoon: 304
- deli turkey breast, 1 ounce: 335 mg

Fresh fruits, vegetables, unsalted nuts, and rice, dried beans and peas are examples of foods that are low in sodium.

Sodium and health

Too high a concentration of sodium in the blood causes a condition called hypernatremia. Too much sodium in the diet almost never causes hypernatremia. Causes include excessive water loss (e.g. severe **diarrhea**), restricted water intake, untreated diabetes (causes water loss), kidney disease, and hormonal imbalances. Symptoms include signs of **dehydration** such as extreme thirst, dark urine, sunken eyes, fatigue, irregular heart beat, muscle twitching, seizures, and **coma**.

Too low a concentration of sodium in the blood causes hyponatremia. Hyponatremia is not usually a problem in healthy individuals, although it has been known to occur in endurance athletes such as ultramarathoners. It is common in seriously ill individuals and can result from vomiting or diarrhea (extreme loss of sodium), severe burns, taking certain drugs that cause the kidney to selectively excrete sodium, extreme overconsumption of water (water intoxication, a problem among the elderly with dementia), hormonal imbalances, kidney failure, and liver damage. Symptoms include nausea, vomiting, headache, tissue swelling (**edema**), confusion, mental disorientation, hallucinations, muscle trembling, seizures, and coma.

Hypernatremia and hyponatremia are at the extreme ends of sodium imbalance. However, high dietary intake of salt can cause less visible health damage in the form of high blood pressure (**hypertension**). Hypertension silently damages the heart, blood vessels, and kidney and increases the risk of **stroke**, **heart attack**, and kidney damage. A low-salt diet significantly lowers blood pressure in 30–60% of people with high blood pressure and a quarter to half of people with normal blood pressure. Some individuals are more sensitive to sodium than others. Those people who are most likely to see a rise in blood pressure with increased sodium intake include people who are obese, have type 2 diabetes, are elderly, female, and African American.

The American Heart Association recommends reducing sodium in the diet to between 1,500 mg and 2,300 mg daily. Below are some suggestions for cutting down on salt.

- Eat more fresh fruits and vegetables.
- Look for processed foods that say "no salt added"
- Limit or eliminate salty snacks such as chips and pretzels.
- Restrict the amount processed meats such as hot dogs, pepperoni, and deli meats.
- Avoid high salt canned soups; choose heart-healthy lower salt soups instead.
- Use spices instead of salt to give foods flavor.

Precautions

People who are salt-sensitive may need to keep their salt intake at levels below the suggested daily amounts to control their blood pressure.

Interactions

Certain drugs cause large amounts of sodium to be excreted by the kidneys and removed from the body in urine. **Diuretics** ("water pills") are among the best known of these drugs. Other types of drugs that may cause low sodium levels, especially in ill individuals, include non-steroidal anti-inflammatory drugs (NSAIDs) such as Advil, Motrin, and Aleve, opiates such as codeine and morphine, selective serotonin-reuptake inhibitors (SSRIs) such as Prozac or Paxil, and **tricyclic antidepressants** such as Elavil and Tofranil.

Complications

Health concerns about sodium have been discussed above. Most problems related to high blood pressure are chronic, slow to develop disorders that do not cause serious complications until the second half of an individual's lifetime. Kidney failure, heart attack, and stroke are all complications of high blood pressure and potentially of high sodium intake.

Resources

BOOKS

American Heart Association. *American Heart Association Low-Salt Cookbook: A Complete Guide to Reducing Sodium and Fat in Your Diet,* 3rd ed. New York: Clarkson Potter Pubs., 2006.

Hawkins, W. Rex. *Eat Right—Electrolyte: A Nutritional Guide to Minerals in Our Daily Diet* Amherst, NY: Prometheus Books, 2006.

James, Shelly V, *The Complete Idiot's Guide to Low-Sodium Meals.* Indianapolis, IN : Alpha Books, 2006.

Pressman, Alan H. and Sheila Buff.*The Complete Idiot&s Guide to Vitamins and Minerals,*3rd ed. Indianapolis, IN: Alpha Books, 2007.

ORGANIZATIONS

American Heart Association. 7272 Greenville Avenue, Dallas, TX 75231. Telephone: (800) 242-8721. Web site: http://www.americanheart.org

International Food Information Council. 1100 Connecticut Avenue, NW Suite 430, Washington, DC 20036. Telephone: 02-296-6540. Fax: 202-296-6547. Web site: http://ific.org

Linus Pauling Institute. Oregon State University, 571 Weniger Hall, Corvallis, OR 97331-6512. Telephone: (541) 717-5075. Fax: (541) 737-5077. Web site: http://lpi.oregonstate.edu

OTHER

American Heart Association. "Sodium." undated, accessed April 27, 2007, http://www.americanheart.org/presenter.jhtml?identifier=4708

Higdon, Jane. "Sodium." Linus Pauling Institute-Oregon State University, February 16, 2004. http://lpi.oregonstate.edu/infocenter/minerals/sodium

Mayo Clinic Staff. "Sodium: Are You getting Too Much?" MayoClinic.com, May 24, 2006. http://www.mayoclinic.com/health/sodium/NU00284

Medline Plus. "Dietary Sodium." U. S. National Library of Medicine, April 23, 2007. http://www.nlm.nih/gov/medlineplus/dietarysodium.html

Murray, Robert. "The Risk and Reality of Hyponatremia." Gatorade Sports Science Institute, 2006. http://www.gssiweb.com/

Northwesternutrition "Nutrition Fact Sheet: Sodium." Northwestern University, September 21, 2006. http://www.feinberg.northwestern.edu/nutrition/factsheets/sodium.html

United States Department of Health and Human Services and the United States Department of Agriculture. "Dietary Guidelines for Americans 2005." January 12, 2005. http://www.healthierus.gov/dietaryguidelines

Tish Davidson A.M.

Spastic colon *see* **Irritable bowel syndrome**

Special dietary needs of cancer patients

Definition

Good **nutrition** is important at any age, but even more so for older adults. As men and women age their dietary needs change. Older adults may face many challenges in maintaining good nutrition. These challenges may become even more difficult during **cancer** treatment

Good nutrition during cancer treatment may help cancer patients keep up their energy levels, prevent infection, cope with side effects of treatment, and help the body heal. In addition to eating a balanced **diet** and consuming enough nutrients, the dietary needs of cancer patients also include addressing challenges to eating such as difficulty chewing and swallowing, nausea and vomiting, **diarrhea** or **constipation**, and changes in smell and taste. Diet that provides adequate nutrition may also help cancer patients to recover more quickly after treatment is complete.

Description

Good nutrition can help cancer patients stay healthy and strong during treatment. Eating a healthy balanced diet is important. Good nutrition during cancer treatment helps build and maintain the body's store of necessary nutrients, decreases the risk of infection, and provides the strength to combat treatment side effects such as nausea, vomiting, **dehydration**, **dry mouth**, constipation, and diarrhea.

A balanced diet includes eating a variety of healthy foods that provide the full amount of nutrients necessary to stay healthy and to fight the cancer. Such a diet includes foods from all the major food groups, including protein, **carbohydrates**, and fat.

Protein helps the body to repair itself and to fight infection. While eating enough protein is generally not a problem for people living in the United States, it may be difficult for older patients fighting cancer. Consuming too little protein can lead to a decrease in the body's ability to fight infection, weakening of the heart and lungs, and, though rare, can be fatal. Examples of foods that contain protein are lean meats, fish, dairy foods (such as cheese and low fat milk), nuts, beans, and soy products.

Carbohydrates provide energy the body needs for the organs to function properly and for the body to move. Carbohydrates are made up of sugars, starches, and fiber. Both sugar and starch are digested by the body and provide energy. Fiber is not digested, but it is important to help the bowel function properly. Fiber can help remove excess fat and can lower the impact of excess sugar in the diet. For people with diabetes, carbohydrate intake may be carefully monitored. While carbohydrates, especially those from refined sugar, may be harmful, carbohydrates from whole grains and high in fiber are helpful. Carbohydrates are found in foods such as bread and baked goods, pasta, cereals, dried beans, rice, and vegetables such as corn, potatoes, and peas.

Fat is essential to the diet. While too much fat may be harmful, fats and oils provide energy for the body and are important in transporting certain **vitamins** throughout the body. Fat also makes many foods taste better and have a creamy or tender texture. Examples of foods containing fat include oils, butter, margarine, meat, poultry, and dairy products.

In addition to these foods groups, a healthy diet includes enough liquids. The American Dietetic Association (ADA) recommends drinking at least eight glasses of water each day. Proper hydration may help prevent constipation and allow nutrients to be digested and absorbed from the foods eaten. To ensure that adequate amounts of vitamins and minerals are consumed, those living with cancer may need to take supplements. Cancer patients should consult a doctor before taking any vitamins, minerals, or other supplements.

Demographics

Rates for all cancers increase as the population ages. Factors such as **smoking**, sun exposure, delayed child bearing, and exposure to carcinogens all increase the risk of developing cancer. According to the National Cancer Institute (NCI), 70 percent of all new cancer diagnoses were anticipated to be made in people age 65 and older and 70 percent of all cancer deaths occur in this age group.

According to the National Institutes of Health (NIH), women over the age of 60 have the highest risk of developing **breast cancer**. While white women are at a greater risk of developing breast cancer, African American women are at a greater risk of **dying** from the disease.

The NIH also reports that more than 65 percent of all prostate cancers occur in men over the age of 65. Men of African American decent are at the greatest risk of developing **prostate cancer**, and Asian men and Native American men have the lowest rate.

In addition to an increased risk for breast and prostate cancer, people over the age of 50 are at a greater risk of developing colorectal cancer.

According to the National Cancer Institutes Cancer Trends Progress Report 2007 update, all cancer deaths continue to decline. Whites and African Americans continue to be the racial groups most likely to develop cancer, and African Americans are more likely to die from cancer than any other racial or ethnic group.

Purpose

In addition to helping to promote good health and healing during cancer treatment, dietary changes and good nutrition may help cancer patients cope with side effects of treatment. Most cancer patients undergo one or more treatment options, including **chemotherapy**, radiation therapy, surgery, and medication. These treatments can cause side effects such as nausea and vomiting, constipation and diarrhea, and dry mouth and difficulty swallowing. These side effects can make getting adequate nutrition difficult. The American Cancer Society advocates the use of nutrition and dietary changes to help cancer patients cope with the side effects of cancer treatment.

Diet and Chemotherapy and Radiation Therapy

The following suggestions may help cancer patients undergoing chemotherapy and radiation therapy:

- avoid fried or greasy foods
- eat small frequent meals
- eat larger, balanced meals when feeling well
- eat throughout the day, smaller regular meals and snacks
- drink plenty of fluids, eight to ten 8-oz glasses per day, sip liquids throughout the day

- eat bland and easy-to-digest foods on days when receiving therapy
- rinse the mouth with baking soda and salt mouthwash before and after meals

Diet and Surgery

Cancer patients may need to follow a specific diet prior to and following surgery. In general, patients are not allowed to eat or drink for several hours prior to surgery. Following surgery, many people are asked to follow a standard diet progression.

A Progression Diet is a three-stage diet:

- Stage one: Consume clear liquids such as clear carbonated beverages; plain gelatin; sports drinks; weak tea; clear, carbonated drinks; juices; popsicles; bouillon; broth; and water.
- Stage two: Eat easy-to-digest foods such as plain crackers, pancakes, cake, fruit juices, lean meat, broths and cream soups, milk, custard or pudding, and frozen yogurt or ice milk.
- Stage three: Eat a regular diet, careful to avoid high fat, fried, greasy foods and foods that produce gas such as beans, melons, cruciferous vegetables (broccoli and cauliflower), and milk products.

Diet and Side Effects of Cancer Treatment

Dietary changes may be very helpful in coping with the side effects of cancer treatment. There are many simple suggestions cancer patients may follow to help ensure they are consuming adequate amounts of food and liquids, and to help relieve side effects. The American Cancer Society offers helpful suggestions to help those coping with the side effects of cancer treatment.

DIARRHEA Cancer treatment, including radiation therapy, chemotherapy, and many medications, may affect the bowels. Some treatment may cause the bowels to work more slowly causing constipation. Other treatment may cause the bowels to move more often causing diarrhea. There are many dietary options cancer patients have to help control the discomfort and inconvenience of constipation and diarrhea.

To help reduce the occurrence of diarrhea, those living with cancer may do the following:

- eat small meals and snacks frequently during the day
- drink plenty of fluids avoiding carbonated beverages and extremely hot or cold liquids and being sure to drink at least one cup of liquid after each loose bowel movement
- consume foods high in potassium and high sodium foods such as fruit juices, sports drinks, broths and soups, peeled potatoes, bananas, pretzels, and crackers
- add soluble fiber to the diet by eating foods such as oatmeal, white rice, applesauce, and canned pears or peaches
- avoid fried, greasy, extremely spicy foods, or very sweet foods.
- avoid foods with sugar alcohols such as sorbitol, mannitol or xylitol, which can cause diarrhea

The following diet may help reduce the number of loose bowel movements:

- Protein: Boiled or baked meat such as beef, pork, fish, poultry, or veal; eggs, dairy products such as cheese, milk, and yogurt. Avoid dried beans, nuts, seeds, peanut butter and greasy or fatty meats.
- Breads: Products made with white flour such as rolls, bread, and pasta; hot cereals such as cream of wheat, cream of rice, and oatmeal; other breads such as waffles, pancakes, muffins, and crackers. Avoid high fiber foods such as bran, whole wheat, shredded wheat, wild rice, popcorn, and granola.
- Fruits and Vegetables: Peeled canned or frozen fruit; baked, boiled, or mashed potatoes without the skins; and soups made from potatoes, vegetables that are peeled and cooked such as asparagus, beets, carrots, mushrooms, celery, and tomato sauces, and pastes. Avoid fresh fruit with the skins on, melons, and most vegetables.
- Beverages: Decaffeinated beverages, sports drinks, and water. Avoid colas, drinks with caffeine, and hot or extremely cold drinks.
- Deserts: Sherbet, gelatin, cookies, angel-food cake, sponge cake, and fruit pies made with canned, skinless fruits. Avoid very sweet deserts, nuts, coconut, dried fruit, chocolate, and licorice.
- Seasonings and condiments: Butter and margarine, mayonnaise, salad dressing, some gravy, salt, cinnamon, and other spices as tolerated. Avoid taco seasoning, hot spices and seasonings, and pickles and relish.

CONSTIPATION To help reduce the occurrence of constipation, those living with cancer may:

- Attempt to have a bowel movement at the same time each day.
- Eat meals at consistent times each day.

- Drink eight to ten glasses of liquid every day.
- Eat high fiber foods and drink hot liquids at breakfast.
- Develop a plan with a doctor and registered dietician that may include a gradual increase of consumption of high fiber foods, taking over-the counter stool softeners, and drinking liquid supplements containing high quality protein, fiber, and calories.
- Increase daily activity levels if possible.
- Discuss laxative use with a doctor, and contact the doctor if it has been over three days without a bowel movement.

The following diet may help increase the frequency of bowel movements:

- Protein: boiled or baked lean meat such as fish and poultry, eggs, milk, and yogurt.
- Breads: Products made with whole grains such as whole wheat breads and rolls, high fiber foods such as bran, whole wheat, shredded wheat, and wild rice, whole grain cereals such as bran flakes, raw wheat bran, and granola, and popcorn.
- Fruits and Vegetables: Fresh fruits with the skins such as apples and pears, other fruits such as bananas, oranges, and berries; dried fruits such as prunes and raisins; vegetables such as potatoes with the skins on, carrots, brussels sprouts, and corn, legumes or beans such as kidney beans, navy beans , and nuts.
- Beverages: Decaffeinated beverages, sports drinks, and water, fruit juices such as prune juice and fresh pressed or squeezed juices, hot drinks such as coffee and tea.
- Desserts: Sherbet, gelatin, whole grain cookies, cakes and cookies with nuts, and fruit pies made with fresh and fruits with the skins on. Seasonings and condiments: Butter and margarine, mayonnaise, salad dressing, some gravies, salt, cinnamon, and other spices as tolerated.

NAUSEA AND VOMITING Nausea and vomiting may be especially troubling for cancer patients undergoing radiation therapy and chemotherapy. These side effects may be quite severe and may severely limit the patient's ability to consume adequate nutrition.

The American Cancer Society suggests the following to help cancer patients suffering from nausea and vomiting:

- eat frequent smaller meals rather than two or three large ones
- drink liquids before or after eating rather than with meals
- try eating foods at room temperature or cold to avoid smells
- drink cool liquids
- suck on ice cubes, mints, or tart candy

Patients may find it helpful to follow this eating plan on days they are receiving radiation or chemotherapy:

- protein: boiled or baked meats, fish or poultry, cold meats, eggs, yogurt, cream soups
- breads: crackers, toast, dry cereal, English muffins, bagels, noodles without sauce, rice
- fruits and vegetables: baked, boiled, or mashed potatoes; canned or fresh fruit; vegetables if tolerated
- beverages: cold fruit drinks, sports drinks, iced tea, decaffeinated colas
- desserts: sherbet, gelatin, angel-food cake, sponge cake, pudding, popsicles, and juice bars
- seasonings: salt, cinnamon, and other spices as tolerated

DIFFICULTY SWALLOWING AND DRY MOUTH For patients who suffer from difficulty swallowing and dry mouth, it may be helpful to consult with a speech pathologist and registered **dietician** to develop a meal plan that helps maintain good nutrition and adapts for difficulty swallowing. A diet that consists of consuming plenty of fluids and semi-thickened liquids may help maintain good nutrition during treatment. Liquid **nutritional supplements** and pureeing food in a food processor or blender may be necessary. Other dietary suggestions for coping with difficulty swallowing include: using thickening agents such as gelatin, pureed fruit or vegetables, flour, cornstarch, tapioca, or baby cereal.

The American Cancer Society suggests the following guidelines may be helpful in relieving the discomfort of difficulty swallowing and dry mouth:

- Consume pureed thick liquids that contain an adequate amount of good quality protein such as dairy products, yogurt without fruit, sour cream, pureed meat, poultry and fish, scrambled eggs, and cream soups
- Make cereals, grains, and breads easier to swallow by adding slurry to them. (Slurry is made by combining flour and water to make a very thin paste. When this paste is added to hot liquids foods it

thickens them slightly.) Slurry may be spread on top of cakes or breads to soften them as well.

- Eat semi-soft breads, grains, and cooked cereals such as oatmeal, Cream of Wheat or Rice, with slurry added.
- Eat pureed fruits and vegetables with the skins and seeds removed
- Consume other sources of nutrition that may be easier to swallow such as milkshakes, eggnog, ice cream, thickened juices, cream soups, thickened broths, pudding and custard, cake and cookies with slurry on top, honey, butter, or spices.

As treatment progresses, patients with difficulty swallowing or dry mouth may find it easier to swallow thick liquids. Once this occurs, it may be possible to consume soft but thicker foods.

Examples of slightly thicker but still soft foods include:

- Proteins include cheese, ground meats, casseroles, fish, and sandwiches made with spreads or ground meats.
- Breads and grains that are thicker but still soft include soft bread, crackers, pasta, cereals with milk, pancakes, and rice.
- Fruits and vegetables that may be eaten without pureeing include bananas, fruit cocktail, canned fruit, and boiled or steamed vegetables, and pureed fruits and vegetables.
- Other nutritional sources that may be easier to swallow include most beverages, ice cream, cream soups, thickened broths, pudding and custard, soft cakes, honey, butter, or spices.

Challenges

Because of diminished immunity, it is especially important to use good food handling practices and avoid exposure to bacteria and food contamination. Always wash hands well before handling food. The United States Department of Agriculture (USDA) advises anyone handling food, but especially those with weakened immune systems such as people battling cancer, to clean, separate, cook, and chill.

- Clean hands well before and after handling food, clean all work surfaces before and after food preparation, wash all fruits and vegetables prior to cooking and eating them, and clean can lids before opening canned goods.
- Separate all raw meat, poultry, fish, and eggs from other foods in the shopping cart, grocery bags, and especially in the kitchen while preparing foods. Use a separate cutting board or surface for raw meats and all other foods, and never use plates or containers that previously held raw meats to hold or serve cooked meats. Never use marinades that have been on raw meats to season cooked meat. Either discard the marinade or boil it prior to serving it with cooked meat.
- Cook foods to a proper temperature to ensure that all bacteria are killed and the food is safe. To be certain food is cooked thoroughly, use a food thermometer. It is impossible to tell if food is completely cooked by looking at it alone.
- Chill foods to prevent or slow the growth of bacteria. Refrigerate or freeze all perishable food within two hours or less of cooking or bringing home from the grocery. Thaw meat in the refrigerator, in cold water, or in the microwave oven, never at room temperature or on the kitchen counter.

SAFE FOOD TEMPERATURES: ACCORDING TO THE USDA

- Steaks and Roast: 145 degrees F
- Fish: 145 degrees F
- Park: 160 degrees F
- Ground Beef 160 degrees F
- Eggs: 160 degrees F
- Chicken Breasts: 165 degrees F
- Whole Poultry: 165 degrees F

Other challenges faced by those living with cancer include difficulty eating well when in **pain**, feeling tired or unwell, or when coping with side effects of treatment such as mouth sores, nausea, vomiting, constipation, diarrhea, and a limited ability to eat. It may be difficult to get to the grocery to purchase nutritious food. Asking friends and family to assist with grocery shopping and meal preparation may be extremely helpful in ensuring the patient has access to fresh, nutritious foods.

Many people fighting cancer must travel away from home to receive treatment. It may be difficult to maintain proper nutrition or deal with side effects that impact nutrition when one lives in an unfamiliar city. Individuals with access to a kitchen may find it helpful to store portioned food that is easy to prepare such as canned soup, frozen foods, and single serving snacks such as cereal, fruit, pudding, or gelatin. If

KEY TERMS

Carbohydrates—A component of food that provides energy for the body. Carbohydrates are broken down into sugar during digestion.

Carcinogens—Any substance that produces cancer in humans or animals.

Chemotherapy—The treatment of disease using chemicals that destroy cells.

Constipation—Inability to pass stool for three or more days. When stool is passed it may be hard, dry, and painful to pass.

Diarrhea—Loose, watery, or frequent bowel movements.

Laxative—Any food, beverage, or medication that stimulates bowel movements or softens stool.

Nutrients—Compounds that are necessary to survival and cannot be made by the body.

Protein—An essential nutrient that helps the body build necessary parts of the body such as muscle, tissue, and blood cells.

Radiation therapy—The treatment of disease using radiation to destroy cells.

Registered dietician—A healthcare professional who has completed an academic program and been accredited to provide advice about proper nutrition.

Speech pathologist—A healthcare profession who has been trained and certified to provide advice and therapy to individuals with disorders of speech, language, swallowing, or eating.

Stool softeners—Medication that causes stool to become softer and easier to pass.

there is no access to a kitchen, it may be helpful to bring snacks that do not require refrigeration or heating such as canned fruit, crackers, cereals, and peanut butter.

Risks

Other medical conditions such as diabetes may require special attention to diet and may be impacted by dietary changes during cancer treatment. It is important to meet with a registered dietician or nurse to be sure dietary needs are met. Healthcare professionals may be able to prescribe medication to treat side effects such as nausea, vomiting, diarrhea, and constipation so that is it easier for patients to maintain a healthy diet during cancer treatment.

Results

Eating a healthy, well-balanced diet is always important, but even more so when undergoing treatment for cancer. Good nutrition can help cancer patients to maintain strength and energy, cope with treatment and side effects, and return to normal activities following treatment and during remission.

Side effects and symptoms such as dry mouth, decreased appetite, difficulty swallowing, and fatigue may persist for a period of time after treatment ends. Continuing to follow dietary guidelines that address these issues may help until these side effects subside.

Resources

BOOKS

Beliveau, Richard, and Denis Gingras. *Foods that Fight Cancer: Preventing Cancer through Diet.* Toronto, Ontario: McClelland and Stewart, 2006.

Keane, Maureen, and Daniella Chace. *What to Eat if You Have Cancer.* New York: McGraw-Hill, 2006.

ORGANIZATIONS

American Cancer Society, PO Box 22718, Oklahoma City, OK, 73123-1718, (800) ACS-2345, https://www.cancer.org/.

National Cancer Institute, 6116 Executive Blvd., Room 3036A, Bethesda, MD, 20892-8322, (800) 422-6237, http://www.cancer.gov/.

National Coalition for Cancer Survivorship, 1010 Wayne Avenue, 5th Floor, Suite 300, Silver Spring, MD, 20910, (888) 650-9127, http://www.canceradvocacy.org/.

Deborah L. Nurmi MS

Speech problems

Definition

Speech problems in seniors may refer either to oral communication itself or to the use of language in general (spoken or written). Language problems (using correct spelling and grammar) and speaking difficulties (using the voice effectively) may both be caused by a range of disorders affecting the brain, cranial nerves, muscles, or the structures of the mouth and throat. Speech problems in seniors are serious because they can interfere with the senior's ability to get help when needed as well as lead to social **isolation** and psychological **depression**.

Description

Human speech is a complex activity that requires the coordination of various areas of the brain, the cranial nerves, the respiratory system, the vocal cords, and several sets of muscles in the face, tongue, jaw, and throat. There are two major types of speech problems in seniors, aphasia and dysarthria. Aphasia, which is the more common type of speech-related disorder in seniors, is an impairment of one's ability to express oneself in language or to understand language. It results from brain damage. Dysarthria is impairment of one's ability to articulate (form) word sounds due to the weakness of the muscles involved in speaking or to problems with the nerves that supply those muscles. It is possible for a senior to have both types of speech problems. Both aphasia and dysarthria should be regarded as conditions associated with various neurological or muscular disorders; they are not diseases in their own right.

Aphasia

Aphasia is caused by damage to the parts of the brain that control language. It may cause difficulties with speaking, listening, reading, or writing. Seniors who have trouble using words and sentences are said to have expressive aphasia, while those who have difficulty understanding language are said to have receptive aphasia. Those who have problems with both using language and understanding it are said to have global aphasia. Aphasia may be mild or severe, depending on the extent of brain damage.

Dysarthria

Dysarthria refers to speech problems caused by difficulties in articulating sounds. It may result from weakness or **paralysis** of the muscles in the respiratory tract, throat, mouth, or jaw caused by **stroke** or by such disorders as Parkinson's, Lou Gehrig's, Huntington's, or Alzheimer's disease. The type and severity of dysarthria depend on the area of the nervous system that is affected and the muscles it controls.

Demographics

Speech and language difficulties are more common in seniors than in younger adults. Between 3 and 4 percent of adults over 65 have a speech or language disorder. Between 20 and 40 percent of stroke patients develop aphasia; it is estimated that about 80,000 new cases of aphasia in the United States each year are due to stroke. There are an estimated 1 million adults in the United States with aphasia as of the early 2000s. About 89 percent of patients diagnosed with Parkinson's disease eventually develop dysarthria.

Speech problems affect men and women equally, as far as is known. It is thought that aphasia may be more common among African Americans than Caucasians because African Americans have a higher risk of stroke.

Causes and symptoms

In addition to specific diseases and disorders, the aging process affects seniors' ability to speak clearly. As people get older, their vocal cords become thinner and less flexible and their throat muscles lose some of their tone. As a result, the voice typically becomes lower in pitch and softer in volume. The senior may have mild difficulty articulating sounds, and speak more slowly, with fewer syllables per breath. These changes due to aging do not, however, affect the senior's ability to understand language.

Aphasia

Aphasia in seniors is caused most often by nonprogressive brain disorders (stroke, head trauma, or encephalitis) but can occasionally be caused by a progressive disorder such as a brain tumor. Aphasia can be classified by the part of the brain that is damaged as well as by severity. In Broca's aphasia, an area in the frontal lobe of the brain known as Broca's area is damaged. Persons with this type of aphasia have difficulty expressing themselves; they may use short but understandable phrases or sentences produced with great effort, such as "go bathroom" instead of "I want to use the bathroom" or "Please help me get to the bathroom." Broca's aphasia is called a nonfluent aphasia because seniors with this type of aphasia cannot form long or complicated sentences. Seniors with Broca's aphasia can usually understand the speech of others to varying degrees and are aware of their own problems with expressing themselves. They may also have weakness or paralysis on the right side of the body because the left side of the brain controls movement on the right side of the body.

Another type of aphasia, called Wernicke's aphasia, results from damage to an area in the temporal lobe of the brain known as Wernicke's area. Seniors with this type of aphasia may speak fluently (speak in long sentences), but what they say may not make sense; they may make up words, substitute one word for another, repeat words, or add unnecessary words to what they say. For example, a person may say, "I was in the rain when the television rang and went to the floor but there was no there there." Wernicke's aphasia is sometimes called jargon aphasia for this reason; it is sometimes mistaken for the language disorders associated with schizophrenia. Seniors with Wernicke's aphasia often have difficulty understanding the speech of others and are often unaware of their mistakes in speech. They do not usually have problems with weakness or paralysis, however, because Wernicke's area is not close to the parts of the brain that control body movement.

Mild aphasia is characterized by difficulty using long or complex sentences and by occasional problems with finding the right word for something, a condition called anomia. For example, a person with anomia may say "the thing you tell time with" instead of "clock" or "watch." A person with only mild aphasia, however, can often carry on a normal conversation in many settings. In severe aphasia, the person may say little or nothing, or may be limited to a few words such as "hi" or "thanks."

Symptoms of expressive aphasia include:

- Speaking only in single words.
- Telegraphic speech. The senior omits such words as "the," "of," and "and," so that their sentences sound like a telegram.
- Words coming out in the wrong order.
- Making up words or using words that make no sense when strung together.

Symptoms of receptive aphasia include:

- Taking a lot of time to understand spoken messages.
- Finding it hard to follow television news reporters or other rapid speakers.
- Misinterpreting figurative speech; taking such metaphors as "sitting pretty" or "growing by leaps and bounds" literally.
- Getting frustrated and depressed when others fail to understand him or her.

Dysarthria

Dysarthria may be caused by disorders that affect the brain directly (Alzheimer's or Parkinson's disease, stroke, cerebral palsy), those that affect motor neurons (**amyotrophic lateral sclerosis** or Lou Gehrig's disease), or those that affect the muscles of the neck, throat, and chest. Any of these disorders interferes with the senior's ability to form words and sounds in a way that others can understand. Some specific symptoms of dysarthria are:

- Slurred speech.
- Inability to speak above a whisper.
- Slow rate of speech.
- Unusually rapid speech with a mumbling quality.
- Limited ability to move the lips, jaw, or tongue.
- Abnormal speech rhythm; the speech may sound staccato, jerky, or speed up toward the end of a sentence.
- Changes in vocal quality, such as a hoarse, nasal, or stuffy quality to the voice.
- Breathiness; difficulty forming certain consonant sounds such as "R,", "B," "F," or "M.".
- Drooling.
- Difficulty in chewing or swallowing as well as speaking.

Diagnosis

The diagnosis of speech problems depends in part on the type of accident or disease that has led to brain damage or weakness of the muscles involved in speech. A senior who has been taken to an emergency room with a **head injury**, brain infection, or stroke will be evaluated by a neurologist as soon as possible to evaluate speech problems as well as body weakness and other symptoms of brain injury. The neurologist may administer a variety of tests at the patient's bedside, such as asking him or her to name objects or to list as many words as possible beginning with a particular letter of the alphabet. In order to pinpoint the senior's speech problems with more precision, however, a speech-language pathologist (a health professional with special training in evaluating and treating speech problems) or a neuropsychologist is usually consulted. These specialists may administer one or more tests to define the senior's aphasia. Common tests of this type include the Boston Diagnostic Aphasia Examination, the Western Aphasia Battery, the Boston Naming Test, the Token Test, and the Action Naming Test. The National Institutes of Health (NIH) Stroke Scale may also be used to evaluate the patient's speech as well as his or her sensory perception and ability to move the limbs..

In addition to tests of speech problems as such, the neurologist will also usually administer a mental status examination and order imaging studies to look for damage to Broca's or Wernicke's area. These studies may include **CT scans**, PET scans, MRIs, or functional **magnetic resonance imaging** (fMRI).

Dysarthria may be more likely to be evaluated initially by the senior's primary care physician. In many cases the fact that the senior has a speech problem is obvious to the doctor because a **caregiver** has had to accompany the senior in order to describe the situation. A primary care physician can administer a mini-mental status examination as well as evaluate the senior for visual or hearing disorders that may be contributing to the speech problems. The doctor will also check the patient's throat and esophagus to rule out infections of the vocal cords or digestive disorders that may be affecting speech.

Since speech problems may be an early indication of Alzheimer's or Parkinson's disease, the primary care doctor may refer the senior to a neurologist for further evaluation. The senior may also be examined by a speech-language pathologist, who will watch the movement of the patient's facial and throat muscles as the patient tries to talk; note the amount of breath support for speaking; and evaluate the quality, pitch, rhythm, and other characteristics of the patient's voice. These observations may help to identify the location of the muscles involved in the dysarthria as well as its underlying cause.

Treatment

Treatment of speech problems depends on their underlying cause. Patients with Parkinson's disease or Alzheimer's are usually managed with medications even though these diseases cannot be cured. **Brain tumors** are usually treated with a combination of surgery and radiation therapy. Speech therapy is usually part of rehabilitation for stroke patients and is recommended for patients with aphasia resulting from head injuries as well.

Speech therapy in the most important part of treatment for seniors with speech problems. The therapist may work with the senior one-on-one or with a group of seniors. The purposes of speech therapy are to maintain the senior's present level of speaking ability, to restore that ability when possible, and to help the senior learn to communicate in other ways when necessary. The senior may be evaluated in a speech laboratory in order to guide individualized therapy. There are a variety of communication methods that seniors with speech problems can use, such as alphabet boards, hand gestures or signs, or various electronic or computer-based devices. In addition, speech therapists can work with family members and caregivers of seniors with dysarthria to help them learn strategies for communicating with the senior.

Stroke clubs and other support groups are recommended as part of treatment for speech problems because these groups help seniors to practice their new or relearned communication skills. The groups are also useful in helping family members and caregivers adjust to the senior's difficulties and to practice better ways of communicating with the senior.

QUESTIONS TO ASK YOUR DOCTOR

- What type of speech problem does my senior friend or family member have?
- What is the prognosis for full or partial recovery of speech?
- How can I help?

Nutrition/Dietetic concerns

Patients with dysarthria should be evaluated by a speech-language pathologist to make certain that they do not have swallowing disorders as well as speech problems.

Therapy

Therapy may consist of medications or surgery as required to treat underlying disorders; however, the mainstay of treatment for speech problems in seniors is speech therapy.

Prognosis

The prognosis of speech problems depends on their cause and severity; it is the underlying disorder and not the aphasia or dysarthria by itself that determines prognoses. There is no cure at present for Parkinson's, Lou Gehrig's, Huntington's, or Alzheimer's disease, and dysarthria related to those diseases usually gets worse over time. Patients with certain types of brain tumors may have a life expectancy of only a few months. The prognosis for speech problems caused by any of these disorders is very poor.

Aphasia caused by stroke may have a favorable prognosis, particularly if the stroke was mild. In general, patients with expressive aphasia have a better prognosis than those with receptive aphasia; patients with Broca's aphasia have a much better

KEY TERMS

Anomia—Difficulty in naming objects.

Aphasia—The loss or impairment of the ability to use and understand words.

Articulation—The process of forming word sounds by using the tongue, lips, jaw, voice box, and other structures in the mouth and throat.

Broca's area—An area in the frontal lobe of the left hemisphere of the brain that governs language processing, speech production, and comprehension. It is named for Paul Broca (1824–1880), a French physician.

Dysarthria—Difficulty in articulating words due to disorders of the central nervous system. It is sometimes called a motor speech disorder.

Encephalitis—Inflammation of the brain caused by a viral or bacterial infection.

Speech-language pathologist—A health professional who evaluates and treats people with speech, language, or swallowing disorders that affect their ability to communicate.

Wernicke's area—An area in the temporal lobe of the brain (on the left side in most people) that governs language comprehension. It is named for Karl Wernicke (1848–1905), a German neurologist and psychiatrist who first recognized its role in the type of aphasia that now bears his name.

chance for recovery of speech than those with Wernicke's aphasia.

Prevention

There is no known way to prevent all the possible diseases or traumatic accidents that can lead to speech problems. Some diseases that affect the brain and the muscles that control speech are known or thought to be hereditary. People can, however, lower their risk of stroke—the most common single cause of speech problems— by watching their weight, eating nutritious food, quitting **smoking**, avoiding alcohol and drug abuse, and getting a healthful level of **exercise**.

Caregiver concerns

The National Institute on Deafness and Other Communication Disorders (NIDCD) makes the following recommendations for caregivers of seniors with speech problems:

- Use short and simple sentences in conversation.
- Talk to the senior as an adult, not as if he or she is a child.
- Include the senior with aphasia in as many activities as possible, and show that his or her opinions are still taken seriously by other family members.
- Turn down the volume of nearby radios or televisions whenever possible so that the senior is not distracted when trying to communicate.
- Encourage all forms of communication, whether speech, drawing, gestures or pointing, or the use of sign boards or other devices.
- Give the senior plenty of time to talk, and avoid correcting his or her mistakes in speech.
- Get the senior involved in activities outside the house, including stroke groups and other support groups for older people with aphasia.

Resources

BOOKS

Beers, Mark H., M. D., and Thomas V. Jones, MD. *Merck Manual of Geriatrics*, 3rd ed., Chapter 45, "Speech and Language Disorders." Whitehouse Station, NJ: Merck, 2005.

Mace, Nancy L., and Peter V. Rabins. *The 36-Hour Day: A Family Guide to Caring for People with Alzheimer Disease, Other Dementias, and Memory Loss in Later Life,* 4th ed. Baltimore, MD: Johns Hopkins University Press, 2006. Includes some helpful advice about communicating with seniors who have speech problems.

National Aphasia Association. *The Aphasia Handbook: A Guide for Stroke and Brain Injury Survivors and Their Families*. New York: National Aphasia Association, 2004.

PERIODICALS

Bakheit, A. M. et al. "The Rate and Extent of Improvement with Therapy from the Different Types of Aphasia in the First Year after Stroke." *Clinical Rehabilitation* 21 (October 2007): 941–949.

Marshall, R. C., and H. H. Wright. "Developing a Clinician-Friendly Aphasia Test." *American Journal of Speech-Language Pathology* 16 (November 2007): 295–315.

Medina, J., and S. Weintraub. "Depression in Primary Progressive Aphasia." *Journal of Geriatric Psychiatry and Neurology* 20 (September 2007): 153–160.

Ogar, J. M., N. F. Dronkers, S. M. Brambati, et al. "Progressive Nonfluent Aphasia and Its Characteristic Motor Speech Deficits." *Alzheimer Disease and Associated Disorders* 21 (October-December 2007): S23–S30.

Santacruz, Karen S., and Daniel Swagerty. "Early Diagnosis of Dementia." *American Family Physician* 63 (February 15, 2001): 703–718.

OTHER

American Speech-Language-Hearing Association (ASHA). *Aphasia.* Available online at http://www.asha.org/public/speech/disorders/Aphasia.htm [cited March 11, 2008].

American Speech-Language-Hearing Association (ASHA). *Dysarthria.* Available online at http://www.asha.org/public/speech/disorders/dysarthria.htm [cited March 11, 2008].

Kirshner, Howard S. "Aphasia." *eMedicine*, February 5, 2008. http://www.emedicine.com/neuro/topic437.htm [cited March 11, 2008].

National Institute on Deafness and Other Communication Disorders (NIDCD). *Aphasia.* Bethesda, MD: NIDCD, 2002. Available online at http://www.nidcd.nih.gov/health/voice/aphasia.htm [cited March 12, 2008].

National Institutes of Health (NIH). *NIH Stroke Scale* (NIHSS). Available online at http://strokecenter.stanford.edu/scales/nihss.html [cited March 12, 2008].

ORGANIZATIONS

American Speech-Language-Hearing Association (ASHA), 2200 Research Boulevard, Rockville, MD, 20850, (800) 638-8255, (301) 296-8580, http://www.asha.org/default.htm.

American Stroke Foundation, 5960 Dearborn, Mission, KS, 66202, (913) 649-1776, (866) 549-1776, (913) 649-6661, http://www.americanstroke.org/component/option,com_frontpage/Itemid,1/.

Aphasia Hope Foundation (AHF), P.O. Box 26304, Shawnee Mission, KS, 66225, (913) 839-8083, sandy-caudell@aphasiahope.org, http://www.aphasiahope.org/index.jsp.

National Aphasia Association (NAA), 350 Seventh Avenue, Suite 902, New York, NY, 10001, (800) 922-4622, http://www.aphasia.org/index.html.

National Institute of Neurological Disorders and Stroke (NINDS) Brain Resources and Information Network (BRAIN), P.O. Box 5801, Bethesda, MD, 20824, (800) 352-9424, http://www.ninds.nih.gov.

National Institute on Deafness and Other Communication Disorders (NIDCD), 31 Center Drive, MSC 2320, Bethesda, MD, 20892, (301) 496-7243, (800) 241-1044, (301) 402-0018, nidcdinfo@nidcd.nih.gov.

Rebecca J. Frey Ph.D.

Spinal cord injury

Definition

Spinal cord injury is damage to the spinal cord that causes loss of sensation and motor control.

Description

Approximately 11,000 new spinal cord injuries (SCIs) occur each year in the United States. About 200,000 people are currently affected. Spinal cord injuries can happen to anyone at any time of life. The typical patient, however, is a man between the ages of 19 and 26, injured in a motor vehicle accident (about 35% of all SCIs), a fall (20%), an act of violence (15%), most often related to firearms use or a sporting accident (14%). According to the Centers for Disease Control, violence-related SCIs have been increasing steadily since 1980, and in 2001, violence was associated with 30% of all SCI cases.

Most SCI patients are white, but the nonwhite fraction of SCI patients is larger than the nonwhite fraction of the general population. In fact, the SCI rate among blacks, who are at higher risk for SCI than whites, has been rising in recent years. Alcohol or other drug abuse plays an important role in a large percentage of all spinal cord injuries. Six percent of people who receive injuries to the lumbar spine die within a year, and 40% of people who sustain the more frequent higher, or rostral injuries, also die within a year.

Short-term costs for hospitalization, equipment, and home modifications are approximately $140,000 for an SCI patient capable of independent living. Lifetime costs may exceed one million dollars. Costs may be three to four times higher for the SCI patient who needs long-term institutional care. Overall costs to the American economy in direct payments and lost productivity are more than $10 billion per year.

Causes and symptoms

Causes

The spinal cord descends from the brain down the back through the spinal canal that lies within the bony spinal column. The spinal cord is composed of neurons and axons (nerve cells). The neurons carry sensory data from the areas outside the spinal cord (periphery) to the brain, and convey motor commands from brain to periphery. Peripheral neurons are bundled together to comprise the 31 pairs of peripheral nerve roots. The peripheral nerve roots enter and exit the spinal cord by passing through the spaces between the stacked vertebrae (the neural foramen). Each pair of nerves is named for the vertebra from which it exits. These are known as:

- C1-8. These nerves enter from the seven cervical or neck vertebrae.
- T1-12. These nerves enter from the thoracic or chest vertebrae.

- L1-5. These nerves enter from the lumbar vertebrae of the lower back.
- S1-5. These nerves enter through the sacral, or pelvic vertebrae.
- Coccygeal. These nerves enter through the coccyx, or tailbone.

Peripheral nerves carry motor commands to the muscles and internal organs, and transmit sensations from these areas and from the body's surface. (Sensory data from the head, including sight, sound, smell, and taste, do not pass through the spinal cord and are not affected by most SCIs. These nerves, called the cranial nerves, pass through the brain stem.) Damage to the spinal cord interrupts these signals. The interruption damages motor functions that enable the muscles to move, sensory functions (e.g., feeling heat and cold), and autonomic functions (e.g., urination, sexual function, sweating, and **blood pressure**).

Spinal cord injuries most often occur where the spine is most flexible, in the regions of C5–C7 of the neck, and T10–L2 at the base of the rib cage.

Several physically distinct types of damage are recognized. Sudden and violent jolts to nearby tissues can jar the cord. This jarring causes a transient neurological deficit, known as temporary spinal concussion. Concussion symptoms usually disappear completely within several hours of injury. A spinal contusion, or bruise, is bleeding within the spinal column. The pressure from the excess fluid may kill spinal cord neurons. Spinal compression is caused by an object, such as a tumor, pressing on the cord. Lacerations, or tears, cause direct damage to cord neurons. Lacerations may be caused by bone fragments or missiles, such as bullets. Spinal transection describes the complete severing of the cord. Most spinal cord injuries involve two or more of these types of damage.

Symptoms

PARALYSIS AND LOSS OF SENSATION The extent to which movement and sensation are damaged depends on the level of the spinal cord injury. Nerves leaving the spinal cord at different levels control sensation and movement in different parts of the body. The distribution is roughly as follows:

- C1–C4: head and neck
- C3–C5: diaphragm (chest and breathing)
- C5–T1: shoulders, arms and hands
- T2–T12: chest and abdomen (excluding internal organs)
- L1–L4: abdomen (excluding internal organs), buttocks, genitals, and upper legs
- L4–S1: legs
- S2–S4: genitals and muscles of the perineum

Damage below T1, which lies at the top of the rib cage, causes **paralysis** and loss of sensation in the legs and trunk below the injury. Injury at this level usually does no damage to the arms and hands. Paralysis of the legs is called paraplegia. Damage above T1 involves the arms as well as the legs. Paralysis of all four limbs is called quadriplegia.

Cervical, or neck injuries, not only cause quadriplegia, but also may cause difficulty in breathing. Damage in the lower part of the neck may leave enough diaphragm control to allow unassisted breathing. Patients with damage at C3 or above, just below the base of the skull, require mechanical assistance from a ventilator or a diaphragmatic nerve stimulation to breathe.

Symptoms also depend on the extent of the SCI. A completely severed cord causes paralysis and loss of sensation below the wound. If the cord is only partially severed, some function will remain below the injury. Damage limited to the front portion of the cord causes paralysis and loss of sensations of **pain** and temperature. Other sensation may be preserved. Damage to the center of the cord may spare the legs, but paralyze the arms. Damage to the right or left half causes loss of position sense, paralysis on the side of the injury, and loss of pain and temperature sensation on the opposite side.

AUTONOMIC DYSREFLEXIA Body organs that self-regulate, such as the heart, gastrointestinal tract, and glands, are controlled by autonomic nerves. Autonomic nerves emerge from three different places: above the spinal column, in the lower back from vertebrae T1-L4, and from the lowest regions of the sacrum at the base of the spine. In general, these three groups of autonomic nerves operate in balance. Spinal cord injury can disrupt this balance, a condition called autonomic dysreflexia or autonomic hyperreflexia. Patients with injuries at T6 or above are at greatest risk.

SPASTICITY AND CONTRACTURE A paralyzed limb is incapable of active movement, but the muscle still has tone, a constant low level of contraction. Normal muscle tone requires communication between the muscle and the brain. Spinal cord injury prevents the brain from telling the muscle to relax. The result is prolonged muscle contraction or spasticity. Since the muscles that extend and those that bend a joint are not usually equal in strength, the involved joint is bent, often severely. This constant pressure causes deformity. As the muscle remains in the shortened position over several weeks or months, the tendons remodel and cause permanent muscle shortening or contracture. When muscles have permanently shortened, the inner surfaces of joints, such as armpits or palms, cannot be cleaned and the skin breaks down in that area.

HETEROTOPIC OSSIFICATION Heterotopic ossification is an abnormal deposit of bone in muscles and tendons that may occur after injury. It is most common in the hips and knees. Initially heterotopic ossification causes localized swelling, warmth, redness, and stiffness of the muscle. It usually begins one to four months after the injury and is rare after one year.

In autonomic dysreflexia, irritation of the skin, bowel, or bladder causes a highly exaggerated response from autonomic nerves. This response is caused by the uncontrolled release of norepinephrine, a hormone similar to adrenaline. Uncontrolled release of norepinephrine causes a rapid rise in blood pressure and a slowing of the heart rate. These symptoms are accompanied by throbbing headache, nausea, **anxiety**, sweating, and goose bumps below the level of the injury. The elevated blood pressure can rapidly cause loss of consciousness, seizures, cerebral hemorrhage, and **death**. Autonomic dysreflexia is most often caused by an over-full bladder or **bladder infection**, impaction or hard, impassable fecal mass in the bowel, or skin irritation from tight clothing, sunburn, or other irritant. Inability to sense these irritants before the autonomic reaction begins is a major cause of dysreflexia.

LOSS OF BLADDER AND BOWEL CONTROL Bladder and bowel control require both motor nerves and the autonomic nervous system (ANS). Both of these systems may be damaged by SCI. When the ANS triggers an urge to urinate or defecate, continence is maintained by contracting the anal or urethral sphincter, respectively. The sphincter is a ring of muscle that contracts to close off a passage or opening in the body. When the neural connections to these muscles are severed, conscious control is lost. In addition, loss of feeling may prevent sensations of fullness from reaching the brain. To compensate, the patient may help empty the bowel or bladder by using physical maneuvers that stimulate autonomic contractions before they would otherwise begin. The patient may not, however, be able to relax the sphincters. If the sphincters cannot be relaxed, the patient will retain urine or feces.

Retention of urine may cause muscular changes in the bladder and urethral sphincter that make the problem worse. **Urinary tract infection** is common. Retention of feces can cause impaction. Symptoms of impaction include loss of appetite and nausea. Untreated impaction may cause perforation of the large intestine and sepsis (rapid overwhelming infection).

Complications

DEEP VENOUS THROMBOSIS Blood does not flow normally through a paralyzed limb that is inactive for long periods. The blood pools in the deep veins and forms clots, a condition known as **deep vein thrombosis**. A clot, or thrombus, can break free and lodge in smaller arteries in the brain (causing a **stroke**), or in the lungs (causing **pulmonary embolism**).

DECUBITUS ULCERS (PRESSURE ULCERS) Inability to move may also lead to decubitus ulcers (pressure ulcers or bedsores). Decubitus ulcers form where skin remains in contact with a bed or chair for a long time. The most common sites of pressure ulcers are the buttocks, hips, and heels. Decubitus ulcers can cause sepsis (infection) and may seriously jeopardize recovery.

Diagnosis

The location and extent of SCI is determined by obtaining a history, performing a physical examination, and ordering appropriate imaging studies. Imaging studies usually include a combination of computed tomography (CT) scans, **magnetic resonance imaging** (MRI) scans, and traditional x rays. Computed tomography or MRI scans may be enhanced with an injected contrast dye. These diagnostic imaging studies are explained to patients by nurses and radiologic technicians. The studies are usually performed by these technicians, and are read, or interpreted, by a radiologist and/or a neuroradiologist.

Treatment

Acute care of SCI

Onlookers should not move a person who may have sustained SCI. Emergency medical personnel are best equipped to transport the injured patient. Treatment of SCI begins with immobilization. This strategy prevents partial injuries of the cord from severing it completely. Since the early 1980s, the use of splints to completely immobilize suspected SCI at the scene of the injury has helped reduce the severity of spinal cord injuries. Intravenous methylprednisolone, a steroidal anti-inflammatory drug, is given during the first 24 hours to reduce inflammation and limit tissue destruction.

Restoration of function and mobility

Rehabilitation after SCI seeks to prevent complications, promote recovery, and make the most of remaining function. Rehabilitation is a complex and long-term process; it requires a team of professionals, including a neurologist, physiatrist (or rehabilitation specialist), **physical therapist**, and occupational therapist. Other specialists who may be needed include a respiratory therapist, vocational rehabilitation counselor, social worker, speech-language pathologist, **nutritionist**, special education teacher, recreation therapist, and clinical psychologist. Support groups provide a critical source of information, advice, and support for SCI patients and their families.

While the possibility of using functional electrical stimulation (FES) for ambulation (outside of the laboratory) remains distant, the use of FES to deal with other aspects of SCI (such as loss of grasp capabilities in quadriplegia) is actually more advanced and more likely to be in common use in the forseeable future.

Instruction in activities of daily living

Physical therapy focuses on mobility to maintain range of motion of affected limbs and reduce contracture and deformity. Additionally, it helps to compensate for lost skills by using those muscles that are still functional, and helps to increase any residual strength and control in affected muscles. Adaptive equipment such as braces, canes, or wheelchairs can be suggested by a physical therapist.

The goal of occupational therapy is to restore the ability to perform the activities of daily living, such as eating and grooming, with tools and new techniques. Modifications of the home and workplace to accommodate and address the individual impairment are also addressed by the occupational therapist.

Treatment of sexual dysfunction

Men who have sustained SCI may be unable to achieve an erection or ejaculate. Sperm formation may be abnormal and fertility may be compromised. Fertility and the ability to achieve orgasm are less impaired for women. Women may still be able to become pregnant and deliver vaginally.

Prevention of complications

DECUBITUS ULCERS (PRESSURE ULCERS) Turning the patient in bed at least every two hours prevents the formation of decubitus ulcers. The patient should be turned more frequently when redness begins to develop in sensitive areas. Special mattresses and chair cushions can distribute weight more evenly to reduce pressure. Skin should be carefully attended to by nurses and other caregivers in order to maintain skin integrity and prevent ulcers from developing. Electrical stimulation is sometimes used to promote muscle movement to prevent decubitus ulcers.

SPASTICITY AND CONTRACTURE Range of motion (ROM) exercises help to prevent contracture. Chemicals can be used to prevent contractures from becoming fixed when ROM **exercise** is inadequate. Phenol or alcohol can be injected into the nerve, or botulinum toxin can be injected directly into the muscle. Botulinum toxin is associated with fewer complications, but it is more expensive than phenol and alcohol. Contractures can be released by cutting the shortened tendon or transferring it surgically to a different site on the bone, where deformity will be lessened by its pull. Such tendon transfers may also be used to increase strength in partially functional extremities.

DEEP VENOUS THROMBOSIS Deep venous thrombosis may be prevented by using passive ROM exercises, sequential compression stockings, intermittent pneumatic compression devices, and kinetic (movement) therapies. Heparin and **aspirin** may also be administered to prevent deep venous thrombosis.

HETEROTOPIC OSSIFICATION Etidronate disodium (Didronel), a drug that regulates the body's use of **calcium**, is used to prevent heterotopic ossification. Treatment begins three weeks after the injury and continues for 12 weeks. Surgical removal of ossified tissue is possible.

AUTONOMIC DYSREFLEXIA Bowel and bladder care and attention to potential irritants prevent autonomic dysreflexia. It is treated by prompt removal of the irritant. Drugs to lower blood pressure are used when necessary. Patients and friends and families of the patient should be educated about the symptoms and treatment of dysreflexia, because immediate intervention is usually necessary.

LOSS OF BLADDER AND BOWEL CONTROL Normal bowel function is promoted through adequate fluid intake and a **diet** rich in fiber. Evacuation is stimulated by deliberately increasing the abdominal pressure, either voluntarily or by using an abdominal binder.

Bladder care involves continual or intermittent catheterization. The full bladder may be detected by feeling its bulge against the abdominal wall. Urinary tract infection is a significant complication of catheterization and requires frequent monitoring.

SEXUAL DYSFUNCTION Counseling can help patients to adjust to changes in sexual function after SCI. Erection may be enhanced through the same means used to treat **erectile dysfunction** in the general population.

Prognosis

The prognosis for SCI depends on the site and extent of injury. Injuries of the neck above C4 with significant involvement of the diaphragm hold the gravest prognosis. Respiratory infection is one of the leading causes of death in long-term SCI. Overall, 85% of SCI patients who survive the first 24 hours are alive ten years after their injuries. Recovery of function is impossible to predict. Partial recovery is more likely after an incomplete wound than after the spinal cord has been completely severed.

Caregiver concerns

Initial medical management, including immobilization and transport of SCI patients, is usually provided by emergency medical personnel. Upon arrival, the physicians and nurses in the hospital emergency department assess the nature and extent of the injury. Imaging studies are performed by radiologic technicians and interpreted by radiologists and neuroradiologists. Consultation with a neurosurgeon determines whether surgical intervention will be beneficial in treating the injury.

Following emergency treatment, assessment and completion of the diagnostic work-up, critical care vigilant monitoring of SCI patients is provided by the nurses. The aim of monitoring is to identify the decreased cardiac output that may result from sympathetic nerve blockade; excessive autonomic nerve responses (i.e., distended bladder or bowel); problems associated with breathing; and the risk of **aspiration**.

Nurses, social workers, physical and occupational therapists, pastoral counselors, and other medical and mental health professionals may be called upon to help patients and families manage their emotional responses to the injury. Feelings of anxiety, anger, and denial may be experienced by hopeless patients and families.

Patient education

Patient education is an essential part of the rehabilitation process. Every member of the treatment team is involved in patient education. Patients and families are taught by nurses to recognize symptoms requiring immediate medical attention, and to provide selected care (e.g., a bowel program to prevent impaction). They may be instructed by physical and occupational therapists to use adaptive devices and equipment. Education may help to reduce feelings of powerlessness and hopelessness, and can assist in the creation of realistic expectations about recovery.

Many SCI patients also benefit from participation in peer support groups. They are enabled by the groups to meet others with comparable conditions, thereby reducing feelings of **isolation**, and allowing them to share experience-tested coping strategies.

KEY TERMS

Autonomic nervous system—The part of the nervous system that controls involuntary functions such as sweating and blood pressure.

Botulinum toxin—Any of a group of potent bacterial toxins or poisons produced by different strains of the bacterium *Clostridium botulinum.*

Computed tomography (CT)—An imaging technique in which cross-sectional x rays of the body are compiled to create a three-dimensional image of the body's internal structures.

Magnetic resonance imaging (MRI)—An imaging technique that uses a large circular magnet and radio waves to generate signals from atoms in the body. These signals are used to construct images of internal structures.

Motor—Of or pertaining to motion, the body apparatus involved in movement, or the brain functions that direct purposeful activity.

Motor nerve—Motor or efferent nerve cells carry impulses from the brain to muscle or organ tissue.

Peripheral nervous system—The part of the nervous system that is outside the brain and spinal cord. Sensory, motor, and autonomic nerves are included.

Postural drainage—The use of positioning to drain secretions from the bronchial tubes and lungs into the trachea or windpipe.

Range of motion (ROM)—The range of motion of a joint from full extension to full flexion (bending) measured in degrees like a circle.

Sensory nerves—Sensory or afferent nerves carry impulses of sensation from the periphery or outward parts of the body to the brain. Sensations include feelings, impressions, and awareness of the state of the body.

Voluntary—An action or thought undertaken or controlled by a person's free will or choice.

Prevention

Risk of spinal cord injury can be reduced through prevention of the accidents that lead to it. Chances of injury from automobile accidents, the major cause of SCIs, can be significantly reduced by driving at safe speeds, avoiding alcohol while driving, not talking on mobile phones while driving, and using seat belts.

Paralysis and loss of sensation

Some limited mobility and sensation may be recovered, but the extent and speed of recovery cannot be predicted with any accuracy. Experimental electrical stimulation has been demonstrated to allow some control of muscle contraction in paraplegia. This experimental technique offers the possibility of unaided walking. Further development of current control systems will be needed before useful movement is possible outside the laboratory.

A pulmonologist, or respiratory therapist, can promote airway hygiene through instruction in assisted coughing techniques and postural drainage. **Ventilators**, facial or nasal masks, and tracheostomy equipment, where necessary, can also be prescribed by the respiratory professional. He or she can provide instruction in their use, as well.

Resources

BOOKS

Bradley, Walter G., et al., eds. *Neurology in Clinical Practice,* 2nd ed. Boston: Butterworth-Heinemann, 1996.

Thelan, Lynne A., et al., eds. *Critical Care Nursing Diagnosis and Management,* 3rd ed. St. Louis: Mosby, 1998 pp.1064-1071.

ORGANIZATIONS

Centers for Disease Control. Accessed May 20, 2001. http://www.cdc.gov/safeusas/home/sci.htm.

The National Spinal Cord Injury Association. 8300 Colesville Road, Silver Spring, Maryland 20910. (301) 588-6959. http://www.erols.com/nscia/.

Barbara Wexler MPH

Spinal stenosis

Definition

Spinal stenosis is the narrowing of spaces in or between the bones that make up the spine (vertebrae) through which the spinal cord and spinal nerves pass.

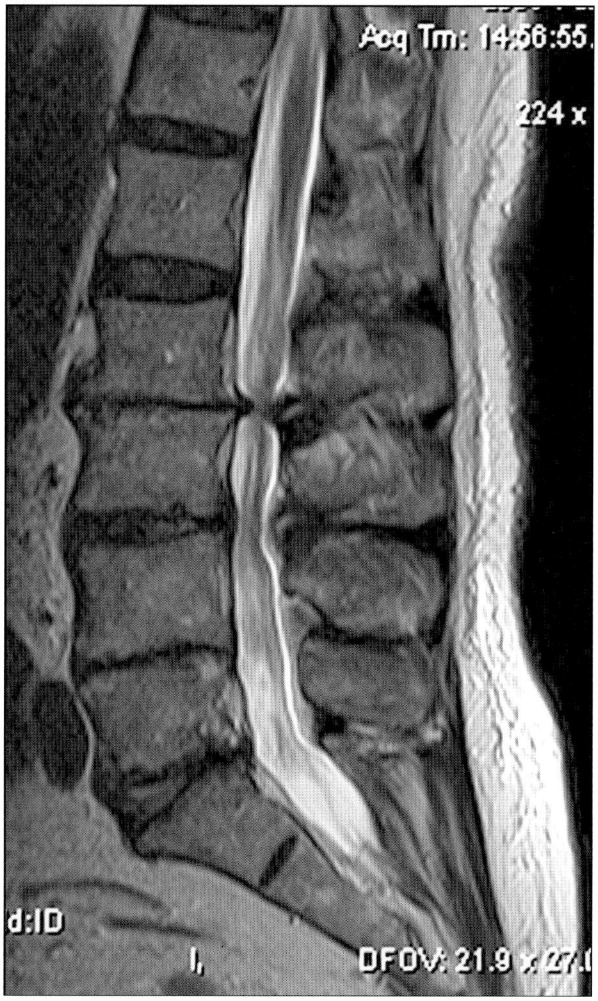

MRI image of the lumbar spine in an elderly person showing multilevel degenerative changes with severe spinal canal stenosis. *(Living Art Enterprises, LLC / Photo Researchers, Inc. Reproduced by permission.)*

As a result of this narrowing, pressure is placed on the nerves that results in **pain** or numbness.

Description

The spinal column is made of bones (vertebrae) that have a large central opening, called the spinal canal, through which the spinal cord passes. When stenosis (narrowing) occurs in the spinal canal, it is called central stenosis. The vertebrae also have openings near their base where nerves serving the rest of the body enter and leave the spinal cord. Spinal stenosis can also occur here or between the vertebrae. No matter where spinal stenosis occurs, it puts pressure on the nerves that can cause pain, numbness, and weakness.

About 75% of the time, spinal stenosis occurs in one of the five lumbar vertebrae in the lower back. This causes symptoms to appear in the back, hip, or leg. Spinal stenosis can also occur in the thoracic (chest) or cervical (neck) vertebrae. Stenosis in these locations causes symptoms to occur in the arm or shoulder.

Degenerative spinal stenosis generally occurs after age 60, and the risk of developing the disease increases with age. Men are about twice as likely to develop spinal stenosis as women. Chances of being affected by this disease are independent of race or ethnicity, but people with **osteoarthritis**, **rheumatoid arthritis**, or curvature of the spine (scoliosis) are more likely to develop symptoms. About five of every 50 Americans over age 50 (roughly 400,000 people) have spinal stenosis.

Causes and symptoms

People can be born with a small spinal canal or deformities in the vertebrae that make them abnormally narrow. This is uncommon, but when it occurs, symptoms of spinal stenosis develop at a fairly young age. Traumatic injuries to the back can also cause spinal stenosis. However, the vast majority of spinal stenosis is caused by degeneration and hardening of cartilage as a normal result of aging. Other uncommon causes of spinal stenosis include spinal tumors, Paget's disease, a condition that causes enlarged and deformed bones, and fluorosis, a condition caused by too much fluorine in the body (usually from industrial inhalation) that causes connective tissue around the vertebrae to harden.

Many people have some stenosis without showing any symptoms. When symptoms do occur, they usually appear gradually, and many people do not seek early medical attention for them because they consider the symptoms a normal condition of aging. Symptoms include:

- pain in the lower back
- pain radiating down the leg (sciatica) or along the shoulder that may temporarily improve when the back is flexed
- numbness, tingling, or sensations of hot and cold in the legs or shoulder
- inability to walk more than a short distance without pain or weakness
- shuffling gait and forward-leaning posture when walking

Diagnosis

Diagnosis is made by either a family physician or **rheumatologist** based on medical history and a physical exam. Physical examination is normally followed by an x ray, **magnetic resonance imaging** (MRI) of the spine, and/or computerized axial tomography (CAT) scan. Less frequently a myelogram or **bone scan** are used as diagnostic tools.

KEY TERMS

Bone scan—A diagnostic test in which radioactive material is injected into the body in a way that shows which areas of bone are active. This test can detect fractures, tumors, bone infections, and arthritis.

Congenital—Present at birth.

Fluorosis—A condition caused by too much fluorine in the body (usually from industrial inhalation) that causes connective tissue around the vertebrae to harden.

Myelogram—A test in which a dye is injected into the spinal column and then the spinal column is x-rayed. This test can show bone spurs, tumors, and herniated (bulging or damaged) discs between the vertebrae.

Osteoarthritis—A noninflammatory wearing away of bone and cartilage most often associated with aging.

Paget's disease—A condition that causes enlarged and deformed bones.

Rheumatoid arthritis—An inflammatory autoimmune disease of the joints.

Rheumatologist—A physician who specializes in non-surgical treatment of bone and joint disorders.

Treatment

Conservative treatment consists of administering pain medications including nonsteroidal anti-inflammatory drugs (e.g., **aspirin**, ibuprophen, naproxen **sodium**) and analgesics (**acetaminophen**, tramadol). Corticosteroid injections (prednisone and cortisone) into the spinal column help reduce pain and inflammation. Injection of anesthetics (a nerve block) offers immediate but temporary relief. Rest, changes in posture, physical therapy, and wearing a lower back brace or corset also help treat symptoms. **Chiropractic** manipulations and **acupuncture** are alternative medicine treatments that appear to substantially benefit some individuals.

When conservative treatment fails and pain, numbness, or weakness persist, surgery may be required. The goal of surgery is to relieve pressure on the nerve. The most common surgical procedure is decompression surgery that either removes some of the cartilage lining the vertebrae or removes a section of the cartilage between the vertebrae. Fusion of the vertebrae may be done at the same time as decompression surgery. Surgery is commonly followed by physical therapy, especially after spinal fusion.

Prognosis

The degree of spinal stenosis dictates whether conservative treatment will improve symptoms. Surgery usually provides substantial improvement, although some pain or numbness may remain if the nerves were badly damaged before surgery occurred. Tissue healing after surgery takes about six to eight weeks, after which rehabilitation can begin.

Caregiver concerns

A **physical therapist** is often involved in conservative treatment, teaching exercises that improve posture and strengthen the back muscles. A standard surgical team supports the neurosurgeon or orthopedic surgeon during surgical treatment. A physical therapist is almost always involved in rehabilitation after surgery. Depending on the age, agility, and working condition of the individual, an occupational therapist and an ergonomist may also participate in rehabilitation.

Prevention

Spinal stenosis cannot generally be prevented, as it is either congenital, the result of trauma, presence of a tumor, or a normal process of aging.

Resources

BOOKS

Parker, James M. and Phillip M. eds. *The Official Patient's Sourcebook on Spinal Stenosis.* San Diego, CA: Icon Health Publications, 2002.

PM Medical Health News. *21st Century Complete Medical Guide to Spinal Cord Diseases, Injuries, and Spinal Stenosis: Authoritative Government Documents, Clinical References, and Practical Information for Patients and Physicians.* CD-ROM electronic book. July 2004.

ORGANIZATIONS

American College of Rheumatology. 1800 Century Place, Suite 250. Atlanta, GA 30345-4300. (404) 633-3777. http://www.rheumatology.org.

National Institute of Arthritis and Musculoskeletal and Skin Disease Information Clearing House. National Institutes of Health, 1 Ames Circle, Bethesda, MD 20892-3675. (877) 226-4267 (toll free). http://www.niams.nih.gov.

National Institutes of Health Osteoporosis and Related Bone Diseases National Resource Center. 2 Ames Circle, Bethesda, MD 20892-3676. (800) 624-BONE. http://www.osteo.org.

OTHER

Hsiang, John N. K. "Spinal Stenosis." February 7, 2005. eMedicine.com. http://www.emedicine.com/med/topic2889.htm(November 10, 2005).

"Questions & Answers About Spinal Stenosis." National Institute of Arthritis and Musculoskeletal and Skin Disease. November 2004. http://www/niams/nih.gov/hi/topics/spinalstenosis/spinal_sten.htm (November 10, 2005).

"Spinal Stenosis." MayoClinic.com. April 19, 2004. http://www.mayoclinic.com/health/spinal-stenosis/DS00515.

Tish Davidson A. M.

Spirituality *see* **Prayer and spirituality**

Squamous cell skin cancer *see* **Skin cancer**

SSRI drugs *see* **Antideprressant drugs, SSRI**

Staphylococcal infections

Definition

Staphylococcus is the name of a genus of Gram-positive bacteria responsible for a number of serious illnesses. There are 31 species of staphylococci that have been identified as of 2008; most of them, however, are harmless to humans. Staphylococci are widespread in all parts of the world; they are

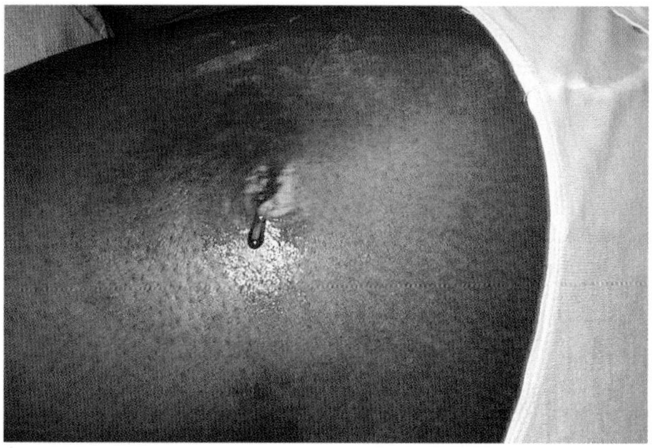

Abscess on hip, caused by staphylococcal infection. *(Science Source / Photo Researchers, Inc. Reproduced by permission.)*

commonly found in the soil as well as on the skin and mucous membranes of humans and domestic animals. The name of the genus comes from two Greek words meaning "bunch of grapes" and "round," as these bacteria look like clumps or clusters of round objects under a microscope.

Description

Staphylococci are usually commensal organisms, which means that they can live on or in humans without necessarily causing harm. They can, however, cause disease in humans and other animals either by direct destruction of tissue or by releasing toxins into the digestive tract or bloodstream.

The following are the species of staphylococci most likely to cause disease in humans:

- *S. aureus*. *S. aureus* is generally considered the most dangerous staphylococcus, causing a range of infections from pneumonia and endocarditis to food poisoning and eye infections. Methicillin-resistant *S. aureus*, or MRSA, has become a major public health concern since the 1990s.
- *S. epidermidis*. *S. epidermidis* usually lives on the skin, as its name suggests, but can also cause infections in indwelling catheters and in HIV-positive patients or others with weakened immune systems. As with *S. aureus*, there are antibiotic-resistant strains of *S. epidermidis*, known as MRSE. This staphylococcus can be additionally difficult to treat because it produces a slimy biofilm that allows it to cling to the surfaces of prostheses and other implanted medical devices.
- *S. saprophyticus*. *S. saprophyticus* is found in the vaginal tract of some women and is a common cause of urinary tract infections in sexually active women, including seniors.
- *S. lugdunensis* and *S. caprae*. These are recently discovered species of staphylococci that have been found to cause endocarditis as well as infections of the bones and joints.

Demographics

Staphylococci are commonplace organisms. In humans, they can be found on the scalp, skin (particularly the armpits and genital areas), or outer nasal passages. Biologists refer to the formation of groups or clumps of bacteria on a human or animal as colonization. Some species of staphylococci colonize the vaginas of about 10 percent of premenopausal women. Staph is found in 80 percent of the general population intermittently and 20–30 percent of the population on an ongoing basis. People who harbor staphylococci most of the time are called "staph carriers." An estimated 2 billion people are colonized by some form of *S. aureus*; of these persons, as many as 53 million, or 2.7 percent of carriers, are thought to carry MRSA, the drug-resistant form of *S. aureus*. It is possible for a senior (or younger adult) to carry staphylococci for many years without becoming sick; in addition, such domestic animals as cats, dogs, chickens, and horses can carry MRSA strains as well as less virulent staphylococci.

As far as is known as of 2008, people of either sex, any age group, or any race are equally likely to carry staphylococci. Newborns may be colonized by staphylococci from the mother during childbirth. Some groups, however, are more susceptible than others to staph infections, including diabetics, African Americans, gay men who practice anal intercourse, and very young children as well as seniors and persons with prosthetic devices.

Causes and symptoms

The causes and symptoms of staphylococcal infections vary somewhat according to the species or strain involved and the tissues or body organs infected.

Skin and soft-tissue infections

Staphylococcal infections of the skin and soft tissues are most commonly caused by *S. aureus*; however, the number of such infections caused by *S. epidermidis* has been rising rapidly since the early 2000s. Skin infections caused by staph often look like spider or other insect bites. Infected wounds or surgical incisions typically ooze pus or another discharge. Many of these skin infections develop from scratching insect bites or patches of eczema; after the skin is broken, the bacteria can enter the tissues beneath the surface and form large pus-filled abscesses. In patients with weakened immune systems, the staphylococci can enter the bloodstream. This condition, which is known as **bacteremia**, can carry the organisms to other parts of the body, including the heart, lungs, and eyes.

Endocarditis

Infective endocarditis is an inflammation of the valves and other tissues lining the heart, caused when staphylococci form colonies on the surface of the valves. Patients with artificial or damaged heart valves have a higher risk of bacterial endocarditis than patients with normal heart valves. The staphylococci typically enter the body through a surgical incision, a **urinary tract infection**, intravenous drug use, or indwelling catheters Although some forms of endocarditis develop slowly, othersmdash;particularly those caused by *S. aureus*—may develop in days or a few weeks. The patient usually runs a fever, and the staphylococci can be detected in a blood culture. The patient will often have a heart murmur or some other abnormality of blood flow in the heart that can be detected on an **echocardiogram**.

Some elderly patients may develop rapid-onset dementia as a symptom of infective endocarditis. About 40 percent of patients will develop skin problems, ranging from small tender nodules in the fingertips to pinpoint hemorrhages in the tissues lining the mouth or on the skin above the shoulder blades. Some patients will develop the signs of a **stroke** if the endocarditis is not detected early; this complication develops when the bacteria growing on the heart tissue form clumps that travel through the bloodstream and block some of the blood vessels in the brain.

Pneumonia

Most cases of **pneumonia** in seniors are caused by streptococci; however, staphylococcal pneumonia accounts for about 3 percent of severe cases acquired outside the hospital. *S. aureus* was identified as the cause of a number of severe cases of pneumonia following **influenza** during the 2003ndash;2004 flu season. The patients had the typical symptoms of pneumonia: fever, chest **pain**, cough, and production of sputum. Community-acquired pneumonia (CAP) following influenza is more likely to affect seniors than younger adults; seniors with diabetes are particularly susceptible.

Joints and prosthetic devices

Infections of the joints may be caused by staphylococci entering the joints from the bloodstream or through contamination of artificial joints. *S. aureus* and *S. epidermidis* are the species usually involved in joint infections. The knee is the most commonly affected joint, but the wrist, ankle, or hip may also be involved; about 20 percent of patients have two or more joints affected by the infection.

The most common symptom of a joint infection is sudden swelling and pain in the affected joint due to the accumulation of pus and tissue fluid. The patient may or may not have a fever.

Endophthalmitis

Endophthalmitis is an inflammation of the tissues on the inside of the eye. It can be caused by bacteria entering these tissues via the bloodstream (endogenous endophthalmitis) or following eye surgery (exogenous endophthalmitis). Endogenous endophthalmitis is rare, accounting for about 15 percent of cases. Most cases of eye infection from staphylococci result from trauma to the eye or following cataract surgery. *S. epidermidis* is the most common staphylococcus involved in bacterial endophthalmitis, followed by *S. aureus*. These organisms usually live on the eyelid and other tissues surrounding the eye, and are introduced into the interior of the eye during surgery or when the eye is injured.

The early symptoms of staphylococcal endophthalmitis include pain, swelling, and redness in the affected eye and partial loss of vision. They usually begin within a week of the injury or operation. The patient may also have a headache and be sensitive to bright light. In some cases there is a noticeable discharge from the affected eye.

Food poisoning

Staphylococcal food poisoning is the result of toxins secreted by the organisms rather than by tissue damage caused by invasion of the bacteria themselves. The staphylococci usually get into food from the hands of food workers or from contaminated cheese or milk products. *S. aureus* is tolerant of salt and can grow in salty foods like ham. The staphylococci produce at least seven different toxins that cannot be destroyed by cooking. Foods most likely to be contaminated are those made by hand and that require little or no cooking, such as sandwiches, cold cuts, and certain types of pastry.

The symptoms of staphylococcal food poisoning include nausea, vomiting, and **diarrhea**. They usually begin between one and six hours after eating the contaminated food, but may cause vomiting in as little as 30 minutes after eating. Most people feel better in one to three days, although seniors may take a few more days to recover fully.

Diagnosis

Diagnosis of a staphylococcal infection in seniors is based on a combination of the patient's medical history, symptoms, an examination of the skin or other affected body parts, and a blood culture that is positive for a specific staphylococcus species. For example, *S. aureus* can be distinguished from *S. epidermidis* by its effects on the blood agar used to culture bacteria in the laboratory. *S. aureus* is a hemolytic bacterium, which means that it destroys the blood cells suspended in the agar and leaves a clear or colorless area beneath and under its colonies.

Another test that is used to distinguish *S. aureus* from other staphylococci is the coagulase test. Coagulase is an enzyme produced by *S. aureus* that causes blood to clot, whereas most other staphylococci do not produce this enzyme. *S. aureus* is thus said to be coagulase-positive while other staphylococci are coagulase-negative. The test is important because *S. aureus* is usually more virulent than other species of staphylococci and early identification is critical.

Samples for a bacterial culture may be obtained from a skin injury, from drawing a blood sample, from a urine sample, or by having the patient cough up sputum (matter from the lungs) if pneumonia is suspected. Although a standard blood culture for a staph infection takes a day or two to yield results, rapid diagnostic methods using amplification and probe-based molecular techniques provide results in hours, thus allowing treatment to be started earlier and improving the patient's chances of recovery.

Although *S. aureus* can be identified in stool samples or vomit from a patient with food poisoning, doctors do not usually test for the organism unless there is an outbreak involving several people. The diagnosis of staphylococcal food poisoning is usually made on the basis of the patient's symptoms.

X-rays and other imaging tests may be performed as part of the diagnosis of joint infections, endocarditis, and pneumonia.

Staphylococcal infections of the eye are diagnosed by an examination of the eye with a slit lamp and a vision test. In most cases the patient will be referred to an ophthalmologist for further testing of the affected eye while a blood culture or **urine culture** is performed to identify the organism involved.

Treatment

Treatment depends on the specific type and location of staphylococcal infection. In most cases the doctor will start antibiotic therapy when a staphylococcal infection is suspected as soon as the sample of tissue, blood, sputum, or urine has been sent to the laboratory. Specific types of infections are treated as follows:

- Skin infections: The doctor will usually make an incision to drain the pus and other infected fluid out of the wound. In some cases a topical antibiotic may be applied after the wound has been cleansed, or the patient may be given systemic oral or intravenous antibiotics.

QUESTIONS TO ASK YOUR DOCTOR

- What is the risk of a staphylococcal infection following surgery on the eye or a joint?
- Should I consider having a flu shot to lower the risk of pneumonia following flu?
- Is it safe for elderly family members to visit friends in the hospital? Should they take any special precautions to lower their risk of contracting an infection?

- Staphylococcal pneumonia following influenza is usually treated with intravenous antibiotics following hospitalization. Severely ill seniors may require treatment with supplemental oxygen in an intensive care unit (ICU).
- Indwelling catheters and similar devices are removed when staphylococcal infection is suspected or proved. If the infection is located in a joint with a prosthetic appliance, the artificial joint must be removed and the patient given a four- to six-week course of antibiotics. Infected joints without a prosthetic appliance are usually drained of fluid and the patient is given a four-week course of antibiotic therapy to clear the infection. Physical therapy is encouraged to maintain the range of motion in the joint.
- Infected artificial heart valves may or may not require removal. Endocarditis does, however, require long-term antibiotic therapy, particularly in seniors.
- Staphylococcal eye infections require emergency treatment. The patient is given antibiotics and the vitreous humor of the eye is removed and replaced with sterile fluid. An ophthalmologist (specialist in eye disorders) usually injects antibiotics into the tissues around the eye as well as giving antibiotics by mouth or intravenously. In extreme cases the entire eye may need to be removed.

Nutrition/Dietetic concerns

Seniors who become sick from staphylococcal food poisoning usually recover with bed rest, plenty of fluids, and antinausea drugs prescribed by the doctor. **Antibiotics** cannot be used to treat food poisoning because the toxins that cause the nausea and vomiting are not affected by these drugs. Seniors who become severely ill from the toxins produced by the bacteria may require hospitalization and treatment with intravenous fluids.

KEY TERMS

Agar—A gel-like substance derived from red seaweed that is used to make a culture medium for growing bacteria on laboratory plates.

Bacteremia—The presence of bacteria in the bloodstream.

Coagulase—An enzyme produced by *S. aureus* that causes blood to clot. Testing for this enzyme can be used to distinguish *S. aureus* from most other species of staphylococci.

Colonization—In biology, the process by which a species moves into and populates a new area. It is also used the describe the process by which bacteria and other microorganisms form colonies in or on the bodies of humans and other animals.

Commensalism—In biology, a relationship in which a member of one species lives on or in a member of another and derives benefit from the relationship while the member of the other species is unharmed. Staphylococci are commensal organisms that can live on or in humans without necessarily causing disease.

Endocarditis—An inflammation of the tissues lining the inside of the heart and its valves.

Endophthalmitis—Inflammation of the tissues inside the eyeball.

Gram-positive—A term that refers to the amount of a crystal violet dye picked up by a bacterium during the Gram stain process. A Gram-positive organism looks blue or violet under a microscope whereas Gram-negative bacteria look red or pink. Staphylococci are Gram-positive bacteria.

Sepsis—The presence of bacteria or their toxic products in the bloodstream or other tissues, causing whole-body inflammation. Sepsis is a serious medical condition.

Sputum—Matter from the lungs or throat that is brought up by coughing.

Strain—A genetic variant or subtype of a bacterium (or other microorganism).

Superbug—Informal term for an antibiotic-resistant bacterium.

Virulence—The relative ability of a disease organism to overcome the body's defenses. A highly virulent organism is one that can readily overcome the immune system.

Vitrectomy—The surgical removal of the vitreous humor. The gel is replaced with saline or another clear fluid.

Vitreous humor—The clear gel that fills the space between the lens and the retina of the eye.

Therapy

Therapy for staphylococcal infections consists of administration of appropriate antibiotics by mouth or intravenously as appropriate, with surgical removal of infected tissue or medical devices as necessary.

Prognosis

The prognosis of staphylococcal infections varies according to the specific illness. Untreated *S. aureus* infections of the bloodstream can have a mortality rate as high as 80 percent. Endocarditis and pneumonia caused by antibiotic-resistant staphylococci have mortality rates around 11 percent in patients without other diseases or disorders, but the rate may be as high as 44 percent in patients with diabetes, HIV infection, or other disorders that weaken the **immune system**. Seniors with staphylococcal pneumonia have a worse prognosis than younger adults. In patients over the age of 70, community-acquired staph infections are associated with a mortality rate of 21 percent in the year following diagnosis.

The prognosis for staphylococcal endophthalmitis depends on timely diagnosis and treatment. In general, patients with postoperative endophthalmitis do better than those with endogenous infections. Seniors with weak immune systems, HIV infection, diabetes, or other disorders have a poor prognosis for full recovery of vision.

Most patients with staphylococcal food poisoning or staphylococcal urinary tract infections recover completely; fatalities are rare except in the very old.

Prevention

Preventive measures against staphylococcal infections include the following:

- Avoid scratching insect bites or other areas of irritated skin; see a doctor about a boil filled with pus or a similar skin lesion that will not heal.

- Wash hands carefully before and after preparing food.
- Cover infected skin or skin draining pus with waterproof dressings, and dispose of soiled dressings carefully. Clean cuts and scratches promptly and keep them bandaged.
- People with infections on their hands or wrists should avoid preparing or serving food until the infection has been cleared.
- Avoid sharing such personal items as combs, brushes, cosmetics, cell phones, razors, and towels. Be particularly careful in gyms and health clubs, as staphylococci prefer warm, moist environments.
- Wipe down kitchen countertops, athletic equipment, and hospital equipment with alcohol-based sanitizers.
- Avoid direct contact with other people's wounds or injuries whenever possible.

Caregiver concerns

Caregivers of seniors should be concerned about the following:

- Carefully monitor all indwelling catheters or similar devices and notify the doctor at once if there are signs of infection.
- If the senior has recently had eye surgery, watch for a discharge or other signs of infection in the eye that was treated This precaution is particularly important if the senior has diabetes.
- Look for signs of skin injury and be careful to keep the senior's skin clean and dry. Notify the doctor at once if even a small wound looks infected or the tissue around it seems to be dying.
- Wash hands carefully before and after giving the senior a bath or other body care, and use a hand sanitizer as well. Clean kitchen countertops and other hard surfaces with an alcohol-based cleaning agent.
- Do not use or serve food that may be contaminated, and do not prepare food for the senior if you have been diagnosed with a skin or eye infection. Keep hot foods hot (over 140°F) and cold foods cold if they must be stored for longer than 2 hours.

Resources

BOOKS

Rhinehart, Emily, and Mary McGoldrick. *Infection Control in Home Care and Hospice*. Sudbury, MA: Jones and Bartlett, Publishers, 2006.

Wilson, Michael. *Bacteriology of Humans: An Ecological Perspective*. Malden, MA: Blackwell Publishing, 2008.

PERIODICALS

Appelbaum, P. C. "Microbiology of Antibiotic Resistance in *Staphylococcus aureus*." *Clinical Infectious Diseases* 45 (September 15, 2007): S165–S170.

Bamberger, David M., and Sarah E. Boyd. "Management of *Staphylococcus aureus* Infections." *American Family Physician* 72 (December 15, 2005): 2474–2481.

Hageman, Jeffrey C., Timothy M. Uyeki, John S. Francis, et al. "Severe Community-Acquired Pneumonia Due to *Staphylococcus aureus*, 2003–04 Influenza Season." *Emerging Infectious Diseases* 12 (June 2006): 894–899.

Liu, G. Y., A. Essex, J. T. Buchanan, et al. "*Staphylococcus aureus* Golden Pigment Impairs Neutrophil Killing and Promotes Virulence through Its Antioxidant Activity." *Journal of Experimental Medicine* 202 (July 18, 2005): 209–215.

Miller, D. M., A. S. Vedula, H. W. Flynn, Jr., et al. "Endophthalmitis Caused by *Staphylococcus epidermidis*: In Vitro Antibiotic Susceptibilities and Clinical Outcomes." *Ophthalmic Surgery, Lasers and Imaging* 38 (November-December 2007): 446–451.

Mody, L., S. Maheshwari, A. Galecki, et al. "Indwelling Device Use and Antibiotic Resistance in Nursing Homes: Identifying a High-Risk Group." *Journal of the American Geriatrics Society* 55 (December 2007): 1921–1926.

Noskin, G. A., R. J. Rubin, J. J. Schentag, et al. "The Burden of *Staphylococcus aureus* Infections on Hospitals in the United States: An Analysis of the 2000 and 2001 Nationwide Inpatient Sample Database." *Archives of Internal Medicine* 165 (August 8-22, 2005): 1756–1761.

OTHER

Centers for Disease Control and Prevention (CDC). *Staphylococcal Food Poisoning*. Available online at http://www.cdc.gov/ncidod/dbmd/diseaseinfo/staphylococcus_food_g.htm [cited March 9, 2008].

Egan, Daniel J., and Jessica R. Peters. "Endophthalmitis." *eMedicine*, December 21, 2007. http://www.emedicine.com/emerg/topic880.htm [cited March 9, 2008].

Fraser, Susan L. "Enterococcal Infections." *eMedicine*, July 5, 2006. http://www.emedicine.com/med/topic680.htm [cited March 8, 2008].

Herchline, Thomas. "Staphylococcal Infections." *eMedicine*, May 8, 2007. http://www.emedicine.com/med/topic2166.htm [cited March 7, 2008].

ORGANIZATIONS

Centers for Disease Control and Prevention (CDC), 1600 Clifton Road, Atlanta, GA, 30333, (404) 498-1515, (800) 311-3435, http://www.cdc.gov/.

Food and Drug Administration (FDA), 5600 Fishers Lane, Rockville, MD, 20857, (888) 463-6332, http://www.fda.gov/default.htm.

National Institute of Allergy and Infectious Diseases (NIAID), 6610 Rockledge Drive, MSC 6612, Bethesda, MD, 20892, (301) 496-5717, (866) 284-4107, (301) 402-3573, http://www3.niaid.nih.gov/.

Rebecca J. Frey Ph.D.

Stasis dermatits *see* **Dermatitis**

STDs *see* **Sexually transmitted diseases**

Stomach cancer

Definition

Stomach **cancer** (also known as gastric cancer) is a disease in which the cells forming the inner lining of the stomach become abnormal and start to divide uncontrollably, forming a mass called a tumor.

Description

The stomach is a J-shaped organ that lies in the left and central portion of the abdomen. The stomach produces many digestive juices and acids that mix with the food and aid in the process of digestion. There are five regions of the stomach that doctors refer to when determining the origin of stomach cancer. These are:

- the cardia, area surrounding the cardiac sphincter which controls movement of food from the esophagus into the stomach
- the fundus, upper expanded area adjacent to the cardiac region
- the antrum, lower region of the stomach where it begins to narrow
- the prepyloric, region just before or nearest the pylorus
- the pylorus, the terminal region where the stomach joins the small intestine.

Cancer can develop in any of the five sections of the stomach. Symptoms and outcomes of the disease will vary depending on the location of the cancer.

Demographics

In 2007,the American Cancer Society estimated that 21,260 Americans would be diagnosed with stomach cancer and approximately 11,210 deaths would result from the disease. The risk for developing stomach cancer in the United States is about 1 in 100. The risk is higher for men than for women. Two-thirds of stomach cancer cases are diagnosed in people older than age 65, but in families with a hereditary risk for stomach cancer, cases in younger individuals are more frequently seen.

Stomach cancer is one of the leading causes of cancer deaths in several areas of the world, most notably Japan and other Asian countries. In Japan it appears almost ten times as frequently as in the United States. The number of new stomach cancer cases is decreasing in some areas, however, especially in developed countries. In the United States, incidence rates of stomach cancer have declined. The use of refrigerated foods and increased consumption of fresh fruits and vegetables, instead of preserved foods with high salt content, may be a reason for the decline. Another reason for the decrease may be that **antibiotics**, which are given to treat childhood illnesses, can kill the bacterium *Helicobacter pylori,* which is a major cause of stomach cancer.

Causes and symptoms

While the exact cause for stomach cancer has not been identified, several potential factors have led to increased numbers of individuals developing the disease and, therefore, significant risk has been associated. **Diet**, work environment, exposure to the bacterium *Helicobacter pylori,* and a history of stomach disorders such as ulcers or polyps are some of these believed causes.

Studies have shown that eating foods with high quantities of salt and nitrites increases the risk of stomach cancer. The diet in a specific region can have a great impact on its residents. Making changes to the types of foods consumed has been shown to decrease likelihood of disease, even for individuals from countries with higher risk. For example, Japanese people who move to the United States or Europe and change the types of foods they eat have a far lower chance of developing the disease than do Japanese people who remain in Japan and do not change their dietary habits. Eating recommended amounts of fruit and vegetables may lower a person's chances of developing this cancer.

A high risk for developing stomach cancers has been linked to certain industries as well. The best proven association is between stomach cancer and persons who work in coal mining and those who work processing timber, nickel, and rubber. An unusually large number of these workers have been diagnosed with this form of cancer.

Several studies have identified a bacterium (*Helicobacter pylori*) that causes stomach ulcers (inflammation in the inner lining of the stomach). Chronic (long-term) infection of the stomach with these bacteria may lead to a particular type of cancer (lymphomas or mucosa-associated lymphoid tissue [MALT]) in the stomach.

Another risk factor is the development of polyps, benign growths in the lining of the stomach. Although polyps are not cancerous, some may have the potential to turn cancerous. People in blood group A are also at elevated risk for this cancer for unknown reasons. Other speculative causes of stomach cancer include previous stomach surgery for ulcers or other conditions, or a form of **anemia** known as pernicious anemia.

A history of **smoking** also increases the risk for developing stomach cancer. Smoking doubles the risk for the development of stomach cancer.

Stomach cancer is a slow-growing cancer. It may be years before the tumor grows very large and produces distinct symptoms. In the early stages of the disease, the patient may only have mild discomfort, indigestion, **heartburn**, a bloated feeling after eating, and mild nausea. In the advanced stages, a patient has loss of appetite and resultant **weight loss**, stomach pains, vomiting, difficulty in swallowing, and blood in the stool. Stomach cancer often spreads (metastasizes) to adjoining organs such as the esophagus, adjacent lymph nodes, liver, or colon.

Diagnosis

Unfortunately, many patients diagnosed with stomach cancer experience **pain** for two or three years before informing a doctor of their symptoms. When a doctor suspects stomach cancer from the symptoms described by the patient, a complete medical history is taken to check for any risk factors. A thorough physical examination is conducted to assess all the symptoms. Laboratory tests may be ordered to check for blood in the stool (fecal occult blood test) and anemia (low red blood cell count), which often accompany gastric cancer.

In some countries, such as Japan, it is appropriate for patients to be given routine screening examinations for stomach cancer, as the risk of developing cancer in that society is very high. Such screening might be useful for all high-risk populations. Due to the low prevalence of stomach cancer in the United States, routine screening is usually not recommended unless a family history of the disease exists.

Whether as a screening test or because a doctor suspects a patient may have symptoms of stomach cancer, **endoscopy** or barium x rays are used in diagnosing stomach cancer. For a barium x ray of the upper gastrointestinal tract, the patient is given a chalky, white solution of barium sulfate to drink. This solution coats the esophagus, the stomach, and the small intestine. Air may be pumped into the stomach after the barium solution in order to get a clearer picture. Multiple x rays are then taken. The barium coating helps to identify any abnormalities in the lining of the stomach.

In another more frequently used test, known as upper gastrointestinal endoscopy, a thin, flexible, lighted tube (endoscope) is passed down the patient's throat and into the stomach. The doctor can view the lining of the esophagus and the stomach through the tube. Sometimes, a small ultrasound probe is attached at the end of the endoscope. This probe sends high frequency sound waves that bounce off the stomach wall. A computer creates an image of the stomach wall by translating the pattern of echoes generated by the reflected sound waves. This procedure is known as an endoscopic ultrasound, or EUS.

Endoscopy has several advantages because the physician is able to see any abnormalities directly. In addition, if any suspicious-looking patches are seen, biopsy forceps can be passed painlessly through the tube to collect some tissue for microscopic examination. This is known as a biopsy. Endoscopic ultrasound (EUS) is beneficial because it can provide valuable information on depth of tumor invasion.

After stomach cancer has been diagnosed and before treatment starts, another type of x-ray scan is taken. Computed tomography (CT) is an imaging procedure that produces a three-dimensional picture of organs or structures inside the body. **CT scans** are used to obtain additional information in regard to how large the tumor is and what parts of the stomach it borders; whether the cancer has spread to the lymph nodes; and whether it has spread to distant parts of the body (metastasized), such as the liver, lung, or bone. A CT scan of the chest, abdomen, and pelvis is taken. If the tumor has gone through the wall of the stomach and extends to the liver, pancreas, or spleen, the CT will often show it. Although a CT scan is an effective way of evaluating whether cancer has spread to some of the lymph nodes, it is less effective than EUS in evaluating whether the nodes closest to the stomach are free of cancer. However, CT scans, like barium x rays, have the advantage of being less invasive than upper endoscopy.

Laparoscopy is another procedure used to stage some patients with stomach cancer. This involves a medical device similar to an endoscope. A laparoscopy is a minimally invasive surgery technique with one or a few small incisions, which can be performed on an outpatient basis, followed by rapid recovery. Patients who may receive radiation therapy or **chemotherapy** before surgery may undergo a laparoscopic procedure to determine the precise stage of cancer. The patient with bone pain or with certain laboratory results should be given a **bone scan**.

Benign gastric neoplasms are tumors of the stomach that cause no major harm. One of the most common is called a submucosal leiomyoma. If a leiomyoma starts to bleed, surgery should be performed to remove it. However, many leiomyomas require no treatment. Diagnosis of stomach cancers should be conducted carefully so that if the tumor does not require treatment the patient is not subjected to a surgical operation.

Other tests that may be performed to diagnosis stomach cancer include **magnetic resonance imaging** scan (MRI), positron emission tomography (PET) scan, and **chest x ray**.

Clinical staging

More than 95% of stomach cancers are caused by adenocarcinomas, malignant cancers that originate in glandular tissues. The remaining 5% of stomach cancers include lymphomas and other types of cancers.

It is important that gastric lymphomas be accurately diagnosed because these cancers have a much better prognosis than stomach adenocarcinomas. Approximately half of the people with gastric lymphomas survive five years after diagnosis.

Treatment for gastric lymphoma involves surgery combined with chemotherapy and radiation therapy.

Staging of stomach cancer is based on how deep the growth has penetrated the stomach lining; to what extent (if any) it has invaded surrounding lymph nodes; and to what extent (if any) it has spread to distant parts of the body (metastasized). The more confined the cancer, the better the chance for a cure.

One important factor in the staging of adenocarcinoma of the stomach is whether the tumor has invaded the surrounding tissue and, if it has, how deep it has penetrated. If invasion is limited, prognosis is favorable. Diseased tissue that is more localized improves the outcome of surgical procedures performed to remove the diseased area of the stomach. This is called a resection of the stomach.

Stomach cancer is staged using the Tumor(T), Node(N), Metastasis(M), classification system. After stage 0, where the cancer has not grown beyond the layers of the tissue lining the stomach, the tumor is labeled stage I through IV. Stage 1 indicates less tumor involvement; stage IV indicates the tumor has spread outside of the stomach and has invaded other tissues or organs in the body.

Treatment

Because symptoms of stomach cancer are so mild, treatment often does not commence until the disease is well advanced. The three standard modes of treatment for stomach cancer are surgery, radiation therapy, and chemotherapy. While deciding on the patient's treatment plan, the doctor takes into account many factors. The location of the cancer and its stage are important considerations. In addition, the patient's age, general health status, and personal preferences are also taken into account.

Surgery

In the early stages of stomach cancer, surgery may be used to remove the cancer. Surgical removal of adenocarcinoma is the only treatment capable of eliminating the disease. Laparoscopy is often used before surgery to investigate whether the tumor can be removed surgically. If the cancer is widespread and cannot be removed with surgery, an attempt is made to remove blockage and control symptoms such as pain or bleeding. Depending on the location of the cancer, a portion of the stomach may be removed, a procedure called a partial gastrectomy. In a surgical procedure known as total gastrectomy, the entire stomach may be removed. However, doctors prefer to leave at least part of the stomach if possible. Patients who have been given a partial gastrectomy achieve a better quality of life than those having a total gastrectomy. Even when the entire stomach is removed, the patients quickly adjust to a different eating schedule, which involves eating small quantities of food more frequently. High protein foods are generally recommended.

Partial or total gastrectomy is often accompanied by other surgical procedures. Lymph nodes are frequently removed and nearby organs, or parts of these organs, may be removed if cancer has spread to them. Such organs may include the pancreas, colon, or spleen.

Preliminary studies suggest that patients who have tumors that cannot be removed by surgery at the start of therapy may become candidates for surgery later. Combinations of chemotherapy and radiation therapy are sometimes able to reduce disease for which surgery is not initially appropriate. Preliminary studies were being performed as of 2008 to determine if some of these patients can become candidates for surgical procedures after such therapies are applied.

Chemotherapy

Whether patients undergoing surgery for stomach cancer should receive chemotherapy is controversial. Chemotherapy involves administering anti-cancer drugs either intravenously (through a vein in the arm) or orally (in the form of pills). This method can either be used as the primary mode of treatment or after surgery to destroy any cancerous cells that may have migrated to distant sites. Most cancers of the gastrointestinal tract do not respond well to chemotherapy; however, adenocarcinoma of the stomach and advanced stages of cancer are exceptions.

Although chemotherapy using a single medicine is sometimes used, the best response rates are often achieved with combinations of medicines. Therefore, in addition to studies exploring the effectiveness of new medicines, as of 2008 there were many clinical trials in progress attempting to evaluate how to best combine existing forms of chemotherapy to bring the greatest degree of help to patients.

Radiation therapy

Radiation therapy is often used after surgery to destroy the cancer cells that may not have been completely removed during surgery. To treat stomach cancer, external beam radiation therapy is generally used. In this procedure, high-energy rays from a machine that is outside of the body are concentrated on the area of the tumor. In the advanced stages of stomach cancer, radiation therapy is used to ease the symptoms such as pain and bleeding. However, studies of radiation treatment for stomach cancer have shown that the way it has been used it has been ineffective for many patients.

As of 2008 researchers were actively assessing the role of chemotherapy and radiation therapy used before a surgical procedure is conducted. They were searching for ways to use both chemotherapy and radiation therapy so that they increase the length of survival of patients more effectively than existing methods were able to do.

Nutrition/dietetic concerns

Following gastrectomy or partial gastrectomy it is important for patients to carefully follow doctor's orders about what foods are eaten and when they should be eaten. In particular, patients may be asked to have small, frequent meals.

QUESTIONS TO ASK YOUR DOCTOR

- Has the cancer spread to the lymph nodes?
- Has the cancer spread to the lungs, liver, or spleen?
- (After endoscopy or barium x-rays and CT scan have been completed)Would I benefit from endoscopic ultrasound or laparoscopy?
- (If surgery is recommended) Do recent studies show that it might be a good idea to also use chemotherapy or radiation therapy?
- (If gastrectomy or partial gastrectomy was performed) How should I alter my diet and eating patterns?
- (Following surgery) What foods should I eat? Is there a registered dietitian I can speak with on a regular basis about what I should eat?

Prognosis

In 2007, the American Cancer Society reported approximately 24% of patients with stomach cancer live at least five years following diagnosis. Patients diagnosed with stomach cancer in its early stages had a far better prognosis than those for whom it is in the later stages. In the early stages, the tumor is small, lymph nodes are unaffected, and the cancer has not migrated to the lungs or the liver. Unfortunately, only about 20% of patients with stomach cancer are diagnosed before the cancer had spread to the lymph nodes or formed a distant **metastasis**.

It is important to remember that statistics on prognosis may be misleading. Therapies are being developed rapidly and five-year survival has not yet been measured with all of these. Also, the largest group of people diagnosed with stomach cancer are between 60 and 70 years of age, suggesting that some of these patients die not from cancer but from other age-related diseases. As a result, some patients with stomach cancer in 2008 may be expected to have longer survival than did patients, for example, in 1998.

Prevention

Avoiding many of the risk factors associated with stomach cancer may prevent its development.

KEY TERMS

Adenocarcinoma—Malignant cancers that originate in the tissues of glands or that form glandular structures.

Anemia—A condition in which iron levels in the blood are low.

Barium x ray (upper GI)—An x-ray test of the upper part of the gastrointestinal (GI) tract (including the esophagus, stomach, and a small portion of the small intestine) after the patient is given a white, chalky barium sulfate solution to drink. This substance coats the upper GI and the x rays reveal any abnormality in the lining of the stomach and the upper GI tract.

Biopsy—Removal of a tissue sample for examination under the microscope to check for cancer cells.

Chemotherapy—Treatment of cancer with synthetic drugs that destroy the tumor either by inhibiting the growth of the cancerous cells or by killing the cancer cells.

Endoscopic ultrasound (EUS)—A medical procedure in which sound waves are sent to the stomach wall by an ultrasound probe attached to the end of an endoscope. The pattern of echoes generated by the reflected sound waves are translated by a computer into an image of the stomach wall.

External radiation therapy—Radiation therapy that focuses high-energy rays from a machine on the area of the tumor.

Infiltrate—A tumor that moves into another organ of the body.

Polyp—An abnormal growth that develops on the inside of a hollow organ such as the colon, stomach, or nose.

Radiation therapy—Treatment using high-energy radiation from x-ray machines, cobalt, radium, or other sources.

Total gastrectomy—Surgical removal (excision) of the entire stomach.

Upper endoscopy—A medical procedure in which a thin, lighted, flexible tube (endoscope) is inserted down the patient's throat. Through this tube the doctor can view the lining of the esophagus, stomach, and the upper part of the small intestine.

Excessive amounts of salted, smoked, and pickled foods should be avoided, as should foods high in nitrates. A diet that includes recommended amounts of fruits and vegetables is believed to lower the risk of several cancers, including stomach cancer. The American Cancer Society recommends eating at least five servings of fruits and vegetables daily and choosing six servings of food from other plant sources, such as grains, pasta, beans, cereals, and whole grain bread. Following a healthy diet and balancing caloric intake with recommended amounts of physical activity may reduce **obesity**, which may itself be a risk for developing stomach cancer.

Abstaining from tobacco and excessive amounts of alcohol reduces the risk for many cancers. In countries where stomach cancer is common, such as Japan, early detection is important for successful treatment.

Treatment for H. pylori infection, especially for those individuals with chronic infections, may reduce the risk for developing stomach cancer.

Caregiver concerns

Many patients experience feelings of **depression**, **anxiety**, and fatigue when dealing with the knowledge of and treatments associated with stomach cancer. Side effects such as nausea and vomiting may also be experienced during treatment. Understanding what to expect as a result of the various treatments and learning about alternative methods for reducing these symptoms may improve the effectiveness of treatments and provide a more positive outlook in regard to the one's situation. A doctor or other health professional should be consulted to develop strategies for managing any negative symptoms or feelings.

Resources

OTHER

"Gastric Cancer Treatment." *National Cancer Institute (NCI)* February 22, 2008 [cited April 9, 2008]. http://www.cancer.gov/cancertopics/pdq/treatment/gastric/HealthProfessional

"Overview: Stomach Cancer." American Cancer Society (ACS) 2008 [cited April 9, 2008]. http://www.cancer.org/docroot/CRI/CRI_2_1x.asp?rnav=criov&dt=40

ORGANIZATIONS

American Cancer Society, PO Box 22718, Oklahoma City, OK, 73123-1718, (800) ACS-2345, https://www.cancer.org/.

National Cancer Institute, 6116 Executive Blvd., Room 3036A, Bethesda, MD, 20892-8322, (800) 422-6237, http://www.cancer.gov/.

National Coalition for Cancer Survivorship, 1010 Wayne Avenue, 5th Floor, Suite 300, Silver Spring, MD, 20910, (888) 650-9127, http://www.canceradvocacy.org/.

Lata Cherath Ph.D.
Bob Kirsch
Melinda Oberleitner R.N., D.N.S.

Stomach flu *see* **Gastroenteritis disease**
Stone removal *see* **Gallstones**

Streptococcal disease

Definition

Streptococcal diseases are **infectious diseases** caused by various types of bacteria belonging to the genus *Streptococcus*. All bacteria classified as streptococci are sphere-shaped Gram-positive organisms that grow in chains or pairs. The name *streptococcus* comes from two Greek words that mean "twisted chain" and "spherical."

Description

Streptococci are classified according to their hemolytic properties. Hemolysis is the process in which bacteria break down red blood cells on an agar plate in the laboratory.

- Alpha-hemolytic streptococci. These bacteria cause a greenish discoloration of the agar plate when they are cultured. This group includes such bacteria as *S. pneumoniae*, a major cause of bacterial pneumonia in the elderly; *S. mutans*, which is involved in tooth decay; and *S. viridans*, which can cause infections of the heart tissue as well as dental abscesses.
- Beta-hemolytic streptococci. These bacteria completely destroy the blood cells in the culture medium, causing the area around them to lose color and become transparent. The four major subgroups of beta-hemolytic streptococci are described in the next paragraph.
- Nonhemolytic streptococci. Bacteria in this group do not cause any change in the appearance of the culture medium. They are rarely implicated in disease in humans.

Beta-hemolytic streptococci are further classified into four groups:

- Group A. The most important Group A beta-hemolytic streptococcus is *S. pyogenes*, which is also known as *GAS*. Infections caused by *GAS* include strep throat, erysipelas, scarlet fever, rheumatic fever, and necrotizing fasciitis, or flesh-eating bacteria disease.
- Group B. Group B hemolytic streptococci include *S. agalactiae*, sometimes known as *GBS*. *GBS* can cause meningitis, cellulitis, pneumonia, or infection of the bloodstream in seniors.
- Group C. These streptococci are unlikely to infect humans; they are primarily responsible for infections in cattle and horses.
- Group D. Group D primarily contains enterococci, which grow in the digestive tract. The most important organism in this group is *S. bovis*, which is responsible for many cases of bacterial endocarditis, an inflammation of the tissue that lines the valves of the heart.

Demographics

The demographics of streptococcal diseases vary widely, depending on their severity and whether there is a vaccine for the specific disease. For example, there are millions of cases of strep throat and mild *GAS* infections of the skin each year. By contrast, there are only about 600 cases of necrotizing fascitiis in the United States each year. About 46 out of every 1000 people over the age of 65 develop streptococcal **pneumonia** each year.

An example of the difference made by the introduction of a vaccine is pneumonia caused by *S. pneumoniae*. Before 2002, *S. pneumoniae* caused between 100,000 and 135,000 hospitalizations for pneumonia each year and 6 million cases of otitis media (infection of the middle ear). Since the introduction of a vaccine in 2002, the number of hospitalizations for pneumonia caused by this specific streptococcus has dropped to 13 cases per 100,000 people in the general population.

With regard to seniors, streptococci are responsible for about 70 percent of cases of endocarditis and 50 percent of all cases of pneumonia in this age group. In many cases, however, the specific organism that causes these illnesses is never identified.

Bacterial endocarditis is on the rise among the elderly population in recent years because of the increased number of seniors who have had heart valves replaced and the increased incidence of hospital-acquired infections. About ¼ of all cases of endocarditis occur in people over 60; elderly men are 8 times as

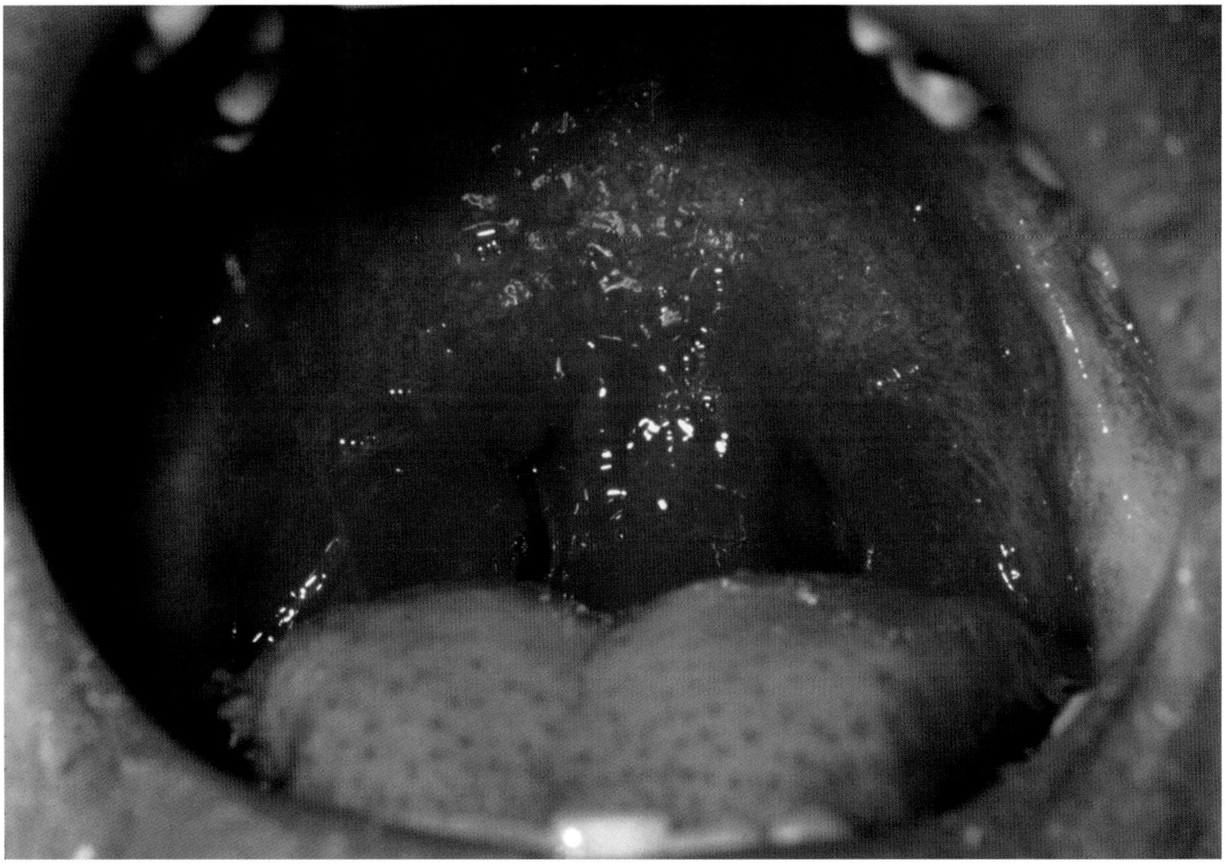

Red and inflamed throat from an infection caused by Streptococcus bacteria. *(Dr. P. Marazzi/Science Photo Library/Photo Researchers, Inc. Reproduced by permission.)*

likely to develop endocarditis as elderly women. In addition to a history of heart surgery, other risk factors for endocarditis include hardening of the arteries and congenital heart malformations.

Streptococcal skin infections are particularly common in seniors; the highest incidence of erysipelas is in people between 60 and 80 years of age.

Causes and symptoms

This section will describe the diseases caused by streptococci that are most likely to affect seniors. It is important to keep in mind, however, that the same species of streptococcus can cause several different diseases, and that some of the diseases described here can be caused by organisms other than streptococci.

Strep throat

Strep throat is caused by Group A streptococci, usually *S. pyogenes*. It is spread by direct contact with the nasal discharges of an infected person or by respiratory droplets in the air; in a few rare cases, seniors have gotten strep throat from contaminated food. The incubation period is between two and five days.

The most noticeable symptom of strep throat is the sudden onset of severe sore throat; the patient may find it hard to talk or even swallow. A fever of 101°F or higher is typical, as are white spots or patches on the tonsils, sore or swollen lymph nodes in the neck, and the absence of a cough. Some patients also develop a headache and skin rash. The patient usually feels better within five days to a week, but may be contagious for several weeks.

Endocarditis

Endocarditis in seniors is most likely to be caused by Group B streptococci or enterococci. The disease develops when the streptococci enter the bloodstream (often through surgical incisions or open sores on the skin) and settle on the tissues lining the valves of the heart. If the surface of the valves has been changed or damaged in some way, it is easier for the streptococci to form a colony on the tissue and multiply.

The symptoms of endocarditis in seniors usually appear about 2 weeks after the bacteria entered the bloodstream. Not all patients have the same symptoms, but a common pattern is fever accompanied by back **pain**, night sweats, loss of appetite, and mental confusion. Some elderly patients may also develop rapid-onset dementia. About 40 percent of patients will develop skin problems, ranging from small tender nodules in the fingertips to pinpoint hemorrhages in the tissues lining the mouth or on the skin above the shoulder blades. Some patients will develop the signs of a **stroke** if the endocarditis is not detected early; this complication develops when the bacteria growing on the heart tissue form clumps that travel through the bloodstream and block some of the blood vessels in the brain.

Pneumonia

About half of all cases of pneumonia in seniors are caused by *S. pneumoniae*. Pneumonia develops when the streptococci are carried into the lungs from the mouth or throat by inhaling air containing the organisms, or more commonly, by **aspiration** (food or oral fluid getting into the airway because of abnormal swallowing). Seniors who are hospitalized are at increased risk of aspiration pneumonia because they often have poor **oral hygiene** and **swallowing problems**. The use of sedatives and painkillers is also a risk factor because these medications often slow down the patient's breathing.

The usual signs of pneumonia are fever, cough, and sputum (matter from the throat or lungs brought up by coughing). Many elderly patients with pneumonia may have **delirium** or mental confusion as the most noticeable symptom, however; only about half of seniors have high fever as an early symptom of streptococcal pneumonia.

Skin and wound infections

Seniors may develop skin infections caused by streptococci belonging to either Group A or Group B. One of the more common skin infections caused by *S. pyogenes* is erysipelas, also known as Saint Anthony's fire. Erysipelas is an infection of the dermis, the portion of the skin lying below the epidermis. It develops when *S. pyogenes* gets beneath the epidermis through a crack in the skin, a surgical incision, a patch of eczema, or an ulcer. Within 48 hours, the area of infection becomes red and swollen, with a sharply raised edge. It is bright red or orange in color and is painful to touch. Erysipelas is most likely to appear on the face, arms or legs, but may affect almost any area of the body. In addition to the rash, the patient typically develops a high fever, chills, headache, nausea and vomiting, and fatigue.

Cellulitis is another infection caused by *S. pyogenes* that is likely to occur in the elderly and in others with weakened immune systems. Like erysipelas, cellulitis develops when streptococci get below the outer layer of skin through insect bites, recent surgical incisions, patches of eczema, or other skin rashes that have been scratched open. Cellulitis differs from erysipelas in that it is usually slower to develop and does not have a sharp border between affected and unaffected skin.

Diagnosis

Diagnosis of streptococcal infections begins with a physical examination of the affected part of the body. In the case of strep throat, the doctor will look inside the patient's throat to examine the tonsils, touch the lymph nodes in the neck, and record the patient's temperature. The next step is a rapid strep test, which involves swabbing the back of the throat to collect a sample of mucus. The test takes about 15 minutes to yield results. Because the rapid test has an error rate of about 20 percent, the doctor will usually send another sample of mucus on a swab to a laboratory for culture. The results of this test take about 2 days.

Infective endocarditis is often diagnosed when the doctor listens to the senior's heart. A heart murmur can be heard in more than 90 percent of cases. The patient's spleen is often enlarged; this can be detected when the doctor palpates (feels) the patient's abdomen. The doctor may order an **echocardiogram**, which is a test that uses ultrasound to detect growths of bacteria on the heart valves as well as other abnormalities. The definitive diagnosis is provided by a culture of the patient's blood.

Streptococcal pneumonia is diagnosed by taking a chest x-ray and making a culture of the patient's blood.

Erysipelas and cellulitis are usually diagnosed by the appearance of the patient's skin. Blood cultures are usually not helpful in diagnosing these conditions.

Treatment

Treatment of streptococcal infections depends on the location of the disease and the type of organism involved.

- Strep throat: Antibiotics are usually given for strep throat, most commonly a 10-day course of penicillin or erythromycin (for patients who are allergic to penicillin.) The patient may also be given ibuprofen or acetaminophen to bring down the fever. It is important for the patient to take the complete course of antibiotic even if the symptoms go away in a day or two in order to prevent possible complications. Complications of *S. pyogenes* throat infections include otitis media (ear infection), rheumatic fever, glomerulonephritis (inflammation of small blood vessels in the kidneys), or meningitis (inflammation of the membranes overlying the brain).

- Endocarditis: Most species of streptococci that cause endocarditis are sensitive to penicillin and ceftriaxone. The usual treatment schedule is four weeks of intravenous penicillin in doses of 12 million to 18 million units every 24 hours or 2 g of ceftriaxone (Rocephin) in a single daily dose given intravenously or intramuscularly. The penicillin can be administered continuously or in six divided doses. In some cases the patient may need surgery after the antibiotic treatment to replace damaged heart valves.
- Pneumonia: Streptococcal pneumonia is treated with a combination of antibiotics and respiratory therapy (suctioning of chest secretions or chest percussion). The antibiotics usually given for streptococcal pneumonia are penicillin, a first-generation cephalosporin, levofloxacin, or a macrolide antibiotic.
- Erysipelas and cellulitis are treated by a 10-day course of penicillin or erythromycin, given either orally or intramuscularly. Cellulitis may also be treated with ceftriaxone given intravenously. The affected limb should be elevated and treated with wet saline dressings to bring down inflammation and swelling. Some patients with cellulites may require surgery to drain the infection if treatment has been delayed. Hospitalization is not usually needed unless the senior has an immune disorder.

Nutrition/Dietetic concerns

Seniors with strep throat should be careful to drink plenty of fluids even if their throat hurts because fever causes the body to lose fluids more rapidly. They should avoid coffee or other beverages containing **caffeine** and drink soup broth or soft drinks containing sugar instead.

Therapy

Therapy for streptococcal infections is intended to kill the organisms causing the infection as well as relieve the patient's symptoms. In most cases the senior will be given **antibiotics** either by mouth or intravenously. Treatment of pneumonia may require suctioning or other forms of treatment to remove secretions from the lungs and airway.

QUESTIONS TO ASK YOUR DOCTOR

- What can I do to protect myself against streptococcal infections?
- If I am allergic to penicillin, what medications can I take for streptococcal infections?
- When should I receive a dose of pneumonia vaccine?

Prognosis

The prognosis of streptococcal infections varies considerably:

- Strep throat: Most seniors will recover completely in a week to 10 days.
- Endocarditis: The prognosis depends on the speed of diagnosis and treatment. The mortality rate for streptococcal endocarditis is about 25 percent.
- Pneumonia: The prognosis depends on the senior's basic health and the presence of other diseases or disorders. Elderly patients who are basically healthy can recover in four to six weeks with appropriate treatment. Those with cancer, heart failure, diabetes, Alzheimer's disease, and chronic obstructive pulmonary disease, however, are likely to have severe complications from pneumonia and may be given end-of-life palliative care. The mortality rate in seniors with bacterial pneumonia runs as high as 47 percent in those with cancer or other systemic diseases.
- Skin infections: The prognosis is usually good, especially if the infection is treated early. The mortality rate for cellulitis in seniors with weakened immune systems is reported to be about 5 percent.

Prevention

Streptococcal infections of the upper respiratory tract can be prevented by avoiding contact with infected persons and by washing one's hands frequently. The risk of endocarditis can be reduced by giving the senior an antibiotic (usually amoxicillin, ampicillin, or clindamycin) an hour before dental work or a procedure involving the mouth, throat, or esophagus. This prophylaxis minimizes the possibility

KEY TERMS

Agar—A gel-like substance derived from red seaweed that is used to make a culture medium for growing bacteria on laboratory plates.

Aspiration—The passage of food from the throat into the airway during swallowing rather than further down the esophagus.

Cellulitis—An infection of the deeper layers of the skin caused by streptococci or other bacteria entering through a break in the skin.

Endocarditis—An inflammation of the tissues lining the inside of the heart and its valves.

Enterococci—Streptococci that live in the digestive tract. Most of these organisms are Group D beta-hemolytic streptococci.

Erysipelas—An acute bacterial infection of the lower layer of the skin, most often caused by *S. pyogenes*. Its name comes from a Greek word meaning "red skin." It is sometimes known as Saint Anthony's fire.

Gram-positive—A term that refers to the amount of a crystal violet dye picked up by a bacterium during the Gram stain process. A Gram-positive organism looks blue or violet under a microscope whereas Gram-negative bacteria look red or pink. Streptococci are Gram-positive bacteria.

Hemolysis—The destruction of red blood cells, whether by bacteria or some other agent.

Necrotizing fasciitis—An infection of the deeper layers of skin and connective tissue caused by bacteria, most commonly *S. pyogenes*. Necrotizing fasciitis is sometimes called flesh-eating bacteria disease.

Prophylaxis—A measure intended to preserve health or prevent the spread of disease. Taking an antibiotic before oral surgery to prevent bacteria from entering the bloodstream is an example of prophylaxis.

Sputum—Matter from the lungs or throat that is brought up by coughing.

of streptococci getting into the senior's bloodstream through small breaks in the tissues of the mouth or throat.

Quitting **smoking** lowers a senior's risk of pneumonia, as does immunization with a vaccine against *S. pneumoniae* that was developed in the early 2000s. The pneumonia vaccine is recommended for all persons over the age of 65. Healthy seniors need only one immunization; those with diabetes, **cancer**, kidney failure, **chronic obstructive pulmonary disease**, or kidney disease should be reimmunized every 6 to 10 years.

The risk of streptococcal skin infections can be lowered by proper care of the skin, proper care of surgical incisions, and prompt treatment of any open sores, insect bites, and other **skin lesions**. In addition, seniors should avoid scratching patches of eczema or other skin rashes.

Caregiver concerns

Care givers for seniors with streptococcal infections should be careful to:

- Make sure that the senior takes any antibiotic that is prescribed according to the doctor's directions and completes the full course of the medication.
- Keep a senior with a streptococcal infection away from other people until he or she is no longer infectious. The senior's clothing, bedding, towels, and food utensils should be washed separately from the rest of the family's laundry or dishes.
- Ask the senior's doctor about antibiotic prophylaxis prior to dental work or other minor surgical procedures.
- Request home health care if necessary for a senior recovering from pneumonia, and keep in close contact with the doctor, particularly if the senior develops delirium.
- Check the senior's skin for any signs of open sores, ulcers, cuts, or other breaks in the skin, and make sure that the skin is kept clean and dry.
- Follow the doctor's instructions for care of surgical incisions and notify the doctor at once if there are signs of infection (warmth, redness, swelling, or pain).

Resources

BOOKS

Beers, Mark H., M. D., and Thomas V. Jones, MD. *Merck Manual of Geriatrics*, 3rd ed., Chapter 76, "Pulmonary Infections"; and Chapter 90, "Infective Endocarditis." Whitehouse Station, NJ: Merck, 2005.

Jevitz, Maria. "Streptococcus." Chapter 13 in Samuel Baron, ed., *Medical Microbiology*, 4th ed. New York: Churchill Livingstone, 1991.

PERIODICALS

Celestin, R., et al. "Erysipelas—A Common Potentially Dangerous Infection." *Acta Dermatolovenerologica Alpina* 16 (September 2007): 123–127.

Giessel, Barton E., Clint J. Koenig, and Robert L. Blake, Jr. "Management of Bacterial Endocarditis." *American Family Physician* 61 (March 15, 2000): 1725–1739.

Knoll, B., I. M. Tleyjeh, J. M. Steckelberg, et al. "Infective Endocarditis Due to Penicillin-Resistant Viridans Group Streptococci." *Clinical Infectious Diseases* 44 (June 15, 2007): 1585–1592.

Maestro, B., and J. M. Sanz. "Novel Approaches to Fight *Streptococcus pneumoniae. Recent Patents on Anti-Infective Drug Discovery* 2 (November 2007): 188–196.

O'Laughlin, R. E., A. Robertson, P. R. Cieslak, et al. "The Epidemiology of Invasive Group A Streptococcal Infection and Potential Vaccine Implications: United States, 2000-2004." *Clinical Infectious Diseases* 45 (October 1, 2007): 853–862.

Stulberg, Daniel L., Marc A. Penrod, and Richard A. Blatny. "Common Bacterial Skin Infections." *American Family Physician* 66 (July 1, 2002): 119–124.

OTHER

Centers for Disease Control and Prevention (CDC). *Group A Streptococcal (GAS) Disease.* Available online at http://www.cdc.gov/ncidod/dbmd/diseaseinfo/groupastreptococcal_g.htm [cited March 2, 2008].

Davis, Loretta. "Erysipelas." *eMedicine*, February 11, 2008. http://www.emedicine.com/derm/topic129.htm [cited March 2, 2008].

Micali, Giuseppe. "Cellulitis." *eMedicine*, October 19, 2006. http://www.emedicine.com/derm/topic464.htm [cited March 2, 2008].

Narayanan, Sharat K., and Charles S. Levy. "Streptococcus Group B Infections." *eMedicine*, March 24, 2006. http://www.emedicine.com/med/topic2185.htm [cited March 1, 2008].

Sharma, Sat, and Godfrey Harding. "Streptococcus Group A Infections." *eMedicine*, May 5, 2006. http://www.emedicine.com/med/topic2184.htm [cited March 1, 2008].

Sinave, Christian P. "Streptococcus Group D Infections." *eMedicine*, May 8, 2007. http://www.emedicine.com/med/topic2186.htm [cited March 1, 2008].

ORGANIZATIONS

Centers for Disease Control and Prevention (CDC), 1600 Clifton Road, Atlanta, GA, 30333, (404) 498-1515, (800) 311-3435, http://www.cdc.gov/.

Food and Drug Administration (FDA), 5600 Fishers Lane, Rockville, MD, 20857, (888) 463-6332, http://www.fda.gov/default.htm.

National Institute of Allergy and Infectious Diseases (NIAID), 6610 Rockledge Drive, MSC 6612, Bethesda, MD, 20892, (301) 496-5717, (866) 284-4107, (301) 402-3573, http://www3.niaid.nih.gov/.

Rebecca J. Frey Ph.D.

Stress

Definition

Stress is defined as an organism's total response to environmental demands or pressures. When stress was first studied in the 1950s, the term was used to denote both the causes and the experienced effects of these pressures. More recently, however, the word stressor has been used for the stimulus that provokes a stress response. One recurrent disagreement among researchers concerns the definition of stress in humans. Is it primarily an external response that can be measured by changes in glandular secretions, skin reactions, and other physical functions, or is it an internal interpretation of, or reaction to, a stressor; or is it both?

Description

Stress in humans results from interactions between persons and their environment that are perceived as straining or exceeding their adaptive capacities and threatening their well- being. The element of perception indicates that human stress responses reflect differences in personality, as well as differences in physical strength or general health.

Risk factors for stress-related illnesses are a mix of personal, interpersonal, and social variables. These factors include lack or loss of control over one's physical environment, and lack or loss of social support networks. People who are dependent on others (e.g., children or the elderly) or who are socially disadvantaged (because of race, gender, educational level, or similar factors) are at greater risk of developing stress-related illnesses. Other risk factors include feelings of helplessness, hopelessness, extreme fear or anger, and cynicism or distrust of others.

Causes and symptoms

Causes

The causes of stress can include any event or occurrence that a person considers a threat to his or her coping strategies or resources. Researchers generally agree that a certain degree of stress is a normal part of a living organism's response to the inevitable changes in its physical or social environment, and that positive, as well as negative, events can generate stress as well as negative occurrences. Stress-related disease, however, results from excessive and prolonged demands on an organism's coping resources. It is now believed that 80–90% of all disease is stress-related.

Recent research indicates that some vulnerability to stress is genetic. Scientists at the University of Wisconsin and King's College London discovered that people who inherited a short, or stress-sensitive, version of the serotonin transporter gene were almost three times as likely to experience **depression** following a stressful event as people with the long version of the gene. Further research is likely to identify other genes that affect susceptibility to stress.

One cause of stress that has affected large sectors of the general population around the world since 2001 is terrorism. The events of September 11, 2001, the sniper shootings in Virginia and Maryland and the Bali nightclub bombing in 2002, the **suicide** bombings in the Middle East in 2003, have all been shown to cause short-term symptoms of stress in people who read about them or watch television news reports as well as those who witnessed the actual events. Stress related to terrorist attacks also appears to affect people in countries far from the location of the attack as well as those in the immediate vicinity. It is too soon to tell how stress related to episodes of terrorism will affect human health over long periods of time, but researchers are already beginning to investigate this question. In 2004 the Centers for Disease Control and Prevention (CDC) released a report on the aftereffects of the World Trade Center attacks on rescue and recovery workers and volunteers. The researchers found that over half the 11,700 people who were interviewed met threshold criteria for a mental health evaluation. A longer-term evaluation of these workers is underway.

A new condition that has been identified since 9/11 is childhood traumatic grief, or CTG. CTG refers to an intense stress reaction that may develop in children following the loss of a parent, sibling, or other loved one during a traumatic event. As defined by the National Child Traumatic Stress Network (NCTSN), "Children with childhood traumatic grief experience the cause of [the loved one's] **death** as horrifying or terrifying, whether the death was sudden and unexpected (for example, due to homicide, suicide, motor vehicle accident,drug overdose, natural disaster, war, terrorism, and so on) or due to natural causes (**cancer**, **heart attack**, and so forth). Even if the manner of death does not appear to others to be sudden, shocking, or frightening, children who perceive the death in this way may develop childhood traumatic grief. In this condition, even happy thoughts and memories of the deceased person remind children of the traumatic way in which the deceased died." More information on the identification and treatment of childhood traumatic grief can be obtained from the NCTSN web site, http://www.nctsnet.org/nccts/nav.do?pid=hom_main.

Symptoms

The symptoms of stress can be either physical or psychological. Stress-related physical illnesses, such as **irritable bowel syndrome**, heart attacks, arthritis, and chronic **headaches**, result from long-term overstimulation of a part of the nervous system that regulates the heart rate, **blood pressure**, and digestive system. Stress-related emotional illness results from inadequate or inappropriate responses to major changes in one's life situation, such as marriage, completing one's education, becoming a parent, losing a job, or retirement. Psychiatrists sometimes use the term adjustment disorder to describe this type of illness. In the workplace, stress-related illness often takes the form of burnout—a loss of interest in or ability to perform one's job due to long-term high stress levels. For example, palliative care nurses are at high risk of burnout due to their inability to prevent their patients from **dying** or even to relieve their physical suffering in some circumstances.

Diagnosis

When the doctor suspects that a patient's illness is connected to stress, he or she will take a careful history that includes stressors in the patient's life (family or employment problems, other illnesses, etc.). Many physicians will evaluate the patient's personality as well, in order to assess his or her coping resources and emotional response patterns. There are a number of personality inventories and psychological tests that doctors can use to help diagnose the amount of stress that the patient experiences and the coping strategies that he or she uses to deal with them. A variation on this theme is to identify what the patient perceives as threatening as well as stressful. Stress-related illness can be diagnosed by primary care doctors, as well as by those who specialize in psychiatry. The doctor will need to distinguish between **adjustment disorders** and **anxiety** or mood disorders, and between psychiatric disorders and physical illnesses (e.g., thyroid activity) that have psychological side effects.

Treatment

Recent advances in the understanding of the many complex connections between the human mind and body have produced a variety of mainstream approaches to stress-related illness. Present treatment regimens may include one or more of the following:

- Medications. These may include drugs to control blood pressure or other physical symptoms of stress, as well as drugs that affect the patient's mood (tranquilizers or antidepressants).

- Stress management programs. These may be either individual or group treatments, and usually involve analysis of the stressors in the patient's life. They often focus on job or workplace-related stress.
- Behavioral approaches. These strategies include relaxation techniques, breathing exercises, and physical exercise programs including walking.
- Massage. Therapeutic massage relieves stress by relaxing the large groups of muscles in the back, neck, arms, and legs.
- Cognitive therapy. These approaches teach patients to reframe or mentally reinterpret the stressors in their lives in order to modify the body's physical reactions.
- Meditation and associated spiritual or religious practices. Recent studies have found positive correlations between these practices and stress hardiness.

Alternative treatment

Treatment of stress is one area in which the boundaries between traditional and alternative therapies have changed in recent years, in part because some forms of physical **exercise** (**yoga**, **tai chi**, aikido) that were once associated with the counterculture have become widely accepted as useful parts of mainstream stress reduction programs. Other alternative therapies for stress that are occasionally recommended by mainstream medicine include aromatherapy, dance therapy, **biofeedback**, nutrition-based treatments (including dietary guidelines and **nutritional supplements**), **acupuncture**, homeopathy, and herbal medicine.

Prognosis

The prognosis for recovery from a stress-related illness is related to a wide variety of factors in a person's life, many of which are genetically determined (race, sex, illnesses that run in families) or beyond the individual's control (economic trends, cultural stereotypes and prejudices). It is possible, however, for humans to learn new responses to stress and, thus, change their experiences of it. A person's ability to remain healthy in stressful situations is sometimes referred to as stress hardiness. Stress-hardy people have a cluster of personality traits that strengthen their ability to cope. These traits include believing in the importance of what they are doing; believing that they have some power to influence their situation; and viewing life's changes as positive opportunities rather than as threats.

KEY TERMS

Adjustment disorder—A psychiatric disorder marked by inappropriate or inadequate responses to a change in life circumstances. Depression following retirement from work is an example of adjustment disorder.

Biofeedback—A technique in which patients learn to modify certain body functions, such as temperature or pulse rate, with the help of a monitoring machine.

Burnout—An emotional condition, marked by tiredness, loss of interest, or frustration, that interferes with job performance,. Burnout is usually regarded as the result of prolonged stress.

Stress hardiness—A personality characteristic that enables persons to stay healthy in stressful circumstances. It includes belief in one's ability to influence the situation; being committed to or fully engaged in one's activities; and having a positive view of change.

Stress management—A category of popularized programs and techniques intended to help people deal more effectively with stress.

Stressor—A stimulus, or event, that provokes a stress response in an organism. Stressors can be categorized as acute or chronic, and as external or internal to the organism.

Prevention

Complete prevention of stress is neither possible nor desirable, because stress is an important stimulus of human growth and creativity, as well as an inevitable part of life. In addition, specific strategies for stress prevention vary widely from person to person, depending on the nature and number of the stressors in an individual's life, and the amount of control he or she has over these factors. In general, however, a combination of attitudinal and behavioral changes works well for most patients. The best form of prevention appears to be parental modeling of healthy attitudes and behaviors within the family.

Resources

BOOKS

Beers, Mark H., MD, and Robert Berkow, MD., editors. "Psychiatry in Medicine. " In *The Merck Manual of Diagnosis and Therapy.* Whitehouse Station, NJ: Merck Research Laboratories, 2004.

Pelletier, Kenneth R., MD. *The Best Alternative Medicine*, Part I, "Spirituality and Healing." New York: Simon & Schuster, 2002.

PERIODICALS

Blumenthal, J. A., M. Babyak, J. Wei, et al. "Usefulness of Psychosocial Treatment of Mental Stress-Induced Myocardial Ischemia in Men." *American Journal of Cardiology* 89 (January 15, 2002): 164-168.

Cardenas, J., K. Williams, J. P. Wilson, et al. "PSTD, Major Depressive Symptoms, and Substance Abuse Following September 11, 2001, in a Midwestern University Population" *International Journal of Emergency Mental Health* 5 (Winter 2003): 15–28.

Centers for Disease Control and Prevention. "Mental Health Status of World Trade Center Rescue and Recovery Workers and Volunteers—New York City, July 2002–August 2004." *Morbidity and Mortality Weekly Report* 53 (September 10, 2004): 812–815.

Gallo, L. C., and K. A. Matthews. "Understanding the Association Between Socioeconomic Status and Physical Health: Do Negative Emotions Play a Role?" *Psychological Bulletin* 129 (January 2003): 10–51.

Goodman, R. F., A. V. Morgan, S. Juriga, and E. J. Brown. "Letting the Story Unfold: A Case Study of Client-Centered Therapy for Childhood Traumatic Grief." *Harvard Review of Psychiatry* 12 (July-August 2004): 199–212.

Hawkley, L. C., and J. T. Cacioppo. "Loneliness and Pathways to Disease." *Brain, Behavior, and Immunity* 17, Supplement 1 (February 2003): S98–S105.

Latkin, C. A., and A. D. Curry. "Stressful Neighborhoods and Depression: A Prospective Study of the Impact of Neighborhood Disorder." *Journal of Health and Social Behavior* 44 (March 2003): 34–44.

Ottenstein, R. J. "Coping with Threats of Terrorism: A Protocol for Group Intervention." *International Journal of Emergency Mental Health* 5 (Winter 2003): 39–42.

Ritchie, L. J. "Threat: A Concept Analysis for a New Era." *Nursing Forum* 39 (July-September 2004): 13–22.

Surwit, R. S., M. A. van Tilburg, N. Zucker, et al. "Stress Management Improves Long-Term Glycemic Control in Type 2 Diabetes." *Diabetes Care* 25 (January 2002): 30-34.

West, P., and H. Sweeting. "Fifteen, Female and Stressed: Changing Patterns of Psychological Distress Over Time." *Journal of Child Psychology and Psychiatry* 44 (March 2003): 399–411.

White, K., L. Wilkes, K. Cooper, and M. Barbato. "The Impact of Unrelieved Patient Suffering on Palliative Care Nurses." *International Journal of Palliative Nursing* 10 (September 2004): 438–444.

ORGANIZATIONS

The American Institute of Stress. 124 Park Avenue, Yonkers, NY 10703 (914) 963-1200. Fax: (914) 965-6267. http://www.stress.org.

Centers for Disease Control and Prevention. 1600 Clifton Rd., NE, Atlanta, GA 30333. (800) 311-3435, (404) 639-3311. http://www.cdc.gov.

National Child Traumatic Stress Initiative. Center for Mental Health Services, Substance Abuse and Mental Health Services Administration, Department of Health and Human Services, 5600 Fishers Lane, Parklawn Building, Room 17C-26, Rockville, MD 20857. (301) 443-2940. http://www.nctsnet.org/nccts/nav.do?pid=hom_main.

National Institute of Mental Health (NIMH). 6001 Executive Boulevard, Room 8184, MSC 9663, Bethesda, MD 20892-9663. (301) 443-4513. http://www.nimh.nih.gov.

OTHER

National Center for Post-Traumatic Stress Disorder, Department of Veterans Affairs. *Fact Sheet: Survivors of Human-Caused and Natural Disasters.* http://www.ncptsd.org/facts/disasters/fs_survivors_disaster.html.

National Institute of Mental Health (NIMH) news release, July 17, 2003. "Gene More Than Doubles Risk of Depression Following Life Stresses." http://www.nimh.nih.gov/events/prgenestress.cfm.

Rebecca J. Frey Ph.D.

Stress test

Definition

A stress test is primarily used to identify coronary artery disease. It requires patients to **exercise** on a treadmill or exercise bicycle while their heart rate, **blood pressure**, electrocardiogram (ECG), and symptoms are monitored.

Purpose

The body requires more oxygen during exercise than when it is at rest. To deliver more oxygen during exercise, the heart has to pump more oxygen-rich blood. Because of the increased stress on the heart, exercise can reveal coronary problems that are not apparent when the body is at rest. This is why the stress test, though not perfect, remains the best initial, noninvasive, practical coronary test.

The stress test is particularly useful for detecting **ischemia** (inadequate supply of blood to the heart muscle) caused by blocked coronary arteries. Less commonly, it is used to determine safe levels of exercise in people with existing coronary artery disease.

Description

A technician affixes electrodes to the patient's chest, using adhesive patches with a special gel that

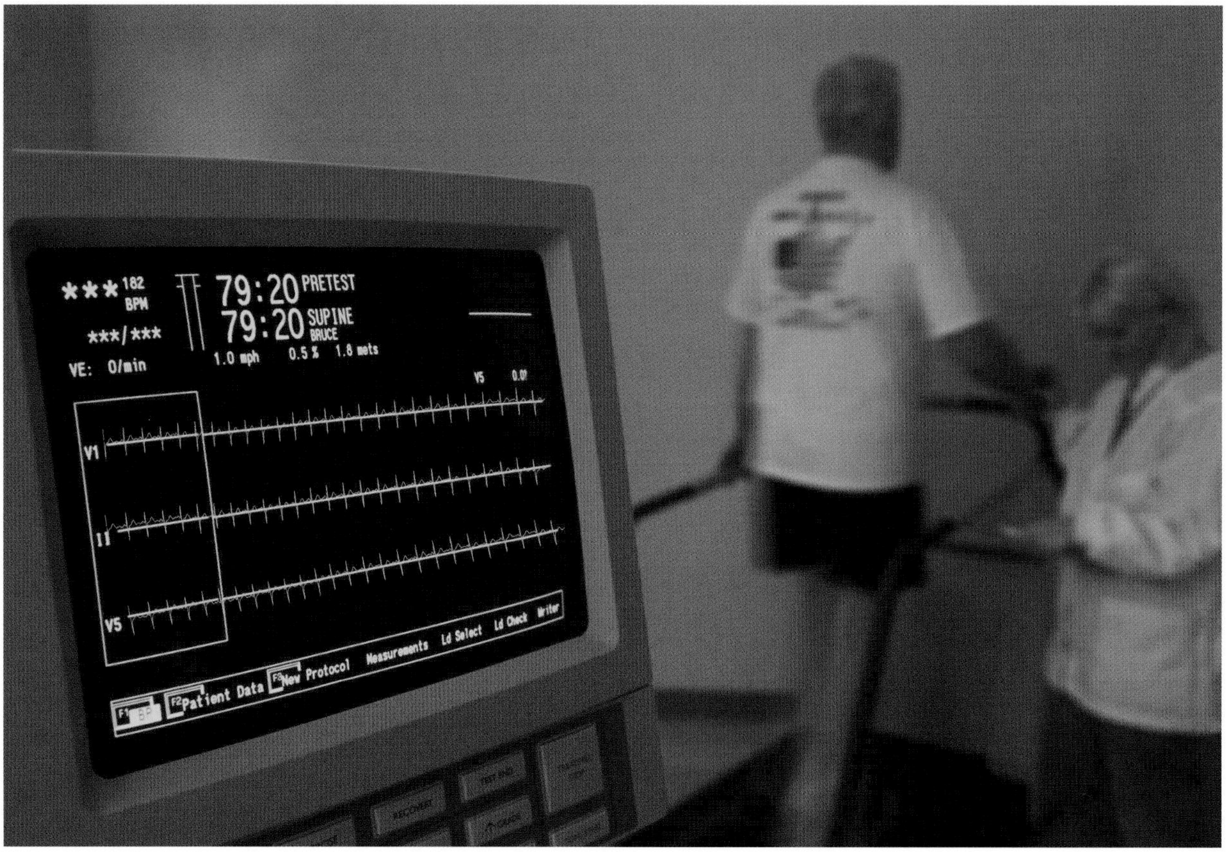

A nurse monitors a patient taking a stress test. *(George Mattei / Photo Researchers, Inc. Reproduced by permission.)*

conducts electrical impulses. Typically, electrodes are placed under each collarbone and each bottom rib, and six electrodes are placed across the chest in a rough outline of the heart. Wires from the electrodes are connected to an ECG, which records the electrical activity picked up by the electrodes.

The technician runs resting ECG tests while the patient is lying down, then standing up, and then breathing heavily for half a minute. These baseline tests can later be compared with the ECG tests performed while the patient is exercising. The patient's blood pressure is taken and the blood pressure cuff is left in place so that blood pressure can be measured periodically throughout the test.

The patient begins riding a stationary bicycle or walking on a treadmill. Gradually the intensity of the exercise is increased. For example, if the patient is walking on a treadmill, then the speed of the treadmill increases and the treadmill is tilted upward to simulate an incline. If the patient is on an exercise bicycle, then the resistance or "drag" is gradually increased. The patient continues exercising at increasing intensity until reaching the target heart rate (generally set at a minimum of 85% of the maximal predicted heart rate based on the patient's age) or experiences severe fatigue, **dizziness**, or chest **pain**. During the test, the patient's heart rate, ECG, and blood pressure are monitored.

Sometimes other tests, such as echocardiography or thallium scanning, are used in conjunction with the exercise stress test. For instance, recent studies suggest that women have a high rate of false negatives (results showing no problem when one exists) and false positives (results showing a problem when one does not exist) with the stress test. They may benefit from another test, such as exercise echocardiography. People who are unable to exercise may be injected with drugs, such as adenosine, which mimic the effects of exercise on the heart, and then given a thallium scan. The thallium scan or **echocardiogram** are particularly useful when the patient's resting ECG is abnormal. In such cases, interpretation of exercise-induced ECG abnormalities is difficult.

Preparation

Patients are usually instructed not to eat or smoke for several hours before the test. They should be

KEY TERMS

Angina—Chest pain from a poor blood supply to the heart muscle due to stenosis (narrowing) of the coronary arteries.

Cardiac arrhythmia—An irregular heart rate (frequency of heartbeats) or rhythm (the pattern of heartbeats).

Defibrillator—A device that delivers an electric shock to the heart muscle through the chest wall in order to restore a normal heart rate.

False negative—Test results showing no problem when one exists.

False positive—Test results showing a problem when one does not exist.

Hypertrophy—The overgrowth of muscle.

Ischemia—Dimished supply of oxygen-rich blood to an organ or area of the body.

advised to inform the physician about any medications they are taking, and to wear comfortable sneakers and exercise clothing.

Aftercare

After the test, the patient should rest until blood pressure and heart rate return to normal. If all goes well, and there are no signs of distress, the patient may return to his or her normal daily activities.

Risks

There is a very slight risk of myocardial infarction (a **heart attack**) from the exercise, as well as cardiac arrhythmia (irregular heart beats), **angina**, or cardiac arrest (about one in 100,000). The exercise stress test carries a very slight risk (one in 100,000) of causing a heart attack. For this reason, exercise stress tests should be attended by health care professionals with immediate access to defibrillators and other emergency equipment.

Patients are cautioned to stop the test should they develop any of the following symptoms:

- unsteady gait
- confusion
- skin that is grayish or cold and clammy
- dizziness or fainting
- a drop in blood pressure
- angina (chest pain)
- cardiac arrhythmias (irregular heartbeat)

Results

A normal result of an exercise stress test shows normal electrocardiogram tracings and heart rate, blood pressure within the normal range, and no angina, unusual dizziness, or shortness of breath.

A number of abnormalities may appear on an exercise stress test. Examples of exercise-induced ECG abnormalities are ST segment **depression** or heart rhythm disturbances. These ECG abnormalities may indicate deprivation of blood to the heart muscle (ischemia) caused by narrowed or blocked coronary arteries. Stress test abnormalities generally require further diagnostic evaluation and therapy.

Caregiver concerns

Patients must be well prepared for a stress test. They should not only know the purpose of the test, but also signs and symptoms that indicate the test should be stopped. Physicians, nurses, and ECG technicians can ensure patient safety by encouraging them to immediately communicate discomfort at any time during the stress test.

Resources

BOOKS

Ahya, Shubhada N., Kellie Flood, and Subramanian Paranjothi. *The Washington Manual of Medical Therapeutics,* 30th ed. Philadelphia: Lippincott Williams & Wilkins, 2001, pp. 96–100.

ORGANIZATIONS

American Heart Association. 7272 Greenville Avenue, Dallas, TX 75231. (214) 373-6300. http://www.amhrt.org.

National Heart, Lung, and Blood Institute. Information Center. PO Box 30105, Bethesda, MD 20824-0105. (301) 951-3260. http://www.nhlbi.nih.gov.

Barbara Wexler MPH
Lee A. Shratter M.D.

Stroke

Definition

Brain cells need oxygen and nutrients to function properly. When blood flow to the brain is interrupted, brain cells can begin to die and a person can experience a stroke, also called a brain attack. Damage from a stroke can temporarily or permanently disable a person's movement, speech, and cognition.

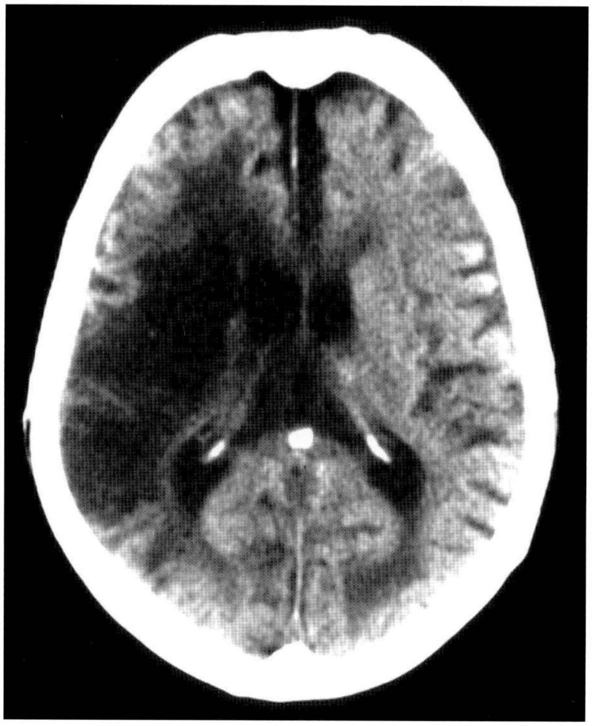

This cross sectional unenhanced CT of the brain in an elderly person shows the typical appearance of a large region of old infarction (stroke), involving the right (on your left) middle cerebral artery vascular territory. *(Living Art Enterprises, LLC / Photo Researchers, Inc. Reproduced by permission.)*

Percentage of people in the United States age 65 and over who reported having a stroke, by sex and by race, 2005–2006

Sex	Percent
Men	10.4%
Women	8.4%
Total	9.3%
Race	**Percent**
White	8.9%
Black	15.6%
Hispanic or Latino	6.5%

Data is based on a 2-year average from 2005–2006.

SOURCE: National Health Interview Survey, National Center for Health Statistics, Centers for Disease Control and Prevention, U.S. Department of Health and Human Services

(Illustration by GGS Information Services. Cengage Learning, Gale)

Description

A stroke occurs when blood flow to the brain is blocked or stopped. Strokes generally fall into two categories: strokes that occur when blood flow is blocked and strokes that occur because of bleeding in the brain.

Ischemic strokes are the most common cause of stroke and occur when a blood vessel in the brain or neck becomes blocked. Ischemic strokes comprise 87 percent of all strokes, and are not generally fatal.

Three conditions may contribute to the **ischemia**, or blockage.

Thrombosis: When a blood clot forms in a blood vessel in the brain or neck. Embolism: When a clot moves from another part of the body to the brain or neck. Stenosis: When an artery in or leading to the brain becomes severely narrowed and impedes blood flow.

Prior to an ischemic stroke, a person may experience mini strokes, also known as **transient ischemic attacks** (TIA). These strokes have symptoms similar to those of a stroke, but the symptoms are temporary and disappear. For most people, TIAs do not precede a stroke, but among people who have had one or more TIAs, more than a third will later have a stroke.

Strokes that occur because of bleeding in the brain are called hemorrhagic strokes. Intracerebral hemorrhages comprise 10 percent of all strokes. This type of hemorrhagic stroke occurs when a diseased blood vessel inside the brain bursts and blood begins leaking inside the brain. Subarachnoid hemorrhages, which occur when a blood vessel outside the brain ruptures and causes the skull surrounding the brain to fill with blood, comprise 3 percent of all strokes.

Treating and rehabilitating stroke victims poses an enormous cost to the U.S. health care system. It is estimated that in 2008, the direct and indirect costs of stroke will reach $65.5 billion.

Demographics

Stroke ranks as the third leading killer in the United States, behind **heart disease** and **cancer**. According to the American Stroke Association, one out of every 16 deaths in 2004 was attributable to stroke. Stroke also leads the list of causes of serious, long-term disability in the United States.

New strokes are more common than recurrent strokes. About 780,000 people experience strokes annually, about 600,000 of which are new strokes and 180,000 of which are recurrent strokes.

Among people ages 55 to 74, men have a slightly higher risk of stroke than women. In people ages 75 to 84, men and women have a similar risk of stroke. In people 85 and older, men are less likely to have a stroke than women. Also, more women die of stroke every year, in part because as a group, women live longer than men. Sixty-one percent of U.S. stroke deaths occur in women.

Stroke incidence also varies depending on racial/ethnic group. Compared to whites, blacks have almost twice the risk of having a first-time stroke and they have a greater risk of **death** due to stroke. Mexican Americans also have an increased incidence of stroke overall, compared to whites, and an increased risk of having a stroke at a younger age.

In the United States, stroke risk and mortality rates may also be tied to geographic region. Researchers have found that people living in the "Stroke Belt," a region in the southwestern part of the United States that includes Alabama, Arkansas, Georgia, Indiana, Kentucky, Louisiana, Mississippi, North Carolina, South Carolina, Tennessee, and Virginia, had stroke death rates more than 10 percent higher than the U.S. average. Men and women in both black and white ethnic groups living in the Stroke Belt had higher stroke death rates than their counterparts in other regions of the country.

Causes and symptoms

Several untreatable and treatable risk factors exist that increase a person's risk of having a stroke.

Risk factors for stroke that cannot be changed include:

- Age: According to the American Stroke Association, the risk of having a stroke doubles for each decade of life after age 55.
- Gender: Overall men have a greater risk of stroke, but women have a greater risk of death due to stroke.
- Family history and ethnicity: If a close relative (parent, grandparent, or sibling) has had a stroke, a person has a greater risk of having one, too. In addition, blacks have a greater stroke risk than whites.
- Having had stroke warning signs or a previous stroke.

The good news for many older adults is that the stroke risk factors that follow can be reduced by making some changes to lifestyle, **exercise** habits, and nutrition.

- High blood pressure, also called hypertension, is one of the main factors that puts a person at risk for stroke.
- Smoking: Dependence on cigarettes damages the cardiovascular system and increases the risk of stroke. The risk of ischemic stroke in smokers is double that of nonsmokers.
- Heart disease: People with atherosclerosis, or fatty deposit buildup on the walls of the arteries, are prone to having narrowed arteries that may become blocked by blood clots. Older adults with heart defects or heart failure also have an increased risk of stroke.
- Atrial fibrillation: This problem with the heart's rhythm raises the risk of blood clots and increases a person's risk of stroke five-fold.
- Taking estrogen plus progestin during menopause: A large clinical trial in women found that taking estrogen plus progestin increased ischemic stroke risk by 44 percent.
- Diabetes: Having diabetes on its own increases a person's risk for stroke, but having high cholesterol, high blood pressure, and being overweight, conditions that often go hand in hand with diabetes, send stroke risk percentages spiraling higher.
- High cholesterol: Having high cholesterol levels increases the risk for stroke.
- Depression: In people under age 65, risk of stroke was more than 5 times higher in people with depressive symptoms.
- Poor diet and physical inactivity: High-fat, high-sodium, high-cholesterol diets and lack of exercise contribute to numerous medical problems and increase the risk of stroke.
- Alcohol and drug abuse: Abusing these substances also increases a person's risk for a stroke.

Stroke symptoms often occur suddenly and without warning. Older adults who experience stroke symptoms or their caregivers should call 911 or go to a hospital emergency department immediately.

Symptoms of stroke, or loss of oxygen and blood flow to the brain, include sudden:

- weakness or numbness in the leg, arm, or face, especially on one side of the body
- confusion or difficulty speaking or understanding
- vision problems in one or both eyes
- dizziness, problems walking, or loss of balance
- severe headache that comes on suddenly and doesn't have another cause
- drowsiness
- nausea or vomiting

In many cases, these warning signs of a stroke occur suddenly and then disappear. If these symptoms go away quickly, they are easy to ignore, but that early resolution does not mean they are not dangerous.

Diagnosis

When making a stroke diagnosis, health care professionals first obtain a complete medical history. A person with stroke symptoms (or a family member or **caregiver**, if the person cannot communicate) will be asked about his current and previous symptoms, medical problems or surgeries he has had previously, and medications he is taking. A person having stroke symptoms will also be examined and health care professionals will check his reflexes, strength, sensation, and overall coordination. Questions may also be asked to determine whether the patient's memory, speech, or cognition is impaired.

Laboratory tests and procedures may also be helpful when making a stroke diagnosis. To look at the brain, skull, or spinal cord, health care professionals may use computed tomography (CT) scans or **magnetic resonance imaging** (MRI) scans. Getting a view of the blood vessels that supply the brain may be accomplished by using ultrasound waves to take a picture of the carotid arteries in the neck (this is called a **carotid ultrasound** or carotid Doppler). Transcranial Doppler or magnetic resonance angiogram may also be used to see the blood vessels in the neck or brain. Another test, called a cerebral arteriogram, uses a catheter inserted in the arm or leg to find any abnormalities of the blood vessels, such as blockages or narrowing.

Other tests, including echocardiograms and electrocardiograms (EKG), may be used to check the heart's function. X-rays, urine samples, and blood oxygen tests may be used to check for infection, and neurologic tests, such as electroencephalogram or nerve conduction tests, may be done if a health care professional suspects a seizure or nerve problem is causing symptoms. Lumbar puncture (LP or spinal tap), the removal of fluid that surrounds the brain and spinal cord, may be used to check for bleeding from a subarachnoid hemorrhage. If doctors think a person has had a stroke, they also usually order blood tests to measure chemicals in the blood, check cholesterol levels, and identify clotting problems that may contribute to stroke.

Treatment

If a person has been diagnosed with a stroke, there are many steps on the road to recovery.

The first stage involves acute care treatment. During this type of treatment, health care professionals work to help the patient survive and prevent another stroke.

People who have had strokes may need to take **antiplatelet drugs** (such as **aspirin**, clopidogrel, ticlopidine, and aspirin/dipyridamole) to prevent blood clotting and reduce the risk of recurrent thrombotic stroke. Others may need to take anticoagulants (such as warfarin and heparin) to prevent clot formation.

Sometimes thrombolytic agents are used to treat an ongoing ischemic stroke. If a person having a stroke gets medical treatment within 3 hours of stroke onset, thrombolytic drugs such as recombinant tissue plasminogen activator (rt-PA) can be used to dissolve the blood clot that is blocking blood flow to the brain. Because these drugs can increase bleeding, they should only be used by a doctor who has carefully examined a suspected stroke patient.

Surgical procedures such as carotid endarterectomy may also be performed to reduce the risk of acute or recurrent stroke. In this procedure, surgeons open the carotid artery in the neck and scrape plaque from the artery's walls, thereby reducing the chance that **blood clots** might lodge in the narrowed artery and cause a stroke.

Devices can also be inserted in the carotid artery to reduce stroke risk. In a procedure called an **angioplasty**, a small tube called a stent is placed over the artery to help keep it open and reduce the risk of blockage that could cause a stroke. Stents are usually used in people who have had TIAs or who have at least half of their arteries blocked. People who have 80 percent blockage but who have never experienced a stroke might also be advised to have a stent placed.

Stroke treatment also involves recovery and rehabilitation. After acute care, some of the abilities a person has may begin to come back, which is called spontaneous recovery. Spontaneous recovery occurs in the days, weeks, and months following the stroke. Rehabilitation involves helping someone who has had a stroke recover some of the abilities that were lost. Rehabilitation can take place in the hospital, at a recovery facility, or at the patient's home.

Nutrition/Dietetic concerns

Eating a **diet** that contains too much fat, cholesterol, and **sodium** (salt) can increase stroke risk. Health care professionals recommend that person who has had a stroke or has stroke risk factors should reduce stroke risk by taking the following steps.

Consume foods lower in fat. Eating a diet filled with saturated fat and cholesterol contributes to **atherosclerosis**, a factor that increases the risk of stroke. Older adults can cut the fat by choosing low-fat or nonfat dairy items, limiting oil or butter used in cooking, avoiding fried foods in favor of broiled or baked versions, and trimming fat or skin from meats and poultry.

Watch sodium intake. Eating too many high-sodium foods (sodium, or salt, is often used to preserve foods and add flavor) can increase **blood pressure** and thereby increase the risk of stroke. To cut back on sodium, instead of highly processed foods, choose fresh fruits, vegetables, whole grains, and lean sources of protein. Also, some evidence suggests that adding fiber to the diet might help reduce cholesterol levels. **High cholesterol** levels are another risk factor for stroke.

Limit alcohol consumption. Research has shown that drinking up to two drinks a day can cut stroke risk in half, but drinking too much does more harm than good. Consuming more than two drinks a day increases stroke risk three-fold. Also, alcohol interacts dangerously with many medicines, so people taking medication should talk to their doctors before consuming any amount of alcohol.

Therapy

Older adults who have experienced a stroke may require a variety of therapies during the rehabilitative process.

Physical therapy, which the National Institute of Neurological Disorders and Stroke calls the "cornerstone of the rehabilitative process," helps people with stroke relearn balance, movement, and coordination. This type of therapy is essential to help stroke victims learn to walk, sit, stand, and lie down, movements that may be difficult after experiencing a stroke.

Occupational therapy is also often used in post-stroke recovery. With this type of therapy, people who have experienced a stroke relearn how to do activities of daily living, such as eating and drinking, cooking, writing, toileting, and bathing.

For stroke victims who experience speech and language problems, speech therapy can help them understand speech and written words, form words themselves, and develop alternative ways of communicating.

Depression, **anxiety**, and frustration are a common aspect of the stroke survivor's experience, and psychological counseling can help survivors deal with these problems. Sometimes, cognitive behavioral therapy or medication might be recommended for the survivor to alleviate post-stroke psychiatric problems.

QUESTIONS TO ASK YOUR DOCTOR

- Do I have any of the risk factors for stroke, such as high cholesterol or high blood pressure?
- If I experience any of the warning signs of stroke, what should I do?
- Is there anything I can do now to reduce my risk of stroke?
- I've had TIAs. What can I expect in terms of stroke risk?
- I've survived a stroke. What can I do to improve my recovery and regain function?
- I'm caring for someone who's had a stroke. Can you recommend a support group for me?

Prognosis

People who experience one stroke often go on to have others. According to the National Stroke Association, of the people who have a stroke every year, 5 to 14 percent will have an additional stroke within 1 year. Within 5 years after an initial stroke, 24 percent of women and 42 percent of men will experience recurrent stroke.

In people between 45 and 64, 8 to 12 percent of ischemic strokes and 37 to 38 percent of hemorrhagic strokes cause death within a month.

Prevention

Lowering stroke risk often involves making lifestyle changes, such as sticking to a low-sodium, **low-fat diet**, to improve circulation and reduce the risk of diseases that can influence stroke risk, such as diabetes, heart disease, high cholesterol, and high blood pressure.

Exercise, especially moderate to high intensity exercise, has also been associated with a lowered risk of stroke. In a large Japanese study of 73,265 men and women, risk of stroke death dropped 29 percent in men and 20 percent in women who got the most intense exercise.

Some older adults might also need to take medication to lower blood pressure and cholesterol, two leading risk factors for stroke. Other adults who are diabetic need to follow their diabetes care plan and

KEY TERMS

Carotid endarterectomy—Procedure to open the carotid artery in the neck and scrape plaque from the artery's walls, thereby reducing the risk of stroke.

Hemorrhage—Bleeding from the blood vessels.

Ischemia—Blockage of blood flow due to obstruction of the blood vessels.

Stent—A small tube placed within an artery to help keep it open and reduce the risk of blockage that could cause a stroke

Transient ischemic attack (TIA)—Mini strokes that cause symptoms similar to those of a stroke, but which are temporary and disappear.

control their blood sugar levels carefully, through diet, exercise, and medications.

Caregiver concerns

Caregivers of people who have experienced a stroke will initially want to familiarize themselves with the physical, emotional, and cognitive changes that might occur in the post-stroke recovery period. Stroke victims may experience **memory loss**, confused behavior or poor judgment, depression, unpredictable or inappropriate emotions (a condition sometimes called involuntary emotional expression disorder), communication problems, problems dressing and grooming themselves and caring for their skin, problems eating, and **pain**.

To help prevent confusion in the stroke survivor, a caregiver needs to ensure that the survivor's environment is orderly and easy to navigate. If the stroke victim is having trouble dressing or feeding himself or herself, talk to the person's health care provider or stroke rehabilitation specialist about adaptive aids that may make independent living easier.

To deal with the emotional changes and depressive symptoms that often accompany the post-stroke recovery period, stroke victims might need behavioral therapy, antidepressant medications, or a combination of both.

Communication problems or difficulty with speech (referred to as aphasia) often occur after stroke because of damage to the areas of the brain that control communication. Caregivers might need to secure professional help to cope with these difficulties.

When caring for someone with a stroke, proper skin care is important, especially for survivors who spend lots of time sitting or in wheelchairs. Caregivers can help prevent bed sores by making sure the person changes position frequently and has pillows or other soft props to support disabled limbs.

Caring for a person who has had a stroke can be frightening, confusing, and frustrating for family members. To get emotional support in the post-stroke journey, caregivers can attend support groups for stroke victims and their families.

ORGANIZATIONS

American Heart Association/American Stroke Association, 7272 Greenville Avenue, Dallas, TX, 75231, 800-AHA-USA-1 (242-8721), http://www.americanheart.org; http://www.strokeassociation.org.

National Institute of Neurological Disorders and Stroke, P. O. Box 5801, Bethesda, MD, 20824, 301-496-5751, 800-352-9424, braininfo@ninds.nih.gov, http://www.ninds.nih.gov.

National Stroke Association, 9707 E. Easter Lane Building B, Centennial, CO, 80112, 800-787-6537, 303-649-1328, info@stroke.org, http://www.stroke.org.

Rehabilitation Institute of Chicago, 345 E. Superior Street, First Floor, Chicago, IL, 60611, 312-238-5433, 312-238-2860, lifecenter@ric.org, http://lifecenter.ric.org.

Stroke Association UK, Stroke House, 240 City Road, London, United Kingdom, EC1V 2PR, 020 7566 0300, info@stroke.org.uk, http://www.stroke.org.uk.

Amy Sutton

Substance abuse and dependence

Definition

Substance abuse is a pattern of drug, alcohol, or other substance use that creates many adverse results from its continual use. The characteristics of abuse are a failure to carry out obligations at home or work, continual use under circumstances that present a hazard (such as driving a car), and legal problems such as arrests. Use of the drug is persistent despite personal problems caused by the effects of the substance on self or others.

Substance dependence has been defined medically as a group of behavioral and physiological symptoms that indicate the continual, compulsive use of a substance in self-administered doses despite the problems related to the use of this substance. Sometimes Increased amounts are needed to achieve the desired effect or level of intoxication. Consequently the patient's tolerance for the drug increases. Withdrawal is a physiological and psychological change that occurs when the body's concentration of the substance declines in a person who has been a heavy user.

Description

Substance abuse and dependence cross all lines of race, culture, education, and socioeconomic status, leaving no group untouched by its devastating effects. A recent survey estimated that about 16 million citizens of the United States had used an illegal substance in the month preceding the study. Substance abuse is an enormous public health problem, with far-ranging effects throughout society. In addition to the toll substance abuse can take on one's physical health, it is considered an important factor in a wide variety of social problems, affecting rates of crime, domestic violence, **sexually transmitted diseases** (including HIV/AIDS), unemployment, homelessness, teen pregnancy, and failure in school. One study estimated that 20% of the total yearly cost of health care in the United States is spent on the effects of drug and **alcohol abuse**.

A wide range of substances can be abused. The most common classes include:

- opioids, including such prescription pain killers as morphine and Demerol, as well as illegal substances such as heroin
- benzodiazapines, including prescription drugs used for treating anxiety, such as Valium
- sedatives or "downers," including prescription barbiturate drugs commonly referred to as tranquilizers
- stimulants or "speed," including prescription amphetamines used for weight loss and in the treatment of attention deficit disorder
- cannabinoid drugs obtained from the hemp plant, including marijuana ("pot") and hashish
- cocaine-based drugs
- hallucinogenic or "psychedelic" drugs, including LSD, PCP or angel dust, and other PCP-type drugs
- inhalants, including gaseous drugs used in the medical practice of anesthesia, as well as such common substances as paint thinner, gasoline, glue
- alcoholic drinks, including beer, liquor, and wine

Those substances of abuse that are actually prescription medications may have been obtained on the street by fraudulent means or may have been a legal, medically indicated prescription that a person begins to use without regard to the directions of his/her physician.

A number of important terms must be defined in order to have a complete discussion of substance abuse. Drug tolerance refers to a person's body becoming accustomed to the symptoms produced by a specific quantity of a substance. When a person first begins taking a substance, he/she will note various mental or physical reactions brought on by the drug, some of which are the very changes in consciousness that the individual is seeking through substance use. Over time, the same dosage of the substance may produce fewer of the desired feelings. In order to continue to feel the desired effect of the substance, progressively higher drug doses must be taken.

Substance dependence is the phenomenon whereby a person becomes physically addicted to a substance. A substance-dependent person must have a particular dose or concentration of the substance in their bloodstream at any given moment in order to avoid the unpleasant symptoms associated with withdrawal from that substance. The common substances of abuse tend to exert either a depressive (slowing) or a stimulating (speeding up) effect on such basic bodily functions as respiratory rate, heart rate, and **blood pressure**. When a drug is stopped abruptly, the person's body will respond by overreacting to the substance's absence. Functions slowed by the abused substance will be suddenly speeded up, while previously stimulated functions will be suddenly slowed. This results in very unpleasant symptoms, known as withdrawal symptoms.

Addiction refers to the mind-state of a person who reaches a point where he/she must have a specific substance, even though the social consequences of substance use are clearly negative (loss of **relationships**, employment, housing). Craving refers to an intense hunger for a specific substance, to the point where this need essentially directs the individual's behavior. Craving is usually seen in both dependence and addiction. Such craving can be so strong that it overwhelms a person's ability to make any decisions which will possibly deprive him/her of the substance. Drug possession and use becomes the most important goal, and other forces (including the law) have little effect on changing the individual's substance-seeking behavior.

Causes and symptoms

There is not thought to be a single cause of substance abuse, though scientists are increasingly convinced that certain people possess a genetic predisposition that can affect the development of addictive behaviors. One theory holds that a particular nerve pathway in the brain, dubbed the "mesolimbic reward pathway," holds certain chemical characteristics that can increase the likelihood that substance use will ultimately lead to substance addiction. Certainly, however, other social factors are involved, including family problems and peer pressure. Primary mood disorders, such as **bipolar disorder**, **personality disorders**, and the role of learned behavior can influence the likelihood that a person will become substance dependent.

The symptoms of substance abuse may be related to its social effects as well as its physical effects. The social effects of substance abuse may include dropping out of school or losing a series of jobs, engaging in fighting and violence in relationships, and legal problems, ranging from driving under the influence to the commission of crimes committed to obtain the money needed to support an expensive drug habit.

Physical effects of substance abuse are related to the specific drug being abused:

- Opioid drug users may appear slowed in their physical movements and speech, may lose weight, exhibit mood swings, and have constricted (small) pupils.
- Benzodiazapine and barbiturate users may appear sleepy and slowed, with slurred speech, small pupils, and occasional confusion.
- Amphetamine users may have excessively high energy, inability to sleep, weight loss, rapid pulse, elevated blood pressure, occasional psychotic behavior and dilated (enlarged) pupils.
- Marijuana users may be sluggish and slow to react, exhibiting mood swings and red eyes with dilated pupils.
- Cocaine users may have wide variations in their energy level, severe mood disturbances, psychosis, paranoia, and a constantly runny nose. Crack cocaine may cause aggressive or violent behavior.
- Hallucinogenic drug users may display dilated pupils and bizarre behavior due to hallucinations. (Hallucinations arc imagincd sights, voiccs, sounds, or smells which seem completely real to the individual experiencing them.) LSD can cause flashbacks.

Other symptoms of substance abuse may be related to the form in which the substance is used. For example, heroin, certain other opioid drugs, and certain forms of cocaine may be injected using a needle and a hypodermic syringe. A person abusing an injectable substance may have "track marks"—outwardly visible signs of the site of an injection, with possible redness and swelling of the vein in which the substance was injected. Furthermore, poor judgment brought on by substance use can result in the injections being made under horrifyingly dirty conditions. These unsanitary conditions and the use of shared needles can cause infections of the injection sites, major infections of the heart, as well as infection with human immunodeficiency virus (HIV) (the virus that causes acquired immunodefiency syndrome, or **AIDS**), certain forms of **hepatitis** (a liver infection), and **tuberculosis**.

Cocaine is often taken as a powdery substance which is inhaled or "snorted" through the nose. This can result in frequent nose bleeds, sores in the nose, and even erosion of the nasal septum, the structure that separates the two nostrils. Cocaine can also be smoked.

Overdosing on a substance is a frequent complication of substance abuse. Drug overdose can be purposeful (with **suicide** as a goal), or caused by carelessness, the unpredictable strength of substances purchased from street dealers, mixing of more than one type of substance, or as a result of the ever-increasing doses which a person must take of those substances to which he or she has become tolerant. Substance overdose can be a life-threatening emergency, with the specific symptoms dependent on the type of substance used. Substances with depressive effects may dangerously slow the breathing and heart rate, drop the body temperature, and result in a general unresponsiveness. Substances with stimulatory effects may dangerously increase the heart rate and blood pressure, increase body temperature, and cause bizarre behavior. With cocaine, there is a risk of **stroke**.

Still other symptoms may be caused by unknown substances mixed with street drugs in order to "stretch" a batch. A health care worker faced with a patient suffering extreme symptoms may have no idea what other substance that person may have unwittingly put into his or her body. Thorough drug screening can help with this problem.

Diagnosis

The most difficult aspect of diagnosis involves addressing and overcoming the patient's denial. Denial is a psychological trait whereby a person is unable to allow him- or herself to acknowledge the reality of a situation. This may lead a person to completely deny his or her substance use, or may cause the person to greatly underestimate the degree of the problem and its effects on his or her life.

One of the simplest and most commonly used screening tools used by nursing staff or allied health professionals to begin the process of diagnosing substance abuse is called the CAGE questionnaire. CAGE refers to the first letters of each word that forms the basis of each of the four questions of the screening exam:

- Have you ever tried to Cut down on your substance use?
- Have you ever been Annoyed by people trying to talk to you about your substance use?
- Do you ever feel Guilty about your substance use?
- Do you ever need an Eye opener (use of the substance first thing in the morning) in order to start your day?

Other, longer lists of questions exist in order to try to determine the severity and effects of a person's substance abuse. Certainly, it is also relevant to determine whether anybody else in a person's family has ever suffered from substance or alcohol addiction.

A physical examination may reveal signs of substance abuse in the form of needle marks, tracks, trauma to the inside of the nostrils from snorting drugs, unusually large or small pupils. With the person's permission, substance use can also be detected by examining an individual's blood, urine, or hair in a laboratory. This drug testing is limited by sensitivity, specificity and the time elapsed since the person last used the drug.

Treatment

Treatment has several goals, which include helping a person deal with the uncomfortable and possibly life-threatening symptoms associated with withdrawal from an addictive substance (called detoxification), helping a person deal with the social effects which substance abuse has had on his or her life, and efforts to prevent relapse (resumed use of the substance). Individual or group psychotherapy is sometimes helpful.

Detoxification may take from several days to many weeks. Detoxification can be accomplished "cold turkey," by complete and immediate cessation of all substance use, or by slowly decreasing (tapering) the dose that a person is taking, to minimize the side effects of withdrawal. Some substances absolutely must be tapered, because "cold turkey" methods of detoxification are potentially life threatening. Alternatively, a variety of medications may be utilized to combat the unpleasant and threatening physical symptoms of withdrawal. A substance (such as methadone in the case of heroin addiction) may be substituted for the original substance of abuse, with gradual tapering of this substituted drug. In practice, many patients may be maintained on methadone and lead a reasonably normal life. Because of the rebound effects of fluctuating blood pressure, body temperature, heart and breathing rates, as well as the potential for bizarre behavior and hallucinations, a person undergoing withdrawal must be carefully monitored and treated appropriately.

A recent discovery for the treatment of opiate addiction is a medication called naltrexone. This medication blocks the receptors involved with the "high" produced by heroin. The drug is useful for many patients since it is does not produce physical dependence and has virtually zero potential for abuse. Scientists have found that unfortunately, many heroin addicts do not like to take naltrexone quite possibly because they enjoy the effects of opiates. Since the medication eliminates the craving for opiates, in one recent study only 15% of heroin addicts were still taking the drug after one month.

Alternative treatments for substance abuse include those specifically designed to aid a person who is suffering from the effects of withdrawal and the toxicities of the abused substance, as well as treatments which are intended to decrease a person's **stress** level, thus hopefully decreasing the likelihood that he or she will relapse.

Additional treatments thought to improve a person's ability to stop substance use include **acupuncture** and hypnotherapy. Ridding the body of toxins is believed to be aided by **hydrotherapy** (bathing regularly in water containing baking soda, sea salt, or Epsom salts). Hydrotherapy can include a constitutional effect where the body's vital force is stimulated and all organ systems are revitalized. Elimination of toxins is aided by hydrotherapy as well as by such herbs as milk thistle *(Silybum marianum)*, burdock *(Arctium lappa)*, a blood cleanser, and licorice *(Glycyrrhiza glabra)*. **Anxiety** brought on by substance withdrawal is thought to be lessened by using other herbs, which include valerian *(Valeriana officinalis)*, vervain *(Verbena officinalis)*, skullcap *(Scutellaria baicalensis)* and kava *(Piper methysticum)*.

Other treatments aimed at reducing the stress a person suffers while attempting substance withdrawal and throughout an individual's recovery process

KEY TERMS

Addiction—The state of being both physically and psychologically dependent on a substance.

Dependence—A state in which a person requires a steady concentration of a particular substance in order to avoid experiencing withdrawal symptoms.

Detoxification—A process whereby an addict is withdrawn from a substance.

Disease model of alcoholism—Also known as the Minnesota model, the disease model contends that alcoholism is a disease that alcoholism is chronic, progressive, and frequently fatal.

High—The altered state of consciousness that a person seeks when abusing a substance.

Street drug—A substance purchased from a drug dealer; it may be a legal substance, sold illicitly (without a prescription, and not for medical use), or it may be a substance which is illegal to possess.

Tolerance—A phenomenon whereby a drug user becomes physically accustomed to a particular dose of a substance, and requires ever-increasing dosages in order to obtain the same effects.

Withdrawal—Those side effects experienced by a person who has become physically dependent on a substance, upon decreasing the substance's dosage, or discontinuing its use.

include **biofeedback**, guided imagery, and various meditative arts, including **yoga** and **tai chi**. Alternative medicine also places a great emphasis on proper **nutrition**, for detoxification, healing, and sustained recovery.

Prognosis

After a person has successfully withdrawn from substance use, the even more difficult task of recovery begins. Recovery refers to the lifelong efforts of a person to avoid returning to substance use. The craving can be so strong, even years and years after initial withdrawal has been accomplished, that a previously addicted person is virtually forever in danger of slipping back into substance use. Triggers for such a relapse include any number of life stressors: problems on the job or in the marriage, loss of a relationship, **death** of a loved one, and financial stresses, in addition to seemingly mundane exposure to a place or an acquaintance associated with previous substance use. While some people remain in counseling indefinitely as a way of maintaining contact with a professional who can help monitor behavior, others find that various support groups or 12-step programs such as Narcotics Anonymous are the most successful and useful way of monitoring the recovery process and avoiding relapse. Research indicates that a good prognosis is more likely for individuals who have a strong support than for those who have little or no support.

Another important aspect of treatment for substance abuse is the inclusion of close family members in treatment. Because substance abuse has severe effects on the functioning of the family, and because research shows that family members can accidentally develop behaviors that inadvertently serve to support a person's substance habit, most good treatment programs will involve all family members.

Caregiver concerns

Nursing staff and allied health professionals can assist in the treatment of substance abuse and dependence by understanding the disease model of alcoholism and addiction.

During the treatment phase, nursing staff and allied health professionals can help patients by providing them with appropriate educational materials and referrals for supportive services such as Alcoholics Anonymous or Narcotics Anonymous.

Prevention

Prevention is best aimed at teenagers, who are at very high risk for substance experimentation. Data reveals that 14% of high school seniors had used an illegal substance other than marijuana in the preceding year. Education regarding the risks and consequences of substance use, as well as teaching methods of resisting peer pressure, are both important components of a prevention program. Furthermore, it is important to identify children at higher risk for substance abuse, including victims of physical or sexual abuse, children of parents who have a history of substance abuse, especially alcohol, and children with school failure and/or attention deficit disorder. These children will require a more intensive prevention program.

Resources

BOOKS

Allen, Frances, et al. *Diagnostic and Statistical Manual of Mental Disorders.* Washington, D.C.: American Psychiatric Association, 1994.

O'Brien, C.P. "Drug Abuse and Dependence." In *Cecil Textbook of Medicine,* edited by J. Claude Bennett and Fred Plum. Philadelphia: W.B. Saunders, 1996.

Shealy, C. Norman. *The Complete Family Guide to Alternative Medicine.* New York: Barnes and Noble, 1996.

Volpicelli, Joseph. *Recovery Options: The Complete Guide.* New York: John Wiley & Sons, 2000.

ORGANIZATIONS

Al-Anon, Alanon Family Group, Inc. PO Box 862, Midtown Station, New York, NY 10018-0862. (800) 356-9996. http://www.recovery.org/aa.

National Alliance On Alcoholism and Drug Dependence, Inc. 12 West 21st St., New York, NY 10010. (212) 206-6770.

National Clearinghouse for Alcohol and Drug Information. http://www.health.org.

Parent Resources and Information for Drug Education (PRIDE). 10 Park Place South, Suite 340, Atlanta, GA 30303. (800) 853-7867.

Bethanne Black

Substance abuse counseling

Definition

Substance abuse counseling refers to a type of intervention (action intended to alter the course of a disease process) to help individuals recover from abuse of alcohol (or other drug) by abstaining completely from the substance or cutting down on its use. With regard to alcohol abuse—which is the most common form of substance abuse in seniors— the most widely used form of counseling is called brief alcohol intervention or BAI.

Physicians and other substance abuse counselors distinguish between substance abuse and substance dependence. The *Diagnostic and Statistical Manual of Mental Disorders*, fourth edition (DSM-IV) defines substance dependence as "a maladaptive pattern of substance use, leading to clinically significant impairment or distress" over a 12-month period. Substance abuse is defined as "a maladaptive pattern of substance use manifested by recurrent and significant adverse consequences related to the repeated use of substances." These consequences may be social or occupational (repeated absences from work), legal (being arrested for driving while drunk), or social (marital separation or divorce). These definitions, however, often complicate the diagnosis of substance-related problems in seniors because they may have retired from work, may have given up driving, and may be living alone. In addition, seniors are less likely to go to bars or participate in other group activities (e. g., office parties, tailgate parties at sports events) that include or encourage drinking.

With alcohol in particular, it is important to define what counts as a "drink": this is usually defined as 0.5 oz of pure alcohol, which is the amount contained in 1.5 oz of whiskey or other distilled liquors; 12 oz of beer; and 5 oz of wine. The National Institute on Alcohol Abuse and Alcoholism (NIAAA) considers one drink per day to be the maximum safe amount for seniors over 65.

Purpose

The purpose of substance abuse counseling in seniors is the same as its purpose in the general population—namely, to improve or maintain health by changing behaviors that are causing present or potential harm to the substance user and others. Alcohol and substance abuse can trigger a number of health-related problems in seniors and worsen those that already exist. A major reason for these negative effects on health is that the human body metabolizes (digests and uses) alcohol much less efficiently as it ages; thus, seniors may get drunk on the same amount of alcohol that they could drink without noticeable effects when they were younger. Studies have shown that a 65-year-old who consumes the same amount of alcohol as a 20-year-old will have a blood alcohol level 20 percent higher, and a 90-year-old will have a blood alcohol 50 percent higher. Some of the specific health risks of substance abuse in the elderly are:

- High blood pressure and increased risk of stroke.
- Increased risk of cancer of the head, neck, or esophagus.
- Increased risk of cirrhosis of the liver.
- Increased risk of falls and fall-related injuries, particularly in women. Studies indicate that heavy drinking in older women increases the risk of osteoporosis.
- Decline in cognitive function. Some researchers think that alcohol abuse increases a senior's risk of Alzheimer's disease, although further research is needed.
- Increased risk of malnutrition.
- High risk of interactions with prescription drugs that the senior may be taking.

Scope of the problem

Alcohol and substance abuse are a greater problem among seniors than many people recognize. The

NIAAA estimates that between 2 and 10 percent of seniors living in the community meet the DSM-IV criteria for substance dependence or abuse. Another study reported that 6 percent of seniors are heavy drinkers, which is defined as having two or more drinks per day. A public health study in upstate New York found in the late 1990s that 62 percent of seniors between the ages of 60 and 94 who were living in the community drank alcohol at least occasionally, and heavy drinking was reported in 13 percent of men and 2 percent of women in this group.

Abuse of other substances is less common in seniors as of the early 2000s, affecting only a small percentage of seniors. Abuse of narcotics and other illicit drugs is rare in persons over 65 as of 2008, although this finding is expected to change as the so-called baby boomers retire. Most seniors who abuse other substances are alcoholics who misuse prescription drugs—most commonly **benzodiazepines** (tranquilizers) and opiates (painkillers). Like alcohol, these drugs are metabolized less quickly by the aging body and tend to remain in the bloodstream longer. Thus, seniors who drink heavily after taking a prescribed tranquilizer may become intoxicated from the combination of substances.

As of 2008, most seniors diagnosed with substance abuse problems are men; the gender ratio is expected to change in the coming years, however, as women tend to outlive men and a higher proportion of women who are middle-aged in the late 2000s are heavy drinkers compared to women in previous generations. In addition, a woman's body at any age metabolizes alcohol less efficiently than a man's; women can become intoxicated on smaller amounts of alcohol than a man of the same height and weight. Last, women progress more rapidly than men from moderate use of alcohol to dependence and abuse of the substance.

Diagnosis

Diagnosis of alcohol or substance abuse in the elderly is complicated by several factors. One is that the signs of alcohol or substance dependence are easy to confuse with age-related changes in muscle coordination, cognition, mood, social functioning, and the like. As noted above, older alcoholics are less likely to be noticed if they no longer drive or work outside the home. In addition, about a third of seniors who abuse alcohol are so-called late-onset drinkers; they are people who did not abuse alcohol previously but have turned to it out of loneliness or bereavement. These late-onset seniors typically have higher levels of education and income than the two-thirds of older substance abusers with previous histories of alcohol or drug dependence.

Primary care physicians are the healthcare professionals most likely to notice signs of alcohol or substance abuse in seniors. These "red flags" include:

- Decline in personal hygiene and self-care.
- Frequent falls or accidents.
- Uncontrolled high blood pressure.
- Unexpected delirium during hospitalization.
- Frequent visits to the hospital emergency department.
- Frequent arguments with or estrangement from family members.
- Gastrointestinal disorders.
- Failure to keep appointments with the doctor or comply with treatment.

Precautions

Medical

Substance abuse counseling should not be offered if individuals are currently having a health crisis, have another psychiatric disorder, or are already in treatment for substance abuse. In addition, rapid cessation of alcohol intake may produce withdrawal symptoms; thus, the doctor needs to be alert for such signs of alcohol withdrawal as trembling, **delirium**, and hallucinations, and take care not to confuse them with symptoms of other medical conditions.

In many cases a primary care physician who suspects a senior may be having problems with alcohol or other substances may need to consult friends or family members. Consultation is particularly important if the senior is already in the early stages of cognitive decline or may be otherwise unable to answer the doctor's questions about alcohol and drug use. In some cases the primary care doctor may consult a psychiatrist to evaluate the patient's behavior or physical symptoms.

Psychological

Beginning substance abuse counseling with a senior requires a good relationship between physician and patient, particularly if the senior has already begun to miss appointments because of substance use. In addition, older alcoholics are more likely than younger ones to feel embarrassed or ashamed by a diagnosis of substance dependence or abuse, and the doctor may need to be tactful and proceed slowly.

Steps of recovery

Substance abuse counseling often has to be conducted during as well as before treatment for problem drinking or drug use. The following sections outline the most common pattern of counseling:

Primary care evaluation and BAI

The first stage of substance abuse counseling for most seniors takes place in their primary care doctor's office. It often takes the form of a brief alcohol intervention or BAI, a five-or ten-minute discussion that has been shown to be successful in spite of its brevity in getting seniors with substance abuse problems to get help. A BAI consists of three steps: an evaluation of the senior's actual consumption of alcohol (more than 1 drink per day for a senior of either sex over 65 is considered risky); an assessment of whether the patient has problems related to alcohol (e. g., days missed from work; arguments with family members); and the intervention itself.

The intervention has six specific steps:

- The doctor expresses concern about the senior's drinking.
- The doctor reviews a list of medical and social reasons for quitting.
- The doctor advises the patient to at least cut down on the amount of drinking (or substance use).
- The doctor and the senior together set a goal of acceptable daily intake, preferably within the safe limit.
- If the senior refuses to make a change, the doctor avoids getting confrontational, recognizing that admitting one has a problem and getting ready to change often takes time.
- The doctor recommends keeping a diary of the senior's drinking or substance use.

Detoxification

If the senior is severely dependent on alcohol, an inpatient detoxification program is often recommended. The senior will be given medications (usually benzodiazepines) in the hospital to manage withdrawal symptoms and be evaluated for nutritional deficiencies and other possible physical disorders. The senior should be referred to an outpatient support group or a community-based group such as Alcoholics Anonymous as soon as he or she completes the detoxification program. Elder-specific therapy groups are reported to be more successful than mixed-age groups.

Treatment options

Treatment options for seniors who do not require detoxification include ongoing counseling with the primary care physician, support groups, and support from family members. The doctor may need to educate the senior's friends and family about the harmful effects of heavy drinking and substance use because they may have been reluctant to interfere on the grounds that the senior had been comforted by the alcohol or drugs.

Naltrexone and acamprosate, two drugs that reduce the desire to drink, appear to reduce the rate of relapse in seniors by 50 percent when the medications are combined with counseling and social support. Disulfiram (Antabuse), the oldest drug given to control the desire to drink, should not be used in seniors because it may cause too-low **blood pressure** as a side effect.

Seniors with dementia who cannot stop drinking or abusing substances may have to be placed in a nursing home for long-term care.

Challenges

The primary challenge that a senior receiving substance abuse counseling confronts is the risk of relapse. Returning to heavy drinking (or drug use) means further risks to physical and mental health. Even limiting one's drinking to smaller amounts is preferable to uncontrolled use.

Risks

There are no physical risks involved with receiving substance abuse counseling by itself, although seniors may have some emotional reactions related to admitting that they have a problem with substance dependence or abuse.

Results

The results of substance abuse counseling for seniors depend on a variety of factors ranging from the person's overall level of physical health and the point at life in which he or she began abusing substances to income level and the amount of available family support. Such statistics as are available indicate that older adults have the same rate of abstinence after counseling as younger substance abusers; about 50 percent remain abstinent 1 year after treatment. As a rule, late-onset alcohol abusers do better than

KEY TERMS

Abstinence—Complete nonuse of alcohol (or other substance). Abstinence is the goal of substance abuse counseling in the elderly.

Detoxification—A program of medical care in which alcoholic or substance abusers are withdrawn from alcohol or other drugs and treated with medications while their body is cleared of the abused substance.

Intervention—A general medical term for any action taken to interrupt a disease process. In the field of substance abuse, it is used in a narrower sense to refer to an attempt on the part of a physician or family members to persuade an alcoholic or substance abuser to get help.

Moderation—Limiting one's drinking to what is considered a safe amount for one's age and sex.

Relapse—Returning to a previous behavior pattern of heavy drinking or substance abuse after treatment.

Withdrawal—A group of physical and psychological symptoms that occur when a person abruptly stops drinking or taking a drug of abuse. Seniors who are abruptly withdrawn from alcohol may become confused, have seizures or hallucinations, vomit, or suffer from insomnia.

seniors with previous histories of substance abuse; one study found that they are twice as likely to avoid relapse as those who had abused alcohol or substances in the past.

Resources

PERIODICALS

Bertholet, Nicolas, Jean-Bernard Daeppen, Vincent Wietlisbach, et al. "Reduction of Alcohol Consumption by Brief Intervention in Primary Care." *Archives of Internal Medicine* 165 (May 9, 2005): 986–995.

Epstein, E. E., K. Fischer-Elber, and Z. Al-Otaiba. "Women, Aging, and Alcohol Use Disorders." *Journal of Women and Aging* 19 (January/February 2007): 31–48.

Simoni-Wastila, L., and H. K. Yang. "Psychoactive Drug Abuse in Older Adults." *American Journal of Geriatric Pharmacotherapy* 4 (December 2006): 380–394.

Zanjani, F., et al. "Predictors of Adherence within an Intervention Research Study of the At-risk Older Drinker: PRISM-E." *Journal of Geriatric Psychiatry and Neurology* 19 (December 2006): 231–238.

OTHER

"Alcohol Use and Abuse." National Institute on Aging (NIA) Age Page. Bethesda, MD: NIA. 2005 [cited March 21, 2008].. http://www.nia.nih.gov/NR/rdonlyres/89CF17D6-ADF4-498A-AD58-F4C85D606E66/7410/Alcohol_Use_And_Abuse.pdf.

Larson, Michael. "Alcohol-Related Psychosis." *eMedicine.* March 30, 2006 [cited March 21, 2008].. http://www.emedicine.com/med/topic3113.htm.

Thompson, Warren. "Alcoholism." *eMedicine.* June 6, 2007 [cited March 21, 2008]. http://www.emedicine.com/med/topic98.htm.

ORGANIZATIONS

American Psychiatric Association, 1000 Wilson Blvd., Suite 1825, Arlington, VA, 22209, (703) 907-7300, apa@psych.org, http://www.psych.org/.

National Institute on Alcohol Abuse and Alcoholism (NIAAA), 5635 Fishers Lane, MSC 9304, Bethesda, MD, 20892, (301) 443-3860, http://www.niaaa.nih.gov/.

Rebecca J. Frey Ph.D.

Sudden confusion *see* **Delirium**

Sugar diabetes *see* **Diabetes mellitus**

Suicide

Definition

Suicide is defined as the intentional taking of one's own life. In some European languages, the word for suicide translates into English as "self-murder." Until fairly recently, suicide was considered a criminal act; legal terminology used the Latin phrase *felo de se*, which means "a crime against the self." Much of the social stigma that is still attached to suicide derives from its former association with legal as well as religious condemnation.

As of the early 2000s, however, suicidal behavior is most commonly regarded as and treated as a psychiatric emergency. Law enforcement personnel may be involved in preventing an attempted suicide or taking suicidal individuals to a hospital emergency department but not in arresting these persons for breaking the law.

Description

Researchers estimate that 8 to 25 people in the general population attempt suicide for every person who completes the act; however, seniors have a lower

U.S. suicide deaths, 2005

Age group	Number of deaths
50–54	3,227
55–59	2,477
60–64	1,733
65–69	1,198
70–74	1,146
75–79	1,143
80–84	1,057
85+	860
Total	**12,841**

SOURCE: National Center for Injury Prevention and Control, Centers for Disease Control and Prevention, U.S. Department of Health and Human Services

(Illustration by GGS Information Services. Cengage Learning, Gale)

rate of suicide attempts than younger Americans. The ratio of attempted suicides to completed suicides among people over 65 is thought to be as low as 4:1. By contrast, according to the National Strategy for Suicide Prevention (NSSP), seniors are more likely than younger persons to use highly lethal means of suicide. According to a Canadian study published in 2008, seniors are most likely to use firearms to commit suicide, followed by hanging, self-poisoning, and leaping from heights.

Demographics

The incidence of suicide and attempted suicide among seniors is widely perceived as a growing public health problem in the United States; as of 2008, older adults represent about 13 percent of the U.S. population but account for 20 percent of suicides. According to the National Institute of Mental Health (NIMH), the highest suicide rate in the nation is for Caucasian men ages 85 and older: 65.3 deaths per 100,000 persons, about six times the national U.S. rate of 10.8 per 100,000.

In the United States, the rate of suicide has continued to rise since the 1950s. More people in the general population die from suicide than homicide in North America. Suicide is the eighth leading cause of **death** in North America; there are over 30,000 suicides per year in the United States, or about one every 17 minutes; and each day about 1,500 people attempt suicide.

Risk factors in seniors

Research conducted by the NIMH indicates that the following factors increase a senior's risk of suicide:

- Male sex; three-fourths of suicides among seniors involve males.
- Age over 65.
- White race. Asian men, Hispanic men, and African American men are less likely to attempt or commit suicide than Caucasians.
- A family history of suicide.
- A history of previous suicide attempts.
- A history of abuse in childhood.
- Recent stressful events: separation or divorce; job loss or financial difficulty; death of spouse, partner, friend, or pet.
- Medical illness. Many elderly people commit suicide when they are diagnosed with a terminal illness.
- Chronic, severe, or intractable pain.
- Loss of mobility or independence.
- Alcohol or substance abuse. Mood-altering substances do not inevitably drive individuals to kill themselves; however, these substances weaken impulse control.
- Presence of a psychiatric illness. Over 90 percent of Americans, including seniors, who commit suicide had a significant mental illness. Major depression accounts for 60 percent of all suicides. Other mental disorders accounting for suicide among seniors include schizophrenia, alcoholism, substance abuse, borderline personality disorder, Huntington's disease, and epilepsy.

Protective factors

Factors that lower seniors' risk of suicide include:

- A significant friendship network.
- Religious faith and practice. Older African American women have a particularly low rate of suicide and a high rate of church membership.
- A stable marriage or close-knit extended family.
- A strong interest in or commitment to a project or cause that brings people together, for example, community service, neighborhood associations, book clubs, and hobby groups.

Treatment of attempted suicide

Suicide attempts can be broadly categorized along a continuum that ranges from planned attempts, involving highly lethal methods that fail by good fortune, to impulsive or poorly planned attempts, using less lethal methods. Suicide attempts that are unlikely to succeed are sometimes referred to as suicide gestures or pseudocide.

A suicide attempt of any kind, however, is treated as a psychiatric emergency by police or other rescue personnel. Treatment in a hospital emergency room includes a complete psychiatric evaluation, a mental status examination, and a detailed assessment of the circumstances surrounding the attempt. The physician will interview the senior's relatives or anyone else who accompanied the patient in order to obtain as much information as possible. As a rule, suicide attempts requiring advance planning and the use of violent or highly lethal methods are regarded as the most serious. The patient will be kept under observation while decisions are made about the need for hospitalization.

Seniors who have attempted suicide and who are considered a serious danger to themselves or to others can be legally hospitalized against their will. The doctor bases the decision on the severity of the patient's **depression** or agitation; the presence of other suicide risk factors, including a history of previous suicide attempts, substance abuse, recent stressful events, and symptoms of psychosis; and the availability of friends, relatives, or other social support. If the attempt is judged to be a nonlethal suicide gesture, and the patient has adequate support outside the hospital, then the patient may be released after the psychiatric assessment is completed.

Viewpoints

Social changes and suicide among seniors

Some observers have identified several changes in the United States since the 1950s that are thought to contribute to the rising rate of suicide among the elderly:

- The loss of a set of moral values held in common by the entire society.
- The lessened effect of religious and other social groups outside the family. In the past, these institutions often provided fellowship and a sense of belonging for the elderly and others living alone.
- Media images that glamorize youth and present negative stereotypes of seniors.
- Frequent geographical moves, which make it hard for seniors to keep in touch or visit members of their extended family.
- Sensationalized treatment of suicide in the mass media. Some research studies have shown a definite risk of so-called contagion suicides from irresponsible reporting.
- The development over the past century of medications that allow relatively painless suicide. For most of human history, the available means of suicide were uncertain, painful, or both.
- The easy availability of lethal methods of suicide, most notably firearms, and so-called suicide magnets such as bridges or tall buildings that do not have suicide barriers and are easy even for seniors who do not drive to reach. The Golden Gate Bridge in San Francisco is the most notorious suicide magnet in the United States; others include the Aurora Bridge in Seattle, the Sunshine Skyway Bridge in Florida, and the Duke Ellington Bridge in Washington, D.C.

A right to suicide?

The idea that suicide is a right among the elderly surfaced with the 1991 publication of Derek Humphry's *Final Exit,* a controversial book described by its author as a how-to manual for suicide and assisted suicide. Humphry is the founder of the **Euthanasia** Research and Guidance Organization (ERGO), known until 2003 as the Hemlock Society. Humphry maintains that people have a right to choose the time, place, and method of their death and that rational suicide is a legitimate and even reasonable choice.

People often overlooked in discussions of the right to commit suicide are the relatives and friends who are bereaved by the suicide. It is estimated that each person who commits suicide leaves six survivors to deal with the aftermath. On the basis of this figure, there are at least 4.5 million survivors of suicide in the United States. In addition to the grief that ordinarily accompanies death, survivors of suicide often struggle with feelings of guilt and shame as well. Some people blamed Humphry and his book for their loved one's decision to commit suicide.

Assisted suicide

Questions pertaining to the legalization of assisted suicide for persons suffering from a terminal illness are connected in part to increases in the average lifespan. Physician-assisted suicide (also known as physician-assisted death or PAD) was legalized in the Netherlands in April 2001 and in the state of Oregon. As of 2008 it was also legal in Belgium and is practiced openly in Switzerland. It is important to distinguish between physician-assisted suicide and euthanasia, or mercy killing. Assisted suicide, which is called "self-deliverance" in Britain, refers to individuals bringing about their own death with the help of another person. Because the other person is often a physician, the act is often called doctor-assisted suicide.

Euthanasia strictly speaking means that the physician or other person is the one who performs the last act that causes death. For example, if a physician injects a patient with a lethal dose of a pain-killing medication, the physician is performing euthanasia. If the physician leaves the patient with a loaded syringe and the patient injects himself or herself with it, the act is an assisted suicide. As of 2008, assisted suicide is illegal everywhere in the United States except Oregon, and euthanasia is illegal in all fifty states. The *Merck Manual of Geriatrics* states: "Physicians can provide treatment intended to minimize [a patient's] physical and emotional suffering, even if a secondary result is the shortening of life, but they cannot specifically intend to hasten death."

Suicide prevention

In the late 2000s research was ongoing to discover better methods of treating depression and other disorders that may influence a senior's decision to commit suicide. In addition, primary care physicians were continually learning how to better identify and intervene when treating suicidal seniors. Too often, physicians and relatives may think that signs of depression and hints that the senior is contemplating suicide are normal signs of aging. An estimated 80 percent of the elderly who committed suicide saw their doctors within a month prior to their deaths. Thus primary care physicians are in a good position to evaluate a senior for signs of depression. The good news is that depression in the elderly is highly treatable, particularly when antidepressant medications are combined with psychotherapy.

Warning signs of suicidal thinking have been identified:

- Reading a lot of books or articles on death and suicide
- Talking a lot about death or suicide or expressing feelings of hopeless
- Stockpiling medications
- Refusing to take care of oneself
- Sudden interest in guns
- Giving away cherished possessions, writing long letters, or making other elaborate farewells
- Disrupted sleep patterns
- Hurriedly revising a will
- Increased intake of alcohol or prescription drugs

People who are concerned about a senior at risk of self-harm should take the following steps:

- Become educated about warning signs and risk factors
- Identify physicians and other healthcare professionals who know the senior and can provide help and keep their telephone numbers readily available
- Talk openly with the senior about the senior's feelings. Although many people are afraid to ask whether the senior is thinking about suicide for fear of angering the person or giving the person an idea, in many cases honest concern is welcomed by the senior.
- Call the local hospital emergency department if the senior seems to be at immediate risk of suicide.

KEY TERMS

Assisted suicide—A form of self-inflicted death in which individuals voluntarily bring about their own death with the help of another, usually a physician, relative, or friend. Assisted suicide is sometimes called physician-assisted death (PAD).

Euthanasia—The act of putting individuals or animals to death painlessly or allowing them to die by withholding medical services, usually because of an incurable disease; also called mercy killing.

Self-deliverance—Another term for assisted suicide, more commonly used in Great Britain than in the United States.

Suicide gesture—Attempted suicide characterized by a low-lethality method, low level of intent or planning, and little physical damage; sometimes called pseudocide.

Suicide magnet—A bridge or tall building that acquires a reputation for attracting people who want to commit suicide and attempt it.

Resources

BOOKS

Beers, Mark H., and Robert Berkow, eds. *Merck Manual of Geriatrics*, 3rd ed. Whitehouse Station, NJ: Merck, 2005.

PERIODICALS

American Academy of Hospice and Palliative Medicine. "Position Statement on Physician-Assisted Death." *Journal of Pain and Palliative Care Pharmacotherapy* 21 (April 2007): 55–57.

Beyer, J. L. "Managing Depression in Geriatric Populations." *Annals of Clinical Psychiatry* 19 (October/December 2007): 221–238.

Centers for Disease Control and Prevention (CDC). "Increases in Age-Group-Specific Injury Mortality—United States, 1999–2004." *Morbidity and Mortality Weekly Report* 56 (December 14, 2007): 1281–1284.

Elison, N. W. "Senior Suicide." *New Jersey Nurse* 37 (September/October 2007): 5–9.

Hamlin, Jesse. "Family Grief: A Suicide Leaves a Legacy of Anguish." *San Francisco Chronicle*, October 31, 2005 [cited April 1, 2008]. Part 2 of a seven-part series on the Golden Gate Bridge as a suicide magnet. http://www.sfgate.com/cgi-bin/article.cgi?f=/c/a/2005/10/31/MNG2NFG1L61.DTL.

Mann, J. J., et al. "Suicide Prevention Strategies." *Journal of the American Medical Association* 294 (October 26, 2005): 2064–2074.

Voaklander, D. C., B. H. Rowe, D. M. Dryden, et al. "Medical Illness, Medication Use, and Suicide in Seniors: A Population-Based Case Control Study." *Journal of Epidemiology and Community Health* 62 (February 2008): 138–146.

OTHER

"At a Glance: Suicide among the Elderly." *National Strategy for Suicide Prevention (NSSP) Fact Sheet.* [cited April 1, 2008]. http://mentalhealth.samhsa.gov/suicideprevention/elderly.asp.

Evans, Garret D., and Heidi L. Radunovich. "Suicide and the Elderly: Warning Signs and How to Help." Gainesville: University of Florida, Family, Youth, and Community Sciences Department, February 28, 2006 [cited April 1, 2008]. *http://edis.ifas.ufl.edu/FY101.*

"Older Adults: Depression and Suicide Facts." NIH Publication No. 4593. *National Institute of Mental Health (NIMH).* April 2007 [cited February 6, 2008].http://www.nimh.nih.gov/health/publications/older-adults-depression-and-suicide-facts.shtml.

Soreff, Stephen. "Suicide." *eMedicine.* September 28, 2006 [cited February 6, 2008]. http://www.emedicine.com/med/topic3004.htm.

ORGANIZATIONS

American Association of Suicidology (AAS), 5221 Wisconsin Ave. NW, Washington, DC, 20015, (202) 237-2280, (202) 237-2282, info@suicidology.org, http://www.suicidology.org/index.cfm.

American Psychiatric Association, 1000 Wilson Blvd., Suite 1825, Arlington, VA, 22209, (703) 907-7300, apa@psych.org, http://www.psych.org/.

Centers for Disease Control and Prevention (CDC), National Center for Injury Prevention and Control (NCIPC), Suicide Prevention, 4770 Buford Hwy NE, MS K-65, Atlanta, GA, 30341, (800) CDC-INFO, (770) 488-4760, cdcinfo@cdc.gov, http://www.cdc.gov/ncipc/dvp/Suicide/default.htm.

National Institute of Mental Health (NIMH), 6001 Executive Blvd., Room 8184, MSC 9663, Bethesda, MD, 20892, (301) 443-4513, (866) 615-6464, (301) 443-4279, nimhinfo@nih.gov, http://www.nimh.nih.gov/index.shtml.

National Suicide Prevention Hotline, (800) 273-8255.

Rebecca J. Frey Ph.D.

Supportive cancer therapy *see* **Cancer therapy, supportive**

Surgical oncology

Definition

Surgical oncology is a specialized area of oncology that engages surgeons in the cure and management of **cancer**.

Purpose

Cancer has become a medical specialty warranting its own surgical area because of advances in the biology, pathophysiology, diagnostics, and staging of malignant tumors. Surgeons have traditionally treated cancer patients with resection and radical surgeries of tumors, and left the management of the cancer and the patient to other specialists. Advances in the early diagnosis of cancer, the staging of tumors, microscopic analyses of cells, and increased understanding of cancer biology have broadened the range of nonsurgical cancer treatments. These treatments include systematic **chemotherapy**, hormonal therapy, and radiotherapy as alternatives or adjunctive therapy for patients with cancer.

Not all cancer tumors are manageable by surgery, nor does the removal of some tumors or metastases necessarily lead to a cure or longer life. The oncological surgeon looks for the relationship between tumor excision and the risk presented by the primary tumor. He or she is knowledgeable about patient management with more conservative procedures than the traditional excision or resection.

Demographics

According to the American Cancer Society, approximately 12 million people were diagnosed with cancer in 2007. The most commonly diagnosed cancers for males were:

- lung
- prostate

KEY TERMS

Biopsy—The surgical excision of tissue to diagnose the size, type, and extent of a cancerous growth.

Cancer surgery—Surgery in which the goal is to excise a tumor and its surrounding tissue found to be malignant.

Resection—Cutting out tissue to eliminate a cancerous tumor; usually refers to a section of the organ, (e.g., colon, intestine, lung, stomach) that must be cut to remove the tumor and its surrounding tissue.

Tumor staging—The method used by oncologists to determine the risk from a cancerous tumor. A number—ranging from 1A–4B— is assigned to predict the level of invasion by a tumor, and offer a prognosis for morbidity and mortality.

- stomach

For women, the leading cancers were:

- breast
- cervical
- colon and rectum

Cancer survival rates vary among developed and developing countries.

Description

Surgical oncology is guided by principles that govern the routine procedures related to the cancer patient's cure, palliative care, and quality of life. Surgical oncology performs its most efficacious work by local tumor excision, regional lymph node removal, the handling of cancer recurrence (local or widespread), and in rare cases, with surgical resection of metastases from the primary tumor. Each of these areas plays a different role in cancer management.

Excision

Local excision has been the hallmark of surgical oncology. Excision refers to the removal of the cancer and its effects. Resection of a tumor in the colon can end the effects of obstruction, for instance, or removal of a breast carcinoma can stop the cancer. Resection of a primary tumor also stops the tumor from spreading throughout the body. The cancer's spread into other body systems, however, usually occurs before a local removal, giving resection little bearing upon cells that have already escaped the primary tumor. Advances in oncology through pathophysiology, staging, and biopsy offer a new diagnostic role to the surgeon using excision. These advances provide simple diagnostic information about size, grade, and extent of the tumor, as well as more sophisticated evaluations of the cancer's biochemical and hormonal features.

Regional lymph node removal

Lymph node involvement provides surgical oncologists with major diagnostic information. The sentinel node biopsy is superior to any biological test in terms of prediction of cancer mortality rates. Nodal biopsy offers very precise information about the extent and type of invasive effects of the primary tumor. The removal of nodes, however, may present **pain** and other morbid conditions for the patient.

Local and regional recurrence

Radical procedures in surgical oncology for local and regional occurrences of a primary tumor provide crucial information on the spread of cancer and prognostic outcomes. However, they do not contribute substantially to the outcome of the cancer. According to most surgical oncology literature, the ability to remove a local recurrence must be balanced by the patient's goals related to aesthetic and pain control concerns. Historically, more radical procedures have not improved the chances for survival.

Surgery for distant metastases

In general, a cancer tumor that spreads further from its primary site is less likely to be controlled by surgery. According to research, except for a few instances where **metastasis** is confined, surgical removal of a distant metastasis is not warranted. Since the rapidity of discovering a distant metastasis has little bearing upon cancer survival, the usefulness of surgery is not time dependent. In the case of liver metastasis, for example, a cure is related to the pathophysiology of the original cancer and level of cancer antigen in the liver rather than the size or time of discovery. While surgery of metastatic cancer may not increase life, there may be indications for it such as pain relief, obstruction removal, control of bleeding, and resolution of infection.

Diagnosis/Preparation

Surgery removes cancer cells and surrounding tissues. It is often combined with radiation therapy and chemotherapy. It is important for the patient to meet with the surgical oncologist to talk about the procedure and begin preparations for surgery. Oncological surgery may be performed to biopsy a suspicious site for malignant cells or tumor. It is also used for tumor removal from organs such as the tongue, throat, lung, stomach, intestines, colon, bladder, ovary, and prostate. Tumors of limbs, ligaments, and tendons may also be treated with surgery. In many cases, the biopsy and surgery to remove the cancer cells or tissues are done at the same time as the biopsy.

The impact of a surgical procedure depends upon the diagnosis and the area of the body that is to be treated by surgery. Many cancer surgeries involve major organs and require open abdominal surgery, which is the most extensive type of surgical procedure. This surgery requires medical tests and work-ups to judge the health of the patient prior to surgery, and to make decisions about adjunctive procedures like radiation or chemotherapy. Preparation for cancer surgery requires psychological readiness for a hospital stay, postoperative pain, sometimes slow recovery, and anticipation of complications from tumor excision or resection. It also may require consultation with stomal therapists if a section of the urinary tract or bowel is to be removed and replaced with an outside reservoir or conduit called an ostomy.

Aftercare

After surgery, the type and duration of side effects and the elements of recovery depend on where in the body the surgery was performed and the patient's general health. Some surgeries may alter basic functions in the urinary or gastrointestinal systems. Recovering full use of function takes time and patience. Surgeries that remove conduits such as the colon, intestines, or urinary tract require appliances for urine and fecal waste and the help of a stomal therapist. Breast or prostate surgeries yield concerns about cosmetic appearance and intimate activities. For most cancer surgeries, basic functions like tasting, eating, drinking, breathing, moving, urinating, defecating, or neurological ability may be changed in the short-term. Resources to attend to deficits in daily activities need to be set up before surgery.

Risks

The type of risks that cancer surgery presents depends almost entirely upon the part of the body being biopsied or excised. Risks of surgery can be great when major organs are involved, such as the gastrointestinal system or the brain. These risks are usually discussed explicitly when surgerical decisions are made.

QUESTIONS TO ASK THE DOCTOR

- Who is recommended for a second opinion?
- What are the alternatives to surgery for this cancer?
- What is the likelihood that this surgery will entirely eliminate the cancer?
- Is this a surgical procedure that is often performed in this hospital or surgical center?

Results

Most cancers are staged; that is, they are described by their likelihood of being contained, spreading at the original site, or recurring or invading other bodily systems. The prognosis after surgery depends upon the stage of the disease, and the pathology results on the type of cancer cell involved. General results of cancer surgery depend in large part on norms of success based upon the study of groups of patients with the same diagnosis. The results are often stated in percentages of the chance of cancer recurrence or its spread after surgery. After five disease-free years, patients are usually considered cured. This is because the recurrence rates decline drastically after five years. The benchmark is based upon the percentage of people known to reach the fifth year after surgery with no recurrence or spread of the primary tumor.

Resources

BOOKS

Abeloff, M.D., Martin D. "Surgical Therapy." In *Clinical Oncology.* 2nd ed. Churchill Livingstone, Inc., 2000.

PERIODICALS

Blake, C. "Multidisciplinary Approach to Cancer: The Changing Role of the Surgical Oncologist." *Surgical Clinics of North America* 80, no. 2 (April 2000).

Jemal, A., et. al. "Cancer Statistics, 2002." *CA: A Cancer Journal for Clinicians* 52, no. 1 (2002): 23–47.

Kemeny, M.M. "Cancer Surgery in the Elderly." *Hematology/Oncology Clinics of North America* 14, no.1 (February 1, 2000): 169–93.

ORGANIZATIONS

American Cancer Society. (800) ACS-2345. http://www.cancer.org/docroot/home/index.asp..

National Alliance of Breast Cancer Organizations. 9 East 37th Street, Tenth Floor, New York, NY 10016. (212) 719-0154. Fax: (212) 689-1213. http://www.nabco.org.

National Cancer Institute's Office of Alternative Medicine. 6120 Executive Boulevard, Suite 450, Bethesda, Maryland, 20892. (800) 4- CANCER, (800) 422-6237.

OTHER

2001 Cancer Progress Report. National Cancer Institute. http://www.progressreport.cancer.gov/.

Nancy McKenzie Ph.D.

Swallowing problems

Definition

Swallowing problems refers to a group of disorders characterized by difficulty in moving food from the mouth into the throat and esophagus, moving food down the esophagus, or having a sensation of **pain** during swallowing. Some swallowing problems are caused by abnormalities in the structure of the senior's mouth and throat, while others are caused by neurological disorders, disorders affecting the muscles that control swallowing, or damage to the tissues lining the esophagus caused by prescription drugs. The general term for swallowing problems is dysphagia, which comes from two Greek words meaning "disordered" and "eating." Painful swallowing is known as odynophagia. Odynophagia can occur with or without dysphagia.

A third sensation related to swallowing is called globus pharyngis, or simply globus. Globus is the persistent feeling of having a lump in one's throat or some other small obstruction when there is nothing present. Globus does not interfere with swallowing, but it can be irritating to the patient, and has to be considered during the diagnosis of a swallowing problem.

Description

It is helpful to review the process of normal human swallowing in order to understand the different types of swallowing problems in seniors. The medical term for swallowing is deglutition. It is a complex process involving the coordination of messages from the brain, skeletal muscles in the mouth and jaw, and smooth muscles in the pharynx (throat) and esophagus.

There are three phases to normal swallowing:

- Oral (sometimes called buccal). In the oral phase of swallowing, the teeth and tongue grind food and mix it with saliva to form a soft mass called a bolus. The muscles in the tongue lift the bolus and push it toward the throat. This phase of swallowing is voluntary. It is controlled by three major cranial nerves: V, VII, and XII.
- Pharyngeal. This phase of swallowing is not voluntary. After the bolus enters the pharynx, it is pushed further downward toward the esophagus by peristalsis, which is the rhythmic contraction of smooth muscles that propels food through the digestive tract. At the same time, another set of muscles temporarily closes the windpipe to prevent the bolus from entering the windpipe and the respiratory system. Skeletal muscles in the throat contract to push the food past the upper esophageal sphincter (a circular muscle) and into the upper portion of the esophagus. This phase of swallowing involves cranial nerves V, X, and XI.
- Esophageal. In the third phase of swallowing, the muscles in the upper esophagus push the food downward toward the stomach. This phase is involuntary; it is controlled by the medulla, a part of the brain stem. Another sphincter at the lower end of the esophagus relaxes and allows the bolus to pass into the stomach. It takes between 8 and 20 seconds for the contractions of the esophagus to push the bolus into the stomach.

From the foregoing description of normal swallowing, the reader can see that any disease or disorder that affects the brain stem and the cranial nerves (such as **stroke**, Parkinson's disease, or Alzheimer's disease); the skeletal muscles of the body (such as polio or muscular dystrophy); the smooth muscles of the digestive tract; or blocks the throat or esophagus (such as foreign objects, malignant tumors, or a swollen thyroid gland) can cause swallowing problems.

Demographics

Swallowing problems are common in seniors; various estimates range from 10 percent of all adults over 50 to as many as 50 percent of seniors in **nursing homes**. It is thought that the actual incidence of swallowing problems in seniors in the community may be higher than 10 percent because many do not seek medical advice for them.

Causes and symptoms

The causes and symptoms of swallowing problems depend on the location of the difficulty. They are usually grouped into two categories, oropharyngeal and esophageal.

Oropharyngeal dysphagia

Oropharyngeal dysphagia is caused by diseases or disorders affecting the mouth and throat. These may include:

- Stroke. Stroke may affect the parts of the brain that control the voluntary phase of swallowing in the mouth. Between 51 and 73 percent of stroke patients develop dysphagia.
- Brain tumors, Parkinson's disease, and Alzheimer's disease. These disorders prevent impulses from the brain and cranial nerves reaching the muscles of the mouth and throat.
- Syphilis. Syphilis is a sexually transmitted disease that causes nerve cells in the spinal cord to degenerate during its third or final stage. The loss of these cells can affect swallowing as well as walking, hearing, and sight.
- Abnormalities of the upper esophageal sphincter. Some people have a sphincter that does not relax normally during swallowing. In others, the sphincter closes too quickly. This overly rapid closure eventually results in the formation of a pouch in the upper esophageal wall known as Zenker's diverticulum. Most patients with Zenker's diverticulum are over 50.
- Cancerous tumors of the throat and esophagus. These cause dysphagia by blocking the passage of food.
- Myasthenia gravis, polio, and muscular dystrophy. Diseases affecting skeletal muscles elsewhere in the body also affect swallowing.
- Esophageal rings and webs of tissue. These are noncancerous membranes along the walls of the esophagus that some people are born with. They cause narrowing of the esophagus that is usually not noticeable until the patient is over 40.

Symptoms associated with oropharyngeal dysphagia include:

- Coughing or choking.
- A nasal quality to the patient's voice.
- Regurgitation. Regurgitation refers to food coming back up through the mouth or nose when swallowing is not proceeding normally.
- Aspiration. Aspiration occurs when the bolus enters the respiratory system (the windpipe and lungs) rather than proceeding down the digestive tract.
- Some seniors experience globus along with the dysphagia.
- Chest pain. This symptom is often found in anxious or depressed patients with dysphagia.
- Bad breath. This is a common symptom of Zenkel's diverticulum.

Esophageal dysphagia

Causes of esophageal dysphagia include:

- Achalasia. Achalasia is a disorder in which the sphincter at the lower end of the esophagus does not relax normally and allow food to enter the stomach.
- Scleroderma. This is a disease characterized by fibrous deposits of collagen in the skin and internal organs. It can cause a narrowing of the esophagus near the point at which it joins the stomach.
- Spontaneous spasms of the muscles of the esophagus.
- Narrowing of the lower portion of the esophagus by tumors.
- Narrowing of the lower end of the esophagus caused by scarring from radiation treatments, certain medications (most commonly antibiotics, NSAIDs, and potassium chloride), or peptic ulcers.

Symptoms of esophageal dysphagia include:

- A sensation of food sticking in the back of the throat or further down the chest. The patient's identification of the trouble spot, however, may not be the actual location of the blockage or narrowing.
- Pain or a feeling of heartburn underneath the breastbone.
- Regurgitation.
- Changing dietary habits, typically eating fewer solid foods and taking in more liquids and soft foods.

Diagnosis

Office examination

In many cases the doctor can narrow the diagnostic possibilities by looking at the patient's medical history and by performing a careful physical examination in the office. The doctor can examine the senior's mouth and throat in the office for evidence of anatomical abnormalities and to test the senior's ability to move and control the tongue, chew, and swallow. The doctor will also check the senior's level of mental alertness and cognitive status.

Other tests that can be performed in the office include the use of a tongue depressor to see whether the gag reflex is working normally; placing two fingers over the patient's throat and asking him or her to swallow; feeling the thyroid gland in the neck for signs of enlargement; and asking the patient to cough or clear the throat. If the patient cannot clear the throat adequately, the risk of **aspiration** is increased. The doctor will also palpate (feel) the patient's abdomen for signs of abnormal masses or enlargement of the internal organs.

The final part of an office examination for dysphagia is to have the patient swallow several different types of solids and liquids while the doctor watches. Delayed swallowing, hoarse voice, coughing, or drooling indicate a problem.

Special tests

Most swallowing problems can be diagnosed on the basis of the patient's history and the office examination. In some cases, however, the doctor may order special tests:

- Laboratory tests. A complete blood count can be used to screen for syphilis or other infectious diseases, and a thyroid function test can be ordered to screen for thyroid disorders.
- Neurological examination. A neurologist may be consulted to check the functioning of the patient's cranial nerves and other parts of the brain that affect swallowing.
- Upper endoscopy. This is a procedure in which the doctor passes a tube called an endoscope through the mouth, over the tongue, and down the throat. The endoscope allows the doctor to see whether there are any tumors or other abnormalities blocking normal swallowing. The doctor can also use the endoscope to remove a piece of tissue for biopsy.
- Barium swallow. This test is used to evaluate the presence of such abnormalities as tumors, webs, or Zenkel's diverticulum. The patient is given a solution of barium sulfate to drink, which coats the inside of the throat and esophagus. While the patient is swallowing, the radiologist takes images with a fluoroscope at the rate of 2 to 3 frames per second. In most cases images will be taken from the side as well as the front and back while the patient drinks the barium.
- Manometry. This test, which takes about 45 minutes, is performed to evaluate the internal pressure at various points along the length of the esophagus. A catheter containing pressure probes is guided through the nose into the patient's stomach and slowly withdrawn. At various points the patient is asked to swallow some water or take a few deep breaths while the catheter records the changes in pressure inside the esophagus during these maneuvers.

QUESTIONS TO ASK YOUR DOCTOR

- What is causing my difficulties in swallowing?
- Where is the problem located?
- Will I need special tests to find the cause?
- Will I need a special diet?
- What other treatments will be needed?

Treatment

Treatment depends on the cause of the dysphagia. It may involve surgery, medications, radiation therapy, physical rehabilitation, or dietary changes.

Nutrition/Dietetic concerns

Nutrition is a major concern with dysphagia because some patients stop eating, or eat only soft foods. **Malnutrition**, **dehydration**, and **weight loss** are common in seniors with swallowing problems. In some cases the patient benefits from a **diet** of soft or pureed foods. In other cases the patient is taught a variety of techniques to train their mouth and throat muscles to hold food in the mouth and swallow more efficiently, or to hold the head in certain positions to assist in swallowing. Patients who are able to improve their swallowing by retraining the muscles of the mouth and throat can gradually be moved from liquid or soft diets to semi-solid foods or even some solid foods.

Patients whose dysphagia is caused by neurological disorders or **cancer** usually require tube feeding.

Therapy

Some patients whose swallowing problems are caused by muscular disorders can be helped by medications. Stroke patients can often be evaluated and retrained to swallow by a speech therapist. Seniors with cancers of the head and neck usually require a combination of surgery, radiation therapy, and **chemotherapy**. Surgery is used occasionally to treat anatomical abnormalities of the throat or

KEY TERMS

Achalasia—A disorder in which the lower esophageal sphincter fails to relax during swallowing.

Aspiration—The passage of food from the throat into the airway during swallowing rather than further down the esophagus.

Bolus—A soft mass of chewed food formed in the mouth during the first stage of swallowing.

Deglutition—The medical term for the act of swallowing.

Dysphagia—The medical term for difficulty in swallowing.

Globus pharyngis—The persistent sensation of a lump or some other small object in the throat even though no obstruction is present.

Medulla—A structure in the brain stem that controls breathing, swallowing, and other vital functions.

Odynophagia—The medical term for painful swallowing. It may be present with or without dysphagia.

Regurgitation—The casting up of undigested food through the nose or mouth.

Sphincter—A ring-shaped muscle that is able to contract or relax in order to close or open a body passage. The esophagus has two sphincters, one at the upper end in the throat, and the other at the lower end where the esophagus joins the stomach.

Zenker's diverticulum—A disorder in which an overly tense sphincter at the upper end of the esophagus leads to the formation of a pouch in the wall of the esophagus.

esophagus, but this approach is effective only in selected patients. In patients with Alzheimer's or Parkinson's disease, changing the diet to soft foods or using tube feeding are usually necessary, as these disorders are incurable.

Prognosis

The prognosis depends on the cause of the swallowing problem.

Prevention

There is no way as of the early 2000s to prevent all the possible causes of difficult swallowing in seniors.

Caregiver concerns

Caregiver concerns include:

- Obtaining advice about maintaining the senior's nutrition.
- Assisting with feeding (if necessary) or with exercises to improve swallowing.
- Watching for signs of aspiration. The major danger associated with food getting into the windpipe and lungs is a type of pneumonia called aspiration pneumonia.
- Making sure that the senior takes any medications prescribed to treat difficult swallowing.
- Making sure that the senior is getting proper dental care. Swallowing disorders can lead to tooth decay and other dental problems.

Resources

BOOKS

Beers, Mark H., M. D., and Thomas V. Jones, MD. *Merck Manual of Geriatrics*, 3rd ed., Chapter 105, "Dysphagia." Whitehouse Station, NJ: Merck, 2005.

Mace, Nancy L., and Peter V. Rabins. *The 36-Hour Day: A Family Guide to Caring for People with Alzheimer Disease, Other Dementias, and Memory Loss in Later Life,* 4th ed. Baltimore, MD: Johns Hopkins University Press, 2006.

Morris, Virginia. *How to Care for Aging Parents*, 2nd ed. New York: Workman Publishing Co., 2004.

Sonies, Barbara C. *Dysphagia: A Continuum of Care*. Austin, TX: Pro-Ed, 2004.

PERIODICALS

Ferreira, L. E., D. T. Simmons, and T. H. Baron. "Zenker's Diverticula: Pathophysiology, Clinical Presentation, and Flexible Endoscopic Management."*Diseases of the Esophagus* 21 (January 2008): 1–8.

Roy, N., et al. "Dysphagia in the Elderly: Preliminary Evidence of Prevalence, Risk Factors, and Socio-emotional Effects." *Annals of Otology, Rhinology, and Laryngology* 116 (November 2007): 858–865.

Spieker, Michael R. "Evaluating Dysphagia." *American Family Physician* 61 (June 15, 2000): 3639–3648.

OTHER

Fisichella, P. Marco. "Achalasia." *eMedicine*, October 10, 2006. http://www.emedicine.com/med/topic16.htm [cited February 27, 2008].

National Institute of Neurological Disorders and Stroke (NINDS). *NINDS Swallowing Disorders Information Page*. Bethesda, MD: NINDS, 2007. Available online at http://www.ninds.nih.gov/disorders/swallowing_disorders/swallowing_disorders.htm?css=print [cited February 27, 2008].

Paik, Nam-Jong. "Dysphagia." *eMedicine*, December 6, 2006. http://www.emedicine.com/pmr/topic194.htm [cited February 27, 2008].

ORGANIZATIONS

Alzheimer's Association, 225 North Michigan Ave., Floor 17, Chicago, IL, 60601, (312) 335-8700, (800) 272-3900, (866) 699-1246, info@alz.org, http://www.alz.org/index.asp.

National Institute of Diabetes and Digestive and Kidney Diseases (NIDDK), Building 31, Room 9A06, 31 Center Drive, MSC 2560, Bethesda, MD, 20892, (301) 496-3583, http://www2.niddk.nih.gov/.

National Institute of Neurological Disorders and Stroke (NINDS) Brain Resources and Information Network (BRAIN), P.O. Box 5801, Bethesda, MD, 20824, (800) 352-9424, http://www.ninds.nih.gov.

Rebecca J. Frey Ph.D.

Syncope *see* **Fainting**

Systemic lupus erythematosus *see* **Lupus**

T

T'ai chi

Definition

T'ai chi, also known as t'ai chi chuan or taiji, is a form of mind/body **exercise** that developed in China about the twelfth century A.D. as a so-called soft martial art. Its name means "supreme ultimate boxing" in Chinese. The word "soft" means that t'ai chi emphasizes the person's internal spiritual power rather than sheer external muscular force. It is sometimes described as a form of moving meditation. In China, t'ai chi is thought to benefit a person by unblocking and improving the flow of chi (or qi) throughout the body. Chi is the Chinese term for vital energy or life force.

Description

Background

According to legend, t'ai chi originated with a Taoist monk named Chang (or Zhang) Sanfeng, variously said to have lived in the tenth or the twelfth

A t'ai chi class for senior adults. *(AP Images. Reproduced by permission.)*

century. One day the monk noticed a snake bobbing and weaving to avoid a crane trying to kill it rather than striking back directly at the bird. After a few minutes the crane became frustrated and flew off, leaving the snake in peace. The monk concluded that the snake's receptive or "soft" pattern of self-defense was a good illustration of a saying attributed to Lao Tzu, the founder of Taoism: "The soft and the pliable will defeat the hard and strong." Chang Sanfeng is credited with developing the 13 basic postures found in all modern forms of t'ai chi.

Until the early nineteenth century, t'ai chi developed within China as a combination of martial art, meditation training, and physical workout for the maintenance of overall good health. It was incorporated into the practice of traditional Chinese medicine, an inclusive system that teaches the importance of regular exercise as well as proper **diet**, the use of herbal remedies, **acupuncture**, and a type of deep tissue massage known as *tui na*. Beginning in the 1820s, five major schools of t'ai chi developed in China, known by the names of their founding families as Yang, Wu, Sun, Chen, and Wu/Hao.

T'ai chi was first popularized as a form of physical exercise for health maintenance (rather than a martial art) in China in the early twentieth century. It did not become widely popular in the West, however, until the 1970s. During that period some Chinese masters came to the United States, while practitioners of alternative medicine began to recommend t'ai chi (along with **yoga**) as a form of low-impact exercise that reduces emotional **stress** and clears the mind as well as maintaining good posture and flexibility of joints and muscles. Since 1990 t'ai chi has been studied by Western researchers as a form of exercise particularly well-suited to seniors because it can be practiced by people who are overweight or have other health limitations. It also has a low risk of injury to muscles and joints.

Basic t'ai chi practice

There are two basic forms of t'ai chi widely taught in the United States, a solo form for overall fitness, balance, and flexibility; and the "pushing hands" form, which requires a partner. Both forms can be practiced by seniors following appropriate instruction.

The solo form most commonly taught in the United States was developed by a teacher named Cheng Man-Ching in the 1940s and is variously known as the Yang Short Form or the Cheng Man-Ching Tai Chi Form. It consists of 37 basic postures that flow into one another in graceful, continuous movements. The person performing t'ai chi practices deep breathing (from the abdomen) and meditating while moving through the series of postures. The postures themselves are performed while keeping the spine straight, but do not require extreme positions or stretching beyond the body's natural range of motion. To encourage participants to hold the body upright, some teachers of solo t'ai chi instruct students to think of a string stretching from the top of their head into the sky and to let their weight sink down to the soles of the feet.

The Yang Short Form was developed for overall health and fitness rather than martial arts skills. It takes about 7 minutes to complete when performed for health benefits, but can be performed more slowly (taking about 10 to 12 minutes) for purposes of meditation and release of emotional stress. The various movements have interesting names, including Undifferentiated Unity (the introductory posture), Single Whip, White Crane Cools Wings, Play Guitar, Embrace Tiger, Diagonal Flying, Wave Hands Like Clouds, Golden Rooster Stands on One Leg (teaches balance), Fair Lady Weaves the Shuttle, Grasping the Sparrow's Tail, and Step Up to the Seven Stars. Most practitioners complete the short form twice a day, usually once in the morning and once in the evening.

"Pushing hands" tai chi requires faster movement and is closer to the practice of t'ai chi as a martial art. The goal of the exercise is to improve one's own coordination and balance while pushing the partner off balance. The two partners face each other at arm's distance and place a hand on the other's elbow at chest height. The participants move their arms, legs, and hands in a circular pattern while maintaining contact with each other; they are not permitted to use brute force to unbalance each other. Pushing hands requires a basic understanding of and experience in practicing solo t'ai chi. It allows people to test and improve upon their **relaxation**, flexibility, timing, and balance, and also provides a form of low-key competition without risking serious injury.

T'ai chi does not require expensive equipment or a uniform. Participants wear loose-fitting unisex-style clothing and soft-soled shoes. A cotton T-shirt loose enough to permit free movement of the arms and wide-legged pants with either an elastic waist or drawstring waist are fine.

Demographics

Some sources claim that t'ai chi is the most widely practiced form of physical exercise in the world. It is common in China and other countries with large Chinese populations to see people of all ages and both sexes performing t'ai chi exercises for health outdoors (usually in the morning), in public squares or parks or other convenient open spaces. T'ai chi is practiced as a competitive sport in China as well as a martial art and a general fitness exercise; in tournament competition, the athlete completes a standardized set of movements known simply as the Competition Form within a time limit of 6 minutes.

In the United States through the 1990s and early 2000s, particularly as the "baby boomer" generation approached retirement age, there was a sharp increase in interest in t'ai chi as a form of exercise with many benefits to seniors, . According to one U.S. sports participation study published in 2007, t'ai chi is one of the fastest-growing fitness activities in the United States. Many senior centers, as well as hospitals, wellness clinics, and general community centers offer classes in t'ai chi. Those who cannot find or get to a class in their area can learn t'ai chi from instructional books or videos intended for seniors; some are listed below. A major advantage of having an instructor, however, is that participants can receive feedback as to whether they are performing the movements safely and correctly.

Purpose

Although Westerners generally think of t'ai chi in terms of its benefits to physical health (particularly flexibility, good posture, better sleep, and better coordination) and emotional stress reduction, the Chinese regard it as part of an overall medical system intended to preserve the body's chi and extend the lifespan. Although some Westerners do value the meditative dimension of t'ai chi and maintain that it helps in focusing the mind as well as keeping the body fit and flexible, relatively few follow the dietary rules and herbal medications of traditional Chinese medicine.

Challenges

There are relatively few physical challenges involved in t'ai chi, since the postures are well within the body's normal range of motion and feel comfortable and natural to most people. Some seniors who are seriously overweight or have weak ankles may find a few of the poses intended to teach balance a bit difficult, but these can be omitted or modified if necessary. A competent teacher of t'ai chi can modify the Yang Short Form to accommodate almost any physical limitation that individuals may have.

Risks

As with any physical exercise program, seniors thinking about t'ai chi as a fitness regimen should consult their primary care physician before taking a class— particularly if they have not been physically active for some time. The most common risk is falling; therefore, seniors with **osteoporosis** or arthritis should be particularly careful to seek a physician's advice.

Many t'ai chi instructors also advise participants not to practice t'ai chi if they are extremely tired or sleepy; are being treated for an active infection; or have just eaten a large meal.

Results

Studies of t'ai chi in various Western countries have claimed that it benefits seniors with a range of health problems:

- A study published in Hong Kong in early 2008 maintained that t'ai chi is beneficial to seniors with osteoporosis in that it retards further bone loss and improves muscular coordination.
- As of 2008 T'ai chi was being studied at a Miami hospital for potential benefits to seniors suffering from frailty syndrome, a condition marked by weight loss, muscular weakness, tiring easily, and difficulty in walking.
- Studies carried out in Germany, the United Kingdom, and Australia evaluated the efficacy of t'ai chi in improving balance and lowering the risk of falls in older adults. Although t'ai chi appears to confer short-term benefits in these areas, the studies disagreed about long-term improvement in seniors' health.
- A study conducted at the University of Pittsburgh in 2007 reported that t'ai chi and yoga are both effective in reducing chronic low back and joint pain in seniors.
- A pilot program at a research institute in Oregon found that t'ai chi is effective in maintaining physical functioning in seniors with Parkinson's disease and that it is a safe and appropriate form of exercise for some PD patients.
- A study in Australia comparing t'ai chi to hydrotherapy for treatment of hip and knee osteoarthritis reported that t'ai chi is only slightly less effective than hydrotherapy in improving range of motion in the affected joints. The study also found that the improvements in joint mobility were sustained for six months.
- Research conducted at the University of Wisconsin in 2006 showed that t'ai chi was helpful in improving

KEY TERMS

Chi (qi)—The Chinese term for vital energy or life force. T'ai chi is said to unblock the flow of chi through the body and, therefore, to support the body's basic store of chi.

Frailty syndrome—A condition of physical weakness that places older adults at increased risk of disability or institutionalization. It is measured by evaluating seniors for muscle weakness, weight loss, low physical activity, exhaustion, and slow walking speed.

Taoism—A traditional Chinese belief system that influenced the development of t'ai chi and Chinese herbal medicine. It holds that the human body is a microcosm (miniature form) of the universe and is connected to it by its chi or vital energy.

seniors' psychological well-being and in enhancing sleep for those with sleep disturbances.

A considerable amount of research has been done on t'ai chi in Western institutions since the 1980s. As of early 2008, the National Institutes of Health (NIH) was conducting five studies of possible health benefits of t'ai chi in patients with the following conditions:

- Women recently diagnosed with breast cancer (to determine the effects of t'ai chi on stress reduction and the immune system).
- A comparative study of t'ai chi and a cardiovascular fitness program in improving fitness and endurance in survivors of cancer.
- Patients with osteoarthritis of the knee (to determine whether t'ai chi reduces pain and improves range of motion)
- Patients with stable heart failure (to evaluate whether t'ai chi improves their quality of life)
- Patients with rheumatoid arthritis (to evaluate the effects of t'ai chi on the immune system and overall health).

Resources

BOOKS

Frantzis, Bruce K. *Big Book of Tai Chi.* Berkeley, CA: Blue Snake Books, 2006.

Hong, Youlian, ed. *Tai Chi Chuan: State of the Art in International Research.* Basel and New York: Karger, 2008.

Koskuba, Eva, and Karel Koskuba. *Tai Chi for Every Body: Easy Low-Impact Exercises for Every Age.* Pleasantville, NY: Reader's Digest Association, 2007.

Pelletier, Kenneth R. *The Best Alternative Medicine,* Chapter 2, "Sound Mind, Sound Body." New York: Fireside Books, 2002.

PERIODICALS

Cherniak, E. P., H. J. Flores, and B. R. Troen. "Emerging Therapies to Treat Frailty Syndrome in the Elderly." *Alternative Medicine Review* 12 (September 2007): 246–258.

Fransen, M., L. Nairn, J. Winstanley, et al. "Physical Activity for Osteoarthritis Management: A Randomized Controlled Clinical Trial Evaluating Hydrotherapy or Tai Chi Classes." *Arthritis and Rheumatism* 57 (April 15, 2007): 407–414.

Greenspan, A. I. et al. "Tai Chi and Perceived Health Status in Older Adults Who Are Transitionally Frail: A Randomized Controlled Trial." *Physical Therapy* 87 (May 2007): 525–535.

Howe, T. E., L. Rochester, A. Jackson, et al. "Exercise for Improving Balance in Older People." *Cochrane Database of Systematic Reviews,* October 17, 2007: CD004963.

Kuramoto, A. M. "Therapeutic Benefits of Tai Chi Exercise: Research Review." *Wisconsin Medical Journal* 105 (October 2006): 42–46.

Li, F., P. Harmer, K. J. Fisher, et al. "Tai Chi-based Exercise for Older Adults with Parkinson's Disease: A Pilot-Program Evaluation." *Journal of Aging and Physical Activity* 15 (April 2007): 139–151.

Lui, P. P., L. Qin, and K. M. Chan. "Tai Chi Chuan Exercises in Enhancing Bone Mineral Density in Active Seniors." *Clinics in Sports Medicine* 27 (January 2008): 75–86.

Morone, N. E., and C. M. Greco. "Mind-Body Interventions for Chronic Pain in Older Adults: A Structured Review." *Pain Medicine* 8 (May/June 2007): 359–375.

Voukelatos, A., et al. "A Randomized, Controlled Trial of Tai Chi for the Prevention of Falls: The Central Sydney Tai Chi Trial." *Journal of the American Geriatric Society* 55 (August 2007): 1185–1191.

OTHER

Backgrounder: Tai Chi for Health Purposes. National Center for Complementary and Alternative Medicine (NCCAM). Bethesda, MD: NCCAM. June 2007 [cited March 21, 2008]. http://nccam.nih.gov/health/taichi/.

ORGANIZATIONS

International Taoist Tai Chi Socicty, 134 D'Arcy St., Toronto, Ontario, Canada, M5T 1K3, +1 (416) 656-2110, +1 (416) 654-3937, headoffice@taoist.org, http://www.taoist.org/content/standard.asp?name=Home.

National Center for Complementary and Alternative Medicine (NCCAM), 9000 Rockville Pike, Bethesda, MD, 20892, (301) 519-3153, (888) 644-6226, (866) 464-3616, info@nccam.nih.gov, http://nccam.nih.gov.

Patience T'ai Chi Association, PO Box 350-532, Brooklyn, NY, 11235, 718-332-3477, staff@patiencetaichi.com, http://www.patiencetaichi.com/public/main.cfm.

T'ai Chi Foundation, PO Box 575, Midtown Station, New York, NY, 10018, (212) 645-7010, http://www.taichifoundation.org/.

Rebecca J. Frey Ph.D.

Talking with your doctor

Definition

Talking with your doctor is perhaps the most important element in receiving safe, effective health care.

Purpose

In order to judge which tests to order, medication to prescribe, or surgery to recommend, your doctor needs to know about you as a person, your health problems, how they affect your life, and how you feel. You have a responsibility to be open and honest with your doctor and your doctor has a responsibility to carefully listen to you.

Description

You tell your mechanic what problems your car has and then trust that he can fix them, and you need to be able to tell your doctor how your body or mind are working so that you can trust her to help you function and feel better. Talking with your doctor can be difficult. Many doctors seem preoccupied, in a hurry, and are not good listeners. And patients, especially seniors, fear being judged negatively because of their physical infirmities and problems, age, size, looks, personal habits or behaviors.

Establishing trust

Your doctor works for you. In a sense, doctor-patient relationships are similar to spousal relationships. Trust relationships take time to build. It is crucial that seniors find doctors they can talk with. When changing doctors, it's a good idea to make a get-acquainted appointment to review your records and **health history** and see whether that doctor is someone you might want to trust your life with. And trust is a two-way street. The doctor wants to know that she can trust you to be open and honest.

Resources

BOOKS

Bickley, L. S., P. G. Szilagyi, and J. G. Stackhouse, eds. *Bates' Guide to Physical Examination & History Taking*, 8th ed. Philadelphia, PA: Lippincott Williams & Wilkins, 2002.

Chan, P. D., and P. J. Winkle. *History and Physical Examination in Medicine*, 10th ed. New York, NY: Current Clinical Strategies, 2002.

Seidel, Henry M. *Mosby's Physical Examination Handbook*, 4th ed. St. Louis, MO: Mosby-Year Book, 2003.

Swartz, Mark A., and William Schmitt. *Textbook of Physical Diagnosis: History and Examination*, 4th ed. Philadelphia, PA: Saunders, 2001.

PERIODICALS

Lee, S. J., A. L. Back, S. D. Block, and S. K. Stewart. "Enhancing Physician-Patient Communication." *Hematology* (2002): 464-483.

Nadelson, C., and M. T. Notman. "Boundaries in the Doctor-Patient Relationship." *Theoretical Medicine and Bioethics* 23 (March 2002): 191-201.

Nebel, E. J. "Malpractice: Love Thy Patient." *Clinical Orthopedics* 407 (February 2003): 19-24.

Thakur, N. M., and R. L. Perkel. "Prevention in Adulthood: Forging a Doctor-Patient Partnership." *Primary Care* 29 (September 2002): 571-582.

ORGANIZATIONS

American Academy of Family Physicians. 11400 Tomahawk Creek Parkway, Leawood, KS 66211-2672. (913) 906-6000. E-mail: fp@aafp.org. http://www.aafp.org.

American Academy of Pediatrics. 141 Northwest Point Boulevard, Elk Grove Village, IL 60007-1098. (847) 434-4000. Fax: (847) 434-8000. E-mail: kidsdoc@aap.org. http://www.aap.org.

American College of Physicians. 190 N. Independence Mall West, Philadelphia, PA 19106-1572. (800) 523-1546, x2600 or (215) 351-2600. http://www.acponline.org.

American College of Surgeons. 633 North St. Clair Street, Chicago, IL 60611-3231. (312) 202-5000. Fax: (312) 202-5001. E-mail: postmaster@facs.org. http://www.facs.org.

American Hospital Association. One North Franklin, Chicago, IL 60606-3421. (312) 422-3000. http://www.aha.org/index.asp.

American Medical Association. 515 N. State Street, Chicago, IL 60610. (312) 464-5000. http://www.ama-assn.org.

OTHER

Cable News Network (CNN). [cited March 2, 2003]. http://www.cnn.com/HEALTH/9906/30/internet.house.calls.

Emory University. [cited March 2, 2003]. http://www.emory.edu/WHSC/HSNEWS/releases/jun98/061898kaleidoscope.html.

University of North Carolina at Chapel Hill. [cited March 2, 2003]. http://www.med.unc.edu/wrkunits/2depts/medicine/fgidc/improving_relationships.htm.

YourDoctorintheFamily.Com. [cited March 2, 2003]. http://www.yourdoctorinthefamily.com/grandtheory/section11.htm.

L. Fleming Fallon Jr., MD, DrPH

Tamoxifen *see* **Anticancer drugs**

TB *see* **Tuberculosis**

Teeth whitening

Definition

Teeth whitening is the process of using bleach or other materials to make teeth look whiter. The materials remove stains or other discoloration from the tooth surface.

Purpose

Teeth whitening is a cosmetic treatment done to improve the appearance of teeth. Teeth are whitened to remove the effects of coffee, cigarettes, and other substances that permanently stain or discolor teeth. Medications such as **antibiotics** like tetracycline may discolor teeth. Fluorosis, a condition caused by absorbing too much fluoride, could affect tooth color. Furthermore, aging also causes teeth to loose their bright color.

Precautions

Teeth whitening is not safe or effective for everyone, so a person should have a dental exam before starting treatment. The dentist can advise the patient about the most appropriate procedure. The oral health professional will also discuss the expected results of treatment. Patients may expect yellow or gray teeth to be replaced with a bright, white color. However, whitening may not work well on some stain colors.

The importance of a check-up

Whitening may not be recommended for people with gum disease, receding gums, or sensitive teeth. The dentist may advise against certain treatments if the enamel is worn. Enamel is the outer layer of the tooth. There is no enamel on an exposed tooth root, so the root cannot be whitened.

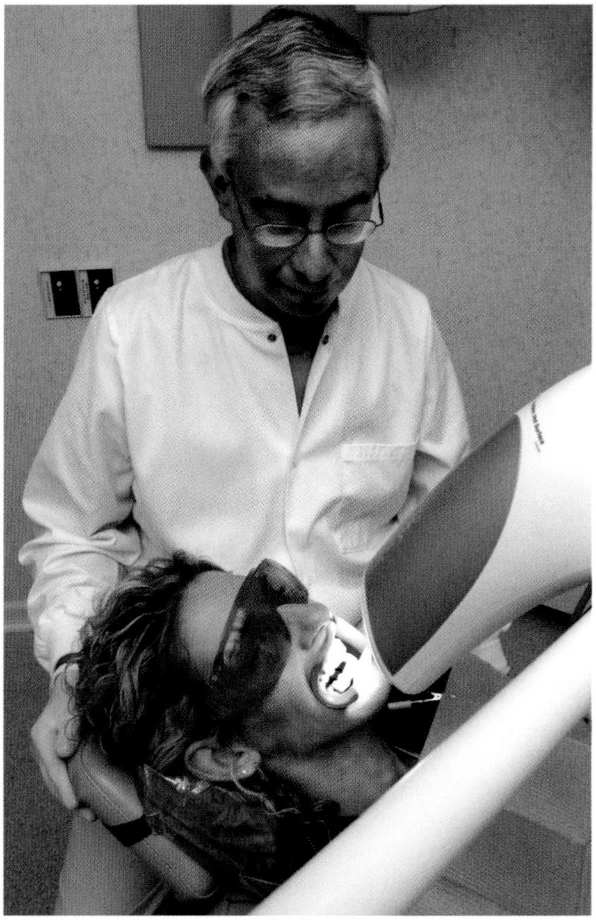

Dentist administers tooth whitening process to patient. *(AP Images. Reproduced by permission.)*

In addition, cavities must be filled before treatment begins. Otherwise, the patient could experience additional mouth sensitivity when treatment material comes into contact with decay or the tooth interior.

When whitening is not recommended

Women who are pregnant and nursing should avoid any whitening treatment except for toothpaste. Oral health care professionals advise that other treatments could contain levels of peroxide that are potentially dangerous to the child. Although no connections have been made between these treatments and harm to the child's health, mothers are urged to take preventive action and delay whitening treatment.

Teenagers should not have their teeth bleached until they are between 14 and 16 years old. In a younger child, the nerve of the tooth called the pulp chamber has not fully developed. Whitening at this point could irritate the pulp and cause sensitivity.

People who are allergic to peroxide should not be treated with this whitening agent.

Cautions about tooth color

Treatments such as bleaching are most effective on yellowish stains, according to the American Dental Association (ADA). Teeth with brown stains may not bleach as well, and the treatment is even less effective on gray-stained teeth.

Furthermore, bleaching will not change the color of tooth-colored fillings, dentures, crowns, porcelain restorations, bonding, or other material used to restore or replace a tooth. If bleaching is done, the newly whitened teeth will stand out in contrast to fillings or other modifications.

Description

Teeth are whitened by the use of bleach or other material. The treatment may be done in the dental office, at home with guidance from a dentist, or at home with the use of over-the-counter products. Tools for self-treatment include bleaching trays, gels or strips that are applied to the teeth, and toothpaste.

Whitening treatments are cosmetic procedures, and are usually not covered by dental insurance.

Products used by oral health professionals such and those sold over the counter may have the ADA Seal of Acceptance. This endorsement indicates that products carrying the seal have met the American Dental Association's criteria for safety and effectiveness. Those standards are based on the patient following directions when the product is used.

The ADA evaluation program is voluntary. That means manufacturers are not required to submit products for review. As a result, the lack of a seal may not indicate that the product is unsafe. However, products on the Accepted list have the ADA endorsement, and the association may take positions on certain unevaluated procedures such as laser treatment.

Dental office treatment

The whitening treatment provided by dentists is known as chairside bleaching, in-office bleaching, or power bleaching. The dentist first protects the patient's gums and tissue by applying a protective gel or a rubber shield. The dentist than applies a whitening solution on the teeth.

The whitening solution contains hydrogen peroxide, which is a bleaching agent that could change the tooth color. The bleach is used to remove surface (extrinsic) and deeper (intrinsic) stains. Professionally applied whiteners, those solutions used by dentists, usually contain hydrogen peroxide. This bleaching agent comes in concentrations ranging from 15% to 35%. As of March of 2005, all solutions with the ADA Seal had a 35% concentration of hydrogen peroxide.

After the gel is applied, a light may be shined on the teeth to accelerate the whitening agent. Some agents are enhanced by lasers. However, no treatments requiring lasers were on the ADA list of accepted products as of March 2005. Although lasers may be safe, the association had not seen published, peer-reviewed data on the safety and effectiveness of laser whitening.

Chairside bleaching treatment may last from thirty minutes to an hour, according to the ADA. In addition, patients may need to return for additional treatments. The cost of treatment for the whole mouth can cost from $500 to $1,000. Factors affecting cost include the patient's location and the number of treatments needed. At the high end of the range is laser treatment, which could cost $1,000 or more.

Dentist-supervised treatment

Supervised treatment combines visits to the dentist with treatment at home. The procedure is also called tray bleaching or nightguard bleaching because the patient wears a tray on the teeth that protects the gums from the whitening solution.

For this treatment, the dentist takes an impression of the patient's teeth and makes a mouthpiece tray, or mouthguard, that will fit over the teeth. The dentist dispenses a whitening gel that the patient will place in the customized mouthguard.

The gel usually contains carbamide peroxide, which comes in concentrations of 10%, 16%, and 22%. Products with the ADA Seal have a 10% concentration. That amount is the equivalent of an approximately 3% concentration of hydrogen peroxide. The ADA endorsement applies only to home systems dispensed by dentists. The association's Seal reflects the importance of consulting with a dentist before undergoing treatment at home, according to the ADA.

The dentist will set up a schedule for wearing the mouthguard. Wearing times vary by product. A patient may we ar the piece overnight for one to two weeks. For other systems, the patient wears the

KEY TERMS

Enamel—The hard, white, outer layer of the tooth.

Fluoride—A compound believed to combat cavities in teeth.

Peroxide—A bleaching agent that is a compound consisting of two atoms of oxygen connected by a single bond.

mouthguard for a set amount of time twice a day. This treatment usually lasts two weeks.

During supervised treatment, the dentist generally schedules appointments to monitor the patient's progress. In addition to checking the whitening process, the dentist may examine the fit of the mouthguard and look for signs of gum irritation.

Supervised home bleaching of the whole mouth costs from $300 to $600.

Over-the-counter (OTC) products

In-home treatments that can be purchased over-the-counter include products that use bleach in mouthguard trays as well as strips and gels. The bleaching agent is usually carbamide peroxide, which is not as strong as the hydrogen peroxide found in solutions that are used in chairside bleaching and supervised home treatment.

OTC treatments range in price from $20 to $150. Treatment lasts 14 days on average. Another treatment is the use of whitening toothpaste, a product that does not contain bleach.

TRAY TREATMENT Mouthguard treatment kits can be bought in stores and over the Internet. The tray kits involve the use of a mouthguard and gel. While similar to dentist-supervised home treatment, the patient does not use a customized tray specifically for her or his mouth. Some kits have mouthguards that patients can mold to their teeth. However, the patient relies on the generic instructions provided by the manufacturer.

GELS AND WHITENING STRIPS Gels are applied directly to the teeth. Whitening strips are thin, clear strips coated with a peroxide-based gel. The strips are applied to the teeth and worn for 30 minutes twice a day. Treatment time varies by product and generally lasts from five to 14 days.

WHITENING TOOTHPASTES Whitening toothpastes do not contain bleach. Instead mild abrasives remove surface stains, but do not change tooth color. Products with the ADA Seal contain special chemicals or polishing agents that remove stains. A tube of whitening toothpaste costs about $5.

Preparation

The ADA advises people to consult with a dentist before beginning any teeth whitening treatment. The dentist can review the patient's oral **health history** and discuss the appropriate treatment. If necessary, the dentist will fill cavities.

Aftercare

During supervised at-home treatment, the dentist may schedule appointments to check on the progress of whitening, side effects, and the tray fit.

After treatment is completed, people need to be aware that **smoking** will cause teeth to discolor. Beverages with **caffeine** should be consumed with a straw to reduce the effects of staining. Another preventive action is brushing the teeth after drinking or eating foods that cause stains.

Risks

Teeth-whitening may cause sensitivity to hot and cold food and beverages. This is a temporary side effect that usually ends when treatment is completed. Some patients also experience gum irritation if the tray does not fit properly.

Results

Dentists use a stronger bleaching agent than that found in commercial products, so in-office whitening treatment produces a more dramatic effect on teeth with yellow stains. Over-the-counter products with bleach provide some change in the tooth color, and whitening toothpaste works only on surface stains.

Bleaching does not leave teeth permanently white. Whitening can last from six months to a year. Sometimes teeth stay white even longer. However, smoking or consumption of food and beverages that stain can cause discoloration within one month.

Resources

PERIODICALS

Caruana, Claudia M. "The Smiles Have It!" *Vegetarian Times*, February 2003, 35-39.

Foley, Denise; Poust, Jenny. "Home Tooth-Whitening Kits." *Prevention*,February 2004, 160 (4 pages)[cited March 21, 2005]. http://search.epnet.com/login. aspx?direct=true&db=hxh&an=11891865.

ORGANIZATION

Academy of General Dentistry. 211 East Chicago Avenue, Suite 900, Chicago, IL 60611-1999. 888-AGD-DENT (888-243-3368). http://www.agd.org.

American Dental Association. 211 East Chicago Avenue, Chicago, IL 60611-2678. 312-440-2500. http://www.ada.org.

American Dental Hygienists' Association. 444 North Michigan Avenue, Suite 3400, Chicago, IL 60611. 312-440-8927.http://www.adha.org.

OTHER

"Teeth Whitening: Is it for you?" Academy of General Dentistry. December 20, 2004 [cited March 21, 2005]. http://www.agd.org/media/2004/dec/whitening.asp.

"Tooth Whitening Systems." American Dental Hygienists' Association 2005 [cited March 21, 2005]. http://www.adha.org/oralhealth/whitening.htm.

"Tooth Whitening Treatments." American Dental Association 2005 [cited March 21, 2005]. http://www.ada.org/public/topics/whitening.asp.

Liz Swain

Tendinitis

Definition

Tendinitis is the inflammation of a tendon, a tough rope-like tissue that connects muscle to bone.

Description

Tendinitis usually occurs in individuals in middle or old age because it is often the result of overuse over a long period of time.

tendons that commonly become inflamed include:

- tendons of the hand
- tendons of the upper arm that effect the shoulder
- achilles tendon and the tendon that runs across the top of the foot

Causes and symptoms

Sudden stretching or repeated overuse injures the connection between the tendon and its bone or muscle. The injury is largely mechanical, but when it appears, the body tries to heal it by initiating inflammation. Inflammation increases the blood supply, bringing nutrients to the damaged tissues along with immunogenic agents to combat infection. The result is swelling, tenderness, pain, heat, and redness if the inflammation is close to the skin.

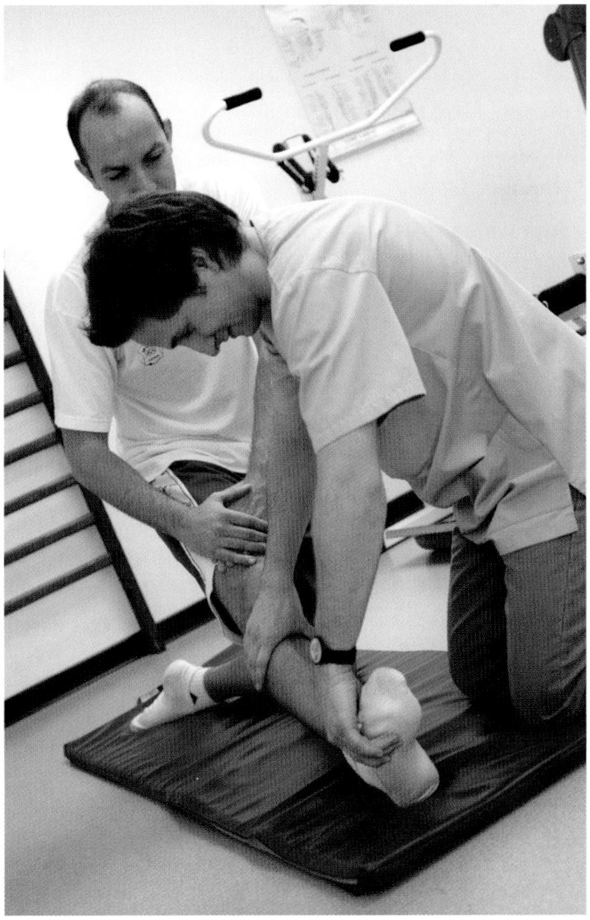

Man with achilles tendonitis stretching, assisted by physical therapist. *(Phanie / Photo Researchers, Inc. Reproduced by permission.)*

Diagnosis

Some tendon injuries are superficial and easy to identify. These include "tennis elbow" (extensor tendinitis) over the outside of the elbow, and Achilles' tendinitis just above the heel of the foot. There are several tendons in the shoulder that can be overused or stretched, and usually a shoulder will have more than one injury at a time. Tendinitis in the biceps, the infraspinatus, or the supraspinatus tendon may accompany a tear of the shoulder ligaments or an impingement of one bone or another. Careful pressure testing and movement of the parts is all that is necessary to identify the tendinitis.

Treatment

Rest, ice, compression, and elevation (RICE) will treat the acute condition. The best way to apply ice is

KEY TERMS

Biceps—The muscle in the front of the upper arm.

Infraspinatus—A muscle at the middle of the shoulder blade.

Supraspinatus—A muscle at the top of the shoulder blade.

in a bag with water. The water applies the cold directly to the skin. Chemical ice packs can get too cold and cause frostbite. Compression using an elastic wrap minimizes swelling and bleeding in an acute sprain. Splinting may help rest the limb. Pain and anti-inflammatory medications (aspirin, naproxen, ibuprofen) will help. Sometimes the inflammation lingers and requires additional treatment. Injections of cortisone-like medicine often relieve chronic tendinitis, but should be reserved for resistant cases since cortisone can occasionally cause problems of its own.

If tendinitis is persistent and unresponsive to nonsurgical treatment, a surgery to remove the afflicted portion of tendon can be performed. Surgery is also conducted to remove calcium buildup that comes with persistent tendinitis.

Alternative treatment

An osteopathic soft-tissue treatment on the tendon may relieve pain and increase mobility. Increasing intake of antioxidant-rich foods and lowering intake of animal fats may help reduce the inflammation. Acupuncture has also been used to combat tendinitis. Hydrotherapies, such as whirlpool baths, help relax the surrounding muscles.

Prognosis

Generally, tendinitis will heal if the provoking activity is stopped.

Prevention

If given enough time, tendons will strengthen to meet the demands placed on them. They grow slowly because of their poor blood supply, so adequate time is required for good conditioning.

J. Ricker Polsdorfer MD

Testicular self-examination

Definition

A testicular self-examination (TSE) is the procedure by which a man checks the appearance and consistency of his testes.

Purpose

Most testicular cancers are first noticed by the man himself. Men should do a TSE every month to find out if the testes contain any suspicious lumps or other irregularities, which could be signs of **cancer** or infection.

Precautions

None.

Description

A TSE should take place during a warm shower or bath, when the skin is warm, wet, and soapy. The man needs to step out of the tub so that he is in front of a mirror. The heat from the tub or shower will relax the scrotum (sac containing the testes) and the skin will be softer and thinner, making it easier to feel a lump. It is important that the exam be done very gently.

The man should stand facing his mirror and look for swelling on the scrotum. Using both hands, the scrotum should be gently lifted so that the area underneath can be checked.

The next step is examination by hand. The index and middle fingers should be placed under each testicle, with the thumbs on top. The testes should be examined one at a time. The man should roll each testicle between his fingers and thumbs. He should feel for lumps of any size (even as small as a pea) particularly on the front or side of each testicle. He should also look for soreness or irregularities. Next, the epididymis and vas deferens, located on the top and back of the testes, should be felt. This area feels like a cord, and should not be tender.

Results

It is normal for one testicle to be larger than the other is, and for them to hang at different levels; but the size should stay the same from one month to the next. The testes should be free from lumps, **pain**, irregularities and swelling.

A TSE is considered abnormal if any swelling, tenderness, lumps, or irregularities are found. Hard,

KEY TERMS

Epididymis—A tube in the back of the testes that transports sperm.

Scrotum—The pouch containing the testes.

Testes—Egg-shaped male gonads located in the scrotum. Testes is the plural form of testis, which is a testicle.

Vas deferens—A tube that is a continuation of the epididymis. This tube transports sperm from the testis to the prostatic urethra.

unmoving lumps are abnormal, even if they are painless. A lump could be a sign of an infection or a cancerous tumor. A change in testicle size from one month to the next is also abnormal. A feeling of heaviness in the scrotum is another abnormal sign. If any abnormality is found, a man is encouraged to check with his doctor as soon as possible because testicular cancer is highly curable if found early.

Resources

BOOKS

Hainsworth, John D., and F. Anthony Greco. "Testis." In *Cancer Treatment,* edited by Charles M. Haskell, 5th ed. Philadelphia: W.B. Saunders, 2001.

OTHER

"Questions and Answers About Testicular Cancer." *National Cancer Institute.* February 2000. http://cis.nci.nih.gov/fact/6_34.htm

Rhonda Cloos R.N.

Tetanus

Definition

Tetanus is a rare but often fatal disease that affects the central nervous system by causing painful muscular contractions. It begins when tetanus bacteria enter the body, usually through a wound or cut exposed to contaminated soil. Tetanus is easily preventable through vaccination.

Description

Tetanus is rare in the United States, with nearly all cases occurring in adults who were not vaccinated as children. About 100 cases are reported each year; 63% of these occur in people over the age of 50. The number of tetanus cases in the United States has steadily decreased since the 1940s (500 to 600 cases per year); the number of reported cases has remained at approximately 50 to 100 cases per year since the mid-1970s.

Tetanus causes convulsive muscle spasms and rigidity that can lead to respiratory paralysis and death. It is sometimes called "lockjaw" because one of the most common symptoms is a stiff jaw, unable to be opened. Sometimes, tetanus affects only the part of the body where the infection began, but in almost all of reported cases, it spreads to the entire body. The incubation period from the time of the injury until the first symptoms appear ranges from two to 50 days. Symptoms usually occur within five to 10 days. When symptoms occur early, the chance of death is increased. Tetanus is not contagious.

Causes and symptoms

Tetanus is caused by a bacteria called *Clostridium tetani*, whose spores (the dormant form) are found in soil, street dust, and animal (or even human) feces. Tetanus spores germinate in the body, producing a highly poisonous neurotoxin in the blood, spreading to the nervous system. The infection is usually transmitted through deep puncture wounds or cuts or scratches that are not cleaned well. Many people associate tetanus with rusty nails and other dirty objects, but any wound can be a source. Less common ways of getting tetanus are animal scratches and bites, surgical wounds, dental work, therapeutic abortion, and as a result of intravenous drug use. Cases have also been reported in people with no known wound or medical condition.

The first symptom of tetanus is often a stiff or "locked" jaw that prevents the patient from opening his/her mouth or swallowing. This is also called trismus and results in a facial expression called a sardonic smile (or risus sardonicus). Stiffness of the neck and other muscles throughout the body and uncontrollable spasms often follow. Sometimes these convulsions are severe enough to cause broken bones. The bacterial toxin (*tetanospasmin*) affects the nerve endings, causing a continuous stimulation of muscles. Other symptoms include fever, loss of appetite, and drooling. People with tetanus that is localized experience pain and tingling only at the wound site and spasms in nearby muscles.

Diagnosis

Tetanus is diagnosed by the clinical symptoms and a medical history that shows no tetanus

KEY TERMS

Clostridium—A genus of deadly bacteria that are responsible for tetanus and other serious diseases, including botulism and gangrene from war wounds. Clostridia thrives without oxygen.

DTaP—Diphtheria and tetanus toxoids and accellular pertussis combination vaccine.

DTP—Diphtheria, tetanus, and whole-cell pertussis vaccine.

Td—Tetanus and diphtheria vaccine.

Toxin—A poisonous substance that flows through the body.

Wound—Any injury that breaks the skin, including cuts, scratches, and puncture wounds.

immunization. Early diagnosis and treatment is crucial to recovery from tetanus.

Treatment

Tetanus is a life-threatening disease that requires immediate hospitalization, usually in an intensive care unit (ICU). Treatment can take several weeks and includes antibiotics to kill the bacteria and shots of antitoxin to neutralize the toxin. It also includes muscle-relaxing drugs to control muscle spasms or barbiturates for sedation. In severe cases, patients are placed on an artificial respirator. Recovery can take six weeks or more. After recovery, since the levels of circulating toxin are too low to stimulate natural antibody production, the patient must still be immunized against this disease to prevent reinfection.

Prognosis

Up to 30% of tetanus victims in the United States die. Early diagnosis and treatment improves the prognosis. Neonatal tetanus has a mortality rate of more than 90%.

Prevention

Pre-exposure vaccination

Tetanus is easily preventable through vaccination. All children should have a series of five doses of DTaP, a combined vaccine that offers protection against diphtheria, tetanus, and pertussis, before the age of seven, according to the Centers for Disease Control and Prevention's national immunization guidelines, the Advisory Committee on Immunization Practices, the Committee on Infectious Diseases of the American Academy of Pediatrics, and the American Academy of Family Physicians. Children will not be admitted to school without proof of this and other immunizations.

The DTaP (diptheria, tetanus, accellular pertussis) vaccine should be given at ages two months, four months, six months, 15 to 18 months, and four to six years. DTaP is the preferred vaccine for children up to the age of seven in the United States; it has fewer side effects than DTP and can be used to complete a vaccination schedule begun with DTP. DTaP was first approved by the Food and Drug Administration (FDA) in September 1996. In December 1996, it was approved for use in infants. Between the ages of 11 and 13, children should have a booster for diphtheria and tetanus, called Td.

Adults should have a Td booster every 10 years. Statistics from the Centers for Disease Control and Prevention (CDC) show that fewer than half of Americans 60 years of age and older have antibodies against tetanus. The CDC suggests adults may be revaccinated at mid-decade birthdays (for example, 45, 55). Adults who have never been vaccinated against tetanus should get a series of three injections of Td over six to 12 months and then follow the 10-year booster shot schedule.

Side effects of the tetanus vaccine are minor: soreness, redness, or swelling at the site of the injection that appear anytime from a few hours to two days after the vaccination and go away in a day or two. Rare but serious side effects that require immediate treatment by a doctor are serious allergic reactions or deep, aching pain and muscle wasting in the upper arms. These symptoms could start from two days to four weeks after the shot and could continue for months.

In early 2001, a shortage of the tetanus vaccine became evident after the pharmaceutical company Wyeth-Ayerst Laboratories decided to stop production of the tetanus vaccine, leaving Aventis-Pasteur as the sole manufacturer of the vaccine. As a result, hospitals were provided with only a minimal amount of the drug on a weekly basis—enough to vaccinate patients with potentially infected wounds and other priority cases. Despite stepped-up production efforts on the part of the manufacturer, however, a spokesperson for Aventis-Pasteur predicted that the shortage would last until the end of 2001, as the vaccine takes 11 months to produce.

Post-exposure care

Keeping wounds and scratches clean is important in preventing infection. Since this organism grows only in the absence of oxygen, wounds must be adequately cleaned of dead tissue and foreign substances. Run cool water over the wound and wash it with a mild soap. Dry it with a clean cloth or sterile gauze. To help prevent infection, apply an antibiotic cream or ointment and cover the wound with a bandage. The longer a wound takes to heal, the greater the chance of infection. If the wound doesn't heal, or, it is red, warm, drains, or swells, consult a doctor.

Following a wound, to produce rapid levels of circulating antibody, a doctor may administer a specific antitoxin (human tetanus immune globulin, TIG) if the individual does not have an adequate history of immunization. The antitoxin is given at the same sitting as a dose of vaccine but at separate sites. Some individuals will report a history of significant allergy to "tetanus shots." In most cases, this occurred in the remote past and was probably due to the previous use of antitoxin derived from horse serum.

Resources

PERIODICALS

"Vaccines:Not Just for Kids.(NEWS & Notes)(Brief article)." *Clinician Reviews*18.2(Feb 2008):38.

DuVal, Tara, Maura Brennan, and Sandra Bellantonio. "Preventive Care in Older Adults: What and When?." *Family Practice Recertification*29.10(Oct 2007):41–49.

Landers, Susan J. "Tetanus vaccine shortage leads to rationing." *American Medical News*. March 19, 2001. http://www.ama-assn.org/sci-pubs/amnews/pick_01/hlsb0319.htm.

OTHER

"Tetanus." Centers for Disease Control and Prevention. http://www.cdc.gov/nip/publications/pink/tetanus.pdf.

Lori De Milto
Lisa M. Piazza M.A.

Tetracyclines *see* **Antibiotics**

Therapeutic exercise

Definition

Therapeutic **exercise** can be defined as a specific program of regular exercise with certain objectives. It refers to physical activity undertaken to treat chronic musculoskeletal, cardiopulmonary, or neurologic conditions as part of a rehabilitation program, as distinct from exercise undertaken for general health maintenance, recreation, or as a social activity. Therapeutic exercise may vary from exercises directed toward a specific body part or muscle group to general workouts intended to restore a patient recovering from illness or surgery to better physical condition.

Description

There are four basic types of therapeutic exercises, aimed at improving the senior's strength (resistance training), flexibility, endurance, and stability or balance. When possible, the doctor or **physical therapist** incorporates activities that the senior enjoys as well as those intended to bring about a specific result; for example, a senior with arthritis who enjoys swimming may be given therapeutic exercises intended to increase range of motion that can be performed in a swimming pool. Therapeutic exercise is always tailored to the fitness needs of the individual senior. Seniors with certain heart conditions or **blood pressure** that drops while exercising should be supervised by a doctor during their exercise period.

Some types of therapeutic exercise can be modified for seniors; for example, weight training to increase muscle strength can be carried out while sitting if the senior has difficulty standing or walking. Patients with **osteoarthritis** may prefer three 10-minute exercise sessions spaced out over the day to one 30-minute session; they will still gain health benefits as long as the shorter sessions add up to 30 minutes per day.

Strength training

Strength training is done to build up muscle tissue; it typically consists of graded exercises involving resistance training. This type of therapeutic exercise is important for seniors because most persons lose between 20 and 40 percent of their muscle tissue as they age. Strength training may be high or moderate in intensity.

Most forms of high-intensity strength training involve free weights that the patient swings or moves through a distance or machines that use either weights or air pressure that the patient must push against. The muscles are trained by repetitions of the pushing or lifting motion. For healthy elderly patients, a fitness machine can be set to 60 to 80 percent of the one-repetition maximum, which is the weight that the person can lift once. Elderly patients who are in good condition can perform two sets of 10 repetitions each on several different machines during a strength training workout. When done twice a week, strength

A senior practicing Qigong. *(AP Images. Reproduced by permission.)*

training can improve a senior's strength by 30 to 150 percent during the first year of exercise.

Moderate-intensity strength training increases a senior's strength by 10 to 20 percent over a period of several months and helps to maintain it. This type of strength training uses calisthenics, which are exercises that employ the body's own weight for resistance; cuff weights, which can be attached to ankles or wrists; or weighted elastic tubing. Calisthenics include such well-known exercises as sit-ups, push-ups, squats, and pull-ups. These moderate-intensity exercises are well suited for weak elderly patients and other seniors because they do not require expensive equipment or a trip to a gym or fitness center; they can easily be done at home.

Flexibility training

Flexibility training is generally low-intensity in terms of the strength or level of aerobic fitness required. Many seniors enjoy flexibility exercises, however, on the grounds that they confer a feeling of overall well-being. Most flexibility exercises consist of stretches, in which seniors slowly move their body into the desired position and hold it for 10 to 30 seconds. Flexibility exercises should be carried out after strength or endurance exercises, when the muscles are already warmed up. Seniors should not bounce or jerk into position but move gently and gradually. Flexibility exercises include such exercises as hamstring stretches, hip and shoulder rotations, calf and ankle stretches, and stretches of the triceps muscle in the upper arm.

T'ai chi and **yoga** are frequently recommended as a form of flexibility training for seniors. Many enjoy these forms of exercise because they can be done with a group of friends or as part of a class.

Endurance training

Endurance exercises provide the best-documented benefits of therapeutic exercise for the elderly. Walking is the most common form of endurance exercise practiced by seniors—about 50 percent of elderly people walk for exercise—and it is the one most frequently recommended by doctors. Walking can be easily incorporated into the senior's daily schedule of errands by going on foot to the post office, store, church, for example, rather than driving. One study showed that seniors who walk at least 2 miles a day on average lower their mortality risk by 50 percent. Other good forms of endurance training are swimming, cycling, dancing, walking up stairs instead of taking the elevator, golf (walking), gardening or heavy yard work, and low-impact aerobics. Jogging is not a good exercise for seniors unless they are already used to it.

The doctor may use a method called the target heart rate to calculate the intensity of endurance exercises that will provide the most health benefits for the senior. The target heart rate for moderate-intensity endurance exercise is 60 to 79 percent of maximal heart rate (measured in beats per minute). Maximal heart rate, which is usually determined by an exercise **stress test**, can also be calculated by subtracting the senior's age from 220. Thus seniors who have 70 years old would have a maximal heart rate of 150, and their target heart rate would be about 90–120 beats per minute during moderate-intensity endurance exercises.

Seniors whose endurance exercise programs are interrupted by a few weeks of illness or inactivity should return to exercising at a lower level of intensity. Strict bed rest leads to loss of muscle mass as well as to loss of muscular strength and aerobic fitness.

Stability or balance

Balance exercises are important for seniors because they lower the risk of falls—a major cause of disability in the elderly. Balance exercises include plantar flexion, in which the senior stands with hands on a table for balance and slowly stands on tiptoe, holding the position for 1 second and repeating the motion 8 to 15 times. After seniors feel steady while performing the exercise, they can gradually work up to holding the table only with a fingertip, then with no hands, then with eyes closed. Other balance exercises include side leg raises and hip or knee flexion. One exercise for balance that can be done while taking a daily walk is to walk heel to toe for short distances. Another is to stand on one foot for a few seconds while waiting in line or waiting for a bus, and alternate the feet every few seconds.

Demographics

According to the *Merck Manual of Geriatrics*, "Physical inactivity is the second leading cause (after tobacco use) of premature death" in the United States. Therapeutic exercise is often prescribed after an injury or diagnosis of a chronic disease or disorder because many elderly people do not get enough physical exercise. Only 20 to 25 percent of elderly persons exercise for more than 30 minutes 5 times or more per week. Women generally exercise less than men; however, low income and low educational level are more influential factors in lack of exercise than gender or advancing age.

Purpose

Therapeutic exercise in seniors serves a number of different purposes:

- Reducing mortality, even in obese persons and smokers. A number of studies have reported that seniors who exercise regularly have mortality rates 20 to 50 percent lower than their sedentary peers.
- Improved general sense of well-being and opportunities for social interaction.
- Improved sleep quality, which is significant because insomnia is a common problem in seniors.
- Preserving muscle strength, bone density, and lung capacity—factors that maintain mobility and hence independence.
- Creating a balanced energy state and reducing the risk of obesity. Excess weight is hard on aging joints and increases the risk of heart disease and type 2 diabetes.
- Maintaining or improving the flexibility and range of motion of joints, which contributes to the senior's functional ability.
- Lowering blood pressure.
- Lowering the risk of such psychiatric disorders as depression.
- Lowering the risk of falls and fall-related injuries, particularly when balance training is part of the exercise regimen.

Challenges

Seniors should be checked for potential health problems before beginning a regimen of therapeutic exercise. Some doctors use a questionnaire called the Physical Activity Readiness Questionnaire, or PAR-Q, as a preliminary to planning a program of therapeutic exercise. The PAR-Q has seven items asking for yes/no answers to such questions as chest pains, a history of high blood pressure, **dizziness**, and the like.

Seniors with any of the following medical conditions should be treated for them and have their condition stabilized before beginning a therapeutic exercise program:

- Unstable angina (chest pain caused by inadequate blood supply to the heart muscle)
- Uncontrolled irregular heart rhythm.
- Cardiomyopathy (disease of the heart muscle; may be genetic or caused by inflammation of the walls of the heart)

KEY TERMS

Aerobic fitness—A measure of the amount of oxygen delivered to muscle tissue to keep it working. Any type of exercise that raises the heart rate and keeps it up for a period of time improves aerobic fitness.

Angina—A severe constricting pain or sense of pressure in the chest caused by an inadequate supply of blood to the heart tissue.

Calisthenics—A type of exercise consisting of simple movements intended to improve body strength and flexibility by using the body's own weight as resistance. The English word comes from two Greek words meaning "beautiful" and "strength."

Deconditioning—Loss of physical fitness due to illness or inactivity.

Diastolic blood pressure—The lowest level of blood pressure in the arteries, which occurs at the point in the heart's cycle when its chambers fill with blood.

Pulmonary artery—The large artery that carries blood from the heart to the lungs to receive oxygen. It is the only artery in the body that carries deoxygenated blood.

Sedentary—Not physically active.

Systolic blood pressure—The highest level of blood pressure in the arteries, which occurs at the point in the heart's cycle when the heart contracts and pushes blood out through the aorta and the pulmonary artery.

- Known or suspected dissecting aneurysm (abnormal blood-filled bulge in the wall of a weakened artery that is spreading along the length of the artery)
- Recent systemic or pulmonary embolus (air bubble or other abnormal particle circulating in the blood)
- Resting systolic blood pressure over 200 mm Hg or resting diastolic blood pressure over 110 mm Hg.
- Severe pulmonary hypertension (high blood pressure in the pulmonary artery).
- Thrombophlebitis (inflammation of the veins caused by blood clot formation).

Seniors with **osteoporosis** should follow very gradual increases in intensity and duration during strength and endurance exercises. While therapeutic exercise has been shown to increase bone density, this is best achieved in seniors with osteoporosis by increasing the number of repetitions for each exercise before increasing the weights used in strength training.

Although seniors are not always given physical fitness tests before starting a program of therapeutic exercise, some doctors and physical therapists use them as a way of evaluating the senior's level of aerobic fitness, or the amount of oxygen delivered to muscle tissue. The most common fitness test given to seniors is a 6-minute walk test. Periodic fitness tests may be given after the senior has started the exercise program as feedback to encourage the senior to continue with the program.

Risks

The most common health risks of therapeutic exercise for seniors are muscle injuries and torn ligaments. **Falls** are also a risk, although the many health benefits of therapeutic exercise are considered to outweigh the risk of falls. There is also a temporary increase in the risk of sudden **death** during exercise if the senior has begun to exercise too vigorously after months or years of being in poor condition.

Results

Participating in an individualized program of therapeutic exercise approved by a doctor is one of the best strategies seniors can follow to maintain overall health and **independence**, speed recovery following surgery or illness, manage a chronic health condition such as osteoarthritis or osteoporosis, participate in social activities, and lower mortality risk. Seniors who are deconditioned, whether by long years of a sedentary lifestyle or by recent injury or illness, can still improve their fitness by modest amounts of low-intensity exercise. The NIA points out that even seniors who have already suffered disabilities or been diagnosed with diseases can benefit from regular long-term exercise; even 2–3 minutes of activity alternating with 2–3 minutes of rest over a 15-minute period is a worthwhile beginning. The most important aspect of therapeutic exercise is keeping up the program, as muscle strength and endurance decline rapidly after only a few weeks of inactivity.

Resources

BOOKS

Beers, Mark H., and Thomas V. Jones. *Merck Manual of Geriatrics*, 3rd ed., Chapter 31, "Exercise." Whitehouse Station, NJ: Merck, 2005.

Hall, Carrie M., and Lori Thein Brody. *Therapeutic Exercise: Moving toward Function*, 2nd ed. Philadelphia: Lippincott Williams and Wilkins, 2005.

Kisner, Carolyn, and Lynn Allen Colby. *Therapeutic Exercise: Foundations and Techniques*, 5th ed. Philadelphia: F. A. Davis, 2007.

PERIODICALS

Fleg, J. L. "Exercise Therapy for Elderly Heart Failure Patients." *Heart Failure Clinics* 3 (October 2007): 529–537.

Herman, T., et al. "Six Weeks of Intensive Treadmill Training Improves Gait and Quality of Life in Patients with Parkinson's Disease: A Pilot Study." *Archives of Physical Medicine and Rehabilitation* 88 (September 2007): 1154–1158.

Netz, Y., S. Axelrad, and E. Argov. "Group Physical Activity for Demented Older Adults: Feasibility and Effectiveness." *Clinical Rehabilitation* 21 (November 2007): 977–986.

Rooks, D. S., S. Gautam, M. Romeling, et al. "Group Exercise, Education, and Combination Self-Management in Women with Fibromyalgia: A Randomized Trial." *Archives of Internal Medicine* 167 (November 12, 2007): 2192–2200.

Sullivan, K. J., D. A. Brown, T. Klassen, et al. "Effects of Task-Specific Locomotor and Strength Training in Adults Who Were Ambulatory after Stroke: Results of the STEPS Randomized Clinical Trial." *Physical Therapy* 87 (December 2007): 1580–1602.

Vizza, J., et al. "Improvement in Psychosocial Functioning during an Intensive Cardiovascular Lifestyle Modification Program." *Journal of Cardiopulmonary Rehabilitation and Prevention* 27 (November/December 2007): 376–383.

OTHER

"Exercise: A Guide from the National Institute on Aging." National Institute on Aging (NIA). NIH Publication No. 01-4258. Bethesda, MD: NIA. 2007. [cited March 21, 2008]. http://www.nia.nih.gov/NR/rdonlyres/8E3B798C-237E-469B-A508-94CA4E537D4C/0/Exercise_Guide907.pdf.

Lieberman, Jesse A. "Therapeutic Exercise." *eMedicine*. June 26, 2007 [cited March 21, 2008]. http://www.emedicine.com/pmr/topic199.htm.

"Physical Activity Readiness Questionnaire (PAR-Q)." July 17, 2006 [cited March 21, 2008]. http://www.d.umn.edu/kmc/student/loon/soc/phys/par-q.html.

ORGANIZATIONS

American Association of Retired Persons (AARP) Fitness Guide to Walking, 601 E St. NW, Washington, DC, 20049, (800) OUR-AARP (687-2277), http://www.aarp.org/health/fitness/walking/.

American Physical Therapy Association (APTA), 1111 North Fairfax St., Alexandria, VA, 22314, (703) 684-APTA (2782), (800) 999-2782, (703) 684-7343, http://www.apta.org/.

National Heart, Lung, and Blood Institute (NHLBI), PO Box 30105, Bethesda, MD, 20824, (301) 592-8573, (240) 629-3246, nhlbiinfo@nhlbi.nih.gov, http://www.nhlbi.nih.gov/index.htm.

Rebecca J. Frey Ph.D.

Thiazides *see* **Diuretics**

Thoracic aneurysm *see* **Aneurysm**

Thoracic surgery

Definition

Thoracic surgery is the repair of organs located in the thorax, or chest. The thoracic cavity lies between the neck and the diaphragm, and contains the heart and lungs (cardiopulmonary system), the esophagus, trachea, pleura, mediastinum, chest wall, and diaphragm.

Purpose

Thoracic surgery repairs diseased or injured organs and tissues in the thoracic cavity. General thoracic surgery deals specifically with disorders of the lungs and esophagus. Cardiothoracic surgery also encompasses disorders of the heart and pericardium. Blunt chest trauma, reflux esophagitis, **esophageal cancer**, lung transplantation, **lung cancer**, and **emphysema** are just a few of the many clinical indications for thoracic surgery.

Precautions

Patients who have blood-clotting problems (coagulopathies), and who have had previous standard thoracic surgery may not be good candidates for video-assisted thoracic surgery (VATS). Because VATS requires the collapse of one lung, potential patients should have adequate respiratory function to maintain oxygenation during the procedure.

Description

Thoracic surgery is usually performed by a surgeon who specializes in either general thoracic surgery or cardiothoracic surgery. The patient is placed under **general anesthesia** and endotracheally intubated for the procedure. The procedure followed varies according to the purpose of the surgery. An incision that opens the chest (thoracotomy) is frequently

KEY TERMS

Blood gas analysis—A blood test that measures the level of oxygen, carbon dioxide, and pH in arterial blood. A blood gas analysis can help a physician assess how well the lungs are functioning.

Electrocardiography—A cardiac test that measures the electrical activity of the heart.

Embolism—A blood clot, air bubble, or clot of foreign material that blocks the flow of blood in an artery. When blood supply to a tissue or organ is blocked by an embolism, infarction, or death of the tissue that the artery feeds, occurs. Without immediate and appropriate treatment, an embolism can be fatal.

Emphysema—A lung disease characterized by shortness of breath and a chronic cough. Emphysema is caused by the progressive stretching and rupture of alveoli, the air sacs in the lung that oxygenate the blood.

Endoscopy—The examination of organs and body cavities using a long, tubular optical instrument called an endoscope.

Intubation—Insertion of an endotracheal tube down the throat to facilitate airflow to the lung(s) during thoracic surgery.

Pericardium—The sac around the heart.

Pleural space—The space between the pleural membranes that surround the lungs and the chest cavity.

Pulmonary angiography—An x-ray study of the lungs, performed by insertion of a catheter into a vein, through the heart, and into the pulmonary artery. Pulmonary angiography is performed to evaluate blood circulation to the lungs. It is also considered the most accurate diagnostic test for detecting a pulmonary embolism.

Sputum culture—A laboratory analysis of the fluid produced from the lungs during coughing. A sputum culture can confirm the presence of pathogens in the respiratory system, and help to diagnose certain respiratory infections, including bronchitis, tuberculosis, and pneumonia.

performed to give the surgeon access to the thoracic cavity. Commonly, the incision is made beginning on the back under the shoulder blade and extends in a curved arc under the arm to the front of the chest. The muscles are cut, and the ribs are spread with a retractor. The surgeon may also choose to open the chest through an incision down the breastbone, or sternum (sternotomy). Once the repair, replacement, or removal of the organ being operated on is complete, a chest tube is inserted between the ribs to drain the wound and re-expand the lung.

Video-assisted thoracic surgery (VATS) is a minimally invasive surgical technique that uses a thoracic endoscope (thoracoscope) to allow the surgeon to view the chest cavity. A lung is collapsed and 3-4 small incisions, or access ports, are made to facilitate insertion of the thoracoscope and the surgical instruments. During the procedure, the surgeon views the inside of the pleural space on a video monitor. The thoracoscope may be extracted and inserted through a different incision site as needed. When the surgical procedure is complete, the surgeon expands the lung and inserts a chest tube in one of the incision sites. The remaining incisions are sealed with adhesive.

The thoracic surgeon may also use a mediastinoscope or a bronchoscope to explore the thoracic cavity. Mediastinoscopy allows visualization of the mediastinum, the cavity located between the lungs. The bronchoscope enables the surgeon to view the larynx, trachea, and bronchi. These instruments may be used in a separate diagnostic procedure prior to thoracic surgery, or during the surgery itself.

Preparation

Except in the case of emergency procedures, candidates for general thoracic surgery should undergo a complete medical history and thorough physical examination prior to surgery. Particular attention is given to the respiratory system. The patient's **smoking** history will be questioned. If the patient is an active smoker, encouragement is always given for the patient to quit smoking prior to the surgery to facilitate recovery and reduce chances of complications.

Diagnostic tests used to evaluate the patient preoperatively may include, but are not limited to, x rays, MRI, **CT scans**, blood gas analysis, pulmonary function tests, **electrocardiography**, **endoscopy**, pulmonary **angiography**, and sputum culture.

Candidates for thoracic surgery should be fully educated by their physician or surgeon on what their surgery will involve, the possible risks and complications, and requirements for **postoperative care**.

Patients are instructed not to eat 10 to 12 hours prior to a thoracic surgery procedure. A sedative may be provided to relax the patient prior to surgery. An intravenous line (IV) is inserted into the patient's arm or neck to administer fluids and/or medication.

Aftercare

After surgery, the patient is taken to the **recovery room**, where vital signs are monitored; depending on the procedure performed, the breathing tube may be removed. The patient typically experiences moderate to severe **pain** following surgery. Analgesics or other pain medication are administered to keep the patient comfortable. Chest tubes are monitored closely for signs of fluid or air accumulation in the lungs that can lead to lung collapse. A urinary catheter will remain in the patient for 24 to 48 hours to drain urine from the bladder.

The hospital stay for thoracic surgery depends on the specific procedure performed. Patients who undergo a thoracotomy may be hospitalized a week or longer, while patients undergoing VATS typically have a shorter hospital stay of 2-3 days. During the recovery period, respiratory therapists and nurses work with the patient on deep breathing and coughing exercises to improve lung function.

Complications

Respiratory failure, hemorrhage, nerve injury, **heart attack**, **stroke**, embolism, and infection are all possible complications of general thoracic surgery. The chest tubes used for drainage after thoracic surgery may cause a build-up of fluid or the accumulation of air in the pleural space. Both of these conditions can lead to total lung collapse. Other specific complications may occur, depending on the procedure performed.

Results

Normal results of thoracic surgery are dependent on the type of procedure performed and the clinical purpose of the surgery.

ORGANIZATIONS

American Thoracic Society, 1740 Broadway, New York, NY, 10019, (212) 315-8700, http://www.thoracic.org.

Paula Anne Ford-Martin

Thrombocytopenia

Definition

Thrombocytopenia (thrombocythemia) is a blood disorder characterized by an abnormally low number of circulating platelets (thrombocytes) in the bloodstream.

General description

Platelets play an important role in the process of coagulation (blood clotting) and in the plugging of damaged blood vessels. Persons with decreased platelets bruise easily and can have episodes of excessive bleeding (hemorrhage). Thrombocytopenia is usually an acquired disorder, but it can also be congenital, as in neonatal rubella (German measles).

Platelets are irregular, disc-shaped fragments of large cells called megakaryocytes, which are found in the spongy center of long bones (bone marrow). They are the smallest cell-like structures in the blood. When a blood vessel is punctured or damaged, normal mature platelets have a tendency to aggregate (group) together at the site, forming a plug that stops the bleeding. The lifespan of platelets in the blood is relatively short (five to ten days), so the bone marrow of healthy individuals is continually producing new platelets to replace the old ones.

Causes and symptoms

Thrombocytopenia occurs when any of the following abnormal conditions exist:

- decreased production of platelets by the bone marrow
- increased destruction of circulating platelets
- increased trapping of platelets by the spleen
- platelet loss from hemorrhage

The most common cause of thrombocytopenia is a decrease in the production of platelets by the bone marrow. When abnormalities develop in the bone marrow, the megakaryocytes (platelet precursors) can lose their ability to produce platelets in sufficient amounts. This is a common side effect of blood cancers such as leukemia, which causes an abnormal growth of white blood cells in the bone marrow. These abnormal cells crowd out the normal bone marrow cells, including the platelets. Other diseases that cause this condition are tumors that spread (metastasize) to the bone, aplastic **anemia** and viral infections such as rubella. Radiation and drugs used in **cancerchemotherapy** and in the treatment of other serious diseases can also cause the bone marrow to malfunction in this way, especially if they are used together. Heparin, an intravenous medication used to reduce the risk of **blood clots**, is known to sometimes cause a drop in the platelet count.

QUESTIONS TO ASK YOUR DOCTOR

- What is the cause of my thrombocytopenia?
- Can this be treated? If so, how?
- How long will my treatment last?
- What are the side effects of my treatment?
- Can I expect to experience episodes of thrombocytopenia once treatment is completed?
- What are the signs I should look for to determine if I have thrombocytopenia again?

Platelets can break down in unusually high amounts in persons with abnormalities in their blood vessel walls, with blood clots, or with man-made replacement heart valves. Devices (stents) placed inside blood vessels to keep them from closing (because of weakened walls or fat build-up) can also cause an increased destruction of platelets. In addition, severe microbial infections; infection with the human immunodeficiency virus (HIV), the virus that causes **AIDS**; and other changes in the **immune system** can speed up the removal of platelets from the circulation.

Normally, the spleen holds about one-third of the body's platelets as part of this organ's function to recycle certain aging or damaged blood cells. When liver disease or cancer of the spleen is present, the spleen can become enlarged (a condition called splenomegaly) and trap many more platelets than normal. Because a greater number of platelets remain in the enlarged organ, fewer platelets are circulating in the bloodstream.

Signs of thrombocytopenia include:

- bleeding(most common symptom)
- nose bleeds
- bleeding gums
- petechiae, small red or purple spots on the skin
- purpura, skin appears purple due to hemorrhage beneath the skin
- ecchymoses, blood escaping from ruptured blood vessels into surrounding tissue forms a purple or black-and-blue spot on the skin

Diagnosis

Doctors usually use a combination of the physical examination, the medical history, and laboratory testing to diagnose this disorder. The platelet count, which is part of a **complete blood count** (CBC), is a key diagnostic tool. It measures the number of platelets in a volume of blood. The blood normally contains between 150,000 and 400,000 platelets per microliter (cubic millimeter or mm3) of blood. (A million microliters is equal to one liter, or about 1.1 quarts.) In adults, a platelet count of less than 100,000/microliter is considered low but might occur without symptoms. Abnormal bleeding often occurs when the platelet count is below 30,000/microliter. If the count falls below 10,000/microliter, abnormal external bleeding is usually evident, and serious internal bleeding can be life threatening.

Treatment

Sometimes this disorder is asymptomatic and does not require any treatment. This is often the case when thrombocytopenia occurs in children following a viral infection. Even when the disorder is a side effect of both radiation therapy and chemotherapy, if the thrombocytopenia is not severe, it is often reversible on its own once the therapies end.

Treatments, when necessary, vary with the severity of the disorder, the abnormal condition that caused the disorder, and any underlying or secondary cause. When possible, the best form of treatment is to eliminate whatever is causing the condition. For example, if a drug is causing the thrombocytopenia, eliminating that drug would be the ideal solution. However, when the disorder is a side effect of chemotherapy, the patient might need to continue the drug therapy. In such cases, the doctor must decide whether it is in the best interest of the patient to continue with the same dosage, to lower the dosage, to try an alternative drug, or to give the patient a platelet transfusion. For diseases other than blood cancers, doctors can sometimes continue the chemotherapy at full dosage by also giving the patient a platelet growth factor called oprelvekin (Neumega) to boost the production of normal platelets in the bone marrow.

If a dysfunctional immune system is destroying the patient's platelets, the doctor might use a corticosteroid (such as prednisone) or gamma globulin to suppress the patient's immune response and to help maintain adequate platelet levels. Corticosteroids can also have unwanted side effects, so doctors usually do not use this treatment for very long.

KEY TERMS

Asymptomatic—Without symptoms.

Congenital—Existing at birth.

Gamma globulin—One of a group of proteins found in the blood that is involved in helping the body to fight infections.

Microliter—Same as a cubic millimeter. One million microliters equals 1 liter, which equals about 1.06 quarts.

Neonatal—Relating to a newborn child.

Stent—A man-made surgical device, usually tube-shaped, that is placed into a blood vessel to keep it from closing.

Transfusion—The transfer of blood from one person to another. Transfusions can be direct, in which blood is transferred from the donor to the recipient; or indirect, in which the blood is taken from the donor, stored in a container, and then given to the recipient.

If an enlarged spleen is the underlying cause of the thrombocytopenia, the doctor might want to try corticosteroids or epinephrine to release platelets from the spleen. If these methods fail, surgical removal of the spleen (splenectomy) can help to raise the platelet level since the spleen is no longer there to capture the platelets. However, the disease that caused the enlarged spleen, such as lymphoma or cancer that spread to the spleen from another area of the body, should be treated as well.

If the patient is having severe external or internal bleeding as the result of injury or disease, a platelet transfusion might be necessary for immediate results. This is especially true if laboratory tests show a decreased production of platelets in the bone marrow.

Alternative and complementary therapies

A natural substance called thrombopoietin shows promise as a regulator of platelet production.

Many over-the-counter medicines, herbal supplements (such as **garlic**, ginger, feverfew, and **ginkgo biloba**) and **vitamins** can affect the ability of platelets to function properly. To determine the best treatment for a patient and to avoid **drug interactions**, the doctor needs to know every drug and remedy a patient is taking.

Caregiver concerns

Individuals who are diagnosed with thrombocytopenia should inspect their skin and other body areas closely for signs of bleeding or oozing of blood. Using electric razors for shaving and soft bristled toothbrushes or gauze sponges to brush teeth with minimal pressure may avoid bleeding. They may also be instructed to avoid products which contain **aspirin** and to avoid activities such as forceful coughing when their platelets are low. During the time that their platelets are below normal they should also avoid the use of **enemas** and suppositories.

Beverly Miller MT(ASCP)
Dominic De Bellis
Melinda Oberleitner R.N., D.N.S.

Thrombocytosis

Definition

Thrombocytosis is a blood disorder in which the body produces a surplus of platelets (thrombocytes).

Description

Thrombocytosis is an abnormally increased number of platelets in the blood. Platelets are blood cells that stick together, helping blood to clot. Thrombocytosis is a condition that may have many causes.

Throbocytosis is classified as one of two types. Secondary thrombocytosis can be traced to another cause, such as inflammation, severe bleeding, iron deficiency, or some cancers. Primary thrombocytosis (or essential thrombocythemia) is a single disease entity, with unique clinical characteristics.

Causes and symptoms

The cause of essential thrombocytosis is unknown.

Secondary thrombocytosis may develop as a result of:

- acute hemorrhage or infection
- anemia
- arthritis and other chronic inflammations
- cancer
- exercise

- iron deficiency
- medication
- csteoporosis
- removal of the spleen (splenectomy)
- polycythemia vera (a disorder affecting other red blood cells, as well as platelets)
- stress
- surgery

Symptoms

Two of every three patients who have thrombocytosis do not have any symptoms of the disease at the time of diagnosis. Younger patients may remain symptom-free for years.

Enlargement of the spleen is detected in 60% of patients with thrombocytosis. The liver may also be enlarged. As many as half of all patients experience bleeding from the skin, gums, or nose; and 20–50% have some blockage of veins or arteries.

Other symptoms of thrombocytosis include:

- bloody stools
- bruising
- dizziness
- headache
- hemorrhage
- prolonged bleeding after having surgery or after having a tooth pulled
- redness or tingling of the hands and feet
- weakness. In rare instances, the lymph nodes become enlarged

The highest platelet counts usually produce the most severe symptoms. Younger patients (especially women) may not have symptoms, even though their platelet counts are very high.

Complications

Complications of thrombocytosis include **stroke**, **heart attack**, and formation of **blood clots** in the arms and legs.

A doctor should be notified whenever bleeding is unexplained or prolonged or the patient develops:

- chest or leg pain
- confusion
- numbness
- weakness

Diagnosis

The patient's symptoms suggest the presence of thrombocytosis. Blood tests confirm the diagnosis.

Bone marrow aspiration (removal of a tissue sample for microscopic examination) may also be performed.

Treatment

The key to treating secondary thrombocytosis is treating the underlying condition.

Any patient who has thrombocytosis should be encouraged not to smoke.

Treatment for patients who do have symptoms focuses on controlling bleeding, preventing the formation of blood clots, and lowering platelet levels. Treatment for secondary thrombocytosis involves treating the condition or disease responsible for excess platelet production.

Anagrelide HCl (Agrylin) has been used to reduce elevated platelet counts and decrease the risk of clot formation. Some patients have also benefited from the use of hydroxyurea, an anti-cancer drug.

Low doses of **aspirin** may prevent clotting, but can cause serious hemorrhages.

If drug therapy does not bring platelet counts down to an acceptable level as rapidly as necessary, plateletpheresis may be performed. Usually combined with drug therapy and used primarily in medical emergencies, this procedure consists of:

- withdrawing blood from the patient's body
- removing platelets from the blood
- returning the platelet-depleted blood to the patient

Prognosis

Many patients with thrombocytosis remain free of complications for long periods.

Prevention

There is no known way to prevent thrombocytosis.

Maureen Haggerty

Thrombolytic therapy

Definition

Thrombolytic therapy is the use of drugs that dissolve **blood clots**.

Purpose

When a blood clot forms in a blood vessel, it may cut off or severely reduce blood flow to parts of the body that are served by that blood vessel. This can cause serious damage to those parts of the body. If the clot forms in an artery that supplies blood to the heart, for example, it can cause a **heart attack**. A clot that cuts off blood to the brain can cause a **stroke**. Thrombolytic therapy is used to dissolve blood clots that could cause serious, and possibly life-threatening, damage if they are not removed. Research suggests that when used to treat stroke, thrombolytic therapy can prevent or reverse **paralysis** and other problems that otherwise might result.

Thrombolytic therapy also is used to dissolve blood clots that form in tubes put into people's bodies for medical treatments, such as dialysis or **chemotherapy**.

Description

Thrombolytic therapy uses drugs called thrombolytic agents, such as alteplase (Activase), anistreplase (Eminase), streptokinase (Streptase, Kabikinase), urokinase (Abbokinase), and tissue plasminogen activator (TPA) to dissolve clots. These drugs are given as injections, only under a physician's supervision.

Recommended dosage

The physician supervising thrombolytic therapy decides on the proper dose for each patient. He or she will take into account the type of drug, the purpose for which it is being used, and in some cases, the patient's weight.

Precautions

For thrombolytic therapy to be effective in treating stroke or heart attack, prompt medical attention is very important. The drugs must be given within a few hours of the beginning of a stroke or heart attack. However, this treatment is not right for every patient who has a heart attack or a stroke. Only a qualified medical professional can decide whether a thrombolytic agent should be used. To increase the chance of survival and reduce the risk of serious, permanent damage, anyone who has signs of a heart attack or stroke should get immediate medical help.

Thrombolytic therapy may cause bleeding. Usually this is not serious, but severe bleeding does occur in some people. This is especially likely in older people. To lower the risk of serious bleeding, people who are given this drug should move around as little as possible and should not try to get up on their own unless told to do so by a health care professional. Following all the instructions of the health care providers in charge is very important.

Thrombolytic therapy may be more likely to cause serious bleeding in people who have certain medical conditions or have recently had certain medical procedures. Before being given a thrombolytic agent, anyone with any of these problems or conditions should tell the physician in charge about it:

- blood disease or current or past bleeding problems in any part of the body
- heart or blood vessel disease
- stroke (recent or in the past)
- high blood pressure
- brain tumor or other brain disease
- stomach ulcer or colitis
- severe liver disease
- active tuberculosis
- recent falls, injuries, or blows to the body or head
- recent injections into a blood vessel
- recent surgery, including dental surgery
- tubes recently placed in the body for any reason
- recent delivery of a baby

In addition, anyone who has had a recent streptococcal (strep) infection should tell the physician in charge. Some thrombolytic agents may not work properly in people who have just had a strep infection, so the physician may want to use a different drug.

People who take certain medicines may be at greater risk for severe bleeding when they are given a thrombolytic agent.

Side effects

Anyone who has fever or who notices bleeding or oozing from their gums, from cuts, or from the site where the thrombolytic agent was injected should immediately tell their health care provider.

People who are given thrombolytic therapy should also be alert to the signs of bleeding inside the body and should check with a physician immediately if any of the following symptoms occur:

- blood in the urine
- blood or black, tarry stools
- constipation

KEY TERMS

Arteries—Blood vessels that carry blood away from the heart to the cells, tissues, and organs of the body.

Blood clot—A hard mass that forms when blood gels.

Chemotherapy—Treatment of an illness with chemical agents. The term is usually used to describe the treatment of cancer with drugs.

Dialysis—A process used in people whose kidneys are not working well. By way of a filtering machine, dialysis separates waste and other useless materials from the blood – a job the kidneys usually do.

Paralysis—Loss of the ability to move one or more parts of the body.

Stroke—A serious medical event in which blood flow to the brain is stopped. This may be because of a blood clot in an artery or because an artery has burst. Strokes may cause paralysis and changes in speech, memory, and behavior.

- coughing up blood
- vomiting blood or material that looks like coffee grounds
- nosebleeds
- unexpected or unusually heavy vaginal bleeding
- dizziness
- sudden, severe, or constant headaches
- Pain or swelling in the abdomen or stomach
- back pain or backache
- severe or constant muscle pain or stiffness
- stiff, swollen, or painful joints

Other side effects of thrombolytic agents are possible. Anyone who has unusual symptoms during or after thrombolytic therapy should tell a health care professional.

Interactions

People who take certain medicines may be at greater risk for severe bleeding when they receive a thrombolytic agent. Anyone who is given a thrombolytic agent should tell the physician in charge about all other prescription or nonprescription (over-the-counter) medicines he or she is taking. Among the medicines that may increase the chance of bleeding are:

- aspirin and other medicines for pain and inflammation
- blood thinners (anticoagulants)
- antiseizure medicines, such as Depakote (divalproex) and Depakene (valproic acid)
- cephalosporins, such as cefamandole (Mandol), cefoperazone (Cefobid), and Cefotetan (Cefotan)

Also, anyone who has been treated with anistreplase or streptokinase within the past year should tell the physician in charge. These drugs may not work properly if they are given again, so the physician may want to use a different thrombolytic agent.

Nancy Ross-Flanigan

Thyroid cancer

Definition

Thyroid **cancer** is a disease in which the cells of the thyroid gland become abnormal, grow uncontrollably and form a mass of cells called a tumor.

Description

The thyroid is a hormone-producing, butterfly-shaped gland located in the neck at the base of the throat. It has two lobes, the left and the right. The thyroid uses iodine, a mineral found in some foods, to make several of its hormones. Thyroid hormones regulate essential body processes such as heart rate, **blood pressure**, body temperature, metabolism, and affect the nervous system, muscles and other organs. These hormones play an important role in regulating childhood growth and development.

Types of thyroid cancer

Thyroid cancer is grouped into four types based on how cells appear under a microscope. The types are papillary, follicular, medullary and anaplastic thyroid cancers. They grow at different rates and can spread to other parts of the body if left untreated. The two most common types are papillary carcinoma and follicular carcinoma.

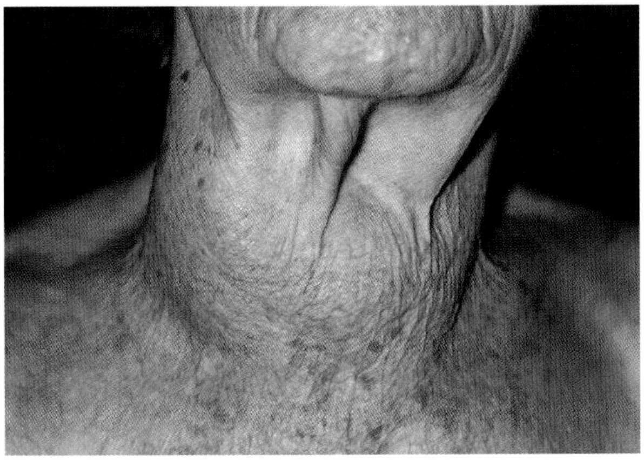

Neck swollen with thyroid cancer. *(Dr P. Marazzi / Photo Researchers, Inc. Reproduced by permission.)*

PAPILLARY The papillary type (60%–80% of all thyroid cancers) is a slow-growing cancer that develops in the hormone-producing cells containing iodine.

FOLLICULAR The follicular type (30%–50% of thyroid cancers) also develops in the hormone-producing cells.

MEDULLARY The medullary type (5%–7% of all thyroid cancers) develops in the parafollicular cells (known as the C cells) that produce calcitonin, a hormone that does not contain iodine.

ANAPLASTIC The fourth type of thyroid cancer, anaplastic (2% of all thyroid cancers), is the fastest growing, most aggressive thyroid cancer type.

Demographics

Diseases of the thyroid gland affect millions of Americans. The most common diseases of the thyroid are hyperthyroidism (Grave's disease) and hypothyroidism, an overactive or an underactive gland, respectively. Sometimes lumps or masses may develop in the thyroid. Although most (95%) of these lumps or nodules are non-cancerous (benign), all thyroid lumps should be taken seriously. The American Cancer Society estimates that in 2007, approximately 33,550 new cases of thyroid cancer were diagnosed in the United States.

Women are three times more likely to develop thyroid cancer than men. Unlike many cancers, thyroid cancers are most often diagnosed in younger people, with almost two-thirds of cases diagnosed in individuals between the ages of 20 and 55. Caucasians are affected more often than African Americans.

Causes and symptoms

The exact cause of thyroid cancer is not known but some risk factors have been identified. Radiation was used in the 1950s and 1960s to treat acne and to reduce swelling in infections of the tonsils, adenoids and lymph nodes. It has been proven that this exposure is a risk factor for thyroid cancer. In some areas of the world, diets are low in iodine. Papillary and follicular cancers occur more frequently in these areas. Iodine deficiency is not a large problem in the United States because iodine is added to table salt and other foods. Approximately 7% of thyroid cancers are caused by the alteration (mutation) of a gene called the RET oncogene, which can be inherited.

Symptoms are rare, and the lump is not usually painful. The following are symptoms of thyroid nodules.

- A lump or nodule that can be felt in the neck is the most frequent sign of thyroid cancer.
- The lymph nodes may be swollen and the voice may become hoarse because the tumor presses on the nerves leading to the voice box.
- Some patients experience a tight or full feeling in the neck and have difficulty breathing or swallowing.

Diagnosis

Physicians use several tests to confirm the suspicion of thyroid cancer, to identify the size and location of the lump and to determine whether the lump is non-cancerous (benign) or cancerous (malignant).

A blood test called the thyroid stimulating hormone (TSH) test checks thyroid function. Blood is drawn by a technician with a needle and the test takes a few minutes. Results take several days to be interpreted by a pathologist.

The calcitonin test may be ordered to evaluate calcitonin levels in blood. Calcitonin is a hormone produced by the C cells (parafollicular cells) of the thyroid gland. The hormone is produced in excess when the parafollicular cells of the thyroid become cancerous. Results of this test are used to confirm the diagnosis of medullary thyroid cancer if it is suspected.

Computed tomography (CT) scan or ultrasonography (an ultrasound scan) are imaging tests used to produce a picture of the thyroid. A radiologist usually interprets the results of these tests within 24 hours. In ultrasonography, high-frequency sound waves are bounced off the thyroid. The pattern of echoes produced by these waves is converted into a computerized image on a television screen. This test can determine whether the lumps found in the thyroid are benign fluid-filled cysts or solid malignant tumors.

A radioactive scan (a **thyroid nuclear medicine scan**) may take several hours and is used to identify abnormal areas in the thyroid. For this test, the patient is given a very small amount of radioactive iodine that can either be swallowed or injected. Since the thyroid is the only gland in the body that absorbs iodine, the radioactive iodine accumulates there. An x-ray image is taken or an instrument called a scanner is used to identify areas in the thyroid that do not absorb iodine normally. These abnormal spots are called cold spots and further tests are performed to check whether the cold spots are benign or malignant tumors. If a significant amount of radioactive iodine is concentrated in the nodule, then it is termed "hot" and is usually benign. A radiologist interprets the results within a day.

The most accurate diagnostic tool for thyroid cancer is a biopsy. In this process, a sample of thyroid tissue is obtained and examined under a microscope by a pathologist. This usually takes a day. The tissue sample can be obtained either by drawing out a sample of tissue through a needle (needle biopsy) or by surgical removal of the nodule (surgical biopsy). A needle biopsy takes a few minutes and can be done by a trained physician, usually a radiologist. The surgical biopsy is done by a surgeon under **general anesthesia** with the help of an anesthesiologist and takes a few hours. If thyroid cancer is diagnosed, further tests may be done to determine the stage of the disease and help doctors plan appropriate treatment.

Staging

The aggressiveness of each type of thyroid cancer is different. Cancer staging considers the size of the tumor, whether it has grown into surrounding lymph nodes and whether it has spread to distant parts of the body (metastasized). Age and general health status are also taken into account. The American Joint Commission on Cancer (AJCC) staging is summarized below for each thyroid cancer type.

PAPILLARY AND FOLLICULAR In patients younger than 45 years:

- Stage I: Patients without evidence of cancer beyond the thyroid.
- Stage II: Patients with spread of cancer outside the thyroid gland to one or more distant sites.

In patients over 45:

- Stage I: Tumors are smaller than 2 cm (0.3 in).
- Stage II: Tumors are 2–4 cm (0.3–0.6 in) across but have not spread to adjacent lymph nodes or distant sites.
- Stage III: Tumors have spread locally to nearby lymph nodes or are larger than 4 cm (0.6 in) and have grown slightly outside of the thyroid but not into lymph nodes or distant sites.
- Stage IV: Tumors have spread outside the thyroid area (distant metastases).

In the case of Stage IV cancer, the places to which thyroid cancer often metastasizes are the lungs and bone.

MEDULLARY The stages of medullary thyroid carcinomas for individuals at any age are the same as for papillary or follicular thyroid cancer in people over age 45.

ANAPLASTIC All cases of anaplastic thyroid cancer are considered Stage IV because this type of cancer is extremely aggressive.

Treatment

Papillary thyroid cancer can be treated successfully. Follicular thyroid cancer also has a good cure rate but may be difficult to control if the cancer invades blood vessels or spreads to nearby structures in the neck. Medullary thyroid cancers are more difficult to control because they often spread to other parts of the body. Anaplastic thyroid cancer is the fastest growing and tends to respond poorly to all treatments.

Like most cancers, cancer of the thyroid is best treated when it is found early by a primary physician. Treatment depends on the type of cancer and its stage. The four types of treatment used are surgical removal, radiation therapy, hormone therapy, and **chemotherapy**.

Surgery

Surgical removal is the usual treatment if the cancer has not spread to distant parts of the body. It is the primary treatment for early stage papillary, follicular, and medullary thyroid cancers. The surgeon may remove the side or lobe of the thyroid where the cancer is found (lobectomy) or all of it (total thyroidectomy). If the adjoining lymph nodes are affected, they may also be removed during surgery.

Radiation

For papillary and follicular thyroid cancers, radioactive iodine may be used in addition to surgery. In this treatment, the patient is asked to swallow a drink containing radioactive iodine. Because the thyroid cells take up iodine, the radioactive iodine collects in any thyroid tissue remaining in the body and

KEY TERMS

Calcitonin—A hormone produced by the parafollicular cells (C cells) of the thyroid. The main function of the hormone is to regulate calcium levels in body serum.

Chemotherapy—Treatment of cancer with synthetic drugs that destroy the tumor either by inhibiting the growth of cancerous cells or by killing them.

Hormone therapy—Treatment of cancer by inhibiting the production of hormones such as testosterone and estrogen.

Hyperthyroidism—A condition in which the thyroid is overactive due to overstimulation of the thyroid cells.

Hypothyroidism—A condition in which the thyroid gland is underactive.

Lobectomy—A surgical procedure that removes one lobe of the thyroid gland.

Radiation therapy—Treatment with high-energy radiation from x-ray machines, cobalt, radium, or other sources.

Total thyroidectomy—A surgical procedure that removes the entire thyroid gland.

kills the cancer cells. External beam radiation may be used if the radioactive iodine is unsuccessful.

For medullary cancers, radioactive iodine is not used. External beam radiation may be used as a palliative therapy. (A palliative therapy is one intended to make the patient more comfortable, not to cure the cancer.)

Hormone therapy

Removal of the thyroid gland causes levels of thyroid hormones to decrease. The pituitary gland then produces TSH, which normally stimulates the thyroid gland to make thyroid hormone. TSH stimulates thyroid cells to grow, and most likely promotes thyroid cancer growth. Hormone therapy uses hormones after surgery to stop this growth and the formation of new cancerous thyroid cells. To prevent cancerous growth, the natural hormones produced by the thyroid are taken in the form of a pill. This maintains normal hormone levels and inhibits the pituitary gland from making TSH. If the cancer has spread to other parts of the body and surgery is not possible, hormone treatment is aimed at killing or slowing the growth of cancer cells throughout the body.

Chemotherapy

For advanced thyroid cancers for which surgery was not an option or that have not responded well to other treatments, chemotherapy may be used. There is no standard chemotherapeutic regimen for advanced papillary, follicular, and anaplastic thyroid cancers. Clinical studies are ongoing for patients with these cancers. Anaplastic thyroid cancer may show an increased local response to the chemotherapeutic agent, doxorubicin, which is used as a radiation sensitizer in combination with hyperfractionated radiation therapy. Paclitaxel may provide some palliative benefit. Patients with anaplastic thyroid cancer may be eligible for ongoing clinical trials.

Clinical trials

As of 2008, approximately 50 clinical trials were in progress for patients diagnosed with various types of thyroid cancer. Information about current clinical trials is available through the National Institutes of Health.

Alternative and complementary treatments

Alternative treatments are treatments used instead of conventional treatments. Complementary therapies are intended to supplement traditional therapies and usually have the objective of relieving symptoms or helping cancer patients cope with the disease or traditional treatments. Common complementary therapies that may be employed by cancer patients are aromatherapy, art therapy, journal therapy, massage, meditation, music therapy, **prayer**, t'ai chi, and **yoga** or other forms of **exercise**, which can reduce **anxiety** and increase a patient's feeling of well-being. A well-balanced **diet** can also enhance a patient's sense of well-being, and can help patients with cancer better manage their treatments and the side effects of those treatments.

Prognosis

As of 2008, the five year relative survival rates for individuals with thyroid cancer are:

- Papillary: Ranges from 100% in Stage I to 45% in Stage IV.

QUESTIONS TO ASK YOUR DOCTOR

- What type of thyroid cancer do I have?
- Has it spread?
- Is my thyroid cancer hereditary? Should other members of my family be tested?
- What treatment do you recommend? Do you recommend a clinical trial?
- What are the advantages, disadvantages, and side effects of this treatment?
- How much experience do you have treating thyroid cancer/performing thyroid surgery?

- Follicular: Ranges from 100% in Stage I to 47% in Stage IV.
- Medullary: Ranges from 100% in Stage I to 24% in Stage IV.
- Anaplastic carcinomas: Approximately 3% since all tumors are classified as Stage IV.

Prevention

It is not possible to prevent this disease completely because most people with thyroid cancer have no known risk factor. The risk for radiation-related thyroid cancer can be reduced by avoiding radiation to the neck when possible. Inherited cases of medullary thyroid cancer can be prevented. If a family member has had this disease, other family members can be tested and treated early. Carriers of the RET mutation may want to consider a prophylactic thyroidectomy at an early age. The National Cancer Institute recommends that every one or two years, a doctor examine anyone who has received radiation to the head and neck during childhood. The neck and thyroid should be carefully examined for any lumps or enlargement of nearby lymph nodes. Ultrasound may be used to screen for the disease in people at risk for thyroid cancer.

Caregiver concerns

After thyroid surgery, some patients experience difficulty swallowing, voice changes, and damage to the parathyroid glands.

After surgery, swallowing may be difficult. Many patients start with soft foods, like milkshakes, bananas, applesauce, yogurt, mashed potatoes, and pureed foods. A consultation with a dietitian before surgery may be helpful, so that the patient can be prepared.

Hoarseness after surgery is usually temporary. Patients may have difficulty hitting high notes when singing, but the voice change and hoarseness is usually not a major issue for most patients. (Professional singers are advised to discuss their surgery in great detail with their surgeons beforehand.)

If all four parathyroid glands are injured or damaged, it may be necessary for patients to take **calcium supplements** for a few weeks. Rarely, these supplements may be prescribed for longer periods of time, or even indefinitely.

After radioiodine treatment, some patients experience neck tenderness, nausea and stomach irritation, and **dry mouth** (xerostomia). These side effects are rare, but if they occur, patients can try to eat foods that are easy to digest, drink plenty of water to keep the mouth and throat moist, keep lips moist with lip balm, and suck on hard candies to alleviate dry mouth.

The side effects of chemotherapy are bone marrow suppression causing **anemia** and low platelets. This causes weakness or bleeding. Other problems are nausea and vomiting, hair loss (**alopecia**), and inflammation of the oral mucosa. The symptoms are improved with medications.

Depression, if it occurs, is often temporary and can be managed by counseling and family support. Medication is usually not necessary.

Complications of surgery are rare with experienced surgeons. Sometimes injury to the nerves in the neck can cause voice changes. This can be improved with **collagen injection** after surgery. Occasionally, there is bleeding after surgery and the incision is reopened to evacuate the clot and stop the bleeding. Patients may have a slightly increased risk of developing another cancer (such as leukemia) in the future after undergoing radioiodine treatment, but this correlation has not been proven. Because thyroid cancers may grow slowly and may recur decades after treatment, follow-up care is important.

Resources

BOOKS

Cameron, John L. *Current Surgical Therapy*. 6th ed. St. Louis: Mosby, Inc., 2001.

ORGANIZATIONS

American Cancer Society. (800) ACS-2345. http://www.cancer.org.

National Cancer Institute, Cancer Information Service. (800) 4-CANCER (800-422-6237). TTY: (800) 332-8615. http://www.nci.nih.gov/.

OTHER

Clinical Trials. National Cancer Institute (NCI). http://www.cancer.gov/clinicaltrials.

Eating Hints for Cancer Patients: Before, During, and After Treatment. National Institutes of Health. NIH Publication #98-2079. Revised July 1997. Also available at: http://cancernet.nci.nih.gov/cancertopics/eatinghints.pdf.

How is Thyroid Cancer Staged? American Cancer Society (ACS). October 3, 2007 [cited March 24, 2008]. http://www.cancer.org/docroot/CRI/content/CRI_2_4_3X_How_is_thyroid_cancer_staged_43.asp?sitearea=.

Practice Guidelines in Oncology Thyroid Cancer v.2.2007. National Comprehensive Cancer Network (NCCN). April 20, 2007 [cited March 24, 2008]. http://www.nccn.org/professionals/physician_gls/PDF/thyroid.pdf.

Lata Cherath Ph.D.
Kulbir Rangi D.O.
Melinda Oberleitner R.N., D.N.S.

Thyroid function tests

Definition

Thyroid functions tests are a variety of blood and nuclear medical tests performed to determine if the thyroid is working correctly and to help diagnose the cause if a problem is found.

Purpose

The first purpose of thyroid function tests is to determine if the thyroid is producing the correct amount of hormone. If not, then it is important to detemrine the cuase of the over- or under-production. Thyroid fucntion tests help the doctor determine whenther the cause of the problem is the thyroid itself of if it is the pituitary or a problem with the **immune system**. Determining the correct cause of the probel mallows the docotr to treat it most effectively.

Precautions

Women who are pregnant or breast feeding should not have a thyroid scan. The very small amount of radioactive substance used has been shown to be safe for adults, but it is not completely clear what effect it might have on a developing fetus. Therefore, women who are pregant should rescheudle the exam for a time after giving birth, or ask their doctor about an alternate imaging test. Women who are breatfeeding should not have thyroid scan because the radioactive material can be passed to the nursing infacnt in the breat milk. If a breastfeeding woman needs a thryodiscan she should make alternate feeding arrangements, such as swithcing to formula, for a few days following the scan until all of the radioactive material has been elimated from her body.

Description

The thyroid is located in the lower part of the neck in the front. It is a gland that is shaped somewhat like a butterfly. It produces thyryd hormones that help the msucles, organs, ans the brain function properly. When the thyroid produces too much horomone it is known ans hyperthyroidism. When the thyroid produces too little hormone it is called hypothyroidism.

The main hormone produced by the thyroid is called thyroxine, also called T4. The reason it is called T4 is because it contains four atoms of iodine. In the body T4 is converted to a hormone called T3 when one of its iodine atoms is removed. Both T4 and T3 levels are important to good health, and separate thyroid funciton tests test for these levels in the blood. Another hormone level improatnt for good heatlh is the level of thryroid stimulating hormone (THS) present in the body. THS is produced by the pituitary gland, and causes the thyroid to relsease T4. THS level can be checked using a blood test.

In some cases when the thryroid appears to not be funcitoning properly it is due to antibodies in the body acting incorrectly. In some people antibodies are produced that attack the thyroid, reducing its hormone output, or stimulate it, increasing its hormone output. Both of these situations can cause serious health consequencse. Antibodies that may be affecitng the thryoid are checked for during a thryroid antibody blood test.

In addition to blood tests, a thyroid scan is sometimes done. This allows the doctor to see an image of the thyroid and how it is working. During a thryroid scan a very small amount of radioactive material, called a radioactive tracer or just a tracer, is either injected into the patinet's arm or swallowed in tablet form. The tracer then enters the bloodstream and ciruclates to the thryoid where it is absorbed.

The tracer gives off a very small amount of gamma radioation. A special camer, called a gamma camera, can detect this radioation, and passes this

QUESTIONS TO ASK YOUR DOCTOR

- If the test shows an abnormality, what is the next step?
- Do I need to stop taking any of my medications before the test?
- Do I need to eat a special diet before the test?

infroamtion to a computer where an image of the tyroid is produced.

Preparation

Certain medications can interfere with the results of the thyroid funciton tests. Which medicaitons may interefere depend on the tests being performed. The paitnet should be sure to tell the doctor all medicaitons that are being taken, inlcyding over-the-counter medications and supplements. The doctor can then determine if any of theses are likely to effect the test results. If so, the patient may be asked to discontinue taking the medication for one or more days before the test.

Paitnets preparing for a thyroid scan should not eat or drink anything for two hours prior to the test. The doctor may tell the patient not to take certain medications for a few days before the test. The patient may be asked to eat a **diet** low in iodine before the test. The patient will be given insturcitons specific to his or her case when the test is schedulted

Aftercare

No special aftercare is required for thyroid function tests.

Complications

Anytime that blood is drawn or an injection is given there is a very small risk of bleeding, swelling, **bruising**, or infection. There is an extremely small chance that an indiuval may have an allergic reaction to the radioactive tracer used in the thyroid scan.

Results

Normal reslults of thyroid function tests occur when all of the tests show results within normal ranges for a healthy adult. Abnormla results can indicacate a variety of different problems. Diagnoses are generally made using the results from a variety of funciton tsts and diagnositc imaing tests, not on the bases of a single test. The results of thyroid function tests may indcatie:

- THS test-Elevated THS levels can indicate primary hypothyroidism, congentical hypothyroidism, thyroid hormone resistance, or tsh-dependent hyperthyroidims. Lowered THS levles can idnicate hyperthyroidism.
- T3 test-Elevated levels of T3 indicate hyperthyroidism, or rarely thyrotoxicosis or thyroid cancer. Lowered levels of T3 can idnicate hypothyroidism, starvation, or a long-term illness.
- T4 test-Elevated T4 levels may indicate many thigns incluing Graves disease, Hasimoto's disease, iodine-induced hyperthyroidism, toxic goiter, or chronic thyroidosis. Lowered T4 levels may indicuate hypothyroidism, starvation, or illness.
- Thyroid anitbody test-Elevated levels in an indivual with hyperthyroidism may indicate autoimmune thyroid disease. Elevated levels in an induval with hypothyroidism may indciate Hashimoto's disease.
- Thyroid scan-Abnmral scan reslults will be shown as lighter, or darker patches on the images indicating elevated or lowered amounts of tracer absorbtion. Theses reulsts indicate thyroid dysfunction or tumor. The thyroid may appear out of place or mishappen, mich may also indicate a tumor.

Caregiver concerns

A doctor determines the need for thyroid function tests. A nurse trained in drawing blood, a phlebotomist, takes a blood sample from the patient, labels it, and sends it to the laboratory. In the laboraty a laboratory technican performs a varieyt of chemcial and other tests on the blood to determine the level of the homromones of intrest. The results are then sent to the doctor who ordered the study who communicates them to the patient and determines the need for additional testing or treatment.

When a thryoid scan is performed a nurse injects the patient with the radioactive tracer. A nulcear medicine technician performs the actual scan, contorling the gamma camera and repositioning the patient as necessary during the scan to get all necessary images. The images from the scan are read by a radiologist or a doctor trained in nuclear meidince. The results are then sent to the doctor who ordered the test who determines the need for treatment or addional diagnostic tests.

Resources

BOOKS

Fischbach, Frances Talaska, and Marshall Barnet Dunnin III. *A Manual of Laboratory and Diagnostic Tests.* Philadelphia: Wolters Kluwer Health/Lippincott Willaims & Wilkins, 2009.

Milton, Carl A., ed. *Trends in Thyroid Cancer Research.* New York: Nova Biomedical Books, 2007.

Rone, James K. *The Thyroid Paradox: How to Get the Best Care for Hypothyroidism.* Languna Beach, CA: Basic Health Publications, 2007.

PERIODICALS

Cardenas-Ibarra, Lilia, et al. "Cross-Sectional Observartions of Thyroid Function in Geriatric Mexican Outpatients With and Without Dimentia." *Archives of Gerontology and Geriatrics* 46.2 (March 2008): 173-181.

Harrison, Pam. "Thyroid Function." *Canadian Living* 31.7 (July 2006): 57.

ORGANIZATIONS

American Clinical Laboratory Association, 1250 H Street, Suite 880, Washington, DC, 20005, (202) 637-9466, (202) 637-2050, info@clinical-labs.org, www.clinical-labs.org.

Robert Bockstiegel

Thyroid nuclear medicine scan

Definition

A thyroid nuclear medicine scan is a diagnostic procedure to evaluate the thyroid gland located in the front of the neck and controls the body's metabolism. A radioactive substance that concentrates in the thyroid is taken orally or injected into a vein (intravenously), or both. A special camera is used to take an image of the distribution of the radioactive substance in and around the thyroid gland. This is interpreted to evaluate thyroid function and to diagnose abnormalities.

Purpose

A thyroid scan may be ordered by a physician when the gland becomes abnormally large, especially if the enlargement is greater on one side, or when hard lumps (nodules) are felt. The scan can be helpful in determining whether the enlargement is caused by a diffuse increase in the total amount of thyroid tissue or by a nodule or nodules.

When other laboratory studies show an overactive thyroid (hyperthyroidism) or an underactive thyroid (hypothyroidism), a radioactive iodine uptake scan is often used to confirm the diagnosis. It is frequently done along with a thyroid scan.

Description

This test is performed in a radiology facility, either in an outpatient x ray center or a hospital department. Most often, the patient is given the radioactive substance in the form of a tasteless liquid or capsule. It may be injected into a vein (intravenously) in some instances. Images will be taken at a specified amount of time after this, depending on the radioisotope used. Most often, scanning is done 24 hours later, if the radioisotope is given orally. If it is given intravenously, the scan is performed approximately 20 minutes later.

For a thyroid scan, the patient is positioned lying down on his or her back, with the head tilted back. The radionuclide scanner, also called a gamma camera, is positioned above the thyroid area as it scans. This takes 30-60 minutes.

The uptake study may be done with the patient sitting upright in a chair or lying down. The procedure is otherwise the same as described for the thyroid scan. It takes approximately 15 minutes. There is no discomfort involved with either study.

A thyroid scan may also be referred to as a thyroid scintiscan. The name of the radioactive substance used may be incorporated and the study called a technetium thyroid scan or an iodine thyroid scan. The radioactive iodine uptake scan may be called by its initials, an RAIU test, or an iodine uptake test.

Preparation

Certain medications can interfere with iodine uptake. These include certain cough medicines, some oral contraceptives, and thyroid medications. The patient is usually instructed to stop taking these medicines for a period of time before the test. This period may range from several days up to three to four weeks, depending on the amount of time the medicine takes to clear from the body.

Other nuclear medicine scans and x ray studies using contrast material performed within the past 60 days may affect this test. Therefore, patients should tell their doctors if they have had either of these types

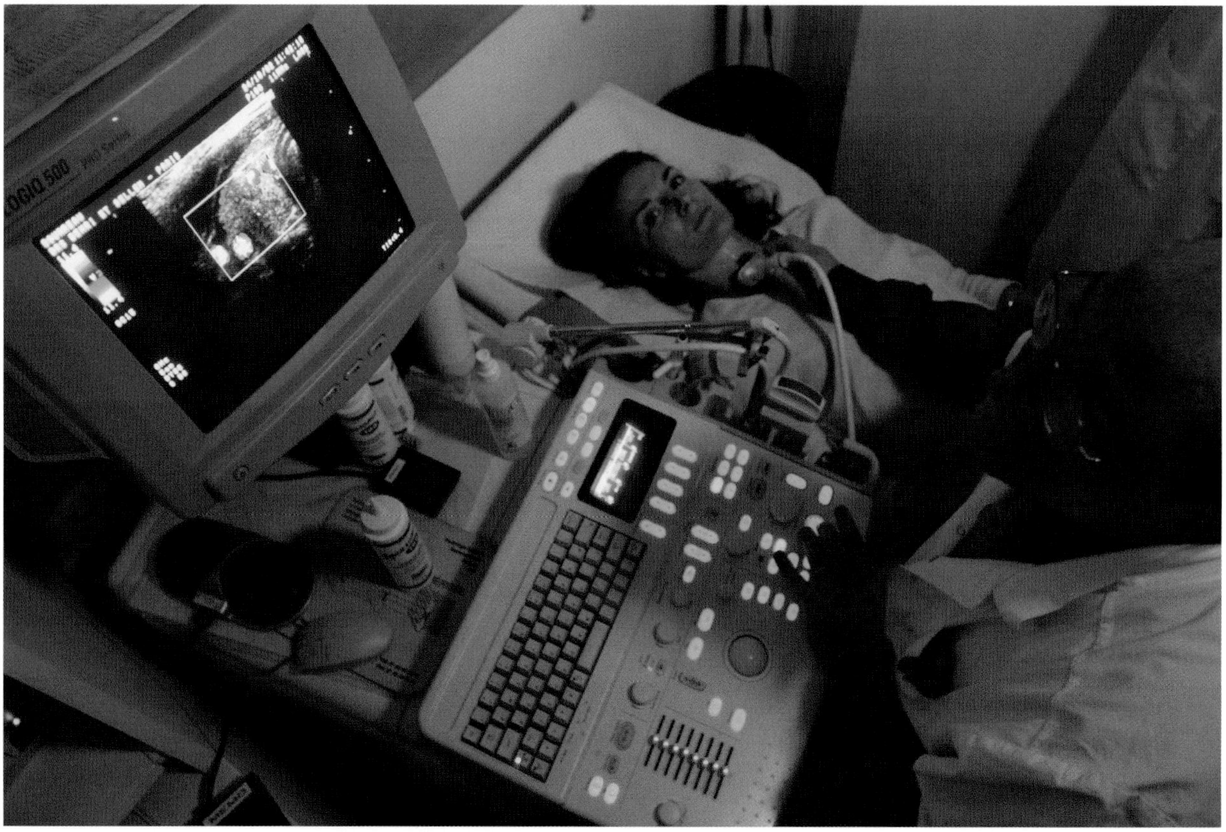

A thyroid scan being performed on a female patient. *(Voisin / Photo Researchers, Inc. Reproduced by permission.)*

of studies before the thyroid scan is begun, to avoid inaccurate results.

Some institutions prefer that the patient have nothing to eat or drink after midnight on the day before the radioactive liquid or capsule is to be taken. A normal **diet** can usually be resumed two hours after the radioisotope is taken. Dentures, jewelry, and other metallic objects must be removed before the scanning is performed. No other physical preparation is needed.

The patient should understand that there is no danger of radiation exposure to themselves or others. Only very small amounts of radioisotope are used. The total amount of radiation absorbed is often less than the dose received from ordinary x rays. The scanner or camera does not emit any radiation, but detects and records it from the patient.

Aftercare

No isolation or special precautions are needed after a thyroid scan. The patient should check with his or her physician about restarting any medications that were stopped before the scan.

Risks

There are no risks with this procedure.

Results

A normal scan will show a thyroid of normal size, shape, and position. The amount of radionuclide uptake by the thyroid will be normal according to established laboratory figures. There will be no areas where radionuclide uptake is increased or decreased.

An area of increased radionuclide uptake may be called a hot nodule or "hot spot." This means that a benign growth is overactive. Despite the name, hot nodules are unlikely to be caused by **cancer**.

An area of decreased radionuclide uptake may be called a cold nodule or "cold spot." This indicates that this area of the thyroid gland is underactive. A variety of conditions, including cysts, nonfunctioning benign growths, localized inflammation, or cancer may produce a cold spot.

A thyroid nuclear medicine scan is rarely sufficient to establish a clear diagnosis. Frequently, the

KEY TERMS

Radioisotope—A radioactive or radiation-emitting form of an element.

Radionuclide—A substance that emits radiation as it disintegrates.

information revealed will need to be combined with data from other studies to determine the problem.

.

Ellen S. Weber MSN

Thyroid storm *see* **Hyperthyroidism**

Thyroid ultrasound

Definition

A thyroid ultrasound is a diagnostic imaging test that uses sound waves to create a picture of the thyroid.

Purpose

A thyroid ultrasound is performed to help diagnose abnormalities of the thyroid. It may be performed when a lump or enlargement is felt during a physical examination of the neck to help provide additional information about the problem. A thyroid ultrasound is also often performed to help guide other procedures. When a biopsy is performed on the thyroid, an ultrasound image can be used to help guide the needle. An ultrasound can also be used to help guide catheter placement when drainage is required.

Thyroid ultrasound can also be performed to help monitor the progress of a disease or treatment. When an element of the thyroid has occurred, thyroid ultrasound can be used to help monitor the success of the treatment being used in shrinking the thyroid to a more normal size. It can also be used to help monitor suspicious growths to determine if they are increasing in size or changing shape, which could indicate intervention or additional diagnostic procedures are required.

Precautions

Thyroid ultrasound does not involve the use of any radiation or radioactive material, unlike x-ray imaging tests and those **thyroid function tests** that use radioactive markers. This means that a thyroid ultrasound is completely safe, even for women who are pregnant or breastfeeding.

Description

The thyroid is a small gland in the neck that weighs less than one ounce. It is butterfly shaped and is located slightly above the collar bone. The thyroid uses iodine to produce two hormones thyroxine (T4) and triiodothyronine (T3). The thyroid hormones are required for regulation of body temperature, metabolism, heartbeat, digestion, and a variety of other necessary body functions.

A thyroid ultrasound is performed with an ultrasound machine. An ultrasound machine consists of a handheld device, called a transducer, and a computer. The transducer is placed in direct contact with the skin and gives of high-frequency sound waves. These sound waves are above the frequency range that can be heard by humans. The sound waves bounce off of body tissues and return to the transducer. The transducer sends information about the angle of the returning waves and how long it took them to return to the computer. The computer then takes this information and uses it to create a visual image of the tissues and organs as the transducer passes over them.

During a thyroid ultrasound the patient is asked to remove any jewelry from the head and heck. He or she may be asked to remove his or her shirt and replace it with a gown. The patient then lies on a table with the neck extended. A gel is often rubbed onto the skin in the area of interest. This gel helps to ensure that there is good contact between the transducer and the skin, allowing for a clear image. The ultrasound technician or radiologist then slowly moves the transducer back and forth across the area of interest.

The procedure usually takes about 30 minutes. The ultrasound technician or radiologist may reposition the patient or turn the head to get a better image or to take images of the thyroid from different angles. After the procedure the gel is wiped off and the patient can return to normal activities.

Preparation

No special preparation is required for a thyroid ultrasound.

Aftercare

No special aftercare is required for a thyroid ultrasound.

QUESTIONS TO ASK YOUR DOCTOR

- Are there any other imaging or diagnostic tests that would help to diagnose my disease or condition?
- If the ultrasound shows abnormal results, what is the next step?
- If the ultrasound shows no abnormal results, what is the next step?

Complications

No complications are expected from a thyroid ultrasound.

Results

A thyroid ultrasound produces images of the thyroid that are interpreted by a radiologist. A normal thyroid will be of a normal size and shape, be in a normal position within the neck, and have no apparent lumps, growths, or nodules.

A thyroid ultrasound could return abnormal results in a variety of situations. The thyroid may appear to have a lump on it. The ultrasound can help determine if the lump is a cyst (a fluid filled sac) or a tumor. In most cases it is not possible to tell if the tumor is cancerous or not using only the ultrasound images. In such cases a biopsy of the tumor is usually taken, which may be guided by an additional thyroid ultrasound procedure. About 90% of nodules of the thyroid are found to be benign (non-cancerous). The thyroid may also appear abnormal if it is enlarged. The ultrasound may also appear abnormal because of enlarged thyroid (goiter).

Thyroid ultrasound can only produce results relating to the image of the thyroid produced by the procedure. These images allow the radiologist to see what the thyroid looks like. They do not, however, provide any information about thyroid function. When a thyroid ultrasound shows an abnormal result other tests, called thyroid function tests, may be performed to help determine if there are any problems with the thyroid's functioning. A nuclear medicine test, called a thyroid scan, can also be used to help determine if the thyroid is absorbing iodine normally. Tests of the thyroid's function can help doctors make a diagnosis when the results of the thyroid ultrasound are not clear.

Caregiver concerns

A doctor determines the need for a thyroid ultrasound based on the patient's symptoms, a physical examination, healthy history, and previous diagnostic tests. The doctor, a nurse, or a member of the radiology team explains the procedure to the patient and answers any questions about the ultrasound and why it is needed. The ultrasound itself is performed by a radiologist or an ultrasound technician. The pictures produced by the procedure are interpreted by a radiologist. The results of the ultrasound, in addition to copies of the images in many cases, are sent to the doctor who ordered the test. The doctor, a member of the doctor's staff, or a member of the radiology team communicates the results to the patient. The doctor then decides which, if any, treatment or additional diagnostic procedures, are indicated.

Resources

BOOKS

Fischbach, Frances Talaska, and Marshall Barnet Dunnin III. *A Manual of Laboratory and Diagnostic Tests.* Philadelphia: Wolters Kluwer Health/Lippincott Williams & Wilkins, 2009.

Milton, Carl A., ed. *Trends in Thyroid Cancer Research.* New York: Nova Biomedical Books, 2007.

Rone, James K. *The Thyroid Paradox: How to Get the Best Care for Hypothyroidism.* Languna Beach, CA: Basic Health Publications, 2007.

PERIODICALS

Bunevicius, Robertas, et al. "Mood and Thyroid Immunity Assessed by Ultrasonographic Imaging in Primary Health Care." *Journal of Affective Disorders* 97.1-3 (January 2007): 85-91.

Stacul, F., et al. "The Radiologist and the Cytologist in Diagnosing Thyroid Nodules: Results of Cooperation." *La Radiologia Medica* 112.4 (June 2007): 597-603.

ORGANIZATIONS

American Institute of Ultrasound in Medicine, 14750 Sweitzer Lane, Suite 100, Laurel, MD, 20707-5906, (301) 498-4100, (800) 638-5352, (310) 498-4450, www.aium.org.

Robert Bockstiegel

Thyroid x ray *see* **Thyroid radionuclide scan**

TIAs *see* **Transient ischemic attack**

Tinnitus

Definition

Tinnitus refers to abnormal sounds heard in one or both ears, including possible swishing, ringing, whistling, roaring or rushing that does not come from the outside environment.

Description

Tinnitus, sometimes called head noise, is not a condition in itself, but is usually a symptom of another condition. It can occur in one or both ears, originating from any part of the ear, including the outer, middle, or inner ear or the part of the brain that controls hearing. Tinnitus is not dangerous, but can be annoying and upsetting to those who experience it, primarily because it is constant and distracting, sometimes interfering with the ability to concentrate. The presence of other sounds in the environment may diminish the sensation of tinnitus, but as soon as it becomes quiet, the swishing, ringing, buzzing or roaring will continue. Some head noise is to be expected in any adult, although normal sounds from the environment typically cover head noises to a great extent. However, the presence of significant sound without an outside source exceeds normal head noises and becomes an irritant to the individual.

The inner ear contains thousand of tiny auditory cells that each carry an electrical charge. When microscopic hairs on the surface of each auditory cell move as sound waves pass over them, the cell will discharge an electrical signal through the auditory nerve and, though the ear does not actually "hear" the electrical signal, the brain interprets it as sound. The hairs on auditory cells can become bent or broken and may respond by moving eratically, simultaneously releasing random or steady electrical signals that the brain will again interpret as noise. Although this mechanism is understood, it is not understood if it is the specific trigger for tinnitus.

Demographics

Tinnitus or head noise is common, particularly in adults over age 60 who have begun to experience age-related **hearing loss** (presbyacusis). One third of all adults report having tinnitus for some period during their lifetime. The prevalence of tinnitus has been estimated to be as low as 7.9 million and as high as 37 million. The range varies because millions of individuals worldwide experience tinnitus and report it, while millions of cases are believed to go unreported.

QUESTIONS TO ASK YOUR DOCTOR

- Is the noise in my ears caused by nerve damage or by any of the medications I've taken?
- Can I expect the tinnitus to diminish or go away entirely at some point?
- What can I do to diminish the sound or avoid hearing it?
- Is my blood pressure a factor in producing ear noises?

Causes and symptoms

Tinnitus can occur as the result of fluid in the ear or in the tube (auditory tube or Eustachian tube) that runs from the space behind the ear (tympanic cavity) into the nose and throat (nasopharynx), or infection or diseases that affect the bones of the middle ear or the membrane called the ear drum (tympanic membrane). Injury to the inner ear can occur with trauma to the head or neck, resulting in tinnitus and hearing loss. The bones of the middle ear can become stiff (otosclerosis), which can cause tinnitus and associated hearing loss. High **blood pressure** can cause a sensation of rushing in the ear. Similarly, the build up of fatty deposits in blood vessels (**atherosclerosis**) close to the middle and inner ear can cause more turbulent blood flow than normal in the narrowed vessels, allowing the beating of the heart to be heard. Meniere's syndrome, a disease that affects the inner ear, can cause tinnitus as well as disrupting normal balance. Prolonged use of **aspirin** or aspirin-containing drugs may lead to head noise. Tinnitus can also be caused by some type of damage to the tiny hearing nerve in the inner ear. Hearing nerve damage is common during aging and may be accompanied by tinnitus. An extremely loud noise or steady exposure to loud noise over a period of time can be the cause of nerve-related tinnitus and hearing can be damaged permanently as a result. In rare instances, tinnitus can be a sign of **aneurysm** or brain tumor. Build up of ear wax can aggravate tinnitus but is not believed to cause it.

The only symptom of tinnitus, the ringing, buzzing, roaring, hissing, whistling or swishing may be noticed suddenly and continue steadily, and can also be intermittent and gradually increase in frequency. Tinnitus can be accompanied by hearing loss.

KEY TERMS

Acoustic neuroma—A non-cancerous tumor caused by growth of abnormal cells on the auditory nerve that governs hearing.

Audiogram—A graph-like tracing that records results of hearing tests performed with an audiometer.

Audiometer—An electrical device designed to measure hearing across a range of frequencies.

Auditory tube (eustachian tube)—A tube joining the tympanic cavity behind the ear to the nasopharynx.

Nasopharynx—The space above the roof of the mouth (soft palate) that opens into the nasal cavity and joins with the tympanic cavity behind the ear drum.

Otosclerosis—Changes in the bones of the ear (stapes) that result in their stiffness and immobility, leading to progressive deafness.

Presbyacusis—Age-related hearing loss as a result of losing the ability to discriminate between sounds.

Tympanic cavity—A mucus-membrane lined cavity behind the ear drum that connects with the auditory (Eustachian) tube.

Tympanic membrane—The ear drum, a thin but firm covering over the tympanic cavity that forms a barrier between the middle ear and the outer ear.

Diagnosis

The physician will take a medical history of previous illnesses, surgeries, injuries and medications, and conduct a physical examination to help determine the likely source of tinnitus. The doctor will want to know the intensity of the sound and if it is steady or pulsing, heard constantly or only heard at certain times, and if any hearing loss or problems with balance were noticed before the tinnitus began. A hearing test (audiogram) will be conducted using an audiometer that measures ability to hear different frequencies. Blood pressure and heart rate will also be part of the physical examination. A special computerized test, the auditory brain stem response (ABR), may be performed to evaluate hearing nerves and pathways in the brain. Diagnostic imaging such as computed tomography (CT) or **magnetic resonance imaging** (MRI) may be conducted to determine if a rare small tumor may be pressing on the auditory nerve (acoustic neuroma).

After examination and testing, the condition may be diagnosed as "subjective tinnitus" if some evidence of nerve damage is found and only the individual can hear sounds. However, if the doctor can hear sounds attributable to high blood pressure or exaggerated heart or blood vessel noise due to atherosclerosis, the condition will be described as "pulsatile tinnitus."

Treatment

There is no standard treatment for tinnitus, especially if it is believed to be part of age-related hearing loss. The individual cause of tinnitus may help direct treatment, however. Reducing blood pressure and decreasing salt intake is sometimes helpful. Avoiding stimulants such as **caffeine** in coffee, tea and colas may diminish tinnitus. Focus on other sounds rather than the tinnitus, such as listening to soft music when relaxing or resting. Other "white noise" such as the ticking of a clock or whirring of a fan may help reduce the sound of tinnitus during sleeping hours. Reducing **stress** and **anxiety** generally can reduce the sensation of tinnitus. Avoiding aspirin or medications containing aspirin may relieve the tinnitus. Drugs such as **tricyclic antidepressants** (amitriptyline, nortriptyline), nervous system depressants (**benzodiazepines**) and **muscle relaxants** (baclofen) are sometimes prescribed and are reported to have provided relief in some cases. A drug used in the treatment of alcoholism (acamprosate)) has relieved tinnitus in some individuals, and a **migraine** medication (gabapentin) showed positive results in a clinical trial.

Prognosis

In most cases, tinnitus will diminish on its own or the individual will become accustomed to the sound and essentially not "hear" it any more. If nerve damage is involved, tinnitus may be a permanent condition that will need to be accepted.

Therapy

Acupuncture has been recommended for treating tinnitus and has shown positive results in some individuals. Hypnosis has also worked for some people, though there is no scientific basis for the results. Electrical stimulation, a physical therapy technique, has shown some positive results as well, coordinating electrical activity of auditory cells.

Herbs and supplements that have been reported to help reduce tinnitus include:

- Ginkgo to help encourage circulation and improve hearing loss and tinnitus related to changes in blood pressure

- B vitamin complex to reduce ear pressure and encourage healing; includes niacin and thiamine that provide direct nutrition for nerves
- Vitamin E to improve circulation and provide antioxidant activity

Prevention

Excessively loud noise such as firearms, industrial equipment noise, chain saws, power mowers, or high intensity music should be avoided. Ear plugs or ear muffs should be worn to protect the ears against exposure to steady loud noise. Individuals should refrain from putting objects into the ears, even Q-tips for cleaning the ear, because ear wax can be pushed against the ear drum in this way, causing or aggravating tinnitus. Blood pressure should be checked regularly in senior adults and blood pressure medication should be taken as prescribed.

Resources

PERIODICALS

Heller AJ. "Classification and epidemiology of tinnitus." *Otolaryngology Clinics of North America 36(2); 2003.*

OTHER

Cunha JP. "Tinnitus (Ringing and Other Ear Noises)" *Medicine Net.*2008. Available at www.medicinenet .com. Accessed March 14, 2008.

"Tinnitus." *Mayo Foundation for Medical Education and Research.*2006. Mayo Clinic. www.mayoclinic.com/ health/tinnitus/DS00365. Accessed March 13, 2008.

ORGANIZATIONS

American Speech/Language Hearing Association, 2200 Research Boulevard, Rockville, MD, 20850-3289, 800-638-8255, actioncenter@asha.org, www.asha.org.

American Tinnitus Association (ATA), PO Box 5, Portland, OR, 97207, www.ata.org.

L. Lee Culvert

Tobacco use *see* **Smoking**

Topical antibiotics *see* **Antibiotics**

Topical antifungal drugs *see* **Antifungal drugs, topical**

Transient blindness

Definition

Transient blindness, also called transient monocular blindness or amaurosis fugax, is a brief loss of vision. Vision loss usually occurs in only one eye and can last anywhere from a few minutes to a few hours. Transient vision loss is often a warning sign that a **stroke** is imminent.

Description

Transient blindness can occur because a blood vessel to the eye is blocked, the eye is damaged, or nerves to the eye are diseased. People who experience transient blindness may feel like their vision is gradually blurring, fogging, or fading out, or they may feel as if a dark curtain has suddenly descended over their field of vision. Most often, transient blindness affects only one eye. The condition can last anywhere from a few seconds to hours. Although vision returns, anyone who experiences transient blindness should see a physician promptly because it can be a symptom of an impending medical emergency.

Demographics

Because transient blindness has many causes, it can happen to people of any age, although it is often linked to cardiovascular disease and is more likely to occur in older individuals. Transient blindness is most common in white men over age 50.

Causes and symptoms

Transient blindness occurs for three main reasons: blockage of a blood vessel going to the eye, damage to the eye, or damage to the nerves that serve eye. Of these, blockage of the blood vessels going to the eye is the most common.

Blood vessel blockage

Amaurosis fugax is the temporary loss of vision caused by debris in the circulatory system that blocks blood flow to the retina. Typically, only one eye is affected at a time. The blockage often occurs because a bit of plaque from **atherosclerosis** breaks off from the lining of a main artery and travels to a smaller artery that delivers blood to the retina. Atherosclerosis is a condition in which arteries narrow because of a build up of debris, called plaque, on the inside of the arterial walls. When loose bits of debris lodge in an artery, blood flow is severely restricted or stops, which causes the retina to be deprived of oxygen and nutrients. The retina then stops functioning and the person loses vision. If the blockage lasts only a short time, vision is lost only temporarily and returns when blood flow to the retina begins again. Plaque that obstructs arteries to the eye most often comes from the internal carotid artery (an artery in the neck),

QUESTIONS TO ASK YOUR DOCTOR

- What caused my vision loss?
- Are there underlying health problems that are likely to have caused this vision loss?
- Do I need to be referred to a specialist?
- Do I need immediate treatment such as surgery?
- What should I do if I experience transient vision loss again?

although it can come from anywhere in the cardiovascular system. Arteries to the retina can also be blocked by **blood clots**. Often these clots arise in the heart from conditions such as atrial fibrillation or heart valve defects.

Amaurosis fugax can also occur when the arteries that serve the retina develop such severe plaque build up that blood flow is substantially reduced. In this case, vision loss is often triggered by sudden exposure to sunlight, which causes the retina to need more nutrients than the reduced flow of blood can deliver. Transient vision loss caused by any kind of blockage is a warning sign that a transient ischemic attack (TIA) or a stroke is likely to occur in the near future.

Occasionally amaurosis fugax occurs in healthy individuals during **exercise**. Vision loss lasts less than five minutes and is thought to be caused by a temporary spasm (vasospasm) of a blood vessel serving the eye, triggered by the release of certain chemicals into the blood. This type of vision loss is not a warning sign of stroke.

Inflammation of the retinal artery (giant cell arteritis) can also cause amaurosis fugax. The inflammation causes the artery to become partially or completely blocked. This condition is usually associated with headache. Various studies found that giant cell arteritis was the cause of temporary vision loss in 2 to 19% of people with amaurosis fugax.

Transient vision loss due to insufficient blood flow has also been reported as an occasional side effect of such drugs as sidenafil (Viagra), vardenafil (Levitra), and tadalafil (Cialis) taken for **erectile dysfunction**. Individuals experiencing this side effect should stop using the drug and be evaluated by their physician.

Sudden vision loss can also be caused by psychological trauma. This condition is sometimes called hysterical vision loss.

Damage to the eye

Infection and inflammation of various parts of the eye can also cause temporary vision loss, as can a transient increase in intraocular pressure (the pressure inside the eye). Disorders such as closed-angle **glaucoma** and the build up of drusen (pigment clumps) can also cause temporary or permanent vision loss. Temporary vision loss has also been reported in young children who have had mild head trauma with no loss of consciousness.

Nerve damage

The optic nerve carries information from the retina to the brain, where the information is processed to create an image. Any event that damages the optic nerve or interferes with nerve impulse transmission can cause transient or permanent blindness. These events include inflammation of the optic nerve, compression of the optic nerve, temporary reduction in blood flow to the optic nerve, **multiple sclerosis** (nerve impulses are disrupted due to degeneration of the myelin sheath surrounding the nerve), tumors that infringe on the optic nerve, psychoactive drug use, and **migraine headaches**.

Symptoms

About one-fourth of patients describe their transient vision loss as a dark curtain descending across their field of vision, while the majority describe it as a dimming, fogging, or blurring of vision.

The sensation of a dark curtain obscuring the field of vision also characterizes a **retinal detachment**. Loss of vision due to a retinal detachment is not temporary. Individuals with sudden vision loss should seek immediate medical care. A retinal detachment is a medical emergency that can result in permanent blindness if not treated promptly.

Diagnosis

Diagnosing the cause of transient vision loss is difficult because by the time the patient sees a physician vision has often returned. Diagnosis begins with a thorough **eye examination**. The eye will be dilated so that interior structures can be seen using an ophthalmoscope and a slit lamp. An ophthalmologist will look for any signs of infection, bleeding, eye disease,

KEY TERMS

Artery—A vessel that carries oxygen-rich blood to the body.

Atherosclerosis—A chronic condition characterized by thickening and hardening of the arteries and the build up of plaque on the arterial walls. Atherosclerosis can slow or impair blood circulation, and be the source of debris that travels to and blocks other arteries.

Balloon angioplasty—A surgical procedure performed to reopen a partially blocked artery so that blood can flow through it again at a normal rate. A tiny tube (catheter) is threaded through blood vessels to the point of the blockage. The catheter contains a balloon that is then expanded to stretch and open the artery.

Drusen—Clumps of pigment that accumulate under the retina when wastes build up faster than they can be removed. Drusen are a sign of dry age-related macular degeneration.

Echocardiogram—A non-invasive imaging procedure used to create a picture of the heart's movement, valves, and chambers.

Electrocardiogram (ECG)—A test that measures electrical impulses in the heart.

Embolism—A blood clot, air bubble, or clot of foreign material that travels in and blocks the flow of blood in an artery. When blood supply to a tissue or organ is blocked by an embolism, infarction (death of the tissue the artery feeds) may occur. Without immediate and appropriate treatment, an embolism in a critical blood vessel can even be fatal.

Glaucoma—An eye disorder in which increased pressure in the eye (intraocular pressure) causes damage to the optic nerve, resulting in vision loss. There are several types of glaucoma, and glaucoma may develop suddenly or gradually.

Plaque—Fatty material that is deposited on the inside of an arterial wall.

Retina—Light-sensitive tissue on the back of the eye that receives images and converts them into nerve impulses to be sent to the brain by way of the optic nerve.

Retinal detachment—Separation of the retina of the eye from its underlying layer of tissue. This separation results in loss of vision. A retinal detachment is a medical emergency.

Stenosis (plural, stenoses)—The narrowing or constriction of an opening or passageway in the body.

or other condition that could have caused the vision loss. A complete eye examination can determine if the cause of vision loss is physical or psychological by the way the eye responds to light and movement. In the case of hysterical vision loss, the patient will be referred to a psychiatrist.

Because transient vision loss may indicate a serious cardiovascular condition, the patient usually needs evaluation by an internal medicine specialist or cardiologist. Screening can include an electrocardiogram (ECG), 24-hour **Holter monitoring** (in which the patient wears a portable monitor that records heart contractions for 24 hours), **echocardiogram**, and an ultrasound or other scan of the head and neck to assess the degree of arterial blockage.

Treatment

Treatment depends on the cause of vision loss. If an artery in the neck is more than 70% blocked, the patient may benefit from surgical unblockage, often by balloon **angioplasty**. If the condition of the patient makes surgery undesirable or the blockage is less than 70%, the patient may be given blood-thinning drugs such as warfarin (Coumadin) and drugs to lower cholesterol to prevent additional plaque build up.

When damage to the eye has occurred or an underlying disease is present, these conditions are treated.

Nutrition/Dietetic concerns

Since transient vision loss is often caused by plaque in the arteries, dietary changes are directed at preventing plaque build up. A low-cholesterol, heart-healthy **diet** low in fats, especially saturated (animal) fats and high in fresh fruits, vegetables, and whole grains is recommended by the American Heart Association. Calorie and portion control is also important in maintaining or reaching a healthy weight.

Prognosis

Although people with transient vision loss regain their vision without any permanent disability, short-term loss of vision is often a forewarning of stroke or other serious medical problem and should not be ignored.

Prevention

Prevention involves preventing the underlying problem that causes the transient loss of vision. If the cause of vision loss is due to narrowed or blocked blood vessels, then following a heart-healthy diet, maintaining a healthy weight, and exercising regularly, controlling blood sugar levels and **blood pressure**, and not **smoking** are all helpful. Some causes of transient vision loss cannot be prevented.

Caregiver concerns

Caregivers should arrange for the person in their care who experiences transient vision loss to see a doctor promptly, even if vision loss is only momentary and vision then returns to normal. Transient vision loss is a warning sign that a more serious health problem is likely to occur in the near future.

Resources

OTHER

"Amaurosis Fugax." *Medline Plus.* September 10, 2006 [cited February 24, 2008]. *http://www.nlm.nih.gov/medlineplus/ency/article/000784.htm.*

Farina, Gino A., and Nicholas Lorenzo. "Sudden Vision Loss." *eMedcinie.com.* November 8, 2005 [cited February 24, 2008]. *http://www.emedicine.com/neuro/topic480.htm*

Sowka, Joseph W., and Alan G. Kabat. "Sudden Vision Loss: Now They See It, Now They Don't." *Review of Optometry Online.* March 15, 2000 [cited February 24, 2008]. *http://www.revoptom.com/archive/FEATURES/ro0300f7.htm.*

ORGANIZATIONS

American Heart Association, 7272 Greenville Ave., Dallas, TX, 75231, (800) 242-8721, http://www.americanheart.org.

American Optometric Association, 243 N. Lindbergh Blvd., St. Louis, MO, 63141, (800) 365-2219, http://www.aao.org.

EyeCare America Foundation of the American Academy of Ophthalmology, PO Box 429098, San Francisco, CA, 94142-9098, (877) 887-6327, (800) 324-3937, (415) 561-8567, pubserv@aao.org, http://www.eyecareamerica.org.

National Eye Institute, 2020 Vision Place, Bethesda, MD, 20992-3655, (301) 496-5248, 2020@nei.nih.gov, http://www.nei.nih.gov.

National Heart, Lung, and Blood Institute Information Center, PO Box 30105, Bethesda, MD, 20824-0105, 301) 592-8573, http://www.nhlbi.nih.gov.

Tish Davidson A. M.

Transient ischemic attacks

Definition

Transient ischemic attacks or TIAs are brief stroke-like episodes, sometimes called mini-strokes or transient **stroke**, that occur when a blood clot temporarily blocks an artery and prevents blood from flowing normally in the brain.

Description

A transient ischemic attack (TIA) is not an actual stroke but gives the individual a serious warning of increased risk for stroke. It should be considered an emergency and requires an immediate visit to a physician or an emergency department. Although a TIA cannot predict when a stroke will occur, clinical evidence from thousands of cases shows that strokes usually follow TIAs within one year, and sometimes as soon as 24 to 48 hours. TIAs happen when a blood clot blocks an artery and interrupts blood flow to a specific part of the brain, producing transient stroke-like symptoms such as numbness in the face or limbs, confusion, difficulty speaking, vision problems, **dizziness** or difficulty maintaining balance and sudden severe headache. The blocked artery is usually between the heart and the brain, often in the carotid artery in the neck, the vertebral arteries or within the brain itself. Although symptoms of stroke and TIA are similar, the difference between a stroke and a TIA is that no permanent damage to the brain usually occurs as a result of TIA. However, TIA is a critical indication that stroke is likely to occur and physicians pay strict attention to TIAs, seeking to prevent stroke, which can lead to permanent disability or **death**. Immediate diagnosis is needed so that treatment of TIA can be provided as quickly as possible to prevent or reduce blood clot formation and reduce the threat of stroke.

Demographics

Between 200,000 and 500,000 individuals experience TIAs every year in the United States; the majority are over age 65 and it is rare for anyone 45 or younger to have TIA. Among emergency room patients with TIAs, 25% have another adverse event such as **heart attack** or stroke within 90 days of the original emergency room visit, and 10% of these are strokes that occur with 48 hours after the visit. Risk for TIA parallels risk for stroke. The National Stroke Association reports that two-thirds of stroke victims are over age 65, with risk doubling in each 10 years over age 55. Men are at greater risk than women and

African-Americans at greater risk than other racial groups. Stroke is the third leading cause of death after **heart disease** and **cancer**. Nearly 700,000 strokes are recorded each year in the United States; most individuals are disabled by the stroke and about 150,000 will die.

Causes and symptoms

The most frequent risk factors for TIA and stroke are high **blood pressure** (**hypertension**), **high cholesterol**, heart disease, carotid artery disease, diabetes, cigarette **smoking** and excess alcohol consumption. Diabetes increases risk because of associated **circulatory problems**. Individuals with high blood pressure are at four to six times greater risk for TIA and stroke. Common to most of these health and lifestyle factors, as well as normal aging, is damage to arteries and the resultant narrowing from buildup of fatty deposits (plaque) on artery walls, making them harder and thicker (**atherosclerosis**). In carotid artery disease, plaque builds up in either one or both of the carotid arteries on each side of the neck, narrowing them significantly (between 50 and 70% blockage), a condition called stenosis. Narrowing of arteries increases blood pressure and reduces blood circulation throughout the body, creating a potentially dangerous condition that robs cells and organs of necessary oxygen (**ischemia**), which can ultimately result in heart attack or stroke. Blockage of an important artery by accumulated deposits or a blood clot can prevent blood and oxygen from flowing to the heart or the brain. Reduced blood flow to the heart can result in cardiac ischemia and heart attack. Lack of blood flow to the brain can precipitate TIA and ischemic stroke.

Symptoms of TIA appear suddenly and are similar to those of stroke but are transient, usually lasting only minutes. Symptoms are derived from lack of oxygen and blood flow to a part of the brain and are therefore typical of nervous system disorders (neurological deficit). TIA must be considered if the individual experiences numbness or weakness on one side of the face, or in an arm or leg on one side. Loss of ability to speak or think clearly, slurring words, feeling confused or having trouble understanding what another person is saying can be signs of TIA. Vision may be disturbed in one eye or both. Sudden severe headache may be the first symptom or may accompany other symptoms. Dizziness and loss of balance or unsteady walking may also indicate TIA. Symptoms can last up to an hour but more typically will pass within five minutes or so; in some cases, certain symptoms may continue into the next day, diminishing gradually. Because the individual or caretaker can not determine if the symptoms are TIA or stroke, immediate emergency attention is needed to diagnose the condition and to obtain fast, appropriate treatment.

Diagnosis

Emergency evaluation of possible TIA should ideally be conducted within 180 minutes of the first appearance of symptoms. The physician will immediately examine the patient for signs of weakness in the face, arms and legs and note any altered speech or presence of confusion. Vital signs such as blood pressure and heart rate will be monitored and an electrocardiogram (ECG) will be done to evaluate heart function. Family history of stroke may be noted. The individual's recent history of symptoms and current and prior diseases or conditions will be reviewed as quickly as possible while beginning laboratory testing to determine if TIA or pending stroke will require immediate medication to reduce risk of **blood clots**. Diagnostic laboratory tests will include a **complete blood count**, platelet count, and coagulation tests (prothrombin time, partial thromboplastin time) to determine likelihood of clotting abnormalities and clot formation. Serum electrolytes (**sodium**, potassium and chloride) will be done to evaluate presence of vascular or heart abnormalities, and blood glucose will be done to determine blood sugar abnormalities, which can be confused with TIA. Computed tomography (CT) of the head may be done to determine if brain hemorrhage or tumor may be present, which can mimic TIA; prior stroke can also be identified with **CT scans**. However, **magnetic resonance imaging** (MRI) may also be performed to examine brain tissue more closely for specific damage; MRI is considered the most accurate imaging technique for identifying TIA.

Treatment

Immediate treatment for TIA will focus on dissolving blood clots or preventing clot formation. Drug therapy with appropriate **anticoagulant drugs** will typically be given intravenously and may include tissue-type plasminogen activator (tPA) in some individuals for whom it is appropriate. A drug that reduces platelet aggregation, a mechanism involved in clot formation, may be given (antiplatelet therapy) or other types of anticoagulant therapy, including heparin or warfarin, depending on the health status of the individual and presence of any concomitant disease. Individuals are monitored extremely closely while receiving drug therapy for TIA, drawing blood

QUESTIONS TO ASK YOUR DOCTOR

- Have I had a TIA or stroke?
- If this is a TIA, what must I do to prevent having a stroke?
- How can I reduce my risk for stroke?
- How many people have you treated for TIA and how many avoided stroke?

frequently to evaluate coagulation processes and conditions of the blood that could lead to hemorrhage.

Because the presence of fatty deposits in the carotid arteries of the neck is the most significant risk factor for ischemic stroke, treatment may involve correcting carotid artery blockage. If carotid artery disease is present and the narrowed artery has resulted in TIA, a carotid endarterectomy (CEA) may be performed to reduce risk of stroke. CEA is a surgical procedure that removes plaque deposits from the carotid arteries in the neck, restoring the flow of blood and oxygen to the brain and preventing risk of stroke. The National Institute of Neurological Disorders and Stroke (NINDS) reports that endarterectomy has proven to be especially protective for people who have already had a stroke or who have had TIAs and are at high risk for stroke.

Nutrition/Dietetic concerns

Lifestyle changes to reduce risk factors for TIA and stroke will necessarily include **diet**. A vegetarian diet has been shown to be associated with lower blood pressure, which is a risk factor for TIA and stroke. The DASH diet, a way of eating shown to reduce blood pressure, is described in Dietary Approaches to Stop Hypertension. It is recommended by the National Institutes of Health (NIH), the American Heart Association, and most heart doctors and is just as beneficial in preventing heart disease and stroke as it is in reducing blood pressure, because salt, fat and sugar content is far below the national average. The DASH diet consists of fruits, vegetables, low-fat dairy, whole grains, poultry, fish and nuts. Most Americans consume about 37% of calories as fat and 300 to 500 milligrams of dietary cholesterol daily. By contrast, the Lifestyle Heart Trial study conducted by noted heart doctor, Dean Ornish, M.D., put participating adults on a vegetarian diet that reduced their fat intake to 10% of total calories and dietary cholesterol to only 5 milligrams daily. When tested, participants were found to have significantly reduced atheroslclerosis, a significant risk factor for TIA and stroke, with greatly improved blood and oxygen flow throughout their bodies.

Prognosis

TIAs provide warning of possible serious stroke that can have debilitating effects. Giving immediate attention to a TIA can lead to appropriate treatment of risk factors, helping to prevent stroke. Ignoring TIAs will almost certainly lead to stroke and serious consequences.

Prevention

Lifestyle habits directly influence the risk factors and causes of TIA and stroke. Eating a balanced, whole foods diet with sufficient intake of nutrients and fiber is essential, including the avoidance of excess salt and not eating prepared, packaged foods that are high in salt and sugar and low in nutritional value. Regular **exercise** and maintaining a healthy weight appropriate for the individual's age and activity level are important as well. Smoking and alcohol consumption are known causes of conditions leading to atherosclerosis, heart disease and stroke and should be avoided; programs to stop smoking and using alcohol are available in most communities. Underlying diseases such as diabetes, atherosclerosis, high blood pressure and vascular disease must be managed through regular care of a physician.

Caregiver concerns

When caring for someone known to have conditions that lead to stroke such as heart disease, high blood pressure, **obesity**, diabetes, or previous stroke, or someone who smokes or consumes excess alcohol, it is necessary to be on the alert for uncharacteristic behavior and movements. Pay particular attention to changes in the face such as one side becoming drawn or drooping, or the presence of confusion or agitation, dizziness or difficulty walking. Ask the individual to move arms and legs and if they have normal feeling in the limbs. Ask the individual to smile and see if the smile is one-sided, and note if speech has changed in any way. Report any changes to the physician or emergency services without delay to ensure immediate diagnosis and treatment of possible TIA, which can help prevent stroke.

KEY TERMS

Atherosclerosis—The buildup of wax-like fatty deposits on the walls of medium and large arteries that later become calcified, narrowing the blood vessels and restricting blood flow.

Endarterectomy—A surgical procedure that removed damaged portions of arteries, including portions with atherosclerotic deposits, to open the vessels and restore unrestricted blood flow.

Ischemia—A type of localized anemia that occurs when blood and oxygen flow is reduced, robbing organ tissues of necessary oxygen.

Neurological deficit—Nervous system or neuromuscular disorders or symptoms.

Stenosis—Narrowing of any tubular-like vessel in the body, such as a cardiac valve (mitral stenosis) or an artery (carotid stenosis).

Vertebral arteries—Arteries that run along the cervical spine through the neck and into the brain stem.

Resources

BOOKS

"Ischemic Stroke" *The Merck Manual of Diagnosis and Therapy,*Section 16. R.S. Porter, ed. White House Station, NJ: Merck Research Laboratories, 2007.

"TIA." *Merck Manual of Diagnosis and Therapy.*Section 16. R.S. Porter, ed. White House Station, NJ: Merck Research Laboratories, 2007.

"Carotid endarterectomy."*Gale Encyclopedia of Surgery.* Michigan: Gale/Thomson, 2001.

Balch P A."Atherosclerosis."*Prescription for Nutritional Healing.*Garden City Park, NY:Avery, 1997.

PERIODICALS

Solenski NJ. "Transient Ischemic Attacks: Part I. Diagnosis and Evaluation.*American Family Physician 69(4); 2004.*

WEBSITES

"Transient Ischemic Attack."*American Heart Association.*2008. Available at www.american heart.org. Accessed March 11, 2008.

"NINDS Transient Ischemic Attack Information." *National Institute of Neurological Disorders and Stroke (NINDS)*March 2008. Available at www.ninds .nih.gov/disorders/tia/tia.htm. Accessed March 11, 2008.

*The DASH Diet Action Plan*Available at www.dashdiet.org/ dash_diet_action_plan.htm. Accessed Feb. 4, 2008.

ORGANIZATIONS

American Heart Association, 7272 Greenville Avenue, Dallas, TX, 75231-4596, 214-373-6300, 800-AHA-8721, inquiries@heart.org, www.americanheart.org.

National Stroke Association, 9707 East Easter Lane, Suite B, Centennial, CO, 801120-3747, info@stroke.org, www.stroke.org.

L. Lee Culvert

Travel *see* **Senior travel**

Trigger finger

Definition

Trigger finger is the popular name of stenosing tenosynovitis, a painful condition in which a finger or thumb locks when it is bent (flexed) or straightened (extended).

Description

Tendons are tough, fibrous cords that connect muscles to bones. Tendons must slide easily through their protective coverings (tendon sheaths). The finger and thumb bones have tendons that are responsible for bending and straightening the fingers. Problems start when a tendon sheath narrows (stenosis) and the outer covering of the tendon becomes inflamed (tenosynovitis). The tendon swells because of the constriction, sometimes forming a nodule, and is no longer able to move smoothly through its sheath. As a result, a finger may lock in an upward position as the person tries to straighten it.

Causes and symptoms

Trigger finger is often an overuse injury because of repetitive or frequent movement of the fingers. Trigger finger may happen because a person performs the same manipulation over and over on a job, from squeezing and gripping during a weekend of heavy pruning and gardening, or from such hobbies as playing a musical instrument or crocheting. Trigger finger may also result from trauma or accident. The symptoms of trigger finger are **pain** in the fingers and "popping" sensations. Sometimes the finger may lock down into the palm or lock out straight. Symptoms are usually worse in the morning and improve during the day.

KEY TERMS

Microcirculation—The passage of blood in the smallest blood vessels of the body, such as the capillaries in the hand and fingers.

Myofascial—The fibrous tissue that encloses and separates layers of muscles.

Nodule—A swelling or knob that may form on a tendon and make it difficult to slide smoothly through its sheath.

Stenosis—Narrowing of a passageway or opening in the body. In trigger finger it is the tendon sheath that narrows.

Synovial tendon sheath—Where the tendons cross joints, they are sheathed in thin membranes known as synovium, which provide lubrication to decrease friction.

Tendon sheath—A membrane covering a tendon.

Tenosynovitis—Inflammation of a tendon and its enveloping sheath, usually resulting from overuse injury.

Diagnosis

The diagnosis of trigger finger and thumb is obvious on physical examination. Often there is a click that can be felt as the nodule passes through the sheath. Most cases are uncomplicated although X rays are often taken to rule out other injuries or disease such as arthritis.

Treatment

Initial treatment for mild or infrequent symptoms of trigger finger include rest, avoiding or modifying those activities that caused the inflammation, and the use of a nonsteroidal anti-inflammatory drug (NSAID) such as ibuprofen. This may relieve the swelling and inflammation that resulted in the constriction of the sheath and the restriction of the tendon. Injection of a steroid medication (cortisone) into the tendon sheath is the next option to treat trigger finger. Depending on the severity, there may be one more injection a week later. Two-thirds of patients improve after one injection. Some physicians will splint the finger in extension after the injection.

In severe cases that do not respond to injections and the finger or thumb remains in a locked position, surgery may be required to relieve the symptoms. A local anesthetic is used for the surgical procedure performed on an outpatient basis. An incision is made by a surgeon in the palm of the hand at the base of the affected finger or thumb to relieve the constriction of the tendon. Recovery may take up to four weeks. Sometimes physical therapy of the hand is required after surgery to regain good use.

Treatment should begin when a person starts having difficulty moving the fingers. If started early, noninvasive measures have a good chance for success. Alternative treatments include **acupuncture** to facilitate healing and microcirculation, pulsed ultrasound, and myofascial release work for the affected area.

Prognosis

At least half of cases can be cured non-surgically. The key to successful treatment is early intervention. A mistake people make is trying to work through the pain. Diabetics have a higher incidence of the condition and are sometimes left with a disability.

Prevention

Taking frequent breaks from a repetitive activity will do much to prevent the condition. Depending on the intensity, that may mean a 10-minute break every hour from the repetitive activity. The break should be spent stretching the hands and arms and generally moving around.

Resources

PERIODICALS

"Ask the Mayo Physician." *HealthOasis MayoClinic* May 4, 2000.

Stroud, R. "Minimally Invasive Surgical Techniques of the Hand andUpper Extremities." *Orthopedic Technology Review* September 2000: 18.

OTHER

Jameson DC, CCSP, Timothy J. "Explanation,Treatment, and Prevention of Trigger Finger."GuitarBase Articles. http://www.gbase.com/articles/med/med4.html.

Ruthan Brodsky

Tube feedings

Definition

Tube feeding is a procedure used for placing food, fluids, and drugs directly into the stomach or small intestine through a tube inserted through the nose or

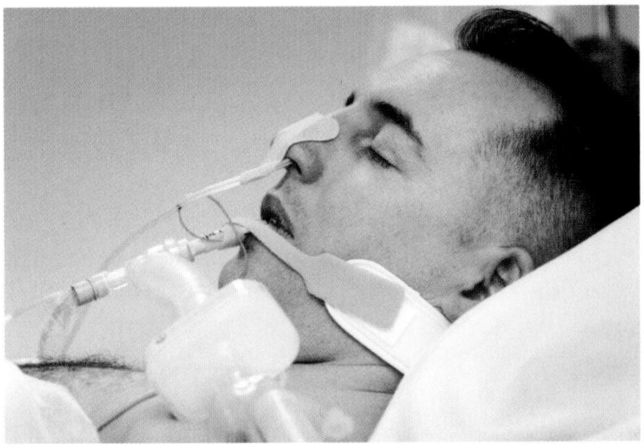

Patient fed with feeding tube. *(Bodenham, LTH NHS Trust / Photo Researchers, Inc. Reproduced by permission.)*

abdomen. Tube feeding is also called enteral feeding or enteral **nutrition**.

Purpose

Tube feeding is used with people who have normally functioning digestive systems, but who cannot or will not take food by mouth. Common reasons to perform tube feeding include:

- stroke resulting in paralysis of the muscles involved in swallowing
- coma
- cancer of the mouth, throat, or esophagus
- trauma or burns to the mouth, throat, or esophagus
- mental illness such as dementia that leads to refusal to eat

Most often people are fed through a nasogastric tube that goes from the nose through the esophagus and into the stomach. This method of tube feeding is preferred for short term feeding problems that do not last longer than about two weeks. There are two choices for tube feeding that is needed on a long term basis. One is the insertion of a nasointestinal tube that passes through the stomach and delivers nutrients directly into the small intestine. A nasointestinal tube is also used after gastric surgery, gastric trauma, or **paralysis** of the stomach muscles. The other option for long term feeding lasting over 30 days is a tube that is surgically placed through the abdomen directly into the small intestine. This is called a percutaneous endoscopic gastrostomy (PEG) tube. PEG tubes are often used for individuals with **oral cancer** as well as for elderly patients who cannot physically pass food through the mouth.

Precautions

Problems can arise in the insertion of the tube. During the actual feeding process, care must be taken to introduce the food at a manageable rate. Also, the tube must be kept clean and flushed after each use.

Description

Tube feedings can be delivered either continuously or intermittently by gravity feed or by pump. Each method has its advantages and disadvantages. The critically ill are often put on continuous feed systems. Each institution has a protocol for starting an individual on tube feedings that specifies the initial rate of flow. A **nutritionist** works with the physician to determine the appropriate caloric, water, and micro-nutrient needs of each individual. Medications can be added to the food if necessary.

In individuals needing long-term tube feeding, a PEG tube is placed through the abdominal wall during a simple surgery that lasts about 20 minutes. The tube has a valve that closes the end outside the body. When the tube is taped to the patient's stomach, it is not particularly noticeable under street clothes. Many patients with PEG tubes, or their caregivers, learn how to care for the tube and feed themselves at home. The feeding tube must be replaced about every six months.

Preparation

A nutritionist should evaluate the individual's nutrient needs before tube feeding begins. Special tube feeding diets exist for a variety of conditions such as kidney failure, liver failure, trauma, glucose intolerance, and other special needs.

Aftercare

Cleaning and maintaining the tube and feeding equipment are necessary after each use. Once the tube is removed, little aftercare is needed. After tube removal, individuals with PEG tubes will need to keep the tube site clean and covered until it heals.

Complications

Tube feeding is a relatively safe procedure. The most serious complications that occur when using a nasogastric tube involve **aspiration** of the nutrients. Other complications from all tube feeding can include **diarrhea**, changes in the absorption rate of drugs, and metabolic (fluid and electrolyte) disturbances related to the composition of the food. Many of these complications can be reduced or eliminated by working

KEY TERMS

Aspirate—To breathe foreign material into the lungs, as when stomach contents back up into the mouth and are breathed into the windpipe.

closely with a nutritionist who has expertise in tube feeding.

Results

Tube feeding is an effective way to provide nutrients, fluids, and drugs to patients who cannot take these things by mouth. The ultimate health of the patient depends largely on the reason the feeding tube was needed.

Caregiver concerns

A nutritionist is a key person on the health care team when caring for someone who is being tube fed. The nutritionist makes an initial needs assessment and helps the physician decide on an appropriate feeding program. Once tube feeding has begun, the nutritionist assess the results and makes recommendations to help control complications such as diarrhea. Besides the physician, other health care workers who may be involved in the care of a person being tube fed include a dietitian, nurses, and a pharmacist experienced in changes in drug metabolism caused by tube feeding. If the individual is going to be tube fed at home, a nurse will educate the patient and **caregiver** about tube care and feeding. A visiting nurse may follow up with a patient being tube fed at home.

Tish Davidson A.M.

Tuberculosis

Definition

Tuberculosis (TB) is a potentially fatal contagious disease that can affect almost any part of the body but is mainly an infection of the lungs. It is caused by a bacterial microorganism, the tubercle bacillus or *Mycobacterium tuberculosis*. Although TB can be treated, cured, and can be prevented if persons at risk take certain drugs, scientists have never come close to wiping it out. Few diseases have caused so much distressing illness for centuries and claimed so many lives.

Description

Overview

Tuberculosis was popularly known as consumption for a long time. Scientists know it as an infection caused by *M. tuberculosis*. In 1882, the microbiologist Robert Koch discovered the tubercle bacillus, at a time when one of every seven deaths in Europe was caused by TB. Because **antibiotics** were unknown, the only means of controlling the spread of infection was to isolate patients in private sanitoria or hospitals limited to patients with TB—a practice that continues to this day in many countries. The net effect of this pattern of treatment was to separate the study of tuberculosis from mainstream medicine. Entire organizations were set up to study not only the disease as it affected individual patients, but its impact on the society as a whole. At the turn of the twentieth century more than 80% of the population in the United States were infected before age 20, and tuberculosis was the single most common cause of **death**. By 1938 there were more than 700 TB hospitals in this country.

GEM_sbtuberculosis.sgm

Tuberculosis spread much more widely in Europe when the industrial revolution began in the late nineteenth century. The disease became widespread somewhat later in the United States, because the movement of the population to large cities made overcrowded housing so common. When streptomycin, the first antibiotic effective against *M. tuberculosis*, was discovered in the early 1940s, the infection began to come under control. Although other more effective anti-tuberculosis drugs were developed in the following decades, the number of cases of TB in the United States began to rise again in the mid-1980s. This upsurge was in part again a result of overcrowding and unsanitary conditions in the poor areas of large cities, prisons, and homeless shelters. Infected visitors and immigrants to the United Stateshave also contributed to the resurgence of TB. An additional factor is the **AIDS** epidemic. AIDS patients are much more likely to develop tuberculosis because of their weakened immune systems. There still are an estimated 8–10 million new cases of TB each year worldwide, causing roughly 3 million deaths.

Demographics

Tuberculosis is more common in elderly persons. More than one-fourth of the nearly 23,000 cases of

Tuberculosis cases, percentages, and case rates per 100,000 population by age group: United States, 1993–2006

Year	Total cases	45–64 No.	45–64 (%)	45–64 Rate	≥65 No.	≥65 (%)	≥65 Rate
1993	12,017	6,197	(25)	12.4	5,820	(23)	17.7
1994	11,664	6,125	(25)	11.9	5,539	(23)	16.6
1995	11,228	5,960	(26)	11.3	5,328	(23)	15.8
1996	10,648	5,572	(26)	10.2	5,076	(24)	14.9
1997	9,940	5,277	(27)	9.4	4,663	(24)	13.6
1998	9,333	4,956	(27)	8.5	4,377	(24)	12.6
1999	8,878	4,858	(28)	8.0	4,020	(23)	11.6
2000	8,153	4,637	(28)	7.4	3,516	(22)	10.0
2001	7,808	4,515	(28)	7.0	3,293	(21)	9.3
2002	7,323	4,182	(28)	6.3	3,141	(21)	8.8
2003	7,277	4,283	(29)	6.2	2,994	(20)	8.3
2004	7,005	4,194	(29)	5.9	2,811	(19)	7.7
2005	6,940	4,125	(29)	5.7	2,815	(20)	7.7
2006	6,729	4,053	(29)	5.4	2,676	(19)	7.2

SOURCE: Reported Tuberculosis in the United States, 2006. Centers for Disease Control and Prevention, U.S. Department of Health and Human Services

(Illustration by GGS Information Services. Cengage Learning, Gale)

TB reported in the United States in 1995 developed in people above age 65. Many elderly patients developed the infection some years ago when the disease was more widespread. There are additional reasons for the vulnerability of older people: those living in **nursing homes** and similar facilities are in close contact with others who may be infected. The aging process itself may weaken the body's **immune system**, which is then less able to ward off the tubercle bacillus. Finally, bacteria that have lain dormant for some time in elderly persons may be reactivated and cause illness.

TB also is more common in blacks, who are more likely to live under conditions that promote infection. At the beginning of the new millennium, two-thirds of all cases of TB in the United States affect African Americans, Hispanics, Asians, and persons from the Pacific Islands. Another one-fourth of cases affect persons born outside the United States. As of 2002, the risk of TB is still increasing in all these groups.

TB is a major health problem in certain specific immigrant communities, such as the Vietnamese in southern California. One team of public health experts in North Carolina maintains that treatment for tuberculosis is the most pressing health care need of recent immigrants to the United States. In some cases, the vulnerability of immigrants to tuberculosis is increased by occupational exposure, as a recent outbreak of TB among Mexican poultry farm workers in Delaware indicates. Other public health experts are recommending tuberculosis screening at the primary care level of all new immigrants and refugees.

The high risk of TB in AIDS patients extends to those infected by human immunodeficiency virus (HIV) who have not yet developed clinical signs of AIDS. Alcoholics and intravenous drug abusers are also at increased risk of contracting tuberculosis. Until the economic and social factors that influence the spread of tubercular infection are remedied, there is no real possibility of completely eliminating the disease.

Causes and symptoms

Transmission

Tuberculosis spreads by droplet infection. This type of transmission means that when a TB patient exhales, coughs, or sneezes, tiny droplets of fluid containing tubercle bacilli are released into the air. This mist, or aerosol as it is often called, can be taken into the nasal passages and lungs of a susceptible person nearby. Tuberculosis is not, however, highly contagious compared to some other **infectious diseases**. Only about one in three close contacts of a TB patient, and fewer than 15% of more remote contacts, are likely to become infected. As a rule, close, frequent, or prolonged contact is needed to spread the disease. Of course, if a severely infected patient emits huge numbers of bacilli, the chance of transmitting infection is much greater. Unlike many other infections, TB is not passed on by contact with a patient's clothing, bed linens, or dishes and cooking utensils. The most important exception is pregnancy. The fetus

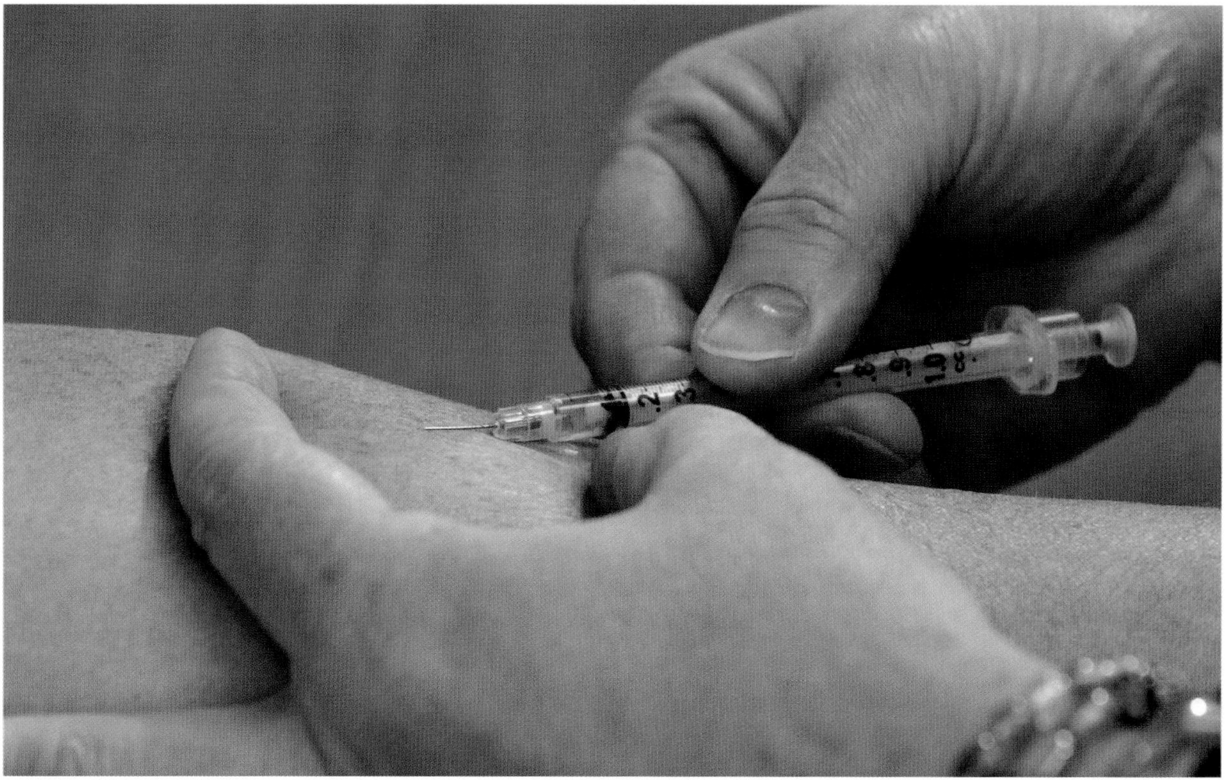

A tuberculosis test being administered. *(AP Images. Reproduced by permission.)*

of an infected mother may contract TB by inhaling or swallowing the bacilli in the amniotic fluid.

Progression

Once inhaled, tubercle bacilli may reach the small breathing sacs in the lungs (the alveoli), where they are taken up by cells called macrophages. The bacilli multiply within these cells and then spread through the lymph vessels to nearby lymph nodes. Sometimes the bacilli move through blood vessels to distant organs. At this point they may either remain alive but inactive (quiescent), or they may cause active disease. Actual tissue damage is not caused directly by the tubercle bacillus, but by the reaction of the person's tissues to its presence. In a matter of weeks the host develops an immune response to the bacillus. Cells attack the bacilli, permit the initial damage to heal, and prevent future disease permanently.

Infection does not always mean disease; in fact, it usually does not. At least nine of ten patients who harbor *M. tuberculosis* do not develop symptoms or physical evidence of active disease, and their x-rays remain negative. They are not contagious; however, they do form a pool of infected patients who may get sick at a later date and then pass on TB to others. It is thought that more than 90% of cases of active tuberculosis come from this pool. In the United States this group numbers 10–15 million persons. Whether or not a particular infected person will become ill is impossible to predict with certainty. An estimated 5% of infected persons get sick within 12–24 months of being infected. Another 5% heal initially but, after years or decades, develop active tuberculosis either in the lungs or elsewhere in the body. This form of the disease is called reactivation TB, or post-primary disease. On rare occasions a previously infected person gets sick again after a later exposure to the tubercle bacillus.

Pulmonary tuberculosis

Pulmonary tuberculosis is TB that affects the lungs. Its initial symptoms are easily confused with those of other diseases. An infected person may at first feel vaguely unwell or develop a cough blamed on **smoking** or a cold. A small amount of greenish or yellow sputum may be coughed up when the person gets up in the morning. In time, more sputum is produced that is streaked with blood. Persons with pulmonary TB do not run a high fever, but they often have a low-grade one. They may wake up in the night drenched with cold sweat when the fever breaks. The patient often loses interest in food and may lose weight. Chest **pain** is sometimes present. If the infection allows air to escape from the lungs into the chest cavity (pneumothorax) or if fluid collects in the pleural space (**pleural effusion**), the patient may have difficulty breathing. If a young adult develops a pleural effusion, the chance of tubercular infection being the cause is very high. The TB bacilli may travel from the lungs to lymph nodes in the sides and back of the neck. Infection in these areas can break through the skin and discharge pus. Before the development of effective antibiotics, many patients became chronically ill with increasingly severe lung symptoms. They lost a great deal of weight and developed a wasted appearance. This outcome is uncommon today—at least where modern treatment methods are available.

Extrapulmonary tuberculosis

Although the lungs are the major site of damage caused by tuberculosis, many other organs and tissues in the body may be affected. The usual progression is for the disease to spread from the lungs to locations outside the lungs (extrapulmonary sites). In some cases, however, the first sign of disease appears outside the lungs. The many tissues or organs that tuberculosis may affect include:

- Bones. TB is particularly likely to attack the spine and the ends of the long bones. If not treated, the spinal segments (vertebrae) may collapse and cause paralysis in one or both legs.
- Kidneys. Along with the bones, the kidneys are probably the commonest site of extrapulmonary TB. There may, however, be few symptoms even though part of a kidney is destroyed. TB may spread to the bladder. In men, it may spread to the prostate gland and nearby structures.
- Female reproductive organs. The ovaries in women may be infected; TB can spread from them to the peritoneum, which is the membrane lining the abdominal cavity.
- Abdominal cavity. Tuberculous peritonitis may cause pain ranging from the vague discomfort of stomach cramps to intense pain that may mimic the symptoms of appendicitis.
- Joints. Tubercular infection of joints causes a form of arthritis that most often affects the hips and knees. The wrist, hand, and elbow joints also may become painful and inflamed.
- Meninges. The meninges are tissues that cover the brain and the spinal cord. Infection of the meninges by the TB bacillus causes tuberculous meningitis, a condition that is most common in young children but is especially dangerous in the elderly. Patients develop headaches, become drowsy, and eventually comatose. Permanent brain damage is the rule unless prompt treatment is given. Some patients with tuberculous meningitis develop a tumor-like brain mass called a tuberculoma that can cause stroke-like symptoms.
- Skin, intestines, adrenal glands, and blood vessels. All these parts of the body can be infected by *M. tuberculosis*. Infection of the wall of the body's main artery (the aorta), can cause it to rupture with catastrophic results. Tuberculous pericarditis occurs when the membrane surrounding the heart (the pericardium) is infected and fills up with fluid that interferes with the heart's ability to pump blood.
- Miliary tuberculosis. Miliary TB is a life-threatening condition that occurs when large numbers of tubercle bacilli spread throughout the body. Huge numbers of tiny tubercular lesions develop that cause marked weakness and weight loss, severe anemia, and gradual wasting of the body.

Diagnosis

The diagnosis of TB is made on the basis of laboratory test results. The standard test for tuberculosis—the so-called tuberculin skin test—detects the presence of infection, not of active TB. Tuberculin is an extract prepared from cultures of *M. tuberculosis*. It contains substances belonging to the bacillus (antigens) to which an infected person has been sensitized. When tuberculin is injected into the skin of an infected person, the area around the injection becomes hard, swollen, and red within one to three days. Today skin tests utilize a substance called purified protein derivative (PPD) that has a standard chemical composition and is therefore is a good measure of the presence of tubercular infection. The PPD test is also called the Mantoux test. The Mantoux PPD skin test is not, however, 100% accurate; it can produce false positive as well as false negative results. What these terms mean is that some people who have a skin reaction are not infected (false positive) and that some who do not react are in fact infected (false negative). The PPD test is, however, useful as a screener. Anyone who has suspicious findings on a **chest x ray**, or any condition that makes TB more likely should have a PPD test. In addition, those in close contact with a TB patient and persons who come from a country where TB is common also should be tested, as should all healthcare personnel and those living in crowded conditions or institutions.

KEY TERMS

Bacillus Calmette-Guérin (BCG)—A vaccine made from a damaged bacillus akin to the tubercle bacillus, which may help prevent serious pulmonary TB and its complications.

Mantoux test—Another name for the PPD test.

Miliary tuberculosis—The form of TB in which the bacillus spreads through all body tissues and organs, producing many thousands of tiny tubercular lesions. Miliary TB is often fatal unless promptly treated.

Mycobacteria—A group of bacteria that includes *Mycobacterium tuberculosis*, the bacterium that causes tuberculosis, and other forms that cause related illnesses.

Pneumothorax—Air inside the chest cavity, which may cause the lung to collapse. Pneumothorax is both a complication of pulmonary tuberculosis and a means of treatment designed to allow an infected lung to rest and heal.

Pulmonary—Referring to the lungs.

Purified protein derivative (PPD)—An extract of tubercle bacilli that is injected into the skin to find out whether a person presently has or has ever had tuberculosis.

Resistance—A property of some bacteria that have been exposed to a particular antibiotic and have "learned" how to survive in its presence.

Sputum—Secretions produced in the infected lung and coughed up. A sign of illness, sputum is routinely used as a specimen for culturing the tubercle bacillus in the laboratory.

Tuberculoma—A tumor-like mass in the brain that sometimes develops as a complication of tuberculous meningitis.

Because the symptoms of TB cover a wide range of severity and affected body parts, diagnosis on the basis of external symptoms is not always possible. Often, the first indication of TB is an abnormal chest x ray or other test result rather than physical discomfort. On a chest x ray, evidence of the disease appears as numerous white, irregular areas against a dark background, or as enlarged lymph nodes. The upper parts of the lungs are most often affected. A PPD test is always done to show whether the patient has been infected by the tubercle bacillus. To verify the test results, the physician obtains a sample of sputum or a tissue sample (biopsy) for culture. Three to five sputum samples should be taken early in the morning. If necessary, sputum for culture can be produced by spraying salt solution into the windpipe. Culturing *M. tuberculosis* is useful for diagnosis because the bacillus has certain distinctive characteristics. Unlike many other types of bacteria, mycobacteria can retain certain dyes even when exposed to acid. This so-called acid-fast property is characteristic of the tubercle bacillus.

Body fluids other than sputum can be used for culture. If TB has invaded the brain or spinal cord, culturing a sample of spinal fluid will make the diagnosis. If TB of the kidneys is suspected because of pus or blood in the urine, culture of the urine may reveal tubercular infection. Infection of the ovaries in women can be detected by placing a tube having a light on its end (a laparoscope) into the area. Samples also may be taken from the liver or bone marrow to detect the tubercle bacillus.

One important new advance in the diagnosis of TB is the use of molecular techniques to speed the diagnostic process as well as improve its accuracy. As of late 2007, four molecular techniques are increasingly used in laboratories around the world. They include polymerase chain reaction to detect mycobacterial DNA in patient specimens; nucleic acid probes to identify mycobacteria in culture; restriction fragment length polymorphism analysis to compare different strains of TB for epidemiological studies; and genetic-based susceptibility testing to identify drug-resistant strains of mycobacteria.

Treatment

Supportive care

In the past, treatment of TB was primarily supportive. Patients were kept in isolation, encouraged to rest, and fed well. If these measures failed the lung was collapsed surgically so that it could "rest" and heal. Today surgical procedures still are used when necessary, but contemporary medicine relies on drug therapy as the mainstay of **home care**. Given an effective combination of drugs, patients with TB can be treated at home as well as in a sanitorium. Treatment at home does not pose the risk of infecting other household members.

Drug therapy

Most patients with TB can recover if given appropriate medication for a sufficient length of time. Three principles govern modern drug treatment of TB:

- Lowering the number of bacilli as quickly as possible. This measure minimizes the risk of transmitting the disease. When sputum cultures become negative, this has been achieved. Conversely, if the sputum remains positive afterfive to six months, treatment has failed.
- Preventing the development of drug resistance. For this reason, at least two different drugs and sometimes three are always given at first. If drug resistance is suspected, at least two different drugs should be tried.
- Long-term treatment to prevent relapse.

Five drugs are most commonly used today to treat tuberculosis: isoniazid (INH, Laniazid, Nydrazid); rifampin (Rifadin, Rimactane); pyrazinamide (Tebrazid); streptomycin; and ethambutol (Myambutol). The first three drugs may be given in the same capsule to minimize the number of pills in the dosage. As of 1998, many patients are given INH and rifampin together for six months, with pyrazinamide added for the first two months. Hospitalization is rarely necessary because many patients are no longer infectious after about two weeks of combination treatment. Follow-up involves monitoring of side effects and monthly sputum tests. Of the five medications, INH is the most frequently used drug for both treatment and prevention.

Surgery

Surgical treatment of TB may be used if medications are ineffective. There are three surgical treatments for pulmonary TB: pneumothorax, in which air is introduced into the chest to collapse the lung; thoracoplasty, in which one or more ribs are removed; and removal of a diseased lung, in whole or in part. It is possible for patients to survive with one healthy lung. Spinal TB may result in a severe deformity that can be corrected surgically.

Prognosis

The prognosis for recovery from TB is good for most patients, if the disease is diagnosed early and given prompt treatment with appropriate medications on a long-term regimen. According to a 2002 Johns Hopkins study, most patients in the United States who die of TB are older—average age 62—and suffer from such underlying diseases as diabetes and kidney failure.

Modern surgical methods have a good outcome in most cases in which they are needed. Miliary tuberculosis is still fatal in many cases but is rarely seen today in developed countries. Even in cases in which the bacillus proves resistant to all of the commonly used medications for TB, other seldom-used drugs may be tried because the tubercle bacilli have not yet developed resistance to them.

Prevention

General measures

General measures such as avoidance of overcrowded and unsanitary conditions are also necessary aspects of prevention. Hospital emergency rooms and similar locations can be treated with ultraviolet light, which has an antibacterial effect.

Vaccination

Vaccination is one major preventive measure against TB. A vaccine called BCG (Bacillus Calmette-Guérin, named after its French developers) is made from a weakened mycobacterium that infects cattle. Vaccination with BCG does not prevent infection by *M. tuberculosis* but it does strengthen the immune system of first-time TB patients. As a result, serious complications are less likely to develop. BCG is used more widely in developing countries than in the United States. The effectiveness of vaccination is still being studied; it is not clear whether the vaccine's effectiveness depends on the population in which it is used or on variations in its formulation.

Prophylactic use of isoniazid

INH can be given for the prevention as well as the treatment of TB. INH is effective when given daily over a period of six to 12 months to people in high-risk categories. INH appears to be most beneficial to persons under the age of 25. Because INH carries the risk of side-effects (liver inflammation, nerve damage, changes in mood and behavior), it is important to give it only to persons at special risk.

High-risk groups for whom isoniazid prevention may be justified include:

- close contacts of TB patients, including health care workers
- newly infected patients whose skin test has turned positive in the past two years
- anyone who is HIV-positive with a positive PPD skin test; Isoniazid may be given even if the PPD results are negative if there is a risk of exposure to active tuberculosis
- intravenous drug users, even if they are negative for HIV

- persons with positive PPD results and evidence of old disease on the chest x-ray who have never been treated for TB
- patients who have an illness or are taking a drug that can suppress the immune system
- persons with positive PPD results who have had intestinal surgery; have diabetes or chronic kidney failure; have any type of cancer; or are more than 10% below their ideal body weight
- people from countries with high rates of TB who have positive PPD results
- people from low-income groups with positive skin test results
- persons with a positive PPD reaction who belong to high-risk ethnic groups (African Americans, Hispanics, Native Americans, Asians, and Pacific Islanders)

Resources

BOOKS

Beers, Mark H., MD, and Robert Berkow, MD., editors. "Infectious Diseases Caused by Mycobacteria." In *The Merck Manual of Diagnosis and Therapy.* Whitehouse Station, NJ: Merck Research Laboratories, 2004.

Pelletier, Kenneth R., MD. *The Best Alternative Medicine,* Part II, "CAM Therapies for Specific Conditions: Tuberculosis." New York: Simon & Schuster, 2002.

PERIODICALS

"Changing Patterns of New Tuberculosis Infections." *Infectious Disease Alert* August 15, 2002: 171–172.

Fielder, J. F., C. P. Chaulk, M. Dalvi, et al. "A High Tuberculosis Case-Fatality Rate in a Setting of Effective Tuberculosis Control: Implications for Acceptable Treatment Success Rates." *International Journal of Tuberculosis and Lung Disease* 6 (December 2002): 1114–1117.

"Guidelines Roll Out Two New Variations: Experts give Both a Thumbs Up." *TB Monitor* August 2002: 85.

Houston, H. R., N. Harada, and T. Makinodan. "Development of a Culturally Sensitive Educational Intervention Program to Reduce the High Incidence of Tuberculosis Among Foreign-Born Vietnamese." *Ethnic Health* 7 (November 2002): 255–265.

Kim, D. Y., R. Ridzon, B. Giles, and T. Mireles. "Pseudo-Outbreak of Tuberculosis in Poultry Plant Workers, Sussex County, Delaware." *Journal of Occupational and Environmental Medicine* 44 (December 2002): 1169–1172.

David A. Cramer MD
Rebecca J. Frey Ph.D.

U

UGI series *see* **Upper gastrointestinal series**

Ulcers

Definition

In general, an ulcer is any eroded area of skin or a mucous membrane, marked by tissue disintegration. In common usage, however, ulcer usually is used to refer to disorders in the upper digestive tract. Peptic ulcers develop on the inside lining of the stomach, upper small intestine (duodenum) or on the esophagus. A peptic ulcer of the stomach is commonly referred to as a gastric ulcer. A duodenal ulcer is a sore that develops on the upper small intestine, and an esophageal ulcer develops on the esophagus.

Description

An ulcer occurs when the lining of the stomach, upper small intestine(duodenum) or the esophagus is eroded by acidic digestive fluids that are secreted by the stomach. It is estimated that 2% of the adult population in the United States has active peptic ulcers, and that about 10% will develop ulcers at some point in their lives. There are about 500,000 new cases of peptic ulcer in the United States every year, with as many as 4 million recurrences. The male/female ratio for ulcers of the digestive tract is 3:1.

The most common forms of peptic ulcer are duodenal and gastric. About 80% of all ulcers in the digestive tract are duodenal ulcers. This type of ulcer may strike people in any age group but is most common in males between the ages of 20 and 45. The incidence of duodenal ulcers has dropped over the past 30 years. Gastric ulcers account for about 16% of peptic ulcers. They are most common in males between the ages of 55 and 70. The single most common cause of gastric ulcers is the use of **nonsteroidal anti-inflammatory drugs**, or NSAIDs. The widespread use of NSAIDs is thought to explain why the incidence of gastric ulcers in the United States is rising.

Causes and symptoms

Causes of peptic ulcers

There are three major causes of peptic ulcers: infection, certain types of medication, and disorders that cause oversecretion or reflux of stomach juices.

***HELICOBACTER PYLORI* INFECTION** *Helicobacter pylori* is a rod-shaped gram-negative bacterium that lives in the mucous tissues that line the digestive tract. Infection with *H. pylori* is the most common cause of

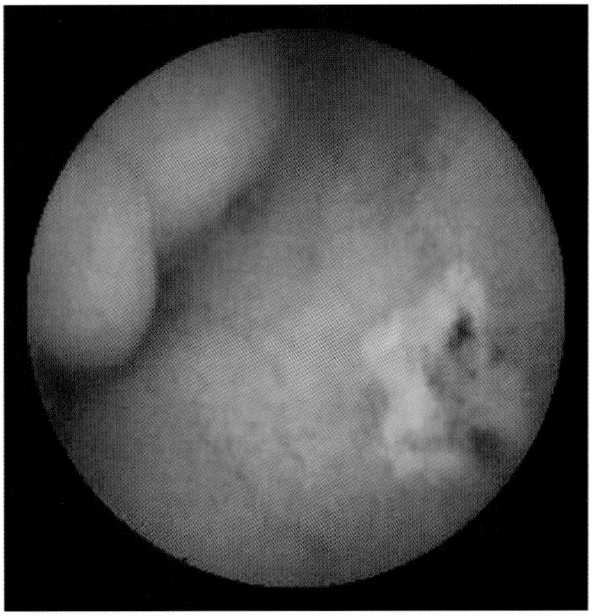

Microscope view of an ulcer. *(David M. Martin, M.D. / Photo Researchers, Inc. Reproduced by permission.)*

duodenal ulcers. About 95% of patients with duodenal ulcers are infected with *H. pylori*, as opposed to only 70% of patients with gastric ulcers.

USE OF NONSTEROIDAL ANTI-INFLAMMATORY DRUGS (NSAIDS) Nonsteroidal anti-inflammatory drugs, or NSAIDs, are painkillers that many people use for headaches, sore muscles, arthritis, menstrual cramps, and similar complaints. Many NSAIDs are available without prescriptions. Common NSAIDs include aspirin, ibuprofen (Advil, Motrin), flurbiprofen (Ansaid, Ocufen), ketoprofen (Orudis), and indomethacin (Indacin). Chronic NSAID users have 40 times the risk of developing a gastric ulcer as nonusers. Users also are three times more likely than nonusers to develop bleeding or fatal complications of ulcers. Aspirin is the NSAID that is most likely to cause ulcers.

MISCELLANEOUS SYNDROMES AND DISORDERS Fewer than 5% of peptic ulcers are due to these disorders. They include Zollinger-Ellison syndrome, a disorder in which small tumors, called gastrinomas, secrete a hormone (gastrin) that stimulates the production of digestive juices. Because of this excess secretion, these disorders are sometimes called hypersecretory syndromes.

OTHER RISK FACTORS **Smoking** is an important risk factor that increases a patient's chance of developing an ulcer, decreases the body's response to therapy, and increases the chances of dying from ulcer complications. Blood type appears to be a predisposing factor for ulcer location; people with type A blood are more likely to have gastric ulcers, while those with type O are more likely to develop duodenal ulcers. The role of emotional stress in ulcer development is currently debated. Present research indicates that an individual's attitudes toward stress, rather than the amount of stress by itself, is a better predictor of vulnerability to peptic ulcers. Preferences for high-fat or spicy foods do not appear to be significant risk factors.

Symptoms

GASTRIC ULCERS The symptoms of gastric ulcers include feelings of indigestion and **heartburn**, weight loss, and repeated episodes of gastrointestinal bleeding. Ulcer **pain** often is described as gnawing, dull, aching, or resembling hunger pangs. The patient may be nauseated and suffer loss of appetite. About 30% of patients with gastric ulcers are awakened by pain at night. Many patients have periods of chronic ulcer pain alternating with symptom-free periods that last for several weeks or months. This characteristic is called periodicity.

DUODENAL ULCERS The symptoms of duodenal ulcers include heartburn, stomach pain relieved by eating or antacids, weight gain, and a burning sensation at the back of the throat. The patient is most likely to feel discomfort two to four hours after meals, or after having citrus juice, coffee, or aspirin. About 50% of patients with duodenal ulcers awake during the night with pain, usually between midnight and three a.m. A regular pattern of ulcer pain associated with certain periods of day or night or a time interval after meals is called rhythmicity.

Not all digestive ulcers produce symptoms; as many as 20% of ulcer patients have so-called painless or silent ulcers. Silent ulcers occur most frequently in the elderly and in chronic NSAID users.

Complications

Between 10–20% of peptic ulcer patients develop complications at some time during the course of their illness. All of these are potentially serious conditions. Complications are not always preceded by diagnosis of or treatment for ulcers; as many as 60% of patients with complications have not had prior symptoms.

HEMORRHAGE Bleeding is the most common complication of ulcers. It may result in anemia, vomiting blood (hematemesis), or the passage of bright red blood through the rectum (melena). About half of all cases of bleeding from the upper digestive tract are caused by ulcers. The mortality rate from ulcer hemorrhage is 6–10%.

PERFORATION About 5% of ulcer patients develop perforations, which are holes in the duodenal or gastric wall through which the stomach contents can leak out into the abdominal cavity. The incidence of perforation is rising because of the increased use of NSAIDs, particularly among the elderly. The signs of an ulcer perforation are severe pain, fever, and tenderness when the doctor touches the abdomen. Most cases of perforation require emergency surgery. The mortality rate is about 5%.

PENETRATION Ulcer penetration is a complication in which the ulcer erodes through the intestinal wall without digestive fluid leaking into the abdomen. Instead, the ulcer penetrates into an adjoining organ, such as the pancreas or liver. The signs of penetration are more severe pain *without* rhythmicity or periodicity, and the spread of the pain to the lower back.

OBSTRUCTION Obstruction of the stomach outlet occurs in about 2% of ulcer patients. It is caused by swelling or scar tissue formation that narrows the opening between the stomach and the duodenum (the pylorus). Over 90% of patients with obstruction have recurrent vomiting of partly digested or undigested food; 20% are seriously dehydrated. These patients also usually feel full after eating only a little food, and may lose weight.

Diagnosis

Physical examination and patient history

The diagnosis of peptic ulcers should rarely be made on the basis of a physical examination alone. The only significant finding may be mild soreness in the area over the stomach when the doctor presses (palpates) it. The doctor is more likely to suspect an ulcer if the patient has one or more of the following risk factors:

- male sex
- age over 45
- recent weight loss, bleeding, recurrent vomiting, jaundice, back pain, or anemia
- history of using aspirin or other NSAIDs
- history of heavy smoking
- family history of ulcers or stomach cancer

Imaging studies

- Upper endoscopy(EGD-esophagogastroduodenoscopy. An endoscopy is considered the best procedure for diagnosing digestive ulcers and for taking samples of stomach tissue for biopsies. An endoscope is a slender tube-shaped instrument that allows the doctor to view the tissues lining the stomach and duodenum. Duodenal ulcers are rarely malignant. If the ulcer is in the stomach, however, the doctor will take a tissue sample because 3–5% of gastric ulcers are malignant.
- Upper gastrointestinal (upper GI) x ray. For this test, the patient swallows a white liquid that coats and then exposes the digestive tract so that an ulcer is detectable. While the UP X-ray involves minimal discomfort for the patient it is less accurate than the endoscopy

Laboratory tests

BLOOD TESTS Blood tests usually give normal results in ulcer patients without complications. They are useful, however, in evaluating anemia from a bleeding ulcer or a high white cell count from perforation or penetration. Serum gastrin levels can be used to screen for Zollinger-Ellison syndrome.

TESTS FOR *HELICOBACTER PYLORI* It is important to test for *H. pylori* because almost all ulcer patients who are not taking NSAIDs are infected. Noninvasive tests include blood tests for immune response and a breath test. In the breath test, the patient is given an oral dose of radiolabeled urea. If *H. pylori* is present, it will react with the urea and the patient will exhale radiolabeled carbon dioxide. Invasive tests for *H. pylori* include tissue biopsies and cultures performed from fluid obtained by endoscopy. Stool sample tests are particularly useful because samples can be used to detect the presence of H. pylori and also to monitor a patient's response to treatment after a diagnosis has been made.

Treatment

Medications

Most drugs that are currently given to treat ulcers work either by lowering the rate of stomach acid secretion or by protecting the mucous tissues that line the digestive tract.

ANTISECRETORY DRUGS Medications that lower the rate of stomach acid secretions fall into two major categories: proton pump inhibitors, which bind an enzyme that secretes stomach acid, and H_2 receptor antagonists, which work by reducing intracellular acid secretion. The proton pump inhibitors include omeprazole (Prilosec) and lansoprazole (Prevacid). The H_2 receptor antagonists include ranitidine (Zantac), cimetidine (Tagamet), famotidine (Pepcid), and nizatidine (Axid). Both types of drugs have few serious side effects and appear to be safe for long-term use.

PROTECTIVE DRUGS The drugs that are currently used to protect the stomach tissues are sucralfate (Carafate), which forms a pastelike substance that clings to the mucous tissues and prevents further damage from stomach acid; and bismuth preparations. A third type of protective drug includes misoprostol (Cytotec), which is often given to patients with ulcers caused by NSAIDs.

Surgery

Surgical treatment of ulcers is generally used only for complications and suspected malignancies. The most common surgical procedures that are used are vagotomies, in which the connections of the vagus nerve to the stomach are cut in order to reduce acid secretion; and antrectomies, which involve the removal of a part of the stomach (the antrum).

Eradication of Helicobacter pylori

Most doctors presently recommend treatment to eliminate *H. pylori* in order to prevent ulcer recurrences. Without such treatment, ulcers recur at the rate of 80% per year. The usual regimen used to eliminate the bacterium is a combination of tetracycline, bismuth subsalicylate (Pepto-Bismol), and metronidazole (Metizol).

Alternative treatment

Alternative treatments can relieve symptoms and promote healing of ulcers. A primary goal of these treatments is to rebalance the stomach's hydrochloric acid output and to enhance the mucosal lining of the stomach.

Food allergies have been pointed to as a major cause of peptic (stomach) ulcers. An elimination/challenge diet can help identify the allergenic food(s) and continued elimination of these foods can assist in healing the ulcer. People with ulcers should not take aspirin. They also should stop smoking, since smoking irritates the mucosal lining of the stomach. Antacids should be avoided by anyone with an ulcer, because they can cause a rebound effect of increasing gastric acid secretion, as well as deplete vital nutrients necessary for healing. Stress reduction is also important for ulcer sufferers.

Botanical medicine offers a variety of remedies that may be helpful in ulcer treatment. Deglycyrrhizinated licorice or DGL, in a chewable or powder form, can help heal the mucous membranes and increase mucous so that it mixes with saliva to protect the membranes. Raw cabbage juice, high in glutanic acid, is very effective in healing an ulcer (one quart per day in divided doses). Soothing herbs, such as plantain (*Plantago major*), marsh mallow (*Althaea officinalis*), and slippery elm (*Ulmus fulva*); astringent herbs, such as geranium (*Pelargonium odoratissimum*); and the anitmicrobial herb goldenseal (*Hydrastis canadensis*) can all be effective. Nutritionists advise taking antioxidant nutrients, including vitamins A, C, and E, zinc, and selenium.

Prognosis

The prognosis for recovery from ulcers is good for most patients. Very few ulcers fail to respond to the medications that are currently used to treat them. Recurrences can be eliminated completely or cut to 5% by eradication of *H. pylori*. Most patients who develop complications recover without problems even when emergency surgery is necessary.

Prevention

Strategies for the prevention of ulcers or their recurrence include the following:

- eradication of *H. pylori* in patients already diagnosed with ulcers
- giving misoprostol to patients who must take NSAIDs
- avoiding unnecessary use of aspirin and NSAIDs
- giving up smoking
- cutting down on alcohol, tea, coffee, and sodas containing caffeine.

KEY TERMS

Duodenum—The first of the three segments of the small intestine. The duodenum connects the stomach and the jejunum. Most peptic ulcers are in the duodenum.

Helicobacter pylori—A gram-negative rod-shaped bacterium that lives in the tissues of the stomach and causes inflammation of the stomach lining.

Zollinger-Ellison syndrome—A disorder characterized by the presence of tumors (gastrinomas) that secrete a hormone (gastrin), which stimulates the production of digestive juices.

Resources

PERIODICALS

"Peptic Ulcers and Bacterial Infections." *Harvard Men's Health Watch* (June 2007):NA.

Harvard Health Publications Group"Digestion Digest." *Harvard Health Commentaries* (2006):NA.

Harvard Health Publications Group"Medical Myths:Does Food Cause Ulcers?." *Harvard Health Commentaries* (2006):NA.

ORGANIZATIONS

American College of Gastroenterology. 4900-B South Thirty-First St., Arlington, VA 22206-1656. (703) 820-7400. http://www.acg.cgi.gi.org/acghome/html.

American Gastroenterological Association. 4930 Del Ray Avenue, Bethesda, MD 20814. (301)654-2055. http://www.gastro.org

International Foundation for Functional Gastrointestinal Disorders. P.O. Box 170864, Milwaukee, WI 53217–8076.(888)964–2001. http://www.iffgd.org

National Digestive Diseases Clearinghouse (NDDIC). 2 Information Way.

National Institute of Diabetes and Digestive and Kidney Diseases (NIDDK). Building 31, Room 9A04, 31 Center Drive, MSC 2560, Bethesda, MD 208792-2560. (301) 496-3583. http://www.niddk.nih.gov.

Rebecca J. Frey Ph.D.
Lisa M. Piazza M.A.

Upper GI exam

Definition

An upper GI examination is a fluoroscopic examination (a type of x-ray imaging) of the upper gastrointestinal tract, including the esophagus, stomach, and upper small intestine (duodenum).

Purpose

An **upper GI series** is frequently requested when a patient experiences unexplained symptoms of abdominal **pain**, difficulty in swallowing (dysphagia), regurgitation, **diarrhea**, or unexplained **weight loss**. It is used to help diagnose disorders and diseases of, or related to, the upper gastrointestinal tract. Some of these conditions are: hiatal hernia, diverticula, tumors, obstruction, **gastroesophageal reflux disease**, pulmonary **aspiration**, and inflammation (e.g., ulcers, enteritis, and Crohn's disease).

Glucagon, a medication sometimes given prior to an upper GI procedure, may cause nausea and **dizziness**. It is used to relax the natural movements of the stomach, which will enhance the overall study.

Description

An upper GI series takes place in a hospital or clinic setting, and is performed by an x-ray technologist and a radiologist. Before the test begins, the patient is sometimes given a glucagon injection, a medication that slows stomach and bowel activity, to provide the radiologist with a clear picture of the gastrointestinal tract. In order to further improve the upper GI picture clarity, the patient may be given a cup of fizzing crystals to swallow, which distends the esophagus and stomach by producing gas.

Once these preparatory steps are complete, the patient stands against an upright x-ray table, and a fluoroscopic screen is placed in front of him or her. The patient will be asked to drink from a cup of flavored barium sulfate, a thick and chalky-tasting liquid, while the radiologist views the esophagus, stomach, and duodenum on the fluoroscopic screen. The patient will be asked to change positions frequently to coat the entire surface of the gastrointestinal tract with barium, move overlapping loops of bowel to isolate each segment, and provide multiple views of each segment. The technician or radiologist may press on the patient's abdomen to spread the barium throughout the folds within the lining of the stomach. The x-ray table will also be moved several times throughout the procedure. The radiologist will ask the patient to hold his or her breath periodically while exposures are taken. After the radiologist completes his or her portion of the exam, the technologist takes three to six additional films of the GI tract. The entire procedure takes approximately 15–30 minutes.

In addition to the standard upper GI series, a physician may request a detailed small bowel follow-through (SBFT), which is a timed series of films. After the preliminary upper GI series is complete, the patient will drink additional barium sulfate, and will be escorted to a waiting area while the barium moves through the small intestines. X rays are initially taken at 15-minute intervals until the barium reaches the colon (the only way to be sure the terminal ileum is fully seen is to see the colon or ileocecal valve). The interval may be increased to 30 minutes, or even one hour if the barium passes slowly. Then the radiologist will obtain additional views of the terminal ileum (the most distal segment of the small bowel, just before the colon). This procedure can take from one to four hours.

Esophageal radiography, also called a barium esophagram or a barium swallow, is a study of the esophagus only, and is usually performed as part of the upper GI series (sometimes only a barium swallow is done). It is commonly used to diagnose the cause of difficulty in swallowing (dysphagia), and to detect a hiatal hernia. The patient drinks a barium sulfate liquid, and sometimes eats barium-coated food while the radiologist examines the swallowing mechanism on a fluoroscopic screen. The test takes approximately 30 minutes.

Preparation

Patients must not eat, drink, or smoke for eight hours prior to undergoing an upper GI examination. Longer dietary restrictions may be required, depending on the type and diagnostic purpose of the test. Patients undergoing a small bowel follow-through exam may be asked to take **laxatives** the day before to the test. Patients are required to wear a hospital gown, or similar attire, and to remove all jewelry, to provide the camera with an unobstructed view of the abdomen.

Aftercare

No special aftercare treatment or regimen is required for an upper GI series. The patient may eat and drink as soon as the test is completed. The barium sulfate may make the patient's stool white for several days, and can cause **constipation**; therefore patients

KEY TERMS

Crohn's disease—A chronic, inflammatory bowel disease usually affecting the ileum, colon, or both.

Diverticula—Pouch-like herniations through the muscular wall of an organ such as the stomach, small intestine, or colon.

Enteritis—Inflammation of the mucosal lining of the small intestine.

Gastroesophageal reflux disease—A painful, chronic condition in which stomach acid flows back into the esophagus causing heartburn and, in time, erosion of the esophageal lining.

Hiatal hernia—Protrusion of the stomach up through the diaphragm.

are encouraged to drink plenty of water to eliminate it from their system.

Risks

Because the upper GI series is an x-ray procedure, it does involve minor exposure to ionizing radiation. Unless the patient is pregnant, or multiple radiological or fluoroscopic studies are required, the small dose of radiation incurred during a single procedure poses little risk. However, multiple studies requiring fluoroscopic exposure that are conducted in a short time period have been known, on very rare occasions, to cause skin **death** (necrosis) in some individuals. This risk can be minimized by careful monitoring and documentation of cumulative radiation doses.

Results

A normal upper GI series shows a healthy, normally functioning, and unobstructed digestive tract. Hiatal hernia, obstructions, inflammation (including ulcers or polyps of the esophagus, stomach, or small intestine), or irregularities in the swallowing mechanism are just a few of the possible abnormalities that may appear on an upper GI series. Additionally, abnormal peristalsis, or digestive movements of the esophagus, stomach, and small intestine can often be visualized on the fluoroscopic part of the exam, and in the interpretation of the SBFT.

Debra Novograd B.S., R.T.(R)(M)
Lee A. Shratter M.D.

Upper GI series

Definition

An upper GI examination is a fluoroscopic examination (a type of x-ray imaging) of the upper gastrointestinal tract, including the esophagus, stomach, and upper small intestine (duodenum).

Purpose

An upper GI series is frequently requested when a patient experiences unexplained symptoms of abdominal **pain**, difficulty in swallowing (dysphagia), regurgitation, **diarrhea**, or **weight loss**. It is used to help diagnose disorders and diseases of, or related to, the upper gastrointestinal tract, including cases of hiatal hernia, diverticuli, ulcers, tumors, obstruction, enteritis, **gastroesophageal reflux disease**, Crohn's disease, and pulmonary **aspiration**.

Precautions

Patients with an obstruction or perforation in their bowel should not ingest barium (a radioactive substance used to show contrast in the images) for an upper GI, but may still be able to undergo the procedure if a water-soluble contrast medium is substituted for the barium.

Glucagon, a medication sometimes given prior to an upper GI procedure, may cause nausea and **dizziness**.

Description

An upper GI series takes place in a hospital or clinic setting and is performed by an x-ray technician and a radiologist. A radiologist typically is in attendance to oversee the procedure and view and interpret the fluoroscopic pictures. Before the test begins, the patient is sometimes administered an injection of glucagon, a medication which slows stomach and bowel activity, to allow the radiologist to get a clearer picture of the gastrointestinal tract. In order to further improve the clarity of the upper GI pictures, the patient may be given a cup of baking soda crystals to swallow, which distend the stomach by producing gas.

Once these preparatory steps are complete, the patient stands against an upright x-ray table, and a fluoroscopic screen is placed in front of him. The patient will be asked to drink from a cup of flavored barium sulfate, a thick and chalky-tasting liquid that allows the radiologist to see the digestive tract, while the radiologist views the esophagus, stomach, and

KEY TERMS

Dysphagia—An inability to swallow, or difficulty with swallowing.

Fluoroscopy—Also called radioscopy, this procedure involves the examination of internal body structures using x-rays and projecting images on a fluorescent screen.

Necrosis—Death of cells in a body tissue.

Radiologist—A doctor who specializes in an area of medicine that focuses on the use of radiation to diagnose and treat disease.

duodenum on the fluoroscopic screen. The patient will be asked to change positions frequently in order to coat the entire surface of the gastrointestinal tract with barium. The technician or radiologist may press on the patient's abdomen in order to spread the barium. The x-ray table will also be moved several times throughout the procedure. The radiologist will ask the patient to hold his breath periodically while exposures are being taken. The entire procedure may take up to 45 minutes.

In some cases, in addition to the standard upper GI series, a doctor may request a detailed intestine, or small bowel, radiography and fluoroscopy series; it is also called a small bowel follow-through (SBFT). Once the preliminary upper GI series is complete, the patient will be escorted to a waiting area while the barium travels down the rest of the small intestinal path. Every 15 to 30 minutes, the patient will return to the x-ray suite for additional x rays. Once the barium has traveled down the small bowel tract, the test is complete. This procedure can take anywhere from one to four hours.

Esophageal radiography, also called a barium esophagram or a barium swallow, is a study of the esophagus only, and is usually performed as part of the upper GI series. It is commonly used to diagnose the cause of difficulty in swallowing (dysphagia) and for detecting hiatal hernia. A barium sulfate liquid, and sometimes pieces of food covered in barium or a barium tablet, are given to the patient to drink and eat while a radiologist examines the swallowing mechanism on a fluoroscopic screen. The test takes approximately 30 minutes.

Preparation

Patients must not eat, drink, or smoke for eight hours prior to undergoing an upper GI examination. Longer dietary restrictions may be required, depending on the type and diagnostic purpose of the test.

QUESTIONS TO ASK YOUR DOCTOR

- What is the purpose of this examination?
- When will I know the results?
- How will I be notified of the results?
- How will the examination results help to determine the next step in management of my condition?
- What are the alternatives to this diagnostic exam?

Patients undergoing a small bowel follow-through exam may be asked to take **laxatives** the day prior to the test. Upper GI patients are typically required to wear a hospital gown, or similar attire, and to remove all jewelry, so the camera has an unobstructed view of the abdomen. Patients who are severely ill may not be able to tolerate the procedure.

Aftercare

No special aftercare treatment or regimen is required for an upper GI series. The patient may eat and drink as soon as the test is completed. The barium sulfate may make the patient's stool white for several days, and patients are encouraged to drink plenty of fluids in order to eliminate it from their system.

Risks

Because the upper GI series is an x-ray procedure, it does involve minor exposure to ionizing radiation. Unless the patient is pregnant, or multiple radiological or fluoroscopic studies are required, the small dose of radiation incurred during a single procedure poses little risk. However, multiple studies requiring fluoroscopic exposure that are conducted in a short time period have been known, on rare occasions, to cause skin **death** (necrosis) in some individuals. This risk can be minimized by careful monitoring and documentation of cumulative radiation doses administered to these patients.

Another risk is barium impaction, which occurs when the patient is unable to completely expel the barium contrast agent before it eventually dries and hardens. The risk of barium impaction is greatest in elderly patients and those with colon obstruction or colon motility disorder.

Results

A normal upper GI series will show a healthy, functioning, and unobstructed digestive tract.

Obstructions or inflammation, including ulcers of the esophagus, stomach, or small intestine, or irregularities in the swallowing mechanism are some of the possible abnormalities that may show up on an upper GI series. Other abnormalities may include polyps, foreign bodies, or congenital anomalies. Upper GI series are helpful in the diagnosis of gastric (stomach) **cancer**.

Resources

PERIODICALS

Froehlich, F., and C. Repond, et al. "Is the Diagnostic Yield of Upper GI Endoscopy Improved by the Use of Explicit Panel-based Appropriateness Criteria?" *Gastrointestinal Endoscopy* 52, no. 3 (September 2000): 333–41.

Paula Anne Ford-Martin

Urge incontinence *see* **Urinary incontinence**

Urinalysis *see* **Urine culture**

Urinary catheterization *see* **Catheterization, female; Catheterization, male**

Urinary incontinence

Definition

Urinary incontinence is a condition characterized by the involuntary loss of bladder control.

Description

Urinary incontinence, the inability to keep urine in the bladder, is a problem of the urinary tract, the organs of the body that produce and discharge urine from the body. They include the kidneys, ureters, bladder, and urethra. A circular muscle system, called the urethral sphincter, controls the retention and release of urine from the bladder. As the bladder fills with urine, the sphincter expands to accommodate the increasing urine volume and holds the urine in the bladder without leakage. When the bladder is full, the brain signals the sphincter and the muscles at the base of the pelvis that support the bladder (pelvic floor muscles) to contract and expel urine through the urethra and out of the body. When the urinary muscle system malfunctions, incontinence can result, almost always due to an underlying medical condition. There are different types of urinary incontinence:

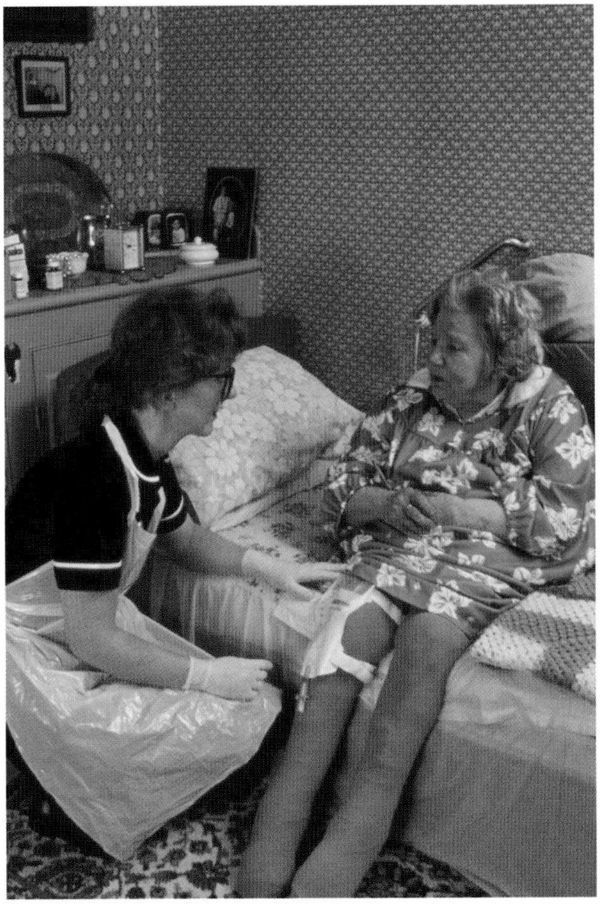

Nurse attending an elderly woman who wears a urinary incontinence bag. *(Hattie Young / Photo Researchers, Inc. Reproduced by permission.)*

- *Stress incontinence.* This type of incontinence is due to a weakened sphincter muscle and occurs when pressure is exerted on the bladder for example by coughing, sneezing, laughing, or lifting something heavy.
- *Urge incontinence.* This type of incontinence, also called "overactive bladder," is characterized by a sudden urge to urinate, and the need to urinate often. Affected persons often also awaken during the night to urinate (nocturia).
- *Overflow incontinence.* This type of incontinence is an inability to empty the bladder, leading to overflow and leakage. Affected persons often dribble urine and feel as if their bladder cannot be emptied.
- *Functional incontinence.* People suffering from this type of incontinence have a physical or mental impairment that prevents them from reaching the bathroom in time.

Demographics

According to the National Association for Continence (NAFC), urinary incontinence affects 200 million people worldwide and some 25 million adult Americans. NAFC estimates that 75–80% of those affected are women, 9–13 million of whom have severe symptoms. 33% of people aged 30–70 years have also experienced loss of bladder control during their adult lives. In this age group, more than 33% who experience nocturia get up twice or more per night, and one in eight persons report that they sometimes lose urine on the way to the bathroom. On average, women wait on average 6.5 years from the first time they experience incontinence to obtain a diagnosis for their bladder control problem. The condition is highly prevalent in the 70–79 age group. At least 50% of all nursing home residents are urine incontinent and many also experience loss of bowel control.

Causes and symptoms

Urinary incontinence is an under-diagnosed and under-treated condition that is falsely thought to be a normal consequence of aging. In fact, it is almost always indicative of some underlying medical condition that can be treated. A broad range of conditions and disorders can cause incontinence, including birth defects, pelvic surgery, injuries to the pelvic region or to the spinal cord, neurological diseases, and urinary tract infections. For example, urge incontinence may be caused by **multiple sclerosis**, Parkinson's disease, Alzheimer's disease, or **stroke**. Overflow incontinence occurs in people with a damaged bladder or blocked urethra, or with nerve damage resulting from diabetes, and in men with prostate problems.

Symptoms of urinary incontinence may include:

- Leakage of urine impacting on activities
- Leakage of urine causing embarrassment
- Urgent need to urinate with loss of urine before reaching the bathroom
- Frequent bladder infections
- Urinating more frequently than usual
- Pain related to filling the bladder and during urination
- Inability to urinate (urinary retention)

Diagnosis

Diagnosis includes a complete medical history and a thorough physical examination to determine the cause of the incontinence. Tests may include x rays, blood analysis, urine analysis, and special tests to determine bladder capacity, sphincter condition, and urethral pressure. A cystoscopic examination may also be performed. In this test, a tube with a small camera on the end (cystoscope) is inserted through the urethra into the bladder to visualize possible abnormalities.

QUESTIONS TO ASK YOUR DOCTOR

- What causes my urinary incontinence?
- Can it be cured?
- What does treatment involve?
- Are medications effective?
- Can exercise help?

Treatment

Since urinary incontinence is a condition and not a disease, treatment depends on diagnostic results to clarify the type of incontinence and its underlying cause. Treatment commonly involves a combination of medications, behavioral techniques, and pelvic muscle exercises. Behavioral techniques include prompting the incontinent person to visit the bathroom every 2–4 hours, and bladder retraining that gradually increases the length of time between bathroom trips.

For patients whose incontinence cannot be cured, devices and products are available to help manage incontinence, including catheters, pelvic organ support devices, urethral plug inserts, external collection systems, and absorbent products.

Nutrition/Dietetic concerns

Including more fiber in the **diet** has been shown to prevent **constipation**, a risk factor for urinary incontinence. Avoiding or limiting certain foods and drinks that may irritate the bladder, such as coffee, may also reduce urinary incontinence.

Therapy

Drug therapy can be used for incontinence. Medications are available to help control an **overactive bladder**, such as olterodine (Detrol), oxybutynin (Ditropan), solifenacin (Vesicare) and darifenacin (Enablex). Imipramine (Tofranil) is occasionally prescribed in combination with other medications to relax the bladder muscle. **Antibiotics** may also be prescribed if the incontinence results from a **urinary tract infection** or an inflamed prostate gland (prostatitis).

KEY TERMS

Alzheimer's disease—Degenerative brain disease resulting in progressive mental deterioration with disorientation, memory disturbance and confusion.

Bladder—Elastic, muscular pouch in which urine collects before being discharged from the body through the urethra.

Catheter—A hollow flexible tube for insertion into a body cavity, duct, or vessel to allow the passage of fluids or distend a passageway.

Cystoscope—Specialized endoscope, a tube with a small camera on the end, inserted through the urethra into the bladder to visualize the inside of the bladder and urethra.

Diuretics—Medications that help the body get rid of excess water and salt.

Kidneys—Pair of bean–shaped organs located below the ribs toward the middle of the back that clean the blood, regulate acid concentration and maintain water balance in the body by excreting urine.

Multiple sclerosis—A chronic degenerative disease of the central nervous system.

Nocturia—Excessive urination at night.

Pelvic floor muscles—Muscles at the base of the pelvis that support the bladder and rectum, and the uterus and vagina in women.

Parkinson's disease—Chronic, progressive disorder of the nervous system.

Ureters—Tubes from the kidneys to the bladder that drain urine.

Urethra—The tube leading from the bladder to discharge urine outside the body. In males, the urethra travels through the penis, and in females, it is shorter than in the male and emerges above the vaginal opening.

Urethral sphincter—The muscle system that controls the retention and release of urine from the bladder.

Urinary incontinence—Inability to keep urine in the bladder.

Urinary retention—Inability to urinate.

Urinary tract—The organs of the body that produce and discharge urine. They include the kidneys, ureters, bladder, and urethra.

Urinary tract infection—Bacterial infection that occurs in any part of the urinary tract.

Urine—Fluid containing water and waste products. Urine is made by the kidneys, stored in the bladder, and leaves the body through the urethra.

Prognosis

According to the NAFC, approximately 80% of those affected by urinary incontinence can be cured or improved. However, people wait on average some seven years before seeking treatment for their incontinence problem, and only one out of every twelve people affected seeks help. Recent surveys performed by the NAFC seem to contradict the 80% improvement rate: after receiving treatment, more people rated their incontinence as "unchanged" or "worse" after treatment than "improved" or "cured."

Prevention

Prevention of incontinence is centered on maintaining a healthy lifestyle since the condition almost always results from an underlying medical disorder. Maintaining a healthy weight, and regular physical **exercise** have been shown to lower the risk of developing incontinence.

Caregiver concerns

Two–thirds of men and women in the 30–70 age group have never discussed bladder health with their physician. Men are also less likely to be diagnosed than women. In women over the age of 60, the high prevalence of urinary incontinence has been associated with a three–fold increase in nursing home admissions, social **isolation**, and psychological distress. This suggests that urinary incontinence should be routinely and more pro–actively evaluated in this age group.

Resources

BOOKS

Ellsworth, Pamela. *100 Questions and Answers about Overactive Bladder and Urinary Incontinence.* Sudbury, MA: Jones and Bartlett Publishers, 2005.

Genadry, Rene, and Jacek L. Mostwin. *A Woman's Guide to Urinary Incontinence.* Baltimore, MD: Johns Hopkins University Press, 2007.

Kaschak Newman, Diane. *Managing and Treating Urinary Incontinence.* Baltimore, MD: Health Professions Press, 2002.

Safir, Michael H., Caly N. Boyd, and Tony E. Pinson. *Overcoming Urinary Incontinence: A Woman's Guide to Treatment.* Omaha, NE: Addicus Books, 2008.

PERIODICALS

Charles, J., et al. "Urinary incontinence in the older patient." *Australian Family Physician* 37, no. 3 (March 2008): 105.

Chiaffarino, F., et al. "Impact of urinary incontinence and overactive bladder on quality of life." *European Urology* 43, no. 5 (May 2003): 535–538.

Couture, J. A., and L. Valiquette. " Urinary incontinence." *Annals of Pharmacotherapy* 34, no. 5 (May 2000): 646–65.

Jackson, R. A., et al. "Urinary incontinence in elderly women: findings from the Health, Aging, and Body Composition Study." *Obstetrics & Gynecology* 104, no. 2 (August 2004): 301–307.

Ko, Y., et al. "The impact of urinary incontinence on quality of life of the elderly." *American Journal of Managed Care* 11, no. 4 (July 2005): S103–S111.

Lusky, K. F. "Real treatment options for incontinence. Condition is no longer a given in the aging process." *Provider* 44, no. 6 (June 1998): 42–47.

MacDonald, C. D., and L. Butler. "Silent no more: elderly women's stories of living with urinary incontinence in long–term care." *Journal of Gerontological Nursing* 33, no. 1 (January 2007): 14–20.

Wagg, A. "Continence, incontinence and the aging male." *Aging Male* 3, no. 3 (September 2000): 143–154.

OTHER

Controlling Urinary Incontinence. FDA, Consumer Magazine (March 20, 2008) http://www.fda.gov/fdac/features/2005/505_incontinence.html

Urinary Incontinence. National Institute on Aging, Age Page (March 20, 2008) http://www.niapublications.org/agepages/urinary.asp

Urinary Incontinence: Embarrasing but Treatable. American Academy of Family Physicians, Family Doctor Information Page (March 20, 2008) http://familydoctor.org/online/famdocen/home/women/gen-health/189.printerview.html

Your Body's Design for Bladder Control. NKUDIC, Information Page (March 20, 2008) http://kidney.niddk.nih.gov/kudiseases/pubs/bodydesign_ez/index.htm

ORGANIZATIONS

American Urological Association (AUA), 1000 Corporate Blvd., Linthicum, MD, 21090, (410)689-3700, (866) 746-4282, (410)689-3800, aua@auanet.org, http://www.auanet.org.

National Association For Continence (NAFC), POB 1019, Charleston, SC, 29402-1019, (843)377-0900, (800) BLADDER, http://www.nafc.org.

National Kidney and Urologic Diseases Information Clearinghouse (NKUDIC), 3 Information Way, Bethesda, MD, 20892–3580 , (800)891–5390, (703) 738–4929, nkudic@info.niddk.nih.gov, http://kidney.niddk.nih.gov.

Monique Laberge Ph.D.

Urinary tract infection

Definition

A urinary tract infection is a bacterial infection that occurs in any part of the urinary tract.

Description

The organs of the body that produce and discharge urine are called the urinary tract. They include the kidneys, ureters, bladder, prostate (in men only), and urethra. Urine contains water and waste products. It is made by the kidneys, and carried through the ureters to the bladder for storage. It leaves the body through the urethra, which carries the urine from the bladder. In men, the urethra travels from the bladder through the prostate and out through the penis. In women, the urethra is shorter than in the male and emerges above the vaginal opening.

Urine is normally sterile, meaning that it is free from infectious organisms such as bacteria. The urinary tract is also built to mechanically resist infections. For example, urine is normally prevented from backing up in the ureters to the kidneys. The flow of urine also flushes out bacteria from the body. However, an infection can occur when bacteria attach to the opening of the urethra and enter the urinary tract, which leads to an inflammatory response of the lining of the urinary tract (urothelium). Infection can affect the urethra (urethritis), the bladder (**cystitis**), and if not treated, can even reach the kidneys (pyelonephritis).

Demographics

According to the National Institute of Diabetes and Digestive and Kidney Diseases (NDDKD), urinary tract infections account for about 8.3 million medical visits each year in the United States. In 2004, these infections required 429,000 hospital stays. *Escherichia coli* is the main culprit, causing approximately 80% of urinary tract infections in adults.

Urinary tract infection is extremely common in women. It is estimated that at least 33% of all women

QUESTIONS TO ASK YOUR DOCTOR

- What causes a urinary tract infection?
- What are the signs of a urinary tract infection?
- How is a urinary tract infection treated?
- Can it be cured?
- What can I do to prevent a urinary tract infection?
- Is a urinary tract infection contagious?

in the United States are diagnosed with a urinary tract infection by the time they reach 24 years of age. Many women also suffer from frequent infections: some 20% of women who have had an infection will have a recurrence.

Causes and symptoms

Most urinary tract infections are caused by *Escherichia coli* bacteria that normally live in the large intestine, and are present in feces. They can enter the urethra from the skin around the anus in the rectal area. Other microorganisms, such as *Chlamydia trachomatis* and *Mycoplasma hominis*, often transmitted from one sexual partner to the other, can also cause infections.

A common source of infection are catheters, the tubes that are placed in the urethra or bladder of patients who cannot urinate or are unconscious. Other people suffering from illnesses also require catheters, sometimes permanently, as for example the elderly or patients with nervous system disorders resulting in loss of bladder control. When catheters are not properly cleaned, bacteria can easily be transferred to the urethra or bladder upon insertion.

Common symptoms of urinary tract infection include:

- a burning sensation or pain when urinating (dysuria)
- frequent need to urinate
- need to urinate during the night (nocturia)
- dark, cloudy urine
- blood in the urine (hematuria)
- pus in the urine (pyuria)
- urge to urinate but only passing small amounts
- abnormal urine smell

Diagnosis

The diagnosis of urinary tract infection is established on the basis of clinical signs and symptoms in combination with urinalysis results. In the urinalysis test, the urine is examined for white and red blood cells and the presence of bacteria (bacteriuria). Cultures may also be obtained to identify the specific organism involved. When an infection does not clear up with treatment, other tests may be performed, such as an intravenous pyelogram, which provides x-ray images of the bladder, kidneys, and ureters.

Treatment

Urinary tract infections are commonly treated with an antibiotic. Other medications may also be prescribed to relieve the burning and the frequent urge to urinate.

Nutrition/Dietetic concerns

Some studies have shown that women who drink cranberry juice have fewer repeat urinary tract infections. However, more research is required to evaluate the amount required to provide effective protection.

Therapy

The drugs most often used to treat mild urinary tract infections include trimethoprim (Trimpex), trimethoprim/sulfamethoxazole (Bactrim, Septra, Cotrim), amoxicillin (Amoxil, Trimox, Wymox), nitrofurantoin (Macrodantin, Furadantin), and ampicillin (Omnipen, Polycillin, Principen, Totacillin). Another class of drugs called quinolones include ofloxacin (Floxin), norfloxacin (Noroxin), ciprofloxacin (Cipro), and trovafloxin (Trovan). Longer treatment is often required by patients with infections caused by *Chlamydia* and *Mycoplasma*, commonly treated with tetracycline, trimethoprim/sulfamethoxazole (TMP/SMZ), or doxycycline.

Prognosis

Urinary tract infections can often be cured with proper treatment if the infection is not complicated by another condition. Women who have had three infections are likely to continue having them. For instance, once a woman has had one cystitis episode, she has a 20% chance of developing a second infection. After the second infection, she has a 30% risk of developing a third.

KEY TERMS

Bacterium—A single-celled microorganism that can cause disease. Pl.: bacteria.

Bacteriuria—Presence of bacteria in the urine.

Bladder—Elastic, muscular pouch in which urine collects before being discharged from the body through the urethra.

Catheter—A hollow flexible tube for insertion into a body cavity, duct, or vessel to allow the passage of fluids or distend a passageway.

Cystitis—Inflammation of the bladder.

Feces—Stool, the excrement discharged from the intestines.

Inflammatory response—The immune system's normal response to tissue injury caused by a physical, chemical, or biological substance.

Kidneys—Pair of bean-shaped organs located below the ribs toward the middle of the back that clean the blood, regulate acid concentration and maintain water balance in the body by excreting urine.

Microorganism—An organism that can be seen only through a microscope. They include bacteria, protozoa, algae, and fungi.

Prostate—In males, a walnut-shaped gland that surrounds the urethra at the neck of the bladder. It supplies fluid that goes into semen.

Pyelonephritis—Bacterial infection of the kidney.

Sterile—Free from infectious organisms such as bacteria.

Ureters—Tubes from the kidneys to the bladder that drain urine.

Urethra—The tube leading from the bladder to discharge urine outside the body. In males, the urethra travels through the penis, and in females, it is shorter than in the male and emerges above the vaginal opening.

Urethritis—Infection of the urethra.

Urinary tract—The organs of the body that produce and discharge urine. They include the kidneys, ureters, bladder, and urethra.

Urine—Fluid containing water and waste products. Urine is made by the kidneys, stored in the bladder, and leaves the body through the urethra.

Urothelium—The lining of the urinary tract, including the renal pelvis, ureters, bladder and urethra.

Inflammatory response—The immune system's normal response to tissue injury caused by a physical, chemical, or biological substance.

Prevention

Urinary tract infections can be prevented with good hygiene, starting with wiping from front to back after using the toilet and keeping the rectal and genital areas clean. Drinking at least six glasses of water every day also maintains the urinary tract in good working order and capable of flushing waste material and bacteria.

Caregiver concerns

Urinary tract infections are common in older community dwellers aged 65 and older, and also in nursing home residents. The challenge involved in diagnosing these infections in this population results from other illnesses that may have symptoms similar to those of urinary tract infection. Some elderly adults who have cognitive impairment are also not able to report their symptoms.

Resources

BOOKS

Icon Health Publications. *Urinary Tract Infections—A Medical Dictionary, Bibliography, and Annotated Research Guide to Internet References.* San Diego, CA: Icon Health Publications, 2004.

Kavaler, Elizabeth. *A Seat on the Aisle, Please!: The Essential Guide to Urinary Tract Problems in Women.* New York, NY: Springer, 2006.

Kilmartin, Angela, and Geoffrey Chamberlain. *The Patient's Encyclopaedia of Urinary Tract Infection, Sexual Cystitis and Interstitial Cystitis.* Chula Vista, CA: New Century Press, 2004.

Parker, James N., and Philip M. Parker. *The Official Patient's Sourcebook on Urinary Tract Infection: A Revised and Updated Directory for the Internet Age.* San Diego, CA: Icon Health Publications, 2002.

Stanton, Stuart L., and Peter L. Dwyer. *Urinary Tract Infection in the Female.* London, UK: Informa Healthcare, 2000.

PERIODICALS

Hazelett, S. E., et al. "The association between indwelling urinary catheter use in the elderly and urinary tract infection in acute care." *BMC Geriatrics* 12 (October 2006): 6–15.

Juthani–Mehta, M. "Asymptomatic bacteriuria and urinary tract infection in older adults." *Clinics in Geriatric Medicine Geriatrics* 23, no. 3 (August 2007): 584–594.

Midthun, S. J. "Criteria for urinary tract infection in the elderly: variables that challenge nursing assessment." *Urological Nursing* 24, no. 3 (June 2004): 157–162.

Nicolle, E. "Urinary tract pathogens in complicated infection and in elderly individuals." *Journal of Infectious Diseases* 183, no. S1 (April 2007): S5–S8.

OTHER

TMP Sulfa/Bactrim. Cleveland Clinic, Information Page (March 20, 2008) http://cms.clevelandclinic.org/transplant/body.cfm?id=248

Urinary Tract Infection (UTI). Women's Health.com, Information Page (March 20, 2008) http://womenshealth.gov/faq/Easyread/uti-etr.htm

Urinary Tract Infections in Women. American Academy of Family Physicians, Family Doctor Information Page (March 20, 2008) http://familydoctor.org/online/famdocen/home/women/gen-health/190.printerview.html

What I need to know about Urinary Tract Infections. NKUDIC, Information Page (March 20, 2008) http://kidney.niddk.nih.gov/kudiseases/pubs/uti_ez

ORGANIZATIONS

American Urological Association (AUA), 1000 Corporate Blvd., Linthicum, MD, 21090, (410)689-3700, (866) 746-4282, (410)689-3800, aua@auanet.org, http://www.auanet.org.

National Institute of Diabetes and Digestive and Kidney Diseases, Building 31, Rm 9A06, 31 Center Drive, MSC 2560, Bethesda, MD, 20892-2560, (301)496.3583, http://www2.niddk.nih.gov/.

National Kidney and Urologic Diseases Information Clearinghouse (NKUDIC), 3 Information Way, Bethesda, MD, 20892–3580, (800)891–5390, (703)738–4929, nkudic@info.niddk.nih.gov, http://kidney.niddk.nih.gov.

Monique Laberge Ph.D.

Urine culture

Definition

A urine culture determines the presence or absence of abnormal amounts of bacteria in urine to diagnoses a urinary tract or **bladder infection**.

Purpose

A urine culture is performed when a **urinary tract infection** or a bladder infection is suspected. Such an infection is indicated by the presence of abnormal amounts of bacteria in the urine. A urine culture grows a sample of the urine in the laboratory for one or more days to determine what quantity of bacteria are present. If enough bacteria are present to indicate an infection, sensitivity testing can be performed. Sensitivity testing tests various **antibiotics** against the bacteria grown in the culture to determine which ones would be most effective for treatment of the infection.

Precautions

If the penis or vagina is not thoroughly cleaned the sample can be contaminated. The sample can also be contaminated if it is collected from the first urine released because bacteria are naturally present in the urethra that would contaminate the sample. A contaminated sample may lead to a false positive. It may also cause the results to be unusable, requiring the test to be repeated. Individuals who are going to collect a sample for urine culture should not drink an unusually large amount of water prior to collecting the ample because this may dilute the bacteria in the sample to such a degree a false negative is reported.

Description

To perform a urine culture a urine sample must be collected. Generally this is done by asking the patient to collect a sample of urine in a plastic container. The patient begins urinating into the toilet, places the cup under the stream to collect urine without touching the cup to the genitals or stopping the stream, removes the cup from the stream when the desired amount ahs been collected, and finishes urinating into the toilet. In cases where voluntary urination is not possible a urine sample for culture can also be collected by using a catheter or by removing a sample or urine directly from the bladder using a needle.

Once the sample is collected it must be refrigerated. Urine samples can generally be refrigerated for up to 24 hours. When the sample is brought tot the lab, a small amount of the sample is placed on a sterile swab which is then rubbed on a sterile petri dish. The culture is then allowed to grow for 24 to 48 hours, or longer in some cases. After the required amount of time the petri dish is examined to determine the extent of bacterial growth. If the extent of bacterial growth indicates an infection, sensitivity testing can be performed. During sensitivity testing the bacteria that grew on the petri dish are exposed to various types of

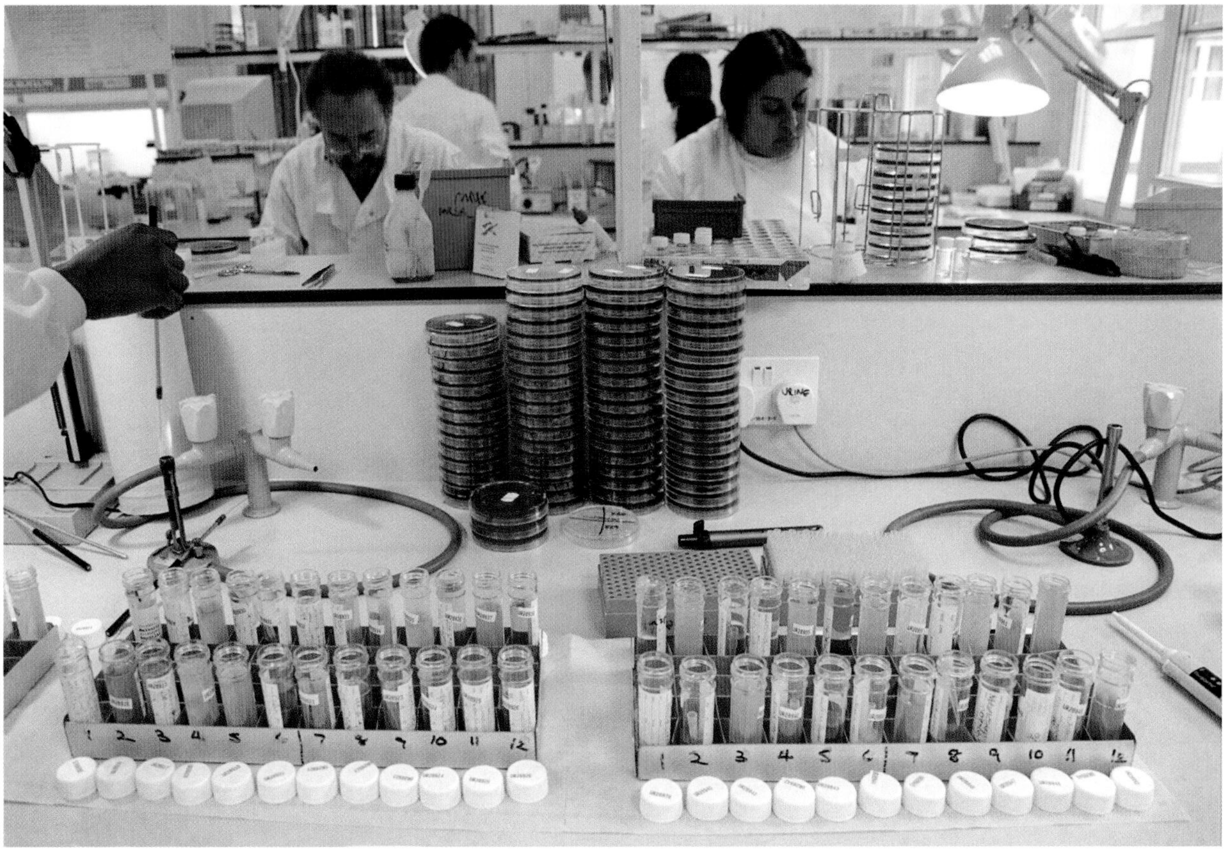

Urine cultures are analyzed in a laboratory. *(Sotiris Zafeiris / Photo Researchers, Inc. Reproduced by permission.)*

antibiotics one at a time. If the bacteria die, then it indicates that the bacteria are sensitive to that type of antibiotic, and that antibiotic would be effective for treatment of the infection.

Preparation

Before collecting a sample for urine culture the area around the genitals should be thoroughly cleaned with sterile wipes or swabs. Men should thoroughly clean the head of the penis, retracting the foreskin if necessary. Women should thoroughly clean the folds of skin around the vagina (labia) and keep them pulled back while urinating to ensure the sample is not contaminated. The patient may be instructed to take the urine sample from the first urine produced during the day.

Aftercare

There is no aftercare required for a urine culture.

Complications

There are no complications expected from a urine culture.

Results

If the culture shows that there is a single bacteria with more than 10,000 colony forming units (CFU) per milliliter of urine after 24 to 48 hours then the culture is positive for an infection. If the culture shows less than 10,000 CFU/ml but still shows a very significant number the test may be considered inconclusive and may be repeated. Very few CFU/ml indicates the absence of an infection.

In some cases the culture will show a large amount of many different kinds of bacteria. Urinary tract infections and bladder infections are usually caused by the overgrowth of a single kind of bacteria, so a large number of many different bacteria usually indicates contamination of the sample. In this case a new sample must be collected.

Caregiver concerns

A patient's doctor determines the need for a urine culture based on the patient's symptoms and history. The doctor then orders the test. A nurse or other member of the healthcare team will provide the urine

QUESTIONS TO ASK YOUR DOCTOR

- In how long should I expect the results of the culture?
- If the culture is positive will a susceptibility testing be performed?
- What is the next step if the culture is negative but I am still experiencing symptoms?

KEY TERMS

sensitivity testing— testing done on a bacterial culture to determine which antibiotics would be most effective at treating the infection.

collection cup, sterile wipes or swabs, and directions about how much urine should be collected. He or she will also accept the completed sample, label it, and store it until it is sent to the laboratory for analysis. At the laboratory a laboratory technician or other member of the laboratory staff will perform the culture and analyze the results. After the laboratory has reported the results to the doctor he or she will prescribe any antibiotics that were indicated by the results of the culture.

Resources

BOOKS

Ricotta, Mary C. *A Consumer's Guide to Laboratory Tests.* Amherst, NY: Prometheus Books, 2005.

Schumann, G. Berry and Sheryl K. Friedman. *Wet Urinalysis: Interpretations, Correlations, and Implications.* Chicago: ASCP Press, 2003.

Strasinger, Susan King and Marjorie Schaub Di Lorenzo. *Urinalysis and Body Fluids*, 5th Ed. Philadelphia, PA: F.A. Davis, 2008.

PERIODICALS

"Urine Sample Collection/Containment System." *Medical Laboratory Observer* 32.11 (Nov 2000): 52.

Lewis, Carol. "Home Diagnostic Test: The Ultimate House Call?" *FDA Consumer* 35.6 (Nov-Dec 2001): 18-23.

ORGANIZATIONS

American Urological Association, 1000 Corporate Boulevard, Linthicum, MD, 21090, 866-746-4282, http://www.auanet.org/.

Robert Bockstiegel

V

VA *see* **Veterans Administration hospital system**

Vaccinations

Definition

Vaccination is the injection of a weakened or dead disease–producing organism in a person to provide immunity against the disease caused by the organism.

Description

Many microorganisms, such as **viruses** and bacteria, can infect humans and produce disease. The body's defense mechanism against these foreign invaders is the *immune system* which can produce *antibodies* to neutralize or destroy the disease-carrying organisms (pathogens) and the toxins that they produce. When a person's **immune system** has produced antibodies against a specific pathogen after being exposed to it, the person is said to have achieved *natural immunity* to that pathogen. If this person comes into contact with that same pathogen in the future, the immune system will immediately recognize it and produce the antibodies required to fight it. Besides having the immune system of a person produce antibodies upon exposure to a real pathogen, another way to provide immunity is to inject a person with a killed or weakened form of the disease organism through *vaccination*. This is called *vaccine-induced immunity*, and will trigger the same antibody-producing immune response from the person's body. A preparation of weakened or killed pathogen is called a *vaccine*. The advantage of vaccination is that it stimulates antibody production against the pathogen and provides immunity, but does not cause severe infection.

Vaccines recommended for adults over 50

Tetanus-diphtheria (Td)	Booster every 10 years, especially after age 50
Influenza (Flu)	After age 50, every year
Pneumonia	A single dose around age 65. If you have lung, heart, or kidney disease, HIV, diabetes, or cancer, you may need this shot sooner
Herpes Zoster (Shingles)	A single dose for adults 60 years old or older who have already had chickenpox but who have not had shingles
Hepatitis A	Recommended if you have long-term liver disease, receive blood products to help your blood clot, or travel to countries with high rates of hepatitis A
Hepatitis B	Recommended if you are a dialysis patient or have end-stage kidney disease, have HIV infection, have chronic liver disease, or travel to countries with intermediate or high rates of hepatitis B virus infection

SOURCE: Centers for Disease Control and Prevention, U.S. Department of Health and Human Services

(Illustration by GGS Information Services. Cengage Learning, Gale)

Antibodies are disease-specific. For example, antibodies produced against the virus that causes measles will protect a person who is exposed to the virus, but will have no effect if the person is exposed to the **hepatitis** virus. This is why there are so many different types of vaccines.

Purpose

The purpose of vaccination is to immunize people against specific pathogens to protect them from disease and also to eliminate disease. As more and more people are vaccinated, specific disease are eradicated, as for example polio and diphtheria in the United States.

Children are routinely given a series of vaccinations starting at birth. Given according to a specific schedule, they immunize against hepatitis A and B,

KEY TERMS

Active immunity—Protection against a disease that results when exposure to a disease organism triggers the immune system to produce antibodies to that disease.

Anthrax—An infectious disease caused by a type of bacterium. The disease can be passed from animals to people and usually is fatal. Symptoms include sores on the skin.

Antibody—Proteins produced by the body to neutralize or destroy toxins or disease-carrying organisms.

Bacteria—Tiny, single-celled forms of life that cause many diseases and infections.

Cholera—An infection of the small intestine caused by a type of bacterium. The disease is spread by drinking water or eating seafood or other foods that have been contaminated with the feces of infected people. It occurs in parts of Asia, Africa, Latin America, India, and the Middle East. Symptoms include watery diarrhea and exhaustion.

Cowpox—A mild disease in cows that is caused by a poxvirus.

Diphtheria—A serious, infectious disease that produces a toxin (poison) and an inflammation in the membrane lining of the throat, nose, trachea, and other tissues.

Encephalitis—Inflammation of the brain, usually caused by a virus. The inflammation may interfere with normal brain function and may cause seizures, sleepiness, confusion, personality changes, weakness in one or more parts of the body, and even coma.

Immune system—The immune system consists of the organs and cells of the lymphatic system that protect the body against infections and other diseases.

Immunization—A technique used to cause an immune response that results in resistance to a specific disease, especially an infectious disease. A vaccination is a type of immunization.

Immune—Resistant to an infectious disease.

Influenza—A serious disease caused by viruses that infect the respiratory tract.

Measles—An acute and highly contagious viral disease marked by distinct red spots followed by a rash that occurs primarily in children.

Meningitis—Inflammation of tissues that surround the brain and spinal cord.

Microorganism—An organism that is too small to be seen with the naked eye.

Mumps—An acute and highly contagious viral illness that usually occurs in childhood.

Natural immunity—Protection against a disease that results when exposure to a real disease organism triggers the immune system to produce antibodies to that disease.

Pathogen—A disease–causing microorganism.

Passive immunity—Protection against a disease that is provided when a person is given antibodies to a disease rather than producing them through his or her own immune system.

Plague—A highly infectious disease that can be fatal if not treated promptly. The bacteria that cause plague mainly infect rats, mice, squirrels, and other wild rodents. The disease is passed to people through fleas. Infected people can then spread the disease to other people.

Rabies—A rare but serious disease caused by a virus carried in saliva. It is transmitted when an infected animal bites a person.

Rubella—A contagious viral disease that is milder than typical measles but is damaging to the fetus when it occurs early in pregnancy. Also called German measles.

Smallpox—A highly contagious viral disease characterized by fever and weakness and skin eruption with pustules that form scabs that slough off leaving scars.

Tuberculosis—An infectious disease that usually affects the lungs, but may also affect other parts of the body. Symptoms include fever, weight loss, and coughing up blood.

Typhoid fever—An infectious disease caused by a type of bacterium. People with this disease have a lingering fever and feel depressed and exhausted. Diarrhea and rose–colored spots on the chest and abdomen are other symptoms. The disease is spread through poor sanitation.

Vaccination—Injection of a killed pathogen in order to stimulate the immune system against the pathogen.

Vaccine—A preparation of a weakened or killed pathogen, such as a bacterium or virus, that upon administration to a person stimulates antibody production against the pathogen but is incapable of causing severe infection.

Vaccine–induced immunity—Protection against a disease that results when exposure to a dead or weakened disease organism triggers the immune system to produce antibodies to that disease.

Virus—A tiny, disease-causing particle that can reproduce only in living cells.

Whooping cough—An infectious disease, also called pertussis, especially of children that is caused by a bacterium and is marked by a convulsive, spasmodic cough, sometimes followed by a shrill intake of breath.

Yellow fever—An infectious disease caused by a virus. The disease, which is spread by mosquitoes, is most common in Central and South America and Central Africa. Symptoms include high fever, jaundice (yellow eyes and skin) and dark–colored vomit, a sign of internal bleeding. Yellow fever can be fatal.

diphtheria, tetanus, whooping cough, measles, mumps, German measles (rubella), chickenpox (varicella), polio, pneumococcus and *Haemophilus influenzae* type b, which causes Hib disease with associated spinal **meningitis**. This series of vaccinations is recommended by the American Academy of Family Physicians (AAFP), the American Academy of Pediatrics (APA), and the Centers for Disease Control and Prevention (CDC). It is required in all states before children can attend school. Exceptions are made for children who have medical conditions such as **cancer** that prevent them from having vaccinations, and some states also will make exceptions for children whose parents object for various reasons. Some vaccines are combined in one injection, such as the measles-mumps-rubella (MMR) or diphtheria-pertussis-tetanus (DPT) combinations.

In addition to the childhood vaccination schedule, vaccines are available for preventing anthrax, cholera, Japanese encephalitis, meningococcal meningitis, plague, pneumococcal infection (meningitis, **pneumonia**), **tuberculosis**, typhoid fever, and yellow fever. Most vaccines are given as injections, but a few are given by mouth.

Vaccines are also given for targeted purposes. Some, such as the rabies vaccine, are given only when a person is likely to have been exposed to the virus that causes the disease—through a dog bite, for example. Others are given to travelers planning to visit countries where certain diseases are common such as typhoid fever or yellow fever. Vaccines such as the **influenza** vaccine, also called "flu shots," are given mainly to specific groups of people—older adults and others, who are considered at high risk of developing influenza or its complications.

Influenza vaccination policy in most high-income countries attempts to reduce the mortality burden of influenza by targeting people aged at least 65 years for vaccination. However, the effectiveness of this strategy is being debated. Trials have shown that influenza vaccine is effective in younger adults, but few trials have included elderly people, and especially those aged at least 70 years, the age group that accounts for 75% of all influenza-related deaths.

Operation

To administer a vaccine, a sterile needle is fitted into a syringe. The vaccine is withdrawn from a single dose vial or a single dose is taken from a multidose vial. The vaccine is always administered shortly after withdrawal from the vial by injection.

Maintenance

Vaccines are stored in refrigerated units at a temperature of 35°46°F (2°–8°C). Before administration, they are carefully checked for extraneous particulate matter and/or discoloration.

Training

Vaccines are administered by trained health practitioners. The Association for Prevention Teaching and Research (APTR), in collaboration with the University of Pittsburgh School of Medicine and the Centers for Disease Control distribute Teaching Immunization for Medical Education (TIME) modules to medical schools that can be integrated into existing medical courses. The modules include vaccine indications and contraindications, immunization schedules, and recommendations on efficient ways to increase vaccination levels.

Resources

BOOKS

Crosby, Molly C. *The American Plague: The Untold Story of Yellow Fever, the Epidemic that Shaped Our History.* New York: Berkley Books (Penguin Group), 2006.

Jenner, Edward, ed. *The Three Original Publications on Vaccination Against Smallpox.* Whitefish: Kessinger Publishing, 2005.

Offit, Paul A. *The Cutter Incident: How America's First Polio Vaccine Led to the Growing Vaccine Crisis.* New Haven: Yale University Press, 2007.

Offit, Paul A. *Vaccinated: One Man's Quest to Defeat the World's Deadliest Diseases.* New York: Collins, 2007.

Romm, Aviva J. *Vaccinations: A Thoughtful Parent's Guide: How to Make Safe, Sensible Decisions about the Risks, Benefits, and Alternatives.* Rochester: Healing Arts Press, 2001.

PERIODICALS

Aspinall, R., Del Giudice, G., Effros, R. B., Grubeck–Loebenstein, B., Sambhara, S. "Challenges for vaccination in the elderly." *Immunity & Ageing* 4, no. 1 (December 2007): 9.

El Yousfi, M., et al. "The inflammatory response to vaccination is altered in the elderly." *Mechanisms of Ageing and Development* 126, no. 8 (August 2005): 874–881.

Kasten, M. J., and G. A. Poland. "Influenza vaccination and the elderly : pandemic preparedness." *Drugs & Aging* 25, no. 3 (2008): 179–186.

Kovaiou, R. D., et al. "Age–related changes in immunity: implications for vaccination in the elderly." *Expert Reviews in Molecular Medicine* 9, no. 3 (February 2007): 1–17.

OTHER

Adults With Asthma Should Receive Flu Vaccination. CDC, Information Page (March 30, 2008) http://www.cdc.gov/asthma/flushot.htm

Combination Vaccines. NNII Immunization Issues, Information Page (March 30, 2008) http://www.immunizationinfo.org/immunization_issues_detail.cfv?id=50

How do I know if the vaccine information I find on the Internet is accurate? NNII Immunization Issues, Information Page (March 30, 2008) http://www.immunizationinfo.org/immunization_issues_detail.cfv?id=102

Immunization. Medline Plus, Health Topics (March 30, 2008) http://www.nlm.nih.gov/medlineplus/immunization.html

Questions and Answers about Vaccination. Health Canada, Information Page (March 30, 2008) http://www.hc-sc.gc.ca/ahc-asc/media/nr-cp/2002/2002_81bk1_e.html

What You Need to Know About Vaccinations and Travel: A Checklist. CDC Vaccinations, Information Page (March 30, 2008) http://wwwn.cdc.gov/travel/contentVaccinations.aspx

ORGANIZATIONS

Centers for Disease Control and Prevention (CDC), 1600 Clifton Road NE, MS-C09, Atlanta, GA, 30333, (404) 498-1515, (800)311-3435, http://www.cdc.gov.

National Institute of Allergy and Infectious Diseases (NIAID), 6610 Rockledge Drive, MSC 6612, Bethesda, MD, 20892-6612, (301)496-5717, (866)284-4107, http://www3.niaid.nih.gov.

National Network for Immunization Information, 301 University Blvd., CH 2.218, Galveston, TX, 77555-0351, (409)772-0199, nnii@i4ph.org, http://www.immunizationinfo.org.

National Vaccine Program Office. U.S. Department of Health & Human Services, 200 Independence Ave., SW, Washington, DC, 20201, (202)619-0257, (877)696-6775, nnii@i4ph.org, http://www.hhs.gov/nvpo.

Monique Laberge Ph.D.

Varicella *see* **Shingles**

Varicose veins

Definition

Varicose veins are veins right below the surface of the skin (superficial veins) that are swollen with blood and which become twisted and painful.

Description

Veins return unoxygenated blood from the body back to the heart and lungs. When the veins lose their elasticity they become thickened and enlarged with twists and turns. Varicose veins occur most often in the legs and thighs but can occur anywhere in the body.

Demographics

Approximately 25 million people in the United States have varicose veins. Varicose veins are more common between the ages of 30 and 70 years. Most elderly individuals have some evidence of varicose veins. Women are two to three times more likely than men to develop varicose veins and about half of women in the United States have varicose veins. Changes in hormones associated with puberty, pregnancy, **menopause**, and taking oral contraceptives may increase a woman's chance of developing varicose veins.

Causes and symptoms

Varicose veins may be due to weakness in the walls of the veins or improper functioning of the valves within the veins. Weakened vein walls lose their elasticity allowing the vein to become wider and

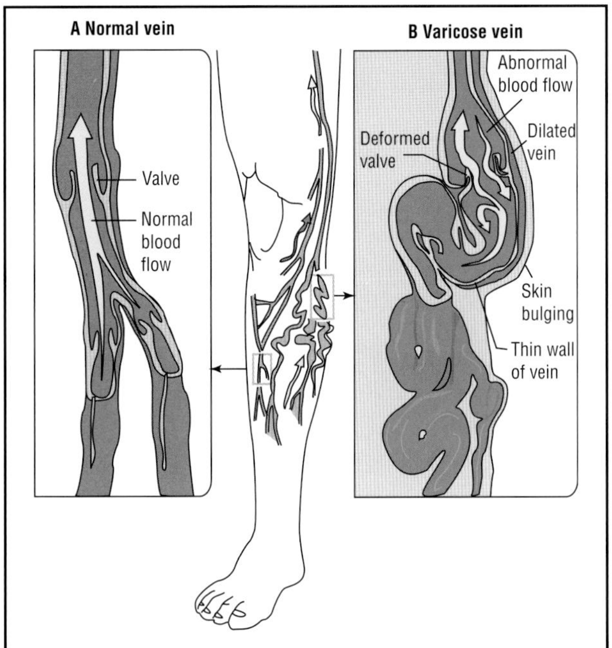

SOURCE: Diseases and Conditions Index (DCI), National Heart, Lung and Blood Institute, National Institutes of Health, U.S. Department of Health and Human Services

Varicose veins on leg. The illustration shows the location of leg veins, which can become varicose veins. Figure A shows a normal vein with working valves and normal blood flow. Figure B shows a varicose vein with deformed valves, abnormal blood flow, and thin, dilated (stretched) walls. *(Illustration by GGS Information Services. Cengage Learning, Gale)*

longer. The swollen vein often twists and turns to remain in its normal position.

Veins have one-way valves that keep blood moving toward the heart. When the valves malfunction, blood backs up and collects in the veins. This abnormal pooling of blood causes the vein to swell resulting in the development of a varicose vein.

Certain conditions are associated with the development of varicose veins including pregnancy, prolonged sitting or standing, **obesity**, history of trauma or surgery to the leg, and age. An increased volume of blood and added weight of the uterus during pregnancy increases pressure on the leg veins contributing to the development of varicose veins. Varicose veins that develop during pregnancy usually get better within three to twelve months after childbirth. Prolonged sitting, especially with the legs bent or crossed, or standing causes the veins to work harder to pump blood back to the heart and varicose veins may result. Obesity places increased pressure on the veins increasing the risk of developing varicose veins. Previous surgery or injury to the leg may disrupt normal blood and contribute to the development of varicose veins.

A family history of varicose veins may also increase the risk of developing them. Age weakens vein valves which increases the likelihood of developing varicose veins.

Symptoms include **pain** and swelling in the legs; visible, enlarged veins; **itching** around one or more veins; and discoloration of the skin around the varicose vein. Pain may be described as burning, throbbing, tingling, soreness, aching, or cramping. Prolonged standing or sitting may aggravate the pain.

Diagnosis

Diagnosis begins with a complete medical history and physical examination. The history will include questions about pain characteristics and physical examination will include observation for any prominent veins. Testing may include ultrasound to evaluate blood flow and structure of the leg veins. Referral to a blood vessel specialist (vascular medicine specialist or vascular surgeon) may be made. If necessary, referral to a **dermatologist** may also be made.

Treatment

Treatment is aimed at reducing symptoms, preventing complications, and improving the physical appearance of the legs. Mild symptoms may respond to self-care treatment including avoiding prolonged sitting or standing, raising the legs above the level of the heart when sitting or lying down, wearing support hose, maintaining adequate **exercise**, losing weight if overweight or obese, and avoiding wearing tight or binding clothes especially around the waist and legs.

Medical or surgical treatment may be needed if self-care measures do not work or symptoms are severe and disrupt activities of daily living. These treatments include sclerotherapy, laser surgery, endovenous ablation therapy, endoscopic vein surgery, ambulatory phlebectomy, and vein ligation and stripping.

Sclerotherapy involves injection of a chemical irritant into the vein causing scarring inside the vein which results in the vein closing off and **dying** away. Several treatments may be needed to completely close off the vein. This procedure is usually done in a doctor's office on smaller varicose veins.

Laser surgery involves light energy to fade away varicose veins. Laser surgery is usually done on smaller varicose veins.

During endovenous ablation therapy, an incision is made into the skin and a small tube is inserted into the vein. A laser or other energy source heats up the inside of the vein causing it to close off. This procedure is usually done in a doctor's office and pain and recovery time may be less than with other procedures.

Endoscopic vein surgery involves a small incision through which a tiny camera at the end of a small tube is used to move through the vein. A surgical instrument at the end of the camera closes off the vein. This type of procedure is usually reserved for severe cases of varicose veins in which skin ulcers have developed.

Ambulatory phlebectomy uses small incisions made into the skin to remove varicose veins. This procedure is usually done to treat superficial varicose veins and the patient usually goes home the same day.

In vein ligation and stripping, veins are ligated (tied off) and stripped (removed) through small skin incisions. This procedure is usually done in cases in which pain is severe or skin ulcers are present. This procedure is usually done on an outpatient basis with anesthesia.

Nutrition/Dietetic concerns

Consume a low-salt **diet** to reduce water retention and swelling. Eat a **high-fiber diet** to decrease **constipation**, which can contribute to varicose veins because of straining. Lose weight if overweight or obese. Avoid alcohol because it can cause the veins in the legs to dilate.

Therapy

Exercise regularly, lose weight if necessary, don't wear tight-fitting clothes, avoid sitting or standing for long periods of time, and elevate the legs when sitting or lying down. Get up and walk at least every hour to help with blood flow in the legs. Don't cross the legs when sitting. Wear support hose. Put hose on in the morning before beginning to walk around and legs become swollen.

Prognosis

Symptoms of varicose veins usually worsen with time but self-care may reduce the symptoms and progression of the condition.

Prevention

Nothing can prevent varicose veins from developing but lifestyle dietary and activity modifications may decrease the chances of developing varicose veins.

QUESTIONS TO ASK YOUR DOCTOR

- Which vein or veins in my legs is causing the problem?
- What is causing my varicose veins?
- What type of treatment is needed?
- Are there treatments I can try at home?
- Will surgery be required?
- Do I need to see a specialist?
- Will my varicose veins get worse?
- Will my varicose veins recur after treatment?

Caregiver concerns

Varicose veins sometimes cause skin problems, **blood clots**, or other complications. Skin complications may include ulcers caused by severe problems with blood circulation. These skin ulcers are difficult to heal and usually recur even if they do heal. Varicose veins may also cause red, scaly, itchy skin usually around the ankle.

Blood clots can be life-threatening because the clot can disrupt blood flow to a major organ. Symptoms including chest pain and shortness of breath require immediate medical attention. Sudden leg swelling may indicate a blood clot in the leg (thrombophlebitis) which also requires immediate medical attention.

June G. Borazjani R.N., B.S.N., C.P.H.Q.

Ventilation management

Definition

Ventilation management involves providing optimal mechanical ventilation in order to promote the patient's recovery and to reestablish spontaneous breathing.

Purpose

Mechanical ventilation is used when a patient is unable to breathe adequately on their own. The purpose of ventilation management is to "breathe for them" until they are sufficiently recovered to initiate respiration. This process is usually a gradual one, and is referred to as weaning. During the ventilatory weaning process, the modes of mechanical ventilation are gradually changed to allow the patient to initiate more breaths while the ventilator provides less.

Precautions

Ventilatory weaning should not be attempted until the patient's respiratory status is stable and they are arousable and able to follow commands. If the patient is unstable or unarousable, attempting to wean may cause unnecessary physical **stress** and may delay recovery.

Description

The ventilatory weaning process is accomplished by decreasing the number of breaths supplied by the ventilator, as well as by changing the way in which those breaths are delivered to the patient. The process also depends on the reason why the patient requires mechanical ventilation. For example, post-operative **cardiac bypass** patients are generally weaned within a few hours after surgery. However, a patient with extensive lung disease may require days or weeks to wean.

There are three primary methods used to wean patients from the ventilator. These include T-piece, synchronized intermittent mandatory ventilation and pressure support ventilation. A short description of each of these is included here. The method chosen depends on the patient's respiratory status and on how long they have been on the ventilator.

T-piece trials consist of alternating intervals of time on the ventilator with intervals of spontaneous breathing. To facilitate spontaneous breathing, the patient is removed from the ventilator and a T-shaped tube is attached to the endotracheal tube or tracheostomy tube. One end of this tubing is attached to an oxygen flowmeter and the other end is open. The amount of oxygen to be used is ordered by the physician. The patient on a T-piece doesn't have the ventilator as back-up if they can't breathe, so they must be monitored closely. If they tire out or their respiratory status becomes unstable, they should be reconnected to the ventilator. The goal of this method of weaning is to gradually increase the amount of time spent off the ventilator.

Synchronized intermittent mandatory ventilation (SIMV) is a ventilator mode that delivers a preset number of breaths to the patient but coordinates them with the patient's spontaneous breaths. Thus, the ventilator may be set to deliver 12 breaths per minute but the patient's respiratory rate may be 16 (12 ventilator-initiated breaths plus four patient-initiated breaths.) The goal of SIMV weaning is to gradually decrease the number of breaths delivered by the ventilator, which allows the patient to take more breaths of their own. The ventilator rate is usually decreased by one to three breaths at a time and an arterial blood gas (ABG) is obtained 30 minutes after the change to assess the patient's respiratory status. The benefits of SIMV weaning are that the patient has the ventilator for back-up if they fail to take a breath and the ventilator alarms will sound if they are not tolerating weaning. However, the patient should still be closely monitored for signs of respiratory fatigue.

Pressure support ventilation (PSV) augments the patient's spontaneous inspiration with a positive pressure "boost." This decreases the resistance created from breathing through ventilator tubing and is used with the SIMV mode to decrease the work of breathing.

If the patient tolerates SIMV weaning, the ventilator mode may be changed to constant positive airway pressure (CPAP) as a final trial of spontaneous breathing prior to removing the endotracheal tube. In this mode, patients will breathe independently but have the benefit of the ventilator alarms if they have difficulty. CPAP maintains constant positive pressure in the airways, which facilitates gas exchange in the alveoli. PSV is often used with the CPAP mode to further decrease the work of breathing. If the patient tolerates CPAP, the endotracheal tube is removed and a face mask with humidified oxygen is applied for a short time. If the patient remains stable, a nasal cannula may be used to deliver oxygen.

If the patient has a tracheostomy, the weaning process is the same as with a endotracheal tube, with the exception that after the ventilator is disconnected, a tracheostomy collar may be used to deliver humidified oxygen instead of a face mask or nasal cannula. This is simply a mask-like device that fits loosely over the tracheostomy and is held in place by an elastic band around the neck.

Preparation

As discussed earlier, the patient's respiratory status must be stable and they must be arousable and able to follow commands prior to initiating weaning. Patients who require mechanical ventilation are often kept sedated or even paralyzed with drugs to facilitate optimal ventilation. These drugs must be tapered off prior to weaning.

Weaning criteria should be done to determine the patient's readiness to wean. The best indicators include a vital capacity of at least 10-15 cc/kg and a negative inspiratory fraction of greater than -30 cm H_2O, however, many other factors are also measured. The patient should be suctioned prior to any weaning attempt, both orally and via the endotracheal tube or tracheostomy. A pulse oximeter and **cardiac monitor** should be applied if they are not already present. Weaning should be done when there is adequate staffing so the patient can be closely monitored.

Aftercare

The patient's respiratory status should be assessed after any period of weaning. The ventilator should be securely reconnected and the patient made comfortable and reassured if necessary.

Complications

The greatest risk of ventilator weaning (especially premature weaning) is respiratory distress. The patient must be closely monitored and the weaning stopped before the respiratory distress becomes too great to control. Patients may also have **anxiety** or fear about weaning, which can complicate their respiratory distress.

KEY TERMS

Alveoli—Saclike structures in the lungs where oxygen and carbon dioxide exchange takes place.

Endotracheal tube—Tube inserted into the trachea via either the oral or nasal cavity for the purpose of providing a secure airway.

Negative inspiratory fraction—The amount of force used to draw air into the lungs during maximal inspiration.

Pulse oximeter—Noninvasive machine that measures the amount of hemoglobin that is saturated with oxygen.

Tracheostomy—Surgically created opening in the trachea for the purpose of providing a secure airway. This is used when the patient requires long term ventilatory assistance.

Ventilator—Device used to provide assisted respiration and positive pressure breathing.

Vital capacity—Maximum volume of air that can be expelled from the lungs after a maximal inspiration.

Results

The goal of ventilation management is to wean the patient from mechanical support and to reestablish spontaneous respiration.

Caregiver concerns

The nurse and respiratory therapist share equal roles in ventilator management. Both are responsible for suctioning and monitoring the patient during weaning periods. Since the nurse is at the bedside the most, they have the primary monitoring role and are often able to predict the best time for a weaning trial. It is the nurse's responsibility to communicate with the respiratory therapist in planning when weaning trials will occur. The respiratory therapist is generally responsible for making the actual ventilator changes. Both the nurse and respiratory therapist document the ventilator change and their assessment of the patient's respiratory status before, during, and after the weaning period. Both are responsible for teaching and reassuring the patient and family regarding the weaning process.

Patients may be fearful about weaning because it is difficult for them to communicate around the endotracheal tube or tracheostomy. They may be afraid no one will know if they're having difficulty breathing. The nurse should explain all procedures before performing them, reassure the patient that they will be closely monitored, and ensure that the patient's call light is within reach. It is important that the patient actually see the nurse enter the room frequently, as this is the only way they will know they are being monitored.

Resources

BOOKS

Thelan, Lynne, et al. *Critical Care Nursing: Diagnosis and Management.* St. Louis, MO: Mosby, 1998.

PERIODICALS

Hanneman, H. "Weaning from Short Term Mechanical Ventilation" *Critical Care Nurse* 19, no. 5 (1999): 86-89.

Abby Wojahn RN, BSN, CCRN

Ventilators

Definition

A ventilator is a device used to provide assisted respiration and positive-pressure breathing.

Actor Christopher Reeve, attached to ventilator. *(AP Images. Reproduced by permission.)*

Purpose

Ventilators are used to provide mechanical ventilation for patients with **respiratory failure** who cannot breathe effectively on their own. They are also used to decrease myocardial gas consumption or intracranial pressure, provide stability of the chest wall after trauma or surgery, and when a patient is sedated or pharmacologically paralyzed.

Description

Different types of ventilators can be programmed to provide several modes of mechanical ventilation. A brief overview of each type and mode follows.

Negative-pressure ventilators

The original ventilators used negative pressure to remove and replace gas from the ventilator chamber. Examples of these include the iron lung, the Drinker respirator, and the chest shell. Rather than connecting to an artificial airway, these ventilators enclosed the body from the outside. As gas was pulled out of the ventilator chamber, the resulting negative pressure caused the chest wall to expand, which pulled air into the lungs. The cessation of the negative pressure caused the chest wall to fall and exhalation to occur. While an advantage of these ventilators was that they did not require insertion of an artificial airway, they were noisy, made nursing care difficult, and the patient was not able to ambulate.

Positive-pressure ventilators

Postive-pressure ventilators require an artificial airway (endotracheal or tracheostomy tube) and use positive pressure to force gas into a patient's lungs. Inspiration can be triggered either by the patient or the machine. There are four types of positive-pressure ventilators: volume-cycled, pressure-cycled, flow-cycled, and time-cycled.

VOLUME-CYCLED VENTILATORS This type delivers a preset tidal volume then allows passive expiration. This is ideal for patients with acute respiratory distress syndrome (ARDS) or bronchospasm, since the same tidal volume is delivered regardless of the amount of airway resistance. This type of ventilator is the most commonly used in critical care environments.

PRESSURE-CYCLED VENTILATORS These ventilators deliver gases at a preset pressure, then allow passive expiration. The benefit of this type is a decreased risk of lung damage from high inspiratory pressures, which is particularly beneficial for neonates who have a small lung capacity. The disadvantage is that the tidal volume delivered can decrease if the patient has poor lung compliance and increased airway resistance. This type of ventilation is usually used for short-term therapy (less than 24 hours). Some ventilators have the capability to provide both volume-cycled and pressure-cycled ventilation. These combination ventilators are also commonly used in critical care environments.

FLOW-CYCLED VENTILATORS Flow-cycled ventilators deliver oxygenation until a preset flow rate is achieved during inspiration.

TIME-CYCLED VENTILATORS Time-cycled ventilators deliver oxygenation over a preset time period. These types of ventilators are not used as frequently as the volume-cycled and pressure-cycled ventilators.

Modes of ventilation

Mode refers to how the machine will ventilate the patient in relation to the patient's own respiratory efforts. There is a mode for nearly every patient situation; plus, many different types can be used in conjunction with each other.

CONTROL VENTILATION (CV) CV delivers the preset volume or pressure regardless of the patient's own inspiratory efforts. This mode is used for patients who are unable to initiate a breath. If it is used with spontaneously breathing patients, they must be sedated and/or pharmacologically paralyzed so they don't breathe out of synchrony with the ventilator.

ASSIST-CONTROL VENTILATION (A/C) OR CONTINUOUS MANDATORY VENTILATION (CMV) A/C or CMV delivers the preset volume or pressure in response to the patient's inspiratory effort, but will initiate the breath if the patient does not do so within a preset amount of time. This mode is used for patients who can initiate a breath but who have weakened respiratory muscles. The patient may need to be sedated to limit the number of spontaneous breaths, as hyperventilation can occur in patients with high respiratory rates.

SYNCHRONOUS INTERMITTENT MANDATORY VENTILATION (SIMV) SIMV delivers the preset volume or pressure and preset respiratory rate while allowing the patient to breathe spontaneously. The vent initiates each breath in synchrony with the patient's breaths. SIMV is used as a primary mode of ventilation as well as a weaning mode. (During weaning, the preset rate is gradually reduced, allowing the patient to slowly regain breathing on their own.) The disadvantage of this mode is that it may increase the effort of breathing and cause respiratory muscle fatigue. (Breathing spontaneously through ventilator tubing has been compared to breathing through a straw.)

POSITIVE-END EXPIRATORY PRESSURE (PEEP) PEEP is positive pressure that is applied by the ventilator at the end of expiration. This mode does not deliver breaths but is used as an adjunct to CV, A/C, and SIMV to improve oxygenation by opening collapsed alveoli at the end of expiration. Complications from the increased pressure can include decreased cardiac output, lung rupture, and increased intracranial pressure.

CONSTANT POSITIVE AIRWAY PRESSURE (CPAP) CPAP is similar to PEEP, except that it works only for patients who are breathing spontaneously. The effect of CPAP (and PEEP) is compared to inflating a balloon but not letting it completely deflate before inflating it again. The second inflation is easier to perform because resistance is decreased. CPAP can also be administered using a mask and CPAP machine for patients who do not require mechanical ventilation but who need respiratory support (for example, patients with sleep apnea).

PRESSURE SUPPORT VENTILATION (PSV) PS is preset pressure which augments the patient's spontaneous inspiration effort and decreases the work of breathing. The patient completely controls the respiratory rate and tidal volume. PS is used for patients with a stable respiratory status and is often used with SIMV during weaning.

INDEPENDENT LUNG VENTILATION (ILV) This method is used to ventilate each lung separately in patients with unilateral lung disease or a different disease process in each lung. It requires a double-lumen endotracheal tube and two ventilators. Sedation and pharmacologic **paralysis** are used to facilitate optimal ventilation and increase comfort for the patient on whom this method is used.

HIGH FREQUENCY VENTILATION (HFV) HFV delivers a small amount of gas at a rapid rate (as much as 60-100 breaths per minute). This is used when conventional mechanical ventilation would compromise hemodynamic stability, during short-term procedures, or for patients who are at high risk for lung rupture. Sedation and/or pharmacologic paralysis are required.

INVERSE RATIO VENTILATION (IRV) The normal inspiratory:expiratory ratio is 1:2, but this is reversed during IRV to 2:1 or greater (the maximum is 4:1). This method is used for patients who are still hypoxic, even with the use of PEEP. Longer inspiratory time increases the amount of air in the lungs at the end of expiration (the functional residual capacity) and improves oxygenation by reexpanding collapsed alveoli. The shorter expiratory time prevents the alveoli from collapsing again. This method requires sedation and therapeutic paralysis because it is very uncomfortable for the patient.

Ventilator settings

Ventilator settings are ordered by a physician and are individualized for the patient. Ventilators are designed to monitor most components of the patient's respiratory status. Various alarms and parameters can be set to warn healthcare providers that the patient is having difficulty with the settings.

RESPIRATORY RATE The respiratory rate is the number of breaths the ventilator will deliver to the patient over a specific time period. The respiratory rate parameters are set above and below this number, and an alarm will sound if the patient's actual rate is outside the desired range.

TIDAL VOLUME Tidal volume is the volume of gas the ventilator will deliver to the patient with each breath. The usual setting is 5-15 cc/kg. The tidal volume parameters are set above and below this number and an alarm sounds if the patient's actual tidal volume is outside the desired range. This is especially helpful if the patient is breathing spontaneously between ventilator-delivered breaths since the patient's own tidal volume can be compared with the desired tidal volume delivered by the ventilator.

OXYGEN CONCENTRATION (FIO_2) Oxygen concentration is the amount of oxygen delivered to the patient. It can range from 21% (room air) to 100%.

INSPIRATORY:EXPIRATORY (I:E) RATIO As discussed above, the I:E ratio is normally 1:2 or 1:1.5, unless inverse ratio ventilation is desired.

PRESSURE LIMIT Pressure limit regulates the amount of pressure the volume-cycled ventilator can generate to deliver the preset tidal volume. The usual setting is 10-20 cm H_2O above the patient's peak inspiratory pressure. If this limit is reached the ventilator stops the breath and alarms. This is often an indication that the patient's airway is obstructed with mucus and is usually resolved with suctioning. It can also be caused by the patient coughing, biting on the endotracheal tube, breathing against the ventilator, or by a kink in the ventilator tubing.

FLOW RATE Flow rate is the speed with which the tidal volume is delivered. The usual setting is 40-100 liters per minute.

SENSITIVITY/TRIGGER Sensitivity determines the amount of effort required by the patient to initiate inspiration. It can be set to be triggered by pressure or by flow.

SIGH The ventilator can be programmed to deliver an occasional sigh with a larger tidal volume. This prevents collapse of the alveoli (atelectasis) that can result from the patient constantly inspiring the same volume of gas.

Operation

Many ventilators are now computerized and have a user-friendly control panel. To activate the various modes, settings, and alarms, the appropriate key need only be pressed. There are windows on the face panel which show settings and the alarm values. Some ventilators have dials instead of computerized keys, e. g., the smaller, portable ventilators used for transporting patients.

The ventilator tubing simply attaches to the ventilator on one end and to the patient's artificial airway on the other. Most ventilators have clamps that prevent the tubing from draping across the patient. However, there should be enough slack so that the artificial airway isn't accidentally pulled out if the patient turns.

Ventilators are electrical equipment so they must be plugged in. They do have battery back up, but this is not designed for long-term use. It should be ensured that they are plugged into an outlet that will receive generator power if there is an electrical power outage. Ventilators are a method of life-support. If the ventilator should stop working, the patient's life will be in jeopardy. There should be a bag-valve-mask device at the bedside of every patient receiving mechanical ventilation so they can be manually ventilated if needed.

Maintenance

When mechanical ventilation is initiated, the ventilator goes through a self-test to ensure it is working properly. The ventilator tubing should be changed every 24 hours and another self-test run afterwards. The bacteria filters should be checked for occlusions or tears and the water traps and filters should be checked for condensation or contaminants. These should be emptied and cleaned every 24 hours and as needed.

Caregiver concerns

The respiratory therapist is generally the person who sets up the ventilator, does the daily check described above, and changes the ventilator settings based on the physician's orders. The nurse is responsible for monitoring the alarms and the patient's respiratory status. The nurse is also responsible for notifying the respiratory therapist when mechanical problems occur with the ventilator and when there are new physician orders requiring changes in the settings or the alarm parameters. The physician is responsible for keeping track of the patient's status on the current ventilator settings and changing them when necessary.

Training

Training for using and maintaining ventilators is often done via hands-on methods. Critical care nurses usually have a small amount of class time during which they learn the ventilator modes and settings. They then apply this knowledge while working with patients on the unit under the supervision of a nurse preceptor. This preceptorship usually lasts about six weeks (depending upon the nurse's prior experience) and includes all aspects of critical care. Nurses often learn the most from the respiratory therapists, since ventilator management is their specialty.

KEY TERMS

Alveoli—Saclike structures in the lungs where oxygen and carbon dioxide exchange takes place.

Bag-valve-mask device—Device consisting of a manually compressible bag containing oxygen and a one-way valve and mask that fits over the mouth and nose of the patient.

Endotracheal tube—Tube inserted into the trachea via either the oral or nasal cavity for the purpose of providing a secure airway.

Hemodynamic stability—Stability of blood circulation, including cardiac function and peripheral vascular physiology.

Hypoxic—Abnormal deficiency of oxygen in the arterial blood.

Intracranial pressure—The amount of pressure exerted inside the skull by brain tissue, blood, and cerebral-spinal fluid.

Peak inspiratory pressure—The pressure in the lungs at the end of inspiration.

Pharmacologically paralyzed—Short-term paralysis induced by medications for a therapeutic purpose.

Tracheostomy tube—Surgically created opening in the trachea for the purpose of providing a secure airway. This is used when the patient requires long-term ventilatory assistance.

Weaning—The process of gradually tapering mechanical ventilation and allowing the patient to resume breathing on their own.

Respiratory therapists complete an educational program that specifically focuses on respiratory diseases, and equipment and treatments used to manage those diseases. During orientation to a new job, they work under the supervision of an experienced respiratory therapist to learn how to maintain and manage the ventilators used by that particular institution. Written resources from the company that produced the ventilators are usually kept in the respiratory therapy department for reference.

Physicians generally do not manage the equipment aspect of the ventilator. They do, however, manage the relation of the ventilator settings to the patient's condition. They gain this knowledge of physiology during medical school and residency.

Abby Wojahn R.N., B.S.N., C.C.R.N.

Ventricular fibrillation

Definition

Ventricular fibrillation is a very rapid, uncoordinated, ineffective series of contractions throughout the lower chambers of the heart. Unless stopped, these chaotic impulses are fatal.

Description

When the ventricles begin to quiver and do not employ coordinated contractions, the heart is said to be fibrillating. In this condition the ventricles cannot pump blood from the heart. Ventricular fibrillation (V-fib) is the worst kind of abnormal heart rhythm, and is a form of cardiac arrest. It involves the pumping of the lower chambers of the heart, while atrial fibrillation involves the upper chambers.

Causes and symptoms

Ventricular fibrillation often is associated with acute ischemic events (**ischemia** involves the deprivation of oxygenated blood to an area of tissue), and with chronic ischemic **heart disease**. It is frequently seen immediately following a **heart attack**. It also may develop during hypoxia, atrial fibrillation, or improper grounding of electrical devices. An extremely low level of potassium in the blood also can cause ventricular fibrillation.

The first, and usually the only, symptom of V-fib is sudden unconsciousness.

Diagnosis

When an individual suddenly collapses, the possibility of ventricular fibrillation should be considered immediately. A quick assessment usually shows no pulse or heartbeat. The diagnosis of ventricular fibrillation is confirmed with an electrocardiogram.

Treatment

Basic life support with standard **cardiopulmonary resuscitation (CPR)** must be started within a few minutes, followed as soon as possible with **cardioversion**. Cardioversion is an electric shock delivered to the heart to stop the fibrillating. Early defibrillation is the key to survival. If left untreated, irreversible brain damage, due to lack of oxygen to the brain, occurs after about five minutes. After the heart resumes its normal rhythm, medications are given to help maintain the rhythm.

KEY TERMS

Atrial fibrillation—A condition in which the upper chambers of the heart quiver instead of contracting effectively

Cardiopulmonary resuscitation (CPR)—Using rescue breathing and chest compressions to help a person whose breathing and heartbeat have stopped

Cardioversion—An electrical shock delivered to the heart to restore a normal rhythm

Electrocardiogram—A visual representation of the heart beat

Heart failure—A term used when the heart is unable to pump enough blood to supply the needs of the body

Hypoxia—Insufficient oxygen in the cells of the body

Ischemic—Insufficient blood reaching the tissues

Research continues into methods to deliver defibrillation as soon as possible to those experiencing ventricular fibrillation. One of the studies addressed in 2003 researched various clinical trials that implanted defibrillators into patients to prevent sudden cardiac **death**. The devices worked in many instances but more proof of their success was needed for widespread use.

Prognosis

Early and effective **CPR** may provide the time necessary for medical personnel to arrive with a defibrillator. If a defibrillator is able to promptly restore a normal rhythm, up to 25% of victims are able to leave the hospital without evidence of brain damage.

If ventricular fibrillation occurs in the hospital in conjunction with a heart attack, defibrillation has a 95% success rate. If shock and heart failure are present at the time, even with immediate defibrillation, only about 30% of those stricken are successfully restored to a normal heart rate.

Prevention

A healthy lifestyle to reduce the risk of heart diseases that lead to ventricular fibrillation is the best prevention. For people who have experienced an episode of V-fib, an internal cardioverter-defibrillator may prevent further episodes.

Resources

PERIODICALS

Ezekowitz, Justin A., et al. "Implantable Cardioverter Defibrillators in Primary and Secondary Prevention: A Systematic Review of Randomized, Controlled Trials." *Annals of Internal Medicine* January 2002: 445.

ORGANIZATIONS

American Heart Association, 7320 Greenville Ave, Dallas, TX, 75231, (214) 373-6300, http://www.americanheart.org.

Dorothy Elinor Stonely
Teresa G. Odle

Ventricular tachycardia

Definition

Ventricular tachycardia (V-tach) is a rapid heart beat that originates in one of the lower chambers (the ventricles) of the heart. To be classified as tachycardia, the heart rate is usually at least 100 beats per minute.

Description

A rapid heart rate can originate in either the left or right ventricle. Ventricular tachycardia which lasts more than 30 seconds is referred to as sustained ventricular tachycardia. A period of three to five rapid beats is called a salvo, and six beats or more lasting less than 30 seconds is called nonsustained ventricular tachycardia. Rapid ventricular rhythms are more serious than rapid atrial rhythms because they make the heart extremely inefficient. They also tend to cause more severe symptoms, and have a much greater tendency to result in **death**.

Although generally considered to be among the life-threatening abnormal rhythms, harmless forms of sustained V-tach do exist. These occur in people without any structural **heart disease**.

Causes and symptoms

Most ventricular tachycardias are associated with serious heart disease such as coronary artery blockage, **cardiomyopathy**, or valvular heart disease. V-tach is often triggered by an extra beat originating in either the right or left ventricle. It also occurs

KEY TERMS

Atrial—Having to do with the upper chambers of the heart.

Cardiomyopathy—A disease of the heart muscle.

Cardioversion—A electrical shock delivered to the heart to restore a normal rhythm.

Coronary artery—The artery that supplies blood to the heart muscle itself.

Electrocardiogram—A visual representation of the heart beat.

Fibrillation—Rapid, uncoordinated, quivering of the heart.

Palpitations—Uncomfortable feeling of the heart beat in the chest.

Valvular—Having to do with the valves inside the heart.

frequently in connection with a **heart attack**. V-tach commonly occurs within 24 hours of the start of the attack. It must be treated quickly to prevent fibrillation. After 48 to 72 hours of the heart attack, the risk of ventricular tachycardia is small. However, people who have suffered severe damage to the larger anterior wall of the heart have a second danger period, because V-tach often occurs during convalescence from this type of heart attack.

Sustained ventricular tachycardia prevents the ventricles from filling adequately so the heart can not pump normally. This results in loss of **blood pressure**, and can lead to a loss of consciousness and to heart failure.

The individual with V-tach almost always experiences palpitation, though some episodes cause no symptoms at all.

Diagnosis

Diagnosis is easily made with an electrocardiogram.

Treatment

Any episode of ventricular tachycardia that causes symptoms needs to be treated. An episode that lasts more than 30 seconds, even without symptoms, also needs to be treated. Drug therapy can be given intravenously to suppress episodes of V-tach. If blood pressure falls below normal, a person will need electric **cardioversion** ("shock") immediately.

Prognosis

With appropriate drug or surgical treatment, ventricular tachycardia can be controlled in most people.

Prevention

A person susceptible to sustained ventricular tachycardia often has a small abnormal area in the ventricles that is the source of the trigger event. This area can sometimes be surgically removed. If surgery is not an option, and drug therapy is not effective, a device called an automatic cardioverter-defibrillator may be implanted.

ORGANIZATIONS

American Heart Association, 7320 Greenville Ave, Dallas, TX, 75231, (214) 373-6300, http://www.americanheart.org.

Dorothy Elinor Stonely

Veterans Affairs hospital system

Definition

The Veterans Affairs hospital system, formerly known as the Veterans Administration hospital system, operates 153 medical centers, more than 700 community clinics, 136 **nursing homes**, and 43 residential rehabilitation treatment programs in the United States, its territories, and abroad, that provide medical care for veterans of the United States armed forces.

Description

Commonly known as VA hospitals, the Veterans Affairs hospital system is part of the U.S. Department of Veterans Affairs, a cabinet-level agency. There is at least one medical center in each state, the District of Columbia, and Puerto Rico. The VA medical system operates clinics in all states and territories along with a clinic in the Philippines. More than 5.3 million people received care in 2005 in VA health care facilities, a 29% increase from 2001. That number was expected to increase due to the wars in Iraq and Afghanistan that were ongoing as of 2008. Projections are that in 2009, the VA system will treat about 6.8

Total number of U.S. veterans age 65 and over who are enrolled in or receiving health care from the Veterans Health Administration, 1990–2006

Year	VA enrollees	VA patients	Total
		Number in millions	
1990	n/a	0.9	7.9
1991	n/a	0.9	8.3
1992	n/a	1.0	8.7
1993	n/a	1.0	9.0
1994	n/a	1.0	9.2
1995	n/a	1.1	9.4
1996	n/a	1.1	9.7
1997	n/a	1.1	9.8
1998	n/a	1.3	9.9
1999	1.9	1.4	10.0
2000	2.2	1.6	10.0
2001	2.8	1.9	9.9
2002	3.2	2.2	9.8
2003	3.3	2.3	9.7
2004	3.4	2.4	9.5
2005	3.5	2.4	9.3
2006	3.5	2.4	9.2

n/a = designates data not available. Department of Veterans Affairs enrollees are veterans who have signed up to receive health care from the Veterans Health Administration. VA patients are veterans who have received care each year through VHA.

SOURCE: Department of Veterans Affairs, Veteran Population 2004 Version 1.0; Fiscal 2006 Year-end Office of the Assistant Deputy Under Secretary for Health for Policy and Planning Enrollment file linked with August 2007 VHA Vital Status data (including data from VHA, VA, Medicare, and SSA)

(Illustration by GGS Information Services. Cengage Learning, Gale)

million people. It is the largest health care system in the United States. VA medical centers are also at the forefront of medical research in such war-related conditions as Agent Orange exposure, Gulf War syndrome, and post-traumatic stress disorder. Its research extends into conditions that affect the general population, including diabetes and HIV/AIDS. Many VA medical centers are affiliated with university medical schools. For example, the VA Medical Center in La Jolla, California, which serves San Diego County, is located adjacent to the University of California, San Diego's (UCSD) School of Medicine. The VA and UCSD medical centers cooperate in numerous research and treatment ventures. A number of new VA facilities and expansions have been approved or proposed for construction through 2012 across the U.S. Of the system's 153 medical centers (as of early 2008), 12 are in New York, 10 are in California, and six are in Texas.

The first hospital for war veterans was Hand Hospital, established in 1778 in Pittsburgh. Other medical facilities followed, including the Naval Home in Philadelphia (1812), and two facilities in Washington, D.C., Soldier's Home (1853) and St. Elizabeth's Hospital (1855). The Veterans Administration was created in 1930 by consolidating several agencies that administered services for veterans. By 1930, there were 54 VA hospitals. Demand for medical care grew substantially in the 1930s, fueled primarily by an epidemic of **tuberculosis**, and the number of VA hospitals continued to grow. In 1946, the VA's Hines Hospital became the first VA facility to partner with medical schools (Northwestern University and the University of Illinois). By 1946, a year after World War II ended, the VA was operating 97 hospitals with a total bed capacity of 82,241. Another 25 VA hospitals were under construction or planned, along with additions to 11 existing facilities. Despite this, VA hospitals were filled to capacity by the end of 1946 and nearly all hospitals had waiting lists for admission. During 1946 and 1947, 29 new VA hospitals opened, bringing the total to 126.

The 1950s and 1960s brought two wars (Korea and Vietnam) and new challenges to health care for veterans. A special medical issue of the Vietnam War was the health problems that resulted from exposure to Agent Orange. Since 1978, the VA has offered special access to medical care, including physical exams, to Vietnam veterans with Agent Orange health concerns. The VA in 1981 established a special eligibility program which provided free follow-up hospital care to Vietnam veterans with any health problems whose cause was unclear.

By the 1970s, burdened with a growing number of casualties from the Vietnam War, the VA hospital system began to break down. Hospitals were aging and were short of doctors, nurses, and specialists and many lacked up-to-date medical equipment. Many hospitals fell into disrepair and were literally falling apart. Infestations of rodents and cockroaches, and unsanitary conditions were reported at many facilities. The problems prominently came to the attention of the American public when a paralyzed Vietnam veteran, Ron Kovic, ended up in the VA's hospital in the Bronx, New York. He documented the dirty, rat-infested hospital and sub-standard medical care in his best-selling 1976 book, *Born on the Fourth of July*, which was later made into a movie of the same name. Over the course of the next decade, the VA began revitalizing its hospitals and making improvements in its medical staff. To meet the special needs of its increasing number of older veteran patients, the VA in 1975 began to train interdisciplinary teams of health-care specialists. Congress in 1980 authorized Geriatric Research, Education and Clinical Centers (GRECCs) to coordinate in the field of geriatric medicine. Late in the 1980s, VA dedicated resources to serving homeless and chronically mentally ill veterans. It also responded to the growing numbers of patients with HIV/AIDS with special treatment units and special training for medical staffs.

Following Operation Desert Storm in 1991, many veterans returning from Iraq, Kuwait, and other war staging areas, complained of symptoms with no readily identifiable cause. The symptoms included fatigue, skin rash, headache, muscle and joint **pain**, **memory loss** and difficulty concentrating, shortness of breath, sleep problems, gastrointestinal problems, and chest pain. Scientists examining symptoms of the undiagnosed Gulf War illnesses concluded that there was no single disease or illness affecting Gulf veterans. VA nevertheless initiated a number of research studies to determine the health consequences to veterans of military service in the Gulf War. A number of possible causes for the symptoms have been under examination, including chemical and biological warfare agents, as well as smoke from oil well fires, **vaccinations** (such as the anthrax vaccine), infections, chemicals, pesticides, microwaves, and depleted uranium which the U.S. military used in munitions. As of 2008, the cause or causes of Gulf War Syndrome were still being disputed by the military and medical researchers.

In 1997, the Women Veterans Health Program Office was established within the Office of Public Health and Environmental Hazards and the first full-time director of the program was appointed. The VA established eight Comprehensive Women's Health Centers and four Stress Disorder Treatment Centers across the country. Also in 1997, the VA began establishing community-based outpatient clinics across the country to increase access to localized health-care. Since 1998, veterans who served in a combat zone or in comparable hostilities have been eligible for free VA hospital care, outpatient services, and nursing **home care** for two years after leaving active duty for illnesses and injuries that may be the result of their military service.

Viewpoints

In the early 1990s, the care at VA hospitals was so bad that Congress was considering closing the facilities and giving veterans vouchers for care at private hospitals and clinics, according to a Sept. 4, 2006, article in *Time* magazine. Since the mid-1990s, services at VA hospitals improved drastically, and from 2000 to 2005, VA hospitals scored higher than private hospitals on a patient satisfaction survey conducted by the University of Michigan. By 2005, the VA hospital system had become recognized as one of the nation's premier health care systems, with top primary care doctors, specialists, researchers, nurses, and support staff. It also provided state-of-the-art medical care with the latest diagnostic equipment and treatment techniques. In 2005 and 2006, three of the nation's top news magazines, *Time*, *Fortune*, and *U.S. News & World Report* all carried articles lauding the VA hospital system as a leader in care and technology.

KEY TERMS

Agent Orange—A toxic herbicide sprayed by the U.S. military during the Vietnam War to defoliate jungle areas and expose enemy forces.

Geriatric medicine—A field of medicine that specializes in the care and treatment of the elderly.

Gulf War syndrome—A multi-symptom illness of unknown causes that affected veterans of Operation Desert Storm, a war to free Kuwait of Iraqi occupation in 1991.

Post-traumatic stress disorder—A psychological condition affecting people who have suffered severe emotional trauma as a result of an experience such as combat and causing sleep disturbances, flashbacks, anxiety, tiredness, and depression.

Resources

BOOKS

Budahn, P.J. *Veteran's Guide to Benefits*Mechanicsburg, PA: Stackpole Books, 2005.

Committee to Review the Health Effects in Vietnam Veterans of Exposure to Herbicides. *Veterans and Agent Orange: Update 2006*Washington: National Academies Press, 2007.

Lee, Harry, and Edgar Jones. *War and Health: Lessons from the Gulf War*Hoboken, NJ: Wiley, 2007.

Roche, John D. *Veteran's PTSD Handbook: How to File and Collect on Claims for Post-Traumatic Stress Disorder*Dulles, VA: Potomac Books, 2007.

PERIODICALS

Gearon, Christopher. "Military Might: Today's VA Hospitals are Models of Top-Notch Care." *U.S. News & World Report*(July 18, 2005): N/A.

Ritter, Ben. "Viva, VA Care!" *Paraplegia News*(August 2007): 12(3).

Stires, David. "Technology Has Transformed the VA." *Fortune*(May 15, 2006): N/A.

Waller, Douglas. "How Veterans' Hospitals Became the Best in Health Care." *Time*(September 4, 2006): N/A.

Zigmond, Jessica. "Fixing Veterans' Care; Payment, Disability Systems Seen as Key." *Modern Healthcare* (August 6, 2007): 14.

ORGANIZATIONS

Veterans Health Administration, 810 Vermont Ave. N.W., Washington, DC, 20420, (202) 273-5400, (800) 827-1000, http://www.va.gov.

Ken R. Wells

Veterans of Foreign Wars *see* **VFW**

VFW

Definition

The Veterans of Foreign Wars of the United States (VFW) is an advocacy organization for the rights of United States veterans who have fought in wars on foreign soil.

Description

The VFW is an American organization composed of men and women who are current or former members of any of the five branches of the United States military: army, navy, air force, Marine Corps, or coast guard. They must have received a campaign medal for overseas service or meet at least one of the following eligibility criteria:

- received a Combat Infantryman Badge
- received a Combat Medical Badge
- received a Combat Action Ribbon
- received a Korea Defense Service Medal
- received an Air Force Expeditionary Service Ribbon with gold border
- received a Navy SSBN (nuclear ballistic missile submarine) Deterrent Patrol Insignia
- served in Korea for 30 consecutive or 60 non-consecutive days from June 30, 1949 to the present.
- received hostile fire or imminent danger pay

Also, membership requirements include being on active duty, in a reserve component, in the National Guard, or receiving an honorable discharge from the U.S. military. Members must also be U.S. citizens. Current members have served in various overseas military campaigns, including World War II, the Korean War, Vietnam War, Gulf War I (Desert Storm), Gulf War II (Iraqi Freedom), and the Afghanistan War (Enduring Freedom). As of 2008, the VFW had about 2.6 million members in 9,000 posts worldwide. The membership includes various auxiliary groups, most notably the Ladies Auxiliary.

A patriotic tablecloth, Veterans of Foreign Wars banner, gavel and Bible decorate the table inside of VFW Harrison-White Post 5048 in Florence, MS. *(AP Images. Reproduced by permission.)*

History

The VFW was founded in 1899 as the American Veterans of Foreign Service following the Spanish American War of 1898. Many veterans returning from the war's fronts (mainly Cuba and the Philippines) were deeply dissatisfied with the treatment they received by the U.S. government after the war ended. Most wounded veterans received scant medical treatment or were denied medical care and rehabilitation services. Many even had to find and pay for their own transportation to return from the battle front to their homes.

The VFW was the result of the merger of two organizations: the American Veterans of Foreign Service founded in 1899 in Columbus, Ohio, and the Colorado Society of the Army of the Philippines founded the same year in Denver, Colorado. Both were established to fight for the rights of war veterans, but they achieved few successes and suffered many defeats. The two groups merged in 1913 and in 1914 adopted the name Veterans of Foreign Wars of the United States. In 1914, the organization achieved its first major victory when Congress and the president approved a pension bill that provided financial payments to widows of Spanish American War veterans. Also in 1914, the VFW established the Ladies Auxiliary. In the 1920s, the group successfully lobbied for creation of the Veterans Bureau of the U.S. government and formation of veterans affairs committees in the House of Representatives and Senate. In the 1930s, the two greatest achievements of the VFW were lobbying Congress to approve legislation that gave cash bonuses totaling nearly $2 billion to 3.5 million veterans, and nullification of the Economy Act, which had drastically cut veterans benefits during the height of the Great **Depression**. Through the ensuing decades, the VFW continued to fight for the rights of war veterans and expanded its efforts into community outreach programs.

Benefits

Annual membership dues are set by individual posts and are usually $20 to $35. A lifetime membership is available and the cost is on a sliding scale based on age. The lowest fee is $170 for veterans born in 1926 or earlier and the highest fee as of 2008 was $425 for veterans born in 1977 and later. Member benefits include:

- subscription to *VFW Magazine*
- help in obtaining government benefits for veterans
- discounts on prescriptions, computers, hotels, and car rentals
- real estate and mortgage services
- group-rate insurance programs that cover personal accidents, vehicles, long-term care, cancer treatment, senior term life, pets, condominiums, and travel

Activities

The VFW encourages local posts to become active in their communities. In addition, the VFW has four major nationwide service programs:

KEY TERMS

Buddy Poppy—A trademarked artificial red poppy that is distributed by the VFW around Memorial Day.

Junior Reserve Officers' Training Corps (JROTC)—A federal program in American high schools that teaches patriotism and prepares students for military careers.

Political Action Committee (PAC)—A type of political committee that raises and spends money on political candidates and causes.

Term life—A life insurance policy that provides coverage for a specific time period (term), usually five, 10, 20, or 30 years.

- National Veterans Service—Provides full-time advocacy for individual veterans and their families. It employs a staff of veteran service officers who are experts at dealing with the Department of Veterans Affairs.
- National Military Services—Provides help to currently deployed military personnel and their families. Services include family group support activities, pre-paid phone cards to overseas service members, and emergency financial aid.
- National Legislative Service—Lobbys Congress in support of legislation that benefits veterans.
- Youth Development Service—A program that offers scholarships and savings bonds to American students. It also supports the Junior Reserve Officers' Training Corps (JROTC) in high schools and scouting programs.

To many Americans, the VFW is best known for its Buddy Poppy program that it started in 1922. The red artificial poppies are made by disabled and needy veterans and distributed during the Memorial Day weekend each year. Donations from the program raises millions of dollars annually and are used for veterans services, including the VFW National Home for orphans and widows of veterans.

Viewpoints

The VFW considers itself a patriotic organization that is an advocacy group for war veterans. It is generally viewed as a politically conservative group, especially regarding military and foreign affairs. It frequently endorses political candidates and causes. In 1979, it established the VFW Political Action Committee. Besides lobbying Congress in support of veterans' benefits and national defense issues, it contributes money to political campaigns.

Resources

BOOKS

Wolin, Jeffrey. *Inconvenient Stories: Vietnam War Veterans.* Brooklyn, NY: Umbrage Editions, 2007.

PERIODICALS

Blankenship, Janie. "VA Adapts to the Newest Wave of Vets." *VFW Magazine* (September 2006): N/A.

Blankenship, Janie. "VFW Makes a Difference in the Lives of Today's Troops." *VFW Magazine* (January 2007): N/A.

Blankenship, Janie. "VFW Members Offer Assistance to Hurricane Victims." *VFW Magazine* (January 2006): N/A.

"Iraq and Afghanistan Vets: A Dominant Theme at VFW's Convention." *VFW Magazine* (October 2005): N/A.

Pope, Tom. "VFW Rebranding: Deeper List Segments Putting Forward a New Face." *The Non-Profit Times* (February 15, 2007): 1(2).

Urban, Kelly. "VFW Project Helps Keep Troops in Touch." *Tribune-Democrat (Johnstown, PA)* (December 31, 2007): 1.

ORGANIZATIONS

Veterans of Foreign Wars (National Headquarters), 406 W. Thirty-fourth St., Kansas City, MO, 64111, (816) 756-3390, (800) 839-1899, (816) 968-1149, info@vfw.org, http://www.vfw.org.

Veterans of Foreign Wars (Washington, DC Office), VFW Memorial Bldg., 200 Maryland Ave. NE, Washington, DC, 20002, (202) 543-2239, (202) 543-6719, cwells@vfw.org, http://www.vfw.org.

Ken R. Wells

Viagra *see* **Sildenafil citrate**

Viruses

Definition

Viruses are not living things but tiny protein-covered parcels of genetic material (either DNA or RNA) that become active only in the cells of living organisms such as the human body. Viruses are not active in the air or on surfaces. Within a human cell or other host cell, a virus releases its DNA or RNA and infects the cell, then reproduces and spreads rapidly to nearby cells resulting in viral infection.

Description

The only purpose viruses have is to reproduce, which depends on taking over a living organism and inserting their genetic material into its cells. Unlike bacteria, which are living organisms that consume and metabolize nutrients, reproduce, and adapt to their environment, viruses are not organisms and, on their own, do not absorb or metabolize nutrients, move around or reproduce unless they are within the cells of a living organism. Once inside living cells of a host, they use the normal functions of the host cells to carry out instructions programmed in their own viral DNA or RNA, including reproducing themselves and occupying the living organism. Although viruses often infect more than one type of organism, including plants, animals, birds and humans, reactions to the virus by each organism are usually different—it may be harmless in one, while infecting and killing another. Viruses infect different parts of the body and the same virus may also affect different people in different ways, depending on the status of their general health and their **immune system**.

Many viruses infect humans, including: viruses that cause common diseases of childhood such as measles (rubella virus) and chicken pox (herpes zoster virus) among others; viruses that cause the **common cold**, respiratory infections (e.g., **influenza** or flu, respiratory syncytial virus, parainfluenza, rhinovirus, and coronavirus), stomach virus (not the same virus that causes influenza or "flu"), **shingles** (herpes zoster virus), and certain types of sexually-transmitted diseases (e.g., human papilloma virus and genital herpes). HIV (human immunodeficiency virus) is an aggressive virus that has affected the immune system of susceptible individuals worldwide. Senior adults who have chronic disease of any kind (e.g., heart, lung or liver disease and diabetes) or whose immune system is weakened (immunodeficiency) may not able to respond to viruses by developing antibodies against them, placing them at higher risk than younger adults of becoming seriously ill or developing complications from certain common viruses.

Viruses Common in Senior Adults

- Influenza virus (flu)is an acute respiratory infection that is highly contagious with possible life-threatening complications in elderly and immunocompromised adults. It is spread by airborne droplets of virus-containing fluids sneezed or coughed into the atmosphere from the nose and throat of infected individuals. Bacterial infection may follow influenza, leading to pneumonia. Influenza viruses are classified as A, B or C, according to prevalence and the presence of complications. Influenza virus A is most prevalent with greatest likelihood of serious complications such as pneumonia, and has been associated with major epidemics; B is a milder virus and rarely occurs in epidemic proportions; C does not cause typical influenza and has never caused epidemics. An increase in deaths from influenza has been noted since the 1990s due to the aging population. Avian influenza (bird flu) is caused by a strain of influenza A that typically infects wild birds, but has only rarely been detected in humans, usually related to direct contact with an infected bird and never in western countries of the world.

- Common cold virus is a relatively minor viral infection of the upper respiratory tract, including nose and throat. Colds are especially contagious, spreading rapidly between individuals when fluid containing the cold virus is passed from one person to another, either by touch or by inhaling fluid droplets from sneezes and coughs. Adults who catch cold frequently, or have colds that last more than two weeks, may have immune system deficiencies that should be investigated.
- Hepatitis C virus causes inflammation of the liver. Hepatitis C virus (HCV) is acquired from direct contact with the blood of someone who has HCV), either through blood transfusions or blood-contaminated needles. It is not believed to be acquired by casual or sexual contact. At highest risk for infection by hepatitis C are people who received blood transfusions before 1992 when U.S. law began to require all donors, units of blood and blood components to be tested for hepatitis C. Older adults are at high risk because hepatitis C virus can be present in the body for years without producing symptoms and can become chronic before symptoms develop, leading gradually to permanent liver damage, cirrhosis and liver failure.(See Hepatitis.)
- Respiratory Syncytial Virus (RSV)is a common contagious virus among children during the winter season but has also been shown through research in 2003 to be as great a threat to senior adults and those with chronic disease as influenza A. Among approximately 177,500 elderly adults hospitalized each year with flu-like symptoms or related pneumonia, 90% are diagnosed with influenza virus and 78% with RSV infection.
- Herpes zoster virus (Shingles) is a nerve infection caused by the same virus (varicella zoster virus) that causes chickenpox, which becomes reactivated either by stress (not "nervousness"), presence of another illness such as cancer, or a weakened immune system. It develops as a red, blotchy rash on the chest, legs, or another part of the body. Because it is a nerve disorder, pain can be the predominant symptom. It is not related to genital herpes or herpes mouth sores.

Demographics

Elder adults, especially those with chronic disease or immune system dysfunction, are at high risk of infections caused by respiratory viruses such as influenza viruses A and B and respiratory syncytial virus (RSV); 35,000 individuals a year die from influenza A alone and as many as 69,000 individuals in an epidemic year. Each year about 14,000 seniors and other high-risk adults die of RSV. Viruses are identified in 0.3 to 30% of cases of community-acquired **pneumonia** and 50% are over age 60. Up to 40% of all viral **hepatitis** cases are hepatitis C occurring in adults age 50 or older. The U.S. Center for Disease Control (CDC) reports that four million people are infected with hepatitis C virus and 2.7 million have chronic infection. Shingles (herpes zoster) can affect anyone who has had chickenpox, but occurs most frequently in senior adults over age 60, resulting in over 500,000 cases each year in the United States.

Causes and symptoms

All virus infections are caused by the presence of a specific virus in the cells of the body. Most respiratory viruses and hepatitis C are spread by direct contact with individuals who already have the virus or contact with their body fluids which contain virus-infected cells. Herpes zoster is caused by reactivation of the chickenpox virus in a period of illness or **stress**.

The common symptoms of influenza virus are fever and chills, headache, body aches and pains, weakness, sore throat and nasal congestion, dry cough, and loss of appetite. Some individuals may have difficulty breathing, reduced levels of oxygen or chest noises (rales or wheezing). Symptoms of RSV are similar to symptoms of a bad cold at first, but commonly progresses to bronchiolitis and pneumonia in older individuals with chronic disease or immunodeficiency. The common cold will begin with nose and throat symptoms, including congestion and mucus production, but is seldom accompanied by fever, with symptoms clearing in a week or two.

Stomach flu symptoms include nausea, vomiting and **diarrhea** for a 24-hour period. Stomach flu virus is not related to the influenza virus that causes respiratory illness.

People with chronic hepatitis C may have no symptoms at all for years, but typical flu-like symptoms or skin rashes can appear suddenly. Characteristic symptoms of hepatitis are similar to flu symptoms, including fever, fatigue, weakness, nausea, vomiting, loss of appetite, abdominal disturbances, diarrhea and aching muscles and joints. Yellowing of the skin, eyes and urine may also occur in some individuals.

Shingles has a characteristic red, blotchy rash with eventual blister-like sores. It is accompanied by intense **pain** as the virus moves along affected nerves to get to the skin surface.

Diagnosis

Physicians diagnose viruses such as influenza or RSV by comparing the affected individual's symptoms to specific symptoms prevalent in the community where the viral infection has spread. Laboratory tests are seldom used, however chest x-rays may be taken to detect possible pneumonia in individuals with influenza-like symptoms. Cell cultures can be done to identify influenza; however, because this type of testing is slow to produce definitive results, it is not often used except to confirm the identity of the virus causing a community-wide infection. Tests for antibodies against RSV found in human serum are available and often performed to distinguish RSV from influenza A. Hepatitis C virus can be identified in the laboratory and a home testing kit is also available to detect presence of the virus even before symptoms appear. Herpes zoster or shingles is diagnosed by the presence of characteristic sores and associated pain.

Treatment

Viruses are difficult to treat because they adapt within host cells and change their DNA/RNA characteristics (gene mutation) before they attack other individuals, always developing new strains so their activity can not be effectively stopped by antibodies developed from prior virus infections. **Antibiotics** are not prescribed for viruses because they only act against bacteria; however, **bacterial infections** such as pneumonia that result from virus infections will be treated with antibiotics. Typical treatment for influenza is to let it run its course; doctors advise staying in bed, drinking plenty of fluids and taking **aspirin** or acetominophen to relieve fever and body aches. Vaccines are available against certain viruses, including influenza type A, which is recommended by most physicians for senior adults or individuals with compromised immune function. No vaccine is yet available for RSV but it is a high priority among researchers. Some adults with RSV may need **oxygen therapy**, and severe disease in immuno-compromised patients may be treated with intravenous immune globulin (IGIV) containing RSV-neutralizing antibodies.

Antiviral drugs approved by the FDA are available but are not prescribed routinely for influenza and other common viruses. Antiviral drugs such as amantadine and rimantadine, which reduce penetration of cells by the virus, may be used in high-risk individuals but resistance develops quickly, making the drugs ineffective. The main clinical benefit of antiviral drugs is slight reduction of symptom duration.

Hepatitis C is treated with bed rest, nutritious food, drinking a lot of water to flush the body and avoiding alcohol or medications that may affect the liver. Oral anti-viral drugs may be given to some individuals. Recovery can be successful although individuals compromised by another chronic disease or a weakened immune system may develop chronic hepatitis C infection and complications leading to **cirrhosis** and liver failure.

The skin rash of shingles is sometimes treated with acyclovir or cortisone taken orally to treat underlying nerve inflammation. Over-the-counter pain killers such as **acetaminophen** may be taken and sometimes stronger pain medications will be prescribed. Patients are advised not to use skin medications or to open the sores; white vinegar in warm water is recommended for gently washing affected areas. When skin eruptions clear up and pain persists, a cream (Zostrix) can be used on painful areas.

Nutrition/Dietetic concerns

Natural, antiviral neutraceuticals and immune system boosters are available that can shorten duration and severity of viral illness, including:

QUESTIONS TO ASK YOUR DOCTOR

- Is my condition caused by a virus? Which virus?
- What can I do to recover?
- How can I avoid viruses?
- Am I at greater than average risk for viral infection? Why?

- DHEA, an adrenal hormone with antiviral and immune-boosting benefits.
- Melatonin, a pineal hormone shown to enhance immune system function.
- Sambucol, black elderberry extract shown in studies to have antiviral activity aginst strains of influenza virus.
- Lactoferrin, a component of whey (non-fat portion of milk) shown to have antiviral, antimicrobial effects as well as ability to enhance immune function.
- Echinacea, known for its immune system boosting properties.
- Garlic, with active component allicin, offers antifungal, antibacterial and antiviral activity with beneficial effects on immune system function.

Prognosis

Most people recover fully from influenza or other respiratory viruses within one to two weeks but viral respiratory illness and related pneumonia can result in serious complications and **death** in high-risk older adults with chronic disease or immune system dysfunction. Viral infections may develop more easily in individuals who do not have full immune response to fight the causative virus. Lack of immune response by the individual may lead to systemic infection, sepsis and death.

Some individuals who have the hepatitis C virus from prior transfusion never develop liver inflammation. Other individuals may develop chronic hepatitis C and progressive liver disease that may lead to cirrhosis, liver failure, transplantation or death.

Most individuals recover within several weeks from the skin eruptions of shingles with no serious consequences. However, pain can continue for up to six months because nerves heal extremely slowly.

Prevention

Annual vaccination against influenza virus is recommended for high-risk groups such as senior adults over age 65, people with chronic disease and reduced immune system function. Researchers and physicians, however, vary in their opinions about the effectiveness of vaccines as protection against influenza virus in vulnerable populations. Individuals should depend on the advice of their own physician. No vaccine is yet available for RSV infection.

Washing hands is still an important preventive method against airborne viruses. Although viruses don't live long on surfaces, nose and throat secretions from infected people contain virus-infected cells that can live for up to 24 hours on door knobs, toilet seats, glassware, telephones, cell phones and other surfaces. Touching the live virus and then placing fingers in the mouth or nose can transmit the viral disease. Infectious disease experts say that washing hands frequently can help prevent acquiring respiratory viral infection such as influenza and RSV.

Individuals at greater risk for infection should obtain good **nutrition** with fresh, whole foods, regular sleep and regular **exercise** to help their immune systems generate cells needed for immune response. Besides practicing good hygiene, individuals with known immune deficiency must reduce the threat of viral infection by avoiding crowds and contact with friends, family members or others who have viral infections, including colds, flu and other viral respiratory infections.

KEY TERMS

DNA—An important genetic determinant, deoxyribonucleic acid (DNA) is found in nuclei of human and plant cells, functioning as the reproducing component of chromosomes, controlling hereditary characteristics; also present in viruses.

genetics—The science of biologic inheritance and the transmission of traits of a single organism through possession of specific genes, which are the units of heredity.

gene mutation—Changes in a gene that may change the way it expresses inherited traits in an organism.

immunodeficiency—Describing the lack of basic functioning of the immune system designed to ward off disease.

RNA—An important genetic determinant, ribonucleic acid (RNA) is found in nuclei of human and plant cells and functions as a reproducing component of chromosomes, controlling hereditary characteristics; also present in viruses.

Caregiver concerns

Caregivers should protect themselves and others in the household while caring for senior adults with contagious viral infection, including washing hands frequently, wearing a protective face mask, and obtaining vaccination if available.

Individuals with chronic disease or whose immune system functioning is reduced should be protected from exposure to viral infection by avoiding crowds and contact with other individuals who may have viral infections, particularly influenza or respiratory infections. Good hygiene should be practiced, including frequent and thorough hand washing.

Resources

BOOKS

"Influenza."*The Merck Manual of Diagnosis and Therapy,* Section 14. R.S. Porter, ed. White House Station, NJ: Merck Research Laboratories, 2007.

"Chronic Hepatitis."*The Merck Manual of Diagnosis and Therapy,*Section 16. R.S. Porter, ed. White House Station, NJ: Merck Research Laboratories, 2007.

"Influenza virus."*Disease Prevention and Treatment.*Expanded 4th ed. M. Segala, Ed. Ft. Lauderdale, FL: Life Extension Foundation; 2003, 1049-1054.

PERIODICALS

Thompson WW, Shay DK, Weintraub E et al. "Mortality Associated with Influenza and Respiratory Syncytial Virus in the United States." *Journal of the American Medical Association.*289(2); 2003.

Falsey A. "Community-Acquired Viral Pneumonia."*Clinics in Geriatric Medicine 23(3); 2007.*

OTHER

"Respiratory Syncytial Virus May Kill as Many Elderly as Flu." *Senior Journal: Senior Citizens Information and News.*Seniorjournal.com, 2003. Available at www.seniorjournal.com/NEWS/Health/6-01-13-RespiratorySyncytialVirus.htm. Accessed March 16, 2008.

"Respiratory Syncytial Virus." *Centers for Disease Control and Prevention.*Available at www.cdc.gov/ncidod/dvrd/revb/respiratory/rsvfeat.htm. Updated Jan. 2005. Accessed March 17, 2008.

Hecht F."Shingles (Herpes Zoster)."*Medicine Net.*Updated March 7, 2008. Available at www.medicinenet.com/. Accessed March 17, 2008.

ORGANIZATIONS

National Institute of Allergy and Infectious Diseases (NIAID), 6610 Rockledge Drive MSC 6612, Bethesda, MD, 301-496-5717, 866-284-4107, 301-402-3573, www3.niaid.nih.gov.

L. Lee Culvert

Vision disorders

Definition

Vision disorders in seniors refer to a group of eye diseases or disorders that cause vision impairment. Deterioration or loss of eyesight is a major problem for seniors as it can interfere with activities of daily living (ADLs) and be a risk factor for **depression**.

Description

The four most common eye disorders in seniors are (in alphabetical order) **age-related macular degeneration** (AMD), cataract, **diabetic retinopathy**, and **glaucoma**.

Age-related macular degeneration

Age-related macular degeneration (AMD) is the single most common cause of vision loss in seniors. It is a disorder of the macula, the central portion of the light-sensitive retina at the back of the eye. The macula is the part of the retina where one's central vision is sharpest.

There are two basic forms of AMD, wet (or exudative) and dry (or atrophic). About 90 percent of seniors diagnosed with AMD have the dry form, which accounts for only 20 percent of cases of blindness caused by AMD. The 10 percent of seniors diagnosed with wet AMD account for 80 to 90 percent of cases of total vision loss caused by the disorder.

Cataract

Cataract is an eye disorder that develops when the lens of the eye develops cloudy or opaque spots, in most cases after age 40. **Cataracts** are classified according to their location within the lens. Nuclear cataracts develop in the center of the lens; cortical cataracts develop along the sides of the lens; and posterior subcortical cataracts form in the central part of the lens on the posterior lens capsule.

Diabetic retinopathy

Diabetic retinopathy is an eye disorder that develops in seniors who have had diabetes for five years or longer. It accounts for almost 7 percent of cases of blindness in the United States. There are two major types of diabetic retinopathy, proliferative and nonproliferative. Nonproliferative diabetic retinopathy (NPDR) is often the first stage of the disorder. In this type, tiny blood vessels in the retina can leak or become blocked. The patient may not notice any changes in his or her vision; on the other hand, fluid leaking from the broken vessels may cause swelling of the macula and blurring of vision. NPDR can progress to proliferative diabetic retinopathy (PDR), as the lack of oxygen supply to the retina causes new blood vessels to form (proliferate) alongside the retina. These new vessels may bleed, cloud vision, or

Prevalence of cataract, Age-Related Macular Degeneration (AMD), and open-angle glaucoma among adults 40 years and older in the United States

Age Years	Cataract Persons	Cataract (%)	Advanced AMD Persons	Advanced AMD (%)	Intermediate AMD Persons	Intermediate AMD (%)	Glaucoma Persons	Glaucoma (%)
40–49	1,046,000	2.5%	20,000	0.1%	851,000	2.0%	290,000	0.7%
50–59	2,123,000	6.8%	113,000	0.4%	1,053,000	3.4%	318,000	1.0%
60–69	4,061,000	20.0%	147,000	0.7%	1,294,000	6.4%	369,000	1.8%
70–79	6,973,000	42.8%	388,000	2.4%	1,949,000	12.0%	530,000	3.9%
≥80	6,272,000	68.3%	1,081,000	11.8%	2,164,000	23.6%	711,000	7.7%
Total	**20,475,000**	**17.2%**	**1,749,000**	**1.5%**	**7,311,000**	**6.1%**	**2,218,000**	**1.9%**

SOURCE: Adapted from *Archives of Ophthalmology, Vol. 122, April 2004*

(Illustration by GGS Information Services. Cengage Learning, Gale)

cause the retina to pull away from underlying tissue (**retinal detachment**).

Glaucoma

Glaucoma is an eye disorder resulting from destruction of the cells in the optic nerve caused (in most cases) by increased intraocular pressure or IOP. Two other classic signs of glaucoma are cupping of the optic disc and loss of the visual field. There are two major types of glaucoma, open-angle and closed-angle. These terms refer to the angle inside the eye where the cornea (the clear curved structure at the front of the eye where light enters the eye) and the iris (the colored part of the eye) meet. In a normal eye, fluid from a chamber at the front of the eye flows through a meshwork of tissue in this angle to nourish the tissues of the eye. If the flow of fluid through the meshwork becomes too slow, pressure inside the eye builds up. If the optic nerve is not able to tolerate the increased pressure, its cells begin to die. This condition is called open-angle glaucoma and accounts for about 80 percent of cases of glaucoma.

In closed-angle glaucoma, which is a less common form, the edge of the iris brushes against the lens and completely closes off the chamber at the front of the eye. Fluid backs up behind the meshwork in the angle and can cause irreversible damage to the eye within 48 to 72 hours. Closed-angle glaucoma is a medical emergency; the patient needs to see an ophthalmologist (doctor who specializes in eye disorders) as soon as possible.

Demographics

Approximately one senior in every three has some eye disorder involving partial or total loss of vision by age 65. Age is considered an independent factor for vision loss in seniors; for this reason, all seniors should be screened for vision problems at least once a year. About 1 million Americans over the age of 40 are blind as of 2008; those who are considered visually impaired number about 3.5 million.

In general, blacks and Hispanics are at increased risk of age-related eye disorders. Alaska has the lowest percentage of visually impaired seniors, while North Dakota has the highest. The rate of eye disorders in all races and ethnic groups increases rapidly after age 75.

The demographics of specific vision disorders are as follows:

- AMD: About 1.6 million Americans over age 40 have a late form of either wet or dry AMD. Black women are at slightly greater risk than black men.
- Cataract: One in six Americans over the age of 40 has a cataract in one or both eyes; more than half of seniors over 80 have cataracts. Women are at slightly greater risk than men for cataract formation.
- Diabetic retinopathy: The risk of diabetic retinopathy increases the longer a person has diabetes. Twenty years after diagnosis, almost all adults with type 1 diabetes and more than 60 percent with type 2 diabetes have some degree of diabetic retinopathy. As of early 2008, about 5.3 million adults in the United States are affected by diabetic retinopathy.
- Glaucoma: About 1 in 200 adults under the age of 50 and as many as 1 in 10 over the age of 80 have some form of glaucoma. With regard to open-angle glaucoma, blacks over the age of 40, Hispanics over the age of 60, and people with a family history of glaucoma are at increased risk. Blacks in the United States are five times as likely as Caucasians to develop open-angle glaucoma. Women, persons

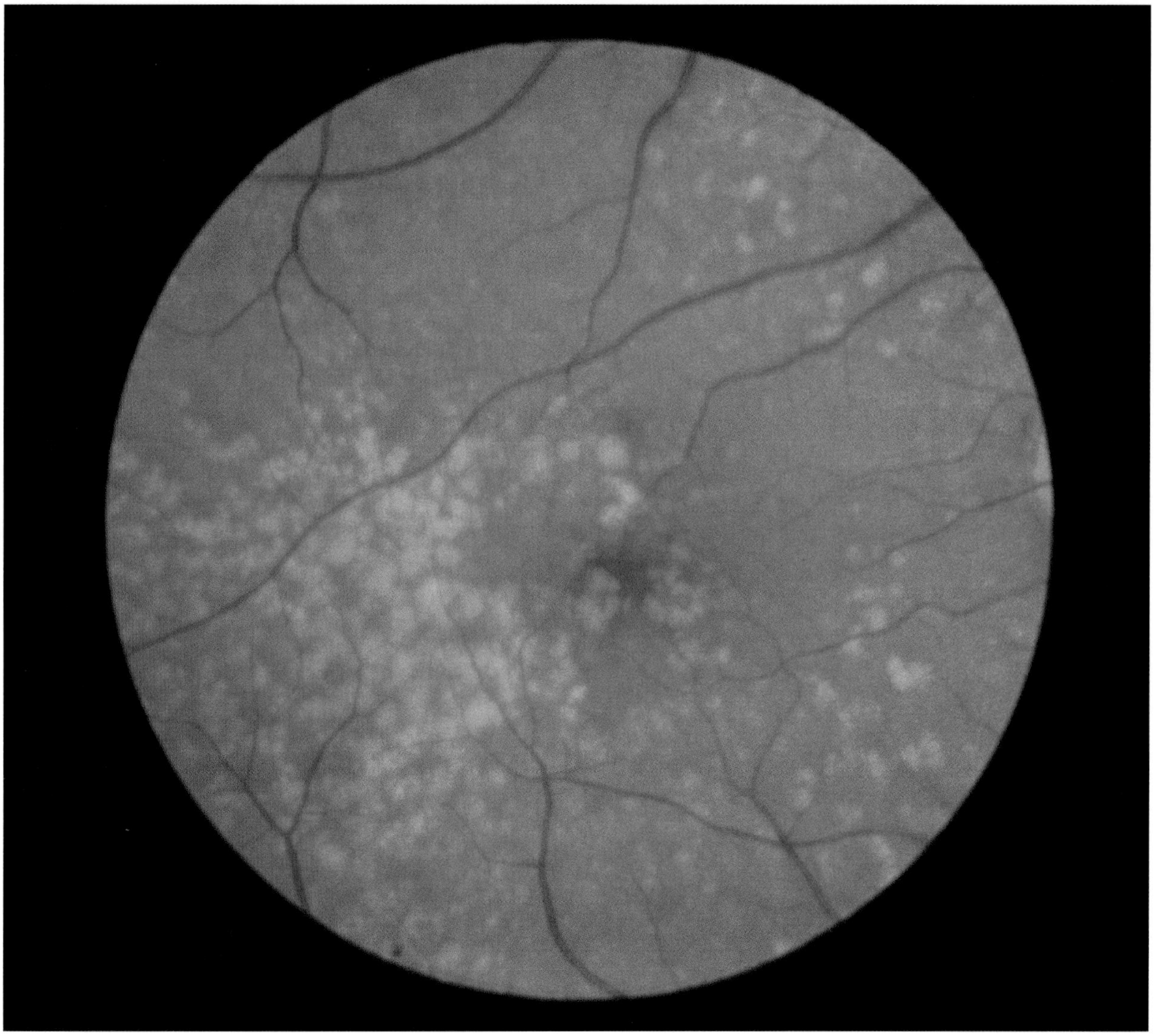

Macular degeneration. *(Paul Parker / Photo Researchers, Inc. Reproduced by permission.)*

of Chinese descent, Eskimos, and people who are farsighted have an increased risk of closed-angle glaucoma.

Causes and symptoms

Causes

The causes of vision disorders in seniors vary:

- AMD: Dry AMD is caused by the buildup of fatty deposits underneath the cells in the retina that sense light. The layer of supportive cells directly under the retina may also start to break down. Wet AMD develops when new tiny blood vessels form underneath the retina, leaking fluid or breaking open and causing scarring of the retina. It is not yet known what triggers the processes leading to either wet or dry AMD; however, risk factors for the disorder include Caucasian race; a history of cigarette smoking; and variations in a specific gene located at chromosome 1q31.
- Cataract: Cataract is caused by the formation of cloudy or opaque spots in the crystalline lens of the eye. Although some children are born with cataracts, in most cases cataracts develop as a result of exposure to ultraviolet light from the sun or from exposure to other forms of radiation. Other risk factors for cataract formation include malnutrition, smoking, alcoholism, treatment with corticosteroid medications, or a history of eye surgery or trauma to the eye.

- Diabetic retinopathy: Diabetic retinopathy is caused by the swelling and breaking of tiny blood vessels in the retina of the eye due to weakness of the walls of these blood vessels. This weakness is caused by high blood sugar levels—which is why it is critical for people diagnosed with diabetes to control their blood sugar.
- Glaucoma: Glaucoma is caused by the buildup of fluid in the interior of the eye resulting from slowed or blocked passage of fluid between the structures in the front of the eye. The increase in intraocular pressure (IOP) can cause irreversible damage to the cells in the optic nerve. The vulnerability of the nerve to increased IOP varies from person to person, however, and is thought to be influenced by genetic factors. Some people can have an increase in IOP without developing glaucoma.

Symptoms

The symptoms of specific vision disorders are as follows:

- AMD: Blurred vision, usually in both eyes; dark areas in the central part of the visual field; distortion of letters or images; difficulty reading. Dry AMD typically develops gradually, while wet AMD is more likely to develop rapidly.
- Cataract: Blurred vision in either one or both eyes; glare; painless; seeing double in the eye that has the cataract.
- Diabetic retinopathy: Blurred vision; floaters; loss of portions of the visual field; poor night vision.
- Glaucoma: Shrinking or narrowing of the visual field; blurred vision (in advanced glaucoma). Patients with open-angle glaucoma may not notice any changes in vision until the disorder is advanced; then they may notice that they are gradually less able to see objects out of the corner of their eye or that they are losing their side vision. Patients with closed-angle glaucoma, however, may become severely nauseated and headachy within hours of the angle closure as well as have blurred vision and pain or redness in the affected eye. Another common symptom of closed-angle glaucoma is seeing halos around lights.

Diagnosis

All seniors should have an **eye examination** that involves dilation at least once a year (twice a year if the senior has been diagnosed with diabetes). Dilation involves the use of eye drops that cause the pupil of the eye to open wider than usual; it allows the doctor to examine the retina and the optic nerve at the back of the eye for signs of disease.

In addition to dilating the eye, the doctor will use the following tests or techniques:

- Visual acuity test. This test involves asking the senior to read an eye chart to determine how well he or she can see at various distances.
- Visual field test. The examiner asks the patient to close one eye; then moves his or her hand to one side, moves it back toward the patient, and asks when the patient can see the hand again. This test evaluates the loss of side vision.
- Tonometry. This test measures IOP. Older types of tonometry required the application of a local anesthetic to the eye followed by the use of a probe or pressure sensor that had to make direct contact with the cornea. Newer devices can measure IOP through the eyelid or by using an air puff.
- Slit lamp examination. The slit lamp is a device that contains a high-intensity light source that can be concentrated into a narrow beam or slit. It can be used to examine the structures in the front of the eye to check for cataracts, or used after dilation to examine the retina and the optic nerve.
- Gonioscopy. The gonioscope is a device containing a mirror that is used together with a slit lamp to measure the angle between the cornea and the iris in the front of the eye. This test is done to check for glaucoma.

Treatment

Treatment varies depending on the specific disorder:

- AMD: There is no generally accepted treatment for dry AMD as of the early 2000s, although quitting smoking helps to slow the progress of the disease in smokers. Wet AMD is treated with laser therapy to stop the development of new blood vessels. Other approaches that have been tried include low-level radiation therapy or transplanting a new retina from a tissue donor.
- Cataract: Patients with small and slow-developing cataracts may not need surgery for some years and usually benefit from a new eyeglass prescription. Surgery is the preferred treatment for cataracts that are large enough to interfere with driving, reading, and other daily activities. About 98 percent of surgical procedures for cataracts in the United States involve removal of the natural lens of the eye and replacing it with a clear plastic lens.

- Diabetic retinopathy: Photocoagulation (destruction of leaking blood vessels) with a laser benefits about 50 percent of patients with diabetic retinopathy. In cases of retinal detachment or clouding of the fluid inside the eye, a surgical procedure called a vitrectomy can be performed. In this procedure the surgeon removes the vitreous humor (a clear gel-like substance that lies between the lens of the eye and the retina) and replaces it with a sterile fluid. In addition to surgery, patients with diabetic retinopathy are usually treated with medications to control high blood pressure, which can make the eye disorder worse.
- Glaucoma: Open-angle glaucoma is treated with medications to lower the IOP; with laser surgery or conventional surgery to create a new opening for fluid to move through the eye; or by a combination of these approaches. Closed-angle glaucoma is treated with drugs in the emergency room to lower the IOP until an ophthalmologist can perform surgery on the eye. The most common procedure involves surgical removal of part of the iris in order to allow fluid pressure to equalize on both sides of the iris. This surgery is usually done with a laser as of 2008.

Nutrition/Dietetic concerns

Good **nutrition** is as important to the health of the eyes as to other parts of the body. With regard to AMD, there is some evidence that antioxidant vitamin supplements, particularly carotenoids (a group of nutrients found in carrots, orange juice, squash, egg yolk, spinach, mango, and other fruits and vegetables), may protect the health of the retina. With regard to diabetic retinopathy, careful attention to blood sugar levels can slow the progress of the disorder.

Therapy

Therapy for age-related eye disorders may involve medications, surgery, laser treatment, corrective lenses, low-grade radiation therapy, or a combination of these approaches.

Prognosis

The prognoses of the various vision disorders vary:

- AMD: Most patients with the dry form of AMD have only mild or moderate loss of vision. The prognosis is less hopeful for patients with wet AMD, as laser therapy is not effective in some patients.
- Cataract: Cataract surgery is very safe, with about 1.5 million procedures performed each year in the United States. About 95 percent of patients have better vision and improved quality of life; fewer than 1 percent have complications.
- Diabetic retinopathy: When diagnosed early, the progress of diabetic retinopathy from the nonproliferative to the proliferative form can be slowed significantly by tight control of blood sugar levels. In proliferative diabetic neuropathy, 95 percent of patients will keep their sight for at least 5 years if treated promptly. If they are treated late, only 50 percent will keep their sight for 5 years.
- Glaucoma: Open-angle glaucoma, if diagnosed early, is treatable. Vision that has already been lost cannot be restored; however, laser surgery and conventional surgery are highly effective in lowering IOP in 60 to 80 percent of patients. Medications to reduce IOP must be taken correctly and regularly. The prognosis for closed-angle glaucoma depends on speed of emergency treatment for the disorder.

QUESTIONS TO ASK YOUR DOCTOR

- How often should I have an eye examination?
- Glaucoma runs in my family. How much will that affect my risk of developing it?
- Can my eye disorder be treated with medications or will I need surgery?
- What can I do to slow the progress of my eye disorder?

Prevention

Genetic factors that increase the risk of vision disorders in seniors cannot be prevented as of the early 2000s.

Quitting **smoking** (or never starting in the first place) reduces the risk of most age-related vision disorders, as does limiting alcohol consumption. Good nutrition lowers the risk of cataract formation in later life, along with protecting the eyes from ultraviolet radiation by wearing sunglasses during outdoor sports or other activities.

Seniors diagnosed with either type 1 or type 2 (adult-onset) diabetes should have an eye examination twice yearly as they are at increased risk of AMD and diabetic retinopathy. They should also take extra care to control their blood sugar levels and **blood pressure**.

KEY TERMS

Cornea—The clear curved structure at the front of the eye that allows light to enter the eye.

Floater—An object in a person's field of vision caused by a tiny particle or deposit in the vitreous humor.

Intraocular pressure (IOP)—The pressure of the fluid inside the eyeball. An increase in IOP is a major factor in the development of glaucoma.

Iris—The colored circular membrane in front of the lens of the eye.

Macula—An area of tissue at the center of the retina that is responsible for the clearest central vision.

Ophthalmologist—A doctor who specializes in diagnosing and treating eye disorders.

Photocoagulation—The use of light from a laser to block or destroy broken blood vessels in the eye.

Retina—The innermost layer of the eye containing light-sensitive nerve cells and fibers. The retina is connected to the brain via the optic nerve.

Vitrectomy—The surgical removal of the vitreous humor. The gel is replaced with saline or another clear fluid.

Vitreous humor—The clear gel that fills the space between the lens and the retina of the eye.

Caregiver concerns

Caregivers should make sure that seniors in their care:

- Have an annual eye examination even if they haven't noticed any changes in their vision.
- Tell the doctor right away if there are changes in vision (blurring, glare, floaters, problems with night driving, etc.)
- Take all medications prescribed for eye care—particularly medications for glaucoma—and wear sunglasses when they are outside in bright sunlight.
- Eat a nutritious diet.
- Quit smoking if they are a smoker.
- See the doctor at once if they have an accident involving injury to the head or eye; if they have pain or redness in one or both eyes; or if they begin to see halos around lights.

Resources

BOOKS

Beers, Mark H., M. D., and Thomas V. Jones, MD. *Merck Manual of Geriatrics*, 3rd ed., Chapter 127, "Ocular Disorders." Whitehouse Station, NJ: Merck, 2005.

Friedman, Neil J., and Peter K. Kaiser. *Essentials of Ophthalmology*, 1st ed. Philadelphia: Saunders Elsevier, 2007.

PERIODICALS

Green, C. M., L. S. Kearns, J. Wu, et al. "How Significant Is a Family History of Glaucoma? Experience from the Glaucoma Inheritance Study in Tasmania." *Clinical and Experimental Ophthalmology* 35 (December 2007): 793–799.

Hassell, J. B., E. L. Lamoureux, and J. E. Keeffe. "Impact of Age-Related Macular Degeneration on Quality of Life." *British Journal of Ophthalmology* 90 (May 2006): 593–596.

Quillen, David A. "Common Causes of Vision Loss in Elderly Patients." *American Family Physician* 60 (July 1, 1999): 99–108.

OTHER

National Eye Institute (NEI). *Age-Related Macular Degeneration: What You Should Know*. Bethesda, MD: NEI, 2008. Available online in PDF format at http://www.nei.nih.gov/health/maculardegen/webAMD.pdf [cited February 28, 2008].

National Eye Institute (NEI). *Facts about Cataract*. Bethesda, MD: NEI, 2008. Available online at http://www.nei.nih.gov/health/cataract/cataract_facts.asp [cited February 28, 2008].

National Eye Institute (NEI). *Facts about Diabetic Retinopathy*. Bethesda, MD: NEI, 2008. Available online at http://www.nei.nih.gov/health/diabetic/retinopathy.asp [cited February 28, 2008].

National Eye Institute (NEI). *Facts about Glaucoma*. Bethesda, MD: NEI, 2006. Available online at http://www.nei.nih.gov/health/glaucoma/glaucoma_facts.asp [cited February 28, 2008].

Prevent Blindness America and the National Eye Institute (NEI). *Vision Problems in the U.S.: Prevalence of Adult Vision Impairment and Age-Related Eye Disease in America*. Chicago, IL: Prevent Blindness America, 2002. Available online in PDF format at http://www.nei.nih.gov/eyedata/pdf/VPUS.pdf [cited February 27, 2008].

ORGANIZATIONS

American Academy of Ophthalmology (AAO), P.O. Box 7424, San Francisco, CA, 94120, (415) 561-8500, (415) 561-8533, http://www.aao.org/aao/.

Macula Vision Research Foundation (MVRF), Five Tower Bridge, 300 Barr Harbor Drive, Suite 600, West Conshohocken, PA, 19428, (610) 668-6705, (866)-4MAC-ULA, (610) 667-1459, lea@mvrf.org, http://www.mvrf.org/.

National Eye Institute (NEI) Information Office, 31 Center Drive, MSC 2510, Bethesda, MD, 20892, (301) 496-5248, 2020@nei.nih.gov, http://www.nei.nih.gov/index.asp.

Prevent Blindness America, 211 West Wacker Drive, Suite 1700, Chicago, IL, 60606, (800) 331-2020, http://www.preventblindness.org/.

Wills Eye (formerly Wills Eye Hospital), 840 Walnut Street, Philadelphia, PA, 19107, (215) 928-3000, (877) AT-WILLS, http://www.willseye.org/.

AMD Alliance International, 1929 Bayview Avenue, Toronto, Ontario, Canada, M4G 3E8, (416) 486-2500 ext. 7505, (877) AMD-7171, (416) 486-8574, info@amdalliance.org, http://www.amdalliance.org/.

Rebecca J. Frey Ph.D.

Vision loss *see* **Visual impairment**

Visual impairment

Definition

Total blindness is the inability to tell light from dark, or the total inability to see. Visual impairment or low vision is a severe reduction in vision that cannot be corrected with standard glasses or **contact lenses** and reduces a person's ability to function at certain or all tasks. Legal blindness (which is actually a severe visual impairment) refers to a best-corrected central vision of 20/200 or worse in the better eye or a visual acuity of better than 20/200 but with a visual field no greater than 20° (e.g., side vision that is so reduced that it appears as if the person is looking through a tunnel).

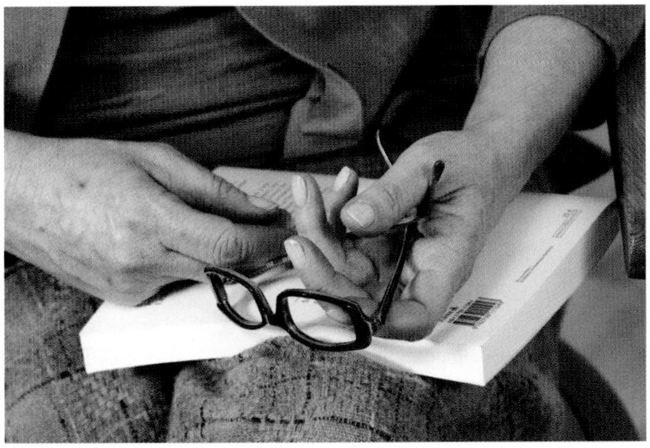

Vision loss is common in older people. *(Lea Paterson / Photo Researchers, Inc. Reproduced by permission.)*

Description

Vision is normally measured using a Snellen chart. A Snellen chart has letters of different sizes that are read, one eye at a time, from a distance of 20 ft. People with normal vision are able to read the 20 ft line at 20 ft—20/20 vision—or the 40 ft line at 40 ft, the 100 ft line at 100 ft, and so forth. If at 20 ft the smallest readable letter is larger, vision is designated as the distance from the chart over the size of the smallest letter that can be read.

Eye care professionals measure vision in many ways. Clarity (sharpness) of vision indicates how well a person's central visual status is. The diopter is the unit of measure for refractive errors such as nearsightedness, farsightedness, and astigmatism and indicates the strength of corrective lenses needed. People do not just see straight ahead; the entire area of vision is called the visual field. Some people have good vision (e.g., see clearly) but have areas of reduced or no vision (blind spots) in parts of their visual field. Others have good vision in the center but poor vision around the edges (peripheral visual field). People with very poor vision may be able only to count fingers at a given distance from their eyes. This distance becomes the measure of their ability to see.

The World Health Organization (WHO) defines impaired vision in five categories:

- Low vision 1 is a best corrected visual acuity of 20/70.
- Low vision 2 starts at 20/200.
- Blindness 3 is below 20/400.
- Blindness 4 is worse than 5/300
- Blindness 5 is no light perception at all.
- A visual field between 5° and 10° (compared with a normal visual field of about 120°) goes into category 3; less than 5° into category 4, even if the tiny spot of central vision is perfect.

Color blindness is the reduced ability to perceive certain colors, usually red and green. It is a hereditary defect and affects very few tasks. Contrast sensitivity describes the ability to distinguish one object from another. A person with reduced contrast sensitivity may have problems seeing things in the fog because of the decrease in contrast between the object and the fog.

According to the WHO there are over forty million people worldwide whose vision is category 3 or worse, 80% of whom live in developing countries. Half of the blind population in the United States is over 65 years of age.

Prevalence of blindness and low vision among adults 40 years and older in the United States

Age	Blindness*		Low Vision*		All Vision Impaired	
Years	Persons	(%)	Persons	(%)	Persons	(%)
40–49	51,000	0.1%	80,000	0.2%	131,000	0.3%
50–59	45,000	0.1%	102,000	0.3%	147,000	0.4%
60–69	59,000	0.3%	176,000	0.9%	235,000	1.2%
70–79	134,000	0.8%	471,000	3.0%	605,000	3.8%
≥80	648,000	7.0%	1,532,000	16.7%	2,180,000	23.7%
Total	**937,000**	**0.8%**	**2,361,000**	**2.0%**	**3,298,000**	**2.7%**

*Blindness is defined as the best-corrected visual acuity of 6/60 or worse (= 20/200) in the better-seeing eye; low vision is defined as the best-corrected visual acuity less than 6/12 (<20/40) in the better-seeing eye.

SOURCE: Adapted from *Archives of Ophthalmology, Vol. 122, April 2004*

(Illustration by GGS Information Services. Cengage Learning, Gale)

Causes and symptoms

The leading causes of blindness include:

- macular degeneration
- glaucoma
- cataracts
- diabetes mellitus

Other possible causes include infections, injury, or **nutrition**.

Infections

Most infectious eye diseases have been eliminated in the industrialized nations by sanitation, medication, and public health measures. Viral infections are the main exception to this statement. Some infections that may lead to visual impairment include:

- Herpes simplex keratitis. A viral infection of the cornea. Repeated occurrences may lead to corneal scarring.
- Trachoma. This disease is responsible for six to nine million cases of blindness around the world, of the third of a billion who have the disease. Trachoma is caused by an incomplete bacterium, *Chlamydia trachomatis*, that is easily treated with standard antibiotics. It is transmitted directly from eye to eye, mostly by flies. The chlamydia gradually destroy the cornea.
- Leprosy (Hansen's disease). This is another bacterial disease that has a high affinity for the eyes. It, too, can be effectively treated with medicines.
- River blindness. Much of the tropics of the Eastern Hemisphere are infested with *Onchocerca volvulus*, a worm that causes "river blindness." This worm is transmitted by fly bites and can be treated with a drug called ivermectin. Nevertheless, twenty-eight million people have the disease, and 40% of them are blind from it.

Other causes

Exposure of a pregnant woman to certain diseases (e.g., rubella or toxoplasmosis) can cause congenital eye problems. Injuries to the eyes can result in blindness. Very little blindness is due to disease in the brain or the optic nerves. **Multiple sclerosis** and similar nervous system diseases, **brain tumors**, diseases of the eye sockets, and head injuries are rare causes of blindness.

Nutrition

Vitamin A deficiency is a widespread cause of corneal degeneration in developing nations. As many as five million develop xerophthalmia from this deficiency each year. Five percent end up blind.

Diagnosis

A low vision exam is slightly different from a general exam. While a case history, visual status, and eye health evaluation are common to both exams, some things do differ. Eye charts other than a Snellen eye chart will be used. Testing distance will vary. A trial frame worn by the patient is usually used instead of the instrument containing the lenses the patient sits behind (phoropter). Because the low vision exam is slightly more goal oriented than a general exam, for example, what specifically is the patient having trouble with (reading, seeing street signs, etc.) different optical and nonoptical aids will generally be tried. Eye health is the last thing to be checked so that the lights necessary to examine the eyes will not interfere with the rest of the testing.

Treatment

There are many options for patients with visual impairment. There are optical and nonoptical aids. Optical aids include:

- Telescopes. May be used to read street signs.
- Hand magnifiers. May be used to read labels on things at the store.
- Stand magnifiers. May be used to read.
- Prisms. May be used to move the image onto a healthy part of the retina in some eye diseases.
- Closed circuit television (CCTV). For large magnification (e.g., for reading).

Nonoptical aids can include large print books and magazines, check-writing guides, large print dials on the telephone, and more.

For those who are blind, there are enormous resources available to improve the quality of life. For the legally blind, financial assistance for help may be possible. Braille and audio books are increasingly available. Guide dogs provide well-trained eyes and **independence**. Orientation and mobility training is available.

Prognosis

The prognosis generally relates to the severity of the impairment and the ability of the aids to correct it. A good low vision exam is important to be aware of the latest low vision aids.

Prevention

Regular eye exams are important to detect silent eye problems (e.g., **glaucoma**). Left untreated, glaucoma can result in blindness.

Corneal infections can be treated with effective **antibiotics**. When a cornea has become opaque beyond recovery it must be transplanted. Good hygiene (e.g., washing hands frequently) to prevent infection, proper use of contact lenses, and not sharing makeup are just some ways to guard against corneal infections.

Cataracts should be removed when they interfere with a person's quality of life.

Primary prevention addresses the causes before they ever begin. Fly control can be accomplished by simple sanitation methods. Public health measures can reduce the incidence of many **infectious diseases**. Vitamin A supplementation (when appropriate) will eliminate xerophthalmia completely. It is possible that protecting the eyes against ultraviolet (UV) light will reduce the incidence of cataracts, macular degeneration, and some other eye diseases. UV coatings can be placed on regular glasses, sunglasses, and ski goggles. Patients should ask their eye care professional about UV coatings.

Secondary prevention addresses treating established diseases before they cause irreversible eye damage. Having general physical checkups can also detect systemic diseases such as diabetes or high **blood pressure**. Control of diabetes is very important in preserving sight.

J. Ricker Polsdorfer MD

KEY TERMS

Cornea—The clear dome-shaped structure that is part of the front of the eye. It lies in front of the colored part of the eye (iris).

Diabetic retinopathy—Retinal disease caused by the damage diabetes does to small blood vessels.

Phoropter—The instrument used to measure refractive status of the eyes. It contains many lenses which are then changed in front of the eyes while the patient is looking at an eye chart. This is when the doctor usually asks, "Which is better, one or two?"

Xerophthalmia—A drying of the cornea and conjunctiva.

Vital signs in the aging

Definition

Vital signs (VS), which are also called simply vitals, are four measurements taken to determine whether a person is alive. The English word *vital* comes from the Latin *vitalis*, which means "pertaining to life" or "alive." There are four standard vital signs: pulse (or heart) rate, **blood pressure**, breathing (or respiratory) rate, and body temperature.

Some health care professionals have suggested adding **pain**, skin color, and blood oxygen concentration to the basic list of vital signs, but these suggestions have not been accepted by most doctors.

Vital sign	Age-related changes and effects
Blood pressure	Blood vessels become less elastic. The average blood pressure increases from 120/70 mm Hg to about 150/90 mm Hg and may remain slightly high even if treated. The blood vessels also respond more slowly to a change in body position. High blood pressure (hypertension) is a common blood pressure problem. Many older people find that they become dizzy if they stand up too suddenly. This is caused by a drop in blood pressure when they stand called orthostatic hypotension. Use of diuretics can cause low blood pressure and aggravate orthostatic hypotension.
Body temperature	Normal body temperature does not change significantly with aging, however, temperature regulation is more difficult. Loss of subcutaneous fat makes it harder to maintain body heat. Many older people find that they need to wear layers of clothing in order to feel warm. Skin changes include the reduced ability to sweat. Therefore, older people find it more difficult to tell when they are becoming overheated. Older people are at greater risk for overheating (hyperthermia or heat stroke). They are also at risk for dangerous drops in body temperature (hypothermia). Fever is an important sign of illness in the elderly. Many times, fever is the only symptom for several days.
Breathing (or respiratory rate)	Although lung function decreases slightly, changes are usually only in the reserve function. The rate of breathing usually does not change. There may be decreased tolerance to exercise. Some elderly people have a reduced response to decreased oxygen or increased carbon dioxide levels (the rate and depth of breathing does not increase as it should). Breathing problems are seldom normal. Although exercise tolerance may decrease slightly, even a very elderly person should be able to breathe without effort under usual circumstances. Use of pain medications can slow breathing.
Pulse (or heart rate)	Because of changes in the heart, the resting heart rate may become slightly slower. It takes longer for the pulse to speed up when exercising, and longer to slow back down after exercise. The maximum heart rate reached with exercise is lowered. Heart rate and rhythm problems are fairly common in the elderly. Excessively slow pulse (bradycardia) and arrhythmias such as atrial fibrillation are also common. Digitalis (used for heart failure) and certain blood pressure medications, such as beta blockers, may cause the pulse to slow.

SOURCE: Adapted from: A.D.A.M. Medical Encyclopedia [Internet]. Atlanta (GA): A.D.A.M., Inc.; © 2005. Aging changes in vital signs; [updated 2006 Nov. 6]. Available from: http://www.nlm.nih.gov/medlineplus/ency/article/003247.htm

(Illustration by GGS Information Services. Cengage Learning, Gale)

Purpose

A senior's vital signs may be taken for a number of different reasons:

- As part of a regular physical checkup.
- As part of a comprehensive geriatric assessment.
- To determine fitness for major surgery.
- As part of inpatient preparation for surgery and to monitor the senior's condition after the procedure.
- To help the doctor in diagnosing the possible cause (s) of the senior's symptoms. For example, an irregular pulse in an elderly patient as well as the location of the irregularity can help the doctor determine whether the senior has a heart condition that requires immediate attention or is simply experiencing a side effect of a medication.
- To monitor the course of a disease or a chronic health condition.
- To evaluate the effectiveness of medications and the need to increase or decrease the dosage.
- To measure the effects of an exercise program or physical therapy.
- To determine time of death.

Precautions

The precautions that should be taken by the health professional taking the vital signs include care to avoid exposing the senior to infection and care in maintaining any equipment used to measure vital signs (to avoid inaccurate measurements).

Precautions that should be taken to ensure the senior's safety during a physical examination include:

- Allowing the senior extra time to undress, move to the examining table, and dress afterward. The table should be a comfortable height for the patient. In some cases, the doctor can take the vital signs with the patient seated in a chair.
- Frail seniors should not be left alone in the examining room as a safeguard against falls.

Description

Temperature

The senior's temperature is taken with a thermometer. Glass thermometers that used to require placement for 3 minutes have now been replaced almost everywhere by electronic thermometers that record temperature accurately within seconds. The doctor should be careful to use a thermometer that will record temperatures below 95°F, as the major change in the aging body is not temperature level but the ability to regulate body temperature. Many seniors feel chilly much of the time because of the loss of body fat under the skin; it is also possible for a senior to have an infection without a noticeable fever. A temperature below 95°F in an elderly person should be rechecked because it may indicate acute illness or a severe medication reaction. Fever in a senior is usually defined as a temperature above 100°F.

In addition to taking the senior's oral temperature, the doctor may take the temperature again in the armpit or rectum. Seniors who breathe more rapidly than 20 breaths per minute may have artificially low oral temperatures. In some medical emergencies it may also be necessary to take the temperature in the armpit or rectum rather than the mouth.

Breathing

Breathing rate is measured by the physician's counting the number of breaths for a full minute and observing the pattern. Although most adults take between 12 and 18 breaths per minute, seniors in long-term care may take 16–25 breaths per minute. If the senior is taking more than 20 breaths per minute, the doctor will consider the possibility of an upper respiratory infection, **congestive heart failure**, lung disease, **asthma**, or **pneumonia**.

If the senior is taking 10 breaths or fewer per minute, the doctor will consider the possibility of heavy drinking, overuse of benzodiazepine tranquilizers, or high doses of painkillers, as these substances depress (slow down) the central nervous system. Another possible explanation for a low breathing rate is **meningitis**.

Pulse

The pulse should be taken in both arms in seniors. The reason for this precaution is that some heart problems result in a difference in volume in the blood flow on the two sides of the body, and the doctor can sometimes feel this difference by taking the pulse on both sides at the same time. When the doctor takes a senior's pulse, he or she will be trying to evaluate the stiffness of the blood vessel wall as well as the rhythm and strength of the pulse, as stiffening of the blood vessels in the aging body is a common development. It is not as easy for the doctor to detect the pulse in a stiff artery.

the most common location for taking the pulse is the radial artery, which runs along the side of the wrist and can be felt just below the thumb. The doctor may also take the pulse using the carotid artery just below the jaw or the femoral artery in the leg.

QUESTIONS TO ASK YOUR DOCTOR

- Are all my vital signs within the normal range for a person my age?
- Can you explain what the numbers indicate?
- Why is blood pressure measured in both arms?
- Can you tell from taking my pulse whether my arteries are stiffening?

Blood pressure

Blood pressure is measured by a device called a sphygmomanometer, which consists of an inflatable cuff to constrict blood flow connected to a mercury tube or digital gauge to record the pressure. The measurements are expressed in millimeters of mercury, or mm Hg. To take blood pressure, the doctor places the cuff around the upper arm at the level of the heart while the patient is sitting upright. The doctor listens with a stethoscope at the inside of the senior's elbow and inflates the cuff until the brachial artery in the upper arm is squeezed shut. The doctor then slowly releases the pressure in the cuff until a whooshing sound is heard when the blood returns to the artery. This is the systolic pressure (the highest level of blood pressure in the arteries). The cuff is then further released until the sound is no longer heard; this is the diastolic pressure (the lowest level of blood pressure in the arteries).

Blood pressure is usually taken in both arms in seniors for the same reason that the pulse is taken on both sides of the body—to screen for possible heart disorders. In addition, the doctor should be careful to note whether a high reading is an accurate measurement of blood pressure or whether it is caused by stiffening of the patient's blood vessels. This condition is called pseudohypertension.

Preparation

There are no special preparations required for the taking of vital signs, although the patient may be asked to roll up sleeves or remove a shirt or blouse if the measurements are taken as part of a routine office visit.

Aftercare

There is no aftercare required for the taking of vital signs.

KEY TERMS

Diastolic blood pressure—The lowest level of blood pressure in the arteries, which occurs at the point in the heart's cycle when its chambers fill with blood.

Pseudohypertension—A condition in which a senior's blood pressure measures higher than it really is because of stiffening of the arteries.

Sphygmomanometer—A device for measuring blood pressure that consists of an inflatable cuff connected to a mercury column or a digital gauge.

Systolic blood pressure—The highest level of blood pressure in the arteries, which occurs at the point in the heart's cycle when the heart contracts and pushes blood out through the aorta and the pulmonary artery.

Complications

It is rare for serious complications to occur as the result of taking vital signs, since these measurements do not involve drawing blood or other invasive procedures. Some elderly persons with very fragile skin, however, may notice **bruising** after the use of a blood pressure cuff.

Results

Normal ranges for vital signs in health adults are as follows:

- Temperature: between 97.8 and 99.1°F. This range is the same in seniors as in younger adults.
- Breathing rate: 12 to 18 breaths per minute. Changes in the senior's lungs do not always affect the rate of breathing; however, some seniors in long-term care with respiratory problems may have a breathing rate as high as 25 breaths per minute.
- Pulse: Between 60 and 80 beats per minute when the person is at rest. In seniors, however, the pulse is often slightly slower than in younger adults. It takes longer for a senior's pulse to speed up during exercise and longer for it to slow down after exercise. In addition, the maximum heart rate with exercise is lower in seniors than in younger adults.
- Blood pressure: systolic 120 mm Hg or less; diastolic 80 mm Hg or less. In seniors, however, blood pressure is often higher than normal values in younger adults; it may be as high as 150/90 mm Hg even when the senior is being treated for high blood pressure.

Caregiver concerns

Taking vital signs is a routine medical procedure that does not require a special request. In most cases, a senior's vital signs will be taken by a physician, physician assistant, or **registered nurse**. In emergencies, vital signs may be taken by an emergency medical technician (EMT), paramedic, member of a rescue squad, firefighter, or police officer.

Resources

BOOKS

Beers, Mark H., M. D., and Thomas V. Jones, MD. *Merck Manual of Geriatrics*, 3rd ed., Chapter 3, "Physical Examination." Whitehouse Station, NJ: Merck, 2005.

Gomella, Leonard, M.D., and Steven A. Haist, M.D. *Clinician's Pocket Reference*, 11th ed. New York: Mc-Graw-Hill, 2007.

PERIODICALS

Cheng, T. O. "Osler Maneuver to Detect Pseudohypertension." *Journal of the American Medical Association* 282 (September 8, 1999): 943.

Summerhill, E. M., et a. "Respiratory Muscle Strength in the Physically Active Elderly." *Lung* 185 (December 2007): 315–320.

OTHER

Bryan, E. David. "Abdominal Pain in Elderly Persons." *eMedicine*, October 5, 2006. http://www.emedicine.com/emerg/topic931.htm [cited February 22, 2008].

Cohen, Sandra, M.D. *Aging Changes in Vital Signs*. Last reviewed November 2006. Available online at http://www.umm.edu/ency/article/004019.htm [cited February 22, 2008].

ORGANIZATIONS

American Academy of Family Physicians (AAFP), 11400 Tomahawk Creek Parkway, Leawood, KS, 66211, (913) 906-6000, (800) 274-2237 , (913) 906-6269, http://www.aafp.org/online/en/home.html.

National Heart, Lung and Blood Institute (NHLBI), P.O. Box 30105, Bethesda, MD, 20824, (301) 592-8573, (240) 629-3246, nhlbiinfo@nhlbi.nih.gov, http://www.nhlbi.nih.gov/index.htm.

Rebecca J. Frey Ph.D.

Vitamin B_{12}

Definition

Vitamin B_{12} is a water-soluble organic compound that the body needs to remain healthy. The only organisms that can make vitamin B_{12} are bacteria, fungi, yeast, molds, and algae. Humans must get it from foods in their **diet**. Vitamin B_{12} is sometimes called cobalamin.

Purpose

Vitamin B_{12} plays major roles in developing healthy red blood cells, creating new deoxyribose nucleic acid (DNA, genetic material), and in maintaining the health of nerve cells. It is also involved in making certain nutrients available to the body.

Description

Vitamin B_{12} is one of the least understood **vitamins**. Although some of its effects were experimentally discovered in the 1930s, Vitamin B_{12}'s structure was not determined until the 1960s. Questions still remain about some of its functions. Vitamin B_{12} is different from other vitamins in several ways. It is the only vitamin not made by any plant or animal, but only by microorganisms. It is the only vitamin to contain the metal cobalt (thus the name cobalamin), and it is the only vitamin that must combine with another substance, called the intrinsic factor (IF), before it can be absorbed by the body.

Although vitamin B_{12} is made only by microorganisms, it is found in association with animal protein. In nature, it comes in a variety of chemical forms that the body converts into two active forms of B_{12}. Most B_{12} **dietary supplements** contain the form called cyanocobalamin. B_{12} is included in over-the-counter multivitamins and in vitamin-B-complex supplements. It is also sold as a stand-alone dietary supplement and in an injectable form available only by prescription.

When people eat animal protein-beef, fish, pork, chicken, eggs, milk, cheese-the stomach is stimulated to secrete hydrochloric acid and enzymes that break down the protein and release vitamin B_{12}. B_{12} then binds with IF, which is made in the stomach. Vitamin B_{12} cannot be absorbed into the body unless it is combined with IF. Therefore, either an absence of B_{12} in diet or inability of the stomach to make IF can result in B_{12} deficiency.

Some fermented bean products such as tofu, tempeh, natto, tamari, and miso may or may not contain vitamin B_{12} depending on which bacteria were used to ferment these products. Nutritional yeast also may or may not contain vitamin B_{12} depending on the type of yeast used. Consumers should read labels of these products carefully. The best source of vitamin B_{12} for people who do not eat meat or animal products is fortified breakfast cereal. Cereals can be fortified at various strengths, ranging from in amounts ranging from 100% of the daily requirement to 25% of the daily requirement. The label must contain information about vitamin fortification.

KEY TERMS

Amino acid—Molecules that are the basic building blocks of proteins.

Dietary supplement—A product, such as a vitamin, mineral, herb, amino acid, or enzyme, that is intended to be consumed in addition to an individual's diet with the expectation that it will improve health.

Enzyme—A protein that change the rate of a chemical reaction within the body without themselves being used up in the reaction.

Vitamin—A nutrient that the body needs in small amounts to remain healthy but that the body cannot manufacture for itself and must acquire through diet.

Water-soluble vitamin—A vitamin that dissolves in water and can be removed from the body in urine.

Vitamin B_{12}'s role in health

Vitamin B_{12} is crucial to the development of healthy red blood cells. As red blood cells mature, they need new DNA. In the absence of adequate vitamin B_{12}, the new DNA is defective. This results in red blood cells that are too large and poorly shaped. These malformed cells have a reduced ability to carry oxygen and result in pernicious **anemia** or megaloblastic anemia.

Vitamin B_{12} also is necessary to maintain healthy nerves. Nerves are covered with a fatty sheath called myelin. The myelin covering is necessary for effective transmission of nerve impulses. When vitamin B_{12} is absent, the myelin sheath does not form correctly.

Proteins in the diet are broken down into small molecules called amino acids that are then used by the body to build new proteins. Vitamin B_{12} helps make amino acid available to the body. High levels of one particular amino acid, homocysteine, are associated with increased risk of **heart disease**. Vitamin B_{12}, along with vitamin B_6 and **folic acid** help reduce the level of homocysteine in the blood. Vitamin B_{12} is also thought to play a role in making **carbohydrates** and fats available to the body. Clinical trials are underway to determine safety and effectiveness of vitamin B_{12} in a variety of situations. Individuals interested in participating in a clinical trial at no charge can find a list of open trials at http://www.clinicaltrials.gov.

Normal vitamin B_{12} requirements

The United States Institute of Medicine (IOM) of the National Academy of Sciences has developed values called Dietary Reference Intakes (DRIs) for vitamins and minerals. The DRIs consist of three sets of numbers. The Recommended Dietary Allowance (RDA) defines the average daily amount of the nutrient needed to meet the health needs of 97–98% of the population. The Adequate Intake (AI) is an estimate set when there is not enough information to determine an RDA. The Tolerable Upper Intake Level (UL) is the average maximum amount that can be taken daily without risking negative side effects.

The following are the RDAs and IAs for vitamin B_{12} for healthy individuals:

- people 14 years and older: RDA 2.4 mcg

Sources of vitamin B_{12}

Vitamin B_{12} is found in food that comes from animals, including meat, fish, poultry, eggs, milk, and cheese. It is also added to fortified breakfast cereals and is found in some fermented bean products. Heating or cooking foods does not reduce their vitamin B_{12} content very much.

The following list gives the approximate vitamin B_{12} content for some common foods:

- calf's liver, cooked, 4 ounces: 41 mcg
- salmon, baked or broiled, 4 ounces: 3.3 mcg
- shrimp, steamed or boiled, 4 ounces: 1.7 mcg
- mollusks or clams, cooked, 3 ounces: 84 mcg
- tuna, white, canned in water, 3 ounces: 1.0 mcg
- beef, top sirloin, broiled, 3 ounces: 2.4 mcg
- cheeseburger, fast food, double patty: 1.9 mcg
- taco, fast food, 1 large: 1.6 mcg
- ham, canned or roasted, 3 ounces: 0.6 mcg
- chicken breast, roasted, 1/2 breast: 0.3mcg
- milk, 1 cup: 0.9 mcg
- egg, 1 whole, cooked: 0.3 mcg
- breakfast cereal, fortified 100%, 3/4 cup: 6.0 mcg
- breakfast cereal, fortified 25%, 3/4 cup: 1.5 mcg

Vitamin B_{12} deficiency

Vitamin B_{12} deficiency is hard to determine, and there is little agreement on how many people are vitamin B_{12} deficient. This is partly because the body can store 5–10 year's worth of vitamin B_{12}, so symptoms of deficiency are slow to show up, especially in adults. Researchers estimate that anywhere from 300,000–3 million Americans are vitamin B_{12} deficient.

Most meat-eating Americans get enough vitamin B_{12} from diet alone. However, the elderly are at higher risk than younger people of developing mild vitamin B_{12} deficiency. Other people at greater risk of vitamin B_{12} deficiency include:

- vegans who eat no animal products
- people who have had part of their stomach or intestine removed
- people with diseases that interfere with the absorption of nutrients such as Crohn's disease, celiac disease, or ulcerative colitis.
- people with alcoholism
- people with liver or kidney damage
- people with HIV/AIDS

Symptoms of vitamin B_{12} deficiency include shaky movements, loss of balance, muscle weakness and spasms, vision problems, reduced mental functioning, and changes in mood and mental state. These symptoms are quite general and have many other causes besides vitamin B_{12} deficiency.

Precautions

Individuals with the eye disorder Leber's optic atrophy should not use vitamin B_{12} supplements. High levels of B_{12} will accelerate degeneration of the optic nerve, leading to blindness.

Folic acid may mask vitamin B_{12} deficiency. Folic acid supplements will reverse anemia symptoms, but they do not stop nerve damage caused by B_{12} deficiency. Permanent nerve damage may result. People with suspected folic acid deficiency who begin taking folic acid supplements should also be evaluated for vitamin B_{12} deficiency.

Interactions

Many drugs used to treat **gastroesophageal reflux disease** (GERD) such as omeprazole (Prilosec), lansoprazole (Prevacid), cimetidine (Tagamet), famotidine (Pepsid), nizatidine (Axid), or ranitidine (Zantac) decrease the amount of hydrochloric acid secreted by the stomach. In turn, this may limit the amount of B_{12}

available from food, but not from dietary supplements. Antacid abuse may also limit the absorption of B_{12}.

Metaformin (Fortamet, Glucophage, Glucophage XR, Riomet), a drug used to treat diabetes, may indirectly decrease vitamin B_{12} absorption by altering **calcium** metabolism. When metaformin is taken for a long time (years), the risk of megaloblastic anemia and cardiovascular disease may increase.

Nitrous oxide ("laughing gas") can inactivate the cobalamin form of vitamin B_{12}. Nervous system symptoms can develop in people exposed to nitrous oxide if they already have with low vitamin B_{12} levels. This is unlikely to occur with people who have normal levels of B_{12}.

Complications

No complications are expected from taking vitamin B_{12}.

Resources

BOOKS

Berkson, Burt and Arthur J. Berkson. *Basic Health Publications User's Guide to the B-complex Vitamins.* Laguna Beach, CA: Basic Health Publications, 2006.

Gaby, Alan R., ed. *A-Z Guide to Drug-Herb-Vitamin Interactions Revised and Expanded 2nd Edition: Improve Your Health and Avoid Side Effects When Using Common Medications and Natural Supplements Together.* New York: Three Rivers Press, 2006.

Lieberman, Shari and Nancy Bruning. *The Real Vitamin and Mineral Book: The Definitive Guide to Designing Your Personal Supplement Program,* 4th ed. New York: Avery, 2007.

Pressman, Alan H. and Sheila Buff. *The Complete Idiot's Guide to Vitamins and Minerals,* 3rd ed. Indianapolis, IN: Alpha Books, 2007.

Rucker, Robert B., ed. *Handbook of Vitamins.* Boca Raton, FL: Taylor & Francis, 2007.

Tish Davidson A.M.

Vitamin C

Definition

Vitamin C, also called ascorbic acid or antiscorbutic vitamin, is a water-soluble organic compound needed to prevent scurvy. Humans cannot make or store vitamin C, so they must get a steady supply of it from foods in their **diet**.

Drug interactions with grapefruit products, tangelos and Seville oranges

- Antiarrhythmic medication
  - Amiodarone (Cordarone)
- Antidepressants
  - Buspirone (BuSpar)
  - Clomipramine (Anafranil)
  - Sertraline (Zoloft)
- Antiseizure medication
  - Carbamazepine (Carbatrol, Tegretol)
- Calcium channel blockers (for high blood pressure)
  - Felodipine (Plendil)
  - Nifedipine (Adalat, Procardia)
  - Nimodipine (Nimotop)
  - Nisoldipine (Sular)
  - Verapamil (Isoptin, Verelan)
- Erectile dysfunction medication
  - Sildenafil (Viagra)
- HIV medications
  - Indinavir (Crixivan)
  - Saquinavir (Invirase)
- HMG-CoA reductase inhibitors (for high cholesterol)
  - Atorvastatin (Lipitor)
  - Lovastatin (Mevacor, Altoprev)
  - Simvastatin (Zocor)
  - Simvastatin-ezetimibe (Vytorin)
- Immunosuppressant drugs
  - Cyclosporine (Neoral, Sandimmune)
  - Sirolimus (Rapamune)
  - Tacrolimus (Prograf)
- Pain relief medication
  - Methadone
- Tranquilizers
  - Diazepam (Valium)
  - Triazolam (Halcion)

List of drugs that interact with grapefruit products, tangelos and Seville oranges. Chemicals in these fruits and their products can interfere with enzymes that break down the drugs in the digestive system, resulting in an increased risk of side effects. *(Illustration by GGS Information Services. Cengage Learning, Gale)*

Purpose

Vitamin C is a powerful antioxidant that helps protect cells from damage. Vitamin C also is needed to make and repair collagen, move fat into cells where it can be converted into energy, and make neurotransmitters. There are also disputed claims that vitamin C, taken in large quantities as a dietary supplement, can prevent **cancer**, **heart disease**, the **common cold**, **cataracts**, and many other diseases.

High dose vitamin C may be used to treat or prevent urinary tract infections. High levels of vitamin C increase the acidity of urine, creating an unhospitable environment for bacteria growing in the urinary tract.

Description

Long before people knew what vitamin C was, they understood that eating certain foods, especially citrus fruit, would prevent a severe disease called scurvy. Vitamin C turned out to be the essential health-promoting compound in these foods. This vitamin was isolated in the early 1930s, and by 1934, a synthetic version of vitamin C was produced by the pharmaceutical company Hoffman-La Roche.

All animals need Vitamin C, but most animals can make their own. However, humans, along with apes, guinea pigs, and a few other animals, have lost that ability. In humans, this occurs because of a gene mutation that controls an enzyme needed to make vitamin C. As a result, humans are completely dependent on getting enough of the vitamin from foods in their diet. In addition, vitamin C cannot be stored in the body. It is a water-soluble vitamin, and any amount that cannot be used immediately is excreted in urine. Vitamin C is not evenly distributed throughout the body. The adrenal glands, pituitary gland, thymus, retina, brain, spleen, lungs, liver, thyroid, testicles, lymph nodes, kidney, and pancreas all contain much higher levels of vitamin C than are found in circulating blood.

Vitamin C's role in health

Vitamin C functions as an antioxidant and as a coenzyme. Molecules called free radicals are formed during normal cell metabolism and with exposure to ultraviolet light or toxins such as cigarette smoke. Free radicals cause damage by reacting with fats and proteins in cell membranes and genetic material. This process is called oxidation. **Antioxidants** like vitamin C are compounds that attach themselves to free radicals so that it is impossible for the free radical to react with, or oxidize, other molecules. In this way, antioxidants protect cells from damage. The antioxidant properties of vitamin C are the basis for many of the controversial health claims made for it.

Vitamin C also functions as a coenzyme. Coenzymes are small molecules that make it possible for metabolic activities to occur in cells. They are needed to break down food into its building-block molecules, build up new molecules from these building blocks, and convert nutrients into energy in cells. Vitamin C functions as a coenzyme in reactions that create collagen. Collagen is a protein that is found in cartilage, ligaments, tendons, bones, skin, and blood vessels. Vitamin C also is required to make the neurotransmitters dopamine, norepinephrine (noradrenaline), and epinephrine (adrenaline). Neurotransmitters are molecules that carry chemical messages from one nerve to another. Epinephrine is also made in the adrenal gland in response to stress. It prepares the body for a fight or flight response. Vitamin C may also be involved in cholesterol metabolism.

Normal vitamin C requirements

The United States Institute of Medicine (IOM) of the National Academy of Sciences has developed values called Dietary Reference Intakes (DRIs) for **vitamins** and minerals. The DRIs consist of three sets of numbers. The Recommended Dietary Allowance (RDA) defines the average daily amount of the nutrient needed to meet the health needs of 97–98% of the population. The Adequate Intake (AI) is an estimate set when there is not enough information to determine an RDA. The Tolerable Upper Intake Level (UL) is the average maximum amount that can be taken daily without risking negative side effects.

The following lit gives the daily RDAs and IAs and ULs for vitamin C for healthy individuals as established by the IOM.

- men age 19 and older: RDA 90 mg; UL 2,000 mg
- women age 19 and older: RDA 75 mg; UL 2,000 mg
- men who smoke: RDA 125 mg; UL 2,000 mg
- women who smoke: RDA 110 mg; UL 2,000 mg

Vitamin C is the most commonly taken dietary supplement taken by Americans. As a single-ingredient supplement, it is available as tablets, capsules, and powder. It is found in multivitamin and antioxidant supplements. It is also combined with minerals such as **calcium** (e.g. Ester-C) to make it less acidic and thus less irritating to the stomach in large doses. Vitamin C can be made synthetically or derived from corn or palm oil (ascorbyl palmate). There is little evidence that one form is more effective than another. Vitamin C is added to some skin creams, throat lozenges, energy drinks, and energy bars, and to some processed foods. In 2007, the two largest American soft drink manufacturers announced that they were going to produce carbonated drinks fortified with vitamins and minerals, including vitamin C.

Vitamin C deficiency produces a disease called scurvy. From the earliest times, scurvy was a problem for sailors on long voyages where there was no way to store fresh fruits and vegetables. In 1746, a doctor in the British navy proved that eating lemons and oranges could prevent scurvy among sailors. Early Spanish explorers planted orange trees in Florida and the Caribbean so that they would have a source of oranges to prevent scurvy on their long voyages back to Europe. Today scurvy occurs infrequently. As little as 10 mg per day of vitamin C can prevent the disease. People with alcoholism, elderly individuals on extremely restricted diets, and malnourished infants in developing countries are at higher risk for developing scurvy. Symptoms include fatigue, easy **bruising**,

KEY TERMS

Alzheimer's disease—An incurable disease of older individuals that results in the destruction of nerve cells in the brain and causes gradual loss of mental and physical functions.

Antioxidant—A molecule that prevents oxidation. In the body antioxidants attach to other molecules called free radicals and prevent the free radicals from causing damage to cell walls, DNA, and other parts of the cell.

Coenzyme—Also called a cofactor, a small non-protein molecule that binds to an enzyme and helps regulate enzyme-mediated reactions.

Collagen—A long fiber-like protein found in skin, bones, blood vessels, and connective tissue such as tendons and ligaments.

Conventional medicine—Mainstream or Western pharmaceutical-based medicine practiced by medical doctors, doctors of osteopathy, and other licensed health care professionals.

Dietary supplement—A product, such as a vitamin, mineral, herb, amino acid, or enzyme, that is intended to be consumed in addition to an individual's diet with the expectation that it will improve health.

Enzyme—A protein that change the rate of a chemical reaction within the body without themselves being used up in the reaction.

Neurotransmitter—One of a group of chemicals secreted by a nerve cell (neuron) to carry a chemical message to another nerve cell, often as a way of transmitting a nerve impulse. Examples of neurotransmitters include acetylcholine, dopamine, serotonin, and norepinephrine.

Osteoporosis—A condition found in older individuals in which bones decrease in density and become fragile and more likely to break. It can be caused by lack of vitamin D and/or calcium in the diet.

Placebo—A pill or liquid given during the study of a drug or dietary supplement that contains no medication or active ingredient. Usually study participants do not know if they are receiving a pill containing the drug or an identical-appearing placebo.

Toxin—A general term for something that harms or poisons the body.

Vitamin—A nutrient that the body needs in small amounts to remain healthy but that the body cannot manufacture for itself and must acquire through diet.

Water-soluble vitamin—A vitamin that dissolves in water and can be removed from the body in urine.

excessive bleeding, hair loss, sore gums, tooth loss, and joint **pain**. Left untreated, **death** can occur, usually through sudden cardiac attack. **Smoking** increases the body&s need for vitamin C, but is not, by itself, a cause of scurvy.

Sources of vitamin C

People need a continuous supply of vitamin C from their diet because of the role it plays in many metabolic processes. Vitamin C is found in many foods. Good natural sources of vitamin C include citrus fruits and their juices, papaya, red bell peppers, broccoli, and tomatoes.

Vitamin C is unstable and is lost when food is exposed to air, temperature changes, and water. About one-quarter of the vitamin C content of vegetables is lost by brief boiling, steaming, or freezing and thawing. Canning fruits and vegetables reduces their vitamin C content by about one-third, as does longer cooking at higher temperatures. However, both the American Cancer Society and the American Heart Association recommend that people meet their vitamin C (and many other vitamin requirements) through a healthy diet that includes eating a minimum of 5 servings of fruits and vegetables daily.

The following list gives the approximate vitamin C content for some common foods:

- orange, 1 medium: 70 mg
- orange juice, 3/4 cup (6 ounces): 75 mg
- grapefruit, 1/2 medium: 44 mg
- grapefruit juice, 3/4 cup (6 ounces): 60 mg
- strawberries, 1 cup: 82 mg
- papaya, 1: 94 mg
- tomato, 1 medium: 23 mg
- red bell pepper, 1/2 cup raw: 141 mg
- broccoli, steamed, 1/2 cup: 62 mg

- cauliflower, boiled, 1/2 cup: 27 mg
- potato, 1 medium, baked: 26 mg

Controversial health claims for vitamin C

Controversy about vitamin C centers on its usefulness in preventing or treating disease when taken in very large quantities as a dietary supplement. Most of these claims have not been substantiated by well-designed, well-controlled studies. Many are still being investigated in government-sponsored clinical trials. Individuals interested in participating in a clinical trial at no charge can find a list of open trials at http://www.clinicaltrials.gov.

COLDS Nobel prize-winning chemist Linus Pauling popularized the idea that large doses (1,000 mg or more) of vitamin C daily, will prevent, shorten the duration, or reduce the severity of symptoms of the common cold. More than 30 trials have compared colds in people taking up to 2,000 mg of vitamin C daily and those taking a placebo (pill with no nutritional value). These studies found no difference in the number or severity of colds in the two groups, with one exception. Skiers, marathon runners, and soldiers training in Arctic conditions who took vitamin C supplements had 50% fewer colds than people who took no extra vitamin C. All the people who benefited from taking vitamin C supplements were putting their bodies under extreme stress. It appears that for elite athletes and others under physical stress, **dietary supplements** of vitamin C may be of value in preventing colds.

CANCER Cancer is thought to arise because of damage to cells caused by free radicals. Health claims that vitamin C prevents cancer are based on its antioxidant properties. Many studies have shown that people who eat a diet low in fats and high in fresh fruits and vegetables have a lower risk of developing cancer, especially cancer of the mouth, esophagus, stomach, colon, and lung. It is not clear that the benefit of this diet is due to vitamin C. Study results using dietary supplements of vitamin C are mixed. The American Cancer Society recommends increasing healthy foods in the diet to reduce cancer risk rather than taking a dietary supplement.

CARDIOVASCULAR HEALTH Because vitamin C is involved in the production of collagen in blood vessels, researchers have examined the relationship between vitamin C intake and cardiovascular health. Some studies found no benefit to vitamin C supplementation, while others reported that a relatively low dose of vitamin C reduced the risk of death from strokes. Vitamin C does not reduce blood levels of cholesterol. The American Heart Association recommends that to improve cardiovascular health individuals should increase their intake of vitamin C (and other vitamins and mineral) by increasing the amount of fresh vegetables in their diet. Research continues in this area.

CATARACTS Cataracts are the leading cause of vision impairment worldwide. They develop, usually in older individuals, because of changes in the proteins in the lens of the eye. Initial studies suggested that vitamin C could prevent these changes because of its antioxidant properties. A recent a 7-year follow-up study found vitamin C supplements to be of no benefit in preventing cataracts.

OTHER HEALTH CLAIMS Claims have been made that vitamin C can treat or prevent lead poisoning, high **blood pressure** (**hypertension**), **asthma**, Alzheimer&s disease, macular degeneration, premature birth, stomach ulcers, autism, and many other diseases and disorders. None of these health claims have been proved to the satisfaction of practitioners of conventional medicine.

Precautions

People who smoke cigarettes need more vitamin C than those who do not. People with cancer also seem to need more vitamin C.

Large doses of vitamin C as a dietary supplement may cause indigestion or **diarrhea** that stops when the dose is reduced.

Interactions

Vitamin C has few interactions with drugs or other vitamins. Large doses of vitamin C increase the amount of iron absorbed from food in the small intestine. In healthy people, this does not cause any problems and may be beneficial.

Large daily doses of vitamin C may interfere with the absorption of **vitamin** $\mathbf{B}_{12}$.

Complications

Vitamin C can be taken in enormous doses without any serious side effects. At very high doses, it causes diarrhea. Some researchers who believe that large doses of vitamin C prevent disease think that the appropriate daily dose is an amount just slightly less than the amount that causes diarrhea. This amount varies considerably form person to person.

Resources

BOOKS

Berkson, Burt and Arthur J. Berkson. *Basic Health Publications User&s Guide to the B-complex Vitamins.* Laguna Beach, CA: Basic Health Publications, 2006.

Gaby, Alan R., ed. *A-Z Guide to Drug-Herb-Vitamin Interactions Revised and Expanded 2nd Edition: Improve Your Health and Avoid Side Effects When Using Common Medications and Natural Supplements Together.* New York: Three Rivers Press, 2006.

Lieberman, Shari and Nancy Bruning. *The Real Vitamin and Mineral Book: The Definitive Guide to Designing Your Personal Supplement Program,* 4th ed. New York: Avery, 2007.

Peel, Thomas, ed. *Vitamin C: New Research.* New York: Nova Science Publishers, 2006.

Pressman, Alan H. and Sheila Buff. *The Complete Idiot's Guide to Vitamins and Minerals,* 3rd ed. Indianapolis, IN: Alpha Books, 2007.

Rucker, Robert B., ed. *Handbook of Vitamins.* Boca Raton, FL: Taylor & Francis, 2007.

PERIODICALS

Kushi, Lawrence H., Tim Byers, Colleen Doyle, et al. "American Cancer Society Guidelines on Nutrition and Physical Activity for Cancer Prevention." *CA: Cancer Journal for Clinicians* , 56 (2006):254-281.

ORGANIZATIONS

Vitamin C Foundation, P. O. Box 73172, Houston, TX, 77273, (281) 443-3634, http://www.vitamincfoundation .org/found.htm.

Tish Davidson A.M.

Vitamin D

Definition

Vitamin D is a fat-soluble steroid compound that the body needs to remain healthy. In some ways, vitamin D is not a true vitamin because the skin can make vitamin D when exposed to sunlight. However, if the body does not make enough vitamin D, additional amounts must be acquired through **diet**.

Purpose

The main role of vitamin D is to regulate amount of **calcium** circulating in the blood. Calcium is a mineral acquired through diet that is involved in building bones, muscle contraction, and nerve impulse transmission. Vitamin D helps regulate the absorption of calcium from the small intestine. Too little vitamin D can cause weak, brittle, deformed bones. There is also evidence that vitamin D plays a role in controlling cell differentiation and may help to protect the body from developing some types of **cancer**.

Description

Vitamin D exists in several forms, two of which are important to humans. Vitamin D2, called ergocalciferol, is made by plants. Vitamin D2 can be manufactured synthetically by irradiating yeast. This type of vitamin D is most often found in **dietary supplements** and foods fortified with vitamin D. Vitamin D3, called cholecalciferol, is made naturally by the skin when it is exposed to ultraviolet rays in sunlight. Neither vitamin D2 nor D3 is active in the body. Both must be converted, first in the liver and then in the kidney, into an active form of vitamin D (1alpha, 25-dihydroxyvitamin D). Vitamin D in this topic means the active form of vitamin D.

Vitamin D's role in health

Although Vitamin D has been known to play a role in bone health for many years, only recently have researchers begun to explore its effects on cell differentiation and the **immune system**.

BONE HEALTH The role of vitamin D and calcium are closely connected. The body needs calcium to build bones and teeth, contract muscles, transmit nerve impulses, and help blood to clot. Vitamin D helps the body get the calcium it needs by increasing the amount of calcium absorbed in the small intestine. Vitamin D is an active part of the feedback loop that maintains a normal level of calcium in the blood.

To maintain health, the amount of calcium in the blood must stay within a very narrow range. When the amount of calcium in the blood falls below normal, the drop is sensed by the parathyroid glands. The parathyroid glands are four separate clusters of specialized cells in the neck. Low blood calcium levels stimulate the parathyroid glands to secrete parathyroid hormone (PTH). PTH travels through the bloodstream and stimulates the kidney to increase the conversion of vitamin D2 and D3 into its active form. Active vitamin D is released into blood and stimulates the cells lining the small intestine to increase the amount of calcium that they absorbed from digesting food. Vitamin D also causes the kidney to conserve calcium so that less is lost in urine. If these actions do not return the level of calcium in the blood to normal, vitamin D activates cells called osteoclasts that break down bone and return calcium from the bone to the bloodstream. People who do not have enough vitamin D absorb less calcium from the food they eat. To make up for this, calcium is taken from their bones and the bones weaken and break more easily.

CANCER PREVENTION AND TREATMENT Vitamin D also helps regulate cell differentiation. During

KEY TERMS

Cell differentiation—the process by which stem cells develop into different types of specialized cells such as skin, heart, muscle, and blood cells.

Fat-soluble vitamin—a vitamin that dissolves in and can be stored in body fat or the liver

Hormone—a chemical messenger that is produced by one type of cell and travels through the bloodstream to change the metabolism of a different type of cell

Mineral—an inorganic substance found in the earth that is necessary in small quantities for the body to maintain a health. Examples: zinc, copper, iron.

Osteoporosis—a condition found in older individuals in which bones decrease in density and become fragile and more likely to break. It can be caused by lack of vitamin D and/or calcium in the diet.

Placebo—a pill or liquid given during the study of a drug or dietary supplement that contains no medication or active ingredient. Usually study participants do not know if they are receiving a pill containing the drug or an identical-appearing placebo.

Steroid—a family of compounds that share a similar chemical structure. This family includes the estrogen and testosterone, vitamin D, cholesterol, and the drugs cortisone and prendisone.

Vitamin—a nutrient that the body needs in small amounts to remain healthy but that the body cannot manufacture for itself and must acquire through diet

development, cells divide over and over again. At some point, they are triggered to specialize (differentiate) into different types of cells, for example, skin, muscle, blood, or nerve cells. Vitamin D joins with other compounds to turn on and off more than 50 different genes that stop cell growth and start cell differentiation.

One characteristic of cancer cells is that they grow wildly, dividing many times more than normal cells without differentiating. Since vitamin D can stimulate cells to stop dividing and begin differentiating, researchers are investigating whether vitamin D can protect people from getting certain cancers, especially colon, prostate, skin, and **breast cancer**. The research has produced mixed results. Some studies found that vitamin D protected against **colon cancer**, while other found it offered no protection. The official position of the American Cancer Society described in their 2006 **Nutrition** and Physical Activity Guidelines states, "There is a growing body of evidence from population studies (not yet tested in clinical trials) that vitamin D may have helpful effects on some types of cancer, including cancers of the colon, prostate, and breast." However, the American Cancer Society makes no recommendations on the amount of vitamin D needed to have a beneficial effect. Clinical trials are underway to determine safety and effectiveness of vitamin D in a variety of situations. Individuals interested in participating in a clinical trial at no charge can find a list of open trials at http://www.clinicaltrials.gov.

OTHER DISORDERS Vitamin D has been proved to successfully to treat a few other disorders. **Psoriasis**, a skin disorder, often responds to ointments that contain synthetic vitamin D3 when other treatment options have failed. When the parathyroid glands fail to function or are removed during surgery, vitamin D supplements help make up for the lack of PTH. Supplements are also used to treat rare inherited familial hypophosphatemia and Fanconi syndrome-related hypophosphatemia. Both of these are characterized by abnormally low levels of phosphate in the blood.

Normal vitamin D requirements

The United States Institute of Medicine (IOM) of the National Academy of Sciences has developed values called Dietary Reference Intakes (DRIs) for **vitamins** and minerals. The DRIs consist of three sets of numbers. The Recommended Dietary Allowance (RDA) defines the average daily amount of the nutrient needed to meet the health needs of 97–98% of the population. The Adequate Intake (AI) is an estimate set when there is not enough information to determine an RDA. The Tolerable Upper Intake Level (UL) is the average maximum amount that can be taken daily without risking negative side effects. The DRIs are calculated for children, adult men, adult women, pregnant women, and breastfeeding women.

The IOM has not set RDA values for vitamin D because of incomplete scientific information and variability in the amount of vitamin D the body makes when the skin is exposed to sunshine. Instead, it has set AI and UL levels. Recently the UL level has become somewhat controversial and has been challenged by some researchers as being set too low. AI and UL levels are measured in both weight (micrograms or mcg) and international units (IU). The IU measurement is the measurement used on dietary supplement labels. For vitamin D, 1.0 mcg equals 40 IU.

The following are the AIs and ULs for vitamin D for healthy individuals:

- adults 19–50 years: AI 200 IU or 5 mcg; UL 2,000 IU or 50 mcg
- adults 51–70 years: AI 400 IU or 10 mcg; UL 2,000 IU or 50 mcg
- adults 71 years and older: AI 600 IU or 15 mcg; UL 2,000 IU or 50 mcg

Exposing the face, arms, and legs to sunshine for 15 minutes three or four times a week meets the dietary requirements for vitamin D for people with fair skin much of the time. However, people who live north of 40° latitude (approximately a line that extends from Philadelphia to San Francisco) may not get enough sun exposure to meet their dietary needs during winter months. Dark-skinned people may need to spend triple the amount of time in the sun as fair-skinned people to synthesize adequate amounts of vitamin D, since the increased amount melanin pigment in dark skin slows vitamin D production. Using sunscreen with an SPF of 8 or higher also slows the production of vitamin D in the skin.

Vitamin D is not found in large amounts in many foods. However, since the 1930s vitamin D has been added to about 99%: of all milk, and to some breakfast cereals, bread, orange juice, and infant formula. In addition, the Food and Drug Administration requires all foods containing olestra, a compound that reduces fat absorption, to be fortified with the fat-soluble vitamins A, D, E, and K.

The following list gives the approximate vitamin D content for some common foods:

- cod liver oil, 1 Tablespoon: 1,360 IU
- salmon, cooked, 3.5 ounces: 360 IU
- mackerel, cooked, 3.5 ounces: 345 IU
- tuna, canned in oil, 3 ounces: 200 IU
- milk, any type fortified, 1 cup: 100 IU
- orange juice, fortified, 1 cup: 100 IU
- cereal, fortified, 1 serving: 40 IU (average, serving sizes vary)
- egg, 1 whole: 20 IU

Precautions

Vitamin D deficiency

Vitamin D deficiency results in rickets in children and osteomalacia in adults. Rickets is a condition in which the bones do not harder because of a lack of calcium deposited in them. Instead they remain soft and become deformed. Osteomalacia is a weakening of bones in adults that occurs when they are broken down (demineralized) and calcium in the bones is returned to the blood. Vitamin D deficiency also can cause joint and muscle **pain**, and muscle spasm. Less severe cases can result in **osteoporosis** in older adults.

The vitamin D fortification program, along with the popularity of daily multivitamins, has greatly reduced the number of people in the United States who are vitamin D deficient. However some groups remain at risk of vitamin D deficiency. These include:

- institutionalized or homebound people who rarely go outside. One study found that 60% of nursing home patients were vitamin D deficient.
- people living in northern latitudes who cover almost all their body for much of the year due to climate or religious requirements
- people with gastrointestinal diseases such as Crohn&s disease, celiac disease, or inflammatory bowel disease that interfere with the absorption of nutrients from the intestine
- people with disorders of the pancreas that interfere with the absorption of nutrients
- people with anorexia nervosa (self-starvation)
- people who have had part of their stomach or intestine surgically removed for weight loss or other reasons

Vitamin D excess

Vitamin D excess in healthy individuals occurs only when large quantities of vitamin D are taken as a dietary supplement over several months. This can result in high calcium levels in the blood (hypercalcemia). Symptoms of vitamin D excess include nausea, vomiting, excessive thirst, weakness, and high **blood pressure**. Calcium deposits may develop in the kidneys, blood vessels, heart, and lungs. The kidneys may be permanently damaged and eventually fail completely.

Interactions

Research suggests that the following types of medications may increase the available amount of vitamin D in the body. People taking these drugs should not take a vitamin D supplement without consulting their healthcare provider.

- hormone replacement therapy/estrogen replacement therapy
- isoniazid (INH) used to treat tuberculosis
- thiazide diuretics

Research suggests that the following types of medications may decrease the available amount of vitamin D in the body. People taking these drugs should discuss with their healthcare provider whether a vitamin D supplement is right for them.

- antacids taken daily for long periods
- calcium-channel blockers used to treat heart conditions and high blood pressure
- certain cholesterol-lowering medications that block fat absorption
- phenobarbitol and similar anticonvulsants
- mineral oil taken on a daily basis
- orlistat, a weight loss drug marketed as Xenical or Alli

Complications

No complications are expected when vitamin D is used in the recommended amounts. The complications resulting from insufficient or excess use are discussed above.

Resources

BOOKS

Gaby, Alan R., ed. *A-Z Guide to Drug-Herb-Vitamin Interactions Revised and Expanded 2nd Edition: Improve Your Health and Avoid Side Effects When Using Common Medications and Natural Supplements Together.* New York: Three Rivers Press, 2006.

Lieberman, Shari and Nancy Bruning. *The Real Vitamin and Mineral Book: The Definitive Guide to Designing Your Personal Supplement Program,* 4th ed. New York: Avery, 2007.

Pressman, Alan H. and Sheila Buff.*The Complete Idiot's Guide to Vitamins and Minerals,* 3rd ed. Indianapolis, IN: Alpha Books, 2007.

Rucker, Robert B., ed. *Handbook of Vitamins.* Boca Raton, FL: Taylor & Francis, 2007.

PERIODICALS

Carpenter, Kenneth J. and Ling Zhao. "Forgotten Mysteries in the Early history of Vitamun D." *Journal of Nutrition*, 129 (1999):923-7.

Tish Davidson A.M.

Vitamin E

Definition

Vitamin E is a antioxidant vitamin found in many foods or can be taken as a supplement.

Description

Vitamin E naturally exists in eight different forms; four tocopherols: alpha tocopherol, beta tocopherol, gamma tocopherol, delta tocopherol and four tocotrienols: alpha tocotrienol, beta tocotrienol, gamma tocotrienol and delta tocotrienol. Each form has a slightly different activity in the body. The most active form in humans is alpha tocopherol and vitamin E supplements are often sold as alpha tocopherol acetate.

Synthetic vitamin E is labeled as "D,L" or "d,l" tocopherol. Since only the "D" or "d" form of the vitamin is active, the D,L or d,l form is only half as active as the naturally occurring form, which is D or d. When vitamin E is supplied as a mixture of different forms it is often referred to as mixed tocopherols, which is considered by many to be the most useful form.

The most important role of vitamin E is as an antioxidant protecting cells against free radical damage. Damage by free radicals can lead to several diseases including **heart disease** and **cancer**. Although vitamin E deficiency in humans is rare, it can occur in several situations:

- People with disorders that affect absorption of fat from the intestines including cystic fibrosis, Crohn's disease or the inherited conditions abetalipoproteinemia, and ataxia and vitamin E deficiency (AVED) may be at risk.
- Premature or low birth weight infants and people on a very low fat diet.
- Deficiencies in vitamin E are associated with unsteady walking or poor coordination, muscle weakness, nerve degeneration in hands and feet.

Prolonged and severe vitamin E deficiencies can lead to blindness, abnormal heart rhythms and dementia.

A number of investigations are underway to evaluate the ability of vitamin E to prevent chronic disease. Vitamin E has been promoted for the following uses:

- as an immune stimulant
- prevention of macular degeneration, cataracts, Parkinson's disease, premenstrual syndrome, and cancer
- treatment for anemia and angina
- prevention or treatment of atherosclerosis
- reducing the side effects of cisplatin for chemotherapy

- as a cancer treatment itself
- prevention of heart disease in dialysis patients
- prevention or slowing of dementia
- prevention or improvement of diabetes
- prevention of scars
- lowering high cholesterol levels

Much of the research remains inconclusive or very preliminary. More significant research has been done in the areas of heart disease, cancer, and dementia or Alzheimer's disease.

Because oxidative injury is thought to play a role in the development of both cancer and heart disease it seems logical that taking **antioxidants** such as vitamin E should reduce the risk of both. Laboratory studies show several small benefits to alpha tocopherol related to cancer and heart disease, such as decreased platelet aggregation and inhibiting cell growth. Several epidemiology studies have also shown a lower risk of heart disease and cancer associated with people who have an increased ingestion of vitamin E either from **diet** or supplements. However, when randomized, controlled, clinical trials have been done to follow up and confirm a role for vitamin E supplementation in reducing cancer risks or cardiovascular disease risks the results have not usually been positive.

A study published in the *Journal of the American Medical Association* (JAMA) in 2005 compared individuals taking 400 IU/d of vitamin E (alpha tocopherol) to volunteers taking no vitamin E. After seven years there was no significant difference between groups in the occurrence of cancer or cardiovascular disease. In fact, researchers noticed a slight increase in heart failure in the vitamin E group. A second study from the same year evaluated all published results from studies involving vitamin E. The study concluded that regular high doses of vitamin E (400 IU/day or more) slightly increased the risk of **death** for any reason compared with individuals who did not take vitamin E. It is, therefore, recommended that doses higher than 400 IU/day be avoided.

In 2008, a review of studies that evaluated the use of vitamin E for Alzheimer's disease was published. The review found that, although fewer patients taking vitamin E progressed to incapacity compared to control groups who took no vitamin E, more patients taking vitamin E experienced **falls**. The review concluded that as of yet there is no evidence that vitamin E is beneficial for those with Alzeheimer's disease or mild cognitive impairment.

QUESTIONS TO ASK YOUR PHARMACIST

- Is vitamin E useful in treating my condition?
- What is the recommended dose for vitamin E supplements?
- How do I know if I have vitamin E deficiency?
- Will vitamin E supplements interact with my other medications?

Although some studies show that deficiencies of vitamin E are linked to increased risk of heart disease, taking vitamin E supplements does not decrease the risk of heart disease or cancer. The best way to get vitamin E is through food. Foods high in vitamin E include vegetable oils, wheat germ oil in particular; nuts including peanuts; green leafy vegetables; eggs; and whole grains and fortified cereals. Food supplies all eight forms of vitamin E and other antioxidants. Eating a variety of foods is important in order to get enough vitamin E and other antioxidants. Cooking and storage of foods can be detrimental to vitamin E content.

Recommended dosage

The recommended daily allowance (RDA) for vitamin E in adults is 15 mg or 22.5 International Units (IU). RDAs for vitamin E are only based on alpha tocopherol. Amounts of vitamin E in foods are typically given as IUs. The upper tolerable limit recommended for vitamin E is 1,000 mg (1,500 IUs) daily. Vitamin E deficiency in North Americans is rare with most people getting adequate levels from foods.

Precautions

Because the FDA does not regulate herbs and supplements, there is no guarantee of strength, purity or safety of these products. **Contact dermatitis** has been reported with topical use. Recent reports indicate that regular doses of 400 IU or greater per day can slightly increase the risk of death. It is wise to study current research on vitamin E and ask a physician about the latest recommendations. Very few long term studies have been done to document risks or benefits of vitamin E supplementation.

Use of vitamin E should be avoided if the patient has a rare eye condition called retinitis pigmentosa. Taking vitamin E with this condition has been

KEY TERMS

Antioxidants—Particles that seek out and destroy free radicals, by-products of oxygen use, to prevent damage to the body.

Contact dermatitis—Rash or irritation of the skin caused by contact with a substance.

Epidemiology—A branch of science that studies the frequency and distribution of disease in a population.

Free radicals—The by-products of oxidation, these molecules can cause damage throughout the body.

Recommended Daily Allowance (RDA)—The amount of a specific nutrient that should be consumed each day for optimal health. This standard is set and periodically updated by U.S. government agencies.

Vitamin E deficiency—Failure to obtain the necessary levels of vitamin E through food.

associated with an increased loss of vision. The absorption of vitamin E is dependent on the presence of other fats so vitamin E supplements are best taken with a meal.

Side effects

Vitamin E supplementation at doses higher than 400 IU/day have been associated with increased risk of bleeding, particularly in patients taking anticoagulants such as warfarin, heparin or **aspirin**. Regular high doses of vitamin E are also linked to increased risk of death from all causes. Caution should be taken when ingesting large amounts of vitamin E.

Side effects for short term use of vitamin E include contact **dermatitis** on the skin, abdominal **pain**, **diarrhea**, nausea, gonadal dysfunction, diminished kidney function, **dizziness**, fatigue, headache, weakness or blurred vision. These side effects are rare.

Interactions

Zinc deficiency may also be related to decreases in vitamin E. Vitamin E can interfere with antidepressant drugs, **antipsychotic drugs**, aspirin, **beta blockers** for high **blood pressure**, chloroquine for malaria, and cyclosporine for cancer. Patients should notify their physician if they take any of these drugs with vitamin E.

Caregiver concerns

Caregivers should monitor the use of vitamin E supplements in older adults. Any adverse side effects from taking supplements should be reported to the patient's physician. Caregivers should also learn to recognize symptoms of vitamin E deficiency and discuss these concerns with the physician.

Resources

PERIODICALS

Lonn, E., et al. "Effects of Long-term Vitamin E Supplementation on Cardiovascular Events and Cancer: A Randomized Controlled Trial." *Journal of the American Medical Association* (JAMA) 293, no. 11 (March 16, 2005): 1338–1347.

Miller, E. R., et al. "Meta-Analysis: High-Dosage Vitamin E Supplementation May Increase All-Cause Mortality." *Annals of Internal Medicine* 142, no. 1 (January 4, 2005).

OTHER

"Possible Interactions With: Vitamin E." *Adam.com*. 2002 [cited April 15, 2008]. http://www.ajc.com/health/altmed/shared/health/alt_medicine/ConsSupplements/Interactions/VitaminEcs.html.

"Vitamin E." *Drugs & Supplements*. November 1, 2005 [cited April 14, 2005]. The Natural Standard Research Collaboration. http://www.mayoclinic.com/health/vitamin-e/NS_patient-vitamin-e.

"Vitamin E." Office of Dietary Supplements, National Institutes of Health. January 23, 2007 [cited April 15, 2008]. http://dietary-supplements.info.nih.gov/factsheets/vitamine.asp.

Cindy L. A. Jones Ph.D.

Vitamin K

Definition

Vitamin K is a fat-soluble organic compound that the body needs to remain healthy. Although bacteria in the human intestine make some vitamin K, it is not nearly enough to meet the body's needs, so people must get most of their vitamin K from foods in their **diet**.

Purpose

The liver needs vitamin K to make factors that regulate blood clotting. Vitamin K may also play a role in maintaining strong bones and preventing **osteoporosis**.

Description

Vitamin K is not a single substance but a collection of chemically similar compounds called naphthoquinones. Vitamin K_1, called phylloquinone, is the natural form of vitamin K. It is found in plants and is the main source of vitamin K in the human diet. Vitamin K_2 compounds, called menaquinones, are made by bacteria that live in the human intestine. Researchers originally thought that bacteria in the gut provided a substantial percentage of human vitamin K needs, but more recent research suggests that these bacteria provide only a small amount and that people should get most of their vitamin K from diet. Vitamin K_1 is manufactured synthetically and sold many brand names as a dietary supplement. Vitamin K is also included in many multivitamins. In addition, a synthetic water-soluble form of vitamin K called K_3 or menadione is not allowed in **dietary supplements** in the United States because of its association with serious side effects.

Normal vitamin K requirements

The United States Institute of Medicine (IOM) of the National Academy of Sciences has developed values called Dietary Reference Intakes (DRIs) for **vitamins** and minerals. The DRIs consist of three sets of numbers. The Recommended Dietary Allowance (RDA) defines the average daily amount of the nutrient needed to meet the health needs of 97–98% of the population. The Adequate Intake (AI) is an estimate set when there is not enough information to determine an RDA. The Tolerable Upper Intake Level (UL) is the average maximum amount that can be taken daily without risking negative side effects.

The IOM has not set RDA values for vitamin K because of incomplete scientific information. Instead, in 2000, it set AI levels for all age groups. AI and levels for vitamin K are measured in by weight (micrograms or mcg). No UL levels have been set for vitamin K. Large amounts of vitamin K_1 do not appear to cause blood clotting or other side effects. However, K_3 is associated with health risks especially to children. It is banned by the United States Food and Drug Administration.

The following are the AIs for vitamin K for healthy adults:

- men age 19 and older: 120 mcg
- women age 19 and older: 90 mcg

KEY TERMS

Coenzyme—Also called a cofactor, a small non-protein molecule that binds to an enzyme and catalyzes (stimulates) enzyme-mediated reactions.

Dietary supplement—A product, such as a vitamin, mineral, herb, amino acid, or enzyme, that is intended to be consumed in addition to an individual's diet with the expectation that it will improve health.

Enzyme—A protein that change the rate of a chemical reaction within the body without themselves being used up in the reaction.

Fat-soluble vitamin—A vitamin that dissolves in and can be stored in body fat or the liver.

Osteoporosis—A condition found in older individuals in which bones decrease in density and become fragile and more likely to break. It can be caused by lack of vitamin D and/or calcium in the diet.

Vitamin—A nutrient that the body needs in small amounts to remain healthy but that the body cannot manufacture for itself and must acquire through diet.

Sources of vitamin K

Vitamin K is found in the largest quantities in green, leafy vegetables. The following list gives the approximate vitamin K_1 content or some common foods. Little vitamin K is lost during cooking, but more is lost when foods are frozen.

- parsley, fresh, 2 Tablespoons: 120 mcg
- spinach, cooked 1/2 cup: 445 mcg
- kale, cooked, 1/2 cup: 530 mcg
- turnip greens, cooked, 1/2 cup: 265 mcg
- Swiss chard, cooked, 1/2 cup: 285 mcg
- brussel sprouts, cooked 1/2 cup: 110 mcg
- broccoli, cooked, 1/2 cup: 77 mcg
- asparagus, cooked, 1/2 cup: 46 mcg
- celery, raw, 1/2 cup: 18 mcg
- carrots, raw, 1/2 cup: 8 mcg
- miso, 1 ounce: 4 mcg
- milk, 2% 1 cup: 5 mcg
- dietary supplements: 10–120 mcg

Vitamin K's role in health

Vitamin K is necessary for normal blood clotting (coagulation). In the liver, it is converted into more than half a dozen coenzymes that are essential to the complex cascade of events that result in the formation of a blood clot.

There is some growing evidence that vitamin K plays a role in maintaining strong bones. Certain proteins that regulate the cells (osteoblasts) that deposit **calcium** and other minerals in bone appear to be dependent on vitamin K. If this is true, vitamin K may play a role in preventing osteoporosis. Clinical trials are currently underway to determine safety and effectiveness of vitamin K in a variety of situations. Individuals interested in participating in a clinical trial at no charge can find a list of open trials at http://www.clinicaltrials.gov.

Vitamin K deficiency

Vitamin K deficiency is extremely rare in healthy people. It can, however, occur in individuals who have disorders that interfere with the absorption of nutrients from the intestine. Signs of vitamin K deficiency include easy **bruising**, excessive bleeding, and slow clotting. People who are at higher risk for vitamin K deficiency include:

- people with gastrointestinal diseases such as Crohn&s disease, cystic fibrosis, inflammatory bowel disease, or ulcerative colitis
- people who have had part of their stomach or intestine surgically removed for weight loss or other reasons
- people with liver damage
- people with alcoholism
- people who take high doses of antibiotics over a long period.

Precautions

People who are taking blood-thinning drugs, especially warfarin (Coumadin), should discuss their vitamin K needs with their healthcare provider. They may need to restrict their intake of vitamin K. The purpose of blood-thinning drugs is to keep the blood from forming clots in the veins and arteries. Since vitamin K helps blood to clot, high levels of vitamin K in the diet may work against blood-thinning drugs and reduce their effect. Individuals taking these drugs are encouraged to keep their daily intake of vitamin K steady at or slightly below the IA level. In addition, they should have their international normalized ratio (INR) and prothrombin time (PT), both measures of blood clotting potential, checked regularly.

Injections of vitamin K_3 (menadione) are banned in the United States because they can cause liver damage and rupture of red blood cells in infants and children.

Interactions

In addition to interfering with blood-thinning drugs mentioned above, vitamin K may interact with the following:

- Some broad-spectrum antibiotics (antibiotics that kill a wide variety of bacteria) may decrease the amount of vitamin K_2 produced in the intestines.
- Aspirin (salicylates) taken in high doses over a long time may increase the body's need for vitamin K.
- Cholestyramine (Questran) and mineral oil may decrease vitamin K absorption.
- Quinine may increase the body's need for vitamin K
- Orlistat (Xenical, Alli) is likely to decrease Vitamin K absorption.
- Vitamin K may decrease the effectiveness of blood thinning herbs such as American ginseng (*P. quinquefolius*), alfalfa (*Medicago sativa*), and angelica (*Angelica archangelica*).
- Olestra, a compound that reduces fat absorption, decreases the absorption of vitamin K. The FDA requires all foods containing olestra to be fortified with the fat-soluble vitamins A, D, E, and K.

Complications

No complications are expected from vitamin K, especially when most of the vitamin K comes from dietary sources. However, pregnant and breastfeeding women should avoid taking vitamin K supplements. In addition, people taking blood-thinning drugs should carefully monitor their intake of vitamin K so that they do not increase the chance of developing **blood clots**.

Resources

BOOKS

Gaby, Alan R., ed. *A-Z Guide to Drug-Herb-Vitamin Interactions Revised and Expanded 2nd Edition: Improve Your Health and Avoid Side Effects When Using Common Medications and Natural Supplements Together.* New York: Three Rivers Press, 2006.

Lieberman, Shari and Nancy Bruning. *The Real Vitamin and Mineral Book: The Definitive Guide to Designing*

Your Personal Supplement Program, 4th ed. New York: Avery, 2007.

Pressman, Alan H. and Sheila Buff.*The Complete Idiot's Guide to Vitamins and Minerals,* 3rd ed. Indianapolis, IN: Alpha Books, 2007.

Rucker, Robert B., ed. *Handbook of Vitamins.* Boca Raton, FL: Taylor & Francis, 2007.

Food and Nutrition Board, Institute of Medicine. *Dietary Reference Intakes for Vitamin A, Vitamin K, Arsenic, Boron, Chromium, Cooper, Iodine, Iron, Manganese, Molybdenum, Nickel, Silicon, Vanadium, and Zinc.* Washington, DC: National Academy Press, 2001, pp. 162-177. http://books.nap.edu/books/0309072794/html.

Tish Davidson A.M.

Vitamins

Definition

Vitamins are micronutrients found in many foods, which are essential to proper bodily function. They act as enzymes or coenzymes, and when they are not consumed in adequate amounts, result in a *deficiency syndrome*. Some vitamins can be produced either by the body, or by bacteria normally resident in the intestines, but some intake from either foods or supplements is still essential. Some vitamins, when taken in large quantities, may have uses other than prevention of the deficiency syndrome.

Description

Vitamins are usually divided into two groups, the oil soluable vitamins, D, E, A and K, and the watwer soluable vitamins C and the B complex.

Vitamin A is an umbrella term for a group of related compounds, all of which can produce the same effects. Although retinol, which is chemically and alcohol, and retinal, an aldehyde, have direct action, there are a number of compounds called provitamin A carotenoids, which can be converted by the body into retinol. Retinol and retinal are called *preformed vitamin A* and are normally ingested in the form of animal products, paerticularly milk and liver. The provitamin compounds are most commonly found in vegetables, including carrots, peppers, tomatoes, peas and many others, however although there are many caotenoid compounds, only about 10% of the known carotenoids can be effectively converted into retinol. Beta-carotene, alpha-carotene, and beta-cryptoxanthin can all be converted into retinol, but with different degrees of efficiency, with beta-carotene being the best.

Although vitamin A would seem to be readily available, either as part of a normal **diet** or in the form of supplements, a deficiency has been reported both in developing nations and among low income familes in Canada. While vitamin A deficiency is relatively rare in the United States, it can be associated with other conditions, such as iron deficiency which leads to inadequate ability to store the vitamin, alcoholism, or diseases of the pancreas, liver or intestines. Chronic **diarrhea** may also lead to vitamin A deficiency. On occasion, vitamin A deficiency is observed among people following a vegan diet, but this can be easily remedied by eating more vitamin A rich vegetables.

The best known symptom of vitamin A deficiency is *night blindness*, a condition in which the ability of the eyes to adapt to low lighting is reduced. Vitamin A deficiency has also been linked to **immune system** impairment, particularly in the lining of the lungs, resulting in increased susceptibility to **pneumonia**. While some data would seem to indicate thsat vitamin A may prevent some forms of **cancer**, a 1996 study comparing male smokers who received vitamin A supplements with a placebo control found an 18% higher rate of **lung cancer** among patients in the study group.

While vitamin A is essential to the diet, it also has potential for toxicity, even in relatively modest excess (see *Precautions*. According to the United States National Library of Medicine, forms of vitamin A have been found useful in acute promyelocytic leukemia and improves median survival in this disease. There have been reports that vitamin A may be useful for control or prevention of **cataracts** and **breast cancer**, but the results and inconclusive. Other established uses for forms of vitamin A include treatment of acne and supportive therapy in measels and malaria.

Vitamin B_1, thiamine is found in whole grains, meat, particularly pork and liver, in nuts, beans and potatoes. It is a water soluable vitamin, which is essential for carbohydrate metabolism and nerve conduction, since it is essential for the production of actylcholine, the primary neurohormone of the parasympathetic nervous system. The deficiency syndrome associated with thiamine is Beri-Beri, and is most often seen in areas where milled rice is the major food source, since milling removes most of the outer, vitamin containing layer. A 2007 report from the Thailand Ministry of Health described an outbreak of the syndrome among fisherman who subsisted on only fish ans rice for a period of 2 months. While the earliest symptoms are known to be tiredness and irritability, followed by peripheral nerve **pain**, the report describes one advanced case: *leg edema scrotal edema or ascites, dyspnea, chest discomfort, chest pain, extremity numbness, or extremity weakness*. The other cases were similar, and 2 crewmembers died as a result of heart failure caused by the vitamin deficiency. *Wernicke-Korsakoff syndrome*, also called Korsakoff psychosis; Alcoholic encephalopathy, and Wernicke's disease is also related to thiamine deficiency, but is caused by inhibition of thiamine utilization by heavy alcohol use, so that it may appear even in the presence of adequate thiamine intake. The initial symptoms are double vision and eye movement problems, later evolving into **memory loss**, which can be severe, and ultimately hallucinations. While alcohol withdrawal and thiamine supplementation may repaier the muscle weakness, brain function does not usually recover. Untreated, Wernicke-Korsakoff syndrome leads to **death**.

A 2006 report from George Washington University indicated that thiamine supplementation might be of some use in control of type 2 diabetes ansd **atherosclerosis**, but this has not been confirmed.

vitamin B_2, riboflavin is found in meat, milk, cheese, eggs, leafy green vegetables, peas and beans. The vitamin is so common that a pure vitamin deficiency is almost never seen, but only as part of general **malnutrition**. Symptoms of the deficiency syndrome include sore throat, swelling of mucous membranes, mouth or lip sores, **anemia**, and skin disorders. There is some, very limited, evidence that riboflavin may be useful in migraine prophylaxis.

Vitamin B_3, niacin has also been called Vitamin P and nicotinic acid. It is found in dairy, poultry, meats, fish, nuts and eggs. The deficiency state is pellagra, and is marked by scaly skin sores, diarrhea, inflamed mucous membranes, mental confusion, and delusions. Beyond its vitamin applications, niacin has been recognized as a treatment for **high cholesterol**, but its use is limited by the frequency of adverse effects. A review, published in 2007, described new formulations that may minimize or eliminate the side effects, but success has been limited.

Vitamin B_5, pantothenic acid derives its name from "pan" meaning "from everywhere", and is found in some quantity in virtually all food, but especially in eggs, fish, dairy products and meat. Because pantothenic acid is so prevalent in nature, a true vitamin deficiency is never seen except as part of the most severe malnutrition, and the dificiency syndrome has not been fully established. Even so, pantothenic acid is recognized as an essential nutrient because it is required for formation of coenzyme A (CoA), a molecule that is essential to the metabolism of **carbohydrates**, proteins, and fats, as well as for the synthesis of hormones and cholesterol. Claijms have been made that pantothenic acid can prevent hair from turning grey, lower cholesterol, relieve aerthritis, and prevent post-surgical sore throat, but none of these reports have been well documented.

Vitamin B_6, pyridoxine beans, nuts, legumes, eggs, meats, fish, whole grains, and dweficiency is extremely rare, although processing of foods does reduce the B6 content. The deficiency syndrome is similar to pellegra, and includes rash, glossitis, and cracks at the corners of the mouth. Pyridoxine deficiency can also cause cause **depression**, confusion, abnormal brain waves, and seizures.

Vitamin B_7, biotin has also been called cadaverine and vitamin H. There is no established deficiency state because biotin deficiency has only been seen in cases of complete malnutrition, but it is recognized as an essential component of several enzyme systems. Metabolic problems including very low blood sugars between meals, high blood ammonia, or acidic blood (acidosis) can occur. Recent studies suggest that biotin is also necessary for processes on the genetic level in cells. Like pantothenic acid, biotin is found in almost all foods.

Vitamin B_9, folic acid has also been called vitamin M, and is found in leafy green vegetables, but the amount is greatly reduced if these vegetables are stored at room temperature or cooked. The Merck Manual notes that the bioavailability of folates is greater in supplements ans enriched foods than in fodstuffs as commonly consumed.

Folate deficiency is common, and may result from inadequate intake, malabsorption, or the effects of drugs, most notably methotrexate which is used to treat cancer and **rheumatoid arthritis**, and trimethoprim/sulfamethoxazole, an antibacterial combination, and metformin, which is used to treat diabetes type 2. Renal dialysis increases the excretion of folates. The deficiency syndrome is a megaloblastic anemia, in which red cells are released before they are mature, and so lack adequate oxygen carrying capacity. The appearance of these cells is identical to the anemia caused by vitamin B_{12}, and so tests are required to determine which supplements are required for treatment. Other symptoms of folate deficiency are diarrhea, depression, and confusion.

Vitamin B_{12}, cyanocobalamine is found only in foods of animal origen, eggs, milk, fish and meat. Vegans are advised to supplement their diets to maintain adequate cobalamine levels. Since the body is capable of storing B_{12}, observed deficiency is rare, and is most often seen in elderly persons.

Vitamin B_{12} deficiency can result in a megaloblastic anemia which is superficially indistinguishable from that caused by folate deficiency. A number of other uses have been studied, but some of the reports are based on epidemiologic data showing that patients with specific pathologic conditions have low B_{12} levels—this does not indicate that the diseases are secondary to B_{12} deficiency. For example, it had been observed that persons with **Alzheimer's Disease** had low B_{12} levels, suggesting that there might be an association, but a 2008 Swedish study was unable to show any relationship between the two. While B_{12} defieicncies may produce some mental confusion, this was overshadowed by the deterioration caused by Alzheimer's. Similarly, low folate levels have been linked to depression, and folate injections have been given to improve the general sense of well-being, but a 2007 review from Harvard Medical School concludes that the evidence for this use is still speculative. The National Library of Medicine has reported that folate supplements are of doubtful, is any, value in **sleep disorders**, lung cancer and **stroke**.

Vitamin C also called ascorbic acid, is required for prevention of scurvy. Symptoms of scurvy include include loss of appetite, diarrhea, shortness of breath, weakness, and fever, followed by irritability, depression, leg pain, pseudoparalysis, swelling over long bones of the body, anemia, paleness, poor wound healing, corkscrew hair, dry eyes, skin thickening (hyperkeratosis), and bleeding (particularly gum bleeding, bleeding behind the eyes causing prominence..., bleeding at the joints of the ribs and sternum causing discoloration under the skin of the chest,,, skin bruising, or blood in the urine or stool).

Because **vitamin C** is acidic and has a high margin of safety, it has been used to acidify urine for the prevention of urinary tract infections, however reports of other uses, which include cold prevention, **asthma** prevention, and cancer prevention and treatment have been inconclusive at best.

Vitamin D is an oil soluable vitamin which, unlike other vitamins, can be synthesized by the human body. The vitamin can be produced by the skin during exposure to ultraviolet-B (UVB) rays in sunlight. Even so, diatary intake is necessary, paerticulaerly among the elderly, obese, and people who routinely use high levels of sun protection including sunscreens. There is also an inherited condition, *familial hypophosphatemia* which causes impaired transport and utilization of phsophate and **vitamin D**, which can be effectively treated with vitamin supplementation. Also, inadequate secretions drom the parathyroid gland or surgical removal of the parathyroid, can result in inadequate vitamin D utilization.

The classic vitamin D deficiency syndrome is rickets, seen among children, and marked by skeletal deformities as a result of failure of **calcium** utilization. In adults, the deficiency syndrome is marked by weakness both of muscles and bones. While the role of vitamin D in prevention or treatment of many bone and muscle disorders has been demonstrated, it has also been hypothesized that it may be useful in other conditions, although as of 2008, the evidence is inconclusive. There is an epidemiologic association between high vitamin D levels and a low incidence of **multiple sclerosis**, but further study is needed before a cause and effect relationship can be drawn. Similarly, vitamin D levels seem to have an inverse relationship to vitamin D levels, and it has been noted that **blood pressure** may rise in the winter, when there is less sun exposure, and decline during warmer months. This too requires additional study.

Vitamin E, tocopherols is a fat soluable vitamin with a rich history. The vitamin was discovered in 1922, when it was found to be essential for reproduction in rats. This led to the name "the antisterility vitamin", and led to the belief that **vitamin E** was not only essential for reproduction, but had aphrodisiac properties. In fact, vitamin E, while essential for reproduction in rats, has no comparable effect in humans. The vitamin is well established as an antioxidant, and plays a role in maintaining the integrity of the cell membranes of red blood cells and in **vitamin K** utilization, but its value beyond that has not been confirmed by well designed studies. Vitamin E apparently inhibits platelet aggregation and causes some degree of vasodilation, which would lower blood pressure ansd reduce the risk of heart attacks and strokes, but clear documentation of the ability of vitamin E to prevent or treat cancer, **heart disease**, dementia, liver disease, and stroke has not been achieved.

In November, 2004, the American Heart Association stated that high amounts of vitamin E can be harmful. Taking 400 IU per day, or higher, may increase the risk of death, however the interpretation of the studies on which this conclusion is based has been questioned. A 2006 report indicated that higher vitamin E levels *within the normal range* were associated with lowered all-cause mortality as compared with a control group. A 2005 report from Harvard Medical School found vitamin E to be neither beneficial nor harmful in the course of their women's health study. The researchers concluded that 600 IU of natural-source vitamin E taken every other day provided no overall benefit for major cardiovascular events or cancer, did not affect total mortality, and decreased cardiovascular mortality in healthy women. These data do not support recommending vitamin E supplementation for cardiovascular disease or cancer prevention among healthy women.

Vitamin K refers to a group of chemically similar compounds which affect blood coagulation. Vitamin K_1 (phytonadione) is the natural form of vitamin K, which is found in plants, and provides the primary source of vitamin K. Vitamin K_2 compounds (menaquinones) are made by bacteria in the intestine, while vitamin K_3 is a water soluable derivative which is useful in treating vitamin K deficiencies caused by problems in fat absorption. Vitamin K is found in green leafy vegetables, cauliflower, green peas, beans, olives, canola, soybeans, meat, cereals, and dairy products. Cooking does not remove significant amounts of vitamin K from these foods.

Vitamin K functions in blood clotting, and to some extent in bone formation. The deficiency syndrome is marked by excess bleeding and **osteoporosis**.

Vitamin K deficiency is rare, although it may be seen in cases of malnutrition. More often it is associated with malabsorption syndromes or surgical procedures which limit the ability to absorb vitamins such as biliary obstruction, **celiac disease** or sprue, ulcerative colitis, regional enteritis, cystic fibrosis, short bowel syndrome or intestinal resection. In addition, some drugs affect the absorption of vitamin K, or destroy the intestinal flora which produce a portion of vitamin K. Coumadin, an anti-coagulant (blood thinner) which is routinely used after heart attacks or vardiovasular surgery to reduce the risks of blood clotting that might result in heart attacks or strokes acts by inhibiting vitamin K, while **antibiotics** may destroy the intestinal bacteria which produce the vitamin. Persons taking **anticoagulant drugs** are advised to maintain a constant diet in order to achieve steady vitamin K levels. For those people taking coumadin or other blood thinners as well as multivitamin preparations, it is important to check the vitamin K content of the vitamins. Some preparations do not include vitamin K, and a change of brands may alter the required dose of anti-coagulant.

Recommended dosage

The following are the recommended daily intakes for healthy persons over the age of 51, and are based on estimated needs of 97-98% of healthy people. Note that in this group, gender differences may be based largely on body size and are not absolute. Because many vitamins are available in different chemical forms, with different potencies, it is adviseable to check the form and RDA labeling on commercial products, and to discuss actual needs with a **nutritionist**, physician or pharmacist. In some cases, vitamins may be labeled in terms of activity units instead of by weight.

- Folate: 400 micrograms
- Niacin: women 14 mg, men 16 mg
- Riboflavin: women 1.1 mg, men 1.3 mg
- Thiamin: women 1.1 mg, men 1.2 mg
- Vitamin A: women 700 micrograms, men 900n micrograms
- Vitamin B6: woman 1.5 mg, men 1.7 mg
- Vitamin B12: 2.4 micrograms
- Vitamin C: women 75 mg, men 90 mg
- Vitamin D: 400 units, higher doses are recommended for people over the age of 70
- Vitamin E: 15 mg
- Vitamin K: women 90 micrograms, men 120 micrograms

QUESTIONS TO ASK YOUR PHARMACIST

- What is best dosage form for me?
- Does the brand matter or can I buy generic vitamin supplements?
- Does the chemical form in which the vitamins are provided have any side effects profiles?
- Are there possible interactions with my OTC and prescription medical drugs?

Precautions

While vitamins are inherently safe in normal doses, some have toxic effects when taken in overdose.

Niacin causes severe facial flushing.

Vitamin A causes a severe hypervitaminosis syndrome which includes peeling of the skin, headache, enlargement of the liver and spleen and bone thickening. The recommended safe limit for vitamin A is 3,000 micrograms/day.

KEY TERMS

Anemia—a condition in which the blood is deficient in red blood cells, in hemoglobin, or in total volume

Atherosclerosis—presence of plaque in the inside of the arteries

Dyspnea—difficulty breathing

Edema—An excess accumulation of fluid in a tissue causing swelling

Glossitis—Inflammation of the tongue

Malnutrition—Inadequate nutrition caused by either inadequate intakwe of one or more nutrients, or failure to absorb or process the nutrients

Megaloblastic anemia—An anemia in which immature red blood cells appear in the peripheral blood

Provitamin—A chemical which can be converted into a vitamin in the body

Sternum—The breastbone

Syndrome—A collection of symptoms and signs that occur together

Type 2 diabetes—Maturity onset diabetes, a condition in which the body produces insulin, but does not use it properly

Vegan—A person who eats only vegetable products

Folate can cause peripheral neuropathy marked by a feeling of numbness. The recommended maximum daily dose is 1,000 micrograms/day

Vitamin D can cause elevated serum calcium, loss of appetite, kidney failure and abnormal bone growth. The maximu recommended daily dose is 2,000 units.

Vitamin E may cause abnormal bleeding. The maximum daily dose is 1,000 milligrams.

Side effects

When taken in normal nutritional doses, vitamins have no adverse effects.

Interactions

Vitamins do not have clinically significant interactions in nutritional doses. There may, however, be purposeful interactions when used with drugs whose mechanism of action is intended to couhteract the vitamins, such as the folate antagonists used in cancer therapy, or the anticoagulant coumadin which prevents blood clotting by inhibting vitamin K. These should be discussed with the prescriber.

Mineral oil, used as a laxative, may inhibit the absorption of oil soluable vitamins D, E, A and K.

While maintenance multi-vitamins present little risk of **drug interactions**, combination products which contain minerals may interact with some drugs. For example, iron, which may be present in some formulations, binds to the tetracycline antibiotics. Most of these interactions can be avoided by taking the two drugs at appropriate intervals so they are not in the digestive system at the same time.

Caregiver concerns

While routine maintenance vitamins are rarely a cause for concern, discuss the use of larger doses with a qualified professional. This is particularly true if the patient is elderly, since the vitamin needs may be higher or lower than the usual recommended dsily intakes.

Resources

BOOKS

Stanton R *Vitamins: What They Do and what They Don't Do*Allen & Unwin, St Leonards, NSW Australia 1999

Reynild J (ed)*Martindale the Extra Pharmacopoeia 30th ed* The Pharmaceutical Press London 1993

Pauling, L *Vitamin C, the Common Cold and the Flu.* W.H. Freeman & Co Ltd 1977

PERIODICALS

Kirkpatrick SI, Tarasuk V *Food insecurity is associated with nutrient inadequacies among Canadian adults and adolescents.* J Nutr. 2008 Mar;138(3):604-12

Albanes D, Heinonen OP, Taylor PR, et al *Alpha-Tocopherol and beta-carotene supplements and lung cancer incidence in the alpha-tocopherol, beta-carotene cancer prevention study: effects of base-line characteristics and study compliance.* J Natl Cancer Inst. 1996 Nov 6;88 (21):1560-70.

Doung-ngern P, Kesornsukhon S, Kanlayanaphotporn J et al *Beriberi outbreak among commercial fishermen, Thailand 2005.* Southeast Asian J Trop Med Public Health. 2007 Jan;38(1):130-5.

Arora S, Lidor A, Abularrage CJ, Weiswasser JM,et al *Thiamine (vitamin B1) improves endothelium-dependent vasodilatation in the presence of hyperglycemia.* Ann Vasc Surg. 2006 Sep;20(5):653-8

Modi S, Lowder DM.*Medications for migraine prophylaxis.* Am Fam Physician. 2006 Jan 1;73(1):72-8

Drexel H.*Nicotinic acid in the treatment of hyperlipidaemia.* Fundam Clin Pharmacol. 2007 Nov;21 Suppl 2:5-6.

Gulhas N, Canpolat H, Cicek M etal *Dexpanthenol pastille and benzydamine hydrochloride spray for the prevention of post-operative sore throat.* Acta Anaesthesiol Scand. 2007 Feb;51(2):239-43

Wahlin A, Fahlander K, Wahlin TB et al *Vitamin B status and cognitive performance in preclinical and clinical Alzheimer's disease: data from the Kungsholmen Project.*Dement Geriatr Cogn Disord. 2008;25(1):23-31

Mischoulon D, Raab MF. *The role of folate in depression and dementia.* J Clin Psychiatry. 2007;68 Suppl 10:28-33.

Patterson C, Feightner JW, Garcia A, et al *Diagnosis and treatment of dementia: 1. Risk assessment and primary prevention of Alzheimer disease.* CMAJ. 2008 Feb 26;178(5):548-56

Buijsse B, Feskens EJ, Kwape L et al *Both alpha- and beta-carotene, but not tocopherols and vitamin C, are inversely related to 15-year cardiovascular mortality in Dutch elderly men.* J Nutr. 2008 Feb;138(2):344-50.

Munteanu A, Zingg JM, Azzi A.

*Anti-atherosclerotic effects of vitamin E–myth or reality?*J Cell Mol Med. 2004 Jan-Mar;8(1):59-76

Wright ME, Lawson KA, Weinstein SJ et al *Higher baseline serum concentrations of vitamin E are associated with lower total and cause-specific mortality in the Alpha-Tocopherol, Beta-Carotene Cancer Prevention Study.* Am J Clin Nutr. 2006 Nov;84(5):1200-7.

Lee IM, Cook NR, Gaziano JM, et al *Vitamin E in the primary prevention of cardiovascular disease and cancer: the Women's Health Study: a randomized controlled trial.* JAMA. 2005 Jul 6;294(1):56-65

Kademian M, Bechtel M, Zirwas M. *Case reports: new onset flushing due to unauthorized substitution of niacin for nicotinamide.*J Drugs Dermatol. 2007 Dec;6 (12):1220-1.

OTHER

http://dietary-supplements.info.nih.gov/

http://findarticles.com/p/articles/mi_g2603/is_0005/ai_2603000575

http://www.quackwatch.org/search/webglimpse.cgi?ID=1&query=vitamin+E

http://www.musc.edu/BCMB/onlinepubs/molecularmedicinejournal/vol2002/folate_pershing.htm

http://online.factsandcomparisons.com/

http://www.hsph.harvard.edu/nutritionsource/vitamins.html HERE

http://lpi.oregonstate.edu/infocenter/vitamins.html

http://clinicaltrials.gov/search/open/intervention=vitamins

http://www.merck.com/mmpe/index.html

http://www.medscape.com

http://www.cfsan.fda.gov/~dms/supplmnt.html

http://www.fda.gov/consumer/updates/vitamins111907.html

Sam Uretsky PharmD

W

Walking problems

Definition

Walking problems result from conditions or disabilities that impair the ability to walk without experiencing discomfort or **pain**.

Description

Besides direct injuries to the spine, legs or feet, almost any disease or condition that affects the nerves or muscles can result in walking problems. Muscle weakness, joint problems, pain, disease, and neurological disorders can all contribute to walking problems. It is also often the case that more than one disease or condition contributes to their development. Walking problems are also much more common in the elderly population than in people younger than 65.

Demographics

Problems with walking are commonly associated with **falls** and disability in senior adults. The American Geriatrics Society estimates that walking problems affect approximately 20% of older adults living in the community and 50% of the elderly, aged 85 years old and older. Most of these problems are associated with underlying diseases, especially severe diseases. In the United States, each year, falls occur in over 33% of persons over age 65, and in 50% of persons over age 75. About a third of the older population reports some difficulty with balance or walking, and this percentage also increases in frequency and severity after age 75.

Causes and symptoms

Many conditions can cause walking problems, and these problems increase with age. Chronic disease conditions often lead to walking problems, such as movement disorders. Though it seems simple and effortless, walking in fact requires an astonishingly complex system of control. Disruption of any portion of this system, resulting from movement disorders, can cause a person to produce movements that are too uncoordinated, or too poorly controlled to maintain the ability to walk without discomfort or pain. Parkinson's disease and ataxia are two movement disorders that can significantly affect walking. As symptoms of Parkinson's disease get worse, patients often experience trouble walking. People with ataxia experience a failure of muscle control in their arms and legs, resulting in a lack of balance and coordination or a disturbance of gait.

The ability to walk can also be impaired by a wide variety of injuries or other illnesses. Common injuries caused by falls include fractures to the spine, legs or feet. Falls are most often caused by home hazards, such as slippery floors and rugs, weak muscles, unstable balance, and side effects from medications, such as **dizziness** and confusion. Common illnesses associated with difficulty walking include **osteoporosis** and arthritis. Osteoporosis is a disease in which the density and quality of bone is reduced, which significantly increases the risk of fracture. Arthritis is a disease that damages the lining of joints and causes pain and swelling in the joints. **Multiple sclerosis** is also associated with muscle weakness and trouble with coordination and balance. Complications after orthopedic surgery or **stroke** can also impair walking. **Vitamin B_{12}** deficiency has also been associated with numbness in the extremities and a disturbed sense of balance, leading to gait problems.

Symptoms of walking problems vary depending on the underlying cause. They may include changes in gait, difficulty negotiating turns or climbing stairs, feelings of numbness, pain, unsteadiness, twitching, muscle stiffness or weakness in the legs, and frequent falls or loss of balance.

Diagnosis

A complete medical history is usually taken to identify health factors that may be causing problems with walking and mobility, such as past medical problems, episodes of acute illness, poor vision, or other conditions that can affect stability, coordination, strength, or posture. The examination may include specific tests to evaluate walking speed, balance, coordination, strength, body position, and gait.

Treatment

Treatment depends on the number, type, and severity of the underlying conditions that contribute to walking problems and will first seek to treat the disorder or disease associated with the walking difficulty. The goal of treatment is usually to improve standing and walking function and often feature therapies that combine a variety of different exercises such as leg resistance training, balance, and flexibility exercises.

Nutrition/Dietetic concerns

Healthy bones are important for walking. Among the nutrients important for bone health are **calcium**, phosphorus, magnesium, fluoride, **vitamins** D, B_{12}, and K, and macronutrients such as protein, carbohydrate, and fat. Calcium is the most critical mineral for a healthy bone mass and is found in milk and other dairy products, green vegetables, and calcium–enriched foods. **Vitamin D** also helps the body absorb calcium and other minerals while **vitamin K** has been shown to increase bone mineral density in osteoporotic people while reducing fracture rates.

Therapy

Therapy can help people who experience difficulty walking. It may involve a combination of services and assistive technology, such as having a **physical therapist** use a special massage to restore a wider range of motion to stiff leg muscles. The use of lift inserts to correct for different leg lengths, ankle braces, and various shoe modifications can also help relieve walking problems. Leg braces can also help maintain proper foot alignment for standing and walking.

Various assistive devices are also available to help people who require assistance to walk or stand:

- Canes: Canes are meant to provide light support to help people maintain balance and avoid falls while walking.
- Crutches: Crutches provide more support than canes as they allow a person to support the entire weight of the body.

QUESTIONS TO ASK YOUR DOCTOR

- What is the cause of my walking problem?
- Is there a cure?
- What treatments are available?
- What kinds of walking aids are available and whom should I contact about getting the right one?
- What type of walker would best help me maintain mobility?
- Are my walking problems permanent?
- How can I improve my strength and fitness level?

- Standing Aids: These are designed to be propelled by the user, and usually support standing from non–weight–bearing to full–weight–bearing.
- Walkers: Walkers provide a higher level of support than canes to help people avoid falls while walking, as they can support up to 50% of a person's weight.

Changes can also be made to the home to adapt living spaces to meet the needs of people with walking problems so that they can continue to live independently and safely. Modifications can range from something as simple as installing handrails in bathrooms to full–scale construction projects that require building wheelchair ramps and widening doorways.

Prognosis

Outcomes for walking problems depend on the underlying cause. Treatment can generally improve some walking problems, such as those associated with vitamin B12 deficiency, knee arthritis, Parkinson's disease, or nerve inflammation. In many cases, physical therapy has proven effective to improve or recover walking function. For example, therapy for knee arthritis or stroke often leads to improvement.

Prevention

Problems with walking can be prevented with good, preventive health care on a routine basis, and lifestyle choices that maintain health. For example, wearing well–fitting walking shoes with low heels and firm soles help maximize balance and prevent falls. Loss of bone density and osteoporosis can be delayed or prevented with a balanced **diet** and regular

KEY TERMS

Arthritis—Disease that damages the lining of joints and causes pain and swelling in the joints.

Ataxia—Disorder that damages the parts of the nervous system that control movement.

Gait—A particular way or manner of moving on foot.

Movement disorders—Group of diseases and syndromes affecting the ability to produce and control movement.

Multiple sclerosis—Chronic inflammatory disease of the central nervous system that primarily affects the myelin sheath, the fatty white matter that covers and protects the nerve cells.

Osteoporosis—Disease in which the density and quality of bone is reduced, which significantly increases the risk of fracture.

Parkinson's disease—Disorder that affects nerve cells, or neurons, in a part of the brain that controls muscle movement.

exercise. The National Osteoporosis Foundation also recommends bone density testing for all women over age 65, and for all women under the age of 65 who have one or more risk factors for osteoporosis in addition to **menopause**. Accidental injuries can also be prevented by removing hazards in the home to reduce the risk of falls. Besides treatment, the health of people who already have a disease can often be improved by regular screening to ensure that treatment options are effective and identify potential walking problems.

Caregiver concerns

It is important to realize that walking problems are not an automatic and irreversible consequence of aging. Rather, they most often result from other conditions that become more common and severe as a person gets older. Proper treatment of any medical condition and appropriate follow–up of patients in this age group is accordingly crucial to ensure that walking problems are identified and addressed before they seriously affect mobility.

Resources

BOOKS

Harrington, Candy B. *Barrier–Free Travel: A Nuts and Bolts Guide for Wheelers and Slow Walkers.* 2nd ed., New York, NY: Demos Medical Publishing, 2005.

Iezzoni, Lisa. *When Walking Fails: Mobility Problems of Adults with Chronic Conditions.* Berkeley, CA: University of California Press, 2003.

PERIODICALS

Cooper, K. M., et al. "Health barriers to walking for exercise in elderly primary care." *Geriatric Nursing* 22, no. 5 (September–October 2001): 258–262.

Ingemarsson, A. H., et al. "Walking ability and activity level after hip fracture in the elderly—a follow–up." *Journal of Rehabilitation Medicine* 35, no. 2 (March 2003): 76–83.

Kubo K., et al. "Effects of 6 months of walking training on lower limb muscle and tendon in elderly." *Scandinavian Journal of medicine & science in sports* 18, no. 1 (February 2008): 31–39.

Lindemann, U., et al. "Distance to achieve steady state walking speed in frail elderly persons." *Gait & Posture* 27, no. 1 (January 2008): 91–96.

Melzer, I., et al. "Effects of regular walking on postural stability in the elderly." *Gerontology* 49, no. 4 (July–August 2003): 240–245.

Rhudy, J. L., et al. "Efficacy of a program to encourage walking in VA elderly primary care patients: the role of pain." *Psychology, Health & Medicine* 12, no. 3 (May 2007): 289–298.

OTHER

Canes and Walkers: Which One Is Right for You? American Geriatrics Society, Foundation for Health in Aging, Information Page (March 08, 2008) http://www.healthinaging.org/public_education/tools/10_canes_walkers.pdf

Crutches: A "How–To" Guide. American College of Foot and Ankle Surgeons, Healthy Feet for an Healthy Life, Information Page (March 08, 2008) http://www.footphysicians.com/footankleinfo/crutches.htm

Falls and Balance Problems. American Geriatrics Society, Foundation for Health in Aging, Information Page (March 08, 2008) http://www.healthinaging.org/public_education/pef/falls_and_balance_problems.php

Home Modification. U.S. Department of Health and Human Services, Administration on Aging Information Page (March 08, 2008) http://www.aoa.gov/press/fact/pdf/fs_home_mod.pdf

How to Choose and Use a Cane. University of Michigan Health System, Information Page (March 08, 2008) http://www.med.umich.edu/1libr/sma/sma_caneuse_sha.htm

Walking Aids. National Institute on Disability and Rehabilitation Research, AbleData Page (March 08, 2008) http://www.abledata.com/abledata.cfm?pageid=19327&top=14223

ORGANIZATIONS

American College of Foot and Ankle Surgeons (ACFAS), 8725 West Higgins Rd., Chicago, IL, 60631-2724, (773) 693-9300, (800)421-2237, (773) 693-9304, info@acfas.org, http://www.acfas.org.

National Center on Physical Activity and Disability (NCPAD), 1640 W. Roosevelt Rd., Chicago, IL, 60608-6904, (800)900-8086, (312)355-4058, ncpad@uic.edu, http://www.ncpad.org.

National Institute of Arthritis and Musculoskeletal Diseases (NIAMS), 1 AMS Circle, Bethesda, MD, 20892-3675, (301)495-4484, (877)22-NIAMS, (301)718-6366, NIAMSinfo@mail.nih.gov, http://www.niams.nih.gov.

Monique Laberge Ph.D.

Wasting *see* **Cachexia and wasting**

Water and nutrition

Definition

Water is essential to life and nutritional health. Humans can live for several weeks without food, but we can survive only a few days without water. Water makes up a large percentage of the body, in muscles, fat cells, blood, and even bones.

Purpose

Every cell, tissue and organ requires water to function properly. Water transports nutrients and oxygen to the cells, provides a medium for chemical reactions to take place, helps to flush out waste products, aids in maintaining a constant body temperature, and keeps the tissues in the skin, mouth, eyes, and nose moist.

Precautions

The body does not store excess water, unlike it does with other nutrients. With physical exertion, water requirements increase; therefore, fluid replacement during **exercise** is critical. The longer the duration and the more physical exertion athletes put into their exercise, the more fluid they lose during workouts. To keep the body working at its best, it is essential to replenish lost fluid after workouts, and to stay well hydrated during exercise.

The body can accommodate extreme changes in water intake when the brain and kidneys are functioning normally. It is usually possible for a person to consume enough water to maintain blood volume and **electrolyte balance** in the blood. However, if a person is unable to consume enough water to equal excessive water loss, **dehydration** may result.

Description

Water for sustaining life

The body works to maintain water balance through mechanisms such as the thirst sensation. When the body requires more water, the brain stimulates nerve centers in the brain to encourage a person to drink in order to replenish the water stores.

The kidneys are responsible for maintaining homeostasis of the body water (i.e. water balance) through the elimination of waste products and excess water. Water is primarily absorbed through the gastrointestinal tract and excreted by the kidneys as urine. Water intake can vary widely on a daily basis, influenced by such factors as: access to water, thirst, habit, and cultural factors. The variation in water volume ingested is dependent on the ability of kidneys to dilute and concentrate the urine as needed. There is a reservoir of water outside of the bloodstream that can replace or absorb excess water in the blood when necessary.

For a normal adult, a minimum daily intake between 700-800 ml (0.74-0.84 US quarts) is required to meet water losses and maintain the body's water balance. To protect against dehydration and developing **kidney stones**, greater water consumption (between 1.4-2 L/day or 1.5-2 US quarts/day) is advised. Water losses occur through evaporation in expired air and through the skin. Sweat losses are usually minimal but can be significant in warmer climates or with accompanying fever.

The following conditions increase water consumption needs. However, the amount of water necessary depends on body size, age, climate, and exertion level.

Water needs are increased by:

- Exercise. Water is lost through perspiration.
- Hot and humid climates.
- High altitudes. The breathing rate is twice as fast as at sea level. At high altitudes, most water loss is due to respiration rather than perspiration.
- Prescription drugs. If adequate water is not available for proper blood flow, medication can become concentrated in the bloodstream and become less effective.
- Dieting. A reduced carbohydrate intake may have a diuretic effect because carbohydrates store water.

- Airplane, bus, or train travel. The re-circulated air causes water to evaporate from skin faster.
- Illness. Fever, diarrhea and vomiting lead to increased water losses.

Individuals should not wait until they are thirsty to replenish water stores. By the time the thirst mechanism signals the brain to encourage a person to drink water, already 1–3% of the body fluids are lost and an individual is mildly dehydrated.

Nutrition for optimal health

Not only is water necessary to sustain life, but proper **nutrition** is also required to ensure optimal health. Consumption of wide variety of foods, with adequate vitamin and mineral intake is the basis of a healthy **diet**. **Vitamins** are compounds that are essential in small amounts for proper body function and growth. Vitamins are either fat soluble: A, D, E, and K; or water soluble: vitamin B and C. The B vitamins include vitamins B_1 (thiamine), B_2 (riboflavin), and B_6 (pyridoxine), pantothenic acid, niacin, biotin, **folic acid** (folate), and **vitamin B_{12}** (cobalamin).

Researchers state that no single nutrient is the key to good health, but that optimum nutrition is derived from eating a diverse diet including a variety of fruits and vegetables. Because there are many more nutrients available in foods such as fruits and vegetables than vitamin supplements, food is the best source for acquiring needed vitamins and minerals. The mineral nutrients are defined as all the inorganic elements or inorganic molecules that are required for life. As far as human nutrition is concerned, the inorganic nutrients include water, **sodium**, potassium, chloride, **calcium**, phosphate, sulfate, magnesium, iron, copper, **zinc**, manganese, iodine, selenium, and molybdenum. Other inorganic nutrients include phosphate, sulfate, and selenium. Inorganic nutrients have a great variety of functions in the body. The electrolytes are affected by fluid balance in particular (sodium, potassium, calcium, phosphate, and magnesium etc.). Water, sodium, and potassium deficiencies are most closely associated with abnormal nerve action and cardiac **arrhythmias**.

Laboratory studies with animals have revealed that severe deficiencies in any one of the inorganic nutrients can result in very specific symptoms, and finally in **death**, due to the failure of functions associated with that nutrient. In humans, deficiency in one nutrient may occur less often than deficiency in several nutrients. A patient suffering from **malnutrition** is deficient in a variety of nutrients.

Complications

Sodium deficiency (hyponatremia) and water imbalances (dehydration) are the most serious and widespread deficiencies in the world. These electrolyte deficiencies tend to arise from excessive losses from the body, such as during prolonged and severe **diarrhea** or vomiting. Diarrheal diseases are a major world health problem, and are responsible for about a quarter of the 10 million infant deaths that occur each year. Nearly all of these deaths occur in impoverished parts of Africa and Asia, where they result from contamination of the water supply by animal and human feces.

Dehydration is a deficit of body water that results when the output of water exceeds intake. Dehydration stimulates the thirst mechanism, instigating water consumption. Sweating and the output of urine both decrease. If water intake continues to fall short of water loss, dehydration worsens.

Causes of dehydration may include:

- vomiting
- diarrhea
- diuretics
- excessive heat
- excessive sweating
- fever
- decreased water intake

Dehydration induces water to move from the reservoir inside cells into the blood. If dehydration progresses, body tissues begin to dry out and the cells start to shrivel and malfunction. The most susceptible cells to dehydration are the brain cells. Mental confusion, one of the most common signs of severe dehydration may result, possibly leading to **coma**. Dehydration can occur when excessive water is lost with diseases such as **diabetes mellitus**, diabetes insipidus, and Addison's disease.

Dehydration is often accompanied by a deficiency of electrolytes, sodium and potassium in particular. Water does not move as rapidly from the reservoir inside of the cells into the blood when electrolyte concentration is decreased. **Blood pressure** can decline due to a lower volume of water circulating in the bloodstream. A drop in blood pressure can cause light-headedness, or a feeling of impending blackout, especially upon standing (orthostatic hypotension). Continued fluid and electrolyte imbalance may further reduce blood pressure, causing shock and damage to many internal organs including the brain, kidneys, and liver.

Consumption of *plain water* is usually sufficient for mild dehydration. However, when both water and electrolyte losses have occurred after vigorous exercise, electrolytes must be replaced, sodium and potassium in particular. Adding a little salt to drinking water or consuming drinks such as Gatorade during or following exercise can replace lost fluids. Individuals with heart or kidneys problems should consult a physician regarding the replacement of fluids after exercise.

Overhydration is an excess of body water that results when water intake exceeds output. Drinking large amounts of water does not typically lead to overhydration if the kidneys, heart, and pituitary gland are functioning properly. An adult would have to drink more than 7.6 L per day (2 US gallons/day) to exceed the body's ability to excrete water. Excessive body water causes electrolytes in the blood, including sodium to become overly diluted. Overhydration occurs in individuals whose kidneys do not function normally, primarily in kidney, heart, or liver disease. People with these conditions may have to limit their water and dietary salt intake. Similar to dehydration, the brain is the most sensitive organ to overhydration. The brain cells can adapt to increased fluid volume when overhydration increases slowly, however, when it occurs rapidly, mental confusion, seizures, and coma can result.

Results

Consuming adequate food and fluid before, during, and after exercise can help maintain blood glucose during exercise and also maximize exercise performance. Athletes should be well-hydrated before exercise commencement and should drink enough fluid during and after exercise to maintain homeostasis. The same rules apply to non-athletes who are participating in physical activity or are in conditions that increase dehydration. Careful attention to water intake and urine output should provide the best results.

Avoiding some beverages such as coffee, tea, alcohol and caffeinated soft drinks may reduce the risk of dehydration. These beverages are all **diuretics** (substances that increase fluid loss). Water in foods, especially fruits and vegetables, is a great source of fluid. Fruits and vegetables can contain up to 95 percent water, so a well-balanced diet is a good way to stay hydrated.

Caregiver concerns

All health care professionals should recognize the importance of promoting proper nutrition and hydration. Encouraging patients to follow nutrition guidelines for adequate vitamin and mineral intakes is critical.

KEY TERMS

Dehydration—A deficit of body water that results when the output of water exceeds intake.

Diuretic—An agent or drug that eliminates excessive water in the body by increasing the flow of urine.

Electrolyte—A substance such as an acid, bases, or salt. An electrolyte's water solution will conduct an electric current and ionizes. Acids, bases, and salts are electrolytes.

Homeostasis—An organism's regulation of body processes to maintain internal equilibrium in temperature and fluid content.

Overhydration—An excess of body water that results when water intake exceeds output.

Patient education

Patients and individuals can be educated regarding the importance of hydration by nutrition experts and physicians as well as the need for good nutrition. Individuals themselves can become familiar with concepts for healthy eating using a number of resources such as the Food Pyramid, which provides a visual guide to healthy eating. In addition, the U.S. Department of Agriculture and the U.S. Department of Health and Human Services have developed official dietary guidelines that include ten basic recommendations for healthy eating:

- Aim for a healthy weight.
- Be physically active each day.
- Let the Food Pyramid guide your food choices.
- Choose a variety of grains daily, especially whole grains.
- Choose a variety of fruits and vegetables daily.
- Keep food safe to eat.
- Choose a diet low in saturated fat and cholesterol, and moderate in total fat.
- Choose beverages and foods to moderate intake of sugars.
- Choose and prepare foods with less salt.
- If you drink alcoholic beverages, do so in moderation.

Resources

BOOKS

Speakman, Elizabeth and Weldy, Norma Jean. *Body Fluids and Electrolytes* 8th ed. London: Mosby Incorporated, 2001.

Workman, M. Linda *Introduction to Fluids, Electrolytes and Acid-Base Balance.* London: W B Saunders Co., 2001.

PERIODICALS

Beck, L.H. "The aging kidney. Defending a delicate balance of fluid and electrolytes." *Geriatrics* 55, no. 4 (2000): 26-28, 31-32.

Sawka, M.N. and Montain, S.J. "Fluid and electrolyte supplementation for exercise heat stress." *American Journal of Clinical Nutrition* 72, no. 2 Suppl. (2000): 564S-572S.

OTHER

Food and Nutrition Professionals Network. http://nutrition.cos.com.

Nr-Space, et al. *Fluids & Electrolytes CD-ROM.* Delmar Publishers, 2001.

ORGANIZATIONS

American Dietetic Association, 216 W. Jackson Blvd, Chicago, IL, 60606-6995, (312) 899-0040, http://www.eatright.org.

Food and Nutrition Information Center Agricultural Research Service, USDA, National Agricultural Library, Room 304, 10301 Baltimore Ave, Beltsville, MD, 20705-2351, (301) 504-5719, (301) 504-6409, fnic@nal.usda.gov, http://www.nal.usda.gov/fnic.

Crystal Heather Kaczkowski MSc.

Patient undergoing hydrotherapy. *(Inga Spence / Photo Researchers, Inc. Reproduced by permission.)*

Water exercise

Definition

Water **exercise** is a type of activity that is done in a body of water, such as a pool, a lake, or the ocean. Sometimes, limited water exercise can be done in a spa or hot tub.

Description

Exercise in the water is a low-impact activity that puts less stress on the joints. When the entire body is underwater, it experiences almost zero gravity since the water carries 90 percent of the body's weight. This buoyancy helps older adults by improving their balance and strength.

Participants in water exercise classes benefit from water resistance exercise and can expect relief from muscle stiffness and pain, as well as increased muscle strength and endurance. *(AP Images. Reproduced by permission.)*

Water, also, offers resistance. It has 12 to 14 percent more resistance than air. This gentle friction aids in strengthening muscles and joints, especially for those recovering from an injury. Some people may choose to increase resistance by wearing wrist or ankle weights in shallow water to offer a more challenging workout.

Like land-based exercise, water exercise can increase cardiovascular fitness, lower **blood pressure** and cholesterol levels, and increase energy. It can also help people lose body fat. Exercising in the water can improve **depression**, **anxiety**, and self-esteem. It enhances flexibility, strengthens muscles, and improves circulation. Moreover, the hydrostatic pressure of the water helps increase heart and lung function. It also can encourage better blood flow to the muscles, especially the legs, much like support hosiery does.

Some activities in the water are done by individuals, such as swimming, water jogging, and water walking. Other activities can be done in a group. Those include water polo, water aerobics, water **yoga**, water **tai chi**, and water Pilates. All of these individual and group activities, except swimming, do not require skill in the water.

Little is needed in order to participate in water exercise besides swimwear. Some people may want to wear a swimming cap or goggles, but usually those are only worn by people who swim laps or engage in water polo. Some swimmers may want to use swim fins or a kickboard.

Water jogging is a deep-water workout that is done in water over the jogger's head. In order to stay afloat and keep the body upright, joggers wear a buoyancy belt with special floats that keep the person's feet off the bottom of the pool or lake and keep the head above the surface of the water. Water jogging can offer a very intense workout as the jogger does jumping jacks or moves the legs in movements that mimic jogging, cycling, or cross-country skiing on land. These activities place added demand on the heart and lungs, as well as on the jogger's ability to keep his or her balance.

Water exercise is often suggested for people who are obese because it puts less stress on the joints and it fosters more active participation because participants find exercising in water is easier to do. Nevertheless, a 2005 study showed that exercising in water to lose weight should be done in warm water, not cold water. The researchers found that participants ate more after exercising in cold water than they did after exercising in warm water.

People who have arthritis often find exercising in warm water easier to do than on land. The warm water soothes stiff joints and muscles and helps people warm-up before activity. Warm water raises body temperature, causing the blood vessels to dilate, thus increasing circulation. Water exercises for these patients can help knees, hips, shoulders, elbows, and even ankles and hands. Whatever body part is affected should be submerged in water, and all movements should be done slowly.

QUESTIONS TO ASK YOUR DOCTOR

- What kinds of water exercise do you recommend?
- What are my limitations?
- Do I need to see a physical therapist?
- Where can I find water exercise programs?

People with **osteoarthritis** often can exercise at much higher intensities than they could on a mat in a gym on land. A study in 2003 found that not only were osteoarthritis patients who exercised in water able to improve their walking ability on land, but they also increased their **independence**.

Some people use a spa or hot tub as an adjunct to water exercise. The jet nozzles massage the body and help relax tight muscles. The size of the hot tub will determine what kinds of exercises can be done. If the feet or hands are of concern, then a smaller sized spa can help work these smaller joints and muscles. Obviously, a small spa would not allow for aerobic activities that work the larger muscles and joints. Also, time in a hot tub should be limited to 10 minutes, and temperatures should not exceed between 98 and 104 degrees F.

Demographics

Anyone can participate in water exercise. Swimming is considered an activity that spans all generations, from infants to octogenarians. Water aerobics, water walking, and water yoga and tai chi, however, are most often activities that older adults enjoy. Young people who have had joint or back injuries may participate for a short time as a rehabilitation activity. Water jogging, though, has become an exercise that even athletes are engaging in because it offers a superior workout with little risk of injury.

Purpose

The purpose of water exercise is to put the body through activity without adding extra stress and strain on the joints. Though people have been swimming and playing water polo for a long time, water exercise grew out of **therapeutic exercise** for people recovering from injury or conditions such as **bursitis** and **sciatica**. It also was and still is used for arthritis patients.

Challenges

Before starting any exercise program, older adults should check with their doctors and explain the types of activities they want to do. It is important when starting a new exercise regime to start slowly and build up gradually. Older adults should go to the pool three times a week and start by doing a few repetitions or a couple of laps, if swimming. Then, gradually the person can increase swimming time to 20 or 30 minutes or exercise to 45 minutes.

Risks

Because exercising in water is easier to do, sometimes beginners can do too much. That is why it is important to warm up prior to the more vigorous part of the exercise session and to cool down afterwards. Those warm-ups should be stretches in the areas that will be exercised. Older adults should learn the difference between muscle **pain** and sore muscles. Muscle pain is more intense and lasts longer than a week. If that occurs, older adults should see their healthcare providers.

Most public or therapeutic pools keep water temperatures in the safe range, usually between 84 to 88 degrees F. Home indoor pools and spas should keep their temperatures in that range also. Though spas are usually hotter, older adults should limit their time in hot water to a few minutes. They may be able to stay in a warm pool safely for far longer. In addition, older adults may not realize that the water is too hot.

It should be noted that for water aerobics or other structured activity, a qualified instructor is essential. If older adults have specific problems, such as arthritis, then the instructor should have some knowledge of the disease. The Arthritis Foundation Aquatic Program has qualified instructors who teach at YMCAs and community pools across the U.S.

In addition, older adults should never engage in water exercise without someone else near the pool. Most community pools, lakes, and beaches have lifeguards. Therapeutic pools also have therapist available to instruct in the proper exercise techniques. These pools also have pool attendants who keep track of people's time in the pool and are available if someone gets into difficulty.

Results

People who participate in water exercise can expect to have better flexibility, stronger muscles, and improved circulation. Participants can also have lower cholesterol and blood pressure readings. Some people can lose weight using this method of exercise. Most importantly, older people who regularly participate in water exercise have less depression and more self-esteem, as well as more independence as they gain confidence in a stronger body. Many people also report fewer **falls** after engaging in regular water exercise.

KEY TERMS

Aerobics—Synchronized movements to strengthen muscles while exercising the heart and lungs.

Hydrostatic pressure—The pressure of the water against the body.

Pilates—A form of exercise that combines yoga, dance, and isometric exercises.

Tai chi—Based on an ancient form of Chinese martial arts, this form of exercise is a series of slow movements that improve balance and strength and also calms the mind.

Water Polo—A game played in the water with two teams trying to get a large ball through a hoop on each side of the pool.

Yoga—An ancient form of exercise that strengthens the spine and the muscles of the body while it calms the mind.

Resources

PERIODICALS

Archer, Shirley. "Tai chi and water exercise relieve arthritis pain."*IDEA Fitness Journal.* (October 2007):95

"Exercise in cold water may increase appetite, University of Florida Study finds."*Ascribe Science News Service* (May 4, 2005):NA

Mancini, Lee. "Swimming and water exercise."*Clinical Reference Systems.*(May 31, 2007):NA

Sato, Daisuke; Kandeda, Koichi; Wakabayashi, Hitoshi; and Nomura, Takeo. "The water exercise improves helath-related quality of life of frail elderly people at day service facility."*Quality of Life Research.* (December 2007):1577-1586

ORGANIZATIONS

National Institute on Aging(NIA), 31 Center Drive, MSC 2292, Building 31, Room 5C27, Bethesda, Maryland, 20892, 301-496-1752, 301-496-1072, www.nia.nih .gov.

United States Water Fitness Association, P.O. Box 243279, Boynton Beach, FL, 33424-3279, 561-732-9908, 561-732-0950, info@uswfa.org, www.uswfa.com.

Janie F. Franz

Water pills *see* **Diuretics**

Weight loss

Definition

Weight loss/management is a term that defines not only a controlled plan for losing weight. It also implies that after individuals have lost the desired amount of weight, they will continue to maintain that weight by managing the weight loss—keeping off the pounds they lost. How many ways, and how many **diet** plans that might assist a senior adult in this venture are as individual as people themselves. Senior adults who suffer from diseases such as diabetes, **heart disease**, or kidney disease, have a vested interest in maintaining a proper weight due to complications that are linked to **obesity**. But this subject is of concern to any senior concerned about maintaining optimum health.

Description

The facts surrounding a diagnosis of obesity can be startling. Nine out of 10 people who are diagnosed with type 2 diabetes, also known as adult onset diabetes, are overweight. The optimum muscle mass that individuals typically have in their 20s is 45 per cent of total body weight. By the time that same population reaches the age of 70, that muscle mass decreased to 27 per cent. Even senior adults who are not overweight can have as much as 50% of their weight as fat.

The health risks that emerge when an individual is overweight, besides diabetes, include high **blood pressure**, high blood cholesterol, coronary heart disease, **stroke**, certain types of **cancer**, and gallbladder disease. Losing excess weight can be crucial to improving health, successful surgery and recovery from surgery, and minimizing the effects of diseases commonly associated with age such as arthritis, **mobility issues**, sleep apnea, **fatty liver** disease, and breathing difficulties—even those that are not directly related to coronary disease, **emphysema**, or **asthma**.

An unexplained, unplanned weight loss is cause for serious investigation. That is when even senior adults who might be overweight should immediately make an appointment to see their physician. Sudden weight loss might be a sign of the onset of diabetes, cancer, or mental health issues such as Alzheimer's, dementia, or **depression** of which a person might not be fully aware. Once a weight loss occurs, either planned or unplanned, being underweight can also pose such health problems as increased risk for **osteoporosis**, decreased immunity, decreased muscle strength, hypothermia, **constipation**, and poor memory.

When any individual decides to lose weight, either at the recommendation of a personal physician or through concern for possible health complications, a careful diet/nutrition plan is addressed. Care must be taken to determine what is the best eating regimen for a person to follow depending on disease factors, medications, lifestyle, genetic and physiological factors, and the amount of excess weight to be lost.

Demographics

According to the National Center for Health Statistics, acting as a division of that Centers for Disease Control and Prevention, based on a 1999–2002 National Health and Nutrition Examination Survey, a population-based survey, 65 percent of adults in the United States over the age of 20 were overweight or obese, and 30 percent of all adults are obese. Institutes of Health Obesity Research Task Force, weight loss and obesity can become issues as people age even when they were not overweight as younger people.

For women in particular, during the years leading up to **menopause**, when increases in weight, and shifts in body weight begin to occur, an average of a pound a year is gained. According to information provided by the Mayo Clinic, however, it is not the normal shifts in hormone levels that are the only cause of weight gain. Factors that are more significant in weight gain include decreased physical activity, eating more, burning fewer calories, and genetic predisposition to certain kinds of weight gain. **Breast cancer** risk has also been found to be reduced when women maintain an appropriate weight.

The groundbreaking Framingham Heart Study, conducted by the National Heart, Lung, and Blood Institute (NHLBI) studied 4,000 white individuals from 1971 through 2001, aged 30 to 59. That study found that in middle age, following menopause, even those women who had maintained a healthy weight and were not considered overweight. For those already overweight, 16 to 23 percent would become obese within 4 years. For men, 12 to 13 percent of them were likely to become obese within that same time period.

As people age, the chances of increasing weight become greater due to decreased physical activity, poor eating habits, and medications.

Purpose

Losing weight during the senior adult years, and maintaining the weight loss provide many health and social benefits. It can decrease difficulty in mobility, the risk for diseases and conditions such as diabetes, coronary artery disease, gallbladder disease, high blood pressure, stroke, certain types of cancer, and high blood cholesterol—determined to be a factor in some heart conditions. A five to 10 percent weight loss alone can lower blood pressure, assist in maintaining lower blood sugar levels in diabetic individuals, increase mobility by easing pressure on otherwise painful joints, and provide more energy and motivation for social activities.

By the late twentieth century the **body mass index**, or BMI index, was developed as one way of determining whether an individual was overweight or obese. A BMI of 25–29.9 is considered overweight; and a calculation of 30 or greater, is obese.

BMI is only one tool in determining whether a person is overweight or obese. Because it does not measure body fat or muscle directly, people might have the same BMI but differ in their percentages of body fat. A muscle builder would typically average greater muscle to body fat percentages than most senior adults. Physicians are also concerned, especially with senior adults with how body fat is distributed. Any excess abdominal fat presents an increased risk factor for health. People who carry excess weight at that body location are more likely to develop obesity–relatd health issues. Women whose waists measure more than 35 inches, and men who measure more than 40 inches, are more likely to suffer health risks than those people with lower waist measurements—indicating that body fat is more evenly distributed throughout the body.

The most accurate measures of obesity involve weighing a person underwater, or in a chamber that uses air displacement to measure body volume, according to the Weight–control Information Network (WIN) of the National Institute of Diabetes and Digestive and Kidney Diseases (NIDDK) of the National Institutes of Health. In addition, an x-ray test known as the dual energy x-ray absorptionmetry, or DEXA. In fact, those most qualified to determine whether or not a person is overweight or obese is the personal physician who has the benefit of professional experience and guidelines that address the issue of weight. Standard charts—once the domain of insurance providers—are also available to present what an appropriate weight for a particular height and body frame might be. Again, though, seeking professional medical advice to determine levels of obesity constitutes the preferable approach.

QUESTIONS TO ASK YOUR DOCTOR

- How much do I have to exercise to lose weight, and maintain my weight loss?
- What harmful affects can any particular "popular" or "fad" diet have on my health?

Challenges

Any weight loss regimen should be discussed with an individual's physician. Hundreds of diets, many of them considered fad diets beckon to people with promises of quick and dramatic weight loss. The issue of losing weight can be particularly difficult in senior adults due to slower metabolisms, economic factors that pose a financial strain when purchasing healthy food items such as organic meats, fish, cheese, and fresh produce. Any diet plan that indicates people can lose a lot of weight quickly should be avoided. Losing two pounds a week during any diet is optimal for the body to adjust to weight loss, and ensures the likelihood of understanding how to maintain that loss throughout the coming years. Yet watching such a slow decrease in weight can provide frustration and temptation to veer off the course of the diet plan. The issue in any healthy weight loss plan is finding what works best for any individual, and what will be most likely to keep a person on a diet for the duration of the necessary weight loss. Dieting that is arduous and makes an individual feel hungry all the time can be a plan of self-sabotage from the beginning. Any individual setting out to lose weight should set a positive, and reasonable goal. The best diet plan is simply a healthy eating pattern, with smaller meals and overall fewer calories. When a person feels deprived, the chances for defeat are greater.

A weight loss study lead by Dr. Laura Svetkey, a professor of medicine at Duke University was published in the March 12, 2008, issue of the *Journal of the American Medical Association.* It followed almost 1,700 overweight or obese people, with the first phase of the program being a six–month weight loss program, with an average weight loss during that time of 19 pounds. The second phase randomly selected for three groups—a "personal contact" group, an "interactive technology" group, and a "self-directed" group. After 30 months, it was the group that had personal contact with other individuals who were either interested also in maintaining a weight loss, or individuals interested in helping the individuals maintain their weight loss, that regained 8.8 pounds less than the self-directed group. The "interactive technology" group regained an average of 3.3 pounds more than the group maintaining personal contacts. What this study might indicate is that support systems, while challenging to maintain, can be essential in maintaining weight loss.

Risks

A diet that emphasizes one particular food group might be tempting when discovering how much weight can be lost in such a short period of time. Seldom does the weight stay off—and the risk of sudden weight loss to health conditions can be life threatening. A decrease in calories should not mean a decrease in necessary nutrients. When approaching any change in eating habits, even when they are an improvement, attention to how those changes might be affected in relation to medications, physical activity, and mental health issues should also be considered. Risks can be minimized if following any diet in the care of a physician or registered **dietician**.

Losing weight is only part of the challenge in weight loss. Maintaining the weight post loss can be at risk if healthy eating patterns that satisfy both nutritional needs and emotional needs are not continued. The risk of a diet of deprivation almost ensures that most people will binge following a weight loss. Not only can that result in gaining back lost weight. It can trigger complications for disease conditions already present, particularly diabetes.

Taking diet pills without the advice of a physician, especially for senior adults with varying medical conditions can prove harmful. **Bariatric surgery**, another weight loss method involving gastrointestinal bypass methods, can pose risks to senior adults. Only can a team of medical professionals that include an individual's personal physician provide the best advice regarding the benefits of such a surgery as opposed to the risks.

Results

The success of any weight loss program offers numerous health and social benefits to senior adults, no matter what medical conditions might exist. Maintaining the weight loss through proper nutrition and healthful eating habits can provide protection for the **immune system**, help regulate diabetes, high blood pressure, and other coronary-related diseases, increase mobility for necessary physical activity, increase overall emotional well-being.

KEY TERMS

BMI—The abbreviation for "Body Mass Index" calculating a figure to determine an individual's weight–height proportion and measure determining level of underweight, normal weight, overweight, or obesity.

Calorie—The unit of measure used to determine the amount of energy is produced by food when oxidized in the human body—every measured portion of food is assigned a certain calorie level. Suggestions for calorie intake for age, gender, and body weight in order to maintain weight are provided by the U.S. Food and Drug Adminstration.

Resources

BOOKS

Zinczenko, David; and, Goulding, Matt.*Eat This, Not That: Thousands of Simple Food Swaps that can save you 10, 20, 30 pounds-or more.* Emmaus, PA and NY: Rodale Books. 2007

PERIODICALS

"Baby Boomers and Arthritis: Increasing Arthritis Linked to Higher Obesity Rates-Beth Israel Deaconess Medical Center study." *American Journal of Public Health.* September 2007.

"Diabetes, Obesity, and Hypertension May Enhance Associations between Air Pollution and Markers of Systemic Inflammation." *Environmental Health Perspectives.* July 2006. pp. 992–998.

"Snacking helps seniors fight weight loss." *NY Daily News.* May 25, 2007.

OTHER

"Calorie restriction: Is this anti–aging diet worth a try?" http://www.mayoclinic.com/print/anti-aging/HQ00223/METHOD=pri...

"Eating Well As We Age." http://www.www.fda.gov/opacom/lowlit/eatage.html

"Embrace Your Health! Lose Weight if You Are Overweight." http://www.win.niddk.nih.gov/health/public/heart/other/chdblack/embrace1.htm

"Good Nutrition: It's a Way of Life." http://www.niapublications.org/agepages/nutrition.asp

"Losing Weight Safely." http://www.www.fda.gov/opacom/lowlit/weightls.html

"Losing Weight: Start By Counting Calories." http://www.www.fda.gov/fadc/features/2002/102_fat.html

"Obesity." http://www.mayoclinic.com/print/obesity/DS00314/METHOD=pri...

"Personal Contact Helps Maintain Weight Loss." http://www.nlm.nih.gov/medlineplus/print/news/fullstory_62090.html

"Understanding Adult Obesity." http://www.win.niddk.nih.gov/publications/understanding.htm

"Weight Control." http://www.nlm.nih.gov/medlineplus/print/weightcontrol.html

"Weight Gain After Menopause:Reverse the Middle age spread." http://www.mayoclinic.com/print/menopause-weight-gain/HQ01072

"Young At Heart, Healthy Eating & Physical Activity Across Your Lifespan." http://www.win.niddk.nih.gov

ORGANIZATIONS

American Diabetes Association, 1701 Beauregard Street, Alexandria, VA, 22311, 800–342–2383, http://www.ada.org.

American Dietetic Association, 120 South Riverside Plaza, Suite 2000, Chicago, IL, 60606–6995, 800–877–1600, http://www.eatright.org.

Mayo Clinic, 200 First Street, NW, Rochester, MN, 55905, 507–284–2511, http://www.mayoclinic.com.

National Institute on Aging, National Institutes of Health, Building 31, Room 5C27, 31 Center Drive, Bethesda, MD, 20892, http://www.nia.nih.org.

U.S. Food and Drug Administration, 5600 Fishers Lane, Rockville, MD, 20857–0001, 888–463–6332, http://www.fda.gov.

Weight-control Information Network (WIN)/National Institute of Diabetes and Digestive and Kidney Diseases of the National Institutes of Health, 1 WIN Way, Bethesda, MD, 20892–3665, 202–828–1025, 877–946–4627, 202–828–1028, win@info.niddk.nih.gov, http://win.niddk.nih.gov.

Jane Elizabeth Spear

Wheelchair prescription

Definition

A wheelchair is a mobile chair used by individuals who have impairments that limit their ability to walk. A wheelchair prescription defines the specifications of a chair according to an individual's particular needs.

Purpose

Wheelchairs are used either as primary or secondary means of mobility, depending upon the extent of an individual's functional limitations. When using a wheelchair as a primary means of mobility, an individual may spend the majority of his or her day in the chair and use it for movement within his or her home, work, school or community setting. As a secondary means of mobility, a chair may be used just for longer distances by an individual who has low endurance or tolerance for walking. The wheelchair prescription is used to define the type of wheelchair required, seating needs, and details about necessary components.

Description

Selection of a type of wheelchair, its fit, and included components depends largely on the following factors:

- What are the patient's disability, medical, and management issues? These can include considerations such as level of independence, pressure relief, orthoses, etc.
- What is the patient's size, weight, and posture? Does the patient need a heavy-duty chair? Is there a fixed scoliosis or kyphosis that needs to be accommodated?
- What is the individual's functional ability? Sitting balance, ability to transfer oneself and provide pressure relief, upper extremity strength and dexterity, and cognitive level are just a few of the things that must be considered.
- What are the patient and family goals for using the chair? What has been tried already? Will the chair be used as a primary or secondary means of positioning and mobility? Will it be used around the house, at school/work, outside, for sports participation?
- What are the environmental concerns? Access to public and private settings, including work, school, libraries, and transportation, must be considered. Is the individual's own home wheelchair-accessible?
- What are the funding issues? The cost of basic and special features, sources of funding, rental/leasing options, future maintenance, and upgrade costs should all be considered.

The prescription should include the following categories of specifications:

Type of wheelchair

There are standard and heavy-duty adult chairs, in addition to junior, youth, and "growing" frames. In a user assessment study in 2000, ultra lightweight chairs with a high degree of adjustability were shown to be preferred over lightweight chairs for ride comfort and ergonomics in long-term wheelchair use. Chairs for people with hemiplegia include a seat that is lower to accommodate for propulsion with a lower extremity. One-hand drive chairs allow a chair to be propelled with one handrim controlling both wheels. Chairs for people with lower-extremity amputations are designed to widen the base of support, compensating for the loss of anterior weight. Sports wheelchairs are lighter and easier to maneuver, for active individuals. They include a lower back, canted wheels for more efficient propulsion, and small handrims. Reclining and tilt wheelchairs offer individuals the opportunity to either recline, opening up the angle at the hips, or tilt their entire position back. Reclining chairs tend to be used for relief from orthostatic hypotension, while tilt chairs address pressure relief and gravity-assisted positioning. Power wheelchairs may be used by individuals who would have difficulty with operating a manual wheelchair. Dependent bases, which allow only for a **caregiver** to push the chair, also exist; however, great care must be taken in choosing this option because it does not allow for the user to self-propel the chair in any capacity.

Standard measurements

Measurements should be taken with the individual seated on a firm surface in an erect posture. The individual may require physical support to maintain this position while being measured. If an additional seat cushion or back will be used with the chair, those measurements also must be figured in to the individual measurements.

Specific formulas exist and should be used to determine: seat height, depth and width; back height and armrest height. The size of a standard adult wheelchair is:

- seat width = 18 in (45 cm)
- seat depth = 16 in (40 cm)
- seat height = 20 in (50 cm)

Standard sizes exist for smaller adults and children as well; custom fabrication also is available but can be costly.

Components

Wheel locks are used to prevent movement of the chair while the user is moving into or out of it. The wheels of the chair may have solid rubber, pneumatic or semi-pneumatic tires. Pneumatic tires provide a smoother ride and are easier to maneuver on rough and soft surfaces, but they also create more friction, increasing the energy expenditure required. The caster wheels are the front, smaller wheels that allow turns to occur. The rear wheels are large and include an outer handrim that is used to propel the chair.

Lap and chest belts are used to prevent the user from falling out of the chair. Several types of armrests exist, including fixed, removable, reversible, desk-length, and adjustable. The front rigging supports the lower leg and foot. The leg rest may be swing-away, removable, or elevating. The footplates may be fixed or adjustable, and may include strapping for proper foot positioning. Antitipping devices often are attached to the lower rear support bar to prevent backward tipping of the chair.

All of these components may be included on the chair with various options that must be specified on the wheelchair prescription according to the patient's needs.

Seating

Seating is an important consideration, especially for users who will spend most of their waking day in the chair or for those with pressure relief concerns. Several cushion types exist: planar, contoured, and molded. A planar surface offers the least support and pressure relief, but may be the least expensive and simplest to maintain. A contoured surface may either assume contour with pressure through the use of foam, air, or gel within the cushion, or it may be preformed. It provides more support than the planar surface, but is more adjustable than the molded surface. A molded seat is created from liquid foam that follows the direct contours of the specific user. It offers the most support for an individual with low trunk control and may be formed to accommodate fixed deformities; however, it also is costly and room for growth is limited.

Operation

Operation of a wheelchair varies depending on the type. A user who is going to be active in self-propelling a manual wheelchair must learn the following techniques, if applicable to his or her individual needs:

- Locking brakes, swinging away or removing front riggings, and adjusting or removing armrests.

- Transferring into and out of the chair, which may include transfers to standing, to the floor, to an automobile seat, to various sitting surfaces, or to bed.
- Wheeling the chair, using the handrims, over various types of terrain including smooth tile, carpeting, gravel, sand, asphalt, and/or grass.
- Maneuvering the chair over curbs and ramps.
- Folding or disassembling the chair for transport in a car or for storage.

The user also should be able to educate another individual on how to assist with or perform any of the above activities, in case the user requires assistance at any time. A caregiver should be able to assist with reclining or tilt-in-space functions as well.

A user of a power wheelchair must learn to maneuver the chair using the control interface selected for his or her individual needs. This may be a joystick, sip-and-puff, tongue touch pad, eye gaze, or chin or head control, depending upon the level of disability. Research has found that in individuals with severe disabilities resulting from high-level **spinal cord injury**, nervous system diseases, cognitive impairment or blindness, 10% find it extremely difficult to perform activities of daily living with power wheelchairs, and up to 40% find many steering and maneuvering situations difficult or impossible. New technology using microprocessors and sensors to assist navigation may help to alleviate this problem in the future.

Maintenance

Maintenance, just like operation, depends on the type of wheelchair used. A solidly built manual chair may require minimal maintenance, while a power chair often requires nightly battery charges. Proper function of wheel locks and other components should be monitored frequently and adjusted as necessary by the wheelchair supplier or with his or her explicit instruction.

Caregiver concerns

A physician, **physical therapist**, occupational therapist, seating specialist, and assistive technology specialist all may be involved in making recommendations for the wheelchair type and specification of components.

Training

Training is required in order for an individual to successfully operate a wheelchair, regardless of the type. A physical therapist often is the health care team member who works with a patient to learn transferring, propulsion, and maneuvering techniques. The occupational therapist and assistive technology practitioner (who may also be an OT or PT) play key roles as well in training the patient for optimum use of hand, head, mouth, or other controls.

Resources

PERIODICALS

Cooper, Rory A. "Wheelchairs and Related Technology for the Millenium." *Journal of Rehabilitation Research and Development* 37 (May/June 2000).

DiGiovine, Michalle M., et al. "User Assessment of Manual Wheelchair Ride Comfort and Ergonomics." *Archives of Physical Medicine and Rehabilitation* 81 (Apr. 2000): 490–3.

Fehr, Linda, et al. "Adequacy of Power Wheelchair Control Interfaces for Persons with Severe Disabilities: A Clinical Survey." *Journal of Rehabilitation Research and Development* 37 (May/June 2000): 353–60.

OTHER

Bergen, Adrienne Falk. "Assessment for Seating and Wheeled Mobility Systems." *WheelchairNet.* Apr. 1998. http://www.wheelchairnet.org.

"Prioritizing and Making Decisions About Wheelchairs." *WheelchairNet.* http://www.wheelchairnet.org/ProdServ/Docs.

Peggy Campbell Torpey

Withdrawing support

Definition

Withdrawing support, or withdrawing life support, refers to stopping or removing various devices or treatments used to sustain vital body processes.

Life support procedures are usually put in place in order to stabilize a patient until he or she can start to breathe, eat and drink, or until his or her heart can start beating normally again. In many cases, when an illness is considered curable or treatable, life support measures are successful in maintaining body processes until the person can continue recovering on their own. At other times, however, life support is considered futile treatment; that is, the patient has an incurable disease or will never recover full functioning, and further treatment is considered useless. At that point, the decision is usually made to withhold life support (not starting it in the first place) or withdrawing it (stopping it once it has been started). Although at one time doctors made a distinction between withholding and withdrawing life support, as of the early 2000s most lawyers and ethicists believe that it is appropriate to try life support if there is even a small chance that it will help the patient. If it becomes clear after a few days that the treatment is not helping, then the doctor can withdraw it without feeling that he or she is causing the patient's death.

Description

Dramatic cases involving withdrawal of life support often receive wide publicity in the media, and many people think that withdrawal of life support is therefore unusual. A Harris survey conducted in 2005, however, found that 28 percent of the adults surveyed had experienced the death of a close friend or family member within the past 10 years who had been on life support before death. Of these deaths, two-thirds had happened after life support was withdrawn; only 34 percent of the patients had died while they were still on life support systems. By extending these figures to the total adult population of the United States, the authors of the survey concluded that "death following the withdrawal of life support happens millions of times [in the United States] every year. This is neither uncommon nor unusual."

There are three major systems or procedures commonly used in life support: artificial nutrition and hydration; cardiopulmonary resuscitation (CPR); and mechanical ventilation.

Artificial nutrition and hydration

Artificial nutrition and hydration refers to giving a patient who cannot eat or drink normally a balanced combination of fluids and nutrients through a tube placed directly into the stomach or the upper intestine, or a vein. This form of nutrition is commonly called tube feeding.

When tube feeding is withdrawn or withheld, the patient dies of dehydration rather than starvation, usually within 5–12 days, as the body can survive longer without food than without fluids. According to doctors, dehydration is not a painful process as long as the patient's mouth is kept moist, because the mouth is the only part of the body that can perceive thirst.

Cardiopulmonary resuscitation

Cardiopulmonary resuscitation is a series of procedures undertaken to provide artificial blood circulation and artificial respiration until a patient whose heart has stopped beating (or who has stopped breathing) regains a normal heartbeat. It is essential to maintain a flow of blood to the brain, because the brain suffers damage if blood flow is interrupted for 4 minutes and may suffer irreversible damage after 7 minutes. For this reason CPR is usually effective only within 7 minutes of cardiac arrest, although it can still double or triple the patient's chances of survival.

Outside a hospital, CPR consists of a series of chest compressions and mouth-to-mouth resuscitation performed until emergency personnel arrive. A defibrillator, or device that delivers a dose of electrical to the heart, is usually needed to restart normal heartbeat. Many emergency vehicles carry defibrillators to use when needed.

Stopping CPR is usually not a controversial decision, particularly if some time has passed since the patient's heart stopped and brain damage has almost certainly occurred.

Mechanical ventilation

Mechanical ventilation is a type of life support in which a machine called a ventilator or respirator is used to force air into the patient's lungs through a tube inserted into the nose or mouth. The tube extends down into the patient's trachea or windpipe. Mechanical ventilation is used to supply oxygen to the body until the patient can breathe on their own again, but it is also used in cases of incurable disease or damage to the central nervous system to prolong life until some other body system fails.

To withdraw this type of life support, the tube is usually removed from the patient's mouth or nose before death; this is called extubation. Before or during extubation, the patient is usually given a combination of opioids (painkillers) and benzodiazepines (tranquilizers) to minimize discomfort and prevent coughing or seizures. In some cases the respirator is adjusted gradually to a series of lower settings while in others, mechanical ventilation is stopped at once.

Viewpoints

Withdrawal of life support is controversial because it raises fundamental and disturbing questions about the nature and value of human life as well as control over one's body at the end of life. It is one of the primary reasons for making advance directives, which are written statements of personal preferences regarding medical care at the end of life and authorizing another person to make decisions about health care in one's stead. Many people would prefer not to

KEY TERMS

Advance directive—A document in which a person describes their wishes regarding medical treatment if they are incapacitated and names another person (proxy) to direct their care.

Cardiac arrest—The medical term for the failure of the heart to contract normally and blood circulation to stop abruptly as a result.

Cardiopulmonary resuscitation (CPR)—The name for a group of treatments, including drugs and electric shocks, intended to clear the passageways to the lungs and restart the heart.

Defibrillator—A machine used by emergency health care personnel to deliver an electric shock to heart muscle in order to restore normal heart beat.

Ethicist—A person who studies and writes about moral principles and questions involving good and evil or human duties and obligations.

Extubation—The removal of the tube that connects a patient to a ventilator.

Futile care—Medical care that is useless or highly unlikely to produce a good outcome.

Prognosis—Prediction of the course of a disease and the patient's chances of recovery.

Ventilator—A machine that moves breathable air in and out of the lungs of a person who cannot breathe on their own.

be kept alive for prolonged periods of time by artificial nutrition or mechanical ventilation, while others are distressed by the possibility of being denied life support measures.

Advance directives do not, however, always resolve the question of withdrawing support in actual situations. In some cases the patient's wishes are not followed, either because family members disregard them or disagree among themselves, or because there has been poor communication between family members and staff. In 95 percent of cases, according to one study, the patient is not conscious or able to communicate clearly. Sometimes it is not clear even to the patient's doctors whether further treatment is futile, or whether the patient has a chance, however small, to improve.

Several doctors offer the following recommendations to help family members and health care professionals resolve disagreements and deal with guilt feelings about withdrawing life support:

- Doctors and nurses should tell family members about the patient's prognosis in clear and understandable language and in a timely fashion.
- They should be available to family members to answer any questions that may arise rather than avoiding the family out of their own discomfort.
- The patient should be kept comfortable and his or her physical symptoms controlled.
- The decision to withdraw support should not be made by only one person, even a family member; it should represent a consensus.
- Health care professionals should always involve the family in decisions about withdrawing support rather than doing it without consultation because they consider further care futile.
- The family should be encouraged to remain with the patient when support is withdrawn and to have a clergyperson or other spiritual leader present for religious end-of-life rituals.

Resources

BOOKS

Beers, Mark H., M. D., and Thomas V. Jones, MD. *Merck Manual of Geriatrics*, 3rd ed., Chapter 13, "Care of the Dying Patient." Whitehouse Station, NJ: Merck, 2005.

Caplan, Arthur, James J. McCartney, and Dominic A. Sisti. *The Case of Terri Schiavo: Ethics at the End of Life.* Amherst, NY: Prometheus Books, 2006.

Wicclair, Marc R.*Ethics and the Elderly*. New York: Oxford University Press, 1993.

PERIODICALS

Mayer, Stephan A., and Sharon B. Kossoff. "Withdrawal of Life Support in the Neurological Intensive Care Unit." *Neurology* 52 (1999): 1602.

Orr, Robert D., M.D., and Gilbert Meilaender. "Ethics and Life's Ending." *First Things*, August/September 2004. Available online at http://www.firstthings.com/article.php3?id_article=371&var_recherche=%22life+support%22 [cited February 23, 2008].

Prendergast, Thomas, M.D., and Kathleen Puntillo, R.N. "Withdrawal of Life Support: Intensive Caring at the End of Life." *Journal of the American Medical Association* 288 (December 4, 2002): 2732–2740. Available online at http://cms.clevelandclinic.org/ccfpulmonary/documents/journals/Withdrawal%20of%20Life%20Support%20Dec.%202002.pdf [cited February 23, 2008].

Way, Jenny, Anthony Back, and J. Randall Curtis. "Withdrawing Life Support and Resolution of Conflict with Families." *British Medical Journal* 325 (December 7, 2002): 1342–1345. Available online at http://cms.clevelandclinic.org/ccfpulmonary/documents/journals/Withdrawing%20Life%20Support%20and%20Resolution%20of%20Conflict%20with%20Families%20Dec.%202002.pdf [cited February 24, 2008].

OTHER

Cleveland Clinic. *Understanding Life Support Measures.* Cleveland, OH: Cleveland Clinic, 2006. Available online at http://www.clevelandclinic.org/health/health-info/docs/3800/3888.asp?index=12362 [cited February 24, 2008].

Harris Poll. "Withdrawal of Life Support Systems Is More Common Than Public May Think." *Harris Interactive*, April 21, 2005. Available online at http://www.harrisinteractive.com/harris_poll/index.asp?PID=560 [cited February 23, 2008].

Johns Hopkins Hospital. "Procedure for Withdrawal of Life Support in the MICU/ICP." *The Johns Hopkins Hospital Medical Nursing Service Standards of Care Manual.* Baltimore, MD: The Johns Hopkins Hospital, 2001. Available online at http://www.aacn.org/PalCare/pdfs/withdrawal_procedure_jhopkins.pdf [cited February 23, 2008].

ORGANIZATIONS

American Medical Association (AMA) Institute for Ethics, 515 N. State Street, Chicago, IL, 60610, (800) 621-8335, http://www.ama-assn.org/ama/pub/category/2558.html.

The Hastings Center, 21 Malcolm Gordon Road, Garrison, NY, 10524, (845) 424-4040, (845) 424-4545, mail@thehastingscenter.org, http://www.thehastingscenter.org/default.asp.

The President's Council on Bioethics, 1425 New York Avenue, NW, Suite C100, Washington, DC, 20005, (202) 296-4669, info@bioethics.gov, http://www.bioethics.gov/.

Rebecca J. Frey Ph.D.

Wound care

Definition

Wound care refers to specific types of treatment for **pressure sores**, skin ulcers and other wounds that break the skin. Pressure ulcers, also called "bed sores" and referred to medically as decubitus ulcers, are wounds that commonly develop at pressure points on the body when the weight of an immobilized individual rests continuously on a hard surface such as a mattress or wheel chair. Uninterrupted pressure is the cause of pressure sores and relieving pressure is the mainstay of wound care. Other wounds that may benefit from specialized wound care techniques are diabetic foot ulcers, traumatic ulcers caused by injury, arterial and vein ulcers caused by lack of circulation, and burns.

Purpose

The purpose of wound care is twofold: 1) to relieve pressure on a weight-bearing part of the body such as a boney prominence (hand, arm, knee, heel, hip or buttocks) that rests on a bed, wheelchair, another body part, a splint or other hard object, and 2) to treat the ulcerated wound itself when skin has become weakened, inflamed and possibly infected. Although the current discussion of wound care relates primarily to pressure ulcers, other skin ulcers and burn wounds may benefit from similar treatment principles and practices.

Pressure sores develop in immobilized individuals who are constantly positioned the same way in a bed, chair or wheelchair or who may be in traction or paralyzed with limited range of motion. Older individuals who are compromised through acute or chronic illness, under heavy sedation or unconscious, or who have reduced mental functioning, typically do not receive normal nerve signals to move as mobile individuals do. Tissue damage may begin as tender inflamed areas over weight-bearing parts of the body that are in contact with a supporting surface such as a bed or wheelchair, or with another body part or a supportive device. Constant contact at these points exerts pressure on the skin and soft tissue, cutting off the normal flow of blood, oxygen and nutrients to tissue (**ischemia**), resulting in **death** of tissue cells

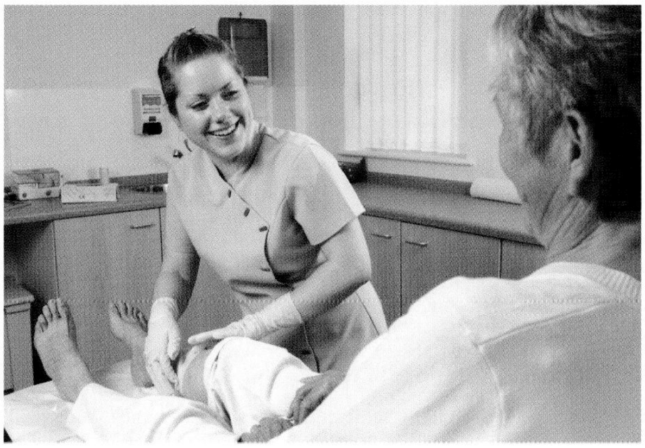

It is important to properly dress and care for wounds. *(Jim Varney / Photo Researchers, Inc. Reproduced by permission.)*

(**anoxia**) and formation of pressure sores. The presence of sores is complicated by rubbing (shear) or friction between the supportive surface and skin over boney prominences. In compromised, immobilized individuals, skin breakdown can happen quickly within hours or days. Regular movement or turning of the individual is needed to relieve pressure, and clinical treatment of pressure sores is required to prevent infection and further breakdown.

Precautions

Physicians orders are required for wound care designed to prevent and treat pressure sores. Alertness to skin condition in immobilized patients is critical among caretakers and medical personal. Individuals at risk for pressure sores may only be aware of discomfort at the points of pressure and may not be aware of the presence of sores or the risk of infection. Caretakers should be informed of pressure sore risk and instructed about typical signs and preventive measures to protect the skin of at-risk individuals in their care.

Steps of recovery

Wound care is usually ordered for any immobilized or bedridden individual with compromised skin integrity in order to prevent pressure sores from developing or to keep red, tender areas from deepening into serious wounds. Care is typically provided by specialized registered nurses called "enterostomal therapists" who are trained in skin and wound care as well as incontinence care and retraining, and care of individuals with surgically diverted urinary or fecal elimination (ostomy). A thorough risk assessment is conducted first and therapy is designed accordingly, employing specific wound care principles and practices shown to be effective for various levels of tissue injury.

Risk Assessment

Enterostomal therapists will note any conditions such as underlying disease, incontinence, or mental confusion that could impede pressure sore recovery. Nutritional status will be evaluated and a specific dietary plan may be designed to provide **nutrition** to benefit skin healing, including **dietary supplements**, intravenous (parenteral) feeding, restoring nitrogen balance and normal protein levels. **Weight loss** may be recommended for obese individuals. Pressure sores will be classified in one of four stages based on wound depth and skin condition: Stage I has intact skin with redness (erythema) and warmth; Stage II has loss of normal skin thickness, possible abrasion, swelling and blistering or peeling of skin; Stage III has full loss of normal skin thickness, an open wound (crater), and possible exposure of deeper layers of skin; Stage IV has full loss of normal skin thickness and erosion of underlying tissue extending into muscle, bone, tendon or joint, along with possible bone destruction, dislocation or pathologic fractures. Therapists will note if wounds are draining, if foul odors are present, or if any debris such as pieces of dead skin are in the wound. Presence of urine or feces from incontinence will be noted as well and regular care personnel will be advised about need for increased hygienic measures.

Pressure Relief

Reducing or eliminating pressure is the first task of wound care and requires the cooperation of the nursing center or family member responsible for onsite care. Recommendations will be made for shifting or turning the patient every two hours or other regular intervals. Some patients may benefit from lying flat on their backs; others may need the head of the bed lowered. Shear can be minimized by placing the patient on a special surface that alternates pressure points. A low-level of pressure relief can be obtained by using egg-crate mattresses or chair cushions. Egg-crate surfaces are constructed of sculpted foam with deep gullies between raised points of cushioning, which alternates pressure on vulnerable areas. Other types of air, foam and gel pressure-relieving surfaces are available. Wheel chair patients may need to be trained to shift their weight or lean side to side to relieve pressure. For deep wounds, burns, or pressure sore prevention, special "low air-loss" or "air-fluidized" beds are available that relieve pressure by constantly moving air within specially designed pillows or within an entire bed surface filled with millions of tiny silicone-coated beads. Many institutions use beds that employ these principles to help heal wounds of all types and to prevent pressure sores from developing in at risk individuals.

Wound Cleansing and Dressing

For more superficial Stage I and II pressure sores, treatment will involve keeping the wound clean and moist, and the area around the sore clean and dry. Saline washes may be used and placement of sterile medicated non-stick gauze dressings that absorb wound drainage and fight infection-causing bacteria. Other bio-protective cleaning solutions include acetic acid, povidone iodine, and **sodium** hypochlorite. Harsh antiseptics, soaps and regular skin cleansers are not used because they can damage newly developing tissue. However, drying agents, lotions or ointments may be applied in a thin film over the wound three or four times daily. Massage of any at-risk area should be avoided because it encourages skin breakdown.

Whirlpool Treatment

Warm-water whirlpool treatments are sometimes used to treat pressure ulcers on arms, hands, feet or legs. This technique removes destroyed tissue fragments (necrotic tissue) by the force of irrigation followed by application of wet-to-dry non-stick dressings. After a wet dressing has been applied to the wound and allowed to dry, its removal picks up necrotic debris and a new dressing of sterile, medicated non-stick gauze or semi-permeable transparent adhesive dressings is applied to keep the area dry and prevent destruction of healthy skin near the wound, reducing risk of infection. Adhesive dressings are not recommended for draining wounds.

Hyperbaric Oxygen Therapy

Treatment of Stage III and IV decubitus ulcers, and other types of skin ulcers or burn wounds, may benefit from treatment that saturates the body with oxygen. The individual rests in a pressurized hyperbaric oxygen chamber, breathing 100% oxygen for 90 to 120 minutes. As the oxygen is absorbed by the blood, extra oxygen is provided to all cells and tissues, increasing healing capability and clearing of bacterial infection. Hyperbaric chambers are available in larger hospitals and medical centers.

Antimicrobial or Antibiotic Therapy

Antimicrobial topical therapy or oral antibiotic therapy may be recommended by the individual's physician to prevent possible bacterial infection or to address existing infection. Silver sulfadiazine is applied topically with good results. **Antibiotics** taken orally include penicillins, cephalospoins, **aminoglycosides**, sulfonamides, metronidazol and trimethoprim. Selection is based on specific bacteria causing infection or on obtaining the broadest possible coverage. Tissue biopsy may be performed to identify the causative bacteria.

Debridement and Debriding Agents

Surgical treatment is often needed for wounds showing poor response to standard wound care. Debridement is a surgical procedure that uses either a scalpel or chemicals to remove dead tissue (necrotic debris) from Stage III and IV wounds. Enzymatic debridement uses proteolytic enzymes that destroy collagen and necrotic wound debris without damaging new tissue. Mechanical debridement or "sharp debridement" perfomed with a scalpel loosens the necrotic tissue and removes it to encourage growth of new tissue. Debridement is accompanied by blood loss and may not be possible in individuals who are anemic or cannot afford to lose blood.

Urinary or Fecal Diversion

Incontinent individuals may require a surgical procedure (urinary or fecal diversion) to redirect the flow of urinary or fecal material to keep the wound clean, reducing likelihood of infection and encouraging positive response to medical treatment.

Reconstructive Surgery

Stage III and IV wounds may require consultation with a plastic surgeon to evaluate benefits of reconstructive surgery. Reconstructive surgery involves completely removing the ulcerated area and surrounding tissue (excision), debriding the bone, flushing the area with saline (lavage) to remove excess bacteria, and placing a drain in the wound for several days until risk of infection is gone and evidence of healing becomes apparent. Smaller wounds may then be sutured closed. Plastic surgery may follow surgical excision of a larger wound area, placing a flap of skin from another part of the body over the area to provide a new tissue surface. Skin grafts and other types of flaps may also be used for surgical closure (secondary closure) of excised wounds.

Challenges

Healing existing pressure sores and preventing recurrence is a long, arduous task for wound care professionals and caretakers, requiring patience and constant care. Impaired mobility is the critical factor in developing pressure sores, but risk in immobilized or bedridden individuals is increased by acute or chronic illnesses or conditions that might weaken muscles or soft tissue or that reduce blood circulation, which robs tissues of needed oxygen and causes skin to be thinner and more likely to break down and become infected. Conditions in immobilized older adults that may compromise skin integrity, increase risk of pressure sore development, or impede healing of pressure sores, include:

- atheroslerosis or peripheral vascular disease
- heart disease
- diabetes

- cancer
- anemia
- incontinence, inability to control urination or bowel movements
- malnutrition
- obesity
- stroke, paralysis (paraplegia) or spinal cord injury
- sensory loss (as in paralysis) with diminished sense of pain
- chronic infection
- smoking tobacco, which compromises skin healing

When therapists are providing regular care for individuals with existing pressure ulcers or at risk for pressure sores, progress may be challenged if caretakers are not able to identify warning signs of skin breakdown on regular inspection, are not providing regular bathing or care for incontinence, or are not consistent in moving patients as needed to support ongoing treatment. Adequate instruction must be provided to caretakers by therapists and consistent care given to the individual in order to achieve good results.

Risks

Risk is high for recurrence of pressure sores and deepening of existing sores into serious infection, especially in individuals compromised by poor nutritional status, chronic disease, or reduced **immune system** function. Complications can occur after pressure sore surgery, including bleeding under the skin (hematoma), bacterial infection, and wound recurrence. **Amputation** may be required if wounds will not heal or reconstructive surgery is not an option due to poor overall health status. Infection in deep wounds can spread to the blood and the entire body, becoming life threatening. Individuals at high risk for pressure ulcers are also at higher risk for chronic infection and death.

Results

When consistent care is provided including removal or reduction of pressure source, attention to the patient's general health and underlying condition, and treatment of existing wounds, pressure sores typically heal between two and four weeks after starting treatment. For successful surgical results, infection and complications must be avoided. Preventing recurrence of pressure sores requires regular surveillance and avoidance of pressure on vulnerable areas.

KEY TERMS

Anoxia—Reduced or almost entire absence of oxygen in the blood, cells and tissues of the body resulting in tissue death.

Debridement—Cutting away or "excising" dead tissue from a wound.

Erythema—Redness and warmth of the skin caused by dilation of small blood vessels (capillaries) under the skin.

Excision—Removal of tissue, organ, limb or other body part by cutting.

Friction—A force exerted when two surfaces move across each other such as moving patients across a bed or other support surface.

Hematoma—An area of blood that has gathered and remains confined under the skin or within an organ or body tissue.

Ischemia—Localized anemia stemming from reduced flow of blood and oxygen to organs and tissue, including skin.

Pathologic fracture—A fracture that occurs spontaneously at a weakened area of bone.

Shear—Mechanical stress experienced at the plane of the affected area such as pressure sores on the lower back or hip.

Ulcer—An inflammed sore or "lesion" that occurs on a surface such as skin or the mucus membrane of an organ, typically breaking the skin or membrane and resulting in loss of tissue.

Resources

BOOKS

"Wound Healing."*Disease Prevention and Treatment.* Expanded 4th ed. M. Segala, Ed. Ft. Lauderdale, FL: Life Extension Foundation; 2003, 1581-1592.

Haggerty M, Culvert LL. "Bedsores."*Gale Encyclopedia of Surgery. Farmington Hills, MI: Gale/Thomson; 2000.*

WEBSITES

Salcido R, Popescu A. "Pressure Ulcers and Wound Care." *eMedicine Specialties.*The Medscape Journal. Available at www.emedicine.com/pmr/topic179 .htm. Updated Aug. 10, 2006. Accessed March 17, 2008.

Revis DR. "Decubitus Ulcers."*eMedicine Continuing Education,* Available at emedicine.com. Updated August 2003. Accessed March 17, 2008.

ORGANIZATIONS

National Pressure Ulcer Advisory Panel, 12100 Sunset Hills Road, Suite 130, Reston, VA, 20190, 703-464-4849, 703-435-4390, rturner@drohanmgmt.com, International Association of Enterostomal Therapists, 27241 La Paz Road, Suite 121, Laguna Niguel, CA, 714-476-0268.

L. Lee Culvert

Wrinkles

Definition

Wrinkles refer to changes in the texture of the skin that appear as lines, creases or folds. It is a normal change in the skin that occurs with aging. Medically, wrinkles are known as rhytides.

Description

Wrinkles in the skin generally begin as fine lines and then deepen. They occur mostly on the face, neck, backs of the hands and the forearms. Although wrinkles are not physically harmful in any way they can influence a person's self-perception, especially in women and lead to lack of confidence.

Wrinkles occur due to changes in the skin that occur with aging. The skin is composed of two layers; the outer epidermis which lies on top of the second layer called the dermis. With age the outer layer of the skin, the epidermis, slows its rate of cellular reproduction and becomes thinner. The under layer of the skin or dermis also becomes thinner and the two layers tend to separate some. This separation decreases the circulation to the upper dermis and the epidermis which decreases the supply of nutrients to cells located there. Other changes that occur in the skin include the decrease of large structural molecules including collagen, elastin and glycosaminoglycans. All of these changes collectively lead to decreases in elasticity, firmness and structure of the skin that result in fine lines and wrinkles.

Fine expression lines that occur from talking, laughing and frowning can begin to occur as early in a person's twenties. These lines are generally seen in areas used in facial expressions such as the forehead, eyes and around the corners of the mouth. These fine lines eventually deepen into wrinkles and folds that affect deeper layers of the skin. Wrinkling of the skin that may be caused by sun exposure can show up in the thirties. In the forties **dry skin** can begin and the expression lines that may have begun in the twenties deepen. These effects progress through the fifties. Developing a basic skin care routine that includes wearing sunscreen and moisturizer early in life can minimize the effects such that they pay off when a person reaches age 60.

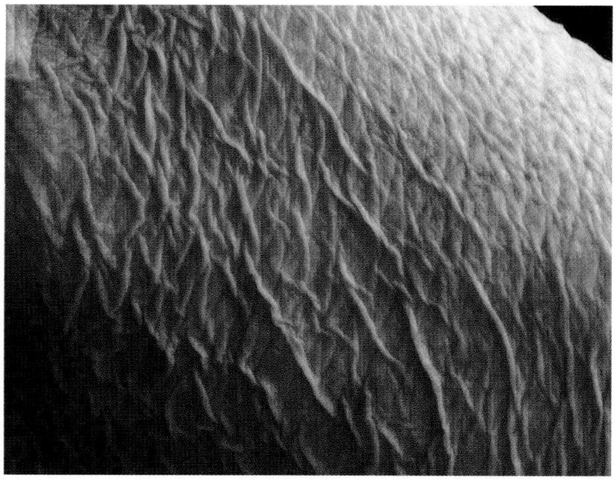

Wrinkled skin. *(Peter Skinner / Photo Researchers, Inc. Reproduced by permission.)*

Demographics

Skin changes that result in wrinkles can start as early in life as the mid-20s. These changes are part of the natural aging process but there can also be a genetic predisposition to early wrinkling. People with overexposure to the sun, particularly those with outdoor jobs or who routinely tan are at a higher risk for developing wrinkles early. Those exposed to environmental pollution as well as smokers are also more at risk. Fair skinned people are also more prone to wrinkles. There is no evidence that **stress** increases the risk of wrinkles, none the less, we often hear people say they have 'earned' their wrinkles.

Causes and symptoms

Normal changes in the skin that occur with age cause wrinkles. These changes include thinning of the skin, loss of moisture and decreased barrier function of the skin. This process of aging skin is accelerated by exposure to excess sunlight, environmental pollutants and cigarette smoke. There are also internal factors that are associated with aging skin. These include decreases in estrogen levels that occur with **menopause** and decreases in metabolic activity of the skin cells. Structural proteins in the skin also decrease.

Diagnosis

Diagnosis of wrinkles is made by visual examination of the skin.

Treatment

Wrinkles do not require treatment as they are not considered a medical illness. Wrinkles are a normal natural process for which there is no real cure. However, there are treatments or procedures that can decrease the appearance of wrinkles. Procedures that can be done at home include the use of products that contain **alpha hydroxy acids** or beta hydroxy acids. These products remove the very outer layer of cells from the skin, which allow it to maintain moisture better and removes superficial lines and wrinkles. Care should be taken with these products because too high of a concentration can cause damage to the skin. Using a good moisturizer on the skin to help maintain water in the skin can also help mask lines. The most important ingredient in a moisturizer or cream is a high quality oil to help prevent loss of moisture from the skin.

There is of course extensive research done each year to investigate possible ingredients for skin creams that can help in the treatment and prevention of wrinkles. Although many ingredients end up being marketing hype, there are a few ingredients that have potential to help decrease the appearance of wrinkles. The trouble is that some of the anti-aging creams are able to garner large price tags and it has to be questioned whether it is worth the price without solid data to back up the claims.

- KTTKS or palmitoyl pentapeptide-3 which goes by the brand name of Matrixyl is a bioactive peptide that can increase the production of collagen and other structural proteins in the skin thus decreasing the appearance of wrinkles.
- Tretinoin is a derivative of vitamin A that works by irritating the skin causing the cells to divide more rapidly. This gives the skin a younger appearance. It is also used to treat acne.
- Alpha-hydroxy acids are fruit acids that penetrate the skin to remove the very outer layer of dead cells. This removed some fine lines and helps to moisturize the skin.
- Vitamin C and other antioxidants including alpha lipoic acid may help the skin's appearance. These vitamins and antioxidants can be both applied to the skin as well as ingested in the form of fruits and vegetables.

Besides over the counter treatments for wrinkles there are also medical procedures used to remove lines. These include chemical peels, resurfacing, fillers and botulinum neurotoxin or Botox. Chemical peels involve the use of phenol, trichloroacetic acid, alpha-hydroxy acids or beta hydroxyl acids. These peels remove some of the outer skin and can be either light peels, medium peels or deep peels. Peels can help remove wrinkles, uneven pigmentation and scars. This treatment lasts a few weeks. There are side effects associated with peels so a physician or other qualified professional should be consulted.

Fillers are substances that are injected directly under the skin to smooth out wrinkles by increasing tissue volume. There is a wide assortment of fillers used including collagen, hyaluronic acid and synthetic polymers. Botox is a brand name for botulinum toxin which is a neurotoxin secreted by a bacteria. This neurotoxin causes **paralysis** of muscle. When injected into the muscles between the eyebrows it diminishes what is called motion wrinkles which are caused from contraction of facial muscles. Botox treatment lasts three to six months. Dermabrasion is a surgical procedure where the skin is sanded away to expose lower layers of the skin. Dermabrasion can remove wrinkles, scars and age spots. A related procedure is laser resurfacing which uses a laser to vaporize the outer layer of skin.

Contour threads are often referred to as a non-surgical **face lift**. This is a relatively new procedure so there is not a lot known about it yet although it is being heavily advertised both on TV and in magazines. In this procedure a surgical thread containing tiny hooks or barbs are injected into the skin to pull up sagging areas. Finally, the most invasive procedure for treating wrinkles of course is the face lift. In this surgical procedure incisions are made in the hair area near the temple to the front of the ear and behind the ear. The sagging tissue is pulled and lifted to remove wrinkles. The skin is then closed with stitches or clips.

Nutrition/Dietetic concerns

The best way for the skin to receive nutrients is through the **diet**. Increased consumption of foods high in **antioxidants** found in fruits and vegetables are most important for skin health. **Vitamin C** is necessary for the production of collagen in the skin and so important in delaying wrinkling. Ingestion of fats, especially essential fatty acids are important in holding moisture in the skin and providing it with its barrier function. Drinking plenty of water is important in keeping the skin moisturized. Using topical moisturizers does not help unless there is plenty of moisture inside the body. **Nutrition** can also be delivered to the surface of the skin to a certain extent.

Many anti-wrinkle creams will contain essential fatty acids, vitamin C, retinoids as well as other antioxidants. These nutrients are important in the diet as well as topically.

Therapy

The influence of societal standards of beauty is often the incentive for wrinkle treatment. Because of this it may be good to really consider the risks and benefits of cosmetic surgeries. Since nothing can remove all of a persons imperfections, looking at other ways to improve self confidence and self-esteem might be a good idea. One's attitude towards aging is most important when determining the effect wrinkles have on quality of life.

Prognosis

Wrinkles will tend to get worse with age. Since wrinkles are not a medical condition, treatment is not necessary. However, one's physical appearance can have an effect on self-image and thus on quality of life. Using a good moisturizer can always diminish the appearance of wrinkles though.

Prevention

Preventing or slowing the progression of wrinkles is something that begins years before wrinkles appear. Establishing a good skin care routine early in life will pay off. The most important points in preventing or delaying wrinkling include keeping the skin well moisturized, wearing a sunscreen with SPF 15 or a hat to prevent sun damage to the face, and not **smoking** or binging on alcohol, which causes **dehydration**. Daily **exercise** helps to increase circulation to the skin and deliver nutrients. It is generally accepted that antioxidants can slow the progression of wrinkles, both topically and in the diet. There are many new products on the market touting their ability to prevent wrinkles. Although there is not much evidence to support claims as of yet, some of the promising ingredients for anti-aging creams include alpha hydroxyl acids, vitamin C, retinoids, lycopene, green tea, oat beta-glucan, niacinamide, coenzyme Q10, alpha lipoic acid and DMAE (dimethylaminoethanol).

Caregiver concerns

Care givers should be aware of what affect signs of aging such as wrinkles have on the patient's quality of life.

Resources

OTHER

British Medical Journal, Wrinkles http://clinicalevidence.bmj.com/ceweb/conditions/skd/1711/1711_background.jsp

Proctor & Gamble The Science of Beauty, Biology of fine lines, wrinkles & texture http://www.pgbeautyscience.com/biology-of-fine-lines-wrinkles-texture1.html

Smart Skin Care.com http://www.smartskincare.com/

Cindy L.A. Jones Ph.D.

XYZ

Yoga

Definition

The term *yoga* comes from a Sanskrit word which means yoke or union. Traditionally, yoga is a method joining the individual self with the Divine, Universal Spirit, or Cosmic Consciousness. Physical and mental exercises are designed to help achieve this goal, also called self-transcendence or enlightenment. On the physical level, yoga postures, called *asanas*, are designed to tone, strengthen, and align the body. These postures are performed to make the spine supple and healthy and to promote blood flow to all the organs, glands, and tissues, keeping all the bodily systems healthy. On the mental level, yoga uses breathing techniques (*pranayama*) and meditation (*dyana*) to quiet, clarify, and discipline the mind. However, experts are quick to point out that yoga is not a religion, but a way of living with health and peace of mind as its aims.

An elderly man performs yoga, in Allahabad, India. *(AP Images. Reproduced by permission.)*

Purpose

Yoga has been used to alleviate problems associated with high **blood pressure**, **high cholesterol**, **migraine headaches**, **asthma**, shallow breathing, backaches, **constipation**, diabetes, **menopause**, **multiple sclerosis**, **varicose veins**, carpal tunnel syndrome and many chronic illnesses. It also has been studied and approved for its ability to promote **relaxation** and reduce **stress**.

Yoga is increasingly recommended for dysmenorrhea, premenstrual syndrome, and other disorders in premenopausal women, in Europe as well as in the United States.

Yoga can also provide the same benefits as any well-designed **exercise** program, increasing general health and stamina, reducing stress, and improving those conditions brought about by sedentary lifestyles. Yoga has the added advantage of being a low-impact activity that uses only gravity as resistance, which makes it an excellent physical therapy routine; certain yoga postures can be safely used to strengthen and balance all parts of the body. A study published in late 2002 summarized recent findings about the benefits of yoga for the cardiovascular and musculoskeletal systems. The review noted that yoga is still viewed as a "trendy" form of exercise rather than one with documented medical benefits.

Meditation has been much studied and approved for its benefits in reducing stress-related conditions. The landmark book, *The Relaxation Response*, by Harvard cardiologist Herbert Benson, showed that meditation and breathing techniques for relaxation could have the opposite effect of stress, reducing blood pressure and other indicators. Since then, much research has reiterated the benefits of meditation for stress reduction and general health. Currently, the American Medical Association recommends meditation techniques as a first step before medication for borderline **hypertension** cases. Some 2002 studies indicate that yogic meditation by itself is effective in lowering serum cholesterol as well as blood pressure.

Modern psychological studies have shown that even slight facial expressions can cause changes in the involuntary nervous system; yoga utilizes the mind/body connection. That is, yoga practice contains the central ideas that physical posture and alignment can influence a person's mood and self-esteem, and also that the mind can be used to shape and heal the body. Yoga practitioners claim that the strengthening of mind/body awareness can bring eventual improvements in all facets of a person's life.

Description

Origins

Yoga originated in ancient India and is one of the longest surviving philosophical systems in the world. Some scholars have estimated that yoga is as old as 5,000 years; artifacts detailing yoga postures have been found in India from over 3000 B.C. Yoga masters (*yogis*) claim that it is a highly developed science of healthy living that has been tested and perfected for all these years. Yoga was first brought to America in the late 1800s when Swami Vivekananda, an Indian teacher and yogi, presented a lecture on meditation in Chicago. Yoga slowly began gaining followers, and flourished during the 1960s when there was a surge of interest in Eastern philosophy. There has since been a vast exchange of yoga knowledge in America, with many students going to India to study and many Indian experts coming here to teach, resulting in the establishment of a wide variety schools. Today, yoga is thriving, and it has become easy to find teachers and practitioners throughout America. A recent Roper poll, commissioned by *Yoga Journal*, found that 11 million Americans do yoga at least occasionally and 6 million perform it regularly. Yoga stretches are used by physical therapists and professional sports teams, and the benefits of yoga are being touted by movie stars and Fortune 500 executives. Many prestigious schools of medicine have studied and introduced yoga techniques as proven therapies for illness and stress. Some medical schools, like UCLA, even offer yoga classes as part of their physician training program.

Classical yoga is separated into eight limbs, each a part of the complete system for mental, physical and spiritual well-being. Four of the limbs deal with mental and physical exercises designed to bring the mind in tune with the body. The other four deal with different stages of meditation. There are six major types of yoga, all with the same goals of health and harmony but with varying techniques: hatha, raja, karma, bhakti, jnana, and tantra yoga. Hatha yoga is the most commonly practiced branch of yoga in America, and it is a highly developed system of nearly 200 physical postures, movements and breathing techniques designed to tune the body to its optimal health. The yoga philosophy believes the breath to be the most important facet of health, as the breath is the largest source of *prana*, or life force, and hatha yoga utilizes *pranayama*, which literally means the science or control of breathing. Hatha yoga was originally developed as a system to make the body strong and healthy enough to enable mental awareness and spiritual enlightenment.

There are several different schools of hatha yoga in America; the two most prevalent ones are Iyengar and ashtanga yoga. Iyengar yoga was founded by B.K.S. Iyengar, who is widely considered as one of the great living innovators of yoga. Iyengar yoga puts strict emphasis on form and alignment, and uses traditional hatha yoga techniques in new manners and sequences. Iyengar yoga can be good for physical therapy because it allows the use of props like straps and blocks to make it easier for some people to get into the yoga postures. Ashtanga yoga can be a more vigorous routine, using a flowing and dance-like sequence of hatha postures to generate body heat, which purifies the body through sweating and deep breathing.

The other types of yoga show some of the remaining ideas which permeate yoga. Raja yoga strives to bring about mental clarity and discipline through meditation, simplicity, and non-attachment to worldly things and desires. Karma yoga emphasizes charity, service to others, non-aggression and non-harming as means to awareness and peace. Bhakti yoga is the path of devotion and love of God, or Universal Spirit. Jnana yoga is the practice and development of knowledge and wisdom. Finally, tantra yoga is the path of self-awareness through religious rituals, including awareness of sexuality as sacred and vital.

A typical hatha yoga routine consists of a sequence of physical poses, or asanas, and the sequence is designed to work all parts of the body, with particular emphasis on making the spine supple and healthy and increasing circulation. Hatha yoga asanas utilize three basic movements: forward bends, backward bends, and twisting motions. Each asana is named for a common thing it resembles, like the sun salutation, cobra, locust, plough, bow, eagle, tree, and the head to knee pose, to name a few. Each pose has steps for entering and exiting it, and each posture requires proper form and alignment. A pose is held for some time, depending on its level of difficulty and one's strength and stamina, and the practitioner is also usually aware of when to inhale and exhale at certain points in each posture, as breathing properly is another fundamental aspect of yoga. Breathing should be deep and through the nose. Mental concentration in each position is also very important, which improves awareness, poise and posture. During a yoga routine there is often a position in which to perform meditation, if deep relaxation is one of the goals of the sequence.

Yoga routines can take anywhere from 20 minutes to two or more hours, with one hour being a good time investment to perform a sequence of postures and a meditation. Some yoga routines, depending on the teacher and school, can be as strenuous as the most difficult workout, and some routines merely stretch and align the body while the breath and heart rate are kept slow and steady. Yoga achieves its best results when it is practiced as a daily discipline, and yoga can be a life-long exercise routine, offering deeper and more challenging positions as a practitioner becomes more adept. The basic positions can increase a person's strength, flexibility and sense of well-being almost immediately, but it can take years to perfect and deepen them, which is an appealing and stimulating aspect of yoga for many.

Yoga is usually best learned from a yoga teacher or **physical therapist**, but yoga is simple enough that one can learn the basics from good books on the subject, which are plentiful. Yoga classes are generally inexpensive, averaging around 10 dollars per class, and students can learn basic postures in just a few classes. Many YMCAs, colleges, and community health organizations offer beginning yoga classes as well, often for nominal fees. If yoga is part of a physical therapy program, its cost can be reimbursed by insurance.

Preparations

Yoga can be performed by seniors of any age and condition, although not all poses should be attempted by everyone. Yoga is also a very accessible form of exercise; all that is needed is a flat floor surface large enough to stretch out on, a mat or towel, and enough overhead space to fully raise the arms. It is a good activity for those who can't go to gyms, who don't like other forms of exercise, or have very busy schedules. Yoga should be done on an empty stomach, and teachers recommend waiting three or more hours after meals. Loose and comfortable clothing should be worn.

Precautions

Seniors with injuries, medical conditions, or spinal problems should consult a doctor before beginning yoga. Those with medical conditions should find a yoga teacher who is familiar with their type of problem and who is willing to give them individual attention.

Beginners should exercise care and concentration when performing yoga postures, and not try to stretch too much too quickly, as injury could result. Some advanced yoga postures, like the headstand and full lotus position, can be difficult and require strength, flexibility, and gradual preparation, so beginners should get the help of a teacher before attempting them.

Yoga is not a competive sport; it does not matter how a person does in comparison with others, but how aware and disciplined one becomes with one's own body and limitations. Proper form and alignment should always be maintained during a stretch or posture, and the stretch or posture should be stopped when there is **pain**, **dizziness**, or fatigue. The mental component of yoga is just as important as the physical postures. Concentration and awareness of breath should not be neglected. Yoga should be done with an open, gentle, and noncritical mind; when one stretches into a yoga position, it can be thought of accepting and working on one's limits. Impatience, self-criticism and comparing oneself to others will not help in this process of self-knowledge. While performing the yoga of breathing (pranayama) and meditation (dyana), it is best to have an experienced teacher, as these powerful techniques can cause dizziness and discomfort when done improperly.

Side effects

Some people have reported injuries by performing yoga postures without proper form or concentration, or by attempting difficult positions without working up to them gradually or having appropriate

KEY TERMS

Asana—A position or stance in yoga.

Dyana—The yoga term for meditation.

Hatha yoga—Form of yoga using postures, breathing methods and meditation.

Meditation—Technique of concentration for relaxing the mind and body.

Pranayama—Yoga breathing techniques.

Yogi (female, yogini)—A trained practitioner of yoga.

supervision. Beginners sometimes report muscle soreness and fatigue after performing yoga, but these side effects diminish with practice.

Although yoga originated in a culture very different from that of modern America, it has been accepted and its practice has spread relatively quickly. Many yogis are amazed at how rapidly yoga's popularity has spread in the United States and Canada. Ongoing research in top medical schools is showing yoga's effectiveness for overall health and for specific problems, making it an increasingly acceptable health practice.

The growing acceptability of yoga as an alternative therapy for certain disorders or conditions is reflected in the fact that the National Center for Complementary and Alternative Medicine (NCCAM) is conducting a series of clinical trials of ypga. As of the summer of 2004, NCCAM has five clinical trials in progress, evaluating yoga as a treatment for chronic **low back pain**; **insomnia**; **depression** in patients diagnosed with HIV infection; and shortness of breath in **chronic obstructive pulmonary disease** (COPD). The fifth clinical trial is an evaluation of yoga in improving attention span in aging and multiple sclerosis.

Resources

BOOKS

Ansari, Mark, and Liz Lark. *Yoga for Beginners.* New York: Harper, 1999.

Pelletier, Kenneth R., MD. *The Best Alternative Medicine*, Chapter 10, "Ayurvedic Medicine and Yoga: From Buddha to the Millennium." New York: Simon & Schuster, 2002.

PERIODICALS

Bielory, L., J. Russin, and G. B. Zuckerman. "Clinical Efficacy, Mechanisms of Action, and Adverse Effects of Complementary and Alternative Medicine Therapies for Asthma." *Allergy and Asthma Proceedings* 25 (September-October 2004): 283–291.

Engebretson, J. "Culture and Complementary Therapies" *Complementary Therapies in Nursing and Midwifery* 8 (November 2002): 177–184.

Gerritsen, A. A., M. C. de Krom, M. A. Struijs, et al. "Conservative Treatment Options for Carpal Tunnel Syndrome: A Systematic Review of Randomized Controlled Trials." *Journal of Neurology* 249 (March 2002): 272–280.

Kronenberg, F., and A. Fugh-Berman. "Complementary and Alternative Medicine for Menopausal Symptoms: A Review of Randomized, Controlled Trials." *Annals of Internal Medicine* 137 (November 19, 2002): 805–813.

Lee, S. W., C. A. Mancuso, and M. E. Charlson. "Prospective Study of New Participants in a Community-Based Mind-Body Training Program." *Journal of General Internal Medicine* 19 (July 2004): 760–765.

Manocha, R., G. B. Marks, P. Kenchington, et al. "Sahaja Yoga in the Management of Moderate to Severe Asthma: A Randomized Controlled Trial." *Thorax* 57 (February 2002): 110–115.

Raub, J. A. "Psychophysiologic Effects of Hatha Yoga on Musculoskeletal and Cardiopulmonary Function: A Literature Review." *Journal of Alternative and Complementary Medicine* 8 (December 2002): 797–812.

Vyas, R., and N. Dikshit. "Effect of Meditation on Respiratory System, Cardiovascular System and Lipid Profile." *Indian Journal of Physiology and Pharmacology* 46 (October 2002): 487–491.

Yoga International Magazine. R.R. 1 Box 407, Honesdale, PA 18431. http://www.yimag.com.

Yoga Journal. P.O. Box 469088, Escondido, CA 92046. http://www.youajournal.com.

OTHER

NCCAM Yoga Clinical Trials. http://nccam.nih.gov/clinicaltrials/yoga.htm.

Douglas Dupler MA

Rebecca J. Frey Ph.D.

Zinc

Definition

Zinc is a trace element considered a micronutrient, meaning a nutrient needed in very small amounts. It is found in almost every living cell. The significance of zinc in human **nutrition** and public health was recognized relatively recently (1961) and it is now considered to have a wide range of essential biological roles in maintaining life and health.

Purpose

Zinc is considered essential to maintain health. It is required for the activity of numerous metalloenzymes involved in metabolism, it maintains the **immune system** that protects the body against disease, and also supports normal growth and development during pregnancy, childhood, and adolescence. It plays three crucial roles:

- Catalytic role: Enzymes are proteins that are vitally important for speeding up the biochemical reactions (catalysis) of cells and organisms and nearly 200 different ones depend on zinc. Zinc-dependent enzymes can be found in all known classes of enzymes.
- Structural role: Zinc also maintains the structure of proteins and cell membranes. A finger-like structure, called a zinc finger motif, strengthens the structure of several important proteins and enzymes. For instance, that of the antioxidant copper-zinc superoxide dismutase enzyme. Copper is required for the catalytic activity of the enzyme, but zinc plays a critical structural role. Zinc also affects the structure and function of cell membranes, which become more likely to be damaged by harmful oxidative species (oxidative stress) with zinc loss.
- Regulatory role: Zinc finger proteins are also involved in the regulation of gene expression by binding to DNA and influencing the copying of specific genes. Zinc also plays a role in the regulation of cell signaling and influences the release of hormones and the transmission of nerve impulses.

Additionally, zinc has the following functions:

- It is required for vision, taste, and smell.
- It maintains healthy a healthy connective tissue in skin.
- It helps tissue repair after burns and wound healing.
- It is needed for bone growth.
- It promotes the production of healthy white blood cells and antibodies, important components of the body's immune system.
- It is involved in the metabolism of carbohydrates, proteins and phosphorus.
- It is involved in the production of insulin in the pancreas.

Recent research reports indicate that zinc has been found to play a role in cell **death** (apoptosis) with implications for growth and development, as well as a number of chronic diseases. Zinc is also actively taken up by synaptic vesicles that store the neurotransmitters released by nerve cells, suggesting a new role in neuronal activity and memory.

Description

Zinc is found in the body in a form bound to proteins within cells, especially in the nucleus, and cell membranes. The adult body contains about 1.5–2.5 g of zinc bound to various proteins. They occur in specialized areas of the brain that produce the chemical substances that can send messages from one nerve cell to another (neurotransmitters). Zinc is also found in the pancreas, adrenal gland, bones, liver, prostate and in the reproductive organs. Most of the zinc (75–88%) in blood is found in a red blood cell metalloenzyme called carbonic anhydrase. In the plasma, zinc is bound to proteins such as alpha-2-macroglobulin, albumin, transferrin and ceruloplasmin.

Zinc is found in a wide variety of foods. Oysters are the richest zinc source per serving, but since they are not consumed regularly in the American **diet**, red meat and poultry provide the majority of dietary zinc. Other good zinc sources include beans, nuts, certain seafood, whole grains, fortified breakfast cereals, and dairy products. Zinc absorption is more efficient from a diet high in animal protein than a diet rich in plant proteins. Phytates, which are found in whole grain breads, cereals, legumes and other products, are believed to decrease zinc absorption. Some good food sources of zinc include (per 1oz–serving or as indicated):

- oysters, 6 medium (16 mg)
- beef shank, lean (3 mg)
- beef chuck, lean (2.7 mg)
- beef tenderloin, lean (1.6 mg)
- pork shoulder, lean (1.4 mg)
- beef, eye of round, lean (1.3 mg)
- pork tenderloin, lean (0.8 mg)
- chicken leg, meat only (0.9 mg)
- chicken breast, meat only (0.9 mg)
- yogurt, plain, low fat (2.2 mg per cup)
- baked beans, canned with pork (0.6 mg)
- cashews, dry roasted, no salt (1.6 mg)
- pecans, dry roasted, no salt (1.4 mg)
- chickpeas, canned (2.6 mg per cup)
- mixed nuts, dry roasted, no salt (1.1 mg)

KEY TERMS

Acrodermatitis enteropathica—A genetic disorder resulting from the impaired uptake and transport of zinc in the body.

Albumin—Water-soluble proteins that can be coagulated by heat and are found in egg white, blood serum, milk.

Amino acid—Organic (carbon-containing) molecules that serve as the building blocks of proteins.

Antibody—A protein produced by the body's immune system that recognizes and helps fight infections and other foreign substances in the body.

Antioxidant enzyme—An enzyme that can counteract the damaging effects of oxygen in tissues.

Ceruloplasmin—A blue copper containing dehydrogenase protein found in serum that is apparently involved in copper detoxification and storage.

Chelating agent—An organic compound in which atoms form more than one bond with metals in solution.

Cofactor—A compound that is essential for the activity of an enzyme.

DNA—The material inside the nucleus of cells that carries genetic information. The scientific name for DNA is deoxyribonucleic acid.

Enzyme—Enzymes are proteins and vitally important to the regulation of the chemistry of cells and organisms.

Gene expression—The process by which the coded information of a gene is translated into the proteins or RNA present and operating in the cell.

High-density lipoprotein (HDL)—HDL is called the "good cholesterol" because it helps remove fat from the body by binding with it in the bloodstream and carrying it back to the liver for excretion in the bile and disposal.

L-cysteine—A sulfur–containing amino acid produced by enzymatic or acid hydrolysis of proteins. Supplements are used as antioxidant.

L-histidine—An essential amino acid, $C6H9N3O2$, important for the growth and repair of tissues.

Lipoproteins—Proteins present in blood plasma. The five major families are: chylomicrons, very low-density lipoproteins (VLDL), intermediate-density lipoproteins (IDL), low-density lipoproteins (LDL), and high-density lipoproteins (HDL).

Metalloenzyme—An enzyme that contains a tightly bound metal ion, such as cobalt, copper, iron or zinc.

Oxidative stress—Accumulation in the body of destructive molecules such as free radicals that can lead to cell death.

Plasma—The liquid part of the blood and lymphatic fluid. Plasma is 92% water, 7% protein and 1% minerals.

RNA—A chemical similar to DNA from which proteins are made. Unlike DNA, RNA can leave the nucleus of the cell.

Short bowel syndrome—Problems related to absorbing nutrients after removal of part of the small intestine.

Sickle cell anemia—Genetic disorder in which red blood cells take on an unusual shape, leading to other problems with the blood.

Synaptic vesicles—Also called neurotransmitter vesicles, these pouches store the various neurotransmitters that are released by nerve cells into the synaptic cleft of a synapse.

Trace minerals—Minerals needed by the body in small amounts. They include: selenium, iron, zinc, copper, manganese, molybdenum, chromium, arsenic, germanium, lithium, rubidium, tin.

Transferrin—A protein synthesized in the liver that transports iron in the blood to red blood cells.

Ulcerative colitis—Inflammation of the inner lining of the colon, characterized by open sores that appear in its mucous membrane.

- walnuts, black, dried (1.0 mg)
- almonds, dry roasted, no salt (1.0 mg)
- milk (1.8 mg per cup)
- cheese, Swiss (1.1 mg)
- cheese, Cheddar (0.9 mg)
- cheese, Mozzarella, part skim (0.9 mg)
- beans, kidney, California red (1.6 mg per cup)
- peas, green, frozen (1.6 mg per cup)
- oatmeal, instant, low salt (0.8 mg per packet)
- flounder, sole (0.2 mg)

The Recommended Dietary Allowance (RDA) for zinc is:

- infants: (0–6 months): 3 mg
- infants: (7–12 months): 3 mg
- children (1–3 y): 3 mg
- children (4–8 y): 5 mg
- children (9–13 y): 8 mg
- adolescents (14–18): males, 11 mg, females, 9 mg
- adults: males, 11 mg, females, 8 mg
- pregnancy: 13 mg
- lactation: 14 mg

Zinc in **nutritional supplements** is available as zinc gluconate, zinc oxide, zinc aspartate, zinc picolinate, zinc citrate, zinc monomethionine and zinc histidine. They are distributed as stand-alone or combination products as tablets, capsules or liquids.

Precautions

Zinc deficiency most often occurs when zinc intake is inadequate or poorly absorbed and it can have serious health consequences. Moderate to severe zinc deficiency is rare in the United States. However, it is highly prevalent in developing countries. The symptoms of severe deficiency include the slowing or cessation of growth and development, delayed sexual maturation, skin rashes, chronic and severe **diarrhea**, immune system deficiencies, poor wound healing, decreased appetite, impaired taste sensation, night blindness, swelling and clouding of the corneas, and behavioral disorders. These symptoms were first accurately described when a genetic disorder called acrodermatitis enteropathica was linked to zinc deficiency. Although mild dietary zinc deficiency is unlikely to cause such severe symptoms, it is known to contribute to several health problems, especially in young children. Zinc deficiency leads to impaired physical and neuropsychological development, and to an increased risk of life–threatening infections in young children. Individuals at risk of zinc deficiency include:

- infants and children
- pregnant and breastfeeding women, especially teenagers
- patients receiving intravenous feeding
- malnourished individuals, including those with anorexia nervosa
- people with severe or persistent diarrhea
- people with malabsorption syndromes, including celiac disease and short bowel syndrome
- people with inflammatory bowel disease, including Crohn's disease and ulcerative colitis
- people with alcoholic liver disease
- people with sickle cell anemia
- elderly people
- strict vegetarians whose major food staples are grains and legumes because the high levels of phytic acid in these foods lower the absorption of zinc

Fortified foods include many types of breakfast cereals that make it easier to consume the RDA for zinc. However, they also make it easier to consume too much zinc, especially if zinc supplements are also taken. Anyone considering zinc supplementation should accordingly first consider whether their needs could be met by dietary zinc sources and from fortified foods. Intakes between 150 and 450 mg of zinc per day lead to copper deficiency, impaired iron function, reduced immune function, and reduced levels of high-density lipoproteins, the "good cholesterol". A few isolated cases of acute zinc toxicity have been reported for food or beverages contaminated with zinc present in galvanized containers. Single doses of 225–450 mg of zinc are known to induce vomiting. Milder gastrointestinal distress has been reported at doses of 50–150 mg/day of supplemental zinc.

Interactions

The simultaneous administration of zinc supplements and certain **antibiotics**, such as tetracyclines and quinolones, may decrease absorption of the antibiotic with potential reduction of their action. To prevent this interaction, it is recommended to take the zinc supplements and antibiotics at least two hours apart. Metal chelating agents like penicillamine, used to treat copper overload in Wilson's disease, and diethylenetriamine pentaacetate (DTPA), used to treat iron overload, can lead to severe zinc deficiency. **Anticonvulsant drugs**, such as **sodium** valproate, may also cause zinc deficiency. The prolonged use of **diuretics** may increase urinary zinc excretion, resulting in increased zinc losses. A medication used to treat **tuberculosis**, ethambutol, has been shown to increase zinc loss in rats.

Interactions of zinc taken with other supplements are as follows:

- Calcium: May lower zinc absorption in postmenopausal women.
- Iron: May reduce the absorption of both iron and zinc.

- Phosphate salts: May lower the absorption of zinc.
- L-cysteine: May increase the absorption of zinc.
- L-histidine: May also enhance the absorption of zinc.

Aftercare

In the case of zinc deficiency, oral zinc therapy usually results in the complete disappearance of symptoms, but it must be maintained indefinitely in individuals with the acrodermatitis enteropathica.

Excessive intake can be corrected by bringing levels back to the RDA values.

Complications

It has been estimated that 82% of pregnant women worldwide are likely to have inadequate zinc intakes. Zinc deficiency has been associated with a number of pregnancy complications, including low birth weight, premature delivery, and labor and delivery complications.

The adverse effects of zinc deficiency on immune system function are also likely to increase complications in children that have infectious diarrhea. Persistent diarrhea contributes to zinc deficiency and **malnutrition**. Recent research has shown that zinc deficiency may also increase the harmful effects of toxins produced by diarrhea-causing bacteria like *E. coli.* Zinc supplementation in combination with drinking plenty of liquids has also been shown to significantly reduce the duration and severity of childhood diarrhea.

Parental concerns

Significant delays in growth and weight gain, known as growth retardation or failure to thrive, are common symptoms of mild zinc deficiency in children. But since many of the symptoms associated with zinc deficiency are general and also observed with other medical conditions, parents should not assume that they are due to a zinc deficiency. It is important to consult with a health care professional concerning medical symptoms so that appropriate care can be given.

Resources

BOOKS

Larson Duyff, R. *ADA Complete Food and Nutrition Guide, 3rd ed.* Chicago, IL: American Dietetic Association, 2006.

Challem, J., Brown, L. *User's Guide to Vitamins & Minerals.* Laguna Beach, CA: Basic Health Publications, 2002.

Bogden, J., ed. *Clinical Nutrition of the Essential Trace Elements and Minerals (Nutrition and Health).* Totowa, NJ: Humana Press, 2000.

Griffith, H. W. *Minerals, Supplements & Vitamins: The Essential Guide.* New York, NY: Perseus Books Group, 2000.

Quesnell, W. R. *Minerals : The Essential Link to Health.* Long Island, NY: Skills Unlimited Press, 2000.

Garrison, R., Somer, E. *The Nutrition Desk Reference.* New York, NY: McGraw–Hill, 1998.

Newstrom, H. *Nutrients Catalog: Vitamins, Minerals, Amino Acids, Macronutrients—Beneficials Use, Helpers, Inhibitors, Food Sources, Intake Recommendations.* Jefferson, NC: McFarland & Company, 1993.

Wapnir, R. A. *Protein Nutrition and Mineral Absorption.* Boca Raton, FL: CRC Press, 1990.

ORGANIZATIONS

American Dietetic Association (ADA). 120 South Riverside Plaza, Suite 2000, Chicago, IL 60606-6995. 1-800/877-1600. http://www.eatright.org.

U.S. Department of Agriculture, Food and Nutrition Information Center. National Agricultural Library,10301 Baltimore Avenue, Room 105, Beltsville, MD 20705. (301) 504-5414. http://www.nal.usda.gov.

American Society for Nutrition (ASN). 9650 Rockville Pike, Bethesda, MD 20814. (301) 634-7050. http://www.nutrition.org.

Office of Dietary Supplements, National Institutes of Health. National Institutes of Health, Bethesda, Maryland 20892 USA. http://ods.od.nih.gov.

Monique Laberge Ph.D.

ORGANIZATIONS

The following is an alphabetical compilation of organizations listed in the *Resources* section of the main body entries. Although the list is comprehensive, it is by no means exhaustive. It is a starting point for further information. Cengage Learning is not responsible for the accuracy of the addresses or the contents of the websites.

A

AARP
601 E St., NW
Washington, DC 20049
Toll free: (888) 687-2277
Web site: http://www.aarp.org

AARP Health Care
PO Box 1017
Montgomeryville, PA 18936
Toll free: (800) 444-6544
Web site: http://www.aarphealthcare.com

Academy of General Dentistry
211 E. Chicago Ave.
Chicago, IL 60611
Phone: (312) 440-4300
Web site: http://www.agd.org

Academy of Orthopaedic Surgeons
6300 North River Rd.
Rosemont, IL 60018-4262
Toll free: (800) 346-AAOS
Web site: http://www.orthoinfo.aaos.org/

Accreditation Association for Ambulatory Health Care (AAAHC)
3201 Old Glenview Rd., Ste. 300
Wilmette, IL 60091-2992
Phone: (847) 853-6060
Web site: http://www.aahc.org

Action on Smoking and Health
2013 H St., NW
Washington, DC 20006
Phone: (202) 659-4310
Web site: http://ash.org

Acupressure Institute
1533 Shattuck Ave.
Berkeley, CA 94709
Phone: (510) 845-1059
Toll free: (800) 442-2232
Web site: http://www.acupressure.com/program/index.htm

Administration on Aging (AoA)
One Massachusetts Ave.
Washington, DC 20201
Phone: (202) 619-0724
Web site: http://www.aoa.gov

Adult Congenital Heart Association
6757 Greene St., Ste. 335
Philadelphia, PA 19119-3508
Phone: (215) 849-1260
Toll free: (888) 921-2242
Fax: (215) 849-1261
Web site: http://www.achaheart.org

Agency for Healthcare Research and Quality (AHRQ)
2101 East Jefferson St., Ste. 501
Rockville, MD 20852
Phone: (301) 594-1364
Web site: http://www.ahcpr.gov

AGS Foundation for Health in Aging
Empire State Bldg., 350 Fifth Ave., Ste. 801
New York, NY 10118
Phone: (212) 755-6810
Toll free: (800) 563-4916
Fax: (212) 832-8646
Web site: http://www.healthinaging.org

Al-Anon Family Group Headquarters
1600 Corporate Landing Parkway
Virginia Beach, VA 23454-5617
Phone: (757) 563-1600
Toll free: (800) 425-2666
Fax: (757) 563-1655
Web site: http://www.al-anon.org

Alcohol and Drug Foundation of Queensland
PO Box 481
Morayfield, QLD 4810
New Zealand
Phone: 07 5428 6244
Toll free: (800) 425-2666
Fax: 07 5428 6544
Web site: http://www.adfq.org

Alcohol Concern
64 Leman St.
London, E1 8EU
United Kingdom
Phone: 020-7264-0510
Toll free: (800) 425-2666
Fax: 020-7488-9213
Web site: http://www.alcoholconcern.org.uk

Alcoholics Anonymous
PO Box 459, Grand Central Station
New York, NY 10163
Phone: (212) 870-3400
Toll free: (800) 425-2666
Fax: (212) 870-3003
Web site: http://www.aa.org

Alcor Life Extension Foundation
7895 East Acoma Dr., Ste. 110
Scottsdale, AZ 85260
Phone: (480) 905-1906
Toll free: (877) 462-5267
Fax: (480) 922-9027
Web site: http://www.alcor.org/index.html

Alden March Bioethics Institute
47 New Scotland Ave., MC 153
Albany, NY 12208-3478
Phone: (518) 262-6082
Web site: http://bioethics.org

Alliance for Aging Research
2021 K St. NW, Ste. 305
Washington, DC 20006
Phone: (202) 293-2856
Fax: (202) 785-8574
Web site: http://agingresearch.org

Alliance for Lupus Research
28 West 44th St., Ste. 501
New York, NY 10036
Phone: (212) 218-2840
Toll free: (800) 867-1743
Web site: http://www.lupusresearch.org/home.html

ALS Association
27001 Agoura Rd., Ste. 150
Calabasas Hills, CA 91301-5104
Phone: (818) 880-9007
Toll free: (800) 782-4747
Fax: (818) 880-9006
Web site: http://www.alsa.org/

The ALS Society of Canada
265 Yorkland Blvd., Ste. 300
Toronto, ON M2J 1S5
Canada
Phone: (416) 497-2267
Toll free: (800) 267-4ALS
Fax: (416) 497-1256
Web site: http://www.als.ca

Alzheimer Society of Canada
20 Eglinton Ave. W, Ste. 1200
Toronto, ON M4R 1K8
Canada
Phone: (416) 488-8772
Toll free: (800) 272-3900
Fax: (416) 488-3778
Web site: http://www.alzheimer.ca

Alzheimer's Association
225 N. Michigan Ave., 17th Fl.
Chicago, IL 60601-7633
Phone: (312) 335-8700
Toll free: (800) 272-3900
Fax: (866) 699-1246
Web site: http://www.alz.org

Alzheimer's Australia
PO Box 4019
Hawker, ACT 2614
Australia
Phone: (02) 6254 4233
Fax: (02) 6278 7225 (Australia only)
Web site: http://www.alzheimers.org.au

Alzheimer's Disease Education and Referral Center
PO Box 8250
Silver Spring, MD 20907-8250
Toll free: (800) 438-4380
Phone: (301) 495-3334
Web site: http://www.nia.nih.gov/alzheimers

Alzheimer's Foundation of America
322 8th Ave., 6th Fl.
New York, NY 10001
Toll free: (866) 232-8484
Phone: (646) 638-1546
Web site: http://www.alzfdn.org

AMD Alliance International
1929 Bayview Ave.
Toronto, ON M4G 3E8
Canada
Phone: (416) 486-2500 ext. 7505
Toll free: (877) AMD-7171
Fax: (416) 486-8574
Web site: http://www.amdalliance.org/

America on the Move Foundation
44 School St.
Boston, MA 02108
Toll free: (800) 807-0077
Web site: http://aom.americaonthe-move.org

America's Health Insurance Plans
601 Pennsylvania Ave., NW
Washington, DC 20004
Phone: (202) 778-3200
Fax: (202) 331-7487
Web site: http://www.ahip.org

American Academy of Acupuncture and Oriental Medicine (AAAOM)
1925 West County Rd., B2
Roseville, MN 55113
Phone: (651) 631-0216
Web site: http://www.aaaom.edu/index.php

American Academy of Allergy, Asthma, and Immunology (AAAAI)
555 E. Wells St., Ste. 1100
Milwaukee, WI 53202-3823
Phone: (414) 272-6071
Toll free: (800) 822-2762
Web site: http://www.aaaai.org

American Academy of Audiology
11730 Plaza America Dr., Ste. 300
Reston, VA 20190
Phone: (703) 790-8466
Toll free: (800) 222-2336
Web site: http://www.audiology.org

American Academy of Cosmetic Surgery
737 N. Michigan Ave., Ste. 820
Chicago, IL 60611
Phone: (312) 981-6760
Web site: http://www.cosmeticsurgery.org

American Academy of Dermatology
1350 I St. NW, #870
Washington, DC 20005-4355
Phone: (202) 842-3555
Fax: (202) 843-4355
Web site: http://www.aad.org

American Academy of Emergency Medicine
611 E. Wells St.
Milwaukee, WI 53202
Toll free: (800) 884-2236
Fax: (414) 276-3349
Web site: http://www.aaem.org

American Academy of Facial Plastic and Reconstructive Surgery
310 S. Henry St.
Alexandria, VA 22314
Phone: (703) 229-9291
Web site: http://www.aafprs.org/

American Academy of Family Physicians
114 Tomahawk Creek Pkwy.
Leawood, KS 66211-2672
Toll free: (800) 274-2237
Phone: (913) 906-6269
Web site: http://www.familydoctor.org

American Academy of Grief Counseling
2400 Niles-Cortland Rd. SE, Ste. #3
Warren, OH 44484
Phone: (330) 652-7776
Fax: (330) 652-7575
Web site: http://www.aihcp.org/aagc.htm

American Academy of HIV Medicine
1705 DeSales St. NW, Ste. 700
Washington, DC 20036
Phone: (202) 659-0699
Fax: (202) 659-0976
Web site: http://www.aahivm.org/index.php?option=com_frontpage&Itemid=1

American Academy of Implant Dentistry
211 E. Chicago Ave., Ste. 750
Chicago, IL 60611
Phone: (312) 335-1550
Fax: (312) 335-9090
Web site: http://www.aaid-implant.org

American Academy of Medical Acupuncture (AAMA)
4929 Wilshire Blvd., Ste. 428
Los Angeles, CA 90010
Phone: (323) 937-5514
Toll free: (800) 442-2232
Web site: http://www.medicalacupuncture.org/index.html

American Academy of Neurology
1080 Montreal Ave.
St. Paul, MN 55116
Phone: (651) 695-2791
Web site: http://www.aan.org

American Academy of Ophthalmology
PO Box 7424
San Francisco, CA 94120-7424
Phone: (415) 561-8500
Toll free: (800) 342-2383
Fax: (415) 561-8533
Web site: http://www.aao.org

American Academy of Optometry
6110 Executive Blvd., Ste. 506
Rockville, MD 20852
Phone: (301) 984-1441
Fax: (301) 984-4737
Web site: http://www.aaopt.org

American Academy of Orthopaedic Surgeons
6300 North River Rd.
Rosemont, IL 60018-4262

Phone: (847) 823-7186
Toll free: (800) 346-2267
Fax: (847) 823-8125
Web site: http://www.aaos.org

American Academy of Otolaryngology—Head and Neck Surgery
One Prince St.
Alexandria, VA 22314-3357
Phone: (703) 836-4444
Toll free: (800) 222-2336
Web site: http://www.entnet.org/

American Academy of Pain Management (AAPM)
13947 Mono Way, #A
Sonora, CA 95370
Phone: (209)533-9744
Fax: (209)533-9750
Web site: http://www.aapainmanage.org

American Academy of Sleep Medicine (AASM)
One Westbrook Corporate Center, Ste. 920
Westchester, IL 60154
Phone: (708) 492-0930
Web site: http://www.aasmnet.org

American Aging Association
The Sally Balin Medical Center, 110 Chesley Dr.
Media, PA 19063
Phone: (610) 627-2626
Toll free: (877) 462-5267
Fax: (610) 565-9747
Web site: http://www.americanaging.org/

American Alternative Medical Association
2200 Market St., Ste. 329
Galveston, TX 77550-1530
Phone: (409) 621-2600
Toll free: (888) 764-2237
Fax: (775) 703-5334
Web site: http://www.joinaama.com

American Association of Cardiovascular and Pulmonary Rehabilitation
401 North Michigan Ave., Ste. 2200
Chicago, IL 60611
Phone: (312) 321-5146
Fax: (312) 673-6924
Web site: http://www.aacvpr.org

American Association for Clinical Chemistry
1850 K St., Ste. 625
Washington, DC 20006-2213
Toll free: (800) 892-1400
Phone: (202) 857-0717
Fax: (202) 833-4576
Web site: http://www.aacc.org

American Association of Clinical Urologists
1100 E. Woodfield Rd., Ste. 520
Schaumburg, IL 60173
Phone: (847) 517-1050
Fax: (847) 517-7229
Web site: http://www.aacuweb.org

American Association of Colleges of Nursing
One Dupont Circle, NW, Ste. 530
Washington, DC 20036
Phone: (202) 463-6930
Web site: http://www.aacn.nche.edu

American Association of Colleges of Osteopathic Medicine (AACOM)
5550 Friendship Blvd., Ste. 310
Chevy Chase, MD 20815
Phone: (301) 968-4100
Fax: (301) 968-4101
Web site: http://www.aacom.org/Pages/default.aspx

American Association of Critical-Care Nurses
101 Columbia
Aliso Viejo, CA 92656-4109
Toll free: (800) 899-2226
Web site: http://www.aacn.org/

American Association for Geriatric Psychiatry
7910 Woodmont Ave., Ste. 1050
Bethesda, MD 20814
Phone: (301) 654-7850
Web site: http://www.aagponline.org

American Association on Intellectual and Developmental Disabilities
444 North Capitol St. NW, Ste. 846
Washington, DC 20001-1512
Toll free: (800) 424-3688
Fax: (202) 387-2193
Web site: http://www.aamr.org

American Association of Kidney Patients
100 S. Ashley Dr., #280
Tampa, FL 33602
Toll free: (800) 749-2257
Web site: http://www.aakp.org

American Association of Managed Care Nurses
4435 Waterfront Dr., Ste. 101
Glen Allen, VA 23060
Phone: (804) 747-9698
Web site: http://www.aamcn.org

American Association of Naturopathic Physicians (AANP)
4435 Wisconsin Ave. NW, Ste. 403
Washington, DC 20016
Phone: (202) 237-8150
Toll free: (866) 538-2267
Fax: (202) 237-8152
Web site: http://www.naturopathic.org/index.php

American Association of Nurse Anesthetists
222 S. Prospect Ave.
Park Ridge, IL 60068-4001
Phone: (847) 692-7050
Web site: http://www.aana.com

American Association of Pastoral Counselors (AAPC)
9504-A Lee Hwy.
Fairfax, VA 22031
Phone: (703) 385-6967
Fax: (703) 352-7725
Web site: http://www.aapc.org/index.cfm

American Association of PPOs
222 South First St., Ste. 303
Louisville, KY 40202
Phone: (502) 403-1122
Fax: (502) 403-1129
Web site: http://www.aappo.org

American Association for Respiratory Care
11030 Ables Ln.
Dallas, TX 75229
Web site: http://www.aarc.org

American Association of Suicidology (AAS)
5221 Wisconsin Ave., NW
Washington, DC 20015
Phone: (202) 237-2280
Fax: (202) 237-2282
Web site: http://www.suicidology.org/index.cfm

American Autoimmune Related Diseases Association (AARDA)
22100 Gratiot Ave.
Detroit, MI 48021
Phone: (586) 776-3900
Toll free: (800) 598-4668
Web site: http://www.aarda.org

American Automobile Association
Public Affairs MS 72, 1000 AAA Dr.
Heathrow, FL 32746
Web site: http://www.aaaexchange.com/Main

American Bar Association (ABA) Commission on Law and Aging
740 Fifteenth St. NW
Washington, DC 20005
Phone: (202) 662-8868
Toll free: (800) 687-2277
Web site: http://www.abanet.org/aging

American Board of Anesthesiology
4101 Lake Boone Trl., Ste. 510
Raleigh, NC 27607-7506
Phone: (919) 881-2570
Web site: http://www.abanes.org/

American Board of Medical Specialties (ABMS)
1007 Church St., Ste. 404
Evanston, IL 60201
Toll free: (866) ASK-ABMS
Web site: http://www.abms.org

American Board of Plastic Surgery
1635 Market St.
Philadelphia, PA 19103-2204
Phone: (215) 587-9322
Web site: http://www.abplsurg.org/

American Board of Surgery (ABS)
1617 John F. Kennedy Blvd., Ste. 860
Philadelphia, PA 19103
Phone: (215) 568-4000
Web site: http://www.absurgery.org

American Board of Urology
2216 Ivy Rd., Ste. 210
Charlottesville, VA 22903
Phone: (434) 979-0059
Web site: http://www.abu.org/

American Cancer Society
1599 Clifton Rd., NE
Atlanta, GA 30329
Phone: (404) 320-3333
Toll free: (800) ACS-2345
Web site: http://www.cancer.org

American Chiropractic Association
1701 Clarendon Blvd.
Arlington, VA 22209
Phone: (703) 276-8800
Fax: (703) 243-2593
Web site: http://www.americhiro.org

American Chronic Pain Association
PO Box 850
Rocklin, CA 95677-0850
Phone: (916) 632-0922
Toll free: (800) 533-3231
Fax: (916) 632-3208
Web site: http://www.theacpa.org

American Clinical Laboratory Association
1250 H St., Ste. 880
Washington, DC 20005
Phone: (202) 637-9466
Toll free: (800) 622-9010
Fax: (202) 637-2050
Web site: http://www.clinical-labs.org

American College of Cardiology
Heart House, 2400 N St., NW
Washington, DC 20037
Phone: (202) 375-6000
Toll free: (800) 253-4636 x8603
Fax: (202) 375-7000
Web site: http://www.acc.org

American College of Chest Physicians
3300 Dundee Rd.
Northbrook, IL 60062
Phone: (847) 498-1400
Fax: (847) 498-5460
Web site: http://www.chestnet.org

American College of Emergency Physicians
PO Box 619911
Dallas, TX 75261-9911
Toll free: (800) 798-1822
Phone: (972) 550-0911
Fax: (972) 580-2816
Web site: http://www.acep.org/

American College of Foot and Ankle Surgeons (ACFAS)
8725 West Higgins Rd.
Chicago, IL 60631-2724
Phone: (773)693-9300
Toll free: (800)421-2237
Fax: (773) 693-9304
Web site: http://www.acfas.org

American College of Gastroenterology (ACG)
4900 B South, 31 St.
Arlington, VA 22206
Phone: (703) 820-7400
Fax: (703) 931-4520
Web site: http://www.acg.gi.org

American College of Nurse Practitioners
503 Capitol Ct. NE, #300
Washington, DC 20002
Phone: (202) 546-4825
Web site: http://www.nurse.org

American College of Nurse-Midwives
818 Connecticut Ave. NW, Ste. 900
Washington, DC 20006
Phone: (202) 738-9860
Web site: http://www.acnm.org

American College of Nutrition (ACN)
300 S. Duncan Ave., Ste. 225
Clearwater, FL 33755
Phone: (727) 446-6086
Fax: (727) 446-6202
Web site: http://www.amcollnutr.org/index.htm

American College of Obstetricians and Gynecologists
409 12th St. SW, PO Box 96920
Washington, DC 20090-6920
Web site: http://www.acog.org

American College of Osteopathic Emergency Physicians
142 E. Ontario St., Ste. 550
Chicago, IL 60611
Phone: (312) 587-3709
Toll free: (800) 521-3709
Fax: (312) 587-9951
Web site: http://www.acoep.org

American College of Physicians
190 N. Independence Mall W
Philadelphia, PA 19106-1572
Toll free: (800) 523-1546, x2600
Phone: (215) 351-2600
Web site: http://www.acponline.org

American College of Prosthodontists
211 E. Chicago Ave., Ste. 1000
Chicago, IL 60611
Phone: (312) 573-1260
Web site: http://www.prosthodontics.org

American College of Rheumatology
1800 Century Place, Ste. 250
Atlanta, GA 30345-4300
Phone: (404) 633-3777
Fax: (404) 633-1870
Web site: http://www.rheumatology.org

American College of Surgeons
633 North Saint Claire St.
Chicago, IL 60611
Phone: (312) 202-5000
Web site: http://www.facs.org

American Council of the Blind
1155 15th St. NW, Ste. 1004
Washington, DC 20005
Phone: (202) 467-5081
Toll free: (800) 424-8666
Fax: (202) 467-5085
Web site: http://www.acb.org

American Dance Therapy Association
2000 Century Plaza, Ste. 108
Columbia, MD 21044-3263
Phone: (410) 997-4040
Web site: http://www.adta.org

American Dental Association
211 E. Chicago Ave.
Chicago, IL 60611
Phone: (312) 440-2500
Fax: (312) 440-7494
Web site: http://www.ada.org

American Dental Hygienists' Association
444 N. Michigan Ave., Ste. 3400
Chicago, IL 60611
Toll free: (800) 243-2342
Web site: http://www.adha.org

American Diabetes Association
1701 North Beauregard St.
Alexandria, VA 22311
Toll free: (800) 342-2383
Web site: http://www.diabetes.org

American Dietetic Association
120 South Riverside Plaza
Chicago, IL 60606-6995
Toll free: (800) 877-1600
Web site: http://www.eatright.org

American Foundation for Urologic Disease
1000 Corporate Blvd.
Linthicum, MD 21090
Phone: (410) 689-3700
Toll free: (866) RING-AUA
Fax: (410) 689-3800
Web site: http://www.auafoundation.org

American Gastroenterological Association
4930 Del Ray Ave.
Bethesda, MD 20814
Phone: (301) 654-2055
Fax: (310) 654-5920
Web site: http://www.gastro.org

American Geriatrics Society (AGS)
Empire State Building, 350 Fifth Ave., Ste. 801
New York, NY 10118
Phone: (212) 308-1414
Fax: (212) 832-8646
Web site: http://www.americangeriatrics.org/index.shtml

American Headache Society (AHS)
19 Mantua Rd.
Mount Royal, NJ 08061
Phone: (856) 423-0258
Fax: (856) 423-0082
Web site: http://www.achenet.org

American Health Assistance Foundation
22512 Gateway Center Dr.
Clarkburg, MD 20871
Phone: (301) 948-3244
Toll free: (800) 437-2423
Fax: (301) 258-9454
Web site: http://www.ahaf.org

American Health Information Management Association
233 N. Michigan Ave., 21st Fl.
Chicago, IL 60601
Phone: (312) 233-1100
Web site: http://www.ahima.org/

American Healthcare Quality Association
1140 Connecticut Ave., Ste. 105
Washington, DC 20036
Phone: (202) 331-5790
Web site: http://www.ahqa.org/

American Hearing Aid Associates
1380 Wilmington Pike
West Chester, PA 19382
Toll free: (800) 984-3272
Toll free: (800) 222-2336
Fax: (610) 455-3018
Web site: http://www.ahaanet.com

American Heart Association
7272 Greenville Ave.
Dallas, TX 75231
Phone: (202) 375-6000
Toll free: (800) 242-8721
Fax: (202) 375-7000
Web site: http://www.americanheart.org

American Hospital Association
One North Franklin
Chicago, IL 60606-3421
Phone: (312) 422-3000
Web site: http://www.aha.org/index.asp

American Insomnia Association (AIA)
One Westbrook Corporate Center, Ste. 920
Westchester, IL 60154
Phone: (708) 492-0939
Web site: http://www.americaninsomniaassociation.org

American Institute for Cancer Research
1759 R St. NW
Washington, DC 20009
Toll free: (800) 843-8114
Web site: http://www.aicr.org

American Institute of Homeopathy
801 N. Fairfax St., Ste. 306
Alexandria, VA 22314
Toll free: (888) 445-9988
Web site: http://www.homeopathyusa.org

American Institute of Ultrasound in Medicine
14750 Sweitzer Ln., Ste. 100
Laurel, MD 20707-5906
Phone: (301) 498-4100
Toll free: (800) 638-5352
Fax: (310) 498-4450
Web site: http://www.aium.org

American Kidney Fund (AKF)
Ste. 1010, 6110 Executive Blvd.
Rockville, MD 20852
Toll free: (800) 638-8299
Web site: http://www.arbon.com/kidney

American Liver Foundation
1425 Pompton Ave.
Cedar Grove, NJ 07009
Toll free: (800) 465-4837
Web site: http://www.liverfoundation.org

American Lung Association
61 Broadway, 6th Fl.
New York, NY 10006
Phone: (212) 315-8700
Toll free: (800) LUNG-USA
Web site: http://www.lungusa.org

American Medical Association (AMA)
515 N. State St.
Chicago, IL 60610
Phone: (703) 385-6967
Toll free: (800) 621-8335
Fax: (703) 352-7725
Web site: http://www.ama-assn.org/

American Nurses Association
600 Maryland Ave., SW, Ste. 100 West
Washington, DC 20024
Toll free: (800) 274-4ANA
Web site: http://www.ana.org

The American Occupational Therapy Association
4720 Montgomery Ln.
Bethesda, MD 20824
Phone: (301) 652-2682
Web site: http://www.aota.org

American Optometric Association
243 N. Lindbergh Blvd.
St. Louis, MO 63141
Phone: (301) 984-1441
Toll free: (800) 365-2219
Fax: (301) 984-4737
Web site: http://www.aao.org

American Organization for Bodywork Therapies of Asia (AOBTA)
1010 Haddonfield-Berlin Rd., Ste. 408
Voorhees, NJ 08043
Phone: (856) 782-1616
Toll free: (800) 442-2232
Fax: (856) 782-1653
Web site: http://www.aobta.org/index.php

American Osteopathic Association (AOA)
142 East Ontario St.
Chicago, IL 60611
Phone: (312) 202-8000
Toll free: (800) 621-1773
Fax: (312) 202-8000
Web site: http://www.osteopathic.org/index.cfm

American Osteopathic College of Dermatology (AOCD)
1501 East Illinois St., PO Box 7525

Kirksville, MI 63501
Phone: (660) 665-2184
Toll free: (800) 449-2623
Fax: (660) 627-2623
Web site: http://www.aocd.org

American Pain Foundation
201 North Charles St., Ste. 710
Baltimore, MD 21201-4111
Toll free: (888) 615-PAIN
Web site: http://www.painfoundation.org

American Pain Society (APS)
4700 W. Lake Ave.
Glenview, IL 60025
Phone: (847) 375-4715
Toll free: (877) 734-8758
Web site: http://www.ampainsoc.org

American Parkinson Disease Association, Inc.
1250 Hylan Blvd., Ste. 4B
Staten Island, NY 10305-1946
Phone: (651) 695-1940
Toll free: (800) 223-2732
Web site: http://www.apdaparkinson.com

American Physical Therapy Association
1111 N. Fairfax St.
Alexandria, VA 22314-1488
Phone: (703) 684-2782
Toll free: (800) 999-2782
Fax: (703) 684-7343
Web site: http://www.apta.org

American Podiatric Medical Association
9312 Old Georgetown Rd.
Bethesda, MD 20814-1698
Toll free: (800) 366-8227
Phone: (301) 571-9200
Email: askapma@apma.org
Web site: http://www.apma.org/

American Prostate Society
PO Box 870
Hanover, MD 21076
Phone: (410) 859-3735
Fax: (410) 850-0818
Web site: http://www.americanprostatesociety.com

American Psychiatric Association
1000 Wilson Blvd., Ste. 1825
Arlington, VA 22209
Phone: (703) 907-7300
Toll free: (888) 35-PSYCH
Fax: (212) 832-8646
Web site: http://www.healthyminds.org

American Psychological Association
750 First St., NE
Washington, DC 20002-4242
Phone: 202-336-5500
Toll free: (800) 374-2721
Web site: http://www.apa.org

American Public Health Association
800 I St., NW
Washington, DC 20001
Phone: (202) 777-2742
Web site: http://www.apha.org

American Registry of Diagnostic Medical Sonographers
51 Monroe St., Plaza One East
Rockville, MD 20850
Phone: (301) 738-8401
Toll free: (800) 541-9754
Fax: (301) 738-0312
Web site: http://www.ardms.org

American Sleep Apnea Association (ASAA)
1424 K St., NW, Ste. 302
Washington, DC 20005
Phone: (202) 293-3650
Web site: http://www.sleepapnea.org

American Social Health Association, National HPV and Cervical Cancer Prevention Resource Center
PO Box 13827
Research Triangle Park, NC 27709
Phone: (919) 361-8400
Toll free: (800) 227-8922
Fax: (919) 361-8425
Web site: http://www.ashastd.org/hpvccrc

American Society for Aesthetic Plastic Surgery
11081 Winners Circle
Los Alamitos, CA 90720
Phone: (312) 202-5000
Toll free: (888) 272-7711
Web site: http://www.surgery.org/

American Society of Anesthesiologists (ASA)
520 N. Northwest Hwy.
Park Ridge, IL 60068-2573
Phone: (847) 825-5586
Fax: (847) 825-1692
Web site: http://www.asahq.org

American Society for Bioethics and Humanities
4700 W. Lake
Glenview, IL 60025
Phone: (847) 375-4745
Web site: http://www.asbh.org

American Society of Colon and Rectal Surgeons (ASCRS)
85 W. Algonquin Rd., Ste. 550
Arlington Heights, IL 60005
Phone: (847) 290-9184
Fax: (847) 290-9203
Web site: http://www.fascrs.org

American Society for Dermatologic Surgery
5550 Meadowbrook Dr., Ste. 120
Rolling Meadows, IL 60006
Phone: (847) 956-0900
Web site: http://www.asds-net.org

American Society of Echocardiography
1500 Sunday Dr., Ste. 102
Raleigh, NC 27607
Phone: (919) 861-5574
Toll free: (800) 541-9754
Fax: (919) 787-4916
Web site: http://www.asecho.org

American Society for Gastrointestinal Endoscopy
1520 Kensington Rd.
Oak Brook, IL 60523
Phone: (630) 573-0600
Web site: http://www.asge.org

American Society of Health-System Pharmacists
7272 Wisconsin Ave.
Bethesda, MD 20814
Phone: (301) 657-3000
Toll free: (866) 279-0681
Web site: http://www.ashp.org/

American Society of Hematology
1900 M St., NW, Ste. 200
Washington, DC 20036
Phone: (202) 776-0544
Fax: (202) 776-0545
Web site: http://www.hematology.org

American Society of Hypertension
148 Madison Ave., Fifth Fl.
New York, NY 10016
Phone: (212) 696-9099
Fax: (212) 696-0711
Web site: http://www.ash-us.org

American Society for Pharmacology and Experimental Therapeutics
9650 Rockville Pike
Bethesda, MD 20814
Phone: (301) 530-7060
Web site: http://www.faseb.org/aspet/

American Society of Plastic Surgeons
444 E. Algonquin Rd.
Arlington Heights, IL 60005
Phone: (847) 228-9900
Toll free: (888) 272-7711
Web site: http://www.plasticsurgery.org

American Speech-Language Hearing Association
2200 Research Blvd.
Rockville, MD 20850-3289
Toll free: (800) 638-8255
Toll free: (800) 222-2336
Fax: (610) 455-3018
Web site: http://www.asha.org

American Stroke Association: A Division of American Heart Association
7272 Greenville Ave.
Dallas, TX 75231-4596
Phone: (414) 272-6071
Toll free: (888) 4STROKE
Fax: (214) 706-5231
Web site: http://www.strokeassociation.org

American Thoracic Society
1740 Broadway
New York, NY 10019
Phone: (212) 315-8700
Web site: http://www.thoracic.org

American Tinnitus Association (ATA)
PO Box 5
Portland, OR 97207
Toll free: (800) 638-8255
Web site: http://www.ata.org

American Urological Association (AUA)
1000 Corporate Blvd.
Linthicum, MD 21090
Phone: (410) 689-3700
Toll free: (866) 746-4282
Fax: (410) 689-3800
Web site: http://www.aocd.org

Amputee Coalition of America
900 East Hill Ave., Ste. 205
Knoxville, TN 37915-2566
Toll free: (888) 267-5669
Web site: http://www.amputee-coalition.org

Anxiety Disorders Association of America (ADAA)
8730 Georgia Ave., Ste.600
Silver Spring, MD 20910
Phone: (240) 485-1001
Fax: (240) 485-1035
Web site: http://www.adaa.org/

AnxietyBC
4th Fl., 402 East Columbia St.
New Westminster, BC V3L 3X1
Canada
Phone: (604) 681-3400
Web site: http://anxietybc.com

Aphasia Hope Foundation (AHF)
PO Box 26304
Shawnee Mission, KS 66225
Phone: (913) 839-8083
Toll free: (866) 549-1776
Fax: (913) 649-6661
Web site: http://www.aphasiahope.org/index.jsp

The Arc of the United States
1010 Wayne Ave., Ste. 650
Silver Spring, MD 20910
Phone: (301) 565-3842
Toll free: (800) 433-5255
Fax: (301) 565-3843/(301) 565-5342
Web site: http://thearc.org

Arthritis Foundation
PO Box 7669
Atlanta, GA 30357-0669
Phone: (404) 872-7100
Toll free: (800) 283-7800
Web site: http://www.arthritis.org

Arthritis Society
393 University Ave., Ste. 1700
Toronto, ON M5G 1E6
Canada
Phone: (416) 979-7228
Toll free: (800) 321-1433
Fax: (416) 979-8366
Web site: http://www.arthritis.ca

Assisted Living Federation of America
1650 King St., Ste. 602
Alexandria, VA 22314-2747
Phone: (703) 894-2747
Fax: (703) 894-1831
Web site: http://www.alfa.org

Association for Applied Psychophysiology and Biofeedback (AAPB)
10200 W. Forty-fourth Ave., #304
Wheat Ridge, CO 80033
Phone: (303) 422-8436
Fax: (303) 422-8894
Web site: http://www.aapb.org/i4a/pages/index.cfm?pageid=1

Association of Black Cardiologists
5355 Hunter Rd.
Atlanta, GA 30349
Phone: (404) 201-6600
Toll free: (800) 753-9222
Fax: (404) 201-6601
Web site: http://www.abcardio.org

Association for Death Education and Counseling (ADEC)
111 Deer Lake Rd., Ste. 100
Deerfield, IL 60015
Phone: (847) 509-0403
Fax: (847) 480-9282
Web site: http://www.adec.org/

Association of Diagnostic Imaging Technologists
13750 Crosstown Dr. NW, Ste. 108
Andover, MN 55304-5855
Phone: (763) 213-8252
Fax: (763) 753-7463
Web site: http://www.aditprofessionals.com

Association for Frontotemporal Dementias
1616 Walnut St., Ste. 1100
Philadelphia, PA 19103
Phone: (267) 514-7221
Toll free: (866) 507-7222
Web site: http://www.ftd-picks.org

Association of Reflexologists (AoR)
5 Fore St.
Taunton, Somerset TA1 1HX
United Kingdom
Phone: 01823 351010
Toll free: (800) 442-2232
Fax: 01823 336646
Web site: http://www.aor.org.uk/index.asp

Asthma and Allergy Foundation of America
1233 20th St., NW, Ste. 402
Washington, DC 20036
Phone: (202) 466-7643
Toll free: (800) 727-8462
Web site: http://www.aafa.org

Australian Homeopathic Association
6 Cavan Ave.
Renown Park, SA 5008
Australia
Phone: (61) 8-8346-3961
Web site: http://www.homeopathyoz.org

Australian Rheumatology Association
145 Macquarie St.
Sydney, NSW 2000
Australia
Phone: 02 9256 5458
Fax: 02 9256 3310
Web site: http://www.rheumatology.org.au

B

Bastyr University
14500 Juanita Dr. NE
Kenmore, WA 98028
Phone: (425) 823-1300
Toll free: (866) 538-2267
Fax: (425) 823-6222
Web site: http://www.bastyr.edu/default.asp

BD
1 Becton Dr.
Franklin Lakes, NJ 07417-1880
Phone: (201) 847-6800
Toll free: (888) 232-2737

Fax: (201) 847-4856
Web site: http://www.bddiabetes.com

Benson-Henry Institute for Mind Body Medicine
824 Boylston St.
Chestnut Hill, MA 02467
Phone: (617) 732-9130
Fax: (617) 732-9111
Web site: http://www.mbmi.org/home/

Better Sleep Council
501 Wythe St.
Alexandria, VA 22314
Phone: (703) 683-8371
Web site: http://www.bettersleep.org

Brain Injury Association
105 North Alfred St.
Alexandria, VA 22314
Phone: (703) 236-6000
Toll free: (800) 444-6443
Web site: http://www.biausa.org/Sportsfs.htm

Brain Trauma Foundation
523 East 72nd St.,8th Fl.
New York, NY 10021
Phone: (212)772-0608
Toll free: (800) 444-6443
Web site: http://www.braintrauma.org

British Epilepsy Association
New Anstey House, Gate Way Dr., Yeadon
Leeds, LS19 7XY
Unitcd Kingdom
Phone: +44 113 210 8850
Toll free: 0808 800 5050 (UK only)
Email: helpline@epilepsy.org.uk
Web site: http://www.epilepsy.org.uk/

British Lung Foundation
73-75 Goswell Rd.
London, EC1V 7ER
United Kingdom
Phone: 08458 50 50 20
Web site: http://www.lunguk.org

Byk-Sangtec Diagnostica GmbH and Co.
von Hevesy-Str. 3D-63128
Dietzenbach
Germany
Phone: +49 (0) 6074/401-0
Web site: http://www.byk-sangtec.de/English2/Products/Autoimmune

C

California Association of Physician Groups
915 Wilshire Blvd., Ste. 1620
Los Angeles, CA 90017
Phone: (213) 624-2274
Web site: http://www.capg.org

Canadian Association of Gastroenterology
2902 S. Sheridan Way, Ste. 201
Oakville, ON L6J 7L6
Canada
Phone: (905) 829-2504
Toll free: (888) 780-0007
Fax: (905) 829-0242
Web site: http://www.cag-acg.org

Canadian Cancer Society
10 Alcorn Ave., Ste. 200
Toronto, ON M4V 3B1
Canada
Phone: (416) 961-7223
Toll free: (888) 939-3333
Fax: (416) 961-4189
Web site: http://www.cancer.ca

Canadian Chiropractic Examining Board
Ste. 238, 2116 Twenty-seventh Ave. NE
Calgary, AB T2E 7A6
Canada
Phone: (403) 230-5997
Fax: (403) 230-3321
Web site: http://www.cceb.ca

Canadian Institute of Musculoskeletal Health and Arthritis
160 Elgin St., 9th Fl., #4809A
Ottawa, ON K1A 0W9
Canada
Phone: (613) 957-8678
Web site: http://www.cihr-irsc.gc.ca

Canadian Medical Association
1867 Alta Vista Dr.
Ottawa, ON K1G 3Y6
Canada
Toll free: (800) 457-4205
Web site: http://www.cma.ca

Canadian Neurological Sciences Federation
7015 Macleod Trail SW, Ste. 709
Calgary, AB T2H 2K6
Canada
Phone: (403) 229-9544
Fax: (403) 229-1661
Web site: http://www.ccns.org

Canadian Urological Association
1155 University, Ste. 1155
Montreal, QC H3B 3A7
Canada
Phone: (514) 395-0376
Fax: (514) 875-0205
Web site: http://www.cua.org

Cancer Research Institute
681 Fifth Ave.
New York, NY 10022
Phone: (301) 654-2055
Toll free: (800) 992-2623
Web site: http://www.cancerresearch.org

Cancer Research and Prevention Foundation
1600 Duke St., Ste. 500
Alexandria, VA 22314
Phone: (703) 836-4412
Toll free: (800) 227-2732
Fax: (919) 361-8425
Web site: http://www.preventcancer.org

Celiac Disease Foundation
13251 Ventura Blvd. #1
Studio City, CA 91604
Phone: (818) 990-2354
Fax: (818) 990-2379
Web site: http://www.celiac.org

Celiac Sprue Association
PO Box 31700
Omaha, NE 68131-0700
Phone: (402) 558-0600
Toll free: (877) CSA-4-CSA
Fax: (818) 990-2379
Web site: http://www.csaceliacs.org

Center for Food Safety and Applied Nutrition
5100 Paint Branch Pkwy.
College Park, MD 20740-3835
Toll free: (888) 723-3366
Web site: http://www.cfsan.fda.gov

Center for Healthy Aging, National Council on Aging
1901 L St.
Washington, DC 20036
Phone: (202) 479-1200
Toll free: (800) 366-1655
Fax: (202) 479-0735
Web site: http://www.healthyagingprograms.org

Centers for Disease Control and Prevention (CDC)
1600 Clifton Rd.
Atlanta, GA 30333
Phone: (404) 498-1515
Toll free: (800) 311-3435
Fax: (212) 832-8646
Web site: http://www.cdc.gov

Centers for Disease Control and Prevention (CDC)—Division of Foodborne, Bacterial and Mycotic Diseases (DFBMD)
1600 Clifton Rd. NE, MS-C09
Atlanta, GA 30333
Phone: (404) 498-1515

Toll free: (800) 311-3435
Web site: http://www.cdc.gov/nczved/dfbmd

Centers for Disease Control and Prevention (CDC)—National Center for Infectious Diseases
1600 Clifton Rd. NE, MS-C14
Atlanta, GA 30333
Phone: (404) 498-1515
Toll free: (800) 311-3435
Web site: http://www.cdc.gov

Centers for Disease Control and Prevention (CDC), National Center for Injury Prevention and Control (NCIPC), Suicide Prevention
4770 Buford Hwy NE, MS K-65
Atlanta, GA 30341
Phone: (703) 907-7300
Toll free: (800) CDC-INFO
Fax: (770) 488-4760
Web site: http://www.cdc.gov/ncipc/dvp/Suicide/default.htm

Centers for Disease Control and Prevention Influenza
Web site: http://www.cdc.gov/flu/

Centers for Disease Control and Prevention National Prevention Information Network (CDC NPIN)
PO Box 6003
Rockville, MD 20849
Phone: (404) 679-3860
Toll free: (800) 458-5231
Toll free: (888) 282-7681
Web site: http://www.cdcnpin.org

Centers for Medicare and Medicaid Services (CMS)
7500 Security Blvd.
Baltimore, MD 21244
Phone: (410) 786-3000
Toll free: (877) 267-2323
Web site: http://www.cms.hhs.gov/

Central School of Practicing Nursing
4600 Carnegie Ave.
Cleveland, OH 44103
Web site: http://www.cspnohio.org

Certification Board for Nutrition Specialists (CBNS)
300 S. Duncan Ave., Ste. 225
Clearwater, FL 33755
Phone: (727) 446-6086
Fax: (727) 446-6202
Web site: http://www.cbns.org

The Coalition to Prevent Deep-Vein Thrombosis
55 Corporate Dr.
Bridgewater, NJ 08807
Phone: (301) 592-8573
Toll free: (800) 981-2491
Web site: http://www.preventdvt.org

College of American Pathologists
325 Waukegan Rd.
Northfield, IL 60093
Toll free: (800) 323-4040
Web site: http://www.cap.org

Coma Recovery Association
Republic Airport, Ste. 106
Farmingdale, NY 11735
Phone: (631) 756-1826
Toll free: (800) 444-6443
Web site: http://www.comarecovery.org

Consumer Consortium on Assisted Living
2342 Oak St.
Falls Church, VA 22046
Phone: (703) 533-8121
Fax: (703) 894-1831
Web site: http://www.ccal.org

Consumers Advancing Patient Safety
One W. Superior St., Ste. 2410
Chicago, IL 60610
Phone: (312) 274-1301
Web site: http://www.patientsafety.org

Contact Lens Association of Ophthalmologists
721 Papworth Ave., Ste. 206
Metairie, LA 70005
Phone: (504) 835-3937
Web site: http://www.clao.org

Cornea Research Foundation of America
9002 N. Meridian St., Ste. 212
Indianapolis, IN 46260
Phone: (317) 844-5610
Fax: (317) 814-2806
Web site: http://www.cornea.org

Cornell Institute for Translational Research on Aging (CITRA)
Beebe Hall, Second Fl., Cornell University
Ithaca, NY 14853
Phone: (607) 254 4336
Fax: (607) 254 2903
Web site: http://www.citra.org/index.php

Council on Chiropractic Education
8049 N. Eighty-fifth Way
Scottsdale, AZ 85258-4321
Phone: (480) 443-8877
Fax: (480) 483-7333
Web site: http://www.cce-usa.org

Council for Homeopathic Certification
PMB 187, 16915 SE 272nd St., Ste. 100
Covington, WA 98042
Toll free: (866) 242-3399
Web site: http://www.homeopathicdirectory.com

Council on Naturopathic Medical Education (CNME)
PO Box 178
Great Barrington, MA 01230
Phone: (413) 528-8877
Toll free: (866) 538-2267
Fax: (413) 528-8880
Web site: http://www.cnme.org/index.html

Council on Optometric Practitioner Education
4401 East West Hwy., Ste. 205
Bethesda, MD 20814-4521
Toll free: (800) 758-COPE (2673)
Phone: (301) 913-0641
Fax: (301) 913-2034
Email: COPE@copeonline.org.
Web site: http://www.copeopt.org

Council for Responsible Nutrition
1828 L St., NW, Ste. 900
Washington, DC 20036-5114
Phone: (202) 776-7929
Toll free: (800) 242-872
Fax: (202) 204-7980
Web site: http://www.crnusa.org

Cushing's Help and Support
Web site: http://www.cushings-help.com/intro.htm

Cushing's Support & Research Foundation
65 E India Row, Ste. 22B
Boston, MA 02110
Phone: (617) 723-3674
Fax: (617) 723-3674
Web site: http://www.csrf.net/index.htm

Cystic Fibrosis Foundation
6931 Arlington Rd.
Bethesda, MD 20814
Toll free: (800) FIGHT-CF
Web site: http://www.cf.org

D

Delta Society
875 124th Ave. NE, Ste. 101
Bellevue, WA 98005
Phone: (425) 679-5500
Fax: (425) 679-5539
Web site: http://www.deltasociety.org/index.htm

Depression and Bipolar Support Alliance
730 N. Franklin St., Ste. 501
Chicago, IL 60610-7224

Phone: (703) 907-7300
Toll free: (800) 826-3632
Fax: (312) 642-7243
Web site: http://www.ndmda.org

Dermatology Foundation
1560 Sherman Ave., Ste. 870
Evanston, IL 60201-4808
Phone: (847) 328-2256
Toll free: (866) 503-SKIN (7546)
Fax: (847) 328-0509
Web site: http://dermatologyfoundation.org/

The Diabetes Insipidus Foundation, Inc.
3742 Woodland Dr.
Columbus, GA 31907
Phone: (706) 323-7576
Toll free: (800) 457-6676
Web site: http://www.diabetesinsipidus.org

The Diabetes Insipidus and Related Disorders Network
535 Echo Court
Saline, MI 48176-1270
Toll free: (800) 457-6676
Web site: http://www.autopenhosting.org

Dignitas (Swiss assisted suicide group)
Postfach 9
Forch, CH 8127
Switzerland
Phone: +41 44 980 44 59
Toll free: (800) 621-8335
Fax: +41 44 980 14 21
Web site: http://www.dignitas.ch/

Direct Care Alliance, Inc., National Clearinghouse on the Direct Care Workforce, and Paraprofessional Healthcare Institute
349 East 149th St., 10th Fl.
Bronx, NY 10451
Phone: (718) 928-2063
Fax: (718) 585-6852
Web site: http://www.directcarealliance.org
Web site: http://www.directcareclearinghouse.org/index.jsp
Web site: http://www.paraprofessional.org

Donate Life America
700 N. Fourth St.
Richmond, VA 23219
Phone: (804) 782-4920
Fax: (804) 782-4643
Web site: http://www.donatelife.net/

Dorot
171 West 85th St.
New York, NY 10024
Phone: (212) 769-2850
Fax: (425) 679-5539
Web site: http://www.dorotusa.org/site/PageServer?pagename=homepage_DOROT

Dysautonomia Foundation
315 W 39th St., Ste. 701
New York, NY 10018
Phone: (212) 279-1066
Fax: (212) 279-2066
Web site: http://www.familialdysautonomia.org

E

e-Healthcare Solutions, Inc.
953 Route 202 N.
Branchburg, NJ 08876
Phone: (908) 203-1350
Fax: (908) 203-1307
Email: info@e-healthcaresolutions.com
Web site: http://www.digitalhealthcare.com/

Emergency Nurses Association
915 Lee St.
Des Plaines, IL 60016-6569
Toll free: (800) 900-9659
Phone: (847) 460-4001
Web site: http://www.ena.org/about/index.htm

Emphysema Anonymous, Inc.
PO Box 3224
Seminole, FL 34642
Phone: (813) 391-9977

Epilepsy Foundation
4351 Garden City Dr.
Landover, MD 20785-7223
Toll free: (800) 332-1000
Phone: (301) 459-3700
Web site: http://www.efa.org

European Alzheimer's Disease Consortium
Dept. of Internal Medicine and Clinical Gerontology, Toulouse University Hospital, 170 Ave. de Casselardit
Toulouse, 31300
France
Phone: 33-5-6177-7649
Fax: 33-5-6149-7109
Web site: http://www.eadc.alzheimer-europe.org

European Association of Nuclear Medicine
Hollandstrasse 14 / Mezzanine
Vienna, A-1020
Austria
Phone: +43-1-2 12 80 30
Fax: +43-1-2 12 80 309
Web site: http://www.eanm.org

European Society of Cardiology
The European Heart House, 2035 Route des Colles, B.P. 179-Les Templiers
Sophia-Antipolis, 06903
France
Phone: 33 4 9294 7600
Fax: 33 4 9294 7601
Web site: http://www.escardio.org

Experience Works
2200 Clarendon Blvd., Ste. 1000
Arlington, VA 22201
Phone: (703) 522-7272
Toll free: (866) EXP-WRKS [397-9757]
Fax: (703) 522-0141
Web site: http://www.experienceworks.org/site/PageServer

EyeCare America
655 Beach St.
San Francisco, CA 94109-1336
Phone: (877) 887-6327
Toll free: (800) 222-3937
Web site: http://www.eyecareamerica.org/eyecare

F

Family Caregiver Alliance (FCA) National Center on Caregiving
180 Montgomery St., Ste. 1100
San Francisco, CA 94104
Phone: (415) 434-3388
Toll free: (800) 445-8106
Web site: http://www.caregiver.org

Federation of State Medical Boards of the United States, Inc.
PO Box 619850
Dallas, TX 75261-9850
Phone: (817) 868-4000
Web site: http://www.fsmb.org

Fetzer Institute
9292 West KL Ave.
Kalamazoo, MI 49009
Phone: (269) 375-2000
Web site: http://www.fetzer.org/default.aspx

Final Exit Network (choice in dying group)
PO Box 965005
Marietta, GA 30066
Toll free: (800) 524-EXIT
Toll free: (800) 621-8335
Phone: (703) 352-7725
Web site: http://www.finalexitnetwork.org/

Food and Drug Administration (FDA)
5600 Fishers Ln.
Rockville, MD 20857
Phone: (404) 679-3860
Toll free: (888) 463-6332
Toll free: (888) 282-7681
Web site: http://www.fda.gov/default.htm

Food and Nutrition Information Center Agricultural Research Service, USDA
National Agricultural Library, Room 304, 10301 Baltimore Ave.
Beltsville, MD 20705-2351
Phone: (301) 504-5719
Fax: (301) 504-6409
Web site: http://www.nal.usda.gov/fnic

G

Geriatric Mental Health Alliance (MHA) of New York City
666 Broadway, Ste. 200
New York, NY 10012
Phone: (212) 614-5753
Fax: (425) 679-5539
Web site: http://www.mhawestchester.org/advocates/geriatrichome.asp

Geriatric Mental Health Foundation
7910 Woodmont Ave., Ste. 1050
Bethesda, MD 20814
Phone: (301) 654-7850
Toll free: (888) 35-PSYCH
Fax: (301) 654-4137
Web site: http://www.gmhfonline.org

Glaucoma Foundation
80 Maiden Lane, Ste. 700
New York, NY 10038
Phone: (212) 285-0080
Web site: http://www.glaucomafoundation.org

Gynecologic Cancer Foundation
230 W. Monroe, Ste. 2528
Chicago, IL 60606
Phone: (312) 578-1439
Toll free: (800) 444-4441
Fax: (312) 578-9769
Web site: http://www.wcn.org/gcf

H

The Hastings Center
21 Malcolm Gordon Rd.
Garrison, NY 10524
Phone: (845) 424-4040
Toll free: (800) 621-8335
Fax: (845) 424-4545
Web site: http://www.thehastingscenter.org/default.asp

Health Canada/Santé Canada
A.L. 0900C2
Ottawa, ON K1A 0K9
Canada
Phone: (613) 957-2991
Web site: http://www.hc-sc.gc.ca

Health Care Financing Administration, United States Department of Health and Human Services
200 Independence Ave. SW
Washington, DC 20201
Web site: http://www.hcfa.gov

Health Resources and Services Administration
5600 Fishers Lane
Rockville, MD 20857
Toll free: (888) 275-4772
Fax: (703) 821-2098
Web site: http://www.hrsa.gov

Heart Failure Society of America
Court International - Ste. 240 S, 2550 University Ave. W
Saint Paul, MN 55114
Phone: 651) 642-1633
Toll free: (800) 242-8721
Fax: (651) 642-1502
Web site: http://www.hfsa.org

Heart Foundation
80 William St., Level 3
Sydney, NSW 2011
Australia
Phone: 02 9219 2444
Fax: 300 36 27 87
Web site: http://www.heartfoundation.org.au

Heart Rhythm Society
1400 K St. NW, Ste. 500
Washington, DC 20005
Phone: (202) 464-3400
Toll free: (800) 242-8721
Fax: (202) 464-3401
Web site: http://www.hrspatients.org

Hepatitis Foundation International
504 Blick Dr.
Silver Spring, MD 20904
Toll free: (800) 891-0707
Web site: http://www.hepfi.org/

HIV InSite
University of California San Francisco, Center for HIV Information
4150 Clement St., Box 111V
San Francisco, CA 94121
Phone: (404) 679-3860
Toll free: (888) 463-6332
Fax: (415) 379-5547
Web site: http://hivinsite.ucsf.edu/InSite

Home Safety Council
1250 Eye St., NW, Ste. 1000
Washington, DC 20005
Phone: (202) 330-4900
Fax: (202) 330-4901
Web site: http://www. homesafety-council.org/

Homeopathic Medical Council of Canada
3910 Bathurst St., Ste. 202
Toronto, ON M3H 3N8
Canada
Phone: (416) 638-4622
Web site: http://www.hmcc.ca

Hospice Foundation of America
2001 S St. NW, Ste. 300
Washington, DC 20009
Toll free: (800) 854-3402
Web site: http://www.hospicefoundation.org

Hospital Infections Program. Centers for Disease Control and Prevention
1600 Clifton Rd.
Atlanta, GA 30333
Web site: http://www.cdc.gov/ncidod/publications/brochures/hip.htm

I

Institute for Family-Centered Care
7900 Wisconsin Ave., Ste. 405
Bethesda, MD 20814
Phone: (301) 652-0281
Web site: http://www.familycentered-care.org

Institute for Religion and Health (IRH)
8100 Greenbriar, Ste. 220
Houston, TX 77054
Phone: (713) 797-0600
Fax: (425) 679-5539
Web site: http://www.religionandhealth.org/default.htm

Institute of Medicine
500 Fifth St. NW
Washington, DC 20001
Phone: (202) 334-2352
Web site: http://www.iom.edu

International Academy of Nutrition and Aging
320 rue Saint-Honoré

Paris, 75001
France
Phone: 33 (0) 5 61 75 79 12
Fax: 33 (0) 5 61 75 11 28
Web site: http://www.healthandage.com/html/min/iananda/index.htm

International Association of Hospice and Palliative Care
UTMD Anderson Cancer Center, 1515 Holcombe Blvd., Box 08
Houston, TX 77030
Web site: http://www.hospicecare.com

International Association for the Study of Pain
111 Queen Anne Ave. North, Ste. 501
Seattle, WA 98109
Phone: (206) 283-0311
Fax: (206) 283-9403
Web site: http://www.iasp-pain.org//AM/Template.cfm?Section=Home

International Brain Injury Association
1150 South Washington St., Ste. 210
Alexandria, VA 22314
Phone: (703) 683-8400
Web site: http://www.international-brain.org

International Confederation of Dietetic Organizations
Illinois
Web site: http://www.internationaldietetics.org

International Diabetes Federation (IDF)
Avenue Emile De Mot 19
Brussels, B-1000
Belgium
Phone: +32-2-5385511 1
Toll free: (888) 232-2737
Fax: +32-2-5385114
Web site: http://www.idf.org

International Federation on Aging
4398 Boul. Saint-Laurent, Ste. 302
Montreal, QC H2W 1Z5
Canada
Phone: (514) 396-3358
Toll free: (800) 537-9728
Fax: (514) 396-3378
Web site: http://www.ifa-fiv.org/en/accueil.aspx

International Food Information Council
1100 Connecticut Ave., NW, Ste. 430
Washington, DC 20036
Phone: (202) 296-6540
Fax: (202) 296-6547
Web site: http://www.ific.org/

International Forgiveness Institute (IFI)
1127 University Ave. #201
Madison, WI 53715
Phone: (608) 251-6484
Web site: http://www.forgiveness-institute.org/index.htm

International Foundation for Functional Gastrointestinal Disorders (IFFGD)
PO Box 170864
Milwaukee, WI 53217-8076
Phone: (414) 964-1799
Toll free: (888) 964-2001
Fax: (414) 964-7176
Web site: http://www.iffgd.org

International Longevity Center-USA
60 E. 86th St.
New York, NY 10028
Phone: (212) 288-1468
Toll free: (877) 462-5267
Fax: (212) 288-3132
Web site: http://www.ilcusa.org/

International Psychogeriatric Association
550 Frontage Rd., Ste. 3759
Northfield, IL 60093
Phone: (847) 501-3310
Toll free: (888) 35-PSYCH
Fax: (847) 501-3317
Web site: http://www.ipa-online.org

International Rosacea Organization
Ste. 200, 800 South Northwest Hwy.
Barrington, IL
Phone: (888) 662-5874
Web site: http://www.internationalrosaceafoundation.org/

International Society of Hematology
5 Revere Dr., Ste. 200
Northbrook, IL 20036
Phone: (312) 238-0900
Fax: (202) 776-0545
Web site: http://www.ishworld.org

International Society for Laboratory Hematology
5 Revere Dr., Ste. 200
Northbrook, IL 20036
Phone: (312) 238-0900
Fax: (202) 776-0545
Web site: http://www.islh.org

International Taoist Tai Chi Society
134 D'Arcy St.
Toronto, ON M5T 1K3
Canada
Phone: +1 (416) 656-2110
Fax: +1 (416) 654-3937
Web site: http://www.taoist.org/content/standard.asp?name=Home

Irritable Bowel Syndrome (IBS) Self-Help Group
1440 Whalley Ave., #145
New Haven, CT 06515
Web site: http://www.ibsgroup.org

J

Jean Mayer USDA Human Nutrition Research Center on Aging
711 Washington St.
Boston, MA 02111
Phone: (617) 556-3000
Fax: (617) 556-3344
Web site: http://hnrc.tufts.edu/

Joint Commission on Accreditation of Healthcare Organizations (JCAHO)
One Renaissance Blvd.
Oakbrook Terrace, IL 60181
Phone: (630) 792-5000
Web site: http://www.jcaho.org

Joint Commission on Allied Health Personnel in Ophthalmology
2025 Woodlane Dr.
St. Paul, MN 55125-2995
Toll free: (888) 284-3937
Web site: http://www.jcahpo.org/

K

Kaiser Commission on Medicaid and the Uninsured
1450 G St. NW, Ste. 250
Washington, DC 20005
Phone: (202) 347-5270
Fax: (202) 347-5274
Web site: http://www.kff.org

L

Leukemia and Lymphoma Society
1311 Mamaroneck Ave., Ste. 130
White Plains, NY 10605
Phone: 914-949-0084
Web site: http://www.leukemia-lymphoma.org/

Lighthouse National Center for Vision and Aging
111 E. 59th St.
New York, NY 10022
Toll free: (800) 334-5497
Web site: http://www.lighthouse.org

Linus Pauling Institute. Oregon State University
571 Weniger Hall,

Corvallis, OR 97331-6512
Phone: (541) 737-5075
Toll free: (800) 242-872
Fax: (541) 737-5077
Web site: http://lpi.oregonstate.edu

Lions Clubs International Headquarters
300 West 22nd St.
Oak Brook, IL 60523
Phone: (630) 571-5466
Toll free: (866) EXP-WRKS [397-9757]
Fax: (703) 522-0141
Web site: http://www.lionsclubs.org/EN/index.shtml

Little Brothers-Friends of the Elderly (LBFE)
28 East Jackson Blvd., Ste. 405.
Chicago, IL 60604
Phone: (312) 786-1032
Fax: (312) 786-1067
Web site: http://www.littlebrothers.org/

Look Good . . . Feel Better
601 E St. NW
Washington, DC 20049
Phone: (312) 335-8700
Toll free: (800) 395-LOOK (24-hour hotline)
Toll free: (866) 699-1246
Web site: http://www.lookgoodfeelbetter.org/index.htm

The Lung Association
1750 Courtwood Crescent, Ste. 300
Ottawa, ON K2C 2B5
Canada
Phone: (613) 569-6411
Toll free: (888) 566-5864
Fax: (613) 569-8860
Web site: http://www.lung.ca

Lupus Foundation of America
2000 L St. NW, Ste. 710
Washington, DC 20036
Phone: (202)349-1155
Toll free: (800) 558-0121
Fax: (202) 349-1156
Web site: http://www.lupus.org/newsite/index.html

Lymphoma Research Foundation
8800 Venice Blvd., Ste. 207
Los Angeles, CA 90034
Phone: (310) 204-7040
Web site: http://www.lymphoma.org

M

Macula Vision Research Foundation (MVRF)
Five Tower Bridge, 300 Barr Harbor Dr., Ste. 600
West Conshohocken, PA 19428
Phone: (610) 668-6705
Toll free: (866) 4MACULA
Fax: (610) 667-1459
Web site: http://www.mvrf.org/

The Macular Degeneration Partnership
8733 Beverly Blvd. #201
Los Angeles, CA 90048
Phone: (301) 496-5248
Toll free: (888) 430-9898
Fax: (301) 623-1837
Web site: http://www.amd.org

Mayo Clinic
200 First St., NW
Rochester, MN 55905
Phone: (507) 284-2511
Toll free: (800) 342-2383
Fax: (202) 843-4355
Web site: http://www.mayoclinic.com

McKenzie Institute USA
600 E. Genesee St., Ste. 124
Syracuse, NY 13202
Toll free: (800) 635-8380
Email: Slyon@mckenziemdt.org
Web site: http://www.mckenziemdt.org

Meals on Wheels Association of America (MOWAA)
203 S. Union St.
Alexandria, VA 22314
Phone: (703) 548-5558
Fax: (703) 548-8024
Web site: http://www.mowaa.org/

Meningitis Research Foundation
Midland Way, Thornbury
Bristol, BS35 2B5
England and Wales
Phone: 01454 281811
Fax: 01454 281094
Web site: http://www.meningitis.org

Meningitis Research Foundation
133 Gilmore Place
Edinburgh, EH3 9PP
Scotland
Phone: 0131 228 3322
Fax: 0131 221 0300
Web site: http://www.meningitis.org

Meningitis Research Foundation
71 Botanic Ave.
Belfast, BT7 1JL
Northern Ireland
Phone: 028 9032 1283
Fax: 028 9032 1284
Web site: http://www.meningitis.org

Meningitis Research Foundation
63 Lower Gardiner St.
Dublin, 1
Republic of Ireland
Phone: 01 819 6931
Fax: 01 819 6903
Web site: http://www.meningitis.org

Michael J. Fox Foundation for Parkinson's Research
Grand Central Station, PO Box 4777
New York, NY 10163
Phone: (212) 509-0995
Toll free: (800) 223-2732
Web site: http://www.michaeljfox.org

Michigan State University College of Veterinary Medicine Pet Loss Support Hotline
111 Deer Lake Rd., Ste. 100
Deerfield, IL 60015
Phone: (517) 432-2696
Fax: (847) 480-9282
Web site: http://cvm.msu.edu/alumni-friends/information-for-animal-owners/pet-loss-support/plsh_brochure.pdf

Multiple Sclerosis Association of America (MSAA)
706 Haddonfield Rd.
Cherry Hill, NJ 08002
Phone: (856) 488-4500
Toll free: (800) 532-7667
Web site: http://www.msaa.com

Multiple Sclerosis Foundation
6350 North Andrews Ave.
Ft. Lauderdale, FL 33309-2130
Phone: (954) 776-6805
Toll free: (888) MSFOCUS
Fax: (660) 627-2623
Web site: http://www.msfocus.org

MyPyramid
3101 Park Center Dr., 10th Fl.
Alexandria, VA 22302
Phone: (703) 305-7600
Fax: (703) 305-3300
Web site: http://www.mypyramid.gov/

N

National Academy on an Aging Society
1220 L St. NW, Ste. 901
Washington, DC 20005
Phone: (202) 408-3375
Toll free: (800) 222-2336
Fax: (202) 842-1150
Web site: http://www.agingsociety.org/agingsociety/index.html

National Aging in Place Council (NAIPC)
1400 16th St. NW, Ste. 420
Washington, DC 20036
Phone: (202) 939-1784
Toll free: (800) OUR-AARP [687-2277]
Fax: (202) 265-4435
Web site: http://www.naipc.org/NAIPCHome/tabid/36/Default.aspx

National Alliance on Alcoholism and Drug Dependence, Inc.
12 West 21st St.
New York, NY 10010
Phone: (212) 206-6770.

National Alliance of Breast Cancer Organizations
9 East Thirty-seventh St., 10th Fl.
New York, NY 10016
Phone: (212) 889-0606
Toll free: (888) 806-2226
Web site: http://www.nabco.org

National Alliance for Caregiving
4720 Montgomery Lane, 5th Fl.
Bethesda, MD 20814
Toll free: (800) 445-8106
Web site: http://www.caregiving.org

National Alliance for Research on Schizophrenia and Depression (NARSAD)
60 Cutter Mill Rd., Ste. 404
Great Neck, NY 11021
Phone: (516) 829-0091
Toll free: (800) 829-8289
Fax: (516) 487-6930
Web site: http://www.NARSAD.org

National Alliance on Mental Illness
Colonial Place Three, 2107 Wilson Blvd., Ste. 300
Arlington, VA 22201-3042
Phone: (703) 524-7600
Toll free: (888) 950-NAMI
Fax: (703) 524-9094
Web site: http://www.nami.org/

National Anemia Action Council (NAAC)
555 E. Wells St., Ste. 1100
Milwaukee, WI 53202
Phone: (414) 225-0138
Fax: (414) 276-3349
Web site: http://www.anemia.org

National Aphasia Association (NAA)
350 Seventh Ave., Ste. 902
New York, NY 10001
Phone: (913) 839-8083
Toll free: (800) 922-4622
Fax: (913) 649-6661
Web site: http://www.aphasia.org/index.html

National Association of Adult Day Services
85 S. Washington, Ste. 316
Seattle, WA 98104
Toll free: (877) 745-1440
Fax: (206) 461-3218
Email: info@nadsa.org
Web site: http://www.nadsa.org

National Association for Chiropractic Medicine
15427 Baybrook Dr.
Houston, TX 77062
Phone: (480) 443-8877
Fax: (480) 483-7333
Web site: http://www.chiromed.org

National Association of Clinical Nurse Specialists
3969 Green St.
Harrisburg, PA 17110-1575
Phone: (717) 234-6799
Toll free: (800) 274-4ANA
Web site: http://www.nacn.org

National Association for Continence (NAFC)
POB 1019
Charleston, SC 29402-1019
Phone: (843) 377-0900
Toll free: (800) BLADDER
Web site: http://www.nafc.org

National Association for Home Care and Hospice
228 Seventh St. SE
Washington, DC 20003
Phone: (202) 547-7424
Fax: (202) 547-3540
Web site: http://www.nahc.org/

National Association of Nephrology Technicians/Technologists (NANT)
PO Box 2307
Dayton, OH 45401-2307
Toll free: (877) 607-6268
Web site: http://www.dialysistech.org

National Association of Professional Geriatric Care Managers (NAPGCM)
1604 North Country Club Rd.
Tucson, AZ 85716
Phone: (520) 881-8008
Toll free: (800) OUR-AARP [687-2277]
Fax: (520) 325-7925
Web site: http://www.caremanager.org/index.cfm

The National Association for the Relief of Paget's Disease
323 Manchester Rd., Walkden, Worsley
Manchester, M28 3HH
United Kingdom
Phone: 0161 799 4646 (International +44 161 799 4646)
Fax: 0161 799 6511
Web site: http://paget.org.uk

National Board for Respiratory Care
830 Nieman Rd.
Lenexa, KS 66214
Phone: (913) 599-4200
Web site: http://www.nbrc.org

National Board of Examiners in Optometry
4340 East West Hwy., Ste. 1010
Bethesda, MD 20814
Phone: (301) 652-5192
Email: nbeo@optometry.org
Web site: http://www.optometry.org

National Breast and Cervical Cancer Early Detection Program, Centers for Disease Control and Prevention, Division of Cancer Prevention and Control
4770 Buford Hwy. NE, MS K-64
Atlanta, GA 30341-3717
Phone: (404) 320-3333
Toll free: (800) CDC-INFO
Fax: (770) 488-4760
Web site: http://www.cdc.gov/cancer/NBCCEDP/about.htm

National Cancer Institute
6116 Executive Blvd., Room 3036A
Bethesda, MD 20892-8322
Phone: (301) 496-8531
Toll free: (800) 422-6237
Fax: (301) 402-0181
Web site: http://www.cancer.gov

National Center for Assisted Living
1201 L St.Washington, DC 20005
Phone: (202) 842-4444
Web site: http://www.ncal.org

National Center for Complementary and Alternative Medicine (NCCAM)
9000 Rockville Pike
Bethesda, MD 20892
Phone: (301) 519-3153
Toll free: (888) 644-6226
Toll free: (866) 464-3616
Web site: http://nccam.nih.gov

National Center for Death Education (NCDE)
Mount Ida College, 777 Dedham St.
Newton, MA 02459
Phone: (617) 928-4500

Fax: (847) 480-9282
Web site: http://www.mountida.edu/sp.cfm?pageid=307

National Center for Injury Prevention and Control. Centers for Disease Control and Prevention, Mailstop
F41, 4770 Buford Hwy. NE
Atlanta, GA 30341-3724
Phone: (770) 488-4031
Fax: (770) 488-4338
Web site: http://www.cdc.gov/ncipc/dacrrdp/tbi.htm

National Center on Physical Activity and Disability (NCPAD)
1640 W. Roosevelt Rd.
Chicago, IL 60608-6904
Toll free: (800) 900-8086
Fax: (312) 355-4058
Web site: http://www.ncpad.org

National Center for Policy Analysis
655 15th St. NW, Ste. 375
Washington, DC 20005
Phone: (202) 628-6671
Fax: (202) 628-6474
Web site: http://www.ncpa.org

National Center on Sleep Disorders Research (NCSDR)
Two Rockledge Centre, Ste. 10038, 6701 Rockledge Dr., MSC 7920
Bethesda, MD 20892-7920
Phone: (301) 435-0199
Web site: http://www.nhlbi.nih.gov/about/ncsdr/index.htm

National Certification Commission for Acupuncture and Oriental Medicine (NCCAOM)
76 South Laura St., Ste. 1290
Jacksonville, FL 32202
Phone: (904) 598-1005
Toll free: (888) 644-6226
Fax: (904) 598-5001
Web site: http://www.nccaom.org/index.html

National Coalition for Cancer Survivorship
1010 Wayne Ave., 5th Fl., Ste. 300
Silver Spring, MD 20910
Toll free: (888) 650-9127
Web site: http://www.canceradvocacy.org/

National Committee for Quality Assurance
1100 13th St., NW, Ste. 1000
Washington, DC 20005
Phone: (202) 955-3500
Web site: http://www.ncqa.org

National Conference of Commissioners on Uniform State Laws (NCCUSL)
111 North Wabash Ave., Ste. 1010
Chicago, IL 60602
Phone: (312) 450-6600
Fax: (312) 450-6601
Web site: http://www.nccusl.org/Update/AboutNCCUSL_desktopdefault.aspx

National Diabetes Information Clearinghouse
1 Information Way
Bethesda, MD 208920
Toll free: (800) 860-8747
Fax: (703) 738-4929
Web site: http://diabetes.niddk.nih.gov

National Digestive Diseases Information Clearinghouse (NDDIC)
2 Information Way
Bethesda, MD 20892-3570
Phone: (310) 654-2055
Toll free: (800) 891-5389
Fax: (301) 654-3810
Web site: http://digestive.niddk.nih.gov

National Eye Institute
2020 Vision Place
Bethesda, MD 20992-3655
Phone: (301) 496-5248
Toll free: (800) 324-EYES [3937]
Fax: (415) 561-8567
Web site: http://www.nei.nih.gov

National Eye Institute (NEI) Information Office
31 Center Dr., MSC 2510
Bethesda, MD 20892
Phone: (301) 496-5248
Toll free: (866)-4MACULA
Fax: (610) 667-1459
Web site: http://www.nei.nih.gov/index.asp

National Family Caregivers Association (NFCA)
10400 Connecticut Ave., Ste. 500
Kensington, MD 20895
Phone: (301) 942-6430
Toll free: (800) 896-3650
Fax: (301) 942-2302
Web site: http://www.nfcacares.org

National Foundation for Celiac Awareness
PO Box 544
Ampler, PA 19002-0544
Phone: (215) 325-1306
Toll free: (877) CSA-4-CSA
Fax: (818) 990-2379
Web site: http://www.celiaccentral.org

National Foundation for the Treatment of Pain
PO Box 70045
Houston, TX 77270-0045
Phone: (713) 862-9332
Fax: (713) 862-9346
Web site: http://www.paincare.org

National Gerentological Nursing Association
7794 Grow Dr.
Pensacola, FL 32514
Toll free: (800) 723-0560
Fax: (850) 484-8762
Email: ngna@puetzamc.com
Web site: http://www.ngna.org

National Guardianship Association
174 Crestview Dr.
Bellefonte, PA 16823
Phone: (877) 326-5992
Toll free: (800) 687-2277
Fax: (814) 355-2452
Web site: http://www.guardianship.org/index.htm

National Headache Foundation
820 N. Orleans, Ste. 217
Chicago, IL 60610
Toll free: (888) NHF-5552
Fax: (913) 906-6269
Web site: http://www.headaches.org

National Health Service of Great Britain
Riverside House, 2a Southwark Bridge Rd.
London SE1 9HA
United Kingdom
Phone: 0845 4647 (UK only Helpline)
Web site: http://www.nhsdirect.nhs.uk/

National Heart Lung and Blood Institute Health Information Center
PO Box 30105
Bethesda, MD 20824-0105
Phone: (301) 592-8573
Toll free: (800) 242-8721
Fax: (240) 629-3246
Web site: http://www.nhlbi.nih.gov

National Highway Traffic Safety Administration
1200 New Jersey Ave., SE, West Bldg.
Washington, DC 20590
Toll free: (888) 327-4236 or TTY for hearing impaired
Toll free: (800) 424-9153
Web site: http://www.nhtsa.dot.gov

National Institute on Aging
350 Fifth Ave., Ste. 801
Washington, DC 10118
Phone: 212-755-6810
Web site: http://www.nia.nih.gov/nutritionforseniors/

National Institute on Aging (NIA)
Building 31, Room 5C27, 31 Center Dr., MSC 2292
Bethesda, MD 20892
Phone: (301) 496-1752
Toll free: (800) 222-4225
Fax: (301) 496-1072
Web site: http://www.nia.nih.gov/

National Institute on Alcohol Abuse and Alcoholism
5635 Fishers Lane, MSC 9304
Bethesda, MD 20892-9304
Phone: (301) 443-3860
Toll free: (800) 222-2225
Fax: (301) 480-1726
Web site: http://www.niaaa.nih.gov

National Institute of Allergy and Infectious Diseases
6610 Rockledge Dr., MSC 6612
Bethesda, MD 20892-6612
Phone: (301) 496-5717
Toll free: (866) 284-4107
Fax: (301) 402-3573
Web site: http://www3.niaid.nih.gov

National Institute of Arthritis and Musculoskeletal and Skin Diseases
1 AMS Circle
Bethesda, MD 20892-3675
Phone: (301) 495-4484
Toll free: (877) 22-NIAMS [226-4267]
Fax: (301) 718-6366
Web site: http://www.niams.nih.gov

National Institute on Deafness and Other Communication Disorders
1 Communication Ave.
Bethesda, MD 20892-3456
Toll free: (800) 241-1044
Web site: http://www.nidcd.nih.gov

National Institute of Dental & Craniofacial Research. National Institutes of Health
Bldg. 45, Room 4AS-18, 45 Center Dr. MSC 6400
Bethesda, MD 20892-6400
Phone: (301) 402-7364
Fax: (301) 480-4098
Email: nidcrinfo@mail.nih.gov
Web site: http://www.nidcr.nih.gov/

National Institute of Diabetes and Digestive and Kidney Diseases (NIDDK)
Building 31, Room 9A06, 31 Center Dr., MSC 2560
Bethesda, MD 20892
Phone: (301) 496-3583
Toll free: (800) 272-3900
Fax: (866) 699-1246
Web site: http://www2.niddk.nih.gov/

National Institute of Mental Health (NIMH)
6001 Executive Blvd., Room 8184, MSC 9663
Bethesda, MD 20892
Phone: (301) 443-4513
Toll free: (866) 615-6464
Fax: (301) 443-4279
Web site: http://www.nimh.nih.gov/index.shtml

National Institute of Neurological Disorders and Stroke
PO Box 5801
Bethesda, MD 20824
Phone: (301) 592-8573
Toll free: (800) 352-9424
Fax: (301) 496-6751
Web site: http://www.ninds.nih.gov

National Institute for Rehabilitation Engineering
PO Box 1088
Hewitt, NJ O7421
Phone: (973) 853-6585
Phone: (928) 832-2894
Fax: (928) 832-2894
Web site: http://www.angelfire.com/nj/nire2

National Institutes of Health
9000 Rockville Pike
Bethesda, MD 20892
Phone: (301) 496-4000
Email: NIHInfo@OD.NIH.GOV
Web site: http://www.nih.gov/

National Institutes of Health Osteoporosis and Related Bone Diseases National Resource Center
2 Ames Circle
Bethesda, MD 20892-3676
Toll free: (800) 624-BONE
Web site: http://www.osteo.org

National Keratoconus Assistance Foundation (NKCAF)
2607 Rockefeller Lane, Ste. 3
Redondo Beach, CA 90278
Phone: (714) 404-8690
Web site: http://www.nkcaf.org

National Keratoconus Foundation
8733 Beverly Blvd., Ste. 201
Los Angeles, CA 90048
Phone: (310) 423-6455
Toll free: (800) 521-2524
Web site: http://www.nkcf.org

National Kidney Foundation
30 East 33rd St.
New York, NY 10016
Phone: (212) 889-2210
Toll free: (800) 622-9010
Fax: (212) 689-9261
www.kidney.org

National Kidney and Urologic Diseases Information Clearinghouse
3 Information Way
Bethesda, MD 20892-3580
Toll free: (800) 891-5390
Fax: (703) 738-4929
Web site: http://www.kidney.niddk.nih.gov

National Long Term Care Ombudsman Resource Center
1828 L St., Ste. 801
Washington, DC 20036
Phone: (202) 332-2275
Fax: (202) 332-2949
Web site: http://www.ltcombudsman.org

National Lymphedema Network
Latham Square, 1611 Telegraph Ave., Ste. 1111
Oakland, CA 94612-2138
Phone: (510) 208-3200
Toll free: (800) 541-3259
Fax: (510) 208-3110
Web site: http://www.lymphnet.org

National Marrow Donor Program
Ste. 500, 3001 Broadway St. NE
Minneapolis, MN 55413-1753
Toll free: (800) 627-7692
Web site: http://www.marrow.org

National Mental Health Association (NMHA)
2000 N. Beauregard St., 6th Fl.
Alexandria, VA 22311
Phone: (703) 684-7722
Toll free: (800) 969-NMHA
Fax: (703) 684-5968
Web site: http://www1.nmha.org/

National Mental Health Information Center
PO Box 42557
Washington, DC 20015
Phone: (703) 524-7600
Toll free: (800) 789-2647

Fax: (240) 221-4295
Web site: http://mentalhealth.samhsa .gov

National Multiple Sclerosis Society
733 Third Ave., 3rd Fl.
New York, NJ 10017
Phone: (212) 986-3240
Toll free: (800) 344-4867
Fax: (212) 986-7981
Web site: http://www.nationalmssoci-ety.org

National Network of Career Nursing Assistants
3577 Easton Rd.
Norton, OH 44203
Phone: (330) 825-9342
Fax: (330) 825-9378
Web site: http://www.cna-network.org

National Network for Immunization Information
301 University Blvd., CH 2.218
Galveston, TX 77555-0351
Phone: (409) 772-0199
Web site: http://www.immunizationin-fo.org

National Organization for Rare Disorders (NORD)
55 Kenosia Ave., PO Box 1968
Danbury, CT 06813-1968
Toll free: (800) 999-6673
Web site: http://www.rarediseases.org

National Osteoporosis Foundation
1232 22nd St. NW
Washington, DC 20037-1202
Phone: (202) 223-2226
Toll free: (800) 231-4222
Web site: http://www.nof.org

National Parkinson Foundation
1501 NW 9th Ave. / Bob Hope Rd.
Miami, FL 33136-1494
Phone: (305) 243-6666
Toll free: (800) 327-4545
Fax: (305) 243-5595
Web site: http://www.parkinson.org

National Patient Advocate Foundation
753 Thimble Shoals Blvd., Ste. A
Newport News, VA 23606
Toll free: (800) 532-5274
Fax: (757) 873-8999
Web site: http://www.npaf.org

National Pressure Ulcer Advisory Panel
1255 Twenty-Third St. NW, Ste. 200
Washington, DC 80013
Phone: (202) 521-6789
Fax: (202) 833-3636
Web site: http://www.npuap.org

National Psoriasis Foundation
6600 SW 92nd Ave., Ste. 300
Portland, OR 97223-7195
Phone: (503) 244-7404
Toll free: (800) 723-9166
Fax: (503) 245-0626
Web site: http://www.psoriasis.org

National Research Center for Women & Families
1701 K St. NW, Ste. 700
Washington, DC 20006
Phone: (202) 223-4000
Toll free: (800) 541-3259
Fax: (510) 208-3110
Web site: http://www.center4research .org

National Right to Life Committee (NRLC)
512 10th St. NW
Washington, DC 20004
Phone: (202) 626-8800
Fax: (312) 450-6601
Web site: http://www.nrlc.org/default .html

National Rosacea Society
Ste. 200, 800 South Northwest Hwy.
Barrington, IL
Toll free: (888) 662-5874
Web site: http://rosacea.org

National Safety Council
1121 Spring Lake Dr.
Itasca, IL 60143-3201
Phone: (630) 285-1121
Fax: (630) 285-1315
Web site: http://www.nsc.org/

National Scoliosis Foundation
5 Cabot Place
Stoughton, MA 02072
Phone: (617) 341-6333
Toll free: (800) NSF-MYBACK
Fax: (617) 341-8333
www.scoliosis.org

National Sleep Foundation
1522 K St. NW
Washington, DC 20005
Phone: (202) 347-3472
Fax: (202) 347-3472
Web site: http://www.sleepfoundation .org

National Stroke Association
9707 East Easter Lane
Englewood, CO 80112-3747
Phone: (303) 649-9299
Toll free: (800) STROKES
Fax: (303) 649-1328
Web site: http//www.stroke.org

National Vaccine Program Office U.S. Department of Health & Human Services
200 Independence Ave. SW
Washington, DC 20201
Phone: (202) 619-0257
Fax: (877) 696-6775
Web site: http://www.hhs.gov/nvpo

Natural Standard
245 First St., 18th Fl.
Cambridge, MA 02142
Phone: (617) 444-8629
Toll free: (888) 644-6226
Fax: (617) 758-4274
Web site: http://www.naturalstandard .com/

Nephrogenic Diabetes Insipidus Foundation
Main St., PO Box 1390
Eastsound, WA 98245
Toll free: (888) 376-6343
Web site: http://www.ndif.org

NIH Neurological Institute
PO Box 5801
Bethesda, MD 20824
Phone: (301) 496-5751
Toll free: (800) 352-9424
Web site: http://www.ninds.nih.gov/ index.htm

NIH Osteoporosis and Related Bone Diseases, National Resource Center
2 AMS Circle
Bethesda, MD 20892-3676
Phone: (202) 223-0344
Toll free: (800) 624-BONE
Fax: (202) 466-4315
Web site: http://www.niams.nih.gov/ Health_Info/bone/default.asp

Not Dead Yet (NDY)
7521 Madison St.
Forest Park, IL 60130
Phone: (708) 209-1500
Toll free: (800) 621-8335
Fax: (708) 209-1735
Web site: http://notdeadyetnewscom-mentary.blogspot.com/

O

Office of Dietary Supplements
31 Center Dr., MSC 2086
Bethesda, MD 20892-2086
Phone: (301) 435-2920
Toll free: (800) 222-2225
Web site: http://dietary-supplements .info.nih.gov

Office of Dietary Supplements, National Institutes of Health
Ste. 3B01, 6100 Executive Blvd.
Bethesda, MD 20892
Phone: (301) 435-2920
Fax: (301) 480-1845
Web site: http://ods.od.nih.gov

Office of Nutritional Products, Labeling, and Dietary Supplements, Center for Food Safety and Applied Nutrition, Food and Drug Administration
5100 Paint Branch Parkway
College Park, MD 20740
Phone: (301) 436-2373
Toll free: (888) 723-3366
Fax: (301) 436-2639
Web site: http://www.cfsan.fda.gov/~dms/onplds.html

One Plus One Marriage and Partnership Research
1 Benjamin St.
London, DC EC1M 5QG
United Kingdom
Phone: +44 (0)20 7553 9530
Fax: +44 (0)20 7553 9550
Web site: http://www.opo.org.uk/MAIN/Index.php

The Oral Cancer Foundation
3419 Via Lido #205
Newport Beach, CA 92663
Phone: (949) 646-8000
Fax: (949) 496-3331
www.oralcancerfoundation.org

P

The Paget Foundation
120 Wall St., Ste. 1602
New York, NY 10005-4001
Phone: (212) 509-5335
Toll free: (800) 23-PAGET
Fax: (212) 509-8492
Web site: http://www.paget.org

Pan American Health Organization
525 Twenty-third St., NW
Washington, DC 20037
Phone: (202) 974-3000
Fax: (202) 974-3663
Web site: http://www.paho.org

Park Ridge Center for Health, Faith, and Ethics
205 West Touhy Ave., Ste. 203
Park Ridge, IL 60068
Phone: (837) 384-3507
Toll free: (888) 644-6226
Fax: (847) 384-3557
Web site: http://www.parkridgecenter.org/index.html

Parkinson's Disease Foundation
710 West 168th St.
New York, NY 10032-9982
Phone: (212)509-0995
Toll free: (800) 457-6676
Web site: http://www.pdf.org

Parkinson's Disease Society (UK)
215 Vauxhall Bridge Rd.
London, NY SW1V 1EJ
United Kingdom
Phone: (020) 7931-8080
Toll free: (800) 457-6676
Web site: http://www.parkinsons.org.uk

Partnership for Caring
1620 Eye St., NW, Ste. 202
Washington, DC 20006
Phone: (202) 296-8071
Toll free: (800) 989-9455
Fax: (202) 296-8352
Web site: http://www.partnershipforcaring.org/

Patience T'ai Chi Association
PO Box 350-532
Brooklyn, NY 11235
Phone: 718-332-3477
Toll free: (888) 644-6226
Fax: (866) 464-3616
Web site: http://www.patiencetaichi.com/public/main.cfm

People Living with Cancer, American Society of Clinical Oncology
19000 Duke St., Ste. 200
Alexandria, VA 22314
Phone: (703) 519-2997
Toll free: (888) 651-3038
Fax: (703) 299-1014
www.plwc.org

Persons United Limiting Substandards and Errors in Health Care (P.U.L.S.E.)
Web site: http://www.pulseamerica.org

Phoenix Project/Head Injury Hotline
Box 84151
Seattle, WA 98124
Phone: (206) 621-8558
Toll free: (800) 444-6443
Web site: http://www.headinjury.com

Planned Parenthood Federation of America
434 West Thirty-third St.
New York, NY 10001
Phone: (212) 541-7800
Toll free: (800) 230-7526
Fax: (212) 245-1845
Web site: http://www.ppfa.org

Prevent Blindness America
211 West Wacker Dr., Ste. 1700
Chicago, IL 60606
Phone: (301) 496-5248
Toll free: (800) 331-2020
Fax: (610) 667-1459
Web site: http://www.preventblindness.org/

The President's Council on Bioethics
1425 New York Ave. NW, Ste. C100
Washington, DC 20005
Phone: (202) 296-4669
Toll free: (800) 621-8335
Fax: (708) 209-1735
Web site: http://www.bioethics.gov/

The Psoriasis and Psoriatic Arthritis Alliance
Unit 3, Horseshoe Business Park, Lye Lane, Bricket Wood
St. Albans, OR AL2 3TA
Phone: 0870-7703212
Toll free: (800) 723-9166
Fax: 0870-7703213
Web site: http://www.papaa.org

Pulmonary Fibrosis Foundation (PFF)
1332 North Halsted St., Ste. 201
Chicago, IL 60622
Phone: (312)587-9272
Fax: (312)587-9273
Web site: http://www.pulmonaryfibrosis.org

Pulmonary Hypertension Association (PHA)
801 Roeder Rd., Ste. 400
Silver Spring, MD 20910
Phone: (301)565-3004
Fax: (301)565-3994
Web site: http://www.phassociation.org

R

Radiological Society of North America
820 Jorie Blvd.
Oak Brook, IL 60523-2251
Toll free: (800) 381-6660
Web site: http://www.rsna.org/

Rehabilitation Institute of Chicago
345 E. Superior St., First Fl.
Chicago, IL 60611
Phone: 312-238-5433
Fax: 312-238-2860
Web site: http://lifecenter.ric.org

Rehabilitation Research and Training Center on Aging with Developmental Disabilities,

Department of Disability and Human Development, College of Applied Health Sciences, University of Illinois at Chicago
1640 W. Roosevelt Rd, Ste. 436 IIDD, MC 626
Chicago, IL 60608
Phone: (312) 413-1647
Toll free: (800) 221-4602
Fax: (312) 413-1630
Web site: http://www.uic.edu/orgs/rrtcamr

Restless Legs Syndrome Foundation
1610 14th St. NW
Rochester, MN 55901-2985
Phone: (507) 287-6465
Fax: (507) 287-6312
Web site: http://www.rls.org

Robert Packard Center for ALS Research at Johns Hopkins
5801 Smith Ave., McAuley Ste. 110
Baltimore, MD 21209-3652
Phone: (410) 735-7678
Web site: http://www.alscenter.org

Rural Center for AIDS/STD Prevention, Indiana University
801 E. Seventh St.
Bloomington, IN 47405-3085
Phone: (812) 855-1718
Toll free: (800) 566-8644
Fax: (812) 855-3717
Web site: http://www.indiana.edu

Rush Arthritis and Orthopedics Institute
1725 West Harrison St., Ste. 1055
Chicago, IL 60612
Phone: (312) 563-2420
Web site: http://www.rush.edu

S

S.L.E. Lupus Foundation
330 Seventh Ave., Ste. 1701
New York, NY 10001
Phone: (212) 685-4118
Fax: (212) 545-1843
Web site: http://www.lupusny.org

Self Help for Hard of Hearing People, Inc.
7910 Woodmont Ave., Ste. 1200
Bethesda, MD 20814
Phone: (301) 657-2248
Phone: (301) 657-2249 (TTY)
Web site: http://www.shhh.org

Senior Corps
1201 New York Ave. NW
Washington, DC 20525
Phone: (202) 606-5000
Toll free: (800) 424-8867
Fax: (703) 522-0141
Web site: http://www.seniorcorps.gov/Default.asp

Seniorresource.com
Web site: http://www.seniorresource.com/hsdc.htm

Sex Information and Education Council of Canada
850 Cozwell Ave.
Toronto, ON M4C 5R1
Canada
Phone: (416) 466-5304
Fax: (416) 778-0785
Web site: http://www.sieccan.org

Sex Information and Education Council of the United States
130 W. Forty-Second St., Ste. 350
New York, NY 10036-7802
Phone: (212) 819-9770
Toll free: (800) 891-5390
Fax: (212) 819-9776
Web site: http://www.siecus.org

Sexual Dysfunction Association
London Bridge Hospital, Rm. 301, Emblem House, 27 Toole St.
London, NY SE1 2PR
United Kingdom
Phone: (44) 0870-7743571
Toll free: (800) 891-5390
Fax: (212) 819-9776
Web site: http://www.sda.uk.net

Shasta County Public Health Department
2650 Breslauer Way
Redding, CA 9600
Phone: (530) 225-5591
Web site: http://www.co.shasta.ca.us/Departments/Public Health/CommunityNutrition

Sjögren's Syndrome Foundation
6707 Democracy Blvd., Ste. 325
Bethesda, MD 20817
Phone: (301) 530-4420
Toll free: (800) 475-6473
Fax: (301) 530-4415
Web site: http://www.sjogrens.org/

Skin Cancer Foundation
149 Madison Ave., Ste. 901
New York, NY 10016
Phone: (212) 725-5176
Toll free: (800) 422-6237
Fax: (212) 725-5751
Web site: http://www.skincancer.org

Society for Nutrition Education
7150 Winton Dr., Ste. 300
Indianapolis, IN 46268
Toll free: (800) 235-6690
Web site: http://www.sne.org

Society of Thoracic Surgeons
633 N. Saint Clair St., Ste. 2320
Chicago, IL 60611
Phone: (312) 202-5800
Toll free: (800) 242-8721
Fax: (312) 202-5801
Web site: http://www.sts.org

Society for Vascular Surgery (SVS)
633 N. St. Clair, 24th Fl.
Chicago, IL 60611
Phone: (312)334-2300
Toll free: (800)258-7188
Fax: (312)334-2320
Web site: http://www.vascularweb.org

Stroke Association UK
Stroke House, 240 City Rd.
London, EC1V 2PR
United Kingdom
Phone: 020 7566 0300
Web site: http://www.stroke.org.uk

Susan G. Komen for the Cure.
5005 LBJ Freeway, Ste. 250
Dallas, TX 75244
Phone: (404) 320-3333
Fax: (877) GO-KOMEN
Fax: (770) 488-4760
Web site: http://ww3.komen.org/home/

Systemic Lupus Erythematosus. National Arthritis and Musculoskeletal and Skin Diseases Information Clearinghouse, NIAMS/National Institutes of Health
1 AMS Circle
Bethesda, MD 20892-3675
Phone: (301) 495-4484
Web site: http://www.nih.gov/niams/

T

T'ai Chi Foundation
PO Box 575, Midtown Station
New York, NY 10018
Phone: (212) 645-7010
Toll free: (888) 644-6226
Toll free: (866) 464-3616
Web site: http://www.taichifoundation.org/

TATLife
PO Box 5192
Mooresville, NC 28117

Phone: (310) 378-7381
Toll free: (877) 674-4344
Fax: (617) 758-4274
Web site: http://www.tatlife.com/

Texas Heart Institute Heart Information Service. PO Box 20345
Houston, TX 77225-0345
Toll free: (800) 292-2221
Web site: http://www.tmc.edu/thi/his.html

U

U.S. Department of Agriculture
1400 Independence, SW
Washington, DC 20250
Phone: (507) 284-2511
Toll free: (800) 342-2383
Web site: http://www.usda.gov

U.S. Department of Health & Human Services
200 Independence Ave. SW
Washington, DC 20201
Phone: (847) 328-2256
Toll free: (877) 696-6775
Fax: (847) 328-0509
Web site: http://www.hhs.gov/

U.S. Food and Drug Administration
5600 Fishers Ln.
Rockville, MD 20857-0001
Phone: (507) 284-2511
Toll free: (888) 463-6332
Web site: http://www.fda.gov

U.S. Living Will Registry
523 Westfield Ave., PO Box 2789
Westfield, NJ 07091
Phone: (202) 626-8800
Toll free: (800) LIV-WILL [548-9455]
Fax: (908) 654-1919
Web site: http://www.uslivingwillregistry.com/default.asp

United Kingdom Homecare Association
Group House, 52 Sutton Court Rd., Sutton
Surrey, SM1 4SL
United Kingdom
Phone: 020 8288 5291
Fax: 020 8288 5290
Email: helpline@ukhca.co.uk
Web site: http://www.ukhca.co.uk

United Network for Organ Sharing
700 North 4th St.
Richmond, VA 23219
Toll free: (888)894-6361
Web site: http://www.unos.org

United Ostomy Associations of America, Inc.
PO Box 66
Fairview, TN 37062-0066
Toll free: (800) 826-0826
Web site: http://www.uoaa.org

United States Centers for Disease Control and Prevention (CDC)
1600 Clifton Rd.
Atlanta, GA 30333
Phone: (404) 639-3534
Toll free: (800) 311-3435
Fax: (301) 402-3573
Web site: http://www.cdc.gov

United States Department of Agriculture, Food and Nutrition Information Center
10301 Baltimore Ave.
Beltsville, MD 20705-2351
Phone: (301) 504-5719
Toll free: (800) 366-1655
Fax: (202) 479-0735
Web site: http://www.nal.usda.gov/fnic

United States Department of Health and Human Services
200 Independence Ave. SW
Washington, DC 20201
Web site: http://www.hhs.gov

United States Department of Veterans Affairs
100 Emancipation Dr.
Hampton, VA 23667
Phone: (757) 722-9961
Fax: (301) 443-4279
Web site: http://www.va.gov

United States Renal Data System (USRDS)
USRDS Coordinating Center, 914 S. 8th St., Ste. D-206
Minneapolis, MN 55404
Phone: (612) 347-7776
Web site: http://www.usrds.org

United States Renal Data System (USRDS)
The University of Michigan, 315 W. Huron, Ste. 240
Ann Arbor, MI 48103
Phone: (734) 998-6611
Toll free: (888) 894-6361
Web site: http://www.med.umich.edu/usrds

United States Water Fitness Association
PO Box 243279
Boynton Beach, FL 33424-3279
Phone: (561) 732-9908
Fax: (561) 732-0950
Web site: http://www.uswfa.com

Urological Society of Australia and New Zealand
180 Ocean St., Ste. 512 Eastpoint
Edgecliff, NSW 2027
Australia
Phone: (61) 2 9362 8644
Fax: (61) 2 9362 1433
Web site: http://www.usanz.org.au

USDA Center for Nutrition Policy and Promotion
3101 Park Center Dr., Rm. 1034
Alexandria, VA 22302-1594
Toll free: (888) 7-PYRAMID
Web site: http://www.mypyramid.gov

USDA Food and Nutrition Service
3101 Park Center Dr.
Alexandria, VA 22302
Web site: http://www.fns.usda.gov/fns/

V

Vascular Disease Foundation
1075 S. Yukon, Ste. 320
Lakewood, CO 80226
Toll free: (866) 723-4636
Web site: http://www.vdf.org/

Veterans of Foreign Wars (National Headquarters)
406 W. Thirty-fourth St.
Kansas City, MO 64111
Phone: (816) 756-3390
Toll free: (800) 839-1899
Fax: (816) 968-1149
Web site: http://www.vfw.org

Veterans of Foreign Wars (Washington, DC Office)
VFW Memorial Bldg., 200 Maryland Ave. NE
Washington, DC 20002
Phone: (202) 543-2239
Fax: (202) 543-6719
Web site: http://www.vfw.org

Veterans Health Administration
810 Vermont Ave. NW
Washington, DC 20420
Phone: (202) 273-5400
Toll free: (800) 827-1000
Web site: http://www.va.gov

Visiting Nurses Association of America
99 Summer St., Ste. 1700
Boston, MA 02110
Phone: (617) 737-3200
Web site: http://www.vnaa.org

Vitamin C Foundation
PO Box 73172
Houston, TX 77273
Phone: (281) 443-3634
Web site: http://www.vitamincfoundation.org/found.htm

VZV Research Foundation (For Research on Varicella Zoster)
21 East Sixty-fourth St., 5th Fl.
New York, NY 10021
Phone: (212) 371-7280
Toll free: (800) 342-2383
Fax: (212) 838-0380
Web site: http://www.vzvfoundation.org

W

Weight-control Information Network (WIN)/National Institute of Diabetes and Digestive and Kidney Diseases of the National Institutes of Health
1 WIN Way
Bethesda, MD 20892-3665
Phone: (202) 828-1025
Toll free: (877) 946-4627
Fax: (202) 828-1028
Web site: http://win.niddk.nih.gov

Wills Eye (formerly Wills Eye Hospital)
840 Walnut St.
Philadelphia, PA 19107
Phone: (215) 928-3000
Toll free: (877) AT-WILLS
Fax: (610) 667-1459
Web site: http://www.willseye.org/

Women's Cancer Network
230 W. Monroe, Ste. 2528
Chicago, IL 60606
Phone: (312) 578-1439
Fax: (312) 578-9769
Web site: http://www.wcn.org

World Community for Christian Meditation
St. Mark's, Myddelton Square
London EC1R 1XX
United Kingdom
Phone: +44 0207 278 2070
Toll free: (888) 644-6226
Toll free: (866) 464-3616
Web site: http://www.wccm.org/home.asp?pagestyle=home

World Confederation for Physical Therapy (WCPT)
Kensington Charity Centre, 4th Fl., Charles House, 375 Kensington High St.
London W14 8QH
United Kingdom
Phone: +44 (0)20 7471 6765
Toll free: (800) 222-4225
Fax: +44 (0)20 7471 6766
Web site: http://www.wcpt.org/index.php

World Health Organization
20 Ave. Appia
1211 Geneva, 27
Switzerland
Phone: +41 (22) 791 4140
Fax: +41 (22) 791 4268
Web site: http://www.who.int/gtb

World Hypertension League
100-1260 Hamilton St., Ste. 52
Vancouver, BC V6B 2S8
Canada
Phone: +1-604-268-7176
Toll free: (800) 242-8721
Fax: +1-604-291-5927
Web site: http://www.worldhypertensionleague.org/

Worldwide Education & Awareness for Movement Disorders (WE MOVE)
204 West 84th St
New York, NY 10024
Phone: (212) 875-8312
Toll free: (866) 546-3136
Fax: (212) 875-8389
Web site: http://www.wemove.org

XYZ

Y-ME: National Breast Cancer Organization
12 W. Van Buren, Ste. 1000
Chicago, IL 60607-3903
Phone: (312) 986-8338
Toll free: (800) 221-2141
Fax: (312) 294-8597
Web site: http://www.y-me.org

GLOSSARY

A

AADC INHIBITORS. Drugs that block the amino acid decarboxylase; one type of enzyme that breaks down dopamine. Also called DC inhibitors, they include carbidopa and benserazide.

ABDOMINAL CAVITY. The hollow part of the body that extends from chest to groin. It is located between the diaphragm, which is the thin muscle below the lungs and heart, and the pelvis, the basin-shaped cavity that contains the reproductive organs, bladder, and rectum.

ABDOMINAL HERNIA. A defect in the abdominal wall through which the abdominal organs protrude.

ABSCESS. A localized collection of pus in the skin or other body tissue.

ABSTINENCE. Complete nonuse of alcohol (or other substance). Abstinence is the goal of substance abuse counseling in the elderly.

ACALCULOUS CHOLECYSTITIS. Inflammation of the gallbladder that occurs without the presence of gallstones.

ACCOMMODATION. The ability of the eye to change its focus from near to distant objects.

ACETABULUM. The socket-shaped part of the pelvis that forms part of the hip joint.

ACETYLCHOLINE. A neurotransmitter that causes cardiac inhibition, vasodilatation, gastrointestinal peristalsis, and other parasympathetic effects.

ACHALASIA. A disorder in which the lower esophageal sphincter fails to relax during swallowing.

ACID INDIGESTION. Indigestion that results from too much acid in the stomach.

ACIDOTIC. Characterized by acidosis, an abnormal increase in the acidity of the body's fluids.

ACINAR CELL CARCINOMA. A malignant tumor arising from the acinar cells of the pancreas.

ACINAR CELL(S). Cells that comprise small sacs terminating the ducts of some exocrine glands.

ACNE. A chronic inflammation of the sebaceous glands that manifests as blackheads, whiteheads, and/or pustules on the face or trunk.

ACOUSTIC NEUROMA. A non-cancerous tumor caused by growth of abnormal cells on the auditory nerve that governs hearing.

ACQUIRED IMMUNE DEFICIENCY SYNDROME (AIDS). A disease that is characterized by the body's inability to fight off infection.

ACRODERMATITIS ENTEROPATHICA. A genetic disorder resulting from the impaired uptake and transport of zinc in the body.

ACTH (ADERENOCORTICOTROPHIN). A hormone secreted by the pituitary gland that causes the adrenal glands to secrete the hormone cortisol.

ACTIVATED PARTIAL THROMBOPLASTIN TIME (APTT). A lab test that detects coagulation defects in the intrinsic clotting cascade. Used to regulate heparin dosing.

ACTIVE IMMUNITY. Protection against a disease that results when exposure to a disease organism triggers the immune system to produce antibodies to that disease.

ACTIVITIES OF DAILY LIVING (ADLS). Activities considered necessary for adequate self-care, such as eating, bathing, dressing, toileting, etc.

ACUPOINT. Any location on the body stimulated in either acupressure or acupuncture in order to redirect or adjust the flow of energy within the body. Some practitioners maintain that the human body has over 2,000 acupoints.

ACUPUNCTURE. The technique of inserting thin needles through the skin at specific points on the body to control pain and other symptoms.

ACUTE CONFUSIONAL STATE. A term that some doctors use as a synonym for delirium.

ACUTE PAIN. Pain that is usually temporary and results from something specific, such as a surgery, an injury, or an infection.

ACUTE PRESCRIBING. Homeopathic treatment for self-limiting illnesses with abrupt onset.

ACUTE RESPIRATORY DISTRESS SYNDROME. A serious reaction to various forms of injuries to the lung, characterized by inflammation of the lung, leading to impaired gas exchange and release of inflammatory mediators causing inflammation and low blood oxygen.

ACUTE RETROVIRAL SYNDROME (ARS). A syndrome that develops in about 30 percent of HIV patients within a few weeks of infection. ARS is characterized by nausea, vomiting, fever, headache, general tiredness, and muscle cramps.

ADAPTATION. Altering a tool used in performing a task so that the individual is better able to function independently or with minimal assistance.

ADAPTIVE IMMUNITY. The response of lymphocytes to specific antigens. After the first response of lymphocytes to a pathogen, B and T cells remain to fight more effectively against the pathogen if it ever returns. Also called acquired immunity.

ADDICTION. Compulsive, overwhelming physical and/or psychological dependence on a specific activity. The activity may be smoking, gambling, alcohol, or may involve the use of almost any substance, such as a drug.

ADENOCARCINOMA. Malignant cancers that originate in the tissues of glands or that form glandular structures.

ADENOVIRUS. One type of virus that can cause upper respiratory tract infections.

ADJUSTMENT DISORDER. A psychiatric disorder marked by inappropriate or inadequate responses to a change in life circumstances. Depression following retirement from work is an example of adjustment disorder.

ADJUVANT THERAPY. Treatment involving radiation, chemotherapy (drug treatment), or hormone therapy, or a combination of all three given after the primary treatment for the possibility of residual microscopic disease.

ADRENAL GLANDS. Two glands located next to the kidneys. The adrenal glands produce the hormones epinephrine and norepinephrine and the corticosteroid (cortisone-like) hormones.

ADRENERGIC. Refers to neurons (nerve cells) that use catecholamines as neurotransmitters at a synapse.

ADRENERGIC RECEPTOR. There are three families of adrenergic receptors, $alpha_1$, $alpha_2$ and beta, and each family contains three distinct subtypes. Each of the nine subtypes are coded by separate genes.

ADRENERGIC-BLOCKING AGENTS. Medications used to treat some types of heart conditions and high blood pressure.

ADVANCE (MEDICAL) DIRECTIVE. A legal document drafted by a patient, in advance, ordering specific medical procedures to be offered or withheld if they are incapacitated. A living will is a type of advance directive.

ADVENTURE TRAVEL. Travel in which the traveler takes an active rather than passive role, such as hiking, cycling, mountain climbing, or white water rafting.

AEROBIC. A type of organism that grows and thrives only in environments containing oxygen.

AEROBIC BACTERIA. Bacteria that require oxygen in order to grow and survive.

AEROBIC FITNESS. A measure of the amount of oxygen delivered to muscle tissue to keep it working. Any type of exercise that raises the heart rate and keeps it up for a period of time improves aerobic fitness.

AFLATOXIN. A substance produced by molds that grow on rice and peanuts. Exposure to aflatoxin is thought to explain the high rates of primary liver cancer in Africa and parts of Asia.

AGAR. A gel-like substance derived from red seaweed that is used to make a culture medium for growing bacteria on laboratory plates.

AGC. Atypical glandular cells; a Pap-test result indicating that mucus-producing cells in the cervix or the lining of the uterus appear abnormal.

AGEISM. Stereotyping of or prejudice against people because of their age.

AGENT ORANGE. A toxic herbicide sprayed by the U.S. military during the Vietnam War to defoliate jungle areas and expose enemy forces.

AGE-RELATED MACULAR DEGENERATION (ARMD). A chronic, painless eye disease occurring in people over age 50 that damages the macula, or central part of the retina causing irreversible loss of central vision.

AGGLUTINATION. Antibody-induced clumping of cells.

AGING IN PLACE. Not having to move from one's present home to secure needed support services as one grows older and one's needs change; also called aging at home.

AGING SCHEDULE. A list of overdue medical accounts calculated from date of original bill to current date.

AGITATION. An emotional condition in which the patient is highly excitable and often physically restless.

AGONIST. A drug which can bind to a receptor protein and produce the same effects as the natural substance that ordinarily binds to that receptor.

AGORAPHOBIA. An irrational fear of venturing outside the home or into open spaces, so pervasive that a large number of activities outside the home are limited or avoided altogether. Agoraphobia is often associated with panic attacks.

AGRANULOCYTOSIS. An acute condition marked by high fever and a sharp drop in the number of some types of white blood cells.

AIDS. Acquired immunodeficiency syndrome, caused by HIV infection.

AIS. Endocervical adenocarcinoma-in-situ; a Pap test result indicating precancerous cells in the glandular or mucus-producing tissue of the cervix.

AKINESIA. A loss of the ability to move; freezing in place.

AKINETIC SEIZURE. Seizure characterized by limp posture and a brief period of unconsciousness; also called a drop attack.

ALBUMIN. Water-soluble proteins that can be coagulated by heat and are found in egg white, blood serum, milk.

ALKALOID. A type of chemical commonly found in plants and often having medicinal properties.

ALLERGEN. Any substance that causes an allergic response. Allergens contain protein, and almost anything can be an allergen. Allergens stimulate the immune system to produce antibodies.

ALLERGENIC. Acting as an allergen, inducing allergy.

ALLERGIC CONJUNCTIVITIS. Inflammation of the conjunctiva, the membrane covering the white part of the eye, due to allergy.

ALLERGIC DERMATITIS. Itching, reddening, and flaking or peeling of the skin resulting from allergen exposure to the skin.

ALLERGIC REACTION. An inappropriate or exaggerated genetically determined reaction to a chemical that occurs only on the second or subsequent exposures to the offending agent, after the first contact has sensitized the body.

ALLERGIC RHINITIS. An allergy affecting the mucus membrane of the nose. Seasonal allergic rhinitis is called hay fever.

ALLERGY. Immune response of the body to a substance which is not necessarily harmful in itself, but results in a reaction that causes symptoms and disease in a predisposed person.

ALLOGRAFT. A graft of bone or other tissue taken from a donor.

ALLOPATHY. The treatment of disease using conventional evidence-based medical or surgical therapies. In recent years allopathy has become a synonym for mainstream Western medicine. Physicians who are doctors of medicine (M.D.s) are sometimes called allopaths.

ALLOPURINOL. A drug that corrects hyperuricemia by inhibiting urate production.

ALPHA HYDROXY ACIDS (AHAS). Acids present in fruit and milk.

ALPHA-FETOPROTEIN. A protein in blood serum that is found in abnormally high concentrations in most patients with primary liver cancer.

ALS. Amyotrophic Lateral Sclerosis (Lou Gehrig's Disease).

ALTERNATIVE OR COMPLEMENTARY MEDICINE. Those healthcare practices that are not considered part of traditional medicine, sometimes used separately and sometimes used in coordination with traditional medicine.

ALVEOLI. Tiny air sacs within the lungs where the exchange of oxygen and carbon dioxide takes place.

ALYKYLATING DRUG. A drug that kills cells by directly damaging DNA.

ALZHEIMER'S DISEASE. Degenerative brain disease resulting in progressive mental deterioration with disorientation, memory disturbance and confusion.

AMBLYOPIA. Decreased visual acuity, usually in one eye, in the absence of any structural abnormality in the eye.

AMBULATE. To move from place to place (walk).

AMBULATORY. Applied to patients who are able to walk or move about. Applied to a clinic or medical center, it is a synonym for "outpatient" or "walk-in."

AMBULATORY MONITORING. EKG recording over a prolonged period during which the patient can move around.

AMINO ACID. Organic (carbon-containing) molecules that serve as the building blocks of proteins.

AMNESIA. Loss of memory often traceable to brain tissue damage.

AMNESIC. Relating to amnesia, the loss of memory.

AMPUTATION. Surgical removal of a limb that is damaged beyond repair due to nerve problems or loss of blood supply.

AMYGDALA. An almond-shaped brain structure made of neurons in the limbic system. It is located in the medial temporal lobe of the brain and is activated to process memories and emotions.

AMYLOID. A waxy, starch-like protein.

AMYLOID PLAQUE. A waxy, translucent substance composed of complex protein fibers and polysaccharides that forms in body tissues in some degenerative diseases, such as Alzheimer's disease.

ANABOLIC STEROIDS. A group of mostly synthetic hormones sometimes taken by athletes to temporarily increase muscle size.

ANAEROBIC. Not requiring oxygen. Anaerobic bacteria are commonly found in the mouth, intestines and vaginal area.

ANALGESIA. A state of insensitivity to pain even though the person remains fully conscious.

ANALGESIC. A medication that can relieve pain by altering perception of pain without producing anesthesia or loss of consciousness.

ANAPHYLACTIC SHOCK. A systemic reaction that is often severe and occasionally fatal due to a second exposure to a specific antigen (i.e., wasp venom or penicillin) after previous sensitization that results in symptoms of allergic reaction.

ANASTOMOSIS. In heart surgery, connection of the bypassing blood vessel to the blocked blood vessel by surgical suture; or, in surgery for colon cancer, surgical reconnection of the ends of the bowel after removal of part of the bowel.

ANATOMIC. Related to the physical structure of an organ or organism.

ANDROGENETIC ALOPECIA. Hair loss that develops into baldness and affects both men and women.

ANEMIA. The condition of having less than the normal number of red blood cells or less than the normal quantity of hemoglobin in the blood. The oxygen-carrying capacity of the blood is, therefore, decreased. The iron levels in the blood are low.

ANEMIA OF CHRONIC DISEASE (ACD). Blood disorder that results from a medical condition that affects the production and lifespan of red blood cells.

ANESTHESIA. A combination of drugs administered by a variety of techniques by trained professionals that provide sedation, amnesia, analgesia, and immobility adequate for the accomplishment of the surgical procedure with minimal discomfort to the patient.

ANESTHESIOLOGIST. A medical specialist who administers an anesthetic to a patient before he is treated.

ANESTHESIOLOGY. The branch of medicine specializing in the use of drugs or other agents that cause insensibility to pain.

ANESTHETIC. A drug that causes loss of sensation. It is used to lessen the pain of surgery and medical procedures.

ANEURYSM. Dilation or ballooning of an artery, stretching artery walls until they become thin and weakened.

ANGINA. Angina pectoris, or chest pain, caused by an insufficient supply of oxygen and decreased blood flow to the heart muscle. Angina is frequently the first sign of coronary artery disease.

ANGIODYSPLASIA. An abnormally formed collection of blood vessels anywhere in the walls of the gastrointestinal tract, but most common in the colon. It often bleeds.

ANGIOGENESIS. The process of forming new blood vessels that supply a tumor with nutrients and help to carry tumor emboli into the larger vessels of the circulatory system.

ANGIOGRAM. An x-ray (radiographic) study of the blood vessels. An angiogram uses a radiopaque substance, or contrast medium, to make the blood vessels visible under x ray.

ANGIOGRAPHY. Injecting dye into blood vessels so they can be seen on an x ray.

ANGIOMA. Tumor-like growth of blood vessels or related structures.

ANGIOPLASTY. A surgical operation to clear a narrowed or blocked artery.

ANGULATION OF THE PENIS. Abnormal bend or angle to the structure of the penis.

ANKLE STRATEGY. An automatic posture response in which the body moves as a unit over the feet to control postural sway.

ANKYLOSING SPONDYLITIS. A form of inflammatory arthritis in which the bones in the spine and pelvis gradually fuse when inflamed connective tissue is replaced by bone. It occurs most commonly in males between 16 and 35.

ANOMIA. Difficulty in naming objects.

ANOREXIA NERVOSA. An eating disorder primarily found in adolescents and young adults, characterized by intense fear of gaining weight, extreme reduction of food intake, and malnutrition.

ANOXIA. Reduced or almost entire absence of oxygen in the blood, cells and tissues of the body resulting in tissue death. Also called anoxemia.

ANTERIOR. Toward the front of the body.

ANTHRAX. An infectious disease caused by a type of bacterium. The disease can be passed from animals to people and usually is fatal. Symptoms include sores on the skin.

ANTI–INFLAMMATORY. A drug used to reduce inflammation, the body's response to surgery, injury, irritation, or infection.

ANTI–NAUSEA. A drug that is effective against vomiting and nausea.

ANTI–REJECTION DRUG. Drug given to transplant patients that suppresses the production of white blood cells and the immune response.

ANTIANDROGEN. A substance that blocks the action of androgens, the hormones responsible for male characteristics. Used to treat prostate cancers that require male hormones for growth.

ANTIARRYTHMIC. Drug that prevents or alleviates irregularities in the force or rhythm of the heart.

ANTIBIOTIC. A chemical substance produced by a microorganism that kills or stops the growth of other microorganisms. The term includes antibiotics chemically modified from their original form, such as the semisynthetic penicillins.

ANTIBODY. Y-shaped protein molecule produced by B cells as part of the primary immune defense; each molecule and its clones have a unique binding site that combines with a complementary site of an antigen, to disable the antigen and signal other immune defenses.

ANTICHOLINERGIC. A drug that blocks the action of acetylcholine, causing many effects including but not limited to reductions in secretions such as tears and saliva, as well as reduction in the movement of the intestines, causing constipation.

ANTICOAGULANTS. Also called blood thinners, these medications decrease the blood's ability to clot. Decreased clotting keeps fewer harmful blood clots from forming and from blocking blood vessels.

ANTICONVULSANT. Medication used to control seizures.

ANTIDEPRESSANTS. Medications prescribed to relieve major depression. Classes of antidepressants include selective serotonin reuptake inhibitors (fluoxetine/Prozac), tricyclics (amitriptyline/Elavil), MAOIs (phenelzine/Nardil), and heterocyclics (bupropion/Zyban).

ANTIDIURETIC HORMONE (ADH). A hormone that encourages the kidney to retain water when body stores are low.

ANTIEMETIC. A medicine that helps control nausea; also called an anti-nausea drug.

ANTIFUNGAL. A drug that treats infections caused by fungi.

ANTIGEN. Any foreign substance, usually a protein, that stimulates the body's immune system to produce antibodies.

ANTIHISTAMINE. A drug used to treat allergic conditions that counteracts histamines—a substance in the body that causes itching, vascular changes, and mucus secretion when released by cells.

ANTIHYPERTENSIVE. Medication used to treat high blood pressure.

ANTIMETABOLITE. A drug that interferes with a cell's growth or ability to multiply.

ANTIMICROBIAL. Having the ability to help the immune system resist or destroy a wide spectrum of disease-causing organisms.

ANTINUCLEAR ANTIBODY (ANA) TEST. A test that measures the amount and pattern of antibodies in the blood that work against a person's own body.

ANTIOXIDANT. A molecule that prevents oxidation. In the body antioxidants attach to other molecules called free radicals and prevent the free radicals from causing damage to cell walls, DNA, and other parts of the cell.

ANTIOXIDANT ENZYME. An enzyme that can counteract the damaging effects of oxygen in tissues.

ANTIPLATELET DRUG. Medication that reduces platelet clumping to form clots inside blood vessels with atherosclerosis.

ANTIPSYCHOTICS. A class of drugs used to control psychotic symptoms in patients with psychotic disorders such as schizophrenia and delusional disorder. Antipsychotics include risperidone (Risperdal), haloperidol (Haldol), and chlorpromazine (Thorazine).

ANUS. The opening at the lower end of the rectum.

AORTA. The main artery that carries blood from the heart to the rest of the body. The aorta is the largest artery in the body.

APHASIA. The loss or impairment of the ability to use and understand words.

APHRODISIAC. Any substance that excites sexual desire.

APLASTIC ANEMIA. Rare and serious blood disorder in which bone marrow stops making enough new blood cells.

APOPTOSIS. The programmed self-destruction of a cell, which takes place when the cell detects some damage to its DNA. Apoptosis is sometimes called "cell suicide."

AQUEOUS HUMOR. The clear, watery fluid in the front of the eyeball.

AROMATASE INHIBITOR. Letrozole, a medication for preventing or treating breast cancer in postmenopausal women by inhibiting the body's production of estrogen.

AROMATHERAPY. A form of alternative medicine that uses essential oils derived from plants or other aromatic compounds to affect mood or improve health.

ARRHYTHMIA. Irregular heartbeat caused by erratic electrical signals or nerve impulses to the cardiac muscles.

ARTERIAL EMBOLISM. A blood clot arising from another location that blocks an artery.

ARTERIES. Blood vessels that carry blood away from the heart to the cells, tissues, and organs of the body.

ARTERIOGRAM. A diagnostic test that involves viewing the arteries and/or attached organs by injecting a contrast medium, or dye, into the artery and taking an x ray.

ARTERIOSCLEROSIS. A chronic condition characterized by thickening and hardening of the arteries and the build-up of plaque on the arterial walls. Arteriosclerosis can slow or impair blood circulation.

ARTERY. A vessel that carries oxygen-rich blood to the body.

ARTHEROSCLEROSIS. The cause of coronary artery disease, in which the walls of the coronary arteries thicken due to the accumulation of plaque in the blood vessels.

ARTHRITIS. A group of diseases that cause joint pain, swelling, and inflammation. The two most common forms are osteoarthritis and rheumatoid arthritis.

ARTHRODESIS. A surgical procedure sometimes used to treat younger patients with hip problems, in which the head of the femur is fused directly to the acetabulum.

ARTHROPLASTY. The medical term for surgical replacement of a joint. Arthroplasty can refer to knee as well as hip replacement.

ARTHROSCOPE. An instrument that contains a miniature camera and light source mounted on a flexible tube. It allows a surgeon to see the inside of a joint or bone during surgery.

ARTHROSCOPIC SURGERY. Surgery of the inside of a joint of the body using an endoscope, a medical instrument consisting of a long, very thin tube inserted into the body.

ARTIFACT. Extra electrical activity typically caused by interference.

ARTIFICIAL NUTRITION. A general term that includes tube feeding and intravenous feeding.

ASANA. A position or stance in yoga.

ASC-H. Atypical squamous cells; a Pap-test finding of atypical cells of unknown significance with the possibility of a precancerous high-grade squamous intraepithelial lesion.

ASC-US. Atypical squamous cells of undetermined significance; a Pap-test result.

ASEPTIC. Without contamination with bacteria or other microorganisms.

ASPIRATE. To breathe foreign material into the lungs, as when stomach contents back up into the mouth and are breathed into the windpipe.

ASPIRATION. The process of removing a gas, fluid, or tissue from the body by suction or drainage methods; also, the passage of food from the throat into the airway during swallowing rather than further down the esophagus.

ASSISTED LIVING FACILITY (ALF). A form of housing for seniors that offers central dining, supervision, and some help with ADLs but does not provide round-the-clock nursing care or medical services.

ASSISTED SUICIDE. A form of self-inflicted death in which a person voluntarily brings about his or her own death with the help of another, usually a physician, relative, or friend. Assisted suicide is sometimes called physician-assisted death (PAD).

ASTHMA. A disease in which the air passages of the lungs become inflamed and narrowed.

ASTIGMATISM. Assymetric vision defects due to irregularities in the cornea.

ATAXIA. Disorder that damages the parts of the nervous system that control movement.

ATHEROMA. Deposits of fat accumulating inside arteries.

ATHEROSCLEROSIS. A chronic condition characterized by thickening and hardening of the arteries and the build-up of plaque on the arterial walls. Atherosclerosis can slow or impair blood circulation.

ATHLETE'S FOOT. A fungal infection between the toes, officially known as tinea pedis.

ATOPIC DERMATITIS. An intensely itchy inflammation often found on the face of people prone to allergies.

ATOPY. Genetic predisposition toward the development of hypersensitivity reactions, such as hay fever, asthma, or hives, upon exposure to specific antigens.

ATRIAL. Having to do with the upper chambers of the heart.

ATRIAL FIBRILLATION. An abnormal rhythm of the heart characterized by rapid, nonproductive contractions of the atria.

ATRIAL FLUTTER. A rapid pulsation of the upper chamber of the heart that interferes with normal function.

ATRIUM. One of the two upper chambers of the heart.

ATROPHY. A wasting or decrease in size of a body organ, tissue, or part owing to disease, injury, or lack of use.

ATYPICAL HYPERPLASIA. An increase in abnormal but noncancerous breast cells.

AUDIOGRAM. A chart or graph of the results of a hearing test conducted with audiographic equipment. The chart reflects the softest (lowest volume) sounds that can be heard at various frequencies or pitches.

AUDIOLOGIST. A person with a degree and/or certification in the areas of identification and measurement of hearing impairments and rehabilitation of those with hearing problems.

AUDIOMETER. An electrical device designed to measure hearing across a range of frequencies.

AUDITORY TUBE (EUSTACHIAN TUBE). A tube joining the tympanic cavity behind the ear to the nasopharynx.

AURA. A distinctive smell, taste, or other unusual sensation that preceeds the onset of a seizure.

AURICULAR. Pertaining to the ear. Auricular acupuncture is based on the theory that the acupoints on the ear correspond to acupoints on other parts of the body and to certain internal disorders.

AUSCULTATION. The act of listening to sounds arising within organs as an aid to diagnosis and treatment.

AUTISM. A spectrum of developmental disorders characterized by impaired social and communication skills and certain behavioral patterns.

AUTOANTIBODY. An antibody produced in the body that attack its own cells, tissues, and/or organs.

AUTOCLAVING. Sterilization by steam under pressure for prescribed time periods.

AUTOGENIC TRAINING (AT). A technique of relaxation developed in Germany in the 1930s, in which the person sits or lies in a comfortable position and silently repeats phrases intended to focus attention on specific organs of the body.

AUTOGRAFT. A graft of bone or other tissue taken from the body of the patient undergoing surgery.

AUTOHEMOTHERAPY. A form of ozone therapy in which a small quantity of the patient's blood is withdrawn, treated with a mixture of ozone and oxygen, and reinfused into the patient.

AUTOIMMUNE DISEASE. A disease in which the immune system makes antibodies that mistakenly attack the body's healthy organs and tissues.

AUTOIMMUNE RESPONSE. A condition in which a person's immune system fails to recognize its own cells as being "self" and attacks its own body.

AUTOIMMUNITY. Condition in which the immune system reacts against the body's own tissue.

AUTOINTOXICATION. Self-poisoning by toxic products formed within the body during intestinal digestion. This term was coined around 1885 as part of a theory that regarded intestinal function as a central aspect of health.

AUTOLOGOUS. From the same person; an autologous breast reconstruction uses the woman's own tissues, while an autologous blood transfusion is blood removed then transfused back to the same person at a later time.

AUTOMATED EXTERNAL DEFIBRILLATOR (AED). A device that analyzes a person's heartbeat and can automatically deliver an electric shock if needed.

AUTOMATED SPHYGMOMANOMETRY. The automatic taking of blood pressure readings at regular intervals.

AUTONOMIC NERVOUS SYSTEM. The part of the nervous system that controls so-called involuntary functions, such as heart rate, salivary gland secretion, respiratory function, and pupil dilation.

AUTOSOMAL. Relating to any chromosome besides the X and Y sex chromosomes. Human cells contain 22 pairs of autosomes and one pair of sex chromosomes.

AVASCULAR NECROSIS. A disorder in which bone tissue dies and collapses following the temporary or permanent loss of its blood supply; it is also known as osteonecrosis.

AVULSE. To pull or tear away forcibly. In some cases, a surgeon must remove a nail by avulsing it from its matrix.

AXILLARY LYMPH NODES. The glands of the lymphatic system located under the arms.

AXON. A long, threadlike projection that is part of a neuron (nerve cell).

AYURVEDA. The traditional system of medicine practiced in India. Ayurveda is the oldest system of natural medicine in the world.

AZT. A drug that inhibits the human immunodeficiency virus (HIV).

B

B CELL (B LYMPHOCYTE). Type of white blood cell that produces antibodies.

BABESIOSIS. A disease caused by protozoa of the genus *Babesia* characterized by a malaria-like fever, anemia, vomiting, muscle pain, and enlargement of the spleen. Babesiosis, like Lyme disease, is carried by a tick.

BABY BOOMERS. Also called boomers, anyone born between 1946 and 1965.

BACILLUS CALMETTE-GUÉRIN (BCG). A vaccine made from a damaged bacillus akin to the tubercle bacillus, which may help prevent serious pulmonary TB and its complications.

BACTEREMIA. Presence of bacteria in the blood. The blood is normally a sterile environment, so the detection of bacteria in the blood is always abnormal. Bacteria can enter the bloodstream as a complication of infections or during surgery.

BACTERIA. The plural of bacterium; unicellular organisms that have a cell wall and multiply by cell fission. Some bacteria cause disease, while others are beneficial to human health. Still other have importance in commercial applications.

BACTERIAL CULTURE. Planting samples of body fluids (e.g., blood, urine or sputum) in a special broth to determine if bacteria are present. Bacteria will then be stained and identified to help select proper antibiotic treatment.

BACTERIAL INFECTION. Infection caused by a bacterium.

BACTERIAL MENINGITIS. A serious bacterial disease in which the membranes lining the brain and spinal cord (the meninges) become infected.

BACTERIUM. A single–celled microorganism that can cause disease. Pl.: bacteria.

BACTERIURIA. The presence of bacteria in the urine.

BAG-VALVE-MASK DEVICE. Device consisting of a manually compressible bag containing oxygen and a one-way valve and mask that fits over the mouth and nose of the patient.

BALLOON ANGIOPLASTY. A procedure used to open an obstructed blood vessel. A small, balloon-tipped catheter is inserted into the vessel and the balloon is inflated to widen the vessel and push the obstructing material against the vessel's walls.

BARBITURATE. A drug with hypnotic and sedative effects.

BARIUM ENEMA. An x-ray test of the bowel after giving the patient an enema of a white chalky substance that outlines the colon and the rectum.

BARIUM SULFATE. A barium compound used during a barium enema to block the passage of x rays during the exam,allowing visualization of the intestinal lining.

BARIUM X RAY (UPPER GI). An x-ray test of the upper part of the gastrointestinal (GI) tract (including the esophagus, stomach, and a small portion of the small intestine) after the patient is given a white, chalky barium sulfate solution to drink.

BASE OF SUPPORT. The location on a body or object where most of the weight is supported.

BASEMENT MEMBRANE. A specialized layer of extracellular matrix that separates epithelial tissue from underlying connective tissue. Cancer cells must break through the basement membrane in order to migrate to other parts of the body and form metastases.

BEHAVIORAL MEDICINE. The branch of medicine that studies mind/body relationships.

BENCE-JONES PROTEIN. Light chain of an immunoglobulin that is overproduced in multiple myeloma and is excreted in the urine.

BENIGN. Mild, nonmalignant. Recovery is favorable with treatment.

BENIGN CYSTS. Non-cancerous tumors.

BEREAVEMENT. The period after the death of a loved one during which grief and mourning take place.

BERG BALANCE SCALE. An assessment tool used to evaluate stability during functional activities. The patient is scored on 14 different tasks.

BETA BLOCKERS. Drugs that lower blood pressure and reduce stress to the heart by blocking the actions of beta receptors that control the speed and strength of heart muscle contractions and blood vessel dilation.

BETA HYDROXY ACIDS. Oil soluble acids, such as salicylic acid, used in cosmetics.

BETA 2-MICROGLOBULIN. Protein produced by B cells; high concentrations in the blood are indicative of multiple myeloma.

BICARBONATE. A salt of carbonic acid produced by neutralizing a hydrogen ion.

BICEPS. The muscle in the front of the upper arm.

BILIARY. Relating to bile.

BILIRUBIN. A reddish-yellow waste product produced by the liver that colors urine and is involved in the formation of some gallstones.

BINGE-EATING DISORDER. Eating disorder characterized by uncontrolled eating.

BINOCULAR VISION. Using both eyes at the same time to see an image.

BIOAVAILABILITY. The portion of a substance that reaches the general circulation and is transported to the target tissue.

BIOFEEDBACK. A relaxation technique that uses electronic devices to help a person learn to control body processes that are normally not consciously controlled, such as heart rate, muscle tension, or breathing.

BIOFEEDBACK THERAPY. Therapy in which people learn to reduce their body's unproductive responses to stress, and thus decrease their sensitivity to pain.

BIOLOGICAL MARKER. Measurable and quantifiable biological parameters that can be used to diagnose a disease accurately.

BIOMARKER. A molecule found in blood, urine, or other body fluids, that is a of a condition or disease. A biomarker also may be used to monitor the progress of treatment for a disease or condition.

BIOMECHANICS. The application of engineering principles to the study of living organisms, particularly in regard to muscular activity and movement.

BIOPSY. The surgical removal and microscopic examination of living tissue for diagnostic purposes.

BIPHOSPHONATES. A class of drugs that bind to the minerals in bone tissue and lessen the amount of bone loss.

BI-RADS. Breast Imaging Reporting and Database System; the American College of Radiology uniform system for reporting mammogram results.

BITE BLOCK. Plastic device inserted into the patient's mouth to prevent him or her from biting on the endotracheal tube.

BLACK LUNG. Black lung disease is the common name for coal workers' pneumoconiosis (CWP) or anthracosis, a lung disease of older workers in the coal industry, caused by inhalation, over many years, of small amounts of coal dust.

BLADDER. Elastic, muscular pouch in which urine collects before being discharged from the body through the urethra.

BLEPHARITIS. An inflammation of the eyelids that causes crusting, swelling, and burning or irritation.

BLOOD CLOT. A hard mass that forms when blood gels.

BLOOD DISEASES. Diseases that affect the production of blood and its components, including blood cells, hemoglobin, blood proteins, and coagulation.

BLOOD GAS ANALYSIS. A blood test that measures the level of oxygen, carbon dioxide, and pH in arterial blood. A blood gas analysis can help a physician assess how well the lungs are functioning.

BLOOD GLUCOSE. A sugar made by the body from food. It moves through the bloodstream to provide energy to the body's cells.

BLOOD POISONING. Infection that has escaped local defenses and spread into the circulation.

BLOOD PRESSURE. The force of blood against the walls of the blood vessels. A vital sign, blood pressure is usually measured in millimeters of mercury (mmHg). Systolic pressure is the peak pressure in the arteries, whereas diastolic pressure is the lowest pressure.

BLOOD THINNER. Medication that prevents the blood from clotting, they are also called anti-coagulants.

BLOOD-BRAIN BARRIER. A blockade of cells separating the circulating blood from elements of the central nervous system (CNS); it acts as a filter, preventing many substances from entering the central nervous system.

BODY MASS INDEX (BMI). A mathematical formula to assess relative body weight. The measure correlates highly with body fat. Calculated as weight in kilograms divided by the square of the height in meters (kg/m^2).

BODYWORK. A general term for body-based therapies that involve touching or manipulation of body tissues. Acupressure is classified as a form of bodywork.

BOLUS. A soft mass of chewed food formed in the mouth during the first stage of swallowing.

BONE LYSIS. The breakdown of old bone matter.

BONE MARROW. Soft tissue that fills the hollow centers of bones. Blood cells and platelets (disk-shaped bodies in the blood that are important in clotting) are produced in the bone marrow.

BONE MINERAL DENSITY (BMD). The number of grams of bone per centimeter of bone. In a DEXA test, BMD numbers equal to or higher than +1 show normal bone mineral density.

BONE RESORPTION. The process by which old bone tissue is broken down and removed by special cells called osteoclasts.

BONE SCAN. A diagnostic test in which radioactive material is injected into the body in a way that shows which areas of bone are active. This test can detect fractures, tumors, bone infections, and arthritis. The test uses imaging such as x ray, MRI or CT.

BONE SPUR. Also called an osteophyte, it is an outgrowth or ridge that forms on a bone.

BOTANICAL. Any supplement that is derived from a plant. This term is often used interchangeably with herb.

BOTULINUM TOXIN. Any of a group of potent bacterial toxins or poisons produced by different strains of the bacterium *Clostridium botulinum.*

BOUCHARD'S NODES. Swelling of the middle joint of the finger.

BOVINE COLLAGEN. Collagen derived from cattle, often made from bone, tendon, or hide.

BOWMAN'S LAYER. Transparent cornea layer directly below the epithelium consisting of strong layered protein fibers called collagen.

BRACHIAL. Of the arm or relating to the arm.

BRADYCARDIA. A slow heart rate. Bradycardia is one of the two types of arrhythmia.

BRADYKINESIA. Extremely slow movement.

BRAIN DEATH. The point at which the flow of oxygen and blood to the brain has stopped and the person's brain no longer functions. The heart and lungs may continue to function for some time after brain death.

BRAIN SCAN. A general term that can include CT scans, MRIs, seldom-used radionuclide scanning (use of radioactive isotopes), or ultrasounds.

BRCA1, BRCA2. Breast-cancer susceptibility genes; specific mutations in these genes greatly increase the risk of breast and ovarian cancers.

BREAST AUGMENTATION. A surgery to increase the size of the breasts.

BROCA'S AREA. An area in the frontal lobe of the left hemisphere of the brain that governs language processing, speech production, and comprehension. It is named for Paul Broca (1824–1880), a French physician.

BRONCHIAL. Any function or condition relating to the bronchi.

BRONCHIAL TUBES. The tubular passages that form part of a network of airways to and within the lungs.

BRONCHIOLE. A small airway within the lungs that is a continuation of the bronchi and connects to the alveoli.

BRONCHITIS. Inflammation of the airway tubes.

BRONCHOALVEOLAR LAVAGE. Washing cells from the air sacs at the end of the bronchioles.

BRONCHODILATORS. Drugs that relax the main air passages in the bronchial tubes that carry air in and out of the lungs. They are often used for people with asthma and are referred to as "inhalers."

BRONCHOSCOPE. A thin, lighted tube used to examine the inside of the trachea and bronchi, the air passages that lead to the lungs.

BRONCHOSCOPY. The examination of the bronchi (the main airways of the lungs) using a flexible tube (bronchoscope). Bronchoscopy helps to evaluate and diagnose lung problems, assess blockages, obtain samples of tissue and/or fluid, and/or help remove a foreign body.

BRONCHUS. One of the large air tubes leading from the trachea to the lungs that convey air to and from the lungs. Pl: bronchi.

BRUXISM. Habitual, often unconscious, grinding of the teeth.

BSW. Baccalaureate degree in social work.

BUDDY POPPY. A trademarked artificial red poppy that is distributed by the VFW around Memorial Day.

BUERGER'S DISEASE. An episodic disease that causes inflammation and blockage of the veins and arteries of the limbs. It tends to be present almost exclusively on men under age 40 who smoke, and may require amputation of the hand or foot.

BURNOUT. An emotional condition, marked by tiredness, loss of interest, or frustration, that interferes with job performance. Burnout is usually regarded as the result of prolonged stress.

BURSA. A fluid-filled sac located near a joint (plural is bursae).

BURSITIS. Inflammation of the tissue around a joint.

C

CAD. Computer-aided detection; software that searches digitized mammogram images for abnormalities.

CALCIFIED. Hardened by calcium deposits.

CALCITONIN. A hormone produced by the parafollicular cells (C cells) of the thyroid. The main function of the hormone is to regulate calcium levels in body serum.

CALCIUM CHANNEL BLOCKERS. Class of blood pressure medications that relax and widen the blood vessels.

CALCULUS. An adherent, calcified deposit of bacteria, fungi, desquamated epithelial cells and food debris, formed on the surface of teeth. Also known as tartar.

CALISTHENICS. A type of exercise consisting of simple movements intended to improve body strength and flexibility by using the body's own weight as resistance. The English word comes from two Greek words meaning "beautiful" and "strength."

CALORIE. One unit of heat energy; also unit of measure used to determine the amount of energy produced by food when oxidized in the human body—every measured portion of food is assigned a certain calorie level.

CANCER SURGERY. Surgery in which the goal is to excise a tumor and its surrounding tissue found to be malignant.

CANDIDIASIS. An infection of the mouth caused by a fungus, *Candida albicans*; also known as thrush.

CANKER SORE. A painful sore inside the mouth.

CANNABINOIDS. The chemical compounds that are the active principles in marijuana.

CANNULA. A tube inserted into a cavity to serve as a channel for the transport of fluid.

CANTEEN. An informal social club, cafeteria, or snack bar, often for a particular group of people, such as soldiers, teenagers, or college students.

CANTHUS. Either of the angles formed by the meeting of an eye's upper and lower eyelids.

CAPACITY. Ability to understand the nature and consequences of one's acts; also, the legal qualification, power, or fitness to take an action.

CAPILLARY. Any of the small blood vessels that connect the arteries with the veins.

CAPILLARY BED. A dense network of tiny blood vessels that enables blood to fill a tissue or organ.

CAPSULAR CONTRACTURE. Thick scar tissue around a breast implant, which may tighten and cause discomfort and/or firmness.

CARBOHYDRATES. Organic substances, usually from plant sources. They are made up of carbon, hydrogen, and oxygen and are the diet's major source of energy. Carbohydrates include sugars, starches, celluloses, and gums; they are broken down into sugar during digestion.

CARBON MONOXIDE. A colorless, odorless, tasteless gas that can be fatal if inhaled for a long period of time. It is emitted by burning fuel from sources such as unvented kerosene heaters and gas space heaters, leaking furnaces and fireplace chimneys, improperly vented gas.

CARBON MONOXIDE DETECTOR. A device that measures the amount of carbon monoxide in the air and sounds an alarm if the level remains high for too long a period of time.

CARBUNCLE. A large, deep skin abscess formed by a group or cluster of boils.

CARCINOGENS. Chemical substances that cause cell mutations and, ultimately, cancer.

CARCINOMA-IN-SITU (CIS). Cancer cells confined to the surface of the cervix.

CARDIAC. Of or relating to the heart.

CARDIAC ARREST. The medical term for the failure of the heart to contract normally and blood circulation to stop abruptly as a result.

CARDIAC ARRHYTHMIA. An irregular heart rate (frequency of heartbeats) or rhythm (the pattern of heartbeats).

CARDIAC CATHETERIZATION. A diagnostic procedure (using a catheter inserted through a vein and threaded through the circulatory system to the heart) which does a comprehensive examination of how the heart and its blood vessels function.

CARDIAC DEATH. The point at which a person's heart stops beating and breathing stops.

CARDIAC REHABILITATION. A structured program of education and activity offered by hospitals and other organizations.

CARDIAC TAMPONADE. A condition in which blood leaking into the membrane surrounding the heart puts pressure on the heart muscle, preventing complete filling of the heart's chambers and normal heartbeat.

CARDIOLOGIST. A physician who specializes in cardiovascular (heart) conditions.

CARDIOMYOPATHY. A disease of the heart muscle. Usually refers to a disease of obscure etiology. Pl.: cardiomyopathies.

CARDIOPLEGIC ARREST. Halting the electrical activity of the heart by delivery of a high potassium solution to the coronary arteries. The arrested heart provides a superior surgical field for operation.

CARDIOPULMONARY. Relating to the heart and the lungs.

CARDIOPULMONARY BYPASS. Use of the heart-lung machine to provide systemic circulation cardiac output and ventilation of the blood.

CARDIOPULMONARY RESUSCITATION (CPR). A set of medical procedures used in an emergency to restart the heart and lungs. Includes breathing, chest compression, drugs and electric shock.

CARDIOVASCULAR. Descriptive term referring to anything related to the heart, blood vessels (veins, arteries), and blood circulation.

CARDIOVASCULAR DISEASE. Diseases of the heart and blood vessels.

CARDIOVERSION. A electrical shock delivered to the heart to restore a normal rhythm.

CARDIOVERTER. A device to apply electric shock to the chest to convert an abnormal heartbeat into a normal heartbeat.

CARIES. Tooth decay.

CARMINATIVE. An agent that will remove gases from the gastrointestinal tract.

CAROTENOIDS. Red to yellow pigments responsible for the characteristic colour of many plant organs or fruits, such as tomatoes, carrots, etc.

CAROTID ARTERY. A blood vessel that supplies the brain with oxygenated blood, located in the neck.

CAROTID DISEASE. Carotid disease occurs when the major arteries of the neck that supply blood to the brain become narrowed or blocked.

CAROTID ENDARTERECTOMY. Procedure to open the carotid artery in the neck and scrape plaque from the artery's walls, thereby reducing the risk of stroke.

CARTILAGE. A tough, elastic material that covers the ends of the bones where they meet to form a joint, such as the knee.

CASUISTRY. A case-based approach to medical ethics.

CATARACT. Opacity or cloudiness of the eye lens, which may prevent a clear image from forming on the retina.

CATASTROPHIC REACTION. An emotional outburst or overreaction to a situation or event. Catastrophic reactions are common in patients with Alzheimer's disease or other dementias.

CATATONIA. Psychomotor disturbance characterized by muscular rigidity, excitement or stupor.

CATECHOLAMINES. Family of neurotransmitters containing dopamine, norepinephrine and epinephrine, produced and secreted by cells of the adrenal medulla in the brain. Catecholamines have excitatory effects on smooth muscle cells of the vessels that supply blood to the skin.

CATEGORICAL IMPERATIVE. The principle that one should act in such a way that one's deeds could become universal rules of conduct.

CATEGORICALLY NEEDY. A term that describes certain groups of Medicaid recipients who qualify for the basic mandatory package of Medicaid benefits. States that participate in Medicaid are required to cover certain categorically needy groups.

CATHARTIC COLON. A poorly functioning colon, resulting from the chronic abuse of stimulant cathartics.

CATHETER. A tubular medical device inserted into canals, vessels, passageways, or body cavities to permit injection or withdrawal of fluids, or to keep a passage open.

CATHETERIZATION. Placement of a flow-directed catheter for measuring pulmonary arterial pressures.

CAUDA EQUINA. The roots of the spinal nerves controlling movement and sensation in the legs. These nerve roots are located in the lower spine and resemble a horse's tail (*cauda equina* in Latin).

CAUTERIZATION. Use of a device that applies heat, cold, electricity, or chemical treatment to seal wounds or to burn or cut body tissues.

CAVERNOSAL FIBROSIS. The formation of abnormal fibrous tissue in the erectile tissue of the penis.

CD4 COUNT. A measure of the strength of the immune system. HIV continually kills CD4 cells. Over time, the body can not replace these lost CD4 cells and their number declines. AS this happens, the body becomes more susceptible to infections. A normal CD4 count is 10.

CD4+ T CELL. A type of helper cell in the human immune system that is attacked and infected by HIV. CD4 is a protein on the surface of these T cells that is used by the HIV virus to gain entry into the cells.

CELIAC DISEASE. An inherited condition in which the body cannot properly absorb nutrients from food (malabsorption) due to an autoimmune response triggered by exposure to gluten proteins found in grains.

CELL DIFFERENTIATION. The shape and arrangement of cells; also, the process by which stem cells develop into specialized cells such as skin, heart, muscle, and blood cells.

CELLULITE. Cellulite is dimply skin caused by uneven fat deposits beneath the surface.

CELLULITIS. An infection of the deeper layers of the skin caused by streptococci or other bacteria entering through a break in the skin.

CENTENARIAN. A person who is 100 years old or older.

CENTER OF GRAVITY. The center of weight in a body or object.

CENTRAL NERVOUS SYSTEM (CNS). The brain, spinal cord, and nerves throughout the body.

CENTRIFUGATION. A technique for separating substances of different densities (such as blood cells and blood serum) by spinning samples at high speed in a laboratory machine known as a centrifuge.

CEREBELLUM. The part of the brain that serves to control and coordinate muscular activity and control balance.

CEREBRAL ARTERIES. The arteries carrying oxygen, carrying blood to the brain.

CEREBRAL CORTEX. The outer layer of the brain, consisting of nerve cells and the pathways that connect them, responsible for cognitive functions including reasoning, mood, and perception of stimuli.

CEREBRAL PALSY. A disability caused by brain damage before, during, or shortly after birth that is characterized by poor muscular coordination and speech difficulties.

CEREBROSPINAL FLUID (CSF). A clear fluid that fills the hollow cavity inside the brain and spinal cord. The cerebrospinal fluid has several functions, including providing a cushion for the brain against shock or impact, and removing waste products from the brain.

CERTIFIED REGISTERED NURSE ANESTHETIST. Advanced practice nurse who administers anesthesia as sole providers or as part of health care teams.

CERULOPLASMIN. A blue copper containing dehydrogenase protein found in serum that is apparently involved in copper detoxification and storage.

CERVICAL INTRAEPITHELIAL NEOPLASIA (CIN). Abnormal growth of cells on the surface of the cervix.

CERVIX. The lower narrow part of the uterus that opens to the vagina.

CHANCRES. Open sores.

CHARACTER DISORDER. An older term for what are now called personality disorders.

CHARGE AGENTS. Nurses who work to make changes within systems to improve the delivery of clinical care.

CHELATING AGENT. An organic compound in which atoms form more than one bond with metals in solution.

CHEMOTHERAPY. Treatment of an illness with chemical agents. The term is usually used to describe the treatment of cancer with drugs.

CHEST PERCUSSION. A method respiratory therapists use to loosen deep lung secretions by beating on a patient's chest in a rhythmic motion with a cupped hand or mechanical vbrator.

CHI (QI). The Chinese term for energy, life force, or vital force.

CHIROPRACTIC. A method of treatment based on the interactions of the spine and the nervous system. Chiropractors adjust or manipulate segments of the patient's spinal column in order to relieve pain.

CHITIN. A transparent horny substance found in the outer coverings of shellfish. Chitin is used to make commercial preparations of glucosamine.

CHOLANGIOGRAPHY. Radiographic examination of the bile ducts after injection with a special dye.

CHOLECYSTECTOMY. Surgical removal of the gallbladder.

CHOLECYSTITIS. Inflammation of the gallbladder, usually due to infection.

CHOLEDOCHOLITHIASIS. The presence of gallstones within the common bile duct.

CHOLELITHIASIS. The presence of gallstones within the gallbladder.

CHOLERA. An infection of the small intestine caused by a type of bacterium. The disease is spread by drinking water or eating seafood or other foods that have been contaminated with the feces of infected people.

CHOLESTASIS. A blockage in the flow of bile.

CHOLESTEROL. A waxy substance made by the liver and also acquired through diet. High levels in the blood may increase the risk of cardiovascular disease.

CHOLESTEROLOSIS. Cholesterol crystals or deposits in the lining of the gallbladder.

CHOLINOMIMETIC. A drug that causes reactions similar to those produced by acetylcholine.

CHOREOGRAPHER. A person who creates the overall plan for a dance, usually with multiple dancers. Some choreographers also consult as movement specialists for speakers and actors and help them create gestures and appropriate body language.

CHRONIC. A word used to describe a long-lasting condition. Chronic conditions often develop gradually and involve slow changes.

CHRONIC BRONCHITIS. A smoking-related respiratory illness in which the membranes that line the bronchi, or the lung's air passages, narrow over time. Symptoms include a morning cough that brings up phlegm, breathlessness, and wheezing.

CHRONIC DISEASE. An illness or medical condition that lasts over a long period of time and sometimes causes a long-term change in the body.

CHRONIC FATIGUE SYNDROME. A poorly understood disorder that produces marked fatigue, poor immune response, digestive disturbances, and a range of other symptoms.

CHRONIC OBSTRUCTIVE PULMONARY DISEASE (COPD). A term referring to two lung diseases, chronic bronchitis and emphysema, that are characterized by obstruction to airflow that interferes with normal breathing.

CHRONIC PAIN. Pain that lasts more than three months and threatens to disrupt daily life.

CILIARY MUSCLES. The small muscles that permit the lens to change its shape in order to focus on near or distant objects.

CIN. Cervical intraepithelial neoplasia; abnormal growth of cells on the surface of the cervix.

CIRCADIAN RHYTHM. A biological process that occurs naturally on a daily basis that signals the body when to sleep.

CIRCULATORY SYSTEM. The circular course followed by the blood when it leaves the heart through arteries and returns through veins.

CIRRHOSIS. A chronic degenerative disease of the liver, in which normal cells are replaced by fibrous tissue. Cirrhosis is a major risk factor for the later development of liver cancer.

CITALOPRAM HYDROBROMIDE. Celexa; a SSRI that is highly specific for serotonin reuptake.

CLAIM. Medical bill.

CLASS EFFECT. A property or therapeutic rersult seen with all members of a chemicaslly related group of drugs.

CLAVICLE. The collarbone.

CLIENT-CENTERED. An approach to counseling associated with Carl Rogers that emphasizes the client's ability to grow and change. The counselor may not assess or evaluate the client, rather, they feed a natural capacity for change through empathy.

CLINICAL MYCOLOGY. A branch of medical microbiology that deals with fungi that are pathogenic to humans.

CLONIC. Referring to clonus, a series of muscle contractions and partial relaxations that alternate in some nervous diseases in the form of convulsive spasms.

CLOSTRIDIUM. A genus of deadly bacteria that are responsible for tetanus and other serious diseases, including botulism and gangrene from war wounds. Clostridia thrives without oxygen.

CLOT. A soft, semi-solid mass that forms when blood gels or clots.

COAGULASE. An enzyme produced by *S. aureus* that causes blood to clot. Testing for this enzyme can be used to distinguish *S. aureus* from most other species of staphylococci.

COCCYX. The tail bone or last four vertebrae of the spine.

COCHLEA. A conical bony structure or the inner ear; perforated by numerous openings for passage of the cochlear division of the acoustic nerve.

COENZYME. Also called a cofactor, a small non-protein molecule that binds to an enzyme and catalyzes (stimulates) enzyme-mediated reactions.

COFACTOR. A compound that is essential for the activity of an enzyme.

COGNITIVE. Relating to the process of acquiring knowledge by the use of reasoning, intuition, or perception.

COGNITIVE BEHAVIORAL THERAPY (CBT). Psychotherapy for depression that attempts to replace negative thought patterns with positive ones.

COGNITIVE IMPAIRMENT. Changes in cognitive function affecting a person's ability to reason, understand, and learn, caused by trauma or disease.

COHABITATION. Living together as a couple without being married.

COLCHICINE. A drug used to treat painful flare-ups of gout.

COLD AGGLUTININS. An autoantibody found on the surface of red blood cells in certain diseases that can cause the cells to clump at temperatures below 37°C and cause red blood cell lysis.

COLD SORE. A small blister on the lips or face, caused by a virus. Also called a fever blister.

COLITIS. Inflammation of the colon (large bowel).

COLLAGEN. A long fiber-like protein found in skin, bones, blood vessels, and connective tissue such as tendons and ligaments.

COLON. The part of the large intestine that lies between the cecum and the rectum, and is divided by name into three parts, the ascending, transverse and descending colon. In a healthy person, the ascending colon rises upward intra-abdominally.

COLONIZATION. In biology, the process by which a species moves into and populates a new area. It is also used the describe the process by which bacteria and other microorganisms form colonies in or on the bodies of humans and other animals.

COLONOSCOPE. A thin, flexible, hollow, lighted tube that in inserted through the rectum into the colon to enable the doctor to view the entire lining of the colon.

COLONOSCOPY. A test that examines the entire colon by inserting a camera on the end of a flexible tube through the anus into the colon.

COLOSTOMY. Surgical creation of an artificial anus on the abdominal wall by cutting into the colon and bringing it up to the surface.

COLPOSCOPY. The use of a magnifying instrument to examine the vagina and cervix.

COMMENSALISM. In biology, a relationship in which a member of one species lives on or in a member of another and derives benefit from the relationship while the member of the other species is unharmed. Staphylococci are commensal organisms that can live on/in humans.

COMMON BILE DUCT. The passage through which bile travels from the cystic duct to the small intestine.

COMMUNE. A group of unrelated adults and children living together on a communal basis, often in a rural area.

COMMUNITY OF INTEREST. An academic or scholarly term for a group of people who share a common interest in an activity or purpose.

CO-MORBIDITY. A disease or condition that coexists with the disease or condition for which the patient is being primarily treated.

COMPETENCE. In law, having the cognitive ability to sufficient to carry out such legal tasks as making a will or completing an advance directive.

COMPLETE BLOOD COUNT (CBC). A lab test that determines the number of red and white blood cells per cubic millimeter of blood.

COMPLICATED GRIEF. A chronic state of intense mourning that lasts for months or years after the loss.

COMPRESSION FRACTURE. Breakage of spinal vertebrae through illness or injury, usually resulting in loss of height.

COMPRESSION STOCKINGS. Support hosiery used by men and women to prevent deep vein thrombosis, swelling, or leg pain.

COMPUTED TOMOGRAPHY (CT). A special radiographic imaging technique that uses a computer to acquire multiple x rays into a two-dimensional sectional image.

COMPUTED TOMOGRAPHY. A radiology test by which images of cross-sectional planes of the body are obtained.

COMPUTERIZED AXIAL TOMOGRAPHY (CAT) SCAN. A procedure in which x rays are passed through the knee at different angles, detected by a scanner, and analyzed by a computer. CAT scan images show soft tissues such as ligaments or muscles more clearly than conventional x rays.

COMPUTERIZED TOMOGRAPHIC ANGIOGRAPHY (CTA). Imaging method that combines the technology of a conventional CT scan with that of traditional angiography to create detailed images of the blood vessels in the body.

COMPUTERIZED TOMOGRAPHY (CT). The use of x rays and computers to create images that show cross-sections, or slices, of the body.

COMT INHIBITORS. Drugs that block catechol-O-methyltransferase, an enzyme that breaks down dopamine. COMT inhibitors include entacapone and tolcapone.

CONCENTRATION. Refers to the amount of solute present in a solution, compared to the total amount of solvent.

CONDUCTIVE HEARING LOSS. Occurs when sound cannot pass through the outer or middle ear to reach the inner ear.

CONGENITAL. Present at the time of birth.

CONGESTIVE HEART FAILURE. A condition in which the heart is weakened and cannot pump all the blood that is returned to it from the body. As a result, fluid builds up in tissues and in the lungs.

CONGREGATE HOUSING. A type of housing arrangement for seniors that offers independent living in separate apartments as well as opportunities to share activities of daily living with other residents. This housing does not usually involve assisted living or skilled nursing.

CONGREGATE SENIOR MEAL PROGRAMS. Hot-lunch programs for groups of seniors served in such community settings as churches, synagogues, senior centers, or general community centers.

CONIZATION. Excision of a cone-shaped tissue from the cervix.

CONJUNCTIVA. The mucous membrane that covers the white part of the eyes and lines the eyelids.

CONJUNCTIVITIS. Inflammation of the thin membrane covering the eye. It is caused by bacteria, virus, allergies, etc.

CONNECTIVE TISSUE. Cells such as fibroblasts, and material such as collagen and reticulin, that unite one part of the body with another.

CONSERVATOR/GUARDIAN. An individual or organization named by order of the court to exercise any or all powers and rights over the person or financial assets of an incapacitated individual.

CONSTIPATION. Either having fewer than three bowel movements a week or having difficulty passing stools that are often hard, small, and dry.

CONSTRICT. To squeeze tightly, compress, draw together.

CONTACT DERMATITIS. Itchy, blistering skin rash typically caused by an allergic reaction to direct contact of a substance with the skin.

CONTAGIOUS. Disease transmissible by direct or indirect contact from one person to another.

CONTAMINATE. To make an item unsterile or unclean by direct contact.

CONTINUOUS POSITIVE AIRWAY PRESSURE (CPAP). A ventilation device that blows a gentle stream of air into the nose during sleep to keep the airway open.

CONTRACTURE. Tissue change that is characterized by shortening of length, usually producing wrinkles or areas of thickening.

CONTRAST MEDIUM (OR AGENT). A substance usually injected, swallowed, or used as an enema, before an x-ray image is taken to increase the visual contrast between an internal area of the body under study from the surrounding tissue.

CONTRECOUP INJURY. Brain damage occurring on the side opposite to the point of impact.

CONVENTIONAL MEDICINE. Mainstream or Western pharmaceutical-based medicine practiced by medical doctors, doctors of osteopathy, and other licensed health care professionals.

CONVULSION. To shake or effect with spasms; to agitate or disturb violently.

COPD (CHRONIC OBSTRUCTIVE PULMONARY DISORDER). Lung diseases that involve narrowing of the small bronchi resulting in reduced expiration of air such as emphysema.

COR PULMONALE. Enlargement of the right ventricle of the heart due to resistance of the passage of blood through the lungs.

CORD BLOOD. Blood from a newborn baby collected from the umbilical cord and placenta after the cord has been clamped.

CORE NEEDLE BIOPSY (CNB). A procedure using a larger diameter needle to remove a core of tissue from the breast.

CORNEA. Transparent front part of the eye that covers the iris, pupil, and anterior chamber and provides most of an eye's optical power.

CORONARY ARTERIES. These are the first arteries to branch off the aorta (the large artery leaving the heart). They take oxygen-rich blood to the heart muscle. Blockage of these arteries can cause atherosclerosis and heart attack.

CORONARY ARTERY DISEASE. Also called atherosclerosis, it is a build-up of fatty matter and debris in the coronary artery wall that causes narrowing of the artery.

CORONARY OCCLUSION. Obstruction of an artery that supplies the heart. When the artery is completely blocked, a myocardial infarction (heart attack) results; an incomplete blockage may result in angina.

CORONARY STENT. An artificial support device used to keep a coronary vessel open.

CORPORA CAVERNOSA. Two chambers in the penis which run the length of the organ and are filled with spongy tissue. Blood flows in and fills the open spaces in the spongy tissue to create an erection.

CORTICO-CEREBELLAR. Pertaining to the cerebellum and the cerebral cortex of the brain.

CORTICOSPINAL TRACT. A tract of nerve cells that carries motor commands from the brain to the spinal cord.

CORTICOSTERIOD. A group of synthetic hormones that are used to prevent or reduce inflammation. Toxic effects may result from rapid withdrawal after prolonged use or from continued use of large doses.

CORTISOL. A steroid hormone released by the cortex (outer portion) of the adrenal gland when a person is anxious.

CORTISONE. A steroid compound used to treat autoimmune diseases and inflammatory conditions. It is sometimes injected into a joint to relieve the pain of arthritis.

COWPOX. A mild disease in cows that is caused by a poxvirus.

COX-2 INHIBITORS. A category of non-steroidal anti-inflammatory drugs (NSAIDs) that blocks a form of cyclooxygenase enzyme known as COX-2 that is believed to be at the root of inflammation and pain. The drugs Vioxx and Celebrex are COX-2 inhibitor.

COXSACKIE B VIRUS. A mild virus belonging to a group of viruses (coxsackievirus) that may produce a variety of illnesses, including myocarditis.

CPAP (CONTINUOUS POSITIVE AIRWAY PRESSURE). The most common treatment for a moderate to severe case of sleep apnea requires a senior to wear a CPAP nasal mask while sleeping.

CPR. Cardiopulmonary resuscitation.

CRABS. An informal or slang term for pubic lice.

C-REACTIVE PROTEIN (CRP). A marker of inflammation circulating in the blood has been proposed as a method to identify persons at risk of these diseases.

CREAM. A semi-solid dosage form for external application, relatively soft and non-greasy.

CREEPING ERUPTION. Itchy irregular, wandering red lines on the foot made by burrowing larvae of the hookworm family and some roundworms.

CREPITUS. A crackling sound.

CROHN'S DISEASE. A chronic inflammatory disease where the immune system starts attacking one's own body. The disease generally starts in the gastrointestinal tract.

CROWN. An artificial replacement tooth.

CRYOABLATION. A technique for removing cancerous tissue by killing it with extreme cold.

CRYOGLOBULIN. A plasma immunoglobulin that is insoluble when cold and dissolved at body temperature.

CRYONICS. The low-temperature preservation of humans and animals after death in liquid nitrogen in the expectation of reviving them at some point in the future for treatment.

CRYOPRECIPITATION. Cold-induced precipitation of a substance from solution.

CRYOSURGERY. Surgery that removes or destroys tissue by freezing.

CRYOTHERAPY. Usually an ice or cold treatment after physical therapy treatment.

CT. Computerized tomography, a test that uses a dye and a computer to image parts of the body.

CUE. A stimulus, either internal body sensations or an external event or object that causes a learned response in an individual. Cues are sometimes called triggers.

CULTURE CHANGE. A term that refers to a movement in the United States to make nursing homes more resident-centered and less like hospitals.

CULTURE. A laboratory method in which microorganisms such as bacteria or fungi from an infected wound, are grown in the laboratory on nutrient-enriched substances and then identified.

CURET. A surgical instrument with a circular cutting loop at one end. The curet is pulled over the skin lesion in repeated strokes to remove one portion of the lesion at a time.

CURETTAGE. Surgical scraping using a spoon-shaped tool called a curette.

CUSHING'S DISEASE (HYPERCORTISOLISM, HYPERADRENOCORTICISM). A condition resulting from a hormonal imbalance in which there are high levels of cortisol, either from medication use or abnormal tumors within the body.

CVD. Cardiovascular disease, includes heart attack, stroke, heart failure and rheumatic heart disease.

CYANOSIS. A bluish tint to the skin that is caused by low oxygen levels in the blood.

CYCLOOXYGENASE. An enzyme, found in most tissues, that helps turn some fatty acids into protaglandins.

CYCLOPLEGIC DROPS. Drops used to dilate the pupil and paralyze the eye's powers of accommodation.

CYCLOTHEMIA. A milder form of bipolar disorder characterized by alternating hypomania and less severe depressive episodes.

CYSTECTOMY. Surgery to remove all or part of the bladder.

CYSTITIS. Inflammation of the bladder.

CYSTOLITHOLAPAXY. Removal of bladder stones by breaking them in the bladder and then irrigating the bladder to flush out the fragments.

CYSTOSCOPE. Specialized endoscope, a tube with a small camera on the end, inserted through the urethra into the bladder to visualize the inside of the bladder and urethra.

CYSTOSCOPY. Examination of the bladder and urethra using a cystoscope, a long, thin tube with a light that is inserted into the urethra. A cytoscope may have a tool to remove tissue for examination under a microscope.

CYTOCHROME. A substance that contains iron and acts as a hydrogen carrier for the eventual release of energy in aerobic respiration.

CYTOKINES. Chemical messengers in the immune system (interferons, interleukins, and growth factors) that coordinate immune system response and turn immune cell activity on and off.

CYTOLOGY. Examination of cells using a microscope.

CYTOSCOPY. Examination of the bladder and urethra using a cystoscope, a long, thin tube with a light and lens that is inserted into the urethra. A cytoscope may have a tool attached for removing tissue for examination under a microscope.

D

DANCE TECHNIQUE. The proper alignment and placement of the arms, legs, and feet, as well as specific dance steps.

DE CHI (DE QI). A Chinese phrase that means "drawing the chi." It refers to the tingling or slightly aching sensation that some patients experience when the acupuncturist inserts the needle.

DEBRIDEMENT. Cutting away or "excising" dead tissue from a wound.

DECIBEL. A unit of measure (ranging from 0 to 130) for expressing the loudness of a sound. Normal speech is typically spoken in the range of about 20-50 decibels.

DECOCTION. An herbal extract produced by mixing an herb in cold water, bringing the mixture to a boil, and letting it simmer to evaporate the excess water. The decoction is then strained and drunk hot or cold.

DECONDITIONING. Loss of physical fitness due to illness or inactivity.

DECUBITUS. This term refers to the position of a patient in a bed, but is rarely used that way. In common usage it applies to a bedsore; skin breakdown caused by continued pressure.

DEEP VEIN THROMBOSIS (DVT). Potentially life-threatening blood clot in one of the deep veins of the body, and often in the legs secondary to immobility after surgery. Symptoms include pain, warmth, swelling, and redness.

DEFIBRILLATION. A procedure to stop the type of irregular heart beat called ventricular fibrillation, usually by using electric shock.

DEFIBRILLATOR. A machine used by emergency health care personnel to deliver an electric shock to heart muscle in order to restore normal heart beat.

DEGLUTITION. The medical term for the act of swallowing.

DEHISCENCE. Separation of a surgical incision or rupture of a wound closure.

DEHYDRATION. Excessive loss of body fluids through frequent urinating, sweating, diarrhea or vomiting.

DELAYED HYPERSENSITIVITY REACTION. T cell responses that do not occur immediately upon exposure to an antigen, but over several days.

DELIRIUM. A disturbance of consciousness marked by confusion, difficulty paying attention, delusions, hallucinations, or restlessness, distinguished from dementia by its relatively sudden onset and variation in the severity of the symptoms.

DELUSION. A persistent false belief held in the face of strong contradictory evidence.

DELUSORY PARASITOSIS. A type of psychoses in which people believe that there are insects crawling over their skin.

DEMENTIA. A usually progressive deterioration of intellectual functions, such as memory, that can occur while other brain functions, such as those controlling movement and the senses, are retained.

DEOXYRIBONUCLEOPROTEINS. A class of proteins associated with DNA, found in the nucleus of the cell.

DEPENDENCE. A state in which a person requires a steady concentration of a particular substance in order to avoid experiencing withdrawal symptoms.

DEPRESSANT. A drug or other substance that soothes or lessens tension of the muscles or nerves.

DEPRESSION. A mental health disorder that interferes with a person's ability to eat, sleep, work, and enjoy everyday activities.

DEPRESSIVE DISORDERS. Mental illnesses characterized by a profound and persistent feeling of sadness or despair and/or a loss of interest in activities that once were pleasurable.

DERMATITIS. Inflammation of the skin, either caused by direct contact with an irritating substance, or an allergic reaction.

DERMATITIS HERPETIFORMIS. A chronic very itchy skin disease with groups of red lesions that leave spots behind when they heal. It is sometimes associated with cancer of an internal organ.

DERMATOPHYTE. Any of various fungi that can cause parasitic skin infections.

DESCEMET'S MEMBRANE. Cornea layer beneath the stroma. It consists of thin but strong collagen fibers that serve as a protective barrier against infection and injuries.

DESENSITIZATION. A technique of pain reduction in which the painful area is stimulated with whatever is causing the pain.

DETOXIFICATION. To remove a poison or toxin or the effect of such a harmful substance; to free from an intoxicating or addictive substance in the body or from dependence on or addiction to a harmful substance.

DETUMESCENCE. The return of the penis to its original flaccid state, following erection.

DEVIATED SEPTUM. An abnormal configuration of the cartilage that divides the two sides of the nose. It can cause breathing problems if left uncorrected.

DHHS. The Department of Health and Human Service. It is a federal agency that distributes funds for Medicaid.

DIABETES. A disease in which the body does not properly control the amount of sugar in the blood. The level of sugar in the blood may become excessively high. This disease occurs when the body does not produce enough insulin or does not use it effectively.

DIABETES INSIPIDUS. A disease that causes frequent urination caused by a pituitary gland or kidney problem.

DIABETES MELLITUS. Also known as "diabetes," a group of metabolic diseases characterized by high blood sugar (glucose) levels, which result from defects in the production or action of insulin, or both.

DIABETIC RETINOPATHY. A complication of diabetes in which the blood vessels of the retina leak and cause permanent vision loss.

DIAGNOSTIC RELATED GROUPS (DRGS). Diagnosis categories that are used when doing physician or hospital billing. Each diagnosis is placed into the appropriate category.

DIALYSATE. A chemical bath used in dialysis to draw fluids and toxins out of the bloodstream and supply electrolytes and other chemicals to the bloodstream.

DIALYSIS. A blood filtration therapy that replaces the function of the kidneys, filtering fluids and waste products out of the bloodstream.

DIALYSIS PRESCRIPTION. The general parameters of dialysis treatment that vary according to each patient's individual needs. Treatment length, type of dialyzer and dialysate used, and rate of ultrafiltration are all part of the dialysis prescription.

DIALYZER. An artificial kidney usually composed of hollow fiber that is used in hemodialysis to eliminate waste products from the blood and remove excess fluids from the bloodstream.

DIAPHORESIS. Perspiration, particularly heavy perspiration caused by drugs or other artificial means.

DIAPHRAGM. The large muscle that is located between the abdomen and the chest area. The diaphragm aids in breathing.

DIARRHEA. Loose, watery, or frequent bowel movements.

DIASTOLIC. The relaxation period of heart cycle during which the chambers fill with blood.

DIASTOLIC BLOOD PRESSURE. The lowest level of blood pressure in the arteries, which occurs at the point in the heart's cycle when its chambers fill with blood.

DIASTOLIC PRESSURE. The pressure on the arteries when the heart relaxes.

DIATHROSES. Synovial joints.

DIETARY ASSESSMENT. An estimation of food and nutrients eaten over a particular time point. Some of the most common dietary assessment methods are food records, dietary recalls, food frequency questionnaires, and diet histories.

DIETARY FIBER. Also known as roughage or bulk. Insoluble fiber moves through the digestive system almost undigested and gives bulk to stools. Soluble fiber dissolves in water and helps keep stools soft.

DIETARY SUPPLEMENT. A product, such as a vitamin, mineral, herb, amino acid, or enzyme, that is intended to be consumed in addition to an individual's diet with the expectation that it will improve health.

DIETETICS. The science of applying the principles of nutrition to the human diet.

DIETITIAN. In the United States, a health care professional with one or more degrees in nutrition who has completed an internship and examination and is registered with the American Dietetic Association (ADA).

DIFFUSION TENSOR IMAGING (DTI). A refinement of magnetic resonance imaging that allows the doctor to measure the flow of water and track the pathways of white matter in the brain. DTI is able to detect abnormalities in the brain that do not show up on standard MRI scans.

DIGESTIVE TRACT. The organs that perform digestion, or changing of food into a form that can be absorbed by the body. They are the esophagus, stomach, small intestine, and large instestine.

DIGITAL MAMMOGRAPHY. Full-field digital mammography, FFDM; electronic images of mammogram x rays that are stored directly on a computer rather than on film.

DIGITAL RECTAL EXAMINATION. A routine screening test that is used to detect any lumps in the prostate gland or any hardening or other abnormality of the prostate tissue. The doctor inserts a gloved and lubricated finger (digit) into the patient's rectum, which lies just behind the p.

DILATED PUPIL. Enlarged pupil, resulting from contraction of the dilator muscle or relaxation of the iris. Occurs normally in dim illumination, or may be produced by certain drugs or trauma.

DILATION AND CURETTAGE (D & C). A procedure in which a physician opens the cervix and uses a special instrument to scrape tissue from the inside of the uterus.

DILUTE. A solution that has comparatively more fluid in it, relative to the quantity of solute.

DIOPTER. A unit of measure of the power of a corrective lens. Negative diopter measurements indicate nearsightedness and positive diopter units indicate farsightedness.

DIPHTHERIA. A serious, infectious disease that produces a toxin (poison) and an inflammation in the membrane lining of the throat, nose, trachea, and other tissues.

DISEASE MODEL OF ALCOHOLISM. Also known as the Minnesota model, the disease model contends that alcoholism is a disease that alcoholism is chronic, progressive, and frequently fatal.

DISEASE-MODIFYING ANTIRHEUMATIC DRUG (DMARD). Medication belonging to a group of medications commonly used in patients with rheumatoid arthritis that acts by lowering the autoimmune response.

DISK (DISC). Soft, flexible, shock-absorbing material between each vertebra.

DISKECTOMY. Surgery to remove part of a herniated disc.

DISORIENTATION. Losing one's sense of time, place, and personal identity.

DISPENSING. The act of providing medication to a patient or their representative. This includes providing consultation on the way in which the medication should be taken or administered.

DISSEMINATED. Scattered or distributed throughout the body. Lyme disease that has progressed beyond the stage of localized EM is said to be disseminated.

DISTAL. Farther from the center of the body.

DISTENTION. Swelling or enlargement of a tissue due to internal pressure.

DIURETIC. An agent or drug that eliminates excessive water in the body by increasing the flow of urine.

DIVERTICULA (PLURAL OF DIVERTICULUM). A sac or pouch in the colon walls which is usually asymptomatic (without symptoms) but may cause difficulty if it becomes inflamed.

DIVERTICULITIS. Inflammation of the diverticula that can form in the weakened muscular wall of the large intestine.

DIVERTICULOSIS. A condition where pouchlike sections that bulge through the large intestine's muscular walls but are not inflamed occur. They may cause bleeding, stomach distress, and excess gas.

DIVERTICULUM. A small bulging sac pushing outward from the colon wall. Plural: diverticula.

DNA. An important genetic determinant, deoxyribonucleic acid (DNA) is found in nuclei of human and plant cells, functioning as the reproducing component of chromosomes, controlling hereditary characteristics; also present in viruses.

DOPAMINE. A chemical in the brain (neurotransmitter) that helps send signals that control movement.

DOPPLER ECHOCARDIOGRAPHY. A testing technique that uses Doppler ultrasound technology to evaluate the pattern and direction of blood flow in the heart.

DOPPLER EFFECT. Change in the frequency of sound or light waves as they bounce off a moving object.

DORSAL ROOT ENTRY ZONE (DREZ). A type of nerve surgery for postherpetic neuralgia occasionally used when the patient can get no other pain relief. The surgery destroys the area where damaged nerves join the central nervous system, thereby interfering with inappropriate pain messages.

DOUGHNUT HOLE. A gap in insurance coverage between the point when the annual regular coverage limit is reached and before catastrophic coverage takes effect.

DOWN SYNDROME. Also called trisomy 21; a congenital condition characterized by an extra partial or complete chromosome 21, mental retardation, and specific physical attributes such as a broad skull, blunt facial features and short stature.

DRESSING STICK. A long rod with a hook attached to the end that a patient uses in place of the hands. Typically a dressing rod would be used to pull on a pair of pants or socks.

DRIS. The abbreviation for Daily Reference Intakes established in 1996 to replace the former term, Recommended Daily Allowances, or RDAs.

DRUSEN. Clumps of pigment that accumulate under the retina when wastes build up faster than they can be removed. Drusen are a sign of dry age-related macular degeneration.

DTAP. Diphtheria and tetanus toxoids and accellular pertussis combination vaccine.

DTP. Diphtheria, tetanus, and whole-cell pertussis vaccine.

DUAL CHAMBER. A type of pacemaker having two leads that are placed in the right atria and the right ventricle.

DUAL ENERGY X-RAY ABSORPTIOMETRY (DEXA). Technique used to measure bone mineral density.

DUCTAL ADENOCARCINOMA. A malignant tumor arising from the duct cells within a gland.

DUCTAL CARCINOMA-IN-SITU (DCIS). Breast cancer that has not spread beyond the lining of the milk duct.

DUCTOGRAM. A test used for imaging the breast ducts and diagnosing the cause of abnormal nipple discharges.

DUODENAL. Pertaining to the first part of the small intestine.

DUODENUM. The first of the three segments of the small intestine. The duodenum connects the stomach and the jejunum. Most peptic ulcers are in the duodenum.

DURABLE MEDICAL POWER OF ATTORNEY. A legal document that empowers a person to make medical decisions for the patient should the patient be unable to make the decisions. In some states, these documents have the full weight of law.

DYANA. The yoga term for meditation.

DYSARTHRIA. Difficulty in articulating words due to disorders of the central nervous system. It is sometimes called a motor speech disorder.

DYSKINESIA. An abnormal involuntary movement. Dyskinesias are common late in PD as L-dopa therapy becomes less effective.

DYSMOTILITY. Reduced or absent movement of the intestinal walls for the purpose of propelling food and waste through the intestines.

DYSPEPSIA. A chronic or recurrent pain or discomfort centered in the upper abdomen.

DYSPHAGIA. An inability to swallow, or difficulty with swallowing.

DYSPLASIA. Growth of abnormal cells.

DYSPNEA. difficulty breathing.

DYSTHYMIA. A milder chronic depression.

DYSURIA. Painful or difficult urination.

E

E. COLI. *Escherichia coli*; a bacterium that usually resides harmlessly in the lower intestine but can spread to cause infection elsewhere; also, some infectious strains produce a toxin that causes intestinal illness.

EARDRUM. A paper-thin covering stretching across the ear canal that separates the middle and outer ears.

EATING DISORDER. Conditions where people have an abnormal attitude towards food, altered appetite control and unhealthy eating habits that affect their health and ability to function normally.

ECCHYMOSIS. Large purple area of skin caused by leakage of blood under the skin, characteristic of certain blood clotting disorders.

ECHOCARDIOGRAM. A non-invasive imaging procedure used to create a picture of the heart's movement, valves, and chambers by bouncing sound waves off the heart.

ECZEMA. A superficial type of inflammation of the skin that may be very itchy and weeping in the early stages; later, the affected skin becomes crusted, scaly, and thick. There is no known cause.

EDEMA. An excess accumulation of fluid in a tissue causing swelling.

EFFICACY. The effectiveness of a drug in treating a disease or condition.

EIGHTH CRANIAL NERVE DISEASE. A disorder affecting the eighth cranial nerve, characterized by a loss of hearing and/or balance.

EJACULATORY INCOMPETENCE. The inability to ejaculate within the vagina.

EKG. Electrocardiogram, used to study and record the electrical activity of the heart.

ELECTIVE PROCEDURE. A surgical procedure that is a matter of choice rather than emergency treatment.

ELECTROACUPUNCTURE. A variation of acupuncture in which the practitioner stimulates the traditional acupuncture points electronically.

ELECTROCARDIOGRAM (ECG). A noninvasive test records the electrical activity of the heart (including heart beat) and is useful is assessing general heart health.

ELECTROCARDIOGRAPHY. A method used to trace and record the heart's electrical activity in order to evaluate heart function.

ELECTROCONVULSIVE THERAPY (ECT). A treatment for depression in which an electric current is applied to the head of an anesthetized person to induce seizures.

ELECTRODES. Adhesive pads which are placed on the skin and attached to the leads.

ELECTROENCEPHALOGRAM (EEG). A record of the tiny electrical impulses produced by the brain's activity.

ELECTROLYTE. Ions in the body that participate in metabolic reactions. The major human electrolytes are sodium ($Na+$), potassium ($K+$), calcium ($Ca\ 2+$), magnesium (Mg_2+), chloride ($Cl-$), phosphate ($HPO_4\ 2-$), bicarbonate (HCO_3-), and sulfate ($SO_4\ 2-$).

ELECTROMYOGRAPHY (EMG). A test that uses electrodes to record the electrical activity of muscle. The information gathered is used to diagnose neuromuscular disorders.

ELECTROPHORESIS. Use of an electrical field to separate proteins in a mixture (such as blood or urine), on the basis of the size and electrical charge of the proteins.

ELECTROPHYSIOLOGIC MAPPING. Diagramming the electrical activity by using a catheter that measures the heart's electrical activity at many different spots.

ELECTROPHYSIOLOGIST. A specially trained physician or cardiologist specializing in the treatment and study of disorders of the heart's electrical conduction system.

ELECTROPHYSIOLOGY STUDY. A test using cardiac catheterization to stimulate an electrical current to provoke an arrhythmia. The test identifies the origin of arrhythmias and is used to test the effectiveness of antiarrhythmic drugs.

ELISA TEST. An ELISA (enzyme–linked immunosorbent assay) test is used to detect IgE levels in the blood.

EMBOLISM. A blood clot, air bubble, or clot of foreign material that blocks the flow of blood in an artery. When blood supply to a tissue or organ is blocked by an embolism, infarction, or death of the tissue that the artery feeds, occurs.

EMBOLUS (PLURAL, EMBOLI). Matter within the body, such as a blood clot or tumor cells, that moves from its primary location to travel to another part of the body. The process of forming emboli is called embolization.

EMESIS BASIN. A basin used to collect sputum or vomit.

EMPHYSEMA. A lung disease characterized by shortness of breath and a chronic cough. Emphysema is caused by the progressive stretching and rupture of alveoli, the air sacs in the lung that oxygenate the blood.

ENAMEL. The hard, white, outer layer of the tooth.

ENCEPHALITIS. Inflammation of the brain, usually caused by a virus. The inflammation may interfere with normal brain function and may cause seizures, sleepiness, confusion, personality changes, weakness in one or more parts of the body, and even coma.

ENDARTERECTOMY. A surgical procedure that removed damaged portions of arteries, including portions with atherosclerotic deposits, to open the vessels and restore unrestricted blood flow.

ENDOCARDITIS. Inflammation of the lining of the heart or the heart valves that can be caused by an infectious microorganism.

ENDOCERVICAL CANAL. The opening at the center of the cervix.

ENDOCRINE. Refers to glands that secrete hormones circulated in the bloodstream.

ENDOCRINE SYSTEM. System of glands in the body that includes the pituitary, pineal, thyroid, thymus, adrenal, pancreas, ovaries (females) and testes (males). These glands secrete special, powerful substances called hormones into the bloodstream.

ENDOCRINOLOGIST. A physician who specializes in diseases of the endocrine (gland) system, including diabetes and thyroid conditions.

ENDOMETRIAL BIOPSY. A procedure in which a sample of the endometrium is removed and examined under a microscope.

ENDOMETRIAL CANCER. Abnormal tissue growth or cancer in the lining of the uterus.

ENDOMETRIUM. The mucosal layer lining the inner cavity of the uterus, shed with each menstrual period. The endometrium's structure changes with age and with the menstrual cycle.

ENDOPHTHALMITIS. Inflammation of the tissues inside the eyeball.

ENDORPHINS. Brain peptides that bind to opiate receptors to produce pain relief and feelings of pleasure.

ENDOSCOPE. An instrument for examining visually the interior of a bodily canal or a hollow organ such as the colon, bladder, or stomach.

ENDOSCOPIC RETROGRADE CHOLANGIOPANCREATOGRAPHY (ERCP). Diagnostic technique used to obtain a biopsy. Also a surgical method of relieving biliary obstruction caused by a tumor.

ENDOSCOPIC ULTRASONOGRAPHY (EUS). Diagnostic imaging technique in which an ultrasound probe is inserted down a patient's throat to determine if a tumor is present.

ENDOSCOPIC ULTRASOUND. A radiology test using high frequency sound waves, conducted via an endoscope.

ENDOSCOPY. Use of a special tubular, telescopic instrument, to which a camera and surgical tools can be attached, to examine and treat the gastrointestinal tract or other hollow organs of the body.

ENDOSTEAL IMPLANTS. Dental implants that are placed within the bone.

ENDOTHELIUM. Extremely thin, innermost layer of the cornea that pumps excess fluid out of the stroma.

ENDOTRACHEAL. Placed within the trachea.

ENDOTRACHEAL TUBE. Flexible tube inserted into the trachea via either the oral or nasal cavity for the purpose of providing an airway and supplemental oxygen, as well as providing access for suctioning.

END-STAGE RENAL DISEASE (ESRD). Total kidney failure; chronic kidney failure is diagnosed as ESRD when kidney function falls to 5–10% of capacity.

ENTERITIS. Inflammation of the mucosal lining of the small intestine.

ENTEROCOCCI. Streptococci that live in the digestive tract. Most of these organisms are Group D betahemolytic streptococci.

ENTEROPATHY. A disease of the intestinal tract.

ENTEROSTOMAL THERAPIST. A health professional trained in the care of persons with stomas, such as colostomies.

ENTITLEMENT. A program that creates a legal obligation on the federal government to any person, business, or government entity that meets the legally defined criteria.

ENZYME. A protein molecule, produced by an organism, which acts as a catalyst to a chemical reaction within the organism and is neither destroyed nor changed as a result of the reaction.

ENZYME-LINKED IMMUNOSORBENT ASSAY (ELISA). A biochemical test used in immunology to detect the presence of antibody or antigen in a sample of blood serum. ELISA was the first screening test commonly used to detect HIV infection.

EPIDEMIC. the occurrence of more cases of a disease than would be expected in a community or region during a given time period; a sudden severe outbreak of a disease.

EPIDEMIOLOGY. A branch of science that studies the frequency and distribution of disease in a population.

EPIDERMIS. The outer protective layer of the skin.

EPIDIDYMIS. A tube in the back of the testes that transports sperm.

EPIDURAL SPACE. The space surrounding the spinal fluid sac.

EPIDURAL. A method of administering anesthesia by injecting it into the lower spine in the space around the spinal cord. Epidural anesthesia blocks sensation in the parts of the body below the level of the injection.

EPILEPSY. A neurological disorder characterized by recurrent seizures with or without a loss of consciousness.

EPILEPTOLOGIST. A physician who specializes in the treatment of epilepsy.

EPINEPHRINE. Hormone released into the bloodstream in response to stress, as from fear or injury. It initiates many bodily responses, including the stimulation of heart action and an increase in blood pressure, metabolic rate, and blood glucose concentration.

EPITHELIUM. The layer of tissue that covers body surfaces and lines the internal surfaces of body cavities, blood vessels, and hollow organs. Most cancer cells arise within epithelial tissue.

ERECTILE DYSFUNCTION. Impotence; the inability of a man to achieve and/or maintain an erection of sufficient quality for sexual intercourse.

ERECTION. Condition of the penis when it fills with blood and becomes rigid.

EROSION. A wearing away of tissue, as by pressure or friction, as may occur to the inside lining walls of the esophagus or stomach.

ERYSIPELAS. An acute bacterial infection of the lower layer of the skin, most often caused by *S. pyogenes*. Its name comes from a Greek word meaning "red skin." It is sometimes known as Saint Anthony's fire.

ERYTHEMA MIGRANS (EM). A red skin rash that is one of the first signs of Lyme disease in about 75% of patients.

ERYTHEMA. Skin that is red because of swelling of tiny veins in the skin called capillaries.

ERYTHRODERMIC PSORIASIS. The least common form of psoriasis that can cause a rash over the entire body, and sometimes triggered by severe sunburn, corticosteroids, or inadequate management of other forms of psoriasis.

ERYTHROPOIETIN. A hormone produced by the kidneys that stimulates the production of red blood cells by bone marrow.

ERYTHROPOISIS. The production of red blood cells in the body.

ESCITALOPRAM OXALATE. Lexapro; a SSRI that is very similar to Celexa but contains only the active chemical form.

ESOPHAGEAL VARICES. Varicose veins at the lowermost portion of the esophagus. These are easily injured. Bleeding from esophageal varices is often difficult to stop.

ESOPHAGITIS. An inflammation of the throat.

ESOPHAGOGASTRODUODENOSCOPY (EGD). A test that involves visually examining the lining of the esophagus, stomach, and upper duodenum with a flexible fiber-optic endoscope.

ESOPHAGUS. The muscular tube that leads from the back of the throat to the stomach. Coated with mucus and surrounded by muscles, it pushes food to the stomach by contraction.

ESR (ERYTHROCYTE SEDIMENTATION RATE). A test for inflammation where the rate at which erythrocytes (red blood cells) settle to the bottom of a tube, which often increases during inflammation.

ESRD. End-stage renal disease; chronic or permanent kidney failure.

ESTIMATED AVERAGE REQUIREMENT (EAR). A daily calorie intake of 1,940 calories per day is recommended for women and 2,550 for men. Factors that affect the personal daily calorie needs include age, height and weight, basic level of daily activity, and body composition.

ESTROGEN. A hormone secreted by the ovaries which affects many aspects of the female body, including a woman's menstrual cycle and normal sexual and reproductive development.

ESTROGEN RECEPTOR (ER). A protein on the surface of cells that binds the female hormone estrogen, initiating estrogenic effects.

ESTROGEN REPLACEMENT THERAPY (ERT). A treatment in which estrogen is used therapeutically during menopause to alleviate certain symptoms such as hot flashes. ERT has been shown to reduce the risk of osteoporosis.

ETHICIST. A person who studies and writes about moral principles and questions involving good and evil or human duties and obligations.

ETHICS. A system or set of moral principles; also, the study of values relating to human conduct.

EUKARYOTIC. A cell with a distinct membrane–bound nucleus.

EUPHORIA. An intense feeling of elation or well-being. Many marijuana users experience temporary euphoria.

EUTHANASIA. The act of putting a person (or animal) to death painlessly or allowing death to occur by withholding medical services, usually because of a painful and incurable disease; also called mercy killing.

EXCISION. Removal of tissue, organ, limb or other body part by cutting.

EXECUTIVE FUNCTION. The ability to be flexible (changing behavior in a changing situation), understand new intentions, or plan actions.

EXOCRINE. Refers to glands which secrete their products through a duct.

EXPECTORANT. A medicinal reparation that promotes thinning of mucus membrane secretions in the upper respiratory system—nose, throat, and airways.

EXTENDED FAMILY. A network of relatives consisting of parents and children along with grandparents, the siblings of the parents and their spouses, cousins, and adopted or foster children.

EXTERNAL RADIATION THERAPY. Radiation therapy that focuses high-energy rays from a machine on the area of the tumor.

EXTRACELLULAR MATRIX. A collection of connective tissue proteins and fibers that supports and nourishes body tissues. The extracellular matrix forms a physical barrier to the movement of tumor cells.

EXTRACORPOREAL CIRCUIT (ECC). The path the hemodialysis patient's blood takes outside of the body. It typically consists of plastic tubing, a hemodialysis machine, and a dialyzer.

EXTRAVASATION. The process of reverse invasion in which tumor cells that have invaded the blood vessels and traveled to other organs force their way back out of the blood vessels and into the tissues surrounding their new site.

EXTUBATION. The removal of the tube that connects a patient to a ventilator.

F

FALLOPIAN TUBES. Slender tubes that carry eggs (ova) from the ovaries to the uterus.

FALSE NEGATIVE. A test result that indicates that a person does not have a specific disease when he or she does in fact have it.

FALSE POSITIVE. A test result that indicates a person has a disease when in fact he or she does not.

FAMILY HEALTH HISTORY. A health history that includes information about disease and conditions that affected blood relatives of the patient.

FASCIA. A sheet of connective tissue that covers and interpenetrates the muscles or other body structures. It provides support and protection for the body and acts as a shock absorber.

FASCICULATION. Visible involuntary contraction or twitching of muscle fibers.

FAST TRACK. A protocol for postoperative patients with projected shorter recovery times. Fast-tracking a patient means that they will either bypass PACU completely, or spend a shorter time there with less intensive staff intervention and monitoring.

FAT. Molecules composed of fatty acids and glycerol. Fats are the slowest source of energy but the most energy-efficient form of food. Each gram of fat supplies the body with about nine calories, more than twice that supplied by proteins or carbohydrates.

FAT-SOLUBLE VITAMIN. A vitamin that dissolves in and can be stored in body fat or the liver.

FATIGUE. Physical or mental weariness.

FATTY ACIDS. Complex molecules found in fats and oils. Essential fatty acids are fatty acids that the body needs but cannot synthesize. Essential fatty acids are made by plants and must be present in the diet to maintain health.

FATTY LIVER. A condition in which liver cells accumulate fat. The condition is associated with alcohol abuse, obesity, and pregnancy and can result in serious damage to the liver.

FECAL. Pertaining to feces or fecal matter discharged from the bowel.

FECES. Stool, the excrement discharged from the intestines.

FEDERAL POVERTY LEVEL (FPL). The federal government's definition of poverty used as the reference point for Medicaid eligibility for certain groups of beneficiaries. The FPL is adjusted every year to allow for inflation.

FEE-FOR-SERVICE. A traditional kind of health care policy in which insurance companies pay fees for the services provided to the insured people covered by the policy. This type of health insurance offers the most choices of doctors and hospitals.

FEMORAL ARTERY. An artery located in the groin area that is the most frequently accessed site for arterial puncture in angiography.

FEMUR. The medical name for the thighbone. The femur is the largest bone in the human body.

FETAL ALCOHOL SYNDROME. A wide range of birth defects, including mental retardation, in children whose mothers consumed large amounts of alcohol during pregnancy.

FIBER. Carbohydrate material in food that cannot be digested.

FIBEROPTIC ENDOSCOPY. A test used to evaluate swallowing. A flexible scope is passed into the hypopharynx, the bottom portion of the throat or through the nose to view the desired structures involved in swallowing.

FIBRILLATION. An irregular heart beat caused by rapid twitching of tiny fibers in the heart muscle; it can occur in the atrial or ventricular portions of the heart (atrial fibrillation, ventricular fibrillation).

FIBRIN. A fibrous protein which is part of a blood clot.

FIBROMA. A usually benign tumor consisting of fiborous tissue.

FIBROMAYALGIA. A group of symptoms, including muscle pain, fatigue, and digestive disturbances, that seriously impact quality of life.

FIBROSIS. A condition characterized by the presence of scar tissue, or reticulin and collagen proliferation in tissues to the extent that it replaces normal tissues.

FIGHT-OR-FLIGHT RESPONSE. The body's reaction to threats.

FINE-NEEDLE ASPIRATION BIOPSY (FNAB). A procedure using a thin needle to remove fluid and cells from a lump in the breast.

FISSURE. A deep slit in body tissue.

FLAP. A section of tissue moved from one area of the body to another.

FLATULENCE. Excess gas in the intestines that may cause bloating, pain, and fowl smelling discharge.

FLAVONOID. Refers to compounds found in fruits, vegetables, and certain beverages that have diverse beneficial biochemical and antioxidant effects.

FLEX. To bend.

FLOATERS. Dark spots in the field of vision caused by the accumulation of proteins in the gel-like material (vitreous) in the eye. They can indicate an eye disorder or be a harmless part of aging.

FLUORESCEIN DYE. An orange dye used to illuminate the blood vessels of the retina in fluorescein angiography.

FLUORESCEIN ISOTHIOCYANATE (FITC). An organic molecule that can be covalently bound to other molecules, and that emits visible light when exposed to ultraviolet radiation.

FLUORIDE. A compound believed to combat cavities in teeth.

FLUOROSCOPIC SCREEN. A fluorescent screen which displays "moving x rays" of the body. Fluoroscopy allows the radiologist to visualize the guide wire and catheter he is moving through the patient's artery.

FLUOROSCOPY. Also called radioscopy, this procedure involves the examination of internal body structures using x rays and projecting images on a fluorescent screen.

FLUOROSIS. A condition caused by too much fluorine in the body (usually from industrial inhalation) that causes connective tissue around the vertebrae to harden.

FLUOXETINE. Prozac; the first SSRI; marketed as Sarafem for treating PMDD.

FLUROSCOPY. A special type of x ray where images are projected on a fluorescent screen. Used to guide lead placement in pacemaker installations.

FLUSHING. A redness of the face and neck, caused by increased blood flow through dilated facial blood vessels. During a flush, a patient with rosacea can turn various shades of red, depending on the amount of blood flowing through the skin.

FLUVOXAMINE. Luvox; a SSRI that is used to treat obsessive-compulsive disorder as well as other conditions.

FOLATE. A vitamin in the B complex needed for the production and maintenance of new cells. Folate is found in leafy green vegetables and some other fruits and vegetables; also called folic acid.

FOLEY CATHETER. A double-channel retention catheter; one channel provides for the inflow and outflow of bladder fluid, the second (smaller) channel is used to fill a balloon that holds the catheter in the bladder.

FOLLICLE. The small sac at the base of a hair shaft. The follicle lies below the skin surface.

FOLLICLE-STIMULATING HORMONE (FSH). The pituitary hormone that stimulates the ovary to mature egg capsules (follicles). It is linked with rising estrogen production throughout the cycle. An elevated FSH (above 40) indicates menopause.

FOOD INTOLERANCE. An adverse food-induced reaction that does not involve the immune system.

FORCE PLATFORM. A large plate, usually mounted in the floor, that records forces when an individual stands or walks on it.

FORMAL CAREGIVER. A phrase sometimes used to describe home health care workers or other paid caregivers.

FORMALIN. A clear solution of diluted formaldehyde that is used to preserve liver biopsy specimens until they can be examined in the laboratory.

FORMULARY. A list of prescription medications that are covered by a particular insurance plan.

FORTIFIED FOODS. A method used to provide the required nutrients in populations where a certain vitamin or mineral is not available or not available in sufficient quantities. The required nutrient(s) are added to a staple food, such as flour or salt.

FRACTIONATION. A laboratory test or process in which blood or another fluid is broken down into its components. Fractionation can be used to assess the proportions of the different types of cholesterol in a blood sample.

FRAGILE X SYNDROME. An inherited disorder caused by repeated sequences on the X chromosome resulting in mental retardation and other abnormalities in males, but few if any problems in females who have a normal second X chromosome.

FRAILTY SYNDROME. A condition of physical weakness that places older adults at increased risk of disability or institutionalization. It is measured by evaluating seniors for muscle weakness, weight loss, low physical activity, exhaustion, and slow walking speed.

FREE FLAP. A section of tissue is detached from its blood supply, moved to another part of the body, and reattached by microsurgery to a new blood supply.

FREE-FLOATING. A term used in psychiatry to describe anxiety that is unfocused or lacking an apparent cause or object.

FREE RADICAL. An unstable molecule that causes oxidative damage by stealing electrons from surrounding molecules, thereby disrupting activity in the body's cells.

FRICTION. A force exerted when two surfaces move across each other such as moving patients across a bed or other support surface.

FROZEN SHOULDER. A shoulder that becomes scarred and cannot move.

FRUCTOSE. Monosaccharide known as fruit sugar.

FULMINANT. Starting suddenly with great severity.

FUNCTIONAL INDEPENDENCE. The ability to carry out or perform actions or activities necessary for everyday life without assistance.

FUNCTIONAL MOVEMENT THERAPY. A type of therapy that has positive physical fitness outcomes.

FUNCTIONAL REACH TEST. A test that evaluates stability when reaching out beyond an individual's base of support. In this test the patient stands and tries to reach out with one hand as far as possible without losing balance. The reach is recorded in inches.

FUNDOPLICATION. A surgical procedure that tightens the lower esophageal sphincter by stretching and wrapping the upper part of the stomach around the sphincter.

FUNGAL INFECTION. Conditions in which fungi pass the resistance barriers of the human or animal body and establish infections.

FUNGUS. Any of numerous eukaryotic organisms of the kingdom Fungi, which lack chlorophyll and vascular tissue and can be single–celled or have a body mass of branched filamentous threads that often produce specialized fruiting bodies.

FURUNCULOSIS. A condition in which the patient suffers from recurrent episodes of boils.

FUTILE CARE. Medical care that is useless or highly unlikely to produce a good outcome.

G

GADOLINIUM. A very rare metallic element useful for its sensitivity to electromagnetic resonance, among other things. Traces of it can be injected into the body to enhance the MRI pictures.

GAIT. A person's characteristic manner of walking. Abnormalities of gait are part of assessing an older adult for mobility problems.

GALACTOSE. Monosaccharide known as milk sugar.

GALLSTONE ILEUS. Obstruction of the large intestine caused by a gallstone that has blocked the intestinal opening.

GAMMA GLOBULIN. One of a group of proteins found in the blood that is involved in helping the body to fight infections.

GAMMA RADIATION. High-energy, short wavelength electromagnetic radiation emitted by the nuclei of an excited atom.

GAMMA-AMINOBUTYRIC ACID. GABA; a neurotransmitter that inhibits postsynaptic neurons.

GANGLIA. Groups of nerve cell bodies in the peripheral nervous system. Also referred to as neuroganglion.

GANGRENE. Death of tissue, frequently caused by a loss of blood flow or wounds that cannot heal, especially in the legs and feet.

GASTRIC. Pertaining to the stomach.

GASTRIC LAVAGE. The inside of the stomach is rinsed with a saline (salt water) solution or regular tap water; also called a stomach pump.

GASTRINOMA. Tumor that arises from the gastrin-producing cells in the pancreas.

GASTROENTEROLOGIST. A physician who specializes in diseases of the digestive system.

GASTROESOPHAGEAL REFLUX DISEASE (GERD). A painful, chronic condition in which stomach acid flows back into the esophagus causing heartburn and, in time, erosion of the esophageal lining.

GASTROINTESTINAL. The digestive organs and structures, including the stomach and intestines.

GASTROPARESIS. Nerve damage of the stomach that delays or stops stomach emptying, resulting in nausea, vomiting, bloating, discomfort, and weight loss.

GASTROPLASTY. A surgical procedure used to reduce the digestive capacity by shortening the small intestine or shrinking the effective side of the stomach.

GASTROSTOMY. Surgical creation of an artificial opening into the stomach through the abdominal wall to allow tube feeding.

GEL. A semi-solid dosage form for external application, usually translucent, non-greasy but may be drying.

GENE EXPRESSION. The process by which the coded information of a gene is translated into the proteins or RNA present and operating in the cell.

GENE MUTATION. Changes in a gene that may change the way it expresses inherited traits in an organism.

GENETIC DISEASE. A disease inherited from one or both parents.

GENETICS. The science of biologic inheritance and the transmission of traits of a single organism through possession of specific genes, which are the units of heredity.

GENUS. A category ranking below a family and above a species and generally consisting of a group of species. Pl.: genera.

GERD (GASTROESOPHAGEAL REFLUX DISEASE). Chronic or recurrent upward movement of gastric juices from the stomach into the lower esophagus, producing pain, belching, nausea and cough and sometimes causing regurgitation of stomach contents into the esophagus.

GERIATRIC ASSESSMENT. A comprehensive evaluation of an elderly person's physical health, functional ability, cognitive function, mental health, and social situation.

GERIATRIC MEDICINE. A field of medicine that specializes in the care and treatment of the elderly.

GERIATRICIAN. Physician specializing in the care and treatment of older adults.

GERONTOLOGY. The medical specialty that studies and treats diseases and disorders related to the aging process as well as diseases and disorders of the elderly population.

GESTATIONAL AGE. The length of time of growth and development of the young in the mother's womb.

GET-UP-AND-GO TEST. Evaluates balance during a functional activity. The test is scored based on the patient's ability to get up from a chair, walk forward about 10 feet (3 m), return to the chair and sit down. The test may be timed to monitor progress.

GIANT CELL ARTERITIS. Also called temporal arteritis. A condition which causes the inflammation of temporal arteries. It can cause blindness when the inflammation effects the ophthalmic artery.

GINGIVITIS. Swollen, bleeding gums, usually not painful.

GLANDULAR TISSUE. The glands or lobules of the breast that produce milk.

GLAUCOMA. An eye disorder caused by damage to the optic nerve resulting in vision loss. Glaucoma is usually accompanied by inflammation and increased pressure in the eye (intraocular pressure). There are several types that may develop suddenly or gradually.

GLOBUS PHARYNGIS. The persistent sensation of a lump or some other small object in the throat even though no obstruction is present.

GLOMERULONEPHRITIS. A disease of the kidney that causes inflammation and scarring and impairs the kidney's ability to filter waste products from the blood.

GLOSSITIS. Inflammation of the tongue.

GLOSSOPHARYNGEAL NEURALGIA. Sharp recurrent pain deep in the throat that extends to the area around the tonsils and possibly the ear. It is triggered by swallowing or chewing.

GLUCAGON. A hormone produced by the pancreas that raises blood sugar levels and has the opposite action of insulin.

GLUCOSE. Also known as dextrose, the main sugar the body makes from proteins, fats, and carbohydrates. Glucose is carried through the bloodstream to provide energy to all cells in the body with the help of insulin.

GLUTAMATE. An excitatory neurotransmitter in the central nervous system.

GLUTEN. A storage protein component of the grains wheat, rye, and barely, and an ingredient in many prepared foods and thickening agents.

GOMPHOSIS. A joint where a bony structure is implanted deep into another bony structure. An example would be the joint between a tooth and the mandible (jaw bone).

GONORRHEA. A sexually transmitted disease (STD) that causes infection in the genital organs and may cause disease in other parts of the body.

GOUT. A metabolic disease causing inflammation of the joints, uric deposits in and around the joints, and excessive uric acid in the blood.

GRAFT. To implant living tissue surgically. Also refers to the tissue that is transplanted.

GRAM-NEGATIVE. Refers to the property of many bacteria in which they do not take or color with Gram's stain, a method which is used to identify bacteria. Gram-positive bacteria that take up the stain turn purple, while Gram-negative bacteria which do not.

GRAM-POSITIVE. A term that refers to the amount of a crystal violet dye picked up by a bacterium during the Gram stain process. A Gram-positive organism looks blue or violet under a microscope whereas Gram-negative bacteria look red or pink.

GRAM STAIN. A staining procedure used to visualize and classify bacteria. The Gram stain procedure allows the identification of purple (Gram-positive) organisms and red (Gram-negative) organisms.

GRANNY SNATCHING. An informal term used to describe taking an incapacitated senior over state lines in order to put him or her into a guardianship.

GRANULOCYTE/MACROPHAGE COLONY STIMULATING FACTOR (GM-CSF). A substance produced by cells of the immune system that stimulates the attack upon foreign cells. Used to treat prostate cancers as a genetically engineered component of a vaccine that stimulates the body to attack prostate tissue.

GRIEF. A collections of reactions to death or other losses. Grief involves thought processes and spiritual considerations as well as emotional reactions.

GROWTH FACTORS (CYTOKINES). Chemicals made by the cells that act on other cells to stimulate or inhibit their function. Cytokines that stimulate growth are called "growth factors."

GUIDE WIRE. A wire that is inserted into an artery to guides a catheter to a certain location in the body.

GUILLAIN-BARRE SYNDROME. A disorder characterized by progressive symmetrical paralysis and loss of reflexes, usually beginning in the legs. The paralysis characteristically involves more than one limb (most commonly the legs) and is progressive.

GULF WAR SYNDROME. A multi-symptom illness of unknown causes that affected veterans of Operation Desert Storm, a war to free Kuwait of Iraqi occupation in 1991.

GYNECOLOGIC ONCOLOGIST. A physician who specializes in the treatment of female reproductive cancers.

H

H2 BLOCKERS. Medications used to treat some GERD symptoms, for example, Tagamet, Pepcid, Axid.

HAIR FOLLICLES. Tiny organs in the skin, each one of which grows a single hair.

HALLUCINATION. A sensory perception that occurs in the absence of a real stimulus. Hallucinations can affect any of the body's senses; however, the most common hallucinations in delirium are visual (seeing things) or auditory (hearing voices).

HANSEN'S DISEASE. Hansen's disease, commonly referred to as leprosy, is a chronic infectious disease that can cause severe deformity of the feet, hands and face.

HATHA YOGA. Form of yoga using postures, breathing methods and meditation.

HAY FEVER. A seasonal allergy to airborne particles characterized by itchy eyes, runny nose, nasal congestion, sneezing, itchy throat, and excess mucus.

HAYFLICK LIMIT. The length of a telomere below which a cell will stop dividing. The Hayflick limit for human cells is about 50–52 divisions, after which the cell is senescent.

HCFA. Health Care Financing Administration. The federal agency that provides guidelines for the Medicare program.

HDL CHOLESTEROL. High-density lipoprotein cholesterol is a component of cholesterol that helps protect against heart disease. HDL is nicknamed "good" cholesterol.

HEALTH CARE POWER OF ATTORNEY. An alternate term for health care proxy.

HEALTH MAINTENANCE ORGANIZATION (HMO). Vertically integrated health-care provider employing many clinical professionals and usually owning or controlling a hospital. This managed care health insurance limits the patient's choice of physicians and hospitals to those participating.

HEARING AID. An electronic and/or digital device worn in the ear to amplify sound.

HEART CATHETERIZATION. A heart catheterization is used to view the heart's chamber and valves. A tube (catheter) is inserted into an artery, usually in the groin. A dye is put into the artery and makes its way to the heart to create an image.

HEART FAILURE. A term used when the heart is unable to pump enough blood to supply the needs of the body.

HEART-LUNG OR CARDIOPULMONARY BYPASS MACHINE. A machine that replaces the function of the heart and lungs during open heart surgery by diverting blood flow away from the right atrium, adding oxygen to the blood, and returning blood beyond the left ventricle, to bypass the heart and lungs.

HEART MURMUR. Sound during the heartbeat caused by a heart valve that does not close properly.

HEARTBURN. A burning sensation, usually in the center of the chest, near the breastbone.

HEAT STROKE. A severe condition caused by prolonged exposure to high heat. Heat stroke interferes with the body's temperature regulating abilities and can lead to collapse and coma.

HEBERDEN'S NODES. Swelling or deformation of the finger joints closest to the fingertips.

HELICOBACTER PYLORI. A gram-negative rod-shaped bacterium that lives in the tissues of the stomach and causes inflammation of the stomach lining.

HEMATEMESIS. Vomit that contains blood, usually seen as black specks in the vomitus.

HEMATOCRIT. An indication of blood volume determined by the percentage of blood composed of red blood cells and hemoglobin compared to the liquid portion called plasma.

HEMATOLOGIST. A specialist who treats diseases and disorders of the blood and blood-forming organs.

HEMATOMA. A pooling of blood inside an organ or beneath organ tissue, usually becoming clotted into a noticeable configuration and sometimes requiring removal to avoid the pressure on adjacent organs.

HEMATURIA. Presence of blood in the urine.

HEME IRON. Iron that is bound to four nitrogen atoms in the center of a ring system of carbon atoms called a porphyrin.

HEMODYNAMIC STABILITY. Stability of blood circulation, including cardiac function and peripheral vascular physiology.

HEMOGLOBIN. Iron-containing protein found in red blood cells that carries oxygen to tissues.

HEMOGLOBINOPATHIES. Group of disorders affecting the red blood cells that contain hemoglobin, the oxygen carrier molecule.

HEMOLYSIS. The destruction of red blood cells, whether by bacteria or some other agent.

HEMOLYTIC ANEMIA. Anemic condition characterized by the destruction of red blood cells.

HEMOPTYSIS. The expectoration of blood or of blood containing sputum.

HEMORRHAGE. Heavy or uncontrolled bleeding.

HEMORRHOIDS. Enlarged veins in the anus or rectum. They are sometimes associated with fecal incontinence.

HEPARIN. A substance found especially in lung and liver tissue that can prevent the clotting of blood.

HEPATIC. Pertaining to the liver.

HEPATITIS. A viral disease characterized by inflammation of the liver cells (hepatocytes). People infected with hepatitis B or hepatitis C virus are at an increased risk for developing liver cancer.

HEPATOCYTE. Liver cell.

HER2. Human epidermal-growth-factor receptor-2, which is overproduced in HER2-positive breast cancers.

HERPES ZOSTER. Shingles; an acute nerve inflammation resulting in a rash and pain, caused by the reactivation of latent chickenpox virus in the body.

HERPES ZOSTER OPHTHALMICUS (HZO). The condition indicating that shingles has affected a person's eyes.

HETEROTOPIC BONE. Bone that develops as an excess growth around the hip joint following surgery.

HIATAL HERNIA. A condition in which part of the stomach protrudes above the diaphragm next to the esophagus.

HIGH. The altered state of consciousness that a person seeks when abusing a substance.

HIGH-DENSITY LIPOPROTEIN (HDL). HDL is called the "good cholesterol" because it helps remove fat from the body by binding with it in the bloodstream and carrying it back to the liver for excretion in the bile and disposal.

HIGHLY ACTIVE ANTIRETROVIRAL THERAPY (HAART). An approach to HIV infection that consists of a combination of three or four separate drugs to treat the infection. It is not a cure for HIV infection but acts to slow the replication of the virus and discourage new mutations.

HIP STRATEGY. An automatic posture response in which control comes from the pelvis and trunk.

HIPPOCAMPUS. A curved ridge in the brain that is part of the limbic system. The hippocampus stores long-term memories of anxiety-provoking experiences.

HIPPOCRATIC OATH. The ethical oath attributed to Hippocrates that is used as a standard for care by physicians worldwide.

HISTAMINE. A natural anti-inflammatory chemical produced by the body, which tightens mucus membranes in the nose, throat, and bronchial tubes and dilates blood vessels.

HISTAMINE H-2 RECEPTOR BLOCKERS. Commonly called H-2 blockers, drugs that prevent or block the production of stomach acid.

PLAQUE PSORIASIS. Refers to the thick, red patches of skin that are covered with silvery, flaky scales, and represents the most common form of psoriasis.

HISTONE. Any of a group of five small alkaline proteins that occur in the nucleus of eukaryotic cells and form molecular complexes with DNA, around which the DNA is wound in the nucleosomes.

HISTOPATHOLOGY. The study of diseased tissues at a minute (microscopic) level.

HISTOPLASMOSIS. A fungal infection that can affect the skin, lungs, and eyes.

HIV. Human immunodeficiency virus, the virus which causes AIDS.

HIVES. A raised, itchy area of skin that is usually a sign of an allergic reaction.

HODGKIN'S DISEASE. A type of cancer characterized by a slowly enlarging lymph tissue; symptoms include generalized itching.

HOLISTIC MEDICINE. Any approach to health care that emphasizes treatment of the whole person, mind and spirit as well as body. Osteopathic medicine has traditionally been holistic.

HOME MODIFICATION. Altering the physical environment of the home so as to remove hazards and provide an environment that is more functional for the individual. Examples of home modification include installing grab bars and no-slip foot mats in the bathroom to prevent falls.

HOME PARENTERAL NUTRITION (HPN). Long-term parenteral nutrition, given through a central venous catheter and administered in the patient's home.

HOMEOSTASIS. An organism's regulation of body processes to maintain internal equilibrium in temperature and fluid content.

HOMOCYSTEINE. An amino acid normally found in small amounts in the blood.

HORMONE. A chemical substance produced in the body that controls and regulates the activity of certain cells or organs.

HORMONE REPLACEMENT THERAPY (HRT). The use of estrogen and progesterone to replace hormones that the ovary no longer supplies.

HORMONE THERAPY. Treatment of cancer by inhibiting the production of hormones such as testosterone and estrogen.

HOSPICE. A program that provides special care for people in the final phase of illness, their families and caregivers. The care may take place in the patient's home or in a homelike facility.

HOSPITAL. An institution that provides medical, surgical, or psychiatric care and treatment for the sick or the injured.

HOUSEKEEPING. A general term for house cleaning, food preparation, laundry, and other chores typically done inside the home.

HPV. Human papillomavirus, some strains of which cause warts and others can cause cervical cancer.

HSIL. High-grade squamous intraepithelial lesion; moderate to severe dysplasia; a Pap-test finding of abnormal or precancerous cells with a higher probability of progressing to invasive cervical cancer.

HUMAN COLLAGEN. Collagen derived from human sources, an alternative to bovine collagen.

HUMAN IMMUNODEFICIENCY VIRUS (HIV). The virus that causes acquired immunodeficiency syndrome (AIDS).

HUMAN PAPILLOMAVIRUS (HPV). A group of viruses that are responsible for genital warts and cervical cancer.

HUMERUS. The arm bone, connecting the shoulder and the elbow.

HUTCHINSON-GILFORD PROGERIA SYNDROME (HGPS). A rare disease that affects about 1 in 8 million children, characterized by accelerated aging. Researchers think that HGPS may yield clues about normal aging.

HYDRATION. Sufficient intake of water, usually by drinking and intravenously when necessary, to maintain fluid levels in the body.

HYDROCEPHALUS. Swelling of the brain caused by an accumulation of fluid.

HYDROGEN. The simplest, most common element known in the universe. It is composed of a single electron (negatively charged particle) circling a nucleus consisting of a single proton (positively charged particle).

HYDROGEN PEROXIDE. A colorless, unstable compound of hydrogen and oxygen (H_2O_2). An aqueous solution of hydrogen peroxide is used as an antiseptic and bleaching agent.

HYDRONEPHROSIS. Swelling of a kidney due to elevated pressure from excess fluid accumulation.

HYDROSTATIC PRESSURE. The pressure of the water against the body.

HYDROTHERAPY. The use of water to relieve pain and treat diseases. Hydrotherapy may involve drinking water (usually mineral or spring water), but more commonly involves the external use of water, as in hot or cold baths, exercising in water, and the use of wet soaks.

HYDROURETER. Swelling of a ureter due to elevated pressure from excess fluid accumulation.

HYDROXYCHALCONE. The substance found in cinnamon that may cause insulin receptors in the body to metabolize glucose more effectively.

HYPERBARIC OXYGEN. Medical treatment in which oxygen is administered in specially designed chambers under pressures greater than that of the atmosphere in order to treat specific medical conditions.

HYPERBARIC OXYGEN THERAPY (HBO). A form of oxygen therapy in which the patient breathes oxygen in a pressurized chamber.

HYPERCALCEMIA. Abnormally high levels of calcium in the blood.

HYPERCHOLESTEROLEMIA. The presence of excessively high levels of cholesterol in the blood.

HYPERGLYCEMIA. An elevated concentration of sugar (glucose) in the blood.

HYPEROSMOTIC. Hypertonic, containing a higher concentration of salts or other dissolved materials than normal tissues.

HYPERSECRETORY. Excessive secretions, over production of stomach acid.

HYPERSENSITIVE. A process or reaction that occurs at above normal levels; overreaction to a stimulus.

HYPERSENSITIVITY. Excessively sensitive, used to describe development of an immune response to a harmless stimulant.

HYPERTENSION. Persistently high arterial blood pressure.

HYPERTENSIVE HEART DISEASE. High blood pressure resulting in a disease of the heart.

HYPERTHYROIDISM. A condition in which the thyroid is overactive due to overstimulation of the thyroid cells.

HYPERTROPHY. Literally means an increase in the muscle mass (or weight) of the heart.

HYPERURICEMIA. High levels of a waste product called uric acid in the blood.

HYPERVENTILATION. Rapid, shallow breathing.

HYPERVISCOSITY. Thick, viscous blood, caused by the accumulation of large proteins, such as immunoglobulins, in the serum.

HYPHAE. Any of the thread-like filaments forming the body of a fungus.

HYPNOTIC. A medicine that causes sleep.

HYPNOTIC AGENT. A drug capable of inducing a hypnotic state.

HYPNOTIC STATE. A state of heightened awareness that can be used to modulate the perception of pain.

HYPOCALCEMIA. Abnormally low blood calcium level.

HYPOCHLORHYDRIA. A deficiency of hydrochloric acid in the gastric juice.

HYPOGLYCEMIA. An abnormally low level of circulating blood sugar (blood glucose).

HYPOKALEMIA. Low serum potassium.

HYPOMANIA. Unusual behavior that is less severe than mania, without delusions or hallucinations.

HYPONATREMIA. An abnormally low concentration of sodium in the blood.

HYPOPARATHYROIDISM. A condition resulting from an absence or deficiency in parathyroid hormone. It is characterized by hypocalcemia and hyperphosphatemia.

HYPOTENSION. Having a low blood pressure: less than 90/60 mmHg.

HYPOTHERMIA. Low core body temperature of 95°F (35°C) or less.

HYPOTHYROIDISM. A condition in which the thyroid gland is underactive.

HYPOVENTILATION. Reduced ventilation in the lungs' air sacs resulting in above normal carbon dioxide pressure.

HYPOXEMIA. A condition in which there is deficient oxygen supply in the blood.

HYPOXIA. Low levels of oxygen in blood, tissue, or air.

HYPOXIC. Abnormal deficiency of oxygen in the arterial blood.

HYSTERECTOMY. Surgical removal of the uterus and cervix through the vagina or abdomen.

I

ICTAL EEG. Used to measure brain activity during a seizure. May be useful in learning more about patients who are not responding to conventional treatments.

ICU PSYCHOSIS. A psychosis that results from being confined in a hospital intensive care unit.

IDEAS OF REFERENCE. The notion that irrelevant or unrelated events are related to the self in a special way. An example would be the thought that a radio announcer is talking directly to or about oneself, or that strangers are laughing about oneself.

IDIOPATHIC. Disease of unknown cause or origin.

ILEUS. Obstruction in or immobility of the intestines. Symptoms include nausea and vomiting, absent bowel sounds, abdominal pain, and abdominal distension.

ILIAC ARTERY. Large blood vessel in the pelvis that leads into the leg.

IMMOBILIZATION. Keeping a joint from moving, i.e. when an individual breaks the lower leg; a cast may be used that covers the knee, thus preventing motion.

IMMUNE. Resistant to a given disease.

IMMUNE GLOBULIN. A type of amino acid protein present in human serum.

IMMUNE RESPONSE. The activity of the immune system to defend the body against antigens, involving primarily the production of antibodies and sensitized T-cells.

IMMUNE SYSTEM. Mechanism that protects the body from foreign substances, foreign cells, and pathogens. The thymus, spleen, lymph nodes, white blood cells, including the B cells and T cells, and antibodies are involved in the immune response.

IMMUNITY. The condition of being immune.

IMMUNIZATION. A technique used to cause an immune response that results in resistance to a specific disease, especially an infectious disease. A vaccination is a type of immunization.

IMMUNOCOMPROMISED. Having an immune system that has been impaired by disease or treatment.

IMMUNODEFICIENCY. Describing the lack of basic functioning of the immune system designed to ward off disease.

IMMUNOFLUORESCENCE. Any of various techniques to detect an antigen or antibody in a sample by coupling its target antibody or antigen to a fluorescent compound and observing its reaction with the sample under an ultraviolet-light.

IMMUNOGLOBULIN (IG). A substance made by B cells that neutralizes specific disease–causing substances and organisms. Also called "antibody." Immunoglobulins are divided into five classes: IgA, IgD, IgE, IgG, and IgM.

IMMUNOGLOBULIN E (IGE). Antibodies produced in the lungs, skin, and mucous membranes and responsible for allergic reactions.

IMMUNOSENESCENCE. Loss of immune system function with age.

IMMUNOSUPPRESSANT. A drug that reduces the body's natural immunity by suppressing the natural functioning of the immune system.

IMMUNOSUPPRESSIVE MEDICATION. Drugs given to a transplant recipient to prevent his or her immune system from attacking the transplanted organ.

IMMUNOTHERAPY. Treatment of cancer by stimulating the body's immune defense system.

IMPACTION GRAFTING. The use of crushed bone from a donor to fill in the central canal of the femur during hip revision surgery.

IMPLANTED CARDIAC DEFIBRILLATORS (ICDS). Small devices placed in the chest below the collar bone that monitor the heart and can send a small jolt of electricity to restore normal rhythm. They are most often prescribed for rapid or irregular heartbeat.

IMPOTENT. Unable to achieve or maintain an erection of the penis.

IN SITU. In place, not having invaded other sites.

INCENTIVE SPIROMETER. Device that is used postoperatively to prevent lung collapse and promote maximum inspiration. The patient inhales until a preset volume is reached, then sustains the volume by holding the breath for three to five seconds.

INCONTINENCE. Inability to control one's urine or feces.

INCUBATE. To maintain an organism in an environment of controlled temperature, humidity, and nutrient concentration to provide optimal conditions for growth.

INDEX OF REFRACTION. A constant number for any material for any given color of light that is an indicator of the degree of the bending of the light caused by that material.

INDIGESTION. A feeling of discomfort or illness that results from the inability to properly digest food.

INFECTION. Invasion of the body by organisms that are able to cause disease.

INFECTIOUS. Caused by an infectious agent, such as a bacteria, or capable of being transmitted by infection, such as an infectious disease.

INFECTIOUS DISEASE. Disease resulting from infection by a pathogen microorganism that subsequently grows and multiplies in the body.

INFILTRATE. A tumor that moves into another organ of the body.

INFLAMED BOWEL. Irritation of the intestinal tract.

INFLAMMATION. A physiological response to stress on the body that is characterized by redness, tenderness, increased temperature, swelling and decrease or loss of function.

INFLAMMATORY BOWEL DISEASE. Inflammation of the colon and rectum. Inflammatory bowel disease includes Celiac disease, Crohn's disease, and ulcerative colitis.

INFLAMMATORY BREAST CANCER (IBC). A rare, very aggressive type of cancer that blocks the lymph vessels in the skin causing redness, warmth, and swelling of the breast.

INFLAMMATORY RESPONSE. The immune system's normal response to tissue injury caused by a physical, chemical, or biological substance.

INFLUENZA. Flu; any of several highly contagious respiratory diseases caused by strains of three different species (A, B, or C) of orthomyxoviruses.

INFORMAL CAREGIVER. A term sometimes used for an unpaid caregiver.

INFRASPINATUS. A muscle at the middle of the shoulder blade.

INJECTION SNOREPLASTY. A technique for reducing snoring by injecting a chemical that forms scar tissue near the base of the uvula, helping to anchor it and reduce its fluttering or vibrating during sleep.

INOCULATION. The introduction of a patient specimen in a culture medium.

INOSITOL. A form of vitamin B_8 that is thought to be beneficial for some patients with panic disorder.

INSTRUMENTAL ACTIVITIES OF DAILY LIVING (IADLS). Activities necessary for independent living within one's community.

INSULIN. A natural hormone made by the pancreas that controls the level of the sugar glucose in the blood.

INSULIN RESISTANCE. The body's inability to respond to and use the insulin it produces.

INSULINOMA. Tumor that arises from the insulin-producing cells in the pancreas.

INTELLIGENCE QUOTIENT (IQ). A number used to express a person's relative intelligence based on a standardized test.

INTERMITTENT CATHETERIZATION. Periodic catheterization to facilitate urine flow. The catheter is removed when the bladder is sufficiently empty.

INTERPERSONAL THERAPY (IPT). Psychotherapy for treating depression that focuses on interpersonal relationships.

INTERSTITIAL LUNG DISEASE. About 180 diseases fall into this category. Injury or foreign substances in the lungs (e.g. asbestos fibers), as well as infections, cancers, or inherited disorders may cause the diseases, which are characterized by scarring and/or inflammation of lungs.

INTERSTITIUM. The tissue layers between the alveoli and capillaries of the lungs.

INTERVENTION. A general medical term for any action taken to interrupt a disease process. In the field of substance abuse, an attempt on the part of a physician or family members to compel the abuser to stop substance abuse.

INTESTINAL DYSBIOSIS. An imbalance among the various microorganisms that live in the digestive tract.

INTESTINAL MICROFLORA. The bacteria and other microorganisms that live in the human gastrointestinal tract.

INTESTINE. Also called the bowels. Divided into large and small intestine, they extend from the stomach to the anus, where waste products exit the body. The small intestine is about 20 ft (6 m) long and the large intestine, about 5 ft (1.5 m) long.

INTIMACY. A condition of emotional closeness and warmth in love and friendship. Intimacy within a given relationship may be emotional, physical, or both.

INTRACRANIAL PRESSURE. The amount of pressure exerted inside the skull by brain tissue, blood, and cerebral-spinal fluid.

INTRAEPITHELIAL. On the surface of the cervix.

INTRAOCULAR PRESSURE (IOP). The inner pressure of the eye. Normal intraocular pressure usually ranges from 12–22 mm Hg, although people with relatively low pressures can still have glaucoma.

INTRAOPERATIVE. During surgery.

INTRAPERITONEAL CHEMOTHERAPY. Treatment performed by injecting anti-cancer drugs directed into the abdomen by a catheter.

INTRATHECAL. Introduced into or occurring in the space under the arachnoid membrane which covers the brain and spinal cord.

INTRAVENOUS. Into a vein; a needle is inserted into a vein in the back of the hand, inside the elbow, or some other location on the body. Fluids, nutrients, and drugs can be injected.

INTRAVENOUS CHEMOTHERAPY. Treatment performed by injecting anti-cancer drugs into a patient's veins.

INTRAVENOUS PYELOGRAM (IVP). A procedure in which a dye is injected into a vein in the arm. The dye travels through the body and concentrates in the urine. It outlines the kidneys, ureters, and the urinary bladder. An x-ray image is then made to observe abnormalities of these organs.

INTUBATION. A procedure in which a tube is inserted through the mouth or nose and into the trachea to keep the airway open and to help the patient breathe.

INVASIVE. Involving entry to a patient's body by an instrument or incision.

ION. An atom or molecule that has an electric charge. In the body ions are collectively referred to as electrolytes.

IONIZING RADIATION. Electromagnetic radiation that can damage living tissue by disrupting and destroying individual cells. All types of nuclear decay radiation (including x rays) are potentially ionizing. Radio waves do not damage organic tissues they pass through.

IRIS. Pigmented tissue lying behind the cornea that gives color to the eye and controls amount of light entering the eye by varying the size of the pupil.

IRON DEFICIENCY ANEMIA. A condition in which too few red blood cells are present resulting from low levels of iron in the blood.

ISCHEMIA (ISCHEMIC). A form of anemia in specific areas where blood flow has been blocked or reduced, such as a blocked artery or reduced blood flow in a specific organ. An ischemic process can cause pain and organ dysfunction.

ISCHEMIC HEART DISEASE. Insufficient blood supply to the heart muscle (myocardium).

ISCHEMIC STROKE. A form of stroke caused by a clot blocking the blood supply to the brain.

ISLET CELLS. Cells of the pancreas that produce and secrete insulin.

ISLETS OF LANGERHANS. Pancreatic cell clusters that make and secrete hormones such as insulin.

ISOENZYME. One of a group of enzymes that brings about the same reactions on the same chemicals, but are different in their physical properties.

ISOMETRIC EXERCISES. A mode of exercise where there is contraction of muscle fibers, yet there is no movement of the limb.

IU. International Unit. A measure of strength based on an accepted international standard for dosages of Vitamins A, D and E.

J

JAUNDICE. Hyperbilirubinemia, or too much bilirubin in the blood. Bilirubin will be deposited in the skin and the mucosal membranes. The whites of the eyes and the skin appear yellow.

JEJUNOSTOMY. Surgical creation of an opening to the middle portion of the small intestine (jejunum), through the abdominal wall.

JESUS PRAYER. A short prayer that started among Greek-speaking Christians in the fifth century as an aid to meditation. The believer may simply repeat the name of Jesus or the short phrase "Lord have mercy," synchronized with his or her heartbeat.

JET LAG. Disruption of the sleep-wake cycle due to travel across several time zones within one day.

JOINT. The point of connection between two bones that allows motion.

JUNIOR RESERVE OFFICERS' TRAINING CORPS (JROTC). A federal program in American high schools that teaches patriotism and prepares students for military careers.

K

KARMA. In Buddhism and Hinduism, the law of spiritual cause and effect; the notion that all of a person's actions actively create present and future experiences.

KERATOPLASTY. Surgical replacement (transplantation) of the cornea.

KIDNEY DISEASE. Any disorder which impairs the kidney's ability to remove waste and toxins from the body.

KIDNEYS. Pair of bean-shaped organs located below the ribs toward the middle of the back that clean the blood, regulate acid concentration and maintain water balance in the body by excreting urine.

KINESIOLOGY. The scientific study of the anatomy and mechanics of human body movement.

KIRTAN. The chanting or singing of sacred hymns, practiced by Hindus and Sikhs.

KNEE EXTENSION. The act of straightening the knee or kicking the leg out, as in kicking a ball.

KYPHOS. A bump that forms on the back.

KYPHOSIS. Presence of a concave rounded bump on the back or curvature of the back, also called hump back or hunchback. Some kyphosis of the thoracic spine and sacral area is normal.

L

LACTOSE. Disaccharide known as milk sugar.

LAPAROSCOPE. A viewing tube with a camera attached to its end that is inserted through the abdominal wall through small incisions.

LAPAROSCOPIC SURGERY. A minimally invasive surgery in which a camera and surgical instruments are inserted through a small incision.

LAPAROSCOPY. Examination of the contents of the abdomen through a thin, lighted tube passed through a small incision.

LARGE INTESTINE. The terminal part of the digestive system, site of water recycling, nutrient absorption, and waste processing located in the abdominal cavity. It consists of the caecum, the colon, and the rectum.

LARYNX. The voice box.

LAVAGE. Washing out.

LAW OF SIMILARS. The basic principle of homeopathic medicine that governs the selection of a specific remedy. It holds that a substance of natural origin that produces certain symptoms in a healthy person will cure those same symptoms in a sick person.

LAXATIVE. Any food, beverage, or medication that stimulates bowel movements or softens stool.

L-CYSTEINE. A sulfur-containing amino acid produced by enzymatic or acid hydrolysis of proteins. Supplements are used as antioxidant.

LDL CHOLESTEROL. Sometimes called bad cholesterol, low density lipid (LDL) cholesterol is found in the blood and can contribute to formation of plaque in the walls of blood vessels. Plaque in blood vessels may cause heart attack or stroke.

LEAD. Color coded wires that connect the electrode to the monitor cable.

LEG ULCERS. loss of skin on the leg or foot that takes more than six weeks to heal; Most leg ulcers are a symptom of diseases of the veins; other causes include arterial insufficiency, diabetes, and rheumatoid arthritis.

LENS (OR CRYSTALLINE LENS). The eye structure behind the iris and pupil that helps focus light on the retina.

LENS. Transparent, biconvex crystalline tissue that helps bring rays of light to a focus on the retina.

LESION. A possibly abnormal change or difference in a tissue or structure, such as the skin.

LESIONECTOMY. Removal of a lesion and surrounding tissue. The term is applied to brain tissue when trying to control seizures.

LEUKOCYTE. White blood cell.

LEWY BODY DEMENTIA. A form of dementia characterized by the formation of abnormal round bodies in regions of the brain involved in thinking and movement; often includes hallucinations.

L-HISTIDINE. An essential amino acid, $C_6H_9N_3O_2$, important for the growth and repair of tissues.

LICENSED PHARMACIST. A pharmacist who has completed the full program of education, and has passed a state licensing examination. Also termed "registered pharmacist.".

LICHEN PLANUS. A noncancerous, chronic itchy skin disease that causes small, flat purple plaques on wrists, forearm, ankles.

LIGAMENTS. Fibrous structures that provide an attachment on bone to bone, and provide stability to joint structures.

LIMITED SCLERODERMA. A subtype of systemic scleroderma with limited skin involvement. It is somestimes called the CREST form of scleroderma, after the initials of its five major symptoms.

LINDANE. A benzene compound that is used to kill body and pubic lice. Lindane works by being absorbed into the louse's central nervous system, causing seizures and death.

LIPID. Any organic compound that is greasy, insoluble in water, but soluble in alcohol. Fats, waxes, and oils are examples of lipids.

LIPODYSTROPHY. The medical term for redistribution of body fat in response to HAART, insulin injections in diabetics, or rare hereditary disorders.

LIPOMA. A usually benign tumor of fatty tissue.

LIPOPROTEIN. A complex molecule that consists of a protein membrane surrounding a core of lipids. Lipoproteins carry cholesterol and other lipids from the digestive tract to the liver and other body tissues. There are five major types of lipoproteins.

LIPOSHAVING. Liposhaving involves removing fat that lies closer to the skins surface by using a needle-like instrument that contains a sharp-edged shaving device.

LITHOTRIPSY. A nonsurgical technique for removing gallstones by breaking them apart with high-frequency sound waves.

LOBECTOMY. A surgical procedure that removes one lobe of the thyroid gland.

LOBULAR CARCINOMA-IN-SITU (LCIS). Breast cancer that is confined to the lobules or milk-producing glands.

LOCALIZED SCLERODERMA. Thickening of the skin from overproduction of collagen.

LONELINESS. An internal feeling of hollowness or emptiness combined with a sense of being cut off from or estranged from other people. It can affect people who share a household with others as well as those who live alone.

LONG-TERM CARE. Placement of client in a facility that provides nursing and basic needs care when client is no longer able to provide that care at home.

LONGEVITY. The length of an organism's lifespan.

LOOP ELECTROSURGICAL EXCISION PROCEDURE (LEEP). A procedure in which an electrical current is passed through a thin looped wire to slice off or destroy a piece of tissue.

LORDOSIS. Normal convex curve of the spine or an abnormal convex curve, usually of the lumbar spine.

LOTION. A liquid dosage form for external application, softer than a cream.

LOW-DENSITY LIPOPROTEIN (LDL). A type of lipoprotein that consists of about 50% cholesterol and is associated with an increased risk of coronary artery disease.

LOWER ESOPHAGEAL SPHINCTER (LES). A muscular ring at the base of the esophagus that keeps stomach contents from entering back into the esophagus.

LSIL. Low-grade squamous intraepithelial lesion; mild dysplasia; a Pap-test finding of early changes in the size and shape of squamous cells.

LUMBAR. Pertaining to the vertebrae in the lower back.

LUMBAR PUNCTURE. A diagnostic procedure in which a needle is inserted into the lower spine to withdraw a small amount of cerebrospinal fluid. This fluid is examined to assess trauma to the brain.

LUMBAR SPINE. The segment of the human spine above the pelvis that is involved in low back pain. There are five vertebrae, or bones, in the lumbar spine.

LUMBOSACRAL SPINE. The lower portion of the spine, including the sacrum and the coccyx.

LUMPECTOMY. Excision of a breast tumor and a limited amount of surrounding tissue.

LUPUS ERYTHEMATOSUS. A chronic autoimmune disease that affects the skin, joints, and certain internal organs.

LUTEINIZING HORMONE RELEASING HORMONE (LHRH) AGONIST. A substance that blocks the action of LHRH, a hormone that stimulates the production of testosterone (a male hormone) in men. Used to treat prostate cancers that require testosterone for growth.

LYME BORRELIOSIS. Another name for Lyme disease.

LYMPH. Clear fluid in body tissues that is produced by the lymph nodes and flows through lymphatic vessels into the bloodstream. It is an important part of the body's immune system.

LYMPH NODE. Small, compact structures lying along the channels that carry lymph, a yellowish fluid. Lymph nodes produce white blood cells (lymphocytes), which are important in forming antibodies that fight disease.

LYMPH-NODE DISSECTION. Removal of underarm lymph nodes to check for the spread of breast cancer.

LYMPHATIC SYSTEM. The tissues and organs, including the bone marrow, spleen, thymus, and lymph nodes, that produce and store cells that fight infection and disease.

LYMPHATIC. Pertaining to lymph or the lymphatic vessels that contain lymph.

LYMPHEDEMA. Accumulation of lymphatic fluid in the soft tissues of the arms, hands, and sometimes the breast area following lymph-node dissection.

LYMPHOCYTES. Type of white blood cells that are part of the immune system. The lymphocytes are composed of three main cell lines: B lymphocytes, T lymphocytes, and natural killer (NK) cells.

LYMPHOID. Tissues relating to the lymphatic system. A thin yellowish fluid, called lymph fluid, travels throughout the body. The lymphatic system helps control fluids in the body.

LYMPHOMA. Any of various usually malignant tumors that arise in the lymph nodes or in other lymphoid tissue.

M

MACRONUTRIENT. A nutrient such as protein, carbohydrate, or fat.

MACULA. The sensitive center of the retina that is responsible for detailed central vision.

MACULAE CERULEAE. Bluish or blue-grey skin eruptions often seen on the trunk or thighs of patients with pubic lice. The Latin words mean blue spots.

MAGICAL THINKING. Thinking that one's words or thoughts can affect the external world. An example would be the notion that being angry with someone will cause them to die.

MAGNETIC FIELD. The three-dimensional area surrounding a magnet, in which its force is active. During

MRI, the patient's body is permeated by the force field of a superconducting magnet.

MAGNETIC RESONANCE IMAGING (MRI). An imaging technique that uses a large circular magnet and radio waves to generate signals from atoms in the body. These signals are used to construct images of internal structures.

MAJOR DEPRESSIVE DISORDER. Five or more symptoms of depression lasting at least two weeks and interfering with daily life.

MAJOR DEPRESSIVE EPISODE. A period of prolonged sadness that interferes with daily life.

MALABSORPTION. Decreased ability to absorb nutrients through the body's normal absorption processes.

MALADAPTIVE. An inability or poor ability to adjust to change.

MALATHION. An insecticide that can be used in 1% powdered form to disinfect the clothes of patients with body lice.

MALEFICENCE. The act of intentionally doing harm or evil. Nonmaleficence is the principle of purposefully not doing harm.

MALIGNANT. A general term for cells and the tumors they form that can invade and destroy other tissues and organs.

MALIGNANT HYPERTHERMIA. A type of reaction (probably with a genetic basis) that can occur during general anesthesia in which the patient experiences a high fever, the muscles become rigid, and the heart rate and blood pressure fluctuate.

MALNOURISHMENT. Lack of adequate nutrition.

MALNUTRITION. Inadequate nutrition caused by either inadequate intakwe of one or more nutrients, or failure to absorb or process the nutrients.

MALPRACTICE. A doctor or lawyer's failure in his or her professional duties through ignorance, negligence, or criminal intent.

MALTOSE. Disaccharide known as malt sugar.

MAMMARY ARTERY. A chest wall artery that descends from the aorta and is commonly used for bypass grafts.

MAMMOGRAM. A set of x rays taken of the front and side of the breast used to help diagnose various breast abnormalities.

MANAGED CARE. Health plans that that coordinate a member's healthcare through a network of healthcare providers that participate in a specific plan, such as a health maintenance organization (HMO) or preferred provider organization (PPO).

MANIA. High, energetic, or irritable moods that interfere with daily life.

MANTOUX TEST. Another name for the PPD test.

MANTRA. A sacred word or formula repeated over and over to concentrate the mind.

MAO-B INHIBITORS. Inhibitors of the enzyme monoamine oxidase B. MAO-B helps break down dopamine; inhibiting it prolongs the action of dopamine in the brain. Selegiline is an MAO-B inhibitor.

MARFAN SYNDROME. An inherited condition that affects connective tissue throughout the body including weakening the connective tissue found in arteries.

MARGINS OF RESECTION. The area between the cancerous tumor and the edges of the removed tissue.

MARTIAL ARTS. Group of diverse activities originating from the ancient fighting techniques of the Orient.

MAST CELL. A cell found in connective tissue that releases substances such as heparin and histamine in response to injury or inflammation of bodily tissues.

MASTECTOMY. Surgical removal of part or all of the breast and possibly associated lymph nodes and muscle.

MASTOPEXY. Surgical procedure to lift up a breast; may be used on opposite breast to achieve symmetrical appearance with a reconstructed breast.

MATRIX. The tissue at the base of the nail, from which the nail grows.

MEASLES. An acute and highly contagious viral disease marked by distinct red spots followed by a rash that occurs primarily in children.

MEDICAID. The federally funded program in the United States for state-operated programs that provide medical assistance to permanently disabled patients and to low-income people. Medicaid is the medical assistance provided in Title XIX of the Social Security Act.

MEDICAL AGENT. A designated representative for the patient who, in advance, is legally empowered to carry out their wishes with respect to medial care.

MEDICAL DIRECTIVES. Legal documents that include a declaration of wishes pertaining to medical treatment (living will) and the stipulation of a proxy decision maker (power of attorney).

MEDICAL ETHICS. Moral standards that regulate the conduct of health care professionals.

MEDICAL SURROGATE. Another name for a medical agent or person legally designated to represent the patient with medical providers.

MEDICALLY NEEDY. A term that describes a group whose coverage is optional with the states because of high medical expenses. These persons meet Medicaid's category requirements (they are children or parents or elderly or disabled) but their income is too high to qual.

MEDICARE. The federally-funded national health insurance program, provided for by Title XVIII of the Social Security Act in the United States for all people over the age of 65.

MEDICARE PART A. Hospital insurance provided by Medicare, provided free to persons aged 65 and older.

MEDICARE PART B. Medical insurance provided by Medicare that requires recipients pay a monthly premium. Part B pays for some medical services Part A does not.

MEDITATION. A conscious spiritual discipline in which a person focuses attention on a specific word, phrase, or image in order to quiet the usual stream of thoughts, clearing the mind and thus relaxing the body.

MEDULLA OBLONGATA. The lowest section of the brainstem, located next to the spinal cord. The medulla is the site of important cardiac and respiratory regulatory centers.

MEDULLA. A structure in the brain stem that controls breathing, swallowing, and other vital functions.

MEGALOBLASTIC ANEMIA. An anemia in which immature red blood cells appear in the peripheral blood.

MEIBOMIAN GLAND. Oil-producing glands in the eyelids that open near the eyelid margins.

MELATONIN. A hormone that promotes sleep.

MENGHINI NEEDLE/JAMSHEDI NEEDLE. Special needles used to obtain a sample of liver tissue by aspiration.

MENIERE'S DISEASE. An abnormality of the inner ear that causes dizziness, ringing in the ears, and hearing loss.

MENINGITIS. Inflammation of the protective membranes covering the central nervous system, known collectively as the meninges. Meningitis may develop in response to a number of causes, most prominently bacteria, viruses and other infectious agents, but also physical i.

MENISCUS. Connective tissue that separates the bones of the knee.

MENOPAUSE. The time in a woman's life when menstrual periods permanently stop and end the female reproductive phase of life.

MERIDIANS. In traditional Chinese medicine, a network of pathways or channels that convey chi, or vital energy, through the body.

METABOLIC. Refers to the chemical processes of an organ or organism.

METABOLIC ACTIVITY. The sum of chemical processes occurring within the body that are necessary to maintain life.

METABOLIC BONE DISEASE. Weakening of bones due to a deficiency of certain minerals, specifically calcium.

METABOLISM. The biochemical processes that occur within any living organism and involve the buildup and breakdown of substances such as food, and the transformation of these substances into energy.

METALLOENZYME. An enzyme that contains a tightly bound metal ion, such as cobalt, copper, iron or zinc.

METAPHYSIS. The widened end of the shaft of a long tubular bone such as the femur.

METASTASIS. The spread of cancer cells from the primary site to distant parts of the body.

METASTASIZE. The spread of a disease, such as a cancer, from its original site to another part of the body.

METASTATIC CANCER. A cancer that has spread to an organ or tissue from a primary cancer located elsewhere in the body.

MICROANEURYSM. Small bulges or protrusions in the retinal blood vessels.

MICROCALCIFICATION. Tiny abnormal deposits of calcium salts in the breast that often indicate breast cancer.

MICROCIRCULATION. The passage of blood in the smallest blood vessels of the body, such as the capillaries in the hand and fingers.

MICROCYTIC ANEMIA. Any type of anemia in which red blood cells are of smaller than normal size.

MICRODISKETOMY. A disketomy using a microscope.

MICROLITER. Same as a cubic millimeter. One million microliters equals 1 liter, which equals about 1.06 quarts.

MICROMETASTASIS (PLURAL, MICROMETASTASES). A term sometimes used to describe malignant tumor cells circulating in the blood or other metastases too small to be detected by a standard clinical examination.

MICRONUTRIENT. A vitamin or mineral that the body must obtain from outside sources. Micronutrients are essential to the body in small amounts because they are either components of enzymes or act as coenzymes in managing chemical reactions.

MICROORGANISM. An organism that can be seen only through a microscope. Microorganisms include bacteria, protozoa, algae, and fungi.

MICROWELL PLATE. A rectangular disposable culture dish constructed with an array of small depressions used to carry out reactions.

MIDDLE EAR. The small cavity between the eardrum and the oval window that houses the three tiny bones of hearing.

MIGRAINE. A condition that is marked by recurrent usually one-sided severe headache often accompanied by nausea and vomiting and followed by sleep.

MIGRAINE NEURALGIA. A variant of migraine pain, also called cluster headache, in which severe attacks of pain affect the eye and forehead on one side of the face.

MILIARY TUBERCULOSIS. The form of TB in which the bacillus spreads through all body tissues and organs, producing many thousands of tiny tubercular lesions. Miliary TB is often fatal unless promptly treated.

MINERAL. An inorganic substance found in the earth that is necessary in small quantities for the body to maintain a health. Examples: zinc, copper, iron.

MINERALIZATION. The process of adding minerals to the bone matrix.

MISO. A fermented paste made from soybeans, salt, and rice or barley, used to flavor soups and sauces in Oriental cooking.

MITE. An insect parasite belonging to the order Acarina. The organism that causes scabies is a mite.

MITOCHONDRION. An organelle in the cytoplasm of cells that functions in energy production.

MITRAL VALVE LEAFLETS. The mitral valve is made up of two valve leaflets (anteromedial leaflet and the posterolateral leaflet) and a ring around the valve, known as the mitral valve annulus. The orientation of the two leaflets resembles a bishop's miter, hence its name.

MIXED EPISODE. A period in which symptoms of both mania and depression are present.

MIXED HEARING LOSS. A combination of conductive and sensorineural hearing loss.

MODALITIES (SINGULAR: MODALITY). Factors that cause a patient's symptoms to improve or worsen; or, passive physical therapies that are done to the patient rather than requiring their active involvement.; or, methods of treatment or approaches to therapy.

MODERATION. Limiting one's drinking to what is considered a safe amount for one's age and sex.

MOHS' MICROGRAPHIC SURGERY. A surgical technique in which successive rings of skin tissue are removed and examined under a microscope to ensure that no cancer is left.

MOLD. Parasitic, microscopic fungus with spores that float in the air like pollen.

MOLE. A benign group of pigmented cells on the surface of the skin. A mole is usually dark and is sometimes raised.

MONOAMINE OXIDASE INHIBITOR (MAOI). An older class of antidepressants.

MONOCLONAL. Pertaining to cells or cellular products that are derived from a single cell; a monoclonal antibody is an immunoglobulin directed against a specific epitope of an antigen, and isolated from a culture of identical cells grown from a single clone.

MONOCLONAL ANTIBODY. A type of protein made in the laboratory that can locate and adhere to substances in the body and on the surface of cancer cells.

MONOCLONAL GAMMOPATHY OF UNDETERMINED SIGNIFICANCE (MGUS). Common condition in which M-protein is present but there are no tumors or other symptoms of disease.

MONOUNSATURATED FAT. A non-animal fat that contains one fatty acid.

MORBID OBESITY. A term used to describe individuals 100 lb (45 kg) or more than 50% overweight and/or who have a body mass index above 40.

MORBIDITY. The relative incidence of sickness and injury occurring among a given group of people.

MORPHEA. The most common form of localized scleroderma.

MOTHER TINCTURE. The first stage in the preparation of a homeopathic remedy, made by soaking a plant, animal, or mineral product in a solution of alcohol.

MOTION ANALYSIS. Use of an instrumented system to record whole body and joint movement for later analysis.

MOTOR. Of or pertaining to motion, the body apparatus involved in movement, or the brain functions that direct purposeful activity.

MOTOR NEURON. A neuron that conveys impulses for muscle contraction or glandular secretion.

MOTOR NEURON DISEASE. Group of progressive neurological disorders that destroy motor neurones, the cells that control voluntary muscle activity such as speaking, walking, breathing, and swallowing.

MOURNING. The process of adjusting to a death or other loss. Mourning is often shaped or affected by the bereaved person's religious or cultural background.

MOVEMENT DISORDERS. Group of diseases and syndromes affecting the ability to produce and control movement.

MOXIBUSTION. A technique in traditional Chinese medicine that involves burning a *moxa*, or cone of dried wormwood leaves, close to the skin to relieve pain.

M-PROTEIN. Monoclonal or myeloma protein; paraprotein; abnormal antibody found in large amounts in the blood and urine of individuals with multiple myeloma.

MRI. Magnetic resonance imaging, a test that uses magnets to film parts of the body.

MSW. Master's degree in social work.

MUCOUS MEMBRANE. Also called mucosa, the thin, moist tissue lining of various organs in the body.

MULTICENTRIC. A type of cancer that appears at several different sites in the patient's body simultaneously.

MULTIPLE SCLEROSIS. A progressive disorder of the central nervous system in which scattered patches of the protective sheath covering the nerves is destroyed. The disease, which causes progressive paralysis, is marked by periods of exacerbation and remission.

MUMPS. An acute and highly contagious viral illness that usually occurs in childhood.

MUSCULOSKELETAL. Pertains to the muscular and skeletal systems, and the relationship between the two.

MUTATION. A change in the genetic makeup of a cell that may occur spontaneously or be environmentally induced.

MYASTHENIA GRAVIS. A chronic disease with symptoms that include muscle weakness and sometimes paralysis.

MYCOBACTERIA. A group of bacteria that includes *Mycobacterium tuberculosis*, the bacterium that causes tuberculosis, and other forms that cause related illnesses.

MYCOPLASMA PNEUMONIA. Also called Eaton-agent pneumonia, primary atypical pneumonia, or walking pneumonia, a contagious lung infection caused by the bacterium *Mycoplasma pneumoniae*.

MYCOSIS. An inflammatory condition caused by a fungus. Pl.: mycoses.

MYCOTIC DISEASE. Diseases caused by fungi.

MYCOTOXINS. A diverse class of poisonous compounds produced by certain mushrooms and other fungi.

MYELIN SHEATH. A fatty white matter surrounding nerves throughout the body that protects them and helps conduct impulses more quickly.

MYELIN. The insulation covering nerve cells. Demyelinating disease causes a breakdown of myelin.

MYELOGRAM. A test in which a dye is injected into the spinal column and then the spinal column is x-rayed. This test can show bone spurs, tumors, and herniated (bulging or damaged) discs between the vertebrae.

MYELOGRAPHY. An x-ray process that uses a dye or contrast medium injected into the space around the spine.

MYELOMA (MULTIPLE MYELOMA). A tumor of plasma cells that originates in bone marrow and usually spreads to more than one bone.

MYELOPATHY. A disorder in which the tissue of the spinal cord is diseased or damaged.

MYELOPROLIFERATIVE DISORDER. A disease in which too many blood cells are made in the bone marrow.

MYOCARDIAL INFARCTION. The medical, technical term for heart attack. Myocardial means heart muscle and infarction means death of tissue from lack of oxygen.

MYOCARDIAL ISCHEMIA. Insufficient blood flow to part of the heart.

MYOCARDIUM. The muscular wall of the heart located between the inner endocardial layer and the outer epicardial layer.

MYOCLONIC SEIZURES. Brief, involuntary spasms of the tongue or muscles of the face, arms, or legs.

MYOCLONUS. Involuntary contractions of a muscle or group of muscles.

MYOFASCIAL. The fibrous tissue that encloses and separates layers of muscles.

MYONECROSIS. The destruction or death of muscle tissue.

N

NAIL BED. The layer of tissue underneath the nail.

NARCAN. A drug that reverses the effects of narcotics.

NARCOTIC. A drug that reduces pain and causing a stupifying effect.

NASAL CANNULA. A piece of flexible plastic tubing with two small clamps that fit into the nostrils and provide supplemental oxygen flow.

NASOPHARYNX. The space above the roof of the mouth (soft palate) that opens into the nasal cavity and joins with the tympanic cavity behind the ear drum.

NASW. National Association of Social Workers.

NATURAL IMMUNITY. Protection against a disease that results when exposure to a real disease organism triggers the immune system to produce antibodies to that disease.

NATURALLY OCCURRING RETIREMENT COMMUNITY (NORC). A community or neighborhood where the residents have grown older as neighbors.

NATUROPATHIC PHYSICIAN. In the United States and Canada, a primary healthcare provider who holds the degree of Doctor of Naturopathic Medicine from an accredited institution, has passed the national licensing examination (NPLEX), and has been licensed by the state or province.

NATUROPATHY. An alternative approach to healing that avoids surgery and prescription medications, relying instead on natural agents and therapeutic techniques.

NEBULIZER. A device that turns liquid forms of medicine into a fine spray that can be inhaled.

NECROSIS. Tissue destruction or death of tissue cells that is caused by injury, infection, or disease.

NECROTIZING FASCIITIS. An infection of the deeper layers of skin and connective tissue caused by bacteria, most commonly *S. pyogenes*. Necrotizing fasciitis is sometimes called flesh-eating bacteria disease.

NEEDLE BIOPSY. The removal of body tissue for examination from a surface or organ. Needle biopsy uses a long needle and syringe device to aspirate (remove by suction) a sample of the target tissue.

NEEDLE EMG. During an EMG test, a fine needle is inserted into the muscle to be tested. Recordings are made while the muscle is at rest, and then during the contraction to test muscle response.

NEEDS ASSESSMENT. Social worker conducts an interview with client and family, reviews charts, interviews other health workers to determine what specific services are required by client.

NEGATIVE INSPIRATORY FRACTION. The amount of force used to draw air into the lungs during maximal inspiration.

NEOPLASIA. Tumor formation.

NEOPLASM. The growth of tissue that does not serve any function in the body, also called a tumor.

NEPHELOMETRY. A method for studying the density of suspended particles in a liquid sample by measuring the amount of light scattered by the particles.

NEPHRECTOMY. A medical procedure in which the kidney is surgically removed.

NEPHRITIS. Inflammation of the kidneys.

NEPHRON. Tube within the kidney that processes filtrate from the blood, reclaiming some substances and creating urine.

NEPHROPATHY. Kidney disease or damage.

NEPHROTIC SYNDROME. Characterized by protein loss in the urine, low protein levels in the blood, and fluid retention.

NERVE CONDUCTION VELOCITY (NCV) TEST. A test that measures the time it takes a nerve impulse to travel a specific distance over the nerve after electronic stimulation.

NERVOUS SYSTEM. The system of cells, tissues and organs that regulates the body's responses to internal and external stimuli.

NEURODEGENERATION. Progressive loss of structure or function of neurons, including death of neurons.

NEURODEGENERATIVE DISEASE. Disorder caused by the deterioration of nerve cells called neurons . Changes in these cells cause them to function abnormally, eventually bringing about their death.

NEURODERMATITIS. An itchy skin disease (also called lichen simplex chronicus) found in nervous, anxious people.

NEUROFIBRILLARY TANGLES. Abnormal structures composed of twisted masses of protein fibers within nerve cells, found in the brains of persons with Alzheimer's disease.

NEUROHORMONE. A chemical which goes from one nerve cell to another, causing an action by the second cell.

NEUROLEPTIC. Synonym for antipsychotic, a major tranquilizer.

NEUROLOGICAL. Referring to the structure and function of the nervous system.

NEUROLOGICAL DEFICIT. Nervous system or neuromuscular disorders or symptoms.

NEUROLOGICAL DISEASE. Disease of the nervous system.

NEUROLOGICAL DISORDER. Disturbance in structure or function of the nervous system resulting from developmental abnormality, disease, injury, or toxin.

NEUROLOGICAL EXAM. A physical examination that focuses on the patient's nerves, reflexes, motor and sensory functions, and muscle strength and tone.

NEUROMUSCULAR. Refers to the relationship between nerves and muscles. Neuromuscular disorders or injuries involve both nerves and muscles.

NEURON. A small component of the nervous system composed of a nerve cell body with branch-like processes called dendrites and an axon that conducts nerve impulses. Also referred to as a neurocyte.

NEUROPATHIC PAIN. Pain initiated or caused by a primary lesion or dysfunction in the nervous system.

NEUROPATHY. An abnormality of the nerves outside the brain and spinal cord.

NEUROTRANSMITTER. One of a group of chemicals secreted by a nerve cell (neuron) to carry a chemical message to another nerve cell, often as a way of transmitting a nerve impulse. Examples of neurotransmitters include acetylcholine, dopamine, serotonin, and norepinephrine.

NEUROVASCULAR. Pertaining to the function of nerves and blood vessels.

NEW AGE. A general term for a group of spiritual movements that emerged in the 1970s and emphasized self-exploration, expansion of consciousness, and an interest in mystical or occult teachings.

NICOTINE. The addictive ingredient of tobacco, it acts on the nervous system and is both stimulating and calming. It is also poisonous and an oily alkaloid.

NICOTINE REPLACEMENT THERAPY. A method of weaning a smoker away from both nicotine and the oral fixation that accompanies a smoking habit by giving the smoker smaller and smaller doses of nicotine in the form of a patch or gum.

N-METHYL-D-ASPARTATE. NMDA; a brain chemical that binds to some glutamate receptors on neurons.

NOCICEPTOR. A nerve organ in the skin, muscles, or internal organs that receives and transmits painful stimuli to the central nervous system.

NOCTURIA. Excessive urination at night.

NOCTURNAL. Occurring at night.

NODULE. A swelling or knob that may form on a tendon and make it difficult to slide smoothly through its sheath.

NON-PHARMACOLOGICAL TREATMENT. Treatments that does not rely on medication to achieve its effect.

NONSTEROIDAL ANTI-INFLAMMATORY DRUG (NSAID). Medication that does not contain cortisone used to reduce the symptoms of the pain and inflammation of arthritis.

NOREPINEPHRINE. A hormone released by nerve cells and the adrenal medulla that causes constriction of blood vessels.

NORMAL WEIGHT. A Body Mass Index less than 25.0.

NOROVIRUS. A type of virus that can cause food poisoning and acute gastroenteritis with stomach pain, diarrhea, and vomiting in humans.

NSAIDS. Non-steroidal anti-inflammatory drugs such as aspirin, ibuprofen, and naproxen.

NUCLEAR FAMILY. A family unit consisting of a married couple and their children. It is also known as a conjugal family or immediate family.

NUCLEAR MEDICINE. A subspecialty of radiology that uses small amounts of radioactive material attached to drugs for the purpose of diagnosing or treating certain medical conditions.

NUCLEUS. A specialized spherical structure, present in most living eukaryotic cells and enclosed in a membrane, that is the center for metabolism of DNA and RNA.

NURSE PRACTITIONER. An advanced practice nurse delivering front-line primary and acute care.

NURSING CARE FACILITY. A residential facility for persons with chronic illness or disability, particularly older people who have mobility and eating problems; Also called a convalescent home, long-term care facility, or nursing home.

NUTRACEUTICAL. A food or food ingredient that is thought to provide medical or health benefits. Glucosamine preparations are classified as nutraceuticals.

NUTRIENT. A food substance that provides energy or is necessary for growth and repair. Examples of nutrients are vitamins, minerals, carbohydrates, fats, and proteins.

NUTRITION. The science of food and the nutrients and other substances contained in food: their action, interaction, and balance in relation to health and disease and the processes by which the person ingests, digests, absorbs, transports, utilizes and excretes food.

NUTRITIONAL SUPPLEMENT. Any capsule, pill, powder, gel tab, extract, or liquid that is orally ingested and not classified as a drug.

NUTRITIONIST. A general term for a person with specialized education or on-the-job training in diet and nutrition, who may or may not be licensed or registered with a professional organization in the field.

O

OBSTRUCTIVE SLEEP APNEA (OSA). A potentially life-threatening condition characterized by episodes of breathing cessation during sleep alternating with snoring or disordered breathing. Low levels of oxygen in the blood of patients with OSA may eventually cause heart problems or stroke.

OCCIPITAL NEURALGIA. Pain on one side of the back of the head caused by entrapment or pinching of an occipital nerve.

OCCULT BLOOD. Presence of blood that cannot be seen with the naked eye.

OCCUPATIONAL THERAPY. Therapy used to learn or relearn how to do everyday activities that may have been impaired due to illness or injury. Therapists may introduce assistive devices and help modify the home to make it safe and easy to maneuver.

OCULAR ROSACEA. Rosacea is a disorder that causes the face to flush and red rash-like breakouts on the skin. Ocular rosacea causes the eyes to become red, irritated, and sometimes painful.

ODYNOPHAGIA. The medical term for painful swallowing. It may be present with or without dysphagia.

OFF-LABEL USE. Use of a drug in the United States to treat a condition other than one for which the drug was approved by the U.S. Food and Drug Administration (FDA).

OINTMENT. A semi-solid dosage form for external application, may be greasy but has a longer duration of action than other semi-solids.

OLIGOCLONAL BANDS. Specific gamma globulin proteins that are increased in 90% of persons with MS.

OMBUDSMAN. A patient representative who investigates patient complaints and problems related to hospital service or treatment. He or she may act as a mediator between the patient, the family, and the hospital.

OMEGA-3 FATTY ACIDS. Substances found in fish and some plant/nut oils that are believed to have multiple health benefits.

ONCOGENE. Any gene that is a factor in triggering the development of cancer. Oncogenes are mutated forms of proto-oncogenes, which are genes that promote the normal process of cell growth and division.

ONCOLOGIST. A physician who specializes in cancer treatment.

ONYCHOLYSIS. The separation of a nail from its underlying bed. Onycholysis is a common symptom of candidal infections of the nail or of exposure to harsh chemicals and detergents.

ONYCHOMYCOSIS. Medical term for nail fungus.

OPAQUE. Impenetrable by light, neither transparent nor translucent, not reflecting light.

OPHTHALMIC SOLUTIONS. Sterile solutions for instillation in the eye.

OPHTHALMOLOGIST. A doctor who specializes in diagnosing and treating eye disorders.

OPHTHALMOSCOPE. An specialized lighted instrument used to view the interior of the eye.

OPIATE. A drug used to treat pain. It contains opium or a substance made from opium (such as morphine).

OPIOID. Any morphine-like synthetic narcotic that produces the same effects as drugs derived from the opium poppy (opiates), such as pain relief, sedation, constipation and respiratory depression.

OPTOMETRIST. A healthcare professional licensed to perform routine eye exams, prescribe corrective lenses, diagnose disorders of the eye and treat or refer for treatment certain disorders.

ORAL CANCER. Abnormal or cancerous growths in the mouth. It may occur any where in the mouth including the tongue and gums.

ORAL HYGIENE. Keeping the mouth, tongue, teeth, and gums clean to prevent disease and promote a healthy mouth.

ORCHIECTOMY. Surgical removal of the testes that eliminates the production of testosterone to treat prostate cancer.

ORGASMIC DISORDER. The impairment of the ability to reach sexual climax.

ORIENTATION. The ability of individuals to sense their own physical presence in a specific space or environment.

OROPHARYNGEAL. Pertaining to the oropharynx, the area of the head and neck that includes the tonsils, soft palate, back of the throat, and the back one-third of the tongue.

OROPHARYNX. The part of the throat that is located below the soft palate and above the larynx.

ORTHOPAEDICS. The branch of surgery that treats deformities or disorders affecting the musculoskeletal system.

ORTHOPEDIC. Related to the musculoskeletal system, including the bones, joints, muscles, ligaments, and tendons.

ORTHOPEDIC SURGEON. A doctor who specializes in the treatment, including surgery, of bones, joints, and soft tissues such as ligaments, tendons, and muscles.

ORTHOSIS. An external device, such as a splint or a brace, that prevents or assists movement.

ORTHOSTATIC HYPOTENSION. Low blood pressure which occurs when the patient stands up. This can be the result of drugs which dilate blood vessels so that blood drains from the head when moving from a recumbent position to a standing position. It often causes dizziness.

ORTHOSTATIC. A term that describes standing erect. Orthostatic hypotension is low blood pressure that occurs in some people on standing up.

ORTHOTICS. Mechanical devices that assist function, such as inserts put into shoes that correct muscles, joints, or skeletal parts.

OSA (OBSTRUCTED SLEEP APNEA). One type of sleep apnea that may be caused by obesity or an obstruction in the mouth or nose that blocks the airway.

OSMOLALITY. A measure of the solute-to-solvent concentration of a solution.

OSTEOARTHRITIS. Degenerative joint disease that affects the hips, knees, or spine. Pain occurs after exercise and the joints can become stiff and swell. This common type of arthritis occurs in 80% of people over 50.

OSTEOBLAST. Bone-forming cell.

OSTEOCLAST. Cell that absorbs bone.

OSTEOCYTES. A branched cell embedded in the matrix of bone tissue.

OSTEOGENESIS. The process of bone formation.

OSTEOID SYNTHESIS. The process of producing osteoid matter.

OSTEOID. Uncalcified bone matrix, the product of osteoblasts.

OSTEOLYSIS. Dissolution and loss of bone resulting from inflammation caused by particles of polyethylene debris from a prosthesis.

OSTEOLYTIC LESION. Soft spot or hole in bone caused by cancer cells.

OSTEOMALACIA. Softening of bone, particularly bone weakened by demineralization (loss of mineral) and most notably by the depletion of calcium from bone. Osteomalacia may be caused by poor dietary intake or poor absorption of calcium and other minerals.

OSTEOPATHIC MANIPULATIVE MEDICINE (OMM). A type of manual therapy used to improve the patient's postural balance and the functioning of his or her bones, joints, surrounding soft tissues, and muscles.

OSTEOPENIA. Mild thinning of the bone mass, but not as severe as osteoporosis. Osteopenia results when the formation of bone is not enough to offset normal bone loss. Osteopenia is generally considered the first step to osteoporosis.

OSTEOPHYTE. Also referred to as bone spur, it is an outgrowth or ridge that forms on a bone.

OSTEOPOROSIS. A condition found in older individuals in which bones decrease in density and become fragile and more likely to break. It can be caused by lack of vitamin D and/or calcium in the diet.

OSTEOTOMY. A surgical alternative to a hip prosthesis, in which the surgeon cuts through the pelvis or femur in order to realign the hip.

OSTOMY. A surgical procedure that creates an artificial opening in the body for the passage of urine or feces.

OTORHINOLARYNGOLOGIST. A physician who specializes in diseases of the ear, nose, and throat.

OTOSCLEROSIS. Changes in the bones of the ear (stapes) that result in their stiffness and immobility, leading to progressive deafness.

OTOSCOPE. A hand-held instrument with a tiny light and a funnel-shaped attachment called an ear speculum, which is used to examine the ear canal and eardrum.

OUTBREAK. Classification used in epidemiology to describe a small, localized group of people infected with a disease.

OVAL WINDOW. A tiny opening at the entrance to the inner ear.

OVARIES. Small organs beside the uterus that produce eggs and the female hormones estrogen and progesterone.

OVERHYDRATION. An excess of body water that results when water intake exceeds output.

OVERWEIGHT. Body Mass Index between 25.0 and 30.0.

OVULATION. The monthly release of an egg from the ovary.

OXIDATIVE STRESS. Accumulation in the body of destructive molecules such as free radicals that can lead to cell death.

OXIMETRY. Measuring the degree of oxygen saturation of circulating blood.

OXYGENATION. To supply with oxygen.

OZONE. A form of oxygen with three atoms in its molecule (O_3), produced by an electric spark or ultraviolet light passing through air or oxygen. A layer of ozone about 15 mi (24 km) above Earth's surface helps protect living things.

P

PACU. The postanesthesia care unit, where the patient is cared for after surgery.

PAGET'S DISEASE. A condition that causes enlarged and deformed bones.

PAIN. An unpleasant sensation that can range from mild, localized discomfort to agony.

PAIN MEDICINE. The medical specialty concerned with the prevention, evaluation, diagnosis, treatment, and rehabilitation of painful disorders.

PAIN RECEPTORS. Free nerve endings of groups of nervous fibers abundantly distributed in the superficial layers of the skin and in some deeper tissues of the body.

PAINFUL INTERCOURSE (DYSPAREUNIA). Generally thought of as a female dysfunction but also affects males. Pain can occur anywhere.

PALATE. The roof of the mouth.

PALLIATION. Easing the pain of disease when cure is impossible.

PALLIATIVE. Treatment that is given to relieve symptoms rather than to cure disease.

PALPITATION. Rapid, forceful, throbbing, or fluttering heartbeat.

PANCREAS. A gland located near the liver, the pancreas produces enzymes and fluids that help to breakdown food. It also produces the hormone insulin that the body must have to utilize sugar (glucose).

PANCREATECTOMY. Partial or total surgical removal of the pancreas.

PANCREATIC CANCER. Abnormal cell growth within the pancreas, the organ that produces insulin and other necessary hormones.

PANCREATITIS. Inflammation of the pancreas.

PANDEMIC. An epidemic (a sudden outbreak) that becomes very widespread and affects a whole region, a continent, or the world.

PANIC ATTACK. An episode of intense fear, abrupt in onset, lasting for several minutes, and accompanied by physical symptoms and/or temporary cognitive disturbances. Panic attacks may be unexpected, or they may be cued.

PANIC DISORDER. A disorder in which people have sudden and intense attacks of anxiety in certain situations. Symptoms such as shortness of breath, sweating, dizziness, chest pain, and extreme fear often accompany the attacks.

PANNUS. Overgrowth of connective tissue on the articular surface of a joint.

PANTON-VALENTINE LEUKOCIDIN (PVL). A toxin produced by a virus integrated into the genetic material of *S. aureus* that increases the virulence of the bacterium.

PAP SMEAR. The common term for the Papanicolaou test, a simple smear method of examining stained cells to detect cancer of the cervix.

PAP TEST. Pap smear; examination of cervical cells for the early detection of cancer.

PAPAIN. An enzyme derived from papaya used for skin exfoliation.

PARALYSIS. Loss of the ability to move one or more parts of the body.

PARAPHERNALIA. Articles of equipment or accessory items.

PARAPHRENIA. A group of mental disorders characterized by paranoia; includes paranoid schizophrenia.

PARAPROTEIN. M-protein; abnormal immunoglobulin produced in multiple myeloma.

PARATHYROID GLANDS. Two oval-shaped glands located behind the thyroid gland in the neck and responsible for regulating calcium levels in the blood.

PARENTERAL NUTRITION. The administration of liquid nutrition through an intravenous catheter placed in the patient's vein.

PARENTERAL. Not in or through the digestive system. Parenteral nutrition is given through the veins of the circulatory system, rather than through the digestive system.

PARIETAL PLEURAE. The membrane that surrounds each lung.

PARKINSON'S DISEASE. A neurological disorder caused by deficiency of dopamine, a neurotransmitter, that is a chemical that assists in transmitting messages between the nerves within the brain. It is characterized by muscle tremor or palsy and rigid movements.

PARKINSONISM. A group of neurological conditions that resemble Parkinson's disease; caused by the deficiency or blockage of dopamine by drugs, toxins, or disease.

PARONYCHIA. Inflammation of the folds of skin that surround a nail.

PAROXETINE HYDROCHLORIDE. Paxil; a SSRI that is used to treat mental depression, OCD, and various other disorders.

PARTIAL PARENTERAL NUTRITION (PPN). A solution, containing some essentail nutrients, is injected into a vein to supplement other means of nutrition, usually a partially normal diet of food.

PASSIVE IMMUNITY. Protection against a disease that is provided when a person is given antibodies to a disease rather than producing them through his or her own immune system.

PASSIVE MOVEMENT. Movement that occurs under the power of an outside source such as a clinician. There is no voluntary muscular contraction by the individual who is being passively moved.

PATCH TEST (SCRATCH TEST). Test in which different antigens (substances that cause an allergic reaction) are introduced into a patient's skin via a needle prick or scratch and then observed for evidence of an allergic reaction to one or more of them.

PATELLA. The knee cap.

PATELLAR TENDON. A tendon in the knee.

PATENCY. The quality or state of being open or unobstructed.

PATHOGEN. A disease-causing microorganism.

PATHOLOGIC FRACTURE. A fracture that occurs spontaneously at a weakened area of bone.

PATHOLOGICAL. Arising from or caused by a disease.

PATHOLOGIST. A medical doctor who specializes in identification and diagnosis of disease by studying cells and tissues under a microscope.

PATIENT-CONTROLLED ANALGESIA (PCA). An approach to pain management that allows the patient to control the timing of intravenous doses of analgesic drugs.

PATIENT-CONTROLLED ANALGESIA PUMP. A pump that the patient uses to self-administer medication to control pain.

PATIENT SELF-DETERMINATION ACT (PSDA). Federal law that ensures that medical providers offer the option of medical directives to patients and include documents in their medical records.

PAYOR. One who pays a medical claim. A third party payor is an entity other than the patient, such as the insurance company.

PBP. Progressive Bulbar Palsy.

PEDICLE FLAP. Also called an attached flap; a section of tissue, with its blood supply intact, which is maneuvered to another part of the body.

PEDICULOSIS (PLURAL, PEDICULOSES). The medical term for infestation with lice.

PELVIC EXENTERATION. Surgical removal of the uterus, cervix, ovaries, nearby lymph nodes, lower colon, rectum, and bladder.

PELVIC FLOOR MUSCLES. Muscles at the base of the pelvis that support the bladder and rectum, and the uterus and vagina in women.

PELVIS. A basin-shaped group of bones that form the pelvic girdle.

PENILE IMPLANT. Surgical insertion of an artificial device in the penis to produce an erection. Implantation of rigid or semi-rigid bars produces a permanent erection; use of an inflatable device allows the man to produce an erection at will.

PENIS. The male organ used for urination and sex.

PEPTIC. Induced by or associated with the action of digestive secretions.

PEPTIC ULCER. A hole in the lining of the stomach, duodenum, or esophagus.

PERCUTANEOUS BIOPSY. A biopsy in which the needle is inserted and the sample removed through the skin.

PERICARDIOCENTESIS. Pericardiocentesis is a procedure used to test for viruses, bacteria, and fungus. The physician puts a small tube through the skin, directly into the pericardial sac, and withdraws fluid. The fluid then is tested for viruses, bacteria, and fungus.

PERICARDITIS. Inflammation of the sac around the heart.

PERICARDIUM. The pericardium is the thin, sac-like membrane that surrounds the heart. It has two layers: the serous pericardium and the fibrous pericardium.

PERINEAL. Pertaining to the area known as the perineum, between the anus and the vulva in women, and between the anus and scrotum in the men.

PERIODONTAL DISEASE. Infection of the gums and tissue surrounding the teeth.

PERIODONTITIS. A gum disease that destroys the structures supporting the teeth, including gums, ligaments, and bone.

PERIOSTAL. A bruise on the bone.

PERIPHERAL ARTERIAL DISEASE. A disease caused by the narrowing or obstruction of the iliac or femoral arteries that supply the flow of blood to the legs.

PERIPHERAL NERVES. Nerves that carry information to and from the spinal cord.

PERIPHERAL NERVOUS SYSTEM. The part of the nervous system that is outside the brain and spinal cord. Sensory, motor, and autonomic nerves are included.

PERIPHERAL VASCULAR DISEASE. Hardening of the arteries, caused by a buildup of plaque.

PERIPHERAL VISION. The seeing of objects displaced from the primary line of site and outside of the central visual field.

PERIPHERY. The part of the body away from the center, the arms and legs.

PERISTALSIS. Wave-like movements of the intestine that propel food and waste toward the colon and rectum for elimination.

PERITONEUM. The lining of the abdominal cavity.

PERMEABLE. Capable of allowing substances to pass through.

PERMETHRIN. A medication used to rid the scalp of head lice. Permethrin works by paralyzing the lice, so that they cannot feed after hatching within the 24 hours required for survival.

PEROXIDE. A bleaching agent that is a compound consisting of two atoms of oxygen connected by a single bond.

PERSONAL CARE ATTENDANT. An employee hired either through a healthcare facility, home-care agency, or private agency to assist a patient in performing ADLs.

PETECHIAE. Small purple spots on the skin caused by leakage of blood from tiny blood vessels; a sign of underlying blood or coagulation disorders.

PETIT-MAL SEIZURE. Absence seizure.

PETRI DISH. Shallow, round transparent dish, with a lid, used for growing cultures in a laboratory.

PEYRONIE'S DISEASE. A disease which causes a hardening of the corpora cavernosa, the erectile tissue of the penis. The penis may become misshapen and/or curved as a result.

PH. A measure of acidity; technically, a measure of hydrogen ion concentration.

PHARMACODYNAMICS. The way a drug acts on tissues and cells in the body.

PHARMACOKINETICS. The route and rate at which a drug gets in and out of the body.

PHARMACOLOGICALLY PARALYZED. Short-term paralysis induced by medications for a therapeutic purpose.

PHARMACOLOGY. The study of the actions and uses of drugs.

PHENOL-SOLUBLE MODULIN (PSM). A protein toxin produced by community-acquired strains of MRSA that destroys white blood cells.

PHENYLKETONURIA (PKU). A genetic disorder in which the body lacks an important enzyme. If untreated, the disorder can lead to brain damage and mental retardation.

PHLEBITIS. An inflammation of a vein.

PHLEBOTOMIST. A health professional trained to draw blood for purposes of diagnosis and treatment.

PHLEBOTOMY. The taking of blood from the body through an incision in the vein, usually in the treatment of disease.

PHOBIA. An intense, abnormal, or illogical fear of something specific, such as heights or open spaces.

PHOROPTER. The instrument used to measure refractive status of the eyes. It contains many lenses which are then changed in front of the eyes while the patient is looking at an eye chart.

PHOSPHOLIPID. Any of a group of fatty biomolecules composed of phosphoric esters.

PHOTOCOAGULATION. The use of light from a laser to block or destroy broken blood vessels in the eye.

PHYSIATRIST. A physician who specializes in physical medicine and rehabilitation.

PHYSICAL THERAPY. Use of physical techniques such as manual manipulation, exercise, and massage to restore or improve body function after injury or illness.

PHYSIOTHERAPIST. An alternate term for physical therapist.

PHYTOCHEMICALS. A nonnutritive bioactive plant substance, such as a flavonoid or carotenoid, considered to have a beneficial effect on human health.

PILATES. A form of exercise that combines yoga, dance, and isometric exercises.

PILGRIMAGE. A long journey to a place regarded as holy by one's faith tradition, usually in search of healing, spiritual purification, or enlightenment.

PIRIFORMIS. A muscle in the pelvic area near the sciatic nerve.

PITUITARY GLAND. The "master gland" at the base of the brain that secretes a number of hormones responsible for growth, reproduction, and other activities. Pituitary hormones stimulate the ovaries to release estrogen and progesterone.

PLACEBO. A substance that has no therapeutic effect. A placebo may be prescribed for the psychological benefit of the patient, or it may be used as a control in testing new drugs.

PLACEBO EFFECT. Placebo effect occurs when a treatment or medication with no known therapeutic value (a placebo) is administered to a patient, and the patient's symptoms improve. The patient believes and expects that the treatment is going to work, so it does.

PLAGUE. A highly infectious disease that can be fatal if not treated promptly. The bacteria that cause plague mainly infect rats, mice, squirrels, and other wild rodents. The disease is passed to people through fleas.

PLAQUE. A transparent material in the mouth that contains bacteria and causes tooth decay; or, A deposit of fatty and other substances that accumulate in the lining of the artery wall; or, Silvery, flaky scales on the skin, as appear with psoriasis.

PLASMA. The liquid part of the blood and lymphatic fluid. Plasma is 92% water, 7% protein and 1% minerals.

PLASMA CELL. Type of white blood cell that produces antibodies; derived from an antigen-specific B cell.

PLATELETS. Small, disk-shaped blood cells that clump together to form plugs that seal off damaged blood vessels. They play an important role in blood clotting.

PLEURISY. Chest pain that occurs when a person takes a deep breath.

PLS. Primary Lateral Sclerosis.

PMA. Progressive Muscular Atrophy.

PNEUMONIA. An infection of the lung that can lead in inflammation of the lungs and to serious illness.

PNEUMOTHORAX. Air inside the chest cavity, which may cause the lung to collapse. Pneumothorax is both a complication of pulmonary tuberculosis and a means of treatment designed to allow an infected lung to rest and heal.

POINT-OF-CARE TESTING (POCT). A term that refers to diagnostic testing (whether for HIV or other diseases) that is carried out at or close to a doctor's office, clinic, or other site of patient care.

POLITICAL ACTION COMMITTEE (PAC). A type of political committee that raises and spends money on political candidates and causes.

POLYCLONAL. Pertaining to cells or cellular products that are derived from several lines of clones; a polyclonal antibody is a mixture of immunoglobulins isolated from antisera that is directed against all epitopes of a single antigen.

POLYNEUROPATHY. A generalized disorder of peripheral nerves.

POLYP. An abnormal growth that develops on the inside of a hollow organ such as the colon, stomach, or nose.

POLYPHARMACY. Taking five or more drugs at the same time.

POLYSACCHARIDES. Long chains of glucose units linked together.

POLYSOMNOGRAM. A sleep study that measures sleep cycles by evaluating eye movements, heart rate, breathing rate, brain waves, electrical activity of the muscles, and levels of blood oxygen.

POLYUNSATURATED FAT. A fat consisting of more than one fatty acid that does not come from animal source and does not contribute to high cholesterol.

POPULATION AGING. A condition in which the median age of a country's population rises. It may be caused by a drop in the birth rate, by increased longevity, or by migration.

PORPHYRIA. A disorder in which porphyrins build up in the blood and urine.

PORPHYRIN. A type of pigment found in living things, such as chlorophyll, that makes plants green and hemoglobin which makes blood red.

PORTAL HYPERTENSION. A condition caused by cirrhosis of the liver. It is characterized by impaired or reversed blood flow from the portal vein to the liver, an enlarged spleen, and dilated veins in the esophagus and stomach.

PORTAL VEIN THROMBOSIS. The development of a blood clot in the vein that brings blood into the liver. Untreated portal vein thrombosis causes portal hypertension.

POSITRON EMISSION TOMOGRAPHY (PET). A radiology test by which images of cross-sectional planes of the body are obtained, using the properties of the positron. The positron is a subatomic particle of equal mass to the electron, but of opposite charge.

POST-EXPOSURE PROPHYLAXIS (PEP). A course of antiretroviral drugs given to people immediately following exposure to HIV infection from rape, unprotected sex, needlestick injuries, or sharing needles.

POST-HERPETIC NEURALGIA (PHN). The pain that continues or recurs after the shingles rash has healed. PHN is generally defined as pain that lingers more than five weeks past the appearance of the first rash.

POST-ICTAL STATE. A period of disorientation usually followed by sleep that occurs after a seizure.

POSTOPERATIVE. After surgery.

POST-POLIO SYNDROME. A motor neuron disease that develops many years after polio.

POST-TRAUMATIC AMNESIA. Loss of memory for events during and after an accident.

POST-TRAUMATIC STRESS DISORDER (PTSD). A specific form of anxiety that begins after a life-threatening event, such as rape, a natural disaster, or combat-related trauma. PTSD may cause sleep disturbances, flashbacks, anxiety, tiredness, and depression.

POSTURAL DRAINAGE. The use of positioning to drain secretions from the bronchial tubes and lungs into the trachea or windpipe.

POSTURAL HYPOTENSION (ORTHOSTATIC HYPOTENSION). A sudden drop in blood pressure when rising from a sitting or lying down position.

POSTUROGRAPHY. The study of posture and its effects on health.

POTASSIUM. A mineral found in whole grains, meat, legumes, and some fruits and vegetables. Potassium is important for many body processes, including proper functioning of nerves and muscles.

POTENTIATION. Making effective or active, or more effective or active; synergistically augmenting the activity of one drug with another.

POTENTIZATION. The process of increasing the power of homeopathic preparations by successive dilutions and succussions of a mother tincture.

PRAGMATISM. A philosophical position that regards practical results, rather than abstract principles or theories, as the essential criterion of moral value.

PRANAYAMA. Yoga breathing techniques.

PRE-DIABETES. Also called impaired glucose tolerance (IGT). Condition characterized by blood glucose levels that are higher than normal but not yet high enough to be diagnosed as diabetes.

PRE-ECLAMSIA. A dangerous condition in pregnancy, involving high blood pressure and protein in the urine.

PREFERRED PROVIDER ORGANIZATION (PPO). A type of managed care health plan similar to an HMO but which offers patients greater choices in selecting physicians, hospitals, and services.

PRELOAD. Relating to the heart: the amount of pressure placed on the heart just before the muscle walls contract.

PREMATURE EJACULATION. Rapid ejaculation before the person wishes it, usually in less than one to two minutes after beginning intercourse.

PREMATURE. Happening early or occurring before the usual time.

PREOPERATIVE. Before surgery.

PRESBYACUSIS. Age-related hearing loss as a result of losing the ability to discriminate between sounds.

PRESBYOPIA. A condition affecting people over the age of 40 where the system of accommodation that allows focusing of near objects fails to work because of age-related hardening of the lens of the eye.

PRESCRIPTION. A written or verbal order for a medication, from professional practitioners, such as a physician, dentist, nurse practitioner, or other health care provider.

PRESSURE ULCER. Any lesion caused by unrelieved pressure resulting in damage to the underlying tissue.

PRIAPISM. A painful, abnormally prolonged erection (i.e., four or more hours).

PRIMARY BILIARY CIRRHOSIS (PBC). A liver disease of unknown origin, found mainly in women 40–60 years old, with swelling of the liver and characterized by intense itching, malabsorption, and jaundice.

PRIMARY CARE PHYSICIAN (PCP). A family practitioner, pediatrician, internist, or gynecologist who takes care of a patient's routine medical needs and refers him or her to a surgeon or other specialist when necessary.

PRIMARY DYSMENORRHEA. Painful menstruation caused by inflammation, new growths, or anatomic factors.

PRIMARY OSTEOARTHRITIS. OA that results from hereditary factors or stresses on weight-bearing joints.

PRIMARY PULMONARY HYPERTENSION. Pulmonary hypertension that is inherited or occurs for no known reason.

PRIMARY SNORING. Simple snoring; snoring that is not interrupted by episodes of breathing cessation.

PRIMARY TUMOR. A cancer's origin or initial growth.

PRINCIPLE OF DOUBLE EFFECT. An ethical principle that holds that an act that causes harm may be morally permissible if the harm is a side effect of promoting a good purpose.

PROBENECID. A drug that corrects hyperuricemia by increasing the urinary excretion of urate.

PROBIOTIC. The presence of normal or so-called friendly bacteria that are beneficial to their host organism such as normal intestinal bacteria in humans that help digest food.

PROGESTERONE. The hormone that is produced by the ovary after ovulation to prepare the uterine lining for a fertilized egg. It is a steroid hormone that is a biological precursor to corticoid (another steroid hormone) and androgen (a male sex hormone).

PROGESTERONE RECEPTOR (PR). A cell-surface protein that binds the female hormone progesterone.

PROGESTIN. Any substance that has the biological effects of the female hormone progesterone.

PROGNOSIS. A medical professional's prediction of the course of a disease and the probability of the patient's recovery.

PROGRESSIVE DISEASE. Disease that increases in scope and severity, from bad to worse.

PROGRESSIVE MUSCLE RELAXATION. A two-step relaxation technique that involves tensing various muscle groups in sequence for about eight seconds and then releasing the tension.

PROGRESSIVE RESISTIVE EXERCISES. The mode of training that involves increasing intensity of exercise over time.

PROHORMONE. A substance the body can convert into a hormone.

PROLAPSED UTERUS. A uterus that has slipped out of place, sometimes protruding down through the vagina.

PROPHYLACTIC OOPHORECTOMY. An operation that removes healthy ovaries in order to prevent disease.

PROPHYLAXIS. A measure intended to preserve health or prevent the spread of disease. Taking an antibiotic before oral surgery to prevent bacteria from entering the bloodstream is an example of prophylaxis.

PROPRIOCEPTION. Internal perception of the position of the body and limbs in space that does not depend on visual information.

PROSPECTIVE REFUSAL. The more common type of living will, in which a person refuses in advance to receive life-sustaining care when there is no hope of recovery and/or their quality of life is severely impaired.

PROSTATE. In males, a walnut–shaped gland that surrounds the urethra at the neck of the bladder. It supplies fluid that goes into semen.

PROSTATE-SPECIFIC ANTIGEN. A protein made by the cells of the prostate that is increased by both BPH and prostate cancer.

PROSTATITIS. Inflammation of the prostate gland.

PROSTHESIS (PLURAL, PROSTHESES). An artificial device that substitutes for or supplements a missing or damaged body part. Prostheses may be either external or implanted inside the body.

PROSTHETIC TOOTH. The final tooth that is held in place by the dental implant anchor.

PROSTHODONTICS. The area of dentistry concerned with the replacement of missing teeth.

PROTEASE INHIBITOR. A drug that inhibits the action of enzymes.

PROTECTED HEALTH INFORMATION (PHI). Any information about health care provision, health status, or payment for health care that can be traced to a specific individual.

PROTEIN. An essential nutrient that helps the body build necessary parts of the body such as muscle, tissue, and blood cells.

PROTEIN-ENERGY MALNUTRITION. Deficiencies in proteins or energy or both as a result of inefficient calorie consumption.

PROTHROMBIN TEST. A common test to measure the amount of time it takes for a patient's blood to clot; measurements are in seconds.

PROTHROMBIN TIME (PT). A lab test that detects coagulation defects in the extrinsic clotting cascade. Used to regulate coumadin dosing.

PROTOCOL. A detailed plan for how a disease or condition should be treated, including the drugs that should be used first.

PROTON PUMP. A structure in the body that produces and pumps acid into the stomach.

PROTON PUMP INHIBITOR. One of a group of drugs that acts to reduce the secretion of stomach acid.

PROVIDER. Health team professional or entity (hospital) that offers care.

PROVITAMIN. A chemical that can be converted into a vitamin in the body.

PROXY. In law, a person with the authority to act for another. In some states a health care proxy may be called an agent, representative, surrogate, attorney-in-fact, or patient advocate.

PRURICEPTORS. Nerve endings specialized to perceive itching sensations.

PRURITUS. The medical term for itching.

PSEUDOHYPERTENSION. A condition in which a senior's blood pressure measures higher than it really is because of stiffening of the arteries.

PSEUDOMEMBRANOUS COLITIS. A potentially life-threatening inflammation of the colon, caused by a toxin released by the Clostridium difficile bacterium that multiplies rapidly following antibiotic treatment.

PSORIASIS. A skin disorder of chronic, itchy scaling most commonly at sites of repeated minor trauma (e.g. elbows, knees, and skin folds). It affects up to 2% of the population in Western countries—males and females equally.

PSYCHIATRIC NURSING. The nursing specialty concerned with the prevention and treatment of mental disorders and their consequences.

PSYCHOACTIVE. Affecting the mind or behavior.

PSYCHONEUROIMMUNOLOGY. The study of the relationships among mind, nervous system, and immune response.

PSYCHOSIS. A general psychiatric term for a mental state in which the patient has lost contact with reality. It is marked by delusions, hallucinations, and disorganized thinking.

PSYCHOSOMATIC. A type of physical illness caused by mental factors.

PSYCHOSTIMULANT. A fast-acting antidepressant.

PTA. Physical therapy assistant or physical therapist assistant.

PULMONARY ANGIOGRAPHY. An x-ray study of the lungs, performed by insertion of a catheter into a vein, through the heart, and into the pulmonary artery. Pulmonary angiography is performed to evaluate blood circulation to the lungs. It is also considered the most accurate diagnos.

PULMONARY ARTERY. The large artery that carries blood from the heart to the lungs to receive oxygen. It is the only artery in the body that carries deoxygenated blood.

PULMONARY EDEMA. The build-up of fluid in the lungs. It often is the complication of heart disease and other conditions.

PULMONARY EMBOLISM. Potentially life-threatening blockage of a pulmonary artery by fat, air, or a blood clot that originated elsewhere in the body. Symptoms include acute shortness of breath and sudden chest pain.

PULMONARY HYPERTENSION. A potentially life-threatening condition in which blood pressure in the pulmonary artery increases to abnormal levels.

PULMONARY. Related to or associated with the lungs.

PULSE OXIMETER. Noninvasive machine that measures the amount of hemoglobin that is saturated with oxygen.

PUNCH BIOPSY. The use of a sharp hollow instrument to pinch off small pieces of cervical tissue.

PUPIL. Variable-sized black circular opening in the center of the iris that regulates the amount of light that enters the eye.

PURIFIED PROTEIN DERIVATIVE (PPD). An extract of tubercle bacilli that is injected into the skin to find out whether a person presently has or has ever had tuberculosis.

PURINE. A substance found in foods that is broken down into urate and may contribute to hyperuricemia and gout.

PUSTULE. A small raised pimple or blister-like swelling of the skin that contains pus.

PYELONEPHRITIS. Bacterial infection of the kidney or upper urinary tract.

Q

QI. Basic life energy, according to traditional Chinese medicine.

QRST COMPLEX. The combined waves of an electrocardiogram for monitoring the heart.

QUADRANTECTOMY. A partial mastectomy that removes the quadrant of the breast that includes the tumor.

QUADRICEPS MUSCLES. A set of four muscles on each leg located at the front of the thigh. The quadriceps straighten the knee and are used every time a person takes a step.

R

RABIES. A rare but serious disease caused by a virus carried in saliva. It is transmitted when an infected animal bites a person.

RADIAL ARTERY. An artery located in the arm and used for bypass grafts.

RADIATION THERAPY. Use of radioisotopes to kill tumor cells. Applied externally through a beam of x rays, intraoperatively (during surgery), or deposited internally by implanting radioactive seeds in tumor tissue.

RADICAL PROSTATECTOMY. Surgical removal of the entire prostate, a common method of treating prostate cancer.

RADICAL RESECTION. Surgical resection that takes the blood supply and lymph system supplying the organ along with the organ.

RADICULAR. Pain that is caused by the root of a nerve.

RADICULOPATHY. Sometimes referred to as a pinched nerve, it refers to compression of the nerve root–the part of a nerve between vertebrae. This compression causes pain to be perceived in areas to which the nerve leads.

RADIO WAVES. Electromagnetic energy of the frequency range corresponding to that used in radio communications, usually 10,000 cycles per second to 300 billion cycles per second. Radio waves are the same as visible light, x rays, and other electromagnetic waves.

RADIOFREQUENCY ABLATION. A technique for removing a tumor by heating it with a radiofrequency current passed through a needle electrode.

RADIOISOTOPE. A radioactive or radiation-emitting form of an element.

RADIOLOGIST. A doctor who specializes in an area of medicine that focuses on the use of radiation to diagnose and treat disease.

RADIONUCLIDE. A substance that emits radiation as it disintegrates.

RADIUS. The bone of the forearm which joins the wrist on the same side as the thumb.

RALOXIFENE. A drug for treating osteoporosis that blocks the effects of estrogen.

RANGE OF MOTION (ROM). The range of motion of a joint from full extension to full flexion (bending) measured in degrees like a circle.

RAPID CYCLING. Four or more manic, hypomanic, mixed, or depressive episodes within a 12-month period.

RASH. A spotted, pink or red skin eruption that may be accompanied by itching and is caused by disease, contact with an allergen, food ingestion, or drug reaction.

RAST TEST. A RAST (radioallergosorbent) test is used detect the amount of IgE in the blood.

RAYNAUD'S SYNDROME. A vascular, or circulatory system, disorder which is characterized by abnormally cold hands and feet. This chilling effect is caused by constriction of the blood vessels in the extremities, and occurs when the hands and feet are exposed to cold weather.

REACTIVE OXYGEN SPECIES (ROS). Damaging molecules, including oxygen radicals and other highly reactive forms of oxygen that can harm cells.

RECEPTOR. A molecular structure in a cell or on the surface of a cell that allows binding of a specific substance that causes a specific physiologic response.

RECOMMENDED DAILY ALLOWANCE (RDA). The amount of a specific nutrient that should be consumed each day for optimal health. This standard is set and periodically updated by U.S. government agencies.

RECONCILIATION. Restoration to a relationship on the part of two people; a coming-together in mutual respect.

RECTUM. The lower section of the large intestine that holds stools before defecation.

RECURRENCE. The return of a sign, symptom or disease after a successful treatment and remission.

RED BLOOD CELL (RBC). A cell found in blood that contains haemoglobin to bind oxygen and carry it to all parts of the body.

REDUCTION. The restoring of bones to their correct alignment.

REFERRAL. The process of directing a patient to a specialist for further diagnostic evaluation or treatment.

REFERRED PAIN. Pain that is experienced in one part of the body but originates in another organ or area. The pain is referred because the nerves that supply the damaged organ enter the spine in the same segment as the nerves that supply the area where the pain is felt.

REFLEX. A response, usually a movement, elicited by tapping on the nerve with a special hammer-like instrument.

REFLEXOLOGY. A form of acupressure that seeks to lower stress or treat other health conditions through the application of pressure to specific points or areas of the feet. It is sometimes called zone therapy.

REFLUX. Backflow, also called regurgitation.

REFRACTED. Bent back as if broken.

REFRACTION. Method of determining the optical status of the eyes. Lenses are placed before the patient's eyes while reading from an eye chart. The result is the eyeglass or contact lens prescription.

REGISTERED DIETICIAN. A healthcare professional who has completed an academic program and been accredited to provide advice about proper nutrition.

REGISTERED NURSE. A nurse who has graduated from a nursing program, including an associate degree, bachelor of science degree or diploma program, and passed a national licensing examination.

REGURGITATION. The casting up of undigested food through the nose or mouth.

REHABILITATION. The process of restoring a patient to a condition of health or useful and constructive activity.

REIKI. A Japanese form of energy medicine in which the practitioner places his hands on or near the person receiving treatment with the intent to transmit life-force energy.

REJECTION. The process in which the immune system attacks foreign tissue such as a transplanted organ.

RELAPSE. Returning to a previous behavior pattern of heavy drinking or substance abuse after treatment.

RELAXATION RESPONSE. The body's inactivation of stress responses and return of stress hormone levels to normal after a threat has passed.

REM SLEEP. Rapid eye movement sleep phase where dreaming occurs.

REMISSION. A period during which symptoms of disease are reduced (partial remission) or disappear (complete remission).

RENAL ARTERY STENOSIS. Narrowing or constriction of the artery that supplies the kidney with blood.

RENAL. Relating to the kidneys.

RENIN. An enzyme, produced by the kidneys that acts as a catalyst, causing separation of the leucine–leucine bond in angiotensin to produce angiotensin.

REPLICATION. The process in which a cell duplicates or copies itself.

RESECT. To remove surgically.

RESECTION. Cutting out tissue to eliminate a cancerous tumor; usually refers to a section of the organ, (e.g., colon, intestine, lung, stomach) that must be cut to remove the tumor and its surrounding tissue.

RESISTANCE. A property of some bacteria that have been exposed to a particular antibiotic and have "learned" how to survive in its presence.

RESORBED. Absorbed by the body because of lack of function. This happens to the jawbone after tooth loss.

RESORPTION. The ongoing process of bone loss as a result of osteoclast activity.

RESPIRATORY FAILURE. Loss of lung (pulmonary) function, which can be an acute or chronic disturbance of breathing ability.

RESPITE CARE. Short-term inpatient or outpatient services intended to give the patient's primary caregiver temporary relief.

RESTLESS LEGS SYNDROME. A neurological disorder characterized by unpleasant sensations in the legs and an uncontrollable urge to move when at rest in an effort to relieve these feelings.

RESTRAINT. A physical device or a medication designed to restrict a person's movement.

RESUSCITATION. Bringing a person back to life after an apparent death.

RETICULAR ACTIVATING SYSTEM (RAS). A network of structures, including the brainstem, medulla, and thalamus, and nerve pathways, which function together to produce and maintain arousal.

RETICULOCYTES. Young red blood cells formed in bone marrow that make up about 1% of all red blood cells circulating in the veins and arteries.

RETINA. Light-sensitive tissue on the back of the eye that receives images and converts them into nerve impulses to be sent to the brain by way of the optic nerve.

RETINAL DETACHMENT. Separation of the retina of the eye from its underlying layer of tissue. This separation results in loss of vision. A retinal detachment is a medical emergency.

RETINITIS PIGMENTOSA. A group of inherited disorders that affect the rod cells of the retina. Retinitis pigmentosa begins with loss of night vision, followed by gradual loss of peripheral vision, the development of tunnel vision, and finally blindness.

RETROGRADE AMNESIA. Memory loss for events in the past that occurs over a period of time.

RETROGRADE EJACULATION. A condition in which the semen spurts backward into the bladder.

RETROVIRUS. A single-stranded virus that replicates by reverse transcription to produce DNA copies that are incorporated into the genome of infected cells. AIDS is caused by a retrovirus.

RF TEST. test for rheumatoid factor, which can be elevated in conditions such as rheumatoid arthritis and Sjorgren's syndrome.

RHEUMATIC. Rheuma was a term first introduced in the first century to describe a substance that flows. It now describes a state of rheumatism, or any condition with inflammation in muscles, joints, and fibrous tissues.

RHEUMATIC FEVER. An illness that sometimes follows a streptococcal infection of the throat.

RHEUMATIC HEART DISEASE. A condition caused by a streptococcus infection which can result in permanent heart damage.

RHEUMATOID ARTHRITIS. A chronic inflammatory autoimmune disease of joints that causes stiffness, swelling, weakness, loss of mobility, and leads to damage and eventual destruction of the joints.

RHEUMATOID FACTOR (RF). An antibody present in the blood serum of many individuals affected by rheumatoid arthritis.

RHEUMATOLOGIST. A physician who specializes in non-surgical treatment of bone and joint disorders.

RHEUMATOLOGY. The medical specialty that studies and treats disorders of the joints and muscles.

RHINITIS. Inflammation of the mucous membrane of the nose, resulting in congestion and sneezing.

RHINOPHYMA. A form of rosacea characterized by chronic redness, inflammation, swelling, and increased tissue growth of the nose. The skin of the nose may thicken and have large pores, resembling the skin of an orange.

RHYTIDECTOMY. Wrinkle excision. It is an older, alternative term for a face lift.

RIBONUCLEOPROTEIN. A class of protein found in the nucleus associated with RNA.

RINGWORM. A fungal infection of the skin, usually known as tinea corporis.

RNA. An important genetic determinant, ribonucleic acid (RNA) is found in nuclei of human and plant cells and functions as a reproducing component of chromosomes, controlling hereditary characteristics; also present in viruses.

ROSACEA. A chronic inflammation of the face, with associated scattered round nodules and increased reactivity of the facial capillaries to heat. It is most common in females, aged 30–50 years.

ROTATOR CUFF. The shoulder muscles and tendons.

RUBELLA. A contagious viral disease that is milder than typical measles but is damaging to the fetus when it occurs early in pregnancy. Also called German measles.

RUPTURE. A tear or break in body tissue of an organ.

S

S-ADENOSYL-L-METHIONINE (SAM-E). A substance in the body that regulates serotonin and dopamine levels and is used as an antidepressant in Europe.

SACCULAR ANEURYSM. A type of aneurysm that resembles a small sack of blood attached to the outer surface of a blood vessel by a thin neck.

SACRUM. Posterior bony wall of the pelvis.

SALICYLATES. A group of drugs that includes aspirin and related compounds. Salicylates are used to relieve pain, reduce inflammation, and lower fever.

SALIVARY DUCT. Tube through which saliva is carried from the salivary gland to the mouth.

SALIVARY GLANDS. The glands in the mouth that produce saliva; the parotid, sublingual, and submandibular glands.

SALMONELLA. A genus of bacteria that causes food poisoning, acute gastrointestinal inflammation, typhoid fever, and septicemia.

SAPHENOUS VEIN. A long vein in the thigh or calf commonly used for bypass grafts.

SARCOIDOSIS. An inflammatory disease characterized by the formation of small nodules of immune cells in the lungs, lymph nodes, and other organs.

SARCOPENIA. A deficiency of muscle or flesh that occurs in the elderly.

SATURATED FAT. A fat that comes from an animal source that contributes to the formation of cholesterol in the blood.

SCABIES. A contagious parasitic skin disease characterized by intense itching.

SCALP. That part of the head that is usually covered with hair.

SCAPULA. The shoulder blade.

SCHIP. State Children's Health Insurance Program. It provides health care insurance for children up to the age of 18 years who do not qualify for Medicaid but are not covered by private insurance.

SCHIZOPHRENIA. Schizophrenia is a psychotic disorder that causes distortions in perception (delusions and hallucinations), inappropriate moods and behaviors, and disorganized or incoherent speech and behavior.

SCIATIC NERVE. The largest and longest nerve in the body, running from the lower back to the foot.

SCIATICA. Pain caused by irritation of the sciatic nerve. Sciatica is felt in the lower back, the buttocks, and the backs of the upper legs.

SCINTIGRAM. A nuclear angiogram; a scintigram involves injection of a radioactive substance into the patient's circulatory system. As the substance travels through the body, a special scanning camera takes pictures.

SCLERA. Tough, opaque tissue that serves as the eye's protective outer coat. Also called "the white of the eye."

SCLERODERMA. A disease of connective tissue characterized by the formation of scar tissue in the skin and sometimes also in other organs of the body.

SCLEROSIS. Hardening.

SCOLIOSIS. An abnormal side-to-side or lateral curvature of the spine.

SCROTUM. The pouch containing the testes.

SCRUB NURSE. Scrub nurses directly assist surgeons in the operating room. They are responsible for setting up sterile instruments and supplies and handing them to the operating surgeon or surgical assistant during the procedure.

SEASONAL AFFECTIVE DISORDER. Depression that tends to recur with the shorter days of fall and winter.

SECONDARY OR OPPORTUNISTIC INFECTION. An infection by a microbe that occurs because the body is weakened by a primary infection caused by a different kind of microbe.

SECONDARY OSTEOARTHRITIS. Osteoarthritis that develops following joint surgery, trauma, or repetitive joint injury.

SECONDARY PULMONARY HYPERTENSION. Pulmonary hypertension that is caused by another medical condition.

SEDENTARY. Not physically active.

SEIZURES. Sudden, uncontrolled electrical activity in the brain resulting in characteristic twitching, or spastic, movements that may be accompanied by loss of consciousness.

SELECTIVE SEROTONIN UPTAKE INHIBITORS (SSRIS). Drugs that regulate depression by blocking the reabsorption of serotonin in the brain consequently raising serotonin levels. SSRIs include fluoxetine (Prozac), sertraline (Zoloft), and paroxetine (Paxil).

SELF-DELIVERANCE. Another term for assisted suicide, more commonly used in Great Britain than in the United States.

SENESCENCE. In biology, the state or process of aging.

SENILE PURPURA. Easy skin bruising in older people; As people age, their skin becomes thinner and more fragile. Hence, bruises (senile purpura) tend to form easily as the blood vessels in the skin are also more fragile.

SENSATION. A perception associated with the stimulation of a sense organ or with a specific condition of the body.

SENSITIVITY. A statistical measure of how well a medical test for a specific disease correctly identifies persons who have the disease; or, An exaggerated response by the immune system to a substance.

SENSITIVITY TEST. A test that determines which antibiotics will kill the bacteria isolated from a culture.

SENSORINEURAL HEARING LOSS. Occurs when there is damage or degeneration of the nerves in the inner ear which reduces the ability to understand what is being said. Generally caused by exposure to loud noise, head or ear injury, medications, disease, tumor(s), or infection.

SENSORY HEARING LOSS. Hearing loss due to disorders of the inner ear.

SENSORY NERVES. Sensory or afferent nerves carry impulses of sensation from the periphery or outward parts of the body to the brain. Sensations include feelings, impressions, and awareness of the state of the body.

SENTINEL LYMPH NODE (SLN). The gland(s) of the lymphatic system that breast cancer is most likely to invade first.

SEPSIS. Presence of various pus-forming and other pathogenic organisms, or their toxins, in the blood or tissues.

SEPTIC SHOCK. A life-threatening drop in blood pressure caused by bacterial infection.

SEPTICEMIA. Blood poisoning; an infection of the bloodstream by a virulent bacterium, virus, or fungus, causing acute systemic illness.

SEPTUM (VENTRICULAR SEPTUM). That portion of the heart wall that divides the right and left ventricles.

SEROCONVERSION. The development of detectable specific antibodies in a patient's blood serum as a result of infection or immunization.

SEROTONIN. 5-Hydroxytryptamine; a substance that occurs throughout the body with numerous effects including neurotransmission.

SEROTONIN AND NOREPINEPHRINE REUPTAKE INHIBITOR (SNRI). An antidepressant that increases serotonin and norepinephrine in the brain.

SEROTONIN SYNDROME. A group of symptoms caused by severely elevated serotonin levels in the body.

SERTRALINE. Zoloft; a SSRI that is used to treat mental depression and a variety of other disorders.

SERUM GLUCOSE. Glucose or sugar in the blood.

SEXUAL AROUSAL DISORDER. The inhibition of the general arousal aspect of sexual response.

SHAVE BIOPSY. A method of removing a sample of skin lesion so it can be examined by a pathologist. A scalpel or razor blade is held parallel to the skin's surface and is used to slice the lesion at its base.

SHEAR. Mechanical stress experienced at the plane of the affected area such as pressure sores on the lower back or hip.

SHEMA. A Hebrew verse recited by devout Jews in the morning and the evening, and traditionally by a dying person as an affirmation of faith. The usual English translation is "Hear, O Israel! The LORD is our God! The LORD is One!"

SHIATSU. A Japanese form of acupressure that combines elements of traditional Chinese massage techniques with Western medical understanding of the structures and functions of the human body.

SHINGLES. Herpes zoster; an acute nerve inflammation resulting in a rash and pain, caused by the reactivation of latent chickenpox virus.

SHORT BOWEL SYNDROME. Problems related to absorbing nutrients after removal of part of the small intestine.

SIALOGOGUE. A medication given to increase the flow of saliva.

SICKLE CELL ANEMIA. Blood disorder in which the body produces abnormally shaped red blood cells that look like a crescent or sickle and also contain an abnormal form of hemoglobin, which interferes with oxygen delivery to tissues.

SIDEROBLASTIC ANEMIA. Disorder in which the body has adequate iron but is unable to incorporate it into hemoglobin.

SIDESTREAM SMOKE. The smoke that is emitted from the burning end of a cigarette or cigar, or that comes from the end of a pipe. Along with exhaled smoke, it is a constituent of second-hand smoke.

SIGMOIDOSCOPY. Procedure to visualize the interior of the colon. A flexible tube is inserted in the anus. An operator looks into the colon that is illuminated by a light at the end of the tube.

SIL. Squamous intraepithelial lesion; abnormal squamous cells on the surface of the cervix.

SILENT REFLUX. An acid reflux problem that does not have marked symptoms but can cause chronic, recurrent respiratory symptoms much like asthma.

SINGLE CHAMBER. A type of pacemaker having one lead that is placed either in the right atria or the right ventricle.

SJÖGREN'S DISEASE. An autoimmune disease characterized by fatigue and malaise, dry gritty eyes and dry mouth, and recurrent gingivitis and respiratory infection.

SKILLED NURSING FACILITY (SNF). Another name for a nursing home.

SLEEP APNEA. Repeated episodes of temporary suspension of breathing during sleep.

SLEEP CENTER. A clinic where doctors diagnose, treat, and do research on sleep disorders.

SMALLPOX. A highly contagious viral disease characterized by fever and weakness and skin eruption with pustules that form scabs that slough off leaving scars.

SMITH'S (SM) ANTIBODIES. A nuclear autoantibody specific for SLE, named for the patient in which first described.

SMOKING CESSATION. To quit smoking or withdrawal from nicotine.

SMUDGING. A Native American spiritual practice in which fragrant herbs or tree bark are burned as part of a cleansing or healing ritual.

SOCIAL MODELING. A process of learning behavioral and emotional response patterns from observing one's parents or other adults. Some researchers think that social modeling plays a part in the development of generalized anxiety disorder in women.

SOCIAL RESTRAINT. A technique for restraining a patient with delirium or dementia by placing the person close to a nursing station or by having relatives or healthcare professionals stay with the patient to monitor the person's behavior.

SOCIALIZATION. The process by which people learn the attitudes, values, and behaviors considered appropriate within their culture.

SOCIOECONOMIC STATUS. A measure based on income, level of education, occupation, and role or status within the community.

SOFT TISSUE/JOINT MOBILIZATION. Application of specific stretching techniques to the body's soft tissues and joints.

SOLITUDE. The condition or situation of being apart from other people, whether short-term or long-term. It is often self-chosen for the sake of privacy or to rest or work undisturbed.

SOLUTE. Solid substances that are dissolved in liquid in order to make a solution.

SOMATIC NERVOUS SYSTEM. The part of the nervous system that controls voluntary motions and sensations of the skin.

SOMATIZATION DISORDER. A type of mental disorder characterized by experiences of pain in various parts of the body that have no identifiable physical cause. The symptoms are thought to result from the patient's conversion of emotional distress into bodily sensations.

SOMATOSENSORY SYSTEM. The components of the central and peripheral nervous systems which process information about the muscles, pain, temperature, pressure and joint position.

SOMNOPLASTY. A technique that uses radiofrequency signals to heat a thin needle inserted into the tissues of the soft palate. The heat from the needle shrinks the tissues, thus enlarging the patient's airway.

SONOGRAPHER. A medical technician trained in performing ultrasound exams.

SORBITOL. An artificial sweetener known to trigger IBS symptoms in some patients.

SORE. An open wound, bruise, or lesion on the skin.

SPASM. Sudden, involuntary tensing of a muscle or a group of muscles.

SPASTICITY. Increased muscle tone that results in a tightening and shortening of a muscle.

SPECIFICITY. A statistical measure of how well a medical test for a specific disease correctly identifies persons who do not have the disease. A specificity of 100% would mean that the test would correctly identify all healthy people as such.

SPECULUM. An instrument used to widen the vagina so that a Pap test can be performed.

SPEECH PATHOLOGIST. A healthcare profession who has been trained and certified to provide advice and therapy to individuals with disorders of speech, language, swallowing, or eating.

SPEECH-LANGUAGE PATHOLOGIST. A health professional who evaluates and treats people with speech, language, or swallowing disorders that affect their ability to communicate.

SPEECH-LANGUAGE PATHOLOGY. Formerly known as speech therapy, speech-language pathology includes the study and treatment of human communication—its development and disorders.

SPHINCTER. A ring-shaped muscle that is able to contract or relax in order to close or open a body passage. The esophagus has two sphincters, one at the upper end in the throat, and the other at the lower end where the esophagus joins the stomach.

SPHYGMOMANOMETER. A device for measuring blood pressure that consists of an inflatable cuff connected to a mercury column or a digital gauge.

SPINA BIFIDA. A neural-tube defect in which the spinal column does not completely enclose and protect the spinal cord.

SPINAL CORD. Part of the central nervous system extending from the base of the skull through the vertebrae of the spinal column.

SPINAL STENOSIS. A form of sciatica that is caused by a narrowing of the spinal canal in the lumbar vertebrae. The narrowing puts pressure on the roots of the sciatic nerve.

SPINAL TAP. A procedure used to isolate cerebrospinal fluid for evaluation or diagnosis of disease.

SPIROCHETE. A spiral-shaped bacterium. The bacteria that cause Lyme disease and syphilis, for example, are spirochetes.

SPIROMETER. An instrument for measuring the capacity of the lungs.

SPLINTING. Preventing movement of a joint.

SPONDYLOLISTHESIS. A condition when one vertebra slips forward over another.

SPORE. A small, usually single–celled reproductive body that can grow into a new organism, produced especially by certain bacteria, fungi, and non-flowering plants.

SPUTUM. Matter from the lungs or throat that is brought up by coughing.

SPUTUM CULTURE. A laboratory analysis of the fluid produced from the lungs during coughing. A sputum culture can confirm the presence of pathogens in the respiratory system and help diagnose respiratory infections including bronchitis, tuberculosis, and pneumonia.

SQUAMOUS. Small scale-like cells on the surface of the cervix.

STABILIZER. A device used to depress the movement of the area around the coronary artery where the anastomosis is made. The stabilizer is used to provide a still, motionless field for suturing.

STANCE PHASE. The point where, when walking, one foot is in contact with the ground.

STAPHYLOCOCCUS. Staph; a genus of bacteria that causes various diseases, including food poisoning, skin infections, and endocarditis.

STATE ANXIETY. The immediate physical sensations associated with perception of a threat and the resulting fear response.

STEATORRHEA. An excess of fat in the stool.

STEM CELLS. Unspecialized cells found in both embryonic and adult tissues in humans that are capable of differentiating themselves into a wide variety of specialized cells.

STENOSIS. A narrowing or constriction of the diameter of a passage or orifice, such as a blood vessel.

STENT. A device made of expandable, metal mesh that is placed (by using a balloon catheter) at the site of a narrowing artery; the stent stays in place to keep the artery open.

STERILE. Free from infective organisms, such as bacteria, viruses or fungi.

STERNOTOMY. A surgical opening into the thoracic cavity through the sternum (breastbone).

STERNUM. Also referred to as the breast bone, this is the long flat bone in the middle of the chest.

STEROID. A family of compounds that share a similar chemical structure. This family includes estrogen and testosterone, vitamin D, cholesterol, and the drugs cortisone and prendisone.

STIMULANT. A drug or other substance that increases the rate of activity of a body system.

STIMULUS. Action performed on an individual that predictably provokes a reaction.

STOMA. Surgically constructed mouth or passage between the intestine and the outside of the patient's body.

STOOL. The solid waste that is left after food is digested. Stool forms in the intestines and passes out of the body through the anus.

STOOL SOFTENERS. Medication that causes stool to become softer and easier to pass.

STRAIN. A genetic variant or subtype of a bacterium (or other microorganism).

STREET DRUG. A substance purchased from a drug dealer; it may be a legal substance, sold illicitly (without a prescription, and not for medical use), or it may be a substance which is illegal to possess.

STREPTOCOCCUS. Strep; a genus of bacteria that causes various diseases; Group B strep organisms cause pneumonia, septicemia, and meningitis.

STRESS HARDINESS. A personality characteristic that enables persons to stay healthy in stressful circumstances. It includes belief in one's ability to influence the situation; being committed to or fully engaged in one's activities; and having a positive view.

STRESS MANAGEMENT. A set of techniques and programs intended to help people deal more effectively with stress in their lives by analyzing the specific stressors and taking positive actions to minimize their effects.

STRESS TEST. A test that involves an electrocardiogram during rest and exercise to determine how the heart responds to stress.

STRESSOR. A stimulus, or event, that provokes a stress response in an organism. Stressors can be categorized as acute or chronic, and as external or internal to the organism.

STROKE. Irreversible damage to the brain caused by insufficient blood flow to the brain as the result of a blocked artery. Damage can include loss of speech or vision, paralysis, cognitive impairment, and death.

STROMA. Cornea layer beneath Bowman's layer that represents 90% of the cornea. Consists mostly of water (78%) and collagen (16%).

STRUCTURAL ALIGNMENT. Refers to the normal longitudinal formation of the individual bones and muscles of the body such as limbs, as well as the formation and structural support of the whole skeleton.

SUBARACHNOID SPACE. The space surrounding the spinal cord that is filled with cerebrospinal fluid.

SUBCHONDRAL CYSTS. Fluid-filled sacs that form inside the marrow at the ends of bones as part of the development of osteoarthritis.

SUBCLAVIAN VEIN. The large vein in the chest that pacemaker leads are threaded through to be implanted in the right atria or ventricle.

SUBCUTANEOUS. Below the skin.

SUBSTANTIA NIGRA. One of the movement control centers of the brain.

SUCCUSSION. The act of shaking diluted homeopathic remedies as part of the process of potentization.

SUCROSE. Disaccharide commonly known as table sugar.

SUICIDE GESTURE. Attempted suicide characterized by a low-lethality method, low level of intent or planning, and little physical damage; sometimes called pseudocide.

SUICIDE MAGNET. A bridge or tall building that acquires a reputation for attracting people who want to commit suicide and attempt it.

SULCUS. Pocket space between tooth and gum.

SULFINPYRAZONE. A drug that corrects hyperuricemia by increasing the urinary excretion of urate.

SULFITE. A type of preservative that causes allergic reactions in some people.

SUPERBUG. Informal term for an antibiotic-resistant bacterium.

SUPEROXIDE–DISMUTASE (SOD). An enzyme that catalyzes the decomposition of a superoxide into hydrogen peroxide and oxygen.

SUPINATION. The twisting motion of the forearm, wrist, and hand that turns the palm upward.

SUPPLEMENTAL SECURITY INCOME (SSI). A federal entitlement program that provides cash assistance to low-income blind, disabled, and elderly people. In most states, people receiving SSI benefits are eligible for Medicaid.

SUPPLEMENTS. Pills, capsules, powders, extracts, or liquids that include vitamins, minerals, herbs, or other additives that purportedly improve diet or nutrition.

SUPPORTIVE. Referring to counseling or psychotherapy intended to provide emotional support and encouragement rather than intellectual exploration of the client's problems or behavioral change.

SUPPOSITORY. A solid medication that slowly dissolves after being inserted into the rectum or other body cavity.

SUPRASPINATUS. A muscle at the top of the shoulder blade.

SURROGATE. A person who represents the wishes of the patient, chosen by the patient and stipulated by a legal document as power of attorney.

SWEAT LODGE. In Native American practice, a low structure containing a fire pit holding hot stones for a healing or purification ceremony. Water is poured on the stones to create steam during the ritual.

SWIMMER'S ITCH. An allergic skin inflammation caused by a sensitivity to flatworms that die under the skin, causing an itchy rash.

SYMPHYSES. Joints where bones are connected by a fibrocartilage disk. An example is the symphesis pubis.

SYNAPSE. A connection between nerve cells, by which nervous excitation is transferred from one cell to the other.

SYNAPTIC VESICLES. Also called neurotransmitter vesicles, these pouches store the various neurotransmitters that are released by nerve cells into the synaptic cleft of a synapse.

SYNCHONDROSES. Joints that connect two bony structures by hyaline cartilage. Examples are the ends of long bones, where the bone growth is not yet complete. As the skeleton matures, the hyaline cartilage eventually ossifies.

SYNDESMOSIS. A joint where two bones are joined by a ligament or membrane. An example is the membrane that joins the shaft of the tibia to the shaft of the fibula in the lower leg.

SYNDROME. A group of signs or symptoms that occur together and characterize a specific disease or condition.

SYNERGISTIC. The combined action of two or more processes is greater than the sum of each acting separately.

SYNOVIAL FLUID. Fluid surrounding the joints which acts as a lubricant, reducing friction between the joints.

SYNOVIAL MEMBRANE. A layer of connective tissue that lines the cavities of joints.

SYNOVIAL TENDON SHEATH. Where the tendons cross joints, they are sheathed in thin membranes known as synovium, which provide lubrication to decrease friction.

SYNOVIUM. A fibrous envelope that produces a fluid to help to reduce friction and wear in a joint.

SYSTEMIC. Affecting all or most parts of the body.

SYSTEMIC DISEASE. A disease that affects the entire body instead of a specific organ.

SYSTEMIC LUPUS ERYTHEMATOSUS (SLE). An autoimmune inflammatory disease of the connective tissue that occurs mainly among middle-aged women, characterized by skin eruptions, joint pain, recurrent pleurisy, and kidney disease.

SYSTEMIC SCLEROSIS. A rare disorder that causes thickening and scarring of multiple organ systems.

SYSTOLIC. The contraction period of the heart cycle during which blood is pumped to the body.

SYSTOLIC BLOOD PRESSURE. The highest level of blood pressure in the arteries, which occurs at the point in the heart's cycle when the heart contracts and pushes blood out through the aorta and the pulmonary artery.

T

T LYMPHOCYTES (T CELLS). Lymphocytes that recognize foreign substances and process them for removal.

TACHYCARDIA. An abnormally rapid beating of the heart. The heart rate can be as high as 100 beats per minute or more.

T'AI CHI. Based on an ancient form of Chinese martial arts, this form of exercise is a series of slow movements that improve balance and strength and also calms the mind.

TAMOXIFEN. A drug that blocks the activity of estrogen and is used to prevent or treat breast cancer.

TAOISM. A traditional Chinese belief system that influenced the development of t'ai chi and Chinese herbal medicine. It holds that the human body is a microcosm (miniature form) of the universe and is connected to it by its chi or vital energy.

TAPAS ACUPRESSURE TECHNIQUE (TAT). A controversial form of acupressure based on TCM that claims to clear hereditary as well as past trauma by putting pressure on four points on the face and head.

TARDIVE DYSKINESIA (TD). A neurological disorder characterized by uncontrollable movements and caused by the prolonged use of antipsychotics.

TD. Tetanus and diphtheria vaccine.

TELANGIECTASIAS. Very small arteriovenous malformations, or connections between the arteries and veins. The result is small red spots on the skin known as "spider veins."

TELEHEALTH. The use of computers, computer networks, and telecommunications systems by health care professionals to reach people in rural areas.

TELOMERE. A region of repetitive DNA at the end of chromosomes that protects the end of the chromosome from damage during the process of cell division.

TEMPERAMENT. The dimension of an individual's personality that is rooted in genetic or biological factors.

TEMPLATING. A term that refers to the surgeon's use of x-ray images of an old prosthesis as a template or pattern guide for a new implant.

TEMPORAL. Referring to the area of the temples on either side of the head.

TEMPOROMANDIBULAR JOINT DISORDER. Inflammation, irritation, and pain of the jaw caused by improper opening and closing of the temporomandibular joint. Other symptoms include clicking of the jaw and a limited range of motion.

TEMPOROMANDIBULAR. Relating to the meeting point of the skull and the lower jaw.

TENDINITIS. Inflammation of tissues that connect muscles to bones. Tendinitis is usually caused by strain or an injury.

TENDON. The flexible but strong connective tissue that attaches muscles to bones.

TENDON SHEATH. A membrane covering a tendon.

TENDONITIS. Inflammation of a tendon usually occurring after excessive use, as in a sports injury or repetitive movement.

TENESMUS. A feeling that a bowel movement is imminent.

TENOSYNOVITIS. Inflammation of a tendon and its enveloping sheath, usually resulting from overuse injury.

TENS. The abbreviation for transcutaneous electrical nerve stimulation, a technique used to control chronic pain. Electrodes placed over the painful area deliver a mild electrical impulse to nearby nerve pathways, thereby easing pain.

TERM LIFE. A life insurance policy that provides coverage for a specific time period (term), usually five, 10, 20, or 30 years.

TESTES. Egg-shaped male gonads located in the scrotum. Testes is the plural form of testis, which is a testicle.

TESTOSTERONE. A male hormone produced in the testes or made synthetically that is responsible for male secondary sex characteristics.

TETANY. A general stiffening and spasms of the muscles that can occur in severe cases of hypocalcemia.

THALAMUS. An area of the brain that helps process information from the senses and transmit it to other parts of the brain.

THALASSEMIA. Inherited blood disorder characterized by abnormal red blood cells that are unable to carry enough oxygen throughout the body.

THANATOLOGY. The study of death and dying and of human reactions to these events.

THIAZIDE. A group of drugs used as oral diuretics especially in the control of high blood pressure.

THORACOSCOPY. Examination of the contents of the chest through a thin, lighted tube passed through a small incision.

THORACOTOMY. A surgical opening into the thoracic cavity.

THORASCOPY. A medical test that allows a physician to see the breathing passages and lungs through a special scope passed through small incisions in the chest. The physician guides the examination by video monitor.

THORAX. The chest area, which runs between the abdomen and neck and is encased in the ribs.

THROMBOPHLEBITIS. Swelling of a vein caused by a blood clot.

THROMBOSIS. The development of a blood clot inside a blood vessel.

THRUSH. Yeast infection (candidiasis) of the oral cavity.

THYMUS. An organ that is part of the lymphatic system and in which T lymphocytes grow and multiply. It is located in the chest behind the breastbone.

TIBIA. The larger, longer bone of the lower leg which articulates or joins with the ankle and knee.

TINCTURE. A liquid extract of an herb prepared by steeping the herb in an alcohol and water mixture. A tincture can also be prepared using vinegar or glycerin, instead of alcohol.

TINEA CAPITIS. Ringworm.

TINEA CRURIS. Fungal infection of the groin area.

TINEA PEDIS. Athlete's foot.

TINEA VERSICOLOR. A skin fungus that is recognized because it causes skin discoloration.

TINNETTI BALANCE TEST. A battery of tests to assess balance and identify individuals at risk for falling.

TINNITUS. A condition in which a person may hear ringing or buzzing in one or both ears when there is no exterior ringing or buzzing present.

TISSUE PLASMINOGEN ACTIVATOR (T–PA). Clot–dissolving medicine approved by the U.S. Food and Drug Administration (FDA).

TITER. The concentration of substance in a solution described in terms of the degree of dilution required to achieve a threshold effect.

T-LYMPHOCYTE. A type of white blood cell, also known as a T-helper cell, a T_h cell, an effector T cell, or a CD4 T cell, whose numbers in a blood sample can be used to monitor the progression of HIV infection.

TOLERANCE. A phenomenon whereby a drug user becomes physically accustomed to a particular dose of a substance, and requires ever-increasing dosages in order to obtain the same effects.

TOMOGRAPHY. A technique of using ultrasound, gamma rays, or x rays to produce a focused image of the structures across a specific depth within the body, while blurring details at other depths.

TONIC. Characterized by tonus, a state of partial contraction that is maintained at least in part by a continuous bombardment of motor impulses.

TOPHI. Stone-like deposits of uric acid crystals that may build up in the joints, ligaments, and tendons, and lead to permanent joint deformity and decreased motion.

TOPICAL. A type of medication applied to the skin or body surface.

TOTAL GASTRECTOMY. Surgical removal (excision) of the entire stomach.

TOTAL PARENTERAL NUTRITION (TPN). A solution containing all the required nutrients including protein, fat, calories, vitamins, and minerals, is injected over the course of several hours, into a vein.

TOTAL THYROIDECTOMY. A surgical procedure that removes the entire thyroid gland.

TOURETTE SYNDROME. A condition in which a person has tics and other involuntary behavior, such as barking, sniffing, swearing, grunting, and making uncontrollable movements.

TOURNIQUET. A tube or pressure cuff that is tightened around a limb in order to compress a vein to stop bleeding.

TOXIN. A general term for something that harms or poisons the body.

TOXOPLASMOSIS. A parasitic infection acquired from cat feces or undercooked meat that can affect the brain.

TRABECULAR MESHWORK. The series of canals or tubes behind the iris that filters the aqueous humor and allows it to drain into the bloodstream.

TRACE MINERALS. Minerals needed by the body in small amounts. They include: selenium, iron, zinc, copper, manganese, molybdenum, chromium, arsenic, germanium, lithium, rubidium, tin.

TRACHEA. The windpipe, or main by which air passes to and from the lungs.

TRACHEOBRONCHIAL. Pertaining both to the tracheal and bronchial tubes or to their junction.

TRACHEOSTOMY TUBE. Surgically created opening in the trachea for the purpose of providing a secure airway. This is used when the patient requires long-term ventilatory assistance.

TRACHEOSTOMY. Surgically created opening in the trachea for the purpose of providing a secure airway. This is used when the patient requires long term ventilatory assistance.

TRACTION. A medical treatment that exerts a pulling or extending force. Used for cervical problems, it relieves pressure on structures between the vertebrae and muscular tension.

TRADITIONAL OR CONVENTIONAL MEDICINE. Medical practice by licensed medical or osteopathic doctors in coordination with other healthcare professionals such as registered nurses, physical therapists, and psychologists.

TRADITIONAL NATUROPATH. A practitioner of alternative medicine who uses some of the alternative or complementary therapies recommended by naturopathic physicians but lacks their training in conventional medicine and is not licensed to offer primary health care.

TRAIT ANXIETY. An aspect of an individual's personality that influences their susceptibility to anxiety in stressful situations.

TRANQUILIZER (MINOR). A drug that has a calming effect and is used to treat anxiety and emotional tension.

TRANSCRANIAL MAGNETIC STIMULATION (TMS). A procedure which uses a strong magnet held outside the head to influence brain activity.

TRANSCUTANEOUS ELECTRICAL NERVE STIMULATION (TENS). Application of a gentle electric current to the skin to relieve pain.

TRANSDERMAL. Through the skin, in context, a patch that delivers medication when it is applied to a skin area.

TRANSDUCER. An electronic device that converts sound wave energy into an electrical signal for interpretation.

TRANSESOPHAGEAL ECHOCARDIOGRAPHY. A diagnostic test using an ultrasound device that is passed into the esophagus of the patient to create a clear image of the heart muscle and other parts of the heart.

TRANSFERRIN. A protein synthesized in the liver that transports iron in the blood to red blood cells.

TRANSFUSION. The transfer of blood from one person to another. Transfusions can be direct, in which blood is transferred from the donor to the recipient; or indirect, in which the blood is taken from the donor, stored in a container, and then given to the recipient.

TRANSIENT ISCHEMIC ATTACK (TIA). Temporary blockage of blood flow to the brain often resulting in slurred speech, vision disturbances, and loss of balance. The episode is brief and the damage often short-term. Also called a mini-stroke or a warning stroke.

TRANSSEXUAL. Person desiring to acquire the external appearance of a member of the opposite gender.

TRANS-TELEPHONIC MONITORING. A method of checking on the function and battery strength of a pacemaker involving a special device that allows signals from an implanted pacemaker to be communicated to health care personnel using the telephone lines.

TRANSURETHRAL RESECTION OF THE PROSTATE (TURP). Surgical removal of a portion of the prostate through the urethra, a method of treating the symptoms of an enlarged prostate, whether from BPH or cancer.

TRASTUZUMAB. Herceptin, a monoclonal antibody that binds to HER2 causing the immune system to destroy the cell; used to treat HER2-positive breast cancer.

TRAUMA. A physical injury or wound caused by an external force.

TRAVELER'S DIARRHEA. Diarrhea caused by ingesting local bacteria to which one's digestive system has not yet adapted.

TREMOR. Shakiness or trembling.

TRIGEMINAL NERVE. The cranial (head) nerve with three branches, which serves one side of the face.

TRIGEMINAL NEURALGIA. Brief episodes of severe shooting pain on one side of the face caused by inflammation of the root of the trigeminal nerve. Also referred to as tic douloureux.

TRIGGER POINT. An area of skeletal muscle tissue that is sore to the touch and contains small lumps or nodules in the muscle fibers. Some practitioners use acupuncture to relieve the pain and loosen the muscle fibers in trigger points.

TRIGLYCERIDE. A substance formed in the body from the breakdown of fat in the diet. Triglycerides are the main fatty materials in the blood. Triglyceride levels are important in the diagnosis and treatment of many diseases, including high blood pressure, diabetes, and.

TRITURATION. The process of diluting a nonsoluble substance for homeopathic use by grinding it to a fine powder and mixing it with lactose powder.

TROPICAL SPRUE. A condition of unknown cause whereby abnormalities in the lining of the small intestine prevent the body from absorbing food normally. This disease is not associated with gluten enteropathy. It has been associated with travel and residing in the tropics.

TRUST. A property interest held by one person (the trustee) for the benefit of another (the grantor).

TUBERCULOMA. A tumor-like mass in the brain that sometimes develops as a complication of tuberculous meningitis.

TUBERCULOSIS. An infectious disease that usually affects the lungs, but may also affect other parts of the body. Symptoms include fever, weight loss, and coughing up blood.

TUI NA. A form of acupressure using tapping, kneading, and pressing motions that is part of traditional Chinese medicine (TCM).

TUMOR MARKERS. Substances that occur in the blood, urine, or tissues of patients with certain types of cancer. Tumor markers may be produced either by the tumor itself or by the body in response to the tumor.

TUMOR NECROSIS FACTOR (TNF). A protein that destroys cells showing abnormally rapid growth. TNF is used in immunotherapy to shrink tumors rapidly.

TUMOR STAGING. The method used by oncologists to determine the risk from a cancerous tumor. A number—ranging from 1A–4B— is assigned to predict the level of invasion by a tumor, and offer a prognosis for morbidity and mortality.

TUMOR SUPPRESSOR GENE. A gene that encodes proteins that inhibit cell division and replication. Tumor suppressor genes are damaged or inactive in many types of cancer cells.

TUMOR. An abnormal growth resulting from a cell that lost its normal growth control restraints and started multiplying uncontrollably.

TWELVE-STEP PROGRAM. A program that uses a set of 12 defining and guiding principles in alcohol abuse recovery.

TWILIGHT ANESTHESIA. An intravenous mixture of sedatives and other medications that decreases one's awareness of the procedure being performed.

TYMPANIC CAVITY. A mucus-membrane lined cavity behind the ear drum that connects with the auditory (Eustachian) tube.

TYMPANIC MEMBRANE. The ear drum, a thin but firm covering over the tympanic cavity that forms a barrier between the middle ear and the outer ear.

TYPE 2 DIABETES. The most common form of diabetes, it occurs when the body does not make enough insulin or does not use the insulin produced by the body to effectively create energy from sugar in the diet.

TYPHOID FEVER. An infectious disease caused by a type of bacterium. People with this disease have a lingering fever and feel depressed and exhausted. Diarrhea and rose–colored spots on the chest and abdomen are other symptoms.

U

ULCER. An inflammed sore or lesion that occurs on a surface such as skin or the mucus membrane of an organ, typically breaking the skin or membrane and resulting in loss of tissue.

ULCERATIVE COLITIS. A chronic condition where recurrent ulcers are found in the colon. It is manifested clinically by abdominal cramping, and rectal bleeding.

ULTRASOUND. A radiology test utilizing high frequency sound waves to view images of internal organs.

ULTRAVIOLET (UV) LIGHT. Part of the electromagnetic spectrum with a wavelength just below that of visible light. It is damaging to living material, especially eyes and DNA.

UNITED STATES CONSUMER PRODUCT SAFETY COMMISSION (CPSC). The United States governmental agency charged with protecting the public from unnecessary risk from consumer products sold in the United States.

UPPER ENDOSCOPY. A medical procedure in which a thin, lighted, flexible tube (endoscope) is inserted down the patient's throat. Through this tube the doctor can view the lining of the esophagus, stomach, and the upper part of the small intestine.

URATE CRYSTALS. Crystals formed by high levels of uric acid in the blood.

URBAN STUDIES. Course work in the sociology of urban areas.

URETER. Tube that connects the kidney and urinary bladder, whose function is to transport urine.

URETHAL. Referring to the tube in humans that carries urine from the bladder out of the body.

URETHRA. The tube leading from the bladder to discharge urine outside the body. In males, the urethra travels through the penis, and in females, it is shorter than in the male and emerges above the vaginal opening.

URETHRAL SPHINCTER. The muscle system that controls the retention and release of urine from the bladder.

URETHRITIS. Inflammation of the urinary bladder.

URINARY INCONTINENCE. Inability to keep urine in the bladder.

URINARY RETENTION. The inability to void (urinate) or discharge urine.

URINARY TRACT INFECTION. Bacterial infection that occurs in any part of the urinary tract.

URINARY TRACT. The organs of the body that produce and discharge urine. They include the kidneys, ureters, bladder, and urethra.

URINE. Fluid containing water and waste products. Urine is made by the kidneys, stored in the bladder, and leaves the body through the urethra.

UROGYNECOLOGIST. A physician that deals with women's health, especially with the health of women's reproductive organs and urinary tract.

UROLITHS. Urinary stones or calculi, crystals of concentrated minerals.

UROLOGIST. A physician who deals with the study and treatment of disorders of the urinary tract in women and the urogenital system in men.

UROTHELIUM. The lining of the urinary tract, including the renal pelvis, ureters, bladder and urethra.

UTERUS. The female reproductive organ that contains and nourishes a fetus from implantation until birth. Also known as the womb.

UTILITARIANISM. An ethical position based on the premise that usefulness is the best measure of moral worth, and that ethical decisions should promote the good of the largest number of persons.

UVEITIS. Inflammation of the uvea. The uvea is a continuous layer of tissue that consists of the iris, the ciliary body, and the choroid. The uvea lies between the retina and sclera.

UVULA. A triangular piece of tissue that hangs from the roof of the mouth above the back of the tongue. Primary snoring is often associated with fluttering or vibrating of the uvula during sleep.

UVULOPALATOPHARYNGOPLASTY (UPPP). An operation to remove the tonsils and other excess tissue at the back of the throat to prevent it from closing the airway during sleep.

V

VACCINATION. Injection of a killed or weakened microbe in order to stimulate the immune system against the microbe, thereby preventing disease. Vaccinations, or immunizations, work by stimulating the immune system, the natural disease-fighting system of the body.

VACCINE. A preparation of a weakened or killed pathogen, such as a bacterium or virus, that upon administration to a person stimulates antibody production against the pathogen but is incapable of causing severe infection.

VACCINE–INDUCED IMMUNITY. Protection against a disease that results when exposure to a dead or weakened disease organism triggers the immune system to produce antibodies to that disease.

VACUTAINER. A glass tube fitted with a rubber stopper from which air is evacuated to produce a slight vacuum, used for blood specimen collection.

VAGINA. The tube-like passage from the vulva (a woman's external genital structures) to the cervix (the portion of the uterus that projects into the vagina).

VAGINISMUS. Muscles around the outer third of the vagina have involuntary spasms in response to attempts at vaginal penetration, not allowing for penetration.

VALIDATION. In counseling, the support for or corroboration of the client's feelings or thoughts.

VALSALVA MANEUVER. Forced expiration or breathing out of air when the airway is closed. It is used to test the heart's response to changes in pressure.

VALVULAR. Having to do with the valves inside the heart.

VALVULAR HEART DISEASE. A disease of any one of the four valves that controls blood flow into, through, and out of the heart.

VARICELLA. The virus that causes chicken pox and remains in a person's system, eventually causing shingles to occur.

VARICELLA-ZOSTER VIRUS. A virus in the herpes family that causes chicken pox during childhood and may reactivate later in life to cause herpes zoster (shingles).

VARICES (SINGULAR, VARIX). Enlarged (dilated) veins that are subject to bleeding.

VARICOSE VEINS. Enlarged, twisted, painful superficial veins resulting from poorly functioning valves; In normal veins, valves in the vein keep blood moving forward toward the heart; With varicose veins, the valves do not function properly, allowing blood to remain in th.

VAS DEFERENS. A tube that is a continuation of the epididymis. This tube transports sperm from the testis to the prostatic urethra.

VASCULAR DEPRESSION. Depression associated with blood vessel damage or brain lesions.

VASCULAR. Pertaining to the circulatory system, the arteries, veins, and microcirculation.

VASCULAR SYSTEM. A specialized network of vessels for the circulation of fluids (blood and lymph) throughout the body tissues; also referred to as the circulatory system.

VASCULARIZATION. Another name for angiogenesis.

VASOCONSTRICTOR. An agent that causes blood vessels to contract.

VASODILATION. The increase in the internal diameter of a blood vessel that results from relaxation of smooth muscle within the wall of the vessel thus causing an increase in blood flow.

VASODILATOR. Anb agent that causes blood vessels to relax.

VASOSPASM. Sudden sustained contraction of the walls of a blood vessel.

VEGAN. A person who eats only vegetable products.

VEIN. A blood vessel that returns oxygen-depleted blood from various parts of the body to the heart.

VENIPUNCTURE. The puncture of a vein for therapeutic purpose or to collect a specimen.

VENOUS THROMBOSIS. A condition in which a vein is clogged off by foreign matter or a blood clot that results in decreased blood flow and oxygen to specific parts of the body.

VENTILATOR. Device used to provide assisted respiration and positive pressure breathing.

VENTRICLE. A lower pumping chambers of the heart. There are two ventricles, right and left. The right ventricle pumps oxygen-poor blood to the lungs to be reoxygenated. The left ventricle pumps oxygen-rich blood to the body.

VENTRICLES OF THE BRAIN. The four fluid-filled chambers, or cavities, found in the two cerebral hemispheres of the brain, at the center of the brain, and between the brain stem and cerebellum, and linked by channels, or ducts, allowing cerebral fluid to circulate through them.

VENTRICULAR FIBRILLATION. An arrhythmia in which the heart beats very fast but blood is not pumped out to the body. Ventricular fibrillation can quickly become fatal if not corrected.

VENTRICULAR TACHYCARDIA. An abnormally rapid heartbeat. It includes a series of at least three beats arising from a ventricular area at a rate of more than 100 beats per minute, usually ranging from 150–200 beats per minute.

VERTEBRAE. The bones, also called discs, that make up the spine or backbone.

VERTEBRAL ARTERIES. Arteries that run along the cervical spine through the neck and into the brain stem.

VESTIBULAR. Pertaining to the apparatus in the inner ear that senses orientation and movement of the body in space.

VESTIBULAR SYSTEM. Interaction among the inner ear structures associated with balance and position sense, and the central nervous system.

VIDEOSCOPE. A surgical camera.

VILLI. The tiny, finger-like projections on the surface of the small intestine that help absorb nutrients.

VIPASSANA. A Buddhist meditative practice that emphasizes deep attentiveness to the present moment.

VIRAL INFECTION. Infection caused by a virus.

VIRULENCE. The relative ability of a disease organism to overcome the body's defenses. A highly virulent organism is one that can readily overcome the immune system.

VIRUS (VIRAL). A type of microscopic infectious organism that causes viral illnesses such as influenza and the common cold. The body does not fight viruses as well as it does bacteria because of differences in composition and behavior.

VISCERAL PLEURAE. The outer surface of each lung.

VISUAL ACUITY. Sharpness or clearness of vision.

VISUAL SYSTEM. Components which transmit information from the retina to the brain.

VISUALIZATION. The use of mental imagery to focus attention and assist relaxation.

VITAL CAPACITY. Maximum volume of air that can be expelled from the lungs after a maximal inspiration.

VITAL SIGNS. A person's essential body functions, usually defined as the pulse, body temperature, and breathing rate.

VITAMIN. A nutrient that the body needs in small amounts to remain healthy but that the body cannot manufacture for itself and must acquire through diet.

VITRECTOMY. The surgical removal of the vitreous humor. The gel is replaced with saline or another clear fluid.

VITREOUS HUMOR. The clear gel that fills the space between the lens and the retina of the eye.

VOLUNTARY. An action or thought undertaken or controlled by a person's free will or choice.

VULVA. The external part of the woman's genital organs, including the vaginal vestibule.

VULVOVAGINAL. Pertaining to the vulva and vagina.

W

WARD. A person who by reason of incapacity is under the protection of a court, either directly or through a guardian or conservator appointed by the court. In some jurisdictions wards are called conservatees or protected persons.

WATER BRASH. The flow of saliva and stomach acid back up the esophagus and into the throat or lungs.

WATER HOMEOSTASIS. A condition of adequate fluid level in the body in which fluid loss and fluid intake are equally matched and sodium levels are within normal range.

WATER POLO. A game played in the water with two teams trying to get a large ball through a hoop on each side of the pool.

WATER-SOLUBLE VITAMIN. A vitamin that dissolves in water and can be removed from the body in urine.

WEANING. The process of gradually tapering mechanical ventilation and allowing the patient to resume breathing on their own.

WERNER SYNDROME. A genetic disorder in which a defective gene on chromosome 8 causes telomeres to shorten too rapidly, thus lowering the number of times the cell can divide.

WERNICKE'S AREA. An area in the temporal lobe of the brain (on the left side in most people) that governs language comprehension. It is named for Karl Wernicke (1848–1905), a German neurologist and psychiatrist who first recognized its role in a type of aphasia.

WESTERN BLOT. A procedure that passes an electrical current through a gel containing a sample of tissue extract in order to break down the proteins in the sample and detect the presence of antibodies for a specific disease. This method is used in HIV testing.

WHEEZING. Difficult breathing because of attempts to force air through narrow airways; usually accompanied by a whistling sound.

WHIPPLE PROCEDURE. Surgical removal of the head of the pancreas, part of the small intestine, and some surrounding tissue.

WHITE BLOOD CELL (WBC) DIFFERENTIAL TEST. Blood test that assesses the ability of the body to respond to and eliminate infection. It also detects the severity of allergic and drug reactions.

WHITE BLOOD CELLS (LEUKOCYTES). Cells of the blood that are responsible for fighting infection.

WHOLE-BODY DONATION. The donation of a person's entire body after death to a medical school or other institution for purposes of education and research.

WHOOPING COUGH. An infectious disease, also called pertussis, especially of children that is caused by a bacterium and is marked by a convulsive, spasmodic cough, sometimes followed by a shrill intake of breath.

WILL-TO-LIVE LIVING WILL. A living will that contains explicit instructions for life-sustaining treatment, regardless of the patient's condition or prognosis.

WINDOW PERIOD. The period of time between a person's contracting an infection and the point at which a laboratory test can detect the infection. Depending on the method of analysis used, the window period in HIV testing is between 12 and 22 days.

WITHDRAWAL. Those side effects experienced by a person who has become physically dependent on a substance, upon decreasing the substance's dosage, or discontinuing its use.

WITHDRAWAL SYMPTOMS. A group of physical or mental symptoms that may occur when a person suddenly stops using a drug to which he or she has become dependent.

WOODS LIGHT. Device that allows only ultraviolet light to pass through it.

WOUND. Any injury that breaks the skin, including cuts, scratches, and puncture wounds.

X

X RAYS. High-energy electromagnetic radiation used in high doses, either to diagnose or treat disease. It has a short wavelength, between ultraviolet and gamma rays.

XEROPHTHALMIA. A drying of the cornea and conjunctiva.

XEROSTOMIA. The medical term for dry mouth.

Y

YELLOW FEVER. An infectious disease caused by a virus. The disease, which is spread by mosquitoes, is most common in Central and South America and Central Africa. Symptoms include high fever, jaundice (yellow eyes and skin) and dark-colored vomit.

YIN AND YANG. In traditional Chinese medicine and philosophy, a pair of opposing forces whose harmonious balance in the body is necessary to good health.

YOGA. An ancient form of exercise that strengthens the spine and the muscles of the body while it calms the mind.

YOGI (FEMALE, YOGINI). A trained practitioner of yoga.

Z

ZENKER'S DIVERTICULUM. A disorder in which an overly tense sphincter at the upper end of the esophagus leads to the formation of a pouch in the wall of the esophagus.

ZOLLINGER-ELLISON SYNDROME. A disorder characterized by the presence of tumors (gastrinomas) that secrete a hormone (gastrin), which stimulates the production of digestive juices.

ZOONOSIS (PLURAL, ZOONOSES). Any disease of animals that can be transmitted to humans under natural conditions. Lyme disease and babesiosis are examples of zoonoses.

INDEX

In the index, references to individual volumes are listed before colons; numbers following a colon refer to specific page numbers within that particular volume. **Boldface** references indicate main topical essays. Photographs and illustration references are highlighted with an *italicized* page number; and tables are also indicated with the page number followed by a lowercase, italicized *t*.

A

A/C (Assist-control ventilation), 3:1047–1048, 5:1822
AAA (American Automobile Association), 2:705, 5:1607
AAAAI (American Academy of Allergy, Asthma and Immunology), 1:70
AAAHC (Accreditation Association for Ambulatory Health Care), 3:806
AAHA (American Hearing Aid Association), 3:919, 920
AAMA (American Academy of Medical Acupuncture), 1:20
AAOS. *See* American Academy of Orthopaedic Surgeons
AARDA (American Autoimmune Related Diseases Association), 1:260
AARP, 1:*1*, **1–3**
  caregivers, 2:454
  conservatorship, 2:567
  driver safety, 2:705
  health insurance, 4:1494
  independence, 3:1028
  low-fat diet, 2:661
  Medicare prescription drug plan, 4:1240
  travel, 5:1607
AARP The Magazine, 1:1
AASECT (American Association of Sexual Educators, Counselors, and Therapists), 5:1619
ABA (American Bar Association), 1:30, 31, 32, 2:567
ABA (American Board of Anesthesiology), 4:1399
Abana, 3:1076
Abbokinase. *See* Urokinase
Abbreviations, medication, 1:26
ABCD rule, 2:451, 5:1642, 1650
Abdominal aortic aneurysm, 1:120–121, 122
Abdominal binders, 1:264
Abdominal hysterectomy, 3:1017
Abdominal pain, 3:1147
Abdominal trauma, penetrating, 3:846
Abdominoplasty, 1:*3,* **3–7,** 4–5, 367, 2:582–584
Abetalipoproteinemia, 5:1856
Abitrate. *See* Clofibrate
Ablation
  alcohol, 3:1141
  cardiac, 1:226–227, 2:423–426, 440
  catheter, 1:226–227, 2:424–426
  endometrial, 3:1019
  endovenous, 5:1817–1818
  laparoscopic radiofrequency, 3:1140
  surgical, 2:424–426
ABMA (American Board of Medical Acupuncture), 1:20
ABMS (American Board of Medical Specialties), 3:805–806, 807, 4:1399
ABR (Auditory brainstem response), 5:1780
ABS (American Board of Surgery), 3:805
Abscess, 1:275, 289, 2:695
Absence seizures, 5:1601–1606
Absolute presbyopia, 4:1485
Absorption problems. *See* Malabsorption
Abstract thought, 2:612
Abuse. *See* Alcohol abuse; Child abuse; Drug abuse; Elder abuse
ACA (American Chiropractic Association), 2:502
Academic medical centers, 5:1610
Acamprosate, 5:1731, 1780
Acarbose, 1:178, 2:640
Acceptance, stages of, 3:995
Access to Recovery vouchers, 2:707
Accessory pathways, 2:424
Accidents, traffic. *See* Traffic accidents
Accommodation, 1:94–95, 2:462
Accreditation Association for Ambulatory Health Care (AAAHC), 3:806
Accreditation, hospital, 3:806
  See also Joint Commission on Accreditation of Healthcare Organizations
Accrediting Commission of Career Schools and Colleges of Technology, 4:1219
Accrediting Council for Continuing Education and Training, 4:1219
Accupril. *See* Quinapril
Accutane. *See* Isotretinoin
ACE inhibitors. *See* Angiotensin-converting enzyme inhibitors
Acebutolol, 1:190–191, 2:580
Aceon. *See* Perindopril
Acetaminophen, 1:**7–8,** 106, 107
  anticonvulsant drug interactions, 1:162
  for diabetic neuropathy, 2:647
  for fever, 3:1037
  for headaches, 3:907
  hepatitis from, 3:950
  hormone replacement therapy interactions, 3:993
  hydroxyzine interactions, 1:142
  for influenza, 5:1833
  isoniazid interactions, 1:211
  for knee injuries, 3:1117
  for liver biopsy pain, 3:1136
  liver function test interactions, 3:1143
  for migraines, 4:1267
  for neuralgia, 4:1318
  for osteoarthritis, 4:1367
  overdose, 1:8, 3:897, 4:1380–1381
  for Paget's disease of bone, 4:1392
  for pain, 4:1395, 1398
  for pericarditis, 4:1432
  for psoriasis, 4:1520
  for rheumatoid arthritis, 4:1574
  rifampin interactions, 1:211
  for shingles, 5:1631, 1833
Acetazolamide, 1:235, 2:690
Acetic acid, 1:236, 5:1885
Acetohexamide, 1:178

Acetylcholine
  Alzheimer's disease, 1:87, 164
  Botox injections, 1:345
  delirium, 2:607
Acetylcholinesterase, 1:163
Acetylcholinesterase inhibitors. *See* Cholinesterase inhibitors
Acetylsalicylic acid. *See* Aspirin
ACG (American College of Gastroenterologists), 3:1071
Achalasia, 2:759, 5:1634, 1740
Achilles tendon, 1:388, 389, 5:1753
Acid breakthrough, 3:857
Acid indigestion. *See* Heartburn
Acid reflux. *See* Antacids; Gastroesophageal reflux disease
Acidophilus, 3:1024
Acidosis, 1:180, 4:1381, 1389
Acinar cell carcinoma, 4:1404
AcipHex. *See* Rabeprazole
ACL (Anterior cruciate ligament), 3:1115, 1117
ACN (American College of Nutrition), 4:1346, 1347
Acne, 1:333, 2:530, 5:1588, 1650, 1861
Acne drugs, 2:715
Aconite, 3:987
Aconitum napellus. See Monkshood
Acoustic neuroma, 2:697
Acoustic reflecting CT scans, 5:1673
Acquired immunity, 3:1021
Acquired immunodeficiency syndrome. *See* AIDS
Acral lentiginous melanoma, 4:1197–1198
Acrodermatitis continua of Hallopeau, 4:1519
Acrodermatitis enteropathica, 5:1898
Acromioclavicular separation, 2:687
Acrylic lenses, 2:772
ACTH (Adrenocorticotropic hormone), 2:590, 591, 3:892
Acthar. *See* Adrenocorticotropic hormone
Actimmune. *See* Interferon-gamma 1-b
Actinic chelitis, 5:1642
Actinic keratosis, 5:1642
Actinic purpura, 1:385, 387
Action T4, 2:763
Activase. *See* Alteplase
Activated charcoal, 4:1382
Active euthanasia, 2:763
Active fixation, 4:1388
Activities, major life, 1:92
Activities of daily living
  adult day care, 1:28
  aging in place, 3:1028
  Alzheimer's disease, 1:86–87, 88–89
  assisted living facilities, 1:236
  community social programs, 2:558
  dementia, 2:610
  exercise, 2:767
  geriatric assessment, 3:866
  home health aides, 3:982, 983
  independence, 3:1027
  instrumental, 1:9–10, 2:767, 3:802, 997–998, 1027, 1028, 4:1283, 1441
  low vision, 3:1164
  mobility, 4:1283
  nursing assistants, 4:1329
  paralysis, 4:1418
  personal hygiene, 4:1441, 1444
  physical therapy, 1:268
  pulmonary rehabilitation, 4:1542
  recovery at home, 4:1555
  spinal cord injuries, 5:1694
  vision disorders, 5:1835
  wheelchairs, 5:1881
Activities of daily living evaluation, 1:**9–11,** *9t*
Actonel. *See* Risedronate
Acu-yoga, 1:14, 15
Acupoints, 5:1628, 1629
Acupressure, 1:*11,* **11–17,** *12,* 4:1217
  energy flow, 4:1546
  gastroesophageal reflux disease, 3:856
  menopause, 4:1253
  meridians, 1:12, 13
  nausea and vomiting, 5:1628
  rheumatoid arthritis, 4:1574
  seizures, 5:1605
  shiatsu, 5:1627–1629
  sleep disorders, 5:1628–1629
Acupuncture, 1:**17–22**
  arrhythmias, 1:227
  bursitis, 1:390
  cancer pain, 2:411–412
  cervical spondylosis, 2:489
  chronic pain, 4:1398
  cystitis, 2:595
  diabetic foot infections, 2:641
  energy flow, 4:1546
  gastroesophageal reflux disease, 3:856
  headaches, 3:907
  itching, 3:1082
  low back pain, 3:1152
  lupus, 3:1181
  menopause, 4:1253
  meridians, 1:17, 18, 5:1628
  naturopathy, 4:1316
  neuralgia, 4:1319
  osteoarthritis, 4:1368, 5:1615
  polymyositis, 4:1468
  rheumatoid arthritis, 4:1574
  sciatica, 5:1594
  seizures, 5:1605
  sexual dysfunction, 5:1620
  smoking cessation, 5:1667
  snoring, 5:1675
  spinal stenosis, 5:1697
  substance abuse, 5:1727
  tendinitis, 5:1754
  tinnitus, 5:1780
  trigger finger, 5:1788
Acute bronchitis, 1:375–378
Acute care nurses, 3:1130
Acute infections, 1:277, 3:1032
Acute leukemia, 1:*22,* **22–23,** 5:1861
Acute pain
  acupressure, 1:15
  acupuncture, 1:19
  analgesics, 1:107
  defined, 4:1393–1394
  low back, 3:1151, 1152
  massage, 4:1218
  multiple sclerosis, 4:1304
  treatment, 4:1396
Acute pericarditis, 4:1432
Acute promyelocytic leukemia, 5:1861
Acute PTSD, 4:1469–1470
Acute respiratory distress, 3:1046, 1047, 5:1821
Acute respiratory failure, 4:1569
Acute stress disorder, 4:1469–1470
Acyclovir, 1:212, 5:1833
ADA. *See* American Dietetic Association
ADA (American Diabetes Association), 1:329, 2:515, 639–640, 645
ADAA (Anxiety Disorders Association of America), 1:215–216
Adaptation, 1:10
Adaptive equipment. *See* Assistive devices
Addiction
  defined, 5:1725
  diazepam, 4:1308
  gambling, 3:840
  marijuana, 4:1213
  nicotine, 5:1659, 1660, 1661, 1664
  pharmacology research, 4:1450
  reconciliation, 4:1553
Addison's disease, 1:258–260
  DHEA for, 2:633, 634
  electrolyte tests, 2:739
  hyperkalemia from, 2:737
ADEA (Age Discrimination in Employment Act), 1:47
Adenocarcinoma
  bladder, 1:307
  ductal, 4:1404
  endocrine pancreatic, 4:1401
  endometrial, 2:743
  esophageal, 2:758, 759
  gallbladder, 3:835

Adenocarcinoma *(continued)*
 lung, 3:1174
 stomach, 5:1706, 1707
Adenocarcinoma-in-situ (AIS), endocervical, 2:482, 4:1414
Adenoids, 3:1022, 5:1673
Adenoma, 2:590, 3:1006
Adenovirus autoantibodies, 1:250
Adenovirus infections, 3:851, 4:1309, 1431
Adequate Intake (AI), 2:398, 5:1679, 1854–1855, 1859
ADH (Antidiuretic hormone), 2:636–637, 734
ADHD (Attention deficit/hyperactivity disorder), 1:168, 302, 3:886
Adiponectin, 1:194
Adjustment, chiropractic, 2:501–502, 504
Adjustment disorders, 1:**23–24,** 4:1218, 5:1715
Adjuvant chemotherapy, 2:489, 536
ADL. *See* Activities of daily living
Administration of medication, 1:*24,* **24–28,** *25*
 chemotherapy, 2:490–491
 forgetting to take, 2:629
 oral, 1:25, 2:490
 See also Inhalation therapy; Injections; Intravenous medication administration; Topical medication
Administration on Aging (AoA)
 caregivers, 2:454–455
 elder abuse, 2:727
 movement therapy, 4:1293
 nutrition, 4:1339
Adolescents
 body mass index, 1:332
 bone marrow biopsy and aspiration, 1:342
 personality disorders, 4:1446
 substance abuse prevention, 5:1728
 teeth whitening, 5:1750
Adrenal glands, 2:634, 5:1793
Adrenal insufficiency, 2:633, 634
Adrenalin. *See* Epinephrine
Adrenergic blockers
 $alpha_1$, 1:81–83, 81*t*
 asthma from, 1:241
 beta, 1:83
 for hypertension, 3:1011
Adrenocorticoids, 1:284
Adrenocorticotropic hormone (ACTH), 2:590, 591, 3:892
Adult children, 2:454, 707, 727, 728
Adult day care, 1:*28,* **28–30**
Adult Protective Services Caseworkers, 2:728–729
Adult scoliosis, 1:271–275
Advance directives, 1:**30–33,** 2:598
 assisted living facilities, 1:238
 vs. conservatorship, 2:567
 DNR orders, 2:598, 699–700
 financial management, 3:803
 living wills, 1:30–33, 2:598, 3:1149–1150
 withdrawal of life support, 5:1883
Advance nomination, 2:567, 3:803
Advanced education
 advanced practice nurses, 1:36, 4:1559
 dietitians, 2:681–682
 licensed practical nurses, 3:1129
 optometrists, 4:1355
 pharmacologists, 4:1451–1452
 social work, 5:1678
Advanced practice nurses, 1:**33–36,** 2:525–527, 3:1129, 4:1559
Advertising, 1:1–2, 3:808, 4:1344
Advil. *See* Ibuprofen
AED (Automated external defibrillators), 2:450
AER (Automated endoscope reprocessing) system, 1:384
Aerobic exercise, 1:**36–39,** *37,* 2:767
 depression, 2:628
 fibromyalgia, 3:801
 heart disease, 3:929
 ischemia, 3:1076
 migraine prevention, 4:1268
 pulmonary rehabilitation, 4:1542–1543
 water exercise, 5:1875
AeroBid. *See* Beclomethasone dipropionate
Aerosols, 2:742
 See also Inhalation therapy
Affect, 4:1321, 1446
Affinity anoxia, 1:137
AFP (Alpha-fetoproteins), 3:1139, 1142, 1143
African Americans
 age-related macular degeneration, 5:1836
 AIDS, 5:1622
 asthma, 1:240–241
 autoimmune disorders, 1:258–260
 bladder cancer, 1:308
 breast cancer, 1:351–352, 355, 5:1682
 breast implants, 1:362
 breast reconstruction, 1:364
 cancer, 2:412–413
 cancer mortality, 5:1682
 cervical cancer, 2:481, 484
 congestive heart failure, 2:562
 coronary artery disease, 2:578
 dementia, 2:611
 diabetes mellitus, 2:639
 diabetic nephropathy, 2:643
 diabetic retinopathy, 2:648–649
 end-stage renal disease, 3:1104
 endometrial cancer, 2:743
 esophageal cancer, 2:759
 exocrine pancreatic cancer, 4:1404
 eye examination, 2:769
 glaucoma, 2:769, 3:880, 1163, 5:1836
 grandparent child care, 3:795
 heart disease, 3:926
 hip revision surgery, 3:972, 974
 hypertension, 1:325, 3:1009
 hysterectomy, 3:1016
 influenza vaccines, 3:1041
 iron-deficiency anemia, 3:1064
 lactose intolerance, 3:819, 1121
 liver cancer, 3:1138
 low vision, 3:1163
 lung cancer, 1:382
 lupus, 3:1179
 melanoma, 4:1198, 1200, 5:1641
 multiple myeloma, 4:1299
 multiple sclerosis, 4:1304
 nutrition, 4:1339
 osteoporosis, 3:992, 4:1371
 panic disorder, 4:1410
 prayer and spirituality, 4:1477
 prostate cancer, 4:1505, 1509, 5:1682
 psoriasis, 4:1519
 sarcoidosis, 5:1581
 scleroderma, 5:1596
 sildenafil citrate, 5:1634
 skin cancer, 5:1642
 snoring, 5:1671
 speech disorders, 5:1687
 spinal cord injuries, 5:1691
 stroke, 5:1721
 suicide, 5:1733
 thyroid cancer, 5:1769
 transient ischemic attacks, 5:1785
 tuberculosis, 5:1791
AGA-IgA test, 2:473
AGC (Atypical glandular cells), 2:482, 4:1414
Age
 breast cancer, 3:1169
 caregivers, 3:795
 dietary intake, 2:673–674
 exercise, 2:766*t*
 heart attacks, 3:922
 heart disease, 3:926
 hip revision surgery, 3:974
 ischemia, 3:1074
 liver cancer, 3:1138
 multiple myeloma, 4:1299
 organ donation, 4:1363
 stroke, 5:1721
 See also Aging
Age Discrimination in Employment Act (ADEA), 1:47
Age-Related Eye Disease Study (ARED), 1:41
Age-related hearing loss, 3:919

Age-related macular degeneration, 1:*39*, **39–43,** 40*t,* 5:1612, 1835–1838, *1837*
- blindness, 1:319
- demographics, 1:40, 5:1836, 1836*t*
- dry, 1:39, 41, 42, 5:1615, 1835, 1837, 1838
- low vision, 3:1163
- treatment, 1:41, 5:1615, 1838
- vitamin E for, 5:1856

Aged, defined, 1:46

Ageism, 1:47–48

Agency for Healthcare Policy and Research, 3:806, 4:1511, 5:1587

Agent Orange, 5:1827

AGG-IgG test, 2:473

Agglutination, particle, 1:252, 253

Agglutinins, cold, 1:251, 253, 254

Aggravation, homeopathic, 3:988–989

Aging, 1:**43–48,** 43*t, 44, 45*
- alcohol, 1:65–66
- aneurysm risk, 1:122
- appetite loss, 2:659, 674, 4:1340
- attitude, 5:1890
- biology, 1:43–44
- body composition, 4:1340
- body weight changes, 4:1340
- caloric intake, 3:869, 4:1335–1336, 1340
- chronic pain, 4:1397
- dehydration, 2:603
- demographics, 1:45–46, 2:616, 3:868, 5:1611
- diet and lifestyle, 2:661–664
- emotional factors, 4:1523
- Harvard Study of Adult Development, 4:1525–1526
- hearing loss, 3:919
- immune response, 5:1612
- lifestyle, 5:1611
- malnutrition, 2:674, 4:1340–1341
- mental retardation, 4:1255
- metabolic rate, 2:658
- neurobiology, 4:1523
- normal, 1:44–45
- nutrition status, 2:673–674
- personality disorders, 4:1446
- physiology, 3:869
- premature, 1:44–45
- prevention, 1:46–47
- skin, 5:1888–1889
- theories, 1:45
- thinking, 5:1613
- vocal cords, 5:1687
- *See also* Healthy aging

Aging in place, 3:1028

Aging population
- demographics, 1:43*t, 44,* 45–46, 2:616, 3:868, 914, 5:1611
- economics, 3:795

Agitation, 2:607, 613

Agoraphobia, 2:396, 4:1409–1410

Agranulocytosis, 1:205

Agriculture Research Service (ARS), 2:658

Agrimonia eupatoria. See Agrimony

Agrimony, 4:1379

Agrylin. *See* Anagrelide HCI

AHA (American Heart Association). *See* American Heart Association

AHA (American Hospital Association), 2:527

AHAF (American Health Assistance Foundation), 1:86, 4:1243

AI (Adequate Intake), 2:398, 5:1679, 1854–1855, 1859

AIDS (Acquired immunodeficiency syndrome), 1:**48–56,** 49*t,* 3:1032, 5:1621–1624
- antiretroviral therapy, 1:51–52, 54, 55, 206–207, 207*t,* 5:1623
- cachexia, 2:393, 394
- cardiomyopathy, 2:445
- causes, 1:50, 57
- demographics, 1:50, 3:1034, 5:1622
- diagnosis, 1:51, 56, 58, 59–64
- eyelid tumors, 2:779
- fungal infections, 3:825
- garlic-drug interactions, 3:847, 849, 850
- Health Resources and Services Administration funding, 3:913–914
- hyponatremia, 2:735
- Kaposi's sarcoma, 5:1641
- marijuana for, 4:1213
- Medicare prescription drug plan, 4:1240
- melanoma, 4:1198–1199
- myocarditis, 4:1309
- non-Hodgkin's lymphoma, 4:1194–1195, 1196
- *Pneumocystitis carinii* pneumonia, 4:1464, 1466
- pneumonia risk, 4:1466
- prevention, 1:54
- prognosis, 1:53–54, 3:1035
- psoriasis, 4:1519
- pulmonary hypertension, 4:1539
- scabies, 5:1590
- skin cancer risk, 5:1642
- stages, 1:49–50
- T cells, 3:1023
- tuberculosis, 1:207–208, 5:1790, 1791
- Veterans Affairs hospital system, 5:1828
- VZV vaccine, 5:1632
- wasting syndrome, 1:53, 54, 2:393, 394, 4:1213

AIDS counseling, 1:**56–59**

AIDS dementia complex, 1:51, 53, 55

AIDS-related cancers, 1:51, 55, 5:1641, 1642

AIDS tests, 1:51, 56, 58, **59–64**

Aikido, 5:1716

Air-fluidized beds, 4:1490, 5:1885

Air pollution, 2:512

Airbags, 3:904

Airplane travel, 5:1608–1609, 1871

Airport security, 4:1389, 5:1608–1609

Airsickness, 5:1609

Airway management
- chest physical therapy, 2:495–498
- chronic obstructive pulmonary disease, 2:511
- endotracheal tubes, 2:750–752
- postoperative, 4:1472
- snoring, 5:1673
- spinal cord injuries, 5:1696

AIS (Adenocarcinoma-in-situ), endocervical, 2:482, 4:1414

Aitken, Paul V., 1:32

AJCC (American Joint Commission on Cancer), 3:1093, 1140

Ajoene, 3:847

Akinesia, 4:1422

Akinetic seizures, 5:1602–1606

Alanine aminotransferase (ALT), 3:1143–1146

Alaska Natives, 1:382, 3:910

Albumin
- food allergies, 3:817
- hypocalcemia, 2:736
- liver function tests, 3:1143, 1144, 1145, 1146
- malnutrition, 4:1202

Albuterol, 1:379, 4:1450

Alcohol ablation, ultrasound-guided, 3:1141

Alcohol abuse, 1:**64–70,** 65*t, 66,* 2:706–707, 5:1724–1729
- brief alcohol intervention, 5:1729, 1731
- demographics, 1:66–67, 3:869, 5:1729–1730
- diagnosis, 1:68, 5:1730
- disulfiram for, 5:1731
- liver cancer risk, 3:1142
- mobility, 4:1284
- panic disorder, 4:1411
- psychoses from, 4:1528
- stroke risk, 5:1721
- substance abuse counseling, 5:1729–1732
- suicide risk, 5:1733
- *See also* Alcoholism

Alcohol-based cleansers, 4:1296

Alcohol consumption
- acetaminophen interactions, 1:8
- anti-insomnia drug interactions, 1:141
- antiangina drug interactions, 1:144
- antibiotic interactions, 1:153
- anticoagulant interactions, 1:158
- anticonvulsant drug interactions, 1:162

Alcohol consumption *(continued)*
antituberculosis drug interactions, 1:210–211
barbiturate interactions, 1:282
benzodiazepine interactions, 1:292
Botox injections, 1:347
breast cancer, 1:359, 4:1204
caffeine interactions, 2:396
calcium channel blocker interactions, 2:402
cancer risk, 2:408, 413
cephalosporin interactions, 2:479
cirrhosis from, 2:524
colon cancer, 2:533
congestive heart failure, 2:563
constipation, 2:569, 570
dehydration, 2:605
driver safety, 2:705
drug interactions, 2:709
dry mouth from, 2:714
edema, 2:726
erectile dysfunction, 2:756
esophageal cancer risk, 2:759, 761
family relationships, 3:795
fibromyalgia, 3:801
gingivitis, 3:877
ginkgo biloba for, 3:878
gluten-free diet, 3:888
gout drug interactions, 3:894
headaches, 3:907
healthy aging, 4:1525
heart disease, 1:66, 3:929
heartburn, 3:933
heavy, 1:67
high-density lipoproteins, 3:929
homeopathic medicine, 3:988
hospital admissions, 1:67
hyperlipoproteinemia, 3:1004
hypertension, 3:1012
influenza contraindications, 3:1039
insomnia, 3:1051, 1052
insulin interactions, 3:1055
iron-deficiency anemia, 3:1065
ischemia, 3:1076
liver function test interactions, 3:1143, 1145, 1146
marijuana interactions, 4:1214
mental health, 2:665
methotrexate interactions, 1:156
oral cancer, 4:1357, 1359
over fifty lifestyle, 2:661
psoriasis, 4:1521
recommendations, 4:1336
seborrheic dermatitis, 5:1600
sleep apnea, 5:1653, 1654
snoring, 5:1670, 1673, 1675
SSRI interactions, 1:172
stomach cancer, 5:1706
stroke, 5:1723
tricyclic antidepressants interactions, 1:175
varicose veins, 5:1818
vision disorders, 5:1839
Alcohol, rubbing, 5:1694
Alcohol withdrawal, 5:1603
Alcoholic cardiomyopathy, 2:445
Alcoholic hepatitis, 3:950, 952
Alcoholics Anonymous, 1:68, 2:707
Alcoholism, 1:67
bacteremia, 1:275
benzodiazepines for, 1:144
cirrhosis from, 1:64, 2:521–522, 524
electrolyte tests, 2:739
epilepsy, 5:1602
fatty liver from, 3:797
GI bleeding from, 3:871
malnutrition, 4:1202
organ donation, 4:1364–1365
SSRIs for, 1:166
tuberculosis, 5:1791
vitamin K deficiency, 5:1860
zinc deficiency, 5:1897
Alcor Life Extension Foundation, 1:47
Aldactone. *See* Spironolactone
Aldesleukin, 3:1093, 4:1264
Aldosterone, 2:739
Alendronate, 4:1372, 1392
Aleve. *See* Naproxen sodium
Alexander technique, 2:489, 4:1291, 1324
Alfalfa, 3:1005, 5:1860
Alfentanil, 1:113
Alfuzosin, 4:1511
Alginic acid, 1:139
Alkaline phosphatase (ALP), 3:1143–1146, 4:1390
Alkaloids, plant, 2:490
Alkalosis, 4:1389
Alkeran. *See* Melphalan
Alkylamines, 1:187
Alkylating agents, 2:490
Allergen extracts, 1:72, 75
Allergen immunotherapy, 1:243
Allergens, 1:71, 74–76, 241, 3:814, 816
Allergic contact dermatitis, 2:571–573
Allergies, 1:**70–74,** 3:1022
acetaminophen, 1:8
administration of medication, 1:26
aloe, 1:78–79
angiotensin-converting enzyme inhibitors, 1:133
antiarrhythmic drugs, 1:148
anticoagulants, 1:158
antihistamines for, 1:186–189
asthma precautions, 1:241
barbiturates, 1:283
benzodiazepines, 1:292–293
beta blockers, 1:298
bovine collagen, 2:530, 531
caffeine, 2:396
cats, 1:241
cephalosporins, 1:153, 2:479
cinnamon, 2:515
contact dermatitis, 2:630
contact lenses, 2:772, 774
contrast media, 1:130, 2:494
corneal diseases, 2:574
diagnosis, 1:71, 2:560
diuretics, 2:692
egg, 3:814–815, 1042
eyelid edema, 2:779, 780–781
general anesthesia, 1:114
ginkgo biloba, 3:879
ginkgo biloba for, 3:878
gold, 2:630
H-2 receptor blockers, 3:899
histamine, 1:186
influenza vaccines, 3:1042
irritable bowel syndrome, 3:1069
latex, 4:1482–1483
marijuana, 4:1214
nonsteroidal anti-inflammatory drugs, 4:1326
penicillin, 1:152, 153
probiotics for, 4:1498
saw palmetto, 5:1588
skin lesions from, 5:1650, 1651
sulfites, 1:379, 380
T-cell delayed, 1:76
treatment, 1:71–72, 3:1024
tricyclic antidepressants, 1:161, 176
See also Food allergies
Allergists, 1:76
Allergy drugs, 1:186–189
barbiturate interactions, 1:282, 284
benzodiazepine interactions, 1:292, 294
heatstroke risk, 3:937
Allergy shots, 1:243, 298, 299
Allergy tests, 1:71, **74–77,** *75,* 3:1024
beta blocker interactions, 1:299
food allergies, 3:816–817
Alli. *See* Orlistat
Allicin, 3:846, 848
Alliin, 3:846
Allinase, 3:846
Allium sativum. See Garlic
Allogenic collagen injections, 2:530
Allogenic stem cell transplantation, 4:1196
Allografts, cardiac valve, 2:443
Allopathic medicine, 2:701, 4:1369
Allopurinol, 3:892, 894, 1103
Aloe, 1:**77–79,** *78*
Aloe arborescens, 1:77
Aloe barbadensis, 1:77, 78
Aloe latex, 1:77, 79
Aloe vera, 1:77
Aloin, 1:77
Alopecia, 1:**79–81,** 155, 4:1277–1279
Alopecia areata, 1:79
Alopecia totalis, 1:79
ALP (Alkaline phosphatase), 3:1143–1146, 4:1390

Alph-hemolytic streptococci, 5:1709
Alpha-25-dihydroxyvitamin D, 5:1853
Alpha-beta blockers, 3:1011
Alpha-blockers
for hypertension, 3:1011
for priapism, 4:1492
for prostate enlargement, 4:1511, 1513
Alpha-carotene, 5:1861
Alpha-fetoproteins (AFP), 3:1139, 1142, 1143
Alpha-glucosidase inhibitors, 1:177*t*, 180
Alpha hydroxy acids, 1:**83–85,** 387, 2:716, 5:1889
Alpha lipoic acid, 5:1889
Alpha-pinenes, 4:1213
Alpha-theta neurofeedback, 1:301
Alpha tocopherol, 5:1856, 1857
Alpha tocotrienol, 5:1856
$Alpha_1$-adrenergic blockers, 1:**81–83,** 81*t*
$Alpha_1$-antitrypsin deficiency, 2:512, 522, 740
Alprazolam
antibiotic interactions, 1:153
for anxiety, 1:144, 145, 291–294
cimetidine interactions, 3:900
for panic disorder, 4:1411
ranitidine interactions, 3:900
SSRI interactions, 1:173
tricyclic antidepressant interactions, 1:177
ALS. *See* Amyotrophic lateral sclerosis
ALT (Alanine aminotransferase), 3:1143–1146
Altacs. *See* Ramipril
Alteplase, 5:1767
Alternative family, 3:794
Alternative therapy
angina pectoris, 3:1076
cancer, 2:411–412
cardiomyopathy, 2:447
cervical spondylosis, 2:488–489
cirrhosis, 2:524
fibromyalgia, 3:801
hospice care, 3:996
irritable bowel syndrome, 3:1071
kidney cancer, 3:1094
kidney stones, 3:1102
liver cancer, 3:1141
menopause, 3:994, 4:1252–1253
osteoarthritis, 5:1615
Parkinson's disease, 4:1424
rosacea, 4:1579
smoking cessation, 5:1661–1662
snoring, 5:1675
stress, 5:1716
substance abuse, 5:1727–1728
ulcers, 5:1800
usage statistics, 4:1270
See also Complementary therapies; specific therapies
Althaea officinalis. See Marsh mallow
Altitude, high, 4:1567, 5:1870
Altocor. *See* Lovastatin
Altoprev. *See* Lovastatin
Altruism, 4:1527
Aluminum, 1:86
Aluminum carbonate, 1:139
Aluminum hydroxide, 1:139, 208
Aluminum prosthesis, 3:1112
Alupent. *See* Metaproterenol
Alveoli, 2:511
Alzheimer, Alois, 1:85
Alzheimer's Association, 2:613, 4:1442
Alzheimer's disease, 1:*85t,* **85–90,** 4:1241–1245, 5:1613
alcohol abuse, 1:64
amyloidosis, 1:100
antipsychotic drugs for, 4:1531
caregivers, 1:88–89, 2:453
delirium, 2:608
dementia, 2:611
demographics, 1:86, 4:1243, 1528, 5:1613
diagnosis, 1:87, 4:1243, 5:1616
diet, 2:660, 668
Down syndrome, 4:1257
drug therapy, 1:87–88, 163–166, 2:613, 4:1244, 5:1613, 1616, 1617
dysarthria from, 5:1687, 1688, 1689
financial management, 3:802
genetic factors, 1:86, 4:1242, 1257
ginkgo biloba for, 3:879
vs. HIV-associated dementia, 5:1623
mental retardation, 4:1255
mortality, 1:85*t,* 86
prevention, 1:88, 2:614, 4:1245
risk factors, 4:1244
sleep disorders, 5:1656
sporadic, 1:86, 4:1242
swallowing disorders, 5:1742
treatment, 1:87–88
vitamin B_{12} for, 5:1863
vitamin E for, 5:1857
AMA. *See* American Medical Association
Amantadine
adverse effects, 1:201
for influenza, 3:1040, 5:1833
for Parkinson's disease, 1:200, 3:832, 4:1424
Amaurosis fugax. *See* Transient blindness
Ambien. *See* Zolipedem
Amblyopia, 1:345, 347, 4:1354
Ambrisentan, 4:1540
Ambulation. *See* Mobility
Ambulatory blood pressure, 1:*90,* **90–92,** 2:425
Ambulatory, defined, 4:1283
Ambulatory electrocardiography. *See* Holter monitoring
Ambulatory esophageal pH monitoring, 3:855, 859–860
Ambulatory phlebectomy, 5:1818
Ambulatory surgery, 4:1557
AMD. *See* Age-related macular degeneration
American Academy of Allergy, Asthma and Immunology (AAAAI), 1:70
American Academy of Dermatology, 1:80, 4:1197, 5:1644
American Academy of Family Physicians
AIDS, 1:54
alcohol abuse, 2:706–707
constipation, 2:570
A Physician's Guide to Nutrition in Chronic Disease Management for Older Adults, 2:659
tetanus, 5:1756
vaccines, 5:1815
American Academy of Medical Acupuncture (AAMA), 1:20
American Academy of Neurology, 3:792
American Academy of Ophthalmology, 2:769
American Academy of Orthopaedic Surgeons (AAOS)
cataract prevention, 2:464
falls, 3:790
hip replacement, 3:964
knee injuries, 3:1116
knee joint replacement, 3:1112
American Academy of Pain Medicine, 4:1397
American Academy of Pediatrics, 3:1157, 5:1756, 1815
American Academy of Plastic Surgeons, 1:4
American Academy of Sleep Medicine, 5:1674
American Aging Association, 1:46
American Association of Critical Care Nurses, 2:526
American Association of Neurologic Surgeons, 1:121
American Association of Retired Persons. *See* AARP
American Association of Sexual Educators, Counselors, and Therapists (AASECT), 5:1619
American Association of Suicidology, 1:66
American Autoimmune Related Diseases Association (AARDA), 1:260
American Automobile Association (AAA), 2:705, 5:1607

American Bar Association (ABA), 1:30, 31, 32, 2:567
American Board of Anesthesiology (ABA), 4:1399
American Board of Dermatology, 2:633
American Board of Internal Medicine, 3:943
American Board of Medical Acupuncture (ABMA), 1:20
American Board of Medical Specialties (ABMS), 3:805–806, 807, 4:1399
American Board of Plastic Surgeons, 1:6–7, 2:584
American Board of Surgery (ABS), 3:805
American Cancer Society
- ABCDE system, 5:1642–1643
- brain and central nervous system tumors, 1:348
- breast cancer, 1:351–352, 3:1169
- breast self-examination, 1:369, 370
- cancer causes, 2:407
- cancer symptoms, 2:408
- cancer treatment side effects, 5:1682
- colon cancer, 2:533, 534, 537, 538
- dietary supplements, 4:1344, 1345
- endometrial cancer, 2:743
- exocrine pancreatic cancer, 4:1408
- gallbladder cancer, 3:835
- hospice care, 2:597
- hyperthermia, 4:1264–1265
- kidney cancer, 3:1092
- liver cancer, 3:1138
- low-fat diet, 3:1157
- lung cancer, 3:1174
- marijuana, 2:419
- melanoma, 4:1198, 1200
- metabolic diets, 2:746
- most common cancers, 5:1736–1737
- multiple myeloma, 4:1299
- nausea and vomiting, 5:1684
- Nutrition and Physical Activity Guidelines, 5:1854
- oral cancers, 4:1357
- prostate cancer, 4:1502, 1509
- smoking cessation, 5:1661
- stomach cancer, 5:1704, 1706, 1707
- swallowing difficulty, 5:1684
- thyroid cancer, 5:1769
- vitamin C, 5:1851, 1852
- vitamin D, 5:1854

American Chiropractic Association (ACA), 2:502
American College of Cardiology, 2:563, 3:1025
American College of Chest Physicians, 3:1175
American College of Gastroenterologists (ACG), 3:1071
American College of Nutrition (ACN), 4:1346, 1347
American College of Radiology, 4:1207
American College of Rheumatology, 3:800–801, 884, 1180
American College of Sports Medicine, 3:1076
American College of Surgeons, 3:806
American College of Toxicology, 3:1124
American Dental Association, 2:616, 620, 621, 5:1751
American Dental Hygienists' Association, 4:1361
American Diabetes Association (ADA), 1:329, 2:515, 639–640, 645
American Dietetic Association (ADA)
- certification, 2:557
- Commission on Accreditation for Dietetics Education, 2:681, 683–684
- Commission on Dietetic Registration, 4:1348
- community nutrition, 2:555
- diet plans, 2:658
- Dietetic Practice Group, 4:1347–1348
- dietetics standards, 2:681
- dietitians, 4:1346
- dysphasia diet, 3:870
- fiber, 2:695
- fluid intake, 5:1682
- food allergies, 3:818
- Meals on Wheels, 4:1227, 1228
- nutrition, 4:1337
- *A Physician's Guide to Nutrition in Chronic Disease Management for Older Adults,* 2:659
- surimi, 3:817

American-European Consensus Group, 5:1638–1639
American Foundation for the Blind, 1:319
American Geriatrics Society, 5:1867
American Health Assistance Foundation (AHAF), 1:86, 4:1243
American Hearing Aid Association (AAHA), 3:919, 920
American Heart Association (AHA)
- alcohol consumption, 3:929
- ankle-brachial index, 1:136
- cardiac monitor, 2:434
- cardiopulmonary resuscitation, 2:449, 451
- DASH Diet, 5:1786
- exercise, 5:1611
- heart healthy diet, 1:247, 5:1783
- high-fiber diet, 3:958
- hypertension, 1:324
- hypertrophic cardiomyopathy, 3:1014
- implantable cardioverter-defibrillator, 3:1025–1026
- ischemia, 3:1073
- low-cholesterol diet, 3:1153, 1156
- low-fat diet, 3:1157
- low-sodium diet, 5:1680
- marijuana, 4:1214
- mitral valve prolapse, 4:1281
- over fifty lifestyle, 2:661
- pulmonary hypertension, 4:1539
- vitamin C, 5:1851, 1852
- vitamin E, 5:1863–1864
- water, 5:1616

American Hospital Association (AHA), 2:527, 4:1430
American Indians. *See* Native Americans
American Joint Commission on Cancer (AJCC), 3:1093, 1140
American Liver Foundation, 3:1135
American Lung Association, 2:511–512, 550
American Medical Association (AMA)
- advertising, 3:808
- Code of Ethics, 2:762, 4:1234
- community health programs, 2:555
- Current Procedural Terminology, 4:1231
- elder abuse, 2:729
- euthanasia, 2:762, 763–764
- Hippocratic Oath, 4:1233–1234
- homeopathic medicine, 3:988, 989
- hypertension, 5:1892
- managed care plans, 4:1210
- osteopathic medicine, 2:701, 702
- patient confidentiality, 4:1425, 1426
- prostate enlargement, 4:1513

American Neurological Association, 3:1185
American Nurses Association (ANA), 2:529
American Nurses Credentialing Center, 1:35, 2:526
American Optometric Association, 4:1355–1356
American Organization of Bodywork Therapies of Asia (AOBTA), 1:15
American Oriental Bodywork Therapy Association, 5:1629
American Osteopathic Association (AOA), 2:702
American Physical Therapy Association (APTA)
- *Guide to Physical Therapist Practice,* 1:269, 4:1323
- patient education, 1:268
- physical therapy assistants, 4:1458, 1460

American Psychiatric Association. *See Diagnostic and Statistical Manual of Mental Disorders*
American Public Health Association (APHA), 2:555
American Red Cross, 2:449, 451, 4:1330

American Registry for Diagnostic Medical Sonography (ARDMS), 2:460
American Sleep Apnea Association (ASAA), 5:1673
American Society for Aesthetic Plastic Surgery, 3:783
American Society for Bariatric Surgery, 1:285
American Society of Anesthesiologists, 1:119
American Society of Colon and Rectal Surgeons (ASCRS), 3:1069
American Society of Plastic and Reconstructive Surgery, 1:362, 364
American Thoracic Society, 4:1537
American Veterans of Foreign Service, 5:1830
Americans with Disabilities Act, 1:**92–95**
Amifostine, 4:1509
Amikacin, 1:95–97, 151
Amiloride, 2:690
Amino acids, 3:846, 1076, 5:1847
Aminoglycosides, 1:**95–97,** 149*t,* 151
  vestibular hypofunction from, 3:832
  for wound care, 5:1886
Aminopenicillins, 1:150
Aminophylline, 1:162, 299, 2:396
Amiodarone, 4:1536
Amitriptyline, 1:175
  bronchodilator interactions, 1:380
  for diabetic neuropathy, 2:647
  overdose, 4:1381
  for postherpetic neuralgia, 4:1319
  for tinnitus, 5:1780
Amlodipine, 1:191, 2:401
Ammonia, 3:1143–1146
Ammonia intoxication, 2:523
Ammonium, quaternary, 4:1296
Amnesia, 3:902, 4:1241
Amnesic dysphasia. *See* Anomic dysphasia
Amnesic MCI, 4:1241
Amoebal diarrhea, 2:652–653
Amoxicillin, 1:150
  for bladder infection, 1:311
  for cystitis, 2:595
  for endocarditis prevention, 5:1712
  for helicobacteriosis, 3:940
  for lyme disease, 3:1184
  for MRSA infections, 4:1294
  for urinary tract infections, 5:1808
Amoxil. *See* Amoxicillin
Amphetamines, 1:177, 4:1539, 5:1726
Amphotericin B, 1:311, 3:826
Ampicillin, 1:149–150
  for bladder infection, 1:311
  for cystitis, 2:595
  for endocarditis prevention, 5:1712
  liver function test interactions, 3:1143
  for urinary tract infections, 5:1808
Ampuku, 5:1627
Amputation, 1:**97–99,** *98*
  blood clots, 1:322
  diabetes mellitus-related, 2:640
  diabetic foot infection-related, 2:641
  diabetic neuropathy-related, 2:647
  foot care, 3:821
  gangrene, 1:97, 3:843, 845
  leg, 1:*98,* 99, 3:1165–1167
  wheelchair, 5:1880
Amsler grid, 1:41
Amygdala, 1:212
Amygdalin, 2:746
Amyl nitrates, 5:1635
Amyloid plaques, 1:85, 86, 87
Amyloidosis, 1:*100,* **100–102,** 2:508, 3:1133
Amyotrophic lateral sclerosis (ALS), 1:**102–106,** *103,* 4:1287–1290
  dysarthria from, 5:1687, 1688, 1689
  end-of-life care, 4:1235
ANA. *See* Antinuclear antibody test
ANA (American Nurses Association), 2:529
Anabolic steroids
  hormone replacement therapy interactions, 3:993
  insulin interactions, 3:1055
  liver function test interactions, 3:1143
  saw palmetto interactions, 5:1588
Anabolin. *See* Nandrolone
Anadrol. *See* Oxymetholone
Anafranil. *See* Clomipramine
Anagrelide HCI, 5:1766
Anal specimens, 5:1626
Anal ultrasonography, 3:799
Anal wink test, 3:798
Analgesia, patient-controlled, 3:967, 996, 4:1473
Analgesia stage, 1:111
Analgesics, 1:**106–108,** 2:709*t*
  antihistamine interactions, 2:709
  barbiturate interactions, 1:282, 284
  benzodiazepine interactions, 1:292, 294
  caffeine content, 2:395
  for cellulitis, 2:478
  for colonoscopy, 2:538, 539
  for common colds, 2:552
  for cosmetic surgery, 2:583
  for diabetic neuropathy, 2:647
  dronabinol interactions, 2:420
  for headaches, 3:907
  for heart attacks, 3:923
  for hip replacement pain, 3:969
  hydroxyzine interactions, 1:142
  marijuana as, 4:1213
  for neuralgia, 4:1318
  for pain, 4:1394, 1395
  for pericarditis, 4:1432
  for polymyositis, 4:1468
  recovery room administration, 4:1556
  shiatsu, 5:1628–1629
  for spinal stenosis, 5:1697
  for tendinitis, 5:1754
  See also Nonsteroidal anti-inflammatory drugs
Anaphase, 1:155
Anaphylaxis, 1:70, 72, 3:815–816, 817, 818
Anaplastic thyroid cancer, 5:1768–1771
Anaprox. *See* Naproxen sodium
Anastomosis
  colectomy, 2:536
  minimally invasive cardiac surgery, 4:1275, 1276, 1277
Ancef. *See* Cefazolin
Androgenic alopecia, 1:79
Androgens, 1:155, 162, 2:506
Andrus, Ethel Percy, 1:2
Anemia, 1:*108,* **108–111**
  anoxia, 1:137
  aplastic, 1:109, 110, 5:1763
  autoimmune hemolytic, 1:250, 253
  bone marrow biopsy and aspiration, 1:340, 343
  causes, 1:109, 3:942
  chemotherapy-induced, 1:155, 2:491
  chronic kidney failure-related, 2:508
  cirrhosis-related, 2:523
  demographics, 1:108, 3:942
  diagnosis, 1:109, 2:560–561, 3:1146
  electrolyte tests, 2:739
  epoetin for, 2:418
  hemolytic, 1:109, 110, 250, 3:1145
  hemorrhoid-related, 3:947
  iron-deficiency, 1:108–111, 2:561, 3:870, 1063–1066, *1064*
  iron supplements for, 1:138, 2:510
  iron tests, 3:1067, 1068
  kidney cancer-related, 3:1092
  liver function tests, 3:1146
  malnutrition-related, 2:665
  megaloblastic, 3:1145, 5:1847, 1862, 1863
  multiple myeloma-related, 4:1299
  pernicious, 3:811, 812, 869, 4:1201, 5:1705, 1847
  polymyalgia rheumatica-related, 4:1467
  sickle cell, 1:109, 110, 2:508, 735, 5:1897
  thrombocytosis from, 5:1765
Anemia of chronic disease, 1:109
Anemic anoxia, 1:137, 138

Anesthesia
aspiration during, 1:232
dental, 1:116, 117–118
epidural, 1:116, 118, 119, 3:965
mortality, 1:120
ophthalmic, 1:116, 118
regional, 1:115–118
spinal, 1:116, 118, 119, 3:965
twilight, 3:783–784
See also General anesthesia; Local anesthesia
Anesthesiologists, 1:**118–120,** *119,* 4:1398–1399
Anesthetics
barbiturate interactions, 1:284
benzodiazepine interactions, 1:294
dronabinol interactions, 2:420
liver function test interactions, 3:1143
topical, 1:116, 117
Anesthetists, certified registered nurse, 1:34, 35, 4:1559
Aneurysm, 1:*120,* **120–123**
angiography, 1:127, 129
arteriovenous malformation-related, 1:230
atherosclerosis-related, 1:245
cardiac surgery, 2:438
cerebral, 1:120, 121, 122, 2:401
headache from, 3:906
hypertension-related, 3:1008
magnetic resonance imaging, 4:1192
mortality, 1:121, 122, 229
therapeutic exercise contraindications, 5:1760
Angel dust, 5:1725
Angelica, 5:1860
Angelica archangelica. See Angelica
Anger
coronary artery disease risk, 2:579
heart attack risk, 3:922
ischemia risk, 3:1074
prayer and spirituality, 4:1478
relaxation techniques, 4:1565
Angina. *See* Angina pectoris
Angina pectoris, 1:**123–126,** 3:1073
alternative therapy, 3:1076
beta blockers for, 1:297
calcium channel blockers for, 1:124, 2:401–403
cardiomyopathy-related, 2:446
causes, 1:124, 2:518, 579, 3:1073
coronary artery bypass graft, 1:124–125, 2:427–428, 430, 440
drug therapy, 1:124, 125, 142–144
heart disease, 3:925
sildenafil citrate for, 5:1634, 1635
stress test-induced, 5:1719
symptoms, 1:124, 3:1074
therapeutic exercise contraindications, 5:1759
treatment, 1:124–125, 3:1075
unstable, 1:123, 234, 235
Angiodysplasia, 3:872
Angiogenesis, 1:41, 4:1260, 1261
Angiogenesis inhibitors, 1:41, 4:1264, 1301
Angiography, 1:**126–130,** *127*
atherosclerosis, 1:246
blood clots, 1:322
cardiac catheterization, 2:432
cardiac surgery, 2:439
cerebral, 1:127, 230
coronary, 1:124, 127–128, 2:428, 580, 3:1075, 4:1276
CT, 4:1405
digital subscription, 2:457
endocrine pancreatic cancer, 4:1402
exocrine pancreatic cancer, 4:1405
fluorescein, 1:41, 129, 2:649
heart disease, 3:926
indocyanine green, 1:41
magnetic resonance, 4:1189, 1192, 5:1722
minimally invasive cardiac surgery, 4:1275
myocarditis, 4:1310
peripheral vascular disease, 4:1437
radionuclide, 2:579
Angiomas, 3:872, 1136
Angioplasty, 1:*130,* **130–132**
balloon, 1:131, 224, 247, 322, 2:427, 432, 457, 3:929, 5:1783
carotid, 2:457, 5:1722
percutaneous transluminal coronary, 1:124, 130–132, 2:580, 3:928, 1075, 4:1277
self-hypnosis, 4:1272
Angiosarcoma, 3:1138
Angiotensin-converting enzyme inhibitors (ACEs), 1:**132–135,** 132*t*
adverse effects, 1:133, 134, 191
for angina pectoris, 1:124
aspirin interactions, 1:235
calcium channel blocker interactions, 2:402
for cardiomyopathy, 2:447
celecoxib interactions, 2:586
for congenital heart disease, 3:928
for congestive heart failure, 2:563
for coronary artery disease, 3:927
diuretic interactions, 2:692
for heart attacks, 1:132, 3:923, 928
hyperkalemia from, 2:737
for hypertension, 1:132, 191, 3:1011
insulin interactions, 3:1056
for myocarditis, 4:1310
for scleroderma-related hypertension, 5:1598
Angiotensin I, 1:132
Angiotensin receptor blockers
calcium channel blocker interactions, 2:402
for congestive heart failure, 2:563
for hypertension, 1:191, 3:1011
Anhedonia, 2:625
Animals, 4:1561
See also Pets
Anisinidione, 2:457
Anistreplase, 5:1767, 1768
Ankle braces, 4:1285
Ankle-brachial index, 1:**136–137,** 247, 2:518
Ankle bursitis, 1:388, 389, 390
Ankylosing spondylitis, 3:964, 1151, 4:1326
Anma, 5:1627
Anomia, 5:1688
Anomic dysphasia, 2:717
Anorectal manometry, 3:799
Anorexia nervosa, 5:1855
Anoxia, 1:**137–138,** 4:1528, 5:1885
Ansaid. *See* Flurbiprofen
Antabuse. *See* Disulfiram
Antacids, 1:**139–140**
angiotensin-converting enzyme inhibitor interactions, 1:134
anticoagulant interactions, 2:709
anticonvulsant drug interactions, 1:162
bisacodyl interactions, 3:1124
calcium absorption, 2:400
calcium supplement interactions, 2:405
cephalosporin interactions, 1:153
cholinesterase inhibitor interactions, 1:165
congestive heart failure effects, 2:564
drug interactions, 1:140, 2:707, 708*t*
for gastroesophageal reflux disease, 3:855, 859
iron absorption, 3:1065
isoniazid interactions, 1:208
macrolide interactions, 1:153
for peptic ulcers, 3:940
ulcer contraindications, 5:1800
vitamin B_{12} interactions, 5:1849
vitamin D interactions, 5:1856
Anterior cruciate ligament (ACL), 3:1115, 1117
Anthocyanins, 1:197
Anthocyanosides, 2:415
Anthraquinone glycosides, 1:77
Anti-DNA autoantibodies, 1:250, 254
Anti-double strand DNA (dsDNA), 3:1180
Anti-inflammatory diet, 1:**193–196**
Anti-inflammatory drugs
for amyloidosis, 1:102
for asthma, 1:379
for back curves, 1:274
for botox injections, 1:347

Anti-inflammatory drugs *(continued)*
for bronchitis, 1:377
GI bleeding from, 3:872
hip replacement preparation, 3:966
marijuana as, 4:1213
for osteoarthritis, 5:1615
for pericarditis, 4:1432
for tendinitis, 5:1754
thrombolytic therapy interactions, 5:1768
See also Nonsteroidal anti-inflammatory drugs
Anti-insomnia drugs, 1:**140–141,** 140*t,* 3:1051
anticoagulant interactions, 2:710
barbiturate interactions, 1:282
benzodiazepine interactions, 1:292, 294
dronabinol interactions, 2:420
drug interactions, 1:141, 2:709*t*
overdose, 4:1381
snoring from, 5:1673, 1675
SSRI interactions, 1:173
Anti-itch drugs, 1:**141–142**
Anti-La /SSB autoantibodies, 5:1639
Anti-oncogenes. *See* Tumor suppressor genes
Anti-reflective coatings, 2:773
Anti-Ro/SSA autoantibodies, 5:1639
Anti-scratch coatings, 2:773
Anti-Smith (anti-SM) antibodies, 1:254, 3:1180
Anti-vascular endothelial growth factor agents, 1:41
Anti-VCA (Anti-viral capsis antigen test), 3:1145
Anti-VEGF antibody, 4:1264
Anti-viral capsis antigen test (anti-VCA), 3:1145
Antiallergy drugs. *See* Allergy drugs
Antiandrogens, 4:1509
Antiangina drugs, 1:**142–144**
Antiangiogenesis drugs. *See* Angiogenesis inhibitors
Antianxiety drugs, 1:**144–145**
for adjustment disorders, 1:24
antibiotic interactions, 1:153
for dementia, 2:613
for generalized anxiety disorder, 3:863
hormone replacement therapy interactions, 3:993
overdose, 4:1381
SSRI interactions, 1:173
tricyclic antidepressant interactions, 1:177
See also Benzodiazepines
Antiarrhythmic drugs, 1:**145–149,** 146*t*
caffeine interactions, 2:397
congestive heart failure contraindications, 2:564
for heart attacks, 3:923
for hypertrophic cardiomyopathy, 3:1015
pulmonary fibrosis from, 4:1536
Antiasthma drugs, 1:242–243, 284, 2:710, 3:854
Antibacterial mouthwash, 3:877
Antibiotic-resistant bacteria
aminoglycoside-resistant, 1:96
gonorrhea, 5:1623
methacillin-resistant, 1:150, 278–279, 4:1293–1298, 5:1699
prophylactic antibiotics, 2:467, 470
tuberculosis, 1:207–212, 207*t,* 3:1035, 5:1794, 1795
Antibiotic sensitivity test. *See* Sensitivity tests
Antibiotics, 1:149–150*t,* **149–154**
aminoglycosides, 1:95–97, 149*t,* 151, 3:832, 5:1866
for amputation, 1:98
anti-insomnia drug interactions, 1:141
anticonvulsant drug interactions, 1:162
antidiarrheal drug interactions, 1:183
antinuclear antibody test interactions, 1:253
antitumor, 2:490
for bacteremia, 1:275, 276
beta-lactam, 1:95, 151
for bladder infections, 1:311
for boils, 1:334
broad-spectrum, 1:152, 5:1860
for bronchitis, 1:377
calcium supplement interactions, 2:405
for cellulitis, 2:478
cholesterol test interactions, 2:506
for cirrhosis-associated anemia, 2:523
combination, 1:150*t*
for corneal diseases, 2:575
for cosmetic surgery, 2:583
for cystitis, 2:595
for dental treatment, 2:616
for dermatitis, 2:631
for diarrhea, 2:655
diarrhea from, 4:1497
for diverticulitis, 2:694
drug interactions, 1:152, 153
for emphysema, 2:741
for face lifts, 3:784
folic acid interactions, 3:813
for fungal cultures, 3:822–823
for gangrene, 3:844
for gastroenteritis, 3:851
for gingivitis, 3:877
for helicobacteriosis, 3:940–941
for hip revision surgery infections, 3:973
for infectious diseases, 3:1035
for influenza, 3:1039
iron supplement interactions, 2:709
liver function test interactions, 3:1143
for lyme disease, 3:1182, 1184
for lymphedema, 3:1187
macrolide, 1:149*t,* 152, 153, 5:1712
for meningitis, 4:1248
for MRSA infections, 4:1295–1296
for myocarditis, 4:1310
oral contraceptive interactions, 2:710
for pneumonia, 1:373, 4:1464
probiotic interactions, 4:1497
pulmonary fibrosis from, 4:1536
for rheumatic heart disease, 3:926
for rosacea, 4:1579, 1580
for scleroderma, 5:1598
for sexually transmitted diseases, 5:1623
for staphylococcal infections, 5:1701, 1702
for strep throat, 5:1711–1712
for streptococcal pneumonia, 5:1712
topical, 1:278, 4:1579, 5:1651
for tuberculosis, 5:1790, 1795
for urinary tract infections, 5:1805, 1808
for viral infection-related bacterial infections, 5:1833
vitamin K interactions, 5:1860
warfarin interactions, 4:1466
for wound care, 5:1886
zinc interactions, 5:1897
See also Prophylactic antibiotics
Antibodies
AIDS, 1:59, 61
allergies, 1:74
anti-gliadin, 2:473
anti-Smith, 1:254, 3:1180
anti-VEGF, 4:1264
autoimmune disorders, 1:257
endomysial, 2:473
immune system role, 3:1021
maternal, 1:257
role, 3:1022
smooth muscle, 3:1143, 1145
tissue translutaminase, 2:473
vaccines, 5:1813
See also Monoclonal antibodies
Antibody tests
antimitochondrial, 1:252, 254, 3:1143, 1145
antinuclear, 1:252, 253–254, 259, 3:1145, 1180, 4:1573–1574, 5:1598, 1639
antiphospholipid, 1:252, 254
celiac disease, 2:473
thyroid, 5:1774
Anticancer drugs, 1:**154–157,** 2:415–416, 418–421, 489–493, 4:1240
See also Chemotherapy
Anticholinergic agents
for chronic obstructive pulmonary disease, 2:513
overdose, 4:1381

Anticholinergic agents *(continued)*
for Parkinson's disease, 1:200, 4:1423–1424
psychoses from, 4:1529
Anticoagulants, 1:**157–159,** 157*t*
angioplasty contraindications, 1:131
antacid interactions, 2:709
anti-insomnia drug interactions, 2:710
antiarrhythmic drug interactions, 1:149
anticonvulsant drug interactions, 1:162
aspirin interactions, 2:709
for atherosclerosis prevention, 1:247
barbiturate interactions, 1:284
for blood clots, 1:322, 323
bruising from, 1:385–386
calcium supplement interactions, 2:405
cardiac catheterization, 2:432
for cardiac valve replacement, 2:443
for cardiomyopathy, 2:447
cephalosporin interactions, 2:480
for deep vein thrombosis, 2:519, 602
face lift contraindications, 3:784
garlic interactions, 3:849, 850
GI bleeding from, 3:872
ginkgo biloba interactions, 3:879
for heart attacks, 3:923
hormone replacement therapy interactions, 3:993
for mechanical heart valves, 1:223
for mitral valve stenosis, 4:1282
nonsteroidal anti-inflammatory drug interactions, 4:1327
post-cardiac surgery, 2:439
for pulmonary embolism, 1:373, 4:1534
for pulmonary hypertension, 4:1540
SSRI interactions, 1:173
for stroke prevention, 2:457, 5:1722
thrombolytic therapy interactions, 5:1768
for transient blindness, 5:1783
for transient ischemic attacks, 3:1076, 5:1785–1786
tricyclic antidepressant interactions, 1:177
vitamin K interactions, 5:1860, 1864, 1865
Anticonvulsant drugs, 1:**159–163,** 159*t*
alcohol interactions, 1:66
analgesic contraindications, 1:106
barbiturate interactions, 1:282, 284
benzodiazepine interactions, 1:292, 294
for bipolar disorder, 1:304–305
calcium absorption, 2:400
celecoxib interactions, 2:587
cephalosporin interactions, 2:480
DHEA interactions, 2:635
for diabetic neuropathy, 2:647
dronabinol interactions, 2:420
folic acid interactions, 3:813
for head injury-related seizures, 3:903
heatstroke risk, 3:937
hormone replacement therapy interactions, 3:993
hypocalcemia from, 2:736
marijuana as, 4:1213
Medicare prescription drug plan, 4:1240
for neuralgia, 4:1318
periodic limb movement disorder from, 4:1434
for post-herpatic neuralgia, 1:212, 4:1319, 5:1631
pulmonary fibrosis from, 4:1536
for seizures, 5:1603, 1605
thrombolytic therapy interactions, 5:1768
tricyclic antidepressant interactions, 1:177
vitamin D interactions, 5:1856
zinc interactions, 5:1897
Antidementia drugs, 1:**163–166,** 163*t,* 2:613
Antidepressants, 1:166–177, 166*t*
for dementia, 2:613
for depression, 2:626
erectile dysfunction from, 2:756, 5:1634
for fibromyalgia, 3:801
gastroesophageal reflux disease from, 3:854
for irritable bowel syndrome, 3:1071
Medicare prescription drug plan, 4:1240
for migraines, 4:1267
for neurocardiogenic syncope, 3:788
overdose, 4:1381
for panic disorder, 4:1411
for postherpetic neuralgia, 1:212, 4:1319
for PTSD, 4:1470
SSRIs, 1:**166–174,** 166*t*
for stress-related disorders, 5:1716
tricyclic, 1:**174–177**
vitamin E interactions, 5:1858
See also Selective serotonin reuptake inhibitors; Tricyclic antidepressants
Antidiabetic drugs, 1:**177–181,** 177*t,* 211, 299, 2:640
Antidiarrheal drugs, 1:**181–183,** 2:654
for gastroenteritis, 3:851–852
for irritable bowel syndrome, 3:1071
Antidiuretic hormone (ADH), 2:636–637, 734
Antidotes, overdose, 4:1382
Antiemetics
for cachexia and wasting, 2:394
for chemotherapy, 2:491, 492
drug interactions, 2:708*t*
marijuana as, 4:1213
for migraines, 4:1267
for nausea and vomiting, 2:537
periodic limb movement disorder from, 4:1434
recovery room administration, 4:1556
Antiepilepsy drugs. *See* Anticonvulsant drugs
Antiestrogens, 4:1251–1252
Antifungal drugs, 1:**180–186,** 184*t,* 3:826–827, 1035
anti-insomnia drug interactions, 1:141
proton pump inhibitors interactions, 4:1517
rifampin interactions, 1:211
for skin lesions, 5:1651
SSRI interactions, 1:173
topical, 1:**183–186,** 184*t,* 4:1312
Antigen tests, 1:59, 3:940
Antigens
cell surface, 3:1022
food allergies, 3:814
immune system role, 3:1021
role, 1:256–257
Antigliadin antibodies, 2:473
Antihistamines, 1:**186–189**
allergies, 1:72
barbiturate interactions, 1:282
caffeine content, 2:395
for common colds, 2:552
for contact dermatitis, 2:573
for dermatitis, 2:631
dronabinol interactions, 2:420
drug interactions, 2:708*t,* 709
dry eye from, 2:711
erectile dysfunction from, 2:756, 5:1634
for insomnia, 1:140
for itching, 1:141–142, 3:1081, 1082
overdose, 4:1381
snoring from, 5:1675
SSRI interactions, 1:173
See also H-2 receptor blockers
Antihyperglycemic drugs. *See* Antidiabetic drugs
Antihypertensive drugs, 1:**189–193,** *190,* 190*t,* 325
for angina pectoris, 1:124
antiarrhythmic drug interactions, 1:149
antinuclear antibody test interactions, 1:253
for aortic dissection, 1:219
aspirin interactions, 1:235
for atherosclerosis, 1:247
for autonomic dysreflexia, 5:1694
depression from, 2:624
digitalis interactions, 2:709
edema from, 2:726
erectile dysfunction from, 2:756, 5:1634
gastroesophageal reflux disease from, 3:854
heatstroke risk, 3:937
kidney nuclear medicine scan interactions, 3:1100

Antihypertensive drugs *(continued)*
for Raynaud's disease, 2:519
for stress-related disorders, 5:1715–1716
for stroke prevention, 5:1723
Antilipemics, 2:506
Antimalarial drugs, 3:1143, 1180
Antimetabolites, 2:490
Antimitochondrial antibody test, 1:252, 254, 3:1143, 1145
Antinausea drugs. *See* Antiemetics
Antineoplastic agents. *See* Anticancer drugs; Chemotherapy
Antinuclear antibody test (ANA), 1:252, 253–254, 259
liver function, 3:1145
lupus, 3:1180
rheumatoid arthritis, 4:1573–1574
scleroderma, 5:1598
Sjögren's syndrome, 5:1639
Antioxidants, 1:**197–198**
age-related macular degeneration, 1:319, 5:1839
aging, 1:46
Alzheimer's disease, 1:88, 4:1244
aneurysm, 1:121
angina pectoris, 3:1076
anti-inflammatory diet, 1:195
atherosclerosis, 1:247
autoimmune disorder, 1:259–260
benefits, 1:197, 3:870
blepharitis, 2:780
cancer prevention, 2:413–418
cataracts, 2:463, 464
garlic, 3:847
gingivitis, 3:877
glucosamine, 3:884
osteoarthritis, 4:1368
oxygen/ozone therapy, 4:1384
Parkinson's disease, 4:1424
polymyositis, 4:1468
skin cancer prevention, 4:1200, 5:1643
ulcers, 5:1800
wrinkles, 5:1889, 1890
See also specific antioxidants
Antiparasitic drugs, 5:1590–1591
Antiparkinsonian drugs, 1:**198–202**, 199*t*, 4:1422, 1423–1424
Antiphospholipid antibody test, 1:252, 254
Antiphospholipid syndrome, 1:252, 253
Antiplatelet drugs, 1:**157–159**, 157*t*
for blood clots, 1:322, 323
for coronary artery disease, 3:927
for heart attacks, 3:928
for stroke, 2:457, 5:1722
for transient ischemic attacks, 5:1785
Antipruritic drugs. *See* Anti-itch drugs
Antipsychotic drugs, 1:**202–206**, 4:1529–1532
atypical, 4:1530–1531, 1532
for bipolar disorder, 1:305
for delirium, 2:609
for dementia, 2:613
DHEA interactions, 2:635
erectile dysfunction from, 5:1634
Medicare prescription drug plan, 4:1240
for mental retardation, 4:1258
overdose, 4:1381
periodic limb movement disorder from, 4:1434
for psychoses, 4:1529–1532
side effects, 4:1530, 1531
tricyclic antidepressant interactions, 1:177
typical, 4:1530, 1532
vitamin E interactions, 5:1858
Antipyretics, 4:1326
Antiretroviral drugs. *See* Antiretroviral therapy (ART)
Antiretroviral therapy (ART), 1:51–52, 54, 55, **206–207**, 207*t*, 5:1623
Antirheumatic drugs, disease-modifying, 4:1367, 1574
Antiscorbutic vitamin. *See* Vitamin C
Antisecretory drugs, 5:1799
Antiseizure drugs. *See* Anticonvulsant drugs
Antisocial personality disorder, 4:1444–1448
Antispasmodic drugs, 3:832
Antithrombotics. *See* Anticoagulants; Thrombolytic therapy
Antithyroid drugs, 3:1013–1014
Antitipping devices, 5:1880
Antituberculosis drugs, 1:95, 96, 151, **207–211**, 207*t*
Antitumor antibiotics, 2:490
Antitussives, 2:552, 708*t*
Antiviral drugs, 1:**211–212**, 211*t*, 5:1833
common cold and, 2:551
for corneal diseases, 2:575
for genital herpes, 5:1623
for influenza, 3:1040, 5:1833
for pneumonia, 4:1464
for shingles, 5:1631
Antrectomies, 5:1799
Antrum, 5:1704
Anturane. *See* Sulfinpyrazone
Anxiety, 1:**212–217**
angina pectoris from, 1:125
benzodiazepines for, 1:144–145, 215, 217, 291–294, 291*t*
breathing problems from, 1:373, 374
caffeine-related, 1:216, 2:396
caregivers, 2:454
Cushing's syndrome-related, 2:592
drug therapy, 1:144–145, 215
erectile dysfunction from, 2:756
geriatric assessment, 3:866
hydroxyzine for, 1:141
irritable bowel syndrome-related, 3:1069
massage, 4:1218–1219
motor neuron disease-related, 4:1289
prayer and spirituality, 4:1477
preoperative, 4:1566
probiotics for, 4:1498
relaxation techniques, 4:1565, 1566
sexual dysfunction from, 5:1618
state, 1:213
trait, 1:213, 217
water exercise, 5:1874
See also Antianxiety drugs; Generalized anxiety disorder
Anxiety Disorders Association of America (ADAA), 1:215–216
Anxiolytics. *See* Antianxiety drugs
Anzemet. *See* Dolasetron
AoA (Administration on Aging), 2:454–455, 727, 4:1293, 1339
AOA (American Osteopathic Association), 2:702
AOBTA (American Organization of Bodywork Therapies of Asia), 1:15
Aorta, 1:218
Aortic aneurysm, 1:120–121
Aortic dissection, 1:**217–221**, *218*
Aortic occlusion, 4:1275
Aortic valve defects, 1:219, 222
Aortic valve replacement (AVR), 1:223–224
Aortic valve stenosis, 1:*221*, **221–225**, 2:428, 3:931–932
APHA (American Public Health Association), 2:555
Aphasia, 2:716–719, 5:1687–1690, 1724
Aphrodisiacs, 5:1587
Apical pulse, 2:434
Apigenin, 4:1200
Aplastic anemia, 1:109, 110, 5:1763
Apnea. *See* Sleep apnea
Apomorphine, 1:199–200, 2:755–756, 4:1423
Apoptosis, 4:1261, 1264, 5:1895
Appearance, 4:1321
Appendix, 3:1022
Appetite loss
aging-related, 2:659, 674, 4:1340
chronic kidney failure-associated, 2:509
drug induced, 2:659
lupus-related, 3:1180
malnutrition, 4:1202
undernutrition, 4:1337
Appetite stimulants, 2:394, 537, 626

Appetite suppressants
erectile dysfunction from, 5:1634
heatstroke risk, 3:937
Medicare prescription drug plan, 4:1240
nicotine, 5:1664
for obesity, 4:1351
precautions, 5:1878
pulmonary hypertension from, 4:1539
tricyclic antidepressant interactions, 1:177
Apples, 1:83
Appointments, follow-up, 4:1555
Appropriateness, 3:910
Apresoline. *See* Hydralazine
APTA (American Physical Therapy Association), 1:268, 269, 4:1323, 1458, 1460
APTR (Association for Prevention Teaching and Research), 5:1756
Aquatic therapy. *See* Hydrotherapy
Aqueous humor, 3:880–881
Arab, Leonore, 2:416
Arava. *See* Lefluonmide
ARBS. *See* Angiotensin receptor blockers
Arctium lappa. See Burdock
Arctostaphylos uva-ursi. See Bearberry
ARDMS (American Registry for Diagnostic Medical Sonography), 2:460
ARED (Age-Related Eye Disease Study), 1:41
Aredia. *See* Pamidronate
Argentine tango, 4:1293
Aricept. *See* Donepezil
Aripiprazole, 1:203, 305, 4:1531
ARMD. *See* Age-related macular degeneration
Arnica, 3:1153
Aromatase inhibitors, 1:358, 359, 360
Aromatherapy, 2:742, 5:1605, 1675
Arousal, 2:545, 5:1664
Arousal disorder, sexual, 5:1618, 1619
Arrhthymias, 1:**225–227**
antipsychotic drug-induced, 1:205
caffeine-related, 2:396
calcium channel blockers for, 1:226, 2:401–403
cardiac ablation for, 1:226–227, 2:423–426, 440
cardiac catheterization for, 2:432
cardiac catheterization-induced, 2:432
cardiac monitor, 2:434
cardiac surgery, 2:438
cardiomyopathy-related, 2:445–448
cardioversion, 2:451–452
carotid artery disease-related, 2:458
congestive heart failure-related, 2:564
drug therapy, 1:145–149, 226
electrocardiography, 3:927
fainting, 3:786
hypertrophic cardiomyopathy-related, 3:1014
implantable cardioverter-defibrillator, 3:1025–1026
myocarditis-related, 4:1309, 1310
orthostatic syncope, 3:787
pacemakers, 1:226, 3:788, 4:1387–1390
polymyositis-related, 4:1468
sildenafil citrate contraindications, 5:1634
stress-induced, 2:661
stress test, 5:1719
therapeutic exercise contraindications, 5:1759
See also Antiarrhythmic drugs; Atrial fibrillation; Tachycardia; Ventricular fibrillation
Arrhythmogenic right ventricular cardiomyopathy (ARVC), 2:445
ARS (Agriculture Research Service), 2:658
Arsenic, 3:1092, 5:1642
ART (Antiretroviral therapy), 1:51–52, 54, 55
Artane. *See* Trihexyphenidyl
Arterial blood gas, 2:513
Arterial puncture, 1:126
Arteriography, 2:457, 3:1107
Arteriosclerosis, 1:245, 3:847, 1008
See also Atherosclerosis
Arteriovenous fistula, 1:**227–228**
Arteriovenous malformations, 1:*228*, **228–231,** *229,* 3:872
Arteritis, giant cell, 1:258–260, 2:517–520, 3:906, 4:1467
Arthotec. *See* Misoprostol
Arthrectomy, 2:580, 3:1075
Arthritis
aspirin for, 1:234, 235
Behcet's syndrome-related, 1:290
general anesthesia, 1:114
juvenile, 4:1326
lyme disease-related, 3:1184
nonsteroidal anti-inflammatory drugs for, 4:1326
psoriatic, 4:1519, 1520
septic, 4:1366
sleep disorders from, 5:1656
t'ai chi, 5:1747
thrombocytosis from, 5:1765
travel, 5:1608
walking problems, 5:1867
water exercise, 5:1874
See also Gout; Osteoarthritis; Rheumatoid arthritis
Arthritis Foundation, 4:1573, 5:1875
Arthrodesis, 3:969
Arthrography, 3:966
Arthroplasty, hip. *See* Hip replacement
Arthroscopy, 3:972, 1117
Artichokes, 3:955
Artifact, cardiac monitor, 2:435
Artificial hydration, 5:1882
Artificial joints. *See* Prosthesis
Artificial nutrition, 5:1882
Artificial sphincter, 3:799
Artificial sweeteners, 3:1070
Artificial tears, 2:712, 5:1639
ARVC (Arrhythmogenic right ventricular cardiomyopathy), 2:445
Asanas, 5:1891, 1893
Asbestos
kidney cancer, 3:1092, 1094–1095
lung cancer, 2:408, 3:1174
multiple myeloma, 4:1299
pulmonary fibrosis, 4:1536
ASC-H (Atypical squamous cells-H), 2:482–483, 4:1414, 1415
ASC-US (Atypical squamous cells of undetermined significance), 2:482–483, 4:1414, 1415
Ascending aorta, 1:218
Ascending colon, 2:532
Ascites, 2:725, 3:1136, 1139
Ascorbic acid. *See* Vitamin C
Ascorbyl palmate, 5:1850
ASCRS (American Society of Colon and Rectal Surgeons), 3:1069
Aseptic necrosis, 3:1045
Aseptic technique, 2:465–467, 471
ASH (Asymmetrical septal hypertrophy), 2:445, 3:1014
Ashkenazi Jews
breast cancer, 1:355
lactose intolerance, 3:1121
ovarian cancer, 4:1375
Ashtanga yoga, 5:1892
Asian Americans
autoimmune disorders, 1:258–260
breast cancer, 1:352
breast implants, 1:362
breast reconstruction, 1:364
endometrial cancer, 2:743
glaucoma, 5:1837
grandparent child care, 3:795
heart disease, 3:926
hip revision surgery, 3:974
isolation, 3:1078
lactose intolerance, 3:819, 1121
liver cancer, 3:1138
lung cancer, 1:382
osteoporosis, 3:992, 4:1371
panic disorder, 4:1410
prayer and spirituality, 4:1477
prostate cancer, 5:1682
snoring, 5:1671
stomach cancer, 5:1704

Asian Americans *(continued)*
suicide, 5:1733
tuberculosis, 5:1791
Asian flu pandemic, 3:1038
Asian ginseng, 3:1005
Aspergillis niger, 3:889–890
Aspergillosis, 3:825, 826
Aspergillus fumigatus, 3:826
Aspheric lenses, 2:773
Asphyxia, 4:1256
Aspiration, 1:**231–234,** *232*
bone marrow, 1:338–343, *339,* 4:1300, 5:1766
breast biopsy, 1:352–353
breathing problems, 1:372–373
hip pain, 3:966
knee injuries, 3:1117
liver biopsy, 3:1135
lung biopsy, 3:1172
nipple, 1:356
pneumonia, 5:1711
swallowing disorders, 5:1741
tube feeding, 5:1789
See also Fine needle aspiration biopsy
Aspiration pneumonia, 1:231, 233, 373, 374, 5:1711
Aspirin, 1:**234–236**
vs. acetaminophen, 1:7–8
for angina pectoris, 1:124, 3:1075
antiangina drug interactions, 1:144
anticoagulant drug interactions, 1:157
anticoagulant interactions, 2:709
anticonvulsant drug interactions, 1:162
asthma from, 1:241
for atherosclerosis prevention, 3:923
bismuth subsalicylate interactions, 1:183
for blood clots, 1:322
for botox injections, 1:347
bruising precautions, 1:386
for bursitis, 1:390
calcium supplement interactions, 2:405
celecoxib interactions, 2:586
for cervical spondylosis, 2:488
coronary artery bypass graft preparation, 2:428–429
for coronary artery disease, 2:580, 3:927, 930
for deep vein thrombosis, 5:1694
for dementia prevention, 1:234
for diabetic neuropathy, 2:647
dietary supplement interactions, 2:680
dosage, 1:234–235
drug interactions, 1:235–236, 2:707
for face lifts, 3:784
gastroesophageal reflux disease from, 3:854
GI bleeding from, 3:872, 874, 1064
ginkgo biloba interactions, 3:879
for gout, 3:892
for headaches, 3:907
for heart attacks, 3:923, 928
for hip replacement, 3:966
hypertension from, 3:1009
for influenza, 5:1833
influenza contraindications, 3:1039
insulin interactions, 3:1055
iron test interactions, 3:1067
for itching, 3:1082
for knee injuries, 3:1117
liver biopsy contraindications, 3:1136
liver function test interactions, 3:1143
for low back pain, 3:1152
for migraines, 4:1267
niacin interactions, 3:955, 1005
for osteoarthritis, 3:1117, 5:1615
overdose, 4:1381
for Paget's disease of bone, 4:1392
for pain, 4:1395, 1398
peptic ulcers from, 5:1798, 1800
for pericarditis, 4:1432
for platelet aggregation, 3:847
for polymyositis, 4:1468
for prostate enlargement, 4:1512
for psoriasis, 4:1520
for spinal stenosis, 5:1697
SSRI interactions, 1:173
for stroke, 5:1722
for tendinitis, 5:1754
for thrombocytosis, 5:1766
thrombolytic therapy interactions, 5:1768
tinnitus from, 1:234, 236, 5:1779, 1780
toxicity, 1:234, 236
for transient ischemic attacks, 3:1076
vitamin E interactions, 5:1858
vitamin K interactions, 5:1860
Aspirin Foundation, 1:234
Aspirin Free Anacin. *See* Acetaminophen
Assessment
balance, 1:*280,* 280–281, 3:829–831, 832, 833, 4:1284
dehydration, 3:870
driver safety, 2:703–705
gait, 3:829–831, 832, 833, 1167, 4:1284, 1322
geriatric, 3:865–868, 998, 4:1444
nursing homes, 4:1331–1332
physical therapy, 1:268–269, 4:1323, 1324, 1454
preoperative cardiac, 4:1480–1481
social, 3:866
See also Dietary assessment
Assist-control ventilation (A/C), 3:1047–1048, 5:1822
Assisted living facilities, 1:**236–239,** *237,* 3:1028, 4:1293
Assisted suicide. *See* Physician-assisted suicide
Assistive devices
amyotrophic lateral sclerosis, 1:104
blindness, 1:319–320
communications, 5:1689
hip replacement, 3:968
low vision, 3:1164
mobility, 4:1285, 5:1616
optical, 3:1164, 5:1843
paralysis, 4:1418
physical therapy, 4:1457
recovery at home, 4:1555
urinary incontinence, 5:1805
walking problems, 5:1868
Assistive technology practitioners, 5:1881
Associate degree, 3:1129, 4:1559
Association for Prevention Teaching and Research (APTR), 5:1756
Associative dysphasia. *See* Conduction dysphasia
Astemizole, 1:173
Asthma, 1:73, 239*t*, **239–245,** *240*
anti-inflammatory drugs for, 1:379
breathing problems, 1:372, 373, 374
bronchodilators for, 1:241, 242, 243, 378–381
chest physical therapy, 2:495
common cold-related, 2:553
demographics, 1:*239,* 240–241
diuretic side effects, 2:692
drug therapy, 1:242–243, 284, 2:710, 3:854
exercise-induced, 1:240, 241, 242
garlic for, 3:850
ginkgo biloba for, 3:878
probiotics for, 4:1498
pulmonary rehabilitation, 4:1542
triggers, 1:240, 241, 242, 243
See also Antiasthma drugs
Asthma and Allergy Foundation of America, 1:72
Astigmatism, 4:1354, 5:1841
Aston-Patterning bodywork, 4:1291, 1324
Astrocytomas, 1:349
Astrovirus infections, 3:851
Asymmetrical septal hypertrophy (ASH), 2:445, 3:1014
Atacand. *See* Candesartan
Atarax. *See* Hydroxyzine
Ataxia, 5:1856, 1867
Atazanavir, 4:1517
Atenolol, 1:190–191, 297–299, 381
Atherosclerosis, 1:*245,* **245–248,** *246,* 3:925
aneurysm, 1:121
angioplasty, 1:130–132
aortic dissection, 1:219
balloon angioplasty, 1:247, 2:427

Atherosclerosis *(continued)*
carotid artery disease-related, 2:455–459
cholesterol tests, 2:505–507
coronary artery bypass graft, 2:426–433
coronary artery disease-related, 2:578
diet, 1:220, 4:1339, 5:1783, 1786
erectile dysfunction from, 2:756, 757
garlic for, 3:846–847
heart attacks from, 3:921–924
heart disease-related, 2:455–459, 3:926
Horner's syndrome from, 1:263–264
hyperlipoproteinemia, 3:1003
ischemia from, 3:*1073,* 1073–1077
low-density lipoproteins, 1:246, 3:953
peripheral vascular disease, 4:1436
peripheral vascular disease-related, 4:1436
prevention, 1:248, 3:923, 1076
pulmonary embolism from, 4:1532
sildenafil citrate contraindications, 5:1634
stroke risk, 5:1723
thiamine for, 5:1862
tinnitus from, 5:1779
transient blindness from, 5:1781, 1783
transient ischemic attacks from, 5:1785, 1786
vitamin E for, 5:1856
Athletes
body mass index, 1:332
dehydration, 2:603
DHEA, 2:633, 635
dislocations and subluxations, 2:687
fluid intake, 5:1870
hydration, 5:1872
hypertrophic cardiomyopathy, 3:1014
low-sodium diet, 3:1162
MRSA infections, 4:1295
vitamin C, 5:1852
Athlete's foot, 1:184, 185, 3:821, 825, 826
Athletic trainers, 2:689
Ativan. *See* Lorazepam
Atomic bomb, 4:1195
Atopic dermatitis, 2:572, 629–632, *630*
Atopy, 1:71
Atorvastatin, 1:247, 3:955
Atrasentan, 4:1263
Atrial fibrillation, 1:227
calcium channel blockers for, 2:401
cardiac ablation, 2:424
cardioversion, 2:452
carotid artery disease-related, 2:458
pacemakers, 4:1388
stroke risk, 5:1721
Atrial flutter, 2:424, 452
Atrial tachycardia, 2:424, 5:1825
Atrioventricular node, 1:225, 2:423–424, 4:1387
Atrophy
muscle, 4:1287, 1322
skin, 5:1650
Atropine, 1:380, 4:1381
Atrovent. *See* Ipratropium
Attached flap reconstruction, 1:366
Attachment and fusion inhibitors, 1:207*t*
Attapulgite, 1:182, 183
Attempted suicide, 5:1732–1734
Attention, 4:1321
Attention deficit/hyperactivity disorder (ADHD)
biofeedback, 1:302
gluten-free diet, 3:886
SSRIs for, 1:168
Attitude to aging, 5:1890
Atypical antipsychotic drugs, 1:203, 204–205, 4:1530–1531, 1532
Atypical glandular cells (AGC), 2:482, 4:1414
Atypical squamous cells-H (ASC-H), 2:482–483, 4:1414, 1415
Atypical squamous cells of undetermined significance (ASC-US), 2:482–483, 4:1414, 1415
Audiograms, 1:249, 5:1780
Audiologists, 1:248, 249, 3:917
Audiometry, 1:*248,* **248–250**
Auditory brainstem response (ABR), 5:1780
Auditory seizures, 5:1601
Augmentation mammoplasty. *See* Breast implants
Aura, 4:1266, 1267, 5:1602, 1605
Auricular acupuncture, 1:18
Australia, 3:805
Authentic movement therapy, 4:1291
Autism, 3:886, 4:1257
Autoantibodies
aging, 1:45
anti-DNA, 1:250, 254
anti-La /SSB, 5:1639
anti-Ro/SSA, 5:1639
autoimmune disease tests, 1:250–256
production, 1:257, 3:1023
Autogenic training, 4:1563, 1564, 1565
Autohemotherapy, 4:1385
Autoimmune disease tests, 1:**250–256**
Autoimmune disorders, 1:**256–262,** *257,* 3:1022–1023
aging, 1:45
alopecia from, 1:80
blood clots from, 1:322
celiac disease, 2:472, 473
demographics, 1:258, 3:1022
diagnosis, 1:250–256, 259, 260, 2:560
gluten-free diet, 3:886
hepatitis, 1:258–260, 3:950, 951
lupus, 3:1178
probiotics for, 4:1498
pulmonary fibrosis from, 4:1536
shingles, 5:1630
Sjögren's syndrome with, 5:1638
treatment, 1:259–260, 3:1024
Autoimmune hemolytic anemia, 1:250, 253
Autoimmune hepatitis, 1:258–260
Autointoxication, 4:1497, 1498
Autologous breast reconstruction, 1:366
Autologous collagen injections, 2:530
Autologous stem cell transplantation, 4:1196
Automated endoscope reprocessing (AER) system, 1:384
Automated external defibrillators (AED), 2:450
Automated sphygmomanometry. *See* Ambulatory blood pressure
Automatic implantable defibrillators. *See* Implantable cardioverter-defibrillator
Automobile accidents. *See* Traffic accidents
Automobile drivers. *See* Driver safety
Autonomic disorders, 1:**262–265**
Autonomic dysreflexia, 5:1692, 1693, 1694
Autonomic nervous system, 1:262, 300, 5:1693
Autonomic neuropathy, 2:645
Autonomy, 2:527, 4:1235
AV node reentry tachycardia, 2:424
Avandia. *See* Rosiglitazone
Avapro. *See* Irbesartan
Avascular necrosis, 3:964
Avastin. *See* Bevacizumab
Aveeno. *See* Oatmeal baths
Avena sativa. See Oats
Averrhoa carambola. See Starfruit
Aversion techniques, 5:1667
Avian influenza, 5:1832
Avocados, 2:415
Avodart. *See* Dutasteride
Avoidant personality disorder, 4:1445–1448
Avonex. *See* Interferon-beta
AVR (Aortic valve replacement), 1:223–224
Awareness, 2:545, 4:1292
Axid. *See* Nizatidine
Axillary lymph node dissection. *See* Lymph node dissection

Aygestin. *See* Progestins
Ayurvedic medicine
  angina pectoris, 3:1076
  breath therapy, 4:1272
  patient confidentiality, 4:1425
  sexual dysfunction, 5:1620
Azalestine, 1:187
Azatadine, 1:187
Azathioprine
  for autoimmune disorders, 1:259
  for Behcet's syndrome, 1:290
  for kidney transplantation, 3:1107
  for polymyositis, 4:1468
  for pulmonary fibrosis, 4:1537
Azelaic acid, 4:1579
Azithromycin, 1:152
Azmacort. *See* Triamcinolone acetonide
Azotoluene, 3:835
AZT. *See* Zidovudine
Azulfidine. *See* Sulfasalazine

B

B cells (Lymphocytes)
  lymphoma, 4:1194, 1196
  role, 1:256–257, 3:1022, 4:1194
B-type natriuetic peptide, 2:563
B vitamin complex. *See* Vitamin B complex
Baby boomers
  AARP, 1:1, 2
  community social programs, 2:558
  financial management, 3:803
  isolation, 3:1077
  sandwich generation, 3:794
BAC (Blood alcohol concentration), 1:65
Bach flower remedies, 5:1657
Bachelors degree, 3:1129, 4:1559
Bacillus Calmette Guerin (BCG), 1:309, 5:1795
Bacillus cereus, 2:652
Back curves, 1:**271–275,** *272,* 5:1697
Back pain
  chiropractic manipulation, 2:*501,* 501–502
  chronic kidney failure-associated, 2:509
  low back, 1:267–271, 273, 3:1150–1153, *1151,* 4:1565, 5:1747, 1894
  massage, 4:1218
  physical therapy, 1:*267,* **267–271**
  sciatica, 3:1150, 1151, 1152, 4:1323, 5:1591–1595, *1592,* 1874
  spinal stenosis, 5:1696
  yoga, 5:1894
Back strain, 5:1591, 1592–1595
Baclofen, 3:832, 4:1308, 5:1780
Bacteremia, 1:**275–276,** 4:1294, 5:1699
Bacteria
  cancer risk, 2:408
  gram-negative, 1:96, 5:1624–1625
  gram-positive, 5:1624–1625
  probiotics, 4:1496–1501
  See also Antibiotic-resistant bacteria
Bacterial cultures, 1:278
  bacteremia, 1:276
  cellulitis, 2:477
  helicobacteriosis, 3:940
  infectious diseases, 3:1035
  sexually transmitted diseases, 5:1624–1625
  skin, 5:1645–1646
  staphylococcal infections, 5:1700–1701
  tuberculosis, 5:1794
  urinary tract infections, 5:1808, 1810
Bacterial endocarditis, 3:1032, 1034, 1035, 1036, 5:1709–1710
Bacterial infections, 1:**276–280,** *277*
  aminoglycosides for, 1:95–97
  bladder, 1:310, 311, 2:593–596
  bone and joint, 3:1032
  cellulitis, 2:476–478
  cephalosporins for, 2:478–480
  common cold-related, 2:553
  drug therapy, 1:278–279, 3:1035
  garlic for, 3:846, 847, 849
  gastroenteritis, 3:851
  headaches from, 3:906
  shingles-related, 5:1631
  viral infection-related, 5:1833
  See also Antibiotics
Bacterial meningitis, 1:279, 3:1032, 4:1246–1249
Bacterial pneumonia, 4:1462–1463, 1464, 1465
Bactericidal drugs, 1:151
Bactrim. *See* Trimethoprim/Sulfamethoxazole
Bactroban. *See* Mupirocin
Bad breath, 2:508
Bagging, ozone, 4:1385
BAI (Brief alcohol intervention), 5:1729, 1731
BAI (Bureau of Animal Industry), 2:658
Bailout, 3:841
Bakalar, James B., 4:1213
Baking soda, 1:140, 5:1651
BAL (Bronchoalveolar lavage), 4:1537, 5:1582
Balance assessment, 1:*280,* **280–281,** 3:829–831, 832, 833, 4:1284
Balance, defined, 1:280
Balance disorders, 3:**831–834**
  antipsychotic drug-induced, 4:1530
  diagnosis, 1:*280,* 280–281, 3:829–831, 832
  dizziness, 2:697
  exercise, 5:1611
  falls, 3:790, 791
  hip fractures, 3:960
  mobility, 4:1284
  Parkinson's disease, 3:832, 834, 4:1422, 1423
  t'ai chi, 5:1747
  therapeutic exercise, 5:1757, 1759
  treatment, 3:830, 832–834
  walking problems, 5:1867–1869
Balance training, 2:767, 3:791, 833
Balanced Budget Act, 4:1238
Baldness. *See* Alopecia
Ball and socket joints, 3:1086
Balloon angioplasty, 1:130–132
  aortic valve stenosis, 1:224
  atherosclerosis, 1:247, 2:427
  blood clots, 1:322
  cardiac catheterization, 2:432
  carotid artery disease, 2:457
  congenital heart disease, 3:929
  transient blindness, 5:1783
Balloon dilation, 1:381
Balloon tamponade ligation, 2:523–524
Balloon valvuloplasty, 3:931–932, 4:1282
Bananas, 3:856
Banting, Frederick, 3:1053
Barbita. *See* Phenobarbital
Barbiturates, 1:**281–284,** 282*t*
  antihistamine interactions, 2:709
  drug abuse, 5:1725, 1726
  drug interactions, 1:282, 284
  folic acid interactions, 3:813
  general anesthesia interactions, 1:112, 114
  hydroxyzine interactions, 1:142
  for insomnia, 1:140
  Medicare prescription drug plan, 4:1240
  side effects, 1:283–284
  for sleep disorders, 5:1657
Bariatric surgery, 1:**284–286,** 3:958, 4:1351, 5:1855, 1878
Barium enema, 1:*287,* **287–290,** 2:752
  colon cancer, 2:534, 535
  diverticular disease, 2:694
  double-contrast, 1:287, 288, 2:534, 535
  hemorrhoids, 3:947
Barium esophogram, 5:1801, 1803
Barium impaction, 5:1803
Barium sulfate
  barium enema, 1:288, 2:752
  bone scan interactions, 1:344
  liver-spleen scan interactions, 3:1147
  parathyroid scan interactions, 4:1419
  upper GI series, 3:854–855, 5:1801–1802
Barium swallow. *See* Upper GI series

Barley
celiac disease, 2:473
gluten-free diet, 3:887, 888
high cholesterol, 3:955
Barlow's syndrome. *See* Mitral valve prolapse
Barrett's esophagus
diagnosis, 3:859–860
esophageal cancer, 2:758, 759
gastroesophageal reflux disease, 3:853, 855, 858
Barthel Index, 1:9, 3:1027
Basal cell carcinoma, 2:780, 5:1640–1645, 1647
Basal ganglia dysfunction, 3:831–832, 833
Basal metabolic rate (BMR), 3:869
Base of support (BOS), 3:831, 833
Basedow's disease, 3:1013
Baseline ECG, 2:731
Basement membranes, 4:1261
Basic activities of daily living, 1:9
Bateman's purpura, 1:385
Bath oils, 4:1520
Bathrooms, 3:985–986
Baths
milk, 3:1082
oatmeal, 2:631, 3:1081, 1082, 5:1651
personal hygiene, 4:1441
whirlpool, 1:104, 3:1000–1001, 4:1490, 5:1886
See also Hydrotherapy
Baxsiliximab, 3:1107
Bayer Healthcare, 1:234
Bayer Select Maximum Strength Headache Pain Relief Formula. *See* Acetaminophen
BCG (Bacillus Calmette Guerin), 1:309, 5:1795
Beans
cancer prevention, 2:415
food pyramid, 2:658
healthy aging diet, 4:1338–1339
vitamin B_{12}, 5:1847
zinc, 5:1897
Bearberry, 2:595
Beauchamp, Tom, 4:1234–1235
Beauty, 5:1890
Beclomethasone dipropionate, 1:379
Beclovent. *See* Beclomethasone dipropionate
Bed changing, 4:1444
Bed rest
back pain, 1:269
hip fractures, 3:961
influenza, 3:1039
pressure sores, 4:1488
sciatica, 5:1594
Bed sores. *See* Pressure sores
Bedrooms, 3:985, 1051, 1052, 5:1657
Beds
air-fluidized, 4:1490, 5:1885
hospital, 3:789
low-air-loss, 4:1490, 5:1885
Bedside monitors, cardiac, 2:433–436
Bedsores. *See* Pressure sores
Beer, 3:888
Beeswax, 3:1082
Behavior assessment, 4:1321
Behavior modification, 3:801, 4:1244
Behavioral medicine. *See* Mind/body medicine
Behavioral pharmacology, 4:1450
Behavioral therapy
irritable bowel syndrome, 3:1071
sexual dysfunction, 5:1619
sleep disorders, 5:1657–1658
stress-related disorders, 5:1716
urinary incontinence, 5:1805
See also Cognitive behavioral therapy
Behcet, Hulusi, 1:290
Behcet's syndrome, 1:**290–291**
Behind-the-ear hearing aids, 3:916
Belgium, 5:1734
Belief systems, 4:1478
Belladonna, 1:334, 4:1381
Bellis perennis, 3:1153
Bell's palsy, 2:711, 3:1184
Belpharospams, 1:345, 347
Benadryl. *See* Diphenhydramine
Benazepril, 1:132
celecoxib interactions, 2:586
for congestive heart failure, 2:563
diuretic interactions, 2:692
for hypertension, 1:191
Bence-Jones proteins, 4:1300
Bendroflumethiazide, 1:189
Beneficence, 2:527–528, 4:1235
Benemid. *See* Probenecid
Benign focal epilepsy, 5:1605
Benign paroxysmal positional vertigo, 3:832
Benign positional vertigo (BPV), 2:697
Benign prostatic hyperplasia (BPH). *See* Prostate enlargement
Benign tumors, 1:155, 2:406–407
bone, 5:1583, 1584, 1586
brain, 1:348
stomach, 5:1706
Benson, Herbert, 4:1270, 1563–1565, 5:1892
Benzaldehyde, 2:415–416
Benzaseride, 4:1423
Benzene, 5:1597
Benzocaine, 1:116
Benzodiazepines, 1:**291–294,** 291*t*
alcohol interactions, 1:66
for anxiety, 1:144–145, 215, 217, 291–294
cimetidine interactions, 3:900
for convulsions, 1:159*t,* 160
for dislocations, 2:688
drug abuse, 2:706, 5:1725, 1726, 1730
drug interactions, 1:145, 292, 293–294
for extubation, 5:1882
for generalized anxiety disorder, 3:863
for insomnia, 1:140, 292
Medicare prescription drug plan, 4:1240
for panic disorder, 4:1411
vs. passion flower, 1:216
for periodic limb movement disorder, 4:1435
psychoses from, 4:1529
ranitidine interactions, 3:900
side effects, 1:293
sildenafil citrate interactions, 5:1634
for sleep disorders, 5:1657
for tinnitus, 5:1780
Bereavement, 1:67, 295, 2:599
Bereavement counseling, 1:**294–297,** 3:996
Berg Balance Scale, 3:830
Bergamot, 1:334
Beri-Beri, 5:1861–1862
Berries, 2:415
Best, Charles, 3:1053
Beta 2-microglobulin, 4:1300
Beta-adrenergic blockers. *See* Beta blockers
Beta blockers, 1:146*t,* **297–299,** 297*t*
for aneurysm, 1:121
for angina pectoris, 1:124, 3:1075
antiasthma drug interactions, 2:710
for arrhythmias, 1:226
aspirin interactions, 1:235
bronchodilator interactions, 1:381
calcium channel blocker interactions, 2:402
for cardiomyopathy, 2:447
for cirrhosis-associated hypertension, 2:523
for congenital heart disease, 3:928
for congestive heart failure, 2:563
for coronary artery bypass graft, 2:428–429
for coronary artery disease, 2:580, 3:927
drug interactions, 1:83, 299
dry eye from, 2:711
erectile dysfunction from, 5:1634
for heart attacks, 3:923
hyperlipoproteinemia from, 3:1004
for hypertension, 1:140–141, 191, 297–299, 297*t,* 325, 3:1011

Beta blockers *(continued)*
for hypertrophic cardiomyopathy, 3:1015
insulin interactions, 3:1055
for migraines, 4:1267
for mitral valve prolapse, 4:1281
for mitral valve stenosis, 4:1282
for myocarditis, 4:1310
for neurocardiogenic syncope, 3:788
post-cardiac surgery, 2:439
side effects, 1:299
vitamin E interactions, 5:1858
Beta-carotene
age-related macular degeneration, 1:41
alcohol abuse, 1:68
anti-inflammatory diet, 1:195
atherosclerosis prevention, 1:247
cancer prevention, 2:415, 417
retinol, 5:1861
sources, 2:417
Beta caryophyllenes, 4:1213
Beta-cryptoxanthin, 5:1861
Beta-glucans, 2:416
Beta-hemolytic streptococci, 5:1709
Beta hydroxy acids, 1:83, 5:1889
Beta-lactam antibiotics, 1:95, 151
Beta-pinenes, 4:1213
Beta receptors, 4:1450
Beta-sitosterol, 3:955
Beta tocopherol, 5:1856
Beta tocotrienol, 5:1856
Beta waves, 1:301
Betaocimene, 4:1213
Betaseron. *See* Interferon-beta
Betaxolol, 1:190–191, 297–299
Bethanechol, 1:264
Bethesda system, 2:482, 4:1414
Betoptic. *See* Betaxolol
Bevacizumab, 1:41, 3:1093
Bextra. *See* Valdecoxib
Bhakti yoga, 5:1892
Biaxial joints, 3:1086
Bicarbonates, 2:604, 734, 738–739
Bicuspid valve, 1:222
Bifidobacteria, 4:1496, 1499
Bifidobacterium bifidum, 4:1499
Bifidobacterium infantis, 3:1071
Bifocal contact lenses, 4:1485
Bifocal eyeglasses, 2:772, 4:1485
Biguanides, 1:177*t*
Bilabolide, 3:879
Bilateral salpingo-oophorectomy, 2:484, 745, 3:1015–1018, *1016*
Bilberry, 3:1076, 5:1662
Bile, 2:422, 3:835, 1144
Bile acid-binding resins, 2:519, 3:955
Bile duct, 3:836, 838
Bile duct diseases, 2:522
Bile duct obstruction, 2:507, 3:1136, 1146
Bile pigments, 3:1137
Bile salt tablets, 3:840
Biliary cirrhosis, 2:522
Bilious headache, 3:905
Bilirubin
direct, 3:1144
exocrine pancreatic cancer, 4:1404
gallbladder cancer, 3:835, 838
liver cancer, 3:1139
liver function tests, 3:1143–1146
total, 3:1144
Billing, medical, 4:**1230–1232**
BIM (Bioelectric impedance measurement), 2:434
Binding agents, 3:1082
Binge eating, 4:1350
Bio-oxidative therapy, 4:1383–1386
Bioelectric impedance measurement (BIM), 2:434
Bioethics, 4:1235
See also Ethics
Biofeedback, 1:**300–303,** 4:1271–1272, 1565
constipation, 2:570
fecal incontinence, 3:799
low back pain, 3:1152
menopause, 4:1253–1254
overactive bladder, 4:1379
relaxation technique, 4:1564
seizures, 5:1605
Biofeedback Certification Institute of America, 1:302
Bioflavonoids, 2:416, 3:879, 4:1368
Biomarkers, 1:308, 2:534, 4:1262
Biopsy
bladder cancer, 1:308
bone, 5:1584
bone marrow, 1:101, 109, 338–343, 4:1195, 1300, 5:1584, 1794
brain tumors, 1:349
breast, 1:*351,* 351–354, 356, 369
bronchoscopy, 1:381, 383, 384
cancer, 2:409
celiac disease, 2:474
cervical cancer, 2:483
colon cancer, 2:535
colonoscopy, 2:539, 540
endocrine pancreatic cancer, 4:1402
endometrial, 2:744
endomyocardial, 4:1310
endoscopy, 2:749
exocrine pancreatic cancer, 4:1405
incisional, 1:352, 356
kidney cancer, 3:1092–1093
knee, 3:1117
liver, 2:523, 3:797, 945, 1133–1137, *1134,* 1140, 5:1794
lung, 3:1171–1173, 1175, 4:1464, 1537, 5:1582
lymph node, 1:357, 3:1122, 1169, 4:1195, 1199
muscle, 4:1468
needle, 1:352–353, 356
oral cancers, 4:1358
ovarian, 4:1376
prostate, 4:*1501,* 1501–1504, 1506, 1514
punch, 2:483, 5:1645, 1646, 1647
sentinel lymph node, 1:357, 3:1169, 4:1222
shave, 5:1645, 1646
skin, 5:1645, 1646, 1647
stomach cancer, 5:1705
surgical, 1:352, 353, 356, 2:410, 3:1172–1173
thyroid, 5:1770, 1777, 1778
tissue, 1:101, 5:1886
See also Aspiration
Biotechnology, 4:1235
Biotin, 2:631, 3:1056, 5:1862
Biotin deficiency, 2:630
Bipartisan Patient Protection Act, 4:1430
Bipolar disorder, 1:**303–307,** 2:665
BIRADS (Breast Imaging Reporting and Data System), 4:1207
Bird flu. *See* Avian influenza
Birth control pills. *See* Oral contraceptives
Birth defects
aneurysm, 1:121
aortic valve, 1:222
arteriovenous fistula, 1:227–228
arteriovenous malformations, 1:*228,* 228–229, *229*
folic acid, 3:811
heart, 2:438, 3:924–931, 4:1255, 1282, 1539
mental retardation, 4:1256
misoprostol-induced, 2:585–586
prevention, 4:1258
Birth rates, 1:45, 3:794
Birthmarks, 5:1650, 1651
Bisacodyl, 1:288, 3:1123, 1124
Bismark, Otto von, 2:452–453
Bismuth subsalicylate
bone scan interactions, 1:344
for diarrhea, 1:182, 183, 2:654
for *Helicobacter pylori,* 5:1800
for helicobacteriosis, 3:940
liver-spleen scan interactions, 3:1147
parathyroid scan interactions, 4:1419
for ulcers, 5:1799
Bisphosphonates
corticosteroid interactions, 1:243
for osteoporosis, 4:1372
for Paget's disease of bone, 4:1392, 1393
Bitters, 2:714

Black cohosh, 4:1252, 1319
Black current, 4:1252
Black elderberry, 5:1834
Black pepper, 5:1662
Black raspberries, 2:415
Black tea, 2:417
Blacks. *See* African Americans
Bladder
  anatomy and function, 3:1109, 5:1804
  kidney, ureter, and bladder x-ray study, 3:1108–1110
  neurogenic, 1:312–313
  overactive, 4:1378–1380, 5:1805
Bladder calculi. *See* Bladder stones
Bladder cancer, 1:*307,* **307–310,** 314, 2:408
Bladder disorders, 4:1306
Bladder infections, 1:**310–312,** 2:593–596, 5:1810–1812
Bladder stones, 1:**312–314**
Bladder training, 1:**314–315,** 4:1379, 5:1805
Bladder ultrasound, 1:*315,* **315–317**
Blasts, 1:22–23
Bleaching, teeth, 5:1750–1752
Bleeding. *See* Hemorrhage
Bleeding disorders, 3:871–875, 5:1635
Blenoxane, 5:1597
Bleomycin, 4:1536, 5:1597
Blepharitis, 2:778–780
Blepharoplasty, 1:**317–319,** *318,* 2:582–584
Blindness, 1:**319–321,** 319*t, 320*
  cataract-related, 2:461
  color, 5:1841
  corneal disease-related, 2:574
  defined, 1:319, 5:1841
  demographics, 1:319, 319*t,* 5:1836, 1841, 1842*t*
  diabetes mellitus-related, 2:640
  diabetic retinopathy-related, 2:648, 650
  glaucoma-related, 3:882, 4:1438, 5:1843
  legal, 3:1162, 1164, 5:1841
  Medicaid, 4:1229
  night, 5:1861
  optical aids, 5:1843
  retinal detachment-related, 4:1572
  river, 5:1842
  total, 5:1841
  transient, 5:1781–1784
Blinking, 2:711
Blisters, 5:1649
Blocadren. *See* Timolol
Blood
  hyperviscous, 4:1302
  osmolality, 2:636
Blood alcohol concentration (BAC), 1:65
Blood-brain barrier, 4:1304
Blood chemistry profiles, 3:788, 873
Blood clots, 1:**321–323,** 5:1767
  cardiac valve surgery-related, 2:443, 444
  cerebral angiography, 1:127
  Cox-2 inhibitor-induced, 2:585
  diagnosis, 1:322, 2:518, 561
  drug therapy, 1:157–159, 157*t,* 322
  garlic for, 3:849
  heart attacks from, 3:921–924
  heart disease-related, 3:925
  hormone replacement therapy effects, 4:1251
  inflammation-related, 1:194
  knee joint replacement-related, 3:1113
  mechanical heart valve-related, 4:1280
  myocardial ischemia-related, 3:1074
  peripheral vascular disease-related, 4:1436
  postoperative, 4:1473, 1484
  prevention, 1:322, 4:1473, 1484
  priapism from, 4:1492
  pulmonary embolism from, 4:1532–1535
  stroke from, 2:457, 458
  thrombolytic therapy for, 5:1766–1768
  tissue plasminogen activator for, 2:457
  transient blindness from, 5:1782
  travel-related, 5:1609
  varicose vein-related, 5:1818
  vitamin K, 5:1858–1859, 1864
  See also Anticoagulants; Deep vein thrombosis (DVT)
Blood clotting factors, 5:1858–1859, 1864
Blood clotting tests, 3:788
Blood cultures
  bacteremia, 1:276
  bacterial infections, 1:278
  cellulitis, 2:477
  helicobacteriosis, 3:940
  MRSA infections, 4:1295
  staphylococcal infections, 5:1700–1701
  streptococcal disease, 5:1711
  See also Bacterial cultures
Blood disorders, 1:385, 3:941–943
Blood donors, 4:1281
Blood flow
  amputation, 1:98
  arteriovenous fistula, 1:227–228
  bone, 1:*343,* 343–345
  legs, 1:136–137
Blood gases, arterial, 2:513
Blood group A, 5:1705, 1798
Blood group O, 5:1798
Blood loss, chronic, 2:561
Blood pressure, 1:*323,* **323–327,** 324*t*
  acupuncture, 1:19–20
  ambulatory, 1:*90,* 90–92, 2:425
  amputation, 1:98
  ankle-brachial index, 1:136–137
  aortic dissection, 1:219
  arteriovenous fistula, 1:227–228
  autonomic nervous system, 1:262
  carotid artery disease, 2:457
  dehydration, 5:1870
  diastolic, 1:189, 324, 2:562, 3:1008–1009, 5:1846
  fainting, 3:786
  normal levels, 1:91, 324*t,* 3:1008, 5:1846
  stress response, 1:212
  systolic, 1:189, 324, 3:1008–1009, 5:1846
  water exercise, 5:1875
  See also Blood pressure measurement; Hypertension; Hypotension
Blood pressure lowering drugs. *See* Antihypertensive drugs
Blood pressure measurement, 1:*323,* 325, 5:1843–1846, 1844*t*
  cardiac monitor, 2:434
  cardiac rehabilitation, 2:436, 437
  diabetic neuropathy, 2:646
  fainting, 3:788
  heart attacks, 3:923
  hormone replacement therapy, 3:994
  hypertension, 3:1007–1008, 1009–1010
  peripheral vascular disease, 4:1437
  preoperative cardiac assessment, 4:1480
  stress test, 5:1716–1719
Blood sugar. *See* Glucose
Blood sugar tests, 1:**327–330,** *328,* 2:639
  antidiabetic drug monitoring, 1:179
  cephalosporin interactions, 2:479
  cinnamon, 2:515
  diabetic retinopathy, 2:649
  gout drug interactions, 3:894
Blood tests
  AIDS, 1:60
  allergies, 1:71, 75, 76
  amyloidosis, 1:101
  angina pectoris, 1:124
  autonomic disorders, 1:264
  bronchitis, 1:377
  bursitis, 1:390
  cancer, 2:409
  cardiac surgery, 2:439
  chemotherapy monitoring, 2:491
  chronic kidney failure, 2:509
  congestive heart failure, 2:563
  Cushing's syndrome, 2:591
  dehydration, 2:604
  edema, 2:726
  electrolyte, 2:738–740

Blood tests *(continued)*
helicobacteriosis, 3:940
hemochromatosis, 3:944–945
hemorrhoids, 3:947
HIV, 1:51, 5:1626
hyperparathyroidism, 3:1006
immune system disorders, 3:1023–1024
implantable cardioverter-defibrillator, 3:1026
infectious diseases, 3:1035
kidney function, 3:1096–1097
liver cancer, 3:1139
lyme disease, 3:1184
mobility, 4:1284
multiple myeloma, 4:1300
multiple sclerosis, 4:1305
myocarditis, 4:1309
oral cancers, 4:1358
overactive bladder, 4:1379
overdose, 4:1381
Paget's disease of bone, 4:1390
pericarditis, 4:1432
pneumonia, 4:1464
polymyositis, 4:1468
psoriasis, 4:1519
psychoses, 4:1529
scleroderma, 5:1598
thrombocytosis, 5:1766
ulcers, 5:1799
See also Complete blood count (CBC)
Blood thinning agents. *See* Anticoagulants
Blood transfusions, 1:50, 57, 2:522, 4:1301
Blood urea nitrogen (BUN)
chronic kidney failure, 2:509
dehydration, 2:604
kidney function, 3:1096, 1097
multiple myeloma, 4:1300
Blood volume, 5:1870
Bloodborne infections, 3:1030, 1031
Bloodborne Pathogen Standard, 3:1030
Bloodstream infections. *See* Bacteremia
Blue Cross/Blue Shield, 4:1495
Blue flag, 1:334
Blueberries, 2:415
Blurred vision, 2:649
BMI. *See* Body mass index
BMR (Basal metabolic rate), 3:869
Board certification. *See* Certification
BOC (Bureau of Chemistry), 2:657, 658
Body composition, 1:44, 3:869, 4:1340
Body compression, 1:264
Body fat. *See* Fat (body)
Body fluids
AIDS transmission, 1:49
dehydration, 2:603–604
infection control, 3:1030, 1031
See also Fluid balance; Fluid intake
Body jackets, 1:274
Body lice, 3:1125–1126
Body mass index (BMI), 1:*330,* **330–332**
age-related changes, 4:1340
geriatric assessment, 3:866
nutrition status, 2:674
obesity, 1:284, 330–332, 4:1349, 1350
overweight, 1:330–332, 5:1877
Body temperature, 1:301, 3:937, 5:1843–1846, 1844*t*
Body types, 1:332, 335
Body weight
age-related changes, 4:1340
charts, 5:1877
demographics, 4:1350*t*
Framingham Heart Study, 5:1876–1877
geriatric assessment, 3:866
healthy, 2:661
heart attack prevention, 3:923
knee injury prevention, 3:1119
measurement, 5:1877
menopause, 5:1876
nutrition status, 2:674
osteoporosis, 1:335
recommendations, 3:870
See also Weight gain; Weight loss
Boils, 1:**332–335,** *333*
Bolus infusion, 3:1060–1062
Bombings, 5:1715
Bone and bones
brittle, 2:508
calcium content, 2:398, 399, 403
cortical, 1:336
healthy, 5:1868
lamellar, 4:1390
osteogenesis, 4:1370–1371
trabecular, 1:336
tuberculosis, 5:1793
vitamin D, 5:1853
vitamin K, 5:1859, 1860
woven, 4:1390
Bone biopsy, 5:1584
Bone bridge amputation, 1:99
Bone cancer
bone scan, 1:345
magnetic resonance imaging, 4:1191
metastasis, 4:1262–1263, 1264, 5:1583
sarcomas, 5:1583–1586
thrombocytopenia from, 5:1763
Bone cement, 3:972, 1112
Bone density
calcium, 2:399
multiple myeloma, 4:1302
osteoporosis, 5:1868–1869
therapeutic exercise, 5:1759, 1760
vitamin D, 5:1853
vitamin K, 5:1868
Bone density test, 1:**335–338,** *336,* 3:792
hip pain, 3:966
mobility, 4:1284
osteoporosis, 1:335–338, *336,* 4:*1370,* 1371–1372
recommendations, 5:1869
Bone disorders, 4:1283–1284
Bone grafts
dental implants, 2:619
hip revision surgery, 3:970, 972
post-rotationoplasty, 5:1585
Bone infections, 3:1032, 1034, 1035
Bone marrow, 4:1298, 5:1763
Bone marrow aspiration, 1:**338–343,** *339,* 4:1300, 5:1766
Bone marrow biopsy, 1:**338–343**
amyloidosis, 1:101
anemia, 1:109
lymphoma, 4:1195
multiple myeloma, 4:1300
sarcomas, 5:1584
tuberculosis, 5:1794
Bone marrow sampling. *See* Bone marrow aspiration
Bone marrow transplantation, 1:102, 339, 2:411
Bone mass
bone density test, 1:335–338
decrease, 3:869, 4:1336
formation, 4:1371
Bone mineral density. *See* Bone density
Bone pain, 4:1299, 1301
Bone remodeling, 2:398, 4:1390–1391
Bone resorption, 4:1390–1393
Bone scan, 1:*343,* **343–345**
airport security, 5:1609
bone metastasis, 4:1262
cellulitis, 2:477
kidney cancer, 3:1092
knee injuries, 3:1117
magnetic resonance imaging, 4:1191
prostate cancer, 4:1506
sarcomas, 5:1584–1585, 1586
Bone spurs, 2:487
Bone tumors, benign, 5:1583, 1584, 1586
Bonine. *See* Meclizine
Boniva. *See* Ibandronate
Bookkeeping, 4:1231
Boomers. *See* Baby boomers
Borderline personality disorder (BPD), 4:1444–1448
Born on the Fourth of July (Kovac), 5:1827
Borrelia burgdorferi, 3:1032, 1182–1186
Borst, Els, 2:599
Bortezomib, 4:1301
BOS (Base of support), 3:831, 833
Bosentan, 4:1537, 1540

Boston Diagnostic Aphasia Examination, 2:718
Botanical medicine. *See* Herbal medicine
Botox injections, 1:**345–348,** *346,* 3:785
for contractures, 5:1694
for prostate enlargement, 4:1512
for wrinkles, 1:345, 347, 2:758
Bouchard's nodes, 4:1366
Bovine collagen, 2:530, 531
Bowel cleansing, 1:288, 4:1483, 1499
Bowel incontinence. *See* Fecal incontinence
Bowel movements, 2:568–570, 4:1253, 1498, 5:1693
Bowel obstruction. *See* Intestinal obstruction
Bowel resection with colostomy, 2:694
Bowen's disease, 5:*1641,* 1642
Bowman's layer, 2:573
BPD. *See* Bipolar disorder
BPD (Borderline personality disorder), 4:1444–1448
BPH. *See* Prostate enlargement
BPV (Benign positional vertigo), 2:697
Bracelets, medical alert, 3:817
Braces
ankle, 4:1285
back curves, 1:274
cervical spondylosis, 2:488
gait and balance disorders, 3:830
osteoarthritis, 4:1367
sciatica, 5:1594
spinal stenosis, 5:1697
walking problems, 5:1868
Brachycardia, 4:1387
Brachytherapy, 3:1176
Bradycardia, 1:225
Bradykinesia, 4:1421, 1422
Bradykinin, 1:194
BRAF gene, 4:1199
Braille, 1:*320,* 5:1843
Brain, 2:717, 718, 4:1523
Brain attack. *See* Stroke
Brain death, 2:732, 4:1363, 1364
Brain disorders
arteriovenous malformations, 1:229
cirrhosis-associated, 2:524
electroencephalography, 2:732
magnetic resonance imaging, 4:1190, 1191
Brain injuries, 3:901–905
coma from, 2:545, *546,* 547
demographics, 3:901
dysphasia from, 2:716–719
electroencephalography, 2:732
low vision from, 3:1163
magnetic resonance imaging, 4:1190
paralysis from, 4:1417
persistent vegetative state from, 4:1439–1441
Brain scans, 4:1190, 1243
Brain tumors, 1:*348,* **348–351**
coma from, 2:545, 547
dysphasia from, 2:718
headaches from, 3:906
low vision from, 3:1163
magnetic resonance imaging, 4:1190, 1193
metastasis, 4:1262, 1264
oropharyngeal dysphagia from, 5:1740
speech disorders from, 5:1689
visual impairment from, 5:1842
Brain waves
biofeedback, 1:301, 302
cardiac monitor, 2:435
electrocardiography, 2:730
Brainstem
arteriovenous malformations, 1:229
coma, 2:545, *546*
gliomas, 1:349
Bran, 2:754, 3:958
Branched DNA test, 1:60
BRAT diet, 3:851
Bravo pH probe, 3:855
Brazil nuts, 2:416
BRCA-1 gene
breast cancer, 1:355, 4:1204, 1221, 1224
endometrial cancer, 2:744
ovarian cancer, 4:1377
BRCA-2 gene
breast cancer, 1:355, 4:1204, 1221, 1224
endometrial cancer, 2:744
ovarian cancer, 4:1377
Breast augmentation, 1:368, 2:582–584, 5:1588
See also Breast implants
Breast biopsy, 1:*351,* **351–354,** 356, 369
Breast cancer, 1:*354,* **354–360**
calcium deposits, 4:1204
cancer fighting foods, 2:415
chemotherapy, 1:358, 359, 360
demographics, 1:351–352, 355, 355*t,* 2:407, 3:1169
diagnosis, 1:351–354, 356–357, *369,* 369–372, 2:409, 4:1204–1208, 1205*t*
endometrial cancer risk, 2:744
estrogens, 1:155, 355–356, 358
garlic prevention, 3:848
gene therapy, 2:490
genetic factors, 1:356–366, 2:407, 4:1204, 1221, 1224
high-fat diet, 2:661
hormone replacement therapy-related, 1:359, 3:992, 4:1204, 1250, 1251, 5:1614
inflammatory, 1:355, 359
low-fat diet, 3:1159
lumpectomy, 1:357, 359, 3:*1168,* 1168–1171, 4:1221–1222
mammogram, 1:356, 4:1204–1208, 1205*t*
mastectomy, 1:5, 357–358, 3:*1168,* 1170–1171, 4:1219–1225, *1220*
metastasis, 1:357, 358, 359, 2:490, 3:1169, 1170, 4:1220, 1262, 1263
mortality, 1:351, 354, 358–359, 3:1170, 4:1204–1205, 5:1682
ovarian cancer risk, 4:1377
overweight, 5:1876
pleural effusion from, 4:1460, 1461
prevention, 1:359–360, 2:412, 416, 417
qigong, 4:1547
risk factors, 2:408, 4:1204, 5:1682, 1876
saw palmetto interactions, 5:1588
sentinel lymph node biopsy, 3:1169
staging, 1:356–357, 3:1170, 4:1220, 1222
tamoxifen for, 1:359, 2:490
teeth whitening, 5:1750
vitamin A prevention, 5:1861
vitamin D prevention, 5:1854
Breast carcinoma in situ, 1:351
Breast-conserving surgery, 1:357–358, 359, 3:1169, 4:1221–1222, 1224
See also Lumpectomy
Breast cysts, 1:353
Breast enlargement, male, 3:899
Breast Imaging Reporting and Data System (BIRADS), 4:1207
Breast implants, 1:**360–364**, *361*
abdominoplasty, 1:4–5, 367
breast reconstruction, 1:365–366, 367, 4:1223, 1224
breast self-examination, 1:370
mammogram, 4:1206
silicone gel, 1:360, 363, 365, 367, 368, 4:1223, 5:1597
Breast lift, 1:4–5, 2:582–584
Breast lumps
breast biopsy, 1:351–354
breast self-examination, 1:*369,* 369–372
mammogram, 4:1205
Breast reconstruction, 1:*364,* **364–369,** 4:1222–1223
abdominoplasty with, 1:5, 367
breast implants, 1:362, 4:1224
Breast reduction, 1:4–5
Breast self-examination, 1:353, *369,* **369–372,** 2:409
Breastfeeding
$alpha_1$ adrenergic blockers, 1:82
antiangina drugs, 1:143
anticancer drugs, 1:156
anticoagulants, 1:158
anticonvulsant drugs, 1:161

Breastfeeding *(continued)*
antidiarrheal drugs, 1:183
barbiturates, 1:283
benzodiazepines, 1:293
bone scan, 1:343–344
bronchodilators, 1:380
DHEA, 2:635
dietary fiber, 3:957
diuretics, 2:692
dronabinol, 2:420
general anesthesia, 1:114
kidney nuclear medicine scans, 3:1098
liver-spleen scan, 3:1147, 1148
nonsteroidal anti-inflammatory drugs, 4:1326
nuclear stress test, 4:1327
parathyroid scan, 4:1419, 1420
probiotics, 4:1499
thyroid function tests, 5:1773
Breath, bad, 2:508
Breath, shortness of. *See* Shortness of breath
Breath tests
hydrogen, 3:1122
urea, 3:940
Breath therapy. *See* Breathing exercises
Breathing
aspiration, 1:231
mouth-to-mouth, 2:449, 450
Breathing exercises, 4:1272
deep, 2:496, 742, 4:1460, 1484, 1568
Do-In, 5:1627
postoperative care, 4:1473
qigong, 4:1545, 1547
relaxation response, 5:1892
respiratory failure, 4:1568
yoga, 5:1891, 1893
Breathing problems, 1:*372,* **372–375**
aspiration, 1:232
bronchodilators for, 1:378–381
chronic obstructive pulmonary disease, 1:372–374, 2:512
lung cancer, 3:1174
qigong, 4:1547
respiratory failure, 4:1569
Breathing rate, 5:1822, 1843–1846, 1844*t*
Breathing-related sleep disorders, 5:1655–1656
Brethine. *See* Terbutaline
Bridges (dental), 4:1361
Brief alcohol intervention (BAI), 5:1729, 1731
British Health Technology Assessment Programme, 1:164
British Sleep Society, 5:1655
Brittle bones, 2:508
Brittle nails, 4:1312
Broad-spectrum antibiotics, 1:152, 5:1860
Broca's aphasia, 2:717, 5:1687, 1688–1690
Broccoli, 2:415
BroccoSprouts, 2:415
Broken bones. *See* Fractures
Bromelain, 1:83
Bromocriptine, 1:199–200
hormone replacement therapy interactions, 3:993
for Parkinson's disease, 4:1423
for periodic limb movement disorder, 4:1435
SSRI interactions, 1:173
Brompheniramine, 1:187
Bronchi, 2:511
Bronchial cancer, 1:382
Bronchial challenge test, 1:242
Bronchial pneumonia, 4:1462
Bronchiectasis, 4:1542
Bronchitis, 1:**375–378,** *376,* 3:1032
acute, 1:375–378
beta blocker contraindications, 1:298–299
chronic, 1:372, 375–378, 379, 2:511–514, 740, 4:1463
common cold-related, 2:553
garlic for, 3:850
ginkgo biloba for, 3:878
Bronchoalveolar lavage (BAL), 1:381, 4:1537, 5:1582
Bronchodilators, 1:**378–381**
anticonvulsant drug interactions, 1:162
for asthma, 1:241, 242, 243, 378–381
beta blocker interactions, 1:299
for breathing problems, 1:373, 378–381
for chronic obstructive pulmonary disease, 2:513
drug interactions, 1:380–381, 2:708*t*
for emphysema, 2:741, 742
Bronchoscopy, 1:**381–385,** *382*
aspiration, 1:233
breathing problems, 1:373
lung biopsy, 3:1172, 1175
mortality, 1:384
pneumonia, 4:1464
pulmonary fibrosis, 4:1537
sarcoidosis, 5:1582
thoracic surgery, 5:1762
Bronze diabetes. *See* Hemochromatosis
Bruising, 1:15, **385–387**
Bryonia, 3:987
Buccal swallowing, 5:1739
Buckthorn, 3:1071
Buddhism
medical ethics, 4:1234
mind/body medicine, 4:1271
palliative care, 2:599–600
prayer and spirituality, 4:1477, 1479
qigong, 4:1546
reconciliation and forgiveness, 4:1551
shiatsu, 5:1627
Buddy Poppy program, 5:1830
Budget, health care, 3:910
See also Costs; Financial management
Budwig diet, 2:416
Budwig, Johanna, 2:416
Bulimia nervosa, 1:166
Bulk-forming laxatives, 2:569, 3:1123
Bullae, 5:1649
Bullous pemphigoid, 1:*257*
Bumetanide, 2:563, 690
Bumex. *See* Bumetanide
BUN (Blood urea nitrogen), 2:509, 604, 3:1096, 1097, 4:1300
Bupronophine, 1:107, 2:626
Burdens, 4:1525
Burdock, 2:631, 3:951, 5:1727
Bureau of Animal Industry (BAI), 2:658
Bureau of Chemistry (BOC), 2:657, 658
Bureau of Dairy Industry, 2:658
Bureau of Health Professions, 3:913
Bureau of Labor Statistics, 2:621
Bureau of Primary Health Care, 3:913
Burgdorfer, Willy, 3:1182
Burkitt's lymphoma, 4:1195
Burnout, 5:1715
Burns
dehydration from, 2:604
diagnosis, 2:561
electrolyte tests, 2:739
physical therapy, 4:1455
wound care, 5:1886
Bursitis, 1:**387–391,** *388,* 4:1326, 5:1608, 1874
Bush, George H. W., 1:92
Bush, George W., 3:914
BuSpar. *See* Buspirone
Buspirone, 1:144, 145, 173
Butamben, 1:116
Butenafine hydrochloride, 1:184
Butler, Robert, 1:47
Butoconazole, 3:826
Bypass. *See* Coronary artery bypass graft

C

C-reactive protein (CRP)
inflammation, 1:193, 195
lupus, 3:1180
rheumatoid arthritis, 4:1574
C28Y gene, 3:944, 945
CA 124 tumor marker, 4:1377

CA 125 tumor marker, 4:1262, 1376, 1377
Cabbage, 2:415, 5:1800
Cabergoline, 4:1423
CABG. *See* Coronary artery bypass graft (CABG)
Cachexia, 2:**393–395,** 537
Cactus grandiflorus, 3:1076
CAD (Computer-aided detection), 4:1207
CADE (Commission on Accreditation for Dietetics Education), 2:681, 683–684
Cadergot. *See* Ergotamine
Cadmium, 3:1092, 1094–1095, 4:1505
Cafe-au-lait spots, 5:1648
Caffeine, 2:**395–397**
  anticonvulsant drug interactions, 1:162
  anxiety, 1:216, 2:396
  cimetidine interactions, 3:900
  constipation, 2:569, 570
  dehydration, 2:605
  dry mouth, 2:714
  edema, 2:726
  electroencephalography interactions, 2:733
  fibromyalgia, 3:801
  gastroesophageal reflux disease, 3:856
  generalized anxiety disorder, 3:863
  headaches, 3:907
  hydration, 5:1872
  hypertension, 3:1011–1012, 4:1534
  insomnia, 3:1051, 1052
  mental health, 2:665
  migraines, 4:1267
  mitral valve prolapse, 4:1281
  nuclear stress test interactions, 4:1327
  osteoporosis, 4:1372
  panic disorder, 4:1411
  peptic ulcers, 5:1800
  psoriasis, 4:1521
  ranitidine interactions, 3:900
  recommendations, 4:1336
  scleroderma, 5:1598
  sleep apnea, 5:1653, 1654
  sleep disorders, 5:1657
  SSRI interactions, 1:173
  teeth whitening, 5:1752
  tinnitus, 5:1780
CAG Functional Foods, 4:1497
CagA, 3:939
CAGE questionnaire, 5:1727
Calamine lotion, 5:1651
Calan. *See* Verapamil
Calcimar. *See* Calcitonin
Calcination. *See* Calcium deposits
Calcinosis, 5:1598
Calcitonin
  electrolyte balance, 2:736
  for osteoporosis, 4:1372
  for Paget's disease of bone, 4:1392
  serum calcium levels, 2:735
  thyroid cancer diagnosis, 5:1769
Calcitriol, 4:1520
Calcium, 2:**397–400**
  absorption, 2:400, 404, 4:1516–1517, 5:1853
  antacids, 1:139–140
  bone density test, 1:336
  bone health, 5:1868
  bone mass, 3:869
  bursitis, 1:390
  celiac disease, 3:889
  Cushing's syndrome, 2:592
  daily recommendations, 2:398, 404, 665, 666, 735
  electrolyte balance, 2:734, 735–736
  falls, 3:791
  food pyramid, 2:658
  gallstones, 3:837–838
  gingivitis, 3:877
  healthy aging, 5:1614
  hyperparathyroidism, 3:1005–1006
  hypertension, 3:1011, 4:1534
  kidney cancer, 3:1092
  knee injury prevention, 3:1118
  metformin interactions, 5:1849
  migraine prevention, 4:1267
  multiple myeloma, 4:1300
  normal levels, 2:403
  parathyroid hormone regulation, 2:735, 4:1419
  proton pump inhibitor interactions, 4:1516–1517
  role, 2:403, 4:1339
  sarcoidosis, 5:1582
  sources, 2:398–399, 416, 417, 3:818, 877, 1122, 4:1339, 5:1614
  vitamin D interactions, 4:1372, 5:1853
  zinc interactions, 5:1897
  See also Calcium supplements; Hypercalcemia; Hypocalcemia
Calcium carbonate, 2:399, 403
Calcium channel blockers, 1:146*t*, 2:**401–403,** 401*t*
  for aneurysm, 1:121
  for angina pectoris, 1:124, 2:401–403, 3:1075
  for arrhythmias, 1:226, 2:401–403
  beta blocker interactions, 1:299
  cimetidine interactions, 3:900
  congestive heart failure precautions, 2:564
  for coronary artery disease, 2:580, 3:927
  drug interactions, 2:402
  gastroesophageal reflux disease from, 3:854
  for hypertension, 1:191, 2:401–403, 3:1011
  for hypertrophic cardiomyopathy, 3:1015
  insulin interactions, 3:1056
  for mitral valve stenosis, 4:1282
  for pulmonary hypertension, 4:1540
  ranitidine interactions, 3:900
  for Raynaud's disease, 2:519
  vitamin D interactions, 5:1856
Calcium citrate, 2:399, 403
Calcium deficiency. *See* Hypocalcemia
Calcium deposits
  angioplasty, 1:130–131
  aortic valve stenosis, 1:222
  arteriovenous malformations, 1:230
  breast cancer, 4:1204
  bursitis, 1:390
  calcium supplements, 2:404
  cardiac valve surgery, 2:442
  carotid artery, 2:456
  coronary artery disease, 2:578
  prostate, 4:1515
  scleroderma-related, 5:1597
  tendinitis-related, 5:1754
  vitamin D, 5:1855
Calcium oxalate, 1:312
Calcium plaques. *See* Calcium deposits
Calcium stones, 3:1101, 1102–1103
Calcium supplements, 2:399, 400, **403–406**
  antibiotic interactions, 1:153
  anticonvulsant drug interactions, 1:162
  calcium channel blocker interactions, 2:402
  for chronic kidney failure, 2:510
  corticosteroid interactions, 3:1180–1181
  daily recommended dosage, 2:678
  healthy aging, 5:1614
  for hypertension, 1:326
  for insomnia, 3:1051
  lactose intolerance, 3:1122
  multiple myeloma interactions, 4:1302
  for osteoporosis prevention, 4:1372
  for Paget's disease of bone, 4:1392
  parathyroid surgery, 3:1007
  for Parkinson's disease, 4:1424
  proton pump inhibitor interactions, 4:1516–1517
  for thyroid cancer, 5:1772
Calculus, 4:1360
Calendula
  dermatitis, 2:631
  dry skin, 2:716
  itching, 3:1082
Calendula officinalis. See Calendula
California, 3:977, 984
California County Public Health Department, 2:556–557
California Labor Market Information Division, 2:652

California Medical Association, 2:549
Calisthenics, 5:1758
Calluses, 3:821
Caloric intake, 2:673–677
aging, 3:869, 4:1335–1336, 1340
cachexia and wasting, 2:393, 394
dietary counseling, 2:671
fats, 3:1156, 1157
malnutrition, 4:1201, 1203
obesity, 4:1349
pressure sores, 4:1491
recommendations, 4:1337, 1351
undernutrition, 4:1337
Calorie restriction, 1:46
Calories, empty, 2:659
CAM (Confusion Assessment Method), 2:608
Campferol, 2:416
Camphor, 3:988
Campylobacter jejuni, 3:851
Campylobacter sp., 2:653
Canada, 3:805
Canadian Medical Association, 1:242, 4:1234
Cancell treatment, 2:746
Cancer, 2:*406,* **406–413**, 407*t*
AIDS-related, 1:51, 55, 5:1641, 1642
blood clots, 1:321
cachexia and wasting, 2:393, 394
causes, 2:407–410
demographics, 1:355*t,* 2:406, 406*t,* 407, 5:1682, 1736–1737
depression, 2:628
diagnosis, 2:409–410
folic acid, 3:811
garlic, 3:847, 848
gingivitis risk, 3:876
high-fat diet, 2:661
hospices, 3:996
kidney transplantation contraindications, 3:1106
mortality, 2:406, 407, 407*t,* 5:1682
most common cancers, 5:1736–1737
over fifty lifestyle, 2:662
personal hygiene, 4:1442
pleural effusion from, 4:1460, 1461
prevention, 2:412, 413
probiotics for, 4:1498
prognosis, 2:412
remission, 2:492
survivors, 4:1469, 5:1748
thrombocytosis from, 5:1765
vitamin C, 2:416, 417, 5:1852
vitamin D, 5:1853–1854
vitamin E, 5:1856, 1857
See also Cancer therapy; specific types of cancer
Cancer drug therapy. *See* Chemotherapy
Cancer fighting foods, 2:412, 413, **413–418**
colon cancer, 2:537
esophageal cancer, 2:759
exocrine pancreatic cancer, 4:1407
oral cancers, 4:1359
skin cancer, 4:1200, 5:1643
Cancer metastasis. *See* Metastasis
Cancer pain, 2:411–412
Cancer staging
bladder cancer, 1:308–309
breast cancer, 1:356–357, 3:1170, 4:1220, 1222
cervical cancer, 2:483
colon cancer, 2:535
endocrine pancreatic cancer, 4:1402
endometrial cancer, 2:745
esophageal cancer, 2:760
exocrine pancreatic cancer, 4:1406
gallbladder cancer, 3:836
kidney cancer, 3:1093
liver cancer, 3:1140
lymphoma, 4:1194
melanoma, 4:1199
ovarian cancer, 4:1376
prostate cancer, 4:1506–1507
sarcomas, 5:1585
skin cancer, 5:1643
stomach cancer, 5:1706
surgical oncology, 5:1738
thyroid cancer, 5:1770
Cancer surgery. *See* Surgical oncology
Cancer therapy, 2:410–412
acupuncture, 1:19
diet, 5:1681–1686
side effects, 3:1095
supportive, 2:**418–421**
surgical, 2:415, 5:1736–1739
Cancer vaccines, 2:411, 4:1264
Candesartan, 1:191, 2:563
Candida albicans, 1:184, 3:825–826
Candida sp., 1:184, 3:825–826
Candidiasis, 3:825–826
Canes, 3:968, 4:1285, 5:1868
Cannabidiol, 4:1211
Cannabinoids, 2:419, 4:1213, 5:1725
Cannabinol (CBN), 4:1213
Cannabis indica. See Indian hemp
Cannabis ruderalis, 4:1211
Cannabis sativa. See Marijuana
Cannon, Walter, 4:1269, 1563
Canola oil, 1:195, 3:1157, 4:1339
CAPD (Continuous ambulatory peritoneal dialysis), 2:509
Capecitabine, 2:536
CapeOX regiment, 2:536
Capillaries, 1:229
Capillary leak syndrome, 1:194
Capoten. *See* Captopril
Capsaicin
for cancer prevention, 2:415
for diabetic neuropathy, 2:647
for postherpetic neuralgia, 4:1319
for psoriasis, 4:1520
Capsium frutecens. See Capsaicin
Capsular contracture, 1:363, 367–368
Capsule endoscopy, 3:873
Captopril, 1:132, 133, 134
celecoxib interactions, 2:586
for congestive heart failure, 2:563
diuretic interactions, 2:692
for hypertension, 1:191
insulin interactions, 3:1056
Carbamazepine
for agitation, 2:613
alcohol interactions, 1:66
allergies, 1:176
barbiturate interactions, 1:284
cimetidine interactions, 3:900
for neuralgia, 4:1318
for postherpetic neuralgia, 4:1319
ranitidine interactions, 3:900
for seizures, 1:160, 5:1603
SSRI interactions, 1:173
tricyclic antidepressant interactions, 1:177
Carbamide peroxide, 5:1751, 1752
Carbapenems, 1:149*t*
Carbenicillin, 1:150
Carbidopa
for Parkinson's disease, 1:199, 200–201, 4:1423, 1424
for periodic limb movement disorder, 4:1435
Carbinoxamine, 1:187
Carbo vegetabilis, 3:856
Carbohydrate intolerance, 3:869
Carbohydrates, 2:**421–423**
antidiabetic drugs, 1:178
cancer patients, 5:1682
complex, 2:421, 422, 3:811, 870, 4:1339
dehydration, 5:1870
diarrhea, 2:654
dietary, 1:178
glucosamine, 3:883
low-carbohydrate diet, 5:1604, 1870
percentage of diet, 3:956
seizures, 5:1604
vitamin B_{12}, 5:1847
Carbon dioxide (CO2) lasers, 5:1648
Carbon dioxide poisoning, 3:1046
Carbon monoxide, 5:1660
Carbon monoxide detectors, 3:985
Carbon monoxide poisoning, 4:1492, 5:1602
Carbonated beverages, 3:856
Carbonic anhydrase inhibitors, 2:690–693
Carboplatin, 1:309, 4:1376
Carbuncles, 1:332–335
Carcinoembryonic antigen (CEA), 2:534, 535

Carcinogenesis, 4:1260
Carcinogens, 4:1260
Carcinoma
- acinar cell, 4:1404
- basal cell, 2:780, 5:1640–1645, 1647
- clear cell, 2:743
- description, 2:407
- ductal, 1:355, 357
- glandular, 1:355
- hepatocellular, 3:1138, 1139, 1141
- large-cell, 3:1174
- lobular, 1:355, 357
- Merkel cell, 5:1641
- non-small cell, 3:1173–1174, 1175
- papillary, 4:1404, 5:1768–1771
- papillary serous, 2:743
- primary peritoneal, 4:1374
- renal cell, 3:1091, 1092, 4:1264
- sebaceous gland, 2:779, 780, 5:1641
- small cell, 1:307, 3:1173–1174, 1175
- squamous cell, 1:307, 2:758, 759, 780, 3:1174, 5:1640–1645, 1647
- transitional cell, 1:307, 3:1092

Carcinoma-in-situ (CIS)
- breast, 1:351
- cervical, 2:482, 4:1414–1415
- ductal, 1:357, 4:1204, 1220, 1222, 1224
- lobular, 1:357

Cardiac ablation, 1:226–227, 2:**423–426,** 440
Cardiac arrest. *See* Heart attacks
Cardiac bypass. *See* Coronary artery bypass graft (CABG)
Cardiac catheterization, 2:**430–433,** *431*
- angioplasty, 1:131
- aortic valve stenosis, 1:223
- arrhythmias, 1:226
- cardiac valve surgery, 2:443
- cardiomyopathy, 2:446
- congenital heart disease, 3:929
- coronary artery disease, 2:580
- mitral valve stenosis, 4:1282
- myocarditis, 4:1310
- pericarditis, 4:1432

Cardiac death, 4:1363
Cardiac disease. *See* Heart disease
Cardiac echo. *See* Echocardiography
Cardiac monitor, 2:**433–436,** 3:927
- cardiac surgery, 2:439
- Holter monitoring, 2:446, 3:977–979
- minimally invasive cardiac surgery, 4:1276
- ventilator weaning, 5:1820

Cardiac rehabilitation, 2:**436–438**
- aortic valve stenosis, 1:224
- cardiac surgery, 2:439–440
- cardiac valve surgery, 2:443–444
- coronary artery disease, 2:581

Cardiac surgery, 2:**438–441**
- aortic dissection, 1:219
- aortic valve replacement, 1:223–224
- cardiac rehabilitation, 2:436
- minimally invasive, 2:428, 439, 442, 4:1273–1277, *1274*
- open heart, 2:428, 438–439, 442, 4:*1274*
- *See also* Coronary artery bypass graft; Heart valve repair

Cardiac tamponade, 1:20, 4:1432, 1433
Cardiac valve surgery, 2:**441–445,** *442*
Cardiomyopathy, 2:**445–448**
- echocardiography, 2:725
- hypertrophic, 2:445, 3:1014–1015
- myocarditis-related, 4:1310
- therapeutic exercise contraindications, 5:1759
- ventricular tachycardia, 5:1825

Cardiomyoplasty, dynamic, 2:447
Cardioplegia, 4:1275
Cardiopulmonary bypass. *See* Heart-lung machine
Cardiopulmonary resuscitation (CPR), 2:**448–451,** 699–700, 5:1824–1825, 1882
Cardioquin. *See* Quinidine
Cardiothoracic surgery, 5:1761
Cardiovascular disease. *See* Coronary artery disease; Heart disease
Cardiovascular health
- exercise, 2:766, 767
- vitamin C, 5:1852
- water exercise, 5:1874
- yoga, 5:1891–1892

Cardiovascular pharmacology, 4:1449
Cardiovascular syncope, 3:786–788
Cardioversion, 2:**451–452**
- arrhythmias, 1:226
- ventricular fibrillation, 5:1824–1825
- ventricular tachycardia, 5:1826

Cardioverter-defibrillator, implantable. *See* Implantable cardioverter-defibrillator
CARDS Database (Computer Access to Research on Dietary Supplements), 2:678
Cardura. *See* Doxazosin
Care managers. *See* Case managers
Care plans
- adult day care, 1:29
- nursing homes, 4:1331–1332
- patient rights, 4:1430

Care team
- chiropractic, 2:503
- doctor of osteopathy, 2:702
- ethics, 4:1236
- hematologists, 3:942–943
- home health aides, 3:983–984
- hospice care, 3:996–997
- interdisciplinary, 4:1236
- naturopathy, 4:1316
- nursing assistants, 4:1330
- nutritionists, 4:1346–1347
- physical therapists, 4:1454, 1455
- rheumatologists, 4:1576–1577
- spinal cord injuries, 5:1694

Caregivers, 2:**452–455,** *453*
- adult day care, 1:28–29
- age, 3:795
- Alzheimer's disease, 1:88–89, 2:453
- amyotrophic lateral sclerosis, 1:105
- cachexia and wasting, 2:395
- death and dying, 2:600
- dementia, 2:613
- depression, 2:628
- family, 3:794–795
- home care, 3:980
- malnutrition, 4:1203
- memory loss, 4:1245–1246
- mental retardation, 4:1258–1259
- mobility, 4:1286
- MRSA infections, 4:1296
- pain, 4:1396
- Parkinson's disease, 4:1424–1425
- peripheral vision loss, 4:1439
- personality disorders, 4:1448
- pneumonia, 4:1466
- pressure sores, 4:1491
- psoriasis, 4:1521–1522
- psychoses, 4:1532
- respiratory failure, 4:1569
- rheumatoid arthritis, 4:1575
- sarcoidosis, 5:1582–1583
- shingles, 5:1632–1633
- Sjögren's syndrome, 5:1640
- smoking cessation, 5:1668
- speech disorders, 5:1690
- spinal cord injuries, 5:1695
- staphylococcal infections, 5:1703
- streptococcal disease, 5:1713
- stroke, 5:1724
- substance abuse, 5:1728
- transient ischemic attacks, 5:1786
- viral infections, 5:1834–1835
- vision disorders, 5:1840

CareOne program, 2:548
CARF (Commission of Accreditation of Rehabilitation Facilities), 2:436
Carfate. *See* Sucralfate
Caries, 4:1360–1362, 5:1750
Carisoprodol, 4:1308
Carminative enemas, 2:752, 753
Carnosol, 2:417
Carotenoids
- age-related macular degeneration, 5:1839
- antioxidant role, 1:197
- benefits, 3:870
- cancer prevention, 2:414
- cataract prevention, 2:463
- daily recommended dosage, 1:198
- glaucoma prevention, 3:881–882
- immune system function, 3:1024
- side effects, 1:198
- skin cancer prevention, 5:1643

Carotenoids *(continued)*
vision, 1:319, 2:575
vitamin A, 5:1861
Carotid angioplasty, 2:457, 5:1722
Carotid arteries, 2:455–456, 5:1845
Carotid artery disease, 2:**455–459,** *456*
atherosclerosis, 1:245
diagnosis, 2:*459,* 459–461
transient ischemic attacks, 5:1786
Carotid artery syncope, 3:787
Carotid duplex ultrasonography. *See* Carotid ultrasound
Carotid endarterectomy, 2:457, 5:1722, 1786
Carotid ultrasound, 2:*459,* **459–461,** 5:1722
Carpal tunnel syndrome, 1:101, 5:1597
Carpenter's elbow, 1:389
Carrots, 1:319, 2:415
Carstensen, Laura, 4:1526
Cartelol, 1:190–191, 297–299
Carter, Ann, 3:919
Cartilage
hyaline, 3:1085, 1086, 1087
knee joint, 3:1112
osteoarthritis, 4:1365–1366
Cartilage supplements, shark, 2:746, 3:884
Cartilage transplantation, 4:1367
Cartilaginous joints, 3:1085
Carvedilol, 1:191, 2:563
Caryophyllene oxide, 4:1213
Cascara, 3:1123
Case managers
assisted living facilities, 1:238
cardiac rehabilitation, 2:437
conservatorship, 2:567
discharge planning, 2:685
financial management, 3:804
geriatric, 3:794
home care, 3:982
household management, 3:998–999
managed care plans, 4:1210
Caseworkers, 2:728–729
Caspofungin, 3:826
Cassia. *See* Cinnamon
Castile soap, 2:752
Castor oil, 2:540, 3:1123
Castration, 4:1513
Casual plasma glucose test, 1:330
Casuistry, 4:1234
CAT scans. *See* CT scans
Catapres. *See* Clonidine
Cataracts, 2:**461–465,** *462,* 462*t,* 5:1612, 1835–1838
blindness from, 1:319
corticosteroid-related, 2:780
demographics, 2:461–462, 5:1836, 1836*t*
diabetic retinopathy-related, 2:650
low vision from, 3:1163
mobility, 4:1285
prevention, 2:464, 3:882, 5:1615
retinal detachment from, 4:1570, 1572
surgery, 2:461–462, *462,* 463–463, 5:1838, 1839, 1843
vitamin A, 5:1861
vitamin C, 2:463, 5:1852
vitamin E, 2:463, 5:1856
Catechol O-methyltransferase (COMT) inhibitors, 1:199, 4:1423
Catecholamines, 1:81, 212
Categorical imperative, 4:1234
Cathartics, 3:1123, 1124
Catheter ablation, cardiac, 1:226–227, 2:424–426
Catheterization. *See* Cardiac catheterization; Urinary catheterization
Catheters
chemotherapy administration, 2:490–491
Foley, 2:466, 470
indwelling, 2:465–467, 468–471, 4:1295, 1461, 5:1701, 1703
intravenous medication administration, 3:1059–1063
intravenous nutrition, 4:1342
latex, 2:466, 470
minimally invasive cardiac surgery, 4:1275
PTFE, 2:466, 470
silastic, 2:466, 470
silicone, 2:466, 470
urinary tract infections from, 5:1808
Catnip, 3:1051
Cats, 1:241
Caucasians
autonomic disorders, 1:258
breast cancer, 1:351–352, 5:1682
breast implants, 1:362
breast reconstruction, 1:364
cancer, 2:412–413
cancer mortality, 5:1682
congestive heart failure, 2:562
dementia, 2:611
end-stage renal disease, 3:1104
endometrial cancer, 2:743
glaucoma, 3:880, 5:1836
grandparent child care, 3:795
heart disease, 3:926
hip revision surgery, 3:972, 974
hysterectomy, 3:1016
influenza vaccines, 3:1041
iron-deficiency anemia, 3:1064
kidney stones, 3:1101
lactose intolerance, 3:1121
liver cancer, 3:1138
lupus, 3:1179
melanoma, 4:1198, 5:1641
multiple myeloma, 4:1299
multiple sclerosis, 4:1304
nutrition, 4:1339
osteoporosis, 1:335, 3:992, 4:1371
ovarian cancer, 4:1375
Paget's disease of bone, 4:1390
panic disorder, 4:1410
prayer and spirituality, 4:1477
prostate cancer, 4:1505, 1509
psoriasis, 4:1519
scleroderma, 5:1596
skin cancer, 5:1642
snoring, 5:1671
speech disorders, 5:1687
spinal cord injuries, 5:1691
stroke, 5:1721
suicide, 5:1733
thyroid cancer, 5:1769
Cauda equina syndrome, 1:268
Cauda equina tumors, 3:1151
Cauliflower, 2:415
Caustic injuries, 2:759
Causticum, 4:1379
Cauterization, 3:873, 874
Caverject, 5:1635
Cavernosal fibrosis, 5:1635
Cayenne, 1:326
CBN (Cannabinol), 4:1213
CBT. *See* Cognitive behavioral therapy
CCNT. *See* Dialysis technologists
CCPD (Continuous cyclic peritoneal dialysis), 2:509
CD4 lymphocytes, 1:48, 50
CEA (Carcinoembryonic antigen), 2:534, 535
Ceclor. *See* Cefaclor
Cecum, 2:532
Cefaclor, 1:151, 2:479
Cefadroxil, 1:150–151, 2:479
Cefamandole, 5:1768
Cefazolin, 1:153, 2:479
Cefdinir, 1:151, 153
Cefditoren, 1:151
Cefixime, 2:479
Cefmetazole, 1:153
Cefobid. *See* Cefoperazone
Cefoperazone, 1:153, 5:1768
Cefotan. *See* Cefotetan
Cefotaxime, 1:151
Cefotetan, 1:153, 5:1768
Cefoxitin, 2:479
Cefpodoxime, 1:151, 4:1517
Cefprozil, 1:151, 2:479
Ceftazidime, 2:479
Ceftin. *See* Cefuroxime
Ceftriaxone
for amyotrophic lateral sclerosis, 1:104
for bacterial infections, 1:151

Ceftriaxone *(continued)*
for endocarditis, 5:1712
for lyme disease, 3:1184
Cefuroxime, 1:151, 2:479
Cefzil. *See* Cefprozil
Celebrex. *See* Celecoxib
Celecoxib, 2:585–587, 4:1326, 1367
Celexa. *See* Citalopram hydrobromide
Celiac angiography, 1:129
Celiac disease, 2:*472,* **472–476**
demographics, 2:472, 3:886
gluten-free diet, 2:474, 475, 3:886–890
irritable bowel syndrome, 3:1070
lactose intolerance, 2:474, 3:1121
refractory, 3:888
vitamin D deficiency, 5:1855
vitamins, 3:889
zinc deficiency, 5:1897
Celiac Sprue Association, 3:887
Cell differentiation, 5:1853–1854
Cell division, 1:43–44
Cell duplication cycle, 1:155
Cell membranes, 5:1895
Cell phones, 4:1388
Cell surface antigens, 3:1022
Cellulite, 3:1130
Cellulitis, 2:**476–478,** *477,* 3:1032
vs. contact dermatitis, 2:572
orbital, 2:779
streptococcal, 2:477, 5:1711, 1712
Celontin. *See* Methsuccinide
Celsus, 1:234
Cemadex. *See* Torsemide
Cement, bone, 3:972, 1112
Cenestin, 5:1588
Census Bureau
aging population, 5:1611
elderly population, 2:616
grandparent childcare, 3:795
life expectancy, 4:1522
marijuana, 4:1212
private health insurance, 4:1494, 1495
Centenarians, 1:46
Center of gravity (COG), 3:831, 833
Centers for Disease Control and Prevention (CDC)
acupressure, 1:14
AIDS, 1:50, 57, 58, 62
allergies, 1:70
bronchoscopy, 1:384
chronic disease, 5:1611
dental health, 2:614, 616
fungal infections, 3:824
gastroenteritis, 3:851
heart disease, 3:929
hepatitis, 3:950, 5:1832
HIV screening, 5:1623
infection control, 3:1030
influenza, 3:1040, 1042
ischemia, 3:1076
lupus, 3:1181
lyme disease, 3:1183
MRSA infections, 4:1294
obesity, 4:1349
scabies, 5:1589
sexually transmitted diseases, 5:1622
spinal cord injuries, 5:1691
tetanus, 5:1756
travel vaccines, 5:1609
vaccines, 5:1756, 1815
voluntary counseling and testing, 1:56
Centers for Medicare and Medicaid Services (CMS), 3:808, 4:1385
Central diabetes insipidus, 2:636, 637
Central lines, 3:1060, 1062
Central nervous system, 1:262, 2:395, 3:831
Central nervous system depressants
anti-insomnia drugs, 1:140
anticonvulsant drug interactions, 1:162
barbiturate interactions, 1:282, 284
benzodiazepine interactions, 1:292, 294
calcium channel blocker interactions, 2:402
tricyclic antidepressant interactions, 1:177
Central nervous system disorders, 4:1284
Central nervous system tumors, 1:*348,* **348–351**
Central sleep apnea, 5:1652
Central spinal stenosis, 5:1696
Central vision, 1:39–43
Centrally acting muscle relaxants, 4:1308
Cephalexin, 1:150–151, 334, 2:479
Cephalosporins, 1:149*t,* 150–151, 2:**478–480,** 479*t*
allergies, 1:153, 2:479
for cystitis, 2:595
drug interactions, 1:153, 2:480
thrombolytic therapy interactions, 5:1768
for wound care, 5:1886
Cephradine, 1:150–151
Ceptaz. *See* Ceftazidime
Ceramic-on-ceramic prosthesis, 3:1112
Ceramic-on-polyethylene prosthesis, 3:1112
Cereals, 5:1847
Cerebellar lesions, 3:831, 833
Cerebral aneurysm, 1:120, 121, 122, 2:401
Cerebral angiography, 1:127, 230
Cerebral cortex, 2:545, *546*
Cerebral palsy
dysarthria from, 5:1688
mental retardation, 4:1255
neuromuscular physical therapy, 4:1323
paralysis from, 4:1417, 1418
Cerebrospinal fluid (CSF), 4:1246–1247
Cerebrospinal fluid (CSF) analysis, 4:1248
Cerebrovascular syncope, 3:786–788
Certification
acupressure, 1:15
acupuncture, 1:20
advanced practice nurses, 1:35–36
allergy tests, 1:76
biofeedback, 1:302
chest physical therapy, 2:498
clinical nurse specialists, 2:526
dermatologists, 2:633
dialysis technologists, 2:651
dietitians, 2:557, 683–684, 4:1346–1348
gerontological nutrition, 4:1348
hematologists, 3:943
home health aides, 3:984
massage, 4:1219
nursing assistants, 4:1330
nutritionists, 4:1347
pharmacy technicians, 4:1453
physical therapy, 4:1458
physical therapy assistants, 4:1460
plastic surgery, 2:584
radiography technologists, 1:289
shiatsu, 5:1629
surgeons, 3:805, 806
ultrasonography, 2:460
See also Licensure
Certified nurse midwives, 1:34, 35–36, 3:1129, 4:1559
Certified nursing assistant (CNA), 4:1330
Certified registered nurse anesthetists (CRNAs), 1:34, 35, 4:1559
Cerument, 2:721–723
Cervical cancer, 2:**480–486,** *481*
causes, 2:408, 481–482
colposcopy, 4:1415
diagnosis, 2:409, 481, 482–483, 485, 4:1414–1415
HPV-related, 2:483, 4:1412–1413, 5:1622, 1623, 1625–1626
hysterectomy, 2:413, 3:1016, 1017
metastasis, 2:483, 4:1415
mortality, 2:481, 484, 4:1412
Pap tests, 2:481, 482, 485, 4:1412–1416
symptoms, 2:482, 5:1661
treatment, 2:483–484
vaccines, 5:1623
Cervical carcinoma in situ, 2:482, 4:1414–1415
Cervical dysplasia, 2:481, 4:1414–1415

Cervical dystonia, 1:345, 347
Cervical intraepithelial neoplasia (CIN), 2:482, 4:1415
Cervical nerve roots, 5:1691–1692
Cervical radiculopathy, 2:487, 489
Cervical specimens, 5:1626
Cervical spondylosis, 2:*486,* **486–489**
Cervical stenosis, 5:1697
Cetirizine, 1:187
Cetuximab, 2:536
Ceylon. *See* Cinnamon
CFU (Colony forming units), 5:1811
Chace, Marian, 4:1290–1291
Chagas disease, 4:1309
Chalazion, 2:778–780
Challenge tests
  diet, 3:817, 820, 4:1468, 1579
  polymyositis, 4:1468
  rosacea, 4:1579
Chamber oxygen therapy. *See* Hyperbaric oxygen therapy
Chamomile
  boils, 1:334
  dry skin, 2:716
  gastroesophageal reflux disease, 3:856
  hypertension, 1:326
  seizures, 5:1605
CHAMPUS. *See* Tricare
Chancroid, 5:1625
Chang Sanfeng, 5:1745–1746
Chapparal, 2:679
Character, defined, 4:1445
Charcoal, activated, 4:1382
Charles Bonnet syndrome, 1:41
Charnley, John, 3:964
Charnley prosthesis, 3:964, 965
Charts
  body weight, 5:1877
  eye, 2:770, 4:1321, 5:1841, 1842
Chaste tree, 4:1252
Cheese, 1:208–209
Chelation therapy, 3:1076
Chelidonium majus. See Rock-poppy
Chemical peels, 1:83, 84, 318, 5:1889
Chemical pneumonia, 4:1464
Chemical restraints, 4:1332
Chemicals
  carcinogenic, 4:1260
  cigarettes, 5:1660
  dermatitis, 2:630
  exocrine pancreatic cancer, 4:1408
  sexual dysfunction, 5:1618
  skin cancer, 5:1642
Chemoembolization, hepatic artery, 3:1141
Chemotherapy, 1:154–157, 2:411, 418–421, **489–493,** 4:1240
  acupressure precautions, 1:14
  acupuncture precautions, 1:19
  adjuvant, 2:489, 536
  adverse effects, 1:155–157
  alopecia from, 1:80
  for amyloidosis, 1:102
  for bladder cancer, 1:309
  boils from, 1:333
  bone marrow biopsy monitoring, 1:339
  for brain and central nervous system tumors, 1:350
  for breast cancer, 1:358, 359, 360
  for cervical cancer, 2:484
  for colon cancer, 2:536
  cycle specific, 1:155
  diet, 5:1682–1685
  for endometrial cancer, 2:745
  for esophageal cancer, 2:760
  for exocrine pancreatic cancer, 4:1406–1407
  for gallbladder cancer, 3:836
  hyperthermia enhancement, 4:1264–1265
  informed consent, 3:1044–1045
  intraperitoneal, 4:1376
  intrathecal, 4:1195, 1262
  for kidney cancer, 3:1093
  for liver cancer, 3:1140–1141
  for lung cancer, 3:1176
  mastectomy after, 4:1220–1221
  for melanoma, 4:1200
  for metastasis, 4:1264
  for multiple myeloma, 4:1301
  nausea and vomiting from, 2:418–419, 491, 492, 4:1213, 5:1684
  neoadjuvant, 2:411
  non-cycle specific, 1:155
  for non-Hodgkin's lymphoma, 4:1195
  for oral cancers, 4:1359
  for ovarian cancer, 4:1376
  pharmacology, 4:1449–1450
  post-lumpectomy, 3:1170
  pulmonary fibrosis from, 4:1536
  for sarcomas, 5:1585
  side effects, 2:412, 418–421, 492, 561, 4:1377, 5:1682–1685
  for skin cancer, 5:1643
  for stomach cancer, 5:1706–1707
  surgical oncology, 5:1738
  thrombocytopenia from, 1:155, 5:1763, 1764
  for thyroid cancer, 5:1771, 1772
Cheng Man-Ching, 5:1746
Chess, Stella, 4:1445
Chess, Thomas, 4:1445
Chest compressions, 2:449, 450
Chest CT scans, 2:*493,* **493–495**
Chest pain. *See* Angina pectoris
Chest percussion, 2:742, 4:1465
Chest physical therapy, 2:**495–498**
Chest surgery. *See* Thoracic surgery
Chest trauma, 1:219
Chest x rays, 2:**498–500**
  AIDS, 1:51
  angina pectoris, 1:124
  aortic dissection, 1:219
  aortic valve stenosis, 1:223
  aspiration, 1:233
  breathing problems, 1:373
  cardiac surgery, 2:439
  cardiac valve surgery, 2:443
  cardiomyopathy, 2:446
  cervical cancer, 2:483
  chronic obstructive pulmonary disease, 2:513
  colon cancer, 2:535
  congestive heart failure, 2:562
  delirium, 2:608
  edema, 2:726
  emphysema, 2:741
  implantable cardioverter-defibrillator, 3:1026
  kidney cancer, 3:1092
  liver cancer, 3:1140
  lung biopsy, 3:1173
  lung cancer, 3:1174, 1175, 4:1263
  melanoma, 4:1199
  mitral valve insufficiency, 4:1280
  mitral valve stenosis, 4:1282
  oral cancers, 4:1358
  pleural effusion, 4:1460
  pneumonia, 4:1464
  preoperative care, 4:1482
  prostate cancer, 4:1506
  pulmonary embolism, 4:1533
  pulmonary fibrosis, 4:1537
  pulmonary rehabilitation, 4:1543
  sarcoidosis, 5:1582
  stomach cancer, 5:1706
  streptococcal pneumonia, 5:1711
  tuberculosis, 5:1793, 1794
Chewing tobacco, 4:1357, 1359, 5:1659, 1660
CHF. *See* Congestive heart failure
Chi, 1:12, 13, 17, 18, 4:1546
Chicken broth, 2:553
Chickenpox, 3:1032
  cellulitis from, 2:477
  drug therapy, 1:212
  myocarditis from, 4:1309
  shingles, 5:1630, 1631, 1832
  vaccine, 5:1632, 1815
Child abuse, 3:862
Child care, grandparent, 3:795
Childbirth, 1:119
Childhood cancers, 1:72, 2:603
Childhood memories, 4:1527
Childhood mortality, 1:45–46
Childhood traumatic grief (CTG), 5:1715
Children
  adult, 2:454, 707, 727, 728
  anticonvulsant drugs, 1:160, 161

Children *(continued)*
antidiarrheal drugs, 1:182–183
blood sugar tests, 1:328
body mass index, 1:332
bone marrow biopsy and aspiration, 1:341–342
cancer fighting foods, 2:418
cardiopulmonary resuscitation, 2:450
common cold, 2:550
cystitis, 2:593
dietary fiber, 3:957
dietary supplements, 2:418
enemas, 2:753
feral, 4:1560
ginkgo biloba, 3:879
local anesthesia, 1:117
low-fat diet, 3:1158
Medicaid, 4:1229
meningitis, 4:1247
obesity, 2:556
overdose, 4:1380, 1383
preoperative care, 4:1483
sarcomas, 5:1584
socialization, 4:1560
SSRIs, 1:168
teeth whitening, 5:1750–1751
vaccines, 5:1813, 1815
Childress, James, 4:1235
Chili peppers, 2:415
Chinese traditional medicine. *See* Traditional Chinese medicine
Chiropractic, 2:*501,* **501–504,** *502,* 4:1369
back and neck pain, 1:269
cervical spondylosis, 2:489
low back pain, 3:1152
sciatica, 5:1594
spinal stenosis, 5:1697
Chitin, 3:883
Chlamydia, 5:1621–1624
coronary artery disease, 2:578
diagnosis, 5:1625
diarrhea, 2:654
Chlamydia trachomatis, 1:310, 5:1625, 1808, 1842
Chlorambucil, 1:290
Chloramphenicol, 1:152, 2:779
Chlordiazepoxide, 1:177, 291–294, 3:900
Chloride, 2:604, 734, 738–739
Chlorinated water, 2:408
Chlorine channel activators, 2:569
Chloroform, 1:112
Chlorophyll, 2:417
Chlorophylones, 2:417
Chloroquine, 3:900, 5:1858
Chlorothiazide, 1:189, 2:690
Chlorphenesin, 4:1308
Chlorpheniramine, 1:187
Chlorpromazine
calcium supplement interactions, 2:405
for dementia, 2:613
hormone replacement therapy interactions, 3:993
Parkinson's disease from, 4:1422
for psychoses, 1:203, 4:1530
tricyclic antidepressant interactions, 1:177
Chlorpropamide, 1:178, 180, 2:549
Chlortetracycline, 1:151
Chlorthalidone, 1:189, 2:690
Chlorzoxazone, 4:1308
Chocolate, 2:395, 726, 3:907
Choctaw tribe, 5:1596
Cholangiocarcinoma, 3:1138
Cholangiography, 3:835
Cholecalciferol, 5:1853
Cholecystectomy, 3:839–840
Cholecystitis, 3:835, 838
Cholecystography, 3:839
Choledocholithiasis, 3:838
Choledyl. *See* Oxtriphylline
Cholelithiasis, 3:838
Cholera, 2:655
Cholestasis, 3:1133, 1146
Cholesterol (dietary)
Cushing's syndrome, 2:592
high cholesterol, 3:953–954
low-cholesterol diet, 3:1153–1156, 5:1722–1723
sources, 3:1154
stroke risk, 5:1722–1723
Cholesterol (serum)
aging, 3:869
atherosclerosis, 1:246
blood clots, 1:322
calcium supplements, 2:404
carotid artery disease, 2:457
cinnamon, 2:515
description, 3:953
dietary counseling, 2:671
gallstones, 3:837, 840
garlic, 3:847
hyperlipoproteinemia, 3:1002–1005
ischemia, 3:1076
low levels, 2:506–607
normal levels, 2:506, 3:954
plaques, 2:456
total serum, 2:505, 3:954
vitamin C, 5:1850
See also High cholesterol
Cholesterol absorption inhibitors, 3:955
Cholesterol levels. *See* Cholesterol (serum)
Cholesterol-lowering drugs
for carotid artery disease, 2:456
for coronary artery disease, 2:580
diuretic interactions, 2:692
dry skin from, 2:715
for high cholesterol, 2:519, 3:953*t*
for hyperlipoproteinemia, 3:1004–1005
vs. low-cholesterol diet, 3:1155
for stroke prevention, 5:1723
for transient blindness, 5:1783
vitamin D interactions, 5:1856
Cholesterol polyps, 3:838
Cholesterol tests, 2:**505–507,** 518, 3:954, 1143–1145, 1154
Cholesterolosis, 3:838
Cholestyramine
acetaminophen interactions, 1:8
for atherosclerosis, 1:247
diuretic interactions, 2:692
for heartburn, 3:935
for irritable bowel syndrome, 3:1071
for itching, 3:1082
vitamin K interactions, 5:1860
Cholinergic drugs, 4:1381
Cholinesterase inhibitors, 1:87–88, 163–165, 4:1244, 5:1616
Chondroitin sulfate, 3:884, 1117, 4:1368
Chondrosarcomas, 5:1583
Chordomas, 5:1583–1584
Chore service programs, 2:558
Choroidal neovascularization (CNV), 1:40
Christianity
death and dying, 2:599
euthanasia, 2:762
medical ethics, 4:1234
mind/body medicine, 4:1269
organ donation, 4:1364
prayer and spirituality, 4:1477–1478, 1479
reconciliation and forgiveness, 4:1551
relationships with God, 4:1561
Chromium, 3:1056
Chromosomal abnormalities, 4:1256, 1260
Chromosome 8, 1:45
Chronic blood loss, 2:561
Chronic bronchitis, 1:375–378
breathing problems, 1:372
bronchodilators for, 1:379
chronic obstructive pulmonary disease, 1:375, 376, 377, 2:511–514
demographics, 1:375, 2:740*t*
emphysema, 2:740, 740*t*
pneumonia from, 4:1463
pulmonary rehabilitation, 4:1542
Chronic disease
aerobic exercise, 1:37, 38
anemia of, 1:109
anti-inflammatory diet, 1:193–196
demographics, 5:1611
depression from, 2:623–624
diet recommendations, 2:659, 669–670

Chronic disease *(continued)*
homeopathic medicine, 3:987
inflammation, 1:193–194
lifestyle, 2:663
malnutrition, 2:665
mind/body medicine, 4:1271
periodic limb movement disorder from, 4:1434
qigong, 4:1546
sleep disorders from, 5:1656
travel, 5:1608
viral infection-related, 5:1831, 1834–1835
vitamin E for, 5:1856–1857
walking problems from, 5:1867
Chronic fatigue syndrome
massage, 4:1219
probiotics for, 4:1498
Chronic infections, 1:277, 3:1024, 1032
Chronic inflammatory demyelinating polyradiculoneuropathy (CIDP), 4:1417
Chronic insomnia, 3:1050, 5:1655
Chronic irritation, 4:1260
Chronic kidney disease, 1:128–129, 2:637
Chronic kidney failure, 2:**507–510**
diabetic nephropathy-related, 2:643
kidney nuclear medicine scans, 3:1100
kidney transplantation, 2:509, 3:1104–1108
Chronic leukemia, 2:**511**
Chronic lymphocytic leukemia, 1:254, 2:511
Chronic myelocytic leukemia, 2:511, 4:1547
Chronic obstructive pulmonary disease (COPD), 2:*511,* **511–514**
beta blocker contraindications, 1:298–299
breathing problems from, 1:372–374, 2:512
chronic bronchitis, 1:375, 376, 377, 2:511–514
electrolyte tests, 2:739
emphysema, 2:740
home oxygen therapy, 4:1385
lung cancer, 3:1175
omega-3 fatty acids, 5:1662
oxygen therapy, 3:1046, 1047, 1049
pulmonary rehabilitation, 4:1541–1544
respiratory failure from, 4:1567, 1568
self-help measures, 2:742
smoking-related, 2:512, 5:1662
yoga, 5:1894
Chronic pain
acupressure, 1:15
acupuncture, 1:19
aging, 4:1397
analgesics, 1:107
cancer, 4:1565
defined, 4:1394
fibromyalgia, 3:800, 802
low back, 3:1151, 1152
malnutrition, 4:1395
massage, 4:1218
multiple sclerosis, 4:1304
relaxation techniques, 4:1565
TENS, 4:1398
treatment, 4:1396, 1397
Chronic PTSD, 4:1469–1470
Chronic renal failure. *See* Chronic kidney failure
Chronulac. *See* Lactulose
Chrysanthellum indicum, 4:1579
Church social programs, 2:558, 3:1079
Chylomicrons, 2:505
Cialis. *See* Tadalafil
Ciclopirox, 1:184, 4:1312
CIDP (Chronic inflammatory demyelinating polyradiculoneuropathy), 4:1417
Cigarette smoking. *See* Smoking
Cimetidine, 3:897–900
anticonvulsant drug interactions, 1:162
benzodiazepine interactions, 1:145
caffeine interactions, 2:397
diazepam interactions, 4:1308
erectile dysfunction from, 5:1634
for gastroesophageal reflux disease, 3:855–856
for heartburn, 3:935
for helicobacteriosis, 3:940
for itching, 3:1082
vs. proton pump inhibitors, 4:1516
SSRI interactions, 1:173
tricyclic antidepressant interactions, 1:177
for ulcers, 2:586, 5:1799
vitamin B_{12} interactions, 5:1848
Cimicifuga racemosa. See Black cohosh
CIN (Cervical intraepithelial neoplasia), 2:482, 4:1415
Cinnamomum aromaticum. See Cinnamon
Cinnamomum vera. See Cinnamon
Cinnamon, 2:**514–516**
Cipro. *See* Ciprofloxacin
Ciprofloxacin, 1:151–152
calcium supplement interactions, 2:405
for diarrhea, 2:655
for urinary tract infections, 5:1808
Circadian rhythm, 5:1653, 1656
Circulatory problems, 2:**516–521**
Circumcision, 2:594
Cirrhosis, 2:*521,* **521–525**
alcoholism-related, 1:64, 2:521–522, 524
angiography, 1:129
biliary, 2:522
demographics, 2:521–522, 3:1135
diagnosis, 2:523, 3:1145, 1146
hemochromatosis-related, 3:943–944
liver cancer risk, 2:524, 3:1139
liver function tests, 3:1145, 1146
pigment, 2:522
portal, 2:522
postnecrotic, 2:522, 523
primary biliary, 1:252, 254
rheumatoid factor test, 1:254
CIS. *See* Carcinoma-in-situ
Cisapride, 1:173, 4:1423
Cisplatin, 1:309, 2:484, 5:1856
Citalopram hydrobromide, 1:167–174, 2:626, 4:1470
CITRA (Cornell Institute for Translational Research on Aging), 3:1077, 1078
Citric acid, 1:83
Citric acid cycle, 4:1384
Citrucel. *See* Fiber supplements
Citrus bergamia. *See* Bergamot
Citrus fruit
alpha hydroxy acids, 1:83
cancer fighting effect, 2:416–417
contact dermatitis from, 2:572
drug interactions, 5:1849*t*
gastroesophageal reflux disease from, 3:856
for scurvy, 5:1850
vitamin C content, 5:1849–1850
Civil rights, 1:93
Civil Rights Act (1964), 1:93
Civil Rights Act (1991), 1:93
Claims, 4:1230–1232
Clapping. *See* Percussion
Clarithromycin, 1:152, 153, 162, 3:940
Classical amyotrophic lateral sclerosis, 1:103
Classical yoga, 5:1892
Claustrophobia, 4:1192
Clean-catch method, 5:1626
Cleaning, terminal, 4:1296
Cleanliness. *See* Personal hygiene
Cleansers
alcohol-based, 4:1296
wound, 5:1885
Cleansing enema, 2:752–753
barium enema, 1:288
colonoscopy, 2:540
colostomy, 2:542
endoscopy, 2:748
Clear cell carcinoma, endometrial, 2:743
Cleavers, 2:631
Clemastine, 1:187
Cleveland Clinic Foundation, 2:414
Client-centered counseling, 1:56

Climara, 5:1588
Climate, 5:1610
Clindamycin, 1:152, 334, 5:1712
Clinical depression. *See* Major depressive disorder
Clinical dietitians, 2:683
Clinical nurse specialists, 1:33, 35, 2:**525–527,** 3:1129, 4:1559
Clinical pharmacology, 4:1450
Clinical Test for Sensory Interaction on Balance, 3:832
Clinical trials
  brain and central nervous system tumors, 1:350
  colon cancer, 2:536
  CREATE, 2:419
  endometrial cancer, 2:745–746
  esophageal cancer, 2:761
  exocrine pancreatic cancer, 4:1407
  gallbladder cancer, 3:836
  kidney cancer, 3:1094
  liver cancer, 3:1141
  mammogram, 4:1207
  metastasis, 4:1265
  multiple myeloma, 4:1302
  pharmacologists, 4:1451
  prostate enlargement, 4:1512
  thyroid cancer, 5:1771
  vitamin D, 5:1854
  yoga, 5:1894
Clinton, Bill, 3:919, 4:1238
Clock-drawing test, 3:866
Clodronate, 4:1263
Clofibrate, 3:955
Clomipramine, 4:1411, 5:1620
Clonazepam
  alcohol interactions, 1:66
  for periodic limb movement disorder, 4:1435
  for seizures, 1:160, 5:1603
Clonidine, 1:177, 4:1381
Clopidogrel, 1:157, 3:927, 5:1722
Clopramide, 3:856
Clorazepate, 1:160
Closed-angle glaucoma, 3:880, 5:1782, 1836, 1839
Closed-circuit television, 3:1164, 5:1843
Closed head injuries, 3:901, 902
Clostridium botulinum, 1:345–348
Clostridium difficile, 4:1497
Clostridium perfingens, 2:652
Clostridium sp., 3:842–843
Clostridium tetani, 5:1755
Clothing, 4:1442
Clotrimazole, 1:184, 3:826
Clots. *See* Blood clots
Clotting disorders. *See* Blood clots
Clotting factors, 3:1145
Clotting time test, 3:1132
Clozapine
  for dementia, 2:613
  for Parkinson's disease, 4:1424
  for psychoses, 1:203, 4:1531
  side effects, 1:205, 4:1531
Clozaril. *See* Clozapine
Cluster headaches, 3:905, 906–908
CMS (Centers for Medicare and Medicaid Services), 3:808, 4:1385
CMV (Cytomegalovirus), 3:1107, 1145
CNA (Certified nursing assistant), 4:1330
CNME (Naturopathic Medical Education), 4:1316
CNV (Choroidal neovascularization), 1:40
Co-payments, 4:1232, 1475
CO2 (Carbon dioxide) lasers, 5:1648
Coagulase test, 5:1701
Coagulation, blood, 5:1859
  See also Blood clots
Coagulation disorders
  GI bleeding from, 3:871, 873
  vitamin K, 5:1859
  vitamin K for, 3:873
Coagulation, thermal, 3:873
Coal, 5:1597, 1642, 1704
Coal-tar, 2:631, 4:1520, 5:1642
Coating agents, 3:856
Cobalamin. *See* Vitamin B12
Cobalt, 5:1847
Cobalt prosthesis, 3:1112
Cocaine
  beta blocker interactions, 1:299
  crack, 1:219, 4:1381
  drug abuse, 2:706, 5:1725, 1726
  marijuana interactions, 4:1214
  myocarditis from, 4:1309
  overdose, 4:1381
  priapism from, 4:1492
  psychoses from, 4:1528
  pulmonary hypertension from, 4:1539
Coccygeal nerve roots, 5:1692
Cochlear implants, 3:916–917
Cocksackie virus, 4:1431
Code for Nurses with Interpretive Statements (ANA), 2:529
Code of Ethics (AMA), 2:762, 4:1234
Code of ethics for nurses, 2:**527–529**
Codeine
  analgesic interactions, 1:107
  dry eye from, 2:711
  liver function test interactions, 3:1143
  overdose, 4:1381
  for pain, 4:1395
  for periodic limb movement disorder, 4:1435
  sodium interactions, 5:1680
Codeine phosphate, 3:799
Coding, 4:1231
Coenzyme Q10, 1:326, 378, 3:1024
Coenzymes, 5:1850, 1860
Coffee, 2:395, 3:988, 1065
  See also Caffeine
Coffee enemas, 4:1407
COG (Center of gravity), 3:831, 833
Cognex. *See* Tacrine
Cognition, 1:38, 2:717
Cognitive behavioral therapy (CBT)
  depression, 2:626
  panic disorder, 4:1411
  personality disorders, 4:1447
  PTSD, 4:1470
  stroke, 5:1723
Cognitive impairment
  alcohol abuse, 1:64, 65
  Alzheimer's disease, 1:86–88
  delirium, 2:606
  dementia, 2:612
  depression, 2:628
  diabetes mellitus, 4:1245
  elder abuse, 2:728, 729
  gait and balance disorders, 3:831, 833
  geriatric assessment, 3:866
  ginkgo biloba, 3:879
  isolation, 3:1078
  Mental Status Examination, 4:1320
  mild, 4:1241, 1242
  multiple sclerosis, 4:1304
  personality disorders, 4:1446
  relaxation response, 4:1565
  SSRIs for, 1:166
  vitamin E, 5:1857
  wheelchairs, 5:1881
Cognitive neurorehabilitation, 2:719
Cognitive therapy
  anxiety, 1:215–216
  generalized anxiety disorder, 3:864
  sleep disorders, 5:1657–1658
  stress-related disorders, 5:1716
  See also Cognitive behavioral therapy
Cohen, Bonnie Bainbridge, 4:1292
Cohen, Gene, 4:1526–1528
Coherent ultrapulse carbon dioxide laser surgery, 3:785
Cola nidtida. See Kola
Colace. *See* Docusate sodium
Colbenemid. *See* Colchicine
Colchicine
  for amyloidosis, 1:102
  ginkgo biloba, 3:879
  for gout, 3:891–892, 894
Cold agglutinins, 1:251, 253, 254

Cold medications, 2:*551,* 551–552
barbiturate interactions, 1:282, 284
benzodiazepine interactions, 1:292, 294
dronabinol interactions, 2:420
heatstroke risk, 3:937
hypertension from, 3:1009
Cold therapy
back and neck pain, 1:270
bruising, 1:386
bursitis, 1:390
contraindications, 1:268
dislocations, 2:688
heatstroke, 3:938
low back pain, 3:1152
physical therapy, 4:1457
restless leg syndrome, 5:1657
tendinitis, 5:1753–1754
Cold turkey, 5:1666, 1727
Colds. *See* Common cold
Colebenemid. *See* Colchicine
Colectomy, 2:535–536
Colestid. *See* Colestipol
Colestipol, 1:247, 2:692
Coleus forshohlii, 3:1011
Colitis
pseudomembranous, 4:1497
ulcerative, 1:289, 2:533, 538, 541, 3:872, 5:1860, 1897
See also Irritable bowel syndrome
Collagen
bone remodeling, 4:1390
bovine, 2:530, 531
scleroderma, 5:1596
vitamin C, 5:1850, 1852
wrinkles, 5:1889
Collagen injections, 2:*529,* **529–531,** 5:1772
Colon
electric stimulation, 3:1123
probiotics, 4:1496–1501
Colon and rectal surgery, 3:805
Colon cancer, 2:*532,* **532–538**
demographics, 2:407, 533
diagnosis, 2:534–535, 538–541
endometrial cancer risk, 2:744
genetic factors, 2:407, 533, 538
hereditary nonpolyposis, 2:533
high-fat diet, 2:661
high-fiber diet, 3:958
low-fat diet, 3:1159
ovarian cancer risk, 4:1377
prevention, 2:412, 415, 416, 537–538
treatment, 2:535–536, *541,* 541–543
vitamin D for, 5:1854
Colon Cancer Alliance, 2:538
Colon polyps. *See* Intestinal polyps
Colonic irrigation, 2:752, 753
Colonography, CT. *See* Virtual colonoscopy
Colonoscopy, 2:534, **538–541,** *539*
diverticular disease, 2:694
hemorrhoids, 3:947
iron-deficiency anemia, 3:1065
irritable bowel syndrome, 3:1070
laxatives, 3:1123
virtual, 2:534, 535, 539
Colony forming units (CFU), 5:1811
Colony stimulating factors, 2:418, 419, 420, 492
Color blindness, 5:1841
Colorado Society of the Army of the Philippines, 5:1830
Colorectal cancer
barium enema, 1:287, 289
cimetidine for, 3:897
colostomy, 2:542
demographics, 2:533, 5:1682
diagnosis, 2:538–541
garlic prevention, 3:848
genetic factors, 4:1260–1261
GI bleeding from, 3:872
prevention, 2:416
See also Colon cancer
Colostomy, 2:*541,* **541–543**
barium enema, 1:287
colon cancer, 2:536, 538
diverticulitis, 2:694
fecal incontinence, 3:799
Colostomy care, 2:**543–544**
Colposcopy, 2:482–483, 4:1415
Coltsfoot, 3:850
Coma, 2:**545–548,** *546,* 4:1440
Commercial prescription programs, 2:**548–550**
Commiphora molmol. See Myrrh
Commiphora mukul. See Guggulipid
Commission of Accreditation of Rehabilitation Facilities (CARF), 2:436
Commission on Accreditation for Dietetics Education (CCADE), 2:681
Commission on Dietetic Registration, 4:1348
Commission on Massage Therapy Accreditation, 4:1219
Commission on Truth and Reconciliation, 4:1551
Common cold, 2:**550–554,** *551,* 3:1032, 5:1832–1834
bronchitis from, 1:375, 377
homeopathic medicine, 3:987
vs. influenza, 3:1039
vitamin C for, 2:552, 5:1852
Common variable immunodeficiency (CVID), 3:1023
Communication
nursing homes, 4:1334
talking with your doctors, 5:1748–1749
verbal, 2:716–719
Communications assistive devices, 5:1689
Communities
connections, 4:1523
of interest, 4:1561
religious, 4:1478, 1523–1524
retirement, 5:1623
Community-aquired infections
MRSA infections, 1:278–279, 4:1293, 1294, 1295, 1296
staphylococcal, 5:1700, 1702
Community dieticians, 2:683
Community health centers. *See* Community health programs
Community health programs, 2:*554,* **554–555,** 3:913
hot-lunch programs, 4:1227
Meals on Wheels, 2:558, 4:1203, 1225–1228, *1226*
Medicaid payments, 4:1229
Community nutrition, 2:**555–557**
Community social programs, 2:**557–559,** 4:1527
Companionship, 2:558, 3:794
Compartment syndrome, 1:386
Compatibility tests, 3:1106
Competency, 2:567, 4:1427
Complementary therapies
AIDS, 1:52
anxiety, 1:216
hospice care, 3:996
iron-deficiency anemia, 3:1064–1065
lyme disease, 3:1185
lymphoma, 4:1196
See also Alternative therapy
Complete blood count (CBC), 2:**559–561**
AIDS, 1:51
anemia, 1:109
cellulitis, 2:477
chemotherapy, 2:491
colon cancer, 2:535
dehydration, 2:604
fainting, 3:788
GI bleeding, 3:873
hemorrhoids, 3:947
iron-deficiency anemia, 3:1065
MRSA infections, 4:1295
priapism, 4:1492
sarcomas, 5:1585
swallowing disorders, 5:1741
thrombocytopenia, 5:1764
transient ischemic attacks, 5:1785
See also Platelet count; Red blood cell count; White blood cell count
Complete dentures, 2:620–621
Complex carbohydrates, 2:421, 422, 3:811, 870, 4:1339
Complex partial seizures, 5:1602–1606
Complex regional pain syndrome, 1:263, 264

Complicated grief, 1:295, 296
Complications of hospitalization, 2:686
Comprehension, 2:717
Comprehensive Geriatric Education programs, 3:913, 914
Comprehensive Women's Health Centers, 5:1828
Compression fractures, 1:272, 3:1151
Compression, nerve. *See* Nerve compression
Compression stockings/bandages
- autonomic disorders, 1:264
- edema, 2:727
- gradient elastic, 2:602
- liposuction, 3:1132
- lymphedema, 3:1187
- postoperative care, 4:1473
- TED (thromboembolic deterrent), 3:967, 968
- tendinitis, 5:1754
- varicose veins, 2:519, 5:1818

Compromised immune system. *See* Immunocompromised patients
Computed tomography. *See* CT scans
Computer Access to Research on Dietary Supplements (CARDS Database), 2:678
Computer-aided detection (CAD), 4:1207
Computer records. *See* Electronic medical records
COMT (Catechol O-methyltransferase) inhibitors, 1:199, 4:1423
Comtan. *See* Entacapone
Concentration, 4:1321
Concussion, 3:903, 5:1692
Condoms, 5:1621
Conduction dysphasia, 2:717–718
Conductive hearing loss, 3:914–915, 918
Condyloid joints, 3:1086
Cone biopsy. *See* Conization
Confession, 4:1551
Confidentiality. *See* Patient confidentiality
Confocal laser ophthalmoscopy, 3:881
Confusion, 2:600
Confusion Assessment Method (CAM), 2:608
Congenital heart disease, 3:924–931
- cardiac surgery, 2:438
- Down syndrome, 4:1255
- mitral valve stenosis, 4:1282
- pulmonary hypertension from, 4:1539

Congenital hypothyroidism, 4:1256, 1258
Congestive cardiomyopathy, 2:445
Congestive heart failure, 2:**561–565**
- angiotensin-converting enzyme inhibitors for, 1:132
- antiarrhythmic drugs for, 1:148
- antidiabetic drug precautions, 1:180
- cardiac rehabilitation, 2:436–438
- chest x rays, 2:500
- edema, 2:726
- fainting, 3:788
- gout, 3:894
- idiopathic scoliosis, 1:274
- myocarditis-related, 4:1309
- relaxation techniques with exercise, 4:1565
- treatment, 2:563–564

Congregate senior meal programs, 4:1227
Conization, 2:483, 484
Conlin, M., 2:729
Connective tissue disease
- collagen injections, 2:530
- dry eye from, 2:711
- mixed, 1:254
- pulmonary fibrosis from, 4:1536
- pulmonary hypertension from, 4:1539

Consciousness
- coma, 2:545
- delirium, 2:606
- dementia, 2:612
- postoperative, 4:1472

Consent
- implied, 4:1426
- informed, 2:527, 3:1043–1045, 4:1426, 1483

Conservatorship, 1:32, 2:**565–568**
- advance directives, 1:32
- avoiding, 3:803–804
- financial management, 3:802
- nursing homes, 4:1334

Constant positive airway pressure (CPAP). *See* Continuous positive airway pressure
Constipation, 2:*568,* **568–570,** 3:869
- cancer treatment-related, 5:1683–1684
- chronic, 2:754
- dehydration-related, 2:604
- diet, 2:754
- enemas, 2:752–755
- high-fiber diet, 3:957, 958
- irritable bowel syndrome-related, 3:1070, 1071
- laxative-related, 2:569, 570
- laxatives for, 3:1123–1124
- probiotics for, 4:1497

Constraint-induced movement therapy, 4:1291
Constrictive pericarditis, 4:1432
Consulting dieticians, 2:683
Consumer Product Safety Commission (CPSC), 3:985
Consumption. *See* Tuberculosis
Contact dermatitis, 2:*571,* **571–573,** 629–632
- allergy tests, 1:74
- diagnosis, 2:572, 5:1650
- itching from, 3:1081
- vitamin E-related, 5:1857

Contact dissolution, 3:840
Contact lenses, 2:**772–775,** 5:1841
- bifocal, 4:1485
- monovision, 4:1485–1486
- optometrists, 4:1354
- presbyopia, 4:1485–1486
- soft, 2:575

Contagion suicide, 5:1734
Contagious diseases. *See* Infectious diseases
Continuous ambulatory peritoneal dialysis (CAPD), 2:509
Continuous cyclic peritoneal dialysis (CCPD), 2:509
Continuous positive airway pressure (CPAP), 3:1046–1049, 5:1616, 1653–1654, 1657, 1675, 1819, 1822
Contour threads, 5:1889
Contracts, nursing home, 4:1333
Contractures, 1:363, 367–368, 5:1692–1693, 1694
Contralateral routing of signal (CROS), 3:916
Contrast hydrotherapy, 3:892
Contrast media
- allergies, 1:130, 2:494
- angiography, 1:126–127
- arteriography, 3:1107
- barium enema, 1:287, 288–289
- chest CT scans, 2:493, 494–495
- CT scans, 2:588
- kidney stones, 3:1102
- liver-spleen scan, 3:1147
- magnetic resonance imaging, 4:1191, 1192
- *See also* Radiopharmaceuticals

Control ventilation (CV), 5:1822
Controlled substances, 1:24
Convallaria majalis. See Lily of the valley
Convulsions. *See* Seizures
Cool downs, 1:38
Coordinated Program (CP), 2:681
Coordination
- defined, 1:280
- exercise, 5:1611
- falls, 3:790
- t'ai chi, 5:1747
- walking problems, 5:1867–1869

Coordination tests, 1:*280,* **280–281,** 4:1320, 1322
Copaxone. *See* Copolymer I

COPD. *See* Chronic obstructive pulmonary disease
Coping behavior, 4:1523, 1526
Copolymer I, 4:1305
Copper
  age-related macular degeneration, 1:41
  garlic, 3:846
  Wilson's disease, 2:522, 524
  zinc interactions, 5:1895
Copper deficiency, 5:1897
Cord blood transplantation, 2:411
Core needle biopsy, breast, 1:352–353
Coreg. *See* Carvedilol
Corgard. *See* Nadolol
Coriolus versicolor, 2:746, 752
Corn, 5:1614
Corn silk, 2:595
Cornea, 2:461, 573–574, 4:1321
Corneal diseases, 2:**573–577,** 3:1163, 5:1842, 1843
Corneal topography, 2:575
Corneal transplantation, 2:575–576
Corneal ulcers, 2:574–575
Cornell Institute for Translational Research on Aging (CITRA), 3:1077, 1078
Corns, 3:821
Coronary angiography, 1:127–128
  angina pectoris, 1:124
  coronary artery bypass graft, 2:428
  coronary artery disease, 2:580, 4:1276
  ischemia, 3:1075
Coronary angioplasty. *See* Percutaneous transluminal coronary angioplasty
Coronary artery bypass graft (CABG), 2:**426–430,** *427*
  angina pectoris, 1:124–125, 2:427–428, 430, 440, 3:1075
  aspirin after, 1:235
  atherosclerosis, 1:247
  blood clots, 1:322
  congestive heart failure, 2:564
  coronary artery disease, 2:426–433, 580, 3:928
  minimally invasive, 2:428, 4:1273–1277, *1274*
  off-pump, 4:1273–1277, *1274*
  qigong, 4:1547
  quality of life, 2:440
Coronary artery disease, 2:**577–582,** 3:924–931
  aspirin for, 3:930
  atherosclerosis, 1:245
  calcium supplements, 2:404
  cardiac surgery, 2:438
  causes, 2:455–459, 578–579, 3:926
  cholesterol tests, 2:505–507
  coronary artery bypass graft, 2:426–433, 580, 3:928
  diagnosis, 2:579–580, 4:1276
  echocardiography, 2:725
  heart attacks from, 3:922
  high cholesterol, 3:953
  minimally invasive cardiac surgery, 4:1273–1277, *1274*
  mortality, 2:577
  nuclear stress test, 4:1327–1329
  physical therapy, 4:1455
  postmenopausal women, 3:992
  prevention, 2:581, 3:923, 930
  risk factors, 2:505–506, 578–579, 3:1074
  smoking-related, 5:1665
  stents, 2:580, 3:1075, 4:1277
  stress test, 5:1717
  surgery, 3:928
  treatment, 2:580, 3:927–928, 1075–1076
  ventricular tachycardia, 5:1825
Coronary heart disease. *See* Coronary artery disease
Coronary thrombosis, 2:578
Corpora cavernosa, 4:1491–1492
Corpus callosotomy, 5:1604
Cortical bone, 1:336
Cortical cataracts, 2:461
Corticosteroids
  allergies, 1:72
  anticonvulsant drug interactions, 1:162
  for autoimmune disorders, 1:259
  for Behcet's syndrome, 1:290
  bisphosphonate interactions, 1:243
  for bronchitis, 1:377
  bruising precautions, 1:386
  calcium channel blocker interactions, 2:402
  cataracts from, 2:780
  cellulitis precautions, 2:477
  for cervical spondylosis, 2:488
  cholesterol test interactions, 2:506
  for contact dermatitis, 2:573
  Cushing's syndrome from, 2:590, 591, 592
  depression from, 2:624
  for dermatitis, 2:631
  DHEA interactions, 2:635
  for emphysema, 2:741
  for eyelid edema, 2:780
  gastroesophageal reflux disease from, 3:854
  for gout, 3:892
  for hepatitis, 3:951
  hormone replacement therapy interactions, 3:993
  inhaled, 1:242, 243
  injections, 1:391
  insulin interactions, 3:1056
  for itching, 5:1651
  for lupus, 3:1180
  for lyme disease, 3:1184
  minoxidil interactions, 4:1277
  for multiple myeloma, 4:1301
  for osteoarthritis, 3:1117, 4:1367
  for pain, 4:1395
  for pericarditis, 4:1432
  for pneumonia, 4:1464
  pneumonia risk, 4:1466
  for polymyositis, 4:1468
  for postherpetic neuralgia, 1:212
  psychoses from, 4:1529
  for pulmonary fibrosis, 4:1537
  for rheumatoid arthritis, 4:1574
  for sarcoidosis, 5:1582
  for scleroderma, 5:1598
  side effects, 3:1180–1181, 5:1582
  for Sjögren's syndrome, 5:1639
  for skin lesions, 5:1651
  for spinal stenosis, 5:1697
  for thrombocytopenia, 5:1764
  VZV vaccine interactions, 5:1632
Corticotropin-releasing hormone (CRH), 2:590, 591
Cortisol, 2:589–591, 4:1478
Cortisone
  boils from, 1:333
  for hip replacement pain, 3:969
  for itching, 3:1081
  for low back pain, 3:1152
  minoxidil interactions, 4:1277
  for polymyalgia rheumatica, 4:1467
  for seborrheic dermatitis, 5:1600
  for tendinitis, 5:1754
  for trigger finger, 5:1788
Corynanthe yohimbe. See Yohimbe
Cosmetic procedures (nonsurgical)
  botox injections, 1:345–346, *346*
  collagen injections, 1:345–346, 2:*529,* 529–531
  demographics, 3:783
Cosmetic surgery, 2:*582,* **582–584**
  abdominoplasty, 1:*3,* 3–7
  blepharoplasty, 1:317–319
  demographics, 3:783
  liposuction, 1:4, 2:582–584, 3:1130–1133
Cosmetic, Toiletry and Fragrance Association, 1:84
Cosmetics, 1:83–85
Costs
  abdominoplasty, 1:5
  adult day care, 1:29
  AIDS tests, 1:58
  allergy tests, 3:816
  Americans with Disabilities Act, 1:93
  assisted living facilities, 1:238
  average percentage of income, 4:1522
  bariatric surgery, 1:286
  Botox injections, 1:346
  breast implants, 1:362
  caregiver services, 2:453, 454
  collagen injections, 2:530
  commercial prescription programs, 2:548–549

Costs *(continued)*
conservatorship, 2:567
delirium, 2:607
dementia, 2:611
dentures, 2:621
euthanasia justification, 2:764
exercise, 5:1614
eye examination, 2:769
health care, 3:908–910, 909*t*
hearing aids, 3:917, 919
hip replacement, 3:966
HIPPA compliance, 4:1427
homeopathic medicine, 3:988
increase, 4:1209
liposuction, 3:1132
liver biopsy, 3:1137
long-term care, 4:1522
massage, 4:1217
Meals on Wheels, 4:1227
Medicaid, 4:1229
Medicare, 3:909*t*
Medicare prescription drug plan, 4:1239–1240
mind/body medicine, 4:1271
MRSA infections, 4:1295
nursing homes, 4:1333, 1334
pneumonia, 4:1462
sildenafil citrate, 5:1635
sleep deprivation, 5:1655
spinal cord injuries, 5:1691
teeth whitening, 5:1751, 1752
VFW, 5:1830
See also Financial management; Socioeconomic factors
Cough medicine, 1:186–187, 2:551–552, 709
Coughing, 1:372–375
chest physical therapy, 2:496
chronic bronchitis, 1:376–377
chronic obstructive pulmonary disease, 2:512
emphysema, 2:742
postoperative, 4:1484
smoking, 5:1661
spinal cord injuries, 5:1696
Coumadin. *See* Warfarin
Counseling
AIDS, 1:56–59
bereavement, 1:294–297, 3:996
client-centered, 1:56
crisis, 1:56
dietary, 2:437, 669–673, 4:1315
genetic, 1:102
hospice care, 2:598
marriage, 4:1561
motor neuron diseases, 4:1289, 1290
sexual dysfunction, 5:1620
sleep disorders, 5:1657
smoking cessation, 5:1668
stroke rehabilitation, 5:1723
substance abuse, 5:1728, 1729–1732
Counter pulsation, 3:928
Court system. *See* Legal issues; Legislation
COX-1 (Cyclooxygenase 1), 2:585, 4:1326
COX-2 (Cyclooxygenase 2), 2:418, 585–587, 4:1326
Cox-2 inhibitors, 2:**585–587**
for chronic pain, 1:107
for osteoarthritis, 4:1367
for pain, 4:1398
Coxsackie B virus, 4:1309
Cozzar. *See* Losartan
CP (Coordinated Program), 2:681
CPAP (Constant positive airway pressure), 5:1819
CPAP (Continuous positive airway pressure), 3:1046–1049, 5:1616, 1653, 1654, 1657, 1675, 1822
CPR (Cardiopulmonary resuscitation), 2:**448–451,** 699–700, 5:1824–1825, 1882
CPSC (Consumer Product Safety Commission), 3:985
CPT (Current Procedural Terminology), 4:1231
CR-39, 2:772
Crack cocaine, 1:219, 4:1381
Cranberries
bladder infection, 1:311
cystitis, 2:595
urinary tract infections, 1:313–314, 5:1808
Cranial nerve examination, 4:1320, 1321–1322
Craniopharyngioma, 1:349
Cratagegus laevigata. See Hawthorn
Craving, 5:1725
Creams. *See* Lotions and creams
CREATE trial, 2:419
Creatine kinase, 4:1468
Creatinine, 2:509, 3:1096, 4:1300
Creatinine clearance test, 3:1097
Creativity, pragmatic, 4:1523
Credit, 4:1232
CREST syndrome, 1:254, 5:1598–1599
Crested scabies, 5:1590
Crestor. *See* Rosuvastatin
Creutzfeldt-Jakob disease, 2:531
CRH (Corticotropin-releasing hormone), 2:590, 591
Cri du chat, 4:1256
Crisis counseling, 1:56
Crithidia luciliae, 1:251
CRNAs (Certified registered nurse anesthetists), 1:34, 35, 4:1559
Crohn's disease
colon cancer risk, 2:533
colonoscopy, 2:538, 541
fecal incontinence, 3:798
GI bleeding, 3:872
glucosamine for, 3:884
vitamin D deficiency, 5:1855
vitamin E deficiency, 5:1856
vitamin K deficiency, 5:1860
zinc deficiency, 5:1897
Cromolyn sodium, 1:72
CROS (Contralateral routing of signal), 3:916
Cross infections. *See* Hospital-acquired infections
Cross-reactivity, allergen, 3:816
Crossed eyes. *See* Strabismus
CRP (C-reactive protein), 1:193, 195, 3:1180, 4:1574
Cruciferous vegetables, 2:415
Cruise ships, 5:1608*t*
Crust, 5:1650
Crutches, 5:1868
Cryoablation, ultrasound-guided, 3:1141
Cryoglobulin test, 1:252–253, 254
Cryoglobulins, 1:251
Cryosurgery
cervical cancer, 2:483, 484
hemorrhoids, 3:947
prostate cancer, 4:1507–1508
skin cancer, 5:1643, 1651
skin lesions, 5:1647
Cryptococcus sp., 3:825
Crystalline lens, 2:461–464, 573, 4:1484–1487
Crystallized intelligence, 4:1523
CSA Recognition Seal Program, 3:887
CSF (Cerebrospinal fluid), 4:1246–1247
CT angiography, 4:1405
CT colonography. *See* Virtual colonoscopy
CT scans, 2:*587,* **587–589**
acoustic reflecting, 5:1673
Alzheimer's disease, 1:87, 4:1243
aortic dissection, 1:219
arteriovenous malformations, 1:230
blood clots, 1:322
bone metastasis, 4:1262
brain tumors, 4:1262
breathing problems, 1:373
cardiomyopathy, 2:446
cervical cancer, 2:483
chest, 2:*493,* 493–495
chronic obstructive pulmonary disease, 2:513
cirrhosis, 2:523
colon cancer, 2:535
coma, 2:547
Cushing's syndrome, 2:591
cystitis, 2:595
deep vein thrombosis, 2:602
dementia, 2:612
dental implants, 2:619
dislocations and subluxations, 2:687
diverticular disease, 2:694

CT scans *(continued)*
dysphasia, 2:718
endocrine pancreatic cancer, 4:1402
exocrine pancreatic cancer, 4:1405
gallbladder cancer, 3:835
gangrene, 3:844
head injuries, 3:903
hip fractures, 3:791
hip pain, 3:966
hip revision surgery, 3:973
hyperthyroidism, 3:1013
irritable bowel syndrome, 3:1070
ischemia, 3:1075
kidney cancer, 3:1092
knee injuries, 3:1117
liver biopsy, 3:1135
liver cancer, 3:1140, 4:1263
lung cancer, 3:1174, 1175
lymphedema, 3:1187
melanoma, 4:1199
migraine, 4:1267
mobility, 4:1284
multiple myeloma, 4:1300
oral cancers, 4:1358
osteoarthritis, 4:1367
ovarian cancer, 4:1376
pericarditis, 4:1432
persistent vegetative state, 4:1440
pleural effusion, 4:1460
prostate cancer, 4:1506
psychoses, 4:1529
quantitative, 1:337
sarcoidosis, 5:1582
sarcomas, 5:1584, 1586
sciatica, 5:1593
spinal cord injuries, 5:1693
spiral, 4:1533
stomach cancer, 5:1705
stroke, 5:1722
thyroid cancer, 5:1769
transient ischemic attacks, 5:1785
virtual colonoscopy, 2:534, 535, 539
CTG (Childhood traumatic grief), 5:1715
Cuff suspension, 3:1166
Culture (diagnostic)
fungal, 3:822–824, 5:1645–1646
gangrene, 3:844
sexually transmitted diseases, 5:1624–1627
skin, 5:1645–1646
stool, 2:654, 655
viral, 5:1625–1626, 1645–1646
See also Bacterial cultures; Blood cultures; Urine cultures
Culture (social), 1:48, 2:599
Culture change movement, 4:1334
Culturelle, 4:1497
Cupping. *See* Percussion
Curcumin, 4:1200
Cure, Laws of, 3:988
Curettage, 2:483, 5:1647
Current Procedural Terminology (CPT), 4:1231
Curved back. *See* Back curves
Cushing's syndrome, 2:**589–593,** *590*
Customs, 5:1609
CV (Control ventilation), 5:1822
CVID (Common variable immunodeficiency), 3:1023
Cyanide poisoning, 1:138
Cyanocobalamin. *See* Vitamin B_{12}
Cycle specific chemotherapy, 1:155
Cyclobenzaprine, 4:1308
Cycloheximide, 3:822–823
Cyclooxygenase 1 (COX-1), 2:585, 4:1326
Cyclooxygenase 2 (COX-2), 2:418, 585–587, 4:1326
See also Cox-2 inhibitors
Cyclophosphamide
for autoimmune disorders, 1:259
for Behcet's syndrome, 1:290
for bladder cancer, 1:309
chemotherapy, 2:490
for kidney transplantation, 3:1107
for lupus, 3:1180
for pulmonary fibrosis, 4:1537
Cycloserine, 1:208–211
Cyclosporine
for autoimmune disorders, 1:259
for Behcet's syndrome, 1:290
diuretic interactions, 2:692
hormone replacement therapy interactions, 3:993
nonsteroidal anti-inflammatory drug interactions, 4:1327
for polymyositis, 4:1468
for psoriasis, 4:1520
for rheumatoid arthritis, 4:1574
vitamin E interactions, 5:1858
Cyclothemia, 1:302
Cygnus GlucoWatch, 1:328
Cyproheptadine, 1:187
Cyropreservation, 1:46–47
Cystectomy, 1:309
Cystic acne, 1:333
Cystic duct, 3:835
Cystic fibrosis
chest physical therapy, 2:495
electrolyte tests, 2:739
pulmonary rehabilitation, 4:1542
vitamin E deficiency, 5:1856
vitamin K deficiency, 5:1860
Cystine stones, 3:1101
Cystitis, 1:310–312, 2:**593–596,** 5:1807, 1808
Cystolitholapaxy, 1:313
Cystoscopy
bladder infection, 1:311
bladder stones, 1:313
overactive bladder, 4:1379
urinary incontinence, 5:1805
Cystourethrogram, voiding, 2:595
Cysts
breast, 1:353
ovarian, 4:1376
pilonidal, 1:333
subchondral, 4:1366
thyroid, 5:1778
Cytochrome P450, 3:900
Cytochrome P450 2A6, 5:1661
Cytokines, 1:193, 3:1022
Cytomegalovirus (CMV), 3:1107, 1145
Cytoreductive surgery, 2:410
Cytoscopy, 1:308, 4:1502, 1503
Cytotec. *See* Misoprostol

D

D-9-tetrahydrocannabinol, 4:1211
D-alpha tocopheraol, 1:68
D-dimer test, 2:601–602, 4:1533
D-fraction, 2:416
D-penicillamine, 5:1598
Daclizumab, 3:1107
Daily living activities. *See* Activities of daily living
Daily value (DV), 2:677, 4:1344
Daily wear soft lenses, 2:774
Dairy products
allergies, 3:814–818
calcium, 2:398, 399, 5:1614
food pyramid, 2:658
lactose intolerance, 3:1122, 1123
pro-inflammatory role, 1:196
probiotics, 4:1499
sarcoidosis, 5:1582
Dalacine. *See* Lidocaine
Dance therapy, 4:1291–1292
Dandelion, 2:524
Dandruff, 2:780
Danish Institute of Agricultural Sciences (DIAS), 2:415
Dantrium. *See* Dantrolene
Dantrolene, 3:832, 4:1307
Daptomycin, 4:1296
Daramide. *See* Dichlorphenamide
Darifenacin, 4:1379, 5:1805
Darvon. *See* Propoxyphene
Darwin, Charles, 2:762–763
DASH Diet, 1:325, 2:672, 4:1534, 5:1786
Databases, dietary supplement, 2:678–679
Day care, adult, 1:*28,* **28–30**
Day of Atonement, 4:1551

Daypro. *See* Oxaprozin
Daytime sleepiness
periodic limb movement disorder, 4:1434
sleep apnea, 5:1652, 1653
snoring, 5:1673
D&C. *See* Dilation and curettage
DCC (Deleted for Colon Cancer) gene, 4:1260–1261
DCIS (Ductal carcinoma-in-situ), 1:357, 4:1204, 1220, 1222, 1224
DDT, 3:1126
De chi, 1:18
DEA (Drug Enforcement Administration), 2:706
Death and dying, 2:**597–601,** 597*t,* 3:790
acceptance, 3:995
bereavement counseling, 1:294–297
brain death, 2:732, 4:1363, 1364
cardiac death, 4:1363
fear of, 4:1527
hospices, 2:597–598, 3:995–997
patient representative, 4:1429
reconciliation and forgiveness, 4:1553
spousal death, 1:67, 295
sudden death, 3:923, 1014, 1015, 4:1310, 5:1760
withdrawal of life support, 5:1881–1884
See also Advance directives; Euthanasia
Death rate. *See* Mortality
Debridement, 4:1490, 5:1886
Debriding agents, 5:1886
Debulking surgery, 4:1376
Decalcification, 2:442
Decarboxylase, 4:1423
Decibels, 1:249
Decision making
advance directives, 1:30–33
incompetent patients, 4:1427
managed care plans, 4:1210
nursing home residents, 4:1333, 1334
patient care, 2:528
patient confidentiality, 4:1427
patient education, 4:1428
patient representatives, 4:1428–1429
withdrawal of life support, 5:1883
Decompression sickness, 3:1046, 1047, 1049
Decompression surgery, 5:1698
Deconditioning, 4:1284
Decongestants
for allergies, 1:72
for bronchitis, 1:377
for common colds, 2:552
congestive heart failure precautions, 2:564
diuretic interactions, 2:709
drug interactions, 2:707, 708*t*
Decubitus ulcers. *See* Pressure sores
Deductibles, 4:1232, 1475
Deep breathing exercises
chest physical therapy, 2:496
emphysema, 2:742
pneumonia, 4:1466
postoperative, 4:1484
respiratory failure, 4:1568
Deep tissue massage, 4:1217
Deep vein thrombosis (DVT), 2:517–520, **601–603**
hip replacement-related, 3:967–968
prevention, 2:602, 4:1534, 5:1609, 1694
pulmonary embolism from, 2:601, 4:1532–1533, 5:1609
spinal cord injury-related, 5:1693, 1694
travel-related, 5:1609
Defibrillators, 5:1608–1609
arrhythmias, 1:226
automated external, 2:450
cardiomyopathy, 2:447
implantable cardioverter-defibrillator, 1:226, 3:1015, 1025–1026, 5:1608–1609, 1825, 1826
ventricular fibrillation, 2:449, 5:1825
See also Cardioversion
Defined contribution plans, 1:46
Degenerative disease, 4:1341
Degenerative joint disease. *See* Osteoarthritis
Degenerative spinal disorders, 5:1592–1595
Deglycerrhizinated licorice (DGL), 5:1800
Dehydration, 2:**603–606,** 603*t,* 5:1870–1872
aging-related, 2:674
air travel-related, 5:1609
antidiarrheal drug-induced, 1:182
assessment, 2:604–605, 3:870
causes, 2:603, 604, 5:1870–1871
diagnosis, 2:561, 604
diarrhea-related, 2:654
diuretic-related, 5:1872
dysphagia-related, 5:1741
electrolyte tests, 2:739
gastroenteritis-related, 3:851
gout, 3:893
hydrotherapy-related, 3:1001
nursing homes, 4:1331–1332
snoring surgery-induced, 5:1674
thirst, 2:603, 665, 5:1871
urinary tract infection-related, 2:594
water balance, 5:1870
withdrawal of life support, 5:1882
Dehydroepiandrosterone (DHEA), 2:**633–636,** 3:1051, 1056, 5:1834
Delayed gastric emptying, 3:859
Deleted for Colon Cancer (DCC) gene, 4:1260–1261
Delirium, 1:111–112, 2:**606–610,** 612
Delta sleep, 5:1613
Delta Society, 3:1079
Delta tocopherol, 5:1856
Delta tocotrienol, 5:1856
Delta waves, 1:301
Delusions, 2:609, 4:1528–1532
Delusory parasitosis, 4:1529
Demeclocycline, 1:151, 153, 2:735
Dementia, 2:**610–618,** *611,* 4:1241–1245, 5:1613
AIDS-related, 1:51, 53, 55, 5:1623
antipsychotic drugs for, 4:1531
caregivers, 2:453
demographics, 2:610–611, 664, 4:1242
dietary assessment, 2:668
Down syndrome, 4:1257
drug therapy, 1:163–166, 163*t,* 2:613
geriatric assessment, 3:866
hormone replacement therapy-related, 3:992, 5:1614
Lewy body, 4:1421, 1528
normal aging, 1:44
personal hygiene, 4:1441–1442
prevention, 1:234, 2:614, 4:1245
psychoses-related, 1:204–205, 4:1528, 1532
rapid-onset, 5:1700
risk factors, 2:611–612, 4:1244
stroke-related, 2:613
substance abuse, 5:1731
undernutrition, 4:1337
vascular, 2:611, 613
vitamin E for, 5:1857
Demerol. *See* Meperidine
Demulcents, 2:595
Demyelinating disorders, 4:1417–1418
Dengue fever, 5:1610
Denial (psychology), 5:1726–1727
Denial of care, 1:30–31, 2:763
Denied claims, 4:1232
Dental anesthesia, 1:116, 117–118
Dental care, 2:616–617, 616*t*
malnutrition prevention, 2:666
Sjögren's syndrome, 5:1639
teeth whitening, 5:1750–1752
See also Oral hygiene
Dental caries, 4:1360–1362, 5:1750
Dental exam, 2:616
Dental health, 2:*614,* **614–618,** 616*t,* 3:876, 4:1202
See also Oral hygiene
Dental hygiene. *See* Oral hygiene
Dental implants, 2:**618–620,** 4:1361
Dental insurance, 2:616, 621
Dental plaque, 4:1360

Dental x rays, 3:876, 4:1358

Dentures, 2:*620,* **620–622**
- cleaning, 2:621, 4:1360–1361
- demographics, 2:614
- geriatric nutrition, 3:869
- Sjögren's syndrome, 5:1639

Depakene. *See* Valproic acid

Depakote. *See* Divalproex

Department of Health and Human Services (DHHS)
- AIDS, 1:52
- antioxidants, 1:197
- Health Resources and Services Administration, 3:913–914
- healthy diet, 5:1872
- influenza vaccines, 3:1043
- Medicare, 4:1238
- patient confidentiality, 4:1426

Department of Labor, 1:28–29

Department of Veterans Affairs, 5:1826

Dependence. *See* Independence; Substance abuse and dependence

Dependent personality disorder, 4:1445–1448

Depersonalization disorder, 4:1214, 1409

Depo-Provera. *See* Progestins

Depressants, central nervous system. *See* Central nervous system depressants

Depression, 2:**622–629,** *623,* 624*t*
- alcohol abuse, 1:66
- angina pectoris-related, 1:125
- anxiety, 1:217
- appetite loss from, 2:659
- autonomic disorder-related, 1:263
- bipolar disorder-related, 1:302–307
- caregivers, 2:454
- Cushing's syndrome-related, 2:592
- cycloserine-associated, 1:209
- dementia, 2:613
- demographics, 2:623–624, 624*t,* 664, 3:869
- DHEA for, 2:634
- diagnosis, 2:625–626, 3:1078–1079
- forgiveness, 4:1552
- geriatric assessment, 3:866, 867
- healthy aging, 4:1525
- heart attack-related, 3:923
- hospice care professionals, 3:997
- insomnia-related, 3:1050
- irritable bowel syndrome-related, 3:1069
- isolation, 3:1078–1079
- late-onset, 2:624, 625, 627
- lifestyle factors, 2:661–662
- major, 1:304, 2:622–629
- massage, 4:1218
- Meals on Wheels, 4:1227
- mobility, 4:1283
- mortality, 2:622, 664
- motor neuron disease-related, 4:1289
- multiple sclerosis-related, 4:1304, 1306
- omega-6 fatty acids, 2:665
- prayer and spirituality, 4:1477, 1478
- prognosis, 2:627–628
- psychoses-related, 4:1528, 1529, 1531
- psychotic, 2:622
- PTSD, 4:1470
- qigong, 4:1546
- relaxation techniques, 4:1565
- restraints, 4:1332
- SSRIs for, 1:166–174, 166*t*
- stroke-related, 5:1715, 1721, 1724
- symptoms, 2:625, 664, 4:1470
- treatment, 2:626–627
- tricyclic antidepressants for, 1:166*t,* 174–177
- undernutrition-related, 4:1337
- vascular, 2:622, 625, 627
- water exercise, 5:1874, 1875
- yoga, 5:1894
- *See also* Antidepressants

Depression and Bipolar Support Alliance, 1:304

Depth perception, 4:1572

DeRitis ratio, 3:1145

Dermabrasion, 5:1643, 1889

Dermadex. *See* Torsemide

Dermatitis, 2:**629–632,** *630*
- atopic, 2:572, 629–632, *630*
- contact, 1:74, 2:*571,* 571–573, 629–632, 3:1081, 5:1650, 1857
- ginkgo biloba-induced, 3:879
- nummular, 2:630
- photocontact, 2:571–573
- seborrheic, 2:630–632, 5:1599–1601, *1600,* 1650
- stasis, 2:629–632

Dermatitis herpetiformis, 3:886–890

Dermatologists, 2:**632–633**

Dermatomyositis, 4:1467–1648

Dermatophytoses, 1:184, 185, 3:824–825, 4:1312

Dermis, 2:476, 4:1488, 5:1888

DES (Diethylstilbestrol), 2:481, 4:1204

Descartes, Rene, 4:1269

Descemet's membrane, 2:573

Descending aorta, 1:218

Descending colon, 2:532

Desensitization, 4:1319

Desferal. *See* Desferrioxamine

Desferrioxamine, 3:945

Desfluorane, 1:113

Desipramine
- anticonvulsant drug interactions, 1:162
- for anxiety, 1:215
- for depression, 1:175
- for generalized anxiety disorder, 3:863
- overdose, 4:1381
- for seizures, 1:161

Desloratidine, 1:187

Desmopressin, 2:637

Desyrel. *See* Trazodone

Detoxification
- polymyositis, 4:1468
- probiotics, 4:1498
- substance abuse, 5:1727, 1731

Detrol. *See* Tolterodine

Developed countries, 1:45–46

Development, human, 4:1523, 1526–1528, 1560

Developmental intelligence, 4:1526

Developmental stages of later life, 4:1526–1528

Devices. *See* Assistive devices

Devil's claw, 4:1368

DEXA (Dual-energy x-ray absorptiometry), 1:336–337, 3:1006, 4:1371–1372, 5:1614, 1877

Dexamethasone, 3:1180

Dexamethasone suppression test, 2:591

Dexchlorpheniramine, 1:187

Dextromethorphan, 1:173, 2:552

Dextrose, 5:1603

DGL (Deglycerrhizinated licorice), 5:1800

DHEA (Dehydroepiandrosterone), 2:**633–636,** 3:1051, 1056, 5:1834

DHHS. *See* Department of Health and Human Services

DHT (Dihydrotestosterone), 4:1512, 5:1587

Diabeta. *See* Glyburide

Diabetes insipidus, 2:**636–638,** 735, 739

Diabetes mellitus, 2:*638,* **638–641**
- abdominoplasty, 1:6
- Alzheimer's disease, 1:88
- amputation, 1:97, 99
- antiarrhythmic drug interactions, 1:148
- anticonvulsant drug interactions, 1:161
- antituberculosis drug interactions, 1:209
- aspirin interactions, 1:235
- bacterial infections, 1:278
- beta blocker interactions, 1:298
- blood sugar tests, 1:179, 327–330
- carbohydrates, 2:422–423
- carotid artery disease, 2:457
- cataracts from, 2:462
- cephalosporin interactions, 2:479
- chronic kidney failure from, 2:508
- cinnamon for, 2:514–516
- circulatory disorders, 2:517–520
- cognitive impairment, 4:1245
- coronary artery disease risk, 2:578
- demographics, 2:517, 638*t,* 639
- dental care, 2:616
- diabetic retinopathy, 2:624, 5:1836

Diabetes mellitus *(continued)*
diagnosis, 1:327–330, *328,* 2:639
diuretic side effects, 2:692
drug therapy, 1:177–181, 177*t,* 211, 299, 2:640
electrolyte tests, 2:739
end-stage renal disease risk, 3:1104
endocrine pancreatic cancer-related, 4:1403
endometrial cancer risk, 2:744, 746
epinephrine interactions, 1:379
erectile dysfunction from, 2:756
exocrine pancreatic cancer risk, 4:1404
eye examination, 5:1839
fatty liver from, 3:797
foot care, 2:641–643, 647, 648, 3:821, 843, 846, 1034
garlic for, 3:847–848
gastroparesis, 5:1634
glucosamine interactions, 3:885, 4:1345
gout drug interactions, 3:894
gout interactions, 3:895
heart attack risk, 3:922
heartburn, 3:933
hyperlipoproteinemia, 3:1003
insulin, 3:1053–1056
ischemia risk, 3:1074
liver cancer risk, 3:1139
low-sodium diet, 3:1159
malnutrition, 4:1202
mortality, 2:640
nail fungus, 4:1313
over fifty lifestyle, 2:662
pressure sores, 4:1488
prognosis, 2:640
scabies, 5:1590
seborrheic dermatitis from, 2:630
skin lesions from, 5:1650
smoking, 3:821, 5:1665
stroke risk, 5:1721, 1723–1724
thiamine, 5:1862
tricyclic antidepressant interactions, 1:176
trigger finger from, 5:1788
type 1, 1:178, 258–260, 2:423, 638–640, 3:1053–1056, 5:1836
type 2, 1:44, 178, 2:423, 514–516, 638–640, 662, 3:1053–1056, 5:1836
visual impairment from, 5:1843
vitamin E for, 5:1857
See also Antidiabetic drugs; Blood sugar tests
Diabetes Prevention Program, 2:641
Diabetic foot infections, 2:**641–643**
demographics, 3:1034
gangrene, 3:843, 846
Diabetic kidney disease. *See* Diabetic nephropathy
Diabetic nephropathy, 2:**643–645**
Diabetic neuropathy, 2:**645–648**
erectile dysfunction, 2:756
fecal incontinence, 3:798, 799
Diabetic retinopathy, 2:**648–650,** 648*t,* 5:1835–1839
low vision, 3:1163
peripheral vision loss, 4:1438
retinal detachment, 2:640, 650, 4:1570
Diabinese, 3:1143
Diagnosis-related groups (DRGs), 4:1231
Diagnostic and Statistical Manual of Mental Disorders (DSM)
anxiety, 1:213
complicated grief, 1:296
gambling, 3:841
generalized anxiety disorder, 3:861, 862
panic disorder, 4:1409
personality disorders, 4:1444–1445, 1446
substance abuse counseling, 5:1729
Diagnostic imaging. *See* Imaging studies
Diallyl sulfide, 2:416
Dialysate, 2:651
Dialysis, 2:650–652
amyloidosis, 1:102
kidney cancer risk, 3:1092
kidney transplantation, 3:1107
peritoneal, 2:509
Dialysis technology, 2:**650–652**
Diamox. *See* Acetazolamide
Diaphragm (contraceptive), 2:594
Diarrhea, 2:**652–657,** *653*
antibiotic-induced, 4:1497
cancer treatment-related, 5:1683
cephalosporin-induced, 2:480
dehydration, 5:1871
diagnosis, 2:561, 654
diet, 5:1683
drug therapy, 1:181–183, 2:654, 3:851–852, 1071
electrolyte tests, 2:739
gastroenteritis-related, 3:851
irritable bowel syndrome, 3:1070, 1071
lactose intolerance-related, 3:1121
mortality, 5:1871
probiotics for, 4:1497
traveler's, 2:*653,* 655, 4:1497
vitamin C-induced, 5:1852
zinc deficiency from, 5:1897, 1898
Diarthrotic joints, 3:1085–1086
Diary, food, 2:524, 668, 3:819
DIAS (Danish Institute of Agricultural Sciences), 2:415
Diastolic blood pressure, 1:189, 324, 2:562, 3:1008–1009, 5:1846
Diastolic heart failure, 2:562
Diazepam, 1:291–294
addiction, 4:1308
antibiotic interactions, 1:153
for anxiety, 1:144
cimetidine interactions, 3:900
for dementia, 2:613
drug abuse, 2:706, 5:1725
drug interactions, 1:293–294, 4:1308
for gait and balance disorders, 3:832
gastroesophageal reflux disease from, 3:854
for insomnia, 3:1051
muscle relaxant effect, 4:1308
ranitidine interactions, 3:900
for seizures, 1:160
SSRI interactions, 1:173
Dibasic sodium phosphate, 3:1123
Dibucaine, 1:116
Dichlorphenamide, 2:690
Diclofenac, 4:1326
Dicloxacillin, 1:334
Dicumarol, 2:457, 3:1143
Didactic Program in Dietetics (DPD), 2:681
Didronel. *See* Etidronate
Diet, 2:**657–660,** 673–677, 3:868–871
AIDS, 1:52–53
alcohol abuse, 1:68
anemia, 1:109
angina pectoris, 1:125
anoxia, 1:138
anti-inflammatory, 1:193–196
antioxidants, 1:197–198
anxiety, 1:216
aspiration, 1:233
atherosclerosis, 1:220, 4:1339, 5:1783, 1786
bipolar disorder, 1:305–306
cachexia and wasting, 2:394
cancer patients, 5:1681–1686
cataract prevention, 2:464
challenge, 3:817, 820, 4:1468, 1579
chemotherapy side effects, 4:1377
chronic kidney failure, 2:510
chronic obstructive pulmonary disease, 2:513
circulatory disorders, 2:520
cirrhosis, 2:523, 524
colon cancer, 2:537
community nutrition, 2:555–557
constipation, 2:569, 754
counseling, 2:437, 669–673, 4:1315
Cushing's syndrome, 2:592
dehydration, 2:605
delirium, 2:608
dental health, 2:617
depression, 2:627
diabetes mellitus, 2:639–640
diabetic nephropathy, 2:644
diabetic retinopathy, 2:649
diarrhea, 2:654, 5:1683
drug interactions, 1:26
dysphagia, 5:1741
dysphasia, 3:870

Diet *(continued)*
elimination, 1:71, 75, 3:817, 819–820, 4:1468, 1579
esophageal cancer, 2:759
exercise, 4:1352
exocrine pancreatic cancer, 4:1407
fads, 4:1351
falls, 3:791
fibromyalgia, 3:801
gallstones, 3:838, 839, 840
gastroesophageal reflux disease, 3:854, 855, 856, 857
generalized anxiety disorder, 3:863–864
gingivitis, 3:876, 877
glaucoma, 3:881–882
gluten-free, 2:474, 475, 3:886–890
gout, 3:892, 893–894
guidelines, 4:1338–1339, 5:1872
headaches, 3:907
health effects, 5:1611–1612
healthy aging, 4:1338–1341, 1523–1526, 5:1613–1614
heart attack prevention, 3:923
heart disease, 3:929, 4:1339
heart healthy, 1:247, 2:437, 563, 564, 5:1783
heartburn prevention, 3:935
hemochromatosis, 3:945
hemorrhoids, 3:948
hepatitis, 3:951
high cholesterol, 3:955, 956
high-fat, 1:88, 2:533, 661, 663, 3:838, 839
hyperlipoproteinemia, 3:1004
hypertension, 1:325, 326, 3:1011–1012, 4:1534
hyperthyroidism, 3:1014
immune system function, 3:1024
insomnia, 3:1051, 1052
iron-deficiency anemia, 3:1066
irritable bowel syndrome, 3:1071
ischemia, 3:1076
itching, 3:1082
ketogenic, 5:1604
kidney stone risk, 3:1101, 1102, 1103
lactose intolerance, 3:1122
low-carbohydrate, 5:1604, 1870
low-cholesterol, 3:1153–1156, 5:1722–1723
low-fiber, 2:693–694
low-protein, 5:1604
lupus, 3:1180–1181
macrobiotic, 2:746
malnutrition, 2:659
memory loss, 4:1244
mental health, 2:661–664, **664–667**
metabolic, 2:746
mobility, 4:1285
motor neuron diseases, 4:1289
neuralgia, 4:1319
vs. nutrition, 4:1335
obstacles to, 2:682–683
oral cancers, 4:1359
osteoarthritis, 5:1614–1615
osteoporosis, 4:1372, 5:1614
overactive bladder, 4:1379
post-gastrectomy, 5:1707
pressure sores, 4:1490, 1491
progression, 5:1683
psoriasis, 4:1520–1521
pulmonary hypertension, 4:1540
recommendations, 4:1336
recovery at home, 4:1554
respiratory failure, 4:1568
rosacea, 4:1580
sarcomas, 5:1586
seizures, 5:1605
self-evaluation, 2:674–675
shingles, 5:1631
skin cancer, 4:1200, 5:1643
stroke prevention, 4:1339, 5:1722–1723
transient ischemic attacks, 5:1786
USDA recommendations, 2:672
varicose veins, 5:1818
vegan, 2:399, 5:1862
vegetarian, 1:325, 4:1478, 5:1786, 1897
wrinkles, 5:1889
See also Cancer fighting foods; Diet plans; Dietary assessment; High-fiber diet; Low-fat diet; Low-sodium diet
Diet pills. *See* Appetite suppressants
Diet plans
American Dietetic Association, 2:658
BRAT, 3:851
Budwig, 2:416
compliance, 2:676
DASH, 1:325, 2:672, 4:1534, 5:1786
Mediterranean-style, 1:88, 196, 3:1159, 4:1245
no-salt-added, 2:564
Therapeutic Lifestyle Changes, 3:956
weight loss, 5:1876–1877, 1878
yo-yo weight loss, 2:671–672, 4:1350
Dietary Approaches to Stop Hypertension (DASH), 1:325, 2:672, 4:1534, 5:1786
Dietary assessment, 2:**667–669**
community nutrition, 2:557
dietary counseling, 2:670, 672
healthy aging, 4:1339–1340
Healthy Eating Index, 2:674, 674*t*
malnutrition, 4:1340–1341
nutrition status, 2:674
undernutrition, 4:1337
Dietary counseling, 2:437, **669–673,** 4:1315
Dietary fiber. *See* Fiber (dietary)
The Dietary Guidelines for Americans (USDA), 2:672, 674, 676–677, 4:1338–1339
Dietary Guidelines for Americans 2005, 3:957, 1157
Dietary intake, 2:**673–677,** 674*t*
Dietary Reference Intakes (DRIs)
calcium, 2:398
dietary counseling, 2:670
fiber, 3:957
sodium, 5:1679
vitamin B_{12}, 5:1848
vitamin C, 5:1850
vitamin D, 5:1854–1855
vitamin K, 5:1859
Dietary Supplement Health and Education Act (DSHEA), DHEA, 2:633–634
Dietary supplements, 2:**677–681,** 4:1343–1346
age-related macular degeneration, 1:41
AIDS, 1:53
alcohol abuse, 1:68
anemia, 1:110
anticoagulant effect, 1:386
antioxidants, 1:198
atherosclerosis prevention, 1:247
cachexia and wasting, 2:394
children, 2:418
cirrhosis, 2:523
common cold, 2:552–553
daily value, 4:1344
drug interactions, 2:680
food intolerance, 3:820
health claims, 2:677, 679
hypertension, 1:326
information sources, 2:678–679, 4:1345
insulin interactions, 3:1056
labeling, 2:677, 679
liquid, 4:1345, 5:1684
lupus, 3:1180–1181
malnutrition, 4:1203
natural, 4:1344–1345
phytochemicals, 2:414
pneumonia risk, 4:1464–1465
polymyositis, 4:1468
post-bariatric surgery, 1:286
preoperative care, 4:1482
recommendations, 2:666, 4:1336
rheumatoid arthritis, 4:1574
side effects, 2:680, 4:1345
tinnitus, 5:1780–1781
Dietary Supplements Labels Database, 2:679
Dietetic Practice Group (DPG), 4:1347–1348
Dietetic technicians (DTR), 2:681–682
Dietetics, 2:**681–682**
Diethylenetriamine pentaacetate (DTPA), 5:1897
Diethylstilbestrol (DES), 2:481, 4:1204
Dieticians, 2:**682–684**
certification, 2:557, 683–684, 4:1346–1348

Dieticians *(continued)*
community nutrition, 2:555, 556
dietary assessment, 2:669
dietary counseling, 2:672
education and training, 2:681–682, 683–684
geriatric, 3:868
licensure, 2:683–684, 4:1347
vs. nutritionists, 2:669, 672, 684, 4:1346–1348
referrals, 2:672
work environment, 2:681, 683
Diffuse pain, 3:1150
Diffuse toxic goiter, 3:1013
Diffusion tensor imaging (DTI), 4:1190
Diflucan. *See* Fluconazole
Digestion
aging, 3:869
bariatric surgery, 1:285
bile, 3:835
carbohydrates, 2:422, 3:811
pancreas, 4:1401
Digestive enzymes, 4:1579
Digestive system, 1:264
Digital hearing aids, 3:915–916, 919
Digital rectal exam (DRE)
colon cancer, 2:534
prostate cancer, 4:1502, 1505, 1507, 1509, 1514
prostate enlargement, 4:1511, 1514
Digital subscription angiography (DSA), 2:457
Digitalis
antihypertensive drug interactions, 2:709
for arrhythmias, 1:226
bronchodilator interactions, 1:381
calcium channel blocker interactions, 2:402
diuretic interactions, 2:693
rifampin interactions, 1:211
SSRI interactions, 1:173
Digitalis purpurea. See Foxglove
Digitoxin, 2:693
Digoxin
bronchodilator interactions, 1:381
calcium absorption, 2:400
calcium supplement interactions, 2:405
for cardiomyopathy, 2:447
cholinesterase inhibitor interactions, 1:165
for congenital heart disease, 3:928–929
for congestive heart failure, 2:563
depression from, 2:624
diuretic interactions, 2:693
hypokalemia from, 2:737
for mitral valve prolapse, 4:1281
for mitral valve stenosis, 4:1282
overdose, 4:1381
psychoses from, 4:1529
Dihydrotestosterone (DHT), 4:1512, 5:1587
Dilantin. *See* Phenytoin
Dilated cardiomyopathy, 2:445
Dilated eye examination, 2:463, 3:881
Dilation and curettage, 2:744
Dilation, balloon, 1:381
See also Balloon angioplasty
Diltiazem, 1:191, 2:580, 3:1056
Dimethicone, 1:139
Dimethydrinate, 5:1609
Diopter, 5:1841
Dioscorea villosa. See Mexican wild yam
Dioscorides, 1:234, 4:1212
Diovan. *See* Valsartan
Dipeptidyl peptidase-4 (DPP-4) inhibitors, 1:179–180
Diphenhydramine, 1:187, 3:1081
Diphenoxylate, 4:1381
Diphenoxylate-atropine, 2:480
Diphtheria, tetanus and accellular pertussis (DTaP) vaccine, 5:1756
Diphtheria, tetanus and pertussis (DTP) vaccine, 5:1756, 1815
Diphtheria vaccines, 3:1036, 5:1756, 1815
Diplegia, 4:1417–1418
Diprivan. *See* Propofol
Dipyridamole, 3:927
Direct bilirubin, 3:1144
Direct immunofluorescence, 1:251
Direct pharyngoscopy, 4:1358
Directly Observed Therapy (DOT), 1:208
Disabled individuals
activities of daily living evaluation, 1:9–11, 9*t*
Americans with Disabilities Act, 1:92–95
disability benefits, 4:1521
isolation, 3:1078
Medicaid, 4:1229
Disaccharides, 2:421, 422
Disalcid. *See* Salsalate
Discharge from the hospital, 2:**684–686**
Discharge planning, 2:684–686
Disciplinary actions, physicians, 3:807
Discoid lupus erythematosus (DLE), 3:1177–1182
Discrimination, 1:47–48, 92–95
Disease-modifying antirheumatic drugs (DMARDs), 4:1367, 1574
Disease transmission
AIDS, 1:49
droplet, 5:1791–1792
infectious diseases, 3:1033
MRSA infections, 4:1295
travel, 5:1610
tuberculosis, 5:1791–1792
vector-borne, 3:1182–1183
See also Sexually transmitted diseases
Disequilibrium, 2:696–698
See also Balance disorders
Diskectomy, 5:1594
Dislocations, 2:**686–689**
hip prosthesis, 3:967, 974
knee joint replacement, 3:1113
Disopyramide, 1:146
Disorientation, 2:607, 612, 4:1321
Disposable lenses, extended-wear, 2:774
Disseminated sclerosis. *See* Multiple sclerosis
Distal pancreatectomy, 4:1406
Distal symmetric polyneuropathy, 2:645
Distance testing, intermediate, 4:1485
Distance vision, 2:770, 4:1485
Distraction, 3:1082
Disulfiram
for alcohol abuse, 5:1731
anticonvulsant drug interactions, 1:162
benzodiazepine interactions, 1:145
caffeine interactions, 2:397
diazepam interactions, 4:1308
tricyclic antidepressant interactions, 1:177
Ditropan. *See* Oxybutynin
Diuretics, 2:**690–693,** 690*t*
angiotensin-converting enzyme inhibitor interactions, 1:133, 134
aspirin interactions, 1:236
bronchodilator interactions, 1:381
bruising precautions, 1:386
calcium channel blocker interactions, 2:402
calcium supplement interactions, 2:405
for cardiomyopathy, 2:447
cholesterol test interactions, 2:506
for cirrhosis-associated anemia, 2:523
for congenital heart disease, 3:928
for congestive heart failure, 2:563
for coronary artery disease, 3:927
decongestant interactions, 2:709
dehydration from, 2:604, 606, 5:1872
for diabetes insipidus, 2:637
drug interactions, 2:692–693
dry eye from, 2:711
for edema, 2:726
erectile dysfunction from, 5:1634
glucosamine interactions, 3:885
gout from, 3:893
for heart attacks, 3:923
heatstroke risk, 3:937

Diuretics *(continued)*
hypernatremia from, 2:735
for hypertension, 1:325, 3:1010
kidney cancer from, 3:1092
for kidney stone prevention, 3:1103
liver function test interactions, 3:1143
loop, 1:153, 2:690–693, 690*t,* 737
for lymphedema, 3:1187
for myocarditis, 4:1310
NSAIDS interactions, 2:710
osmotic, 2:690–693
potassium-sparing, 2:690–693, 690*t,* 709
for pulmonary hypertension, 4:1540
for scleroderma, 5:1598
side effects, 2:692
sleep disorders from, 5:1656
sodium interactions, 5:1680
thiazide-like, 2:690
zinc interactions, 5:1897
See also Thiazide diuretics
Diuril. *See* Chlorothiazide
Divalproex
cephalosporin interactions, 2:480
hormone replacement therapy interactions, 3:993
isoniazid interactions, 1:211
for migraines, 4:1267
rifampin interactions, 1:211
thrombolytic therapy interactions, 5:1768
Divers, 3:1046, 1047, 1049
Diverticulitis, 2:**693–696**
barium enema, 1:289
colonoscopy, 2:541
GI bleeding from, 3:872
high-fiber diet, 3:958
Diverticulosis, 2:*693,* **693–696**
Divorce, 2:453, 3:793–794, 795
Dizziness, 2:**696–698**
diagnosis, 1:280, 2:697–698
falls, 2:698, 3:790, 5:1615
gait and balance disorders, 3:832
sildenafil citrate-induced, 5:1634
DLE (Discoid lupus erythematosus), 3:1177–1182
DMARDs (Disease-modifying antirheumatic drugs), 4:1367, 1574
DNA
error accumulation theory, 1:45
folic acid, 3:811
telomeres, 1:43–44
viruses, 5:1831, 1833
vitamin B_{12}, 5:1847
zinc, 5:1895
DNA testing
HPV, 4:1413
human papilloma virus, 4:1415, 5:1625–1626
liver function, 3:1143
multicentric tumors, 4:1262
DNR orders, 2:598, *699,* **699–700,** 763, 4:1441
D.O. *See* Doctor of osteopathy
Do-In breathing exercises, 5:1627
Do-not-resuscitate (DNR) orders, 2:598, *699,* **699–700**
euthanasia, 2:763
persistent vegetative state, 4:1441
Dobutamine, 2:447
Docetaxel, 1:309
Doctor of osteopathy (D.O.), 2:**701–703,** 4:1368–1370
Doctors. *See* Physicians; Surgeons
Doctors of Optometry. *See* Optometrists
Documentation, medication, 1:27
Docusate sodium, 3:1123, 1124
Dogs
bereavement counseling, 1:296
scabies, 5:1590
service, 3:1164, 5:1843
Dolasetron, 2:418, 419, 420
Domestic Volunteer Service Act (1973), 2:558
Donepezil, 1:88, 163–165, 4:1244, 5:1616
Donnagel. *See* Attapulgite
Donors, blood, 4:1281
Donors, organ. *See* Organ donation
Dopa decarboxylase inhibitors, 1:199
Dopamine
antipsychotic drugs, 1:203
bipolar disorder, 1:305
Parkinson's disease, 1:199, 4:1422, 1423
vitamin C, 5:1850
Dopamine agonists, 1:199–200
adverse effects, 1:201
for Huntington's chorea, 3:832
for Parkinson's disease, 4:1423
psychoses from, 4:1529
Dopergine. *See* Lisuride
Doppler ultrasonography
carotid artery, 2:457, 459–461
echocardiography, 2:724
peripheral vascular disease, 4:1437
Doral. *See* Quazepam
Dorot, 3:1079
Dorsal root zone (DREZ) surgery, 4:1319
Dossey, Larry, 4:1477
Dostinex. *See* Cabergoline
DOT (Directly Observed Therapy), 1:208
Double-barrel reverse colostomy, 2:542
Double-contrast barium enema, 1:287, 288, 2:534, 535
Double effect, principle of, 2:762
Double vision, 2:769
Dowager's hump, 1:271
Down syndrome, 1:86, 4:1255–1259
Downers. *See* Sedatives
Doxazosin, 1:81–83, 4:1511, 5:1589
Doxepin, 2:647
Doxorubicin, 1:309, 4:1403, 5:1771
Doxycycline
for bacterial infections, 1:151
insulin interactions, 3:1055
for lyme disease, 3:1184
for urinary tract infections, 5:1808
DPA. *See* Durable power of attorney
DPA (Dual-photon absorptiometry), 1:337
DPD (Didactic Program in Dietetics), 2:681
DPG (Dietetic Practice Group), 4:1347–1348
DPP-4 inhibitors, 1:179–180
Dr. Dean Ornish Diet, 3:1156, 1157
Drainage
chest physical therapy, 2:495–498
lymph, 4:1219
postural, 2:497, 742, 4:1568, 5:1696
Dramamine. *See* Dimethydrinate
DRE. *See* Digital rectal exam
Dressings
pressure, 5:1651
pressure sores, 4:1490, 5:1885–1886
DREZ (Dorsal root zone) surgery, 4:1319
DRGs (Diagnosis-related groups), 4:1231
Drinking water. *See* Water
DRIs. *See* Dietary Reference Intakes
Driver safety, 2:**703–706,** 703*t,* *704*
geriatric assessment, 3:866–867
government regulation, 3:998
independence, 3:1028
peripheral vision loss, 4:1439
recovery at home, 4:1554
Dronabinol, 2:419–420, 421
Droplet disease transmission, 5:1791–1792
Drug abuse, 2:**706–707,** 5:1724–1729
family relationships, 3:795
stroke risk, 5:1721
substance abuse counseling, 5:1729–1732
tuberculosis, 5:1791
Drug Enforcement Administration (DEA), 2:706
Drug-induced lupus, 3:1177–1182
Drug insurance, 2:548–550
Drug interactions, 1:26, 2:**707–710,** 708–709*t*
alcohol abuse, 1:64, 65*t,* 66
caffeine, 2:397
calcium supplements, 2:405

Drug interactions *(continued)*
dietary supplements, 2:680, 4:1345
folic acid, 3:813, 5:1862
garlic, 3:847
glucosamine, 3:885
supportive cancer therapy, 2:421
vitamin C, 5:1849*t*
vitamin D, 5:1855–1856
vitamin E, 5:1858
vitamin K, 5:1860, 1864
vitamins, 5:1865
zinc, 5:1897–1898
See also Food-drug interactions; specific drugs and classes of drugs
Drug overdose. *See* Overdose
Drug resistance
antibiotics, 1:96, 278–279, 2:467, 470, 3:1035, 5:1623
gonorrhea, 5:1623
influenza, 5:1833
lice infestation, 3:1127
tuberculosis, 5:1794, 1795
Drug testing, 5:1727
Drugs
abbreviations, 1:26
allergies, 1:70
appetite loss from, 2:659
bactericidal, 1:151
commercial prescription programs, 2:548–550
constipation from, 2:569
contact dermatitis from, 2:572
contraindications, 1:26
delirium from, 2:607
depression from, 2:624
dizziness from, 2:698
driver safety, 2:704
efficacy, 4:1451
electrocardiography interactions, 2:731
fainting from, 3:789
falls from, 3:790
forgetting to take, 2:629
generic, 2:549, 4:1240, 5:1610
international travel, 5:1609–1610
non-prescription, 2:*551,* 551–552
osteoporosis from, 1:335–336
reference handbooks, 1:26
safe use tips, 1:*25*
street, 1:115, 117, 173, 2:706–707
tolerance, 1:26, 5:1725
See also Administration of medication; Over-the-counter drugs; specific drugs and classes of drugs
Drusen, 1:40, 5:1782
Dry age-related macular degeneration, 1:39, 41, 42, 5:1615, 1835, 1837, 1838
Dry cleaning solvents, 3:1092
Dry eye, 2:**710–714**
blepharoplasty-induced, 1:318–319
corneal infections, 2:574
Sjögren's syndrome, 5:1638, 1639
Dry gangrene, 3:842, 843, 844
Dry mouth, 1:148, 2:**714–715**
geriatric nutrition, 3:869
malnutrition, 4:1202
postoperative, 4:1473
Sjögren's syndrome, 5:1638, 1639
tricyclic antidepressant-induced, 1:176
Dry skin, 2:**715–716**
antihistamine-induced, 1:187
dermatitis, 2:630
itching from, 3:1081–1082
wrinkles from, 5:1888
DSA (Digital subscription angiography), 2:457
dsDNA (Anti-double strand DNA), 3:1180
DSHEA (Dietary Supplement Health and Education Act), 2:633–634
DSM. *See Diagnostic and Statistical Manual of Mental Disorders*
DTaP (Diphtheria, tetanus and accellular pertussis) vaccine, 5:1756
DTI (Diffusion tensor imaging), 4:1190
DTP (Diphtheria, tetanus and pertussis) vaccine, 5:1756, 1815
DTPA (Diethylenetriamine pentaacetate), 5:1897
DTR (Dietetic technicians), 2:681–682
Dual chamber pacemakers, 4:1388
Dual-energy x-ray absorptiometry (DEXA), 1:336–337, 3:1006, 4:1371–1372, 5:1614, 1877
Dual-photon absorptiometry (DPA), 1:337
Dualistic thinking, 4:1526
Ductal adenocarcinoma, pancreatic, 4:1404
Ductal carcinoma, 1:355, 357
Ductal carcinoma-in-situ (DCIS), 1:357, 4:1204, 1220, 1222, 1224
Dulcolax. *See* Bisacodyl
Duodenal ulcers, 5:1797–1800
gastric acid, 3:940
GI bleeding, 3:872
H-2 receptor blockers for, 3:897–898
helicobacteriosis-related, 3:940
Duphalac. *See* Lactulose
Durable power of attorney (DPA), 1:30–33, 2:598
conservatorship, 2:567
financial management, 3:803
informed consent, 4:1483
living wills, 3:1149
nursing homes, 4:1333
Duraquin. *See* Quinidine
Duricef. *See* Cefadroxil
Durie-Salmon staging system, 4:1300
Dust mites, 1:241
Dutasteride, 4:1512
DV (Daily Value), 2:677, 4:1344
DVT. *See* Deep vein thrombosis
Dyana, 5:1891
Dyazide, 2:690–691, 692, 693
Dychtwald, Ken, 1:2
Dyes, contrast. *See* Contrast media
Dyes, industrial, 5:1584
Dying. *See* Death and dying; End-of-life care
Dynamic cardiomyoplasty, 2:447
Dynamic testing, 3:829
Dynapen. *See* Dicloxacillin
Dyphylline, 1:299, 2:396
Dyrenium. *See* Triamterene
Dysarthria, 5:1687–1690
Dysautonomia. *See* Autonomic disorders
Dysbiosis, intestinal, 4:1498
Dysesthesias, 4:1433
Dyskinesia
gait and balance disorders, 3:833
hormone replacement therapy for, 1:201
levodopa-induced, 1:201, 4:1424
Parkinson's disease-related, 4:1423, 1424
tardive, 1:204
Dyslipidemia, 3:1002
Dyslipoproteinemia, 3:1003
Dysmenorrhea, 2:586–587, 4:1326, 5:1891
Dyspepsia, 4:1515
Dysphagia, 5:1739–1743
aspiration, 1:232–233, 374
autonomic disorders, 1:265
cancer treatment-related, 5:1684–1685
demographics, 3:870, 5:1739
esophageal, 5:1740
esophageal cancer-related, 2:759, 761
gastroesophageal reflux disease-related, 3:853
geriatric nutrition, 3:870
motor neuron disease-related, 4:1289
oropharyngeal, 5:1740
undernutrition, 4:1337
Dysphasia, 2:**716–719,** 3:870
Dysplasia, cervical, 2:481, 4:1414–1415
Dyspnea, 4:1464
Dysreflexia, autonomic, 5:1692, 1693, 1694
Dysthymia, 2:622–629
Dystonia, cervical, 1:345, 347
Dystrophy, corneal, 2:574, 575

E

E. coli. *See Escherichia coli*
Ear infections, 2:697, 4:1247
Ear irrigation, 2:*721,* **721–723**
Ear wax, 2:721–723
Ears
  acupuncture, 1:18
  administration of medication, 1:25
  anatomy and function, 3:918, 5:1779
EARs (Estimated average requirements), 4:1349
Eastern movement therapy, 4:1292
Eating disorders
  general anesthesia, 1:114
  undernutrition, 4:1337
Eating habits. *See* Diet
Eating Well As We Age (FDA), 2:659
ECC (Extracorporeal circuit), 2:650–651
ECG. *See* Electrocardiography
Echinacea, 2:552, 3:1024, 5:1834
Echocardiography (ECG), 2:*723,* **723–725,** 5:1783
  aortic dissection, 1:219
  aortic valve stenosis, 1:223
  atherosclerosis, 1:247
  cardiac surgery, 2:439
  cardiac valve surgery, 2:443
  cardiomyopathy, 2:446
  congestive heart failure, 2:563
  coronary artery bypass graft, 2:428
  coronary artery disease, 2:579
  exercise, 5:1718
  heart disease, 3:926–927
  heart valve repair, 3:932
  ischemia, 3:1075
  mitral valve insufficiency, 4:1280
  mitral valve prolapse, 4:1281
  mitral valve stenosis, 4:1282
  myocarditis, 4:1309
  streptococcal disease, 5:1711
  stress, 1:124
  transesophageal, 2:439, 724, 4:1295
Economics. *See* Costs; Financial management; Socioeconomic factors
Economy class syndrome, 2:601
Ecstasy. *See* Mehylenedioxymethamphetamine
ECT (Electroconvulsive therapy), 2:627
Ectropion, 1:318, 2:778–780, 781
Eczema, 2:629–632, *630*
  cellulitis, 2:477
  dry skin, 2:716
  irritant contact dermatitis, 2:572
  itching, 3:1081
  vs. lice infestation, 3:1126
  See also Atopic dermatitis
Edecrin. *See* Ethacrynic acid
Edema, 2:**725–726,** *726*
  chronic kidney failure-related, 2:508
  eyelid, 2:779–781
  macular, 2:648, 650
  peripheral, 2:725, 727
  pulmonary, 2:562, 725, *726*
  See also Lymphedema
Eden Alternative, 4:1334
Education and training
  advanced practice nurses, 1:35–36
  anesthesiologists, 1:118–119
  chest physical therapy, 2:498
  chiropractic, 2:503–504
  clinical nurse specialists, 2:526
  community social programs, 2:558
  dermatologists, 2:633
  dialysis technologists, 2:651
  dieticians, 2:681–682, 683–684, 4:1347
  fungal culture, 3:823–824
  hematologists, 3:943
  home care, 3:981–982
  home health aides, 3:984
  infection control, 3:1029
  isolation prevention, 3:1079
  licensed practical nurses, 3:1128–1129
  massage, 4:1219
  naturopathy, 4:1316
  nursing assistants, 4:1330
  optometrists, 4:1355
  osteopathic medicine, 2:701, 702
  osteopathy, 4:1369
  oxygen/ozone therapy, 4:1385–1386
  pacemakers, 4:1389–1390
  pain management, 4:1398–1399
  pharmacologists, 4:1451–1452
  pharmacy technicians, 4:1453
  physical therapists, 4:1455, 1458
  physical therapy assistants, 4:1455, 1460
  qigong, 4:1547
  registered nurses, 4:1558–1559
  respiratory therapists, 5:1824
  rheumatologists, 4:1577
  shiatsu, 5:1629
  social workers, 5:1677–1678
  ultrasonography, 2:460
  vaccinations, 5:1756
  ventilator management, 5:1823–1824
  See also Advanced education; Health education; Patient education
EEG. *See* Electroencephalography
Effexor. *See* Venlafaxine
Efficacy, drug, 4:1451
Efficiency, 3:910
Egg allergies, 3:814–818, 1042
Eggshell mattresses, 2:600, 5:1885
eHealth, 4:1235
EIA. *See* Enzyme-linked immunosorbent assay
Eicosapentaenoic acid (EPA), 1:194, 3:1082
Eight Figures for Every Day, 4:1547
18-Methoxycoronaridine (18-MC), 5:1661
Eisenhower, Dwight, 2:658
Ejaculation
  premature, 5:1618–1619
  prostate enlargement, 4:1510
  retarded, 5:1618
  retrograde, 4:1511
  SSRI precautions, 1:166, 171
  See also Erectile dysfunction
Ejaculatory incompetence, 5:1618
Ejection fraction, 2:428
EKG. *See* Electrocardiography
Elastin, 1:229
Elavil. *See* Amitriptyline
Elber papyrus, 1:234
Elbow
  bursitis, 1:388, 389
  carpenter's, 1:389
  nursemaid's, 2:688
  tennis, 5:1753
Elder abuse, 2:**727–730,** *728*
  conservatorship, 2:567
  isolation, 3:1078
  nursing homes, 4:1334
  payback, 3:795
  PTSD, 4:1469
Elder neglect, 2:567
Elderberry, black, 5:1834
Elderly, defined, 3:868
Elderly-onset rheumatoid arthritis, 4:1575
Elderly population. *See* Aging population
Elecampane, 2:742
Elective surgery, 3:806, 807
Electrical muscle stimulation (EMS), 1:270
Electrical stimulation, 4:1368
  colon, 3:1123
  contraindications, 1:268
  functional, 5:1694, 1696
  mobility, 4:1285
  Parkinson's disease, 4:1424
  physical therapy, 4:1457
  pressure sores, 4:1490
  seizures, 5:1604
  tinnitus, 5:1780
  transcutaneous, 1:270, 274, 3:1082, 4:1319, 1368, 1398
  vagus, 5:1604
Electroacupunture, 1:18
Electrocardiography (ECG), 2:437, *730,* **730–732**
  angina pectoris, 1:124
  aortic valve stenosis, 1:223
  arrhythmias, 1:226
  atherosclerosis, 1:247
  autonomic disorders, 1:263

Electrocardiography (ECG) *(continued)*
breathing problems, 1:373
cardiac ablation, 2:425
cardiac monitor, 2:433–436, 3:927
cardiac rehabilitation, 2:436
cardiac surgery, 2:439
cardiac valve surgery, 2:443
cardiomyopathy, 2:446
congestive heart failure, 2:562–563
coronary artery bypass graft, 2:428
coronary artery disease, 2:579
delirium, 2:608
diabetic neuropathy, 2:646
edema, 2:726
emphysema, 2:741
fainting, 3:788
heart attacks, 3:923
heart disease, 3:927
Holter monitoring, 2:446, 3:977–979
hypertrophic cardiomyopathy, 3:1015
implantable cardioverter-defibrillator, 3:1026
ischemia, 3:1074–1075
mitral valve insufficiency, 4:1280
mitral valve stenosis, 4:1282
myocarditis, 4:1309–1310
nuclear stress test, 4:1328
pericarditis, 4:1432
preoperative cardiac assessment, 4:1480, 1481
preoperative care, 4:1482
pulmonary embolism, 4:1533
sarcoidosis, 5:1582
scleroderma, 5:1598
transient blindness, 5:1783
transient ischemic attacks, 5:1785
See also Stress test
Electroconvulsive therapy (ECT), 2:627
Electrodes, cardiac monitor, 2:434, 435
Electroencephalography (EEG), 2:**732–734,** *733*
biofeedback, 1:301
coma, 2:547
delirium, 2:607, 608
head injuries, 3:903
seizures, 5:1602
Electrolyte balance, 2:**734–738**
dehydration, 2:603–605, 5:1870
enemas, 2:752
geriatric nutrition, 3:870
heatstroke, 3:938
overdose, 4:1381, 1382
overhydration, 5:1872
sodium, 5:1678–1679
water, 5:1870
Electrolyte tests, 2:**738–740,** 3:938, 5:1785
Electromagnetic fields, 4:1388
Electromyography (EMG)
amyotrophic lateral sclerosis, 1:104
biofeedback, 1:301
cervical spondylosis, 2:488
gait and balance assessment, 3:830
paralysis, 4:1418
polymyositis, 4:1468
sciatica, 5:1593
Electronic medical records, 4:1426, 1430–1431
Electronic protected health information (EPHI), 4:1426
Electronic thermometers, 5:1844–1845
Electrophoresis, protein, 4:1300
Electrophysiologic studies
arrhythmias, 1:226
cardiac ablation, 2:425
cardiac surgery, 2:439
cardiomyopathy, 2:446–447
implantable cardioverter-defibrillator, 3:1026
Electrophysiologists, 4:1389
Electrosurgery, 5:1647
Elimination diet
food allergies, 1:71, 75, 3:817
food intolerance, 3:819–820
polymyositis, 4:1468
rosacea, 4:1579
ELISA (Enzyme-linked immunosorbent assay), 1:51, 60, 251–252, 253
Elizabeth I (Queen of England), 4:1212
Ellagic acid, 2:415, 416
EMA-IgA test, 2:473
Emancipated minors, 2:529
Embolism, 1:321, 322, 5:1720
See also Pulmonary embolism
Embolization
arteriovenous malformations, 1:231
hepatic artery, 3:1141
priapism, 4:1492
uterine artery, 3:1019
EMDR (Eye movement desensitization and reprocessing), 4:1471
EMEA (European Medicines Agency), 4:1398
Emergency medical care
cardiopulmonary resuscitation, 2:449
dislocations and subluxations, 2:688
overdose, 4:1382
panic disorder, 4:1410–1411
spinal cord injuries, 5:1693
transient ischemic attacks, 5:1785
travel, 5:1609
ventricular fibrillation, 5:1824–1825
EMG. *See* Electromyography
Eminase. *See* Anistreplase
Emollient laxatives, 3:1123
Emotional abuse, 2:727–729
Emotional factors
healthy aging, 4:1523, 1526
itching, 3:1080–1081
personal hygiene, 4:1441
relationships, 4:1562
stroke rehabilitation, 5:1724
Emotional lability, 2:607
Emphysema, 2:**740–743**
beta blocker precautions, 1:298–299
breathing problems, 1:372
bronchodilators for, 1:379
chronic bronchitis, 1:375
chronic obstructive pulmonary disease, 2:511–514
demographics, 2:740, 740*t*
diagnosis, 2:513, 741
electrolyte tests, 2:739
lung cancer, 3:1175
oxygen therapy, 3:1046
pulmonary rehabilitation, 4:1542
respiratory failure, 4:1567
Employer-based health insurance, 3:908–909, 4:1496
Employer-sponsored prescription programs, 2:549
Employers, patient confidentiality, 4:1426
Employment
advanced practice nurses, 1:36
ageism, 1:47–48
Americans with Disabilities Act, 1:92–95
clinical nurse specialists, 2:525–526
community social programs, 2:558
dialysis, 2:651–652
dialysis technologists, 2:651
dieticians, 2:681, 683
doctor of osteopathy, 2:702
hematologists, 3:942
home health aides, 3:983
independence, 3:1028–1029
licensed practical nurses, 3:1128, 1130
optometrists, 4:1355–1356
pharmacologists, 4:1452
pharmacology, 4:1451
pharmacy technicians, 4:1453, 1454
physical therapists, 4:1455, 1457, 1458–1459
physical therapy assistants, 4:1460
recovery at home, 4:1554
registered nurses, 4:1558, 1559
rheumatologists, 4:1576
social work, 5:1678
See also Occupational exposure; Work environment
Empty calories, 2:659
EMS (Electrical muscle stimulation), 1:270
Enablex. *See* Darifenacin
Enalapril, 1:132
celecoxib interactions, 2:586
for congestive heart failure, 2:563
diuretic interactions, 2:692
for hypertension, 1:132, 191
terzosin interactions, 1:83
Enamel (tooth), 5:1750

Encephalopathy
- hepatic, 3:1145, 1146
- hypoxic, 5:1602
- metabolic, 5:1602

Encore stage, 4:1526

End colostomy, 2:542

End-of-life care, 2:597–599
- ethics, 4:1235
- pain management, 2:762
- reconciliation and forgiveness, 4:1553
- *See also* Hospices; Palliative care

End-stage renal disease (ESRD), 2:507–508, 509
- causes, 2:508, 3:1104
- diabetic nephropathy-related, 2:643, 644
- dialysis, 2:650–651, 652
- kidney transplantation, 3:1104–1108

Endarterectomy, 1:247, 2:457, 5:1722, 1786

Endocarditis, 5:1710–1713
- bacterial, 3:1032, 1034, 1035, 1036, 5:1709–1710
- MRSA infection-related, 4:1295, 1296
- prevention, 2:444
- staphylococcal, 5:1699–1700, 1701, 1702
- streptococcal, 5:1709–1710

Endocervical adenocarcinoma-in-situ (AIS), 2:482, 4:1414

Endocervical curettage, 2:483

Endocrine disorders, 1:114

Endocrine glands, 2:590, *590*

Endocrine pancreatic cancer, 4:**1400–1403,** *1401,* 1404

Endocrine pharmacology, 4:1449

Endometrial ablation, 3:1019

Endometrial cancer, 2:**743–748**
- estrogens, 4:1253
- high-fat diet, 2:661
- hormone replacement therapy, 4:1251
- hysterectomy, 3:1017
- prevention, 2:412, 746–747

Endometrial hyperplasia, 3:1016

Endometrial resection, 3:1019

Endometriosis, 3:1016

Endomyocardial biopsy, 4:1310

Endomysial antibodies, 2:473

Endophthalmitis, 5:1700, 1701, 1702

Endorphins, 1:19, 4:1253, 5:1666–1667

Endoscopic retrograde cholangiopancreatography (ERCP), 4:1405

Endoscopic ultrasonography, 4:1402, 1405, 5:1705

Endoscopy, 2:**748–750**
- capsule, 3:873
- colon cancer, 2:534
- esophageal cancer, 2:761
- fiberoptic, 1:233
- gallstones, 3:839
- gastroesophageal reflux disease, 3:855, 856, 859–860
- GI bleeding, 3:873
- heartburn, 3:934
- helicobacteriosis, 3:940
- iron-deficiency anemia, 3:1065
- upper, 3:859–860, 5:1705, 1741, 1799
- vein surgery, 5:1817

Endoskeletal shanks, 3:1166

Endostatin, 4:1264

Endosteal implants, 2:618

Endothelial growth factor (VEGF), 4:1261, 1264

Endothelium, corneal, 2:573

Endotracheal tubes, 2:**750–752,** *751*

Endurance training, 5:1757, 1758–1759

Enemas, 2:**752–755,** *753*
- barium, 1:*287,* 287–290, 2:534, 535, 694, 752, 3:947
- carminative, 2:752, 753
- cleansing, 1:288, 2:540, 542, 748, 752–753
- coffee, 4:1407
- constipation, 2:570
- high, 2:753
- low, 2:753
- oil-retention, 2:753–754
- probiotics, 4:1499

Energy drinks, 4:1345

Energy therapies
- acupressure, 1:12
- acupuncture, 1:17, 19
- ovarian cancer, 4:1377
- qigong, 4:1546, 1547
- reflexology, 1:13
- sexual dysfunction, 5:1620
- shiatsu, 5:1627, 1628

Enflurane, 1:113

Enlarged heart. *See* Cardiomyopathy

Enoxacin, 4:1517

Enright, Robert, 4:1552

Entacapone, 1:199, 201, 4:1423

Enteral nutrition. *See* Tube feeding

Enteric fever, 2:653, 654

Enteric nervous system, 1:262

Enterobacter sp., 2:594

Enterococcus sp., 5:1710

Enteropathy-associated T cell lymphoma, 3:888–889

Enterostomy therapists, 2:542, 544, 5:1885

Enterovirus, 4:1248

Enteryx procedure, 3:856

Entrances, 3:986

Entropion, 2:778–780, 781

Environmental factors
- aging, 1:44
- Alzheimer's disease, 1:86
- amyotrophic lateral sclerosis, 1:103
- asthma, 1:240
- autoimmune disorders, 1:258
- breast cancer, 1:355–356
- cancer, 2:408, 413
- colon cancer, 2:533
- delirium, 2:609–610
- dry eye, 2:711, 712
- dry skin, 2:715
- generalized anxiety disorder, 3:862
- insomnia, 3:1051, 1052
- liver cancer, 3:1139
- mobility, 4:1284
- motor neuron diseases, 4:1288
- multiple sclerosis, 4:1304
- osteoporosis, 4:1371
- pacemakers, 4:1389
- Parkinson's disease, 4:1421, 1422
- polymyositis, 4:1467
- pulmonary fibrosis, 4:1536
- seborrheic dermatitis, 5:1600
- sexual dysfunction, 5:1618

Enzymatic debridement, 5:1886

Enzyme inhibitors, 4:1423

Enzyme-linked immunoassay. *See* Enzyme-linked immunosorbent assay

Enzyme-linked immunosorbent assay (ELISA)
- AIDS, 1:51, 60
- autoimmune diseases, 1:251–252, 253

Enzymes
- alcohol abuse, 1:66
- digestive, 4:1579
- pancreatic, 4:1407
- proteolytic, 5:1886
- zinc interactions, 5:1895

EOB (Explanation of benefits), 4:1232

EPA (Eicosapentaenoic acid), 1:194

Ependymomas, 1:349

Ephedra, 3:1076

Ephedrine, 1:379, 4:1389

EPHI (Electronic protected health information), 4:1426

Epidemics
- diarrhea, 2:655
- influenza, 3:1038, 1041
- obesity, 4:1349

Epidermis, 2:476, 4:1488, 5:1888

Epidermophyton floccosum, 3:825

Epidural anesthesia, 1:116, 118, 119, 3:965

Epidural hematomas, 3:906

Epilepsy, 5:1601–1607
- benign focal, 5:1605
- benzodiazepines for, 1:144
- cerebral palsy-related, 4:1255
- demographics, 5:1601

Epilepsy *(continued)*
drug therapy, 1:159–163, 159*t*
electroencephalography, 2:732–734
head injury-induced, 3:902, 5:1602
marijuana for, 4:1213
shiatsu, 5:1628
temporal lobe, 5:1604
See also Anticonvulsant drugs; Seizures
Epilepticus, 5:1601
Epinephrine
allergies, 1:72
for anaphylaxis, 3:817
anger-related, 4:1478
bronchodilator interactions, 1:379
for congestive heart failure, 2:563
for GI bleeding, 3:873
insulin interactions, 3:1056
for liposuction, 3:1131
liver function test interactions, 3:1143
local anesthesia interactions, 1:116
smoking, 5:1659
thiamine interactions, 5:1861
vitamin C interactions, 5:1850
EpiPen, 3:817
Epithelial cell lung cancer, 3:1174
Epithelium, 2:573, 4:1261
Epoetin, 2:418, 419, 420–421, 510
Epogen. *See* Epoetin
Epoprostenol, 4:1540
Epoxy resins, 5:1597
Eprosartan, 1:191
Epstein-Barr virus, 1:250, 3:1145, 4:1195
Epworth Sleepiness Scale (ESS), 5:1673
Equisetum arvense. See Horsetail
Erbital, 4:1536
ERCP (Endoscopic retrograde cholangiopancreatography), 4:1405
Erectile dysfunction, 2:*755,* **755–758,** 5:1618–1619, 1694–1695
aerobic exercise, 1:38
demographics, 2:755–756, 4:1492, 1493, 5:1633–1634
drug-induced, 5:1634
drug therapy, 1:264, 2:756–757, 5:1620
ginkgo biloba for, 3:878
Medicare prescription drug plan, 4:1240
PDE-5 drugs for, 2:647
priapism, 4:1491–1494
prostatectomy-related, 4:1507
sildenafil citrate for, 1:264, 2:647, 755, 757, 4:1507, 5:1620, 1633–1637
tadalafil for, 1:264, 2:647, 755, 757, 5:1635
treatment, 2:757, 5:1635
ERGO (Euthanasia Research and Guidance Organization), 5:1734
Ergocalciferol, 5:1853
Ergoloid mesylates, 1:381
Ergostate. *See* Ergotamine
Ergot, 1:144
Ergotamine, 1:381, 3:907
Erosion (skin), 5:1650
Error accumulation theory, 1:45
Errors
ethics, 4:1235
medication, 1:27
Erysipelas, 5:1711, 1712
Erythema migrans, 3:1183, 1184
Erythrocyte sedimentation rate (ESR)
lupus, 3:1180
polymyalgia rheumatica, 4:1467
Sjögren's syndrome, 5:1639
Erythrocytes. *See* Red blood cells
Erythrocytosis, 3:1092
Erythrodermic psoriasis, 4:1519
Erythromycin, 1:152, 153
anticonvulsant drug interactions, 1:162
for boils, 1:334
buspirone interactions, 1:145
for diarrhea, 2:655
for erysipelas, 5:1712
sildenafil citrate interactions, 5:1635
SSRI interactions, 1:173
for strep throat, 5:1711
for streptococcal disease, 5:1712
Escherichia coli
bacteremia, 1:276, *277*
bladder infection, 1:310
diarrhea, 2:652, 653, 654
food poisoning, 3:1032
gastroenteritis, 3:851
insulin, 3:1053
urinary tract infections, 2:594, 5:1808
Escherichia coli O157:H7, 2:654
Escitalopram, 1:144, 167–174, 2:626
Esidrix. *See* Hydrochlorothiazide
Eskalith. *See* Lithium
Eskimos, 5:1837
Esomeprazole, 4:1515–1517, *1516*
for gastroesophageal reflux disease, 3:856, 4:1515–1517
for heartburn, 3:935
for ulcers, 2:586
Esophageal cancer, 2:**758–762**
garlic prevention, 3:848
gastroesophageal reflux disease-related, 3:853
oropharyngeal dysphagia from, 5:1740
Esophageal dysmotility, 2:759, 5:1598, 1634
Esophageal dysphagia, 5:1740
Esophageal manometry, 3:855, 859–860, 935
Esophageal pH monitoring, 3:855, 859–860, 934
Esophageal rings, 5:1740, 1741
Esophageal stenosis, 5:1740
Esophageal strictures, 3:858, 859–860
Esophageal swallowing, 5:1739
Esophageal ulcers, 5:1797
Esophageal varices, 3:872
Esophageal webs, 2:759, 5:1740, 1741
Esophagectomy, 2:760
Esophagitis, 3:826, 872, 4:1515
Esophagogastrectomy, 2:760
Esophagogastroduodenoscopy, 3:855, 5:1799
Esophagography, 3:859–860
Esophagram, barium, 5:1801, 1803
See also Upper GI series
Esophagus
anatomy and function, 3:933
Barrett's, 2:758, 759, 3:853, 855, 858, 859–860
ESR (Erythrocyte sedimentation rate), 3:1180, 4:1467, 5:1639
ESRD. *See* End-stage renal disease
Essential fatty acids
dry skin, 2:716
hypertension, 1:326
immune system function, 3:1024
wrinkles, 5:1890
Estazolam, 1:140, 5:1657
Estimated average requirements (EARs), 4:1349
Estrace. *See* Estradiol
Estraderm. *See* Estradiol
Estradiol, 3:990–994
Estratest. *See* Estrogen/testosterone combination therapy
Estrogen receptors, 1:356, 359, 2:415
Estrogen replacement therapy, 3:990–995, 991*t,* 4:1250–1251
endometrial cancer risk, 2:743, 4:1253
high-density lipoproteins, 3:1003
liver cancer risk, 3:1139
ovarian cancer risk, 4:1375
saw palmetto interactions, 5:1588
stroke risk, 5:1721
vitamin D interactions, 5:1855
See also Hormone replacement therapy
Estrogen/testosterone combination therapy, 3:991
Estrogen/tranquilizer combination therapy, 3:991
Estrogens
anticonvulsant drug interactions, 1:162
atherosclerosis prevention, 1:245
breast cancer, 1:155, 355–356, 358

Estrogens *(continued)*
caffeine interactions, 2:397
calcium supplement interactions, 2:405
cervical cancer risk, 2:482
cholesterol test interactions, 2:506
dantrolene interactions, 4:1308
DHEA interactions, 2:634
dry eye, 2:711
endometrial cancer risk, 4:1253
face lift, 3:784
gout, 3:891
heart disease, 4:1250
insulin interactions, 3:1056
liver cancer risk, 3:1139
menopause, 3:991, 4:1250–1252
migraine trigger, 4:1268
osteoporosis, 4:1250, 1371
plant, 4:1253
probiotics, 4:1498
prostate cancer, 4:1508
saw palmetto interactions, 4:1512
Estrone, 3:990–994
Eszopiclone, 3:1051, 5:1657
Ethacrynic acid, 2:690
Ethambutol, 1:208–211, 5:1795, 1897
Ethanolamines, 1:187
Ether, 1:112
Ethics
codes of, 2:527–529, 4:1234
euthanasia, 2:762
four principles approach, 4:1234–1235
home care, 3:981
informed consent, 3:1043
Internet, 2:529, 4:1235
medical, 4:1233–1236
nurses, 2:527–529
organ donation, 4:1364–1365
patient confidentiality, 4:1425–1428
patient rights, 4:1429–1431
withdrawal of life support, 5:1882–1883
Ethics committees, 2:528
Ethics consultations, 2:528
Ethionamide, 1:208–211
Ethnicity and race
age-related macular degeneration, 5:1836
AIDS, 5:1622
asthma, 1:240–241
autonomic disorders, 1:258
bladder cancer, 1:308
body mass index, 1:332
breast cancer, 1:351–352, 5:1682
breast implants, 1:362
breast reconstruction, 1:364
cancer mortality, 5:1682
dementia, 2:611
diabetes mellitus, 2:639
diabetic nephropathy, 2:643
end-stage renal disease, 3:1104
endometrial cancer, 2:743
exocrine pancreatic cancer, 4:1404
gallbladder cancer, 3:835
gallstones, 3:838
glaucoma, 3:880, 5:1836–1837
heart disease, 3:926
hip revision surgery, 3:972, 974
hysterectomy, 3:1016
influenza vaccines, 3:1041, 1041*t*
iron-deficiency anemia, 3:1064
lactose intolerance, 3:819, 1121
liver cancer, 3:1138
lung cancer, 1:382
lupus, 3:1179
melanoma, 4:1198, 5:1641
multiple myeloma, 4:1299
multiple sclerosis, 4:1304
osteoporosis, 1:335, 3:992, 4:1371
ovarian cancer, 4:1375
panic disorder, 4:1410
prayer and spirituality, 4:1477
pressure sores, 4:1488
prostate cancer, 4:1505, 1509, 5:1682
psoriasis, 4:1519
rosacea, 4:1578
sarcoidosis, 5:1581
scleroderma, 5:1596
sildenafil citrate, 5:1634
skin cancer, 5:1641, 1642
snoring, 5:1671
speech disorders, 5:1687
spinal cord injuries, 5:1691
stroke, 5:1721
suicide, 5:1733
thyroid cancer, 5:1769
transient ischemic attacks, 5:1785
tuberculosis, 5:1791, 1796
See also African Americans; Asian Americans; Caucasians; Hispanics
Ethosuximide, 1:160, 5:1603
Ethrane. *See* Enflurane
Ethylenediamine, 1:187
Ethylenediaminetetracetric acid, 3:1076
Ethyol. *See* Amifostine
Etidronate, 2:405, 4:1392, 5:1694
Etodolac, 4:1326
Etrentinate, 4:1520
Eucalyptus, 2:552, 742
Eugenics, 2:763
European Medicines Agency (EMEA), 4:1398
European Respiratory Society, 4:1537
EUS. *See* Endoscopic ultrasonography
Euthanasia, 2:599, **762–765,** 5:1734–1735
Euthanasia Research and Guidance Organization (ERGO), 5:1734
Evaporative dry eye, 2:711
Evening primrose oil, 2:631, 746, 4:1252
Evoked potentials, 2:488, 4:1305
Evolution, 2:762–763
Evoxac, 5:1639
Ewing's sarcoma, 5:1583, 1585–1586
Examinations. *See* Licensure; Neurologic examination; Physical examination
Exanatide, 1:178–179, 2:640
Excision, local, 5:1737
Excisional biopsy. *See* Surgical biopsy
Excoriation, 5:1650
Executive function, 3:866, 4:1243
Exelon. *See* Rivastigmine
Exercise, 2:**765–769,** 765*t, 766,* 766*t,* 4:1268
Alzheimer's disease, 1:88
anoxia, 1:138
anti-inflammatory role, 1:194
anxiety, 1:216
back and neck pain, 1:269
back curves, 1:274
benefits, 2:765, 768
blood clot prevention, 1:322
body composition, 3:869
breast cancer risk, 1:360
breathing problems, 1:374
cachexia and wasting, 2:394
cancer prevention, 2:412, 413
cardiac rehabilitation, 2:436–437
cervical spondylosis, 2:488
circulatory disorders, 2:520
colon cancer prevention, 2:537
congestive heart failure, 2:563, 564
constipation, 2:569
coronary artery disease risk, 2:578
costs, 5:1614
deep breathing, 2:496, 742, 4:1466, 1484
deep vein thrombosis, 4:1534
delirium, 2:609
demographics, 2:765*t,* 767, 5:1759
diabetic neuropathy, 2:647
dietary counseling, 2:671
dislocations, 2:688
fall prevention, 3:792, 5:1615
fibromyalgia, 3:801
fluid intake, 5:1870
healthy aging, 4:1523, 5:1611–1612, 1614
heart attack prevention, 3:922
high cholesterol, 3:955
hip replacement, 3:966, 967
hypertension, 1:325, 326, 3:1010, 1012, 5:1759
hypertrophic cardiomyopathy from, 3:1015
ischemia, 3:1076
ischemia risk, 3:1074
isometric, 3:785
knee injuries, 3:1117, 1118
low back pain, 3:1152, 1153
low-impact, 5:1873
lupus, 3:1181

Exercise *(continued)*
malnutrition, 4:1203
memory loss, 4:1244
menopause, 1:38, 3:994, 4:1253
mobility, 4:1285
obesity, 4:1351–1352
osteoarthritis, 4:1367, 5:1614
osteoporosis, 1:38, 3:969, 994, 4:1371, 1372
over fifty lifestyle, 2:661
Parkinson's disease, 4:1422–1423
periodic limb movement disorder, 4:1435
peripheral vascular disease, 4:1437
physical therapy, 4:1456–1457
postural awareness, 3:830
preparation, 5:1616
pulmonary rehabilitation, 4:1542–1543
qigong, 4:1545, 1546–1547
recovery at home, 4:1554
reduction in, 2:659
relaxation techniques, 4:1565
respiratory, 4:1473
rosacea, 4:1580
sciatica prevention, 5:1595
scleroderma, 5:1598
sleep disorders, 5:1657
smoking cessation, 5:1666
snoring, 5:1670
stress, 5:1716
stroke prevention, 5:1723
therapeutic, 5:1757–1761, *1758*
transient blindness during, 5:1782
transient ischemic attacks, 5:1786
travel preparation, 5:1609
USDA recommendations, 2:672
varicose veins, 5:1818
vestibular rehabilitation, 2:698
warm-up, 5:1616, 1875
water, 5:*1873*, 1873–1876
weight-bearing, 3:791, 4:1372
weight-shifting, 3:830
wrinkle prevention, 5:1890
See also Aerobic exercise; Therapeutic exercise
Exercise echocardiography, 5:1718
Exercise hydrotherapy, 3:1000–1001
Exercise-induced asthma, 1:240, 241, 242
Exercise stress test. *See* Stress test
Exertion headache, 3:906
Exfoliants, 1:83–84, 4:1295
Exits, 3:986
Exocrine pancreatic cancer, 4:1401, **1404–1408**
Exonazole nitrate, 1:184
Exoskeletal shanks, 3:1166
Expectorants, 2:551–552, 741, 742
Experience Works Program, 2:558
Explanation of benefits (EOB), 4:1232
Exposure therapy, 1:216, 4:1411, 1471
Expressive dysphasia, 2:717
Extended family, 3:793, 794
Extended-wear disposable lenses, 2:774
Extended-wear soft lenses, 2:774
External radiation therapy. *See* Radiation therapy
Extra-temporal resection, 5:1604
Extracapsular cataract extraction, 2:463
Extracellular fluid, 2:734, 5:1679
Extracellular matrix, 4:1261
Extracorporeal bypass circuit. *See* Heart-lung machine
Extracorporeal circuit (ECC) (dialysis), 2:650–651
Extrapulmonary tuberculosis, 5:1793
Extravasation, 4:1261–1262
Extubation, 5:1882
Exubera, 3:1053–1054
Exudative retinal detachment, 4:1571
Eye charts, 2:770, 4:1321, 5:1841, 1842
Eye diseases
congenital, 5:1842
corneal, 2:573–577
dry eye, 1:318–319, 2:574, 710–714, 5:1638, 1639
mobility, 4:1284
See also Eye infections
Eye examination, 2:**769–771,** 772, 5:1842–1843
age-related macular degeneration, 1:41
annual, 5:1840
corneal diseases, 2:575, 576–577
cranial nerve, 4:1321
diabetes mellitus, 5:1839
diabetic retinopathy, 2:649
dilated, 2:463, 3:881
dry eye, 2:712
glaucoma, 2:769, 3:881
low vision, 3:1163–1164
optometry, 4:1353–1356
peripheral vision loss, 4:1438, 1439
presbyopia, 4:1485
sarcoidosis, 5:1582
transient blindness, 5:1782–1783
vision disorders, 5:1838
Eye glasses. *See* Eyeglasses
Eye infections
shingles-related, 5:1631
staphylococcal, 5:1700, 1701, 1702, 1703
visual impairment from, 5:1842
Eye injuries, 3:1163
Eye movement and tracking, 2:770
Eye movement desensitization and reprocessing (EMDR), 4:1471
Eye strain, 4:1318
Eye surgery
cataracts from, 2:462
retinal detachment, 4:1571–1572
staphylococcal infections, 5:1703
Eyedrops
beta blockers, 1:297–299
eye examination, 2:770–771
instillation, 1:25, 2:**775–777,** *776*
Eyeglasses, 2:**772–775,** 5:1841
bifocal, 2:772, 4:1485
hearing aids, 3:916
low vision, 3:1164
presbyopia, 4:1485, 5:1615
prismatic field-expanding, 4:1438
retinal surgery, 4:1572
safety, 1:320
trifocal, 4:1485
Eyelashes, 3:1126
Eyelid disorders, 2:**777–781,** *778*
Eyelid edema, 2:779–781
Eyelid tumors, 2:779–780
Eyelids
anatomy, 2:778
blepharoplasty, 1:317–319, *318*, 2:582–584
Botox injections, 1:345, 347
shingles, 5:1631
Eyes
anatomy, 2:461, 573
local anesthesia, 1:116, 118
Eyesight. *See* Vision
Eyestrain headache, 3:905
Eysenck Personality Inventory, 4:1447
Ezetimibe, 3:955

F

FAAN (Food Allergy & Anaphylaxis Network), 3:817–818
Face lift, 2:582–584, 3:*783,* **783–786,** 5:1889
Facial asymmetry, 4:1321–1322
Facial disfigurement, 5:1670
Fad diets, 4:1351
Fainting, 2:697–698, 3:**786–789**
Fair Debt Collection Act, 4:1230
Faith. *See* Religious beliefs; Spirituality
Faith communities. *See* Religious communities
Falcarinol, 2:415
Falls, 3:**789–793,** *790*, 791*t*, 4:1372
alcohol abuse, 1:64, 66
autonomic disorders, 1:265
back curves, 1:274
circulatory disorders, 2:520
demographics, 3:789–790, 791*t*, 4:1372
dislocations and subluxations, 2:687
dizziness, 2:698, 3:790, 5:1615

Falls *(continued)*
- fatal/nonfatal, 3:791*t*
- gait and balance assessment, 3:829
- hip fractures, 3:790, 960
- hip pain, 3:965
- home safety, 3:985
- mobility, 4:1283, 1284, 1286
- prevention, 3:792, 5:1611, 1615
- spinal cord injuries, 5:1691
- t'ai chi, 5:1747
- therapeutic exercise, 5:1759, 1760
- walking problems, 5:1867, 1869
- water exercise, 5:1875

False-negative results, 4:1206, 1413, 5:1718

False-positive results, 4:1205–1206, 1413

Famcyclovir, 1:212

Familial adenomatous polyposis (FAP), 2:533, 586

Familial amyloidosis, 1:101, 102

Familial amyotrophic lateral sclerosis, 1:103

Familial dysautonomia, 1:263

Familial hemochromatosis. *See* Hemochromatosis

Familial hypercholesteremia, 3:953

Familial hypophosphatemia, 5:1854, 1863

Familial Mediterranean fever, 1:100, 102

Familial pulmonary hypertension, 4:1539

Family
- caregivers, 2:453–454
- driver safety, 2:703, 705
- drug abuse, 2:707
- elder abuse, 2:727
- extended, 3:793, 794
- generalized anxiety disorder, 3:864
- home care, 3:980
- hospice care, 3:996
- independence, 3:1027
- naturopathy, 4:1316–1317
- nontraditional (alternative), 3:794
- nuclear, 3:793, 794
- nursing homes, 4:1333–1334
- nutritionists, 4:1348
- patient representative, 4:1428–1429
- persistent vegetative state, 4:1441
- socialization, 4:1560
- substance abuse therapy, 5:1728
- suicide prevention, 5:1733, 1734
- withdrawal of life support, 5:1883

Family education, 4:1455–1456, 1577
- *See also* Patient education

Family history, 3:912, 5:1721, 1817
- *See also* Genetic factors; Health history

Family relationships, 3:**793–796,** 802–803

Family therapy
- anxiety, 1:216
- generalized anxiety disorder, 3:864
- PTSD, 4:1471

Famotidine, 3:898–900
- for gastroesophageal reflux disease, 3:855–856
- for heartburn, 3:935
- for helicobacteriosis, 3:940
- *vs.* proton pump inhibitors, 4:1516
- for ulcers, 2:586, 5:1799
- vitamin B_{12} interactions, 5:1848

FANA. *See* Antinuclear antibody test

Fanconi syndrome, 5:1854

FAP (Familial adenomatous polyposis), 2:533, 586

Farmer's lung, 4:1536

Farsightedness, 5:1841

Fasciitis, necrotizing, 5:1709

Fast heart rate. *See* Tachycardia

Fast tracking, 4:1557

Fasting plasma glucose test (FPG), 1:328, 329, 330, 2:639

Fat (body)
- adverse effects, 4:1339
- age-related macular degeneration, 5:1837
- angioplasty, 1:130–131
- body mass index, 1:330–332
- distribution, 5:1877
- eyelid, 1:317–319
- high cholesterol, 3:953
- lipodystrophy, 1:53
- liposuction, 1:4, 5, 2:582–584
- obesity, 4:1350, 1352

Fat deposits. *See* Fat (body)

Fat-free label, 3:1158

Fat rebalancing, 3:785

Fatigue
- chronic kidney failure, 2:508
- fibromyalgia, 3:800
- lyme disease, 3:1184

Fats (dietary)
- caloric intake, 3:1156, 1157
- cancer, 2:408, 413, 5:1682
- coronary artery disease, 2:581
- description, 3:1154, 1156–1157
- food pyramid, 2:658
- gastroesophageal reflux disease, 3:856
- healthy aging diet, 4:1339
- heart disease, 3:929
- liver function, 3:797
- low-cholesterol diet, 3:1154
- monounsaturated, 3:929, 956, 1004, 1154, 1157, 4:1339
- multiple sclerosis, 4:1305
- polyunsaturated, 3:929, 956, 1004, 1154, 1155, 1157, 4:1339
- skin cancer prevention, 4:1200
- sources, 3:1155, 1157–1158
- stroke risk, 5:1722–1723
- trans, 1:196, 3:929, 953–954, 1154, 1157, 4:1339
- unsaturated, 3:1154, 1157, 1159
- vitamin E absorption, 5:1858
- *See also* Low-fat diet; Saturated fats

Fats (lipids), 3:797, *1002,* 1002–1005

Fatty acids. *See* Essential fatty acids; Omega-3 fatty acids; Omega-6 fatty acids

Fatty liver, 3:**796–797,** 4:1500

FBI (Federal Bureau of Investigation), 4:1212

FBUT (Fluorescein break up time), 2:712

FDA. *See* Food and Drug Administration

Fear, 3:786, 792, 4:1527

Fecal diversion, 5:1886

Fecal immunochemical test (FIT), 2:535

Fecal impaction
- barium, 5:1803
- delirium, 2:607, 608
- enemas, 2:752–755
- spinal cord injuries, 5:1693

Fecal incontinence, 2:653, 3:**797–800**
- personal hygiene, 4:1441
- spinal cord injury-related, 5:1693, 1694

Fecal occult blood test
- colon cancer, 2:534, 535
- GI bleeding, 3:872, 873
- stomach cancer, 5:1705

Federal Bureau of Investigation (FBI), 4:1212

Federal Claims Act, 4:1232

Federal poverty level (FPL), 4:1229

Federation of State Medical Boards, 3:807

Fee-for-service plans, 2:548, 4:1209, 1239, 1494, 1496

Fee-setting, 4:1231

Feedback, positive, 2:671

Fees. *See* Costs

Feinbloom low vision chart, 3:1163

Felbamate, 1:160

Felbatol. *See* Felbamate

Feldenkrais method, 2:489, 4:1324

Fellowship, 2:558, 3:806

Female urinary catheterization, 2:**465–468**

Feminization, 2:635

Femoral implants, 3:972

Femoral neck, 3:960

Femoral shaft, 3:960

Fempatch. *See* Estrogen replacement therapy

Fennel, 4:1252

Fenofibratet, 3:955
Fentanyl, 1:113, 2:688, 4:1395
Fenugreek, 3:1005
Feral children, 4:1560
Fermented food, 4:1496–1501
Ferritin, 3:945, 1067, 1068
Ferrous fuconate, 3:1065
Ferrous fumarate, 3:1065
Ferrous sulfate, 3:1065
Fertility, 5:1694
Fertility drugs, 2:744, 4:1375
Fertility rates, 2:554
FES (Functional electrical stimulation), 5:1694, 1696
Fetal alcohol syndrome, 4:1256, 1258
Fetal nigral cell transplantation, 4:1424
FEV (Forced expiratory volume), 1:377, 2:512
Fever
  acetaminophen for, 1:7–8
  common cold-related, 2:552
  dehydration, 5:1871
  infectious disease-related, 3:1034
  nonsteroidal anti-inflammatory drugs for, 4:1326
  travel-related, 5:1610
  treatment, 3:1037
Fexofenadine, 1:187
FFDM (Full-field digital mammography), 4:1206–1207
Fiber (dietary), 3:948, 957–959
  carbohydrates, 2:421, 422
  constipation, 2:569
  Dietary Reference Intakes, 3:957
  diverticular disease, 2:693–694, 695–696
  hemorrhoids, 3:948
  high cholesterol, 3:956
  insoluble, 2:422, 3:957
  irritable bowel syndrome, 3:1071
  ischemia, 3:1076
  laxatives, 3:1123
  low-cholesterol diet, 3:1155
  Parkinson's disease, 4:1423
  recommended intake, 2:695, 3:957, 4:1336
  soluble, 2:422, 3:957–958, 1155
  sources, 2:417, 695, 3:957–958
  stroke prevention, 5:1723
  See also High-fiber diet
Fiber supplements, 3:1123
Fiberoptic endoscopy, 1:233
Fibrates, 2:519, 3:955
Fibric acid derivatives, 3:1004
Fibrillation. *See* Atrial fibrillation; Ventricular fibrillation
Fibrin, 4:1261
Fibrinogen, 3:1143
Fibroadenoma, 1:353
Fibrocartilage, 3:1085
Fibroids, uterine, 3:1016–1017, 1019
Fibromyalgia, 3:**800–802**
  drug therapy, 1:215, 3:801, 863
  massage, 4:1218
  neuromuscular physical therapy, 4:1323
  relaxation techniques, 4:1565
Fibrosarcomas, 5:1583
Fibrosis
  bonc marrow biopsy, 1:340
  cavernosal, 5:1635
  liver, 3:1137
  pulmonary, 1:254, 372, 373, 3:1171, 4:1535–1539, *1536*
Fibrositis. *See* Fibromyalgia
Fibrous joints, 3:1085
Fight-or-flight reaction
  discovery, 4:1563
  isolation-related, 3:1077–1078
  mind/body medicine, 4:1269
  relaxation response, 4:1270
  stress response, 1:212–213
  vitamin C, 5:1850
FIGO staging system, 2:745
Figs, 2:415–416
Figurative speech, 5:1688
Filaria, 3:1187, 1188
Fillers, wrinkle, 5:1889
Filtering microsurgery, 3:882
Final Exit (Humphrey), 5:1734
Financial exploitation, 2:727–729
Financial management, 2:567, 3:**802–804,** 802*t,* 997, 998
Financing, health care. *See* Health care financing
Finasteride
  for alopecia, 1:80
  erectile dysfunction from, 5:1634
  for hair growth, 5:1588
  for prostate enlargement, 4:1512
  saw palmetto interactions, 5:1589
Finding a surgeon, 3:**804–809**
Fine needle aspiration biopsy
  breast, 1:352–353, 356
  exocrine pancreatic cancer, 4:1405
  liver, 3:1135
  lung, 3:1172, 1175
  oral cancers, 4:1358
Finger joints, 3:1086, 4:1366
Finger, trigger, 5:**1787–1788**
Fingernails. *See* Nails
Fingerstick tests, 1:61
FIO_2 (Oxygen concentration), 5:1823
First-generation antihistamines, 1:186–188
First International Congress of Qigong, 4:1546
Fish
  allergies, 3:814–818
  anti-inflammatory diet, 1:195
  food pyramid, 2:658
Fish oils
  Alzheimer's disease, 1:88
  anticoagulant interactions, 1:386
  calcium, 5:1614
  lupus, 3:1181
  multiple sclerosis, 4:1305
  See also Omega-3 fatty acids
Fistula, diverticulitis-related, 2:695
FIT (Fecal immunochemical test), 2:535
FITC (Fluorescein isothiocyanate), 1:251
Fitzgerald, William, 1:13–14
Five Rhythms technique, 4:1291–1292
5-A-Day Week, 2:556
5-Alpha reductase, 5:1588
5 Alpha-reductase inhibitors, 4:1512, 1513
5-Fluorouracil. *See* Fluorouracil
5-FU. *See* Fluorouracil
Flaps (surgical)
  breast reconstruction, 1:366, 367
  latissimus dorsi, 1:367
  pressure sores, 4:1490
Flashbacks, 5:1726
Flavonoids, 1:197, 3:879, 4:1200, 5:1662
Flavoxate, 2:595
Flax, 2:416
Flaxseed oil, 2:631, 4:1252
Fleet enemas, 2:540
Fleming, Alexander, 1:150
Fleming, Tapas, 1:14
Flexeril. *See* Cyclobenzaprine
Flexibility (psychological), 4:1526
Flexibility training, 2:766, 5:1757, 1758, 1875
Flexible sigmoidoscopy, 2:534, 535
Floaters, 3:**809–811,** 4:1571, 1572
Flomax. *See* Tamsulosin
Floppy valve. *See* Mitral valve prolapse
Flossing, 2:616, 4:1360, 1361
Flour, white, 4:1521
Flow-cycled ventilators, 5:1821
Flow rate, 5:1823
Floxin. *See* Ofloxacin
Flu. *See* Influenza
Flu mist vaccine, 3:1042
Fluconazole, 2:587, 3:826, 4:1312
Flucytosine, 1:311
Fludrocortisone, 1:264, 3:788
Fluid balance
  dehydration, 2:603, 5:1870
  diabetes insipidus, 2:636

Fluid intake
athletes, 5:1870
cancer patients, 5:1682
chronic kidney failure, 2:510
common cold, 2:552
congestive heart failure, 2:564
constipation, 2:569, 570
daily amount, 2:658–659, 4:1336
dehydration, 2:605–606
diabetes insipidus, 2:637
diarrhea, 2:654
dietary assessment, 2:667–669
dry eye, 2:712–713
dry mouth, 2:714
exercise, 5:1870
heatstroke, 3:938, 939
hyponatremia, 2:735
infectious diseases, 3:1037
influenza, 3:1039
kidney stone prevention, 3:1102
rehydration, 5:1872
urinary tract infection prevention, 5:1809
Fluid overload, 3:1059
Fluid regulation, intravenous, 3:**1057–1059,** 4:1382
Fluid replacement. *See* Rehydration
Fluid retention, 2:563, 726
See also Edema
Flunisolide, 1:379
Fluorescein angiography, 1:41, 129, 2:649
Fluorescein break up time (FBUT), 2:712
Fluorescein isothiocyanate (FITC), 1:251
Fluorescent antinuclear antibody test (FANA). *See* Antinuclear antibody test
Fluoride, 4:1360
Fluoroquinolones, 1:151–152, 4:1406
for bladder infection, 1:311
calcium supplement interactions, 2:405
for cystitis, 2:595
for diarrhea, 2:655
Fluoroscopy
angioplasty, 1:131
barium enema, 1:288
cardiac catheterization, 2:432
gallstones, 3:839
pacemakers, 4:1388
upper GI series, 5:1801–1802
See also Immunofluorescence
Fluorosis, 5:1697, 1750
Fluorouracil, 2:490
for colon cancer, 2:536
for endocrine pancreatic cancer, 4:1403
for gallbladder cancer, 3:836
Fluorquinolones, 2:400
Fluothane. *See* Halothane
Fluoxetine, 1:167
anticonvulsant drug interactions, 1:162
for anxiety, 1:144
benzodiazepine interactions, 1:145
for bipolar disorder, 1:305
diazepam interactions, 4:1308
for panic disorder, 4:1411
for personality disorders, 4:1447
for premature ejaculation, 5:1620
for PTSD, 4:1470
Fluphenazine, 1:203, 4:1530
Flurazepam, 3:1051
Flurbiprofen, 4:1326, 1367, 5:1798
Flutter, atrial, 2:424, 452
Fluvastatin, 1:247, 3:955
Fluvoxamine, 1:167–174
Flying, 5:1608–1609
fMRI (Functional magnetic resonance imaging), 1:19
Focalyst, 5:1607
Foeniculum vulgare. See Fennel
Folacin. *See* Folic acid
Folate. *See* Folic acid
Foley catheters, 2:466, 470
FOLFOX regimen, 2:536
Folic acid, 3:**811–814,** 5:1862
anemia, 1:110
birth defect prevention, 4:1258
daily recommended dosage, 5:1864
drug interactions, 5:1862
hearing loss prevention, 3:919
mobility, 4:1285
overdose, 5:1865
probiotics, 4:1498
role, 4:1339
skin cancer prevention, 4:1200
smoking-induced lung damage, 5:1662
sources, 3:812, 4:1339, 5:1862
vitamin B_{12} deficiency, 5:1848
Folic acid deficiency, 3:811–812, 5:1862
anemia from, 1:109, 5:1862
diagnosis, 2:561
supplements for, 4:1336
vitamin B_{12} deficiency, 5:1848
Follicle stimulating hormone (FSH), 3:991, 4:1250, 1253
Follicular thyroid cancer, 5:1768–1771
Follow-up appointments, 4:1555
Folstein Mini-Mental State Examination (MMSE), 3:866
Fontaine, J. A., 4:1384
Food
cancer treatment side effects, 5:1682–1685
dietary assessment, 2:667–669
fermented, 4:1496–1501
light, 3:1158
living wills, 3:1149
organic, 2:658
plant-based, 2:413–418
pro-inflammatory, 1:195–196
processed, 3:1160, 4:1339, 5:1605
refined, 4:1349–1350
refusal, 2:600
smoked, 5:1706
sodium content, 3:1161, 5:1679–1680
vitamins and minerals, 5:1871
See also Cancer fighting foods; Diet; specific foods
Food additives, 1:326, 2:658
Food allergies, 1:70, 71, 72, 3:**814–818**
bursitis from, 1:390
demographics, 3:814–815
vs. food intolerance, 3:814, 818–819
peptic ulcers from, 5:1800
polymyositis-related, 4:1468
pro-inflammatory foods, 1:196
probiotic contraindications, 4:1499
Food Allergy & Anaphylaxis Network (FAAN), 3:817–818
Food and Agricultural Organization, 4:1496
Food and Drug Act (1906), 2:657–658
Food and Drug Administration (FDA)
acetaminophen, 1:8
acupuncture, 1:20
AIDS tests, 1:61
allergy tests, 1:75
alpha hydroxy acids, 1:84
Alzheimer's disease, 1:87–88, 163, 164, 4:1244, 5:1613
amyotrophic lateral sclerosis, 1:104
antidementia drugs, 1:163
blood sugar tests, 1:328
botox injections, 1:345, 3:785
Cancell treatment, 2:746
capsaicin, 4:1319
carvedilol, 2:563
collagen injections, 2:530
COX-2 inhibitors, 4:1398
DHEA, 2:633–634
dietary supplements, 1:78, 2:679, 4:1343
Eating Well As We Age, 2:659
erectile dysfunction drugs, 2:755–756
folic acid, 3:811
food allergies, 3:817
food safety, 2:658
fungal infections, 3:826
gastric banding, 1:285
glucosamine, 3:885
gluten-free diet, 3:889
gluten-free label, 2:474
Good Manufacturing Practice, 2:679
herpes simplex culture, 5:1625
homeopathic medicine, 3:989
HPV culture, 5:1625–1626
implanted contact lenses, 2:774

Food and Drug Administration (FDA) *(continued)*
insulin, 3:1053
knee joint replacement, 3:1112, 1113
kola, 2:396
low-sodium diet, 3:1160
lyme disease, 3:1184
mammogram, 4:1208
MedWatch program, 2:680, 4:1345
meningitis, 4:1248
multiple sclerosis, 4:1305
omega-3 fatty acids, 2:666
oral contraceptives, 4:1252
oxygen/ozone therapy, 4:1384
paroxetine, 3:863
PC-SPES, 4:1509
pharmacologists, 4:1451
probiotics, 4:1499
prostate enlargement, 4:1512
pulmonary hypertension, 4:1540
radiofrequency volumetric tissue reduction, 5:1672
rheumatoid arthritis drugs, 4:1574
rofecoxib, 2:585
shingles vaccine, 5:1631–1632
silicone gel breast implants, 1:363, 365, 367
smoking, 5:1659
SSRIs, 1:166
A Status Report on Breast Implant Safety, 1:367
tamoxifen, 1:360
tazarotene, 4:1520
telithromycin, 1:152
teriparatide, 5:1614
vagus nerve stimulation, 5:1604
weight loss drugs, 4:1351
Food-borne disorders, 1:86, 5:1610
Food challenge tests, 3:817, 820, 4:1468, 1579
Food diary, 2:524, 668, 3:819
Food, Drug, and Insecticide Administration, 2:658
Food-drug interactions, 1:26, 2:707–710
angiotensin-converting enzyme inhibitors, 1:134
garlic, 3:847, 849, 850
isoniazid, 1:208–209
Food frequency questionnaire, 2:668
Food Guide Pyramid (Tufts University), 2:666
Food intake. *See* Caloric intake
Food intolerance, 1:74, 3:**818–821**
vs. food allergies, 3:814, 818–819
irritable bowel syndrome, 3:1070
osteoarthritis, 4:1368
polymyositis, 4:1468
See also Lactose intolerance
Food labeling. *See* Labels
Food poisoning
AIDS, 1:53
E. coli, 3:1032
staphylococcal, 5:1700, 1701, 1702, 1703
Staphylococcus aureus, 4:1296
Food preparation
cancer patients, 5:1685
diarrhea prevention, 2:655–656
gastroenteritis prevention, 3:852
Food preservatives, 3:1160
Food pyramid, 2:422, 658, 666, 674, 677, 5:1872
Food record, 2:524, 668, 3:819
Food safety, 2:657–658
Foot-ankle assembly, 3:1166
Foot care, 3:**821–822**
circulatory disorders, 2:520
diabetic, 2:647, 648, 3:821
Foot infections, diabetic, 2:**641–643,** 3:843, 846, 1034
Foot pain, 3:790
Foot ulcers, 2:641
Footwear
bursitis, 1:390–391
fall prevention, 3:792, 5:1615
foot care, 3:821
gait and balance disorders, 3:830
knee injury prevention, 3:1119
mobility, 4:1285
orthopedic shoes, 5:1594
walking problems, 5:1868
Forane. *See* Isoflurane
Forced expiratory volume (FEV), 1:377, 2:512
Forced vital capacity (FVC), 1:377, 2:512
Forehead lift, 2:582–584
Foreign bodies, 2:500, 721, 722
Forgetfulness, 4:1241
Forgiveness, 4:1551–1554
Formal caregivers, 2:452
Forssmann, Werner, 2:431
Fortamet. *See* Metformin
Fortaz. *See* Ceftazidime
Fosamax. *See* Alendronate
Fosinopril, 1:132, 134, 191, 2:586
Foster grandparents, 2:559
Four principles approach, 4:1234–1235
Foxglove, 1:227, 2:447, 563
FPG (Fasting plasma glucose test), 1:328, 329, 330, 2:639
FPL (Federal poverty level), 4:1229
Fractures
bone scan, 1:343, 345
compression, 1:272, 3:1151
diet, 2:660
fall-related, 4:1372
massage therapy, 5:1628
multiple myeloma-related, 4:1300
neuromuscular physical therapy, 4:1323
osteoporosis-related, 1:335, 338, 4:1371, 1372, 5:1612
rib, 2:500
skull, 3:902, 903
sternum, 2:500
See also Hip fractures
Fragile X syndrome, 4:1255, 1256
Frail elderly, 1:28–29, 2:728
Frailty syndrome, 5:1747
Frames, eyeglass, 2:773
Framingham Heart Study, 5:1876–1877
Francis, T. Jr., 1:193
Fraud, Medicare, 4:1232, 1238
Freckles, 5:1650, 1651
Free flap breast reconstruction, 1:366, 367
Free radical scavengers. *See* Antioxidants
Free radicals
aging, 1:46
amyotrophic lateral sclerosis, 1:103
antioxidants, 1:197
cancer fighting foods, 2:414
garlic, 3:847
Parkinson's disease, 4:1422
smoking, 5:1660
vitamin C, 5:1850
Freud, Sigmund, 4:1445
Friedman School of Nutrition Science and Policy, 2:658
Friendship, 5:1733
Frostbite, 3:843
Fructooligosaccharides, 4:1496
Fructose, 2:422, 3:1070, 1124
Fruit
anti-inflammatory diet, 1:195
antioxidants, 1:197–198
cancer prevention, 2:412, 413–418
citrus, 2:416–417, 572, 3:856, 5:1849–1850, 1849*t*
community nutrition programs, 2:556
food pyramid, 2:658
healthy aging diet, 4:1338–1339
Healthy Eating 2010, 2:557
hypertension, 1:326
recommendations, 4:1336
vitamin C content, 5:1851
FSH (Follicle stimulating hormone), 3:981, 4:1250, 1253
Fuch's dystrophy, 2:574
Fucosyltransferase, 2:594
Full-field digital mammography (FFDM), 4:1206–1207
Full thickness tissue loss, 4:1488
Fulvicin. *See* Griseofulvin
Functional electrical stimulation (FES), 5:1694, 1696
Functional independence, 3:1027

Functional magnetic resonance imaging (fMRI), 1:19
Functional movement therapy, 4:1291
Functional presbyopia, 4:1485
Functional reach test, 3:830
Functional status assessment, 3:865–866
Functional urinary incontinence, 5:1804
Funding. *See* Health care financing
Fundoplication, 3:856, 935
Fundus, 5:1704
Funeral services, 2:599–600
Fungal culture, 3:**822–824,** 5:1645–1646
Fungal infections, 3:**824–828**
  alopecia, 1:79
  bladder, 1:311
  cellulitis, 2:477
  diagnosis, 3:822–824, 1035
  drug therapy, 1:183–186, 184*t,* 3:826–827, 1035
  garlic for, 3:846
  hospital-acquired, 3:825
  hypdrogen peroxide for, 4:1385
  marijuana-related, 4:1214
  nail, 4:*1311,* 1311–1314
  See also Antifungal drugs
Fungal meningitis, 3:825, 4:1246–1249
Furadantin. *See* Nitrofurantoin
Furosemide, 2:563, 587, 690, 3:1056
Furuncles. *See* Boils
Furunculosis, 1:333, 334, 335
Fusion, spinal, 5:1698
Futility, 5:1883
FVC (Forced vital capacity), 1:377, 2:512

G

GABA (Gamma-aminobutyric acid), 1:304
GABA analogues, 1:159*t*
Gabapentin
  for bipolar disorder, 1:304
  for diabetic neuropathy, 2:647
  for post-herpatic neuralgia, 5:1631
  for seizures, 1:160, 5:1603
  for tinnitus, 5:1780
GAD. *See* Generalized anxiety disorder
GAD-Q-IV (Generalized Anxiety Disorder Questionnaire for DSM-IV), 3:863
Gag reflex, 1:232, 383, 5:1741
GAIT (Glucosamine Chondroitin Arthritis Intervention Trial), 3:884
Gait assessment, 3:**829–831,** 832, 833
  lower limb prosthesis, 3:1167
  mobility problems, 4:1284
  neurologic examination, 4:1322
Gait, defined, 4:1283
Gait problems, 3:**831–834**
  falls, 3:791
  hip fractures, 3:960
  mobility, 4:1283–1287
  Parkinson's disease, 3:832, 834, 4:1422, 1423
  treatment, 3:830, 832–834
Galactooligosaccharides, 4:1496
Galactose, 3:1122, 1124, 4:1496
Galactosemia, 2:522, 4:1256, 1258
Galantamine, 1:88, 163–165, 4:1244, 5:1616
Galatose, 2:422
Galen, 1:234
Galium sp. *See* Cleavers
Gallbladder cancer, 3:**835–837,** 4:1251
Gallbladder disorders, 3:1157
Gallium scan, 5:1582
Gallstones, 3:*837,* **837–840**
  gallbladder cancer, 3:835
  liver function tests, 3:1146
  low-fat diet, 3:1157
Galton, Francis, 2:762–763
Galvanic skin response (GSR), 1:301
Gambling, 3:**840–842**
Gamma-aminobutyric acid (GABA), 1:304
Gamma camera, 3:1098–1099, 1147, 4:1328, 5:1775
Gamma globulin, 5:1764
Gamma-glutamyltransferase (GGT), 3:1143–1146
Gamma tocopherol, 5:1856
Gamma tocotrienol, 5:1856
Gangrene, 3:*842,* **842–846**
  amputation, 1:97, 3:843, 845
  cellulitis-related, 2:478
  diabetic foot infection-related, 2:641, 3:843, 846
  diabetic neuropathy-related, 2:647
  foot care, 3:821
  peripheral vascular disease-related, 4:1436
Gardasil, 5:1623
Gargling, 2:553
Garlic, 3:**846–850**
  anticoagulant action, 1:386
  bronchitis prevention, 1:378
  cancer fighting effect, 2:416, 3:847, 848
  common cold, 2:553
  cystitis, 2:595
  drug interactions, 3:847
  gout, 3:892
  high cholesterol, 3:955
  hyperlipoproteinemia, 3:1005
  hypertension, 1:326
  immune system function, 3:1024
  lice infestation, 3:1126
  viral infections, 5:1834
Gas exchange, 2:511, 4:1567
Gas gangrene, 3:842–843, 844–845
Gastrectomy, 5:1706, 1707
Gastric acid
  antacids, 1:139–140
  antisecretory drugs, 5:1799
  duodenal ulcers, 3:940
  H-2 receptor blockers, 3:897–901
  proton pump inhibitors, 4:1515–1516
Gastric acid inhibitors, 1:139
Gastric banding, 1:285, 4:1351
Gastric cancer. *See* Stomach cancer
Gastric emptying, delayed, 3:859
Gastric lavage, 4:1382
Gastric ulcers. *See* Peptic ulcers
Gastrin, 5:1798, 1799
Gastrinomas, 4:1401–1403, 5:1798
Gastritis, 3:872, 933
Gastroduodenal ulcers, 2:585
Gastroenteritis, 3:**850–853,** 1032
  demographics, 3:850–851, 1034
  vs. influenza, 5:1833
  lactose intolerance, 3:1121
Gastroesophageal reflux disease (GERD), 3:**853–858**
  antacids for, 1:139
  causes, 3:854, 858–859
  demographics, 3:853–854, 858
  diagnosis, 3:854–855, 858–861
  esophageal cancer risk, 2:759, 761
  H-2 receptor blockers for, 3:855–856, 857, 897–898
  proton pump inhibitors for, 3:856, 857, 4:1515–1517
  scleroderma-related, 3:854, 5:1597, 1598
  smoking-related, 5:1665
Gastroesophageal reflux scan, 3:**858–861**
Gastrograffin, 1:288–289
Gastrointestinal bleeding. *See* GI bleeding
Gastrointestinal cancers
  GI bleeding from, 3:872
  gluten-free diet, 3:888–889
  pleural effusion from, 4:1461
Gastrointestinal disorders, 4:1565, 5:1855, 1860
Gastroparesis, 5:1634
Gastroplasty, vertical banded, 1:285, 4:1351
Gastrostomy, 2:537, 5:1789
Gatifloxacin, 1:151–152
GC-1008, 4:1537
GDS (Geriatric Depression Scale), 3:1079

Gefilus, 4:1497
Gemcitabine, 1:309, 4:1406–1407
Gemfibrozil, 3:955
Gemifloxacin, 1:151–152
Gender differences
 abdominoplasty, 1:4
 age-related macular degeneration, 1:40, 5:1836
 ALS, 1:103
 anemia, 1:108
 aneurysm, 1:121
 angina pectoris, 1:124
 aortic dissection, 1:218
 atherosclerosis, 1:245
 autoimmune diseases, 1:258
 back curves, 1:258
 body mass index, 1:332
 coronary artery disease, 2:578
 dementia, 2:611
 dry eye, 2:711
 esophageal cancer, 2:759
 exercise, 5:1759
 exocrine pancreatic cancer, 4:1404
 fecal incontinence, 3:798
 fibromyalgia, 3:800
 gallstones, 3:838
 generalized anxiety disorder, 3:862
 glaucoma, 5:1836–1837
 gout, 3:891
 hearing loss, 3:919
 heart attacks, 3:922
 high cholesterol, 3:953
 hip revision surgery, 3:972, 974
 hypertension, 1:325, 3:869, 1009
 incontinence, 5:1805
 insomnia, 5:1655–1658
 iron-deficiency anemia, 3:1064
 irritable bowel syndrome, 3:1069
 ischemia, 3:1074
 isolation, 3:1078
 knee joint replacement, 3:1112
 life expectancy, 2:662
 liver cancer, 3:1138
 longevity, 2:662
 lupus, 3:1178–1179
 multiple myeloma, 4:1299
 multiple sclerosis, 4:1304
 nail infections, 4:1311
 nutrition, 4:1339
 nutrition status, 2:675
 obesity, 2:662, 4:1337, 1349
 osteoporosis, 1:335
 panic disorder, 4:1410
 psoriasis, 4:1518
 pulmonary fibrosis, 4:1535
 pulmonary hypertension, 4:1539
 recovery at home, 4:1555–1556
 rheumatoid arthritis, 4:1573
 sarcoidosis, 5:1581
 scleroderma, 5:1596
 sleep apnea, 5:1652–1653
 snoring, 5:1670–1671
 spousal death, 1:295
 stress test, 5:1718
 stroke, 5:1720–1721
 substance abuse counseling, 5:1730
 suicide, 5:1733
 thyroid cancer, 5:1769
 transient ischemic attacks, 5:1784–1785
 urinary tract infections, 5:1807–1808
 varicose veins, 5:1816
 vision disorders, 5:1836
Gene expression, 5:1895
Gene therapy, 2:490, 4:1264
Genealogy, 4:1527
General anesthesia, 1:**111–115**
 abdominoplasty, 1:4
 anti-itch drug interactions, 1:141
 bronchoscopy, 1:383
 colostomy, 2:542
 complications, 1:114
 cosmetic surgery, 2:583
 hip replacement, 3:965
 hypothermia from, 4:1556
 interactions, 1:115
Generalized anxiety disorder (GAD), 1:213, 3:**861–865**
 antianxiety drugs for, 1:144, 3:863
 demographics, 1:214, 3:862
 drug therapy, 1:215, 3:863
 SSRIs for, 1:166, 167, 3:863
Generalized Anxiety Disorder Questionnaire for DSM-IV (GAD-Q-IV), 3:863
Generalized pustular psoriasis, 4:1518
Generalized seizures, 5:1601–1606
Generativity, 4:1525–1526
Generic drugs, 2:549, 4:1240, 5:1610
Genetic counseling, 1:102
Genetic disorders, 1:339
Genetic factors
 aging, 1:44, 45
 allergies, 1:71
 Alzheimer's disease, 1:86, 4:1242, 1257
 amyloidosis, 1:101
 amyotrophic lateral sclerosis, 1:103
 aneurysm, 1:121
 asthma, 1:240, 241
 autoimmune disorders, 1:258
 autonomic disorders, 1:263
 bipolar disorder, 1:302
 blood clots, 1:321
 breast cancer, 1:355–356, 2:412, 4:1204, 1221, 1224
 cancer, 2:406–408
 carcinogenesis, 4:1260–1261
 chronic obstructive pulmonary disease, 2:512
 colon cancer, 2:412, 533, 538
 colorectal cancer, 4:1260–1261
 coronary artery disease, 2:578
 depression, 2:624
 dermatitis, 2:630
 diabetes mellitus, 2:639
 emphysema, 2:740, 743
 endometrial cancer, 2:744
 epilepsy, 5:1602
 food allergies, 3:815
 generalized anxiety disorder, 3:862, 864
 glaucoma, 3:881
 gluten-free diet, 3:888
 heart attacks, 3:922
 hemochromatosis, 3:943–944, 945–946
 high cholesterol, 3:953
 hip revision surgery, 3:974
 hyperlipoproteinemia, 3:1003, 1004, 1005
 immune system disorders, 3:1022
 ischemia, 3:1074
 longevity, 1:44
 lung cancer, 3:1174
 melanoma, 4:1199
 mental retardation, 4:1255
 motor neuron diseases, 4:1288
 multiple myeloma, 4:1299
 multiple sclerosis, 4:1304
 osteoporosis, 4:1371
 ovarian cancer, 2:412, 4:1375, 1377
 panic disorder, 4:1410
 Parkinson's disease, 4:1421
 polymyositis, 4:1467
 pulmonary hypertension, 4:1539, 1540
 rosacea, 4:1578
 sarcomas, 5:1584
 seborrheic dermatitis, 5:1600
 skin cancer, 5:1642
 skin lesions, 5:1650
 smoking, 5:1660
 snoring, 5:1670
 stress, 5:1715
 thyroid cancer, 5:1769, 1772
 tuberculosis, 5:1794
 varicose veins, 5:1817
Genetic mutations, 2:411, 4:1260–1261
Genetic testing
 cancer, 2:410
 cardiomyopathy, 2:446
 gluten-free diet, 3:888
 hemochromatosis, 3:945–946
 HPV, 4:1413
 human papilloma virus, 4:1415, 5:1625–1626
 liver function, 3:1143
 multicentric tumors, 4:1262
 pulmonary hypertension, 4:1540
 sarcomas, 5:1585
Genistein, 1:197, 2:417
Genital herpes, 5:1622–1624
Genital ulcers, 1:290
Genital warts, 5:1622
Gentamicin, 1:95–97, 151
Gentian violet, 1:184
Geranium, 5:1800

GERD. *See* Gastroesophageal reflux disease
Gerda Alexander Eutony therapy, 4:1292
Gerhardt, Charles, 1:234
Geriatric assessment tests, 3:**865–868,** 998, 4:1444
Geriatric case managers, 3:794
Geriatric Depression Scale (GDS), 3:1079
Geriatric dieticians, 3:868
Geriatric nurses, 3:867–868
Geriatric nutrition, 3:**868–871**
  See also Diet; Nutrition
Geriatric optometry, 4:1354
Geriatric Research, Education and Clinical Centers (GRECCs), 5:1827
Germ cell tumors, 1:349, 3:1146, 4:1374
German measles. *See* Rubella
Germanium, 3:846
Germany, 1:19
Germinomas. *See* Germ cell tumors
Gerota's fascia, 3:1093
Gerotranscendence, 4:1527
Gerson therapy, 2:746
Gestational oral glucose tolerance test, 1:330
Get-up-and-go test, 3:830, 4:1284
GFCO (Gluten-Free Certification Organization), 3:887
GGT (Gamma-glutamyltransferase), 3:1143–1146
Ghee, 3:817
GI bleeding, 3:**871–875**
  iron-deficiency anemia, 3:1064, 1065
  nonsteroidal anti-inflammatory drug-induced, 3:872, 874, 1064, 4:1326
GI bleeding studies, 3:**875–876**
Giant cell arteritis, 1:258–260, 2:517–520, 3:906, 4:1467
Giant cell tumors, 5:1583
Giardia lamblia, 2:652–653
GINA (Global Initiative for Asthma), 1:241
Ginger, 1:386, 2:553, 3:1071
Gingivitis, 3:**876–878,** 4:1361–1362
Ginkgo biloba, 3:**878–879**
  Alzheimer's disease, 1:88
  angina pectoris, 3:1076
  anticoagulant action, 1:386
  drug interactions, 2:680
  erectile dysfunction, 2:757
  memory loss, 4:1244
  menopause, 4:1252
  smoking-induced lung damage, 5:1662
  tinnitus, 5:1780
Ginkgolides, 3:879
Ginseng
  Asian, 3:1005
  Korean red, 2:757
  menopause, 4:1252
  vitamin K interactions, 5:1860
Glandular carcinoma, 1:355
Glasgow Coma Scale, 2:545, 547, 3:903
Glasses, eye. *See* Eyeglasses
Glaucoma, 3:**880–883,** 880*t,* 882, 5:1612, 1836–1839
  beta blockers for, 1:297, 297*t*
  blindness from, 3:882, 4:1438, 5:1843
  closed-angle, 3:880, 5:1782, 1836, 1839
  demographics, 3:880, 880*t,* 1163, 5:1836–1837, 1836*t*
  diabetic retinopathy-related, 2:650
  eye examination, 2:769, 3:881
  eyedrops, 2:775, 777
  glucagon, 1:288, 289
  headaches from, 3:906
  intraocular pressure, 3:880–881, 882, 5:1836, 1837, 1839
  low vision from, 3:1163
  marijuana for, 4:1213
  mobility, 4:1285
  open-angle, 5:1836, 1836*t,* 1839
  peripheral vision loss from, 4:1438, 1439
  treatment, 3:881–882, 5:1615, 1839
Glaucoma Research Foundation, 3:881–882
Gleason Grading System, 4:1503–1504, 1506
Gleevec. *See* Imatinib mesylate
Gliadan, 2:473
Glimepiride, 1:178, 2:549
Gliomas, 1:349, 2:407
Glipizide, 1:178, 2:549, 640
Global bioethics, 4:1235
Global dysphasia, 2:718
Global Initiative for Asthma (GINA), 1:241
Global warming, 1:71
Globulins, 3:817
Globus pallidus (GPi), 4:1424
Globus pharyngis, 5:1739
Glomerulonephritis, 2:508, 3:1104
Glossopharyngeal neuralgia, 4:1318
GLP-1 (Glucagen-like peptide-1), 1:179–180
Glucagen-like peptide-1 (GLP-1), 1:179–180
Glucagon
  endocrine pancreatic cancer, 4:1401
  glaucoma, 1:288, 289
  upper GI series, 5:1801, 1802
Glucagonoma, 4:1401–1403
Glucocorticoids
  calcium absorption, 2:400
  calcium supplement interactions, 2:405
  pacemaker interactions, 4:1389
  stress response, 1:212
Glucophage. *See* Metformin
Glucoraphanin, 2:415
Glucosamine, 3:**883–886**
  diabetes mellitus interactions, 4:1345
  for osteoarthritis, 3:883–884, 1117, 4:1368
Glucosamine Chondroitin Arthritis Intervention Trial (GAIT), 3:884
Glucosamine hydrochloride, 3:883, 884
Glucosamine sulfate, 3:883, 884
Glucose
  aging, 1:46
  cinnamon, 2:514–516
  for coma, 2:547
  Cushing's syndrome, 2:592
  diabetes mellitus, 2:638–640
  diabetic nephropathy, 2:644, 645
  diabetic retinopathy, 5:1839
  digestion, 2:422
  garlic interactions, 3:847–848
  glucosamine interactions, 3:885
  insulin, 2:638–639, 3:1052–1057
  lactose intolerance, 3:1122
  nicotine interactions, 5:1664
  role, 3:1053
  tricyclic antidepressants interactions, 1:176
  weight loss, 5:1877
Glucose intolerance, 1:44, 330
Glucose tests. *See* Blood sugar tests
Glucotrol. *See* Glipizide
Glutathione, 2:415
Gluten, 2:472–476, 3:817, 886, 4:1521
Gluten-Free Certification Organization (GFCO), 3:887
Gluten-free diet, 2:474, 475, 3:**886–890**
Gluten intolerance, 3:886
Gluten Intolerance Group, 3:887
Gluten sensitive enteropathy. *See* Celiac disease
Glyburide
  celecoxib interactions, 2:587
  commercial prescription programs, 2:549
  for diabetes, 1:178, 2:640
  insulin interactions, 3:1056
Glycemic control, 1:179
Glycerin, 3:1123
Glycerol, 2:690
Glycogen, 1:327, 2:422
Glycogen storage disease, 2:522
Glycolic acid, 1:83
Glycosaminoglycans, 3:884

Glycosides, 2:447
Glycyrrhizin, 2:416
Glynase. *See* Glyburide
Glyset. *See* Miglitol
GMP (Good Manufacturing Practice), 2:679
Gnostics, 4:1269
Goats milk, 4:1496
God, 4:1551, 1560–1561
Goggles, swimming, 2:712
Goiter, diffuse toxic, 3:1013
Gold allergies, 2:630
Gold miners, 5:1597
Golden lock tea, 4:1379
Goldenseal
- boils, 1:334
- common cold, 2:553
- cystitis, 2:595
- ulcers, 5:1800

Goldin, Barry, 4:1497
Gomphosis joints, 3:1085
Gonioscopy, 3:881, 5:1838
Gonorrhea, 5:1621–1624, 1625
Good Manufacturing Practice (GMP), 2:679
Good Samaritan Law, 2:451
Goodpasture's syndrome, 1:257–260
Gorbach, Sherwood, 4:1497
Gout, 3:*890,* **890–893,** 893–894
- bladder stones, 1:313
- bursitis, 1:389
- drug therapy, 3:891–892, 893–895
- joint function, 3:1086
- kidney stones, 3:1101
- nonsteroidal anti-inflammatory drugs for, 4:1326
- osteoarthritis from, 4:1366

Gout drugs, 3:891–892, **893–895**
Government health insurance, 3:795, 4:1494, 1495–1496
Government regulations. *See* Legislation
GPi (Globus pallidus), 4:1424
Grach, Michael, 1:14
Gradient elastic stockings, 2:602
Grafts, bone, 2:619, 3:970, 972, 5:1585
Grains
- celiac disease, 2:472, 473
- gluten-free diet, 3:886–887
- refined, 1:195–196, 2:693–694
- zinc, 5:1897
- *See also* Whole grains

Gram-negative bacteria, 1:96, 5:1624–1625
Gram-positive bacteria, 5:1624–1625
Gram stain, 5:1624
Grand-mal seizures. *See* Tonic-clonic seizures
Grandparents, 2:559, 3:795
Granisetron, 2:418, 419, 420, 491
Granny snatching, 2:567
Granulomas, 1:343, 5:1581
Granulomatosis, Wegener's, 1:258–260
Granulomatous ileitis, 1:100
Grapefruit
- anti-insomnia drug interactions, 1:141
- calcium channel blocker interactions, 2:402
- cancer fighting action, 2:416
- drug interactions, 5:1849*t*

Grapes, 1:83, 2:416
Grave's disease, 1:258–260, 3:1013
GRECCs (Geriatric Research, Education and Clinical Centers), 5:1827
Green House Project, 4:1334
Green leafy vegetables, 2:415
Green tea, 2:417, 4:1579
Gretter, Lystra, 2:527
Grief
- adjustment disorders, 1:23
- childhood traumatic, 5:1715
- complicated, 1:295, 296
- death and dying, 2:597, 599
- *vs.* depression, 2:625–626
- hospice care professionals, 3:997

Grief counseling. *See* Bereavement counseling
Grief therapy, 1:294, 295, 296
Grindelia, 2:631
Grinspoon, Lester, 4:1213
Griseofulvin, 3:826, 4:1517
Grispeg. *See* Griseofulvin
Grooming, 4:1442
Group A Streptococcus, 2:477, 3:843, 5:1709, 1711
Group B Streptococcus, 3:1033–1034, 1035, 5:1710, 1711
Group C Streptococcus, 5:1709
Group D Streptococcus, 5:1709
Group model HMOs, 3:976, 4:1209
Group therapy
- anxiety, 1:216–217
- bipolar disorder, 1:306
- dysphasia, 2:718
- generalized anxiety disorder, 3:864
- personality disorders, 4:1447
- PTSD, 4:1471

Growth hormones, 2:564
GSR (Galvanic skin response), 1:301
Guafensin, 2:551–552
Guanethidine monosulfate, 1:177, 191, 3:1055
Guardianship. *See* Conservatorship
Guggulipid, 3:1005
Guide dogs, 3:1164, 5:1843
Guide to Physical Therapist Practice (APTA), 1:269
Guided imagery, 4:1377, 1468
- *See also* Visualization

Guillain-Barre syndrome, 1:257–260, 3:1042, 1043, 4:1417
Gulf War syndrome, 5:1828
Gum disease. *See* Gingivitis; Periodontal disease
Gum, nicotine replacement, 5:1667
Gut permeability, 4:1497
Guttate psoriasis, 4:1518
Gymnema sylvestre, 3:1056
Gynecologic surgery, 1:3–4
Gynecologists, 5:1619

H

H-1 receptor blockers, 1:186
H-1 receptors, 3:897
H-2 receptor blockers, 1:186, 3:**897–901,** 897*t*
- for gastroesophageal reflux disease, 3:855–856, 857, 897–898
- for heartburn, 3:935
- for helicobacteriosis, 3:940
- for peptic ulcers, 5:1799
- *vs.* proton pump inhibitors, 4:1515–1516
- for ulcers, 2:586

H. pylori. See Helicobacter pylori
H1N1, 3:1038, 1042
H3N2, 3:1038, 1042
H63D gene, 3:944, 945
Habitrol. *See* Nicotine replacement therapy
Haemophilus ducreyi, 5:1625
Haemophilus influenzae
- antibiotics for, 1:152
- bacteremia, 1:276
- drug resistance, 5:1833
- meningitis, 4:1248, 1256
- pericarditis, 4:1431
- pneumonia, 4:1463
- types A, B and C, 5:1832
- *See also* Influenza

Hahnemann, Samuel, 3:987
Hair follicles, 1:332–335
Hair growth, 5:1588
Hair loss. *See* Alopecia
Hair transplantation, 1:80
Halcion. *See* Triazolam
Half Tablet Program, 2:549
Hallucinations
- age-related macular degeneration, 1:41
- delirium, 2:609
- psychoses, 4:1528–1532
- visual impairment, 4:1529

Hallucinogenics, 5:1725, 1726
Haloperidol, 1:203
  for bipolar disorder, 1:305
  cholesterol test interactions, 2:506
  for delirium, 2:609
  for dementia, 2:613
  Parkinson's disease from, 4:1421–1422
  periodic limb movement disorder from, 4:1434
  for psychoses, 4:1530
Halothane, 1:113
Halsted radical mastectomy, 4:1222
Hamilton Anxiety Scale, 3:863
Hamilton Depression Rating Scale, 2:608
Hamstring muscles, 3:1115, 1117
Hand-assisted laparoscopic nephrectomy, 3:1104
Hand Hospital, 5:1827
Hand sanitizers, 4:1296
Hand washing
  cancer patients, 5:1685
  common cold prevention, 2:553
  diarrhea prevention, 2:655
  infection control, 3:1030–1031
  infectious disease prevention, 3:1035–1036
  MRSA infections, 4:1296
  staphylococcal infections, 5:1703
  travel, 5:1610
  viral infection prevention, 5:1834, 1835
  See also Hygiene
Handedness, 2:719
Hangovers, 1:68
Hansen's disease, 5:1590, 1842
Hardship, undue, 1:94
Harpagophytum procumbens. See Devil's claw
Harris Survey, 5:1882
Harvard Mind/Body Medical Institute, 4:1270
Harvard Study of Adult Development, 4:1525–1526
Hashashins, 4:1211
Hashish, 4:1211, 1212, 5:1725
Hatha yoga, 5:1892, 1893
Hawaiians, 1:382
Hawking, Stephen, 1:*103*
Hawthorn
  angina pectoris, 3:1076
  arrhythmias, 1:227
  cardiomyopathy, 2:447
  hypertension, 3:1011
  menopause, 4:1252
  osteoarthritis, 4:1368
  smoking-induced lung damage, 5:1662
Hawthorne, Fran, 1:2
Hay fever, 1:70
Hayflick, Leonard, 1:43–44
Hayflick's limit, 1:43–44, 45
HCC. *See* Hepatocellular carcinoma
HCFA (Health Care Financing Administration), 4:1237, 1238
HDL. *See* High-density lipoproteins
HE4 test, 4:1377
Head and neck cancers, 5:1668, 1741
Head injuries, 3:**901–905**
  epilepsy, 3:902, 5:1602
  fall-related, 4:1372
  floaters, 3:810
  gait and balance disorders, 3:832
  low vision, 3:1163
  mental retardation, 4:1256
  neuromuscular physical therapy, 4:1323
  visual impairment, 5:1842
  See also Brain injuries
Head lice, 3:1125, 1126
Headaches, 3:**905–908**
  antiangina drug-induced, 1:143
  arteriovenous malformation-related, 1:230
  chronic kidney failure-related, 2:508
  cycloserine-induced, 1:209
  demographics, 3:906
  ginkgo biloba-induced, 3:879
  H-2 receptor blocker-induced, 3:899
  nonsteroidal anti-inflammatory drugs for, 4:1326
  osteopathic manipulation, 4:1369
  prevention, 3:907–908
  snoring-related, 5:1670
  spinal, 1:118
  tension, 3:905, 906–908
  vascular, 4:1266
  See also Migraine
Headgear, protective, 3:904
Healing. *See* Wound healing
Healing and the Mind (Moyers), 4:1270
Health
  eye examination, 2:769
  lifestyle, 2:661
  poor, 1:67
  seniors', 5:1611–1617
Health Aging DPG, 4:1348
Health care
  increased cost, 4:1209
  national, 3:805
  quality of, 3:**910–911**, 4:1334
  right to, 2:555
  travel, 5:1610
  universal, 4:1495
Health care costs. *See* Costs
Health care financing, 3:**908–910,** 909*t*, 4:1522
  Health Resources and Services Administration, 3:913–914
  home care, 3:980
  Medicare, 4:1238
  See also Costs
Health Care Financing Administration (HCFA), 4:1237, 1238
Health care proxy. *See* Durable power of attorney
Health care reform, 4:1430
Health centers, community, 3:913
Health education, 2:555
  See also Patient education
Health history, 3:**911–912**
  anxiety, 1:214
  chiropractic, 2:501
  dehydration, 2:604
  dementia, 2:612
  dislocations and subluxations, 2:687
  drug interactions, 2:710
  fecal incontinence, 3:798
  insomnia, 3:1050–1051
  mobility, 4:1284
  naturopathy, 4:1315
  neuromuscular physical therapy, 4:1324
  pain, 4:1394
  preoperative cardiac assessment, 4:1480–1481
  preoperative care, 4:1482
Health information, electronic, 4:1426, 1430–1431
Health insurance, 3:908–910
  AARP, 1:2
  AIDS tests, 1:58
  bariatric surgery, 1:286
  breast implants, 1:366
  breast reconstruction, 1:366
  commercial prescription programs, 2:548–550
  demographics, 4:1495
  emphysema, 2:741
  employer-based, 3:908–909, 4:1496
  government, 3:795, 4:1494, 1495–1496
  hip replacement, 3:966
  history, 3:908, 4:1495–1496
  vs. HMOs, 3:975–976
  home care, 3:979, 980
  homeopathic medicine, 3:988
  mammogram, 4:1205
  massage, 4:1217
  patient confidentiality, 4:1426
  patient satisfaction, 4:1475
  private, 4:1494–1496, 1494*t*
  sildenafil citrate, 5:1635
  supplemental, 4:1494*t,* 1495
  travel, 5:1610
  underinsurance, 3:910, 913
  See also Managed care plans; Medicaid; Medicare
Health Insurance Portability and Accountability Act (HIPAA), 4:1230, 1426, 1427
Health maintenance organizations. *See* HMOs

Health outcomes, 3:910
Health programs, community, 2:*554,* **554–555,** 3:913, 4:1227, 1229
Health promotion, 2:555, 4:1459
Health Resources and Services Administration (HRSA), 3:**913–914**
Healthcare Systems Bureau, 3:913
Healthy aging, 1:44–45, 47, 2:467
- exercise, 4:1523, 5:1611–1612, 1614
- nutrition, 4:1338–1341, 1523–1526, 5:1613–1614
- psychological and social issues, 4:1523–1526
- sexual activity, 5:1617–1618
- Weil, Andrew, 4:1525

Healthy Aging Project:, 4:1238
Healthy Eating 2010, 2:557
Healthy Eating Index (HEI), 2:674, 674*t*
Healthy People 2010, 3:959
Hearing aids, 3:**914–918,** *915,* 916*t,* 919, 5:1615
Hearing loss, 3:**918–921,** 918*t,* 5:1612–1613
- age-related, 3:919
- balance tests, 1:281
- conductive, 3:914–915, 918
- cranial nerve examination, 4:1322
- demographics, 3:918*t*
- falls, 3:790, 792
- mixed, 3:918
- noise-induced, 3:919
- sensorineural, 3:914–915, 918
- terminal illness, 2:600
- tinnitus, 5:1779–1780
- treatment, 3:920, 5:1615

Hearing tests, 1:*248,* 248–250
Heart anatomy and function, 1:*221,* 221–222, 2:427, 438, 441, *442,* 561, 3:924–925
Heart attacks, 3:*921,* **921–924,** 924–931
- angina pectoris, 1:123
- angiography-induced, 1:130
- angiotensin-converting enzyme inhibitors for, 1:132, 3:923, 928
- antiplatelet drugs for, 3:928
- arrhythmias, 1:225
- aspirin for, 1:234, 235, 3:928
- atherosclerosis, 1:248
- calcium supplements, 2:404
- cardiac catheterization-induced, 2:432
- cardiac monitor, 2:434
- cardiac rehabilitation, 2:436–438
- cardiopulmonary resuscitation, 2:448–451
- causes, 3:847, 922
- coronary artery disease-related, 2:579, 581
- diabetes mellitus-related, 2:640
- diuretic interactions, 2:692
- echocardiography, 2:723
- hypertension-related, 3:1010
- ischemia-related, 3:1073
- liver function tests, 3:1146
- low-fat diet, 3:1159
- marijuana-related, 4:1214
- mitral valve insufficiency from, 4:1280
- nitrates for, 3:923, 928
- nitroglycerin for, 1:143
- nuclear stress test, 4:1327
- orthostatic syncope, 3:787
- *vs.* panic disorder, 4:1409
- prevention, 1:143, 3:923
- psoriasis-related, 4:1521–1522
- sildenafil citrate-induced, 5:1637
- stress test-induced, 5:1719
- thrombolytic therapy for, 3:923, 928, 5:1767
- transient ischemic attacks, 5:1784–1785
- treatment, 3:923, 928
- ventricular fibrillation, 5:1824, 1825
- ventricular tachycardia, 5:1826

Heart block, 4:1387
Heart disease, 3:**924–931,** *925*
- alcohol consumption, 1:66
- amyloidosis, 1:101, 102
- blood clots, 1:321
- blood pressure, 1:324
- caffeine, 2:396
- cardiac rehabilitation, 2:436–438
- chest x rays, 2:499, 500
- congenital, 2:438, 3:924–931, 4:1255, 1282, 1539
- demographics, 3:924*t,* 925–926
- diabetes mellitus-related, 2:640
- diagnosis, 2:723–725, 730–732, 3:926–927
- diet, 3:929, 4:1339
- dizziness from, 2:698
- drug therapy, 3:927
- estrogens, 4:1250
- garlic for, 3:846–847
- general anesthesia, 1:114
- heatstroke risk, 3:937
- high-fiber diet, 3:958
- hormone replacement therapy, 3:991, 992, 4:1250, 5:1614
- hypokalemia, 2:737
- ischemic, 1:123–125, 324, 5:1824
- kidney transplantation contraindications, 3:1106
- lifestyle, 2:661
- low-fat diet, 3:1159
- low-sodium diet, 3:1159, 1161
- mortality, 3:925–926
- neuromuscular physical therapy, 4:1323
- nicotine-related, 5:1659–1660
- nuclear stress test, 4:1327–1329
- over fifty lifestyle, 2:662
- physical therapy, 4:1455
- postmenopausal women, 3:992
- preoperative cardiac assessment, 4:1480
- prevention, 2:416, 3:929–930
- rheumatic, 3:801, 924–931
- sildenafil citrate contraindications, 5:1634, 1636–1637
- sleep apnea, 5:1658
- smoking, 5:1661
- stroke risk, 5:1721
- vitamin E, 5:1857
- *See also* Coronary artery disease; Heart attacks

Heart failure
- calcium channel blocker-induced, 2:402
- cardiomyopathy-related, 2:445
- diastolic, 2:562
- myocarditis-related, 4:1309, 1310
- systolic, 2:562
- t'ai chi, 5:1748
- *See also* Congestive heart failure

Heart friction rub, 3:1179
Heart healthy diet
- atherosclerosis, 1:247, 5:1783
- cardiac rehabilitation, 2:437
- congestive heart failure, 2:563
- congestive heart failure prevention, 2:564

Heart-healthy lifestyle, 2:581
Heart-lung machine
- coronary artery bypass graft, 2:428, 580
- heart valve repair, 2:442, 443, 3:931
- minimally invasive cardiac surgery, 4:1273, 1275, 1276, 1277
- open heart surgery, 2:438–439

Heart monitor. *See* Cardiac monitor
Heart murmur, 5:1711
Heart rate, 5:1843–1846, 1844*t*
- autonomic nervous system, 1:262
- biofeedback, 1:301
- cardiac monitor, 2:433–436
- heart attacks, 3:923
- maximal, 5:1759
- normal, 1:225, 5:1846
- rapid, 5:1825
- stress test, 5:1716–1719
- target, 5:1759

Heart rhythm, irregular. *See* Arrhthymias
Heart scans, 1:124, 2:579, 5:1609
Heart surgery. *See* Cardiac surgery
Heart transplantation
- cardiomyopathy, 2:447
- congestive heart failure, 2:564
- myocarditis, 4:1310
- smoking after, 5:1668
- surgery, 2:438

Heart ultrasound. *See* Echocardiography
Heart valve disease
- aortic valve stenosis, 1:*211,* 221–225, 2:428, 3:931–932
- cardiac catheterization, 2:432
- cardiac surgery, 2:438

Heart valve disease *(continued)*
- echocardiography, 2:725
- mitral valve insufficiency, 2:441, 4:*1279,* 1279–1280
- mitral valve prolapse, 4:1280–1281
- mitral valve stenosis, 3:932, 4:1281–1282
- stenosis, 2:441
- treatment, 2:428, 441–445, 540, 564, 3:788, 931–933, *932*
- ventricular tachycardia, 5:1825

Heart valve repair, 2:441–445, 3:**931–933,** *932*
- aortic valve, 1:223–224, 2:428, 3:931–932
- cardiomyopathy, 2:447
- cardiovascular syncope, 3:788
- congestive heart failure, 2:564
- minimally invasive, 4:1274
- mitral valve, 2:428, 440, 447, 3:932, 4:1280
- mitral valve stenosis, 4:1282
- prophylactic antibiotics, 2:540
- pulmonary valve, 3:931–932
- staphylococcal infections, 5:1699–1700, 1701

Heart valves
- mechanical, 1:223, 224, 2:443, 444, 4:1280, 1295, 5:1699–1700, 1701, 1764
- MRSA infections, 4:1295
- tissue, 1:223–224, 2:443, 4:1280

Heartbeat. *See* Heart rate

Heartburn, 1:139–140, 3:**933–936,** *934*
- antacids for, 1:139–140
- gastroesophageal reflux disease, 3:853–858, 859
- H-2 receptor blockers for, 3:897–898
- proton pump inhibitors for, 4:1515
- scleroderma-related, 5:1597

Heat therapy
- amyotrophic lateral sclerosis, 1:104
- back and neck pain, 1:270
- boils, 1:334
- bursitis, 1:390
- contraindications, 1:268
- hydrotherapy, 3:1001
- low back pain, 3:1152
- mobility, 4:1285
- physical therapy, 4:1457
- psoriasis, 4:1520
- restless leg syndrome, 5:1657

Heatstroke, 3:**936–939,** *937*

Heavy alcohol consumption, 1:67

Heavy metals, 4:1299

Heberden's nodes, 4:1366

HEI (Healthy Eating Index), 2:674, *674t*

Heidelberg retinal tomography, 3:881

Height loss, 1:44

Helicobacter pylori, 3:939–941
- drug therapy, 3:940–941, 5:1799–1800
- garlic, 2:416
- peptic ulcers, 3:873, 939–941, 5:1797–1798, 1799
- probiotics, 4:1498
- stomach cancer, 5:1704, 1705, 1706

Helicobacteriosis, 3:**939–941**

Hellerwork, 4:1324

Helper T cells, 1:71

Hemangioma, 5:1648

Hemangiosarcoma, 3:1138

Hematemesis, 3:871

Hematocrit, 1:109, 2:560–561, 3:947, 1065

Hematologists, 2:412, 3:**941–943**

Hematomas
- epidural, 3:906
- retrobulbar, 1:318
- skin lesion removal-related, 5:1648
- subdural, 3:906
- venipuncture-related, 1:62

Hematoxylin-eosin stain, 1:341

Hematuria, 3:1092

Heme, 1:108, 109

Hemiplegia, 3:832, 833, 4:1417–1418, 5:1603, 1880

Hemispherectomy, 5:1604

Hemlock Society, 5:1734

Hemochromatosis, 3:**943–946,** *944*
- cirrhosis from, 2:522, 524
- iron tests, 3:1067
- liver biopsy, 3:1133
- liver cancer from, 3:1142

Hemodialysis, 2:650–651
- arteriovenous fistula from, 1:227–228
- chronic kidney failure, 2:509, 650–651
- itching from, 3:1082
- overdose, 4:1382

Hemoglobin
- iron binding function, 3:1067
- iron-deficiency anemia, 1:108, 3:1064, 1065
- liposuction, 3:1132
- multiple myeloma, 4:1300

Hemoglobin A1C, 1:179, 2:649

Hemoglobin tests, 2:560–561, 649, 3:1067

Hemoglobinopathies, 4:1539

Hemolytic anemia, 1:109, 110, 250, 3:1145

Hemolytic disease of the newborn, 3:1146

Hemophila, 3:849

Hemorrhage
- arteriovenous malformations, 1:229, 230–231
- GI bleeding, 3:871–875, 1064, 1065
- intracerebral, 5:1720
- intracranial, 3:902
- subarachnoid, 3:906
- thrombolytic therapy-related, 5:1767
- ulcer-associated, 5:1798
- vitreous, 2:650

Hemorrhagic cystitis, 2:594

Hemorrhagic shock, 3:873

Hemorrhagic stroke, 3:878, 5:1720, 1723

Hemorrhoidectomy, 3:798, 947

Hemorrhoids, 3:872, *946,* **946–949,** 958

Hemostatic clips, 3:873

Hepar sulphuris, 1:334

Heparin
- for cardiomyopathy, 2:447
- for deep vein thrombosis, 2:602, 5:1694
- GI bleeding from, 3:872
- nonsteroidal anti-inflammatory drug interactions, 4:1327
- for pulmonary embolism, 4:1534
- for stroke, 5:1722
- thrombocytopenia from, 5:1763
- for transient ischemic attacks, 5:1785

Heparin lock, 3:1061

Hepatectomy, 3:1140, 1141

Hepatic artery embolization, 3:1141

Hepatic cancer. *See* Liver cancer

Hepatic encephalopathy, 3:1145, 1146

Hepatitis, 3:*949*, **949–952**
- alcoholic, 3:950, 952
- autoimmune, 1:258–260, 3:950, 951
- autoimmune disease tests, 1:254
- avocados, 2:415
- dantrolene-induced, 4:1308
- demographics, 3:950
- diagnosis, 3:950–951, 1145, 1146
- drug-induced, 3:950, 952
- GI bleeding from, 3:871
- hypercholesterolemia from, 2:507
- isoniazid-induced, 1:209
- kidney transplantation contraindications, 3:1106
- liver cancer from, 3:951, 1138, 1139, 1142
- liver function tests, 3:1145, 1146
- myocarditis from, 4:1309
- prevention, 3:951–952
- treatment, 3:951
- vaccines, 3:951, 952, 5:1813

Hepatitis A, 3:949–952

Hepatitis B, 3:*949*, 949–952
- cirrhosis from, 2:522, 523, 524
- infection control, 3:1030
- liver function tests, 3:1145

Hepatitis C, 3:949–952, 5:1832–1834
- cirrhosis from, 2:522, 523, 524
- liver biopsy, 3:1133
- liver cancer from, 2:524, 3:1138, 1139
- liver function tests, 3:1145

Hepatitis D, 3:949–952

Hepatitis E, 3:950–952
Hepatoblastoma, 3:1138
Hepatocellular carcinoma, 3:1138, 1139, 1141
Hepatomas, 3:1139
Hepatomegaly, 1:101, 3:1133
HER-2 (Human epidermal growth factor receptor 2), 1:356, 358
Herbal medicine, 2:678, 4:1343
- adverse effects, 2:679
- anti-inflammatory diet, 1:195
- anxiety, 1:216
- arrhythmias, 1:227
- boils, 1:334
- cancer treatment side effects, 2:412
- cardiomyopathy, 2:447
- cirrhosis, 2:524
- cystitis, 2:595
- dermatitis, 2:631
- drug interactions, 2:709
- dry skin, 2:716
- erectile dysfunction, 2:757
- generalized anxiety disorder, 3:864
- hepatitis, 3:951
- high cholesterol, 3:955
- hyperlipoproteinemia, 3:1005
- hypertension, 1:326, 3:1011
- insomnia, 3:1051
- irritable bowel syndrome, 3:1071
- low back pain, 3:1152–1153
- menopause, 4:1252–1253
- naturopathy, 4:1315
- overactive bladder, 4:1379
- prostate cancer, 4:1509
- rheumatoid arthritis, 4:1574
- seizures, 5:1605
- sexual dysfunction, 5:1620
- smoking cessation, 5:1662
- substance abuse, 5:1727
- ulcers, 5:1800
- *See also* specific herbs

Herbicides, 4:1299
Herceptin. *See* Trastuzumab
Hereditary nonpolyposis colon cancer (HNPCC), 2:533
Hering, Constantine, 3:988
Hernia, hiatal, 3:854, 933
Herniated disks
- low back pain, 3:1151, 1152
- magnetic resonance imaging, 4:1190
- paralysis, 4:1417
- sciatica, 5:1592, 1593
- surgery, 5:1594

Herodotus, 4:1212
Heroin, 2:706, 4:1381, 5:1727
Herpes simplex
- cultures, 5:1625
- diarrhea, 2:654
- genital, 5:1622–1624
- ocular, 2:574

Herpes simplex-1 (HSV-1), 5:1622
Herpes simplex-2 (HSV-2), 5:1622, 1625
Herpes simplex keratitis, 5:1842
Herpes zoster. *See* Shingles
Herpes zoster ophthalmicus (HZO), 5:1630
Heterosexuality, 1:56–57
Heterotrophic ossification, 5:1693, 1694
HFE gene, 3:943, 944, 945
HFV (High frequency ventilation), 3:1048, 5:1822
HGPS (Hutchinson-Gilford progeria syndrome), 1:44–45
Hiatal hernia, 3:854, 933
Hib vaccine, 4:1248, 1256, 1258
Hibiclens, 4:1483
Hidradenitis suppurativa, 1:333
High altitude, 4:1567, 5:1870
High blood pressure. *See* Hypertension
High blood sugar. *See* Hyperglycemia
High calcium levels. *See* Hypercalcemia
High cholesterol, 2:516–520, 3:**953–956**
- causes, 3:953–954
- coronary artery disease risk, 2:578
- DASH Diet, 1:325, 2:672
- demographics, 3:953
- diabetic nephropathy risk, 2:643
- diagnosis, 2:505–507, 3:954
- diet, 3:955, 956
- dietary counseling, 2:671
- drug therapy, 2:519, 3:953*t,* 955, 1004–1005
- exercise, 3:955
- heart attack risk, 3:922
- high-fiber diet, 3:958
- hyperlipoproteinemia, 3:*1002,* 1002–1005, 1003
- ischemia risk, 3:1074
- niacin for, 5:1862
- probiotics for, 4:1498
- stroke risk, 5:1721, 1723
- treatment, 2:519, 3:954–955
- vitamin C for, 5:1852
- vitamin E for, 5:1857
- water exercise, 5:1874, 1875
- *See also* Cholesterol-lowering drugs

High-density lipoproteins (HDL)
- alcohol consumption, 3:929
- atherosclerosis, 1:246
- cholesterol tests, 2:518, 3:954
- coronary artery disease, 2:578
- DHEA interactions, 2:635
- exercise, 3:955
- garlic, 3:847
- hyperlipoproteinemia, 3:1002–1005
- low-cholesterol diet, 3:1154, 1155
- niacin, 3:955
- normal/high levels, 3:954
- role, 2:505, 3:953
- zinc, 5:1897

High enemas, 2:753
High-fat diet
- adverse effects, 2:663
- Alzheimer's disease risk, 1:88
- cancer risk, 2:661
- colon cancer risk, 2:533
- gallstone risk, 3:838, 839
- prostate cancer risk, 4:1505
- seborrheic dermatitis risk, 5:1600
- for seizures, 5:1604

High-fiber diet, 3:**957–959**
- autonomic disorders, 1:264
- colon cancer prevention, 2:533, 537
- constipation, 2:569, 570, 754
- diverticular disease, 2:694, 695–696
- hemorrhoids, 3:948
- high cholesterol, 3:956
- osteoarthritis, 4:1368
- varicose veins, 5:1818
- *See also* Fiber (Dietary)

High frequency hearing loss, 3:919
High frequency ventilation (HFV), 3:1048, 5:1822
High-grade squamous intraepithelial lesion (HSIL), 2:482–483, 4:1414, 1415
High potassium levels. *See* Hyperkalemia
Higher power, 4:1476
Highly active antiretroviral therapy (HAART), 1:52, 54
Hinge joints, 3:1086
HIP (Hospital Infections Program), 3:1030
Hip bursitis, 1:388, 389, 390, 391
Hip fractures, 3:**959–961**
- alcohol abuse, 1:66
- diagnosis, 3:791
- fall-related, 3:790, 960
- hip replacement, 3:964
- proton pump inhibitor-related, 3:857, 4:1516–1517
- rehabilitation, 3:**959–961**
- smoking, 5:1660

Hip joint
- anatomy and function, 3:959, 960, 1086
- osteoarthritis, 4:1366
- pain, 3:962–963, 965–966, 969
- polymyalgia rheumatica, 4:1466–1467
- sciatica, 5:1592

Hip replacement, 3:*962,* **962–970**
- acupuncture, 1:19
- deep vein thrombosis from, 2:602
- demographics, 3:964
- hip fractures, 3:960, 961
- lifespan, 3:968
- minimally invasive, 3:964, 965
- mobility, 4:1285
- osteoarthritis, 5:1615, 1617
- postoperative care, 3:967

Hip replacement *(continued)*
preoperative preparation, 3:966–967
recovery at home, 4:1555–1556
revision surgery, 3:964, 965, 968, 970–975
wound healing, 5:1664
Hip revision surgery, 3:964, 965, 968, **970–975,** *971*
HIPAA (Health Insurance Portability and Accountability Act), 4:1230, 1426, 1427
Hippocampus, 1:212
Hippocrates, 1:234, 2:501, 3:987, 4:1215, 1269
Hippocratic Oath, 2:762, 4:1233–1234, 1425
Hirsutism, 3:897
Hismanal. *See* Astemizole
Hispanics
AIDS, 5:1622
angina pectoris, 3:1073
breast cancer, 1:352
cervical cancer, 2:481
community health programs, 2:554
dementia, 2:611
diabetes mellitus, 2:639
diabetic nephropathy, 2:643
end-stage renal disease, 3:1104
gallbladder cancer, 3:835
gallstones, 3:838
glaucoma, 3:880, 5:1836
grandparent child care, 3:795
heart disease, 3:926
influenza vaccines, 3:1041
iron-deficiency anemia, 3:1064
lactose intolerance, 3:819
low vision, 3:1163
lung cancer, 1:382
lupus, 3:1179
osteoporosis, 1:335
prayer and spirituality, 4:1477
sildenafil citrate, 5:1634
snoring, 5:1671
stroke, 5:1721
suicide, 5:1733
tuberculosis, 5:1791
Histamine
allergies, 1:70, 72, 76
antihistamines, 1:186
common cold, 2:552
food allergies, 3:815
H-1 receptors, 3:897
inflammation, 1:194
itching, 1:141
See also Antihistamines
Histamine receptor blocking agents, 3:855–856
cephalosporin interactions, 1:153
for gastroesophageal reflux disease, 3:857
for helicobacteriosis, 3:940
See also H-1 receptor blockers; H-2 receptor blockers
Histiocytomas, malignant fibrous, 5:1583
Histoplasma capsulatum, 3:825, 826
Histoplasmosis, 3:825, 826, 1163
History. *See* Health history
Histotoxic anoxia, 1:138
Histrionic personality disorder, 4:1445–1448
Hitler, Adolf, 2:763
HIV (Human immunodeficiency virus), 1:48–56, 49*t*
blood tests, 5:1626
chlamydia, 5:1621
counseling, 1:56–59
demographics, 1:50, 3:1034, 5:1622
garlic-drug interactions, 3:847, 849, 850
gingivitis risk, 3:876
Health Resources and Services Administration funding, 3:913–914
human papilloma virus, 2:481
infection control, 3:1030
melanoma, 4:1198–1199
misdiagnosis, 5:1621
myocarditis from, 4:1309
pulmonary hypertension from, 4:1539
screening tests, 5:1623
T cells, 3:1023
tests, 1:51, 56, 58, 59–64
thrombocytopenia from, 5:1764
transmission, 1:50, 57, 5:1621
tuberculosis prevention, 5:1795
Veterans Affairs hospital system, 5:1828
See also AIDS
HIV-AIDS Bureau, 3:913–914
HIV-associated dementia, 5:1623
Hives, 1:70, 74, 3:815
HLA (Human leukocyte antigen), 2:472
HMG-CoA reductase inhibitors, 3:953*t*, 955, 1004
HMOs (Health maintenance organizations), 3:**975–977,** 4:1209, 1496
commercial prescription programs, 2:548
home care, 3:980
Medicare prescription drug plan, 4:1239
patient rights, 4:1430
vs. preferred provider organizations, 4:1475
referrals, 3:805, 4:1475
HNPCC (Hereditary nonpolyposis colon cancer), 2:533
Hoarseness, 5:1772
Hobbies, 4:1523
Hobby groups, 3:1079
HOCM (Hypertrophic obstructive cardiomyopathy), 2:445
Hodgkin's disease, 1:100, 339, 3:1146, 4:1193–1197
Holistic health, 4:1317
Holocaust survivors, 4:1469
Holter monitoring, 2:446, 3:**977–979,** 5:1783
Home Access System, 1:61
Home care, 3:**979–982**
discharge planning, 2:685–686
emphysema, 2:741
hip replacement, 3:966–967
hip revision surgery, 3:974
hospice care, 2:597–598
hospices, 3:995–996
licensed practical nurses, 3:1130
oxygen therapy, 2:741, 3:1047, 1048, 4:1385
teeth whitening, 5:1751–1752
Home health aides, 3:979, **982–984,** 4:1444
Home health nurses, 4:1558, 1559
Home maintenance, 3:998
Home modifications
activities of daily living, 1:10
dementia, 2:613
fall prevention, 3:792, 960, 5:1615
hip replacement, 3:966–967
mobility, 4:1285, 1286
personal hygiene, 4:1444
spinal cord injuries, 5:1691, 1694
walking problems, 5:1868
Home parenteral nutrition (HPN), 4:1342
Home safety, 3:**984–986**
See also Home modifications
Home tests
AIDS, 1:61
blood sugar, 1:179, 328
hepatitis, 3:950–951
Homelessness, 5:1828
Homemakers, 4:1444
Homeopathic medicine, 3:**986–990**
arrhythmias, 1:227
cancer treatment side effects, 2:412
cirrhosis, 2:524
cystitis, 2:595
dermatitis, 2:631
gastroesophageal reflux disease, 3:856
itching, 3:1082
kidney stones, 3:1102
low back pain, 3:1153
neuralgia, 4:1319
overactive bladder, 4:1379
polymyositis, 4:1468
sexual dysfunction, 5:1620
snoring, 5:1675
Homeostasis, electrolyte, 2:734
Homicide, 4:1426
Homocysteine, 3:811, 847, 5:1847
Homografts, cardiac valve, 2:443

Homosexuality, 1:56, 57, 3:794
Honey, 3:1082
Hong Kong flu pandemic, 3:1038
Hops, 3:1051
Hormone replacement therapy (HRT), 3:*990*, **990–995,** 991*t,* 4:1250–1251, 1254
- blood clot risk, 1:321
- breast cancer risk, 1:359, 3:992, 4:1204, 1250, 1251, 5:1614
- dementia risk, 3:992, 5:1614
- DHEA interactions, 2:635
- for dyskinesia, 1:201
- heart disease precautions, 3:991, 992, 4:1250, 5:1614
- for menopause, 3:900–905, 4:1250–1251, 1254, 5:1614
- for osteoporosis, 3:991, 992, 993, 4:1251, 1372, 5:1616
- ovarian cancer risk, 4:1375
- post-hysterectomy, 3:1018
- for sexual dysfunction, 5:1620
- stroke risk, 5:1721
- vitamin D interactions, 5:1855
- *See also* Estrogen replacement therapy

Hormone therapy
- for breast cancer, 1:358
- for cancer, 2:411
- for endometrial cancer, 2:745
- post-lumpectomy, 3:1170
- for prostate cancer, 4:1508
- for thyroid cancer, 5:1771

Hormones
- edema from, 2:726
- growth, 2:564
- irritable bowel syndrome, 3:1069
- sex, 1:155
- varicose veins, 5:1816

Horner's syndrome, 1:263–264
Horsetail, 4:1379
Horton's disease, 1:*257*
Hospice Foundation of America, 3:995
Hospices, 3:**995–997**
- bereavement counseling, 1:296
- death and dying, 2:597–598, 3:995–997
- lung cancer, 3:1177

Hospital-acquired infections
- bronchoscopy equipment, 1:384
- fungal, 3:825
- infection control, 3:1029–1032
- MRSA, 1:278, 4:1293, 1294, 1295, 1296
- staphylococcal, 5:1699

Hospital beds, 3:789
Hospital Infections Program (HIP), 3:1030
Hospitalization
- alcohol-related, 1:67
- attempted suicide, 5:1734
- complications after, 2:686
- discharge planning, 2:685–686
- length of stay, 3:979

Hospitals
- accreditation, 3:806
- acute care, 3:1130
- discharge from, 2:684–686
- infection control, 3:1029
- infectious diseases, 3:1033
- Medicaid payments, 4:1229
- preferred provider organizations, 4:1475
- registered nurses, 4:1557, 1558, 1559
- smoke-free, 5:1666
- social workers, 5:1677
- Veterans Affairs, 5:1826–1829

Hot climates, 5:1870
Hot compresses. *See* Heat therapy
Hot flashes, 4:1250, 1251, 1252, 1253
- aerobic exercise, 1:38
- rosacea, 4:1578–1579
- sleep disorders, 5:1655

Hot-lunch programs, 4:1227
Hot tubs, 5:1874
Hotlines, pet grief, 1:296
Household management, 3:**997–999**
- *See also* Home modifications; Home safety

Housekeeping, 3:997–998
Housing, social issues, 4:1523
HPN (Home parenteral nutrition), 4:1342
HPV. *See* Human papilloma virus
HRSA (Health Resources and Services Administration), 3:**913–914**
HRT. *See* Hormone replacement therapy
HRT II, 3:881
HSIL (High-grade squamous intraepithelial lesion), 2:482–483, 4:1414, 1415
HSV-1 (Herpes simplex-1), 5:1622
HSV-2 (Herpes simplex-2), 5:1622, 1625
Huffing, 2:496
Humalog, 3:1054
Human development, 4:1523, 1526–1528, 1560
Human epidermal growth factor receptor 2 (HER-2), 1:356, 358
Human growth factors, 4:1490
Human immunodeficiency virus. *See* HIV
Human leukocyte antigen (HLA), 2:472
Human Nutrition Research Center, 4:1465
Human papilloma virus (HPV), 2:481–482
- cervical cancer risk, 2:408, 483, 4:1412–1413, 5:1622, 1623, 1625–1626
- cultures, 5:1625–1626
- demographics, 2:481, 5:1622
- DNA testing, 4:1413, 1415, 5:1625–1626
- oral cancer risk, 4:1359
- sexually transmitted, 5:1621–1624
- vaccines, 2:485, 5:1623

Humphry, Derek, 5:1734
Humules, 4:1213
Hunchback, 1:271
Hunger headache, 3:905
Huntington's chorea
- dysarthria from, 5:1687, 1689
- gait and balance disorders, 3:832
- psychoses from, 4:1528

Hutchinson-Gilford progeria syndrome (HGPS), 1:44–45
Hutchinson v. United States, 3:1045
Hyalgan. *See* Hyaluronan
Hyaline cartilage, 3:1085, 1086, 1087
Hyaluronan, 4:1367
Hyaluronic acid, 2:523, 3:1117, 4:1367
Hydantoins, 1:159*t,* 160
Hydergine, 1:381
Hydralazine, 1:191, 2:563, 3:1178
Hydrastis canadensis. See Goldenseal
Hydration, 2:603–604, 5:1870–1873, 1882
Hydrazine sulfate, 2:746
Hydrocephalus, 3:903
Hydrochloric acid, 3:811, 5:1800, 1847
Hydrochlorothiazide, 2:690, 691
- for congestive heart failure, 2:563
- for diabetes insipidus, 2:637
- for hypertension, 1:189, 3:1010
- insulin interactions, 3:1056

Hydrocortisone, 3:1180, 4:1520, 5:1600
HydroDIURIL. *See* Hydrochlorothiazide
Hydrogen, 4:1191
Hydrogen breath test, 3:1122
Hydrogen peroxide therapy, 4:*1383,* **1383–1386**
- pressure sores, 4:1490
- teeth whitening, 5:1751

Hydrogenated oils, 3:1154
Hydrotherapy, 3:**999–1002,** *1000*
- back and neck pain, 1:269
- contrast, 3:892
- itching, 2:631, 3:1081, 1082
- mobility, 4:1285
- naturopathy, 4:1316
- pressure sores, 4:1490
- substance abuse, 5:1727
- *vs.* t'ai chi, 5:1747
- tendinitis, 5:1754

Hydrotherapy *(continued)*
water exercise, 5:1873–1876
whirlpool, 1:104, 3:1000–1001, 4:1490, 5:1886
Hydroureter, 3:1101
Hydroxy acids, 1:83–85
Hydroxychalcone, 2:515
Hydroxychloroquine, 3:1180, 4:1574
Hydroxyurea, 5:1766
Hydroxyzine, 1:141–142, 187
Hygiene
gastroenteritis prevention, 3:852
immunocompromised patients, 3:1025
meningitis prevention, 4:1248
sleep, 5:1657, 1658
See also Hand washing; Oral hygiene; Personal hygiene
Hygroton. *See* Chlorthalidone
Hylan G-F20, 4:1367
Hyothalamic-pituitary-adrenal system, 1:212
Hyperactive delirium, 2:607
Hyperadrenocorticism. *See* Cushing's syndrome
Hyperbaric oxygen therapy, 3:1046–1049, 4:1384, 1385
gangrene, 3:844
pressure sores, 4:1490
wound care, 5:1886
Hyperbilirubinemia, neonatal, 3:1144
Hypercalcemia, 2:399
calcium supplement-induced, 2:404
diabetes insipidus from, 2:637
electrolyte balance, 2:736
hyperparathyroidism-related, 3:1006–1007
multiple myeloma-related, 4:1299–1300
parathyroid cancer-related, 4:1419
symptoms, 4:1299–1300
Hypercapnia, 4:1567
Hypercholesteremia. *See* High cholesterol
Hypercortisolism. *See* Cushing's syndrome
Hyperglycemia
blood sugar tests, 1:327–330
carbohydrates, 2:423
coma from, 2:545
Cushing's syndrome, 2:592
symptoms, 3:1055
Hyperhydrosis, 1:345, 347
Hyperkalemia, 2:737
Hyperlipidemia. *See* Hyperlipoproteinemia
Hyperlipoproteinemia, 3:*1002*, **1002–1005**
Hypermagnesemia, 2:737, 3:1124
Hypernatremia, 2:735, 5:1680
Hyperopia, 4:1354
Hyperosmotic laxatives, 3:1123
Hyperoxia, 4:1389
Hyperparathyroidism, 3:**1005–1007,** *1006,* 4:1392, 1419
Hyperplasia
endometrial, 2:743, 3:1016
parathyroid, 3:1006
Hypersecretory syndromes, 3:897–898, 5:1798
Hypersensitivity disorders. *See* Allergies
Hypersensitivity, food. *See* Food allergies
Hypersplenism, 2:561
Hypertension, 1:324–326, 2:516–520, 3:**1007–1012,** *1010*
alcohol abuse, 1:64
$alpha_1$ adrenergic blockers for, 1:81–83
aneurysm, 1:121
angiotensin-converting enzyme inhibitors for, 1:132
aortic dissection, 1:219
arteriovenous malformations, 1:229
atherosclerosis risk, 1:245, 246
beta blockers for, 1:140–141, 191, 297–299, 297*t,* 325
blood clots, 1:322
caffeine precautions, 2:396
calcium channel blockers for, 1:191, 2:401–403
cataracts from, 2:462
causes, 3:1009, 5:1680–1681
chronic kidney failure from, 2:508, 510
coronary artery disease risk, 2:578
Cushing's syndrome, 2:592
demographics, 1:324–325, 2:517, 3:1008*t,* 1009
DHEA precautions, 2:635
diabetic nephropathy risk, 2:643
diagnosis, 1:189, 325, 3:1009–1010
diet, 1:325, 326, 3:1011–1012, 4:1534
drug therapy, 1:189–193, *190,* 190*t,* 325, 3:1010–1011, 1011*t*
end-stage renal disease risk, 3:1104
exercise, 1:325, 326, 3:1010, 1012, 5:1759
forgiveness, 4:1552
garlic for, 3:847
gender differences, 1:325, 3:869, 1009
gout, 3:894
headache from, 3:905, 906
heart attack risk, 3:922
ischemia risk, 3:1074, 1076
isolated systolic, 3:1008–1009
kidney cancer risk, 3:1092
low-sodium diet, 3:1161, 5:1680
meditation, 5:1892
minoxidil for, 4:1277–1279
orthostatic syncope, 3:787
portal, 1:129, 2:523, 3:1148
postmenopausal women, 3:992
prayer and spirituality, 4:1478
prevention, 1:326, 2:520, 3:1012
probiotics for, 4:1498
pulmonary, 2:401, 4:1534, 1539–1541, 1569
pulmonary embolism from, 4:1534
relaxation techniques, 4:1564, 1565
risk factors, 3:1009
scleroderma-related, 5:1598
shiatsu, 5:1628
sleep apnea, 5:1653
smoking-related, 5:1665
sodium, 5:1680–1681
stroke risk, 3:1010, 5:1721, 1723
symptoms, 2:518
therapeutic exercise contraindications, 5:1760
tinnitus from, 5:1779, 1780
treatment, 1:189, 325–326, 2:519, 3:1010–1012
water exercise, 5:1874
white-coat, 1:90–91, 3:1009
See also Antihypertensive drugs
Hyperthermia
malignant, 1:117, 4:1307
for metastasis, 4:1264–1265
Hyperthermic isolated limb perfusion, 4:1200
Hyperthyroidism, 3:**1013–1015**
alopecia from, 1:80
beta blocker precautions, 1:299
demographics, 3:1013, 5:1769
electrolyte tests, 2:739
low cholesterol, 2:507
thyroid function tests, 5:1773, 1774
thyroid nuclear medicine scans, 5:1775
Hypertonicity, 3:833
Hypertriglyceridemia, 3:1002
Hypertrophic cardiomyopathy, 2:445, 3:**1014–1015**
Hypertrophic obstructive cardiomyopathy (HOCM), 2:445
Hypertrophy, 4:1322
Hyperuricemia, 3:891–892
Hyperventilation, 2:739
Hyperviscous blood, 4:1302
Hyphae, 3:822, 824, 825
Hypnosis
polymyositis, 4:1468
self-hypnosis, 4:1272
smoking cessation, 5:1662, 1667
substance abuse, 5:1727
tinnitus, 5:1780
Hypnotics, 1:140
Hypoactive delirium, 2:607
Hypocalcemia, 2:399, 403–404, 4:1339
calcium supplements for, 4:1336

Hypocalcemia *(continued)*
- electrolyte balance, 2:736
- Paget's disease of bone, 4:1392

Hypocapnia, 4:1389

Hypochlorhydria, 3:869

Hypochondriacs, 1:260

Hypodermic syringes, 5:1608, 1609

Hypoglycemia
- antiarrhythmic drug-induced, 1:147, 148
- blood sugar tests, 1:327, 330
- cinnamon-induced, 2:515–516
- insulinoma-related, 4:1403
- sulfonylurea-induced, 1:179
- symptoms, 2:516, 3:1055

Hypogonadism, 5:1652

Hypokalemia, 1:191, 2:737

Hypomagnesemia, 2:737

Hypomania, 1:302, 304

Hyponatremia, 2:735, 3:1162, 5:1680, 1871

Hypoparathyroidism, 2:736

Hypophosphatemia, familial, 5:1854, 1863

Hypoproteinemia, 2:736

Hypotension, 1:324–326
- angiotensin-converting enzyme inhibitor-related, 1:133, 191
- demographics, 1:325
- falls, 3:790
- GI bleeding-related, 3:872
- hypoxia, 1:326
- orthostatic, 1:263, 264, 265, 3:787
- portal, 1:134–135
- postural, 1:324
- sildenafil citrate-induced, 5:1634, 1636
- tizanidine-induced, 4:1308

Hypothalmus, 2:590, 636–637

Hypothermia, 4:1556

Hypothyroidism
- alopecia from, 1:80
- blood clots, 1:322
- congenital, 4:1256, 1258
- demographics, 5:1769
- depression, 2:624
- headaches from, 3:906
- hypercholesterolemia from, 2:507
- hyperlipoproteinemia-related, 3:1003
- thyroid function tests, 5:1773, 1774
- thyroid nuclear medicine scans, 5:1775, 1776
- triglyceride levels, 3:953

Hypoventilation, 3:1048

Hypoxemia, 3:1047, 4:1567

Hypoxemic anoxia, 1:137

Hypoxemic respiratory failure, 4:1567

Hypoxia, 1:137–138, 326, 4:1528

Hypoxic encephalopathy, 5:1602

Hypromellose, 2:780

Hyssop, 5:1605

Hysterectomy, 3:**1015–1019,** *1016*
- endometrial cancer, 2:745, 3:1016, 1017
- estrogen replacement therapy after, 4:1250
- laparoscopic, 2:484
- radical, 2:484, 3:1017
- subtotal, 3:1015–1018, *1016*
- testosterone after, 4:1252
- total, 2:483, 484, 3:*1016,* 1016–1017, 4:1413

Hysteroscopic myomectomy, 3:1019

Hysteroscopy, 2:745

Hytrin. *See* Terazosin

HZO (Herpes zoster ophthalmicus), 5:1630

I

IADLs. *See* Instrumental activities of daily living

Ibandronate, 4:1372

IBIDS lDatabase (International Bibliographic Information on Dietary Supplements), 2:678

IBS. *See* Irritable bowel syndrome

Ibuprofen, 4:1326
- for bursitis, 1:390
- for cervical spondylosis, 2:488
- for common colds, 2:552
- gastroesophageal reflux disease from, 3:854
- for gout, 3:891
- for hip replacement pain, 3:969
- hydroxyzine interactions, 1:142
- hypertension from, 3:1009
- for inflammation, 1:194
- for knee injuries, 3:1117
- liver biopsy contraindications, 3:1136
- for low back pain, 3:1152
- for lupus, 3:1180
- for migraines, 4:1267
- for osteoarthritis, 3:883–884, 1117, 4:1367, 5:1615
- for Paget's disease of bone, 4:1392
- for pain, 4:1395
- for pericarditis, 4:1432
- for polymyositis, 4:1468
- for prostate enlargement, 4:1512
- for sciatica, 5:1593
- for spinal stenosis, 5:1697
- SSRI interactions, 1:173
- for strep throat, 5:1711–1712
- for tendinitis, 5:1754
- terzosin interactions, 1:83
- for trigger finger, 5:1788

ICD (International Classification of Diseases), 4:1231

Ice packs. *See* Cold therapy

Ichthyosis. *See* Dry skin

ICU psychoses, 4:1528, 1529

Idiopathic hypertrophic subaortic stenosis (IHSS), 2:445, 3:1014

Idiopathic pulmonary fibrosis, 4:1536

Idiopathic pulmonary hemochromatosis, 3:943, 944, 945

IDL (Intermediate-density lipoproteins), 2:505, 3:1002

IF (Intrinsic factor), 5:1847

IFA (Immunofluorescent assay), 1:60, 5:1650

IFFGD (International Foundation for Functional Gastrointestinal Disorders), 3:1069, 1070, 1071

Ifosfamide, 1:309

IgE (immunoglobulin E), 1:70, 74, 75, 3:815, 816, 817

IgG (Immunoglobulin G), 1:252, 254, 257, 3:1023

IgM (Immunoglobulin M), 1:252, 254, 257

IGT (Impaired glucose tolerance), 1:330, 2:641

IHSS (Idiopathic hypertrophic subaortic stenosis), 2:445, 3:1014

Ileitis, granulomatous, 1:100

Ileus, gallstone, 3:838

Iloprost, 4:1537, 1540

ILV (Independent lung ventilation), 5:1822

Imagery
- guided, 4:1377, 1468
- mind/body medicine, 4:1272
- movement therapy, 4:1291
- relaxation techniques, 4:1564
- *See also* Visualization

Imaging studies
- amyotrophic lateral sclerosis, 1:104
- aneurysm, 1:121
- anxiety, 1:215
- bladder cancer, 1:308
- bladder stones, 1:313
- brain and central nervous system tumors, 1:349
- cancer, 2:409
- chiropractic, 2:501
- cirrhosis, 2:523
- colon cancer, 2:535
- Cushing's syndrome, 2:591
- exocrine pancreatic cancer, 4:1405
- gangrene, 3:844
- headache, 3:907
- liver cancer, 3:1139–1140
- low back pain, 3:1152
- lymphoma, 4:1195
- oral cancers, 4:1358
- osteoarthritis, 4:1366–1367
- Paget's disease of bone, 4:1390

Imaging studies *(continued)*
paralysis, 4:1418
persistent vegetative state, 4:1440
prostate cancer, 4:1506
speech disorders, 5:1688–1689
spinal cord injuries, 5:1693
spinal stenosis, 5:1697
staphylococcal infections, 5:1701
tinnitus, 5:1780
ulcers, 5:1799
See also specific types
Imatinib mesylate, 4:1537
Imbalance, 2:696–698
Imidazopyrines, 5:1657
Imipramine, 1:175
anticonvulsant drug interactions, 1:162
for anxiety, 1:215
bronchodilator interactions, 1:380
for generalized anxiety disorder, 3:863
for panic disorder, 4:1411
for seizures, 1:161
for urinary incontinence, 5:1805
Imitrex. *See* Sumatriptan
Immigration, 2:554
Immune globulin. *See* Immunoglobulins
Immune response, 1:256–257, 3:1021, 1024
aging, 5:1612
allergies, 1:70, 71
allergy tests, 1:74
bacterial infections, 1:277, 278
chronic infections, 3:1024
effectiveness, 3:1033
massage, 4:1219
Immune system, 3:*1021*, **1021–1025**
depression, 2:628
description, 1:256–257
diet, 2:659
nervous system interactions, 4:1270
oxygen/ozone therapy, 4:1384
probiotics, 4:1498
stress response, 1:212–213
T and B cells, 4:1194
zinc deficiency, 5:1898
Immune system disorders, 1:114, 3:1022–1025
Immune system stimulation, 5:1627
Immunity
acquired, 3:1021
natural, 3:1021, 5:1813
Immunization. *See* Vaccinations
Immunoblot test, 1:60
Immunochromatographic assay, 1:60–61
Immunocompromised patients
bacteremia, 1:275
bruising, 1:386
cellulitis, 2:477
common cold, 2:550
fungal infections, 3:824, 826
infections, 3:1025
lymphoma, 4:1195
melanoma, 4:1198–1199
meningitis, 4:1247–1248
MRSA infections, 4:1296
Pneumocystitis carinii pneumonia, 4:1464, 1466
psoriasis, 4:1519
sexually transmitted diseases, 5:1621
shingles, 5:1630
skin cancer, 5:1642
staphylococcal infections, 5:1702
tuberculosis, 5:1790
viral infections, 5:1831, 1834–1835
VZV vaccine, 5:1632
Immunodeficiency
common variable, 3:1023
primary, 3:1022
viral infections, 5:1834–1835
See also AIDS; Immunocompromised patients
Immunofluorescence assay (IFA), 1:60, 5:1650
Immunofluorescence, direct/indirect, 1:251, 253
Immunoglobulin E (IgE)
allergies, 1:70, 74, 75
food allergies, 3:815, 816, 817
Immunoglobulin G (IgG)
autoimmune disease tests, 1:252, 254
common variable immunodeficiency, 3:1023
infectious diseases, 1:257
Immunoglobulin M (IgM), 1:252, 254, 257
Immunoglobulins
for hepatitis, 3:951
for polymyositis, 4:1468
for respiratory syncytial virus, 5:1833
role, 3:1022
Immunohistochemistry, 5:1585
Immunologic disease. *See* Immune system disorders
Immunologic therapies. *See* Immunotherapy
Immunologists, 1:76
Immunoprecipitation, 1:252
Immunosenescence, 3:1033
Immunosorbent assay, D-dimer, 4:1533
Immunosuppression. *See* Immunocompromised patients
Immunosuppressive agents
for autoimmune disorders, 1:259
bacterial infection risk, 1:278
cellulitis risk, 2:477
for hepatitis, 3:951
infection precautions, 3:1025
for kidney transplantation, 3:1106, 1107
for lupus, 3:1180
lymphoma from, 4:1195
Medicare, 3:1106, 4:1240
side effects, 3:1107
for Sjögren's syndrome, 5:1639
Immunotherapy
allergen, 1:243
bladder cancer, 1:309
cancer therapy, 2:411
exocrine pancreatic cancer, 4:1407
kidney cancer, 3:1093
melanoma, 4:1200
metastasis, 4:1264
skin cancer, 5:1643
Imodium-AD. *See* Loperamide
Impaired glucose tolerance (IGT), 1:330, 2:641
Implantable cardioverter-defibrillator, 1:226, 3:1015, **1025–1026**
airport security, 5:1608–1609
arrhythmias, 1:226
hypertrophic cardiomyopathy, 3:1015
ventricular fibrillation, 5:1825
ventricular tachycardia, 5:1826
Implants
cochlear, 3:916–917
contact lenses, 2:774
dental, 2:618–620, 4:1361
endosteal, 2:618
femoral, 3:972
metal, 4:1191
penile, 2:757
subperiosteal, 2:619
See also Breast implants
Implied consent, 4:1426
Impotence. *See* Erectile dysfunction
Improvisational dance, 4:1291–1292
Impulse control, 4:1446
IMT (Intermittent motorized traction), 1:269–270
In-the-canal hearing aids, 3:916
In-the-ear hearing aids, 3:916
Incentive spirometry, 2:496–497, 3:1046–1049
Incipient presbyopia, 4:1485
Incision care, 4:1555
Incisional biopsy. *See* Surgical biopsy
Inclusion body myositis, 4:1467
Income
community health programs, 2:554–555
health care costs, 4:1522
over fifty lifestyle, 2:662
See also Socioeconomic factors
Incompetent patients
advance directives, 1:32
euthanasia, 2:763
financial management, 3:803
informed consent, 4:1483
patient confidentiality, 4:1427
patient representative, 4:1428–1429

Incontinence. *See* Fecal incontinence; Urinary incontinence
Indacin. *See* Indomethacin
Indapamide, 1:189
Independence, 3:**1026–1029,** 1027*t*
driver safety, 2:703, 705
exercise, 2:767
falls, 3:792
family relationships, 3:793, 794
financial management, 3:803
functional, 3:1027
home care, 3:980
Independent living facilities, 1:236–237
Independent lung ventilation (ILV), 5:1822
Independent practice associations (IPA), 3:976, 4:1209
Inderal. *See* Propranolol
Indian Health Service, 3:909–910
Indian hemp, 4:1211
Indian tobacco. *See* Lobelia
Indians. *See* Native Americans
Indigestion, acid, 1:139–140
Indirect immunofluorescence, 1:251, 253
Indirect pharyngoscopy, 4:1358
Individualism, 3:793
Indocyanine green angiography, 1:41
Indole-3-carbinol, 1:358, 2:415
Indoles, 2:416
Indomethacin
angiotensin-converting enzyme inhibitor interactions, 1:134
for gout, 3:891
liver function test interactions, 3:1143
for pain, 4:1395
peptic ulcers from, 5:1798
Industrialization, 2:657
Indwelling catheters
MRSA infections, 4:1295
pleural effusion, 4:1461
staphylococcal infections, 5:1701, 1703
urinary, 2:465–467, 468–471
Infants
bone marrow biopsy and aspiration, 1:341
cardiopulmonary resuscitation, 2:450
diarrhea, 2:655
enemas, 2:752, 753
low birth weight, 5:1856
massage, 4:1218
newborn, 3:1048, 4:1247, 5:1756
premature, 4:1218
relationships, 4:1560
Infection control, 3:**1029–1032**
Infections
acute, 1:277, 3:1032
amputation-related, 1:99
bladder, 1:310–312
bloodborne, 3:1030, 1031
bone and joint, 3:1034
chemotherapy-related, 1:156, 2:492
chronic, 1:277, 3:1024, 1032
community-aquired, 1:278–279, 4:1293, 1294, 1295, 1296, 5:1700, 1702
corneal, 2:574
diagnosis, 2:560
garlic for, 3:847
latent, 3:1032
opportunistic, 1:51, 53, 3:1023, 1107
postoperative, 3:1113, 1132
upper respiratory, 1:375
See also Bacterial infections; Fungal infections; Hospital-acquired infections; Viral infections
Infectious diseases, 3:**1032–1038**
common cold, 2:550
epilepsy from, 5:1602
immunoglobulins, 1:257
mobility, 4:1284
probiotics for, 4:1498
Infectious hepatitis. *See* Hepatitis A
Infectious mononucleosis, 1:254, 3:1145, 1146
Infertility, 5:1634, 1660
Infinitesimal Dose, Law of, 3:987
Inflammation, 1:194
anti-inflammatory diet, 1:193–196
autoimmune diseases, 1:250
carcinogenesis, 4:1260
chronic, 1:194
fibromyalgia, 3:800
lupus-associated, 3:1180
nonsteroidal anti-inflammatory drugs for, 4:1325–1327
omega-6 fatty acid-related, 2:665
osteoarthritis, 4:1366
pro-inflammatory foods, 1:195–196
TNF-238A gene, 3:974
Inflammatory bowel disease
GI bleeding from, 3:872
hemorrhoids, 3:947
high-fiber diet, 3:958
lactose intolerance, 3:1121
massage, 4:1219
vitamin D deficiency, 5:1855
vitamin K deficiency, 5:1860
zinc deficiency, 5:1897
Inflammatory breast cancer, 1:355, 359
Inflammatory diarrhea, 2:653, 654, 655
Influenza, 3:1032–1036, *1038,* **1038–1041,** 5:1831–1834
avian, 5:1832
bronchitis, 1:375
demographics, 3:1033, 1039
diagnosis, 3:1039, 5:1832, 1833
drug resistance, 5:1833
drug therapy, 1:211–212, 3:1039–1040, 5:1833
epidemics, 3:1038, 1041
homeopathic medicine, 3:987
mortality, 3:1035, 1038, 1040, 1041, 4:1462
myocarditis from, 4:1309
pneumonia, 4:1463, 1466, 5:1700
prevention, 3:1040, 5:1834
treatment, 3:1039–1040, 5:1833
Influenza type A, 3:1038, 1042
Influenza type B, 3:1038, 1042
Influenza type C, 3:1038
Influenza vaccines, 3:**1041–1043**
demographics, 3:1041, 1041*t*
effectiveness, 5:1815
pneumonia prevention, 4:1466
recommendations, 3:1036, 1040, 5:1833, 1834
virus strains, 3:1038
Information
dietary supplements, 2:678–679, 4:1345
elective surgery, 3:807
health, 4:1426, 1430–1431
informed consent, 3:1044
Mental Status Examination, 4:1321
nutrition, 2:682
patient education, 4:1428
travel, 5:1607
Information services, community, 2:558
Informed consent, 2:527, 3:**1043–1045,** 4:1426, 1483
Ingham, Eunice, 1:14
INH. *See* Isoniazid
Inhalation therapy, 1:25, 3:**1046–1050**
asthma, 1:242–244, 243
chronic bronchitis, 1:377
chronic obstructive pulmonary disease, 2:513
general anesthesia, 1:112
insulin, 3:1053–1054
substance abuse, 5:1725
Inhalers, metered dose, 1:25, 377, 2:741–742
Inheritance, 3:803
Injection snoreplasty, 5:1672, 1674
Injections, 1:25
botox, 1:345–348, *346*
collagen, 2:*529,* 529–531
corticosteroids, 1:391
erectile dysfunction, 2:757
intra-articular, 4:1385
Injuries. *See* Trauma
Inner Classic of the Yellow Emperor, 1:17
Inner ear, 5:1779
Inner ear infections, 2:697
Inner Smile, 4:1547
Innocent VIII, 4:1212
Inositol, 4:1411
INR (International normalized ratio), 5:1860

Insect bites and stings, 1:70, 3:1081
Insight, 4:1321
Insoluble fiber, 2:422, 3:957
Insomnia, 3:**1050–1052,** 5:1613, 1655–1658
benzodiazepines for, 1:140, 292
caffeine-related, 2:396
chronic, 3:1050, 5:1655
demographics, 3:1050
depression-related, 2:624, 625
drug therapy, 1:140–141, 3:1051
periodic limb movement disorder-related, 4:1434
prayer and spirituality, 4:1478
relaxation techniques, 4:1565
shiatsu, 5:1627
situational, 5:1655
treatment, 3:1051, 5:1616
yoga, 5:1894
See also Anti-insomnia drugs
Inspections, nursing home, 4:1332–1333
Institute for Religion and Health, 4:1478
Institute of Medicine (ION)
Dietary Reference Intakes, 2:398, 5:1848, 1850, 1854–1855
folic acid, 3:812
high-fiber diet, 3:957
sodium, 5:1679
Institute of Physical and Chemical Research, 2:416
Instrumental activities of daily living (IADLs), 1:9–10
aging in place, 3:1028
exercise, 2:767
financial management, 3:802
household management, 3:997–998
independence, 3:1027
mobility, 4:1283
personal hygiene, 4:1441
Insulin, 3:**1052–1057,** *1053*
aging, 3:869
antidiabetic drugs, 1:177*t,* 2:640
beta blocker interactions, 1:299
blood sugar levels, 1:327
carbohydrates, 2:422–423
cinnamon, 2:514–516
DHEA interactions, 2:635
diabetes mellitus, 2:638–640
drug interactions, 3:1055–1056
garlic interactions, 3:848
glucosamine interactions, 3:885
nicotine interactions, 5:1664
role, 1:178, 2:638–639, 3:1053
Insulin-dependent diabetes. *See* Type 1 diabetes mellitus
Insulin resistance, 1:88, 4:1339
Insulinomas, 4:1401–1403
Insurance
dental, 2:616, 621
drug, 2:548–550
long-term care, 1:238, 4:1333
private, 4:1494–1496, 1494*t*
See also Health insurance
Insurance claim forms, 4:1453
Intelligence
crystallized, 4:1523
developmental, 4:1526
Mental Status Examination, 4:1321
Intelligence quotient (IQ), 4:1255
Interactions. *See* Drug interactions
Interactive technology, 5:1878
Intercourse
HIV transmission, 1:50
painful, 5:1618, 1619
urinary catheterization, 2:467, 471
urinary tract infections, 2:594
See also Sexual activity
Interdisciplinary teams, 4:1236
Interests, communities of, 4:1561
Interferon-alpha, 1:290, 4:1200
Interferon-beta, 4:1305
Interferon-gamma 1-b, 4:1537
Interferons
for kidney cancer, 3:1093
for metastasis, 4:1264
oxygen/ozone therapy, 4:1384
for postnecrotic cirrhosis, 2:523
Interleukin-2, 4:1264
Interleukin-6, 4:1298
Intermediate-acting insulin, 3:1054
Intermediate-density lipoproteins (IDL), 2:505, 3:1002
Intermediate distance testing, 4:1485
Intermittent catheterization, 2:465–467, 468–471
Intermittent claudication, 3:878
Intermittent motorized traction (IMT), 1:269–270
Intermittent peritoneal dialysis (IPD), 2:509
International Bibliographic Information on Dietary Supplements (IBIDS lDatabase), 2:678
International Classification of Diseases (ICD), 3:861, 4:1231
The International Classification of Sleep Disorders, 5:1655
International Federation of Gynecologists and Obstetricians (FIGO), 2:745
International Foundation for Functional Gastrointestinal Disorders (IFFGD), 3:1069, 1070, 1071
International National Osteoporosis Foundation, 4:1372–1373
International normalized ratio (INR), 5:1860
International Staging System, 4:1300
International travel. *See* Travel
Internet
ethics, 2:529, 4:1235
gambling, 3:840, 841
isolation prevention, 3:1079
nursing homes, 4:1333
nutrition information services, 2:682
patient education information, 4:1428
sildenafil citrate, 5:1637
Interpersonal relationships. *See* Relationships
Interpersonal therapy (IPT), 2:626
Interstitial lung disease, 2:500, 4:1535
Intertrochanteric hip fractures, 3:960
Intervertebral disks, 2:487
Intestinal bypass, 1:285–286
Intestinal cancer. *See* Colon cancer
Intestinal diseases
colonoscopy, 2:538, 541
probiotics, 4:1496–1501
tuberculosis-related, 5:1793
Intestinal dysbiosis, 4:1498
Intestinal obstruction, 2:537, 569, 695
Intestinal perforation, 2:695
Intestinal polyps
barium enema, 1:287, 289
benign, 2:535
colon cancer, 2:534
colonoscopy, 2:538–541
GI bleeding from, 3:872
Intestinal transplantation, 4:1363
Intestines
large, 1:*287,* 287–290, 2:532, *532*
peristalsis, 1:262, 2:752, 3:1123
small, 2:532
Intimate relationships, 4:1560–1562
Intolerance
carbohydrate, 3:869
food, 1:74, 3:814, 818–821, 1070, 4:1368
gluten, 3:886
See also Lactose intolerance
Intra-articular injections, 4:1385
Intracerebral hemorrhage, 5:1720
Intracranial hemorrhage, 3:902
Intradermal medication, 1:25
Intradermal test, 1:75
Intrahepatic bile duct diseases, 2:522
Intrahepatic cholestasis, 3:1133
Intramuscular injections, 1:25, 2:490
Intraocular lens (IOL), 2:463–464, 774, 3:880–881
Intraocular melanoma, 4:1197
Intraocular pressure (IOP)
eye examination, 2:770
glaucoma, 3:880–881, 882, 5:1836, 1837, 1839
marijuana for, 4:1213
peripheral vision loss, 4:1438
transient blindness, 5:1782

Intraoperative magnetic resonance imaging, 4:1189
Intraperitoneal chemotherapy, 2:491, 4:1376
Intrathecal chemotherapy, 2:491, 4:1195, 1262
Intravenous fluid regulation, 3:**1057–1059,** 4:1382
Intravenous medication administration, 1:25, 27, 3:**1059–1063,** *1060*
  chemotherapy, 2:490
  dehydration, 2:605
  general anesthesia, 1:112
  shock, 3:873
Intravenous nutrition, 4:**1341–1343**
Intravenous pyelogram (IVP)
  bladder cancer, 1:308
  bladder stones, 1:313
  kidney cancer, 3:1092
  kidney stones, 3:1102
Intrinsic factor (IF), 5:1847
Intubation, 3:1049
Inverse psoriasis, 4:1519
Inverse ratio ventilation (IRV), 5:1822
Involuntary euthanasia, 2:763, 764
Iodine, 2:417, 4:1490, 5:1769
Iodine radioisotopes
  hyperthyroidism, 3:1014
  intravenous pyelogram, 3:1102
  thyroid cancer, 5:1770–1771, 1772
  thyroid function tests, 5:1773–1774
  thyroid nuclear medicine scans, 5:1775–1777, 1778
Iodine uptake test, 5:1775
Iodiopathic pulmonary hypertension, 4:1539
Iodiopathic scoliosis, 1:272
IOL (Intraocular lens), 2:463–464, 774, 3:880–881
ION. *See* Institute of Medicine
Ionizing radiation, 4:1195, 1260
IOP. *See* Intraocular pressure
IPA (Independent practice associations), 3:976, 4:1209
IPD (Intermittent peritoneal dialysis), 2:509
Ipecac, 4:1382
Ipratropium, 1:379, 380
IPT (Interpersonal therapy), 2:626
IQ (Intelligence quotient), 4:1255
Irbesartan, 1:191, 2:563
Irinotecan, 4:1406
Iris (eye), 2:573
Iris versicolor. See Blue flag
Iron
  dietary, 1:109, 110
  garlic, 3:846
  healthy aging, 5:1614
  malabsorption, 3:1064–1065, 1066
  metabolism defects, 2:522
  role, 3:1067
  sources, 2:417
  See also Iron supplements
Iron deficiency, 2:669, 4:1434, 5:1766
Iron-deficiency anemia, 1:108–111, 3:**1063–1066,** *1064*
  diagnosis, 2:561, 3:1065
  diet, 3:870
Iron ferritin tests, 3:1065
Iron overload. *See* Hemochromatosis
Iron salts, 4:1517
Iron supplements
  for anemia, 2:510
  for anemic anoxia, 1:138
  antibiotic interactions, 2:709
  caffeine interactions, 2:397
  calcium supplement interactions, 2:405
  for chemotherapy patients, 2:419
  for cirrhosis-associated anemia, 2:523
  for iron-deficiency anemia, 3:1065
  tetracycline interactions, 5:1865
  zinc interactions, 5:1897
Iron tests, 1:109, 3:1065, **1066–1068**
Irregular heartbeat. *See* Arrhthymias
Irrigation
  colonic, 2:752, 753
  ear, 2:*721,* 721–723
Irritable bowel syndrome, 3:**1068–1073,** *1069*
  high-fiber diet, 3:958
  vs. ovarian cancer symptoms, 4:1375
  probiotics for, 4:1497, 1498
Irritant contact dermatitis, 2:571–573
Irritant laxatives, 3:1123
Irritation, chronic, 4:1260
IRV (Inverse ratio ventilation), 5:1822
Ischemia, 3:*1073,* **1073–1077**
  angiography, 1:129
  myocardial, 1:124, 3:906, *1073,* 1073–1077, 5:1717
  pressure sores, 5:1884
  scleroderma-related, 5:1596–1597
Ischemic cardiomyopathy, 2:445
Ischemic heart disease, 1:123–125, 324, 5:1824
Ischemic priapism, 4:1491–1492
Ischemic stroke, 1:234, 235, 3:1073, 5:1720, 1722, 1723
Ischial bursitis, 1:388, 389
Islam, 2:599
Islet cell cancers, 4:1401–1403
Islets of Langerhans, 3:1053, 4:1401
Ismelin. *See* Guanethidine monosulfate
Isoflavones, 1:195, 2:417
Isoflurane, 1:113
Isolated perfusion, 4:1264
Isolated systolic hypertension, 3:1008–1009
Isolation, 3:**1077–1080**
  alcohol abuse, 1:67
  anxiety, 1:216
  community social programs, 2:559
  companionship, 3:794
  demographics, 3:869, 1078
  elder abuse, 2:728, 729
  generalized anxiety disorder, 3:864
Isolation syndrome. *See* Transcortical dysphasia
Isometric exercises, 3:785
Isoniazid, 1:208–211
  acetaminophen interactions, 1:8
  benzodiazepine interactions, 1:145
  diazepam interactions, 4:1308
  insulin interactions, 3:1056
  for tuberculosis, 3:1036, 5:1795–1796
  vitamin D interactions, 5:1855
Isordil. *See* Isosorbide dinatrate
Isosorbide dinatrate, 1:143, 5:1635
Isosorbide mononitrate, 5:1635
Isothiocyanates, 2:416
Isotretinoin, 2:715, 4:1520
Isradipine, 1:191
Itching, 3:**1080–1083**
  chronic kidney failure-related, 2:509
  contact dermatitis-related, 2:571
  corticosteroids for, 5:1651
  drug therapy, 1:141–142, 3:1081–1082
  dry skin-related, 2:715, 3:1081–1082
  scabies-related, 5:1589
Itraconazole, 1:145, 3:826, 4:1517
IV fluids. *See* Intravenous fluid regulation
IV medication. *See* Intravenous medication administration
Ivermectin, 3:1126, 5:1590–1591, 1842
IVP (Intravenous pyelogram), 1:308, 313, 3:1092, 1102
Ixodes sp., 3:1183
Iyengar yoga, 5:1892

J

J. D. Powers and Associates, 3:977
Jacksonian Seizures, 5:1602–1606
Jalapenos, 2:415
Jamshidi trephine needles, 1:341, 3:1135
Japan, 5:1704, 1706
Japanese Americans. *See* Asian Americans
Japanese meridian acupuncture, 1:18

Japanese traditional massage, 5:1627–1629
Jaundice
  exocrine pancreatic cancer, 4:1404
  gallbladder cancer, 3:835, 836
  gallstones, 3:839
  hepatitis, 3:950
  liver function tests, 3:1145
JCAHO (Joint Commission on Accreditation of Healthcare Organizations), 3:806, 1029, 4:1332, 1431
Jefferson, Thomas, 4:1212
Jenner, Edward, 3:987
Jet lag, 5:1656
Jews, Ashkenazi, 1:355, 3:1121, 4:1375
Jnana yoga, 5:1892
Job training, 2:558
Jobs. *See* Employment; Occupational exposure; Work environment
Jock itch, 1:184, 3:825, 826
Jogging, water, 5:1874
John Paul II, 4:1552
Johns, Murray, 5:1673
Johnson, Lyndon, 2:658
Johnson, Magic, 1:56
Joint capsules, 2:686
Joint Commission on Accreditation of Healthcare Organizations (JCAHO), 3:806, 1029, 4:1332, 1431
Joint disorders, 3:1086–1087
  dislocations and subluxations, 2:686–689
  hypdrogen peroxide for, 4:1385
  magnetic resonance imaging, 4:1190–1191
  mobility, 4:1283–1284
  osteopathic manipulation, 4:1369–1379
  t'ai chi, 5:1747
  water exercise, 5:1873, 1874
Joint function, 3:**1085–1087**
  glucosamine, 3:883–884
  hip replacement, 3:963
Joint immobilization, 5:1615
Joint infections
  bacterial, 3:1032, 1034, 1035
  staphylococcal, 5:1700, 1701
  tuberculosis-related, 5:1793
Joint integrity, 3:**1085–1087**
Joint manipulation, 3:**1087–1089**
Joint mobilization, 3:**1087–1089**
  back and neck pain, 1:269
  gait and balance disorders, 3:830
  osteopathic medicine, 2:702
  t'ai chi, 5:1747
Joint ownership, 2:567, 3:804
Joint replacement. *See* Hip replacement; Knee joint replacement
Joint thrusts. *See* Joint manipulation
JROTC (Junior Reserve Officers' Training Corps), 5:1830
Judaism
  death and dying, 2:599
  euthanasia, 2:762
  medical ethics, 4:1234
  organ donation, 4:1364
  prayer and spirituality, 4:1477–1478
  reconciliation and forgiveness, 4:1551
  relationships with God, 4:1561
Judgment, 2:612, 4:1321
The Jungle (Sinclair), 2:657
Junior Reserve Officers' Training Corps (JROTC), 5:1830
Jury duty, 3:998
Justice, 2:528, 4:1235
Juvenile arthritis, 4:1326
Juvenile-onset diabetes. *See* Type 1 diabetes mellitus
Juvenile rheumatoid arthritis, 1:234, 235

K

Kabat-Zinn, Jon, 4:1271, 1552–1553, 1564
Kabikinase. *See* Streptokinase
Kaiser Family Foundation, 4:1475
Kaiser Permanente, 2:549
Kale, 2:415, 416
Kamami, Yves-Victor, 5:1672
Kanamycin, 1:95–97
Kant, Immanuel, 4:1234
Kaopectate. *See* Attapulgite
Kaposi's sarcoma, 1:51, 2:779, 5:1641, 1642
Karma yoga, 5:1892
Katz Index, 1:9, 3:1027
Kava kava, 3:1051, 5:1662, 1727
Keflex. *See* Cephalexin
Kefzol. *See* Cefazolin
Kelley therapy, 2:746
Kelp, 3:1024
Kenalog, 1:41
Kenny, Elizabeth, 4:1454
Keratectomy, phototherapeutic, 2:575, 576
Keratin, 1:184
Keratitis, herpes simplex, 5:1842
Keratoacanthoma, 5:1642
Keratoconus, 2:574
Keratomileusis, laser-assited in-situ, 4:1486
Keratoplasty, 2:575, 4:1486
Kernicterus, 3:1146, 4:1256, 1258
Ketalar. *See* Ketamine
Ketamine, 1:113
Ketoconazole
  benzodiazepine interactions, 1:145
  celecoxib interactions, 2:587
  diazepam interactions, 4:1308
  for fungal infections, 1:184
  isoniazid interactions, 1:211
  proton pump inhibitors interactions, 4:1517
Ketogenic diet, 5:1604
Ketone tests, 1:209
Ketones, 2:422, 5:1604
Ketoprofen, 4:1367, 5:1798
Ketorolac, 1:107, 4:1326
Ketosis, 2:422
Kevorkian, Jack, 4:1235
Ki, 5:1627–1628
Kidney angiography, 1:128–129
Kidney artery stenosis, 2:508
Kidney cancer, 3:848, *1091,* **1091–1096,** 1110
Kidney dialysis. *See* Dialysis
Kidney disease
  $alpha_1$ adrenergic blockers, 1:82
  chronic, 1:128–129, 2:637
  diabetic, 2:643–645
  diagnosis, 3:1096–1100
  diuretic precautions, 2:692
  edema, 2:726
  electrolyte tests, 2:739
  gout, 3:895
  hyperlipoproteinemia, 3:1003
  low-sodium diet, 3:1159, 1161
  polycystic, 2:508, 3:1092
  scleroderma-related, 5:1597
  smoking, 5:1665
  tuberculosis, 5:1793
Kidney failure
  amyloidosis, 1:101, 102
  chronic, 2:507–511, 643, 3:1100, 1104–1108
  diabetes mellitus-related, 2:640
  dialysis, 2:650–651
  hyperkalemia from, 2:737
  hypertension from, 3:1008
  hypocalcemia-induced, 2:736
  kidney nuclear medicine scans, 3:1100
  smoking, 5:1665
Kidney function tests, 3:**1096–1098**
  cardiac surgery, 2:439
  congestive heart failure, 2:563
  kidney transplantation, 3:1107
Kidney infections. *See* Pyelonephritis
Kidney nuclear medicine scans, 3:**1098–1100,** *1099*
Kidney stones, 3:**1100–1103,** *1101*
  calcium supplement-related, 2:404
  hyperuricemia-related, 3:891
  kidney, ureter, and bladder x-ray study, 3:**1108–1110**

Kidney stones *(continued)*
Paget's disease of bone-related, 4:1393
probiotics for, 4:1498
Kidney transplantation, 3:**1104–1108,** *1105*
amyloidosis, 1:102
chronic kidney failure, 2:509
end-stage renal disease, 2:510
kidney nuclear medicine scans, 3:1100
living donors, 3:1106, 1107, 4:1363
Kidney, ureter, and bladder x-ray study, 3:**1108–1110**
Kidneys
aminoglycoside precautions, 1:95
anatomy and function, 2:643–644, 3:1096, 1100, 1109
sodium, 3:1160
water balance, 5:1870
Kinetic awareness therapy, 4:1292
Kinship, 3:793–796
Kitchens, 3:985
Klebsiella sp., 1:310, 2:594
Klonopin. *See* Clonazepam
Knee biopsy, 3:1117
Knee bursitis, 1:388, 389
Knee injuries, 3:**1114–1119,** *1115*
dislocation, 2:686, 687–688
mobilization and manipulation, 3:1087
Knee joint
anatomy and function, 3:1085, 1086, 1087, 1112, 1115
osteoarthritis, 4:1366
Knee joint replacement, 3:**1110–1114,** *1111*
acupuncture, 1:19
joint mobilization, 3:1089
mobility, 4:1285
osteoarthritis, 5:1615, 1617
prosthesis, 3:*1111,* 1111–1114, 1166
staphylococcal infections, 5:1700
wound healing, 5:1664
Kneipp, Sebastian, 4:1315
Koch, Robert, 5:1790
Koch, William, 4:1384
Koho anma, 5:1627
Kola, 2:395, 396
Koning, Fritz, 3:889–890
Konsil. *See* Psyllium
Korean Americans. *See* Asian Americans
Korean hand acupuncture, 1:18
Korean red ginseng, 2:757
Korean War, 5:1827
Korsakoff psychosis. *See* Wernicke-Korsakoff syndrome
Kovic, Ron, 5:1827
KUB (Kidney, ureter, and bladder x-ray study), 3:**1108–1110**
Kubler-Ross, Elisabeth, 3:995
Kwell. *See* Lindane
Kyphosis, 1:271–275
Kytril. *See* Granisetron

L

L-cysteine, 5:1898
L-dopa. *See* Levodopa
L-glutamine, 1:68
L-histidine, 5:1898
Labels
dietary supplements, 2:677, 679
food, 2:474, 475, 658
food allergies, 3:817
gluten-free, 2:474, 475, 3:888
history, 2:658
lactose intolerance, 3:1123
low-cholesterol diet, 3:1154–1155
low-fat diet, 3:1158
nutritional content, 2:658
sodium content, 3:1160
Labetolol, 1:191, 3:900
Lacerations, spinal cord, 5:1692
Lachesis, 1:227
Lactase, 3:1121, 1122
Lactate, 1:138
Lactate dehydrogenase (LDH), 3:1143–1146, 5:1585
Lactated ringer's solution, 2:654
Lactic acid, 1:83, 3:1122
Lactic acid test, 1:138
Lactic acidosis, 1:180
Lactic dehydrogenase, 3:1139
Lactobacillus acidophilus, 3:1185, 4:1497, 1499
Lactobacillus bulgaricus, 4:1499
Lactobacillus GG (LGG), 4:1497, 1499, 1500
Lactobacillus plantarum 299v, 4:1500
Lactobacillus reuteri, 4:1497
Lactobacillus sp., 3:1143, 4:1496, 1497
Lactoferrin, 5:1834
Lactose, 3:817, 1121
Lactose hydrogen breath test, 3:1122
Lactose intolerance, 3:819, 820, *1121,* **1121–1123**
calcium requirements, 2:399
celiac disease, 2:474, 3:1121
geriatric nutrition, 3:870
irritable bowel syndrome, 3:1070
probiotics for, 4:1498
Lactose tolerance test, 3:1122
Lactulose, 3:1123, 1124
Lady's mantle, 4:1252
Laennec's cirrhosis. *See* Portal cirrhosis
Laetrile. *See* Amygdalin
LAIV (Live, attenuated influenza vaccine), 3:1042
Lamellar bone, 4:1390
Lamictal. *See* Lamotrigine
Laminectomy, 4:1263
Lamisil. *See* Terbinafine
Lamotrigine, 1:305, 5:1603
Langslands, Alan, 3:1045
Language, 3:1078
Language centers, 2:717, 718, 719
Language disorders, 1:87, 2:612, 5:1686–1691
Laniazid. *See* Isoniazid
Lanoxin. *See* Digoxin
Lansoprazole, 4:1515–1517
for gastroesophageal reflux disease, 3:856, 4:1515–1517
for helicobacteriosis, 3:940
for ulcers, 2:586, 5:1799
vitamin B_{12} interactions, 5:1848
Laparoscopic radiofrequency ablation (RFA), 3:1140
Laparoscopic surgery. *See* Laparoscopy
Laparoscopy
cholecystectomy, 3:839–840
colostomy, 2:542
fundoplication, 3:856
gastric banding, 1:285
hysterectomy, 2:484, 745, 3:1018
kidney cancer, 3:1093
liver cancer diagnosis, 3:1140
nephrectomy, 3:1104
stomach cancer, 5:1705–1706
Large-cell carcinoma, 3:1174
Large intestines
anatomy, 2:532, *532*
barium enema, 1:*287,* 287–290
peristalsis, 1:262, 2:752, 3:1123
Laryngeal cancer, 3:848
Laser-assisted uvulopalatoplasty (LAUP), 5:1671–1672, 1674
Laser-assited in-situ keratomileusis (LASIK), 4:1486
Laser resurfacing, 5:1889
Laser surgery
age-related macular degeneration, 5:1838
amputation, 1:98
carbon dioxide lasers, 5:1648
cervical cancer, 2:483, 484
coherent ultrapulse carbon dioxide, 3:785
coronary artery disease, 3:1075–1076
esophageal cancer, 2:761
glaucoma, 3:882
Nd:YAG lasers, 5:1648
presbyopia, 4:1486
refractive, 4:1355

Laser surgery *(continued)*
rosacea, 4:1579
skin cancer, 5:1651
skin lesions, 5:1648
varicose veins, 2:519, 5:1817
Laser therapy, smoking cessation, 5:1666–1667
Laser thermal keratoplasty (LTK), 4:1486
LASIK (Laser-assited in-situ keratomileusis), 4:1486
Lasix, 2:447
Lat Tzu, 5:1746
Late-onset depression, 2:624, 625, 627
Latent infections, 3:1032
Later life development, 4:1526–1528
Lateral collateral ligament (LCL), 3:1115
Latex allergies, 1:70
Latex, aloe, 1:77, 79
Latex catheters, 2:466, 470
Latinos. *See* Hispanics
Latissimus dorsi flaps, 1:367
Laughing gas. *See* Nitrous oxide
Laundry, 4:1442, 1444
LAUP (Laser-assisted uvulopalatoplasty), 5:1671–1672, 1674
Lavender, 1:334, 2:742, 5:1605
Law of Infinitesimal Dose, 3:987
Law of Similars, 3:987
Laws. *See* Legal issues; Legislation
Laws of Cure, 3:988
Lawton IADL scale, 3:1027
Laxatives, 3:**1123–1124**
aloe, 1:77
barium enema, 1:288
bulk-forming, 2:569, 3:1123
calcium absorption, 2:400
for cirrhosis, 2:523
colonoscopy preparation, 2:539
constipation from, 2:569, 570
drug interactions, 2:708*t*, 3:1124
emollient, 3:1123
endoscopy, 2:748
heatstroke risk, 3:937
hyperosmotic, 3:1123
for irritable bowel syndrome, 3:1071
irritant, 3:1123
marijuana, 4:1213
saline, 2:569, 3:1123
stimulant, 3:1124
Lazy eye. *See* Amblyopia
LBFE (Little Brothers-Friends of the Elderly), 3:1079
LCIS (Lobular carcinoma-in-situ), 1:357, 4:1204, 1221
LCL (Lateral collateral ligament), 3:1115
LDH (Lactate dehydrogenase), 3:1143–1146, 5:1585
LDL. *See* Low-density lipoproteins
Lead poisoning, 5:1602
Leaflets, 2:441, 442
Learning, 3:1167, 5:1613
Learning System (AHA), 2:449
Leber's optic atrophy, 5:1848
Lebov, Myrna, 2:763
Lecithin, 1:68
Lectin, 2:416
LEEP (Loop electrosurgical excision procedure), 2:483
Lefluonmide, 4:1574
Left anterior thoracotomy, 4:1275
Left-handed individuals, 2:719
Left-sided brain functioning, 4:1321
Left Ventricular Assist Device (LVAD), 2:447
Leg length, 3:968
Legal blindness, 5:1841
Legal issues
conservatorship, 2:566, 567
home care, 3:981
informed consent, 3:1043, 1044–1045
patient confidentiality, 4:1425–1428
patient representative, 4:1428–1429
patient rights, 4:1429–1431
Legionella pneumophila, 4:1463
Legionnaire's disease, 1:152, 4:1463
Legislation
administration of medication, 1:24
Americans with Disabilities Act, 1:93
Balanced Budget Act, 4:1238
civil rights, 1:93
conservatorship, 2:565–568
driver safety, 3:998
elder abuse, 2:729
food safety, 2:657–658
health insurance, 4:1230
jury duty, 3:998
marijuana, 4:1212
nurse practice, 2:529
nursing homes, 4:1332
Older Americans Act (1965), 2:454
organ donation, 4:1363–1364
patient confidentiality, 4:1426
patient rights, 1:366, 3:1149, 4:1429–1430
physician-assisted suicide, 2:599
Social Security, 4:1228
Legs
amputation, 1:*98,* 99, 3:1165–1167
aneurysm, 1:120
blood flow, 1:136–137
lower limb prosthesis, 3:*1165,* 1165–1167
short, 4:1370
Legumes, 1:195, 2:415, 658, 5:1897
Leiomyoma, submucosal, 5:1706
Leisure time, 2:454, 765*t*
Lemon balm, 3:1071
Lemon juice, 1:314
Lemons, 2:416–417
Lenalidomide, 4:1301
Length of stay, 3:979
Lenses
contact, 2:575, 772–775, 4:1354, 1485–1486, 5:1841
crystalline, 2:461–464, 573, 4:1484–1487
intraocular, 2:463–464, 774, 3:880–881
photosensitive, 2:773
plastic, 2:772–773
polycarbonate, 2:772
Lentigo maligna melanoma, 4:1197–1198
Lentinan, 2:416
Leonurus cardiaca. See Motherwort
Leprosy, 5:1590, 1842
LES. *See* Lower esophageal sphincter (LES)
Lesch-Nyhan syndrome, 3:1101
Lescol. *See* Fluvastatin
Lesionectomy, 5:1604
Letrozole, 1:358
Leucovorin, 2:536
Leukemia, 2:407
acute, 1:*22,* 22–23, 5:1861
acute promyelocytic, 5:1861
bone marrow biopsy, 1:339, 343
chronic, 2:511
chronic lymphocytic, 1:254, 2:511
diagnosis, 2:560, 561
Down syndrome-related, 4:1255
liver function tests, 3:1145
lymphocytic, 1:22–23
myelocytic, 1:22–23, 2:511
ovarian cancer risk, 4:1377
PAP tumor marker, 4:1262
pleural effusion from, 4:1461
scabies risk, 5:1590
Leukine, 2:492
Leukoplakia, 5:1642
Leukotriene modifiers, 1:72
Leukotrienes, 1:193
Levamisole, 1:290
Levitra. *See* Vardenafil
Levo-dihydroxy-phenylalanine. *See* Levodopa
Levodopa
liver function test interactions, 3:1143
for Parkinson's disease, 1:199, 200–201, 3:832, 4:1423
for periodic limb movement disorder, 4:1435
psychoses from, 4:1529

Levodopa *(continued)*
SSRI interactions, 1:173
vitamin B interactions, 4:1424
Levofloxacin, 1:151–152, 5:1712
Levothyroxine, 2:400, 405, 3:1056
Lewy body dementia, 4:1421, 1528
Lexapro. *See* Escitalopram
LGG (Lactobacillus GG), 4:1497, 1499, 1500
Liberation, 4:1526
Librium. *See* Chlordiazepoxide
Lice infestation, 3:**1124–1127,** *1125*
Licensed practical nurses (LPNs), 3:**1127–1130**
Licensed vocational nurses. *See* Licensed practical nurses
Licensure
acupuncture, 1:20
adult day care, 1:29
chiropractic, 2:503–504
dieticians, 2:683–684, 4:1347
homeopathic medicine, 3:988
licensed practical nurses, 3:1129
naturopathy, 4:1316
nursing homes, 4:1332
optometrists, 4:1355
physical therapy, 4:1455, 1458
surgeons, 3:806
See also Certification
Lichen simplex chronicus, 2:573
Lichenificaiton, 5:1650
Lichtenstein, Alice H., 2:658
Licorice
cancer prevention, 2:416
deglycerrhizinated, 5:1800
hepatitis, 3:951
smoking cessation, 5:1662
substance abuse, 5:1727
ulcers, 5:1800
Lidocaine
antiarrhythmic drug interactions, 1:148
cimetidine interactions, 3:900
for diabetic neuropathy, 2:647
local anesthesia, 1:116
ranitidine interactions, 3:900
Life expectancy, 1:45–46
gender differences, 2:662
health care costs, 4:1209
increase, 2:453, 3:913
mental retardation, 4:1258
population aging, 1:45–46
rheumatoid arthritis, 4:1575
social issues, 4:1522
See also Longevity
Life quality. *See* Quality of life
Life support treatment
advance directives, 1:32
denial, 1:30–31, 2:763
living wills, 3:1149
palliative care, 2:600
ventricular fibrillation, 5:1824–1825
withdrawal, 5:1881–1884
Lifespan. *See* Life expectancy
LIFESPAN (movement), 4:1334
Lifestyle, 2:**661–664**
aging, 5:1611–1612
angina pectoris, 1:124, 125
atherosclerosis, 1:245, 247
bipolar disorder, 1:306
breast cancer prevention, 1:359–360
cardiac rehabilitation, 2:436, 437
carotid artery disease, 2:457–458
chronic disease, 2:663
congestive heart failure, 2:563
constipation, 2:569, 570
depression, 2:628
erectile dysfunction, 2:757
gastroesophageal reflux disease, 3:854, 855
gluten-free diet, 3:889
healthy aging, 1:47
heart attack, 3:923
heart disease, 3:930
heart-healthy, 2:581
high cholesterol, 2:519, 3:954–955
hip replacement preparation, 3:966–967
hyperlipoproteinemia, 3:1004
hypertension, 1:325, 3:1010
insomnia, 3:1051
irritable bowel syndrome, 3:1071
ischemia, 3:1076
liver cancer, 3:1142
low back pain, 3:1152
obesity, 2:556, 4:1349–1350, 1351–1352
osteoporosis, 1:335, 4:1371
over age fifty, 2:661–664
post-cardiac surgery, 2:439
sedentary, 2:578, 3:922, 5:1721, 1759
sleeping disorders, 1:141
snoring, 5:1675
stroke, 5:1723–1724
transient ischemic attacks, 5:1786
urinary incontinence, 5:1806
varicose veins, 5:1818
walking problems, 5:1868
Lifestyle Heart Trial, 5:1786
Lifting, 5:1595
Ligaments
dislocations and subluxations, 2:686
hip, 3:1086
joint function, 3:1086
knee, 3:1115, 1116–1117
Ligation and stripping, vein, 5:1818
Light-chain-related amyloidosis, 1:100
Light food, 3:1158
Lightheadedness, 2:697–698
Lignans, 2:416
Lily of the valley, 2:447
Limb girdle muscular dystrophy, 4:1468
Limb movement disorder, periodic, 4:**1433–1436,** 5:1613, 1616, 1656, 1657
Limonene, 2:416–417, 4:1213
Lincoln, Abraham, 2:657
Lindane, 3:1126
Linezolid, 1:173, 4:1296
Ling, Per Henrik, 4:1215
Lingonberries, 1:311, 313–314
Linozolid. *See* Linezolid
Lioresal. *See* Baclofen
Lip collagen injections, 2:529–531
Lipid-lowering drugs, 3:1004–1005
Lipid metabolism disorders, 2:507
Lipid profile. *See* Cholesterol tests
Lipids. *See* Fats (lipids); Hyperlipoproteinemia
Lipitor. *See* Atorvastatin
Lipodystrophy, 1:53, 54
Lipoproteins
cholesterol tests, 2:505–507
classification, 2:505
description, 3:953
hyperlipoproteinemia, 3:1002–1005
intermediate-density, 2:505, 3:1002
liver function tests, 3:1145
low-cholesterol diet, 3:1154
very low-density, 2:505, 3:955, 1002
See also High-density lipoproteins; Low-density lipoproteins
Liposhaving, 3:1130, 1131
Liposuction, 2:582–584, 3:**1130–1133,** *1131*
vs. abdominoplasty, 1:4, 5
face lift, 3:784
Liquid dietary supplements, 4:1345
Liquid nutritional supplements, 5:1684
Liquids. *See* Fluid intake; Water
Lisinopril
celecoxib interactions, 2:586
for congestive heart failure, 2:563
for hypertension, 1:132, 191
Lissamine Green, 5:1639
Listeria monocytogenes, 4:1247, 1248
Lisuride, 4:1423
Lithium
angiotensin-converting enzyme inhibitor interactions, 1:134
for bipolar disorder, 1:304, 305
diabetes insipidus from, 2:637
diuretic interactions, 2:693
hypernatremia from, 2:735
nonsteroidal anti-inflammatory drug interactions, 4:1327
SSRI interactions, 1:173
Lithotripsy, 3:840, 1102
Litigation. *See* Legal issues
Little Brothers-Friends of the Elderly (LBFE), 3:1079

Live, attenuated influenza vaccine (LAIV), 3:1042
Livedo reticularis, 1:252
Liver
 anatomy and function, 3:797, 1144
 fatty, 3:796–797, 4:1500
 high cholesterol, 3:954
Liver biopsy, 3:**1133–1137,** *1134*
 cirrhosis, 2:523
 fatty liver, 3:797
 hemochromatosis, 3:945
 liver cancer, 3:1133, 1136, 1140
 tuberculosis, 5:1794
Liver cancer, 3:*1138,* **1138–1143,** 1140
 cirrhosis-related, 2:524, 3:1139
 demographics, 3:1138
 diagnosis, 3:1133, 1136, 1137, 1139–1140, 4:1263
 hepatitis-related, 3:951, 1138, 1139, 1142
 liver function tests, 3:1145, 4:1263
 liver-spleen scan, 3:1147
 metastasis, 3:1138, 1140, 4:1263
Liver cirrhosis. *See* Cirrhosis
Liver disease
 acetaminophen-induced, 1:8
 $alpha_1$ adrenergic blockers, 1:82
 antituberculosis drug-induced, 1:209, 210
 caffeine precautions, 2:396
 demographics, 3:1135
 DHEA precautions, 2:635
 diagnosis, 3:1133–1137
 diuretic-induced, 2:692
 edema, 2:726
 GI bleeding from, 3:871
 hormone replacement therapy precautions, 4:1251
 hyperlipoproteinemia, 3:1004
 liver-spleen scan, 3:1147–1149
 pulmonary hypertension from, 4:1539
 vitamin K deficiency, 5:1860
 zinc deficiency, 5:1897
Liver failure, 1:200–201, 2:739
Liver function tests, 3:**1143–1147**
 colon cancer, 2:535
 hepatitis, 3:950
 liver cancer, 3:1139, 4:1263
Liver-spleen scan, 3:**1147–1149**
Liver transplantation
 cirrhosis, 2:524
 hepatitis, 3:951
 liver biopsy, 3:1133
 liver cancer, 3:1141
 living donors, 4:1363
Living alone
 family relationships, 3:794
 isolation, 3:1078
 vs. isolation, 3:1077
 malnutrition, 4:1202
 nutrition, 4:1339
 social issues, 4:1523
 See also Independence; Isolation
Living arrangements, 3:1026–1027, 1027*t*
 assisted living facilities, 1:236–239, *237,* 3:1028
 social issues, 4:1523
 See also Home modifications; Home safety
Living donors, 3:1106, 1107, 4:1362–1363
Living rooms, 3:985
Living wills, 1:30–33, 2:598, 3:**1149–1150**
Lloyd, John, 5:1587
Lobar pneumonia, 4:1462
Lobectomy
 liver cancer, 3:1140
 lung cancer, 3:1176
 thyroid cancer, 5:1770
Lobelia, 3:850, 1153, 5:1662
Lobelia inflata. See Lobelia
Lobeline, 5:1662
Lobular carcinoma, 1:355, 357
Lobular carcinoma-in-situ (LCIS), 1:357, 4:1204, 1221
Local anesthesia, 1:**115–118**
 bronchoscopy, 1:383
 endoscopy, 2:748
 face lift, 3:783–784
 liposuction, 3:1131, 1132
 pacemakers, 4:1388
Local recurrence, 5:1737
Localized scleroderma, 5:1596
LoCholest. *See* Cholestyramine
Lockjaw. *See* Tetanus
Lodine. *See* Etodolac
Lomotil. *See* Diphenoxylate-atropine
Loneliness
 alcohol abuse, 1:67
 vs. isolation, 3:1077
 malnutrition prevention, 2:666
 over fifty lifestyle, 2:662
 vs. solitude, 4:1562
 undernutrition, 4:1337
Long-acting insulin, 3:1054
Long-term care
 costs, 4:1522
 dementia, 2:613
 infection control, 3:1029
 shortage, 3:1028
 social workers, 5:1677
 See also Nursing homes
Long Term Care Accreditation Program, 4:1332
Long-term care insurance, 1:238, 4:1333
Longevity
 aerobic exercise, 1:38
 gender differences, 2:662
 genetic factors, 1:44
 increase, 2:453
 lifestyle, 2:661
 population aging, 1:45–46
 positive outlook, 2:661–662
Look Good...Feel Better program, 4:1442
Loop colostomy, 2:542
Loop diuretics, 1:153, 2:690–693, 690*t,* 737
Loop electrosurgical excision procedure (LEEP), 2:483
Loose cannon theory, 1:45, 46
Loperamide, 1:182–183
 for diarrhea, 2:654
 for fecal incontinence, 3:799
 for gastroenteritis, 3:851–852
 for irritable bowel syndrome, 3:1071
Lopid. *See* Gemfibrozil
Lopressor. *See* Metoprolol
Lopurin. *See* Allopurinol
Lorastidine, 1:187
Loratidine, 1:187
Lorazepam, 1:291–294
 for anxiety, 1:144, 145
 for dislocations, 2:688
 for status epilepticus, 5:1603
Lordosis, 1:273
Losartan, 1:191, 2:563
Lotensin. *See* Benazepril
Lotions and creams
 aloe, 1:77–79
 antihistamine, 1:187
 breast augmentation, 1:368
 dermatitis, 2:631
 dry skin, 2:715–716
 itching, 3:1081
 psoriasis, 4:1520
 rosacea, 4:1579
 vaginal, 3:990–991, 993
 wrinkles, 5:1889, 1890
Lou Gehrig disease. *See* Amyotrophic lateral sclerosis
Louse infestation. *See* Lice infestation
Lovastatin, 1:247, 3:955
Lovingkindness meditation, 4:1552–1553
Low-air-loss beds, 4:1490, 5:1885
Low back pain, 3:**1150–1153,** *1151*
 back curves, 1:273
 neuromuscular physical therapy, 4:1323
 physical therapy, 1:267–271, 3:1152
 relaxation techniques, 4:1565
 sciatica, 3:1150, 1151, 1152, 4:1323, 5:1591–1595, *1592,* 1874
 t'ai chi, 5:1747
 yoga, 5:1894
Low birth weight infants, 5:1856
Low blood sugar. *See* Hypoglycemia

Low calcium. *See* Hypocalcemia
Low-carbohydrate diet, 5:1604, 1870
Low-cholesterol diet, 3:**1153–1156,** 5:1722–1723
Low-density lipoproteins (LDL), 2:505
 atherosclerosis, 1:246, 3:953
 carbohydrates, 2:422
 carotid artery disease, 2:457
 cholesterol tests, 2:506, 3:954
 coronary artery disease, 2:578
 drug therapy, 3:955
 exercise, 3:955
 fiber, 3:1155
 garlic, 3:847
 heart attack prevention, 3:923
 hyperlipoproteinemia, 3:1002–1005
 liver function tests, 3:1145
 low-cholesterol diet, 3:1154
 niacin, 1:247
 normal/high levels, 3:954
 saturated fats, 3:1157
Low enemas, 2:753
Low-fat diet, 3:**1156–1159**
 benefits, 2:661, 663
 breast cancer, 1:358
 cancer prevention, 2:412
 heart disease, 3:929
 hepatitis, 3:951
 high cholesterol, 3:955, 956
 hypertension, 3:1011
 low-cholesterol diet, 3:1155–1156
 naturopathy, 4:1315
 prostate cancer, 4:1509
 recommendations, 4:1336
 stroke risk, 5:1722–1723
 vitamin E deficiency, 5:1856
Low-fiber diet, 2:693–694
Low frequency hearing loss, 3:919
Low-grade squamous intraepithelial lesion (LSIL), 2:482–483, 4:1414, 1415
Low-impact exercise, 5:1873
Low-income Americans, 3:913–914, 4:1229
 See also Life expectancy; Poverty; Socioeconomic factors
Low parity, 2:744
Low platelet count. *See* Thrombocytopenia
Low potassium levels. *See* Hypokalemia
Low-protein diet, 5:1604
Low-salt diet. *See* Low-sodium diet
Low-sodium diet, 3:**1159–1162**
 amyloidosis, 1:102
 antacids, 1:140
 congestive heart failure, 2:563, 564, 565
 diabetes insipidus, 2:637
 heart disease, 3:929
 hypertension, 1:326, 3:1011, 4:1534, 5:1680
 ischemia, 3:1076
 stroke, 5:1722–1723
 varicose veins, 5:1818
Low-tar cigarettes, 5:1660
Low vision, 3:**1162–1165,** 1163*t,* 4:1354, 5:1841, 1842*t*
Lower esophageal sphincter (LES)
 gastroesophageal reflux disease, 3:853, 854, 856, 858
 heartburn, 3:933, *934,* 935
Lower extremity amputation, 1:*98,* 99
Lower GI bleeding, 3:871–875
Lower GI exam. *See* Barium enema
Lower limb prosthesis, 3:*1165,* **1165–1167**
Lower urinary tract infections, 2:593
Loxapine, 1:203, 4:1530
Lozenges, nicotine replacement, 5:1667
LPNs (Licensed practical nurses), 3:**1127–1130**
LSD (Lysergic acid diethylamide), 2:706, 5:1725, 1726
LSIL (Low-grade squamous intraepithelial lesion), 2:482–483, 4:1414, 1415
LTK (Laser thermal keratoplasty), 4:1486
Lubricants, 2:569, 5:1619, 1620
 See also Lotions and creams
Lucentis. *See* Ranibizumab
Luconazole, 1:311
Ludwick, Ruth, 2:529
Lufyllin. *See* Dyphylline
LUMA Cervical Imaging System, 2:483, 4:1415
Lumbar nerve roots, 5:1692
Lumbar puncture
 arteriovenous malformations, 1:230
 lymphoma, 4:1195
 meningitis, 4:1248
 migraine, 4:1267
 multiple sclerosis, 4:1305
 stroke, 5:1722
Lumbar spine osteoarthritis, 4:1366
Lumbar stenosis, 5:1697
Lumbosacral radiculopathy, 5:1591
Lumbosacral spine, 5:1592
Lumpectomy, 3:**1168–1171**
 breast cancer, 1:357, 359, 3:*1168,* 1168–1171, 4:1221–1222
 radiation therapy, 3:1169, 1170, 4:1223, 1224
Lumps, breast, 1:*351,* 351–354, 369–372, 4:1205
Lunesta, 1:140
Lung anatomy and function, 2:511, 4:1535, 1567
Lung biopsy, 3:**1171–1173,** 1175
 pneumonia, 4:1464
 pulmonary fibrosis, 4:1537
 sarcoidosis, 5:1582
Lung cancer, 3:**1173–1177**
 breathing problems, 1:373
 causes, 2:408, 3:1174
 chest CT scans, 2:493
 chest x rays, 2:499, 500
 demographics, 1:382, 2:407, 3:1174
 diagnosis, 3:1171–1173, 1175, 4:1263
 metastasis, 3:1173, 1175, 1176, 1177, 4:1262, 1263
 pleural effusion from, 4:1460, 1461
 prevention, 2:416, 3:1177
 smoking-related, 2:407, 3:1174, 1177, 5:1660, 1665
 symptoms, 5:1661
 treatment, 3:1175–1177
Lung capacity, 5:1759
Lung collapse, 5:1763
Lung disease
 chest physical therapy, 2:495
 chest x rays, 2:498–500
 general anesthesia, 1:114
 interstitial, 2:500, 4:1535
 kidney transplantation contraindications, 3:1106
 pulmonary hypertension from, 4:1539
 pulmonary rehabilitation, 4:1542
 respiratory failure from, 4:1567
Lung function tests. *See* Pulmonary function tests
Lung resection, 3:1049
Lung scan, 4:1533
Lung suctioning, 4:1568
Lung transplantation, 2:513, 4:1363, 1541–1542
Lung volume reduction surgery, 2:742, 4:1541–1542
Lupus, 1:257–260, 2:561, 3:**1177–1182,** *1178,* 5:1638
 See also Systemic lupus erythematosus
Lupus Foundation of America, 3:1179, 1181
Luskin, Frederic, 4:1552
Lust, Benedict, 4:1315
Lutein
 age-related macular degeneration, 1:41, 319
 cancer, 2:415
 cataracts, 2:463
 glaucoma, 3:881–882
Luteinizing hormone-releasing hormone (LHRH) agonists, 4:1509
Luvox. *See* Fluvoxamine
LVAD (Left Ventricular Assist Device), 2:447
Lycopene, 1:197, 2:414, 417

Lying, 3:841
Lyme disease, 3:1032, *1182*, **1182–1186**
LYMErix, 3:1185
Lymph drainage massage, 4:1219
Lymph node biopsy, 1:357, 3:1169, 4:1195, 1199, 1222
Lymph node dissection
- lumpectomy with, 3:1168, 1169, 1170, 4:1222
- lymphedema from, 3:1187, 4:1223
- ovarian cancer, 4:1376
- regional, 5:1737
- stomach cancer, 5:1706
- thyroid cancer, 5:1770

Lymph nodes
- anatomy and function, 4:1194
- colon cancer, 2:532, 535
- immune system role, 3:1022, 1186
- kidney cancer, 3:1093
- nervous system interactions, 4:1270
- prostate cancer, 4:1507

Lymph system, 4:1194
Lymphadenitis, 1:333
Lymphangiography, 2:483, 3:1187
Lymphatic channels, 3:1186
Lymphedema, 3:**1186–1188,** *1187*
- lymph node dissection-related, 3:1170, 1187
- massage contraindications, 4:1219
- mastectomy-related, 4:1223

Lymphocele, 3:1107
Lymphocytes
- role, 1:256–257, 3:1022, 4:1194
- Sjögren's syndrome, 5:1638
- *See also* B cells; T cells

Lymphocytic leukemia, acute, 1:22–23
Lymphoid organs, 3:1022
Lymphoid tissue, 3:1022
Lymphoid vessels, 3:1022
Lymphokines, 1:194
Lymphoma, 2:407, 4:**1193–1197**
- bone marrow biopsy and aspiration, 1:339, 343
- Burkitt's, 4:1195
- chest x rays, 2:499
- demographics, 4:1194
- enteropathy-associated T cell, 3:888–889
- liver function tests, 3:1145
- non-Hodgkin's, 3:942, 4:1193–1197, 1263
- pleural effusion from, 4:1460, 1461
- Sjögren's syndrome-related, 5:1640
- stomach, 5:1705, 1706
- *See also* Hodgkin's disease

Lyrica. *See* Pregabalin
Lysergic acid diethylamide (LSD), 2:706, 5:1725, 1726

M

M-proteins, 4:1300–1302
Macroalbuminuria, 2:645
Macrobiotic diet, 2:746
Macrodantin. *See* Nitrofurantoin
Macroglobulinaemia, Waldenström's, 1:254
Macrolide antibiotics, 1:149*t,* 152, 153, 5:1712
Macrophages, 1:194, 3:1022
Macugen. *See* Pegaptanib
Macular degeneration. *See* Age-related macular degeneration
Macular edema, 2:648, 650
Macules, 5:1649
Mad-cow disease, 2:531
Madopar, 4:1423
Magnesium
- alcohol abuse, 1:68
- electrolyte balance, 2:734, 737
- garlic, 3:846
- hypertension, 1:326, 4:1534
- insomnia, 3:1051
- kidney stones, 3:1102
- migraine, 4:1267
- Parkinson's disease, 4:1424
- sources, 2:416, 417, 3:818
- *See also* Hypermagnesemia; Hypomagnesemia

Magnesium ammonium phosphate, 3:1101
Magnesium citrate, 1:288, 3:1123, 1124
Magnesium deficiency, 1:390, 2:736, 4:1528
Magnesium hydroxide, 1:139, 3:1123, 1124
Magnesium salt antacids, 1:139–140
Magnesium sulfate, 3:1123
Magnet therapy, 4:1368
Magnetic resonance angiography (MRA), 4:1189, 1192, 5:1722
Magnetic resonance imaging (MRI), 4:**1189–1193**, *1190*
- Alzheimer's disease, 1:87, 4:1243
- aortic dissection, 1:219
- arteriovenous malformations, 1:230
- blood clots, 1:322
- bone metastasis, 4:1262
- brain tumors, 1:349, 4:1262
- breast cancer, 1:356
- cardiomyopathy, 2:446
- carotid artery disease, 2:457
- cervical cancer, 2:483
- cervical spondylosis, 2:488
- coma, 2:547
- Cushing's syndrome, 2:591
- deep vein thrombosis, 2:602
- dementia, 2:612
- dysphasia, 2:718
- endocrine pancreatic cancer, 4:1402
- exocrine pancreatic cancer, 4:1405
- fecal incontinence, 3:799
- functional, 1:19
- gangrene, 3:844
- head injuries, 3:903
- hemochromatosis, 3:945
- hip pain, 3:966
- Horner's syndrome, 1:263–264
- hyperthyroidism, 3:1013
- intraoperative, 4:1189
- ischemia, 3:1075
- kidney cancer, 3:1092
- knee injuries, 3:1117
- low back pain, 3:1152
- lumpectomy, 3:1169
- lung cancer, 3:1175
- lymphedema, 3:1187
- mechanical heart valves, 1:224, 2:444
- melanoma, 4:1199
- migraine, 4:1267
- mobility, 4:1284
- multiple myeloma, 4:1300
- multiple sclerosis, 4:1304
- nuclear, 2:483
- oral cancers, 4:1358
- osteoarthritis, 4:1367
- pacemakers, 4:1388
- persistent vegetative state, 4:1440
- post-mammogram, 4:1207
- prostate cancer, 4:1506
- psychoses, 4:1529
- rheumatoid arthritis, 4:1574
- sarcomas, 5:1584
- sciatica, 5:1593
- seizures, 5:1603
- snoring, 5:1673
- spinal cord injuries, 5:1693
- stomach cancer, 5:1706
- stroke, 5:1722
- transient ischemic attacks, 5:1785

Magnetic resonance spectroscopy (MRS), 4:1189, 1191
Magnets, 4:1191
Magnifiers, 3:1164, 5:1843
Maharishi Mahesh Yogi, 4:1563–1564
Maidenhair tree. *See* Ginkgo biloba
Maine Woman's Health Study, 3:1018
Maintenance, home, 3:986, 998
Maitake mushrooms, 2:416
Maize, 4:1379
Major affective disorder. *See* Major depressive disorder
Major depressive disorder, 1:304, 2:622–629, 665
Major life activities, 1:92
Major tranquilizers. *See* Antipsychotic drugs
Malabsorption
- aging, 3:869

Malabsorption *(continued)*
calcium, 2:400, 404, 4:1516–1517, 5:1853
celiac disease, 2:472, 473, 474
iron, 3:1064–1065, 1066
malnutrition, 4:1201, 1203
vitamin E, 5:1858
zinc deficiency, 5:1897
Malabsorptive procedures, 1:285–286
Malanga, G. A., 1:269
Malaria, 5:1610, 1861
Malassezia fufur, 1:184
Malathion, 3:1126, 1127
Male pattern baldness, 1:79
Male-to-female transsexuals, 1:362
Male urinary catheterization, 2:**468–472,** *469*
Malic acid, 1:83
Malignant fibrous histiocytomas, 5:1583
Malignant hyperthermia, 1:117, 4:1307
Malignant lymphoma, 4:**1193–1197**. *See also* Lymphoma
Malignant melanoma, 2:407, 4:**1197–1201,** *1198,* 5:1640–1645
causes, 2:408, 4:1199
eyelid, 2:780
intraocular, 4:1197
metastasis, 4:1199, 1263, 1264, 5:1641, 1644
mortality, 4:1200, 5:1644
skin lesion removal, 5:1647
Malignant tumors. *See* Cancer
Mallory-Weiss tear, 3:872
Malnutrition, 4:**1201–1204,** 1336–1337, 5:1871
aging, 2:674, 4:1340–1341
alcohol abuse, 1:64
Alzheimer's disease, 1:88
anxiety, 1:216
bacteremia, 1:275
chronic pain, 4:1395
cirrhosis from, 2:522
demographics, 2:675, 4:1201–1202
dental health, 2:617
diet, 2:659
dysphagia, 5:1741
edema, 2:726
fatty liver, 3:797
gluten-free diet, 3:889
low cholesterol, 2:507
Meals on Wheels, 4:1227
memory loss, 4:1245
mental health, 2:664–665
mobility, 4:1284
myocarditis, 4:1309
nursing homes, 2:675, 4:1331–1332
pneumonia risk, 4:1464
prevention, 4:1203
protein, 3:870
protein-calorie, 3:870
protein-energy, 4:1339
risk factors, 2:676, 3:870
stroke, 5:1721
treatment, 2:666, 4:1203
zinc deficiency, 5:1897, 1898
MALT (Mucosa-associated lymphoid tissue), 3:940, 5:1705
Maltose, 2:422
Mammogram, 4:**1204–1208**
breast cancer, 1:356, 4:1204–1208, 1205*t*
breast implants, 1:362
full-field digital, 4:1206–1207
Mammoplasty, augmentation. *See* Breast implants
Mammotomy, 1:352
Managed care plans, 4:**1209–1211,** 1494
billing, 4:1232
commercial prescription programs, 2:548
denial of care, 1:30–31
employer-based, 4:1496
fee-setting, 4:1231
Medicaid payments, 4:1229
patient rights, 4:1430
patient satisfaction, 3:976–977, 4:1475–1476
physician satisfaction, 3:976, 4:1475, 1496
preventive medicine, 3:977, 4:1476
surgeon referral, 3:805
vision plans, 4:1356
See also HMOs; Preferred provider organizations
Management dieticians, 2:683
Mandol. *See* Cefamandole
Manerex. *See* Moclobemide
Mania, 1:166, 302–307
Manic depression. *See* Bipolar disorder
Manipulation
back and neck pain, 1:269
chiropractic, 1:269, 2:489, 501–502, 504, 3:1152, 4:1369, 5:1594
contraindications, 1:268
dislocations, 2:688
joint, 3:1087–1089
naturopathy, 4:1316
osteopathic, 2:701–703, 4:1369–1370
physical therapy, 4:1369
spinal, 4:1316, 1369
tendinitis, 5:1754
See also Massage therapy
Manner metabolic therapy, 2:746
Mannitol, 2:690
Manometry
anorectal, 3:799
esophageal, 3:855, 859–860, 935
swallowing disorders, 5:1741
Mantle, Mickey, 4:1364–1365
Mantoux test, 5:1793
Mantras, 4:1271, 1477
Manual therapy
back and neck pain, 1:269
joint mobilization, 3:1087–1089
osteopathic medicine, 2:701
See also Manipulation
Maolate. *See* Chlorphenesin
Maprotiline, 1:176, 381
Margarine, 3:955
Marijuana, 4:**1211–1215**
drug abuse, 2:706, 4:1214, 5:1725, 1726
lung cancer risk, 3:1174
nausea and vomiting prevention, 2:418–420, 4:1213
priapism from, 4:1492
Marijuana Tax Act (1937), 4:1212
Marijuana Transfer Tax Bill (1937), 4:1212
Marinol. *See* Dronabinol
Marital status, 4:1560*t,* 1561
Marquiset, Armand, 3:1079
Marriage counseling, 4:1561
Marsh mallow, 2:595, 5:1800
Martial arts, 4:1546, 5:1745
Masculinization, 2:635
Masked face, 4:1422
Mass media, 1:48
Massage therapy, 4:**1215–1219,** *1216*
back and neck pain, 1:269
bursitis, 1:390
cervical spondylosis, 2:488
fibromyalgia, 3:801
fractures, 5:1628
headaches, 3:907
healthy aging, 4:1525
insomnia, 3:1051
Japanese traditional, 5:1627
low back pain, 3:1152, 1153
lupus, 3:1181
lymph drainage, 4:1219
menopause, 4:1253
naturopathy, 4:1316
osteoporosis, 5:1628
restless leg syndrome, 5:1657
rheumatoid arthritis, 4:1574
scleroderma, 5:1598
sexual dysfunction, 5:1620
shiatsu, 5:1627–1629
stress-related disorders, 5:1716
tui na, 1:13, 14, 15, 3:1152
vs. visualization, 4:1565
walking problems, 5:1868
Mast cells, 3:815, 897
Mastectomy, 1:357–358, 359, 4:**1219–1225,** *1220*
breast reconstruction, 1:5
vs. lumpectomy, 3:1170–1171
modified radical, 1:358, 3:*1168,* 4:1222
prophylactic, 1:360, 4:1221, 1224
radical, 4:1222
total, 4:1222

Master clock theory, 1:45
Masters of social work. *See* Social work
Mastopexy. *See* Breast lift
Matcher (device), 3:1080
Materialism, 4:1527
Maternal and Child Health Bureau, 3:914
Maternal antibodies, 1:257
Matricaria recutita. See Chamomile
Matrixyl. *See* Palmitoyl pentapeptide-3
Mattresses, eggshell, 2:600, 5:1885
Maturity, 4:1523
Mavik. *See* Trandolapril
Maximal heart rate, 5:1759
Maxzide, 2:690–691, 692, 693
Mayo Clinic, 3:1160
Maze procedure, 1:227, 2:425
McCartney, Paul, 1:2
MCI (Mild cognitive impairment), 4:1241, 1242
MCL (Medial collateral ligament), 3:1115
MCMI-III (Millon Clinical Multiaxial Inventory-III), 4:1447
McMonnies & Ho Dry Eye Questionnaire, 2:712
MCTD (Mixed connective tissue disease), 1:254
MDI (Metered dose inhalers), 1:25, 377, 2:741–742
MDMA (Mehylenedioxymethamphetamine), 2:706
M:E ratio, 1:340, 342
Meal delivery programs. *See* Meals on Wheels
Meal planning, 2:670, 676, 4:1346, 1349
Meals on Wheels, 2:558, 4:1203, **1225–1228,** *1226*
Mean corpuscular hemoglobin, 2:560–561
Meaning, 4:1525
Measles, 4:1256, 1309, 5:1815, 1861
  See also Rubella
Measles-mumps-rubella (MMR) vaccine, 5:1815
Meat
  food pyramid, 2:658
  high cholesterol, 3:956
  low-cholesterol diet, 3:1155
  low-fat diet, 3:1158
  pro-inflammatory role, 1:196
  red, 2:413, 533
  sodium content, 3:1160
Meat Inspection Act (1906), 2:657–658
Mechanical debridement, 5:1886
Mechanical heart valves
  MRSA infections, 4:1295
  staphylococcal infections, 5:1699–1700, 1701
  surgery, 1:223, 224, 2:443, 444, 4:1280
  thrombocytopenia from, 5:1764
Mechanical ventilation, 3:1046–1049, 5:1820–1824, *1821*
  cardiac surgery, 2:439
  endotracheal tubes, 2:750–752
  minute, 2:434
  modes, 5:1821–1822
  respiratory failure, 4:1568–1569, 5:1821
  tracheostomy, 3:1048, 1049, 5:1819
  types, 5:1819, 1821
  weaning, 3:1048, 4:1569, 5:1818–1820
  withdrawal, 5:1882
Meclizine, 5:1609
Medial collateral ligament (MCL), 3:1115
Mediastinoscopy, 5:1762
Mediators, 1:70
Medicago sativa. See Alfalfa
Medicaid, 3:909, 4:**1228–1230,** 1237
  adult day care, 1:29
  AIDS, 1:58
  commercial prescription programs, 2:548
  demographics, 4:1229, 1495
  end-stage renal disease, 2:510
  home care, 3:980
  kidney transplantation, 3:1106
  nursing homes, 4:1332, 1333
Medical alert bracelets, 3:817
Medical billing, 4:**1230–1233**
Medical errors. *See* Errors
Medical ethics, 4:**1233–1236**
Medical examination. *See* Physical examination
Medical futility, 5:1883
Medical history. *See* Health history
Medical insurance. *See* Health insurance
Medical records
  electronic, 4:1426, 1430–1431
  patient confidentiality, 4:1426
Medicare, 3:909, 4:**1236–1238,** *1237,* 1237*t*
  adult day care, 1:29
  antipsychotic drugs, 4:1531
  bariatric surgery, 1:286
  chiropractic, 2:502–503
  costs, 3:909*t*
  demographics, 4:1236, 1495
  drug abuse, 2:707
  emphysema, 2:741
  end-stage renal disease, 2:510, 3:1106
  eye examination, 2:769
  fraud, 4:1232, 1238
  hip replacement, 3:966
  hip revision surgery, 3:972
  HMOs, 3:976
  home care, 3:980
  hospices, 3:996
  immunosuppressive agents, 3:1106
  influenza vaccines, 3:1040, 1042
  kidney transplantation, 3:1106
  mammogram, 4:1205
  motor neuron diseases, 4:1290
  nursing assistants, 4:1330
  nursing homes, 4:1332, 1333
  Part D (drug plan), 2:548, 4:**1238–1241**, 1239*t*
  preferred provider organizations, 4:1475
  psychoses, 4:1528
  retinal detachment, 4:1572
  seizures, 5:1605
  Streptococcus pneumoniae vaccine, 4:1466
  supplemental insurance, 4:1494*t*, 1495
  travel, 5:1610
  VZV vaccine, 5:1632
Medicare Advantage, 4:1239, 1474
Medicare prescription drug plan (Part D), 2:548, 4:**1238–1241**, 1239*t*
Medicare supplemental insurance, 4:1333
Medication. *See* Administration of medication; Drugs
Medication errors, 1:27
Medication interactions. *See* Drug interactions
Medication profiles, patient, 4:1452
Medicine
  allopathic, 2:701, 4:1369
  osteopathic, 2:701–703, 4:1368–1370
Medigap, 4:1333
Meditation, 4:1271
  chronic pain, 4:1565
  hypertension, 5:1892
  insomnia, 3:1052
  lovingkindness, 4:1552–1553
  mindfulness, 4:1271, 1564, 1565
  New Age movement, 4:1565
  ovarian cancer, 4:1377
  qigong, 4:1545, 1547
  relaxation response, 4:1270, 5:1892
  spiritual, 4:1564
  spirituality, 4:1476
  stress-related disorders, 5:1716
  transcendental, 4:1271, 1563–1564
  yoga, 5:1891, 1892, 1893
Mediterranean-style diet
  Alzheimer's disease, 1:88
  anti-inflammatory role, 1:196
  low-fat diet, 3:1159
  memory loss prevention, 4:1245
Medline Plus, 2:678
MEDSTAT Group, 3:977
Medullary paralysis, 1:112
Medullary thyroid cancer, 5:1768–1771

Medulloblastoma, 1:349
MedWatch program, 2:680, 4:1345
Mefoxin. *See* Cefoxitin
Megakaryocytes, 1:342, 5:1763
Megaloblastic anemia, 3:1145, 5:1847, 1862, 1863
Meglitinides, 1:177*t*
Mehylenedioxymethamphetamine (MDMA), 2:706
Meibomian gland dysfunction (MGD), 2:711
Meibomian glands, 2:711, 779
Melaleuca. *See* Tea tree oil
Melanin, 4:1197, 1198
Melanocytes, 4:1197
Melanoma. *See* Malignant melanoma
Melatonin
  for insomnia, 4:1478
  for sleep disorders, 4:1525, 5:1657
  for viral infections, 5:1834
Melatonin receptor agonists, 5:1657
Mellaril. *See* Thioridazine
Mellon, Andrew, 4:1212
Melphalan, 1:102
Memantine, 1:88, 164–165, 5:1616
Memories, childhood, 4:1527
Memory aids, 4:1244
Memory cells, 1:257
Memory loss, 4:*1241,* **1241–1246,** 1242*t,* 5:1613
  aerobic exercise, 1:38
  Alzheimer's disease, 1:86
  Cushing's syndrome, 2:592
  delirium, 2:607
  dementia, 2:610–612
  demographics, 3:869, 4:1242–1243
  dietary assessment, 2:668
  financial management, 3:802
  folic acid for, 3:811
  geriatric assessment, 3:866
  ginkgo biloba for, 3:878–879
  Mental Status Examination, 4:1320, 1321
  mild, 4:1241, 1243, 1244
  normal aging, 1:44
  prevention, 4:1245
  relaxation response, 4:1565
Men
  age-related macular degeneration, 5:1836
  ALS, 1:103
  aneurysm, 1:121
  angina pectoris, 1:124
  aortic dissection, 1:218
  breast cancer, 1:355
  breast enlargement, 3:899
  caloric intake, 4:1351
  cancer risk, 4:1505*t*
  cystitis, 2:593–596
  dietary fiber, 3:957
  exocrine pancreatic cancer, 4:1404
  hip revision surgery, 3:972
  insomnia, 5:1655
  isolation, 3:1078
  kidney cancer, 3:1092
  kidney stones, 3:1101
  liver cancer, 3:1138
  most common cancers, 5:1736–1737
  obesity, 4:1349, 1350*t*
  osteoporosis, 4:1371
  psoriasis, 4:1518
  recovery at home, 4:1555–1556
  saw palmetto, 5:1587
  sexual dysfunction, 5:1618–1620
  sleep apnea, 5:1652–1653
  snoring, 5:1670–1671
  stroke, 5:1720–1721
  substance abuse counseling, 5:1730
  transient ischemic attacks, 5:1784–1785
  See also Gender differences
MEN (Multiple endocrine neoplasia syndromes), 4:1401, 1403
Menaquinones, 5:1859, 1864
Menghini needles, 3:1135
Meniere's disease
  gait and balance disorders, 3:833
  mobility, 4:1284
  tinnitus from, 5:1779
  vertigo, 2:697, 698
Meninges, 4:1246–1247
Meningioma, 1:349
Meningitis, 4:**1246–1249,** *1247*
  bacterial, 1:279, 3:1032, 4:1246–1249
  epilepsy from, 5:1602
  fungal, 3:825, 4:1246–1249
  Hib, 4:1256
  lyme disease-related, 3:1184
  tuberculosis-related, 5:1793
  viral, 4:1246–1249
Meningococcal meningitis, 4:1248
Meniscal injuries, 3:1115–1117
Menisci, 3:1087, 1115
Menopause, 4:**1249–1254**
  alternative therapy, 3:994
  average age, 4:1249
  biofeedback, 1:302
  body weight changes, 5:1876
  Down syndrome, 4:1256, 1257
  endometrial cancer risk, 2:744
  estrogens, 3:991
  exercise, 1:38, 3:994, 4:1253
  follicle stimulating hormone, 3:991
  hormone replacement therapy for, 3:990–995, 4:1250–1251, 1254, 5:1614
  osteoporosis, 4:1372
  probiotics, 4:1498
  probiotics for, 4:1498
  raloxifene for, 4:1251–1252, 5:1613
  rosacea, 4:1578–1579
  sleep disorders, 5:1655, 1658
  surgical, 3:991
  See also Postmenopausal women
Menrium. *See* Estrogen/tranquilizer combination therapy
Menstrual cycle, 2:744, 4:1250, 1266
Menstruation disorders, 1:335, 5:1588
Mental disorders
  elder abuse, 2:728
  generalized anxiety disorder, 3:862
  marijuana-related, 4:1214
  mental retardation, 4:1257–1258
  neurologic examination, 4:1320–1323
  probiotics for, 4:1498
  suicide, 5:1733
  therapeutic exercise, 5:1759
  Veterans Affairs hospital system, 5:1828
Mental health, 4:1522–1527, 5:1611–1612
  diet, 2:664–667
  driver safety, 2:705
  geriatric assessment, 3:866, 867
  maintaining, 5:1616, 1617
  prayer and spirituality, 4:1477
  retirement, 5:1613, 1616
Mental imagery. *See* Imagery; Visualization
Mental retardation, 4:**1255–1260**
Mental status, 4:1446
Mental Status Examination (MSE), 4:1320–1321, 1322–1323, 1447
Mentastics, 4:1291
Mentholated ointments, 4:1312
Meperidine
  analgesic action, 1:107
  calcium supplement interactions, 2:405
  hydroxyzine interactions, 1:142
  SSRI interactions, 1:173
Mephenytoin, 1:160
Meprobamate, 3:991
Merck Manual of Diagnosis and Therapy, 1:186, 5:1862
Merck Manual of Geriatrics
  AIDS, 1:50, 57
  denial of care, 1:30
  pain, 4:1394
  panic disorder, 4:1410
  physician-assisted suicide, 5:1735
  sedentary lifestyle, 5:1759
  substance abuse, 3:795
Mercurius vivus, 1:334
Mercury, 5:1602
Mercy killing. *See* Euthanasia
Meridians
  acupressure, 1:12, 13
  acupuncture, 1:17, 18
  qigong, 4:1546, 1547
  shiatsu, 5:1628

Merkel cell carcinoma, 5:1641
Mesantoin. *See* Mephenytoin
Mesenteric aneurysm, 1:120
Mesenteric angiography, 1:129
Mesolimbic reward pathway, 5:1726
Mesoridazone, 1:205, 4:1530
Metabolic acidosis, 4:1381
Metabolic diets, 2:746
Metabolic disorders
- coma from, 2:545, 547
- Cushing's syndrome, 2:592
- magnetic resonance imaging, 4:1191
- mental retardation from, 4:1256
- osteoarthritis from, 4:1366
- paralysis from, 4:1417

Metabolic encephalopathy, 5:1602
Metabolic rate, 2:658, 3:869, 4:1335–1336, 1352
Metal detectors, 4:1389
Metal dust, 4:1536
Metals, 3:835, 4:1191, 1299
Metamucil. *See* Psyllium
Metaphase, 1:155
Metaprel. *See* Metaproterenol
Metaproterenol, 1:379
Metastasis, 1:155, 4:**1260–1266**
- bone, 4:1262–1263, 1264, 5:1583
- bone scan, 1:343, 345
- brain and central nervous system tumors, 1:348–349
- brain tumors, 4:1262, 1264
- breast cancer, 1:357, 358, 359, 2:490, 3:1169, 1170, 4:1220, 1262, 1263
- cervical cancer, 2:483, 4:1415
- chest x rays, 2:499
- colon cancer, 2:532
- esophageal cancer, 2:760, 761
- exocrine pancreatic cancer, 4:1406
- gallbladder cancer, 3:836
- kidney cancer, 3:1092, 1093
- liver cancer, 3:1138, 1140, 4:1263
- liver-spleen scan, 3:1147
- low back pain from, 3:1151
- lumpectomy, 3:1170
- lung cancer, 3:1173, 1175, 1176, 1177, 4:1262, 1263
- lymphoma, 4:1193–1197
- melanoma, 4:1199, 1263, 1264, 5:1641, 1644
- ovarian cancer, 4:1262
- prognosis, 2:413
- prostate cancer, 4:1262, 1505, 1507
- stomach cancer, 4:1263, 5:1705, 1706, 1707
- surgical oncology, 5:1737
- thyroid cancer, 5:1770, 1771

Metaxalone, 4:1308
Metered dose inhalers (MDI), 1:25, 377, 2:741–742
Metformin, 1:179–180, 2:640
- commercial prescription programs, 2:549
- folic acid interactions, 3:813, 5:1862
- vitamin B_{12} interactions, 5:1849

Methacholine, 1:242
Methacillin-resistant *Staphylococcus aureus* (MRSA), 1:150, 278–279, 4:**1293–1298,** 5:1699, 1702
Methacillin-resistant *Staphylococcus epidermis* (MRSE), 5:1699, 1702
Methadone, 1:173, 4:1435, 5:1727
Methamphetamines, 2:706
Methazolamide, 2:690
Methicillin, 1:150
Methocarbamol, 4:1308
Methotrexate
- adverse effects, 1:156
- aspirin interactions, 1:236
- for autoimmune disorders, 1:259
- for bladder cancer, 1:309
- folic acid interactions, 3:813, 5:1862
- liver function test interactions, 3:1143
- for polymyositis, 4:1468
- for psoriasis, 4:1520
- pulmonary fibrosis from, 4:1536
- for rheumatoid arthritis, 4:1574

Methsuccinide, 1:160
Methyclothiazide, 1:189
Methylcellulose. *See* Fiber supplements
Methyldopa
- depression from, 2:624
- gallbladder cancer risk, 3:835
- hepatitis from, 3:950
- for hypertension, 1:191

Methylphenidate, 2:626
Methylprednisolone, 3:1180
Methyltestosterone, 3:1055
Metoclopromide, 4:1434
Metolazone, 1:189, 2:563
Metoprolol, 1:190–191, 297–299
- benzodiazepine interactions, 1:145
- cimetidine interactions, 3:900
- diazepam interactions, 4:1308
- ranitidine interactions, 3:900

Metronidazole hydrochloride
- cimetidine interactions, 3:900
- for helicobacteriosis, 3:940, 5:1800
- ranitidine interactions, 3:900
- for trichomoniasis, 5:1623
- for wound care, 5:1886

Metropolitan Life Insurance Co., 4:1494
Mevacor. *See* Lovastatin
Mexican-Americans. *See* Hispanics
Mexican wild yam, 4:1252
Mexiletine, 2:397, 405
Mexitil. *See* Mexiletine
MGD (Meibomian gland dysfunction), 2:711
MGUS (Monoclonal gammopathy of undetermined significance), 4:1300–1301, 1302
Miacalcin. *See* Calcitonin
Micardis. *See* Telmisartan
Micatin, 3:826
Miconazole, 1:184
Microalbuminuria, 2:644, 645
Microcalcifications, 4:1204
Microcirculation, 1:98
Micrografts, hair, 1:80
Micrographic surgery, Mohs, 5:1643, 1648
Micrometastasis, 4:1261
Micronase. *See* Glyburide
Micronization, 3:994
Micronutrients, 2:678
Microorganisms, 3:1030–1031
Microphones, 3:915, *915*
Microscopic Orbit Meditation, 4:1547
Microsporum sp., 3:825
Microsurgery, filtering, 3:882
Microwave ovens, 4:1389
Midamor. *See* Amiloride
Midazolam, 2:688
MIDCAB (Minimally invasive coronary artery bypass), 2:428, 4:1273–1277, *1274*
Middle old, defined, 1:46
Midlife obesity, 2:661
Midlife reevaluation, 4:1526
Midodrine, 1:264, 3:788
Midwives, certified nurse, 1:34, 35–36, 3:1129
Miglitol, 1:178, 2:640
Migraine, 3:905, 906–908, 4:**1266–1269**
- calcium channel blockers for, 2:401
- demographics, 3:906, 4:1266
- *vs.* floaters, 3:810
- prevention, 3:908, 4:1268
- relaxation techniques, 4:1565
- rosacea, 4:1579
- triggers, 4:1266–1267
- tunnel vision from, 4:1438
- vestibular, 2:697

Mild cognitive impairment (MCI), 4:1241, 1242
Mild intermittent asthma, 1:241
Mild memory loss, 4:1241, 1243, 1244
Mild persistent asthma, 1:241
Miliary tuberculosis, 5:1793, 1795
Milk
- allergies, 3:814–818
- alpha hydroxy acids, 1:83
- goats, 4:1496
- lactose intolerance, 3:1122, 1123
- probiotics, 4:1499

Milk baths, 3:1082
Milk of magnesia. *See* Magnesium hydroxide
Milk sugar. *See* Lactose intolerance
Milk thistle, 2:524, 3:951, 5:1727
Miller, Neal, 1:300
Millon Clinical Multiaxial Inventory-III (MCMI-III), 4:1447
Milrinone, 2:447
Mind/body medicine, 4:**1269–1273**
 demographics, 4:1565
 ovarian cancer, 4:1376–1377
 prayer and spirituality, 4:1476
 relaxation techniques, 4:1563
 yoga, 5:1892
Mindfulness meditation, 4:1271, 1564, 1565
Mineral deficiency, 3:870
Mineral oil
 calcium absorption, 2:400
 calcium supplement interactions, 2:405
 hemorrhoids, 3:948
 laxatives, 3:1123, 1124
 vitamin D interactions, 5:1856, 1865
 vitamin K interactions, 5:1860, 1865
Minerals, 4:1343
 alcohol abuse, 1:68
 dietary counseling, 2:670
 optimal health, 5:1871
 recommendations, 2:665, 678
 trace, 3:846
Miner's elbow, 1:389
Mini-Mental State Examination (MMSE), 2:608, 3:866
Mini Nutritional Assessment, 4:1337
Mini-strokes. *See* Transient ischemic attacks
Minimally invasive coronary artery bypass (MIDCAB), 4:1273–1277, *1274*
Minimally invasive surgery
 cardiac, 2:439, 4:1273–1277, *1274*
 coronary artery bypass graft, 2:428, 4:**1273–1277**, *1274*
 endoscopy, 2:748
 heart valve repair, 2:442, 4:1274
 hip replacement, 3:964, 965
Mining industry, 3:1174
Minipress. *See* Prazosin
Minnesota Multiphasic Personality Inventory (MMPI), 4:1447
Minocycline, 1:151, 4:1296
Minority groups, 3:913–914
 See also Ethnicity and race
Minors, defined, 2:529
Minoxidil, 1:80, 4:**1277–1279**
Mint, 3:856
Minute ventilation, 2:434
Minute ventilation rate-adaptive pacemakers, 2:434
Miradon. *See* Anisinidione
Mirapex. *See* Pramipexole
Misoprostol, 2:585–586, 5:1799, 1800
Mistletoe, 3:1011
Mitral valve insufficiency, 2:441, 4:*1279*, **1279–1280**
Mitral valve prolapse, 4:**1280–1281**
Mitral valve regurgitation. *See* Mitral valve insufficiency
Mitral valve repair
 cardiomyopathy, 2:447
 mitral valve insufficiency, 4:1280
 mitral valve stenosis, 3:932
 prognosis, 2:440
Mitral valve stenosis, 3:932, 4:**1281–1282**
Mitroxantrone, 4:1305
Mixed connective tissue disease (MCTD), 1:254
Mixed delirium, 2:607
Mixed hearing loss, 3:918
Mixed HMOs, 3:976
Mixed pain, 4:1394
MMPI (Minnesota Multiphasic Personality Inventory), 4:1447
MMR (measles-mumps-rubella) vaccine, 5:1815
MMSE (Mini-Mental State Examination), 2:608, 3:866
MOA-B (Monoamine oxidase B) inhibitors, 1:200, 4:1423
Mobility, 4:**1283–1287**
 aerobic exercise, 1:38
 assistive devices, 4:1285, 5:1616
 multiple sclerosis, 4:1306
 neuromuscular physical therapy, 4:1325
 physical therapists, 4:1454
 population, 3:794
 postoperative, 4:1484
 recovery at home, 4:1554
Mobility and orientation training, 3:1164, 5:1843
Mobilization, joint, 1:269, 3:**1087–1089**
Moclobemide, 1:173
Moderate persistent asthma, 1:241
Modern Maturity (magazine), 1:1
Modified radical mastectomy, 1:358, 3:*1168*, 4:1222
Moexipril, 1:132, 133, 191, 2:586
Mohs micrographic surgery, 5:1643, 1648
Moist gangrene. *See* Wet gangrene
Moisturizers
 aloe, 1:77–79
 dry skin, 2:715–716
 psoriasis, 4:1520
 rosacea, 4:1579
 wrinkles, 5:1889, 1890
 See also Lotions and creams
Molds, 3:822–824, 4:1312
Molecular pharmacology, 4:1450
Moles, 5:1649–1651
 ABCDE system, 5:1642–1643
 melanoma, 4:1197, 1198, 1199
 skin cancer, 5:1642
 skin lesion removal, 5:1646–1649
Molindone, 1:203, 4:1530
Money management. *See* Financial management
Monkshood, 1:227
Monoamine oxidase (MOA) inhibitors, 1:166*t*
 anticonvulsant drug interactions, 1:162
 beta blocker interactions, 1:299
 bronchodilator interactions, 1:380
 buspirone interactions, 1:145
 caffeine interactions, 2:397
 for depression, 2:626
 insulin interactions, 3:1055
 SSRI interactions, 1:173
 vs. SSRIs, 1:168
 tricyclic antidepressant interactions, 1:177
Monoamine oxidase B (MOA-B) inhibitors, 1:200, 4:1423
Monoclonal antibodies
 for colon cancer, 2:536
 for exocrine pancreatic cancer, 4:1407
 for kidney cancer, 3:1093
 for kidney transplantation, 3:1107
 for metastasis, 4:1264
Monoclonal gammopathy of undetermined significance (MGUS), 4:1300–1301, 1302
Mononucleosis, infectious, 1:254, 3:1145, 1146
Monoplegia, 4:1417–1418
Monopril. *See* Enalapril
Monosaccharides, 2:421, 422
Monoterpenes, 2:416
Monounsaturated fats
 heart disease, 3:929
 high cholesterol, 3:956
 hyperlipoproteinemia, 3:1004
 low-cholesterol diet, 3:1154, 1155
 recommendations, 4:1339
 sources, 3:1157
Monovision, 2:774
Monovision contact lenses, 4:1485–1486
Montelukast, 1:242
Mood disorders
 depression-related, 2:625
 isolation, 3:1078
 Mental Status Examination, 4:1321

Mood disorders *(continued)*
mobility, 4:1283
omega-3 fatty acids for, 2:665
psychoses-related, 4:1528
substance abuse-related, 5:1726
Morbid obesity, 1:4, 331, 4:1349, 1351
Mormons, 4:1478
Morning sickness, 5:1628
Morphea, 5:1598
Morphine
analgesic action, 1:106
analgesic effects, 1:107
for dislocations, 2:688
dry eye from, 2:711
overdose, 4:1381
for pain, 4:1395
for physician-assisted suicide, 2:762
sodium interactions, 5:1680
Mortality
Alzheimer's disease, 1:85*t,* 86
anesthesia, 1:120
aneurysm, 1:121, 122, 229
aortic dissection, 1:218, 220
arteriovenous malformation hemorrhage, 1:229
breast cancer, 1:351, 354, 358–359, 3:1170, 4:1204–1205, 5:1682
bronchoscopy, 1:384
cancer, 2:406, 407, 407*t,* 5:1682
cardiac valve surgery, 2:444
cervical cancer, 2:481, 484, 4:1412
childhood, 1:45–46
chronic obstructive pulmonary disease, 2:512
cirrhosis, 2:521–522
colon cancer, 2:533
coronary artery disease, 2:577
delirium, 2:610
depression, 2:622, 664
diabetes mellitus, 2:640
diarrhea, 2:655, 5:1871
elder abuse, 2:729
emphysema, 2:740
epilepsy, 5:1605
faith communities, 4:1478
falls, 3:791*t*
gallbladder cancer, 3:835
GI bleeding, 3:874
heart disease, 3:925–926
hepatitis, 3:951
hip revision surgery, 3:974
hysterectomy, 3:1018
infectious diseases, 3:1032–1033
influenza, 3:1035, 1038, 1040, 1041, 4:1462
kidney transplantation, 3:1108
liver biopsy, 3:1137
liver cancer, 3:1138
liver disease, 3:1135
lung cancer, 3:1174, 1177
lupus, 3:1181
lymphoma, 4:1196
melanoma, 4:1200, 5:1644
mental retardation, 4:1258
minimally invasive cardiac surgery, 4:1276–1277
mobility, 4:1283
morbid obesity, 4:1349
MRSA infections, 4:1294–1295, 1296
multiple myeloma, 4:1298
nonsteroidal anti-inflammatory drugs, 2:585
obesity, 2:661
oral cancer, 4:1359
ovarian cancer, 4:1375
pneumonia, 3:1035, 4:1462
prostate cancer, 4:1502, 1505, 1509
pulmonary embolism, 4:1533
respiratory failure, 4:1567
SARS, 3:1035
scleroderma, 5:1599
selenium, 4:1344
sleep disorders, 5:1655
smoking, 5:1660, 1665
snoring surgery, 5:1674
spinal cord injuries, 5:1695
stomach cancer, 5:1704
streptococcal pneumonia, 5:1712
stroke, 3:925–926, 5:1720, 1723, 1785
suicide, 5:1733, 1733*t*
tetanus, 5:1756
therapeutic exercise reduces, 5:1759
top causes, 2:597*t*
tuberculosis, 1:207, 5:1790, 1795
vitamin E, 5:1857, 1858, 1863–1864
Mosquitoes, 3:1187
Motherwort, 4:1252
Motility, digestive system, 1:264
Motion sickness, 5:1609
Motor attacks, 5:1601
Motor learning, 3:1167
Motor nerves, 4:1320, 1322, 5:1693
Motor neuron diseases, 1:102, 4:**1287–1290,** *1288*
Motor pathway, 4:1416–1417
Motor planning, 3:831
Motrin. *See* Ibuprofen
Mourning, 1:294–297, 2:599
Mouth
cranial nerve examination, 4:1322
dry, 1:148, 176, 2:714–715, 4:1202, 5:1638, 1639
nutrition, 4:1337
ulcers, 1:290
See also Oral hygiene
Mouth cancer. *See* Oral cancers
Mouth-to-mouth breathing, 2:449, 450
Mouthguard, 5:1751–1752
Mouthwash, 3:877, 5:1667
Movement disorders, 5:1656, 1867
Movement therapy, 4:1273, **1290–1293**
hip joint pain, 3:969
relaxation techniques, 4:1563
sleep disorders, 5:1657
Moxibustion, 1:18
Moxifloxacin, 1:151–152
Moyers, Bill, 4:1270
MRA (Magnetic resonance angiography), 4:1189, 1192
MRS (Magnetic resonance spectroscopy), 4:1189, 1191
MRSA infections, 1:150, 278–279, 4:**1293–1298,** 5:1699, 1702
MRSE (Methacillin-resistant *Staphylococcus epidermis*), 5:1699, 1702
MSE (Mental Status Examination), 4:1320–1321, 1322–1323, 1447
MTX. *See* Methotrexate
Mucosa-associated lymphoid tissue (MALT), 3:940, 5:1705
Mucus
asthma, 1:240
chest physical therapy, 2:495–498
chronic obstructive pulmonary disease, 2:511
common cold, 2:551–552, 553
terminal illness, 2:600
Mucus membranes, 3:1022
MUGA (Multiple-gated acquisition) scan, 2:439, 563
Multicentric tumors, 4:1262
Multiple endocrine neoplasia syndromes (MEN), 4:1401, 1403
Multiple-gated acquisition (MUGA) scan, 2:439, 563
Multiple myeloma, 4:*1298,* **1298–1302**
amyloidosis, 1:100
bone marrow biopsy, 1:339, 340, 343
Multiple sclerosis, 1:258–260, 4:*1303,* **1303–1307**
gait and balance disorders, 3:834
gluten-free diet, 3:886
neuromuscular physical therapy, 4:1323
paralysis, 4:1417, 1418
pulmonary rehabilitation, 4:1542
visual impairment, 5:1842
vitamin D, 5:1863
walking problems, 5:1867
Multiple Sclerosis Association, 4:1304
Multiple sleep latency test, 5:1656–1657
Multiple subpial transection, 5:1604
Mumps vaccine, 5:1815
Mupirocin, 1:334
Muscle. *See* Muscles
Muscle biopsy, 4:1468
Muscle contractions, 1:262, 345–347
Muscle mass, 5:1876
Muscle relaxants, 4:**1307–1308,** 1307*t*
barbiturate interactions, 1:282

Muscle relaxants *(continued)*
benzodiazepine interactions, 1:144, 292, 294
centrally acting, 4:1308
for cervical spondylosis, 2:488
dronabinol interactions, 2:420
for fibromyalgia, 3:801
for low back pain, 3:1152
peripherally acting, 4:1308
for pressure sores, 4:1490
for sciatica, 5:1593
for tinnitus, 5:1780
Muscle stiffness, 3:800
Muscle strength, 5:1611
Muscle tension, 3:862
Muscle weakness, 4:1287
Muscles
atrophy, 4:1287, 1322
body mass index, 1:332
decrease, 4:1336
paralysis, 4:1417
striated, 4:1307
water exercise, 5:1873, 1874
Muscular dystrophy, 3:1146, 4:1468, 5:1740
Musculoskeletal disorders
acupressure, 1:14, 15
acupuncture, 1:19
aging, 3:869
chiropractic, 2:501
gait and balance, 3:831
joint mobilization and manipulation, 3:1087–1089
osteopathy, 4:1368–1370
pain, 4:1394
physical therapy, 4:1455
water exercise, 5:1873
yoga, 5:1891–1892
Musculoskeletal examination, 1:269
MUSE suppositories, 5:1635
Mushrooms
cancer fighting effect, 2:416
endometrial cancer, 2:746
fungal infections, 3:824
hypertension, 1:326
reishi, 4:1509
Music therapy, 3:1082
Mutations, genetic, 2:406, 4:1260–1261
MVP. *See* Mitral valve prolapse
Myambutol. *See* Ethambutol
Myasthenia gravis, 1:250, 5:1740
Mycelia, 3:822
Mycobacterium avium complex, 1:152, 208
Mycobacterium tuberculae, 1:207, 3:1032, 1034, 5:1790–1796
See also Tuberculosis
Mycobutin. *See* Rifabutin
Mycology, 3:822
Mycophenolate mofetil, 3:1107, 1180
Mycoplasma genitialium, 5:1625
Mycoplasma hominis, 5:1625, 1808
Mycoplasma pneumoniae, 1:254, 4:1462, 1463
Mycoplasmal pneumonia, 1:250, 4:1462, 1463
Mycoses. *See* Fungal infections
Myelin basic protein, 4:1305
Myelin sheath, 4:1303, 5:1847
Myelocytic leukemia, 1:22–23, 2:511
Myelofibrosis, 1:343
Myelogenous leukemia. *See* Myelocytic leukemia
Myelography, 5:1593
Myeloma. *See* Multiple myeloma
Myelopathy, spondyltic, 2:487
Myeloproliferative diseases, 4:1539
Myocardial infarction. *See* Heart attacks
Myocardial ischemia, 1:124, 3:906, **1073–1077,** 5:1717
Myocardial perfusion scintigraphy, 3:1075
Myocarditis, 1:205, 4:**1308–1310,** *1309*
Myocardium, 2:445
Myoclonic seizures, 5:1602–1606
Myofascial release, 2:702, 5:1788
Myomectomy, 2:447, 3:1019
Myonecrosis. *See* Gas gangrene
Myositis, inclusion body, 4:1467
Myotherapy, 4:1217
Myotomy-myectomy, 3:1015
MyPyramid, 2:658
MyPyramid for older adults, 4:1336*t,* 1337, 1338–1339
Myrcene, 4:1213
Myrrh, 1:334, 3:1153
Myxomatous degeneration, 4:1280

N

N-acetyl-glycosamine (NAG), 3:883, 884
N-methyl D-aspartate (NMDA) receptor antagonists, 1:163, 163*t,* 5:1616
N-telopeptide, 4:1390
Na+. *See* Sodium
Nabumetone, 4:1326, 5:1605
NACM (National Association for Chiropractic Medicine), 2:502
Nadler, S. F., 1:269
Nadolol, 1:190–191, 297–299
NADSA (National Adult Day Service Association), 1:29
NAFC (National Association for Continence), 5:1805, 1806
Nafcillin, 1:149–150
Naftifine, 1:184
NAG (N-acetyl-glycosamine), 3:883, 884
Nail polish, 4:1311, 1312
Nails
brittle, 4:1312
care, 4:1313
fungal infections, 1:183–186, 184*t,* 3:825, 826, 4:*1311,* **1311–1314**
psoriasis, 4:**1311–1314,** 1518
removal, 4:**1314–1315**
Nalbuphine, 1:107
Nalidixic acid, 2:405
Naltrexone, 1:68, 5:1727, 1731
Namenda. *See* Memantine
Namikoshi, Tokujiro, 1:13
Naming, 2:717
Nandrolone, 3:993
Naprelan. *See* Naproxen sodium
Naprosyn. *See* Naproxen
Naproxen, 4:1326
for pain, 4:1395
for polymyositis, 4:1468
for sciatica, 5:1593
for tendinitis, 5:1754
Naproxen sodium, 4:1326
for bursitis, 1:390
for common colds, 2:552
vs. Cox-2 inhibitors, 2:585
gastroesophageal reflux disease from, 3:854
GI bleeding from, 3:1064
for gout, 3:891
for headaches, 3:907
hypertension, 1:326
for lupus, 3:1180
for spinal stenosis, 5:1697
SSRI interactions, 1:173
Narcan, 2:547
Narcissistic personality disorder (NPD), 4:1445–1448
Narcotics, 1:106–108
depression from, 2:624
for dislocations, 2:688
drug abuse, 5:1725, 1726, 1730
dry eye from, 2:711
for extubation, 5:1882
general anesthesia, 1:113
hydroxyzine interactions, 1:142
liver function test interactions, 3:1143
overdose, 4:1381
for pain, 4:1395
for periodic limb movement disorder, 4:1435
for pneumonia, 4:1464
psychoses from, 4:1528
for shingles, 5:1631
side effects, 4:1396
for terminal illness, 2:762
travel precautions, 5:1608
Narcotics Anonymous, 2:707

Nardil. *See* Phenelzine
NASA (National Aeronautical and Space Administration), 1:300
Nasal congestion, 5:1673
Nasal decongestants. *See* Decongestants
Nasal regurgitation, 5:1674
Nasal spray, 1:25
Nasogastric tubes, 5:1789
Nasointestinal tubes, 5:1789
Nasopharyngoscopy, 5:1673
NASW (National Association of Social Workers), 5:1677, 1678
NAT (Nucleic acid testing), 1:59–60, 5:1794
Nateglinide, 1:179–180, 2:640
National Academy on an Aging Society, 3:919
National Adult Day Service Association (NADSA), 1:29
National Aeronautical and Space Administration (NASA), 1:300
National Association for Chiropractic Medicine (NACM), 2:502
National Association for Continence (NAFC), 5:1805, 1806
National Association for Home Care and Hospice, 3:984
National Association of Social Workers (NASW), 5:1677, 1678
National Board for Respiratory Care, 2:498
National Cancer Institute (NCI)
  alternative therapy, 3:1141
  cancer demographics, 5:1682
  cancer fighting foods, 2:414
  clinical trials, 4:1265
  exocrine pancreatic cancer, 4:1407, 1408
  kidney cancer, 3:1094
  lung cancer, 1:*382*
  ovarian cancer, 4:1375
  periodontal disease, 2:616
  prostatectomy, 4:1507
  skin cancer, 5:1641
  thyroid cancer, 5:1772
  Trends Progress Report 1007, 5:1682
National Center for Complementary and Alternative Medicine (NCCAM)
  acupuncture, 1:19
  AIDS, 1:52, 53
  DHEA, 2:634
  dietary supplements, 2:678–679
  metastasis trials, 4:1265
  mind/body medicine, 4:1565
  oxygen/ozone therapy, 4:1385
  PC-SPES, 4:1509
  prayer and spirituality, 4:1476, 1477, 1478
  qigong, 4:1547
  shingles, 5:1632
  yoga, 5:1894
National Center for Health Statistics (NCHS)
  HMOs, 3:976
  home health aides, 3:983
  overweight, 5:1876
  prayer and spirituality, 4:1478
National Center for Infectious Diseases, 3:1030
National Center on Elder Abuse, 2:727, 728
National Certification Board for Therapeutic Massage and Bodywork (NCBTMB), 4:1219
National Child Traumatic Stress Network (NCTSN), 5:1715
National Cholesterol Education Program (NCEP), 2:505–506, 672, 3:954, 956, 1153
National Coalition for Sleep Disorders in Older People, 5:1655
National Combustion on Marihuana and Drug Abuse, 4:1214
National Commission for Certifying Agencies, 4:1219
National Committee for Quality Assurance (NCQA), 4:1209
National Committee for the Prevention of Elder Abuse, 2:728–729
National Comprehensive Cancer Network (NCCN), 3:1094, 4:1509
National Conference of Commissioners on Uniform State Laws (NCCUSL), 1:32, 2:567
National Council Licensure Examination, 3:1129
National Council on the Aging, 1:29
National Digestive Diseases Information Clearinghouse (NDDIC), 3:850
National Elder Abuse Incidence Study, 2:727
National Eye Institute (NEI), 2:574, 575–576, 3:880
National Family Caregiver Support System, 2:454
National Family Caregivers Association (NFCA), 1:105
National Gambling Impact Study, 3:840
National Headache Foundation, 4:1266
National Health and Nutrition Examination Survey, 5:1876
National health care, 3:805
National Health Interview Survey, 1:19, 2:616
National Health Service Corps, 3:913
National Heart, Lung and Blood Institute (NHLBI)
  body mass index, 1:332
  Framingham Heart Study, 5:1876–1877
  hypertension, 1:189, 2:517, 3:1008, 1009, 1011
  low-cholesterol diet, 3:1153
  oxygen/ozone therapy, 4:1385
  pulmonary embolism, 4:1533
  pulmonary fibrosis, 4:1535
National Home and Hospice Study, 3:983
National Institute for Allergy and Asthma, 1:186
National Institute for Rehabilitation Engineering, 4:1438
National Institute of Allergy and Infectious Diseases (NIAID)
  autoimmune disorders, 1:258
  food allergies, 3:814, 815, 816
  lyme disease, 3:1185
National Institute of Arthritis and Musculoskeletal and Skin Diseases (NIAMS), 3:1110, 1113, 1179, 1185, 4:1371
National Institute of Diabetes, Digestive and Kidney Diseases (NIDDKD), 2:756, 5:1807, 1877
National Institute of Mental Health (NIMH)
  anxiety, 1:213–214, 215–216
  generalized anxiety disorder, 3:862
  panic disorder, 4:1410
  suicide, 5:1733
National Institute of Neurological Disorders and Stroke (NINDS), 4:1394, 5:1723, 1786
National Institute on Aging (NIA)
  DHEA, 2:634–635
  diet recommendations, 2:666
  financial management, 3:803
National Institute on Alcohol Abuse and Alcoholism (NIAAA), 1:66, 67, 68, 5:1729, 1730
National Institute on Deafness and Other Communication Disorders (NIDCD), 5:1690
National Institute on Drug Abuse, 2:707
National Institutes of Health (NIH)
  acupuncture, 1:19
  amyotrophic lateral sclerosis, 1:104
  autoimmune disorders, 1:258–260
  breast cancer, 5:1682
  DASH Diet, 5:1786
  dietary supplements, 2:678
  erectile dysfunction, 2:755
  folic acid, 3:811
  fungal infections, 3:825
  glucosamine, 3:884
  gluten-free diet, 3:889
  high-fiber diet, 3:958–959
  hyperthermia, 4:1265
  knee joint replacement, 3:1113
  low-fat diet, 2:661, 3:1157
  marijuana, 2:419
  Obesity Research Task Force, 5:1876

National Institutes of Health (NIH) *(continued)*
  Office of Dietary Supplements, 2:678
  osteoporosis, 5:1612
  overweight, 1:331
  patient education information, 4:1428
  sciatica, 5:1594
  shingles, 5:1630
  Stroke Scale, 5:1688
  t'ai chi, 5:1748
  thyroid cancer, 5:1771
National Legislative Service, 5:1830
National Library of Medicine (NLM), 2:678, 679
National Military Services, 5:1830
National Multiple Sclerosis Society, 4:1305
National Nephrology Technology Certification Organization (NNCO), 2:651
National Nosocomial Infections Surveillance (NNIS) System, 3:1030
National Nutrition Month, 2:556
National Organ Transplantation Act (NOTA), 4:1363–1364
National Osteoporosis Foundation, 1:335, 338, 4:1372, 5:1869
National Practitioner Data Bank., 3:913
National Pressure Ulcer Advisory Panel (NPUAP), 4:1487
National Psoriasis Foundation (NPF), 4:1519, 1521
National Retired Teachers Association (NRTA), 1:2
National Rosacea Society, 4:1578, 1580
National Sleep Foundation, 5:1613, 1656
National Strategy for Suicide Prevention (NSSP), 5:1733
National Stroke Association, 5:1723, 1784–1785
National Vaccine Injury Compensation Program, 3:1043
National Veterans Service, 5:1830
Native Americans
  autoimmune disorders, 1:258–260
  diabetic nephropathy, 2:643
  end-stage renal disease, 3:1104
  endometrial cancer, 2:743
  gallbladder cancer, 3:835
  gallstones, 3:838
  grandparent child care, 3:795
  heart disease, 3:926
  Indian Health Service, 3:909–910
  lactose intolerance, 3:819, 1121
  lupus, 3:1179
  peripheral vision loss, 4:1438
  prostate cancer, 5:1682
  saw palmetto, 5:1587
  scleroderma, 5:1596
  snoring, 5:1671
  spirituality, 4:1476, 1477, 1479
Natriuetic peptide, B-type, 2:563
Natural disasters, 4:1469
Natural immunity, 3:1021, 5:1813
Natural progesterone, 3: 94
Nature, 4:1527
Naturopathic Medical Education (CNME), 4:1316
Naturopathic Physicians Licensing Examination (NPLEX), 4:1316
Naturopathy, 4:**1315–1317**
  AIDS, 1:52
  boils, 1:334
  hydrotherapy, 3:1001
  menopause symptoms, 3:994
  osteoarthritis, 4:1367–1368
  scleroderma, 5:1598
Nausea
  acupressure, 1:14, 5:1628
  antiretrovial drug-induced, 1:53, 54
  biofeedback, 1:300
  chemotherapy-induced, 2:418–419, 491, 492, 4:1213, 5:1684
  chronic kidney failure-associated, 2:509
  marijuana for, 2:418–420, 4:1213
  prevention, 2:418–420, 537, 4:1213
  radiation therapy-induced, 5:1684
  shiatsu, 5:1627
  sildenafil citrate-induced, 5:1634
  undernutrition from, 4:1337
Navajos, 4:1438
Nazis, 2:763
NCBTMB (National Certification Board for Therapeutic Massage and Bodywork), 4:1219
NCCAM. *See* National Center for Complementary and Alternative Medicine
NCCN (National Comprehensive Cancer Network), 3:1094, 4:1509
NCCUSL (National Conference of Commissioners on Uniform State Laws), 1:32, 2:567
NCEP (National Cholesterol Education Program), 2:505–506, 672, 3:954, 956, 1153
NCHS (National Center for Health Statistics), 3:976, 983, 5:1876
NCI. *See* National Cancer Institute
NCQA (National Committee for Quality Assurance), 4:1209
NCTSN (National Child Traumatic Stress Network), 5:1715
NCV tests. *See* Nerve conduction velocity tests
NDDIC (National Digestive Diseases Information Clearinghouse), 3:850
Nd:YAG lasers, 5:1648
Near aids, 3:1164
Near fainting, 2:697–698
Nearsightedness, 4:1570, 5:1841
Nebulizers, 1:377
Neck cancer, 5:1668, 1741
Neck circumference, 5:1653
Neck injuries, 5:1692
Neck pain, 1:*267*, 267–271, 2:487, 489
Necrosis, aseptic, 3:1045
Necrotizing fascitiis, 5:1709
Needle biopsy, breast, 1:352–353, 356
Needle core biopsy. *See* Bone marrow biopsy
Needle sticks, 1:25
Needles
  acupuncture, 1:17, 18, 20
  intravenous, 1:25
  Jamshidi trephine, 1:341, 3:1135
  Menghini, 3:1135
  shared, 5:1726
  travel precautions, 5:1608
Nefazodone, 1:145, 173
Negative for intraepithelial lesion or malignancy, 4:1414
Negative-pressure ventilators, 5:1821
Neglect, 2:567, 727–729
NEI (National Eye Institute), 2:574, 575–576, 3:880
Neighbors, 4:1561
Neisseria gonorrhoeae, 1:310, 2:654, 5:1625
Neisseria meningitidis, 4:1248
Neoadjuvant chemotherapy, 2:411
Neomycin, 1:95–97, 151, 5:1632
Neonatal hyperbilirubinemia, 3:1144
Neoral. *See* Cyclosporine
Neosynephrine, 4:1492
Neovascularization, choroidal, 1:40
Nepatazane. *See* Methazolamide
Nephelometry, 1:252
Nephrectomy, 3:1093, 1104
Nephrogenic diabetes insipidus, 2:636, 637
Nephroliths. *See* Kidney stones
Nephrons, 3:1100
Nephropathy, 2:508, 643–645
Nephrotic syndrome, 2:507
Nerve blocks, 1:116, 5:1697
Nerve cells. *See* Neurons
Nerve compression, 4:1318, 1417, 5:1591, 1593, 1692
Nerve conduction velocity tests
  amyotrophic lateral sclerosis, 1:104
  cervical spondylosis, 2:488
  paralysis, 4:1418
  sciatica, 5:1593
Nerve damage, 5:1779, 1780
Nerve regeneration, 4:1417, 1418

Nerve roots, 5:1591, 1691–1692
Nerve-sparing prostatectomy, 4:1507
Nerve stimulation. *See* Electrical stimulation
Nervous colon. *See* Irritable bowel syndrome
Nervous system
autonomic, 1:262, 300, 5:1693
central, 1:262, 2:395, 3:831
enteric, 1:262
immune system interactions, 4:1270
parasympathetic, 1:262
sympathetic, 1:262
Netherlands, 2:599, 764, 3:1079, 5:1734
Netilmicin, 1:95–97
Nettles, 2:631
Network
extended family, 3:793
preferred provider organizations, 4:1475
social, 2:662, 3:1078
Network model HMOs, 3:976
Neumega. *See* Oprelvekin
Neupogen, 2:492
Neural tube defects, 3:811, 4:1258
Neuralgia, 4:**1317–1319,** *1318*
postherpetic, 1:212, 3:1035, 4:1318, 1319, 5:1631
trigeminal, 4:1318, 1319
Neuritis, optic, 4:1304
Neurobiology of aging, 4:1523
Neuroblastoma, 4:1263
Neurocardiogenic syncope, 3:786–788
Neurochem (company), 1:164
Neurodegenerative disorders, 4:1417
Neurodermatitis, 2:573
Neurofeedback, 1:301, 302
Neurofibrillary tangles, 1:85, 87
Neurogenic bladder, 1:312–313
Neurohormomes, 1:19–20
Neurokinetics, 4:1291
Neuroleptics. *See* Antipsychotic drugs
Neurologic disorders
amyloidosis, 1:101
diagnosis, 4:1320–1323
general anesthesia, 1:114
lyme disease, 3:1184
physical therapy, 4:1455
psychoses from, 4:1528
Neurologic examination, 4:**1320–1323**
amyotrophic lateral sclerosis, 1:104
arteriovenous malformations, 1:230
cervical spondylosis, 2:488
head injuries, 3:903
lupus, 3:1179–1180
polymyositis, 4:1468
speech disorders, 5:1688
stroke, 5:1722
Neurologic screening examination (NSE), 4:1320
Neurological surgery, 3:805
Neuroma, acoustic, 2:697
Neuromuscular disorders
chest physical therapy, 2:495
muscle relaxants for, 4:1307–1308
physical therapy, 4:1323–1325
pulmonary rehabilitation, 4:1542
Neuromuscular massage, 4:1217
Neuromuscular physical therapy, 4:**1323–1325**
Neuromuscular response, 3:831
Neurons, 1:112, 116, 5:1847, 1848
Neurontin. *See* Gabapentin
Neuropathic pain, 4:1394
Neuropathy
autonomic, 2:645
diabetic, 2:645–648, 756, 3:798, 799
leg amputation, 3:1165
occipital, 4:1318
peripheral, 2:645–648
Neuropathy target esterase (NTE), 4:1288
Neuropharmacology, 4:1449
Neuropsychological tests, 5:1602
Neurorehabilitation, cognitive, 2:719
Neurotransmitters
acupuncture, 1:19–20
delirium, 2:607
depression, 2:624
stress response, 1:212
vitamin C, 5:1850
zinc, 5:1895
Neurotrophin-3, 3:1123
Neurovascular pain syndrome, 3:906
Neutropenia, chemotherapy-related, 1:155, 156
Nevus. *See* Moles
New Age movement, 4:1315, 1565
New onset angina pectoris, 1:123
New York City, 3:1078, 4:1535–1536, 5:1623
New York Heart Association, 2:563
Newborns, 3:1048, 4:1247, 5:1756
Newman, Paul, 3:919
Nexium. *See* Esomeprazole
NFCA (National Family Caregivers Association), 1:105
NHLBI. *See* National Heart, Lung and Blood Institute
NIA. *See* National Institute on Aging
NIAAA (National Institute on Alcohol Abuse and Alcoholism), 1:66, 67, 68, 5:1729, 1730
Niacin, 5:1862
aspirin interactions, 3:955, 1005
for atherosclerosis prevention, 1:247
cholesterol test interactions, 2:506
daily recommended dosage, 5:1864
gingivitis, 3:876
for high cholesterol, 2:519, 3:955
for hyperlipoproteinemia, 3:1004–1005
insulin interactions, 3:1056
probiotic interactions, 4:1498
sources, 3:818
Niacinamide, 4:1579
NIAID (National Institute of Allergy and Infectious Diseases), 1:258, 3:814, 815, 816, 1185
NIAMS (National Institute of Arthritis and Musculoskeletal and Skin Diseases), 3:1110, 1113, 1179, 1185, 4:1371
Niaspan. *See* Niacin
Nicardipine, 1:191, 2:405
Nickel, 5:1704
Nicoderm. *See* Nicotine replacement therapy
Nicotine, 5:1659–1660
action, 5:1664
addiction, 5:1659, 1660, 1661, 1664
anxiety, 1:216
heartburn, 3:933
withdrawal, 1:166, 5:1661, 1662, 1664–1668
Nicotine replacement therapy, 2:708*t,* 5:1661, 1665, 1667
Nicotinic acid. *See* Niacin
Nicotrol. *See* Nicotine replacement therapy
NIDCD (National Institute on Deafness and Other Communication Disorders), 5:1690
NIDDKD (National Institute of Diabetes, Digestive and Kidney Diseases), 2:756, 5:1807, 1877
Niemann-Pick disease, 4:1256
Nifedipine, 1:191, 5:1598
Night blindness, 5:1861
Night terrors, 5:1656, 1657
Night vision, 2:649
Nightingale, Florence, 2:527
Nightingale Pledge, 2:527
Nigral cell transplantation, fetal, 4:1424
Nigral cells, 4:1421–1422
NIH. *See* National Institutes of Health
NIMH. *See* National Institute of Mental Health
Nimodipine, 1:191, 2:405
NINDS (National Institute of Neurological Disorders and Stroke), 4:1394, 5:1723, 1786
Nisoldipine, 1:191
Nissen, Hartwig, 4:1215

Nitrates
for angina pectoris, 3:1075
for coronary artery disease, 2:580, 3:927
gastroesophageal reflux disease from, 3:854
for heart attacks, 3:923, 928
sildenafil citrate interactions, 3:930, 5:1635, 1636
tadalafil interactions, 3:930
vardenafil interactions, 3:930
Nitric oxide, 2:756–757, 5:1634, 1635
Nitrites, 1:196, 5:1704
Nitro-Bid. *See* Nitroglycerin
Nitro-Dur. *See* Nitroglycerin
Nitrofurantoin
for cystitis, 2:595
hepatitis from, 3:950
pulmonary fibrosis from, 4:1536
for urinary tract infections, 5:1808
Nitroglycerin
for angina pectoris, 1:124, 125, 143, 3:1075
for coronary artery disease, 2:580, 581, 3:927
for heart attacks, 3:928
sildenafil citrate interactions, 5:1635
Nitrolingual spray. *See* Nitroglycerin
Nitrosamines, 2:415, 3:835, 847
Nitrostat. *See* Nitroglycerin
Nitrous oxide, 1:113, 4:1214, 5:1849
Nix. *See* Permethrin
Nizatidine, 3:898–900
for heartburn, 3:935
for helicobacteriosis, 3:940
vs. proton pump inhibitors, 4:1516
for ulcers, 2:586, 5:1799
vitamin B_{12} interactions, 5:1848
NLM (National Library of Medicine), 2:678, 679
NMDA receptor antagonists, 1:163, 163*t*, 5:1616
NMRI (Nuclear magnetic resonance imaging), 2:483
NNCO (National Nephrology Technology Certification Organization), 2:651
NNIS (National Nosocomial Infections Surveillance) System, 3:1030
NNRTIs (Non-nucleoside reverse transcriptase inhibitors), 1:207*t*
No-salt-added diet, 2:564
Nociceptive pain, 4:1394
Nocturia, 5:1805
Nocturnal myoclonus. *See* Periodic limb movement disorder
Nocturnal presbyopia, 4:1485
Nodular melanoma, 4:1197–1198
Nodules, 5:1649
Noise-induced hearing loss, 3:919
Noise, white, 5:1780
Nolvadex. *See* Tamoxifen
Nomination, advance, 2:567, 3:803
Non-cycle specific chemotherapy, 1:155
Non-Hodgkin's lymphoma, 3:942, 4:1193–1197, 1263
Non-inflammatory diarrhea, 2:652–653, 655
Non-insulin-dependent diabetes. *See* Type 2 diabetes mellitus
Non-line bifocal eyeglasses, 2:772
Non-nucleoside reverse transcriptase inhibitors (NNRTIs), 1:207*t*
Non-obstructive cardiomyopathy, 2:445
Non-productive pain, 1:106
Non-proliferative diabetic retinopathy, 2:648, 650
Non-self-cells, 3:1021
Non-small cell carcinoma, lung, 3:1173–1174, 1175
Non-viral hepatitis, 3:950–952
Nonfluent aphasia, 5:1687
Nonheme iron, 1:109
Nonhemolytic streptococci, 5:1709
Nonischemic priapism, 4:1492
Nonmaleficence, 2:527–528, 4:1235
Nonoptical aids, 5:1843
Nonprescription drugs. *See* Over-the-counter drugs
Nonproliferative diabetic retinopathy, 5:1835
Nonselective NSAIDS, 4:1326
Nonseminoma germ cell tumors, 1:234, 236
Nonslip surfaces, 4:1444
Nonsteroidal anti-inflammatory drugs (NSAIDS), 1:106–108, 4:**1325–1327**, 1326*t*
acetaminophen interactions, 1:8
angiotensin-converting enzyme inhibitor interactions, 1:134
asthma from, 1:241
for bursitis, 1:390
for cervical spondylosis, 2:488
for common colds, 2:552
congestive heart failure precautions, 2:564
vs. Cox-2 inhibitors, 2:585
for diabetic neuropathy, 2:647
diuretic interactions, 2:710
drug interactions, 4:1327
edema from, 2:726
for fibromyalgia, 3:801
gastroesophageal reflux disease from, 3:854
GI bleeding from, 3:872, 874, 1064, 4:1326
for gout, 3:891
for headaches, 3:907
for hip replacement pain, 3:966, 969
hypertension from, 3:1009
for inflammation, 1:194
for knee injuries, 3:1117
for low back pain, 3:1152
for lupus, 3:1180
for migraines, 4:1267
mortality, 2:585
nonselective, 4:1326
for osteoarthritis, 3:883–884, 1117, 4:1367
for Paget's disease of bone, 4:1392
for pain, 4:1395, 1397–1398
peptic ulcers from, 5:1797, 1798, 1800
for pericarditis, 4:1432
for polymyalgia rheumatica, 4:1467
for psoriasis, 4:1520
for rheumatoid arthritis, 4:1326, 1574, 1575
for sciatica, 5:1593
for shingles, 5:1631
side effects, 1:391, 2:585, 4:1326
for Sjögren's syndrome, 5:1639
sodium interactions, 5:1680
for spinal stenosis, 5:1697
SSRI interactions, 1:173
terzosin interactions, 1:83
for trigger finger, 5:1788
Nontraditional (alternative) family, 3:794
Norepinephrine
for congestive heart failure, 2:563
lafaxine interactions, 1:144
vitamin C interactions, 5:1850
vitamin D interactions, 2:665
Norflex. *See* Orphenadrine
Norfloxacin, 1:151–152, 311, 5:1808
Norlutate. *See* Progestins
Norlutin. *See* Progestins
Normal aging, 1:44–45
Normal tension glaucoma (NTG), 3:880
Norms, social, 4:1527
Norovirus infections, 3:851
Noroxin. *See* Norfloxacin
Norpace. *See* Disopyramide
Norpramin. *See* Desipramine
Nortriptyline
for anxiety, 1:215
for depression, 1:175
for generalized anxiety disorder, 3:863
overdose, 4:1381
for tinnitus, 5:1780
Norwalk virus, 3:851
Norwegian scabies, 5:1590
Nose deformities, 5:1673
Nose infections, 4:1318
Nose surgery, 2:582–584
Nosocomial infections. *See* Hospital-acquired infections
NOTA (National Organ Transplantation Act), 4:1363–1364
Nothing by mouth (NPO), 4:1473

Novantrone. *See* Mitroxantrone
Novocaine. *See* Procaine
NovoLog, 3:1054
NPF (National Psoriasis Foundation), 4:1519, 1521
NPLEX (Naturopathic Physicians Licensing Examination), 4:1316
NPO (nothing by mouth), 4:1473
NPUAP (National Pressure Ulcer Advisory Panel), 4:1487
NRTA (National Retired Teachers Association), 1:2
NRTIs (Nucleoside reverse transcriptase inhibitors), 1:207*t*
NSAIDS, 1:134
NSE (Neurologic screening examination), 4:1320
NSI (Nutrition Screening Initiative), 2:659
NSSP (National Strategy for Suicide Prevention), 5:1733
NTE (Neuropathy target esterase), 4:1288
NTG (Normal tension glaucoma), 3:880
Nuclear cataracts, 2:461
Nuclear family, 3:793, 794
Nuclear magnetic resonance imaging (NMRI), 2:483
Nuclear medicine scans
  brain, 4:1190, 1243
  gallstones, 3:839
  GI bleeding, 3:875–876
  heart, 1:124, 2:579, 5:1609
  ischemia, 3:1075
  kidney, 3:1098–1100, *1099*
  liver-spleen, 3:1147–1149
  myocardial, 2:579
  parathyroid, 4:*1419,* 1419–1421
  stress test, 4:1327–1329, 5:1718
  thyroid, 3:1013, 5:1609, 1770, 1773–1774, 1775–1777, *1776,* 1778
  See also Bone scan
Nuclear stress test, 4:**1327–1329,** 5:1718
Nucleic acid testing (NAT), 1:59–60, 5:1794
Nucleoside reverse transcriptase inhibitors (NRTIs), 1:207*t*
Nulliparity, 2:744
Nummular dermatitis, 2:630
Nuremberg Trials, 3:1044
Nurse midwives, 1:34, 35–36, 3:1129, 4:1559
Nurse practice laws, 2:529
Nurse practitioners, 1:34, 35, 3:1129, 4:1559
  geriatric, 3:867–868
  prescription writing, 1:24–25
Nursemaid's elbow, 2:688
Nurses
  acute care, 3:1130
  advanced practice, 1:33–36, 2:525–527, 3:1129, 4:1559
  clinical nurse specialists, 1:33, 35, 2:525–527
  code of ethics, 2:527–529
  endotracheal tubes, 2:752
  enemas, 2:754
  enterostomal therapists, 5:1885
  gangrene care, 3:845
  geriatric, 3:867–868
  HMOs, 4:1209
  home care, 3:979, 981–982
  home health, 4:1558, 1559
  informed consent, 3:1045
  intravenous fluid regulation, 3:1057–1058
  licensed practical, 3:1127–1130
  managed care plans, 4:1210
  occupational health, 4:1558
  office, 4:1557
  overdose management, 4:1383
  public health, 4:1558
  registered, 1:33–36, 2:525, 3:1129, 4:1210, 1346, 1557–1559
  scrub, 3:1128
  shortage, 4:1559
  staff, 4:1557, 1558, 1559
  triage, 4:1210
  ventilator management, 5:1820, 1823
Nurses aides, 3:1128
Nursing assistants, 3:1128, 4:**1329–1330**
Nursing Home Compare website, 4:1333
Nursing homes, 4:**1330–1335,** 1331*t*
  alcohol abuse, 1:67
  antipsychotic drugs, 4:1531
  vs. assisted living facilities, 1:236–237
  caregivers, 2:454
  demographics, 4:1331, 1331*t*
  diet plans, 2:676
  dysphagia, 5:1739
  elder abuse, 2:729
  falls, 3:789
  fecal incontinence, 3:798
  hip fractures, 3:961
  incontinence, 5:1805
  infection control, 3:1029
  infectious diseases, 3:1033
  inspections, 4:1332–1333
  licensed practical nurses, 3:1128
  malnutrition, 2:675
  Medicaid payments, 4:1229
  MRSA infections, 4:1294
  pain, 4:1394
  pressure sores, 4:1488, 1489
  registered nurses, 4:1557–1558
  sexual activity, 5:1623
  shortage, 3:1028
  underweight, 2:682
Nutrient content, 2:677, 5:1871
Nutrition, 4:**1335–1338,** 1336*t*
  artificial, 5:1882
  cancer patients, 5:1681–1686
  community, 2:555–557
  vs. diet, 4:1335
  food intolerance, 3:820
  geriatric, 3:868–871, 4:1348
  healthy aging, 4:**1338–1341,** 5:1613–1614
  information services, 2:682
  intravenous, 4:**1341–1343**
  optimal health, 5:1871
  water, 5:1870–1873
  See also Diet
Nutrition and Physical Activity Guidelines (American Cancer Society), 5:1854
Nutrition and Vision Project (NVP), 2:463
Nutrition assessment. *See* Dietary assessment
Nutrition labels. *See* Labels
Nutrition Screening Initiative (NSI), 2:659
Nutrition status, 2:**673–677,** 674*t*
Nutritional cirrhosis. *See* Portal cirrhosis
Nutritional counseling. *See* Dietary counseling
Nutritional supplements, 4:**1343–1346**
  See also Dietary supplements
Nutritionists, 4:**1346–1348,** *1347*
  community nutrition, 2:555, 556
  vs. dieticians, 2:669, 672, 684, 4:1346–1348
  tube feeding, 5:1789, 1790
Nuts, 1:195, 2:416, 3:814–818
Nux vomica, 3:856
NVP (Nutrition and Vision Project), 2:463
NX-1207, 4:1512
Nydrazid. *See* Isoniazid
Nystatin, 1:184, 3:826

O

Oat bran, 3:955
Oatmeal baths, 2:631, 3:1081, 1082, 5:1651
Oats, 2:473, 3:888, 958, 4:1252
Obesity, 4:**1349–1353,** *1351,* 5:1817
  abdominoplasty, 1:6
  adverse effects, 5:1611
  asthma, 1:243
  bariatric surgery, 1:284–286, 3:958, 4:1351, 5:1855, 1878
  blood clots, 1:321
  body mass index, 1:284, 330–332, 4:1349, 1350

Obesity *(continued)*
cancer risk, 2:408
causes, 4:1349–1350
cirrhosis from, 2:522
colon cancer risk, 2:537
community nutrition, 2:556
continuous positive airway pressure, 3:1046, 1049
coronary artery disease risk, 2:579
defined, 1:284, 4:1349
demographics, 4:1337, 1349, 1350*t*, 5:1876–1877
diabetes mellitus, 1:178, 2:639
diagnosis, 4:1350
endometrial cancer risk, 2:743, 746
erectile dysfunction risk, 2:757
fatty liver from, 3:797
Framingham Heart Study, 5:1876–1877
gallstone risk, 3:840
gender differences, 2:662
global, 4:1349
heart attack risk, 3:922
heartburn from, 3:933
hip pain, 3:965
hip revision surgery, 3:974
hypertension risk, 3:1009
ischemia risk, 3:1074
kidney cancer risk, 3:1092
knee joint replacement contraindications, 3:1112
lifestyle, 2:556
liver cancer risk, 3:1139
magnetic resonance imaging, 4:1191
mental retardation, 4:1255
midlife period, 2:661
morbid, 1:4, 331, 4:1349, 1351
mortality, 2:661
multiple myeloma, 4:1299
nutrition, 4:1336
osteoarthritis, 3:1119, 4:1366
prevention, 2:556, 4:1352
respiratory failure from, 4:1567
sleep apnea, 3:1049, 5:1613, 1652, 1653
sleep disorders, 5:1613
snoring, 5:1613, 1670, 1673
therapeutic exercise, 5:1759
water exercise, 5:1874
weight loss, 4:1337, 5:1876–1879
Obesity Prevention Center, 4:1352
Obesity Research Task Force, 5:1876
Obsessive-compulsive personality disorder, 1:166–168, 213, 214, 4:1445–1448
Obstetric and gynecologic surgery, 3:805
Obstructive nephropathy, 2:508
Obstructive sleep apnea, 5:1652, 1670, 1672, 1674
Occipital neuropathy, 4:1318
Occlusive vascular disease, 1:130–132
Occult blood test. *See* Fecal occult blood test
Occupational exposure
cancer risk, 2:408
chronic obstructive pulmonary disease, 2:512
contact dermatitis, 2:572
gallbladder cancer risk, 3:835
hospice care, 2:598
kidney cancer risk, 3:1092
multiple myeloma, 4:1299
pulmonary fibrosis, 4:1536
scleroderma, 5:1598, 1599
stroke, 5:1723
wheelchairs, 5:1881
Occupational health nurses, 4:1558
Occupational Outlook Handbook (OOH), 4:1460
Occupational Safety and Health Administration (OSHA), 3:1030
Occupational therapy
activities of daily living, 1:10–11
aneurysm, 1:122
back and neck pain, 1:271
back curves, 1:274
blindness, 1:319–320
cardiac rehabilitation, 2:437
falls, 3:791
gangrene, 3:845
paralysis, 4:1418
rheumatoid arthritis, 4:1574
sciatica, 5:1594
OCD. *See* Obsessive-compulsive personality disorder
OCT (Optical coherence tomography), 1:41, 2:649, 3:881
Octreoscans, 4:1402
Ocufen. *See* Flurbiprofen
Ocular herpes, 2:574
Ocular rosacea, 4:1579
Ocular Surface Disease Index, 2:712
Oculoplethysmography, 2:457
Ocupress. *See* Cartelol
Odynophagia, 3:853, 5:1739
Odyssey House, 2:707
Oenothera biennis. See Evening primrose
Off-pump CABG, 2:428, 4:1273–1277
Office nurses, 4:1557
Office of Dietary Supplements, 2:678
Office of Public Health and Environmental Hazards, 5:1828
Office of Rural Health Policy, 3:914
Office of Technology Assessment, 4:1242
Ofloxacin, 1:152, 5:1808
Ogen. *See* Estrone
Ogston, Alexander, 4:1293
OGTT (Oral glucose tolerance test), 1:328–329, 330, 2:639
Oil-retention enemas, 2:753–754
Oils
anti-inflammatory diet, 1:195
food pyramid, 2:658
hydrogenated, 3:1154
ozonated, 4:1385
wrinkles, 5:1889
See also Olive oil
Ointments. *See* Lotions and creams
Olanzapine, 1:203, 305, 4:1531
Old old, defined, 3:868
Old Testament, 4:1561
Older Americans Act (1965), 2:454
Older eye. *See* Presbyopia
Oldest old
defined, 1:46, 3:868
emotional factors, 4:1526
hip fractures, 3:961
nursing homes, 4:1331
population increase, 1:46
Olecranon bursitis, 1:388, 389
Olestra, 5:1855, 1860
Oligodendrogliomas, 1:349
Olive oil
anti-inflammatory diet, 1:195
dermatitis, 2:631
healthy aging diet, 4:1339
heart healthy diet, 3:929
hyperlipoproteinemia, 3:1004
itching, 3:1082
low-fat diet, 3:1157
Oliver, T. H., 4:1384
Olmesartan, 1:191
Omalizumab, 1:242, 3:818
Omega-3 fatty acids
Alzheimer's disease, 1:88, 4:1244
bipolar disorder, 1:305–306
chronic obstructive pulmonary disease, 5:1662
daily recommended dosage, 2:666
dry eye, 2:713
hyperlipoproteinemia, 3:1005
immune system function, 3:1024
inflammation, 1:194
low-cholesterol diet, 3:1155
low-fat diet, 3:1157
lupus, 3:1181
mental health, 2:665–666
multiple sclerosis, 4:1305
sources, 1:305–306, 2:416
Omega-6 fatty acids, 2:665, 713, 3:1024
Omeprazole, 4:1515–1517
for gastroesophageal reflux disease, 3:856, 4:1515–1517
for GI bleeding, 3:873
for heartburn, 3:935
for helicobacteriosis, 3:940
for ulcers, 2:586, 5:1799
vitamin B_{12} interactions, 5:1848
Omnipen. *See* Ampicillin
On-the-body hearing aids, 3:916
Oncogenes, 4:1260, 1261, 1264

Oncologists, 2:412
Oncology, surgical, 2:410, 5:1736–1739
Ondansetron, 2:418, 419, 420, 491
Onions, 1:378, 3:848, 1005
OOH *(Occupational Outlook Handbook),* 4:1460
Oophorectomy, 1:376, 4:1377
Open-angle glaucoma, 5:1836, 1836*t,* 1839
Open biopsy. *See* Surgical biopsy
Open heart surgery, 2:428, 438–439, 442, 4:*1274*
Open nephrectomy, 3:1104
Open reduction with internal fixation (ORIF), 3:960, 961
Operating room, 4:1471–1472
Operative reduction of dislocations, 2:688
Ophthalmic anesthesia, 1:116, 118
Ophthalmic examination. *See* Eye examination
Ophthalmic medication. *See* Eyedrops
Ophthalmic surgery, 3:805
Ophthalmicus, herpes zoster, 5:1630
Ophthalmologists, 2:771, 772, 3:1163–1164, 4:1354, 1355
Ophthalmoscopy
- confocal laser, 3:881
- corneal diseases, 2:575
- diabetic retinopathy, 2:649
- eye examination, 2:770
- glaucoma, 3:881
- peripheral vision loss, 4:1438

Opiates. *See* Narcotics
Opioids, 1:19
Opportunistic infections, 1:51, 53, 3:1023, 1107
Oprelvekin, 5:1764
Optic nerve, 3:880, 5:1782, 1836, 1842
Optic neuritis, 4:1304
Optical aids, 3:1164, 5:1843
Optical coherence tomography (OCT), 1:41, 2:649, 3:881
Optical colonoscopy, 2:539
OPTN (Organ Procurement and Transplantation Network), 2:510, 3:1106
Optometric Admissions Test, 4:1355
Optometrists, 2:771, 772, 3:1164, 4:1353–1356
Optometry, 4:**1353–1356**
Oral administration, 1:25, 2:490
Oral appliances, 5:1674–1675
Oral cancers, 4:**1356–1360,** *1360*
- diagnosis, 2:616, 4:1357–1358
- gallstone risk, 3:838
- garlic prevention, 3:848
- smoking-related, 4:1357, 1359, 5:1665

Oral contraceptives
- acetaminophen interactions, 1:8
- antibiotic interactions, 2:710
- anticonvulsant drug interactions, 1:162
- antinuclear antibody test interactions, 1:253
- benzodiazepine interactions, 1:145
- breast cancer risk, 1:359
- caffeine interactions, 2:397
- cholesterol test interactions, 2:506
- DHEA interactions, 2:635
- diazepam interactions, 4:1308
- dry eye from, 2:711
- endometrial cancer risk, 2:747
- face lift precautions, 3:784
- gallbladder cancer risk, 3:835
- hip replacement preparation, 3:966
- iron test interactions, 3:1067
- isoniazid interactions, 1:211
- liver function test interactions, 3:1143
- for menopause, 4:1252
- rifampin interactions, 1:211
- varicose veins risk, 5:1816

Oral fluid tests, 1:61, 62
Oral glucose tolerance test (OGTT), 1:328–329, 330, 2:639
Oral hygiene, 2:*614,* 614–618, 4:**1360–1362**
- dentures, 2:621
- dry mouth, 2:714
- gingivitis, 3:876, 877
- malnutrition, 4:1202
- oral cancers, 4:1359
- personal care, 4:1442

Oranges, 2:416–417, 5:1849*t*
OraQuick Advance, 1:61
Orbital cellulitis, 2:779
Orchiectomy, 4:1508
Orders, medication, 1:24–25
Oregon, 2:599, 762, 763, 4:1235, 5:1734, 1735
Organ donation, 2:764, 4:**1362–1365**
- kidney, 3:1106–1107
- living, 3:1106, 1107, 4:1362–1363

Organ Procurement and Transplantation Network (OPTN), 2:510, 3:1106
Organ rejection, 3:1107
Organ transplantation. *See* Transplantation
Organic food, 2:658
Organismal senescence, 1:44
Orgasm, 5:1694
Orgasmic disorder, 5:1618, 1619
Orientation assessment, 4:1321
Orientation training, 3:1164, 5:1843
ORIF (Open reduction with internal fixation), 3:960, 961
Orlistat, 4:1351, 5:1856, 1860
Ornish, Dean, 5:1786
Ornish Diet, 3:1156, 1157
Oropharyngeal cancer, 4:1356–1360
Oropharyngeal dysphagia, 5:1740
Oropharynx specimens, 5:1626
Orphenadrine, 4:1308
ORSA (Oxaxillin-resistant *Staphylococcus aureus*), 4:1293
Orthopedic shoes, 5:1594
Orthopedic surgery, 3:805, 968
Orthostatic hypotension, 1:263, 264, 265, 3:787
Orthostatic syncope, 3:786, 787–788
Orthotics, 1:391, 4:1285
Orudis. *See* Ketoprofen
Oscillatory mobilization, 3:1088
Oseltamivir, 3:1040
OSHA (Occupational Safety and Health Administration), 3:1030
Osmolality, blood, 2:636
Osmotic diuretics, 2:690–693
Ossification, heterotrophic, 5:1693, 1694
Osteitis deformans. *See* Paget's disease of bone
Osteoarthritis, 4:**1365–1368,** *1366,* 1372
- aspirin for, 1:234, 235
- celecoxib for, 2:586–587, 4:1367
- exercise, 1:38, 5:1757
- glucosamine for, 3:883–884, 1117, 4:1368
- hip fractures, 3:959–960
- hip pain, 3:965
- hip replacement, 3:964
- hyaluronic acid for, 3:1117, 4:1367
- hypdrogen peroxide for, 4:1385
- ibuprofen for, 1:117, 3:883–884, 4:1367, 5:1615
- joint function, 3:1086–1087
- joint mobilization and manipulation, 3:1088
- knee injuries, 3:1115–1117
- knee joint replacement, 3:1110
- neuromuscular physical therapy, 4:1323
- nonsteroidal anti-inflammatory drugs for, 3:883–884, 4:1326, 1367
- obesity, 3:1119
- pain from, 4:1394
- pain management, 3:969
- prevention, 5:1614–1615
- spinal stenosis from, 5:1697
- surgery, 5:1617
- t'ai chi, 5:1748
- treatment, 3:1117, 4:1367–1368, 5:1614
- water exercise, 5:1874

Osteoblasts
- bone remodeling, 2:398
- osteoporosis, 4:1371, 1372

Osteoblasts *(continued)*
Paget's disease of bone, 4:1390
vitamin K, 5:1860
Osteoclasts
multiple myeloma, 4:1298, 1299
osteoporosis, 4:1371, 1372
Paget's disease of bone, 4:1390
vitamin D, 5:1853
Osteocyts, 4:1371
Osteogenesis, 4:1370–1371
Osteogenic sarcomas, 4:1392, 5:1583, 1584, 1585, 1586
Osteoid synthesis, 4:1371
Osteolytic lesions, 4:1298, 1300
Osteomalacia, 3:889, 5:1855
Osteomyelitis, 1:100
Osteopathy, 2:701–703, 4:**1368–1370,** 5:1754
Osteopenia, 1:338, 3:889, 4:1371
Osteophytes, 2:487
Osteoporosis, 4:*1370,* **1370–1374**
alcohol abuse, 1:64
antacids for, 1:139
back curves, 1:272
bone density test, 1:335–338, *336,* 4:*1370,* 1371–1372
calcium supplements, 2:403, 404
causes, 2:399, 4:1371, 5:1612
demographics, 3:992, 4:1371, 5:1612
diagnosis, 1:335–338, 3:792, 4:1371–1372, 5:1614
diet, 4:1372, 5:1614
Down syndrome, 4:1256
estrogens, 4:1250
exercise, 1:38, 3:969, 994, 4:1371, 1372
falls, 3:789
fractures from, 1:335, 338, 4:1371, 1372, 5:1612
gluten-free diet, 3:889
hip fractures, 3:791, 959–960
hormone replacement therapy for, 3:991, 992, 993, 4:1251, 1372, 5:1616
joint mobilization and manipulation, 3:1088
lupus-related, 3:1181
massage therapy, 5:1628
multiple myeloma-related, 4:1298, 1300
neuromuscular physical therapy, 4:1323
prevention, 3:969, 4:1372, 5:1611, 1614, 1868–1869
raloxifene for, 4:1252, 5:1613
risk factors, 1:335–336, 3:992
systemic lupus erythematosus-related, 3:1179
t'ai chi, 5:1747
teriparatide for, 5:1614
therapeutic exercise contraindications, 5:1760
thrombocytosis from, 5:1766
treatment, 4:1372
vitamin D for, 5:1855
vitamin K for, 5:1859, 1860
walking problems, 5:1867
Osteosarcoma. *See* Osteogenic sarcomas
Osteotomy, 3:969, 972, 4:1392
Ostomy
bacteremia, 1:275–276
colostomy, 1:287, 2:536, *541,* 541–543
Ostomy care, 2:542, 543–544
Ostosclerosis, 5:1779
OTC drugs. *See* Over-the-counter drugs
Otolaryngology, 3:806
Ouchterlony double diffusion test, 1:252
Out-put focused therapy, 2:718–719
Outcomes, health, 3:910
Outpatient surgery, 3:806
Ovarian cancer, 4:**1374–1378,** *1375*
CA 125 tumor marker, 4:1262, 1376, 1377
chlamydia, 5:1621
diagnosis, 2:409, 4:1375–1376, 1377
endometrial cancer risk, 2:744
garlic prevention, 3:848
genetic factors, 2:407, 4:1375, 1377
hysterectomy, 3:1016
metastasis, 4:1262
pleural effusion from, 4:1461
risk factors, 2:408, 4:1375
treatment, 4:1376–1377
Ovarian cysts, 4:1376
Ovaries, 5:1793, 1794
Over-exertion, 5:1616
Over-the-counter drugs
caffeine, 2:395, 396
common cold, 2:*551,* 551–552
diuretics, 2:691
drug interactions, 2:707–710
for gastroesophageal reflux disease, 3:855–856
ginkgo biloba interactions, 3:879
for heartburn, 3:935
for hemorrhoids, 3:947
for hip replacement pain, 3:969
for osteoarthritis, 5:1615
See also specific drugs
Overactive bladder, 4:**1378–1380,** 5:1805
Overdentures, 2:621
Overdose, 4:**1380–1383,** 5:1726
acetaminophen, 1:8, 3:897, 4:1380–1381
coma from, 2:545, *546,* 547
folic acid, 5:1865
niacin, 5:1864
sildenafil citrate, 5:1637
vitamin A, 5:1864
vitamin C, 5:1852
vitamin D, 5:1855, 1865
vitamin E, 5:1865
zinc, 5:1897
Overdue payments, 4:1232
Overflow incontinence, 5:1804, 1805
Overhydration, 5:1872
Overuse injuries, 5:1787, 1788
Overweight
angina pectoris, 1:125
body mass index, 1:330–332, 5:1877
bursitis, 1:391
defined, 1:331
demographics, 5:1876
gastroesophageal reflux disease, 3:854
health risks, 5:1876
healthy aging, 4:1340
heart attack risk, 3:923
hypertension, 3:1010
ischemia, 3:1076
malnutrition, 4:1201
pulmonary rehabilitation, 4:1543
See also Weight loss
Ovide, 3:1127
Ovomucin, 3:817
Ownership, joint, 2:567, 3:804
Oxacillin, 1:149–150
Oxalate stones, 3:1101, 1103
Oxaliplatin, 2:536, 4:1407, 1536
Oxaprozin, 4:1326
Oxaxillin-resistant S*taphylococcus aureus* (ORSA), 4:1293
Oxazepam, 5:1657
Oxcarbazepine, 1:305
Oxiconazole, 1:184
Oxidation reactions, 1:197
Oxide of mercury, 3:1126
Oxtriphylline, 1:162, 299, 2:396
Oxybutynin, 1:264, 4:1379, 5:1805
Oxycodone, 1:142, 4:1395, 1435
Oxygen chamber therapy. *See* Hyperbaric oxygen therapy
Oxygen concentration (FIO_2), 5:1823
Oxygen delivery, 4:1384
Oxygen deprivation, 5:1652
Oxygen saturation, 4:1556, 1567
Oxygen tension measurements, 1:98
Oxygen therapy, 3:1046–1049, 4:*1383,* **1383–1386**
breathing problems, 1:373–374
bronchitis, 1:377
chronic obstructive pulmonary disease, 2:513
emphysema, 2:741
heart attacks, 3:923
home care, 2:741, 3:1047, 1048, 4:1385
home health services, 2:741
hyperbaric, 3:844, 1046–1049, 4:1384, 1385, 1490, 5:1886

Oxygen therapy *(continued)*
pulmonary fibrosis, 4:1537
pulmonary hypertension, 4:1540
recovery room, 4:1556
respiratory failure, 4:1568
for respiratory syncytial virus, 5:1833
Oxygen toxicity, 3:844
Oxygenation, 1:137–138
Oxymetholone, 3:993
Oxyphenbutazone, 2:405
Oxytetracycline, 1:151
Ozone therapy, 4:*1383,* **1383–1386**

P

P-DEXA (Peripheral DEXA), 1:337
P waves, 2:730
p24 antigen test, 1:59
p53 gene, 4:1199, 1262, 1264
P54, 2:418
Pacemaker system analyzer (PSA), 4:1388
Pacemakers, 4:**1387–1390**
airport security, 5:1608–1609
arrhythmias, 1:226, 3:788
biofeedback, 1:301
cardiac monitor interference, 2:434
cardiomyopathy, 2:447
cardiovascular syncope, 3:788
hypertrophic cardiomyopathy, 3:1015
minute ventilation rate-adaptive, 2:434
Pacific Islanders, 5:1791
Paclitaxel, 1:309, 4:1376, 5:1771
PACU (Post-anesthesia care unit), 4:1471, 1472–1473, 1556–1557
PAD. *See* Peripheral arterial disease
Paget, James, 4:1390
Paget's disease of bone, 4:*1390,* **1390–1393,** 5:1697
Pain, 4:**1393–1397**
abdominal, 3:1147
bone, 4:1299, 1301
cancer, 2:411–412
chest, 1:123–126, 142–144
defined, 4:1393
diabetic neuropathy, 2:645, 646
diffuse, 3:1150
foot, 3:790
hip joint, 3:962–963, 965–966, 969
mixed, 4:1394
neck, 1:*267,* 267–271, 2:487, 489
neuropathic, 4:1394
nociceptive, 4:1394
non-productive, 1:106
phantom limb, 1:99
postoperative, 1:19, 5:1629
productive, 1:106
psychogenic, 3:1151, 1152
psychological, 4:1394
radicular, 3:1151
referred, 3:1151
research, 4:1397
vasovagal syncope from, 3:786
See also Acute pain; Back pain; Chronic pain
Pain management, 4:1395, *1397,* **1397–1400,** *1398*
acetaminophen, 1:7–8
acupuncture, 1:19
analgesics, 1:106–108
back curves, 1:274
dental treatment, 2:616
vs. euthanasia, 2:762, 764
exocrine pancreatic cancer, 4:1406
fibromyalgia, 3:801
forgiveness, 4:1552
hospices, 3:995, 996
hydrotherapy, 3:999, 1000
joint mobilization, 3:1088
kidney stones, 3:1102
living wills, 3:1149
low back pain, 3:1152
lung cancer, 3:1177
marijuana, 4:1213
mind/body medicine, 4:1271
nonsteroidal anti-inflammatory drugs, 4:1326
osteoarthritis, 3:969
osteopathic medicine, 2:701
osteopathy, 4:1369
postoperative, 4:1473, 1484
rheumatoid arthritis, 3:969
sciatica, 5:1593–1594
shiatsu, 5:1627, 1628–1629
terminal illness, 2:598, 764
Pain relievers. *See* Analgesics
Pain scales, 4:1394–1395, *1398*
Painful intercourse, 5:1618, 1619
Paints, 5:1584
Palliative care
acupuncture, 1:19
cachexia and wasting, 2:393
death and dying, 2:600
esophageal cancer, 2:760
vs. euthanasia, 2:762
hospices, 3:995–997
lung cancer, 3:1176, 1177
pleural effusion, 4:1462
vs. suicide, 5:1735
thyroid cancer, 5:1771
tuberculosis, 5:1795
withdrawal of life support, 5:1883
Palliative surgery, 2:410
Pallidotomy, 4:1424
Palmer, Daniel David, 2:501
Palmitoyl pentapeptide-3, 5:1889
Palomar-plantar pustulosis (PPP), 4:1518–1519
Pamelor. *See* Nortriptyline
Pamidronate, 4:1392
Panadol. *See* Acetaminophen
Panax ginseng. See Asian ginseng
Pancreas, 3:1053, 4:1400–1401, 1404
Pancreatectomy, 4:1402, 1406
Pancreatic cancer
endocrine, 4:**1400–1403**, *1401,* 1404
exocrine, 4:1401, **1404–1408**
metastasis, 4:1263
periodontal disease, 2:616
Pancreatic disorders, 2:507, 5:1855
Pancreatic enzymes, 4:1407
Pancreatitis, 3:835, 1146, 4:1404
Pancreatoblastoma, 4:1404
Pancytopenia, 1:340
Pandemics, influenza, 3:1038
Panel of reactive antibody (PRA), 3:1106
Panendoscopy, 4:1358
Panic attacks, 1:373, 4:1409, 1410
Panic disorder, 1:213, 4:**1408–1412**
caffeine precautions, 2:396
demographics, 1:214, 4:1410
generalized anxiety disorder, 3:862
marijuana-related, 4:1214
SSRIs for, 1:166, 167, 168
Panitumumab, 2:536
Panniculectomy, 1:3
Pannus, 1:3
Panothenic acid. *See* Vitamin B_5
Panton-Valentine leukocidin (PVL), 4:1294, 1295
Pantoprazole, 4:1515–1517
for gastroesophageal reflux disease, 3:856, 4:1515–1517
for heartburn, 3:935
for ulcers, 2:586
Pantothenic acid, 4:1267
PAP (Prostatic acid phosphatase), 4:1262
Pap tests, 4:**1412–1416,** *1413, 1414*
cervical cancer, 2:481, 482, 485, 4:1412–1416
HPV DNA test with, 5:1625–1626
Papain, 1:83
Papanicolaou test. *See* Pap tests
Papaverine, 5:1620
Papaya, 1:83, 2:417
Papillary carcinoma
pancreatic, 4:1404
thyroid, 5:1768–1771
Papillary serous carcinoma, endometrial, 2:743
Papules, 5:1649
PAR-Q (Physical Activity Readiness Questionnaire), 5:1759
Para-aminosalicyclic acid (PAS), 2:405
Paraasomnias, 5:1656

Paracetamol, 4:1398
Paraflex. *See* Chlorzoxazone
Paralysis, 4:**1416–1418**
  medullary, 1:112
  motor neuron disease-related, 4:1287
  quadriceps, 3:1112
  spinal cord injury-related, 5:1692, 1696
Paranoia, 4:1532
Paranoid personality disorder (PPD), 4:1444–1448
Paraphrenia, 4:1528, 1529
Paraplatin. *See* Carboplatin
Paraplegia, 4:1417–1418, 5:1692, 1696
Parasites, 2:408, 654
Parasitosis, delusory, 4:1529
Parasympathetic nervous system, 1:262
Parathyroid cancer, 3:1006, 4:*1419,* 1419–1421
Parathyroid glands, 2:398, 3:1005, 4:1419
Parathyroid hormone (PTH)
  calcium levels, 2:735, 4:1419
  hyperparathyroidism, 3:1005
  vitamin D, 5:1853, 1854
Parathyroid hyperplasia, 3:1006
Parathyroid scan, 4:*1419,* **1419–1421**
Parent-child relationships, 4:1561
Parenteral administration of medication, 1:25
Parenteral nutrition, 4:**1341–1343**
Parents, 3:794
Parepectolin. *See* Attapulgite
Paresis, 4:1417
Paresthesias, 4:1433
Parkinsonism, 4:1421–1422, 1530
Parkinson's disease, 4:*1421,* **1421–1425**
  demographics, 4:1421
  drug therapy, 1:198–202, 199*t,* 4:1422, 1423–1424
  dysarthria from, 5:1687, 1688, 1689
  gait and balance disorders, 3:832, 834, 4:1422, 1423
  headaches from, 3:906
  levodopa for, 1:199, 200–201, 3:832, 4:1423
  malnutrition, 4:1202
  movement therapy, 4:1293
  neuromuscular physical therapy, 4:1323
  physical therapy, 4:1422–1423
  psychoses from, 4:1528
  pulmonary rehabilitation, 4:1542
  swallowing disorders from, 5:1742
  t'ai chi, 5:1747
  treatment, 4:1422–1424
  vitamin E for, 4:1432, 5:1856
  walking problems, 5:1867
Parlodel. *See* Bromocriptine
Parnate. *See* Tranylcypromine
Paromycin, 1:95–97
Paroxetine, 1:144, 167–174
  for anxiety, 1:215
  for generalized anxiety disorder, 3:863
  for itching, 3:1082
  for panic disorder, 4:1411
  for PTSD, 4:1470
Parry's disease, 3:1013
Parsley, 1:326
Partial abdominoplasty, 1:4
Partial dentures, 2:620, 621
Partial gastrectomy, 5:1706, 1707
Partial hepatectomy, 3:1140
Partial mastectomy. *See* Lumpectomy
Partial nephrectomy, 3:1093
Partial parenteral nutrition (PPN), 4:1342
Partial seizures, 1:215, 5:1602–1606
Partial thromboplastin time, 5:1785
Particle agglutination, 1:252, 253
Particle repositioning maneuvers, 3:832
Passiflora incarnata. See Passionflower
Passionflower, 1:216, 3:864, 1051
Passive euthanasia, 2:763
Passive fixation, 4:1388
Passive range of motion, 1:269, 2:436
Passive relaxation techniques, 4:1563, 1564
Passive smoking, 5:1660
Pasteur, Louis, 3:846, 987
Pastoral care, 4:1483
Patch tests. *See* Skin patch test
Patellar dislocation, 2:687–688, 5:1695
Patellar tendon, 3:1116, 1117–1118
Patient care
  decision making, 2:528
  rationing, 2:528
  registered nurses, 4:1557
Patient care team. *See* Care team
Patient confidentiality, 2:528, 4:**1425–1428**
  AIDS tests, 1:58
  electronic records, 4:1426, 1430–1431
Patient-controlled analgesia, 3:967, 996, 4:1473
Patient education, 4:**1428**
  anxiety, 1:215
  back and neck pain, 1:270
  boils, 1:335
  cardiac rehabilitation, 2:436
  chest physical therapy, 2:497, 498
  chest x rays, 2:500
  chiropractic, 2:504
  coronary artery disease, 2:581
  dementia, 2:614
  dermatologists, 2:633
  dietary counseling, 2:670
  drug interactions, 2:710
  fibromyalgia, 3:801, 802
  gait and balance disorders, 3:834
  home health aides, 3:984
  hydration, 5:1872
  informed consent, 3:1043
  licensed practical nurses, 3:1128
  liver function tests, 3:1146
  lung cancer, 3:1176
  naturopathy, 4:1316–1317
  nutritionists, 4:1346, 1348
  osteoarthritis, 4:1367
  osteopathic medicine, 2:702
  patient rights, 4:1430
  physical therapists, 4:1455–1456
  physical therapy, 1:268
  postoperative care, 4:1474, 1483–1484
  preoperative, 4:1483–1484
  presbyopia, 4:1487
  pulmonary rehabilitation, 4:1543
  rheumatologists, 4:1577
  surgery, 3:807
  urinary catheterization, 2:467
Patient history. *See* Health history
Patient medication profiles, 4:1452
Patient positioning, 4:1489
Patient representative, 4:**1428–1429**
Patient rights, 2:527, 528, 4:1333, **1429–1431,** *1430*
Patient satisfaction
  HMOs, 3:976–977
  preferred provider organizations, 4:1475–1476
  quality of care, 3:910–911
  Veterans Affairs hospital system, 5:1828
Patient Self-Determination Act (PSDA), 3:1149
Patient's Bill of Rights, 2:527, 4:1430
Paxil. *See* Paroxetine
Payback, 3:795
Payee, representative, 2:567, 3:804
Payments, overdue, 4:1232
PBP (Progressive bulbar palsy), 1:103, 4:1287
PC-SPES, 4:1265, 1509
PCL (Posterior cruciate ligament), 3:1115
PCP, 2:706, 5:1725
PCR (Polymerase chain reaction), 1:60
PCV7 vaccine, 4:1248
PDE (Personality Disorder Examination), 4:1447
PDE-5 (Phosphodiesterase type 5) drugs, 2:647, 756–757
PDNOS (Personality disorder not otherwise specified), 4:1444
PDR for Herbal Medicine, 4:1214
Peanut oil, 3:1157

Peanuts, 1:72, 3:814–818
Pecid AC. *See* Famotidine
Pediatric glaucoma, 3:880
Pediatric optometry, 4:1354
Pediatric surgery, 3:806
Pediculicides, 5:1651
Pediculoses. *See* Lice infestation
Pediculosis humanus capitis, 3:1125
Pediculosis humanus corporis, 3:1125–1126
PEEP (Positive-end expiratory pressure), 5:1822
PEG (Percutanious endoscopic gastrostomy), 5:1789
Pegaptanib, 1:41
Pelargonion odoratissimum. See Geranium
Pellagra, 5:1862
Pelvic examination
  cancer diagnosis, 2:409
  cystitis, 2:594
  ovarian cancer, 4:1376, 1377
Pelvic exenteration, 2:484
Pelvic inflammatory disease, 3:1016
Pen T'sao, 4:1211
Penbutolol sulfate, 1:190–191
Peneocytomas, 1:350
Penetrating abdominal trauma, 3:846
Penetrating head injuries, 3:901, 902, 903
Penetrex. *See* Enoxacin
Penicillamine, 5:1897
Penicillin G, 1:149–150, 152
Penicillin V, 1:149–150
Penicillinase, 1:150
Penicillins, 1:149–150, 149*t*
  allergies, 1:70, 152, 153
  calcium supplement interactions, 2:405
  for cellulitis, 5:1712
  vs. cephalosporins, 2:479
  for cystitis, 2:595
  for endocarditis, 5:1712
  for erysipelas, 5:1712
  for *Staphylococcus aureus,* 4:1294
  for strep throat, 5:1711
  for syphilis, 5:1623
  for wound care, 5:1886
Penile implants, 2:757
Penis, 2:755, 5:1635
Pennyroyal, 3:1126
Pension plans, 1:46
Pentazocine, 1:107, 173
Pentobarbital, 2:405
Pentothal. *See* Thiopental
Pentoxifylline, 2:480
Pepcid. *See* Famotidine
Peppermint, 3:988, 1071
Peppers, chili, 2:415
Peptic ulcers, 5:1797–1800
  caffeine precautions, 2:396
  GI bleeding, 3:872
  H-2 receptor blockers for, 3:897–898
  heartburn from, 3:933
  helicobacteriosis-related, 3:939–941
  proton pump inhibitors for, 4:1515
  risk factors, 5:1797–1798
  sildenafil citrate contraindications, 5:1635
  smoking-related, 5:1665
  treatment, 3:873, 940–941, 5:1799–1800
Pepto-Bismol. *See* Bismuth subsalicylate
Perception, 2:608, 4:1321, 5:1714
Percival, Thomas, 4:1234
Percocet. *See* Oxycodone
Percussion, chest, 2:497, 742, 4:1465
Percutaneous liver biopsy. *See* Liver biopsy
Percutaneous transluminal coronary angioplasty (PTCA), 1:130–132
  angina pectoris, 1:124, 3:1075
  coronary artery disease, 2:580, 3:928
  vs. minimally invasive cardiac surgery, 4:1277
Percutanious endoscopic gastrostomy (PEG), 5:1789
Perforation, ulcer-associated, 5:1798
Pergolide, 4:1423, 1435
Pericardiectomy, 4:1432
Pericardiocentesis, 4:1432
Pericarditis, 4:*1431,* **1431–1433**
  myocarditis-related, 4:1310
  scleroderma-related, 5:1597
  tuberculosis-related, 5:1793
Perimenopause, 3:990–995
  See also Menopause
Perindopril, 1:132, 191, 2:586
Periodic limb movement disorder, 4:**1433–1436**
  healthy aging, 5:1613, 1616
  sleep disorders, 5:1656
  treatment, 4:1434–1535, 5:1657
Periodic limb movement index, 4:1434
Periodontal disease, 2:616, 3:876–878, 4:1360, 1361–1362
Periodontitis, 3:877, 4:1362
Peripheral arterial disease (PAD), 2:517–520
  amputation, 1:97
  ankle-brachial index, 1:136–137, 2:518
  atherosclerosis, 1:245
Peripheral DEXA (P-DEXA), 1:337
Peripheral edema, 2:725, 727
Peripheral intravenous medication administration, 3:1060, 1061
Peripheral joint mobilization and manipulation, 3:1088
Peripheral nerve injuries, 1:263, 4:1417
Peripheral nerve roots, 5:1691–1692
Peripheral neuropathy, diabetic, 2:645–648
Peripheral vascular disease, 3:1112, 1165, 4:*1436,* **1436–1437**
Peripheral vestibular hypofunction, 3:832
Peripheral vision, 1:39
Peripheral vision loss, 4:**1437–1439**
Peripherally acting muscle relaxants, 4:1308
Peristalsis, 1:262, 2:752, 3:1123
Peritoneal dialysis, 2:509
Peritonitis, 2:695, 5:1793
Periwinkle, 2:490
Permax. *See* Pergolide
Permeability, gut, 4:1497
Permethrin, 3:1126, 5:1590
Pernicious anemia, 1:109
  causes, 3:869
  folic acid, 3:811, 812
  malnutrition from, 4:1201
  stomach cancer risk, 5:1705
  vitamin B_{12}, 3:869, 4:1201, 5:1847
Peroxidase, 1:251
Peroxide, 5:1751
Perphenazine, 1:203, 4:1530
Persantine. *See* Dipyridamole
Persistent vegetative state, 2:547, 4:**1439–1441**
Personal care, 4:1442
Personal care attendants, 3:979
Personal growth therapies, 4:1291–1292
Personal hygiene, 2:594, 4:**1441–1444**
  cancer patients, 5:1685
  diarrhea prevention, 2:655
  lice infestation, 3:1127
  mobility, 4:1283
  scabies prevention, 5:1591
  skin lesion prevention, 5:1651
  travel, 5:1610
  urinary tract infection prevention, 5:1809
  viral infection prevention, 5:1834, 1835
  See also Hand washing; Oral hygiene
Personality changes, 2:612
Personality Disorder Examination (PDE), 4:1447
Personality disorder not otherwise specified (PDNOS), 4:1444
Personality disorders, 4:**1444–1449**
Personality types, 4:1270
Persons United Limiting Substandards and Errors in Health Care (PULSE), 4:1430

Perspiration, underarm, 1:345, 347
Pertussis, 4:1258, 5:1756, 1815
Peruvian bark, 3:987
Pes anserine bursitis, 1:388, 389
Pesticides, 4:1195, 1299
PET scans. *See* Positron emission tomography
Pet therapy, 3:1079, 4:1561
Petroleum jelly, 3:948, 1126, 4:1277
Petroleum products, 4:1299, 1384, 1408, 5:1642
Pets
  bereavement counseling, 1:296
  care of, 3:998
  pet food delivery programs, 4:1227
  relationships, 4:1561
Peyronie's disease, 5:1619, 1635
PGE2 (Prostaglandin E2), 4:1326
pH level, 4:1381, 1382
pH probe study, 3:855, 859–860, 934
Phacoemulsification, 2:463
Phagocytes, 3:1022
Phantom limb pain, 1:99
Pharmaceutical companies, 4:1451
Pharmacies, 4:1449, 1453
Pharmacists, 4:1449*t, 1450,* 1451–1452
Pharmacodynamics, 1:26, 4:1450–1451
Pharmacokinetics, 4:1450, 1451
Pharmacologists, 4:1451–1452
Pharmacology, 4:**1449–1452,** 1449*t, 1450*
Pharmacy Technician Certification Board (PTCB), 4:1453
Pharmacy technicians, 4:**1452–1454**
Pharyngeal cancer, 3:848
Pharyngeal swallowing, 5:1739
Pharyngoscopy, 4:1358
Phase II step-down unit, 4:1557
Phenacetin, 3:1092
Phenazopyridine, 1:311, 2:595
Phenelzine
  anticonvulsant drug interactions, 1:162
  beta blocker interactions, 1:299
  bronchodilator interactions, 1:380
  buspirone interactions, 1:145
  insulin interactions, 3:1055
Phenindamine, 1:187
Pheniramine, 1:187
Phenobarbital, 1:282
  hydroxyzine interactions, 1:142
  liver function test interactions, 3:1143
  for seizures, 1:160, 5:1603
  SSRI interactions, 1:173
  for status epilepticus, 5:1603
  vitamin D interactions, 5:1856
Phenol, 5:1694, 1889
Phenol-soluble modulin (PSM), 4:1294
Phenothiazines, 1:187, 4:1434
Phenylbutazone, 2:405
Phenylketonuria (PKU), 2:479, 4:1256, 1258, 5:1602
Phenylpropanolamine, 2:397
Phenytoin, 1:160
  acetaminophen interactions, 1:8
  alcohol interactions, 1:66
  celecoxib interactions, 2:587
  cimetidine interactions, 3:900
  folic acid interactions, 3:813
  hormone replacement therapy interactions, 3:993
  liver function test interactions, 3:1143
  for neuralgia, 4:1318
  nonsteroidal anti-inflammatory drug interactions, 4:1327
  periodic limb movement disorder from, 4:1434
  for postherpetic neuralgia, 4:1319
  pulmonary fibrosis from, 4:1536
  ranitidine interactions, 3:900
  for seizures, 5:1603
  SSRI interactions, 1:173
  for status epilepticus, 5:1603
  tricyclic antidepressant interactions, 1:177
Philadelphia chromosome, 4:1260
Phimosis, 2:470
Phlebectomy, ambulatory, 5:1818
Phlebitis, 4:1251
Phlebotomy, 3:945
Phobia disorders
  antianxiety drugs for, 1:144–145
  social, 1:166, 167, 213, 214, 216
  specific, 1:213, 216
Phone fast victims, 2:449, 450
Phoropters, 4:1485
Phosphates
  chronic kidney failure, 2:509
  electrolyte balance, 2:734, 737–738
  kidney stones, 3:1101
  sources, 2:738
  zinc interactions, 5:1898
Phosphodiesterase type 5 (PDE-5) drugs, 2:647, 756–757
Phospo-Soda. *See* Dibasic sodium phosphate
Photochemotherapy (PUVA), 4:1520
Photocoagulation therapy, 1:41, 5:1839
Photocontact dermatitis, 2:571–573
Photodynamic therapy
  age-related macular degeneration, 1:41
  bladder cancer, 1:309
  esophageal cancer, 2:761
  skin cancer, 5:1643
Photographic dietary assessment, 2:668
Photosensitive lenses, 2:773
Photosensitivity
  diuretics, 2:692
  methotrexate, 1:156
  tetracyclines, 1:153
  tricyclic antidepressant, 1:176
Phototherapeutic keratectomy (PTK), 2:575, 576
Phototherapy, 2:627
Phthalazinone, 1:187
Phthirus pubis, 3:1126
Phylloquinone, 5:1859
Physical abuse, 2:727–729, 4:1256
Physical activity. *See* Exercise
Physical Activity Readiness Questionnaire (PAR-Q), 5:1759
Physical examination
  Americans with Disabilities Act, 1:93–94
  anxiety, 1:214
  cancer diagnosis, 2:409
  dehydration, 2:604
  delirium, 2:608
  dementia, 2:612
  dislocations and subluxations, 2:687
  fecal incontinence, 3:798
  generalized anxiety disorder, 3:863
  GI bleeding, 3:873
  liver cancer, 3:1139
  low back pain, 3:1152
  mobility, 4:1284
  osteoarthritis, 4:1366
  pain, 4:1394
  physical therapists, 4:1454
  preoperative cardiac assessment, 4:1480, 1481
  preoperative care, 4:1482
  psychoses, 4:1529
  pulmonary fibrosis, 4:1537
  substance abuse, 5:1727
  swallowing disorders, 5:1740–1741
  ulcers, 5:1799
Physical fitness test, 5:1760
Physical health. *See* Health
Physical inactivity. *See* Sedentary lifestyle
Physical restraints, 4:1332
Physical therapists, 1:268, 4:**1454–1456,** 1457–1459
Physical therapy, 4:*1456,* **1456–1459**
  activities of daily living, 1:10–11
  amputation, 1:98–99
  amyotrophic lateral sclerosis, 1:104
  aneurysm, 1:122
  assessment, 1:268–269, 4:1323, 1324, 1454
  autonomic disorders, 1:264
  back curves, 1:274

Physical therapy *(continued)*
back pain, 1:*267,* 267–271
burns, 4:1455
bursitis, 1:390
cachexia and wasting, 2:394
cardiac rehabilitation, 2:437
cervical spondylosis, 2:488
chest, 2:495–498
coronary artery disease, 4:1455
diabetic nephropathy, 2:644, 647
dislocations, 2:688, 689
dizziness, 2:698
falls, 3:791
gait and balance disorders, 3:832, 833–834
gangrene, 3:845
heart disease, 4:1455
hip fractures, 3:961
hip replacement, 3:967
hospice care, 2:598
hydrotherapy, 3:1001
joint mobilization and manipulation, 3:1087–1089
knee joint replacement, 3:1113
low back pain, 3:1152
lower limb prosthesis, 3:1167
manipulation, 4:1369
mobility, 4:1285
musculoskeletal disorders, 4:1455
neck pain, 1:*267,* 267–271
neurologic disorders, 4:1455
neuromuscular, 4:1323–1325
orthopedic disorders, 4:1455
osteoarthritis, 5:1615
paralysis, 4:1418
Parkinson's disease, 4:1323, 1422–1423
patient education, 1:268
personal hygiene, 4:1444
pressure sores, 4:1490
pulmonary rehabilitation, 4:1542–1544
sciatica, 5:1594
soft tissue injuries, 4:1455
spinal cord injuries, 5:1694
spinal stenosis, 5:1698
stroke, 5:1723
trigger finger, 5:1788
walking problems, 5:1868
wheelchairs, 5:1881
Physical therapy aides, 4:1457, 1459
Physical therapy assistants (PTAs), 1:271, 4:1454, 1455, 1457, **1459–1460**
Physician assistants, 1:24–25
Physician-assisted suicide
ethics, 4:1235
vs. euthanasia, 2:762, 763
HMOs, 3:977
legislation, 2:599
suicide, 5:1734–1735
Physician-patient relations, 4:1235–1236, 5:1748–1749
Physicians
disciplinary actions, 3:807
HMO satisfaction, 3:976, 4:1209, 1475
informed consent, 3:1043–1045
medical ethics, 4:1233–1236
nursing home residents, 4:1334
patient education, 4:1428
preferred provider organizations, 4:1475
prescription writing, 1:24–25
satisfaction with managed care, 3:976, 4:1475, 1496
talking with, 5:1748–1749
Physician's Desk Reference, 1:26
A Physician's Guide to Nutrition in Chronic Disease Management for Older Adults (American Academy of Family Physicians), 2:659
Physiology of aging, 3:869
Physiotherapy. *See* Physical therapy
Phytates, 5:1895
Phytic acid, 2:399–400, 5:1897
Phytochemicals, 2:413–418
Phytoestrogens, 2:416, 417, 418, 4:1253
Phytonadione, 5:1864
Pickles, 5:1706
Pigment cirrhosis, 2:522
Pigmentation changes, 3:1132
Piles. *See* Hemorrhoids
Pill-roll tremors, 4:1422
Pill splitting, 2:549
Pilocarpine, 2:714, 4:1570
Pilonidal cysts, 1:333
Pimozide, 1:149, 4:1530
Pindolol, 1:190–191
Pine, 2:742
Pineal tumors, 1:349–350
Pineapple, 1:83
Pineoblastomas, 1:350
Pioglitazone, 1:179–180
Pioneer Network, 4:1334
Piper methysticum. See Kava kava
Piperacillin, 1:150
Piperadines, 1:187
Piperazine, 1:187
Pirant, Gary, 2:502
Pirfenidone, 4:1537
Piriformis syndrome, 5:1593–1595
Pituitary adenoma, 2:590
Pituitary gland, 2:590, 636–637
Pityrosporum ovale, 5:1600
Pivot joints, 3:1086
PKU (Phenylketonuria), 2:479, 4:1256, 1258, 5:1602
Placebo effect, 4:1269–1270
Plague, 1:151
Plan of care. *See* Care plans
Planned–replacement soft lenses, 2:774
Plant alkaloids, 2:490
Plant-based foods, 2:413–418
Plant estrogens. *See* Phytoestrogens
Plantago major. See Plantain
Plantain, 4:1379
Plantar flexion, 5:1759
Plantar warts, 3:821
Plants, poisonous, 2:572
Plaque psoriasis, 4:1518, 1520
Plaquenil. *See* Hydroxychloroquine
Plaques
amyloid, 1:85, 86, 87
calcium, 1:130–131
cholesterol, 3:1154
coronary artery disease, 2:577–578
dental, 4:1360
fatty, 3:953
gingivitis, 3:876–878
See also Atherosclerosis
Plasma cell labeling index, 4:1300
Plasma cell myeloma. *See* Multiple myeloma
Plasma cells, 3:1022, 4:1298
Plasmablastic multiple myeloma, 4:1300
Plasmablasts, 4:1298
Plasmacytomas, 4:1298, 1299, 1301, 1302
Plasmapheresis, 3:1106, 4:1301
Plastic lenses, 2:772–773
Plastic surgeons, 1:6–7
Plastic surgery, 2:584, 3:806, 808, 4:1358
See also Cosmetic surgery
Plastics, 4:1299
Platelet aggregation, 3:847
Platelet count, 2:560–561
chemotherapy, 2:491, 492
GI bleeding, 3:873
liver biopsy, 3:1136
lymphoma, 4:1194
multiple myeloma, 4:1299
normal values, 5:1764
priapism, 4:1492
thrombocytopenia, 5:1763, 1764
transient ischemic attacks, 5:1785
Platelet deficiency. *See* Thrombocytopenia
Platelet growth factor, 5:1764
Platelets, 2:585, 5:1763
Platensimycin, 4:1296
Plavix. *See* Clopidogrel
Playdough, 3:888
Pleural effusion, 4:**1460–1462,** *1461*
Pleurectomy, 4:1461
Pleurisy, 1:234, 235
Pleurodesis, 4:1461

Pleuroperitoneal shunts, 4:1461–1462
Pliny the Elder, 1:234
PLS (Primary lateral sclerosis), 1:103, 4:1287
Plugs, punctal, 2:712
PMA (Progressive muscular atrophy), 1:103, 4:1287
PMB. *See* Meprobamate
PMDD (Premenstrual dysphoric disorder), 1:166, 167
PMMA contact lenses, 2:774
PMR (Progressive muscle relaxation), 4:1564, 1565
Pneumatic retinoplexy, 4:1571
Pneumococcal meningitis, 4:1248
Pneumococcus vaccines, 5:1815
Pneumocystitis carinii pneumonia, 4:1463–1464, 1466
Pneumocystitis jiroveci, 4:1463–1464
Pneumonia, 3:1032–1036, 4:**1462–1466**
  aspiration, 1:231, 233, 373, 374, 5:1711
  bacterial, 4:1462–1463, 1464, 1465
  bronchial, 4:1462
  chemical, 4:1464
  common cold-related, 2:553
  community-aquired, 5:1700
  demographics, 3:1033, 4:1462
  diagnosis, 4:1464
  electrolyte tests, 2:739
  influenza-related, 4:1463, 1466, 5:1700
  lobar, 4:1462
  lung cancer from, 3:1174
  lupus-related, 3:1178
  mortality, 3:1035, 4:1462
  MRSA infection-related, 4:1294, 1296
  mycoplasmal, 1:250, 4:1462, 1463
  oxygen/ozone therapy, 4:1384
  Pneumocystitis carinii, 4:1463–1464, 1466
  postoperative, 4:1473, 1484
  prevention, 4:1465–1466, 1473, 1484
  pulmonary fibrosis from, 4:1536
  risk factors, 4:1462–1463
  shingles-related, 5:1631
  staphylococcal, 5:1700, 1702
  Streptococcus pneumoniae, 4:1463, 1463*t,* 5:1709, 1711–1713
  treatment, 1:373, 4:1464
  viral, 4:1462, 1463
  viral infection-related, 5:1834
Pneumothorax, 1:20, 3:1137, 5:1795
POAG (Primary open angle glaucoma), 3:880, 880*t,* 882
Podiatrists, 3:821
Podiatry. *See* Foot care
Poignancy, 4:1526
Point-of-care tests, 1:60
Point-of-service (POS) plans, 4:1209
Poison control centers, 4:1344, 1381–1382
Poison ivy, 2:630
Poison oak, 2:630
Poison sumac, 2:630
Poisoning
  cathartics for, 3:1124
  mental retardation, 4:1256
  paralysis from, 4:1418
  scleroderma, 5:1597
Poisonous plants, 2:572
Polaroid lenses, 2:773
Polio
  oropharyngeal dysphagia from, 5:1740
  pericarditis from, 4:1431
  physical therapists, 4:1454
  vaccine, 5:1815
Polish, nail, 4:1311, 1312
Pollution, 2:408, 512
Polyacethylen, 2:415
Polycillin. *See* Ampicillin
Polycystic kidney disease, 2:508, 3:1092
Polycystic ovary disease, 2:744
Polycythemia vera, 5:1766
Polyethylene, 3:1112
Polymerase chain reaction (PCR)
  AIDS tests, 1:60
  reverse transcriptase, 1:60, 5:1585
  tuberculosis, 5:1794
Polymorphism, restriction fragment length, 5:1794
Polymyalgia, 1:258–260
Polymyalgia rheumatica, 4:**1466–1467**
Polymyositis, 1:254, 4:**1467–1469**
Polymyxin, 1:334
Polyneuropathy, distal symmetric, 2:645
Polypeptides, 1:149*t*
Polypharmacy, 4:1284
Polyphenols, 2:417
Polyps
  cholesterol, 3:838
  endoscopy, 2:748
  intestinal, 1:287, 289, 2:534, 535, 538–541, 3:872
  stomach, 5:1705
Polyradiculoneuropathy, chronic inflammatory demyelinating, 4:1417
Polysaccharide krestin (PSK), 2:746
Polysaccharides, 2:421
Polysomnogram, 3:1051, 5:1653, 1656, 1673–1674
Polyunsaturated fats, 3:1157
  heart disease, 3:929
  high cholesterol, 3:956
  hyperlipoproteinemia, 3:1004
  low-cholesterol diet, 3:1154, 1155
  low-fat diet, 3:1157
  recommendations, 4:1339
Polyvinyl chloride, 5:1597
Pontocaine. *See* Tetracaine
Pool temperature, 5:1875
Poperadines, 1:187
Popliteal artery aneurysm, 1:120
Popular culture, 1:48
Population. *See* Aging population
Population mobility, 3:794
Porch Index of Speech Ability, 2:718
Porin, 1:95
Portal cirrhosis, 2:522
Portal hypertension, 1:129, 2:523, 3:1148
Portal hypotension, 1:134–135
POS (Point-of-service) plans, 4:1209
Positioning, patient, 4:1489
Positive-end expiratory pressure (PEEP), 5:1822
Positive feedback, 2:671
Positive outlook, 2:661–662, 4:1523, 1526
Positive-pressure ventilators, 5:1821
Positron emission tomography (PET)
  Alzheimer's disease, 1:87, 4:1243
  bone metastasis, 4:1262
  brain tumors, 1:349
  head injuries, 3:903
  ischemia, 3:1075
  lung cancer, 3:1175
  melanoma, 4:1199
  oral cancers, 4:1358
  persistent vegetative state, 4:1440
  seizures, 5:1603
  single, 4:1440, 5:1603
  stomach cancer, 5:1706
Posse, Nils, 4:1215
Post-anesthesia care unit (PACU), 4:1471, 1472–1473, 1556–1557
Post-concussion syndrome, 3:902–903
Post-exposure prophylaxis, 1:51
Post-polio syndrome, 4:1287
Post-traumatic knee care, 3:1114
Post-traumatic stress disorder (PTSD), 1:23–24, 166, 213, 214, 4:**1469–1471**
Post-void residual (PVR) measurement, 4:1379
Posterior cruciate ligament (PCL), 3:1115
Posterior vitreous detachment (PVD), 3:809–810
Postherpetic neuralgia, 1:212, 3:1035, 4:1318, 1319, 5:1631
Postmenopausal women
  bone density test, 1:337
  breast cancer, 1:355, 356, 358, 4:1204
  calcium supplements, 2:403

Postmenopausal women *(continued)*
dry eye, 2:711
dry skin, 2:715
heart disease, 3:992
hormone replacement therapy-related problems, 5:1614
hyperlipoproteinemia, 3:1003
iron-deficiency anemia, 3:1064
migraines, 4:1268
osteoporosis, 1:335, 3:992, 4:1371, 1372, 1373
ovarian cancer, 4:1374, 1375
rosacea, 4:1578–1579
See also Menopause
Postnecrotic cirrhosis, 2:522
Postoperative care, 4:**1471–1474**
anesthesiologists, 1:119
hip replacement, 3:967
hip revision surgery, 3:973
patient education, 4:1483–1484
prayer and spirituality, 4:1478
recovery at home, 4:1554–1556
recovery room, 4:1471, 1472–1473, 1556–1557
Postoperative complications
abdominoplasty, 1:6
deep vein thrombosis, 2:602
diet, 2:660
hip replacement, 3:967–968
knee joint replacement, 3:1113
liposuction, 3:1132
Postoperative pain, 1:19, 5:1629
Posttraumatic stress disorder. *See* Post-traumatic stress disorder (PTSD)
Postural awareness exercises, 3:830
Postural control, 3:831
Postural drainage, 2:497, 742, 4:1568, 5:1696
Postural hypotension, 1:324
Postural kyphosis, 1:271–275
Posture, 4:1366
Potassium
antihypertensive drug interactions, 1:189
chronic kidney failure, 2:509
dehydration, 2:604, 5:1870
diuretics, 2:691
electrolyte balance, 2:734, 736–737
electrolyte tests, 2:738–739
heatstroke, 3:938
hypertension, 1:326
liver function test interactions, 3:1143
sources, 2:416, 417, 736–737
ventricular fibrillation, 5:1824
See also Hyperkalemia; Hypokalemia; Potassium supplements
Potassium channel blockers, 1:146*t*
Potassium chloride, 3:1062
Potassium-sparing diuretics, 2:690–693, 690*t*, 709
Potassium supplements
angiotensin-converting enzyme inhibitor interactions, 1:133, 134
diuretic interactions, 2:692–693
for hypertension, 1:326, 3:1010
thiazide diuretic interactions, 1:189
Pouch, ostomy, 2:544
Poultry, 1:195, 2:658
Poverty
community nutrition programs, 2:556
isolation, 3:1078
malnutrition, 4:1201
Medicaid, 4:1229
social issues, 4:1523
tuberculosis, 5:1790, 1796
See also Socioeconomic factors
Povidone iodine, 5:1885
PPD (Paranoid personality disorder), 4:1444–1448
PPD (Purified protein derivative), 5:1793, 1794, 1796
PPIs. *See* Proton pump inhibitors
PPN (Partial parenteral nutrition), 4:1342
PPOs (Preferred provider organizations), 2:548, 4:1209, 1239, **1474–1476,** 1496
PPP (Palomar-plantar pustulosis), 4:1518–1519
PPV vaccine, 4:1248
PRA (Panel of reactive antibody), 3:1106
Practice standards. *See* Standards
Prader-Willi syndrome, 4:1256
Pragmatic creativity, 4:1523
Pramipexole, 1:199–200, 4:1423
Pramlintide acetate, 1:178, 179–180, 2:640
Pramoxine, 1:116
Pranayama, 4:1272, 5:1892
Prancreas transplantation, 4:1363
Prandin. *See* Repaglinide
Pravachol. *See* Pravastatin
Pravastatin, 1:247, 3:955
Prayer, 2:662, 4:1377, **1476–1480,** 1552
Prazosin, 1:81–83, 4:1511
Pre-eclampsia, 3:1009
Pre-hospital DNR orders, 2:699–700
Prealbumin, 3:1143, 4:1202
Prebiotics, 4:1496
Prebycusis. *See* Hearing loss
Precancerous skin lesions, 5:1642
Precose. *See* Acarbose
Prediabetes, 1:330, 2:641, 4:1339
Prednisone
for amyloidosis, 1:102
boils from, 1:333
for cervical spondylosis, 2:488
Cushing's syndrome from, 2:590
for gout, 3:892
insulin interactions, 3:1056
for kidney transplantation, 3:1107
for lupus, 3:1180
for polymyositis, 4:1468
for pulmonary fibrosis, 4:1537
side effects, 3:1045
for thrombocytopenia, 5:1764
Preferred provider organizations (PPOs), 2:548, 4:1209, 1239, **1474–1476,** 1496
Pregabalin, 1:215, 2:647, 3:863
Pregnancy
$alpha_1$ adrenergic blockers, 1:82
antiangina drugs, 1:143
anticancer drugs, 1:156
anticoagulants, 1:158
anticonvulsant drugs, 1:161
antidiarrheal drugs, 1:183
aortic dissection, 1:219
arteriovenous malformations, 1:229
barbiturates, 1:283
bariatric surgery, 1:285
benzodiazepines, 1:293
bone scan, 1:343–344
bronchodilators, 1:380
cardiac valve surgery, 2:441
celiac disease, 3:889
chest CT scans, 2:493
chest x rays, 2:499
community health programs, 2:554
CT scans, 2:588
DHEA, 2:635
dietary fiber, 3:957
diuretics, 2:692
dronabinol, 2:420
edema, 2:726
gallstones, 3:838
gastroesophageal reflux disease, 3:854
general anesthesia, 1:114
ginkgo biloba, 3:879
H-2 receptor blockers, 3:899
heartburn, 3:933
hemorrhoids, 3:947–948
hypertension, 3:1009
kidney nuclear medicine scans, 3:1098
kidney, ureter, and bladder x-ray study, 3:1109
liver-spleen scan, 3:1147
low-fat diet, 3:1158
magnetic resonance imaging, 4:1192
nicotine, 5:1665
nonsteroidal anti-inflammatory drugs, 4:1326
nuclear stress test, 4:1327
parathyroid scan, 4:1419
sciatica, 5:1592
SSRIs, 1:169
teeth whitening, 5:1750
thyroid function tests, 5:1773
tuberculosis, 5:1791–1792
upper GI series, 5:1802, 1803

Pregnancy *(continued)*
varicose veins, 5:1817
visual impairment, 5:1842
zinc deficiency, 5:1897, 1898
Prehypertension, 3:1008, 1009, 1010
Prejudice, 1:47–48
Premarin, 5:1588
Premature aging, 1:44–45
Premature ejaculation, 1:166, 5:1618–1619
Premature infants, 4:1218
Premature presbyopia, 4:1485
Premenstrual dysphoric disorder (PMDD), 1:166, 167
Premenstrual syndrome
biofeedback, 1:302
caffeine, 2:396
edema, 2:726
nonsteroidal anti-inflammatory drugs for, 4:1326
vitamin E, 5:1856
yoga, 5:1891
Preoperative cardiac assessment, 4:**1480–1481**
Preoperative care, 4:**1482–1484**
anxiety, 4:1566
hip replacement, 3:966–967, 973
Prepatellar bursitis, 1:388, 389
Prepyloric region, 5:1704
Presbycusis, 3:919
Presbyopia, 4:**1484–1487,** 5:1612, 1615
contact lenses, 2:774
eye examination, 2:770
eyeglasses, 4:1485, 5:1615
optometrists, 4:1354
Prescriptions, 1:24–25
commercial programs, 2:548–550
dietary supplement interactions, 2:680
drug abuse, 2:706, 5:1725, 1730
drug interactions, 2:707–710
forgetting to take, 2:629
Medicare prescription drug plan, 4:1238–1241
pharmacy technicians, 4:1452
travel precautions, 5:1608
wheelchair, 5:1879–1881
Preservatives, food, 3:1160
Pressure-control ventilation, 3:1048
Pressure-cycled ventilators, 5:1821
Pressure dressings, 5:1651
Pressure limit, 5:1823
Pressure sores, 4:**1487–1491**
bacteremia, 1:275
demographics, 3:1034, 4:1488–1489
malnutrition, 3:870
palliative care, 2:600
prevention, 2:520, 4:1491
reconstructive surgery, 4:1490, 5:1886
recurrence, 5:1887
spinal cord injury-related, 5:1693, 1694
wheelchair-related, 5:1880, 1885
wound care, 4:1489–1490, 5:1884–1887
Pressure support ventilation (PSV), 5:1819, 1822
Pressure ulcers. *See* Pressure sores
Prevacid. *See* Lansoprazole
Prevalite. *See* Cholestyramine
Preventive medicine
aging, 1:46–47
lifestyle, 5:1611–1612
managed care plans, 3:977, 4:1476
Medicare, 4:1238
osteopathic medicine, 2:701
PreVue, 3:1184
Priapism, 4:**1491–1494,** 5:1636
Prick test, 1:75, 3:816
Prilosec. *See* Omeprazole
Prilosec OTC, 4:1515, 1516
Primary biliary cirrhosis, 1:252, 254
Primary bowel resection, 2:694
Primary care physicians
enemas, 2:754
HMOs, 3:976, 4:1209, 1210
preferred provider organizations, 4:1475
substance abuse counseling, 5:1730, 1731
surgeon referral, 3:805
Primary care providers, 4:1209, 1210
Primary generalized seizures, 5:1601–1606
Primary headache, 3:905
Primary hypertension, 3:1008, 1010
Primary immunodeficiency, 3:1022
Primary lateral sclerosis (PLS), 1:103, 4:1287
Primary open angle glaucoma (POAG), 3:880, 880*t,* 882
Primary osteoarthritis, 4:1366
Primary peritoneal carcinoma, 4:1374
Primary pulmonary hypertension, 4:1539
Primary skin lesions, 5:1649
Primary systemic amyloidosis, 1:100
Primatene. *See* Epinephrine
Primidone, 3:813, 5:1603
Principen. *See* Ampicillin
Principle of double effect, 2:762
Prinivil. *See* Lisinopril
Prinzmetal's angina pectoris, 1:123
Prismatic field-expanding eyeglasses, 4:1438
Prisms, 5:1843
Pritikin diet, 3:1156, 1157
Privacy, 2:454, 528
Privacy Rule, 4:1426, 1427, 1430–1431
Private health insurance, 4:**1494–1496,** 1494*t*
Pro-inflammatory foods, 1:195–196
Proanthocyanidins, 3:879
Probalan. *See* Probenecid
Probenecid, 1:102, 3:894
Probiotics, 3:1071, 4:**1496–1501**
Problem-solving therapy, 2:626–627
Procainamide
allergies, 1:148
antinuclear antibody test interactions, 1:253
for arrhythmias, 1:146, 226
liver function test interactions, 3:1143
lupus from, 3:1178
side effects, 1:147
Procaine, 1:116, 148
Procan SR. *See* Procainamide
Processed food, 3:1160, 4:1339, 1349–1350, 1521, 5:1605
Prochlorperazine, 1:202, 3:993, 4:1434
Procrit. *See* Epoetin
Prodium. *See* Prednisone
Productive pain, 1:106
Progesterone
breast cancer, 1:358
bruising, 1:387
for endometrial cancer, 2:745
heartburn, 3:933
hormone replacement therapy, 3:991
hyperlipoproteinemia, 3:1004
menopause, 4:1250–1252
natural, 3:994
plant-based, 4:1253
saw palmetto interactions, 4:1512
Progesterone challenge test, 3:994
Progesterone receptors, 1:356, 359
Progestins, 3:990–994, 991*t,* 4:1253, 1375
Progestogens. *See* Progestins
Progression diet, 5:1683
Progressive bulbar palsy (PBP), 1:103, 4:1287
Progressive muscle relaxation (PMR), 4:1564, 1565
Progressive muscular atrophy (PMA), 1:103, 4:1287
Prohormones, 2:634
Prokinetic drugs, 3:935
Prolamins, 2:473
Prolapsed uterus, 3:1016
Proliferative diabetic retinopathy, 2:648, 649, 650, 5:1835
Promethazine, 1:187, 202
Prometrium. *See* Natural progesterone

Pronestyl. *See* Procainamide
Propaesmolol, 1:190–191
Propanolol, 1:173
Propecia. *See* Finasteride
Property maintenance. *See* Home maintenance
Prophylactic antibiotics
  bacterial resistance, 2:467, 470
  for bladder stones, 1:313
  for cardiac valve surgery, 2:444, 540
  chemotherapy-related, 1:156
  for endocarditis prevention, 5:1712
  for infectious disease prevention, 3:1036
  for kidney stones, 3:1103
  for kidney transplantation, 3:1105
  for liposuction, 3:1132
  for mitral valve prolapse, 4:1281
  for prostate biopsy, 4:1502–1503
Prophylactic mastectomy, 1:360, 4:1221
Prophylactic oophorectomy, 4:1377
Prophylactic surgery, 2:410
Prophylaxis, post-exposure, 1:51
Propofol, 1:113
Propoxyphene
  analgesic action, 1:107
  benzodiazepine interactions, 1:145
  diazepam interactions, 4:1308
  for periodic limb movement disorder, 4:1435
Propranolol, 1:297–299
  benzodiazepine interactions, 1:145
  bronchodilator interactions, 1:381
  caffeine interactions, 2:397
  cimetidine interactions, 3:900
  for coronary artery disease, 2:580
  diazepam interactions, 4:1308
  drug interactions, 1:83, 299
  for hypertension, 1:190
  insulin interactions, 3:1055
  for mitral valve prolapse, 4:1281
  pulmonary fibrosis from, 4:1536
  ranitidine interactions, 3:900
Proprioception, 3:829, 830, 832
Propulsid. *See* Cisapride
Propylene glycol, 4:1277
Proscar. *See* Finasteride
ProSom. *See* Estazolam
Prostaglandin E2 (PGE2), 4:1326
Prostaglandin synthetase inhibitors, 4:1325–1326
Prostaglandins, 1:193, 194, 2:585, 5:1620
Prostate biopsy, 4:*1501,* **1501–1504,** 1506, 1514
Prostate cancer, 4:*1504,* **1504–1510,** 1505*t*
  androgens, 1:155
  calcium supplements, 2:404
  demographics, 2:407, 4:1502, 5:1682
  diagnosis, 2:409, 4:1501–1504, 1505–1506, 1511, 1514–1515, 5:1587
  digital rectal exam, 4:1502, 1505, 1514
  garlic prevention, 3:848
  high-fat diet, 2:661
  metastasis, 4:1262, 1505, 1507
  mortality, 4:1502, 1505, 1509
  prevention, 2:414, 416, 417, 4:1509, 1512
  prostate biopsy, 4:*1501,* 1501–1504, 1506, 1514
  prostate ultrasound, 4:1514–1515
  PSA marker, 4:1262, 1502, 1505–1506, 1509, 1511, 5:1587
  risk factors, 4:1505
  vitamin D, 5:1854
  watchful waiting, 4:1508
Prostate disease, 3:1034
Prostate enlargement, 4:*1510,* **1510–1514**
  $alpha_1$ adrenergic blockers for, 1:81–83
  bladder stones, 1:312
  diagnosis, 4:1505, 1511
  prostate ultrasound, 4:**1514–1515**
  saw palmetto for, 4:1512, 5:1587, 1588
  TURP for, 4:1506
Prostate gland, 4:1514
Prostate-specific antigen (PSA)
  5 alpha-reductase inhibitor interactions, 4:1512
  prostate cancer diagnosis, 4:1262, 1502, 1505–1506, 1509, 1511, 1514, 5:1587
  prostate ultrasound indications, 4:1514
Prostate ultrasound, 4:**1514–1515**
Prostatectomy, 4:1507
Prostatic acid phosphatase (PAP), 4:1262
Prostatitis, 2:596, 5:1805
Prostep. *See* Nicotine replacement therapy
Prosthesis
  airport security, 5:1608–1609
  amputation, 1:99
  dislocations, 3:967
  infections from, 3:1034
  knee joint, 3:1110–1114, *1111,* 1166
  lifespan and wear, 3:968, 1113
  lower limb, 3:1165–1167
  materials used, 3:1112
  post-mastectomy, 4:1223
  post-rotationoplasty, 5:1585
  staphylococcal infections, 5:1700, 1701
  tooth, 2:618–620, 4:1361
  See also Hip replacement
Prosthetic devices. *See* Prosthesis
Prosthetists, 3:1167
Protease inhibitors, 1:207*t*
  garlic interactions, 3:847, 849, 850
  for multiple myeloma, 4:1301
Protective headgear, 3:904
Protein (dietary)
  cancer patients, 5:1682, 1683, 1684, 1685
  healthy aging diet, 4:1338–1339
  high cholesterol, 3:956
  need for, 3:869–870
  pressure sores, 4:1491
  seizures, 5:1604
  skin cancer prevention, 4:1200
  sources, 3:818
  vitamin B_{12}, 5:1847–1848
Protein-calorie malnutrition, 3:870
Protein electrophoresis, 4:1300
Protein-energy malnutrition, 4:1339
Protein malnutrition, 3:870
Protein tests, 4:1202, 1300
Proteins
  allergens, 1:71
  cancer, 2:406
  chronic disease, 1:193
  dietary, 1:326
  liver function tests, 3:1143
  zinc, 5:1895
Proteolytic enzymes, 5:1886
Protestants, 4:1477
Proteus mirabilis, 1:310
Proteus sp., 2:594
Prothrombin, 3:1143
Prothrombin time test
  GI bleeding, 3:873
  liver biopsy, 3:1136
  transient ischemic attacks, 5:1785
  vitamin K, 5:1860
Proton pump inhibitors, 4:**1515–1517,** *1516*
  drug interactions, 4:1517
  for gastroesophageal reflux disease, 3:856, 857, 4:1515–1517
  vs. H-2 receptor blockers, 3:897
  for heartburn, 3:935
  for helicobacteriosis, 3:940
  side effects, 4:1517
  for ulcers, 2:586, 5:1799
Protonix. *See* Pantoprazole
Protriptyline, 1:175
Proventil. *See* Albuterol
Provera. *See* Progestins
Provitamins, 5:1861
Provocation tests, 1:71, 75
Proxy, health care. *See* Durable power of attorney
Prozac. *See* Fluoxetine
Prucalopride, 3:1123
Pruritus. *See* Itching
Pruritus ani, 3:1081

Pruritus vulvae, 3:1081
Prussian blue stain, 1:341
PSA. *See* Prostate-specific antigen
PSA (Pacemaker system analyzer), 4:1388
PSDA (Patient Self-Determination Act), 3:1149
Pseudarthrosis, 3:969
Pseudo-allergic reactions, 1:74
Pseudoephedrine, 2:405, 3:1009
Pseudomembranous colitis, 4:1497
Pseudomonas aeruginosa, 1:151
PSK (Polysaccharide krestin), 2:746
PSM (Phenol-soluble modulin), 4:1294
Psoriasis, 4:**1517–1522,** *1518*
  cellulitis from, 2:477
  dry skin from, 2:716
  hypdrogen peroxide for, 4:1385
  vitamin D for, 5:1854
Psoriasis vulgaris, 4:1518
Psoriatic arthritis, 4:1519, 1520
Psuedomonas sp., 1:276
PSV (Pressure support ventilation), 5:1819, 1822
Psychiatric disorders. *See* Mental disorders
Psychiatric interview, 4:1446
Psychiatric syncope, 3:787
Psychodynamic psychotherapy, 2:627, 4:1447
Psychogenic itching, 3:1081
Psychogenic pain, 3:1151, 1152
Psychogenic polydipsia, 2:637
Psycholinguistic therapy, 2:719
Psychological abuse, 2:727–729
Psychological development, 4:1523
Psychological issues, 4:**1522–1527**
  post-stroke, 5:1723
  preoperative preparation, 4:1483
  reconciliation and forgiveness, 4:1551–1554
  rosacea, 4:1578
  sexual dysfunction, 5:1619
  substance abuse counseling, 5:1730
Psychological pain, 4:1394
Psychological trauma, 5:1782
Psychophysiological feedback. *See* Biofeedback
Psychoses, 4:**1528–1532**
  dementia-related, 1:204–205, 2:612, 4:1528
  drug therapy, 1:202–206, 4:1529–1532
  ICU, 4:1528, 1529
  See also Antipsychotic drugs
Psychosocial changes, 3:869
Psychosomatic conditions, 3:800, 4:1270
Psychostimulants, 2:626
Psychotherapy
  adjustment disorders, 1:24
  anxiety, 1:215–216
  behavioral, 5:1619
  bipolar disorder, 1:306
  for depression, 2:626–627
  fibromyalgia, 3:801
  generalized anxiety disorder, 3:863, 864
  Mental Status Examination, 4:1321
  movement therapy, 4:1291, 1292–1293
  osteoarthritis, 4:1367
  overdose, 4:1382
  pain, 4:1395
  panic disorder, 4:1411
  personality disorders, 4:1447
  psychodynamic, 2:627, 4:1447
  psychogenic pain, 3:1152
  PTSD, 4:1470–1471
  sexual dysfunction, 5:1619, 1620
Psychotic depression, 2:622
Psyllium, 3:948, 1123
PTAs (Physical therapy assistants), 1:271, 4:1454, 1455, 1457, **1459–1460**
PTCA (Percutaneous transluminal coronary angioplasty), 1:124, 130–132, 2:580, 3:928, 1075, 4:1277
PTCB (Pharmacy Technician Certification Board), 4:1453
Pteroglyglutamic acid. *See* Folic acid
PTFE catheters, 2:466, 470
PTH. *See* Parathyroid hormone
PTK (Phototherapeutic keratectomy), 2:575, 576
Ptosis, 2:*778*
PTSAgs (Pyrogenic toxic superantigens), 4:1295
PTSD. *See* Post-traumatic stress disorder (PTSD)
Puberty, 4:1250
Pubic lice, 3:1124, 1126
Public health nurses, 4:1558
Public policy, 1:46, 3:1078–1079
Pulmonary angiography, 1:128
Pulmonary edema, 2:562, 725, *726*
Pulmonary embolism, 4:**1532–1535,** *1533*
  angiography, 1:128
  anticoagulants for, 1:373, 2:519
  breathing problems from, 1:372
  deep vein thrombosis-related, 2:601, 4:1532–1533, 5:1609
  hypertension-related, 4:1534
  liver function tests, 3:1146
  symptoms, 2:518, 4:1533
  therapeutic exercise contraindications, 5:1760
Pulmonary fibrosis, 4:**1535–1539,** *1536*
  breathing problems from, 1:372, 373
  lung biopsy, 3:1171
  rheumatoid factor test, 1:254
Pulmonary function tests
  breathing problems, 1:373
  bronchitis, 1:377
  chronic obstructive pulmonary disease, 2:512–513
  emphysema, 2:741
  inhalation therapy, 3:1048
  pulmonary fibrosis, 4:1537
  pulmonary rehabilitation, 4:1543
  sarcoidosis, 5:1582
  scleroderma, 5:1598
Pulmonary hypertension, 4:**1539–1541**
  calcium channel blockers for, 2:401
  pulmonary embolism from, 4:1534
  respiratory failure-induced, 4:1569
Pulmonary rehabilitation, 1:374, 2:513–514, 4:**1541–1544**
Pulmonary tuberculosis, 5:1792–1793, 1795
Pulmonary valve stenosis, 3:932
Pulsatile tinnitus, 5:1780
Pulse, 5:1843–1846, 1844*t*
  acupuncture, 1:18
  apical, 2:434
  cardiac rehabilitation, 2:436, 437
  See also Heart rate
PULSE (Persons United Limiting Substandards and Errors in Health Care), 4:1430
Pulse oximetry
  cardiac monitor, 2:434
  pulmonary rehabilitation, 4:1543
  recovery room, 4:1556
  ventilator weaning, 5:1820
Pulsed light therapy, 4:1579
Pulsers (ultrasound), 2:459
Punch biopsy, 2:483, 5:1645, 1646, 1647
Punctal plugs, 2:712
Pupils (eye), 2:461, 573, 4:1321
Purified protein derivative (PPD), 5:1793, 1794, 1796
Purine, 3:891, 893
Purpura. *See* Bruising
Pusatilla, 4:1379
Pushing hands t'ai chi, 5:1746
Pustular psoriasis, 4:1518–1519, 1520
Pustules, 5:1649
Putnam, Robert, 1:2
PUVA (Photochemotherapy), 4:1520
PVD (Posterior vitreous detachment), 3:809–810
PVL (Panton-Valentine leukocidin), 4:1294, 1295
PVR (Post-void residual) measurement, 4:1379
PVS. *See* Persistent vegetative state

Pyelogram, intravenous. *See* Intravenous pyelogram
Pyelonephritis, 2:595, 3:1101, 5:1807
Pylorus, 5:1704
Pyrazinamide, 1:208–211, 5:1795
Pyridostigmine bromide, 1:264
Pyridoxine. *See* Vitamin B_6
Pyrilamine, 1:187
Pyrogenic toxic superantigens (PTSAgs), 4:1295

Q

Q fever, 1:151
Q waves, 2:435, 730
QCT (Quantitative computed tomography), 1:337
Qi. *See* Chi
Qigong, 4:1292, *1545,* **1545–1549,** 5:*1758*
  hip joint pain, 3:969
  spirituality, 4:1476
QRST complex, 2:435
Quadrantectomy, 1:358, 3:1169, 4:1221
Quadraplegia, 5:1692
Quadriceps muscles, 3:1112, 1115, 1117
Quadriceps tendon, 3:1116
Quadriplegia, 4:1417–1418
Quality of health care, 3:**910–911,** 4:1334
Quality of life
  dental health, 2:617
  euthanasia, 2:763
  geriatric assessment, 3:865, 866
  nursing homes, 4:1332
  over fifty lifestyle, 2:662–662
  post-cardiac surgery, 2:440
  pulmonary rehabilitation, 4:1542
  t'ai chi, 5:1748
Quantitative computed tomography (QCT), 1:337
Quaternary ammonium, 4:1296
Quazepam, 1:140
Quercetin, 1:197, 2:416, 3:1024, 4:1200
Questions to Ask Your Doctor Before You Have Surgery (Agency for Healthcare Quality and Research), 3:806
Questran. *See* Cholestyramine
Quetelet Index. *See* Body mass index
Quetelet, Lambert Adolphe, 1:331
Quetiapine, 1:203, 305, 4:1531
Quinapril, 1:132, 191, 2:586
Quinidex. *See* Quinidine
Quinidine
  for arrhythmias, 1:146, 226
  caffeine interactions, 2:397
  calcium supplement interactions, 2:405
  cimetidine interactions, 3:900
  ranitidine interactions, 3:900
  side effects, 1:148
Quinine
  cimetidine interactions, 3:900
  homeopathic medicine, 3:987
  vs. quinidine, 1:146
  ranitidine interactions, 3:900
Quinolones, 1:149*t,* 5:1808, 1897
Quitting smoking. *See* Smoking cessation
Qunnabu, 4:1211

R

R waves, 2:730
Rabeprazole, 2:586, 3:856, 4:1515–1517
Rabies vaccine, 5:1756
Race. *See* Ethnicity and race
Radial artery, 5:1845
Radiation detectors, 5:1609
Radiation exposure
  angiography, 1:130
  chest CT scans, 2:494
  chest x rays, 2:499
  CT scans, 2:589
  kidney, ureter, and bladder x-ray study, 3:1109–1110
  lymphoma from, 4:1195
  mammogram, 4:1206
  multiple myeloma from, 4:1299
  paralysis from, 4:1417
  probiotics for, 4:1498
  thyroid cancer from, 5:1769, 1772
Radiation, ionizing, 4:1195, 1260
Radiation oncologists, 2:412
Radiation therapy, 2:410–411
  adverse effects, 3:1176
  age-related macular degeneration, 5:1838
  aortic valve stenosis from, 1:222
  arteriovenous malformations, 1:231
  bone metastasis, 4:1263
  brain and central nervous system tumors, 1:350
  breast cancer, 1:358, 359
  breast cancer from, 4:1204
  cervical cancer, 2:484
  colon cancer, 2:536
  diet, 5:1682–1685
  dietary supplement interactions, 4:1345
  dry mouth from, 2:714–715
  endocrine pancreatic cancer, 4:1403
  endometrial cancer, 2:745
  esophageal cancer, 2:760
  exocrine pancreatic cancer, 4:1406
  external, 2:484
  gallbladder cancer, 3:836
  hyperthermia precautions, 4:1264–1265
  internal, 2:484
  kidney cancer, 3:1093
  liver cancer, 3:1141
  lung cancer, 3:1176
  lymphedema from, 3:1187
  melanoma, 4:1199–1200
  metastasis, 4:1264
  multiple myeloma, 4:1301
  non-Hodgkin's lymphoma, 4:1195–1196
  oral cancers, 4:1359
  ovarian cancer, 4:1376
  pleural effusion, 4:1462
  post-lumpectomy, 3:1169, 1170, 4:1223, 1224
  post-mastectomy, 4:1222
  prostate cancer, 4:1508, 1509
  pulmonary fibrosis from, 4:1536
  sarcomas, 5:1585
  side effects, 2:412, 418–421, 5:1682–1685
  skin cancer, 5:1642, 1643
  stomach cancer, 5:1706–1707
  surgical oncology, 5:1737–1738
  thrombocytopenia from, 5:1763, 1764
  thyroid cancer, 5:1769, 1770–1771, 1772
  VZV vaccine interactions, 5:1632
Radiation, ultraviolet. *See* Ultraviolet light
Radical cystectomy, 1:309
Radical hysterectomy, 2:484, 3:1017
Radical mastectomy, 1:358, 4:1222
Radical nephrectomy, 3:1093
Radical prostatectomy, 4:1507
Radiculopathy
  cervical, 2:487, 489
  lumbosacral, 5:1591
Radioactive iodine. *See* Iodine radioisotopes
Radioactive iodine uptake (RAIU), 5:1775
Radioactive isotopes. *See* Radiopharmaceuticals
Radioactive tracers. *See* Radiopharmaceuticals
Radioallergosorbent test (RAST), 3:816
Radiofrequency volumetric tissue reduction (RFTR), 5:1672
Radiography technologists, 1:289, 3:845
Radioimmunoassay, 3:1006, 1013
Radioisotope scans. *See* Nuclear medicine scans
Radiologists, 2:412

Radionuclide angiography, 2:579
Radionuclide scans. *See* Nuclear medicine scans; Radiopharmaceuticals
Radionuclide ventriculography, 2:446
Radiopharmaceuticals
- airport security, 5:1609
- bone scan, 1:344
- ischemia, 3:1075
- kidney scans, 3:1098–1100
- nuclear stress test, 4:1327, 1328
- parathyroid scan, 4:1419–1420
- thyroid function tests, 5:1773–1774
- thyroid scans, 5:1775–1777, 1778
- *See also* Iodine radioisotopes; Nuclear medicine scans

Radon, 3:1174
RAIU (Radioactive iodine uptake), 5:1775
Raja yoga, 5:1892
Raloxifene
- for breast cancer prevention, 1:360
- for menopause, 4:1251–1252, 5:1613
- for osteoporosis, 4:1252, 5:1613

Ramelteon, 5:1657
Ramipril, 1:132, 191, 2:563, 586
Range of motion
- gait and balance assessment, 3:830
- hip fractures, 3:961
- joint mobilization, 3:1088
- knee injuries, 3:1118
- passive, 1:269, 2:436
- spinal cord injuries, 5:1694
- therapeutic exercise, 5:1759

Ranibizumab, 1:41
Ranitidine, 3:897–900
- for gastroesophageal reflux disease, 3:855–856, 897
- for heartburn, 3:897, 935
- for helicobacteriosis, 3:940
- *vs.* proton pump inhibitors, 4:1516
- for ulcers, 2:586, 5:1799
- vitamin B_{12} interactions, 5:1848

Rapid-acting insulin, 3:1054
Rapid eye movement (REM) sleep, 5:1652, 1653, 1654
Rapid-onset dementia, 5:1700
Rapid screening, HIV, 1:51, 60–61
Rapid strep test, 5:1711
RAS (Reticular activating system), 2:545, *546*
Ras oncogene, 4:1264
Rasagline, 1:200
Rash, erythema migrans, 3:1183, 1184
Raspberries, 2:415
RAST (Radioallergosorbent test), 3:816
Rate of living theory, 1:45
Rate-responsive pacemakers, 4:1388
Rationing, 2:528
Rauwolfia, 3:1011
Raynaud's disease, 2:517–520
- autoimmune disease tests, 1:253
- calcium channel blockers for, 2:401
- CREST syndrome, 5:1598
- ginkgo biloba for, 3:878
- mind/body medicine, 4:1272
- nifedipine for, 5:1598
- scleroderma-related, 5:1597

Razadyne. *See* Galantamine
RBRVS (Resource-Based Relative Value Scale), 4:1231
RDA. *See* Recommended daily allowance
Reactions, 1:44
Reactive oxygen species, 1:103, 197
Reading, 3:1164
Reagan, Ronald, 1:86
Real Age: Are You as Young as You Can Be? (Roizen), 2:662
Reasonable accommodation, 1:94–95
Rebif. *See* Interferon-beta
Rebound effect, 5:1727
Receivers, hearing aid, 3:915, *915*
Receptive dysphasia, 2:717
Reclast. *See* Zoledronate
Reclining wheelchairs, 5:1880
Recoil thrust, 2:501–502
Recombinant tissue plasminogen activator. *See* Tissue plasminogen activator
Recommended daily allowance (RDA), 2:670
- calcium, 2:398, 404
- carotenoids, 1:198
- folic acid, 3:812
- selenium, 1:198
- vitamin A, 1:198
- vitamin C, 1:198
- vitamin E, 1:198, 5:1857

Reconciliation, 4:**1551–1554**
Reconstructive surgery
- breast, 1:362, *364,* 364–369, 4:1222–1223, 1224
- cosmetic, 2:582
- pressure sores, 4:1490, 5:1886

Records. *See* Medical records
Recovery at home, 3:966–967, 974, 4:**1554–1556**
Recovery room, 4:1471, 1472–1473, **1556–1557**
Rectal bleeding, 3:948
Rectal cancer, 2:533
- *See also* Colorectal cancer

Rectal examination, digital. *See* Digital rectal exam
Rectal insufflation, 4:1385
Rectal prolapse, 3:798
Rectal swabs, 2:654
Rectum, 2:532
Recurrence, cancer, 5:1737
Red blood cell count, 2:560
- chemotherapy-induced, 2:491
- iron-deficiency anemia, 3:1064, 1065
- kidney cancer, 3:1092
- lymphoma, 4:1194
- multiple myeloma, 4:1299
- stomach cancer, 5:1705

Red blood cell distribution width, 2:560
Red blood cells
- anemia, 1:108–110
- iron-deficiency anemia, 3:1064, 1065
- oxygen/ozone therapy, 4:1384
- vitamin B_{12}, 5:1847

Red clover, 4:1252
Red meat, 2:413, 533
Red wine, 1:88, 2:417, 3:929
Reduction, dislocations and subluxations, 2:688
Reed, Gregory, 3:879
Reeve, Christopher, 5:*1821*
Refecoxib, 1:107
Reference handbooks, drug, 1:26
Referral services
- community social programs, 2:558
- HMOs, 3:976, 4:1475
- preferred provider organizations, 4:1475
- surgeons, 3:805

Referred pain, 3:1151
Refined food. *See* Processed food
Refined grains, 1:195–196, 2:693–694
Reflex incontinence, 4:1378
Reflex tears, 2:712
Reflex tests, 1:281
Reflexes
- arousal, 2:545
- falls, 3:789, 4:1372
- neurologic examination, 4:1320, 1322
- persistent vegetative state, 4:1440

Reflexology, 1:13–14, 15
Refractive errors, 5:1841
Refractive laser surgery, 4:1355
Refractory celiac disease, 3:888
Refusal of treatment, 4:1430
Regeneration, nerve, 4:1417, 1418
Regional anesthesia, 1:115–118
Regional lymph node dissection, 5:1737
Regional recurrence, 5:1737
Registered dieticians. *See* Dieticians
Registered nurses (RNs), 4:1346, **1557–1560**
- advanced practice, 1:33–36
- associates degree, 3:1129

Registered nurses (RNs) *(continued)*
 bachelors degree, 3:1129
 clinical nurse specialists, 2:525
 licensed practical nurses, 3:1129
 managed care plans, 4:1210
 See also Nurses
Reglan. *See* Clopramide
Regurgitation, 2:441
Rehabilitation
 amputation, 1:98–99
 cardiac, 1:224, 2:436–438, 439–440, 443–444, 581
 hip fractures, 3:959–961
 pulmonary, 1:374, 2:513–514, 4:1541–1544
 spinal cord injuries, 5:1694
 stroke, 5:1720, 1723
 vision, 4:1354
 visual, 3:1164
Rehabilitation facilities, 2:437
Rehydration, 2:603, 605, 654, 5:1872
Reiki, 4:1476
Reimbursement, 4:1334, 1475
Reishi mushrooms, 4:1509
Rejection, 3:1107
Relafen. *See* Nabumetone
Relapsing fever, 3:1124
Relationships, 4:**1560–1563,** 1560*t*
 alcohol abuse, 1:67
 family, 3:793–796
 gambling, 3:841
 healthy aging, 4:1527
 intimate, 4:1560–1562
 isolation, 3:1078, 1079
 maintaining, 5:1617
 malnutrition prevention, 2:666
 over fifty lifestyle, 2:661, 662
 personality disorders, 4:1445, 1446
 physician-patient, 5:1748–1749
 suicide prevention, 5:1733
 virtual, 4:1561
 visitation programs, 3:1079
 weight loss, 5:1878
Relativistic thinking, 4:1526
Relaxation response, 4:1270
The Relaxation Response (Benson), 4:1563–1565, 5:1892
Relaxation techniques, 4:**1563–1567**
 acupressure, 1:14
 angina pectoris, 3:1076
 anti-inflammatory role, 1:194
 anxiety, 1:215–216
 dermatitis, 2:632
 fibromyalgia, 3:801
 generalized anxiety disorder, 3:864
 insomnia, 3:1051, 1052
 itching, 3:1082
 menopause symptoms, 3:994
 passive, 4:1563, 1564
 sexual dysfunction, 5:1620
 sleep disorders, 5:1657
 See also Massage therapy; Stress management
Religious beliefs
 death and dying, 2:599–600
 euthanasia, 2:764
 healthy aging, 4:1523
 mind/body medicine, 4:1269
 organ donation, 4:1364
 prayer and spirituality, 4:1476–1480
 reconciliation and forgiveness, 4:1551–1554
 relationships with God, 4:1561
 stress-related disorders, 5:1716
 suicide prevention, 5:1733, 1734
Religious communities, 4:1478, 1523–1524
REM (Rapid eye movement) sleep, 5:1652, 1653, 1654
Reminiscence therapy, 2:627
Remission, spontaneous, 3:1094
Renal artery stenosis, 3:1100
Renal cell carcinoma, 3:1091, 1092, 4:1264
Renal disease. *See* End-stage renal disease; Kidney disease
Renal failure. *See* Kidney failure
Renal scans. *See* Kidney nuclear medicine scans
Reno, Janet, 4:1213
Repaglinide, 1:179–180, 2:640
Repetition, 2:717
Repetitive motion injuries, 4:1366, 5:1787, 1788
Repose system, 5:1672
Representative, patient, 4:**1428–1429**
Representative payee, 2:567, 3:804
Reproductive health services, 2:554
Requip. *See* Ropinirole
Rescue workers, 5:1715
Research ethics, 4:1235–1236
Resection, tumor, 5:1737
Reserpine, 1:191, 2:624
Resident microorganisms, 3:1030–1031
Resistance. *See* Drug resistance
Resource allocation, 4:1235
Resource-Based Relative Value Scale (RBRVS), 4:1231
Resource review, 4:1210
Respiratory arrest, 2:448–451
Respiratory diseases, 4:1284
Respiratory distress
 acute, 3:1046, 1047, 5:1821
 ventilator weaning-associated, 5:1820
Respiratory distress syndrome, 4:1567
Respiratory exercises. *See* Breathing exercises
Respiratory failure, 1:377, 4:**1567–1570,** 5:1821
Respiratory infections
 pulmonary fibrosis from, 4:1536
 smoking-related, 5:1665
 spinal cord injury-related, 5:1695
 upper, 1:375, 377, 5:1670
Respiratory rate, 5:1822, 1843–1846, 1844*t*
Respiratory sensors, 1:301
Respiratory syncytial virus (RSV), 5:1832–1834
Respiratory therapists, 2:752, 5:1820, 1823, 1824
Respiratory therapy
 pneumonia, 4:1465
 respiratory failure, 4:1568
 spinal cord injuries, 5:1696
 streptococcal pneumonia, 5:1712
Respite care, 2:598
Responsibility, societal, 4:1426–1427
Rest, ice, compression, and elevation (RICE), 5:1753–1754
Restenosis, 4:1276
Restless leg syndrome
 insomnia, 3:1050, 1051, 5:1613
 vs. periodic limb movement disorder, 4:1433, 1434
 sleep deprivation, 5:1656
 treatment, 3:1051, 5:1616, 1657
Reston, James, 1:17
Restorative yoga, 1:274
Restoril. *See* Temazepam
Restraints, chemical/physical, 4:1332
Restriction fragment length polymorphism, 5:1794
Restrictive bariatric surgery, 1:285–286
Resurfacing, laser, 5:1889
Resuscitation. *See* Cardiopulmonary resuscitation
Resveratrol, 2:416, 4:1200
RET oncogene, 5:1769, 1772
Retail chains, optometry, 4:1356
Retarded ejaculation, 5:1618
Reticular activating system (RAS), 2:545, *546*
Retin A. *See* Tretinoin
Retina
 age-related macular degeneration, 1:39
 anatomy, 2:461
 anatomy and function, 4:1570
 fluorescein angiography, 1:129
 peripheral vision loss, 4:1437
Retinal binding protein, 4:1202
Retinal detachment, 4:*1570,* **1570–1573**
 diabetic retinopathy-related, 2:649, 650, 4:1570
 floaters, 3:810, 4:1571, 1572
 peripheral vision loss from, 4:1438
 transient blindness from, 5:1782

Retinal pigment epithelium (RPE), 1:39–40, 4:1570–1571
Retinal transplantation, 5:1838
Retinitis pigmentosa
low vision from, 3:1163
peripheral vision loss from, 4:1438, 1439
sildenafil citrate contraindications, 5:1634
vitamin E interactions, 5:1857–1858
Retinoblastoma, 5:1584
Retinoids, 5:1890
Retinol, 2:575, 5:1861
Retinopathy. *See* Diabetic retinopathy
Retinoplexy, pneumatic, 4:1571
Retinoscopy, 4:1485
Retirement
alcohol abuse, 1:67
mental health, 5:1613, 1616
savings, 3:803
social security system, 2:453
Retirement communities, 5:1623
Retrobulbar hematomas, 1:318
Retrograde amnesia, 3:902
Retrograde ejaculation, 4:1511
Retrovir. *See* Zidovudine
Retroviruses, 4:1195
Reverse transcriptase polymerase chain reaction (RTPCR), 1:60, 5:1585
ReVia. *See* Naltrexone
Reviewing, 4:1526
Revised Kenny Self-Care Evaluation, 1:9
Revision surgery, hip, 3:964, 965, 968, **970–975,** *971*
Reward systems, 2:671
Reye's disease, 3:797, 1145, 1146
RF test. *See* Rheumatoid factor test
RFA (Laparoscopic radiofrequency ablation), 3:1140
RFTR (Radiofrequency volumetric tissue reduction), 5:1672
RGB (Roux-en-Y gastric bypass), 1:285–286
RGP daily-wear lenses, 2:774
RGP extended-wear lenses, 2:774
Rhegmatogenous retinal detachment, 4:1570–1571
Rheumatic fever
aortic valve stenosis from, 1:222
heart disease from, 3:925
mitral valve insufficiency from, 4:1279–1280
mitral valve prolapse from, 4:1281
mitral valve stenosis from, 4:1282
Rheumatic heart disease, 3:801, 924–931
Rheumatoid arthritis, 1:258–260, 4:**1573–1576**
amyloidosis-related, 1:100
aspirin for, 1:234, 235
bursitis-related, 1:388–389
celecoxib for, 2:586–587
collagen injections, 2:530
demographics, 4:1573
diagnosis, 1:253, 254, 4:1519, 1573–1574
drug therapy, 4:1367, 1574
elderly-onset, 4:1575
hip replacement, 3:964
homeopathic medicine, 3:987
hypdrogen peroxide for, 4:1385
knee joint replacement, 3:1110
neuromuscular physical therapy, 4:1323
nonsteroidal anti-inflammatory drugs for, 4:1326, 1574, 1575
pain management, 3:969
paralysis from, 4:1417
pulmonary fibrosis from, 4:1536
Sjögren's syndrome-related, 5:1638
spinal stenosis from, 5:1697
t'ai chi, 5:1748
Rheumatoid factor test
autoimmune disorders, 1:259
immunodeficiency, 3:1023
rheumatoid arthritis, 1:253, 254, 4:1573
Sjögren's syndrome, 5:1639
Rheumatologists, 4:1573, **1576–1577**
Rheumatrex. *See* Methotrexate
Rhinoplasty, 2:582–584
Rhus aromatica. See Sweet sumac
Rhus toxicodendron, 3:1153
Rhytidectomy. *See* Face lift
Rhytides. *See* Wrinkles
Rhytidoplasty. *See* Face lift
Rib fractures, 2:500
Riboflavin, 3:818, 870, 5:1862, 1864
Ribonucleoprotein (RNP), 1:254
Ribosomes, 1:95
Rice, 3:815, 4:1499
RICE (Rest, ice, compression, and elevation), 5:1753–1754
Rickets, 5:1855, 1863
Rifabutin, 1:208–211
Rifadin. *See* Rifampin
Rifampin, 1:208–211
for furunculosis, 1:334
hormone replacement therapy interactions, 3:993
for tuberculosis, 5:1795
Right ventricular failure, 5:1653
Rights
health care, 2:555
patient, 2:527, 528, 4:1333, 1429–1431, *1430*
wards, 2:567
Rigid gas-permeable (RGP) daily-wear lenses, 2:774
Rigid gas-permeable (RGP) extended-wear lenses, 2:774
Rigidity, 3:833
Rilutek. *See* Riluzole
Riluzole, 1:104, 4:1289
Rimactane. *See* Rifampin
Rimantadine, 3:1040, 5:1833
Ringer's solution, lactated, 2:654
Ringing in the ears. *See* Tinnitus
Ringworm, 1:184, 3:825
Riomet. *See* Metformin
Risedronate, 4:1372, 1392
Risperidone
for bipolar disorder, 1:305
for delirium, 2:609
for dementia, 2:613
for mental retardation, 4:1258
for psychoses, 1:203, 4:1531
for schizophrenia, 1:203
side effects, 4:1531
Risus sardonicus, 5:1755
Ritonavir, 5:1635
Rivastigmine, 1:88, 163–165, 4:1244, 5:1616
River blindness, 5:1842
RNA, 3:811, 1013, 5:1831, 1833
RNP (Ribonucleoprotein), 1:254
RNs. *See* Registered nurses
Robaxin. *See* Methocarbamol
Robitussin. *See* Dextromethorphan
Robot-guided surgery, 2:428
Rock-poppy, 2:524
Rocky Mountain spotted fever, 1:151
Rod cells, 4:1437
Rofecoxib, 2:585, 4:1326, 1367
Rogaine. *See* Minoxidil
Rogers, Carl, 1:56
Roizen, Michael, 2:662
Role loss, 3:1078
Roman Catholics, 4:1477, 1551
Romberg test, 3:830
Rome II criteria, 3:1070
Roosevelt, Theodore, 2:657–658
Roper Poll, 5:1892
Ropinirole, 1:199–200, 4:1423, 1435
Rosacea, 1:84, 2:780, 4:**1577–1580,** *1578*
Rose Bengal, 5:1639
Rosemary, 1:326, 2:417, 742, 5:1605
Rosemary Conley's Hip and Thigh Diet, 3:1156
Rosiglitazone, 1:88, 179–180
Rosuvastatin, 1:247, 3:955
Rotational thrust, 2:501–502
Rotationoplasty, 5:1585
Rotavirus infections, 3:851, 4:1497

Roth, Gabrielle, 4:1291–1292
Rotigotine, 1:199–200
Routine ophthalmic examination. *See* Eye examination
Roux-en-Y gastric bypass (RGB), 1:285–286
Royal College of Physicians and Surgeons of Canada, 2:584
RPE (Retinal pigment epithelium), 1:39–40, 4:1570–1571
RSV (Respiratory syncytial virus), 5:1832–1834
RSVP (program), 2:558–559
rt-PA. *See* Tissue plasminogen activator
RTPCR (Reverse transcriptase polymerase chain reaction), 1:60, 5:1585
Rubber band ligation, 3:947
Rubber industry, 3:835, 4:1505, 5:1704
Rubbing alcohol, 4:1296
Rubella
- mental retardation, 4:1256, 1258
- pericarditis from, 4:1431
- thrombocytopenia from, 5:1763
- vaccines, 5:1815
- visual impairment, 5:1842

Rufen. *See* Ibuprofen
Rural areas, 2:728, 3:914
Rush, Benjamin, 4:1234
Rye, 2:473, 3:887

S

S-adenosyl-L-methionine (SAM-e), 2:627, 5:1614
S waves, 2:730
Saccharomyces boulardii, 4:1497
Saccharomyces sp., 4:1496
S.A.C.E. (Serum Angiotensin Converting Enzyme) test, 5:1582
SACH (Solid-ankle-cushion-heel) foot, 3:1166
Sacral nerve roots, 5:1692
Sacroiliac joint dysfunction, 5:1593–1595
Saddle joints, 3:1086
Safety
- dietary supplements, 2:679
- food, 2:657–658
- home, 3:984–986
- home care, 3:981
- pacemakers, 4:1388–1389
- personal hygiene, 4:1444
- *See also* Driver safety

Safety eyewear, 1:320
Sage, 1:334, 4:1252, 5:1605
Sagging skin, eyelid, 1:317–319, *318*
Saint Anthony's fire. *See* Erysipelas
Salagen. *See* Pilocarpine
Salaries
- dieticians, 2:683
- home health aides, 3:983
- licensed practical nurses, 3:1128
- nursing assistants, 4:1329
- physical therapy, 4:1458
- registered nurses, 4:1558

Salicylates
- analgesic effects, 1:106
- bismuth subsalicylate interactions, 1:183
- for gout, 3:892
- insulin interactions, 3:1055
- overdose, 4:1381

Salicylic acid, 1:83, 4:1520
Saline laxatives, 2:569, 3:1123
Saline lock, 3:1060
Saline solution
- breast implants, 1:360, 363, 4:1223
- enemas, 2:752
- intravenous, 3:1061
- pressure sores, 4:1490
- pulmonary embolism, 4:1534
- wound care, 5:1885

Saliva
- dry mouth, 2:714–716
- gingivitis, 3:876
- immune system role, 3:1022
- Sjögren's syndrome, 5:1637–1638

Saliva tests, 1:61, 2:591
Salivary glands, 5:1639
Salmonella paratyphi, 2:653
Salmonella typhimurium, 2:653, 3:851
Salmonellosis, 2:655
Salpingo-oophorectomy, bilateral, 2:484, 745, 3:1015–1018, *1016*
Salsalate, 3:1055
Salt. *See* Sodium
Salt gargling, 2:553
Salt retention, 1:132
Salt substitutes
- angiotensin-converting enzyme inhibitor interactions, 1:133, 134
- congestive heart failure, 2:564
- diuretic interactions, 2:709
- low-sodium diet, 3:1160

Salvia officinalis. See Sage
SAM-e (S-adenosyl-L-methionine), 2:627, 5:1614
Sambucol, 5:1834
Samuel, Michael, 4:1376
Sandimmune. *See* Cyclosporine
Sandwich generation, 3:794
Sangre de drago, 3:1082
Sanitizers, hand, 4:1296
Sapovirus infections, 3:851
Saquinavir, 3:847
Sarcoidosis, 5:*1581,* **1581–1583**
- diabetes insipidus, 2:637
- liver biopsy, 3:1133
- lung biopsy, 3:1171, 5:1582
- rheumatoid factor test, 1:254

Sarcomas, 5:**1583–1586**
- description, 2:407
- Ewing's, 5:1583, 1585–1586
- Kaposi's, 1:51, 2:779, 5:1641, 1642
- metastasis, 4:1263, 5:1583
- osteogenic, 4:1392, 5:1583, 1584, 1585, 1586

Sarcopenia, 3:869
Sarcoptes scabiei. See Scabies
Sardonic smile, 5:1755
SARS (Severe acute respiratory syndrome), 3:1035, 5:1611–1612
Sassafras, 2:631
Satisfaction
- patient, 3:910–911, 976, 4:1475–1476, 5:1828
- physician, 3:976, 4:1209, 1475

Saturated fats, 3:1156–1157
- healthy aging diet, 4:1339
- heart disease, 3:929
- high cholesterol, 3:953–954, 956
- hyperlipoproteinemia, 3:1004
- ischemia, 3:1076
- low-cholesterol diet, 3:1154, 1155–1156
- Mediterranean-style diet, 3:1159
- pro-inflammatory foods, 1:196
- recommendations, 4:1336

Sauna hydrotherapy, 3:1000–1001
Saunders, Cicely, 3:995
Savings, retirement, 3:803
Saw palmetto, 5:**1586–1589,** *1587*
- iron test interactions, 3:1067
- for prostate enlargement, 4:1512, 5:1587, 1588

SBFT (Small bowel follow-through test), 5:1801, 1803
Scabies, 3:1126, 5:**1589–1591,** *1590,* 1651
Scale, 5:1650
Scalp psoriasis, 4:1518
Scandinavians, 5:1581
Scanning laser polarimetry, 3:881
Scars, 5:1650
- collagen injections, 2:529–531
- injection snorplasty, 5:1672
- liposuction, 3:1132
- sarcoidosis, 5:1581
- smoking, 2:583
- vitamin E, 5:1857

Scarsdale diet, 3:1156
Scheel, John, 4:1315
Schistosomiasis, 1:308
Schizoid personality disorder, 4:1444–1448

Schizophrenia, 4:1528
drug therapy, 1:202–206
marijuana-related, 4:1214
neurofeedback, 1:302
ziprasidone for, 4:1531
Schizotypal personality disorder, 4:1444–1448
Schrimer's I test, 2:712
Schultz, Johannes, 4:1563
Schwannoma, 1:349
Schweitzer, Albert, 3:846
Sciatic nerve, 5:1591–1592
Sciatica, 3:1150, 1151, 1152, 5:**1591–1595,** *1592*
neuromuscular physical therapy, 4:1323
water exercise, 5:1874
Scientific Registry of Transplant Recipients (SRTR), 3:1106
Scintigraphy, 3:1075, 4:1402
Sclemm's canal, 3:881
Scleral buckle, 4:1571–1572
Sclerodactyly, 5:1598
Scleroderma, 1:258–260, 5:**1595–1599,** *1596*
bursitis from, 1:389
diagnosis, 1:254, 5:1598
esophageal dysphagia from, 5:1740
gastroesophageal reflux disease from, 3:854, 5:1597, 1598
pulmonary fibrosis from, 4:1536
Sclerosis, 4:1536
Sclerotherapy
cosmetic surgery, 2:582–584
hemorrhoids, 3:947
varicose veins, 2:519, 5:1817
Scoliosis, 1:271–275, 389, 4:1323
Scopolamine, 4:1381
Scratch test, 3:816
Scratching, 3:1080
Screening tests
cancer, 2:409
colon cancer, 2:534
depression, 3:1078–1079
hemochromatosis, 3:945
HIV, 5:1623
isolation, 3:1078–1079
oral cancers, 2:616
prostate cancer, 4:1509
stomach cancer, 5:1705
Scrub nurses, 3:1128
SCSEP (Senior Community Service Employment Program), 2:558
Scurvy, 5:1849, 1850–1851, 1863
sDNA (Stool DNA test), 2:535
Sea cucumber, 3:884
Seafood, 1:70, 195
Seasonal affective disorder, 2:622
Seat belts, 3:904
Seaweed, 2:417
Sebaceous gland carcinoma, 2:779, 780, 5:1641
Seborrheic dermatitis, 2:630–632, 5:**1599–1601**, *1600,* 1650
Secobarbital, 1:142, 282
Seconal. *See* Secobarbital
Second-generation antihistamines, 1:186–188
Second opinion, 3:808
Secondary glaucoma, 3:880
Secondary headache, 3:907, 908
Secondary hypertension, 3:1008
Secondary osteoarthritis, 4:1366
Secondary pulmonary hypertension, 4:1539
Secondary skin lesions, 5:1649
Secondary tumors, 4:1261–1262
Secondhand smoke, 3:1177
Security Rule, 4:1426
Sedation
antihistamines for, 1:186, 188
barbiturates for, 1:281–284
benzodiazepines for, 1:144
muscle relaxants for, 4:1308
shiatsu, 5:1628–1629
Sedatives
antihistamine interactions, 2:709
barbiturate interactions, 1:284
for colonoscopy, 2:538, 539
drug abuse, 5:1725
for endoscopy, 2:748
gastroesophageal reflux disease from, 3:854
for itching, 3:1082
marijuana, 4:1213
for oxygen therapy, 3:1046
for sleep apnea, 5:1652, 1653, 1654
SSRI interactions, 1:173
Sedentary lifestyle
adverse effects, 5:1759
coronary artery disease risk, 2:578
heart attack risk, 3:922
stroke risk, 5:1721
Sedimentation rate, erythrocyte, 3:1180, 4:1467, 5:1639
Seeds, 1:195, 2:696
Segmental cystectomy, 1:309
Segmental excision, breast. *See* Lumpectomy
Seizures, 5:**1601–1607**
absence, 5:1601–1606
akinetic, 5:1602–1606
from arteriovenous malformations, 1:230, 231
auditory, 5:1601
barbiturates for, 1:281–284
benzodiazepines for, 1:292
cardiovascular syncope-related, 3:787
clozapine-induced, 1:205
coma from, 2:545
cycloserine-induced, 1:209
demographics, 5:1601
diagnosis, 5:1602–1603
Down syndrome, 4:1257
electroencephalography, 2:732–734
first aid, 5:1605
generalized, 5:1601–1606
head injury-related, 3:903
isoniazid-induced, 1:209
Jacksonian, 5:1602–1606
myoclonic, 5:1602–1606
partial, 1:215, 5:1602–1606
visual, 5:1601
See also Anticonvulsant drugs
Seldane. *See* Terfenadine
Selective estrogen receptor modulators (SERMS), 1:358
Selective serotonin reuptake inhibitors (SSRIs), 1:144, **166–174,** 166*t*
for anxiety, 1:215, 217
for dementia, 2:613
for depression, 2:626
dosage, 1:168–169
erectile dysfunction from, 2:756
for generalized anxiety disorder, 3:863
interactions, 1:172–173
for itching, 3:1082
for panic disorder, 4:1411
for personality disorders, 4:1447
side effects, 1:170–172
sildenafil citrate interactions, 5:1634
sodium interactions, 5:1680
suicidal behavior precautions, 3:864
tricyclic antidepressant interactions, 1:177
Selegiline, 4:1423, 1435
Selenium
aneurysm, 1:121
antioxidant role, 1:197
benefits and risks, 4:1344
daily recommended dosage, 1:198
garlic, 3:846
immune system function, 3:1024
osteoarthritis, 4:1368
polymyositis, 4:1468
side effects, 1:198
skin cancer prevention, 5:1643
smoking-induced lung damage, 5:1662
ulcers, 5:1800
Selenium-based shampoos, 2:631
Selenium sulfide, 5:1600
Self-acceptance, 4:1526
Self care, 4:1306
Self-catheterization, 2:466, 467, 469
Self-cells, 3:1021, 1023
Self-determination, 4:1428
Self-employment, 3:1029
Self-esteem, 5:1874, 1875
Self-evaluation, dietary, 2:674–675

Self-examination
- breast, 1:353, *369,* 369–372, 2:409
- testicular, 5:1754–1755

Self help groups. *See* Support groups
Self-hypnosis, 4:1272
Self-neglect, 2:727, 728
Self-sufficiency, 3:793, 1027
- *See also* Independence

Selver, Charlotte, 4:1292
Selye, Hans, 4:1269, 1563
Semantic dysphasia. *See* Wernicke's aphasia
Semen, 4:1505
Senescence, organismal, 1:44
Senior centers, 2:557–559, 4:1227
Senior Community Service Employment Program (SCSEP), 2:558
Senior Companions Program, 2:558
Senior Corps, 2:558
Senior travel. *See* Travel
Seniors EyeCare Program, 2:464
Seniors' health, 5:**1611–1617**
Sensitivity tests
- sexually transmitted diseases, 5:1625
- skin culture, 5:1645, 1646
- urinary tract infections, 5:1808
- urine culture, 5:1810–1811

Sensitivity trigger, 5:1823
Sensorineural hearing loss, 3:914–915, 918
Sensory awareness, 4:1292
Sensory dysphasia. *See* Receptive dysphasia
Sensory integration tests, 3:830
Sensory loss
- gait and balance disorders, 3:831, 832, 833
- neurologic examination, 4:1320, 1322
- spinal cord injuries, 5:1692, 1696

Sensory processing, 3:831
Sentinel lymph node (SNL) biopsy, 1:357, 3:1169, 4:1222
Sepsis, 1:277, 4:1294
Septal myomectomy, 2:447
Septic arthritis, 4:1366
Septic bursitis, 1:389, 390
Septic shock, 1:275, 276, 2:736
Septicemia, 1:277, 3:1032–1036
Septra. *See* Trimethoprim/Sulfamethoxazole
Serenoa repens. See Saw palmetto
SERMS (Selective estrogen receptor modulators), 1:358
Seromycin. *See* Cycloserine
Serotonin, 1:168, 194, 305, 2:665
Serotonin and norepinephrine reuptake inhibitors (SNRIs), 2:626
Serotonin receptors, 1:203
Serotonin syndrome, 1:173
Sertaconazole, 1:184
Sertraline, 1:167
- for anxiety, 1:144
- for itching, 3:1082
- for personality disorders, 4:1447
- for PTSD, 4:1470

Serum Angiotensin Converting Enzyme (S.A.C.E.) test, 5:1582
Serum creatinine test, 3:1096–1097
Serum hepatitis. *See* Hepatitis B
Service dogs, 3:1164, 5:1843
Serzone. *See* Nefazodone
Sestamibi, 2:579
Seventh-day Adventists, 4:1478
Severe acute respiratory syndrome (SARS), 3:1035, 5:1611–1612
Severe asthma, 1:241, 243
Seville oranges, 5:1849*t*
Sevofluorane, 1:113
Sex hormones, 1:155
Sex therapy, 5:1619
Sexual abuse, 2:727–729
Sexual activity
- after heart attacks, 3:923
- cancer risk, 2:408
- healthy aging, 4:1525, 5:1617–1618
- HIV transmission, 1:50, 57
- nursing homes, 5:1623
- retirement communities, 5:1623
- risky, 5:1621
- urinary catheterization, 2:467, 471

Sexual arousal disorder, 5:1618, 1619
Sexual desire, 5:1619, 1635
Sexual dysfunction, 5:**1617–1620**
- multiple sclerosis, 4:1304
- sildenafil citrate for, 5:1634
- spinal cord injury-related, 5:1694–1695
- SSRI-induced, 1:171
- *See also* Erectile dysfunction

Sexual response, 1:262
Sexually transmitted diseases, 3:1124, 1126, 5:**1620–1624,** 1624–1627
Sexually transmitted diseases cultures, 5:**1624–1627**
Shampoos
- lice, 3:1126
- seborrheic dermatitis, 5:1600
- selenium-based, 2:631

Shanks, 3:1166
Shark cartilage, 2:746, 3:884
Shasta County community nutrition, 2:556–557
Shave biopsy, 5:1645, 1646
Sheikhouni, Soudon, 4:1212
Shellfish allergies, 3:814–818
Shen-Nung, 4:1211
Shiatsu, 1:13, 15, 4:*1216,* 5:**1627–1629**
Shiatsu Therapists Association, 5:1627
Shigella sp., 3:851
Shigellosis, 2:655
Shingles, 3:1032, 5:*1629,* **1629–1633,** 1832–1834
- acupressure-induced, 1:15–16
- cellulitis from, 2:477
- corneal infection from, 2:574
- demographics, 3:1034, 5:1630, 1832
- drug therapy, 1:211–212, 5:1631, 1833
- neuralgia from, 4:1318, 5:1631
- prognosis, 3:1035
- vaccines, 1:212, 5:1631–1632

SHIP (State Children's Health Insurance Program), 2:548, 3:909, 4:1237
Shirmer's test, 5:1639
Shiva, 2:599
Shock, hemorrhagic, 3:873
Shoes. *See* Footwear
Shopping, 4:1337, 1444
Short-acting insulin, 3:1054
Short bowel syndrome, 5:1897
Short leg, 4:1370
Shortness of breath, 1:372–375, 2:562, 5:1661, 1894
- *See also* Breathing problems

Shoulder bursitis, 1:388, 389
Shoulder dislocation, 2:686–687
Shoulder polymyalgia rheumatica, 4:1466–1467
Shoulder separation, 2:687
Shrines, 4:1477
Shunts, 4:1461–1462
Sialogogues, 2:714
Siblings, 3:794
Sibutramine, 4:1351
Sick sinus syndrome, 4:1387
Sickle cell anemia, 1:109, 110
- chronic kidney failure from, 2:508
- hypernatremia from, 2:735
- zinc deficiency, 5:1897

Sidestream smoke, 5:1660
Sietan, 3:817
Sigh (ventilator), 5:1823
Sigmoid colon, 2:532
Sigmoidoscopy
- diarrhea, 2:654
- flexible, 2:534, 535
- hemorrhoids, 3:947
- irritable bowel syndrome, 3:1070

SIL (Squamous intraepithelial lesion), 2:482
Silastic catheters, 2:466, 470
Sildenafil citrate, 5:**1633–1637**

for erectile dysfunction, 1:264, 2:647, 756–757, 4:1507, 5:1620, 1633–1637
nitrate interactions, 3:930
priapism from, 4:1492
for prostate enlargement, 4:1512
for pulmonary hypertension, 4:1540
transient blindness from, 5:1782
Silent ischemia, 3:1073
Silent kidney stones, 3:1100
Silent ulcers, 5:1798
Silica, 1:334
Silica dust, 5:1597
Silicone catheters, 2:466, 470
Silicone gel breast implants
breast augmentation, 1:368
breast reconstruction, 1:360, 363, 365, 367, 4:1223
scleroderma from, 5:1597
Silva, Mary C., 2:529
Silver sulfadiazine, 5:1886
Silybum marianum. See Milk thistle
Silymarin, 3:951
Similars, Law of, 3:987
Simple carbohydrates, 2:421, 422
SIMV (Synchronized intermittent mandatory ventilation), 5:1819, 1822
Simvastatin, 1:247, 3:955
Sinclair, Upton, 2:657
Sinemet, 4:1423
See also Levodopa
Singer, Peter, 2:763
Single chamber pacemakers, 4:1387–1388
Single-contrast barium enema, 1:287, 288
Single-photon absorptiometry (SPA), 1:337
Single photon emission computed tomography (SPECT), 4:1440, 5:1603
Singulair. *See* Montelukast
Sinoatrial node, 2:423–424, 4:1387
Sinus headache, 3:905
Sinus infections, 4:1247
Sinus node, 1:225
Sirolimus, 3:1107
Sitagliptin phosphate, 1:179–180
Sitostanol, 3:955
Sitting, 5:1595, 1817, 1880
Situational insomnia, 5:1655
Situational syncope, 3:786–788
Situationally bound panic attack, 4:1409
Situationally predisposed panic attack, 4:1409
Six Healing Sounds, 4:1547
Sjögren, Henrick, 5:1638
Sjögren's syndrome, 1:252–254, 258–260, 5:**1637–1640**
Skelaxin. *See* Metaxalone
Skeletal muscle relaxants. *See* Muscle relaxants
Skelid. *See* Tiludronate disodium
Skilled nursing facilities, 4:1331
Skin
aging, 5:1888–1889
exfoliants, 1:83–84
peeling, 3:1132
sagging, 1:317–319, *318*
See also Dry skin
Skin biopsy, 5:1645, 1646, 1647
Skin breakdown, 3:870
Skin cancer, 5:**1640–1644,** *1641,* 1650
causes, 2:408, 4:1260, 5:1642
demographics, 2:407, 5:1641
diagnosis, 2:409, 5:1642–1643
eyelid, 2:779
genetic factors, 2:407
melanoma, 4:1197–1201
prevention, 2:416, 4:1200, 5:1643, 1651
risk factors, 5:1642
rosacea, 4:1579
skin lesion removal, 5:1646–1649, 1651
Skin care, 1:83–85, 5:1888, 1890
Skin culture, 5:**1645–1646**
Skin disorders
aloe, 1:77–79
amyloidosis, 1:101
dermatologists, 2:632–633
itching from, 3:1081
Skin infections
cellulitis, 2:476–478
diagnosis, 5:1645–1646
fungal, 1:183–186, 184*t*
MRSA, 4:1295
staphylococcal, 5:1699, 1701, 1703
streptococcal, 5:1710, 1711–1713
tuberculosis-related, 5:1793
Skin lesion removal, 5:**1646–1649,** 1651
Skin lesions, 5:*1649,* **1649–1651**
ABCDE system, 5:1642–1643
Behcet's syndrome, 1:290
diagnosis, 5:1645–1646, 1650
precancerous, 5:1642
Skin patch test
allergies, 1:71, 73, 75
contact dermatitis, 2:573
dermatitis, 2:631
skin lesions, 5:1650
tuberculosis, 5:1793
Skin patches
cannabinoids, 2:419
hormone replacement therapy, 3:990–994
nicotine replacement, 5:1667
Skin perfusion measurement, 1:98
Skin preparation, preoperative, 4:1483
Skin ulcers, 5:1649, 1818, 1884, 1886
See also Pressure sores
Skull, 4:1369, 1390
Skull fractures, 3:902, 903
Skullcap, 3:1051, 5:1727
SLE. *See* Systemic lupus erythematosus
Sleep apnea, 5:**1651–1654,** *1652,* 1655–1656
breathing problems, 1:372
causes, 5:1652–1653
central, 5:1652
continuous positive airway pressure, 3:1046, 1047, 1049, 5:1653, 1654, 1657, 1675
demographics, 5:1652
diagnosis, 3:1051, 5:1653, 1674
heart disease risk, 5:1658
insomnia, 3:1050
obesity, 3:1049, 5:1613, 1653
obstructive, 5:1652, 1670, 1672, 1674
prevention, 1:374, 5:1654
prognosis, 3:1052
snoring, 3:1051, 5:1653, 1655–1656, 1670
stroke risk, 5:1658
treatment, 3:1051, 5:1615, 1653–1654
Sleep deprivation, 5:1655
Sleep disorder clinics, 5:1615–1616
Sleep disorders, 5:1613, **1654–1659**
acupressure, 5:1628–1629
benzodiazepines for, 1:292
breathing-related, 5:1655–1656
caffeine-associated, 2:396
circadian rhythm, 5:1656
delirium-related, 2:608
demographics, 5:1656
depression, 2:625
diagnosis, 5:1656–1657
drug therapy, 1:140–141, 5:1657
fibromyalgia-related, 3:800, 801
forgiveness, 4:1552
healthy aging, 4:1525
lifestyle, 1:141
menopause, 5:1655
periodic limb movement disorder, 4:1433–1436
psychoses from, 4:1531
relaxation techniques, 4:1565
therapeutic exercise, 5:1759
treatment, 5:1615–1616, 1657–1658
valerian for, 4:1525
See also Insomnia
Sleep hygiene, 5:1657, 1658
Sleep patterns, 5:1613
Sleep, rapid eye movement, 5:1652, 1653, 1654
Sleep restriction therapy, 5:1658
Sleep-wake cycles, 4:1440, 5:1655
Sleepiness, daytime, 4:1434, 5:1652, 1653, 1673
Sleeping pills. *See* Anti-insomnia drugs

Sleeping position, 5:1673, 1675
Sleepwalking, 5:1656, 1657
Sleeves, prosthetic, 3:1166
Slipped disc, 5:1592
Slippery elm, 1:334, 5:1800
Slit-lamp biomicroscopy, 2:770, 779
  diabetic retinopathy, 2:649
  peripheral vision loss, 4:1438
  Sjögren's syndrome, 5:1639
  vision disorders, 5:1838
Slow heart rate. *See* Bradycardia
Small bowel follow-through test (SBFT), 5:1801, 1803
Small cell carcinoma
  bladder, 1:307
  lung, 3:1173–1174, 1175
Small intestines, 2:532
Smell, 2:659
Smile, sardonic, 5:1755
Smoke detectors, 3:985
Smoke-free hospitals, 5:1666
Smoked food, 5:1706
Smoking, 5:**1659–1664,** 1659*t*
  abdominoplasty, 1:6
  adverse effects, 5:1611
  age-related macular degeneration, 1:40
  aneurysm risk, 1:122
  atherosclerosis, 1:246
  blood clots, 1:321
  breathing problems, 1:372
  cancer risk, 2:413
  cataracts, 2:464
  chronic bronchitis, 1:375–376
  chronic obstructive pulmonary disease, 2:512, 5:1662
  colon cancer, 2:533
  common cold, 2:550
  coronary artery disease, 2:578
  demographics, 5:1659*t*, 1665*t*
  diabetes mellitus, 3:821, 5:1665
  diabetic nephropathy risk, 2:643
  drug interactions, 2:710
  emphysema, 2:740, 743
  erectile dysfunction, 2:756
  esophageal cancer, 2:759, 761
  exocrine pancreatic cancer, 4:1404, 1408
  general anesthesia, 1:114
  generalized anxiety disorder, 3:863–864
  gingivitis, 3:876
  head and neck cancer, 5:1668
  heart attacks, 3:922
  heart disease, 5:1661
  heart transplantation, 5:1668
  hyperlipoproteinemia, 3:1004
  influenza contraindications, 3:1039
  insomnia, 3:1052
  insulin interactions, 3:1056
  ischemia, 3:1074, 1076
  kidney cancer, 3:1092, 1094
  lung cancer, 2:407, 3:1174, 1177, 5:1660, 1665
  menopause, 4:1250
  mortality, 5:1660, 1665
  nicotine replacement therapy, 5:1665
  oral cancer, 4:1357, 1359, 5:1665
  oxygen therapy, 3:1046
  passive, 5:1660
  peripheral vascular disease, 4:1436, 1437
  pressure sores, 4:1489
  pulmonary fibrosis, 4:1537
  scar formation, 2:583
  snoring, 5:1670
  stomach cancer, 5:1706
  streptococcal pneumonia, 5:1713
  stroke, 5:1721
  teeth whitening, 5:1752
  ulcer risk, 5:1798
  vitamin C, 5:1852
  wound healing, 5:1664
  wrinkles, 5:1888
Smoking cessation, 5:1661–1663, **1664–1668**, 1665*t*
  acupuncture, 1:20
  cardiac rehabilitation, 2:437
  chronic bronchitis, 1:377
  chronic obstructive pulmonary disease, 2:513, 514
  cold turkey, 5:1666
  congestive heart failure, 2:563
  COPD, 1:374
  coronary artery disease, 2:581
  demographics, 5:1660
  emphysema, 2:741
  face lift, 3:784
  gingivitis, 3:877
  hip replacement preparation, 3:966
  nicotine replacement therapy, 2:708*t*, 5:1661, 1665, 1667
  over fifty lifestyle, 2:661
  pulmonary rehabilitation, 4:1542, 1543
  vision disorders, 5:1839
Smooth muscle antibodies, 3:1143, 1145
Smooth muscle cell leiomyosarcoma, 1:229
Sneddon's syndrome, 1:252
Snellen eye chart, 2:770, 4:1321, 5:1841, 1842
Sniper shootings, 5:1715
SNL(Sentinel lymph node) biopsy, 1:357, 3:1169, 4:1222
Snoreplasty, injection, 5:1672, 1674
Snoring, 5:1670–1671
  alternative therapy, 5:1675
  demographics, 5:1670–1671
  diagnosis, 5:1673–1674
  obesity, 5:1613, 1670, 1673
  risk factors, 5:1670
  sleep apnea, 3:1051, 5:1653, 1655–1656, 1670
  socially unacceptable, 5:1670
  treatment, 5:1671–1672, 1674–1675
Snoring surgery, 5:*1669*, **1669–1677**
SNRIs (Serotonin and norepinephrine reuptake inhibitors), 2:626
Snuff, 4:1357
Soap suds enemas, 2:752–753
Soap, super-fatted, 2:716
Social assessment, 3:866
Social isolation. *See* Isolation
Social issues, 4:**1522–1527,** 1554, 5:1734
Social modeling, 3:862
Social network, 2:662, 3:1078
Social norms, 4:1527
Social phobia, 1:166, 167, 213, 214, 216
Social programs, community, 2:**557–559,** 4:1527
Social relationships. *See* Relationships
Social Security, 1:46, 2:453
Social Security Act (1965), 4:1228, 1236
Social Security Administration, 4:1236–1237, 1238, 1521
Social work, 5:**1677–1678**
  back and neck pain, 1:271
  cardiac rehabilitation, 2:437
  discharge planning, 2:685
  gangrene, 3:845
Social workers. *See* Social work
Socialization, 4:1560
Socializing, 5:1614
Socially unacceptable snoring (SUS), 5:1670
Societal responsibility, 4:1426–1427
Society for Vascular Surgery, 2:456
Society of Actuaries, 1:2
Socioeconomic factors
  aging population, 3:795
  decision making, 2:528
  family relationships, 3:793
  hip revision surgery, 3:974
  home care, 3:980
  isolation, 3:1078
  malnutrition, 4:1201
  Medicaid, 4:1229
  mental retardation, 4:1255
  nutrition, 4:1339
  type 2 diabetes, 2:662
Sockets, prosthetic, 3:1166
Socks, prosthetic, 3:1166
SOD (Superoxide-dismutase), 1:103, 5:1598
Sodium, 5:**1678–1681**
  antibiotic interactions, 1:153
  chronic kidney failure, 2:509
  Cushing's syndrome, 2:592
  daily recommended dosage, 3:1161
  dehydration, 2:604, 5:1870

Sodium *(continued)*
- diabetic nephropathy, 2:644
- dietary Reference Intake, 5:1679
- edema, 2:726
- electrolyte balance, 2:734–735
- electrolyte tests, 2:738–739
- general anesthesia, 1:112
- heatstroke, 3:938
- hypertension, 1:326, 3:1011
- ischemia, 3:1076
- local anesthesia, 1:116
- rehydration, 5:1872
- role, 3:1160, 5:1678
- sources, 3:1161, 5:1679–1680
- stomach cancer risk, 5:1704, 1706
- stroke risk, 5:1722–1723
- tinnitus, 5:1780
- *See also* Hypernatremia; Hyponatremia

Sodium bicarbonate
- antacids, 1:139, 140
- for gastroesophageal reflux disease, 3:856
- local anesthesia interactions, 1:116

Sodium biphosphate, 3:1123

Sodium channel blockers, 1:146*t*

Sodium chloride, 3:1160, 5:1678

Sodium deficiency. *See* Hyponatremia

Sodium ferric gluconate, 3:1065

Sodium hypochlorite, 5:1885

Sodium pentothal, 1:112

Sodium tetradecyl sulfate, 5:1672

Sodium valproate, 5:1603, 1897

Soft contact lenses, 2:575

Soft drinks, 2:395

Soft lenses, 2:774

Soft martial arts, 5:1745

Soft palate, 5:1673

Soft tissue infections, 5:1699

Soft tissue injuries, 4:1455

Soft tissue stretching, 2:702

Solanaceae, 4:1368

Solar purpura, 1:385

Soldier's Home, 5:1827

Solid-ankle-cushion-heel (SACH) foot, 3:1166

Solifenacin succinate, 4:1379, 5:1805

Solitude, 3:1077, 4:1562

Soluble fiber, 2:422, 3:957–958, 1155

Somatosensory evoked potentials, 2:488, 3:833

Somatostatin receptor scintigraphy, 4:1402

Somatostatinoma, 4:1401–1403

Somax. *See* Carisoprodol

Somnoplasty, 5:1672, 1674

Somophyllin. *See* Aminophylline

Somophyllin-T. *See* Theophylline

Sonata. *See* Zalopon

Song of Solomon, 4:1561

Sonohysterography, 2:745

Sorafenib, 3:1093

Sorbitol, 3:1070

Sorbitrate. *See* Isosorbide dinatrate

Sore throat, 1:375

Sotalol, 1:190–191

South Africa, 4:1551

Soy products
- allergies, 3:814–818
- anti-inflammatory diet, 1:195
- calcium, 5:1614
- cancer fighting action, 2:417
- menopause, 4:1253
- oil, 4:1339

SPA (Single-photon absorptiometry), 1:337

Space sickness, 1:300

Spas, 5:1874

Spasms, 4:1323, 5:1740

Spastic bowel. *See* Irritable bowel syndrome

Spastic colon. *See* Irritable bowel syndrome

Spastic quadriplegia/quadriparesis, 4:1255

Spasticity
- multiple sclerosis-related, 4:1306
- muscle relaxants for, 4:1307, 1308
- spinal cord injury-related, 5:1692–1693, 1694

Special Commission on Aging, 2:567

Special dietary needs of cancer patients, 5:**1681–1686**

Specialists
- HMOs, 3:976
- managed care plans, 4:1475–1476
- referrals, 4:1475
- registered nurses, 4:1558, 1559
- surgical, 3:805–806

Specific phobias, 1:213, 216

Specimen collection, 5:1626

SPECT (Single photon emission computed tomography), 4:1440, 5:1603

Spectroscopy, magnetic resonance, 4:1189, 1191

Speech, 4:1321, 5:1688

Speech audiometry, 1:249

Speech disorders, 5:**1686–1691**
- Alzheimer's disease-related, 1:87
- dysphasia, 2:716–719
- snoring surgery-related, 5:1674
- stroke-related, 5:1724

Speech-language pathologists
- aspiration, 1:232, 233
- dysphasia, 2:718
- polymyositis, 4:1468
- speech disorders, 5:1688

Speech therapy, 5:1689
- amyotrophic lateral sclerosis, 1:104
- aneurysm, 1:122
- dysphasia, 2:718
- stroke, 5:1723

Speed. *See* Stimulants

Sphincter, 3:798, 799

Sphygmomanometry, 1:325, 3:1007–1008, 5:1845
- *See also* Ambulatory blood pressure; Blood pressure measurement

Spices, 1:195

Spider vein removal, 2:582–584

Spielberger, C. D., 1:213

Spilanthes, 3:1185

Spina bifida, 4:1255, 1256, 1258

Spinal anesthesia, 1:116, 118, 119, 3:965

Spinal concussion, 5:1692

Spinal cord, 1:229, 5:1691–1692

Spinal cord injuries, 5:**1691–1696**
- autonomic disorders, 1:263
- bacterial infections, 1:278
- muscle relaxants for, 4:1307
- neuromuscular physical therapy, 4:1323
- paralysis, 4:1417, 1418
- pressure sores, 4:1490
- wheelchairs, 5:1881

Spinal cord tumors, 5:1697

Spinal disorders, 4:1190, 5:1592–1595

Spinal fusion, 5:1698

Spinal headache, 1:118

Spinal manipulation, 4:1316, 1369

Spinal stenosis, 5:*1696*, **1696–1698**
- cervical spondylosis, 2:487
- degenerative, 5:1697
- low back pain from, 3:1151
- sciatica, 5:1592, 1593

Spinal tap. *See* Lumbar puncture

Spinal transection, 5:1692

Spine
- anatomy, 5:1696
- chiropractic manipulation, 2:*501*, 501–502
- lumbar, 4:1366
- lumbosacral, 5:1592
- tuberculosis, 5:1793, 1795

Spiral computed tomography, 4:1533

Spirituality, 4:**1476–1480**
- healthy aging, 4:1523
- meditation, 4:1564
- over fifty lifestyle, 2:661, 662
- reconciliation and forgiveness, 4:1553
- stress-related disorders, 5:1716

Spirometry
- asthma, 1:242
- chronic obstructive pulmonary disease, 2:512–513

Spirometry *(continued)*
incentive, 2:496–497, 3:1046–1049
pulmonary rehabilitation, 4:1543
sarcoidosis, 5:1582
Spironolactone
for cardiomyopathy, 2:447
for congestive heart failure, 2:563
diuretic action, 2:690
hyperkalemia from, 2:737
Spleen, 3:1022
Spleen disorders, 3:1147–1149
Spleen, enlarged. *See* Splenomegaly
Splenectomy, 5:1765, 1766
Splenomegaly
amyloidosis, 1:101
thrombocytopenia, 5:1764, 1765
thrombocytosis, 5:1766
Splenoportography, 1:129
Splinting
bursitis, 1:390
dislocations, 2:688
gait and balance disorders, 3:830
sciatica, 5:1594
tendinitis, 5:1754
Spondyloarthritis, 1:234, 235
Spondylosis, 2:*486,* 486–489, 4:1417
Spondyltic myelopathy, 2:487
Spontaneous remission, 3:1094
Sporadic Alzheimer's disease, 1:86, 4:1242
Sporonox. *See* Itraconazole
Sports. *See* Athletes
Sports beverages, 3:938
Sports massage, 4:1217
Spouses
caregivers, 2:453, 454
companionship, 3:794
death of, 1:67, 295
elder abuse, 2:727, 728
isolation, 3:1078
patient representative, 4:1428–1429
snoring, 5:1670
Sprains, knee, 3:1116
Sputum analysis
breathing problems, 1:373
cancer, 2:409
pneumonia, 4:1464
tuberculosis, 5:1794
Sputum secretion, 2:495–498, 511, 512
Squamous cell carcinoma
bladder, 1:307
esophageal, 2:758, 759
eyelid, 2:780
lung, 3:1174
skin, 5:1640–1645, 1647
Squamous intraepithelial lesion (SIL), 2:482
Srsenicum album, 3:856
SRTR (Scientific Registry of Transplant Recipients), 3:1106
SSRIs. *See* Selective serotonin reuptake inhibitors
St. Elizabeth's Hospital, 5:1827
St. John's wort, 1:173, 2:680, 3:1067
ST segment, 2:435, 5:1719
Stability. *See* Balance
Stable angina pectoris, 1:123
Staff model HMOs, 3:976, 4:1209
Staff nurses, 4:1557, 1558, 1559
Staff-to-patient ratio, 4:1334
Stages of change model, 2:671
Staghorn stones, 3:1102
Staging. *See* Cancer staging
Stagnant anoxia, 1:137–138
Stains, bone marrow aspiration, 1:341
Stairs, 3:986
Standards
adult day care, 1:29
dietary intake, 2:676–677
dietetics, 2:681
fibromyalgia, 3:800–801
nursing homes, 4:1332
Standing, 5:1817
Standing aids, 5:1868
Stanford Forgiveness Project, 4:1552
Staph carriers, 4:1294, 5:1699
Staphylococcal infections, 5:*1698,* **1698–1704**
bacteremia, 1:276
community-aquired, 5:1700, 1702
gangrene, 3:843
hospital-acquired, 3:1029, 5:1699
marijuana for, 4:1213
prevention, 5:1702–1703
styes, 2:779
Staphylococcus aureus, 5:1699–1701
boils, 1:333
bursitis, 1:389
cellulitis, 2:477
description, 4:1293–1294
diarrhea, 2:652
food poisoning, 4:1296
methacillin-resistant, 1:150, 278–279, 4:1293–1298, 5:1699, 1702
oxaxillin-resistant, 4:1293
Staphylococcus caprae, 5:1699
Staphylococcus epidermis, 1:389, 5:1699–1701, 1702
Staphylococcus lugdunensis, 5:1699
Staphylococcus saprophytis, 1:310, 2:594, 5:1699
Staples, 3:1132
Starch, 2:421, 3:888, 5:1682
Starfruit, 3:1102
Starlix. *See* Nateglinide
Stasis dermatitis, 2:629–632
Stasis ulcers, 2:632
STAT, 1:26
State anxiety, 1:213
State Board of Pharmacy, 4:1453
State Children's Health Insurance Program (SHIP), 2:548, 3:909, 4:1237
Static testing, 3:829
Statins
for atherosclerosis, 1:247
for high cholesterol, 2:519, 3:955
post-cardiac surgery, 2:439
Statistics Division (U.N.), 5:1611
Status epilepticus, 5:1602, 1603
Status migrainosus, 4:1266
A Status Report on Breast Implant Safety (FDA), 1:367
STDs. *See* Sexually transmitted diseases
Steady traction, 1:269, 270
Steatosis. *See* Fatty liver
Stem cell transplantation
amyloidosis, 1:102
cancer, 2:411
multiple myeloma, 4:1301
non-Hodgkin's lymphoma, 4:1196
Stem cells, 1:80
Stenosis
aortic valve, 1:*221,* 221–225, 2:428, 3:931–932
bronchoscopy, 1:381
coronary artery disease, 2:577
esophageal, 5:1740
heart valve, 2:441
idiopathic hypertrophic subaortic, 2:445
kidney artery, 2:508
mitral valve, 3:932, 4:1281–1282
pulmonary valve, 3:932
renal artery, 3:1100
spinal, 2:487, 3:1151, 5:1592, 1593, *1696,* 1696–1698
stroke from, 5:1720
vaginal, 2:747
Stents
balloon angioplasty, 1:131
bile duct, 3:836
bronchoscopy placement, 1:381
cardiac catheterization, 2:432
coronary artery disease, 2:580, 3:1075, 4:1277
stroke, 5:1722
thrombocytopenia from, 5:1764
Step-down unit, phase II, 4:1557
Stereotactic core biopsy, 1:352
Stereotypes, 1:47–48
Sterman, Barry, 1:300
Sternocleidomastoid muscle, 4:1322
Sternotomy, 4:1275
Sternum fractures, 2:500
Steroids
for age-related macular degeneration, 1:41
anabolic, 3:993, 1055, 1143, 5:1588

Steroids *(continued)*
- antinuclear antibody test interactions, 1:253
- for brain and central nervous system tumors, 1:350
- for cancer, 2:490
- for chronic obstructive pulmonary disease, 2:513
- edema from, 2:726
- for emphysema, 2:741
- for inflammation, 1:194
- for pneumonia, 1:373
- for psoriasis, 4:1519–1520
- rosacea from, 4:1578
- for sciatica, 5:1593–1594
- for shingles, 5:1631
- for temporal arteritis, 2:519
- *See also* Corticosteroids

Stethoscope examination, 1:226, 228, 377

Stevens-Johnson syndrome, 1:180, 2:585

Still, Andrew Taylor, 2:701

Still's disease, 1:254

Stimulant laxatives, 3:1124

Stimulants, 2:709*t,* 5:1725

Stimulation-response therapy, 2:718–719

Stings, insects, 1:70

Stockings. *See* Compression stockings/bandages

Stoma, 2:541, 543
- *See also* Ostomy

Stomach acid. *See* Gastric acid

Stomach anatomy, 5:1704

Stomach cancer, 5:**1704–1709**
- diagnosis, 3:899, 5:1705–1706
- helicobacteriosis-related, 3:939–941
- metastasis, 4:1263, 5:1705, 1706, 1707
- prevention, 2:415, 5:1707–1708
- proton pump inhibitors mask, 4:1516

Stomach flu. *See* Gastroenteritis

Stomach obstruction, 5:1798–1799

Stomach polyps, 5:1705

Stomach pumping, 4:1382

Stomach stapling, 1:285–286

Stomach tumors, benign, 5:1706

Stomach ulcers. *See* Peptic ulcers

Stone, Edward, 1:234

Stoneyfield yogurt, 4:1497

Stool acidity test, 3:1122

Stool analysis
- cancer diagnosis, 2:409
- colon cancer, 2:534
- diarrhea, 2:654, 655
- helicobacteriosis, 3:940
- hemorrhoids, 3:947
- *See also* Fecal occult blood test

Stool cultures, 2:654, 655

Stool DNA test (sDNA), 2:535

Stool softeners, 2:569, 3:1123

Stool weights, 2:652

Stools, 2:568–570

Strabismus, 1:345, 347, 4:1354

Straight-leg-raising test, 5:1593

Strains
- back, 5:1591, 1592–1595
- muscle relaxants for, 4:1307

Strawberries, 1:83, 2:415

Street drugs, 1:115, 117, 173, 2:706–707

Strength-related falls, 3:790

Strength training, 2:766, 768, 5:1757–1758
- gait and balance disorders, 3:830
- hip fractures, 3:961
- knee injuries, 3:1117, 1118
- water exercise, 5:1873

Strep throat, 5:1709, *1710,* 1710–1712
- antibiotics for, 1:279, 5:1711–1712
- heart disease from, 3:925, 926
- rheumatic fever from, 4:1280, 1282

Streptase. *See* Streptokinase

Streptococcal disease, 3:1033–1034, 1035, 5:**1709–1714,** *1710*
- bacteremia, 1:276
- cellulitis, 2:477, 5:1711, 1712
- gangrene, 3:843
- marijuana for, 4:1213
- thrombolytic therapy interactions, 5:1767

Streptococcus agalactiae, 5:1709

Streptococcus faecalis, 1:310

Streptococcus pneumoniae
- meningitis, 4:1248
- pneumonia, 4:1463, 1463*t,* 5:1709, 1711–1713
- vaccines, 3:1036, 4:1463*t,* 1466, 5:1709, 1713

Streptococcus pyogenes, 5:1711, 1712

Streptococcus sp. *See* Streptococcal disease

Streptokinase, 5:1767, 1768

Streptomyces griseus, 1:95

Streptomycin, 1:95–97, 151, 5:1790, 1795

Streptozocin, 4:1403

Stress, 5:**1714–1717,** *1720*
- adjustment disorders from, 1:23–24
- anxiety from, 1:212–213
- arrhythmias from, 2:661
- autonomic nervous system, 1:262
- caregivers, 2:454
- circulatory disorders from, 2:520
- coronary artery disease risk, 2:579
- demographics, 5:1720*t*
- erectile dysfunction from, 2:756
- generalized anxiety disorder, 3:862
- heart attack risk, 3:922
- hospice care professionals, 3:997
- immune system function, 3:1024
- irritable bowel syndrome, 3:1070
- ischemia risk, 3:1074, 1076–1077
- isolation-related, 3:1077–1078
- itching from, 3:1080–1081
- mind/body medicine, 4:1269, 1270
- naturopathy, 4:1315
- over fifty lifestyle, 2:661
- prayer and spirituality, 4:1478
- relaxation techniques, 4:1563–1567
- seizures from, 5:1605
- travel-related, 5:1607, 1608
- vitamin C for, 5:1852

Stress Disorder Treatment Centers, 5:1828

Stress incontinence, 5:1804

Stress management, 5:1716
- lifestyle, 2:661
- migraines, 4:1267
- shingles, 5:1631
- t'ai chi, 5:1748
- yoga, 5:1891
- *See also* Relaxation techniques

Stress-related disorders, 2:454, 5:1714–1717

Stress test, 5:**1717–1719,** *1718*
- angina pectoris, 1:124
- arrhythmias, 1:226
- atherosclerosis, 1:247
- cardiac ablation, 2:425
- cardiac rehabilitation, 2:436
- cardiac surgery, 2:439
- congestive heart failure, 2:563
- coronary artery bypass graft, 2:428
- coronary artery disease, 2:579
- echocardiography, 1:124, 2:724
- electrocardiography, 2:731
- ischemia, 3:1074–1075
- maximal heart rate, 5:1759
- nuclear, 4:1327–1329, 5:1718
- preoperative cardiac assessment, 4:1481
- pulmonary rehabilitation, 4:1543

Stretching
- bursitis, 1:390
- fibromyalgia, 3:801
- gait and balance disorders, 3:830
- joint mobilization, 3:1087, 1088
- shiatsu, 5:1627–1629
- soft tissue, 2:702
- warm-up, 5:1616
- wheelchair patients, 2:768
- yoga, 5:1892

Stretta procedure, 3:856

Striated muscles, 4:1307

Strictures
- bile duct, 3:838
- esophageal, 3:858, 859–860

Strohl, Kingman, 5:1670

Stroke, 5:**1719–1724,** *1720t*
- angiography-induced, 1:130
- antiplatelet drugs for, 2:457, 5:1722

Stroke *(continued)*
- aphasia from, 5:1687, 1689
- aspiration, 1:232
- aspirin for, 1:235
- bipolar disorder-related, 1:306
- calcium supplements, 2:404
- cardiac catheterization-induced, 2:432
- carotid artery disease-related, 2:456, 457, 458
- coma from, 2:545
- dementia from, 2:613
- demographics, 2:456, 5:1720–1721
- diagnosis, 5:1722
- diet, 4:1339
- dysarthria from, 5:1688
- dysphasia from, 2:718
- gait and balance disorders from, 3:832, 833
- ginkgo biloba for, 3:878
- headaches from, 3:906
- hemorrhagic, 3:878, 5:1720, 1723
- hormone replacement therapy-related, 3:992
- hypertension-related, 3:1010, 5:1721, 1723
- ischemic, 1:234, 235, 3:1073, 5:1720, 1722, 1723
- low-fat diet, 3:1159
- low-sodium diet, 3:1161
- magnetic resonance imaging, 4:1192
- mental retardation from, 4:1256
- mortality, 3:925–926, 5:1720, 1723, 1785
- muscle relaxants for, 4:1307
- neuromuscular physical therapy, 4:1325
- oropharyngeal dysphagia from, 5:1740
- over fifty lifestyle, 2:662
- paralysis from, 4:1417, 1418
- peripheral vision loss from, 4:1438
- postmenopausal women, 3:992
- prevention, 2:457, 458, 5:1690, 1722–1724
- psychoses from, 4:1528
- rehabilitation, 5:1720, 1723
- risk factors, 5:1721, 1785
- sleep apnea-related, 5:1658
- speech therapy, 5:1689
- staphylococcal infection-related, 5:1700
- symptoms, 5:1721–1722
- thrombolytic therapy for, 5:1767
- tissue plasminogen activator for, 2:457, 5:1722, 1767
- transient blindness, 5:1782
- transient blindness from, 5:1781
- transient ischemic attacks, 5:1784–1785
- treatment, 5:1722–1723
- vitamin C for, 5:1852
- warfarin for, 2:457, 5:1722
- *See also* Transient ischemic attacks

Stroke Belt, 5:1721

Stroke Scale, 5:1688

Stroma layer, 2:573

Stromectol. *See* Ivermectin

Struvite, 1:312, 3:1101, 1102, 1103

Study of Efficacy of Nosocomial Infection Control (SENIC), 3:1030

Stuttering priapism, 4:1492

Styes, 2:778–780

Subacromial bursitis, 1:388, 389

Subarachnoid hemorrhage, 3:906

Subcapsular cataracts, 2:461

Subchondral cysts, 4:1366

Subcutaneous administration of medication, 1:25

Subdeltoid bursitis, 1:388, 389

Subdural hematomas, 3:906

Subjective tinnitus, 5:1780

Subluxations, 2:**686–689**

Submucosal leiomyoma, 5:1706

Subperiosteal implants, 2:619

Subpial transection, multiple, 5:1604

Substance abuse and dependence, 5:**1724–1729,** *1725*
- anxiety, 1:214
- counseling, 5:1728, 1729–1732
- demographics, 5:1729–1730
- depression, 2:625
- family relationships, 3:795
- generalized anxiety disorder, 3:863
- mobility, 4:1284
- stroke risk, 5:1721
- suicide, 5:1733
- *See also* Alcohol abuse; Drug abuse

Substance Abuse and Mental Health Services Administration, 2:707

Substance abuse counseling, 5:1728, **1729–1732**

Substantia nigra, 4:1421–1422

Subtotal hysterectomy, 3:1015–1018, *1016*

Succinimides, 1:159*t,* 160

Suconazole, 1:184

Sucralfate, 3:856, 5:1799

Suction thrombectomy, 4:1534

Suctioning, 4:1568

Sudden death
- heart attack, 3:923
- hypertrophic cardiomyopathy, 3:1014, 1015
- myocarditis, 4:1310
- therapeutic exercise, 5:1760

Sudomotor axon reflex test, 1:264

Sufentanil, 1:113

Suffering, 4:1393, 1525

Sufism, 4:1561

Suflamethoxazole, 2:595

Sugar
- alpha hydroxy acids, 1:83
- cancer patients, 5:1682
- Cushing's syndrome, 2:592
- cystitis, 2:595
- diet, 2:422
- dietary, 1:196
- fungal infections, 3:826
- psoriasis, 4:1521

Sugar diabetes. *See* Diabetes mellitus

Sugar tests. *See* Blood sugar tests

Suicidal behavior, 5:1732
- alcohol abuse-related, 1:66
- amantidine-induced, 1:201
- anxiety-related, 1:217
- cycloserine-induced, 1:209
- demographics, 5:1733
- depression, 2:628–629
- generalized anxiety disorder-related, 3:864
- multiple sclerosis-related, 4:1306
- overdose, 4:1382, 5:1726
- patient confidentiality, 4:1426
- personality disorders, 4:1448
- SSRI-associated, 1:169–170, 3:864
- warning signs, 5:1735

Suicide, 5:**1732–1736,** 1733*t*
- attempted, 5:1732–1734
- contagion, 5:1734
- depression-related, 2:622, 664
- physician-assisted, 2:599, 762, 763, 3:977, 4:1235, 5:1734–1735
- seizure-related, 5:1605

Suicide magnets, 5:1734

Sulfa drugs. *See* Sulfonamides

Sulfadiazine, 3:1056

Sulfasalazine, 3:813, 4:1536, 1574

Sulfinpyrazone, 3:892, 894

Sulfisoxazole, 2:595

Sulfites, 1:379

Sulfonamides, 1:149*t*
- anticonvulsant drug interactions, 1:162
- contact dermatitis from, 2:572
- insulin interactions, 3:1056
- for wound care, 5:1886

Sulfonylurea, 1:177*t,* 178, 179, 180, 2:640, 3:900

Sulforaphane, 2:415

Sulfur, 3:846, 847, 849

Sumatriptan, 1:173, 3:907

Summary Health Statistics for U.S. Adults, 2:616

Summers, Elaine, 4:1292

Summing up, 4:1526

Sun exposure
- alpha hydroxy acids, 1:84
- melanoma from, 4:1200
- photocontact dermatitis from, 2:572
- for psoriasis, 4:1520
- skin cancer from, 5:1642, 1644

Sun exposure *(continued)*
vitamin D, 5:1644, 1853, 1855, 1863
wrinkles from, 5:1888
See also Photosensitivity
Sunburns, 5:1642, 1644
Sunglasses, 2:464, 712, 773, 781
Sunitinib malate, 3:1093
Sunlight sensitivity. *See* Photosensitivity
Sunscreen, 4:1200, 1579, 5:1651, 1890
Super-fatted soap, 2:716
Superficial spreading melanoma, 4:1197–1198
Superoxide-dismutase (SOD), 1:103, 5:1598
Supplemental health insurance, 4:1494*t*, 1495
Supplements. *See* Dietary supplements
Support garments, 3:1132
Support groups
adjustment disorders, 1:24
alcohol abuse, 1:68
Alzheimer's disease, 1:89
anxiety, 1:216–217
bipolar disorder, 1:306
celiac disease, 2:475
generalized anxiety disorder, 3:864
smoking cessation, 5:1661, 1668
speech disorders, 5:1689
spinal cord injuries, 5:1695
substance abuse, 5:1728, 1731
Support stockings. *See* Compression stockings/bandages
Supportive cancer therapy, 2:**418–421**
Supportive care. *See* Palliative care
Supportive therapies. *See* Complementary therapies
Suppositories, 1:25, 3:849, 5:1635
Supracondylar suspension, 3:1166
Suprane. *See* Desfluorane
Supraventricular tachycardia, 1:226–227
Suprax. *See* Cefixime
Supreme Court, 2:762, 4:1235
Surgeons
advertising, 3:808
finding, 3:804–809
plastic, 1:6–7, 3:808
Surgery, 5:**1736–1739**
alternatives, 3:806
ambulatory, 4:1557
anesthesiologist's role, 1:118–120
aneurysm, 1:121
angina pectoris, 1:124–125
aortic dissection, 1:219
arteriovenous malformations, 1:230–231
back curves, 1:274
bariatric, 1:284–286, 3:958, 4:1351, 5:1855, 1878
bladder cancer, 1:309
blood clots, 1:322
brain and central nervous system tumors, 1:350
breast-conserving, 1:357–358, 359
cataracts, 2:461–462, *462,* 463–464, 5:1838, 1839, 1843
cervical cancer, 2:484
cervical spondylosis, 2:488, 489
cirrhosis, 2:523–524
colon cancer, 2:535–536
congestive heart failure, 2:564
cytoreductive, 2:410
debulking, 4:1376
delirium after, 2:607
diet, 5:1683
dislocations, 2:688
diverticulitis, 2:694
dorsal root zone, 4:1319
elective, 3:806, 807
endocrine pancreatic cancer, 4:1402
endometrial cancer, 2:745
entropion and ectropion, 2:780
esophageal cancer, 2:760
exocrine pancreatic cancer, 4:1406
eye, 2:462
gallbladder cancer, 3:835–836
gallstones, 3:839–840
gastroesophageal reflux disease, 3:856
general anesthesia, 1:111–115
gynecologic, 1:3–4
hemorrhoids, 3:947
hyperparathyroidism, 3:1007
informed consent, 4:1483
kidney stones, 3:1102
liver cancer, 3:1140
local anesthesia, 1:115
lung volume reduction, 2:742
magnetic resonance imaging, 4:1189
maze, 1:227
metastatic cancer, 4:1263–1264
minimally invasive, 2:428, 439, 442, 748, 3:964
oral cancers, 4:1358
orthopedic, 3:805, 968
osteoarthritis, 4:1367
outpatient, 3:806
ovarian cancer, 4:1376
pacemakers, 4:1388
palliative, 2:410
Parkinson's disease, 4:1424
plastic, 2:584
preferred provider organizations, 4:1475
prophylactic, 2:410
prostate cancer, 4:1507–1508
prostate enlargement, 4:1512
regional anesthesia, 1:115
robot-guided, 2:428
sciatica, 5:1594
seizures, 5:1603–1604
skin cancer, 5:1643
snoring, 5:*1669,* 1669–1677
stomach cancer, 5:1706–1707
thoracic, 3:806, 5:1761–1763
tissue-flap, 4:1223, 1224
tuberculosis, 5:1795
ulcers, 5:1799
volume reduction, 4:1541–1542
See also Cardiac surgery; Cosmetic surgery; Postoperative care; Reconstructive surgery
Surgical ablation, 2:424–426
Surgical biopsy
breast, 1:352, 353, 356
cancer diagnosis, 2:410
lung, 3:1172–1173
skin, 5:1645, 1646
Surgical menopause, 3:991
Surgical oncology, 2:415, 5:**1736–1739**
Surgical specialties, 3:805–806
Surgical wound infections, 5:1699
Surimi, 3:817
Surrogates. *See* Durable power of attorney
Survivors, 4:1469, 5:1748
SUS (Socially unacceptable snoring), 5:1670
Susceptibility tests, tuberculosis, 5:1794
Suspension devices, 3:1166
Suture joints, 3:1085
Svetkey, Laura, 5:1876–1877
Swallowing, 1:231, 5:1739
Swallowing disorders, 5:**1739–1743**
aspiration, 1:233
cancer treatment-related, 5:1684–1685
esophageal cancer-related, 2:759, 761
pressure sore-related, 4:1491
radiation therapy-related, 3:1176
snoring surgery, 5:1674
thyroidectomy-related, 5:1772
See also Dysphagia
Sweat test, 1:264
Sweating
antiarrhythmic drug-induced, 1:147
autonomic disorders, 1:264
dehydration, 2:603, 5:1871
dermatitis, 2:632
electrolyte tests, 2:739
heatstroke, 3:937
water loss, 5:1870
Swedish massage, 4:1217
Sweet fennel, 5:1605
Sweet potatoes, 2:417
Sweet sumac, 4:1379
Sweeteners, artificial, 3:1070
Sweigart, Lulu, 4:1291
Swimming, 1:37
Swimming goggles, 2:712
Swine influenza vaccine, 3:1043
Switzerland, 5:1734
Symlin. *See* Pramlintide acetate

Symmetrel. *See* Amantadine
Sympathetic nervous system, 1:262
Synagogues, 2:558, 3:1079, 4:1477–1478
Synarthrotic joints, 3:1085, 1086
Synchronized intermittent mandatory ventilation (SIMV), 5:1819, 1822
Syncope. *See* Fainting
Syndesmotic joints, 3:1085
Synovial fluid, 3:1085, 1087
Synovial joints, 3:1085, 1086
Synthroid. *See* Levothyroxine
Synvisc. *See* Hylan G-F20
Syphilis, 1:219, 5:1621–1624, 1740
Syringomyelia, 5:1590
Systematic thinking, 4:1526
Systemic lupus erythematosus (SLE), 3:1177–1182
  autoimmune disease tests, 1:250, 252–254
  chronic kidney failure from, 2:508
  DHEA for, 2:633, 634
  myocarditis, 4:1309
  osteoporosis risk, 3:1179
  pleurisy, 1:234, 235
  pulmonary fibrosis from, 4:1536
Systemic scleroderma, 5:1596, 1597
Systolic blood pressure, 1:189, 324, 3:1008–1009, 5:1846
Systolic heart failure, 2:562

T

T-cell delayed hypersensitivity reactions, 1:76
T cells (Lymphocytes)
  AIDS tests, 1:60, 61
  autoimmune disorders, 1:260
  CD4, 1:48, 50
  helper, 1:71
  lymphoma, 4:1194, 1196
  role, 1:256–257, 3:1022, 4:1194
t-PA (Tissue plasminogen activator), 2:457, 5:1722, 1767, 1785
T-piece trials, 5:1819
T score, 1:337, 4:1371
T waves, 2:435, 730
T3 (Triiodothyronine), 3:1013, 5:1773, 1774, 1777
T4 (Thyroxine), 3:1013, 5:1773, 1774, 1777
Tachycardia
  atrial, 2:424, 5:1825
  AV node reentry, 2:424
  supraventricular, 1:226–227
  ventricular, 1:225, 2:452, 3:788, 1025, 5:1825–1826
Tacrine, 1:88, 163–165, 4:1244, 5:1616
Tacrolimus, 3:1107
Tadalafil
  for erectile dysfunction, 1:264, 2:647, 756–757, 5:1635
  nitrate interactions, 3:930
  for prostate enlargement, 4:1512
  transient blindness from, 5:1782
Tagamet. *See* Cimetidine
T'ai chi, 4:1292, 5:*1745*, **1745–1750**
  demographics, 4:1565, 5:1746–1747
  flexibility training, 5:1758
  hip joint pain, 3:969
  history, 4:1563, 5:1745–1746
  menopause, 3:994
  shingles, 5:1632
  spirituality, 4:1476
  stress, 5:1716
Talcum powder, 4:1377
Talk therapy, 1:306
Talking with your doctors, 5:**1749–1750**
Talwin. *See* Pentazocine
Tamai, Tenpaku, 1:13
Tamoxifen
  for amyotrophic lateral sclerosis, 1:104
  for breast cancer, 1:358, 360, 2:490
  endometrial cancer from, 2:744
  side effects, 1:156
Tamsulosin, 4:1511
Tangelos, 5:1849*t*
Tango, Argentine, 4:1293
Tanning beds, 4:1200, 5:1642, 1644
Tantra yoga, 5:1892
Tapas acupressure technique (TAT), 1:14
Tar, 2:631, 5:1642, 1660
Tarasoff decision, 4:1426
Taraxacum officinale. *See* Dandelion
Tardive dyskinesia, 1:204, 4:1530
Target (company), 2:549
Target heart rate, 5:1759
Targeted therapies, 2:411, 536
Tartar, 4:1360
Tasmar. *See* Tolcapone
Taste alterations, 2:659, 3:869
TAT (Tapas acupressure technique), 1:14
Tattersall, Martin, 3:1044–1045
Tax credits, 1:93
Taxol. *See* Paclitaxel
Taylor, Andrew, 4:1369
Taylor, Charles, 4:1215
Taylor, George, 4:1215
Tazarotene, 4:1520
Tazicef. *See* Ceftazidime
Tazideme. *See* Ceftazidime
Tazorac. *See* Tazarotene
TB. *See* Tuberculosis
Tc 99m DTPA, 3:1100
TCM. *See* Traditional Chinese medicine
Tea, 2:395, 417, 3:1065
Tea tree oil, 1:334, 2:553, 3:1126
Teaching, 4:1526
  See also Patient education
Teaching Immunization for Medical Education (TIME), 5:1756
Tear-deficient dry eye, 2:711
Tear film supplements, 2:780
Tears
  artificial, 5:1639
  dry eye, 2:710–714
  immune system role, 3:1022
  Sjögren's syndrome, 5:1637–1638, 1639
Tebrazid. *See* Pyrazinamide
Technetium DTPA, 3:1100
Technetium MAG3, 3:1100
Technology, assistive. *See* Assistive devices
Technology, interactive, 5:1878
TED (thromboembolic deterrent) stockings, 3:967, 968
TEE (Transesophageal echocardiography), 2:439, 724, 4:1295
Teeth. *See entries beginning with Tooth*
Teeth whitening, 5:**1750–1753**
Tegaserod, 3:1123
Tegison. *See* Etrentinate
Tegretol. *See* Carbamazepine
Teicoplanin, 4:1296
Telangiectasias, 5:1597, 1598, 1649
Telegraphic speech, 5:1688
Telemedicine, 2:594
Telephone Interview for Cognitive Status (TICS), 2:608
Telescopic devices, 3:1164, 5:1843
Television, closed-circuit, 3:1164, 5:1843
Telithromycin, 1:152, 153
Telmisartan, 1:191, 2:563
Telomeres, 1:43–44
Temazepam, 1:140, 5:1657
Temperament, 4:1445
Temperature, body. *See* Body temperature
Temperature, pool, 5:1875
Temperature sensors, 1:301
Temporal arteritis. *See* Giant cell arteritis
Temporal headache, 3:906
Temporal lobe resection, 5:1604
Temporal mandibular joint syndrome, 3:906

Temporalis muscle, 4:1321
Temsirolimus, 3:1093
TEN (Toxic epidermal necrolysis), 2:585
Tendinitis, 5:*1753*, **1753–1755**
 knee, 3:1116
 nonsteroidal anti-inflammatory drugs for, 4:1326
Tendon injuries
 knee, 3:1116–1118
 ruptures, 1:153, 3:1116, 1117–1118
Tendons, 3:1115, 5:1787
Tennis elbow, 5:1753
Tenormin. *See* Atenolol
TENS (Transcutaneous electrical nerve stimulation), 1:270, 274, 3:1082, 4:1319, 1368, 1398
Tension, 4:1218–1219, 1565
 See also Stress
Tension headaches, 3:905, 906–908
Terazosin, 1:81–83, 4:1511, 5:1589
Terbinafine, 3:826
Terbinafine hydrochloride, 1:184, 4:1312
Terbutaline, 1:379
Terfenadine, 1:173, 187
Teriparatide, 4:1372, 5:1614
Terminal care. *See* End-of-life care; Palliative care
Terminal cleaning, 4:1296
Terminal illness
 advance directives, 1:30
 death and dying, 2:597–599
 hospices, 3:995–997
 pain management, 2:598, 762, 764
Terrorist attacks, 4:1536, 5:1715
Testicles, removal, 4:1508
Testicular cancer, 2:409, 4:1262, 5:1754–1755
Testicular self-examination, 5:**1754–1755**
Testosterone
 DHEA interactions, 2:634
 estrogen/testosterone combination therapy, 3:991
 glycyrrhizin, 2:416
 menopause, 4:1250, 1252
 prostate cancer, 4:1508
 saw palmetto interactions, 4:1512, 5:1587, 1588
Tetanus, 5:**1755–1757**
 autonomic disorders, 1:263
 muscle relaxants for, 4:1307, 1308
 vaccines, 3:1036, 5:1815
Tetanus immune globulin (TIG), 5:1757
Tetracaine, 1:116
Tetracyclines, 1:150*t,* 151
 adverse effects, 1:153
 angiotensin-converting enzyme inhibitor interactions, 1:134
 calcium absorption, 2:400
 calcium supplement interactions, 2:405
 contact dermatitis from, 2:572
 dairy product interactions, 2:710
 diabetes insipidus from, 2:637
 folic acid interactions, 3:813
 for helicobacteriosis, 3:940, 5:1800
 insulin interactions, 3:1055
 iron interactions, 5:1865
 liver function test interactions, 3:1143
 nonsteroidal anti-inflammatory drug interactions, 4:1327
 tooth stains from, 5:1750
 for urinary tract infections, 5:1808
 zinc interactions, 5:1897
Tetrahydrocannabinol (THC), 4:1211, 1213
TH1 cells, 1:71
TH2 cells, 1:71
Thalassemia, 2:561
Thalidomide, 1:104, 290, 4:1301
Thallium, 2:579, 5:1718
THC (Tetrahydrocannabinol), 4:1211, 1213
Theo-Dur. *See* Theophylline
Theobromine, 2:396
Theophylline
 anticonvulsant drug interactions, 1:162
 beta blocker interactions, 1:299
 caffeine interactions, 2:396
 cimetidine interactions, 3:900
 gastroesophageal reflux disease from, 3:854
 ranitidine interactions, 3:900
 SSRI interactions, 1:173
Therapeutic exercise, 4:1285, 1395, 1422–1423, 5:**1757–1761,** *1758*
 See also Exercise
Therapeutic Lifestyle Changes (TLC) Diet, 3:956
Therapeutic touch, 4:1368, 1377
TheraSense, 1:328
Thermal coagulation, 3:873
Thermometers, 5:1844–1845
Thermoregulation, 5:1845
Thiamine, 2:547, 5:1603, 1861–1862, 1864
Thiamine deficiency, 5:1861–1862
Thiazide diuretics, 2:690–693, 690*t*
 adverse effects, 1:191, 2:692
 antinuclear antibody test interactions, 1:253
 calcium absorption, 2:400
 celecoxib interactions, 2:587
 contact dermatitis from, 2:572
 hyperlipoproteinemia from, 3:1004
 for hypertension, 1:189
 hypokalemia from, 2:737
 insulin interactions, 3:1056
 vitamin D interactions, 5:1855
Thiazide-like diuretics, 2:690
Thiazolidinediones, 1:177*t,* 179–180
Thinking, 2:612, 4:1321, 1526, 5:1613
Thinking tests, 3:866
Thiopental, 1:113
Thioridazine
 adverse effects, 1:203, 205, 4:1530
 for bipolar disorder, 1:305
 hormone replacement therapy interactions, 3:993
 for psychoses, 4:1530
 SSRI interactions, 1:173
 tricyclic antidepressant interactions, 1:177
Thiothixene, 1:203, 4:1530
Third parties, 4:1426
Thirst
 decreased sense of, 2:665
 dehydration, 2:603, 665, 5:1871
 diabetes insipidus-related, 2:636
 electrolyte balance, 2:734
 fluid intake needs, 2:658–659
 heatstroke, 3:939
 withdrawal of life support, 5:1882
Thomasson, Randy, 3:977
Thoracentesis, 4:1461
Thoracic nerve roots, 5:1691–1692
Thoracic stenosis, 5:1697
Thoracic surgery, 3:806, 5:**1761–1763**
Thoracostomy, 3:1172, 4:1461
Thoracotomy, 4:1275, 5:1761–1762
Thorazine. *See* Chlorpromazine
Thoresen, Carl, 4:1552
Thorium dioxide, 3:1139
Thought processes. *See* Thinking
Thought stopping, 5:1667
THR (Total hip replacement). *See* Hip replacement
Throat cancer, 5:1740
Thrombectomy, suction, 4:1534
Thrombocythemia. *See* Thrombocytopenia
Thrombocytopenia, 5:**1763–1765**
 bone marrow biopsy, 1:340
 chemotherapy-related, 1:155, 5:1763, 1764
Thrombocytosis, 5:**1765–1766**
Thromboembolic deterrent (TED) stockings, 3:967, 968
Thromboembolism, venous. *See* Deep vein thrombosis
Thrombolytic agents. *See* Thrombolytic therapy

Thrombolytic therapy, 5:**1766–1768**
for heart attacks, 3:923, 928, 5:1767
for pulmonary embolism, 4:1534
for stroke, 2:457, 5:1722, 1767
Thrombophlebitis, 2:601, 4:1532, 5:1760
Thrombopoietin, 5:1765
Thrombosed hemorrhoids, 3:947
Thrombosis
angiography, 1:129
coronary, 2:578
stroke from, 5:1720
treatment, 1:322
venous, 1:321
See also Deep vein thrombosis (DVT)
Thrush, 3:826
Thumb joint, 3:1086
Thyroid antibody tests, 5:1774
Thyroid biopsy, 5:1770, 1777, 1778
Thyroid cancer, 5:**1768–1773,** *1769*
chest x rays, 2:499
diagnosis, 2:409, 5:1769–1770
thyroid nuclear medicine scans, 5:1776
thyroid ultrasound, 5:1777, 1778
Thyroid cysts, 5:1778
Thyroid disorders, 2:726, 4:1539, 5:1769
Thyroid drugs, 3:937
Thyroid function tests, 5:1741, 1769, **1773–1775**
Thyroid gland, 5:1768, 1773
Thyroid nuclear medicine scans, 3:1013, 5:1609, 1770, 1773–1774, **1775–1777,** *1776,* 1778
Thyroid-stimulating hormone (TSH)
Grave's disease, 1:259
hyperthyroidism, 3:1013
thyroid cancer, 5:1769, 1771
thyroid function tests, 5:1773, 1774
Thyroid storm, 3:1013
Thyroid ultrasound, 5:**1777–1778**
Thyroidectomy, 3:1014, 5:1770, 1772
Thyrotoxicosis, 3:1013
Thyroxine (T_4), 3:1013, 5:1773, 1774, 1777
TIAs. *See* Transient ischemic attacks
TIBC (Total iron-binding capacity), 1:109, 3:1067, 1068
Tic douloureux, 4:1318
Ticarcillin, 1:150
Ticks, 3:1182–1186
Ticlid. *See* Ticlopidine
Ticlopidine, 3:927, 5:1722
TICS (Telephone Interview for Cognitive Status), 2:608
Tidal volume, 5:1822–1823
TIG (Tetanus immune globulin), 5:1757
Tigecycline, 4:1296
Tillett, W. S., 1:193
Tilt wheelchairs, 5:1880
Tiludronate disodium, 2:405, 4:1392
TIME (Teaching Immunization for Medical Education), 5:1756
Time-cycled ventilators, 5:1821
Timeliness, 3:910
Timolol, 1:190–191, 297–299
Timoptic. *See* Timolol
Tinea barbae, 1:184
Tinea captis, 1:184, 3:825, 826
Tinea corporis, 1:184
Tinea cruris, 1:184, 3:825, 826
Tinea pedis, 1:184, 3:825, 826
Tinea unguium, 3:825, 826
Tinea versicolor, 1:184
Ting, Paul H., 3:1044
Tinnetti Balance Test, 3:830
Tinnitus, 1:234, 236, 5:**1779–1781**
Tissue biopsy, 1:101, 5:1886
Tissue-flap surgery, 4:1223, 1224
Tissue heart valves, 1:223–224, 2:443, 4:1280
Tissue plasminogen activator (t-PA), 2:457, 5:1722, 1767, 1785
Tissue translutaminase antibodies, 2:473
Titanium, 3:1112
TLC (Therapeutic Lifestyle Changes) Diet, 3:956
TMP/SMZ. *See* Trimethoprim/Sulfamethoxazole
TNF-238A gene, 3:974
TNX-901, 3:817
Tobacco, chewing, 4:1357, 1359, 5:1659, 1660
Tobacco smoking. *See* Smoking
Tobramycin, 1:95–97
Tocopherol, 1:197, 5:1856, 1857
Tocotrienol, 5:1856
Toe osteoarthritis, 4:1366
Toe-touch weight-bearing (TTWB), 3:961
Toenails
care, 3:821
fungal infections, 4:*1311,* 1311–1314
Tofranil. *See* Imipramine
Tofu, 2:417, 5:1614
Toileting, 4:1441
Tolazamide, 1:178
Tolbutamide, 1:178
bismuth subsalicylate interactions, 1:183
Tolcapone, 1:199, 200–201, 4:1423
Tolerable Upper Intake Level, 2:398
Tolerance
caffeine, 2:396
drug, 1:26, 5:1725
gambling, 3:841
Tolnaftate, 1:185
Tolterodine, 1:264, 4:1379, 5:1805
Toluene, 5:1597
Tomatoes, 2:414, 417, 3:856
Tomography
Heidelberg retinal, 3:881
optical coherence, 1:41, 2:649, 3:881
See also CT scans; Positron emission tomography; Single photon emission computed tomography
Tongue examination, 4:1322
Tongue suspension procedure, 5:1672
Tonic-clonic seizures, 5:1601–1606
Tonometry, 2:463, 3:881, 5:1838
Tonsillectomy, 5:1673
Tonsils, 3:1022, 5:1673
Tooth brushing, 2:614–615, 621, 3:877, 4:1360, 1361
Tooth decay, 2:616, 4:1318
Tooth disease, 1:114
Tooth loss, 2:614, 617
dental implants, 2:618–620
dentures, 2:620–622
oral hygiene, 4:1362
Tooth prosthesis, 2:618–620, 4:1361
Tooth stains, 5:1750–1752
Tooth whitening, 5:**1750–1753**
Toothpaste, whitening, 5:1752
Toothpicks, 4:1361
Topamax. *See* Topiramate
Tophi, 3:891, 892
Topical medication, 1:25–26
allergies, 1:73
anesthetics, 1:116, 117
antibiotics, 1:278, 4:1579, 5:1651
antifungal, 1:183–186, 184*t,* 4:1312
chemotherapy, 2:491
contact dermatitis from, 2:572
for diabetic neuropathy, 2:647
minoxidil, 4:1277–1279
for postherpetic neuralgia, 4:1319
for pressure sores, 4:1490
for psoriasis, 4:1519–1520
for rosacea, 4:1578
for scabies, 5:1590–1591
for skin lesions, 5:1650–1651
for wound care, 5:1886
Topiramate, 1:160, 304
Topography, corneal, 2:575
Toradol. *See* Ketorolac
Tornstam, LArs, 4:1527
Torsemide, 2:563, 690
Totacillin. *See* Ampicillin
Total bilirubin, 3:1144
Total blindness, 5:1841

Total gastrectomy, 5:1706
Total hepatectomy, 3:1141
Total hip replacement (THR). *See* Hip replacement
Total hysterectomy, 3:*1016,* 1016–1017
  cervical cancer, 2:483, 484
  Pap tests after, 4:1413
Total iron-binding capacity (TIBC), 1:109, 3:1067, 1068
Total knee replacement, 3:1089, *1111,* 1112–1113
Total lung capacity, 2:741
Total mastectomy, 1:358, 4:1222
Total pancreatectomy, 4:1406
Total parenteral nutrition (TPN), 4:1342
Total protein, 3:1144
Total serum cholesterol, 2:505–507
Total thyroidectomy, 5:1770
Touch
  healthy aging, 4:1525
  massage, 4:1217
  osteoarthritis, 4:1368
  therapeutic, 4:1368, 1377
Tourette disorders, 1:203
Toxic epidermal necrolysis (TEN), 2:585
Toxic psychoses. *See* Dementia
Toxicity, oxygen, 3:844
Toxins
  food-borne, 1:86
  paralysis from, 4:1418
  Parkinson's disease from, 4:1422
Toxoplasmosis, 3:1163, 4:1256, 5:1842
TPN (Total parenteral nutrition), 4:1342
Trabecular bone, 1:336
Trace minerals, 3:846
Traceleer. *See* Bosentan
Tracheostomy, 3:1048, 1049, 5:1819
Trachoma, 5:1842
Traconazole, 4:1312
Traction, 1:269–270, 2:488
Traditional Chinese medicine (TCM)
  acupressure, 1:12
  acupuncture, 1:17, 19
  breath therapy, 4:1272
  cancer treatment side effects, 2:412
  cirrhosis, 2:524
  cystitis, 2:595
  ginkgo biloba, 3:878
  irritable bowel syndrome, 3:1071
  low back pain, 3:1152
  marijuana, 4:1211, 1212
  massage, 4:1215
  osteoarthritis, 4:1368
  overactive bladder, 4:1379
  PC-SPES, 4:1265
  polymyositis, 4:1468
  prostate cancer, 4:1509
  qigong, 4:1546
  sexual dysfunction, 5:1620
  t'ai chi, 5:1746, 1747
  tui na massage, 1:13
Traffic accidents
  alcohol abuse, 1:66
  dislocations and subluxations, 2:687
  driver safety, 2:703–705, 703*t,* 3:867
  head injuries, 3:904
  PTSD, 4:1469
  spinal cord injuries, 5:1691
Trager integration bodywork, 4:1291, 1324
Train travel, 5:1871
Training. *See* Education and training
Trait anxiety, 1:213, 217
TRAM (Transverse rectus abdominis myocutaneous), 1:5
Tramadol, 1:173, 2:647
Trandolapril, 1:132, 134, 191, 2:586
Tranquilizers
  antihistamine interactions, 2:709
  antinuclear antibody test interactions, 1:253
  barbiturate interactions, 1:282, 284
  benzodiazepine interactions, 1:292, 294
  dronabinol interactions, 2:420
  erectile dysfunction from, 2:756, 5:1634
  estrogen/tranquilizer combination therapy, 3:991
  for extubation, 5:1882
  for heart attacks, 3:923
  for itching, 3:1082
  major, 1:177
  overdose, 4:1381
  snoring from, 5:1673, 1675
  SSRI interactions, 1:173
  for stress-related disorders, 5:1716
Trans fats, 3:1157
  heart disease, 3:929
  high cholesterol, 3:953–954
  low-cholesterol diet, 3:1154
  low-fat diet, 3:1157
  pro-inflammatory foods, 1:196
  recommendations, 4:1339
Transcendental meditation, 4:1271, 1563–1564
Transconjunctival blepharoplasty, 1:317
Transcortical dysphasia, 2:717
Transcutaneous electric nerve stimulation (TENS)
  back and neck pain, 1:270
  back curves, 1:274
  itching, 3:1082
  osteoarthritis, 4:1368
  pain, 4:1398
  postherpetic neuralgia, 4:1319
Transderm-Nitro. *See* Nitroglycerin
Transducers, 2:459, 460
Transesophageal echocardiography (TEE), 2:439, 724, 4:1295
Transfemoral sockets, 3:1166
Transferrin, 3:944–945, 1065
Transient blindness, 5:**1781–1784**
Transient ischemic attacks (TIAs), 5:1720, **1784–1787**
  aspirin for, 1:234, 235
  carotid artery disease-related, 2:456
  demographics, 5:1784–1785
  dysphasia from, 2:718
  ischemia-related, 3:1073
  risk factors, 3:1074, 5:1785, 1786
  symptoms, 3:1074, 5:1785
  transient blindness from, 5:1782
  treatment, 3:1076, 5:1722, 1785–1786
  vascular depression from, 2:622
Transient microorganisms, 3:1030
Transitional cell carcinoma, 1:307, 3:1092
Transmission. *See* Disease transmission
Transperineal prostate biopsy, 4:1502
Transplantation
  bone marrow, 1:102, 339, 2:411
  cartilage, 4:1367
  cord blood, 2:411
  corneal, 2:575–576
  hair, 1:80
  heart, 2:438, 447, 564, 4:1310, 5:1668
  intestinal, 4:1363
  liver, 2:524, 3:951, 1133, 1141, 4:1363
  lung, 2:513, 4:1363, 1541–1542
  nigral cell, 4:1424
  organ donors, 2:764, 4:1362–1365
  pancreas, 4:1363
  retinal, 5:1838
  stem cell, 1:102, 2:411, 4:1196, 1301
  See also Kidney transplantation
Transportation services, 2:558
Transrectal ultrasound (TRUS), 4:1502, 1506
Transsexuals, male-to-female, 1:362
Transtelephonic monitoring, 1:226
Transtheoretical model, 2:671
Transthoracic echocardiography (TTE), 2:724
Transthyretin, 3:1143, 1144, 1145
Transtibial sockets, 3:1166
Transurethral incision of the prostate (TUIP), 4:1512
Transurethral microwave thermotherapy (TUMT), 4:1512
Transurethral prostate biopsy, 4:1502
Transurethral resection (TUR), 1:309
Transurethral resection of the prostate (TURP), 4:1506, 1507, 1512
Transvaginal ultrasonography, 2:744–745
Transverse colostomy, 2:542

Transverse rectus abdominis myocutaneous (TRAM), 1:5

Tranxene. *See* Clorazepate

Tranylcypromine

anticonvulsant drug interactions, 1:162
beta blocker interactions, 1:299
bronchodilator interactions, 1:380
buspirone interactions, 1:145

Trastuzumab, 1:358

Trauma

aneurysm, 1:121
bursitis, 1:388
chest, 1:219
gangrene, 3:843, 846
hip replacement, 3:964
home safety, 3:985
leg amputation, 3:1165
neurologic examination, 4:1320–1323
osteoarthritis, 4:1366
paralysis, 4:1417
psychological, 5:1782
PTSD, 4:1469–1471

Travel, 5:*1607,* **1607–1611**

cruise ships, 5:1608*t*
deep vein thrombosis, 2:601, 5:1609
dehydration, 5:1871
infectious diseases, 3:1033, 1036
influenza vaccines, 3:1042
international, 5:1609–1611
vaccines, 3:1036, 5:1609, 1756

Traveler's diarrhea, 2:*653,* 655, 4:1497

Tray treatment kits, 5:1752

Trazodone, 1:173, 176

Treadmill test. *See* Stress test

Treatment

denial of, 1:30–31
futility, 5:1883
refusal, 4:1430

Trecator-SC. *See* Ethionamide

Tree nuts. *See* Nuts

Tregretol. *See* Clonazepam

Tremors, 4:1422

Trench fever, 3:1124

Trental. *See* Pentoxifylline

Trephine needles, 1:341, 3:1135

Treponema pallidum, 5:1625

Treprostinil, 4:1540

Tretinoin, 4:1277, 5:1889

Triage nurses, 4:1210

Triamcinolone acetonide, 1:379

Triamterene

cimetidine interactions, 3:900
diuretic action, 2:690
diuretic interactions, 2:693
folic acid interactions, 3:813
hyperkalemia from, 2:737
ranitidine interactions, 3:900

Triaxial joints, 3:1086

Triazolam

antibiotic interactions, 1:153
for insomnia, 1:140, 3:1051
SSRI interactions, 1:173

Tricare, 3:909

Trichinosis, 2:779

Trichlormethiazide, 1:189

Trichloroacetic acid, 5:1889

Tricholorethylene, 3:1092

Trichomoniasis, 5:1622–1624

Trichophyton sp., 3:825

Trichotillomania, 1:80

Tricor. *See* Fenofibratet

Tricyclic antidepressants, 1:166*t,* **174–177**

allergies, 1:161
analgesic action, 1:106
anticonvulsant drug interactions, 1:162
for anxiety, 1:215
bronchodilator interactions, 1:380
for cervical spondylosis, 2:488
cimetidine interactions, 3:900
for depression, 2:626
for diabetic neuropathy, 2:647
drug interactions, 1:177
dry eye from, 2:711
for generalized anxiety disorder, 3:863
for itching, 3:1082
for panic disorder, 4:1411
for personality disorders, 4:1447
for post-herpatic neuralgia, 5:1631
ranitidine interactions, 3:900
sodium interactions, 5:1680
SSRI interactions, 1:173
vs. SSRIs, 1:168
for tinnitus, 5:1780

Trifluoperazine, 1:203, 305, 4:1530

Trifocal eyeglasses, 4:1485

Trifolium pratense. See Red clover

Trigeminal neuralgia, 4:1318, 1319

Trigger finger, 5:**1787–1788**

Trigger point therapy

fibromyalgia, 3:801
massage, 4:1217
neuromuscular physical therapy, 4:1323
osteopathic medicine, 2:702

Triglycerides, 3:953

atherosclerosis, 1:246
cholesterol tests, 2:505, 3:954
fatty liver, 3:796–797
fibrates for, 3:955
hyperlipoproteinemia, 3:1002, 1003
liver function tests, 3:1143, 1145
normal/high levels, 3:954

Trigonella foenum-graecum. See Fenugreek

Trihexyphenidyl, 1:200, 4:1424

Triiodothyronine (T_3), 3:1013, 5:1773, 1774, 1777

Trilactonic diterpenes, 3:879

Trimethoprim, 5:1808, 1886

Trimethoprim/Sulfamethoxazole

for bladder infection, 1:311
for cystitis, 2:595
for diarrhea, 2:655
folic acid interactions, 5:1862
MRSA infections, 4:1296
for urinary tract infections, 5:1808

Trimox. *See* Amoxicillin

Trimpex. *See* Trimethoprim

Triple therapy, 3:940–941

Triprolidine, 1:187

Trismus, 5:1755

Trobramycin, 1:151

Trochanteric bursitis, 1:388, 389

Trofranil. *See* Imipramine

Trovafloxacin, 1:152, 5:1808

Trovan. *See* Trovafloxacin

TRUS (Transrectal ultrasound), 4:1502, 1506

Trust (psychology), 2:764

Trusts (legal), 2:567, 3:803

Truth-in-lending, 4:1232

Tryptophan, 1:173

TSH (Thyroid-stimulating hormone), 1:259, 3:1013, 5:1769, 1771, 1773, 1774

TTE (Transthoracic echocardiography), 2:724

tTGA-IgA test, 2:473

TTWB (Toe-touch weight-bearing), 3:961

Tube feeding, 4:1337–1338, 5:**1788–1790,** *1789*

cancer-related dysphagia, 5:1741
cirrhosis, 2:523
motor neuron diseases, 4:1289
swallowing disorders, 5:1742
withdrawal, 5:1882

Tube thoracostomy, 4:1461

Tubercle bacillus. *See Mycobacterium tuberculae*

Tuberculin skin test, 5:1793

Tuberculosis, 3:1032, 5:**1790–1796,** *1792*

AIDS-associated, 1:207–208, 5:1790, 1791
aminoglycosides for, 1:96
demographics, 3:1034, 5:1790–1791, 1791*t*
diagnosis, 3:1175, 5:*1792,* 1793–1794
drug-resistant, 1:279, 3:1035, 5:1794, 1795
drug therapy, 1:207–212, 207*t,* 3:1035, 5:1790, 1794–1795

Tuberculosis *(continued)*
extrapulmonary, 5:1793
history, 5:1790
isoniazid for, 3:1036, 5:1795–1796
liver biopsy, 3:1133
lung cancer from, 3:1174
miliary, 5:1793, 1795
mortality, 1:207, 5:1790, 1795
prevention, 5:1795–1796
prophylactic antibiotics for, 3:1036
pulmonary, 5:1792–1793, 1795
pulmonary fibrosis from, 4:1536
rheumatoid factor test, 1:254
streptomycin for, 1:95, 151, 5:1790, 1795
Veterans Affairs hospital system, 5:1827
Tubules, 3:1100
Tufts University Food Pyramid, 2:666
Tui na massage, 1:13, 14, 15, 3:1152
TUIP (Transurethral incision of the prostate), 4:1512
Tumeric, 2:417–418
Tumescent technique, 3:1131, 1132
Tummy tuck. *See* Abdominoplasty
Tumor debulking, 1:381
Tumor markers, 1:308, 2:534, 4:1262
Tumor necrosis factor, 4:1264, 1384
Tumor, Node, Metastasis classification system, 5:1706
Tumor suppressor genes, 4:1260–1261, 1264
Tumors
angiogenesis, 4:1260, 1261
benign, 1:155, 348, 2:406–407, 5:1583, 1584, 1586, 1706
brain and central nervous system, 1:*348*, 348–351
depression, 2:628
eyelid, 2:779–780
multicentric, 4:1262
secondary, 4:1261–1262
stabilization, 2:492
See also Cancer
TUMT (Transurethral microwave thermotherapy), 4:1512
Tunnel vision, 4:1438
TUR (Transurethral resection), 1:309
Turner syndrome, 1:219
Turning, 2:496
TURP (Transurethral resection of the prostate), 4:1506, 1507, 1512
12-Step programs, 5:1728
24 Hour food questionnaire, 2:668
24-Hour urine sample, 2:604
Twilight anesthesia, 3:783–784
Two-hour postprandial blood glucose test, 1:329
Tylectomy. *See* Lumpectomy
Tylenol. *See* Acetaminophen
Tylosis, 2:759
Type 1 diabetes mellitus, 1:178, 258–260, 2:638–640
carbohydrates, 2:423
diabetic retinopathy, 5:1836
insulin, 3:1053–1056
Type 2 diabetes mellitus, 1:178, 2:638–640
aging, 1:44
carbohydrates, 2:423
cinnamon for, 2:514–516
diabetic retinopathy, 5:1836
insulin, 3:1053–1056
socioeconomic factors, 2:662
Type A aortic dissection, 1:218
Type A personality, 4:1270
Type B aortic dissection, 1:218, 219
Type B personality, 4:1270
Type C personality, 4:1270
Typhus, 3:1124
Typical antipsychotic drugs, 4:1530, 1532
Tzanck smear, 5:1625

U

UAGA (Uniform Anatomical Gift Act), 4:1364
UCR (Usual, reasonable, and customary), 4:1231
Udecyline acid, 1:185
UGDP (University group diabetes program), 1:180
UGI series. *See* Upper GI series
UK General Practice Database, 4:1516–1517
UL (Upper intake level), 3:812, 5:1679, 1850, 1854–1855, 1857
Ulcerative colitis
barium enema, 1:289
colon cancer risk, 2:533
colonoscopy, 2:538, 541
GI bleeding from, 3:872
glucosamine for, 3:884
vitamin K deficiency, 5:1860
zinc deficiency, 5:1897
Ulcers, 5:*1797*, **1797–1800**
antacids for, 1:139
bacteremia from, 1:275
Behcet's syndrome-related, 1:290
corneal, 2:574–575
Cox-2 inhibitor-induced, 2:585–586
decubitus, 1:275
duodenal, 3:872, 897–898, 940, 5:1797–1800
esophageal, 5:1797
foot, 2:641
gastroduodenal, 2:585
gastroesophageal reflux disease-related, 3:853
genital, 1:290
mouth, 1:290
scleroderma-related, 5:1597, 1598
silent, 5:1798
skin, 5:1649, 1818, 1884, 1886
stasis, 2:632
See also Peptic ulcers; Pressure sores
Ulmus fulva. See Slippery elm
Ultane. *See* Sevofluorane
Ultram. *See* Tramadol
Ultrasonography
alcohol ablation, 3:1141
anal, 3:799
back and neck pain, 1:270
bladder, 1:*315,* 315–317
blood clots, 1:322
bone density test, 1:337
breast biopsy, 1:353
breast cancer, 1:356
bursitis, 1:390
carotid, 2:*459,* 459–461, 5:1722
certification, 2:460
cervical cancer, 2:483
cirrhosis, 2:523
contraindications, 1:268
corneal diseases, 2:575
cryoablation, 3:1141
deep vein thrombosis, 2:601
Doppler, 2:457, 459–461, 724
education and training, 2:460
endoscopic, 4:1402, 1405, 5:1705
gallstones, 3:839
hepatitis, 3:951
hyperthyroidism, 3:1013
kidney cancer, 3:1092
liposuction, 3:1131, 1132
liver biopsy, 3:1135
liver cancer, 4:1263
lumpectomy guidance, 3:1170
lymphedema, 3:1187
physical therapy, 4:1457
post-mammogram, 4:1207
prostate, 4:1514–1515
thyroid, 5:1777–1778
thyroid cancer, 5:1772
transrectal, 4:1502, 1506
transvaginal, 2:744–745
trigger finger, 5:1788
Ultraviolet A (UVA), 4:1520
Ultraviolet B (UVB), 4:1520, 5:1642, 1863
Ultraviolet light
cataracts, 2:464
eyelid tumors, 2:779
folic acid depletion, 3:812
melanoma, 2:408, 4:1200
skin cancer, 4:1260, 5:1642
UV coatings, 2:773
visual impairment, 5:1843
vitamin D, 5:1863

Ultraviolet light therapy
itching, 3:1082
psoriasis, 4:1520, 1521
scleroderma, 5:1598
Uncued panic attack, 4:1409
Underarm perspiration, 1:345, 347
Underinsurance, 3:910, 913
Undernutrition, 4:1336–1337
See also Malnutrition
Underweight, 1:330–332, 2:682–683, 4:1201
See also Weight loss
Undue hardship, 1:94
Unexplained weight loss, 3:866, 5:1876
Uniaxial joints, 3:1086
Uniform Anatomical Gift Act (UAGA), 4:1364
Uniform Crime Reports for the United States, 4:1212
Uninsured Americans, 3:910, 913, 4:1495
Unipolar mood disorder. *See* Major depressive disorder
United HealthCare Insurance Co., 4:1494
United Kingdom, 1:70, 4:1516–1517
United Nations, 4:1496, 5:1611
United Network for Organ Sharing (UNOS), 2:509, 3:1106, 4:1363, 1364
United States Census. *See* Census Bureau
United States Department of Agriculture. *See* U.S. Department of Agriculture
United States, Hutchinson v., 3:1045
United States Preventive Services Task Force, 1:122
United States Renal Data System (USRDS), 2:510
United Way, 2:597
UnitedHealth Group, 2:549
Univasc. *See* Moexipril
Universal health care, 4:1495
Universal precautions, 1:61, 3:1030, 1031
University group diabetes program (UGDP), 1:180
UNOS (United Network for Organ Sharing), 2:509, 3:1106, 4:1363, 1364
Unsaturated fats, 3:1154, 1157, 1159
Unstable angina pectoris, 1:123, 234, 235
Upper endoscopy, 3:859–860, 5:1705, 1741, 1799
Upper esophageal sphincter, 5:1740
Upper gastrointestinal series. *See* Upper GI series
Upper GI bleeding, 3:871–875, 897–898
Upper GI series, 5:**1801–1804**
esophageal cancer, 2:759–760, 761
gastroesophageal reflux disease, 3:854–855, 859–860
heartburn, 3:934
oral cancers, 4:1358
stomach cancer, 5:1705
swallowing disorders, 5:1741
ulcers, 5:1799
Upper intake level (UL)
folic acid, 3:812
sodium, 5:1679
vitamin C, 5:1850
vitamin D, 5:1854–1855
vitamin E, 5:1857
Upper respiratory infections (URI), 1:375, 377, 5:1670
UPPP (Uvulopalatopharyngoplasty), 5:*1669,* 1671, 1674
Uprima. *See* Apomorphine
Urea breath test, 3:940
See also Blood urea nitrogen
Ureaplasma urealyticum, 5:1625
Urease, 3:939, 1101
Ureter
anatomy and function, 3:1109
kidney stones, 3:1101
kidney transplantation, 3:1107
kidney, ureter, and bladder x-ray study, 3:1108–1110
Urethra, 2:465–466, 469, 594
Urethral meatus, 2:465–466, 470
Urethral obstruction, 4:1510
Urethral specimens, 5:1626
Urethral sphincter, 5:1804
Urethral suppositories, 5:1635
Urethritis, 1:310, 5:1807
Urge incontinence, 1:314–315, 5:1804, 1805
URI (Upper respiratory infections), 1:375, 377
Uric acid
chronic kidney failure, 2:509
gout, 3:891–892, 893
kidney stones, 3:1101, 1102, 1103
Uricosuric drugs, 3:892
Urinalysis
AIDS tests, 1:61–62
amyloidosis, 1:101
autonomic disorders, 1:264
bladder stones, 1:313
cancer, 2:409
cystitis, 2:594
dehydration, 2:604
diabetic nephropathy, 2:644
edema, 2:726
heatstroke, 3:938
implantable cardioverter-defibrillator, 3:1026
kidney cancer, 3:1092
kidney function, 3:1097
mobility, 4:1284
multiple myeloma, 4:1300
overactive bladder, 4:1379
overdose, 4:1381
Urinary catheterization
colostomy, 2:542
female, 2:**465–468**
infections, 2:594, 3:1034
male, 2:**468–472**, *469*
Urinary diversion, 5:1886
Urinary incontinence, 5:*1804,* **1804–1807**
biofeedback, 1:300
bladder training, 1:314–315
catheterization, 2:465–467, 468–472, *469*
causes, 1:315, 5:1805
dehydration, 2:606
drug therapy, 1:264, 5:1805
fecal incontinence, 3:798
functional, 5:1804
overflow, 5:1804, 1805
personal hygiene, 4:1441
prevention, 5:1806
reflex, 4:1378
spinal cord injury-related, 5:1693, 1694
stress, 5:1804
urge, 1:314–315, 5:1804, 1805
Urinary retention
autonomic disorders, 1:263, 264
delirium, 2:607, 608
spinal cord injuries, 5:1693
Urinary tract, 5:1804, 1807
Urinary tract infections (UTIs), 3:1032, 5:**1807–1810**
antibiotics for, 5:1805
bladder stone-related, 1:312, 313–314
causes, 2:594, 3:1034, 5:1808
delirium-related, 2:607, 608
demographics, 1:310, 3:1034, 5:1807–1808
diagnosis, 5:1808, 1810–1812
kidney stone-related, 3:1101
lower, 2:593
male, 2:594
saw palmetto for, 5:1588
spinal cord injury-related, 5:1693
staphylococcal, 5:1702
urinary catheter-related, 2:467
urinary incontinence from, 5:1805
vitamin C for, 5:1849, 1863
Urination problems
overactive bladder, 4:1378–1380
prostate cancer, 4:1505
prostate enlargement, 4:1510
saw palmetto, 5:1587
Urine, 3:1022, 1109, 5:1807
Urine cortisol test, 2:591
Urine cultures, 5:**1810–1812,** *1811*
bladder cancer, 1:308
bladder infection, 1:311
staphylococcal infections, 5:1701

Urine cultures *(continued)*
tuberculosis, 5:1794
urinary tract infections, 5:1808, 1810–1812
See also Bacterial cultures
Urine output, 2:636–638, 692
Urine protein test, 3:1097
Urine specimens, 5:1626, 1810, 1811
Urodynamic testing, 4:1379
Urokinase, 5:1767
Uroliths. *See* Bladder stones; Kidney stones
Urologic surgery, 3:806
Urologists, 5:1619
Uroxatral. *See* Alfuzosin
Urtica, 4:1379
Urtica dioica. See Nettles
Urtica urens. See Urtica
Urticaria. *See* Hives
U.S. Census. *See* Census Bureau
U.S. Department of Agriculture (USDA)
antioxidants, 1:197
The Dietary Guidelines for Americans, 2:672, 674, 676–677, 4:1338–1339
food pyramid, 2:658
healthy diet, 5:1872
Healthy Eating Index, 2:674, 674*t*
history, 2:657–658
Human Nutrition Research Center, 4:1465
insulin, 3:1053
MyPyramid for older adults, 4:1336*t,* 1337, 1338–1339
Nutritional Immunology Laboratory, 4:1465
U.S. Department of Health and Human Services (DHHS). *See* Department of Health and Human Services
U.S. Department of Labor, 1:28–29
U.S. Department of Veterans Affairs, 5:1826
U.S. Public Health Service, 1:324–325, 3:1030
U.S. Supreme Court, 2:762, 4:1235
USDA. *See* U.S. Department of Agriculture
USRDS (United States Renal Data System), 2:510
Usual, reasonable, and customary (UCR), 4:1231
Uterine artery embolization, 3:1019
Uterine cancer
demographics, 2:743
diagnosis, 2:409
endometrial, 2:415, 661, 743–748
genetic factors, 2:407
hormone replacement therapy-related, 3:991, 993, 994
hysterectomy, 3:1016
tamoxifen-related, 1:156
Uterine fibroids, 3:1016–1017, 1019
Uterus, 2:743, 3:1016
Utilitarianism, 4:1234
Utilization review, 4:1210
UTIs. *See* Urinary tract infections
UV coatings, 2:773, 781
UV light. *See* Ultraviolet light
UVA (Ultraviolet A), 4:1520, 5:1642
UVB (Ultraviolet B), 4:1520, 5:1642, 1863
Uvea, 1:290
Uveitis, 2:775, 4:1570
Uvula, 5:*1669,* 1671–1672, 1673
Uvulopalatopharyngoplasty (UPPP), 5:*1669,* 1671, 1674
Uvulopalatoplasty, laser-assisted, 5:1671–1672, 1674

V

V-fib. *See* Ventricular fibrillation
V-tach. *See* Ventricular tachycardia
VA. *See* Veterans Affairs hospital system
VacA, 3:939
Vaccinations, 5:**1813–1816,** 1813*t*
acquired immunity, 3:1021
adverse effects, 3:1043
BCG, 1:309, 5:1795
cancer, 2:411, 4:1264
chicken pox, 5:1632, 1815
diphtheria, 3:1036, 5:1756, 1815
DTaP (diphtheria, tetanus and accellular pertussis), 5:1756
DTP (diphtheria, tetanus and pertussis), 5:1756, 1815
hepatitis, 3:951, 952, 5:1813
Hib, 4:1248, 1256, 1258
human papilloma virus, 2:485, 5:1623
infectious disease prevention, 3:1036
influenza, 3:1036, 1038, 1040–1043, 1041*t,* 4:1466, 5:1815, 1833, 1834
Law of Infinitesimal Dose, 3:987
live, attenuated influenza, 3:1042
lyme disease, 3:1185
measles, 5:1815
MMR (measles-mumps-rubella), 5:1815
mumps, 5:1815
PCV7, 4:1248
pneumococcus, 5:1815
polio, 5:1815
PPV, 4:1248
rabies, 5:1756
rubella, 5:1815
shingles, 1:212, 5:1631–1632
Streptococcus pneumoniae, 3:1036, 4:1463*t,* 1466, 5:1709, 1713
tetanus, 3:1036, 5:1756
travel, 3:1036, 5:1609, 1756
VZV, 1:212, 5:1631–1632
Vaccine Adverse Event Reporting Service, 3:1043
Vaccinium myrtillus. See Bilberry
Vacuum pump therapy, 2:757, 5:1635
Vagina, 5:1621
Vaginal bleeding, 3:1016
Vaginal cancer, 2:409, 4:1413
Vaginal creams, 3:990–991, 993
Vaginal hysterectomy, 3:1017–1018
Vaginal infections, 3:825–826, 849
Vaginal specimens, 5:1626
Vaginal stenosis, 2:747
Vaginismus, 5:1618, 1619, 1620
Vaginosis, 4:1498
Vagotomy, 5:1799
Vagus nerve, 3:786, 5:1799
Vagus nerve stimulation, 5:1604
Vaillant, George E., 4:1525–1526
Valcyclovir, 1:212
Valdecoxib, 2:585
Valerian
insomnia, 3:1051
menopause, 4:1252
sleep disorders, 4:1525, 5:1657
substance abuse, 5:1727
Valeriana officinalis. See Valerian
Valio, Ltd., 4:1497
Valium. *See* Diazepam
Valproate, 2:647, 4:1319
Valproic acid, 1:160
barbiturate interactions, 1:284
benzodiazepine interactions, 1:145
for bipolar disorder, 1:304
cephalosporin interactions, 2:480
cimetidine interactions, 3:900
diazepam interactions, 4:1308
hormone replacement therapy interactions, 3:993
isoniazid interactions, 1:211
ranitidine interactions, 3:900
rifampin interactions, 1:211
for seizures, 1:160, 5:1603
thrombolytic therapy interactions, 5:1768
Valsalva maneuver, 3:1015
Valsartan, 1:191, 2:563
Valvuloplasty, balloon, 3:931–932, 4:1282
Valvulotomy, 3:931
Vanceril. *See* Beclomethasone dipropionate
Vancomycin, 1:95, 4:1296
Vane, John, 1:234

Vantin. *See* Cefpodoxime
Vaporizers, 2:552
Vardenafil
for erectile dysfunction, 1:264, 2:647, 756–757
nitrate interactions, 3:930
for prostate enlargement, 4:1512
transient blindness from, 5:1782
Varicella zoster virus, 2:574, 3:1032, 1107, 5:1629–1630, 1832
See also Chickenpox; Shingles
Varices, esophageal, 3:872
Varicose veins, 2:517, 518, 519, 5:**1816–1818,** *1817*
vs. arteriovenous fistula, 1:228
ginkgo biloba for, 3:878
Varivax, 5:1632
Vascular access port, 3:1060, 1062
Vascular dementia, 2:611, 613
Vascular depression, 2:622, 625, 627
Vascular disease
hematologists, 3:942
occlusive, 1:130–132
pressure sores, 4:1488
Vascular ectasia, 3:872
Vascular occlusion, 2:650
Vascularization. *See* Angiogenesis
Vasoconstrictors, 2:523
Vasodilation, 1:81, 194
Vasodilators
calcium channel blocker interactions, 2:402
for cardiomyopathy, 2:447
for hypertension, 3:1011
for Raynaud's disease, 2:519
sildenafil citrate, 5:1635
Vasospasm, 2:401, 5:1782
Vasotec. *See* Enalapril
Vasovagal syncope, 3:786–788
VATS (Video-assisted thoracoscopic surgery), 3:1172, 5:1761, 1762, 1763
VBG (Vertical banded gastroplasty), 1:285, 4:1351
VCT (Voluntary counseling and testing), 1:56–58
Vector-borne diseases, 3:1182–1183
Vegan diets, 2:399, 5:1862
Vegetables
anti-inflammatory diet, 1:195
antioxidant role, 1:197–198
calcium, 5:1614
cancer prevention, 2:412, 413–418
community nutrition programs, 2:556
cruciferous, 2:415
food pyramid, 2:658
green leafy, 2:415
healthy aging diet, 4:1338–1339
Healthy Eating 2010, 2:557
hypertension, 1:326
recommendations, 4:1336
vitamin C content, 5:1851–1852
Vegetarian diet
hypertension, 1:325
Seventh-day Adventists, 4:1478
transient ischemic attacks, 5:1786
zinc deficiency, 5:1897
Vegetative state. *See* Persistent vegetative state
VEGF (Endothelial growth factor), 4:1261, 1264
Vein ligation and stripping, 5:1818
Vein surgery, 5:1817–1818
Veins, varicose. *See* Varicose veins
Vena cava filter, 1:322
Venipuncture complications, 1:62
Venlafaxine, 1:144
for anxiety, 1:144, 215
for depression, 2:626
for generalized anxiety disorder, 3:863
SSRI interactions, 1:173
Venography, 2:602
Venous insufficiency, 2:725–726
Venous thromboembolism. *See* Deep vein thrombosis
Ventavis. *See* Iloprost
Ventilation management, 5:**1818–1820,** 1823–1824
See also Mechanical ventilation
Ventilator weaning, 3:1048, 4:1569, 5:1818–1820
Ventilators, 5:**1820–1824,** *1821*
Ventilatory failure, 4:1567
Ventilatory training, 4:1542–1543
Ventolin. *See* Albuterol
Ventricular fibrillation, 1:225, 5:**1824–1825**
cardioversion, 2:452
defibrillators, 2:449, 450
implantable cardioverter-defibrillator, 3:1025
Ventricular tachycardia, 1:225, 5:**1825–1826**
cardioversion, 2:452
fainting, 3:788
implantable cardioverter-defibrillator, 3:1025
Ventriculography, radionuclide, 2:446
Verapamil, 1:83, 191, 2:580, 3:1143
Verbal communication, 2:716–719
Verbena officinalis. See Vervain
Verelan. *See* Verapamil
Vertebrae, 2:487, *501,* 3:1085, 4:1369
Verteporfin, 1:41
Vertical banded gastroplasty (VBG), 1:285, 4:1351
Vertigo, 2:696–698
Vervain, 5:1727
Very low-density lipoproteins (VLDL), 2:505, 3:955, 1002
Vesicare. *See* Solifenacin succinate
Vesicles, 5:1649
Vesicoureteral reflux, 4:1272
Vestibular hypofunction, 3:832
Vestibular migraine, 2:697
Vestibular rehabilitation exercises, 2:698
Vestibular system, 3:829, 830, 831, 832, 833
Veterans, 4:1469, 5:1827*t, 1829,* 1829–1831
Veterans Administration, 3:1069
Veterans Affairs hospital system, 5:**1826–1829,** 1827*t*
Veterans of Foreign Wars (VFW), 5:*1829,* **1829–1831**
Veterinary medicine, 1:19
VFW (Veterans of Foreign Wars), 5:*1829,* **1829–1831**
VHL (Von Hipple-Lindau) syndrome, 4:1401–1402, 1403
Viagra. *See* Sildenafil
Vibration therapy, 2:497
Video-assisted thoracoscopic surgery (VATS), 3:1172, 5:1761, 1762, 1763
Videofluoroscopy, 1:232–233
Videos
dietary assessment, 2:668
gait and balance assessment, 3:830
Vietnam War, 4:1469, 5:1827
Vietnamese Americans. *See* Asian Americans
Villa, Pancho, 4:1211
Vinblastine, 1:309, 2:490
Vincristine, 2:490
Vinegar, 4:1312
Vinyl chloride, 3:1139
Vioxx. *See* Rofecoxib
Vipassana, 4:1271
Vipoma, 4:1401–1403
Viral cultures, 5:1625–1626, 1645–1646
Viral infections, 5:1831–1835
Alzheimer's disease from, 1:86
asthma during, 1:240
bacterial infections with, 5:1833
bladder, 1:310, 311
carcinogenesis, 4:1260
cardiomyopathy from, 2:445
demographics, 5:1832
diagnosis, 3:1035, 5:1833
diarrhea from, 2:652–653
drug therapy, 1:211–212, 211*t,* 5:1833
eye, 5:1842
garlic for, 3:846, 847

Viral infections *(continued)*
gastroenteritis, 3:851
myocarditis from, 4:1309
oxygen/ozone therapy, 4:1384
See also Antiviral drugs
Viral meningitis, 4:1246–1249
Viral pneumonia, 4:1462, 1463
Virtual colonoscopy, 2:534, 535, 539
Virtual relationships, 4:1561
Viruses, 2:408, 5:**1831–1835**
Vis medicatrix naturae, 4:1216
Vision
accommodation, 2:462
blurred, 2:649
central, 1:39–43
distance, 2:770
double, 2:769
floaters, 3:809–811
gait and balance assessment, 3:829, 830
gait and balance disorders, 3:833
low, 3:1162–1165, 1163*t,* 4:1354, 5:1841, 1842*t*
night, 2:649
normal, 3:1162, 5:1841
peripheral, 1:39
tunnel, 4:1438
vitamin A, 1:319, 2:575
Vision disorders, 4:1304, 5:**1835–1841,** 1836*t, 1837*
See also Age-related macular degeneration; Cataracts; Glaucoma; Visual impairment
Vision l, 3:1162–1165
Vision loss. *See* Visual impairment
Vision plans, 4:1356
Vision rehabilitation, 4:1354
Vision therapy, 4:1354
Visitation programs, 2:558, 3:1079
Visiting Nurses Association (VNA), 2:597, 3:979–980
Visitors, recovery room, 4:1556–1557
Vistaril. *See* Hydroxyzine
Visual acuity tests, 2:769–771, 5:1838
cataracts, 2:463
low vision, 3:1163
presbyopia, 4:1485
Visual field measurement, 2:770, 5:1838
glaucoma, 3:881
low vision, 3:1163
peripheral vision loss, 4:1437, 1438
Visual impairment, 4:1372, 5:*1841,* **1841–1843**
age-related macular degeneration, 1:39–43
aging, 1:44
balance tests, 1:281
cataract-related, 2:461
corneal diseases, 2:573–577
cranial nerve examination, 4:1321
demographics, 2:464, 5:1841, 1842*t*
diagnosis, 5:1842–1843
ethambutol-induced, 1:209
falls, 3:790, 792
hallucinations from, 4:1529
hypertension-related, 3:1008
low vision, 3:1162–1165
mobility, 4:1284
peripheral, 4:1437–1439, 5:1841
presbyopia, 2:770, 774, 4:1354
terminal illness, 2:600
transient blindness, 5:1781–1784
treatment, 5:1615, 1843
See also Blindness; Vision disorders
Visual rehabilitation, 3:1164
Visual seizures, 5:1601
Visualization, 4:1376–1377
autogenic training, 4:1563
vs. massage therapy, 4:1565
New Age movement, 4:1565
polymyositis, 4:1468
relaxation techniques, 4:1564
Visudyne. *See* Verteporfin
Vital capacity, 2:741
Vital gluten, 3:817
Vital signs, 4:1472, 1473, 5:**1843–1846,** 1844*t*
Vitamin A, 5:1861
alcohol abuse, 1:68
antioxidant role, 1:197
boils, 1:334
bronchitis prevention, 1:378
daily recommended dosage, 1:198, 3:870, 5:1864
dry skin, 2:716
garlic, 3:846
gingivitis, 3:877
immune system function, 3:1024
itching, 3:1082
liver function test interactions, 3:1143
osteoarthritis, 4:1368
overdose, 5:1864
polymyositis, 4:1468
side effects, 1:198
sources, 2:416, 3:877
ulcers, 5:1800
vision, 1:319, 2:575
xerophthalmia, 5:1843
Vitamin A deficiency, 2:575, 742, 5:1842, 1861
Vitamin B complex, 5:1861–1863
alcohol abuse, 1:68
gingivitis, 3:876
hypertension, 1:326
insomnia, 3:1051
neuralgia, 4:1319
osteoarthritis, 4:1368
Parkinson's disease, 4:1424
recommendations, 2:678
rosacea, 4:1579
sources, 3:818
tinnitus, 5:1781
Vitamin B_1. *See* Thiamine
Vitamin B_2. *See* Riboflavin
Vitamin B_3. *See* Niacin
Vitamin B_5, 4:1368, 5:1862
Vitamin B_6, 5:1862
antituberculosis drug interactions, 1:208
daily recommended dosage, 2:665, 3:870, 5:1864
hypertension, 1:326
levodopa interactions, 4:1424
osteoarthritis, 4:1368
probiotics, 4:1498
Vitamin B_6 deficiency, 2:665, 5:1862
Vitamin B_7. *See* Biotin
Vitamin B_8, 4:1411
Vitamin B_9. *See* Folic acid
Vitamin B_{12}, 5:**1846–1849,** 1862–1863
absorption, 4:1203, 5:1847, 1849
anemia, 1:110
daily recommended dosage, 2:665, 666, 3:812–813, 870, 5:1848, 1864
drug interactions, 5:1848–1849
folic acid interactions, 3:811, 812–813
food pyramid, 2:658
generalized anxiety disorder, 3:863
helicobacteriosis, 3:940
mobility, 4:1285
pernicious anemia, 3:869, 4:1201, 5:1847
proton pump inhibitors interactions, 4:1517
role, 4:1339, 5:1847–1848
smoking-induced lung damage, 5:1662
sources, 2:417, 4:1339, 5:1848, 1862
supplements, 5:1847
vitamin C interactions, 5:1852
Vitamin B_{12} deficiency, 5:1847, 1848, 1863
adverse effects, 2:665, 4:1339
anemia, 1:108, 109
anxiety, 1:216
causes, 4:1339, 5:1848
diagnosis, 2:561
folic acid, 3:813
supplements, 4:1336
walking problems from, 5:1867
Vitamin C, 2:709, 5:**1849–1853,** 1849*t,* 1863
age-related macular degeneration, 1:41
alcohol abuse, 1:68
aneurysm, 1:121
angina pectoris, 3:1076
anti-inflammatory diet, 1:195
antioxidant role, 1:197, 5:1850
atherosclerosis prevention, 1:247
benefits, 3:870
blepharoplasty, 1:318
bronchitis prevention, 1:378

Vitamin C *(continued)*
cancer prevention, 2:416, 417, 5:1852
cataract prevention, 2:463, 5:1852
common cold, 2:552, 5:1852
daily recommended dosage, 1:198, 5:1850, 1864
diabetic foot infections, 2:641
drug interactions, 5:1849*t*
face lift healing, 3:784
folic acid with, 3:811
garlic, 3:846
gingivitis, 3:877
health claims, 5:1852
high dosage, 5:1849, 1852
hypertension, 1:326
immune system function, 3:1024
iron supplements with, 3:1065
liver function test interactions, 3:1143
osteoarthritis, 4:1368, 5:1614
overdose, 5:1852
polymyositis, 4:1468
pressure sores, 4:1490
role, 5:1850
side effects, 1:198
skin cancer prevention, 5:1643
smoking-induced lung damage, 5:1662
sources, 2:416, 417, 3:877, 5:1851–1852
supplements, 5:1850
wrinkles, 5:1889, 1890
Vitamin C deficiency, 3:876, 5:1850–1851, 1863
Vitamin D, 5:**1853–1856,** 1863
bone health, 5:1868
bone mass, 3:869
calcium channel blocker interactions, 2:402, 5:1856
calcium interactions, 2:399, 403, 405, 735, 4:1372, 5:1853
celiac disease, 3:889
chronic kidney failure, 2:510
corticosteroid interactions, 3:1180–1181
daily recommended dosage, 2:665, 666, 678, 3:870, 5:1854–1855, 1864
drug interactions, 5:1855–1856
falls, 3:791
food pyramid, 2:658
healthy aging, 5:1614
hypercalcemia, 2:736
hyperparathyroidism, 3:1007
hypertension, 3:1011
knee injury prevention, 3:1118
lactose intolerance, 3:1122
multiple myeloma, 4:1302
multiple sclerosis, 4:1305
osteoporosis, 4:1372
overdose, 5:1855, 1865
Paget's disease of bone, 4:1392
psoriasis, 4:1520
role, 4:1339
scleroderma, 5:1598
sources, 4:1339, 5:1855
sun exposure, 5:1644, 1853, 1855
Vitamin D deficiency, 2:736, 4:1336, 5:1644, 1855, 1863
Vitamin D_2, 5:1853
Vitamin D_3, 5:1853
Vitamin deficiencies, 5:1861
Vitamin E, 5:**1856–1858,** 1863–1864
absorption, 5:1858
age-related macular degeneration, 1:41
aneurysm, 1:121
angina pectoris, 3:1076
antioxidant role, 1:197, 5:1856
atherosclerosis, 1:247
benefits, 3:870
bronchitis, 1:378
cataracts, 2:463, 5:1856
common cold, 2:552
daily recommended dosage, 1:198, 5:1857, 1864
drug interactions, 2:680, 5:1858
gingivitis, 3:877
high dosage, 5:1857, 1858
immune system function, 3:1024
insulin interactions, 3:1056
itching, 3:1082
mortality, 5:1857, 1858, 1863–1864
natural progesterone, 3:994
osteoarthritis, 4:1368, 5:1614–1615
overdose, 5:1865
Parkinson's disease, 4:1423, 5:1856
periodic limb movement disorder, 4:1435
polymyositis, 4:1468
side effects, 1:198
skin cancer, 5:1643
sources, 3:818, 877, 5:1857
supplements, 4:1336
tinnitus, 5:1781
ulcers, 5:1800
Vitamin E deficiency, 4:1336, 5:1856
Vitamin K, 5:**1858–1861,** 1864
anticonvulsant drug interactions, 1:161
blepharoplasty, 1:318
blood clots, 1:323
bone density, 5:1868
coagulation disorders, 3:873
daily recommended dosage, 5:1859, 1864
drug interactions, 5:1860, 1864, 1865
face lift healing, 3:784
liver function tests, 3:1145
sources, 5:1859, 1864
Vitamin K deficiency, 5:1860, 1864
Vitamin K_1, 5:1859, 1864
Vitamin K_2, 5:1859, 1864
Vitamin supplements, 2:678, 4:1343
See also Dietary supplements
Vitamins, 5:**1861–1866**
AIDS, 1:53
alcohol abuse, 1:68
colon cancer prevention, 2:537
dietary counseling, 2:670
optimal health, 5:1871
pneumonia risk, 4:1464–1465
recommendations, 2:665
smoking, 5:1660
Vitex agnus-castus. See Chaste tree
Vitrectomy, 2:649, 3:810, 4:1572, 5:1839
Vitreous gel, 3:809, 880–881, 4:1570–1571, 1572, 5:1839
Vitreous hemorrhage, 2:650
Vivactil. *See* Protriptyline
Vivekananda, 5:1892
Vivelle, 5:1588
VLDL (Very low-density lipoproteins), 2:505, 3:955, 1002
VNA (Visiting Nurses Association), 2:597, 3:979–980
Vocal cords, 5:1687
Voice changes, 5:1772
Voiding cystourethrogram, 2:595
Voltaren. *See* Diclofenac
Volume-cycled ventilators, 5:1821
Volume reduction surgery, lung, 4:1541–1542
Volume therapy, 3:873
Voluntary associations, 4:1561
Voluntary caregivers, 2:452
Voluntary counseling and testing (VCT), 1:56–58
Voluntary euthanasia, 2:763
Volunteers
community social programs, 2:558–559
healthy aging, 4:1523
visitation programs, 3:1079
Vomiting
acupressure, 5:1628
antiretrovial drug-induced, 1:53, 54
blood, 3:871
chemotherapy-induced, 2:492, 4:1213, 5:1684
chronic kidney failure-related, 2:509
dehydration, 5:1871
electrolyte tests, 2:739
induced, 4:1382
marijuana for, 4:1213
prevention, 2:418–420
radiation therapy-induced, 5:1684
shiatsu, 5:1627
See also Nausea
Von Hipple-Lindau (VHL) syndrome, 3:1092, 4:1401–1402, 1403
Von Zumbusch pustular psoriasis, 4:1518

Voriconazole, 3:826
Vytorin, 3:955
VZV vaccine, 1:212, 5:1631–1632

W

Waist circumference, 1:332
Waksman, Selman, 1:151
Wal-Mart drug plan, 2:548–549
Waldenström's macroglobulinaemia, 1:254
Walford, Roy, 1:46
Walkers, 3:968, 4:1285, 5:1868
Walking
  aerobic exercise, 1:37
  demographics, 4:1349–1350
  endurance training, 5:1758–1759
  exercise, 2:767
  fall prevention, 5:1615
  healthy aging, 5:1614
  mobility, 4:1283
Walking problems, 5:**1867–1870**
  falls, 5:1867, 1869
  gait and balance assessment, 3:829–831
  peripheral vision loss, 4:1439
  See also Gait problems
WALOP (We All Love Our Pets) program, 4:1227
War veterans. *See* Veterans
Wards, 1:32, 2:567
Warfarin, 1:157
  acetaminophen interactions, 1:8
  antibiotic interactions, 1:153, 4:1466
  aspirin interactions, 1:235
  for atherosclerosis prevention, 1:247
  bruising with, 1:385–386
  cardiac catheterization, 2:432
  for cardiac valve replacement, 2:443
  for cardiomyopathy, 2:447
  celecoxib interactions, 2:587
  cephalosporin interactions, 2:480
  cholinesterase inhibitor interactions, 1:165
  cimetidine interactions, 3:900
  dietary supplement interactions, 2:680
  garlic interactions, 3:850
  GI bleeding from, 3:872
  mechanical heart valves, 1:223
  for mitral valve stenosis, 4:1282
  nonsteroidal anti-inflammatory drug interactions, 4:1327
  for pulmonary embolism, 4:1534
  for pulmonary hypertension, 4:1540
  ranitidine interactions, 3:900
  SSRI interactions, 1:173
  for stroke, 2:457, 5:1722
  for transient blindness, 5:1783
  for transient ischemic attacks, 5:1785
  vitamin K interactions, 5:1860, 1864
Warm climates, 5:1610
Warm-up, 5:1616, 1875
Warts
  genital, 5:1622
  plantar, 3:821
Washing, 4:1441
  See also Hand washing; Personal hygiene
Washington, George, 4:1212
Washington State, 3:1044
Wasting syndrome, 2:**393–395**
  AIDS-related, 1:53, 54, 2:393, 394, 4:1213
  colon cancer-related, 2:537
  marijuana for, 4:1213
Watchful waiting, 3:839, 4:1508
Water, 5:**1870–1873**
  anti-inflammatory diet, 1:195
  chlorinated, 2:408
  common cold, 2:552
  daily amount, 2:603, 605, 658–659, 712–713, 3:870, 5:1616, 1870
  diabetes insipidus, 2:637
  diarrhea prevention, 2:656
  dry eye, 2:712–713
  dry mouth, 2:714
  dry skin, 2:716
  food pyramid, 2:658
  living wills, 3:1149
  mitral valve prolapse, 4:1281
  ozonated, 4:1385
  urinary tract infection prevention, 5:1809
  wrinkles, 5:1889
  See also Fluid intake
Water-borne disorders, 5:1610
Water deprivation test, 2:637
Water exercise, 5:*1873,* **1873–1876**
Water pills. *See* Diuretics
Water retention, 1:132
Watermelon, 2:414
Wax, ear, 2:721–723
WBAT (Weight-bearing as Tolerated), 3:961
We All Love Our Pets (WALOP) program, 4:1227
Weak link theory, 1:45
Weakened immune systems. *See* Immunocompromised patients
Weaning, ventilator, 3:1048, 4:1569, 5:1818–1820
Wedge resection, liver, 3:1140
Wegener's granulomatosis, 1:258–260
Weight-bearing as Tolerated (WBAT), 3:961
Weight-bearing exercise, 3:791, 4:1372
Weight-Control Information Network (WIN), 5:1877
Weight gain, 1:44, 2:422, 3:1132, 1180
Weight loss, 5:**1876–1879**
  abdominoplasty, 1:3, 5
  aerobic exercise, 1:38
  aging, 1:44
  AIDS, 1:53, 54
  angina pectoris, 1:125
  bariatric surgery, 1:284–286, 3:958
  benefits, 4:1353
  cachexia and wasting, 2:393–395
  circulatory disorders, 2:520
  community nutrition programs, 2:557
  congestive heart failure, 2:563
  dehydration-related, 2:604
  DHEA, 2:634
  dietary counseling, 2:671
  dysphagia-related, 5:1741
  hip replacement preparation, 3:966
  hypertension, 1:325, 3:1010, 1012
  low-fat diet, 3:1158
  lupus-related, 3:1180
  maintaining, 5:1878
  obesity, 4:1337, 1350–1351
  preparation, 5:1616
  rheumatoid arthritis, 4:1574
  tapas acupressure technique, 1:14
  unexplained/unintentional, 3:866, 5:1876
  varicose veins, 5:1818
  water exercise, 5:1874, 1875
  yo-yo, 2:671–672, 4:1350
Weight loss drugs. *See* Appetite suppressants
Weight-shifting exercise, 3:830
Weil, Andrew, 4:1525
Well-being
  diet, 2:664–667
  lifestyle, 2:661
  qigong, 4:1546
  stress, 5:1714
  t'ai chi, 5:1748
  therapeutic exercise, 5:1759
Werner syndrome, 1:45
Wernicke-Korsakoff syndrome, 5:1862
Wernicke's aphasia, 2:717, 5:1687–1688, 1689–1690
West Nile virus, 3:1032
Westerman-Jamshidi trephine needles, 1:341
Western blot, HIV, 1:51, 60
Western medicine acupuncture, 1:18
Wet age-related macular degeneration, 1:40, 41, 42, 5:1615, 1835, 1837, 1838
Wet gangrene, 3:842–843, 844–845
Wetherill, Charles, 2:657
Wheals, 5:1649
Wheat, 2:473, 3:814–818, 887
  See also Gluten
Wheelchairs, 2:768, 4:1488, 5:**1879–1881,** 1885

Wheezing, 1:372–375
Whey, 3:817
Whipple procedure, 4:1406
Whirlpool hydrotherapy, 3:1000–1001
amyotrophic lateral sclerosis, 1:104
pressure sores, 4:1490
wound care, 5:1886
Whistle-blowers, 4:1232
White blood cell count, 2:560
bacterial infections, 1:278
chemotherapy, 2:491
clozapine administration, 1:205
infectious diseases, 3:1035
lupus, 3:1180
multiple myeloma, 4:1299
priapism, 4:1492
White blood cell deficiency. *See* Neutropenia
White blood cell differential, 2:560, 4:1492
White blood cells, 4:1384
White-coat hypertension, 1:90–91, 3:1009
White flour, 4:1521
See also Refined grains
White noise, 5:1780
Whitehouse, Mary Start, 4:1291
Whitening, teeth, 5:**1750–1753**
Whites. *See* Caucasians
WHO. *See* World Health Organization
Whole grains
anti-inflammatory diet, 1:194
cancer fighting foods, 2:418
community nutrition programs, 2:556
diverticulitis, 2:694
food pyramid, 2:658
healthy aging diet, 4:1338–1339
low-cholesterol diet, 3:1155
naturopathy, 4:1315
Wide excision, 4:1221
Widowers, 1:67
Widows, 3:1078
Wild yam, Mexican, 4:1252
Will to live living wills, 1:30–31
Williams, Samuel, 2:763
Willow bark, 1:234
Wills, living, 1:30–33, 2:598, 3:1149–1150
Wilm's tumor, 4:1263
Wilson's disease, 2:522, 524
WIN (Weight-Control Information Network), 5:1877
Windless sunglasses, 2:712
Window period, 1:61
Wine, red, 1:88, 2:417, 3:929
Winter itch. *See* Dry skin
Wisdom, 4:1526
Witch hazel, 1:334, 3:948
Withdrawal (substance)
alcohol, 5:1603
barbiturates, 1:283
caffeine, 2:396
delirium, 2:607
gambling, 3:841
marijuana, 4:1214
nicotine, 1:166, 5:1661, 1662, 1664–1668
SSRIs, 1:170
substance abuse, 5:1725, 1727, 1730
Withdrawal of life support, 1:30–31, 5:**1881–1884**
Withholding life support, 5:1882
Wolff, Albert, 4:1384
Women
abdominoplasty, 1:4
age-related macular degeneration, 5:1836
atherosclerosis, 1:245
bone density test, 5:1869
caloric intake, 4:1351
cancer demographics, 1:355*t*
caregivers, 2:453, 454
celiac disease, 3:889
chronic obstructive pulmonary disease, 2:512
cystitis, 2:593–596
dietary fiber, 3:957
Down syndrome, 4:1256
exercise, 5:1759
fecal incontinence, 3:798
fibromyalgia, 3:800
generalized anxiety disorder, 3:862
glaucoma, 5:1836–1837
gout, 3:891
hip revision surgery, 3:972
hypertension, 3:1009
incontinence, 5:1805
insomnia, 5:1655
isolation, 3:1078
knee joint replacement, 3:1112
life expectancy, 2:662
lupus, 3:1178–1179
most common cancers, 5:1737
nail infections, 4:1311
obesity, 4:1349, 1350*t*, 5:1836
panic disorder, 4:1410
psoriasis, 4:1518
pulmonary hypertension, 4:1539
recovery at home, 4:1555–1556
rheumatoid arthritis, 4:1573
sarcoidosis, 5:1581
saw palmetto, 5:1587–1588
scleroderma, 5:1596
sexual dysfunction, 5:1618–1620
sildenafil citrate, 5:1634
stress test, 5:1718
stroke, 5:1720–1721
substance abuse counseling, 5:1730
thyroid cancer, 5:1769
urinary incontinence, 5:1806
urinary tract infections, 5:1807–1808
varicose veins, 5:1816
working, 2:453
See also Gender differences; Postmenopausal women; Pregnancy
Women Veterans Health Program Office, 5:1828
Women's Health and Cancer Rights Act (1998), 1:366
Women's Health Initiative, 3:992, 1003, 5:1614
Woods light, 5:1650
Word recall, 3:866
Work environment, 4:1329–1330
activities of daily living, 1:9–10
clinical nurse specialists, 2:526
dialysis technologists, 2:651
dieticians, 2:681, 683
doctor of osteopathy, 2:702
hematologists, 3:942
home health aides, 3:983
licensed practical nurses, 3:1128
optometrists, 4:1355
pharmacology, 4:1451
pharmacy technicians, 4:1453
physical therapists, 4:1455, 1457
physical therapy assistants, 4:1460
reasonable accommodation, 1:94–95
registered nurses, 4:1558
relationships, 4:1561
rheumatologists, 4:1576
sleep deprivation, 5:1655
stress, 5:1715
See also Occupational exposure
Working women, 2:453
World Confederation for Physical Therapy, 4:1454
World Conferences for Academic Exchange of Medical Qigong, 4:1546, 1547
World Health Organization (WHO)
anemia, 1:108
dehydration, 2:605
depression, 2:622
diabetes mellitus, 2:639
heart disease, 3:925–926
herbs, 2:678
hypertension, 1:324–325
marijuana, 4:1213
migraine, 4:1266
movement therapy, 4:1291
obesity, 4:1349
osteoporosis, 4:1371
overweight, 1:331
rheumatoid arthritis, 4:1573
stroke, 3:925–926
visual impairment, 5:1841
World Trade Center, 4:1536, 5:1715
World Wide Web. *See* Internet
Wound care, 2:478, 5:1757, *1884*, **1884–1888**

Wound healing
aerobic exercise, 1:38
blood clots, 1:321
garlic, 3:846
pressure sores, 4:1490
skin lesion removal, 5:1648
smoking, 5:1664, 1665
Wound infections, 5:1699, 1711–1713
Woven bone, 4:1390
Wright-Giemsa stain, 1:341
Wright stain, 1:341
Wrinkles, 5:*1888*, **1888–1890**
alpha hydroxy acids for, 1:83, 5:1889
Botox injections, 1:345, 347, 2:758
chemical peels, 1:318, 5:1889
collagen injections, 2:*529*, 529–531
face lift, 3:*783*, 783–786, 5:1889
isometric exercises, 3:785
smoking, 5:1661
Wrist point, 1:14
Writing, 3:1164
Wymox. *See* Amoxicillin

X

X-Prep. *See* Magnesium citrate
X rays, 2:**498–500**
angiography, 1:127, 130
breast biopsy, 1:352, 353
bursitis, 1:390
cellulitis, 2:477
cervical spondylosis, 2:488
chiropractic, 2:501
colon cancer, 2:534
dental, 3:876, 4:1358
dislocations and subluxations, 2:687
gangrene, 3:844
hip fractures, 3:791
hip pain, 3:966
hip revision surgery, 3:973
kidney stones, 3:1102
kidney, ureter, and bladder, 3:1108–1110
knee injuries, 3:1117
low back pain, 3:1152
lumpectomy guidance, 3:1170
mobility, 4:1284
multiple myeloma, 4:1300
osteoarthritis, 4:1366–1367
Paget's disease of bone, 4:1390
pericarditis, 4:1432
prostate cancer, 4:1506
rheumatoid arthritis, 4:1574
sarcomas, 5:1584, 1586
scleroderma, 5:1598
See also Chest x rays
Xanax. *See* Alprazolam
Xanthine-oxidase inhibitors, 3:892
Xenical. *See* Orlistat
Xenon 133 studies, 1:98
Xerophthalmia, 5:1842, 1843
See also Dry eye
Xerostomia. *See* Dry mouth
Xolair. *See* Omalizumab
Xostrix. *See* Capsaicin
Xpert EV test, 4:1248
Xylocaine, 1:148

Y

Y-port, 3:1061
Yang, 1:12, 17, 4:1546
Yang Short Form, 5:1746
Yeast cultures, 3:822–824
Yeast infections, 3:824, 825–826
nail, 4:1312
Sjögren's syndrome-related, 5:1639
vaginal, 3:849
Yersini sp., 2:653
Yin, 1:12, 17, 4:1546
Ylang ylang, 5:1605
YMCA, 5:1875
Yo-yo weight loss, 2:671–672, 4:1350
Yoga, 5:*1891*, **1891–1894**
acupressure, 1:14, 15
breath therapy, 4:1272
breathing exercises, 5:1891
bursitis, 1:390
cervical spondylosis, 2:488
chronic pain, 4:1565
demographics, 4:1565, 5:1892
dermatitis, 2:632
flexibility training, 5:1758
hip joint pain, 3:969
history, 4:1563
low back pain, 3:1153
menopause, 4:1253
menopause symptoms, 3:994
movement therapy, 4:1292
osteoarthritis, 4:1368
qigong, 4:1546
relaxation response, 4:1270
restorative, 1:274
sciatica, 5:1594
seizures, 5:1605
side effects, 5:1893–1894
spirituality, 4:1476
stress, 5:1716
Yogurt, 3:1071, 1185, 4:1497
Yohimbe, 2:679, 757
Yom Kippur, 4:1551
Youk, Thomas, 4:1235
Young old, 1:46, 3:868, 4:1331
Youth Development Service, 5:1830
Yucca, 4:1368

Z

Z score, 1:337, 4:1371–1372
Z-track injections, 1:25
Zaleplon, 3:1051, 5:1657
Zalopon, 1:140
Zanamivir, 3:1040
Zantac. *See* Ranitidine
Zarontin. *See* Ethosuximide
Zaroxolyn. *See* Metolazone
Zea mays. *See* Maize
Zeaxanthin
age-related macular degeneration, 1:41, 319
cataract prevention, 2:463
glaucoma, 3:881–882
sources, 2:415
Zegerid. *See* Omeprazole
Zelnorm. *See* Tegaserod
Zenker's diverticulum, 5:1740, 1741
Zestril. *See* Lisinopril
Zetia. *See* Ezetimibe
Zidovudine, 1:8, 211, 4:1327
Zinc, 5:**1894–1898**
absorption, 5:1895, 1897–1898
age-related macular degeneration, 1:41
Alzheimer's disease risk, 1:86
aneurysm, 1:121
boils, 1:334
common cold, 2:553
daily recommended dosage, 3:870
dermatitis therapy, 2:631
drug interactions, 5:1897–1898
garlic, 3:846
immune system function, 3:1024
osteoarthritis, 4:1368
overdose, 5:1897
pneumonia prevention, 4:1465
polymyositis, 4:1468
pressure sores, 4:1490
rosacea, 4:1579
smoking-induced lung damage, 5:1662
sources, 5:1895–1897
supplements, 5:1897, 1898
ulcers, 5:1800
vitamin E interactions, 5:1858
Zinc deficiency, 5:1897, 1898
Zinc pyrithione, 5:1600
Ziprasidone, 1:203
for bipolar disorder, 1:305
for mental retardation, 4:1258
for psychoses, 1:203, 4:1531
side effects, 4:1531
Zirconium, 3:1112
Zocor. *See* Simvastatin
Zofran. *See* Ondansetron

Zoledronate, 4:1392
Zolicef. *See* Cefazolin
Zolipedem, 1:140
Zollinger-Ellison syndrome, 4:1401, 1515, 5:1798, 1799
Zoloft. *See* Sertraline
Zolpidem, 3:1051, 5:1657
Zone therapy. *See* Reflexology
Zonisamide, 1:304
Zoonotic infections, 3:826
Zostavax. *See* VZV vaccine
Zostrix, 5:1833
Zyban, 5:1661, 1665, 1667
Zyloprim. *See* Allopurinol
Zyvox. *See* Linezolid